Stories to Awaken the World

醒世恒言

Stories to Awaken the World

A MING DYNASTY COLLECTION

VOLUME 3

Compiled by Feng Menglong (1574–1646)
Translated by Shuhui Yang and Yunqin Yang

UNIVERSITY OF WASHINGTON PRESS
SEATTLE AND LONDON

The publication of *Stories to Awaken the World* has been generously supported by grants from Bates College and from the Chiang Ching-Kuo Foundation for International Scholarly Exchange.

University of Washington Press
P.O. Box 50096, Seattle, WA 98145, USA
www.washington.edu/uwpress

Library of Congress Cataloging-in-Publication Data
Feng, Menglong, 1574–1646.
[Xing shi heng yan. English]
Stories to awaken the world / compiled [and authored] by Feng Menglong ; translated by Shuhui Yang and Yunqin Yang.
p. cm. — (Ming dynasty collection ; vol. 3)
Includes bibliographical references.
ISBN 978-0-295-99371-3 (pbk. : alk. paper)
I. Feng, Menglong, 1574–1646—Translations into English.   I. Yang, Shuhui.
II. Yang, Yunqin.   III. Title.
PL2698.F48313   2009
895.1'346—dc22
                                                              2008051941

The paper used in this publication is acid-free and meets the minimum requirements of American National Standard for Information Sciences—Permanence of Paper for Printed Library Materials, ANSI Z39.48-1984.

To our parents and sisters

Contents

Acknowledgments

We are profoundly grateful to Lorri Hagman, without whose indefatigable enthusiasm, staunch support, and guidance the publication of a three-volume translation of *Sanyan* would not have been possible. Our thanks are also due to the two anonymous readers of this volume for their valuable suggestions as well as to our copy editor, Kerrie Maynes.

Foreword

Stories to Awaken the World (Xingshi hengyan) is a collection of forty short stories in vernacular Chinese compiled by Feng Menglong and published in Suzhou in 1627. Feng Menglong (1574–1646) was a well-known writer and celebrated bon vivant in his time; he compiled and published two other successful vernacular-language story collections, anthologies of poems and jokes, several plays, a lengthy volume of classical-language love stories called *A History of Attachments, Categorized* (Qing shi leilue), his extensive commentaries on the classic text he chose for his "major" for the civil service examinations, the *"Spring and Autumn" Annals* (Chunqiu; reportedly compiled by Confucius), other examination preparation textbooks, and two or three novels. Certain of his books were as avidly read by scholars as others were by gamblers.

Only in 1631 did he win appointment to the National Academy in Beijing, from which he might obtain lower-level appointments in local government. Thus he began his official career late in life: in 1634, at the age of sixty, he was appointed to be the magistrate of a poor and out-of-the-way county in the southeastern province of Fujian. By his own estimation, his administration was fair and lenient; before completing his term of office in 1638 he wrote the first history of the county. Feng was seemingly a loyal follower of the Chinese Ming ("Bright") imperial house; he survived only two years after it was overthrown by bandits the Ming rulers had been unable to control. Then the Manchu armies waiting on the northern frontier swept across China, nominally to rid the land of brigands but in fact establishing a new dynasty, the Qing ("Pure"), that was to hold power until 1911. The cause of Feng's death is not known; he probably died during his seventy-second year having finished compiling a historical account of the momentous events of that year of transition, 1644.

Some scholars credit Feng Menglong with the creation of "popular literature" in China. Certainly his first collection of vernacular fiction, *Stories Old and New* (Gujin xiaoshuo), published in 1621, set new standards for breadth of theme and motif, detail in characterization, and cleverness in the creation of dialogue. Later scholars point out the several narrative voices Feng created in his explicit narrator (using the guise of a professional storyteller) and in the editor's poems inserted regularly to comment on events in the tale. Many of these comments are ironic. Given the immediate success of this collection, it was soon reprinted, and followed by a second collection of forty stories entitled *Stories to Caution the World* (Jingshi tongyan), probably in 1624. The present anthology was his third and last. Together these collections drove all earlier compilations of vernacular fiction from the market, and when within a decade another enterprising editor (or perhaps Feng himself) compiled a forty-story selection from Feng's stories along with several by another creative story writer, Ling Mengchu (1580–1644), the canon of short vernacular fiction was established. Even though Feng Menglong certainly did not invent the form, his creative and editorial work assuredly brought the vernacular story to a very high level of development, as well as preserved the most imaginative fiction by his predecessors.

Individual entries in *Stories to Awaken the World*, like those in his previous collections, were largely rewritten by Feng and several still unidentified collaborators[1] on the basis of terse historical and fictional accounts then in circulation. Feng Menglong was tremendously well read; this explains his familiarity with some of the more rare sources uncovered by the modern scholars Tan Zhengbi and Sun Kaidi.[2] But some were developed from the tales in his own *History of Attachments* collection, fleshed out with the circumstantial details and lively dialogue that prefigured the fictional realism to emerge in Europe well over a century later. A few of these stories retold notorious events from earlier in the Ming period.[3] Standard wisdom about the collection was that it was Feng's desperate attempt to earn more money to support his spendthrift ways. It was a big book, then as now, made even more so by large, easy-to-read print and graced with two illustrations for every story. The high quality of its printing, especially of these pictures, guaranteed that it was a fairly expensive item compared to other books of its time—not a luxury edition, of course, but well beyond the meager incomes of shopkeeper's assistants and legal clerks. Instead, it was probably intended for purchase by members of the social elite, as entertaining reading for the men in their off hours and the less-busy educated women and youngsters of the house. For the former, Feng included several risqué tales often omitted from modern editions, including story 23 here.

Especially in retrospect, it is usual to see Feng's time as a period of high culture, easy living, and widespread prosperity. Senior historian of the period, Frederick W. Mote, sums up this vision:

> [F]or several specific reasons the age of Ming could be looked back upon with nostalgia by seventeenth-century Chinese: they remembered (or heard their seniors tell) that it had been an age of great promise, when cities grew, trade expanded, and all the arts of peace flourished. From the time of [idealistic Confucian philosopher] Wang Yangming (d. 1529) to the end of the dynasty in 1644 there was vigorous intellectual activity, whether seen in disputatious Confucian debates, in a revitalized Buddhism, or, above all, in literary and artistic realms. Books were edited and published in greater number than ever before. Entertainment literature flooded the bookstalls. Travel for sightseeing was in great vogue. A prosperous urban environment was found in the dozens

of large cities throughout the realm. Life held excitement and a sense of engage-
ment for many. All manner of memorable events could be recalled by those who
remembered the Ming.

As Mote concludes, so too do most other historians: "The late Ming was a roman-
tic period, marked by imagination, humor, and passion," even though China's last
imperial rulers, the Manchu monarchs, considered the late Ming "decadence" as
the cause of its political weakness.[4]

Thinking in these ways about Feng Menglong's stories, and about the writer's
age, Feng has conventionally been characterized as self-indulgent and yet, through
the voice of his "storyteller" narrators, as a moralist offering instruction on proper
behavior to unsophisticated readers. But if this collection were truly meant as a
profit-making gambit, it was only partially so, as a reading of the stories them-
selves reveals. The collection appeared during a darkening time, politically: in the
1620s the imperial house was weak, and forces loyal to the dictatorial eunuch Wei
Zhongxian (1568–1627)—who had won the emperor's confidence—were system-
atically removing all opposition, with numerous officials resigning throughout the
country in order to avoid arrest or worse. (Wei and his followers were rounded up
and Wei himself died in 1627, the year that this collection of stories was first printed.)[5]
It may be for this reason that morality and ethical choices are highlighted in so
many of these stories—either because strict standards are being upheld in them,
or because morality is being flouted by characters at all levels of society who assume
that they can get away with anything they wish.

Rather than simple teachings for simple readers, when read against their con-
text these stories appear instead to embody discussions of public behavior and the
rationales behind individual choices. Indeed, some characters in the stories here
are utterly self-centered and stop at nothing to achieve gratification. Surely par-
ents of the late Ming would not want their children to read about the open sexu-
ality in several of these stories. In this regard the stories speak to, and about, their
time. Even so, no strident didactic voice is present here; instead many tales are
shot through with irony: both the narrator/storyteller and commentator voices
share amusement with the reader over human foibles far more than they express
outrage or scorn at the shortcomings of these fictional characters. Indeed, short-
sightedness and absurdity in thought, word, and deed are repeatedly featured here,
and many stories incorporate strange coincidences described, ironically at times,
as "destiny" when they really illustrate the contingencies that shape human affairs.
One might argue that these tricks at the expense of the reader's expectations reflect
the ethically inexplicable moves of China's rulers at that time. We might also dis-
cover bleak views of humanity and of prospects for success in the world behind
these stories if we read them as social documents rather than primarily as works
of art and entertainment.

Even though these stories are unambiguously fictional in their present form, several stories raise sensitive social issues including emotional relationships within families, sexual mores (including what constitutes sexual predation), and situations that contrast public face with private guilt. The collection represents the literary fashions of that interesting time: a taste for sexy tales, as always, and a perennial interest in human motivations, to be sure, but enthusiasm for courtroom confrontations, the workings of religious institutions, and the consequences of indulging one's fantasies—sensual, financial, and otherwise. Genres of fiction become clearly identified here through the parodies of more standard examples from earlier texts, including Feng's own fiction collection, *Stories Old and New*.

I suspect that there is also a substantial measure of literary prankishness behind many if not all of these stories. Throughout most of the twentieth century, China's scholars sought evidence for the kind of developmental sequences then in fashion in the West. To show that China's fiction had "evolved," literary historian and writer Lu Xun (1881–1936) and others posited a beginning stage in which all narratives were oral—the imaginative products of China's "masses" of working people and articulated by popular professional storytellers. But subsequent research has invalidated this "promptbook" theory of composition (that the storytellers based their performances on script outlines or that scholars copied down their recitations as a means to make commercial profit for themselves). It is true that entertaining stories circulated among the educated elite and the unlettered masses alike—in both textual and oral forms—but historical evidence suggests that the borrowing apparently went in both directions. However, China's most respected specialists in this literary form have convincingly traced the origins of Feng's vernacular stories to earlier written fiction.[6] If there were oral origins for these narratives, they can only be considered the indirect progenitors of the mature vernacular short story, and the tie between this form and oral entertainments for illiterates is ambiguous at best. This is why we should expect sophisticated complex literary artistry in these texts, and why we should not be surprised when we find it.

Translators Yang Shuhui and Yang Yunqin have insightfully argued that the true nature of the collection can only be appreciated when reading all of the stories in their original order. I could not agree more. What one perceives, then—in the sequence that Feng Menglong intended—is extensive play between stories, the rhythm of slyly changing themes through a number of them, and the extent to which the compiler exploited clever variations in characterization, plot, and subject matter as the reader proceeds from one to the next. Stories here appear in pairs that may be on the same theme but often reflect on each other in a variety of ways; some second stories are ironic inversions of the first in the pair. In some parts of the collection, pairs themselves form parallels to comment on each other. Indeed, only when these stories are read in their original, very deliberate, order do such masterful juxtapositions and ironic reflections become visible.

A case in point is the sequence of stories in which disguise and hidden or changed identity form core scenes. Story 7 is an iteration of a staple of vernacular Chinese fiction, the homely suitor who sends his handsome relative in his place to impress his future in-laws and, should she peek, his intended. Such stories lead to slapstick; the extended scene of everyone beating everyone else serves just that purpose here. Its paired story, number 8, begins with a poem affirming that if marriages are already made in heaven, matchmakers are useless. The story itself is a farce to match number 7; a boy is sent in place of his sister to bolster her dying betrothed by her presence. Since they are not yet formally married, the "bride-to-be" is encouraged to sleep with the sick young man's sister. After some innocent "frolicking between sisters-in-law," the "bride" makes love to the sister, and they become inseparable. This story, too, ends happily, improbable as that might have been. At the center of story 9 is another sick groom-to-be. From the grotesque appearance of leprosy, a handsome young man emerges after poisoning himself (like Shakespeare's Juliet, his betrothed takes the remaining poison to join him in death—but a timely antidote saves them both) to be married to a beautiful young woman and to live happily ever after. In story 10 two helpless "boys" sheltered by a generous but childless old couple devote themselves to caring for the elders until they pass away; then they build up the family business. Finally one reveals to the other that "he" has been a girl in disguise all along, so they marry and produce numerous children of their own.

Through this sequence we see situations that border on absurdity followed by more problematic situations: fatal and disfiguring illness, and orphans stranded far from home. The stories in the second pair are hardly farcical: potentially heart-wrenching disasters are only averted by the devotion of individuals to each other—a young couple in number 9 and adoptive parents and children in number 10. The next two stories have as a central character the famous poet Su Shi (Su Dongpo, 1037–1101). In the first, a brilliant young poet disguises himself to spy on Su's sister to see if she's really as plain in appearance as he has heard; she wins him over by her poetic talent, and he becomes devoted to her. In the second, Su disguises his handsome friend as a Buddhist acolyte in order to afford the young man a rare chance to see the emperor in person; when the emperor plays along with the deception, the youth can only go ahead to become a monk in fact. But in contrast to other stories in this sequence, the monk steadfastly, and with humor, resists seduction by a woman Su sent to win him back to lay life.

With story 12, the series of romantic tales is broken by a handsome monk for whom the disguise becomes real, with no return to his life as lived before the joke that backfired. The following two stories embody a much darker aspect of sexuality. In story 13 a conjurer disguises himself as a god in order to seduce a lonely young woman who languishes from physical desire; for his transgressions he is sentenced to death by dismemberment, the worst possible punishment. And in story 14 the frustrations of "spring longing" bring about a young woman's death, a case of necrophilia, an accidental homicide (the young man sees his revived beloved and throws a pot at her, thinking she is a ghost), conjugal dreams, executions, and the establishment of a new shrine. As each story is built upon the one before, and each pair on its predecessors, in new and clever variations on a common theme, the sequence of events begins with a chance encounter between young people (a situation immortalized the first story in Feng's first collection, *Stories Old and New*) followed by ever more bizarre situations.

And then the collection shifts direction. In stories 13 and 14 we read of hearings and legal proceedings; stories 15 and 16 have investigations of crime and interrogations of malefactors as their central attraction. And in these stories, too, the sexual misbehavior of the earlier sequence has lost its romantic qualities: they are all about lust and brutality, with none of the pretty innocence with which the sequence of love stories began. Other patterns emerge when reading the stories in sequence; I will leave their discovery to the readers of these fine translations.

About one fourth of these stories have attracted the attention of earlier translators, but most have seen fit to produce incomplete or inadequate renditions of the original in order to shape them to fit modern expectations. Patrick Hanan is a noteworthy exception. For his recent anthology of Chinese vernacular love stories, *Falling in Love*, Hanan chose several from this collection. He takes pains to point out in his introduction that the stories he selected are unambiguously about love.[7] But when one reads them in their original context and in the intended sequence as they are here, even Hanan's choices are less straightforward stories about human affections than they are ironic commentaries on human egocentrism and emotional attachments in general—all played out through clever variations on conventional situations. This simply strengthens the Yangs' assertion that the art of Feng Menglong as author and compiler of fiction can only be fully appreciated when one engages the entire collection as a single, complex work of art.

Shuhui and Yunqin Yang are highly experienced translators, having produced excellent renditions of Feng Menglong's earlier story collections, *Stories Old and New* (2000) and *Stories to Caution the World* (2005). Their versions are eminently readable, accurate, and lively; they have managed to hit just the right tone in their translations to convey simultaneously the fun of entertainment and the seriousness of Feng Menglong's moral engagement with the social problems of the day. Their decision to include the commentary from the original edition was especially commendable: it conveys seventeenth-century values shared among the Chinese cultural elite while pointing out what original readers of the collection were being asked to appreciate in the writer's art. This collection is a fine complement to the two volumes of this series the translators have already published. Shuhui and Yunqin Yang have provided a rare treat for English readers: an unparalleled view of the art of short fiction from seventeenth-century China. Unquestionably, their translations rank among the very finest English versions of Chinese fiction from any period.

Robert E. Hegel
Washington University in St. Louis
June 12, 2008

Introduction

Stories to Awaken the World (Xingshi hengyan), more commonly known in English as Constant Words to Awaken the World, was published in Suzhou in 1627. It is the third of three celebrated Ming dynasty (1368–1644) collections of stories; the first is Stories Old and New (Gujin xiaoshuo; 1620 or 1621), and the second is Comprehensive Words to Caution the World (Jingshi tongyan; 1624). Each collection contains forty stories, and since Stories Old and New is also known as Illustrious Words to Instruct the World (Yushi mingyan), the three books are most often referred to collectively as the Sanyan (Three words), from the Chinese character yan at the end of each title.[1]

The Sanyan collections were edited by Feng Menglong (1574–1646), the most knowledgeable connoisseur of popular literature of his time. He came from a well-to-do, educated family in the exceptionally prosperous Suzhou Prefecture, one of the great cultural centers of Ming China. Feng acquired the preliminary academic degree of shengyuan when he was about twenty but apparently had no further luck in the civil service examinations, in spite of his erudition and great literary fame. Finally, in 1630, at the age of fifty-six or fifty-seven, he seems to have lost hope that he would pass the examinations and decided instead to take the alternative route to office by accepting the status of tribute student.[2] He then served one term as assistant instructor in Dantu County (about ninety miles northwest of Suzhou), probably from 1631 to 1634, before he was promoted to a minor position as magistrate of Shouning County, Fujian.[3] He held this office for four years and proved to be an honest, caring, and efficient administrator, as is registered in the County History of Shouning (Shouning xian zhi), compiled in the early Qing period (1644–1911). The county history also tells us that Feng "venerated literary studies more than anything else" (shou shang wenxue) during his service.[4] Feng's last political involvement, toward the end of his life, was his association with the Southern Ming government in its desperate resistance against the crushing forces of the Manchus. He died soon afterward in 1646 at the age of seventy-two.

Feng Menglong was one of the most prolific writers of his time. The books he published could literally be "piled up to reach his own height" (zhuzuo dengshen), a phrase traditionally used by critics to praise exceptionally productive writers,[5] and they covered such a wide range of interests and literary genres that Feng has been described as "presenting himself in two distinct personae, or . . . in a range of personae between two extremes."[6] At one extreme, he appears in some of his works as the wit, the ribald humorist, the bohemian, the drinker, and the romantic lover. This is the Feng Menglong who compiled *Treasury of Jokes* (Xiaofu) and published two volumes of folk songs (*Guazhir* and *Hill Songs*), mostly on erotic or ribald themes, and whose passionate love affair with the famous Suzhou courtesan Hou Huiqing is revealed in some of his poems. At the other extreme is Feng Menglong the patriot, orthodox scholar, and ardent examination candidate, who authored at least three handbooks on the Confucian classic *The Spring and Autumn Annals,* wrote a similar handbook on the *Four Books*, and published many patriotic tracts as a consequence of his participation in Southern Ming resistance activities. These two personae may seem to be mutually exclusive, yet in his fiction as well as in his plays, Feng Menglong often reveals elements of both in a single text.[7]

Modern scholars generally agree, however, that Feng Menglong's greatest contribution to literature is in the field of vernacular fiction, particularly his collecting and editing of the three *Sanyan* books of 120 vernacular short stories. This genre, known as *huaben*, is believed to have developed, along with the vernacular novel, during the Song (960–1279) and Yuan (1260–1368) dynasties and reached maturity in the late Ming. As a passionate champion of popular literature, Feng managed to rescue from oblivion a significant proportion of the early *huaben* stories by making them available to the public again. But preservation of existing stories was by no means Feng Menglong's only concern—he was probably more interested in giving prestige to this new literary genre and establishing it socially. In the preface to *Stories Old and New*, he places vernacular fiction on a par with the highly esteemed classical tales of the Tang dynasty (618–907):

> *Literature and the arts have been so vigorously advanced by the imperial court of this Ming dynasty that each and every school is flourishing; in vernacular fiction alone, there is no lack of writings of a quality far above those of the Song. It is a mistake to believe, as some do, that such works lack the charm of those of the Tang. One who has a love for the peach need not forsake the apricot. Fine linen, silk gauze, plush, brocade—each has its proper occasion for wear.*

In order to elevate the status of the vernacular story, Feng Menglong also claims, in the same preface, that the origin of all fiction is the grand tradition of historiography, and he ascribes more educational and moral power to the *huaben* story than to *The Analects of Confucius* (Lunyu).[8] With the aim of substantiating such claims, Feng is believed, not surprisingly, to have extensively modified some of the stories he had collected and incorporated many of his own stories and those of his friends into the *Sanyan* collections, although he does not acknowledge authorship in the preface.[9] According to Patrick Hanan, who applied rigorous stylistic criteria in his studies of the dating and authorship of Chinese vernacular stories, Feng Menglong is the probable author of nineteen stories in *Stories Old and New*, sixteen in *Stories to Caution the World*, and one or two in *Constant Words to Awaken the World*.[10]

A less drastic but more obvious aspect of Feng's "editing" is his rearrangement into pairs of the stories in the three collections. The thematically and grammatically parallel pairing of titles may be an attempt to parody the parallelism of classical poetry and belles lettres prose (the two most honored literary genres of Feng's time) or may simply represent his effort to elevate the vernacular short story.[11] However, on the textual level, it is clear that the stories were composed with their pairings in mind.[12] The paired stories often share features of subject matter or plot line, and they occasionally contrast or comment on each other.

One of the most interesting and controversial characteristics of Chinese vernacular fiction is its "storyteller's rhetoric." This is part of what Patrick Hanan refers to as the "simulated context" or "the context of situation in which a piece of fiction claims to be transmitted."[13] In the *Sanyan* stories (and in other Chinese vernacular fiction as well), this simulacrum almost always takes the form of a professional storyteller addressing his audience. The storyteller-narrator asks questions of his simulated audience, converses with them, makes explicit references to his own stories, and intersperses his narrative with verses and poems. The narrator usually begins his talk with one or more prologue stories or poems, which supposedly allows time for his audience to gather before he presents the main piece in his performance.

Of course, in written literature, this storyteller's pose is only a pretense in which "the author and reader happily acquiesce in order that the fiction can be communicated."[14] It was a way to "naturalize, by reference to the familiar situation of hearing stories told in the vernacular by professional storytellers, the unfamiliar process of writing and reading fiction in vernacular Chinese."[15] But this formal feature, plus a misunderstanding of the term *huaben*, led many scholars of Chinese literature to subscribe, until a couple of decades ago, to the "promptbook" theory, which held that the Chinese vernacular story developed directly from the promptbooks of marketplace storytellers in the Song dynasty and that the pre-*Sanyan* texts were genuine promptbooks written for performance in the Song and Yuan or early Ming periods.[16] W. L. Idema, however, argues that the storyteller's manner was developed deliberately in literati imitations by Feng Menglong and others. According to Idema, the conspicuous use of this rhetorical stance in the *Sanyan* collections was "a consequence mainly of Feng Menglong's reinterpretation of the genre and due to his overall rewritings."[17] In other words, Feng's editing of the collections included a systematic elaboration of the storyteller's rhetoric, which became a hallmark of the *huaben* story as he conceived of it.

This, however, is not to deny the presence of elements of oral folk literature in the *Sanyan* stories. Most contain anecdotes or episodes known even to the illiterate, which suggests that the editor looked to storytelling for raw materials as well as for rhetorical formulas. And we may assume that traces of the marketplace storyteller and the values he represented would unavoidably have remained in these *huaben* stories in spite of Feng Menglong's often meticulous editing. Idema argues that professional storytelling was but one of the many factors that helped to shape traditional Chinese fiction.[18] Small wonder that the *Sanyan* collections provide for us such a vivid panoramic view of the bustling world of imperial China before the end of the Ming; we see not only scholars, emperors, ministers, and generals but also a gallery of ordinary men and women in their everyday surroundings—merchants and artisans, prostitutes and courtesans, matchmakers and fortunetellers, monks and nuns, servants and maids, thieves and impostors. We learn about their joys and sorrows, likes and dislikes, their view of life and death, and even their visions of the netherworld and the supernatural.

Thus, the *Sanyan* stories are necessarily overdetermined texts—historically, ideologically, and formally. They can justifiably be taken as an intersection of complex cultural determinations, with generic mixture and multiple voices making different and sometimes conflicting claims. This complexity of multiple voices in *Stories to Awaken the World* has never been fully presented to the English reader. Of the forty stories in this collection, only thirteen have been published in English translation, appearing separately in journals and anthologies of Chinese literature instead of being arranged in pairs and in the original sequence. Moreover, in some of these previous translations, the storyteller's rhetoric, the verses, and the prologue stories were often deleted.[19] The interlinear and marginal comments, generally believed to have been made by Feng Menglong himself, are omitted even in modern Chinese editions of the collection.[20] This volume represents the first effort to translate the third, and the last, of the seventeenth-century *Sanyan* collections in its entirety. In doing so, we hope not only to provide the English reader with a fuller picture of the complex social environment of imperial China but, more important, to show the intricate interactions among different voices in the texts, especially between the voice of the conventional storyteller-narrator and that of the literati editor Feng Menglong.[21]

Shuhui Yang

Translators' Note

This translation follows the text of the 1627 Ye Jingchi edition of *Xingshi heng-yan* as reprinted in the 1987 facsimile edition by Shanghai Guji Chubanshe. In this translation, the interlinear and marginal comments in the original text appear in italic within parentheses in roman text and in roman within parentheses in italic text.

The fact that the order of the stories in almost all of the modern editions differs slightly from that of the Ye Jingchi edition needs some explanation. There was a more easily available Yanqingtang edition in premodern China, published some time after the Ye Jingchi edition. The major difference between these two seventeenth-century editions is that the Yanqingtang edition deleted story 23 and split story 20 into two parts, listing them as stories 20 and 21, and renumbering the original story 21 (Zhang Shu'er) as 23 while keeping story 22 (Lü Dongbin) in the original order. In the twentieth century, Gu Xuejie's 1936 Dingwen shuju edition, the earliest modern edition, relies heavily on the Yanqingtang edition: the original story 23 (King Hailing) is marked out as "deleted," and story 20 is back in its entirety, but the Lü Dongbin story still precedes Zhang Shu'er. The subsequent modern editions of Xingshi hengyan, including the 1956 Renmin wenxue edition, follow that order.

Chinese proper names are rendered in the pinyin system. For the convenience of those readers who are more accustomed to the Wade-Giles system of romanization, we have provided the following short list of difficult consonants:

c = ts'
q = ch'
x = hs
z = tz
zh = ch

Information about previous translations of stories in this collection (in varying degrees of completeness and accuracy) is provided in the endnotes for individual stories.

Frequently Encountered Chinese Terms

chi, a unit of measurement, translated as "foot"
jin, translated as "catty," equals half a kilogram

jinshi, one who passed the imperial civil service examinations at the national level

li, approximately one third of a mile

liang, translated as "tael," equals one sixteenth of a *jin*

mu, roughly one sixth of an acre

shi, a married woman known by her maiden name (e.g., Wang-shi)

xiucai, translated as "scholar," a successful candidate at the county level

zhuangyuan, a *jinshi* who ranked first in the palace examination, in which the emperor interviewed those who had passed the imperial civil service examination at the national level

zi, translated as "courtesy name," the name by which an educated person was addressed by people of his or her own generation, probably used more often than an official name

Chronology of Chinese Dynasties

Xia	ca. 2100–ca. 1600 B.C.E.
Shang (Yin)	ca. 1600–ca. 1028 B.C.E.
Zhou	ca. 1027–ca. 256 B.C.E.
Western Zhou	ca. 1027–771 B.C.E.
Eastern Zhou	770–256 B.C.E.
Spring and Autumn	770–476 B.C.E.
Warring States	475–221 B.C.E.
Qin	221–207 B.C.E.
Han	206 B.C.E.–220 C.E.
Western Han (or Former Han)	206 B.C.E.–8 C.E.
Xin	9–25
Eastern Han (or Later Han)	25–220
Three Kingdoms	220–80
Wei	220–65
Shu	221–63
Wu	222–80
Six Dynasties (Wu, Eastern Jin, Former Song, Southern Qi, Southern Liang, and Southern Chen)	222–589
Jin	265–420
Western Jin	265–316
Eastern Jin	317–420
Southern and Northern Dynasties	420–589
Southern Dynasties	
Former Song	420–79
Southern Qi	479–502
Southern Liang	502–57
Southern Chen	557–89
Northern Dynasties	
Northern Wei	386–534
Eastern Wei	534–50
Western Wei	535–56

Northern Qi	550–77
Northern Zhou	557–81
Sui	581–618
Tang	618–907
Five Dynasties and Ten Kingdoms	907–79
Five Dynasties	
Later Liang	907–23
Later Tang	923–36
Later Jin	936–46
Later Han	947–50
Later Zhou	951–60
Ten Kingdoms	907–79
Liao (Khitan)	916–1125
Song	960–1279
Northern Song	960–1126
Southern Song	1127–1279
Xixia (Tangut)	1038–1227
Jin (Jurchen)	1115–1234
Yuan (Mongol)	1260–1368
Ming	1368–1644
Qing (Manchu)	1644–1911

Stories to Awaken the World

醒世恒言

Preface [to the 1627 edition]

All texts other than the Six Classics and the official histories are light reading.[1] However, expositions of moral principles tend to be too tedious, and pursuit of literary grace may result in overly florid rhetoric. Neither style appeals to popular taste and inspires constancy of purpose and will. The forty stories contained in this collection, entitled *Constant Words to Awaken the World*, constitute a sequel to *Illustrious Words to Instruct the World* and *Comprehensive Words to Caution the World*—"Illustrious Words" because they enlighten the obtuse; "Comprehensive Words" because they reach the wide public; and "Constant Words" because they do not wear out with frequent reviews and can be passed on from generation to generation.

The three collections bear different titles but the gist is the same. Those who otherwise talk and act normally will, under the influence of wine, whoop and howl and strut about, taking a moat to be a ditch and a city to be a cage. Why? Because wine addles the wits. But if drinking is done in moderation, even Minister Bi or Chamberlain Liu would not have found themselves in a besotted condition at all times of the day.[2] Isn't it true, then, that wakefulness and sobriety are a constant state whereas inebriation is only a transient one? It can thus be deduced that those who fear for the safety of a child about to fall into a well are sober; those who drop stones on someone down in a well are drunk. One who rejects food that is handed out contemptuously is sober; one who accepts it is drunk. One who appreciates fine jade is sober; one who takes it for rock is drunk. It can be further deduced that a person with the virtues of loyalty and filial piety is sober; one who is rebellious and disobedient is drunk. One who is chaste and frugal is sober; one who is lewd and dissipated is drunk. One with discerning ears and eyes, civil speech, and sterling character is sober; one who is ignorant and benighted and persists in foolish ways is drunk.

It should thus be clear where constancy of purpose and will should be directed. Those who follow that direction will be blessed. Those who go astray will come to grief. If you attain constancy in your heart, your speech, and your actions, you will not cause scandals in your conjugal relationship or have reason to feel ashamed when answering to heaven and earth. With such constancy, even those in lowly professions will gain insight into the ways of the good-hearted, the noble-minded, and the sages. Thus, constancy is a word of immense import. It has always been said that turmoil in the world occurs only because heaven happens to be drunk. If heaven does not voluntarily get inebriated, man will try to make it so. Similarly, if heaven does not wake up on its own, man should try to awake it. If man is the medium for awakening heaven, words are the medium for awakening man. If words can inspire constancy in man, man can in his turn bring about constancy in heaven, leading to the boundless bliss of eternal peace.

I hope that this collection, like the songs "Broad Road" and "Drumming with an Earth Clod," will be handed down to posterity.[3] In dynasties when Confucianism is revered, Daoism and Buddhism are not renounced, because of their role in edifying the benighted and appealing to popular taste. These two teachings can very well serve as supplements to Confucianism. In the same vein, *Illustrious Words, Comprehensive Words,* and *Constant Words* can very well serve as supplements to the Six Classics and the official histories. If they are compared with bawdy works that gain transient popularity but go down in history in infamy—works that are composed in a drunken state and then fed to the public as intoxicants, I wonder from which ones the reader derives more benefit.

Recluse Keyi of Longxi [in present-day Gansu], at the House on the Hill amid Rosy Clouds, Nanjing, in midautumn, the seventh year of the Tianqi reign period [1627]

I

Two High-Minded County Magistrates Vie to Take On an Orphan Girl as Daughter-in-Law

Granted that feng shui cannot be ignored,
It works only when backed up with good deeds.
Those who are blind to the will of heaven
Get nowhere for all their plots and schemes.

As the story goes, in Quzhou Prefecture, Zhejiang, in a previous dynasty, there lived a man named Wang Feng who had an older brother, Wang Chun. They each had a daughter. Wang Chun's daughter was Qiongying, and Wang Feng's daughter, Qiongzhen. Both girls were betrothed at an early age, the former to Pan Hua, son of Millionaire Pan of the same county, and the latter to Xiao Ya, son of Assistant Prefect Xiao, also of the same county. Qiongying was only ten years old when her mother passed away. Her father died immediately thereafter. On his deathbed, Wang Chun had asked his younger brother to take care of Qiongying, saying, "Please treat this only child of mine as your own daughter and marry her with all due ceremony to the Pan family after she comes of age. Her mother's dowry, clothes, and jewelry all go to her. The farmland that I bought with the Pan family's betrothal gifts also goes to her for her personal expenses. Do not fail me!" After giving these instructions, he breathed his last. As soon as the funeral was over, Wang Feng took his niece Qiongying home as a companion for his own daughter, Qiongzhen.

One New Year's Day, both Pan Hua and Xiao Ya went to Wang Feng's house, as if by prior agreement, to extend New Year greetings. Pan Hua, with the fair complexion and ruby lips of a beautiful girl, was called by all and sundry the Jade Boy, whereas Xiao Ya, with his pockmarked face, sunken eyes, and buckteeth, looked like a veritable *yaksha*.[1] By comparison, the handsome one seemed to dazzle with even greater splendor, whereas the ugly one looked as ghastly as if plastered all over with mud. In addition, being a man much given to ostentation, Pan Hua was arrayed in finery and had brought along a whole wardrobe of clothes in which to parade

5

himself. Xiao Ya, on the contrary, was a down-to-earth sort of man who took lit-
tle interest in clothes. As the saying goes, "Clothes to men are what gilt is to a statue
of Buddha." Most people lack the wisdom to look underneath appearances into
the heart. All the members of the Wang family, male and female, old and young,
admired the handsome Young Master Pan as they would have admired Pan An[2]
and, among themselves, set their tongues a-wagging about the unprepossessing looks
of the "*yaksha*." Wang Feng himself also found the latter too unsightly and felt
grievously disappointed.

Before many days had passed, Mr. Xiao Senior died at his duty station. Xiao
Ya hastened there for the funeral and then escorted the coffin back home. Though
a family of distinguished lineage, the Xiaos had little savings to fall back on because,
generation after generation, those in the clan who had served as officials had all
been righteous and incorrupt. After Assistant Prefect Xiao's death, the Xiao fam-
ily circumstances went on the decline, whereas the nouveau-riche Millionaire Pan's
fortunes grew by the day. All of a sudden, an evil thought struck Wang Feng: "The
Xiao family is so poor, and my future son-in-law so ugly. The Pan family is rich,
and the young man handsome. Why don't I secretly switch the two girls? Who's
going to know? I'm not going to let my own flesh and blood throw in her lot with
that miserable pauper!"

His mind thus made up, he married his own daughter, Qiongzhen, to the Pan
family, presenting her as his niece, and gave her all the possessions left by his older
brother. As for Qiongying, he passed her off as his own daughter and married her
to the "*yaksha*," with a modest dowry. Qiongying resented the decisions her uncle
made on her behalf but dared not protest.

After the wedding, Pan Hua turned out to be a man who, smug about his fam-
ily's wealth, spent his time gambling and whoring instead of devoting himself to
study or other serious pursuits. His father's words of admonition consistently fell
on deaf ears. Soon Mr. Pan Senior died of sheer rage, which suited Pan Hua all the
better, for the young man was now free to fool around with his ne'er-do-well friends
day in and day out, giving himself up to drinking, feasting, and making merry.

In less than ten years, he had squandered away his vast inheritance and was left
without an inch of land. His father-in-law's handouts to him were as helpful as a
few flakes of snow to a raging fire. In the end, cold and hunger getting the better
of him, he offered without his father-in-law's knowledge to sell his wife as a ser-
vant to a rich family. As soon as Wang Feng heard about this, he took his daugh-
ter Qiongzhen back to his own home, where she would be supported for the rest
of her life, and closed the door to his son-in-law. Pan Hua then left his hometown,
going none knew whither, to lead a vagabond's existence.

In the meantime, Xiao Ya applied himself assiduously to his studies and won
honors at the civil service examinations on the first try. He then rose steadily in
status until finally becoming a cabinet minister, and Qiongying gained the title of
Lady of the First Grade. There is a poem in evidence:

Rich or poor, your current status does not count;
Who knows what your future holds in store?
You may think you can get away with vice,
But the gods never err in their judgments fair and wise.

Dear audience, you may wonder why I tell you this story about Wang Feng marrying off his daughter. It is to remind you of how people think only of the present, to the neglect of the future, and gain advantages for themselves at the expense of others. Little do they know that for all their little plots and schemes, Heaven is the final disposer. You may very well plan out a smooth path for yourself, but Heaven may not let you have everything your way. The best option is to make a habit of doing good works.

Now the following story, entitled "Two High-Minded County Magistrates Vie to Take On an Orphan Girl as Daughter-in-Law," is about people who did exactly the reverse of what Wang Feng did. It takes place during the Five Dynasties [907–60]. On the throne sat Guo Wei, first emperor of Later Zhou [951–60], who had changed the name of the reign period to Guangshun.[3] His royal status notwithstanding, he had not yet unified the land, which remained divided into five kingdoms and three territories. Which five kingdoms?

Later Zhou under Guo Wei [904–54]
Southern Han, under Liu Sheng [917–71]
Northern Han, under Liu Min [895–954]
Southern Tang, under Li Bian [888–943]
Shu, under Meng Zhixiang [874–934]

Which three territories?

Wu-Yue, under Qian Liu [852–932][4]
Hunan, under Zhou Xingfeng [d. 962]
Jingnan, under Gao Jichang [Gao Jixing; 858–928]

Of the above, I shall tell only about Southern Tang of the house of Li, which had jurisdiction over Jiangzhou [present-day Jiangxi], of which I shall focus on Dehua County [present-day city of Jiujiang]. The county magistrate, Shi Bi, was a native of Linchuan County, Fuzhou, and had lived in Jiankang [present-day Nanjing]. A widower in his forties now, he had no son. Only his eight-year-old daughter Yuexiang [Moon Fragrance] and a maid were with him at his duty station. He was an honest and incorrupt official who had taken nothing but water from Dehua County since he assumed office there. Being also a wise judge, he redressed wrongs and cleared the backlog of outstanding cases. Indeed, administrative work was rendered simple, and punishments were reduced to a minimum. The local people lived in peace in an environment free of crime. In his spare time, the magistrate often held Yuexiang on his knees and taught her to read. Sometimes he had the maid play chess or ball with her and he himself coached her as she played. Indeed, he loved the motherless child with all his heart.

One day, the maidservant and Yuexiang were in the courtyard, kicking a little ball around, when the maid gave it a kick slightly harder than usual, and the ball bounced and rolled all the way into a two- or three-foot-deep pit that had once held a water vat. Her arms being too short to reach the ball, the maid was about to jump into the pit to retrieve it when Shi Bi said, "Stop!" Turning to his daughter, Yuexiang, he asked, "Can you think of a way to make the ball come out by itself?"

The girl thought for a while and said, "I've got it!" She had the maid bring over a bucket of water and empty it into the pit. The ball immediately rose to the surface of the water. Another bucketful of water, and the ball came out with the excess water that spilled over the edge of the pit. (*So, Sima Guang, the child prodigy, had a prototype.*)[5] Shi Bi had meant to test his daughter's resourcefulness and was beside himself with joy at her brilliance.

But let us get on with the story. In less than three years after Shi Bi assumed his post, it turned out, in a way no one would have predicted, that his "career star" faded out and disaster befell him. One night, a fire broke out in the county government granary. Even though action was quickly taken to put it out, more than a thousand piculs of grain were consumed in the flames. The price of grain in those days being as high as fifteen hundred cash per picul, and army provisions being of first importance in times of war, loss of as many as three hundred piculs of army provisions was a capital offense under the law of the Southern Tang. But in Shi Bi's case, his superiors all pleaded on his behalf to the king because he was a good official and, in addition, the fire was an act of providence rather than the result of mismanagement. However, the king's wrath remained unabated. He dismissed Shi from office and demanded repayment for the loss. The estimated total amount came to more than fifteen hundred taels of silver, but the proceeds from the sale of all of Shi Bi's family possessions only added up to less than half of it. The prefectural authorities therefore put Shi Bi under house arrest. The demands for payment so depressed him that he fell ill and died before many days had passed. His daughter and the maid, as was usually the case under such circumstances, were sold off by a middlewoman, acting on behalf of the government, in repayment of the debt. Such was their misery! It was indeed a case of

> An all-night rain wrecks a hut already leaking;
> A head wind thwarts a boat already too slow.

Now, there lived in the same county a man of humble status, Jia Chang, who had been falsely accused of homicide and thrown into prison on a death sentence. Luckily for him, the new magistrate, Mr. Shi, had come on the scene. After looking into the case and concluding that an injustice had been done to him, the magistrate set him free. Lacking an opportunity to repay the magistrate for having saved him and his family, Jia Chang left town as a traveling merchant. Upon returning to his hometown and learning that Magistrate Shi had just died, he went to see the corpse and cried his heart out. He then bought burial clothes for the deceased as well as a coffin. His whole family put on mourning clothes, and a piece of land was bought for the burial.

Upon hearing that the deceased was still heavily in debt to the government, Jia Chang was more than willing to help out but dared not be implicated in a case that involved government grain. As word reached him that the young lady and the maid were to be sold off by a middlewoman on behalf of the government, he hastened to Middlewoman Li's house, equipped with silver, and asked about the price. Li produced a note on government stationery bearing words of approval written in red ink. The maid, sixteen years of age, was approved for sale for only thirty taels of silver, whereas Yuexiang, ten years of age, was to sell for fifty taels. Why the difference? Well, in spite of her tender years, Yuexiang was pretty and lovely, whereas the older girl was but a lowly servant. Hence the difference in price.

Without the least hesitation, Jia Chang took out his package of silver, weighed out eighty taels of sterling silver, and handed them to the woman, with five taels thrown in as a token of gratitude to her. He then took the two girls home. After Middlewoman Li submitted the money to the government, the local headman wrote a note testifying to the fact that all of Magistrate Shi's family possessions and both surviving members of his household had been sold. The superiors of the deceased had to direct funds from other sources to make up for the shortfall, but that is no part of our story.

Let us turn now to Yuexiang, who never stopped sobbing after her father's death. And now, with no idea who Jia Chang was, she wept every step of the way, because she knew that the status of one bought with money could not be other than lowly and base. The maid said, "Miss, now that you're going to another family, it won't be like the old days when the master was alive. If you cry all the time like this, you'll surely be beaten and yelled at." These words plunged Yuexiang into even greater despair.

But Jia Chang turned out to be all kindness. Upon arriving at home, he said to his wife as he introduced them to her, "This is the daughter of my benefactor, Mr. Shi, and this is the maid serving the young lady. If it were not for Mr. Shi, I would have died in prison. The very sight of the young lady reminds me of my benefactor. Now, you get a nice room ready for them and serve them well with our best tea and food. Don't be negligent in any way. If any kinsmen of hers come to see her in the future, we can return her to them by way of showing our gratitude for her father's kindness. Otherwise, we'll wait until she comes of age and then marry her to a local young man of matching family background as his one and only wife, so that my benefactor will have his own kith and kin to look after his grave. (*This is exactly what will happen later.*) The maid will continue to serve the young lady and keep her company. Just give the maid some needlework to do. Don't make her run errands outside the house."

Being the clever and sensible girl she was, Yuexiang quickly stepped forward when Jia Chang had finished giving these instructions to his wife, and said with a deep curtsy, "Since I've been sold here, it's only right that I should do my duty as a servant. My benefactor being so kind as to give me a new lease on life, please accept a bow from me and take me on as an adopted daughter." With that, she fell to her knees.

Abhorring the thought of receiving homage from her, Jia Chang turned around to his wife and told her to raise the girl to her feet. "I was a humble subject of your father's," said he, addressing the girl. "To him I owe everything, including this worthless life of mine. I wouldn't even dream of being less than a perfect host to this maid, let alone you, Miss Shi! How would I dare give myself airs! As long as you are with us in this humble house, you are a distinguished guest to us. My wife and I will be honored if you don't think ill of us for not being generous enough." (*Jia Chang is indeed an honorable man who appreciates and returns favors done to him.*)

Yuexiang said her thanks over and over again. Jia Chang then directed all members of the household, male and female, to address the young lady as Miss Shi. The young lady addressed Jia Chang and his wife as Uncle Jia and Aunt Jia, but of this, no more.

In fact, Jia Chang's wife was not a kind-hearted woman. She was impressed by Yuexiang's refined looks and good sense and therefore had a mind to adopt her as a daughter because she herself was childless. So she was overjoyed at first, but when she was told to treat the girl as a distinguished guest, she began to be somewhat displeased. However, the debt of gratitude to Magistrate Shi was not something for her to write off easily, so she had no choice but to follow her husband's instructions and play along, however reluctantly.

Later, on his business trips away from home, Jia Chang often sent back the finest silk and fabric he could lay his hands on, for Miss Shi to make clothes with. As soon as he returned home, he would first inquire after Miss Shi. His wife grew resentful. As time wore on, she began to drop her pretenses. Whenever Jia Chang was home, she served the young lady her daily meals regularly in observance of proper etiquette and managed to say a few nice words false-heartedly. But when Jia Chang was away, it was a different story. No decent meals and tea were to be had, and the maid was kept busy all the time doing chores around the house. Every day Miss Shi had a needlework quota to fulfill. If the young lady was not quick enough, Mrs. Jia would vent her spleen on one pretext or another and burst into very audible expletives. Truly,

> No act of kindness lasts a thousand days;
> No flower stays in bloom for a hundred days.

Resenting the way they were being treated, the maid advised the young lady to let Uncle Jia know the truth the next time he returned home. Yuexiang rejected the idea outright, saying, "I've never expected any royal treatment since the day he bought me. Aunt Jia may be less than a perfect hostess, but this has nothing to do with Uncle Jia. If you complain about her, we'll lose even Uncle Jia's good will. You and I are born to suffer. The best thing to do is put up with it." (*This girl is of high moral character.*)

One day, on his way back home from a business trip, Mr. Jia ran into the maid as she was drawing water outside the house. Noticing her changed appearance, with her face thin and sallow, Jia said, "I told you to take care of Miss Shi only. You are not supposed to do chores like drawing water. Put the bucket down and have someone else do it."

As she put down the water bucket, the girl was seized with a pang of grief and a few teardrops stole down her cheeks. Mr. Jia was about to ask her why, but she rushed back into the house, wiping her tears with a hand. Feeling apprehensive, Mr. Jia asked his wife as soon as he saw her, "Is there anything the matter with Miss Shi and the maid?"

"No," answered his wife.

There being too many things for him to attend to upon first returning home, Mr. Jia put the matter aside. A few days later, when he came back home from a visit to some neighbors and didn't see his wife around, Mr. Jia headed for the kitchen to look for her for a chat. On his way there, he ran into the maid, who had just emerged from the kitchen, carrying no tray but just a big bowl of rice in her right hand and, in her left hand, an inverted empty bowl topped by a dish of pickles. Jia purposely stepped back out of her line of vision and watched her as she entered Miss Shi's room. Wondering whom this meatless humble meal was meant for, he turned away from the kitchen and went noiselessly to Miss Shi's room to peer through the chink between the double doors. Lo and behold! it was Miss Shi who was eating the rice and the pickles. (*Mr. Jia is a man who keeps his eyes open.*)

Mr. Jia was incensed. When he berated his wife, she retorted, "I've got plenty of meat and fish dishes and I don't begrudge them, but if that girl doesn't come to get them, do I have to go and personally deliver them?"

"I told you that the maid's job is just to keep Miss Shi company in her room. We have enough servants to work in the kitchen. Why would you need her to leave Miss Shi's room to fetch and carry? A couple of days ago, when I saw her tearfully drawing water outside, I suspected that she must be having a hard time at home, but I was too busy at the time to ask her what the matter was. Now I see what's going on. You know nothing of gratitude and loyalty. How dare you mistreat Miss Shi! With plenty of meat and fish dishes in the house, why give her only plain rice? And this happens when I'm at home, too! When I was away, you must have begrudged even the rice and starved them, which is why I find them so thin and sallow."

"She's another man's daughter," said his wife. "Why do you dote on her like that? Do you mean to feed her until she's all rosy-cheeked and aglow with health so that you can take her on as a concubine?"

"What nonsense is this! I'm not going to bandy words with someone as unreasonable as you are. Starting from tomorrow, I'll have the butler buy an extra portion of meat and vegetables every day for them and tell him not to charge the expense to the family account, so as not to take from you and make you unhappy."

Feeling that she was indeed somewhat in the wrong, the wife mumbled something before she fell silent. (*Vivid.*) Henceforth, Mr. Jia had the butler divide the daily purchases of meat and vegetables into two portions and told the kitchen maids to deliver the meals separately. For a time, everything went well. Truly,

> *Would that feelings on first acquaintance remain unchanged,*
> *So that no rancor could ever raise its ugly head!*

Worried about Miss Shi's well-being, Jia Chang forsook his business trips and stayed at home for more than a year. His wife went out of her way to make up with him. Nothing further was said about the matter, and all unpleasantness was forgotten.

After living with the Jias for five years, Yuexiang came of age. Jia Chang's plan was to discreetly find a good match for her. Only after she was married off would he put his mind at ease and resume his business trips. He went about quietly to relieve himself of this weight on his mind without informing his wife, for he believed it useless to consult that wicked woman. If things worked out and the girl could be married off along with a dowry, wouldn't that be quite a relief? However, a good match was not easy to come by, and with reason: Mr. Jia refused to marry the girl beneath her station to some candidate of humble background, so as not to insult the memory of Magistrate Shi. But those from families with even the slenderest claim to distinction would never stoop to take as wife someone living on the charity of a commoner. And so, no marriage offers came his way.

Since his marriage plans were not working, his wife appeared subdued and meek, and rules for the distribution of family provisions were well established, Mr. Jia felt he could not afford to neglect his business any longer but had to undertake another journey. Several days before his departure, he reminded his wife about ten times to take good care of Miss Shi and the maid. He also asked Miss Shi to come out of her room and comforted her with kind words. He had many nice words even for the maid. To his wife, he said, "She has much more strength of character than you have. Don't you ever treat her with disrespect! If you don't do as I say, I'll divorce you next time I come back." He then summoned the butler and the kitchen maids and gave them proper instructions before taking to the road.

> *He took pains leaving instructions behind*
> *To pay an old debt of profound kindness.*

To get on with our story, Jia Chang's wife resented the respectful way her husband treated Miss Shi and the maid, but she had not been able to do otherwise than let him have his way. Thus pent up with silent fury, she began to assert herself as the mistress of the house three days after her husband's departure. When a kitchen maid was late in serving tea and meal, Mrs. Jia took advantage of the minor offense and gave her a quick succession of slaps across the face by way of testing the waters, saying, "You cheap hussy! Don't you eat out of my hands? How dare you put on such airs? How dare you not wait on me hand and foot just because you have the backing of your little mistress? The master pampered you when he was home. Now that he's away, what I say goes, just as before! Who's there to wait on apart from me? At mealtime, let them come out and get the food themselves. You need not shower attentions on them at my expense!"

After this outburst, she called the butler to her amid the commotion and told him to stop buying food for the two girls separately but to put the money that Mr. Jia had earmarked for them back into the family budget. The butler dared not object. Luckily, Yuexiang was the kind of person who could put up with hardships, and she took everything in stride.

One day some time later, Yuexiang's maid went out to fetch warm water for washing. Being a little late, she found the water already cold. She mumbled something, as she should not have done. Upon hearing her, Mrs. Jia called the girl over and exploded, "You did not help carry this water into the house. Why don't you just make do with whatever water someone else happens to be heating? When you were staying with the middlewoman, who ever bothered to heat up water for you to wash your face with?"

Unable to curb her own tongue, the maid shot back, "Who wanted them to carry water and heat it for me? I've carried water before, and I know how to build a fire. Next time, I'll carry water and heat it myself without having to bother my sisters in the kitchen."

What the girl said about having carried water before put words in Mrs. Jia's mouth. "Little slut!" she cursed. "You carried just a few loads of water, and you had to make a fuss about it and complain to the master, all tears. What humiliation you put me through! Now, it's time we get even! Since you say you can carry water and build a fire, well, I'll let you do these things. You will carry all the water needed in the house every day and make sure we don't run short. And you will take care of the kitchen fire. If you use too much firewood, I won't let you off easy. You can wait until your tender loving daddy returns home to sob out your story to him. He can't turn me out of the house!" (*Exactly the tone of a vicious woman.*)

Hearing this stream of verbal abuse from Mrs. Jia at her personal maid, Yuexiang rushed over and bowed in apology. Putting the blame squarely on herself, she begged for Aunt Jia's forgiveness. The maid said, "But it's all my fault! Please don't take offense, for the sake of my mistress!"

This remark added to the woman's fury. "Mistress my foot! If she were a mistress, she shouldn't have come to this family in the first place! I'm too lowly to know her ladyship's exact rank, but don't you try every so often to scare me off with that grand title! I may be a humble woman, but I don't take that kind of bullying! Now let's make things abundantly clear. Even if she *were* some kind of a mistress, she is not to be referred to as such. She was bought with a lot of money. *I am the mistress of the house, not she! She's no Mrs. Jia!*" (*She does have a quick answer to everything.*)

Distressed by Mrs. Jia's reaction, Yuexiang returned to her room with tears in her eyes. Mrs. Jia ordered the kitchen maids not to call her "Miss Shi" but just plain "Yuexiang," and told Yuexiang's maid that she was not to go into Yuexiang's room but only to carry water and attend to the fire in the kitchen, and that Yuexiang was to fetch her own meals from the kitchen. That evening, Mrs. Jia had one of her servants carry the bedding of Miss Shi's maid to her, Mrs. Jia's, room. Yuexiang stayed up late that night, waiting in vain for her maid to return, and in the end resignedly closed the door and went to sleep alone. A few days later, Mrs. Jia called Yuexiang out of her room and then ordered a maid to lock up the door. Without a room to return to, Yuexiang had to walk up and down outside. At night, she shared her maid's bed. As soon as Yuexiang rose in the morning, Mrs. Jia began to order her around and make her fetch and carry. How would someone standing under low eaves dare not to keep the head lowered, as the proverb goes? Yuexiang had no choice but to submit humbly to Mrs. Jia's will. Inwardly rejoicing over Yuexiang's submission, Mrs. Jia suddenly had the girl's room unlocked and everything in it removed. All the fine silk and satin that her husband had sent home to the girl, including clothes already made out of them, went into her own trunks. She even had the girl's bedding taken away. Yuexiang moaned to herself in despair but dared not say anything out loud.

One day, a letter came from Mr. Jia, along with a good many gifts for Miss Shi. The letter said, among other things, "Take good care of her. I'll be coming back soon." When putting the gifts away, the woman thought, "I've been making the two girls' lives miserable enough. He won't let me off easy after he comes back. But I'm not going to pander to them all over again out of fear of that husband of mine! Who knows what that old turtle's going to do with those two hussies, supporting them like that? He said before he left that if I didn't do as he said, he would divorce me the next time he came back. He must be up to something evil. That Yuexiang is quite a young woman now, and a very pretty one, too. He may be thinking of keeping her for himself. It'll be too late if I try to fight it out with her by then. As the saying goes, 'He who doesn't plan for the future will run into trouble soon enough.' Since I've already come so far, why don't I make a final move and sell the two of them off to some faraway place? What can the old turtle do after he comes back other than give me a good talking-to? Having a violent scene is the worst that can happen. He can hardly go so far as to buy them back. What a brilliant plan!" Truly,

> The shortsighted lack a noble spirit;
> The small-minded are prone to hatching schemes.

Right away, the woman called the butler to her and said, "Get Middlewoman Zhang here for me. I need to talk with her." Soon the butler brought Madam Zhang to her. After introducing the guest to Yuexiang and the maid, Mrs. Jia dismissed the two girls and said to Zhang, "We bought those two girls six years ago. Now the older one is too old and the younger one is too pampered and delicate to be of much use around the house. So I'd like to sell them off. Please find me a buyer, and be quick about it!"

Mrs. Li had been the middlewoman acting on behalf of the government, but she had died, and Madam Zhang was now looked up to as the best one in that line of business. Madam Zhang said, "It just so happens that I have here a good candidate for the younger one. I'm only afraid you will object."

"Why would I object?" said Mrs. Jia.

"The magistrate of our county, Mr. Zhongli Yi, a native of Shouchun, has promised his daughter to the oldest son of Magistrate Gao of De'an County. The betrothal gifts have been delivered, and the bridegroom will soon come to get the bride. Magistrate Zhongli has prepared the dowry. Everything is ready now except that they still need a maidservant for the bride. Yesterday, the magistrate told me to find one for him, but I didn't have anyone in mind. Now, your girl is just the right person. I'm only afraid that you might hate to send her off to such a faraway place."

Mrs. Jia thought, "A buyer from a faraway place is exactly what I've been hoping for. This offer can't suit me better! Also, since it's a county magistrate's son, my man won't dare say anything after he comes back." Aloud, she said, "To be part of the dowry of an official's daughter is ten times better than being stuck with me. Why would I refuse to let her go? There's one thing though: don't pay me less than what I paid for her."

"How much did you pay?"

"Fifty taels of silver when she was about ten, plus all the money spent on food."

"Money spent on food doesn't count, but I'll sure take care of the fifty taels."

"And then there's that older maidservant. Please also find a family for her. The two came together. With one gone, I can't very well keep the other. What's more, she's over twenty now, old enough to want to marry. Why would I want to keep her?"

"How much do you ask for her?"

"I paid thirty taels for her."

"A lowly maid like that is not worth that much. If you could knock off half of it, I have a thirty-year-old nephew for her. I've promised him a wife, but I've been dragging my feet because I'm short of money. They'll make a nice couple."

"Since it's your nephew, I'll take off five taels."

"Take off ten, and that includes payment to me for the younger girl's disposal."

"All right, nothing to it. You just go ahead and pull the job off."

"I'll go and report to the county magistrate first. If he agrees, money and goods can change hands."

"Are you coming back this evening?"

"I need to talk to my nephew this evening. I won't have time to come back. I'll let you know the answer early tomorrow morning. Both deals will most likely pull through." With that, she took her leave and went her way. More of this later.

Let us rather talk now of County Magistrate Zhongli Yi, who had been in office for fifteen months. He was successor to Magistrate Ma, who had been, in his turn, successor to Magistrate Shi. (*Clear and straightforward.*) Magistrate Zhongli and Magistrate Gao of De'an County had come from the same village. Magistrate Gao had two sons. The older one, Gao Deng, was eighteen years old now, and the younger one, Gao Sheng, was sixteen. Gao Deng was Magistrate Zhongli's betrothed son-in-law. Magistrate Zhongli had no son but only one daughter, called Ruizhi. Seventeen years of age now, she was to be married on the fifteenth day of the tenth month that year. The end of the ninth month was already approaching at this point in our story, bringing the wedding day nearer and nearer. Magistrate Zhongli having approached Madam Zhang in his eagerness to find a maid for the bride, the middlewoman now went for a report about Mrs. Jia's offer.

"If the girl is good, fifty taels is not too much," said the magistrate. "Come tomorrow to claim the money from the treasury. Be sure to bring her over tomorrow evening."

"I will do as you wish, sir," said Madam Zhang.

Upon returning home that evening, Madam Zhang told her nephew, Zhao Er, about the good marriage deal for him. The news kept him in jubilance throughout the night. The next morning, he set about preparing the clothes for his wedding. At home Madam Zhang put together the twenty taels of silver that had been settled on and went to the county yamen to get the magistrate's note of authorization, with which she then claimed fifty taels from the county treasury. Upon arriving at the Jia residence, she handed the two piles of silver to Mrs. Jia with clear explanations. Mrs. Jia put them away. A few moments later, two yamen runners and two men carrying a small sedan-chair, sent by the county yamen, appeared at the gate of the Jia residence. No one in the Jia family had let on any of this to Yuexiang beforehand. When she was so abruptly told to mount the sedan-chair without being given a clue as to where she was going, she and her maid cried with abandon at the top of their voices. Ignoring their wails of grief, Mrs. Jia and Madam Zhang pushed and shoved Yuexiang all the way out of the gate. It was only then that Madam Zhang explained, "Now, young lady, stop crying. Your mistress has sold you to the county magistrate to be part of his daughter's dowry. It's a gorgeous place you're going to! Now that the deal has been made, crying won't help, and a government yamen is no playground." In resignation, Yuexiang held back her tears, mounted the sedan-chair, and let herself be carried into a rear chamber in the yamen.

When brought into the presence of Magistrate Zhongli Yi, Yuexiang merely dropped a curtsy. Madam Zhang, who was off to one side, said, "This is the magistrate himself. Get down and kowtow!"

Yuexiang had to comply. When she rose to her feet, tears fell thick and fast down her cheeks without her knowing it. Madam Zhang had her wipe her face dry and led her to the private quarters of the yamen to see the magistrate's wife and daughter Ruizhi. When asked her name, she said, "Yuexiang."

"What a nice name—Moon Fragrance!" said Mrs. Zhongli. "It doesn't need to be changed. All right, let her serve my daughter."

Mr. Zhongli gave Madam Zhang a handsome reward, but this is no concern of ours here.

> *How sad that the pampered daughter of an official*
> *Now takes orders from another.*

It was already late in the afternoon when Madam Zhang left the yamen. When she arrived at the Jia residence, Yuexiang's maid, sorely missing Yuexiang, was sobbing in the kitchen. Mrs. Jia was saying to her, "I've married you to Madam Zhang's nephew. It's a regular one-husband, one-wife marriage. So you're better off than Yuexiang. Stop crying!"

Madam Zhang offered the girl some comforting words.

Zhao Er took a bath in a public bathhouse and, well decked-out from head to toe, went to meet his bride, a lantern in his hand. Madam Zhang had the girl bid farewell to Mrs. Jia and, the girl's feet having never been bound, Madam Zhang took her arm and walked with her all the way home for the wedding.

Let us not encumber our story with unnecessary details but come back to Yuexiang. The very second day after she entered Magistrate Zhongli's household, Mrs. Zhongli told her, as the newly acquired maidservant, to sweep the middle hall. Yuexiang obediently took a broom and went off. In the meantime, Zhongli Yi washed himself, did his hair, took care of some business for his morning court session, and stepped out of the middle hall, only to see the new maidservant standing in the courtyard, as if in a trance, with a broom in hand. Mr. Zhongli felt intrigued. (*A wonderful story that moves one to tears.*) He stole up and saw that Yuexiang, her face awash in tears, was staring at an earthen pit in the courtyard. A bewildered Mr. Zhongli went back into the middle hall, summoned Yuexiang to him, and asked her to explain. All the more distraught, Yuexiang said that she would not dare do so. It was only at Mr. Zhongli's insistence that she fought back her tears and said, "This is the very place where my father had taught me how to kick a ball when I was a child. Once when the ball fell into this pit, my father asked me, 'Can you think of a way to make the ball come out by itself without anyone reaching down for it?' I said that I knew what to do. I had my maid fill the pit with water, and the ball rose to the surface. My father said I was smart and was very pleased. That happened a long time ago, but I still remember it. It's the sight of this pit that saddens me. Please have pity and forgive me!"

Mr. Zhongli was flabbergasted. "Who is your father? How did you get here when you were a child? Tell me everything."

"My father, Shi Bi, was the magistrate of this county six years ago. Because a fire of natural cause burned down the county granary, the imperial court removed my father from his post and ordered him to pay for the loss. He died from illness and sorrow. The government sold me and my maid to Mr. Jia of the same county. Mr. Jia is grateful to my father for having once saved him from a false charge and therefore provided for me and treated me most kindly. But while he was away on business, his wife, who hates to keep me in the house, sold me off here. Everything I've said is true."

> *At this sad story poured out from the heart,*
> *Even a man of iron or stone would melt in tears.*

As the saying goes, "Just as a fox mourns the death of a hare, one grieves for one's own kind." Magistrate Zhongli thought, "Shi Bi was a county magistrate, and so am I. It was all because disaster befell him at a luckless moment in his life that his daughter has now been reduced to a lowly servant. It wouldn't have mattered if I had never learned of this, but now that heaven has sent her to me, I would be insulting the dignity of a fellow official if I didn't do anything for her. And Mr. Shi under the Nine Springs will hold me in contempt."[6]

Right away, he called his wife to him and gave her a full account of Yuexiang's background. His wife said, "So she's the daughter of a county magistrate. How can we treat her as a lowly maid? (*Mrs. Zhongli is also a kind person.*) But our daughter's wedding day is approaching. What are you going to do?"

Mr. Zhongli replied, "From now on, we must not let Yuexiang do any chores around the house. She and our daughter will address each other as sister. I know what to do next." There and then, he wrote a letter and had it delivered to Magistrate Gao, his daughter's future father-in-law. Magistrate Gao opened it and found that it was a request for a postponement of the wedding. The letter read as follows:

> *However parents may wish to see their children married, sacrifice of self-interest in the service of others is a nobler undertaking. In preparation for my daughter's wedding, I recently purchased for her a maid by the name of Yuexiang. Quite surprised by her delicate beauty and graceful manners, I asked about her background and learned that she is the daughter of Mr. Shi, magistrate of this county before my immediate predecessor. Mr. Shi was a good and honest official.* (If he were not a good and honest official, there wouldn't have been such compassion for him.) *A fire in the granary cost him his job and his life, and his daughter was sold by the government. And later, by another sale, she came to my humble home. Being the daughter of a fellow official, she is also like my daughter, and, having come of age, she must not be reduced to the status of a maid, nor should my daughter marry before she does. My pressing priority for the moment is to select a husband for her, and I shall provide her with my own daughter's modest dowry.* (Who else would

be willing to do this?) *Therefore, your son's wedding day will have to be slightly postponed. I plead to be forgiven.*

Humbly yours,
Zhongli Yi

After reading the letter, Magistrate Gao said, "I see! Well, I'm not going to let Mr. Zhongli get all the credit in this act of kindness to a venerable predecessor!" Straightaway he wrote a letter of reply:

Even though a date has indeed been set for the wedding, the grief of the fox for the hare is a shared sentiment. If you, sir, treat a fellow official's daughter as your own, how can I not be of one mind with you? Your letter which I have read over and over again fills my heart with grief. This young lady being the daughter of a good official and worthy of any eminent clan, I propose that she be granted to my son and that the wedding take place on the date already chosen. (Who else would be willing to do this?) *Your daughter will thus be free to find a better match. Wouldn't that work out nicely in more ways than one? In the old days, Qu Boyu thought it a shame to claim to himself all the credit for gentlemanly integrity.[7] And now, this humble servant wishes to join you in this act of kindness.*

Yours humbly,
Gao Yuan

After reading the letter presented by the messenger, Mr. Zhongli said, "It is all very magnanimous for Mr. Gao to take an orphan as daughter-in-law, but my daughter and his son have been betrothed to each other for a long time now. How can that be changed? We'd better not rush things but wait until I marry off Miss Shi before preparing another dowry for my own daughter's wedding." Right away he wrote a reply and had it delivered to Mr. Gao, who unsealed the letter and read as follows:

It is a noble act to marry an orphan girl, but it is hardly right and proper to change a pledge of marriage. My daughter and your son have long been betrothed to each other and are destined for a harmonious union. On the part of your son, to abandon his intended wife and marry another would be to violate a time-honored code of conduct; on the part of my daughter, to give up her intended husband in favor of another would be to invite denunciation. Please think again. I trust that you will agree to what I proposed in my last letter.

Respectfully yours,
Yi

(These four letters are absent from all collections of morally edifying letters of correspondence.)

After reading the letter, Mr. Gao said to himself with a sigh, "I didn't think carefully in the rush of the moment. These words of Mr. Zhongli's are enough to make me want to sink into the ground in shame. Now I've got an idea that's perfect every way we look at it. It will fulfill Mr. Zhongli's wish and, at the same time, let me share his credit, and pass on our reputation to posterity." Then and there, he wrote a reply that read,

My proposal for switching the two young ladies was made out of the best intentions, but you were absolutely right in saying that to abandon an intended wife and marry another would be a violation of a time-honored code of conduct. I have a younger son, Gao Sheng, seventeen years of age, who is yet unbetrothed. If your daughter marries my eldest son and Miss Shi marries my younger son, we will bring about blissful marriages of two fine couples and a noble friendship between the dead and the living that transcends all time. Dowries can be dispensed with in celebration of the joyous occasion. (Good choice of words in a lyrical style.) But I humbly defer to you. The chosen date need not be changed.

Respectfully yours,
Yuan

Mr. Zhongli was overjoyed upon reading the letter. "Now this is a solution that will satisfy everyone. Mr. Gao is indeed as much of a man of honor as the ancients. I am not his equal." Immediately he talked to his wife and set about dividing the dowry into two equal portions. Some clothes and jewelry were added to each portion in equal amounts. No favoritism was shown to either of the two girls.

Two days before the fifteenth day of the tenth lunar month, Mr. Gao engaged two nicely adorned sedan-chairs, and the procession, complete with a band of musicians that included players of *sheng* pipes and *xiao* flutes, set off to the brides' house to bring the brides over. Mr. Zhongli sent the dowry procession on its way first before summoning the two girls, Ruizhi and Yuexiang, so that his wife could give them a lecture on wifely duties. The two girls then bade them farewell and set out on the journey.

Overwhelmed by her gratitude to Mr. Zhongli and his wife for their kindness, Yuexiang could not bear parting with them, and it was with loud wails of grief that she mounted her sedan-chair. How the journey went need not be gone into here, but it so happened that the procession arrived at Mr. Gao's residence in the county yamen at a most auspicious hour of the horoscope. The two young couples, arrayed in finery, made bows to the grooms' parents and drank the nuptial wine, to the boundless joy of Magistrate Gao and his wife. Truly,

Their hundred-year unions start from today
In blissful matches made by destiny.

Let us get on with the story. On the third night after the wedding, Mr. Zhongli had a dream in which an official with a scarf over his head and an ivory tablet in his hand appeared before him and said, "I am Shi Bi, Yuexiang's father, former magistrate of this county. I died in grief because I was not able to pay for the loss caused by a fire in the granary. The Lord on High, recognizing my integrity as an official and my innocence of any wrongdoing, took pity on me and made me the tutelary god of this county. *(Have good officials ever been shortchanged?)* Yuexiang is my beloved daughter. It was most kind of you to have freed her from her dire circumstances and given her a good marriage. This is a good deed that earns you credit in the netherworld. I have already reported as much to the Lord on High. You were not destined to have any male issue, but, in view of your kind deed, the Lord on High has granted you a son, so that your family line will continue and prosper. You yourself will attain high office and live to a ripe old age. Mr. Gao, magistrate of your neighboring county, has also gained the favor of the Lord on High by sharing your thoughts and taking an orphan girl as daughter-in-law. Both his two sons will therefore attain high office with matching remuneration as a reward for his kind deed. You will spread this story among the public and exhort people to perform acts of kindness wherever they are, never to bully the weak and vulnerable or profit themselves at the expense of others, for Heaven has eyes that never miss even the minutest detail."

With that, he took a bow. Mr. Zhongli bowed deeply in return.

When rising to his feet, Mr. Zhongli tripped over the front part of his long robe and fell. Upon waking up with a start, he realized that it had all been a dream. Without losing a moment, he told his wife about it, and she also sighed with emotion. After daybreak, Mr. Zhongli went by sedan-chair to the temple of the local god and held an incense-offering ceremony. He also donated one hundred taels from his government salary and asked the priests to renovate the temple and have the story written and inscribed on a monument to acquaint the public with it. Then he wrote a letter to Mr. Gao, informing him about the dream in detail. Mr. Gao, in his turn, showed the letter to his two sons, much to their amazement. Mrs. Zhongli, already past forty years of age, suddenly conceived and in due time gave birth to a son, whom they named Tianci [Granted by Heaven]. Later, Zhongli pledged allegiance to the imperial court of the Song dynasty and rose in rank until he became Grand Academician of the Dragon Diagram Hall[8] and died in his nineties. His son Tianci became a *zhuangyuan* of the Song dynasty. Gao Deng and Gao Sheng both attained official posts and rose to be ministers in the imperial court. But all of this happened later.

Now let us come back to the point when Jia Chang, back from his travels, could not find Yuexiang and the maid. After he found out what had happened, he made quite a few violent scenes with his wife. Later, he learned that Mr. Zhongli had taken Yuexiang on as a daughter and married her as well as his own daughter to the Gao family. Without a better way of showing his good will, Jia Chang offered twenty taels of silver to redeem the maid so as to return her to Miss Shi, but the maid and her husband Zhao Er had come to love each other so much that they could not bear to separate from each other and preferred to go together to serve Yuexiang. Middlewoman Zhang tried to stop them, but to no avail. Jia Chang took Zhao Er and his wife all the way to De'an County to see Magistrate Gao. After a thorough questioning of the visitors, the magistrate went to the private quarters of the yamen to ask his daughter-in-law Yuexiang if what Zhao Er and his wife said was true, and she confirmed their words. He kept Zhao Er and his wife, and offered Jia Chang a handsome reward, but Jia turned down the offer and went back home. Jia Chang hated his wife for her treachery and vowed never to be with her again. He took another wife, who bore him two sons. This is also a reward for acts of kindness. A poet of later times had this to say:

> All want to marry to their advantage;
> Who would wish to take an orphan girl?
> Consider how Heaven rewards those two;
> Heaven never betrays the good at heart.

Three Devoted Brothers Win Honor by Yielding Family Property to One Another

The redbud tree held the clan together;
The Calyx quilt covered all five brothers.
Siblings share the same breath of life;
The age-old "Beanstalks" poem still evokes shame.

This poem uses three stories to exhort brothers to live in harmony with one another. Dear audience, please allow me to present the stories one by one. The first line "The redbud tree held the clan together," alludes to the story about three brothers of a Tian family who lived under the same roof ever since they were born. The eldest one took a wife, who came to be called Big Sister Tian. The second brother also married, and his wife came to be called Second Sister Tian. The two sisters-in-law lived in harmony with never an unkind word for each other. The third son, much younger than the first two, lived with his older brothers and sisters-in-law. Later, after coming of age, he also took a wife, who came to be called Third Sister Tian. Now, this Third Sister Tian was a wicked one. Made presumptuous by her abundant dowry, she felt entitled to be displeased at the way the whole family, brothers and sisters-in-law, ate at the same table from the same pot of rice. With no private accounts or scales to weigh out separate portions of provisions, she could not very well have anything to eat for her own personal enjoyment. Day and night, she kept urging her husband to do something about it, saying, "The ancestral hall, the treasury, and the land properties are all in the hands of your brothers. And you have absolutely no idea what's in those account books. They know everything but you're in the dark. How can you tell if they are playing games with the numbers? We may be living together under the same roof now, but eventually we'll go our separate ways. If the family fortune goes on the decline, you, the youngest son, will be the hardest hit! (*The evil-minded are always ready to confuse right and wrong.*) As I see it, the best thing to do is divide the family property into three portions as soon as possible, so that each brother can do what he wants with his portion. Wouldn't that be nice?"

Third Brother fell for her clever words. Convinced that she was right, he asked a relative to put to his brothers the idea of dividing the family property and living as separate families. They rejected the idea at first, but Third Brother and his wife, in alliance with people outside the family, kept up the pressure on them. Finally they gave in and divided the family property, including the house, the cash, and the grain in storage, into three exactly equal portions. But what was to be done about the large flourishing redbud tree that had been standing in the yard for generations? If everything else was to be divided, to whom should this tree belong? Even though it was in full blossom, which was all the more unfortunate, Tian the Eldest proposed, with his usual selflessness, to cut it down and divide the trunk into three sections, one for each brother. The branches and the foliage were to be weighed out and also divided into three portions. Having reached agreement, they decided to take action the next day. At daybreak, Tian the Eldest took his two brothers to the yard to cut the tree. When drawing near it, they saw that its branches had withered and its leaves had all shrunk. It looked more dead than alive. As Tian the Eldest gave it a push, it fell down, exposing all its roots. Tian the Eldest withdrew his hand and, facing the tree, burst into loud sobs. His two younger brothers said, "Is this tree worth your tears? Why grieve so much?"

"I'm crying not because of this tree," said Tian the Eldest, "but because the three of us, sharing the same family name and born of the same parents, are just like this tree whose branches and leaves grow from the same roots and are inseparable. The tree flourished because from the roots grew the trunk, from the trunk the branches, and from the branches the leaves. After we agreed yesterday to cut the tree into three portions, it was so grief-stricken that it withered and died in the night. If we three brothers split, we'll go the way of this tree. What prosperity will there be to speak of? That's why I cry." (*Words that are sincere and moving.*)

The two younger brothers were deeply moved by these words. "How can human beings have even less sense than a tree?" said they as all three of them fell on one another's shoulders and burst into loud sobs. Loathing the thought of separation, they decided to continue living together in the same house. Hearing the sobs outside the house, the three wives went out to see what it was all about. Big Sister and Second Sister were overjoyed upon learning what had happened, but Third Sister was displeased and raised protests. Third Brother wanted to drive her out, but the two older brothers talked him out of the idea. Third Sister returned to her room in shame and hanged herself. This is a case of "those creating trouble for themselves being doomed to self-destruction." But so much for her.

Let us get on with our story. Worried about the redbud tree, Tian the Eldest went again to look at it and found that even without anyone taking care of it, it was standing up again. The withered branches had regained life, and the flowers were blooming in greater splendor than before. He called over his two brothers, and everyone marveled at the sight. Henceforth, the Tian clan lived together under the same roof from generation to generation, as evidenced by the following poem:

> *The redbud blossoms and the Tian brothers*
> *Share the same lot, together or apart.*
> *They're born as one, the brothers and the branches;*
> *The words of that woman are best left unheeded.*

Now, the second line of the poem, "The Calyx quilt covered all five brothers," refers to Calyx Tower built in Chang'an [present-day Xi'an], Shaanxi, by Emperor Xuanzong, also known as Emperor Ming of Tang [r. 712–56]. Being a member of the imperial Tang house, he raised an army, killed Empress Wei, who had brought chaos to the court in collusion with the power-abusing Wu Sansi, and later assumed the throne.[1] All five of his brothers gained titles of nobility and came to be called the Five Princes. Out of love for his brothers, the emperor built a tower which he called Calyx Tower, alluding to the poem "The Bush Cherry" in the *Book of Songs*,[2] and often invited the five princes to the tower for feasts. He also had an oversize canopy hung up over the bed that he often shared with his five brothers on the same long pillow and under the same large quilt. The canopy came to be called the Five Princes' Canopy." There is a poem in evidence:

> *The Jie drums and jade flutes send the day on its way;[3]*
> *The feast in the grand tower ends with sunset.*
> *The palace maids sit through the night by the candles*
> *In disbelief that the monarch would not return.*

The fourth line of the poem, "The age-old 'Beanstalks' poem still evokes shame," is a reference to Cao Pi [187–226], eldest son of Cao Cao [155–220], who was Duke of Wei toward the end of the Han dynasty. Cao Pi, who betrayed the Han court and declared himself Emperor of Wei, had a younger brother Cao Zhi [192–232], courtesy name Zijian. Cao Zhi, with his peerless talent, was Cao Cao's favorite son, and the father had tried several times in his lifetime to make Cao Zhi his successor, but to no avail. Nursing a grudge against Cao Zhi, Cao Pi tried, after their father's death, to find some excuse and have this younger brother killed. One day, he called Zijian to him and asked, "The late duke often spoke highly of your quickness in composing poems. However, I have never tested you. Now, walk seven paces and finish a poem. If you fail, you will be convicted of fraud." Before taking the seventh step, Zijian had already made up a poem, which was full of admonition and sarcasm. This is how it goes:

> *As the beanstalks are lit to make a fire,*
> *The beans in the pot burst into sobs:*
> *Didn't we spring from the very same root?*
> *Why torment us with such ruthlessness?*

The poem moved Cao Pi to tears and dissolved all the pent-up rancor in his heart. A later poet had this to say:

The high and mighty never trust others;
The seven-step poem gave little protection.
How sad that while fratricidal hatred lasted,
Six rulers of the clan were all wiped out.[4]

Storyteller, why are you telling us these three stories? Well, because they lead to my story about three devoted brothers who won honor by yielding the family property to one another. These brothers had none of the deviousness of the jealous Cao Pi, nor were they blessed with the talent and grace of Cao Zhi, but they were more devoted to one another than even the three Tian brothers by the red-bud tree and the Li brothers in Calyx Tower. I advise those who fall out with their own brothers to listen to this story and mend their ways. Truly,

To know all that happens under the sun,
Be sure to read books by our ancestors.

Our story takes place during the reign of Emperor Guangwu [r. 25–58] of the Eastern Han dynasty [25–220], at a time when peace reigned throughout the land and the people lived in contentment. The court was filled with worthy ministers, and the public had no complaints about failure to appoint able men to office. The selection of officials in the Han dynasty was different from our times. Instead of our civil service examinations, the Han system was for prefectural and county authorities to recommend candidates for official posts. Criteria for recommendation included erudition, literary talent, personal integrity, and, in particular, filial piety and incorruptibility—filial piety because this quality ensures loyalty to the sovereign, and incorruptibility because it ensures devotion to the interests of the people. Those recommended on grounds of filial piety and incorruptibility were thus eligible for official posts.

The way things are nowadays, even a candidate for civil service examinations at the prefectural level would ask thousands of people to write letters for him to the examiner. If appointment for official posts were to be based on recommendations alone, goodness knows how many people would pull strings to get themselves recommended. When all is said and done, it's the sons of the rich and the powerful who would land all the posts. The poor may have the filial piety of Zeng Shen[5] and the incorruptibility of Boyi,[6] but gaining fame for themselves would be nothing more than a daydream. (*If a recommendation system could be implemented strictly, free of chicanery, there would be no lack of worthy men serving the country.*)

But the Han dynasty system was ingenious: if those recommended for being filial and incorrupt proved themselves to be indeed able and virtuous, they would be promoted rapidly regardless of their present status, and those who wrote the recommendation would also be rewarded and have their names entered in the records. On the other hand, if those recommended later turned out to be unworthy of the posts by taking bribes and bending the law, they would be stripped of their posts and, in more severe cases, their property would be confiscated, and those who had recommended them would be punished in the same way. Since those who put forward recommendations and those who received recommendations were thus bound together and therefore dared not act recklessly, justice prevailed throughout the land and rigorous discipline was maintained in the court. (*Records of this system should be copied and circulated among our contemporaries, so that readers can refer to it at all times of the day and know the good from the bad.*) But let me return to our story.

In Yangxian County, Huiji Prefecture [in present-day Jiangsu],[7] there lived a young man called Xu Wu, courtesy name Changwen. His parents died when he was fifteen. Even though they had left behind some land property and a few servants, family circumstances remained modest, and there was no one he could turn to for help. In addition, he had two younger brothers, one called Xu Yan, only nine years old, and the other called Xu Pu, only seven years old, who didn't know better than to follow him around all day, sobbing. By day, Xu Wu led the servants in tilling the fields and tending the vegetable garden. By night, he read his books by the lamp. His brothers were too young to take up the hoe, but he made sure that they watched him work in the fields. And when he did his reading, he sat the little boys by his desk, read aloud to them with detailed, sentence-by-sentence explications, and taught them the virtue of the willingness to yield and the gentleman's proper ways of behavior. Whenever the boys misbehaved, Xu Wu would fall on his knees in front of the family shrine, reproach himself bitterly for not having a strong enough moral character to influence the boys, and tearfully ask for his parents' spirits to enlighten them. He would not rise until his brothers were contrite and sobbingly asked for pardon, and he never said a harsh word to them or gave them a fierce look. With only one set of bedding in the house, the three brothers shared the same bed.

After some years went by in this way, the two younger brothers came of age and family circumstances gradually began to improve. To words of advice for him to marry, Xu Wu replied, "If I do, I'll have to live apart from my brothers. It would be too painful for me to abandon them in favor of conjugal happiness." And so he continued to till the land with them by day and study with them by night, sharing with them the same food utensils and the same bed. He began to be known throughout the area as Xu Wu the Devoted Brother. There also came into circulation the following four-line song:

> *Brother Xu Wu of Yangxian County*
> *Reads by night and works by day;*
> *The way he teaches his two brothers,*
> *He is nothing less than a parent.*

Upon hearing of his fame, officials of various prefectures submitted letters of recommendation to the imperial court, which accordingly decided to employ him as a court advisor. When the imperial edict was delivered to Huiji Prefecture, the prefect, in compliance with the edict, gave the magistrate of Yangxian County a deadline, ordering him to urge Xu Wu to accept the post. Knowing he could not very well reject an order from the emperor, Xu Wu gave his two brothers these instructions: "You go on working in the fields and applying yourself to your studies, just as before. Be sure never to slack off and abandon what you have accomplished, so as not to let our ancestors down."

To the servants, he said, "Do your job with care and follow the two masters' orders. Rise early and go to sleep late and help build up the family fortune." With that, he began packing for his journey. Dispensing with government vehicles, he hired a draft animal and a cart and, bringing along only a page boy, set off for Chang'an. Before many days had passed, he arrived in the capital and took up his post. Those in the city of Chang'an who had heard about Xu Wu the Devoted Brother came in droves to see him. Indeed, he was held in high esteem by the court, and his fame spread far and wide among the populace. A good number of court ministers, having found out that Xu Wu was still a bachelor, offered him marriage proposals on behalf of their daughters. Xu Wu thought, "My two brothers and I are all of marriageable age but still unbetrothed. If I marry before they do, I wouldn't be behaving like an older brother. In addition, it's only by a stroke of good luck that I, from a family of generations of scholar-farmers, get to be an official in the government. If I marry someone from a distinguished family, she is likely to give herself airs because of her impressive family background. This will not only disrupt our Xu family's way of life as simple scholar-farmers but also lead to discord among the sisters-in-law after my brothers marry, because their wives will be from poor and lowly families. Most fraternal fights are caused by the women. I must not let that happen to us."

Whatever his thoughts, he could not very well voice them aloud. So he resorted to subterfuges, saying that he had already been betrothed in his humble "chaff and husks" days and therefore dared not abandon his intended and marry another woman, so as not to become a laughingstock in the eyes of Song Hong.[8] (*This is a subterfuge rather than an outright lie.*) As a result, he rose even higher in people's esteem. As he was also well versed in the classics, court ministers often went to seek his guidance in matters of the court that they were unable to solve, and he would discuss key issues with them and cite cases past and present to support his arguments. He was so convincing that the court ministers set great store by his opinions. In a few years, he rose through a series of promotions to be censor-in-chief.

One day, Xu Wu wondered why his two younger brothers, in their assiduous studies over the years, had not received any recommendations from their district and prefecture. Afraid that they might have slackened their efforts and deviated from proper pursuits, he wanted to return to his home village for a visit. So he wrote a memorandum to the emperor, a shortened version of which reads as follows:

> *Being as unworthy as I am, I owe my eminent post solely to Your Majesty in your sagely wisdom. Before I repay Your Majesty's kindness, I should not presume to ask*

for leave. But, as the ancients said, "Of all human pursuits, filial piety and frater-
nal duty come first," and "Of the three kinds of unfilial offenses, the greatest is not
to have a son to carry on the family line." My parents having passed away a long
time ago, their graves have fallen into disrepair. My two younger brothers have not
yet been established in their academic careers, and I remain a bachelor at the age of
thirty. Of the five cardinal relationships [those between sovereign and subject, father
and son, husband and wife, among brothers, and among friends], three are missing
in my case. I therefore request that I be granted a brief sojourn to my home village.
I stand ready to resume my humble service at a later time.

After reading the memorandum, the emperor granted him his request and ordered that government courier stations provide him with means of transportation on his journey home. It was a journey of someone who had made his fortune returning in all his glory to his humble place of origin. The emperor also gave him twenty *jin*[9] of gold for his wedding expenses. Xu Wu thanked the emperor for his largesse before leaving the court. All the court officials accompanied him as far as the outskirts of the city. Truly,

> *Word spread that he was returning home in glory;*
> *All praised the one who had risen from humble roots.*

After returning home and attending to his parents' graves, Xu Wu sent back the emperor's letter of appointment, pleading illness, but in fact, he was unwilling to serve as an official anymore. After some time, he casually called his two brothers to him and tested them on their knowledge. To his immense joy, Xu Yan and Xu Pu answered his questions with fluent ease, sound reasoning, and good diction. When he checked the family account books, he saw that the land and the real estate of the family had increased several times, thanks to the two brothers' hard work and frugality. He began to search in the neighborhood for good and decent families with eligible young women, and found good matches for his two brothers. Only then did he himself marry. Soon thereafter, he held wedding ceremonies for his two brothers.

One day a few months later, he suddenly said to his brothers, "I understand that brothers should live apart. Now that you and I are all married and in possession of sizable land property, we should, by rights, establish our separate households." The two younger brothers respectfully voiced their willingness to do his bidding.

On a chosen day, a feast was laid out, to which all the elders in the neighborhood were invited. After three rounds of wine, Xu Wu declared that the brothers were to live apart. He summoned the servants and began to announce his plan for the division of the family property. Giving himself the largest house, he said, "Being a high-ranking official entitled to armed guards of honor at my gate, I must keep up appearances. As for farmers like the two of you, humble thatched cottages should suffice."

Going over the land book, he gave all the fertile farmland to himself, and poorer farmland to his two brothers, saying, "I have so many friends to entertain that anything less than this won't be enough to meet my needs. Since your two families won't suffer from cold and hunger as long as you work hard, I'm not going to let too much wealth compromise your moral character."

He then went on to take his pick of the stronger and smarter servants, saying, "I need them to follow me and take my orders wherever I go. Those of slower wit are just the right people to keep you company as you labor in the fields, and the older and weaker ones are just the right people to cook for you and serve you meals. And they don't cost you much, either!"

Having always known Xu Wu to be a man of filial devotion, the neighbors at the feast thought he would surely give more than he would take in the division of the family property. They never expected him to gain such advantages over his brothers in everything, with the two brothers getting less than half of what he kept for himself. The way he bullied his brothers rather than showing them any generosity so enraged the audience that several older men known for their bluntness left in a huff. (*If this happened in our day, everyone would be fawning upon the one wearing an official's hat. Who would be willing to say anything against the injustice of it all? This affords us a glimpse of the mores of the Han times.*) One man prone to speaking his mind freely was about to say something in defense of the two younger brothers when a more prudent man unobtrusively pinched him and told him not to speak up. And so the man remained silent.

The prudent one was not without insight. His reasoning went as follows, "The rich and the poor don't think alike. Xu Wu is a high-ranking official now. He's not the same man as before. As the saying goes, 'Blood is thicker than water.' Who are we to meddle in their family affairs? We may be offering advice out of the best intentions, but I don't think he will listen. We'll be wasting our breath—or worse, set the brothers against one another. If the younger ones are willing to yield to the oldest one, well and good. Why should we get all worked up? If the younger ones won't have it, they'll surely raise objections. We can wait until then to offer them ideas. Won't that be better?" (*Words of a wise man.*) Truly,

> Don't meddle in affairs not your own;
> Say no more if the talk turns sour.

As a matter of fact, being the kind of well-read and decorum-observing young men that the oldest brother had taught them to be, Xu Yan and Xu Pu gave the first importance to the virtues of filial piety and fraternal duty and fully accepted their brother's way of property division without the least bit of resentment. (*These brothers of the same sorry fate share the same nobility of mind.*)

After Xu Wu had finished his announcements, the crowd dispersed. Xu Wu took the grand house in the middle. Xu Yan and Xu Pu moved into smaller houses, one on the left and one on the right. Every day the two of them led the servants to the fields to till the soil and they took up their books when they had time to spare. Every so often, they would go to their oldest brother for explanations of things they didn't understand in their reading, and this became their settled way of life. The sisters-in-law followed their husbands' examples and enjoyed a harmonious relationship with one another, just as the three brothers did. Henceforth, the elders in the neighborhood held Xu Wu in contempt for his behavior and felt sorry for the two younger brothers. Among themselves they commented, "Xu Wu may have been recommended to the court for being filial and incorrupt, but he's a phony! Xu Yan and Xu Pu are the real filial and incorrupt ones. For their parents' sake, they are of one mind and eagerly obey the oldest one without ever doing anything against his will. Isn't this filial devotion? They put family values above money and don't argue over the division of property. Isn't this incorruptibility?"

Xu Wu had been known throughout the neighborhood as Xu Wu the Devoted Brother, but now the epithet was changed to the Devoted Xus. Xu Yan and Xu Pu came to be household names, and public opinion in those days in the Han dynasty carried enormous weight. There also came into circulation the following song:

> The phony one wins a title and a rank;
> The real, deserving ones pay the taxes.[10]
> The phony one takes the grand house;
> The real ones get tumbledown huts.
> The phony one owns all the rich farmland;
> The real ones wield hoes and sickles.
> The phony one is as worthless as a brick;
> The real ones are as good as jade.
> The worthless brick enjoys glory;
> The real jade is tossed away.
> Why bother to be genuine
> When phony ones get everything? (Nice song of early times.)

Upon ascending the throne, Emperor Ming [r. 58–76] issued a decree to seek the services of worthy men, ordering incumbent officials to find men of learning and moral integrity, visit them at their homes, offer them posts with all due ceremony, and send them by government means of transportation to the capital. When the decree reached Huiji Prefecture, the prefect notified the various counties, and the magistrate of Yangxian County submitted the names of Xu Yan and Xu Pu to the prefecture because he had already heard about how Xu Yan and Xu Pu had readily yielded portions of family property that rightfully belonged to them. Moreover, the local elders had recommended the two to him on account of their genuine scholarship and moral integrity, which was more than could be said for their older brother. The prefect and the district magistrate, both having also long heard about them, joined the county magistrate in the recommendation. The county magistrate personally went to their house. After he dismounted his carriage and asked to be admitted, he offered a gift of five bolts of black silk and conveyed to them the emperor's wish for the services of worthy men. Xu Yan and Xu Pu demurred.

Xu Wu said, "A gentleman is duty bound to put to use what he has learned from childhood on. My brothers, you must not decline."

The two younger men thus felt obliged to accept the offer. They bade Xu Wu and his wife farewell and undertook the journey to Chang'an by government-provided means of transportation. After the customary prostrations to the emperor were over, the Son of Heaven said, "Are you Xu Wu's younger brothers?"

Yan and Pu kowtowed and said yes. The emperor said, "We have heard that you are well known for your filial devotion. You surpass your oldest brother in your willingness to yield what rightfully belongs to you. (*In ancient times, good deeds were reported all the way from the village on up to the top, which was why people fell over one another trying to do good.*) We are very pleased to know that."

Yan and Pu said with a kowtow, "Your Majesty's search for worthy men at the start of the new reign is an act of boundless grace. It is too kind of the prefect and the magistrates to recommend us to Your Majesty in spite of our unworthiness. Since we lost our parents early in our childhood, we have been assiduously working in the fields and applying ourselves to our studies under the guidance of our oldest brother, Wu. We have done nothing more than that. We are far inferior to our oldest brother, Wu."

Upon hearing these words, the emperor praised them for their modesty. That very day, both of them were appointed as civil affairs administrators of the capital. In less than five years, they rose to the rank of cabinet ministers of the central government. Even though they did not gain as much fame as their oldest brother did, they were known throughout the imperial court for their willingness to yield.

One fine day, they received a letter from Xu Wu. Upon opening the envelope, they saw that on the stationery were written these words:

"No honor can be greater for a man of humble background than that of being appointed by the emperor as an official and rising through the ranks to be a court minister. As Shu Guang said to his nephew Shu Shou,[11] 'He who knows when to be content will be spared humiliation; he who knows when to stop will know no danger.' Since you are not in possession of outstanding talent, you would do well to retire while your career is still at its height, so as not to block the advance of worthier people."

After receipt of the letter, Yan and Pu handed in their resignation that very day, but the emperor rejected the request. When their resignation letter was submitted a third time, the emperor said to Song Jun, the prime minister, "We did not treat Xu Yan and Xu Pu shabbily. They started their careers at the prime of life and have risen to the rank of court ministers. Why do they insist on resigning?"

Song Jun replied, "The three Xu brothers are most devoted to one another. Yan and Pu, who are now serving in the court, may feel somewhat ill at ease because their brother is not."

"Shall We summon Xu Wu back and have the three brothers serve Us at the same time?"

"As I see it," said Song Jun, "Yan and Pu are sincere in their wish to resign. Your Majesty might as well approve their request now so as to gratify them in their noble-mindedness, but summon them to serve again sometime in the future. Another option is to follow the practice of the previous dynasty and assign each of them a large prefecture in the vicinity of their hometown so that they can do full justice to their talent, which would otherwise be underutilized. If their posts are so conveniently located, Your Majesty's desire for the services of worthy men and Yan and Pu's devotion to their brother will both be satisfied."

The emperor agreed. Right away, he appointed Xu Yan as prefect of Danyang Prefecture and Xu Pu as prefect of Wu Prefecture, and bestowed upon each of them twenty *jin* of gold and a three-month-long leave of absence, so that they could spend some time with their oldest brother. Xu Yan and Xu Pu thanked the emperor for his bounty and left the imperial court. The assembly of officials seeing them off went all the way out of the city gate to a wayside pavilion ten li from the city and offered them farewell toasts.

Yan and Pu hurried posthaste back to Yangxian County and, after saluting their brother Wu, offered him the entire amount of the gold bestowed by the court. Xu Wu said, "How would I presume to take what His Majesty gave you!" And so he told his brothers to keep the gold for themselves. The next day, Xu Wu prepared sacrificial offerings of pig, sheep, and ox, and led the two brothers to their parents' graves for a memorial service. He then laid out a feast to which all the elders in the neighborhood were invited. The three Xu brothers now being high-ranking officials, even though they didn't put on airs, theirs were names that inspired awe. No one declined the invitation, especially when the invitation was issued in all politeness. Xu Wu personally filled the wine cups of all the assembled elders of the neighborhood. The guests said, "This is a dinner Master Changwen laid out to welcome Second Older Brother and Third Older Brother. How would this bunch of old men presume to be the first ones to drink?"

Those were times when social customs were devoid of pretentiousness. Even though Xu Wu had been appointed a court official long ago, he was still addressed by his courtesy name, Master Changwen, as determined by his rank of seniority among the villagers. His two younger brothers were still called Older Brothers, even though they had attained high status as court officials. (*A clear explanation of the customs of the day.*)

Xu Wu said, "I humbly invited all of you here because I have something from the bottom of my heart to tell you. But you must first each finish three full cups of wine."

Thus exhorted, the guests felt obliged to drink. Xu Wu offered each guest one cup of wine and made his two brothers do the same by turn. After drinking up the wine, the guests said in unison, "In return for your kindness, let us 'present the

Buddha with borrowed flowers,' so to speak, and offer toasts to you." Whereupon Xu Wu and his brothers also drained their cups. The guests went on to say, "We are still waiting for you to tell us what you have in mind."

Raising two fingers, Xu Wu said something that soon made the guests' hair stand on end. Truly,

> *The sparrow understands not the roc;*
> *The river god understands not the sea god.*
> *The pains taken by a sage*
> *Are beyond the ken of lowly knaves.*

In fact, Xu Wu dissolved into tears before he even started to speak. Everyone present was flabbergasted. The two younger brothers fell on their knees in consternation and asked, "Why do you grieve so, brother?"

Xu Wu said, "There's something that has been weighing on my mind for several years now. I have to come out with it today." Pointing at Yan and Pu, he continued, "Because the two of you had not yet made your mark in the world, I did things against my conscience, risking condemnation. I brought disgrace to my ancestors and became the laughing stock of the neighborhood. That's why I cry." (*The neighbors see Xu Wu's tears only now. Little do they know that for all the pains he has taken, he could have shed tears at all times of the day!*) He took out a book and showed it around. It was an account book in which were recorded the amounts of the family farmland and real estate property and the sums of rice, millet, cloth, and silk collected over the years. As everyone was still trying to understand the meaning of this, Xu Wu continued, "I had taught my two brothers ways to conduct themselves properly and to gain fame and bring honor to the family. To my surprise, I rose in the world before they did, on the basis of undeserved fame. However assiduously the two of them were in their farming and their studies, the prefecture and the county did not recommend them for service. I felt inclined to imitate Grand Master Qi and 'shun not one's relatives when making recommendations for official posts.'[12] But, without knowing how they were coming along in their studies and their moral conduct, I was afraid that if they were spoken ill of for having got their posts through their brother, their reputation would be tarnished for life. (*His foresight is also something people of today are in lack of.*) That was why I proposed a division of the family property and took for myself the big house, the good farmland, and the abler of the servants, believing that my gentle and kind brothers would never fight with me over them. So, by pretending to be greedy, I thought I could help establish my brothers' fame for their willingness to yield. And indeed, they won recommendations from the neighborhood and entered His Majesty's service. Now that they have attained high posts and maintained an unsullied reputation, my wish has been fulfilled. The land, the house, and the servants belong to the family. How can I keep them all for myself? I have kept intact the crops and fabrics I have collected as family income over these last few years and recorded everything in that account book. Today, I present the account book to my brothers, to make my heart known to them as well as to you all."

Only then did the neighbors come to appreciate all the pains Xu Wu had taken in dividing up the family property. Feeling ashamed for not having known better and guessed at the truth, they praised him profusely. Xu Yan and Xu Pu, however, wept so bitterly that they collapsed onto the floor (*They could hardly do otherwise.*), saying, "It was all thanks to your teachings that we got as far as we have. We had no idea you had given yourself such trouble. Your worthless brothers were not able to attain official posts on our own but became a burden to you. If you hadn't enlightened us today, we would still have been in the dark. Kindness of such magnitude is unprecedented in all history. However, our unworthiness is beyond redemption. What little family possessions there are were accumulated by you through hard work and therefore rightfully belong to you. We have enough to live on. Don't worry about us."

Xu Wu said, "I've been managing the estate for so long that I know how to turn a profit. Moreover, my career as an official is over, so it's only right for me to continue with farming until I live out my span of life. You two, being at the prime of your lives and in public service, need the backing of the family fortune so as to preserve your good names as incorruptible officials." (*Wise remarks.*)

Yan and Pu rejoined, "You sought to have your own name tarnished for our sake. If we enjoy our fame while also coveting wealth, we would be the greediest people on earth. We'll bring disgrace not only to our ancestors but also to you. Please take back the account book by all means, so as to lessen our offense ever so slightly."

Witnessing how the three brothers yielded to one another, the guests stepped forward and offered this advice, "What the three of you said all makes sense. If Master Changwen keeps everything to himself, all the pains he has taken for the two brothers will be in vain, and if the two younger brothers take Master Changwen's offer, they wouldn't be doing justice to his good intentions, either. In our humble view, it would be better to divide the family property into three equal portions, without anyone getting more or less than the others. Only thus will each of you devoted brothers be doing the right thing."

As the three of them continued to demur, the aforementioned more blunt ones among the guests stepped forward and said sharply, "The three-way division that we proposed is the right one. If you continue to decline what is yours, we'll take you to be hypocrites fishing for fame. Now, give us the account book and let us do the division for you." (*Such men could be found only in the Han dynasty.*)

The three Xu brothers dared not say another word but let them have their way. The land was thus divided into three portions, with each to be managed by one brother. Xu Wu was to keep the grand house in the middle. The houses that flanked it being too small, extra amounts of crops and fabrics were allocated, by way of compensation, to Yan and Pu, who were free to renovate the houses later on. The male and female servants were also reassigned. All the assembled guests praised the fairness of the division. Xu Wu and his brothers saluted the guests in gratitude and invited them to dinner and wine. The guests did not leave until after they had thoroughly enjoyed themselves. Still apologetic for the way he had divided up the property, Xu Wu proposed to donate half of his portion of fertile farmland to the village to be jointly managed by the village for the benefit of the poor. As word of this got to Xu Yan and Xu Pu, they also chipped in. In admiration, the villagers made up another song:

> *Who deserves a title and a rank?*
> *Xu Wu, for his filial devotion.*
> *Who followed in his footsteps?*
> *His brothers Yan and Pu.*
> *Yan and Pu don't fight for their fair share;*
> *Wu doesn't take what isn't his.*
> *They offer their land to the village*
> *As a gift for the local poor.*
> *Ah! None can measure up to them*
> *In devotion and in honor!*

Inspired by their brother's noble-mindedness, Yan and Pu used the gold they had received from the imperial court to buy liberal amounts of meat and wine and invited their brother and the elders in the neighborhood to feasts on a daily basis. Three months went by in this fashion, and their leave of absence came to an end. Being loath to part with their brother, Yan and Pu wanted to hand in their resignation to the court. It was only after Xu Wu's repeated admonitions and lectures about the larger principles that the two of them felt obliged to comply, and away they went with their wives and children to resume their posts.

The elders in the neighborhood told the county and prefectural authorities about the Xu brothers' devotion to one another, and the county and prefectural authorities, in their turn, reported the matter all the way on up to the imperial court. By an imperial decree, a board bearing the inscription "The Village of Filial Piety" was put over the village gate. Later, the highest-ranking officials of the empire all submitted memorandums to the court to propose that Xu Wu, with his peerless moral integrity, not be allowed to remain idle, whereupon the court issued one decree after another to have Xu Wu reinstated, but he refused to comply. When asked why, he said, "I had advised my brothers to know when to be content and when to stop. If I comply with the decree and re-enter the civil service, I would be going back on my own word. What's more, there's so much discord and strife in the court that I'm afraid a landed gentleman who had once served in the court would be better off engaging in farming and finding joy in adhering to his principles." Everyone admired him for his wisdom.

Let us turn to Yan and Pu. Once in their posts, they followed their brother's teachings and built a good reputation in their careers by constantly reminding them-selves to be honest and incorruptible. Later, upon hearing about Xu Wu's high-minded decision to decline offers of posts, they handed in their resignations at the same time, by prior agreement, and returned to their home village. They spent their days touring the mountains and rivers with Xu Wu, and lived to a ripe old age. Their descendants enjoyed prosperity, and the Xu clan, still honored to this day as "the Xu clan of filial devotion," has never been short of high-ranking officials. A later poet had this to say,

> *Brothers of today divide up family property;*
> *Brothers of old did the same, but only*
> *For the benefit of their brothers,*
> *While those of today tussle in ugly fights.*
> *The ancients stooped low out of filial devotion;*
> *People of today stoop low for petty profits.*
> *Filial piety leads to fame and glory;*
> *Fights over petty profits ruin all.*
> *The worthy live in Filial Piety Village,*
> *Shaming to death those brothers at strife.*

The Oil-Peddler Wins the Queen of Flowers

Young men vie in boasting of their conquests
Over the choppy sea of romance.
Money without looks breeds no tender feelings;
Good looks without money get one nowhere, either.

Even those with money and looks
Must keep paying little thoughtful attentions.
Only a dashing young man eager to please
Can beat all others and win the beauty's heart.

This lyric to the tune of "Moon over West River" captures the essence of life in the courtesans' quarters. As the saying goes, "The girls love a good-looking face; the madams love the sight of cash." Among the patrons, those with Pan An's looks[1] and Deng Tong's money[2] naturally win the good graces of all and sundry and become kings of the establishment. However, there is also another attribute called "attentiveness," which is to a girl as the lining is to a garment or the upper is to a shoe. One who otherwise doesn't have much to be said about him will soar in the girl's estimation if he dances attendance on her, goes to great lengths to cover up her flaws, humbly attends to her needs in weather hot or cold, and caters to her likes and steers clear of her dislikes. (*A list of do's and don'ts to keep in mind.*) The object of such affection will find it unthinkable not to love him back. This is what attentiveness can do. In the courtesans' quarters, it is such patrons who get the best deals. What they may want in looks and money is easily made up. A case in point: When Zheng Yuanhe was reduced to begging and lived in a poorhouse sponsored by a Buddhist temple, Li Yaxian [a courtesan whom he had known in his better days] saw him on a snowy day and took pity on him in his penniless and emaciated state.[3] She bundled him in embroidered robes, fed him fine food, and married him. Was she enamored of his money and his looks? No! It was only because Zheng Yuanhe had been affectionate, considerate, and attentive that Yaxian had lost her heart to him. Consider the time when Yaxian had craved horse-tripe soup in her illness. Zheng Yuanhe killed his fancy horse whose mane was fashioned to look like five flower petals, and with the tripe made soup for her. This alone was enough to make her remember his love. Later on, Zheng Yuanhe came out first in the imperial examinations and Li Yaxian was granted the title of Lady of Qianguo. So the beggars' song "Lotus Petals" led to government policies that were to stand the test of time, and the poorhouse gave way to a marble mansion. A "brocade quilt" covered up Yaxian's past, and their story gained wide circulation in the courtesans' quarters. Truly,

> When luck goes, even gold glitters no more;
> When luck comes, even iron takes on luster.

Our story takes place in the Song dynasty. Emperor Taizu [r. 960–75], who founded the great Song dynasty, and the six succeeding emperors—Emperor Taizong [r. 976–97], Emperor Zhenzong [r. 998–1022], Emperor Renzong [r. 1023–63], Emperor Yingzong [r. 1064–67], Emperor Shenzong [r. 1068–85], and Emperor Zhezong [r. 1086–1100]—all favored culture and the arts over military activities. The empire and its people enjoyed peace and prosperity. However, after Emperor Huizong the Daoist [r. 1101–25] assumed the throne, he placed his trust in evil ministers like Cai Jing [1047–1126], Gao Qiu [d. 1126], Yang Jian [d. 1121], and Zhu Mian [1075–1126], and spent his days reveling in the fancy palaces and gardens built for his pleasure, to the neglect of government affairs. As resentment seethed among the populace, the Jurchens, seeing their chance, invaded the empire and brought chaos to this land of splendor and beauty. Then Emperor Huizong and his son Emperor Qinzong [r. 1126] were captured, and Emperor Gaozong [r. 1127–62] crossed the Yangzi River on a clay horse and started the Southern Song dynasty in the south, thus dividing the country in half.[4] It was only then that the turmoil subsided. Goodness knows how much misery the people went through in those few decades. Truly,

> They hung on to life amid armor and horses;
> They made their homes among spears and swords.
> Killing was like a child's game;
> Looting became a way of life.

Let me now tell of a man named Shen Shan who lived in Peace and Happiness Village outside the city gate of Bianliang [present-day Kaifeng in Henan]. He and his wife, née Ruan, owned a grain store, selling mostly rice but also wheat, beans, tea, wine, oil, salt, and other sundry goods. They made a comfortable living. In their forties now, they had only one child, a daughter named Yaoqin [Zither Inlaid with Jade] who was as pretty as she was talented from childhood on. At age seven, she was sent to the village school, where she learned to read a thousand sentences per day. At age ten, she was able to write poems. Her poem "In the Boudoir," which came to be widely circulated, is as follows:

> *Quietly the red curtains come off the golden hooks;*
> *Coldly stands the incense burner in the painted tower.*
> *She moves her pillow but hates to awaken the embroidered lovebirds;*
> *She trims the lamp but is loath to break the pair of wicks.*

Twelve years of age at this point in our narration, Yaoqin excelled in music, chess, calligraphy, and painting, and her dexterity in needlework exceeded everyone's expectations. All these accomplishments came not from practice but from her innate talents. Shen Shan, who had no male issue, wanted to have a live-in son-in-law to support him and his wife in their old age. But the girl was too talented and versatile for him to find a suitable match. And so he declined the many offers of marriage proposals that came his way. As bad luck would have it, the ferocious Jurchen troops laid siege to the city of Bianliang. Even though there was no lack of loyal troops all over the land ready to do battle, the prime minister was determined to make peace and gave the order not to fight. Thus emboldened, the Jurchen invaders took the capital and kidnapped the incumbent emperor and his father. The terror-stricken civilians outside the city abandoned their homes and, helping along the elderly and the children, took to the road and fled for their lives.

Shen Shan took his wife, Ruan-shi, and their twelve-year-old daughter and joined the stream of refugees carrying bundles and parcels on their backs.

> *They hurried along like frightened stray dogs;*
> *They pressed on like fish that escaped the net.*
> *Thirsty, hungry, they bore all manner of hardships;*
> *Where would they have a home to call their own again?*
> *They prayed to heaven, earth, and their ancestors,*
> *Not to let them run into the Jurchens.*
> *Truly, better be a dog in days of peace*
> *Than a human in times of war!*

While they were thus pushing on, they did not see any Jurchens but ran into a group of defeated Song soldiers. At the sight of so many refugees carrying baggage on their backs, the soldiers cried out purposely, "The Jurchens are here!" And they set things on fire as they went. (*This often happens in times of war and separation. Army discipline is therefore of first importance.*) As it was growing dark, the refugees ran helter-skelter in too much panic to watch out for one another. The soldiers took advantage of the situation to rob and loot. Those who resisted were killed. Indeed, to chaos was added chaos; to misery was added misery.

Yaoqin of the Shen family tripped and fell in the onrush of the imperial troops. After she rose to her feet, her parents were lost to sight. She dared not call out loud but hid herself among grave mounds by the roadside, and there she stayed throughout the night. When she ventured out for a look the next morning, all she saw was windblown dust and a road strewn with corpses. Those who had traveled with her the day before were nowhere to be seen. She missed her parents so much that she burst into bitter tears. She wanted to look for them, but without knowing which way to go, she finally headed south, weeping as she went along.

After walking for about two li in agony and hunger, she saw an adobe hut. Thinking there must be someone inside, she headed straight for it to ask for a drink of water. But it turned out to be an abandoned and dilapidated hut. The residents had taken to the road as refugees. Yaoqin sank to the ground to sit against the wall and burst into another flood of tears.

As an ancient saying goes, "No coincidence, no story." It so happened that a man named Bu Qiao, a neighbor of the Shens, went by the wall. Not the sort to abide by his lot, he was a loafer used to sponging off people for meals and cash. Called by all and sundry Big Brother Bu, he was walking all alone at this moment because he had also been separated from his companions by the onrush of the soldiers, and had come over when he heard the sobs. At a time when she had no one to turn to for help in her distress, Yaoqin was as happy to see this neighbor as if she had seen a member of her own family, because she had known him since her childhood. Holding back her tears, she stood up to greet him.

"Uncle Bu," said she, "have you seen my parents?"

Bu Qiao thought, "The soldiers robbed me of my bundle yesterday and I have no money left. Now isn't this a rice bowl sent from heaven? This girl is a rare commodity worth hoarding." Lying through his teeth, he said, "Your parents were heartbroken because they couldn't find you. They said to me before they moved on, 'If you see our daughter, be sure to bring her to us,' and they promised me a nice reward." However smart Yaoqin was, she was in desperate straits, and, as the saying goes, "A trusting gentleman is easily fooled." Without the slightest suspicion, Yaoqin went with Bu Qiao. Indeed,

> Knowing he was not the right companion,
> She followed him in a desperate moment.

Bu Qiao gave her some of his provisions and said to her, "Your parents didn't stop for the night. If we don't catch up with them along the way, we won't be able to see them until we cross the river and get to Jiankang [present-day Nanjing]. While we're on the road, I will call you 'daughter' and you will call me 'father'. Otherwise, people will think I keep lost children, and that won't look good."

Yaoqin agreed. Henceforth, as they traveled by land and by water, they addressed each other as "father" and "daughter." Upon reaching Jiankang, they heard that Jin Wuzhu, the fourth son of the Jurchen emperor,⁵ was leading his troops across the river toward Jiankang, which meant that the city would soon be plunged into turmoil. Then news came that Prince Kang had assumed the throne and was staying temporarily in Hangzhou, which he had renamed Lin'an. So Bu Qiao took Yaoqin to Runzhou [present-day Zhenjiang] by boat and passed through Suzhou, Changzhou, Jiaxing, and Huzhou, until finally arriving at Lin'an, where they found lodging at an inn.

It was to Bu Qiao's credit that he had brought the girl over three thousand li from Bianliang to Lin'an. By this time, he had spent his last few pieces of loose silver. Even the outer layers of his clothes went to the innkeeper to pay the bill. He was now left with only Yaoqin, a live commodity that he was determined to sell. After being informed that a procuress by West Lake, Madam Wang the Ninth, was looking for a new girl, he led the madam to the inn to show her his merchandise and strike a deal. Impressed by Yaoqin's good looks, Wang offered fifty taels of silver. Bu Qiao pocketed all the silver and escorted Yaoqin to the Wang establishment.

Being the crafty man that he was, Bu Qiao said these words to Madam Wang, "Yaoqin is my very own daughter. Now that she is unfortunately with you in this kind of a house, you need to teach her patiently. She'll surely give in. Don't rush things." To Yaoqin, he said, "Madam Wang is a close relative of mine. I'm putting you under her care for now, so that I can take my time looking for your parents. I'll come back for you as soon as I've found them."

Having heard this, Yaoqin merrily went to Madam Wang. (*This is the way most swindlers operate.*)

> *How sad that such a jewel of a girl*
> *Ended up in a house of ill fame.*

Having thus acquired Yaoqin, Madam Wang had her change into new clothes, inside and out, and put her up in a room in a discreet inner chamber. She served the girl nice meals to help her regain health and showered her with honeyed words to win her heart. Yaoqin thought that she might as well stay put for now. A few days went by without any news from Bu Qiao. Longing for her parents, she asked Madam Wang tearfully, "Why doesn't Uncle Bu come to see me?"

"What Uncle Bu?"

"Mr. Bu who took me here."

"He said he was your father."

"But he is a Bu. I am a Shen." She then gave a detailed account of how she had become separated from her parents while fleeing from Bianliang, how she had run into Bu Qiao on the road, how he had taken her to Lin'an, and what he had said to fool her.

"So, that's what happened," said Madam Wang. "Now that you are all alone by yourself and can't very well go outside, like a crab without legs, let me tell you something. That man Bu sold you to me for fifty taels of silver. This is a brothel. I make a living out of my girls. I already have a few, but none of them is any good. I like you for your good looks. I've been treating you like a daughter of my own. After you come of age, I'll make sure that you live in comfort for the rest of your life."

Realizing that she had been tricked by Bu Qiao, Yaoqin burst into sobs. Madam Wang tried hard to pacify her, and it was a long time before Yaoqin finally calmed down. Madam Wang then changed Yaoqin's name to Wang Mei [Beautiful] and had everyone in the establishment call her Sister Mei. She was taught to play musical instruments and to sing and dance, all of which she did to perfection. By age fourteen, she had grown into a ravishing beauty. Rich young men in the city of Lin'an, laden with gifts, descended upon the Wang establishment to see her fair face. Those interested in literature and art, hearing about her talent, also came every day, asking for her poems and calligraphy, and her fame spread far and wide. Instead of Sister Mei, she became known as "The Queen of Flowers." A song to the tune of "Hanging Branch" in praise of her came to circulate among the young men of West Lake:

> *Who among the girls has Wang Mei's beauty?*
> *She writes, she paints, she makes poems,*
> *She plays the flute and the zither,*
> *She sings and dances—all with the greatest ease.*
> *The West Lake is often compared to Xishi[6]*
> *But even Xishi was in no way her equal!*
> *Those lucky enough to touch her body*
> *Find the experience worth dying for.*

With her kind of fame, there were men who made offers for her first night as soon as she reached fourteen years of age, but Wang Mei refused, and Madam Wang dared not go against her wishes, for the madam treasured her as if she were made of gold and therefore obeyed her as she would obey an imperial decree. Another year went by, and Wang Mei was now fifteen. Among the courtesans' quarters there is this convention: The first patron of a thirteen-year-old girl, too young to start working in the profession, is said to be a "tester of the flower." This happens because the madams are too greedy to care if the girl suffers, and the patron wins only false fame rather than real pleasure. At age fourteen, the flower "blooms" and begins to menstruate. This is the right time for the male and the female to give and take. At fifteen, the flower is ready to be "picked." A girl of fifteen in an ordinary home is still considered very young, but in the courtesans' quarters, a fifteen-year-old is considered to have already passed her prime. Since Wang Mei had not yet taken a patron at age fifteen, the young men of West Lake came up with another song to the tune of "Hanging Branch":

> *Wang Mei is like a quince, pretty but only for show;*
> *At fifteen, she hasn't been with a man.*
> *What good is a courtesan in name only?*
> *If not a "girl of stone,"[7] she must be in fact a "he!"*
> *If her you-know-what is in good condition,*
> *How can she put up with the itching?*

Having heard such words, Madam Wang tried to talk the girl into taking a patron, afraid that her business would suffer. Wang Mei adamantly refused, saying, "If you want me to take patrons, you must bring me my parents. They have to agree first."

43

Madam Wang was exasperated but didn't have the heart to come down hard on her. (*This madam is not a bad sort.*) And so life went on as before. Quite some time later, an immensely rich Squire Jin Er offered three hundred taels of silver for Sister Mei's first night. Tempted by such an impressive amount of money, Madam Wang devised a plan. She told Squire Jin to do thus-and-so if he wanted to have his way. Squire Jin took the advice. On the fifteenth day of the eighth lunar month, Jin invited Wang Mei to West Lake to watch the tidal bore. Once she was in his boat, he and three or four of his accomplices engaged her in finger-guessing games and did everything they could to make her pay forfeit by drinking. When they had gotten her quite drunk, they took her to Madam Wang's house and put her in bed. The weather being warm, she had few pieces of clothing on. As she lay there unconscious, Madam Wang personally undressed her. Squire Jin was thus free to do whatever he wanted with the now stark-naked girl. That member of his being of none too brave a size, Squire Jin applied some saliva, softly pushed apart her thighs, and drove it in. By the time Sister Mei woke up from the pain, Squire Jin had already had his way with her. She tried to struggle herself free, but her limbs were too weak. The man took his pleasure of her until his lust abated, just as "the green darkens and the red fades [with the departure of spring]." Truly,

> The flowers wilted in the rain after blooming;
> The eyebrows lost their charm in the mirror.

As the night drum struck the fifth watch, Sister Mei woke up from her wine-induced sleep and realized that the madam had schemed to take her virginity. Lamenting that she who was blessed in looks but not in fate should be subjected to such brutality, she rose to go to the toilet. Then she put on her clothes, lay down on a speckled-bamboo couch by the bed, and turned her face toward the wall to hide her tears. When Squire Jin came up to seek intimacy, she scratched him right in the face, leaving trails of blood on his cheeks. Very much put out, he waited miserably until daybreak to bid the madam good-bye and was out the door before the madam could try to keep him.

The established practice in cases of first-night patronage is for the madam to go to the girl's room early the next morning to offer her congratulations. Other courtesans would follow to do the same. Then a celebration feast would be laid out, and the feasting would continue for several days. The patron would stay on for a month or two or at least fifteen to twenty days. No patron had ever left so early the very next morning, as did Squire Jin. In amazement, Madam Wang threw some clothes over her shoulders and went upstairs, only to see Sister Mei lying on the couch, her face awash in tears. In her eagerness to coax the girl into practicing her profession, Madam Wang apologized over and over again, but with Sister Mei keeping her mouth tightly shut, she could do nothing but go back downstairs. Sister Mei wept the whole day without touching any food or drink. From that day on, she refused to go downstairs or receive visitors on plea of illness.

Madam Wang was exasperated. If she were to rough Sister Mei up, the girl with her fiery temper, would most likely turn more bitter against her rather than submit. But if she were to let Sister Mei have her way, she would have no money to rake in. And if the girl was determined not to take on patrons, even keeping her for one hundred years wouldn't serve any useful purpose. So the madam debated with herself for several days in a row without coming up with a plan.

All of a sudden, she thought of a sworn sister of hers called Madam Liu the Fourth, with whom she had frequent mutual visits. This Madam Liu had the gift of the gab and was friends with Sister Mei. Why not invite her over and have her talk to the girl? If the girl could be brought around, she would thankfully make generous offerings to the gods. Right away, she sent a male servant to invite Madam Liu over.

The two women sat down in the front hall, and Madam Wang poured out her heart to her guest. Madam Liu the Fourth said, "I'm a woman Sui He and a female Lu Jia.[8] I can talk an arhat into falling in love and Chang'e the moon goddess into thoughts of marriage. Just leave everything to me!"

"If so," said Madam Wang, "I'll kowtow to you, even though I'm older than you are. Now drink more tea so you won't talk yourself thirsty."

"I was born with a sea of saliva that won't run short even if I talk nonstop from now on until tomorrow!"

After a few more cups of tea, Madam Liu went around to the room in the back of the house but found the door tightly shut. With a gentle tap, she cried, "My dear niece!"

Recognizing Auntie Liu's voice, Sister Mei opened the door. After an exchange of greetings, Madam Liu sat down at the guest's end of the table and Sister Mei sat down by her side. Noticing that spread out on the table lay a scroll of fine silk on which was drawn a yet uncolored sketch of a woman's face, Madam Liu said in praise, "Good job! What clever hands you have! Ninth Sister is so lucky to have a girl as smart and pretty and skillful as you are! Even if one searches through the whole city of Lin'an with an offer of thousands of taels of gold, one wouldn't find another girl like you!"

"Surely you jest," said Sister Mei. "Now, what wind brought you here today, auntie?"

"I've often wanted to come and see you. It's just that I'm too busy with household chores. Well, I heard that you've had your first patron. What a happy occasion! I took some time off today and came here to offer Ninth Sister my congratulations."

At the words "first patron," Sister Mei blushed furiously. She lowered her head and said nothing. Aware of the girl's shyness, Madam Liu hitched her chair forward and, taking Mei's hand into her own, said, "My child! Girls in this line of business can't be as tender as soft-shelled eggs. How can you ever make big money if you're so shy?" (*What a skillful talker!*)

"Why would I want money?"

"My child! You may not want money, but wouldn't your mother want to get back all that she spent in bringing you up? The ancients said, 'Live on the mountain, live off the mountain; live by the water, live off the water.' Sister Ninth has quite a few girls, but which of them is as good as you are? Of all the melons in the garden, you are the seed melon. And Sister Ninth treats you best. You are a smart girl. You should know better. I heard that you refuse to take on patrons after what happened that night. What's the meaning of that? If everybody is like you, who's going to feed mulberry leaves to this family of silkworms? For each favor that your mother does you, you need to make a good showing for her sake, rather than go the other way around and draw unkind words from the other girls." (*Every argument of hers appeals to the emotions. She's gradually getting there.*)

"They can say all the unkind things they want, for all I care!"

"Good gracious! Unkind words may not mean much to you, but do you know what this line of business is all about?"

"What?"

"We owners of the businesses live off the girls. If we get a nice girl by a stroke of luck, it's as if a large family has acquired a piece of fertile land or valuable property. When the girl is still small, we wish the wind would blow her into puberty. After she's had her first patron, it's as if the crops are ready for reaping. And we expect the money to come in every day. A good, famous house of pleasure is a busy one where new patrons are led in through the front door as old ones are escorted out through the back door, where Mr. Zhang brings in rice and Mr. Li brings in firewood."

"How shameful!" said Sister Mei. "I will not do such things!"

Covering her mouth, Madam Liu the Fourth giggled and said, "Will not do such things indeed! You think it's up to you? It's the madam who calls the shots in the family. If the girls don't do as she says, she can flog them any time she wants until they are more dead than alive. They will then do whatever she tells them to. Sister Ninth has never made life hard for you because you are smart and pretty, and you've been pampered since childhood. She respects your feelings and sensibilities. She just told me a lot of things, saying you don't know what's good for you, that you can't tell which one weighs more—a goose feather or a millstone. She was so upset she wanted me to talk you around. If you don't change your stubborn ways, you'll only get her back up. If she turns against you, yells at you, and beats you, where do you think you can go? To the sky? If there's a first time, there's going to be more. If you have to be beaten every day into accepting patrons, wouldn't you be cheapening yourself? You would otherwise be worth a thousand pieces of gold, you know! And you'll become a laughing stock among the sisters, too. As I see it, now that the water bucket has already fallen to the bottom of the well and can't be pulled up again, you might as well throw yourself happily into your mother's arms and just enjoy yourself."

"I'm from a decent family, in this place of sin by a quirk of fate. If you, Auntie, could help me marry and get out of this life, you'll be doing a better deed than building a nine-story stupa, but if you want to make me ingratiate myself with the patrons and lead new ones in and escort old ones out, I'd rather die than comply."

"My child! To marry and get out of this business is what any girl with any pride would want to do. How can I say no to that? (*Maneuvering tactfully to get to her point.*) But there are different ways of doing it."

"What different ways?"

"There are the real getting-out, the false getting-out, the miserable getting-out, the happy getting-out, the well-timed getting-out, the last-resort getting-out, the once-and-for-all getting-out, and the short-lived getting-out. My child, be patient and listen. What is the real getting-out? Generally speaking, if a bright young man marries a beautiful girl and a beautiful girl marries a bright young man, that's a good match, but the journey to happiness never goes smoothly, as they say. What happens most often is that one may seek but doesn't find the right match. If, by a stroke of good luck, a man and a woman meet, fall in love, can't tear themselves apart, want to marry, and won't let go of each other even in death, like a pair of moths, that's the real getting-out.

"What's a false one? A patron may love one of the girls, but the girl doesn't love him back. She doesn't want to marry him but, with the promise of marriage, lures him into spending money like water on her. By the time the promise is to be delivered, she turns him down on one pretext or another. There are also foolhardy men who know perfectly well that the girls don't love them but they take them home as wives anyway. They pay the madam so handsomely that she will make sure the girls comply. After the girls reluctantly enter the household, they will sulk and deliberately violate household rules. In minor cases, they make scenes. In more serious cases, they brazenly commit adultery until their husbands find it impossible to keep them. After six months to a year, the girls will be let go to pick up their old profession. So, marriage is used just as a pretext to make money. These are cases of a false getting-out.

"What's a miserable getting-out? Well, when a patron loves a girl but the girl doesn't care for him, the man will use his power to bully her. Afraid of getting involved in any trouble, the madam gives him her consent, and the girl goes in tears against her own will. Once she joins the rich family with its strict rules, she can't even hold her head high. She's somewhere between a concubine and a maidservant and wishes herself dead as her life drags on day after day. This is a case of a miserable getting-out.

"What's a happy getting-out? A girl on the lookout for a husband gets to know a patron of gentle temperament from a rich family, whose wife, kind but childless, hopes that the girl would join the family and bear children. If she does bear children, she will become a mistress of the family. So she gets to enjoy a peaceful life and a higher status after childbirth. This is a happy getting-out.

"What's a well-timed getting-out? Well, the girl has had her fill of romances. So, while her reputation is at its highest and her suitors numerous, she picks one whom she finds most satisfactory and marries him. By leaving this business while the going is still good for her, she beats a timely retreat so that she won't be cold-shouldered later on. This is a well-timed getting-out.

"What's a last-resort getting-out? The girl has no wish to marry her way out of the profession but does so nonetheless because she is forced to by the authorities, or because she is bullied or duped into doing so, or because she is in more debt than she can ever repay. And so in desperation she marries whomever happens to be available, to get herself a safe haven. This is a last-resort getting-out.

"What's a once-and-for-all getting-out? Having gone through everything that comes with this profession, the girl now reaches a certain age. It so happens that she meets a patron who is older and more mature, and they hit it off. She pulls in the ropes, so to speak, and lives with him to a ripe old age. This is a once-and-for-all getting-out.

"What's a short-lived getting-out? The girl and a patron fall passionately in love and she marries him on the spur of the moment without any long-term commitment. Then, either because his parents reject her or his wife is jealous of her and makes a few scenes, she is sent back to the madam's house for a refund. Or the man falls on hard times and can't support her anymore. So, unable to bear the hardships of such a life, she picks up her old profession again. This is a short-lived getting-out." (*A thorough and detailed exposé of the different ways to marry and get out of the business. Madam Liu and Granny Wang form a perfect pair in this line of profession.*)[9]

"I certainly would like to marry my way out of here," said Sister Mei. "How do I go about it?"

"My child, I have a surefire plan for you."

"If you can teach me how to do it, I'll never forget your kindness."

"As they say in this profession, a girl is not clean until she marries. Now, your body has already been sullied anyway. Even if you marry tonight, you won't pass as a virgin. (*Getting closer to the point.*) Of all mistakes, none is greater than to be in this place. This is your fate. Your mother has gone to such trouble for your sake. If you don't help her out for a few years and make a thousand taels of silver for her, how will she ever let you go out the door? And there's another thing: if you want out, you must pick a good man. You can't just go off with some disgusting guy. But if you don't take on patrons, how do you know which one is a good candidate and which one is not? (*By now, even a person made of iron will follow Madam Liu's baton wherever it leads.*) If you stand your ground, your mother will have no choice but to sell you off as a concubine to anyone willing to cough up the money. That's also a way out, but if the man is old or ugly or an illiterate country bumpkin, wouldn't you be doomed for life? That's even worse than if you throw yourself into the river, because at least you'll be making a splash and onlookers will cry out 'What a pity!' As I see it, you'd better follow your mother's wishes and receive patrons. With your talent and your looks, ordinary men won't dare ask for you. And men from royal and eminent families don't exactly bring you disgrace, do they? First, you should enjoy the romances this life has to offer while you're young; second, help your mother build up some family fortune; and third, have some private savings, so as not to have to ask for other people's help in the future. In five to ten years, if you meet someone who understands you and gets along with you well, let me be the matchmaker and marry you off in style. By that time, your mother won't stop you. Wouldn't that be nice for both of you?"

Sister Mei smiled but said nothing.

Detecting a slight thaw in the girl's position, Madam Liu said, "I mean well in everything I say. If you follow my advice, you'll have much to thank me for in the future." With that, she got up to go.

Madam Wang the Ninth, in the meantime, had been hiding by the door, listening to everything being said. Sister Mei bumped straight into her when walking Madam Liu out of the room. Painfully embarrassed, the girl shrank back into her room. (*A vivid detail that captures the girl's mind.*) Madam Liu followed Madam Wang the Ninth back to the front hall, where they sat down.

"She's a most stubborn girl," said Madam Liu, "but after I talked my head off, that piece of iron began to melt. Now you must quickly find her another patron. She'll surely take him. I'll then come to offer my congratulations."

Madam Wang the Ninth said her thanks over and over again and set out a fine meal in Liu's honor. They didn't part company until they were roaring drunk.

Later, another song to the tune of "Hanging Branch" about this episode came to circulate among the young men of West Lake:

> *Madam Liu the Fourth, what a tongue you have!*
> *No diplomat measures up to you!*
> *You leave no loopholes in your tittle-tattle.*
> *You sober up the drunk and stupefy the wise;*
> *Even a girl with the most fiery temper*
> *Yields to you and has a change of heart.*

To resume our story, upon further reflection, Sister Mei found much sense in Madam Liu's words. Henceforth, she began to take on patrons readily, and the patrons came in droves, keeping her busy and driving up her price. A night with her cost as much as ten taels of silver. Even so, the men fought with one another for their turns. Madam Wang the Ninth was beside herself with joy at the stream of silver coming in. Sister Mei, on her part, kept her eyes open for a candidate who was just right for her, but this was something that would take time. Truly,

> *It's easier to acquire a priceless treasure*
> *Than to find a man after her own heart.*

Our story forks at this point. By Clear Waves Gate of the city of Lin'an, there lived a Zhu the Tenth, owner of an oil shop. Three years earlier, he had adopted a boy, also a refugee from Bianliang, named Qin Zhong. The boy's mother having passed away long ago, his father, Qin Liang, had sold him when he was thirteen and gone to Upper Tianzhu Monastery to serve as an acolyte.

Zhu the Tenth had no children of his own. Being advanced in years and having just lost his wife, he treated Qin Zhong as his own son and changed his surname to Zhu. So Zhu Zhong began to learn the trade. In the beginning, things went well for the father and son as they went about their business, but then Mr. Zhu Senior began to be afflicted with a backache and had to lie in bed or sit most of the time. Unable to work, he hired a man called Xing Quan to help out in the shop.

Time flew by like an arrow. Quite unnoticeably, four years elapsed. Zhu Zhong was now a handsome young man of seventeen. Though old enough to wear a hat, he remained a bachelor. A maidservant of the family, called Orchid, now over twenty years of age, had her eye on Young Master Zhu and repeatedly made advances to him. But Zhu Zhong was an honorable and well-behaved young man. Besides, he found Orchid disgusting and ugly. This was a case of "The flowers falling into the water, seeking love/ But the water flowing on, untempted." Young Master Zhu being unresponsive, Orchid turned her eyes to Xing Quan, a bachelor in his late thirties. The two immediately hit it off. Finding Young Master Zhu too much of a hindrance in their many amorous adventures, they conspired to drive him out. So Xing Quan and Orchid worked in coordination to carry out their plan. To Mr. Zhu the Tenth, Orchid said in affected demureness, "The young master made passes at me several times. What a dirty man!" Mr. Zhu the Tenth could hardly suppress his jealousy because he, too, had had an affair with Orchid.

Xing Quan, on his part, stole some pieces of silver belonging to the shop and said to Zhu Senior, "Young Master Zhu gambles. What a good-for-nothing! He's stolen several times from the shop."

At first Zhu the Elder didn't believe what he heard, but after the two complained a few more times, the old addlehead who didn't know better called Zhu Zhong to him and gave him a good lecture. Being a smart young man, Zhu Zhong knew that this was the doing of Xing Quan and Orchid. He wanted to defend himself but gave up the idea, because if the old man did not believe him, he would only stir up a lot of trouble and offend them without doing himself any good. Then an idea came to him. He said to Zhu the Tenth, "With the business as slow as it is, you don't need two people in the shop. Mr. Xing can take care of the shop. I'll be glad to take up a carrying pole and a load of oil to peddle on the streets. Every day, I'll turn in every penny I make. Wouldn't that be another source of income for the shop?"

Zhu the Elder had a mind to say yes, but Xing Quan said, "He doesn't really want to peddle oil. The fact is, he has now saved up a tidy sum from years of stealing and he's mad at you for not finding him a wife. He doesn't want to work here anymore and is looking for a way out, so that he can get himself a wife and set up his own household."

With a sigh, Zhu the Elder said, "I treat him like my own son, but he is full of ill will towards me. Heaven will not protect such people. Oh well, he's not my own flesh and blood after all. There's no bond between us. I'll just let him be!" He told Zhu Zhong to leave but gave him three taels of silver, along with his clothes for every season and his bedding. This was an act of generosity to the credit of Zhu the Tenth. Knowing the latter would not relent, Zhu Zhong kowtowed four times to him and bade him farewell with bitter sobs. Truly,

> *Prince Xiaoji died of words of slander;[10]*
> *Shensheng of Jin met the same fate.[11]*
> *Such tragedies befall even birth sons,*
> *Let alone adopted ones, however innocent.*

As a matter of fact, Qin Liang [the boy's birth father] had joined Upper Tianzhu Monastery as an acolyte without telling his son about this. Now, after leaving Zhu the Tenth, Zhu Zhong rented a small room by All Peace Bridge, put down his baggage, bought a padlock, locked up the door, and took to the streets in search of his father. After several days went by without any news, he saw nothing for it but to give up the attempt. In all the four years he had lived with Zhu the Tenth, in his utter devotion to his adoptive father, he had not saved one penny for himself. The three taels of silver he received upon dismissal was all the money he had, but what line of business could he go into with such meager capital? He turned his thoughts this way and that before finally settling on oil, the only business he knew well. Being familiar with the oil dealers in the area, he thought that peddling oil would be a secure way for him to make a living. Right away, he bought the necessary equipment and gave the balance to an oil shop for a supply of oil. The owner of the shop knew Young Master Zhu to be good and honest, and was indignant that this young man, who had been working in Mr. Zhu's shop for all these years, was now reduced to peddling oil on the streets, all at the instigation of Clerk Xing. Determined to help, the shop owner offered the purest of his oil, measuring out more than he charged the young man for. With these advantages, Zhu Zhong, in his turn, gave his clients good deals. Therefore, he sold his oil faster than others and turned a profit every day. Being a frugal man, he saved up some money with which he bought himself some housewares and clothes, but not more than was necessary. The only thing preying on his mind was the whereabouts of his father. He thought, "I've been called Zhu Zhong for so long that nobody knows that my surname is actually Qin. If Father comes looking for me, he won't have a clue as to who I am." And so he changed his surname back to Qin. (*Remember well the two surnames, Zhu and Qin, that have been changed back and forth.*)

Storyteller, when those of the upper classes with bright career prospects want to change back to their original surnames, they need to request permission from the imperial court or notify the Ministry of Rites, the Imperial Academy, the National University, and other departments, so that the registry books can be updated and the corrections made public. But how is a lowly oil-peddler to make his change of name known to the public? Well, this one had his own way of doing it. He painted on one side of each of his oil buckets a large character "Qin" and, on the other side, the two characters for "Bianliang." The bucket thus became an eye-catching mark of his identification. He came to be called "Qin the Oil-peddler" by all and sundry in the marketplaces of Lin'an.

One day in the second lunar month, when the weather was neither too hot nor too cold, Qin Zhong heard that monks of Zhaoqing Monastery were having a prayer service that was to last nine days and nights. Since they would be using a lot of oil, Qin Zhong carried his load there to make a sale. Having heard about Qin the Oil-peddler, who sold good-quality oil at a low price, the monks bought oil exclusively from him. For nine days in a row, Qin Zhong did his business only with this monastery. Indeed,

> *Pettiness doesn't bring in gains;*
> *Honesty doesn't lead to losses.*

On the ninth day, which was a glorious day, after having disposed of his oil at the monastery, Qin Zhong was carrying his empty load and walking along the water's edge through crowds of sightseers when he saw, some distance off, Ten-Scene Dyke with its pink peach blossoms and green willows. On the lake floated painted pleasure boats amid the music of flutes and drums. There was more to admire than his eyes could take in. Feeling tired after all this walking, he went back to an open space to the side of Zhaoqing Monastery, put down his load, and sat down on a rock to rest. Nearby stood a house facing the lake with a gilded gate and a clump of thin bamboo showing through the vermilion-colored balustrades inside. The interior of the house was not visible, but the doorway and the courtyard were certainly well kept. He saw three or four men wearing hats coming out and a girl behind them seeing them off. Upon reaching the gate, the men folded their hands and said good-bye, whereupon the girl turned back into the house. Qin Zhong fixed his eyes on her and found her to be the prettiest and the most lithe and graceful girl he had ever seen. He stood transfixed. Being as innocent as he was, he had no idea that this was a brothel. As he was wondering what kind of people lived in this house, a middle-aged woman and a young maidservant emerged from within. They leaned against the gate and looked around.

Her eyes falling upon the oil load, the middle-aged woman said, "Aya! I've been meaning to buy some oil, and here comes an oil peddler! Why don't we buy some from him?"

The maid went in and reemerged with an oil bottle. It was not until she was by the side of the oil load and cried out "Oil-Peddler!" that Qin Zhong became aware of her. "Oh, I have no oil left," he replied. "If your mistress needs oil, I'll deliver to her tomorrow."

Being somewhat literate, the maid recognized the character "Qin" written on the oil buckets and told the woman, "The oil peddler's surname is Qin."

Having heard that there was a Qin the Oil-Peddler known for his honest ways of doing business, the woman said to Qin Zhong, "I need oil every day in the house. If you are willing to deliver, you can count on me as a regular client."

"Thank you so much, ma'am. I won't fail you."

After the woman and the maid went back into the house, Qin Zhong thought, "I wonder who this woman is to the young lady. It'll be a stroke of predestined good luck if I can deliver oil to this house every day and get a look at the young lady. I don't care whether I make a profit or not." He was about to shoulder the load and set off when he saw two carriers of a blue-curtained sedan-chair, followed by two page boys, running as fast as they could toward the house. Upon reaching the gate, the carriers put down the sedan-chair and the page boys disappeared into the house. Qin Zhong said to himself, "How strange! I wonder whom they're picking up." Soon two maids came out, one carrying a scarlet felt bag, the other carrying a speckled-bamboo visiting-card box with carved designs. They handed both objects to the sedan-chair carriers, who put them under the seat. Then the girl he had seen before came out of the house, followed by the two page boys, one carrying a zither case and the other holding in his arms several scrolls with a jade flute dangling from his wrist. After the girl mounted the sedan-chair, the carriers raised it and went the way they had come. The maids and the page boys followed on foot. After having thus laid his eyes a second time on that girl, Qin Zhong felt even more intrigued. His load hanging from the pole over his shoulders, he went away slowly.

After a few steps, he caught sight of a wineshop by the river. He was not a drinker, but today, both delighted and saddened by the sight of the girl, he put down his load, entered the wineshop, and sat down by a small table. The waiter asked, "Are you treating friends or are you drinking by yourself?"

"I'm drinking alone. Give me three cups of your best wine and a couple of dishes of fresh fruit but no meat."

While the waiter was pouring out the wine for him, Qin Zhong asked, "Who lives in that house with the gilded fence gate?"

"That's Young Master Qi's property, now occupied by Madam Wang the Ninth."

"I just saw a young lady go off in a sedan-chair. Who's she?"

"She's Sister Wang Mei, a famous courtesan. Everybody calls her Queen of Flowers. She's a native of Bianliang but got stranded here. She's good at playing musical instruments, singing and dancing, chess, calligraphy, and painting. She takes only rich clients. It costs ten taels of silver to spend one night with her. Those who can't come up with the money have no chance. She used to live outside Yongjin Gate, but the house was too small. So about six months ago, her friend Young Master Qi lent her this house with its garden."

When Qin Zhong heard that she was also a native of Bianliang, a feeling of fellowship welled up in him, and his heart grew doubly fonder of her. After a few more cups, he paid his bill and picked up his load. As he walked along, he thought, "What a shame that such an out-of-this-world beauty should have ended up in a brothel!" Then he laughed at himself, "If she were not in this line of business, an oil-peddler like me would never have gotten to see her." Pursuing these thoughts, he indulged in another flight of fancy and said to himself, "A man has only one life to live, and grass dies in autumn. I would die content if I could hold such a beauty in my arms for one night." He went on thinking (*His thoughts do go everywhere.*) and said, "Bah! How can I have such fanciful ideas when I make only a few pennies a day out of my oil load! This is like a toad in a ditch craving the flesh of a swan. Impossible! She takes only rich patrons. She won't take an oil-peddler like me, even if I have the money." Then he thought again, "I've heard that the madams are only after money. They'll even accept a beggar if he can pay. I am a man with an honest business. If I can pay, why would they reject me? But where am I going to find the money?"

And so he indulged in these wild thoughts as he walked along, talking to himself. Isn't it a wonder that there are such fools in this world? A peddler who had started his business with only three taels of silver wanted to spend ten taels for a night with a celebrated courtesan. Isn't this an impossible dream? Well, as the ancients said, "Where there is a will, there is a way." He racked his brains and came up with a plan: "Starting from tomorrow, I'll save up whatever profit I make. Even if I put aside only one penny a day, I'll have three taels and six maces in one year. Another two years, and I'll be able to do it. If I put away two pennies a day, it'll take me only one and a half years. If I can put away more, one year will do." (*So long as one works hard at it, an iron pestle can be ground down to a needle.*) Preoccupied with these thoughts, he arrived at home before he knew it. His head was filled with such a jumble of thoughts all along the way that after he opened the lock on his door and went inside, he was overwhelmed by a feeling of misery at the sight of his own bed. Without even bothering to eat supper, he went to bed, but thoughts about the beauty kept him tossing and turning all through a wakeful night.

> *The one as fair as flowers and the moon*
> *Made his fancy run away with him.*

When daybreak came at last, he rose, filled his oil buckets, made breakfast, ate it, and locked the door. Carrying his load, he headed straight for Madam Wang's house. After going through the gate, he dared not barge into the house but craned his neck for a look inside. Madam Wang had just risen from bed and, her hair disheveled, was telling a male servant what food to buy. Recognizing the voice, Qin Zhong cried out, "Madam Wang!"

Turning her eyes toward the door, Madam Wang the Ninth said with a smile at the sight of Qin the Peddler, "What an honest young man! You kept your word."

She summoned him in with his load of oil and had a bottle of about five catties filled up, for which she paid him a price she thought was fair. Qin Zhong did not haggle. Greatly pleased, Madam Wang said, "This bottle of oil can only last us two days. If you can come every other day, I won't buy from anyone else."

Qin Zhong promised and left with his load, regretting not to have seen the Queen of Flowers. He thought, "It's a good thing Madam Wang is now my regular customer. If I don't see her this time, there'll be a second time. If I still don't get to see her the second time, there'll be a third time. But there's one problem. To carry the load over such a long distance for Madam Wang alone isn't the right way to do business. Zhaoqing Monastery is on my way. Even though there's no prayer service there today, I'm sure they use oil for everyday purposes also. Let me go over and ask them. If the monks in the various halls can all buy from me, one trip to Qiantang Gate will be enough for me to dispose of all my oil."

It so happened that when Qin Zhong went to the monastery with his load to ask, the monks of the various halls were just thinking of Qin the Peddler. His timing was most opportune. All the monks bought oil from him in varying amounts and they arranged to have him make deliveries every other day. That day being an even-numbered day, they agreed that, henceforth, Qin Zhong would ply his trade elsewhere on odd-numbered days but make a special trip through Qiantang Gate on even-numbered days. Once outside the gate, he would first head for Madam Wang's house, ostensibly to sell oil, but actually to see the Queen of Flowers. He didn't get to see her every time. When he didn't, he would miss her sorely, but when he did, he would long for her even more. Indeed,

The sky and earth will end some day;
But his love will live on forever.

After many deliveries to Madam Wang, everyone in the house, old or young, came to know Qin the Peddler. Time flew by. Quite unnoticeably, another year had elapsed. Every day he put by pieces of the finest silver worth three pennies, or two pennies, or at least one penny. After he put together a certain amount, he would have the small pieces melted and made into a larger piece. As the days and months went by, his silver grew into a pile, which he wrapped up with a piece of cloth. Having saved them in a piecemeal fashion, he had no idea of the exact amount. One odd-numbered day with a pouring rain, he took the day off and stayed at home. The sight of the parcel of silver filled him with joy. He thought, "With all this time on my hands today, let me have the silver weighed out to get an exact figure." Holding an oilcloth umbrella, he went to the silversmith's shop across the street to use their scales.

This silversmith was a snob. He thought, "How much silver can an oil-peddler have to need my scales? Let me give him a small five-tael weight. He may not even need the largest cord." (*A petty man.*)

Qin Zhong untied the knot of his parcel to reveal all his loose pieces of silver.

Generally speaking, a pile of loose pieces of silver may appear to be worth more than one ingot of equal weight. The silversmith being a petty man without having seen much of the world, his facial expression changed as he saw so much silver. Thinking to himself, "As they say, you can't judge a man by his looks, nor measure the sea with a pitcher," he hastened to set up the scales and took out many weights of varying sizes. Qin Zhong put his parcel onto the scale pan and saw that it weighed exactly sixteen taels, or one catty. Qin Zhong said to himself, "If I take off the three taels of capital, I still have more than enough for one night at that house." Then again, he thought, "I can't pay with these loose pieces of silver. They'll look down on me. While I'm in the silversmith's shop, why don't I have them made into nicer-looking ingots?"

Right away, he had some loose pieces weighing ten taels melted and made into a fine large ingot. A few pieces weighing one tael and eight maces were made into a small ingot. Then he picked a small piece from the remaining four taels and two maces and paid the silversmith. With a few maces, he bought himself a pair of white socks and a pair of shoes with fortified copper soles, and had a new square hat made. Back at home, he washed and starched his clothes and scented them over and over again with a few benzoin joss sticks.[12] On a chosen fine day, he rose bright and early and fitted himself out for the occasion.

> *He may not be a rich patron,*
> *But he does cut a dashing figure.*

All spruced up now, Qin Zhong put some silver in his sleeve, locked the door, and, in high spirits, headed straight for Madam Wang's house. Upon gaining the door, however, he was again gripped with a sense of his inadequacy. He said to himself, "I've always been the oil peddler to them. What am I going to say today as a patron?" Before he could make up his mind, the door opened with a creak, and out came Madam Wang.

At the sight of Qin Zhong, she said, "Young Master Qin, why aren't you doing business today but all dressed up like this? Where are you going?"

Now that things had come to this, Qin Zhong forced himself to step forward and make a bow. Madam Wang returned the courtesy.

"I am here to see you, madam."

Being an old hand in the business, the madam had the sharpest eyes. Noticing the young man's outfit and hearing his stated purpose of the visit, she thought, "He must be fancying one of my girls, and wants to spend some time or a night with her. Granted that he's no fat cat, whatever comes into my basket can be served on the table, be it veggies or crabs. Even if what money he brings in is enough for only a handful of green onions, it'll be better than nothing." Switching on an obsequious smile, she said, "Young Master Qin must be thinking of doing this old woman a favor."

"I have an impertinent request but I just can't bring myself to say it."

"It's all right. Let me hear it. Let's go to the sitting room. Feel free to say what you've got to say."

As an oil-peddler, Qin Zhong had been to the house a hundred times, but this was the first time his bottom had ever made acquaintance with a chair in that sitting room.

Once in the sitting room, Madam Wang had the young man take the seat of honor. She herself took the host's seat and called out for tea. Before long, a maid came in with tea. Recognizing Qin the Peddler, she lowered her head and giggled at the way the madam was treating him. Madam Wang said sharply to her, "What's so funny? Have you forgotten your manners?"

The maid stifled her giggles, collected the used teacups, and left. Only at this point did Madam Wang ask, "Young Master Qin, what is it you want to say to me?"

"Nothing much, really. It's just that I'd like to invite a sister of this house to a cup of wine."

"Just wine and nothing else? You must be thinking of spending some time with her in bed, too. You're not a wild one. Why this sudden interest in girls?"

"I've had this wish for quite some time now."

"You know all the girls in this house. Which one do you have in mind?"

"None other than the Queen of Flowers."

The madam's face hardened, for she thought the young man was making fun of her. "What a thing to say! You can't be teasing me?"

"I'm an honest man. I mean what I say."

"Even a night-soil bucket has ears [handles]. Haven't you heard that Sister Mei is expensive? Even if you sell off your oil business, you won't be able to come up with enough money for half a night. (*The procuress has a lot of nerve.*) Why don't you just pick a cheaper one?"

In mock surprise, Qin Zhong drew his head into his shoulders, stuck his tongue out, and said, "My goodness! You can't be bluffing? May I venture to ask, how many thousands of taels a night for your Queen of Flowers?"

His jocular tone dissolved Madam Wang's anger. Breaking into a smile, she said, "How can I ask for that much? It's ten taels of the finest silver, plus dinner treats and other expenses."

"I see. That's not a problem." He retrieved from his sleeve a large, smooth, and shining ingot of high-grade silver and handed it to the procuress, saying, "This one weighs a full ten taels and is of the finest quality. Please take it." Then he produced a small ingot and gave it to her as well, adding, "This two-tael piece is for a simple dinner. Please do me this favor. I'll never forget you. I'll have more gifts for you in the future."

The madam hated the thought of parting with the silver, especially that larger ingot, but she was also afraid that he might regret later on for having spent all he had on an impulse. She felt obliged to remind him, "It's not easy for someone in your business to come by ten taels. Think well before you do anything."

"I have made up my mind. Please don't worry."

The madam slipped the two ingots of silver into her sleeve and said, "All right, I'll do it, but it won't be an easy job."

"Aren't you the mistress of the house? Why do you say it won't be an easy job?"

"Sister Mei associates only with sons of the nobility, and with the rich and the powerful. She 'talks and laughs with great scholars and associates with no illiterates.'[13] How can she not know that you are Young Mr. Qin the peddler? How will she condescend to take you?"

"Could you please tactfully put it to her? If you can pull this off, I'll never forget your great kindness!"

Impressed by his determination, Madam Wang the Ninth knitted her eyebrows and hit upon a plan. With a smile, she said, "I've got a plan for you, but I don't know if this is in your fate. If I succeed, don't jump for joy. If I don't, don't hold me to blame. Sister Mei went to a dinner party at Academician Li's house yesterday and hasn't come back yet. Today, she's scheduled to go on a tour of the lake with Young Master Huang. Tomorrow she's invited by Hermit Zhang and others to a meeting of their poetry club, and the day after tomorrow, she'll be taken up with Minister Han's son, who made the arrangements a few days ago. You can come back for a look the day after that. Another thing: In the next few days, don't deliver oil to this house, so as to prepare everyone for your change of status. Also, you don't look like an upper-class patron in your cotton clothes. Next time you come, wear silk, so that the maids won't recognize you, and it'll be easier for me to cover up for you."

"I understand." With that, Qin Zhong bade her good-bye and went off. He suspended his business for three days and went to a pawnshop and bought a silk robe that was far from new, though not shabby. He put it on and walked leisurely around the neighborhood to practice ways of behaving like a gentleman. Truly,

> Before he learned much about the brothel,
> He first practiced Confucian manners.

Let us skip those three days but come to the fourth day. Qin Zhong rose at first light and went to Madam Wang's house. He was so early that he found the gate still closed. He had a mind to go for a walk, but, wearing such fancy clothes, he dared not go to Zhaoqing Monastery for fear of the monks' disapproval, and went instead for a walk by Ten-Scene Dyke. When he returned quite some time later, the gate was open, but a horse carriage was parked in front and many servants were sitting idly by. However unsophisticated he was, he had enough sense not to go in. Quietly, he signaled to the groom and asked, "Whose horse carriage is this?"

"We are sent by the Han establishment to pick up the young master."

Qin Zhong realized that Mr. Han had stayed overnight and had not yet left. So he turned away again and went to a restaurant, where he ordered some tea and food. He sat a while longer before returning to the Wang house for another look.

Finding the horse carriage gone, he walked in. Madam Wang came up to greet him and said, "I'm sorry, but she's busy again today. Mr. Han just took her to East Manor to see the early plum blossoms. He's a regular customer. I can't say no to him. I heard that he'll take her tomorrow to Soul's Retreat Monastery for a few games of chess with a chess master. And Young Master Qi has asked for her a few times. Since he owns this house, I can't turn him down, either. Every time he comes, he stays for three to five days. Even I can't tell for sure how long he's going to stay. Now, Young Master Qin, if you really want her, you'll have to be patient and wait a little longer. Otherwise, I can give you back every penny of what you gave me the other day."

Qin Zhong said, "I'm just afraid that you won't be able to pull this off. Better late than never. I'll gladly wait even if it takes ten thousand years." (*Number-One lover.*)

Madam Wang said, "In that case, I'll surely be able to do it for you."

Qin Zhong was about to leave when the madam said again, "Young Master Qin, there's one more thing. Don't be too early next time you come to check with me. Let's make it sometime late in the afternoon. I'll surely let you know if she's free or not. Remember to be as late as possible. I have good reasons for saying so. Don't misunderstand me."

"I wouldn't dare! I wouldn't dare!"

That day, Qin Zhong did not do any business. The following day, he rearranged his load and plied his trade away from the Qiantang Gate area. Every evening, after his business of the day was over, he would dress up and go to Madam Wang's house for a reply, but to no avail. More than a month went by without any progress.

On the fifteenth day of the twelfth month, after a heavy snowstorm had cleared up and the west wind had dropped, the accumulated snow iced over in the bone-chilling air, but at least the ground was dry. After spending the better part of the day plying his trade, Qin Zhong put on his finer clothes as usual, and went again to hear a reply. Madam Wang greeted him and said, her face wreathed in smiles, "Today is your lucky day. Your chances are ninety-nine out of a hundred."

"What's that one out of a hundred?"

"Well, she's not in."

"Is she coming back?"

"Marshal Yu invited her to enjoy the snow scene. The feast is laid out in a boat on the lake. Marshal Yu is over seventy now, and is surely not in for that kind of thing. He said he would have her sent back at dusk. You can go to the bridal chamber, have a cup of warm wine, and wait for her."

"Would you please take me there, then?"

Madam Wang led Qin Zhong through many twists and turns to a bungalow of three spacious and airy rooms. The one on the left was a room for the maids, now unoccupied. It was furnished with a bed, a couch, and a table and chairs for the use of guests. The one on the right, the Queen of Flower's bedroom, was locked.

On each side of the bungalow was a small side room. Hanging over the seat of honor in the living room in the middle was a landscape painting by a famous artist. On a side table stood an antique bronze incense burner with ambergris incense sticks aglow. On the tables on both sides were placed some antiques. On the wall were posted many scrolls of poetry. Feeling ashamed that he was not an educated man, Qin Zhong dared not look at them closely. He thought, "Even the living room is so nice. The bedroom must be really elegant. If I can get to enjoy all this luxury tonight, ten taels is not too much." (*Right.*)

Madam Wang offered him the seat for the guest of honor and sat down herself in the host's seat. Presently, some maids came in with a lit lamp and a big square table on which they laid out six bowls of seasonal fruit and a partitioned box filled with assorted delicacies. The aroma of the food and the fine wine assailed the nostrils. A wine cup in her hand, the madam said, "My girls are all occupied today. You'll have to put up with me as a drinking companion. Please drink to your heart's content."

With little capacity for wine and something weighing on his mind, Qin Zhong drank only half a cup of wine and, after a while, said he was not going to drink anymore.

The madam said, "Young Master Qin, you must be hungry. Eat something and then drink some more."

A maid laid down in front of Qin Zhong two bowls of snow-white rice, one for him to eat right away and the other for his second helping, along with a bowl of soup with mixed ingredients. Madam Wang, with her large capacity for wine, did not need the rice but went on drinking to keep him company. After finishing one bowl of rice, Qin Zhong put down his chopsticks. The madam said, "It's going to be a long night. Please eat some more," whereupon Qin Zhong helped himself to another half bowlful of rice. Then the maid came over with a lantern and said, "Your bath is ready, sir."

Qin Zhong had already taken a bath before he came, but, not daring to turn down the offer, he went to the bathroom and washed himself again with soap and perfumed water before putting his clothes back on and returning to his seat. Madam Wang ordered that the food be taken away and the wine be warmed up in a chafing dish. By this time, dusk had deepened into evening and the bells in Zhaoqing Monastery had been struck, but Sister Mei had still not returned.

> *Where is the fair one enjoying herself?*
> *He wears his eyes out awaiting her return.*

As the saying goes, "Waiting tries one's patience." Qin Zhong was quite distraught over the girl's absence. With the procuress talking her head off and plying him with wine, two more hours went by. Then a commotion was heard outside. The Queen of Flowers was back. As soon as a maid came to announce her arrival, Madam Wang hastened to rise and go out to greet the girl. Qin Zhong also stood up from his seat. Sister Mei, very much the worse for drink, was being helped into the house by a maid. Upon gaining the door, she stopped in her tracks at the sight, through her bleary eyes, of the litter of cups and plates in the brightly lit room. "Who's been drinking here?" she asked.

"My child," said the madam, "this is the Young Master Qin I've been telling you about. He's such an admirer of yours, he keeps sending gifts over. But you've been busy, so he's been waiting for more than a month now. Luckily you are free tonight. So I've kept him here for you."

"I've never heard of any Young Master Qin in Lin'an. I don't want to see him." With that, she turned to go. Spreading out her arms, Madam Wang blocked her way and said, "He is a good man, and very sincere. Trust me."

Sister Mei had no choice but to turn back into the room. As she stepped into the room, she raised her head and saw Qin Zhong. She found his face familiar, but, in her drunken condition, she couldn't recall his name on the spur of the moment. "Mother," said she, "I know this man. He's not an upper-class gentleman. I'll be laughed at if I take him."

"My child, this is Young Master Qin, owner of a fabric shop at Yongjin Gate. You must have seen him when we were living there. That's why he looks familiar to you. Don't mistake him for someone else. I was so impressed by his sincerity that I gave him my promise, and I can't very well go back on it. Why don't you just let him stay tonight, if only for my sake? I know I'm in the wrong. I'll make it up to you tomorrow." While saying this, she pushed Sister Mei forward by her shoulders. Hardly able to fight back, Sister Mei had to go into the room and greet the patron. Truly,

> A procuress' tongue has the sharpest bite;
> A procuress' hand just never lets go.
> Thousands of plans you may have in your head,
> But the best one is to bend to her will.

Qin Zhong had heard every word but pretended to have heard nothing. After greeting him with a curtsey, Sister Mei sat down on one side and scrutinized him suspiciously. After sitting in gloomy silence for a while, she asked a maid for some warm wine. When the wine was brought to her and she began to fill a large cup with it, Madam Wang thought she was going to offer the cup to Qin Zhong, but, in fact, she drank it all up herself.

"My child, you're already drunk. You mustn't drink anymore."

Turning a deaf ear to her pleas, Sister Mei said, "I'm not drunk!" After more than ten cups in a row, which further added to her drunkenness, she felt her legs giving way under her. She had a maid open the door of her bedroom and light the lamps. Without bothering to remove the jewelry from her hair or untie her sash, she kicked off her embroidered shoes and lay down in bed fully clothed. Feeling apologetic for the girl's behavior, Madam Wang said to Qin Zhong, "My girl is used to throwing temper tantrums. She's a little upset today for some reason, but it has nothing to do with you. Don't take offense!"

"Oh I won't!"

The madam refilled Qin Zhong's cup a few more times. It was only at his firm insistence that she stopped. When walking him into the bedroom, the procuress whispered into his ear, "She's drunk. Be gentle." Aloud, she called out, "My child! You should get up and take off your clothes before going properly to sleep!"

Being already fast asleep, Sister Mei made no response. The madam had to take her leave. After clearing away the cups and plates and wiping the table, the maid said, "Young Master Qin! You can retire now."

"Could you give me a pot of hot tea?" said Qin Zhong.

The maid made a pot of strong tea and delivered it into the room. She then closed the door after her and withdrew into one of the side-rooms for the night. Qin Zhong saw that Sister Mei was fast asleep, lying on top of her brocade quilt with her face to the wall. Afraid that one in a drunken state would be susceptible to cold, he wished to do something but didn't want to disturb her lest she wake up. He saw that over the bedstead hung a scarlet silkfloss-padded and brocade-covered quilt. Noiselessly he took it down and spread it over her. He then picked the lamp wick until the lamp shone brightly, took off his shoes, got into bed with the pot of hot tea, and nestled up against her. With his left hand holding the teapot against his bosom and his right hand on Sister Mei, he dared not close his eyes even for one instant. Truly,

> He did not enjoy the clouds and rain,
> But he did nestle against fragrant jade.

In the middle of the night, Sister Mei woke up and felt the power of the wine getting the better of her. Feeling on the verge of vomiting, she struggled up to a sitting position, her head hanging low, and she retched over and over again. Qin Zhong also rose quickly. Realizing that she was about to vomit, he put down the teapot and stroked her back. After a while, Sister Mei could not hold out any longer. In less time than it takes to tell, she let go of herself and threw up. Afraid that the quilt would get soiled, Qin Zhong spread out the sleeve of his robe under her mouth. Unaware of his move, Sister Mei vomited with abandon. With her eyes closed, she then asked for tea to rinse her mouth with. Qin Zhong got down from the bed, quietly took off his robe, and laid it on the floor. Finding the teapot still warm, he filled a bowl with the savory strong tea and handed it to her. After finishing two bowls of the tea in quick succession, she lay down, feeling slightly better but still exhausted. Turning her face toward the wall, she went back to sleep. Qin Zhong rolled up his robe tightly around the soiled sleeve and put the bundle by the side of the bed. He then got onto the bed again and held her in his arm as before.

Sister Mei did not wake up until daybreak. Turning over, she saw a man sleeping by her side. "Who are you?" she asked.

"My name is Qin."

Vaguely recalling what had happened in the night, she said, unsure of herself, "I must have been dead drunk last night."

"No, you were not all that drunk."

"Did I throw up?"

"No."

"That's better," said she. But, after a few moments of thinking, she continued, "I remember I did. I also remember drinking some tea. Can I have dreamed everything?"

It was only then that Qin Zhong said, 'Yes, you did throw up. Because you had a drop too much, I had taken precautions by holding a teapot against my bosom to keep it warm for you. Then, when you threw up and asked for tea, I offered you some. You obliged me by drinking two cups."

Appalled, Sister Mei said, "But that was filthy stuff! What did I vomit into?"

"I was afraid that the quilt would be soiled, so I held up my sleeve for you."

"Where is your robe now?"

"I rolled it up and put it over there."

"Too bad your robe is ruined."

"I'm only too lucky to have something from you on my clothes."

Hearing these words, Sister Mei thought, "What a sweet man!" And she became more than a little favorably disposed toward him.

It being broad daylight by now, Sister Mei got off the bed to relieve herself. Looking at Qin Zhong, she suddenly realized that he was Qin the Oil Peddler. "Tell me the truth," said she. "Who are you? Why were you here last night?"

"I wouldn't dare to say anything but the truth to you, Queen of Flowers. Yes, I am Qin Zhong, often in this house to deliver oil." He then proceeded to tell her how he was smitten when he first saw her walking patrons to the gate and later mounting a sedan-chair, and how he had saved money to be with her. "Now that I've spent a night by your side, the happiness of it will suffice for three lifetimes. I can't be more content."

These words touched Sister Mei even more deeply. "I was too drunk last night to take care of you," said she. "Don't you regret that you got nothing for your money?"

"You are a fairy from heaven. My only worry is that I may not have served you well. I'm already happy enough that you are not angry with me. How would I dare to ask too much?"

"You have a business to take care of, so why don't you use your savings to support your family? This is not the kind of place for you."

"I'm a bachelor. I have no wife or children."

After a pause, Sister Mei continued, "Will you come back again?"

"My happiness last night is enough to comfort me throughout the rest of my life. How would I dream of the impossible?"

Sister Mei thought, "Such a good man is hard to come by. He's so honest and kind and considerate. He says only nice things about me and overlooks my faults. He's one in a thousand. Too bad he is of low class. If he were from a respectable family, I'd gladly marry him." While she was in the midst of these thoughts, the maids brought in water for them to wash their faces with, along with two bowls of ginger soup. Qin Zhong washed his face but he needed not comb his hair because he hadn't undone his hair the night before. After a few sips of the ginger soup, he said he was ready to go.

"Why don't you stay a while longer?" said Sister Mei. "I want to talk to you."

"I admire you so much, Queen of Flowers, that I'd be more than happy to be with you for as long as I can. But one must know one's place. I was impudent enough to have come here last evening. If others get to know this, I'm afraid your reputation will suffer. I'd better go as soon as possible."

With a nod, Sister Mei dismissed the maids. She then hurriedly opened her make-up box and took out twenty taels of silver. Handing them over to Qin Zhong, she said, "Last night was tough for you. This money is for your business. Don't tell anyone about it."

Qin Zhong stoutly declined her offer.

"Money comes easily to me," said she. "This little trifle is just to show my gratitude to you for your kindness last night. Don't turn me down. Any time you're short of money for your business in the future, I'll help you out. As for that soiled robe, I'll have a maid wash it clean before returning it to you."

"That worthless piece of clothing doesn't deserve your attention. I'll wash it myself. And I can't take your money."

"Nonsense!" So saying, Sister Mei stuffed the silver into his sleeve and turned him around. Realizing that he would not be able to prevail, he saw nothing for it but to accept. After making a deep bow, he put the rolled-up robe under his arm and walked out the door. When he passed by Madam Wang's room, a male servant saw him and exclaimed, "Ma'am! Young Master Qin is leaving!"

Sitting on her chamber pot at the time, Madam Wang cried out, "Young Master Qin! Why are you leaving so early?"

"I have a few things to take care of," replied Qin Zhong. "I'll come to thank you another day."

Let us not follow Qin Zhong as he left but stay with Sister Mei, who was moved by his sincerity and felt deeply sorry for this man whom she hardly knew. For the rest of the day, she turned away all visitors and stayed in her room to recover from her hangover. Of the entire legion of her patrons, her thoughts were with Qin Zhong alone throughout the day, as attested to by the following song to the tune of "Hanging Branch":

> *My sweet foe is no frequenter of brothels,*
> *But a petty trader, a decent man.*

Tender, gentle, you know my heart and mind;
You are neither hot-tempered nor fickle.
I try to dismiss you from my heart,
But my thoughts keep wandering back to you.

Let us follow another thread of the story and come back to Xing Quan, who was living in Zhu the Tenth's house. Xing was having an affair with Orchid, and, with Zhu confined to bed in his illness, they threw all caution to the winds. After several outbursts of anger from Zhu, the two of them worked out a plan. One night, taking advantage of the darkness, they took all the money of the shop and fled none knew whither. Zhu did not learn about this until the next morning. He had neighbors help him draw up a list of stolen items and go on a search for the two missing persons, but all to no avail. He deeply regretted having been misled by Xing Quan into dismissing Zhu Zhong. As the saying goes, "It takes time to know a person." Having heard that Zhu Zhong was now living in a rented place by All Peace Bridge and peddling oil for a living, he had a mind to take the young man back, so that he could have someone to look after him in his old age and to take care of the funeral after his death. But afraid that Zhu Zhong might still be bearing a grudge against him, he asked some neighbors to talk the young man into coming back home, and to advise him to remember only good things about people and banish bad memories. As soon as he heard these words, Qin Zhong packed his belongings and returned to Zhu the Tenth's house. Upon seeing each other, they burst into bitter sobs. Zhu gave all his savings to Qin Zhong. Throwing in his own savings of more than twenty taels of silver, Qin Zhong renovated the shop and resumed his position behind the counter.

Because he had returned to Mr. Zhu's house, he changed his name back to Zhu Zhong from Qin Zhong. Within a month, Mr. Zhu Senior's illness took a turn for the worse. Medicine failed to work, and he died. Zhu Zhong thumped his chest and wailed in grief as if the deceased were his own birth father. He took care of the funeral and held seven memorial services in all, one on every seventh day after the death. The Zhu family's ancestral grave site was located outside Clear Waves Gate. Zhu Zhong went about all the ceremonies strictly in accordance with etiquette and won praises from the neighbors for his kindness. After the rituals were over, the shop was reopened for business. This oil shop was one of long standing. Business had always been good, but because Xing Quan had been stealing from the shop to fatten his own pocket, the shop had lost many clients. However, now that Young Master Zhu was the owner of the shop, who would not come to patronize? Therefore the business grew to be even more prosperous than before.

Working all by himself, Zhu Zhong was anxious to find an experienced person to help him out. One fine day, a middleman called Jin Zhong led into the shop a man around fifty years old. It turned out that he was none other than Shen Shan (*Good plot.*), who had lived in Peace and Happiness Village outside the city of

Bianliang. He was the one who had lost his daughter, Yaoqin, in their flight south when the government troops scattered the crowd of refugees. He and his wife spent the next few years of their lives on the road, fleeing in panic from one place to another. Having recently heard that Lin'an was a prosperous city where most of the refugees from the north had taken up residence, they made their way there to look for their daughter, but no clue was found. Their travel money all spent, they were reduced to their wits' end as the innkeeper kept pressing them to leave unless they paid the bills for room and board. Quite by accident, they heard Jin Zhong the middleman mention that the Zhu family oil shop needed an assistant. Shen Shan had been owner of a grocery store, and oil retailing was very much in his line. In addition, Young Master Zhu was a fellow native of Bianliang. So he had Jin Zhong take him to the shop. Zhu Zhong asked him some questions and was overcome with emotion upon learning that they were from the same place.

"Since you have nowhere else to go," said he, "you and your wife can stay with me, a fellow townsman. You can take your time looking for your daughter before deciding what to do next." Right away, he offered Shen Shan two strings of cash to pay the innkeeper with. Shen's wife Ruan-shi was also brought over to Zhu Zhong. After an exchange of greetings, Zhu Zhong had an unoccupied room cleaned up for the elderly couple to stay in. Much to Zhu Zhong's delight, the husband and wife did their best to help him out in every way they could in the shop and around the house.

Time flew like an arrow. Quite unnoticeably, more than one year elapsed. As Young Master Zhu remained a bachelor, many people were willing to offer their daughters to him and forgo the betrothal gifts, because they were impressed by his financial status as well as his honesty and sincerity. However, remembering the beauty of the Queen of Flowers, Zhu Zhong had no interest in those of mediocre looks and was determined not to marry until he found a girl with outstanding qualities. And so he dragged his feet as time wore on day by day. (*A clear explanation of why Zhu Zhong remains a bachelor.*) Truly,

> *One who has sailed the vast seas*
> *Is not impressed by just any body of water.*
> *One who has been to the Wu Mountains*
> *Is not easily awed by just any cloud.*

Let us come back now to Sister Mei in Madam Wang's establishment. Enjoying her reputation, she indulged in pleasure day and night. Indeed, she had more exquisite food and clothing than she could ever desire. And yet, every time things didn't turn out right, every time her patrons went too far or fought with one another over her or passed her over for some other girl, and every time she got ill or woke up in the middle of the night after a wine-induced sleep to find no one there to take care of her, she would recall Young Master Qin's kindness and regret that there was no way for her to see him again. Well, her life as a courtesan being predestined to come to an end around this time, a change in her fortunes was about to occur. One year later, something happened.

In the city of Lin'an, there lived a Young Master Wu the Eighth, whose father Wu Yue was the incumbent prefect of Fuzhou. Young Master Wu had recently returned home from his father's duty station with a liberal amount of gold and silver. With a penchant for gambling and drinking, he was also a frequenter of houses of pleasure. Having heard of the fame of the Queen of Flowers but never laid eyes on her, he sent over invitations time and again, but Wang Mei did not want to take him because she had heard unfavorable comments about his character. More than once she turned him down on one excuse or another. He also went several times in person to Madam Wang's house with his good-for-nothing friends to see her, but in vain.

It being the season of the Clear and Bright Festival,[14] every family went out to sweep their family graves and enjoy the sights and sounds of spring. Sister Mei was tired after all the spring excursions day after day. Moreover, she still owed some patrons quite a number of poems and paintings she had promised them. So she instructed the servants to turn away all visitors. Behind closed doors, she lit some joss sticks of superior quality and laid out the four treasures of the scholar's study.[15] She had barely picked up her brush-pen when she heard a commotion outside. It was Mr. Wu, followed by more than ten fierce-looking lackeys, here to take her on an outing to the lake. Because Madam Wang had turned him away each time, he and his men broke everything they saw and smashed their way from the main hall to Sister Mei's room, which they found to be locked. The truth of the matter was that the courtesans' way of rejecting patrons was for the girl to stay in her room with her door locked from the outside, and the patron would be told that she was not there. A naïve patron would be taken in by the trick but Young Master Wu, being a frequenter of houses of ill repute, was not to be deterred. He had his lackeys wrench off the padlock and kick open the door.

Sister Mei dodged but was not quick enough. Wu saw her, and, before she could protest, had two of his men drag her, one by each arm, out of her room. While Wu was spouting a stream of curses, Madam Wang wanted to go up and apologize to him to calm him down, but seeing that things had taken an ugly turn, she shrank back to get out of his way. All the members of the establishment hid themselves out of sight. And so Mr. Wu's lackeys dragged Sister Mei out the gate and tore with all speed down the streets, with total disregard for her small bound feet. Young Master Wu triumphantly brought up the rear. The two lackeys did not let go of Sister Mei until they got to the bank of West Lake, where they put her down into a boat.

Since joining the Wang establishment at age twelve, Sister Mei had enjoyed a pampered life in the lap of luxury. Never had she been subjected to such violence. Once in the boat, she covered up her face and burst into loud sobs, her face turned toward the bow of the boat. Young Master Wu did not relent but sat in anger in his chair facing the lake, in the pose of the valiant Guan Yunchang,[16] with his lackeys standing behind him. After giving the order for the boat to get on its way, he lashed out at Sister Mei, "Cheap little hussy! Little whore! You don't appreciate a favor when you see one! If you cry again, you'll be beaten up!"

Fearlessly, Sister Mei went on crying. Upon reaching the Mid-Lake Pavilion, Wu ordered some food set out in the pavilion. He himself went up first into the pavilion, saying to his men, "Bring that little hussy up for a drink with me."

Sister Mei clung to the railing of the boat and adamantly refused to budge, while crying at the top of her voice. Very much out of countenance, Wu drank a few cups of wine listlessly by himself, had the place cleaned up, and went back down into the boat. As his hands reached out for Sister Mei, she stamped her feet and wailed even more loudly. In a rage, Wu had his men pull off her hairpins and earrings. Her hair disheveled, she ran up to the bow and made as if to throw herself into the water, but the servants held her back. Mr. Wu said, "You think you can get away with your antics? Even if you die, it'll just be a matter of a few taels of silver as far as I'm concerned. Big deal! But I don't want to have a death on my hands. The moment you stop crying, I'll let you go back. I won't be hard on you."

Upon hearing that he would let her go, the Queen of Flowers stopped crying. By Wu's order, the boat moved to a quiet spot by Clear Waves Gate, where Sister Mei's embroidered shoes and foot-bindings were taken off, to reveal a pair of golden-lotus feet shaped like white bamboo shoots. After instructing his men to help her ashore, Wu said crossly, "Whore! Walk home if you can! I can't spare anyone to escort you." (*What a brute!*) With that, the boat was poled away from the shore toward the middle of the lake. Truly,

> *All too many burn zithers and cook cranes;*
> *All too few show kindness to the fair sex.*

Her feet now bare, Sister Mei could not take even one step. She thought, "With my talents and my looks, I got to be so humiliated only because I was driven to this profession. None of my rich and powerful patrons comes to my aid when I need them. Even if I make it back, how can I get on with my life in such humiliation? I'd be better off dead, and yet such a death would be worthless. All this reputation of mine will be for nothing. The way I am now, any village woman is far more fortunate than I am. This is all Madam Liu the Fourth's fault. It was her glib tongue that got me into this pass. The proverb says, 'Pretty face, sorry fate.' But no beauty since ancient times had a fate as sorry as mine!" Her grief deepening with these thoughts, she broke out into another violent fit of sobbing.

As coincidence would have it, it so happened that Zhu Zhong passed by at this moment. He had just paid his respects to Zhu the Tenth's grave by Clear Waves Gate and was heading for home on foot after having loaded the sacrificial offerings onto the boat. Upon hearing sobs, he went up for a look. However unkempt she was now, her one-of-a-kind beauty shone through. How would he fail to recognize her? (*Good detail.*) Much taken aback, he said, "Queen of Flowers, what happened to you?"

Hearing a familiar voice through her sobs, Sister Mei stopped crying to take a look. Lo and behold, it was that affectionate and considerate Young Master Qin. Feeling as if she had seen someone from her own family, she poured her heart out to him and told him everything.

Zhu Zhong's heart ached. With tears in his eyes, he pulled out from his sleeve a white silk kerchief more than five feet in length, tore it in half, and gave her both pieces to bind her feet with. He then wiped off her tears and gathered up her hair, all the while comforting her with soothing words. (*For someone truly in love, these actions are not disgusting.*) After Sister Mei had had her cry, he hastened to hire a curtained sedan-chair for her. Walking on foot, he escorted her all the way to Madam Wang the Ninth's house.

Having heard nothing about the girl's whereabouts, Madam Wang had been running around, making inquiries. It was at this anxious moment that she saw Young Master Qin escorting her girl back. She was overcome with joy at the return of her precious pearl. She had not seen Qin Zhong with his load of oil for a long time, and had heard from various sources that he had inherited Mr. Zhu's shop. In easy circumstances now, he was not the same man as before, and so she looked at him in a new light. (*Such is human nature. Procuresses are not the only ones to be snobbish, although those who are may be justifiably regarded as being as bad as a procuress.*) She asked why the girl was in such a state and, upon learning what an ordeal she had gone through and that Young Master Qin was the one who saved her, bowed deeply to him in gratitude and set out wine in his honor. The hour being late, Qin Zhong drank only a few cups before he stood up to leave, but Sister Mei was not about to let go of him. She said, "I've always liked you and hoped to see you again. I'm certainly not going to let you go this time without doing something for you."

Madam Wang also persuaded him to stay, to his great delight. That evening, Sister Mei played her musical instruments, sang, and danced, trying to please him to the best of her ability. (*A scholar dies for one who appreciates his worth; a woman makes herself pretty for one who strikes her fancy.*) Qin Zhong was thrown into raptures and almost danced for joy, feeling as if he were in a dream, roaming the fairyland. When night came and the wine was finished, the two of them went to bed in each other's arms. Their game of clouds and rain was as blissful as could be.

> *He was a young man in his prime;*
> *She a girl skillful in the art of love.*
> *He had dreamed about this for three long years;*
> *She had wished for this moment for one full year.*
> *She thanked him for his patronage last time,*
> *Which deepened all the more her gratitude now.*

He thanked her for obliging him tonight,
Which added to the love he had in his heart.
The courtesan overturned her powder box;
The silk handkerchief was stained.
The oil peddler knocked over his oil jar;
The quilt became wet and soiled.
The village boy who foolishly squandered his money
Now became a figure of romance.

The clouds and rain over, Sister Mei said, "I have something from the bottom of my heart to say to you. Don't turn me down."

"I'll do anything you want me to do, even if I have to go through boiling water and raging fire. How could I ever turn you down?"

"I want to marry you," said Sister Mei.

Qin Zhong laughed. "Even if you marry ten thousand men, I won't be able to make the list. Don't tease me. You'll only make the gods cut my life short."

"I mean it. How can you say I'm teasing you? I was fourteen when the madam got me drunk and made me take my first patron. Ever since then, I've wanted to marry and get out of this business. But because I had met too few people to tell the good from the bad, I was afraid I might marry the wrong man and ruin my future. Later, even though I took on many patrons, they were all big spenders and libertines. They buy pleasure with money. They care nothing about me. Of all the men I've met, you are the only trustworthy one. I've also heard that you are still single. If you don't look down on me because of my lowly profession, I will be more than happy to serve you as your wife for the rest of my life. If you turn me down, I will strangle myself with a three-foot-long piece of white silk and die at your feet to prove my sincerity. This will be better than dying at the hands of that bumpkin yesterday and getting laughed at for a worthless death." So saying, she started to weep.

Qin Zhong said, "Don't feel so bad. You are too kind. To have your love is more than anything I can ever wish for. Far be it from me to turn you down. But with my limited means, much as I want to, I won't be able to afford you at your high price."

"That's all right. To tell you the truth, in preparation for marriage to get out of this business, I have saved up some things which I've deposited elsewhere. So you don't have to pay a penny for my redemption." (*Thanks to Madam Liu the Fourth's advice.*)

Qin Zhong said, "Even if you redeem yourself with your own money, how are you going to put up with my way of life, after having lived in such grand style for so many years?"

"I'll be content with plain cotton clothes and simple food. I won't have regrets."

"You may be willing to do so, but I'm afraid the madam won't have it."

"I'll come up with something," said Sister Mei. The two of them talked until daybreak about what to do.

The truth of the matter was that Sister Mei had deposited many trunks and boxes with some patrons she knew well, such as the sons of Academician Huang, Secretary Han, and Marshal Qi. Now she took them back one by one, saying that she had a need for them. (*Sister Mei has the potential to do great things.*) Secretly she had Qin Zhong keep these possessions in his house. Then she went to Madam Liu's house in a sedan-chair and told the latter about her plan to marry.

"I did talk to you about this once," said Madam Liu. "But you're still too young to marry. And whom do you have in mind?"

"Auntie, never mind who he is. I did as you said. This is a case of a real getting-out, a happy one and the once-and-for-all kind. It's not a false one, nor a short-lived one. (*A wonderful reply, echoing Madam Liu's own words.*) If you, Auntie, could bring this up to Mother, she'll surely agree. I have nothing much to offer you, Auntie, but here are ten taels of gold for you to make some hairpins with. Please talk to Mother on my behalf. If you can talk her around, I'll have more gifts for you, the matchmaker."

At the sight of the gold, Madam Liu smiled until her eyes all but vanished. "You are like my own daughter. And this is a good thing, too. How can I take money from you? I'll just keep it for you for the time being. You can leave this job to me. I'm only afraid that your mother won't let you go off lightly because you are her money tree. She'll probably ask for a thousand taels of silver. Is your man willing to pay that much? I'd better see him and settle things with him first."

"Auntie, you don't have to concern yourself with this. Just look on it as if I'm paying for my own redemption."

"Does your mother know you are here?"

"No."

"All right. You stay here for lunch. I'll go talk to her. If she changes her mind, I'll come back to let you know."

In a hired sedan-chair, Madam Liu the Fourth went to see Madam Wang. After Madam Wang showed her in, she asked about what Young Master Wu the Eighth had done. After hearing Madam Wang's account, Madam Liu said, "For those of us in this business, it's better to have girls of the middling sort, because they bring in money but don't cause trouble. They don't pick and choose their patrons, and they bring in business every day. But this girl has got too much of a name for herself. She's like a piece of dried fish that has fallen onto the ground: all the ants will swarm up to take a piece of her. Business is good, but there's also a down side to it. She's expensive all right, but she brings you only hollow reputation. Those rich young patrons come with their lackeys who stay the whole night, and that's a lot of work for you because every one of them has to be served well. One slip, and they'll curse you with their foul mouths and break your furniture on the sly. You can't very well complain to their master about them. You just have to swallow the humiliation. (*What a glib tongue! This is only the beginning of much more to come.*) And then, there are those patrons with literary interests and those members of poetry societies and chess clubs, and, several times each month, those girls on the government roster have to provide free entertainment services. With all the rivalry going on among the rich young men, if you give Sister Mei to Mr. Zhang, you offend Mr. Li. When one man is pleased, the other will surely complain. The row kicked up by Young Master Wu was frightening enough. If something had happened to her, you would have lost your capital, and you can't very well sue an official's family. There's nothing for it but to put up with the insult. Thanks to the gods' blessings, nothing much happened to you this time. It was like a thunderstorm that has blown over. But if something unfortunate happened, regrets would have been too late. (*A roundabout way of getting to her purpose: make the madam free Sister Mei from the cage.*) I heard that Young Master Wu the Eighth is up to some mischief and still wants to pick a quarrel with you. That girl of yours has quite a temper. Her refusal to play up to the patrons is the first source of trouble."

Madam Wang said, "Yes, this is exactly what I worry deeply about. This Young Master Wu is not just anybody. He's no lowly sort. It was just because that girl would rather die than receive him that she got into all this trouble. She used to listen to me when she was small. Now that she has built a name for herself, with all those rich young men praising her, coddling her, and spoiling her, she does things her own way all too often. She gets to decide whether to take a patron or not. If she happens to be unwilling, even a team of nine oxen won't be able to pull her around."

"Girls with some status all act like this," said Liu. (*Another push.*)

"Now, listen. If there's an offer for her, I'd rather sell her off and be done with it, so that I won't have to live in fear anymore."

"Wonderful!" said Liu. "With the money you get for her, you can buy five or six girls. If lucky, you may even get ten. It's such a good deal! Why don't you go for it?"

"I've been doing some thinking. Those with money and power hate to part with their money. Instead, they are always out to get a good deal. As for those willing to cough up some money, that girl is so picky she turns them down with that high and mighty air of hers. If there's a good offer for her, could you please make the match? If she's not willing, I'll have to ask you to talk to her. She doesn't listen to me. She believes only in you. You can talk her around."

Bursting into laughter, Madam Liu said, "The purpose of my visit is precisely to make a match for her. How much would you ask for her?"

"Sister, you are a sensible person. In our line of business, we buy cheap, but have you heard of any cheap sales? Also, Sister Mei has been well known for years throughout Lin'an. Who hasn't heard of the Queen of Flowers? She can hardly be let go with just three or four hundred taels. A thousand taels is the minimum."

"I'll do the asking. If I can get that much, I'll come back to let you know. If not, I won't be back." Before leaving, she asked, feigning ignorance, "Where is she?"

"Oh, don't even get me started on this! Ever since that day when she was roughed up by Wu the Eighth, she's been afraid that he'd come again to make more trouble. So she's been going around in her sedan-chair from house to house to complain. The day before yesterday, she went to Marshal Qi's house; yesterday, to Academician Huang's. I have no idea where she went today."

"Since you've made up your mind, she'll have to do as you say. In case she says no, I'll talk to her. But if I produce a buyer, be sure you don't put on airs."

"I won't go back on my word," said Wang, who then walked her guest to the gate. Madam Liu said good-bye and mounted her sedan-chair. Truly,

> She had the tongue of a diplomat;
> She was endowed with the gift of the gab.
> If all tongues wag like a procuress's,
> Huge waves can rise from a puddle.

After returning home, Madam Liu said to Sister Mei, "I told your mother thus-and-so, and she has agreed. As long as she sees the money, this will be done."

"I've got the money," said Sister Mei. "Tomorrow, please be sure to come to see me and close the deal. Don't let it cool off, so that we won't have to start the whole thing over again."

"A promise is a promise," said Liu. "I'll surely be there."

Sister Mei bade Madam Liu good-bye and went home. She did not breathe a word to anyone about the matter.

Around noon the next day, Madam Liu made an appearance, as promised. Madam Wang asked, "Any news?"

"It's as good as settled. I just haven't spoken to the girl yet."

Madam Liu then went to Sister Mei's room. After an exchange of greetings and amenities, Liu asked, "Is the client here? And where's the you-know-what?"

Pointing at the head of her bed, Sister Mei replied, "Everything's in those leather trunks." Whereupon she opened all five or six of them and took out thirteen or fourteen packages, each containing fifty taels of silver. Together with her jewelry items, they amounted to a thousand taels.

Madam Liu was flabbergasted. Her eyes spitting fire, her mouth drooling, she thought, "How can such a young girl be so crafty! How did she manage to put aside so much? Don't those girls of mine take patrons just as she does? But they don't come anywhere close! They don't make as much, of course, but even if they have a few pennies in their purses, they spend them on dried melon seeds and candies, and have me buy fabric for them when their foot-bindings wear out. Sister Wang is the lucky one. She already made a fortune out of this girl over the years, and now here comes along this windfall as the girl gets out. And the money is right here in the house, too, so Sister Wang is spared the trouble of going out to get it." But the words remained unsaid.

Taking Liu's silence to mean that she was trying to make things difficult for her and hit her up for a reward, Sister Mei hastened to take out four lengths of fine silk, two hairpins inlaid with jewels, and a pair of jade hairpins with phoenix patterns. Laying them out on the table, she said, "These are a token of my gratitude to you for what you've done for me."

Merrily, Liu went to Madam Wang and said, "Your girl is buying her own way out. You get the full amount, not a penny less. This is better than having a patron redeem her. Otherwise, you would have to thank the middlemen with feasts and a ten or twenty percent commission." (*Madam Liu never fails to make her point drive home. There's hardly anything she can't sell.*)

When Madam Wang heard about all the riches contained in the girl's leather trunks, her face fell. You may well ask why. Well, of all people in this world, procuresses are the most ruthless. They are not satisfied until their girls surrender everything they make. If the madams hear of any girl with private savings stashed away in a trunk, they would wait until the girl is away to break the locks and ransack the boxes and trunks until they empty them of everything of worth. (*An aside as a lull in the thickening plot.*) In this case, Madam Wang had never dared provoke Sister Mei because the girl had fame, and her patrons were all rich and powerful men who brought in money for the procuress, and because the girl was a little eccentric. Madam Wang had never even set foot in Sister Mei's bedroom. How could she have known that the girl had that kind of money!

Guessing from Madam Wang's dark brows what was in her mind, Madam Liu hastened to say, "Sister Ninth, you're not going to have second thoughts, are you? Those are her private savings. They didn't rightfully belong to you anyway. If she'd spent them, they'd be all gone now. Or, she might have been stupid enough to subsidize a patron who strikes her fancy, for all you know! It's a good thing that she has been frugal. Also, if a girl doesn't have any money of her own, can you drive her out naked when she marries? You'll have to deck her out from head to toe, so that she can hold her head up in her new family. Now, Mei has come up with all these things without ever having to trouble you the least bit. This money is yours, every penny of it. Even after she gets out, she'll still be a daughter to you. If she makes a good living, she'll surely come back with gifts to see you at festivals. After she marries, she'll still be without parents. You can be a grandmother to her children. Won't that be quite nice for you?" These words so pleased Madam Wang that she gave her consent then and there.

Madam Liu went and brought over the packages of silver, which she weighed one by one before handing them over to Madam Wang. She also appraised the jewelry piece by piece. She said to Madam Wang, "I deliberately marked down the price. If you sell them, you should be able to make dozens of taels extra." Though they were both procuresses, Madam Wang was more simpleminded and hung on every word of Liu's.

After witnessing Madam Wang put away everything, Madam Liu had Mr. Wang write a note permitting the girl to marry, and transmitted it to Sister Mei.

"While you're here, Auntie," said Mei, "I'd like to say good-bye to Father and Mother and stay in your home for a couple of days before I choose a lucky day for the wedding. Would you be willing to do that?"

Having accepted the many gifts from Sister Mei, Madam Liu was afraid that Madam Wang the Ninth would back out of the deal. She would be only too happy to get the girl out of the house and be done with it. "Yes, of course," said she in reply.

Right away, Sister Mei began to pack up her toilette boxes, leather trunks, and bedding, but left untouched everything that belonged to the procuress. Her packing finished, she followed Liu out of her room and bade farewell to the madam and her husband and all the other girls. Madam Wang the Ninth gave a few sobs, as befitted the occasion. Sister Mei told the servants to carry her baggage and merrily mounted a sedan-chair with Madam Liu. Upon arrival at Liu's house, Madam Liu put up Sister Mei, along with her baggage, in a nice and quiet room, and Madam Liu's girls all came to offer their congratulations. That evening, Zhu Zhong sent Shen Shan to Madam Liu's house to ask how things were going and learned that Sister Mei had already gotten out. On a chosen auspicious day, the wedding took place amid the music of *sheng* pipes, *xiao* flutes, and drums, with Madam Liu as the matchmaker giving the bride away. Zhu Zhong and the Queen of Flowers spent the night in boundless joy in the bridal chamber decorated with carved candles.

> *Their romance of the past*
> *Did not reduce their joy as groom and bride.*

The following day, when Shen Shan and his wife came to greet the bride, all three of them were dumbstruck upon seeing one another. After some questions and answers, the three of them fell on one another's shoulders and cried. Only then did Zhu Zhong realize that the elderly couple were in fact his parents-in-law. He offered them seats of honor and, together with his bride, bowed to them anew. The neighbors who heard about this were all amazed. On that very day, a feast was laid out in celebration of the doubly happy occasion. All drank and enjoyed themselves thoroughly before the party broke up. Three days later, Sister Mei had her husband prepare some nice gifts and offered them to her former patrons to thank them for their kindness in allowing her to deposit her trunks and boxes, as well as to let them know that she had gotten out and married. This goes to show that she was not a person to leave things at loose ends. She also offered gifts to Madam Wang the Ninth and Madam Liu the Fourth, who were filled with gratitude. After a month had gone by, she opened her trunks and boxes to reveal gold, silver, and silk from the Wu region and brocade from the Shu region, which all came to more than three thousand taels in value. She handed all the keys to her husband for him to acquire land and property and expand the family possessions. The oil shop came to be run by her father, Mr. Shen. In less than a year, the business boomed and the family grew rich enough to hire servants and live in grand style.

Out of gratitude for the blessings of the gods of heaven and earth, Zhu Zhong decided to donate a three-month supply of candles and oil to the various monasteries in the area. He observed a Buddhist diet, took a bath, and went to the monasteries to pay homage. He started from Zhaoqing Monastery and went on to the monasteries of Soul's Retreat, Faxiang, Clear Mercy, and Tianzhu. Let us focus our attention on Tianzhu Monastery. Dedicated to the Bodhisattva Guanyin, it consisted of the Upper Tianzhu, the Middle Tianzhu, and the Lower Tianzhu monasteries, with all their crowds of worshipers, but they were located in the mountains and were inaccessible by boat. Zhu Zhong had some men carry one load of candles and three loads of clear oil while he himself took a sedan-chair. He went to the Upper Tianzhu first, where the monks greeted him and led him into the main hall. Mr. Qin, the old acolyte, lit the candles and took care of the incense.

In changed circumstances now, Zhu Zhong had taken on a dignified look, a far cry from the way he had looked in his childhood. Small wonder that Mr. Qin Senior did not recognize his very own son. He did feel intrigued by the big characters "Qin" and "Bianliang" on the oil buckets. What a coincidence that those very two oil buckets had been brought to Upper Tianzhu Monastery!

After Zhu Zhong had finished burning joss sticks, Mr. Qin Senior brought in tea on a tray and the abbot served the tea to the guest.

Mr. Qin Senior said, "May I venture to ask the benefactor the reason for those three characters on the buckets?"

Detecting a Bianliang accent, Zhu Zhong hastened to ask, "Why do you ask, sir? Might you be a native of Bianliang, also?"

"Yes, I am indeed."

"What is your name? Why did you join the Buddhist order in this temple? How many years have you been here?"

Mr. Qin Senior told him his name and where he was from. "I came here years ago to flee from the soldiers. I had no means of livelihood, so I gave up my thirteen-year-old son, Qin Zhong, for adoption by a Zhu family. It's been eight years now. I'm so old and frail that I haven't gone down the mountain to make inquiries about him."

Zhu Zhong flung himself upon the acolyte and cried bitterly. "I am Qin Zhong, your son," said he. "I used to peddle oil for the Zhu family and I wrote those three characters on the buckets in order to seek you out. Who would have thought that we would meet here! This is indeed a blessing from heaven!"

The monks all marveled at this reunion of father and son after eight years of separation. That night, Zhu Zhong stayed in Upper Tianzhu Monastery with his father and they filled each other in on what had happened to them in these years. The next day, Zhu Zhong changed his name back to Qin Zhong on the prayer sheets of Middle Tianzhu and Lower Tianzhu monasteries. After the incense-burning services in both places were over, they turned back to Upper Tianzhu Monastery. Qin Zhong wanted to have his father live with him so that he could support and look after him. But, having joined the Buddhist order many years before, Mr. Qin Senior had become used to a vegetarian diet and did not want to go and live with his son.

"After an eight-year separation," said Qin Zhong, "I should make up for lost time and provide for you, Father. In addition, I've just married. My wife should also pay her respects to her father-in-law." Mr. Qin Senior felt obliged to consent. Qin Zhong yielded his sedan-chair to his father. He himself walked all the way home. Once in his house, Qin Zhong took out new clothes for his father to change into, had him take the seat of honor in the main hall, and bowed with his wife, Shen-shi, to him. His parents-in-law, Mr. Shen and Ruan-shi, also came to greet Mr. Qin. A grand feast was laid out later in the day. Mr. Qin declined offers of meat and had vegetables and wine only. The next day, the neighbors came with gifts of money to congratulate them on the wedding, the bride's family reunion, the reunion of the father and son, and the resumption of Young Master Qin's original family name. It was thus a four-fold joyous occasion. The feast of celebration lasted for several days.

Mr. Qin Senior was not willing to stay on. He wished to go back to Upper Tianzhu Monastery to lead a quiet Buddhist life. Qin Zhong did not want to go against his father's wishes. With two hundred taels of silver, he had a separate house built for his father there. Once every month, he had supplies of daily necessities sent over and every tenth day he personally went to see his father. Once every three months, he took his wife Shen-shi along to see him. Mr. Qin Senior lived to be over eighty years of age, until one day he sat down solemnly and passed away. In accordance with his will, he was buried on that very mountain, but this happened later and is not part of our story.

Now let us come back to Qin Zhong and Shen-shi. They had two sons. Husband and wife lived together to a ripe old age, and the two sons later gained fame as scholars. Even to this day, when praising a lover who is affectionate and considerate, those in the houses of pleasure will refer to him as "Young Master Qin" or "Oil peddler." There is a poem in testimony:

> When spring is here and the flowers are in bloom,
> Bees and butterflies busily cull their essence.
> Pity those sons of wealthy families,
> Who lost to the oil-peddler in romance.

4

The Old Gardener Meets Fairy Maidens

The cottage gate stood closed in the night-long rainstorm;
The willows survived, but not the flower blossoms.
My broom to sweep the moss halts in midair,
For the steps are strewn with fallen petals.

This poem was written out of a love for flowers. Back in the Tang dynasty, there lived a hermit scholar, Cui Xuanwei by name, who was devoted to Daoism. A bachelor, he lived in seclusion east of Luoyang. He had a large garden in which he grew flowers, bamboo, and trees. In the middle of the flowerbeds, he had a hut built for his own exclusive use. The servants lived outside the garden and were not allowed in without a good reason. For more than thirty years, he never took a step out of the garden. In spring when the flowers were at their best, he would wander among them day and night.

One balmy and moonlit night in spring, loath to tear himself away from the flowers and go to sleep, Xuanwei was strolling among them when suddenly he saw in the moonlight a woman in blue slowly approaching him. In surprise, he said to himself, "How can there be a woman here at this hour?" Intrigued, he thought, "Let me see where she's going."

Heading neither east nor west, the woman walked straight up to Xuanwei and bowed deeply. Xuanwei returned the greeting and asked, "Which family are you from? Why are you here at this time of night?"

The woman replied, her pearly white teeth showing between her red lips, "I live nearby. My female companions and I are on our way to Upper East Gate to visit our auntie. May we take a rest in your garden?"

Marveling at this mysterious visit, Xuanwei readily gave his consent. The woman thanked him and went back the way she had come. Before long, she reemerged, leading a group of women through the flowers and the willows. As they exchanged greetings with Xuanwei, he peered intently at them by the moonlight and found all of them to be graceful and lithesome. Some were more richly adorned than others, and each was dressed in her own style. Their maidservants were also all bewitchingly charming. He wondered where they could have come from. After the exchange of greetings, he invited them into his hut, where everyone sat down, he as the host and the women as guests.

"May I ask your names, ladies?" said he. "So, are you on your way to see a relative? Is that why you honor this humble garden with your presence?"

A woman in green answered, "My surname is Yang [willow]." Pointing at a companion in white, she continued, "This is Li [plum]." Pointing at another one, in crimson, she said, "This is Tao [homophone of peach]." And so she went on. Coming to the last one, a younger woman in scarlet, she said, "This is Shi Acuo [pomegranate]. We have different surnames, but we are sisters in the same calling. Our Auntie Feng the Eighteenth said a few days ago that she would come to see us, but she hasn't shown up. So we sisters are taking advantage of the bright moon tonight to go visit her. Our second purpose for this trip is to thank you, sir, for your kindness to us."

Before Xuanwei could say anything in reply, the woman in blue announced, "Auntie Feng is here."

Pleasantly surprised, all the women rose to greet her. Xuanwei withdrew to one side to watch.

After an exchange of greetings, one of the women said, "We were on our way to see you, Auntie, when our host asked us to sit down here. And now you're here, too, which goes to show that we are of the same mind." With that, all of them stepped forward and saluted Auntie Feng.

Auntie Feng the Eighteenth said, "Quite a few times I wanted to come and see you, but each time, I was detained by my work. I'm free tonight, so here I am."

The young women said, "It is such a glorious night, Auntie. Please sit and let us offer you some wine and wish you longevity." The woman in blue was told to fetch wine.

"Is it all right for us to sit here?" asked Auntie Feng.

"Yes," said Yang. "Our host is most kind and the ambience most pleasant."

"Where's the host?" asked Auntie, whereupon Xuanwei stepped forward to greet her. There was something ethereal about the gracefully lissome Auntie, with her melodious voice, but as he drew near her, he felt a chilliness that sent shivers down his spine. In all politeness, he invited the guests into the main hall, where the maidservants had already arranged the tables and the chairs. Auntie was offered the seat designated for the most honorable guest, and the young women also sat down one by one in order of seniority. Xuanwei took the host's seat. Before long, wine was set out on the table, along with a fine spread of delicacies and exotic fruits. The mellow wine had an otherworldly sweetness. The moon had grown doubly lambent, and the room was as bright as day. Amid the fragrance that permeated the room, the host and the guests toasted each other back and forth. When they were well warmed with wine, a woman in red offered to Auntie a large vessel filled to the brim with wine and said, "I'd like to sing a song for you, Auntie." The lyrics of the song are as follows:

> *Drops of dew glitter on my red gown;*
> *The rouge on my cheeks is light as a cloud.*
> *My beauty, alas, is not here to stay;*
> *Blame not the spring breeze for its cruelty.*

Rendered in a clear and sweet voice, the song saddened everyone. A woman in white offered a toast, saying, "Let me also sing a song for you, Auntie."

> *My face may be still fairer than white snow,*
> *Just as when I was in the bloom of youth.*
> *Joyless, I dare not fault the spring breeze, but*
> *Lament alone that my charm is fading.*

This song was even more doleful than the previous one. Skittish by nature, with a penchant for wine, Auntie Feng the Eighteenth grew more exuberant with each additional cup of wine she took. After listening to the two songs, she said, "While the host and the rest of us are enjoying the glorious night and the beautiful scenery, why did you have to come up with such sad lines? And there's a sharp sting against me in the songs. Where are your manners? You should be penalized. Finish a large vessel, each one of you, and make up a nicer song!" So saying, she filled a vessel with wine and reached out for them. However, being as inebriated as she was, she had little control of her shaking hand. As she raised the vessel, her sleeve swept against her chopsticks and brought the vessel down. If the wine had been spilled on someone else, all would have been well. But it splashed on Acuo. A beautiful young woman fastidious about cleanliness, Acuo happened to be wearing a scarlet floral-pattern dress of the kind of fabric whose color would change at the tiniest drop of wine. Imagine what such a large vessel of wine would do to it! Worse still, Acuo was also very much under the influence of wine. At the sight of the stain on her dress, she said, her face hardening, "My sisters may want something from you, but I am not afraid of you!" With that, she rose and headed for the door.

Auntie also lost her temper and said, "Is this little girl so emboldened by wine that she dares to challenge me?" She flicked at her dress angrily and also rose to her feet.

Unable to hold her back, the other women pleaded as they followed her down the steps, "Acuo is just a girl, and the wine made her forget her manners. Please don't take this to heart. We'll bring her to you tomorrow to apologize." As Auntie Feng headed east in a huff, the women bade Xuanwei farewell and went their separate ways through the flowers. Xuanwei followed behind in order to see where they were going, but, in his haste, he slipped on some moss and fell. By the time he struggled up to his feet, the women had vanished from view. He thought, "Could I have been dreaming? But I didn't lie down to sleep. Could they be ghosts? But they were certainly all nicely dressed and spoke clearly. But if they were humans, how could they have all disappeared without a trace?" These thoughts kept churning his bewildered mind. He turned back to the main hall, only to find the tables and chairs in the same positions as before the visit, and none of the wine vessels and dishes was there anymore. Only the fragrance that permeated the hall remained. Though he marveled at the event, he had no fear, because he didn't think it was the work of evil spirits.

The next evening when he was taking another walk among the flowers, he saw that company of women again. They were urging Acuo to go to Auntie Feng the Eighteenth and apologize to her. Acuo replied in irritation, "Why do we have to be so nice to that old hag? Why don't we simply ask the hermit scholar for anything we need?"

In delight, the others said, "You're right!" Turning to Xuanwei, they said as if with one voice, "We sisters live right here in your garden, sir. Whenever we are harassed by evil winds, we go to Auntie Feng for protection. But after Acuo gave her offense yesterday, we may not be able to do so again. If you would be willing to protect us, we'll surely repay you for your kindness."

"But what power do I have to give you protection?"

Acuo said, "We ask that every New Year's Day, you make a red banner with drawings of the sun, the moon, and the five stars, and stand the banner in the eastern corner of the garden. That will ensure our safety. Now that New Year's Day is already behind us, please do this at dawn on the twenty-first day of this month at the first stir of the east wind. We will thus be spared of a disaster that will otherwise befall us on that day."

"That's easy to do. I won't fail you," said Xuanwei.

The young ladies said gratefully in chorus, "We will never forget your generosity and kindness." That said, they bade him farewell and took off with such speed that before Xuanwei could go after them, they disappeared with a gust of fragrant wind. In order to find out if all this was real, Xuanwei made the banner the very next day. When the twenty-first day of the month finally came, he rose at the first light of dawn. There was indeed a gentle easterly breeze. Quickly he stood the banner in the eastern corner of the garden. In an instant, there sprang up from south of the city a furious gust of wind that shook the earth, whirled up sand and stones, and knocked down trees along its path. Only the flowers in his garden were unscathed. Xuanwei now realized that the women were the spirits of the flowers. Acuo, the one in scarlet, was the spirit of the pomegranate. Auntie Feng the Eighteenth was none other than the goddess of wind.

The next evening, the women came to thank him, each carrying a large bouquet of peach and plum blossoms, and said, "We are ever so grateful to you for having protected us from a major disaster. Lacking a better present to offer to you, we've brought you some flowers. If you eat them, you'll get to live longer and stay young. Should you be willing to go on protecting us, you will be able to live forever." Xuanwei ate the flowers as instructed and, indeed, regained the youthful look of a thirty-year-old man. Later, he acquired the Dao and became an immortal. There is a poem in testimony:

> The Hermit of Luoyang loved growing flowers;
> He raised the red banner year after year.
> The flowers he ate gave him longevity;
> He didn't need gourd-sized dates to be an immortal.

Dear audience, do not dismiss my story about the wind goddess and the spirits of flowers as nonsense. This empire with its nine regions and four seas abounds in strange things that you may not have seen or heard—things that have not found their way into history books or the classic canon. Even the encyclopedia of Zhang Hua recorded only a fraction of them, and there was only so much that Yu Shinan, the walking library, knew.[1] In fact, what I narrated above is nothing out of the ordinary and should come as no surprise. Be all this as it may, I will not pursue this point any further, because Confucius never talked of wonders and extraordinary things. However, loving flowers does lead one to fortune, and destroying flowers does reduce one's life span. These are facts, not fabrications. If you don't believe me, please listen to my next story, about an old gardener meeting fairy maidens. After listening to this story, those who love flowers will cherish them even more dearly; those who don't care for flowers will do so under my persuasion. Even though you may not acquire the Dao and become an immortal as a result, you will find the story entertaining enough.

You may well ask, in which dynasty and what place does the story take place? Well, it takes place in Eternal Happiness Village outside East Gate, Pingjiang Prefecture [present-day Suzhou], south of the Yangzi River, during the reign of Emperor Renzong [r. 1023–63] of the Song dynasty. In the village, located only about two li from the city, lived an old man named Qiu Xian, an erstwhile farmer with several *mu* of land and a thatched hut. His wife, Shui-shi, had passed away, leaving him childless. As he had loved growing flowers and fruits ever since childhood, he gave up farming to devote himself to horticulture. Whenever he chanced upon some rare flower, he was happier than if he had found a jewel. Whatever pressing business he had, if he happened to pass by a house and saw trees or flowers in the yard, he would maneuver his way into the garden with an apologetic smile to take a better look at them, regardless of whether the host was willing or not. If they turned out to be common varieties or if he had the same plants blooming in his own garden, he would quickly take his leave, but if he saw a prized specimen that he did not have, or if he had the same plant in his garden but the blossoms had already faded, he would put on hold what he had set out to do and linger on for the rest of the day, unable to tear himself away. He was called by all and sundry the Flower Maniac.

Whenever Qiu Xian saw a flower vendor with a good plant, he just had to buy it, whether he had money on him or not. In the latter case, he would take off his clothes and pawn them. Some flower-vendors, well aware of this weakness of his, demanded high prices, and he could not do otherwise than brace himself and pay. There were also unsavory characters who, knowing his love of flowers, went looking for good flowers far and near and when they found some, they cut them, stuck them into balls of mud to make them look as if they had roots, and palmed them off on him. And he couldn't help but buy them. Now, isn't it a wonder that they always grew after he planted them in soil? As the days and months went by, he built up an impressive collection.

Around his garden stood a bamboo fence over which climbed roses, roseleaf raspberries, banksia roses, thorned plums, hibiscus, kerria, and broom. By the fence were hollyhocks, touch-me-nots, coxcombs, mallows, and poppies. There were also daylilies and lilies, campions and crown campions, creeping phlox, gladioli, cannas, azaleas, galangals, irises, purple-red pentapetes, twisting-stem peonies, and whatnot. When in bloom, they were a dazzling riot of colors. A few paces from the fence were the more expensive and exotic flowers that blossomed one after another.

The double wicket gate facing south led to a footpath fringed with bamboo and cypresses. Beyond the footpath stood a three-section thatched cottage. For all its humbleness, it was spacious and airy with large windows. The main hall, in which was hung a small scroll of painting by an unknown artist, was furnished with a plain wooden couch, a table, and a few chairs. Everything in the hall was spotlessly clean, and the floor was dustless. Behind the hall were several rooms, including the bedroom, all furnished with exquisite taste. In the garden, a profusion of flowers of all kinds bloomed throughout the seasons. There were:

> *Dainty mei plum blossoms, elegant orchids,*
> *Graceful camellias, demure li plum blossoms,*
> *Apricot flowers that could hardly stand the rain,*
> *Chrysanthemums that defied frosty chills,*
> *Narcissuses in all their refinement,*
> *Tree peonies in all their grandeur,*
> *Scholartrees that towered over the steps,*
> *Water lilies that graced the pond,*
> *Garden peonies nonpareil in their elegance,*
> *Pomegranate blossoms unrivaled in their charm,*
> *Cassia whose fragrance rose to the moon,*
> *Lotuses whose icy beauty chilled the river,*
> *Pear blossoms aglow in the moonlight,*
> *Peach blossoms aflame under the sun,*
> *Mountain camellias shaped like precious pearls,*
> *Wintersweets in the form of alms bowls,*

Crabapple flowers of the best dwarf species,
Winter daphnes of the choicest, gold-rimmed kind,
Roses and azaleas resplendent as scrolls of brocade,
Hydrangeas and brush cherries adding charm to the scene:
The list of flowers goes on with no end;
There were more of them than one could ever count.

The garden gate opened onto a big lake called Skyward Lake but known popularly as Lotus Lake. It merged into Wusong River in the east, Tai Lake in the west, and Pangshan Lake in the south. It was beautiful in all four seasons, rain or shine. Qiu Xian built an earthen causeway along which he planted many peach trees and willows. In spring, the red and green colors rivaled the scenery of West Lake. Lotuses grew all along the margin of the lake, and the center of the lake was bestrewn with water lilies of all colors; when they were in full bloom in all their luxuriance, their fragrance assailed the nostrils. People out to pick water caltrops sang as they oared their small boats. When a light wind sprang up, they would engage in a boat race and skid across the water as if flying. The fishermen rowed their boats to shore to dry out their nets under the willow trees. There were people playing, weaving fishing nets, or lying drunk on the bows of the boats. There were also contests to see who could hold his breath the longest underwater. The air echoed with merry laughter.

Sightseers out to view the water lilies gathered on the painted boats filled with the sound of music. By the time they were ready to go home, dusk had fallen. The thousands of lanterns mixed with the glow of the fireflies and the reflection of stars in the water until one could hardly tell them apart. In late autumn, when chilly winds began to blow and the maple foliage was dyed red and yellow, the withered willows and the lotuses along the shore set off the white duckweeds and the red knotweeds on the water's surface. The mournful cries of the bevies of swan geese among the reeds rose to the clouds. In the depths of winter, with snowflakes whirling around, the water and the clouds shared the same color. The sights and sounds of the four seasons defy description. There is a poem in testimony:

Skyward Lake joins the sky at the horizon;
Some sing fisherman's songs, some pick lotus roots.
With thousands of flowers around the cottage,
He sleeps facing them day after day.

Enough of this idle talk. Early every morning after rising from bed, Qiu Xian swept away fallen leaves from under his flowers, watered the plants one by one, and watered them again in the evening. Whenever he found a plant about to burst into bloom, he would jump for joy. With a warm pot of wine or tea, he would bow deeply to it, pour a libation, call out, "A long life to you!" three times, and sit down by the plant to sip what was left in the pot and eat some light refreshments. When exhilarated by the wine, he would sing with abandon. When tired out, he would lie down by the roots, with a rock as his pillow, and stay there until the buds opened fully. If the sun was beating down too harshly, he would dip a palm-fiber whisk in water and sprinkle the plants. If it was a moonlit night, he would keep himself awake throughout the night. If a rainstorm came on, he would throw a straw poncho over his shoulders, put a bamboo hat on his head, and go on a patrol to inspect the flowers. If a stem was bent, he would prop it up with a bamboo stick, and he would get up from bed and check several times throughout the night.

Whenever flowers wilted, the old man would heave sigh after sigh all day long, often shedding tears. Loath to part with the fallen petals, he would gently sweep them together with his palm-fiber whisk, put them on a plate, and look at them from time to time. After they dried up, he would put them in a clean jar. The day the jar was filled up, he would make a sacrificial offering of tea or wine, saddened by the thought of bidding them farewell. He would then pick up the jar with his hands and bury it deep under the causeway in a ceremony he called "burying the flowers." When fallen flower petals were splashed with mud in the rain, he would wash them with clean water and put them in the lake in a ceremony he called "bathing the flowers."

There was nothing he hated more than the plucking of flowers. His argument went as follows: "A plant blossoms only once a year, in only one season out of the four, and for only a few days in that season. It suffers from three seasons of neglect just to enjoy these few days of glory. But when it is dancing sprightly in the breeze and smiling merrily at people like a human in a moment of triumph, it is suddenly mutilated. It has waited for these few days for so long, only to be snapped off in a trice. If flowers could talk, don't you agree that they would cry out and bemoan their fate? (*These comments remind one of* The History of Vases *by Yuan Hongdao [1568–1610, courtesy name Shigong]*). What's more, budding and wilting take up quite a chunk of these few days, leaving very little time for the real blooming. And then, there's the harassment from butterflies, bees, birds, insects, the sun and the wind, and the fog and the rain. They need humans to take care of them, and yet some people pluck them at will. How can such brutes have the heart to do this?

"Goodness knows how many months and years it takes for a seedling to grow roots, branches, and stems. What's so bad about admiring them while they're in bloom? Why pluck them? Once a blossom is off the stalk, it can't be put back on again. Once a stalk is broken off, it can't go back on the branch again, just as a dead man can't come back to life and separate body parts can't be rejoined. Wouldn't a plant weep if it had a voice?

"Now, about one who plucks flowers, he picks a sprig he likes, puts it in a vase, which he then sets on the table for the enjoyment of a guest sipping wine, or for his woman to wear for the day. The thought never crosses his mind that guests can enjoy their wine outdoors among the flowers and women can deck themselves out with artificial flowers. One stalk in hand means one stalk fewer on the tree. One branch cut off this year means one branch fewer next year. If the life of plants can be extended, wouldn't our enjoyment last longer from year to year? (*This logic applies to everything under the sun. Reckless waste of what heaven provides must be strictly prohibited.*) And then there are the buds that are taken along with the flowers. Aren't they like children who die untimely deaths?

"There are also those who don't enjoy flowers but just pluck them on an impulse. Then they give the good ones away to anyone asking for them or carelessly toss them by the roadside. Aren't these flowers like humans who die unjustly in unforeseen disasters and have no one to redress their wrongs? Wouldn't the flowers burst into angry words if they could talk?"

Such being his philosophy, Qiu Xian never broke off a stalk or hurt a bud in his life. If flowers in someone else's garden struck his fancy, he would rather hang around and look at them all day long. If the owner of the garden offered to cut a spray or a blossom for him, he would say, "What a thing to do!" and refuse to take it. When there were people plucking flowers, all would be well if Qiu Xian was not there to witness the act, but if he were, he would try to talk them out of it. If he was ignored, he would lower his head and sink to his knees to beg for the flowers' lives. Though people ridiculed him and called him the Flower Maniac, many did stop out of regard for his earnestness. In such cases, he would bow deeply to them in gratitude. To boys who wanted to pick flowers and sell them, he offered his own money so as to protect the flowers. If the flowers were damaged in his absence, he would turn sick at heart upon seeing them and try to seal the damaged spots with soil in what he called an act of "curing the flowers." Therefore he did not show his garden to just anyone. He would let in only those relatives, neighbors, and friends whom he found hard to turn away, though not without first giving them the requisite words of admonition. Afraid of any potential offensive odor assailing the flowers, he would tell them to keep their distance and view the flowers from afar. If he caught someone lacking good sense picking a blossom or two, he would make a terrible scene, reddening to the tips of his ears, and would never admit that person again, even if he was sworn at and beaten. People gradually came to know his ways and dared not touch even one leaf.

Birds usually nest in dense foliage and, even more frequently, where they find flowers and fruit. It would not have mattered much if they just fed on fruit, but, sadly, they make it a habit to attack flower blossoms as well. So Qiu Xian fed the birds with rice and cereals that he spread out in open spaces, and prayed to them. And the birds, after eating their fill, had the good sense to flit gently among the flowers and warble, without ever doing the slightest harm to the flowers and the fruit. Qiu Xian was thus able to reap more fruit—all large and delicious—than anyone else. After the fruit ripened, he would first make a sacrificial offering toward the sky to the flower gods before taking a bite himself. He would then offer some to his neighbors before selling what was left, to make enough money to last him through the year.

Finding such delight in his flowers, he never wearied of working in his garden, which he had done for over fifty years. In fact, he found himself in ever-better physical condition as the years went by. Content with his simple lifestyle, he donated whatever he had to spare to help out the poor, which won him respect throughout the village. He came to be called Master Qiu, but he called himself the Old Gardener. There is a poem in testimony:

> *The Old Gardener labored from dawn to dusk*
> *In his garden amid the lovely flowers.*
> *Never tired of the sight of the blossoms,*
> *He forsook sleep to be with his dear ones.*

Our story forks at this point. In the city there lived a certain Zhang Wei, son of a highly placed official. A perfidious, crafty, cruel, and ruthless man emboldened by his family's influence, he bullied the neighbors and brought affliction to innocent people. Those who happened to offend him would come to grief. He would not let go of them until they were completely ruined. With lackeys as ferocious as wolves and tigers, he hung out day and night with several good-for-nothing young men who helped him stir up trouble wherever they went, doing harm to countless people. However, it turned out, in a way no one would have expected, that he was captured by someone more of a terror than he was and beaten within an inch of his life. He brought a lawsuit against the man, but the latter pulled a few strings, and Zhang Wei lost the case. Too ashamed to show his face in public again, he took four or five servants and that gang of young ruffians to his family manor, located in Eternal Happiness Village, not far from Master Qiu's house.

One day, after breakfast, Zhang Wei and his cohorts went out for a walk in the village in a rather besotted state. Their feet led them to Master Qiu's house. At the sight of the luxuriant flowers over the fence embowered in rich foliage, they exclaimed in chorus, "What a nice place! Who lives here?"

A servant of Zhang's replied, 'It's Master Qiu, the gardener. He's better known as the Flower Maniac."

Zhang Wei said, "Yes, I've indeed heard about an old man Qiu nearby who grows wonderful flowers. So this is where he lives. Why don't we go in for a look around?"

"The old man is a little eccentric. He doesn't let people in," replied the servant.

"He may not let other people look around, but he can't treat me the same way. Go knock at the gate!"

This was at a time when the tree peonies in the garden were in bloom. Having just finished watering them, Qiu was seated beside the flowers with a pot of wine and two dishes of tidbits, sipping the wine and enjoying himself. He was into his third cup when he heard poundings on the gate. He put down his cup and went to open the gate, only to see five or six men standing there, reeking with alcohol. Guessing that they must be there to look at his flowers, he blocked the gateway and asked, "How can I help you gentlemen?"

"Don't you know who I am, old man?" said Zhang Wei. "I'm the celebrated Young Master Zhang! That Zhang family manor over there belongs to my family. I'm here because I heard about your nice flowers."

"Young Master," said Qiu, "actually, this old man doesn't have nice flowers. I've only got some peach and apricot trees and the like, and their blossoms are all gone now. There are no other flowers at this time."

Zhang Wei said, his eyes flashing fire, "You old scoundrel! How can looking at the flowers do you any harm? What's the big deal? How can you say you don't have any? Do you think I'm going to eat them?"

"I'm not lying. I don't have any. That's the truth."

Turning a deaf ear to him, Zhang Wei stepped forward and gave the old man a push in the chest, sending him toppling and reeling to one side. The whole gang stormed in. Things having taken such an ugly turn, Master Qiu saw nothing for it but let them enter. Then he closed the fence gate and followed behind. He picked up his wine pot and dish of tidbits and stood off to one side. The men saw that, of the many flowers all around them, the tree peonies were blooming the best, and those were tree peonies not of common varieties like Spring on the Jade Tower but of five rare kinds. Which five? Yellow Tower, Green Butterfly, Red-Fleshed Watermelon, Dancing Green *Suanni* Beast, and Scarlet Lion Head.

The tree peony is the queen of flowers, and the Luoyang tree peony is the queen of queens. One plant of Yao Yellow or Wei Purple costs five thousand cash. You may well ask, Why do peonies bloom best in Luoyang? Well, back in the Tang dynasty, the debauched Empress Wu Zetian [r. 684–704] showered favors on two young officials named Zhang Yizhi and Zhang Changzong. One wintry day, wishing to take a walk in the imperial garden, she wrote a four-lined decree which said,

> *Tomorrow we shall stroll in the royal garden.*
> *Send word at once to the god of Spring:*
> *Make all flowers bloom overnight,*
> *Before the advent of the morning wind.*

Empress Wu being a sovereign preordained by destiny, the flowers dared not resist her order but all bloomed overnight. The following day, when the empress went to the imperial garden, she found all the flowers in bloom in a blaze of color— all except the tree peony, which, in its pride, refused to please the empress and her favorites. Not even one single leaf could be seen. In a rage, Empress Wu banished all tree peonies to Luoyang, hence the fame of the Luoyang tree peony. There is a lyric to the tune of "Spring on the Jade Tower" devoted to the tree peony:

> *The prized flower in its grace*
> *Stands in splendor as the east wind blows by,*
> *Its tender heart arousing pity,*
> *Its beauty partly washed off by the sad rain.*

The fair lady in her boredom
Wakes with a start at the strains of music.
She goes to her mirror, demure and meek,
Her spring sorrows not as deep as the peony's.

The tree peony bed was opposite the thatched cottage, marked off all around by Taihu rocks. A wooden frame stood over the bed, supporting a cotton awning that protected the flowers from the sun. The plants were about six to ten feet tall, and the blossoms, as large as platters, dazzled the eye in their radiant colors. "What wonderful flowers!" exclaimed the men. To Qiu Xian's horror, Zhang Wei stepped onto a rock to sniff at the fragrance. "Young Master," he called out. "Stay away from the flowers, and don't go up there!"

Zhang Wei had been waiting for a chance to pick a fight for having been denied admission. Upon hearing these words, he said, "You live right by my family manor. Don't you know who Young Master Zhang is? You have such beautiful flowers and yet you lied, saying you didn't have any. You should have been satisfied that I let you off easy, and yet you yell at me like that! One little sniff won't hurt! I'm going to do exactly what you say I can't do!" So saying, he bent the blossoms one by one toward himself and reached over to press his nose against them.

Master Qiu was furious but dared not protest. He had expected the brute to be gone in a moment or two. But now, with an exaggerated show of interest, Zhang Wei said, "How can I enjoy such beautiful flowers without wine?" Whereupon he told his servants to fetch wine.

Even more upset now that wine was to be brought over for a longer stay, Master Qiu stepped forward and said, "My cottage is too small. There's no place for you to sit. Could you just look at the flowers and then enjoy your wine in your own house?"

Pointing at the ground, Zhang Wei said, "I can sit on the ground."

"But the ground is too dirty, Young Master."

"That's all right. I just need a rug."

Before long, wine and food were brought over and a rug was spread out on the ground. The men sat down in a circle and, playing finger-guessing games as they drank, they whooped and cheered in a deliberate show of triumph while Qiu sat on one side, fuming.

As Zhang Wei looked at the luxuriant vegetation, an evil thought came to his mind. He wanted to own the place. Squinting his wine-sodden eyes, he said to Qiu, "I'd never have guessed that a dumb-looking old man like you would turn out to be such a good gardener. Here's a cup of wine to reward you for the good job!"

As angry as he was, Qiu snapped, "I don't drink. You help yourself to it."

"Is this garden of yours for sale?"

At this ominous tone, an astounded Qiu answered, "This garden is my life. How would I ever have the heart to sell it?"

"Spare me this nonsense of a garden being your life! Sell it to me! If you don't have a place to go, I can take you in. I won't ask you to do other things. Just take care of the flowers and trees for me. Won't that be nice?"

Zhang's followers chimed in and said, "What a lucky old man you are! The Young Master doesn't give out such favors every day, you know. Come on, say your thanks!"

The way they browbeat him and tried to push their advantage so infuriated him that his hands and feet went numb. He said nothing.

Zhang Wei said, "This old man be cursed! Answer me! Yes or no?"

"I've told you I'm not selling. Why keep asking?"

"What crap! If you say again that you're not selling, I'll write up a complaint and send it to the county yamen."

An incensed Master Qiu was about to lash out at him when he thought better of it. He should not be stooping to the level of one who was the worse for drink, and the man had powerful backing, too. So, thinking he had better humor Zhang for the time being before deciding on the next course of action, he said, swallowing his anger, "If the Young Master wants to buy this place, please give me one day to think about it. This is not something to be done in a rush."

"Right. Let's make it tomorrow, then," said the men. Very much inebriated by now, they all rose to go, and the servants cleared away the utensils. Afraid that the men would walk off with his flowers, Master Qiu positioned himself in front of the peonies to protect them. Sure enough, Zhang Wei walked up to the rock to pick the flowers. Before he could get on the rock, Qiu grabbed him and said, "Young Master, flowers may not mean a lot to you, but these few blossoms are the result of goodness knows how much work throughout the year. It'll be too bad if they are broken off. What's more, after they are plucked, they'll wither in just a couple of days. Such an unkind act is quite uncalled for."

"Nonsense!" roared Zhang Wei. "Unkind act indeed! The garden will be mine tomorrow. So even if I destroy everything here, it's none of your business!" So saying, he put out a hand to push Master Qiu away, but the latter held him in a tight grip and said, "Even if you kill me, I'm still not going to let you pluck these flowers!"

"What a horrible old scoundrel!" cried Zhang's lackeys. "What's the big deal about the Young Master picking a few flowers? Imagine making such a fuss! Do you think we're so afraid of you that we're not going to do it?" So saying, they all went up and plucked the flowers with abandon. Crying out in protest, the old man let go of Zhang Wei and threw himself upon the others, but he couldn't stop every hand at the same time. In the twinkling of an eye, a good many of the blossoms were gone. His heart aching, Qiu cursed, "You swine! Bullying me like this when I've done nothing to provoke you! What's there left for me to live for?" With that, he charged at Zhang Wei and ran smack into him. (*For every lover of the good, there is someone bent on doing evil. For everyone drawn to talent, there is someone bent on killing it. This is the principle of yin and yang at work.*) Being already tipsy with wine, Zhang Wei teetered and fell. "Oh no!" cried his followers. "The Young Master is hurt!" Tossing away the flowers, they pounced on Master Qiu.

An older and wiser man in the crowd, afraid that the violence might be too much for a man of Qiu's age, stopped the others and helped Zhang Wei to his feet. In a mixture of anger and shame because of the fall, Zhang Wei swiped at the flowers left and right until every petal was on the ground. Still not gratified, he trampled them underfoot back and forth. How tragically the flowers perished! Truly,

> *The fists aided by the wine took their toll;*
> *The leaves and the blossoms came to grief.*
> *In the aftermath of a vicious storm,*
> *The fallen petals lay strewn, unpicked.*

Master Qiu burst into loud wails of grief as he rolled in agony on the ground. Hearing the commotion in Master Qiu's garden, the neighbors came running in, only to see flowers and twigs lying all over the ground and a group of men doing violence to them. Appalled, the neighbors stopped them and asked what had happened. Two or three of the neighbors, who happened to be Zhang Wei's tenants, apologized to him on behalf of Master Qiu and humbly saw Zhang off as far as the garden gate.

"Tell that old thing," said Zhang Wei. "If he gives the garden to me and does it nicely, I'll let him off the hook. If there's even a hint of a 'no' from him, he'd better watch out!" That said, he left in a huff.

Seeing Zhang Wei in an intoxicated state, the neighbors did not take his threat seriously. They turned back and helped Master Qiu up to sit on the curb of the pavement. The old man cried his heart out. After saying some comforting words to him, the neighbors bade him good-bye and closed the garden gate after them. As they walked along, one man with a grudge against Qiu for closing his garden to viewers said, "This old man is indeed way too eccentric. That's why this happened. He needs this lesson. It's a warning, so that such a thing won't happen again."

A fair-minded neighbor objected, "What a horrible thing to say! As the ancients said, 'It takes a year's work to make a flower bloom for ten days.' People may admire the flowers and burst into praise, but what do they know about all the hard work that has gone into them? Goodness knows how much trouble he has gone through to make those flowers flourish and bloom. How can you blame him for cherishing them?"

Let us leave them and come back to Master Qiu. Heartbroken over the trodden flowers, he stepped forward and picked them up. The sight of the scattered and soiled petals that had been brutally trampled upon so grieved him that he burst into another fit of sobbing. "Oh my flowers," he cried, "All my life I have taken good care of you. Never have I hurt even one petal or one leaf. I never thought you would come to such grief!" Through his sobs he heard someone saying behind him, "Master Qiu, why are you crying so bitterly?"

Master Qiu turned around and saw a beautiful girl of about sixteen, dressed with quiet, good taste. Not knowing who she was, Qiu held back his tears and asked, "Which family are you from, young lady? What brought you here?"

"I live nearby. I'm here to look at your tree peonies that I've heard so much about. But I see that they're all gone."

The mention of the tree peonies triggered off another fit of weeping from him.

The young lady said, "What is it that makes you cry like this?" Whereupon Master Qiu told her how Zhang Wei had destroyed the flowers.

"I see," said she with a smile. "Would you want to have the blossoms put back onto the stems?"

"You jest! How can fallen blossoms be put back on?"

"I have a magic formula handed down by my ancestors. It works every time."

His grief turning to joy, Master Qiu asked, "Really?"

"Of course."

Sinking to his knees in a bow, Master Qiu said, "If you can work this miracle, I will invite you over each time I have new blooms, for lack of a better way to repay you."

"Don't bow to me. Bring me a bowl of water."

Master Qiu jumped up to get the water, but he thought, "How can there be such magic? Maybe she's making fun of me because she saw me crying." But then he thought again, "I've never seen this girl before. Why should she make fun of me? I think she means it." Hurriedly he filled a bowl with water and rushed back, but the young woman was gone. The fallen flowers were all back on their stems. Not even one petal remained on the ground. Each plant had been uniform in color, but now red and purple were mixed in gradations of shade. With each plant now a patch of colors, the peonies looked even more gorgeous than before, as attested by these lines:

> Apart from Xiangzi the flower dyer,[2]
> There's the fairy who puts blooms back on their stems.
> Faith, when sincere, moves even nonhumans;
> Only a fool would call the gardener a fool.

In happy astonishment, Master Qiu said, "I didn't expect that young lady to work such wonders." Believing that she must still be among the flowers, he put down the bowl of water and went to look for her to thank her. After searching throughout the garden without finding her, he said to himself, "How can she have disappeared just like that?" Then he thought again, "She must still be at the gate. Let me go ask her to pass on her formula to me." And so he rushed all the way to the gate but found it closed. He opened it, only to see two old men, a Mr. Yu and a Mr. Shan, both neighbors of his, sitting there and watching fishermen spreading out their fishnets to dry. At the sight of Master Qiu, both men stood up and said, their hands respectfully folded in front of them, "We heard that Young Master Zhang was here, making trouble. We were in the fields and therefore didn't come to see how you were."

"Don't talk to me about those swine! They made me mad! Luckily, a young lady came and rescued the flowers with a magic formula, but she was gone before I could thank her. Have you seen her?"

In amazement, the two old men said, "Can flowers be rescued? How? And how long has the young lady been gone?"

"She left just a moment ago."

"We've been sitting here for quite some time now. We've seen no one, and certainly no young lady."

Light dawned on Master Qiu. He said, "So, might that young lady be a fairy?"

"Tell us how she rescued the flowers," said the old men.

After Master Qiu gave an account of what had happened, they exclaimed, "How extraordinary! Let's go and see."

Master Qiu asked them in, bolted the gate, and led them to the flowers.

"That young lady must be a fairy!" exclaimed the two men. "No mortal being can work such wonders!"

Without delay, Master Qiu lit some fine joss sticks in his censer and kowtowed to heaven in gratitude.

The two neighbors said, "It's your deep devotion to the flowers that moved the fairy into coming down here. Why don't you show this tomorrow to Young Master Zhang and his bunch of thugs? They'll be ashamed to death!"

"No, no! These thugs are like mad dogs and should be kept at a safe distance. I'm not going to invite them over!"

"You're right," said the neighbors.

Joyfully, Master Qiu warmed up his pot of wine and kept the two neighbors in the garden to enjoy the flowers. They didn't part company until evening. After Mr. Yu and Mr. Shan got back home and spread the story, all the villagers wanted to take a look for themselves on the morrow but were afraid that Master Qiu would not let them.

Now, Qiu had always been a man with a mind of his own. The advent of the fairy stirred up in him the wish to renounce the mortal world. Throughout the wakeful night, he sat by his flowers, lost in thought. When his mind moved on to his clash with Zhang Wei, he gasped with revelation. "It was my own selfishness that brought such humiliation upon myself. If I had been as magnanimous and tolerant as the fairies, this would never have happened."

The next morning, he opened the gate wide to the public. To the first few visitors trying their luck, he said as he sat facing the flowers, "You can go ahead and look at the flowers as long as you don't pluck them." With this assurance, the visitors spread the word around, and all the men and women of the village flocked to the garden.

Let us leave them there for the moment and turn our attention to Zhang Wei. The next morning, he said to his followers, "Yesterday, that old scoundrel knocked me down. I'm not going to let him off the hook so easily. Let's go and demand the garden from him. If he refuses, let's get more men. I won't feel vindicated until we smash up the whole place."

"His garden is right next to your manor. He won't dare refuse to let us in. But we shouldn't have crushed all the flowers yesterday. We should have spared a few for ourselves to enjoy."

"That's all right," said Zhang Wei. "They'll grow back next year. Let's go now, before he comes up with ideas." At these words, all the men got up to go. They were hardly out of the gate of the manor when they heard that a fairy had come down to Qiu's garden and put all the flowers back onto the stems again, and that the flowers had become multicolored, too.

Zhang Wei didn't believe what he heard. "What's so good about that old lowlife that can make a fairy come down to him? And it was good timing, too—coming right after we smashed them up! Does that fairy live in his house? This must be a story he has people spread around because he's afraid we might go back. He thinks we won't bother him if he is protected by a fairy."

"Exactly, exactly, Young Master," said his men.

In a moment, they arrived at Master Qiu's house. The double wicket gate was wide open, through which came and went men and women whose words all confirmed the story.

"So this really happened!" exclaimed Zhang Wei's followers.

"I can't care less!" said Zhang Wei. "Even if the fairy is there right now, I'm still taking over the garden."

They walked along the winding path to the thatched cottage and, upon getting there, realized that what they had heard was true. Strangely enough, whenever there were viewers, the flowers radiated with greater charm and splendor, looking as if they were smiling to people. However astonished he was, Zhang Wei remained unshaken in his resolve to seize the garden. A few moments later, another evil thought came to him. "Let's get out of here," said he to his followers.

Once outside the gate, they asked, "Why didn't you ask him for the garden?"

"I've got a better idea. The garden will be mine tomorrow, and I don't even have to say a word to him."

"What plan have you got?"

"Rebel Wang Ze of Beizhou practices black magic.[3] The Supreme Military Council has issued an order that prohibits sorcery throughout the country and demands the arrest of those who practice black magic. Our prefectural yamen is offering a reward of three thousand strings of cash to anyone with information. Tomorrow, I'll have Zhang Ba go to the yamen and accuse the old man of fooling people with black magic. Didn't he put flowers back on their stems? That old one will surely break down under torture and confess. When he's in prison, the garden will be sold off by the government. Who will dare to buy it? So it'll be given to me for free. And I'll get the three thousand strings of reward cash, too!"

"Good idea!" said his followers. "There's not a moment to lose. Let's get started!"

Right away, they went into the city and wrote up an indictment. The next morning, Zhang Ba was told to bring the charge to the Pingjiang prefectural yamen. Now, this Zhang Ba was Zhang Wei's number-one henchman, who had connections in the yamen, which was why Zhang Wei assigned the job to him.

Upon hearing of this case, the prefectural magistrate, already on the lookout for black magicians, was convinced of the validity of the charge, because all the villagers were witnesses. Immediately, he had the police chief bring along several assistants and go to arrest Qiu Xian, with Zhang Ba leading the way. Having paid bribes, Zhang Wei trailed behind Zhang Ba and the police, along with his followers. The police marched right into the garden, but Master Qiu did not pay attention because he thought they had come to view the flowers. With a mighty shout, the police rushed forward and bound him with a rope.

"What crime have I committed?" asked Qiu in horror. "Please tell me!"

Calling him a sorcerer and a rebel, the police dragged him out of the gate without bothering to hear what he had to say. The neighbors, much taken aback at the sight, went up to ask what was afoot. The police chief said, "Why even ask? It's a big crime that I'm afraid involves all of you in the village." Thus intimidated, the stupid villagers all went their separate ways, afraid to be implicated in the case. Only Mr. Yu, Mr. Shan, and several of Master Qiu's good friends followed at a distance.

After Qiu was gone, Zhang Wei and his followers descended upon the garden to lock up the gate. In case there was still anyone inside, they searched around before they locked the gate and rushed over to the yamen, where the police chief had already brought in Mr. Qiu and made him kneel in the hall. The old gardener saw someone else kneeling next to him but had no idea who he was. The yamen runners, having all pocketed Zhang Wei's bribes, were standing by, ready to put the various instruments of torture to use.

"What kind of a black magician are you?" roared the magistrate. "How dare you fool the local people with your sorcery? How many accomplices do you have? Out with the truth now!"

This accusation was to Master Qiu like a cannon shot out of pitch darkness— he was at a total loss as to where it could have come from. He said, "My family has lived in Eternal Happiness Village for generations. I am a local, not from elsewhere, and I am no sorcerer."

"The other day you used your black magic to put fallen flowers back on their stems. How dare you deny that?"

At the mention of flowers, Master Qiu realized that Zhang Wei was behind all this. And so he gave a detailed account of how Zhang Wei had tried to seize his garden and destroyed the flowers, and how a fairy maiden had descended. To his dismay, the magistrate was a stubborn man and did not believe one word of his deposition. Laughingly, the magistrate said, "Many people infatuated with immortality practice Daoism all their lives without ever meeting a fairy. Why would a fairy be willing to come to you the moment you start crying over some flowers? Even if a fairy did come, she should have told you her name, and how could she have disappeared without even saying good-bye? Whom are you trying to fool? Nothing further need be said. This is a sorcerer, and no mistake! Apply the ankle-squeezer on him!"

With a collective cry, the runners swarmed up like wolves and tigers and threw the old gardener to the ground. They got his ankles and were about to put the squeezer on him when the magistrate had a dizzy spell and almost fell off his seat. Feeling heavy in the head and unable to hold himself upright, he ordered that a cangue be put on Qiu and that he be taken to the lockup to await another interrogation the next day.

Master Qiu wept all the way as the runners took him to the lockup. His eyes falling on Zhang Wei, he said, "Young Master Zhang, you and I had never had any grudges against each other before. Why would you want my life?"

Without bothering to answer him, Zhang Wei turned away and went off with Zhang Ba and the other young thugs.

At this point, Yu and Shan arrived and asked Qiu Xian what had happened. After having learned the details, they said, "How can there be such injustice! But don't worry. We'll have all the villagers write a joint petition tomorrow to bail you out."

Master Qiu said sobbingly, "I certainly hope you will!"

"Hey, you damn criminal!" snapped a lockup warden. "Get a move on! Crying won't get you anywhere!"

Tearfully Master Qiu went to the lockup. His neighbors put together some wine and food and delivered them there. Instead of serving them to him, the wardens kept the wine and food for their own enjoyment. When night fell, they chained him to his bed, where he lay like a dead man, unable to move his hands or feet. In his agony, he thought, "I wonder which fairy rescued the flowers. Now that I'm here on a trumped-up charge because of this, Oh Fairy, please save me if you have any compassion for me. I'll gladly give up my home and enter the Daoist order." He was in the midst of these thoughts when he saw the fairy maiden who had appeared to him the other day approaching him unhurriedly.

"Great Fairy!" he cried out frantically. "Please help this disciple of yours!"

The fairy said with a smile, "So you want to be delivered from your misery?" As she pointed a finger at him, his cangue fell apart. Scrambling to his feet, Qiu Xian said with a kowtow, "May I ask your name, Great Fairy?"

"I am a flower maiden serving Queen Mother of the Jasper Pool.[4] It was out of pity for your profound love of flowers that I made the blossoms return to their stems. I had no idea you would be accused so unjustly by that scoundrel because of this. However, you are predestined to go through an ordeal at this time, but it will be over tomorrow. As for Zhang Wei, who smashed your flowers and plotted against your life, the Lord on High has decided to shorten his life span upon the request of the flower gods. And major misfortunes will befall all his accomplices. You would do well to devote yourself to self-cultivation. In a few years' time, I will surely come to deliver you."

With another kowtow, Qiu Xian said, "Please enlighten me on the ways of self-cultivation."

"There are many ways. It all depends on one's own nature. Since you earned credit by taking good care of flowers, you will attain the Dao through flowers. If you nourish yourself with all kinds of flowers, you will become weightless and fly to heaven." She then taught him the right flower diet.

As Qiu Xian busily kowtowed to her in gratitude, the fairy vanished out of sight. He raised his eyes and saw that she was in fact atop the wall of the lockup, beckoning to him and saying, "Come! Follow me out of here." Qiu Xian found it quite an effort to climb up the wall and began to feel exhausted when he was only halfway up. When he was approaching the top, he heard a gong go off below him and a voice shouting, "The sorcerer is trying to escape! Get him, quick!" In his alarm, his hands and feet went limp and he fell headfirst. With a start he woke up, only to find himself lying in bed in the lockup but he recalled distinctly what he had heard in his dream and, knowing that he would soon be out of harm's way, he breathed a little easier. Truly,

> With nothing against his conscience to hide,
> He trusted that the gods would come to his aid.

Now that the magistrate had determined that Qiu Xian was a sorcerer, Zhang Wei was beside himself with joy. He said, "Let that old freak enjoy his prison bed while we have some fun in the garden!"

His followers said, "The other day when the garden was still his, we didn't get to enjoy ourselves to the full. Now that it's yours, let's go there and have as much fun as we want!"

"Well said!" exclaimed Zhang Wei.

And so they left the city together and ordered Zhang's servants to prepare wine and food. They then went straight to Qiu's house. Witnessing Zhang Wei open the gate and enter the garden, the neighbors were seized with indignation and fear at the same time. None dared to speak up.

As Zhang Wei and his men approached the cottage, they found the tree peony stems bare of blossoms and the ground strewn with fallen petals, just as on the day they smashed up the garden. As everyone stood mystified, Zhang Wei said, "It looks like that old dog is indeed a sorcerer. Otherwise, how can everything have changed again in so little time? Can a fairy have knocked the flowers down?"

One of his followers said, "He knew the Young Master would be looking at the flowers and so he did this trick to humiliate us."

"I don't care what tricks he plays," said Zhang Wei. "The flowers on the ground will do just as well for our enjoyment." Right away, they spread a rug on the ground as before, and they sat down and began to drink with gusto. Zhang Ba was rewarded with two bottles of wine and told to drink off to one side. When they were all half inebriated, the moon began to sink into the west. Suddenly a strong gust of wind sprang up, and a blustering wind it was.

> It rustles the grass in the yard;
> It blows apart the duckweeds on the water.
> It reeks of the foul smell of tigers;
> It drowns the soughing of ten thousand pines.

That gust of wind made the flowers on the ground stand upright and, in a trice, each changed into a one-foot tall young woman. Astounded at the sight, the men exclaimed, "Well, wonders never cease!" Before they had quite gotten the words out, the miniature young women turned around in the wind and grew to full size, each radiant with beauty and dressed in finery. The men were dumbfounded at the sight of this assembly of beautiful young women. A woman in red spoke up, "We sisters have been living here for decades under the tender care of Master Qiu. We certainly never expected to be subjected to violence from thugs whose filthiness poisons the air and whose evil hands commit savage acts, thugs who framed Master Qiu in a scheme to take over this place. Now that our enemies are right in front of us, let us attack them in full force, to repay our benefactor and to avenge ourselves!"

In unison, the young women shouted, "Right! Let's act before they have time to escape!" With that, they raised their arms and swung at the men with sleeves that appeared to be several feet long, fluttering and flapping as if blown by wind and emitting a bone-chilling iciness.

"Ghosts! Ghosts!" cried the men. They threw down their wine cups and ran helter-skelter out of the garden with nary a thought about one another. Some stumbled over rocks, some were scratched by tree twigs in the face, some fell and scrambled back to their feet and fell again. When the commotion came to an end quite some time later, a roll call found everybody present except Zhang Wei and Zhang Ba. By this time, the wind had died down and dusk had set in. The men went their separate ways home, clasping their heads and scurrying along like rats, as if they had just been spared their lives. After the servants had gotten their breath back, they asked several young tenants to join them and go back with torches on a search for the missing. Upon reaching the garden, they heard groans from under a tall plum tree. They raised their torches and saw that it was Zhang Ba, who had tripped over the roots of the tree and, with a wound in his head, was trying futilely to struggle up to his feet. Two of the tenants helped him home. The rest of the men searched all through the garden. In the stillness of the night, they saw that the tree peonies were blooming as flamboyantly as before under the awning, with no petal on the ground, and the thatched cottage was littered with cups and plates with leftovers in them. As they put things in order, clicking their tongues in amazement, they checked all around again. It was not a very large garden, but they went all around it several times without finding a trace of Zhang Wei. Could he have been borne away by a high wind? Or did the female ghosts make a meal of him? Where could he be hiding himself?

They stayed a while longer, but, lacking a better choice, they resignedly decided to go home for the night before thinking about what to do next. They were about to go through the gate when they saw another group of people coming in, carrying lanterns, and led by none other than Mr. Yu and Mr. Shan. Having heard about the encounter with the ghosts and then about the search in the garden for the missing Zhang Wei, Yu and Shan had gathered some neighbors together to see for themselves. As the tenants' testimony bore out the story, the two elderly gentlemen were astounded.

"Don't go yet," said they to the tenants. "Let's join you and search one more time."

Again they searched carefully everywhere. Feeling that they had done a thorough job, they sighed and left the garden. Mr. Yu and Mr. Shan asked, "Will you all be coming again later tonight? May we lock up the gate? In the absence of the gardener, the garden is now the responsibility of us neighbors."

Without a leader now, Zhang Wei's tenants had lost some of their insolence. They declared, "Whatever you say, whatever you say."

Before the crowd had dispersed, one tenant was heard crying out from the east corner of the wall, "The master is here!" As the crowd rushed over, the tenant added, pointing, "Isn't that the master's headscarf hanging on that scholartree branch?"

"If his headscarf is here, he should be nearby," said others. Before they had taken many steps along the wall with their torches and lanterns, one of them exclaimed, "Oh no!" From the cesspool at the east corner stuck out the two legs of a man who had fallen headlong into it. The tenants recognized the shoes, stockings, and trousers as Zhang Wei's. In spite of the foul smell, they went ahead and pulled him out. Yu and Shan silently intoned the Buddha's name as they went their separate ways home, along with the other neighbors. The tenants carried Zhang Wei to the lake and washed the body clean while someone went to inform his family. The entire family, old and young, sobbingly made arrangements for his coffin and his funeral, but that is no part of our story. That very night, Zhang Ba's head wound got worse, and he died at the fifth watch, just before dawn. This was a case of vice getting its due. Indeed,

> Two evil men left the mortal world;
> A pair of monsters went down to hell.

The next day, the magistrate recovered from his indisposition and called a court session to order. He was about to try Master Qiu again when a runner reported,

"Both plaintiffs, Zhang Ba and his master Zhang Wei, died last night." And he went on to give an account of everything that had happened. The magistrate was appalled. He did not believe such things possible. A moment later, about a hundred villagers came to him to present their jointly signed petition, which stated that Master Qiu was no sorcerer but a doer of good deeds with a passion for flowers. The statement also described in detail how Zhang Wei had falsely charged him and how the fairies had administered divine justice.

Because of his sudden dizzy spell the day before, the magistrate had been wondering if Qiu was wronged after all, and now a weight was taken off his mind. He was glad that he had not applied torture to the defendant. Right away he summoned Qiu to the court from the lockup and set him free then and there. He also ordered to have an official poster put up by Qiu's gate prohibiting any action that might damage the trees and flowers. Everyone bowed in gratitude and left the court. Master Qiu thanked his fellow villagers and went home with them. Mr. Yu and Mr. Shan opened the gate and went in with Master Qiu. The sight of the tree peonies blooming as cheerfully as before filled the old gardener with emotion. The neighbors treated him to feasts to help him get over the shock. He reciprocated, and the wining and dining lasted for several days.

But let us not encumber our story with unnecessary descriptions. Master Qiu started a daily flower diet and, after he gradually got used to it, he stopped taking all cooked food and gave away as alms what money he made by selling his fruit. In a few years, his hair turned from white to black and his complexion turned as rosy as a child's. (*Zhang Wei and the Flower Maniac form a contrast. One who admires and takes care of flowers to such an extent does deserve reciprocation from the flowers.*)

One sunny and cloudless day, the fifteenth day of the eighth month one year, Master Qiu was in his room sitting cross-legged in a lotus position when there came a gentle breeze, bearing strains of resounding music from midair, where multicolored clouds appeared. As an extraordinary fragrance assailed his nostrils, green phoenixes and white cranes with outstretched wings glided their way into his garden. On a cloud stood the flower maiden, on both sides of whom were banners, canopies, and fairy maidens playing musical instruments. Master Qiu sank to his knees in prostration. The flower maiden said, "Qiu Xian, you have accumulated enough merit. Upon my request, the Lord on High has made you Protector of All the Flowers on Earth. You are hereby ordered to rise to heaven, along with your house. Those who love and cherish flowers will be blessed. Those who injure and destroy flowers will be punished."

Master Qiu kowtowed toward the sky in gratitude and followed the fairies onto the cloud, along with his cottage and his trees and flowers. Together they rose in air and headed south, as witnessed by Yu, Shan, and the other villagers, who all knelt down in prostration. As he stood on the cloud, Master Qiu was seen raising his hands in acknowledgment of his gratitude to the villagers. He did not vanish from sight until a considerable while later. The village was later renamed Where Fairies Rose to Heaven, and also came to be called the Village of a Hundred Flowers.

> *The old gardener's love of flowers*
> *So touched the fairies they came down to earth.*
> *His plants and house rose with him to heaven;*
> *Liu An need not have made pills of gold.[5]*

5

The Grateful Tiger Delivers the Bride at Big Tree Slope

In this universe boundless and vast,
Life is as short as the foam on the sea.
Those laying plans for a thousand years to come,
Be advised that justice is eternal.
Who can hold the sun from sinking in the west?
Water going east never flows backward.
The average man knows not the will of heaven,
But frets and worries throughout wakeful nights.

The above eight lines exhort people of this world to keep divine justice in mind and refrain from harming others in the pursuit of one's own interests. As the proverb goes, "The schemer ends up the loser." If you flout the will of heaven, you will certainly lose heaven's blessing.

Once upon a time, there was a man called Wei De, a native of Quanzhou, Fujian. Very early in life, he traveled with his father to Shaoxing Prefecture, where his father opened a shop for the smelting of silver into ingots. Mr. Wei Senior being a fair-minded man to whom profit was not of major concern, the shop attracted a large clientele and business prospered. In a few years after opening the shop, Mr. Wei built up a considerable family fortune. After Wei De came of age, Mr. Wei Senior took in as daughter-in-law the daughter of Mr. Shan the tailor who lived nearby. Miss Shan was quite a beauty. She had been offered more than a hundred strings of cash to be a concubine of a rich man in the area, but Mr. Shan the tailor turned him down. Knowing Mr. Wei and his son to be honest men in easy financial circumstances, and considering the fact that they were neighbors and, moreover, that it was going to be a one-husband-one-wife marriage, Mr. Shan married his daughter to Wei De.

It turned out, in a way no one would have expected, that Mr. Shan the tailor died of an illness soon after the wedding. In less than two years, Mr. Wei Senior also died of illness. Wei De suggested to his wife that, without any kith and kin to turn to now, they might as well escort his father's coffin back to Fujian and settle down there. Shan-shi rejected the idea at first but, failing to convince her husband, she yielded to him. Wei De sold the bulkier items in the shop, packed, and chartered a boat for the long journey. On a chosen auspicious day, he loaded his father's coffin onto the boat and set out with his wife.

It so happened that the boatman, called Zhang Shao, was not a decent sort. He regularly robbed his clients. He hired a mute to help him out on the boat so that no word about his doings would get out. Now, he believed that Wei De, a silversmith of many years' standing, must be a rich man. Moreover, he, a bachelor, was smitten at the sight of the beautiful Shan-shi. His greed and his lust thus stirred, a malicious thought crossed his mind, at the very moment they boarded his boat, but the right opportunity did not present itself. One day, the wind being too strong for them to press on, he moored the boat at the foot of Mount Jianglang. And then he hit upon a plan. He claimed that he was out of firewood and needed to go up the mountain to cut some, but because there were tigers that often came out to do harm to humans, he must have Wei De accompany him. The unsuspecting Wei De obliged him. Zhang Shao deliberately took him through many twists and turns to a secluded spot in the depths of the mountain, where he could strike without being seen. He cut some branches from the bushes and told Wei De to bundle them up. While Wei De was bent down, picking up the branches, Zhang Shao swung his ax down from behind, hitting Wei De on his left shoulder. Wei De fell with a thud. With another hack of the ax on the head, Wei De died, his blood gushing like a fountain. Zhang Shao said, "Good job! Good job! This time next year, I'll have your widow observe the anniversary of your death." That said, he stuck the ax in his waist-belt and, leaving the firewood behind, ran down the mountain back to the boat.

At the sight of Zhang Shao back on the boat alone, Shan-shi asked where her husband was. Zhang Shao replied, "Bad luck! A tiger carried your poor husband off in its mouth. I'm a fast runner and got away. I didn't even take the firewood I had already cut down."

At these words, Shan-shi thumped her chest and burst into heartbreaking sobs. Zhang Shao said, trying to calm her down, "He must have been destined to be killed by a tiger. Crying doesn't help."

While sobbing, Shan-shi thought, "I've heard that tigers in the mountains come out only at night. I don't believe they come out to prey on humans in broad daylight. What's more, the two of them were together. How come the tiger picked my husband and left Zhang Shao unhurt in any way? How very strange!" Aloud, she said to Zhang Shao, "The tiger may have picked up my husband in its mouth, but he may also have struggled himself free."

"Even a cat won't give up what's already in its mouth, let alone a tiger."

"That may very well be so, but I didn't witness it. Even if he was really eaten by a tiger, he should still have a few bones left. Please take me there, so that I can do my wifely duties and bring his bones back."

"I'm afraid of tigers. I'm not going."

Again Shan-shi burst into a flood of bitter tears. Zhang Shao told himself, "It looks like she won't give up unless I take her there." Aloud, he said, "All right, I'll take you there, ma'am. Stop crying."

Shan-shi went ashore and followed Zhang Shao on a footpath up the mountain. He had taken the eastern path the previous time, but, afraid that she would see the corpse, he took her on the western path. Shan-shi wept every step of the way. Without seeing the slightest trace of a tiger all along, Zhang Shao tried to strike up a conversation in the hope of distracting her and tiring her out so that she would want to return, but she remained unshaken in her resolve not to stop until she saw her husband's bones and blood. Vexed by her stubbornness, Zhang Shao pointed ahead and said, lying, "Ma'am, do you want to keep going? Don't you see that tiger over there?"

Raising her eyes, Shan-shi asked, "Where's the tiger?" Even as she spoke, a tiger with bulging eyes and a white forehead sprang out from the woods as a rustling eerie wind blew past. It pounced with deadly aim upon Zhang Shao. Before he could dodge, Zhang Shao yelled "Aya!" The tiger carried him off in its mouth and trotted back into the woods to enjoy its prey.

Shan-shi collapsed to the ground in shock. Upon waking up after a long while and failing to see Zhang Shao anywhere in sight, she realized that the tiger had taken him. Now she was convinced that there were indeed tigers in the mountain and that her husband had been eaten by one. Seized with fear, she dared not press ahead but turned back the way she had come, sobbing as she went along. Before she was clear of the mountain, she saw something resembling the shape of a man charging toward her from the other path. Believing it to be a tiger, Shan-shi shrieked, "I'm done for!" With that, she fell backwards. All of a sudden, she heard a voice speaking into her ear, "Wife, why are you here?" And two hands helped her up. She opened her eyes and saw that it was her husband, Wei De. With blood all over his face, he looked a mere semblance of a human being. The fact of the matter was that Wei De was not destined to die at this time after all. The blow of the ax had just knocked him unconscious. After Zhang Shao had left, he had come to, struggled to his feet, and torn off his leggings to dress the wound in his head. He was on his way down the mountain to confront Zhang Shao when he ran into his wife. She thought he had been mangled by a tiger. It was only when Wei De told her what had really happened that she realized that Zhang Shao had plotted to kill her husband and had fooled her with the story of a tiger. It was the gods who then sent a tiger to rid the world of an evil man. The husband and wife were overwhelmed with gratitude to heaven and earth.

When they were back in the boat, the mute gestured with his hands to ask why the owner of the boat was missing. After Wei De and his wife explained the situation to him, he joined his palms and burst out exclaiming, "Namo Amita Buddha!" With that, he began to talk and enumerated all of the evil deeds Zhang Shao had committed. When they asked him further, he was bereft of speech again. This was another most extraordinary thing.

Wei De helped the mute at the helm all along the journey. After arriving at home, he sold the boat and had a Buddhist shrine built for the mute to live in. They burned joss sticks day and night. Throughout the rest of their lives, Wei De and his wife remained devout Buddhists. A poet of later times had this to say:

> He claimed there were tigers when none existed;
> The one that appeared came out of his mind.
> Had Zhang Shao's heart been in the right place,
> Even if there were tigers, they would not have shown themselves.

We just related how a tiger was sent by the gods to rid the world of an evil man, which is the way things should be. It thus appears that the tiger is indeed the king of beasts and an animal with a soul. There are records in the annals of history of tigers helping a good official and a Buddhist monk.[1] I shall now tell of another righteous tiger, one that reciprocated an act of kindness and helped bring about the reunion of a devoted couple. This has become a much-told tale through the ages. Truly,

> This story delights women of honor,
> And terrifies men of vice.

Our story proper takes place in the Tianbao reign period [742–56] of the great Tang dynasty. There lived in Zhangpu County of Fuzhou a man named Qin Zili who lived with his parents in easy circumstances. He had been betrothed from an early age to Chaoyin, daughter of Lin Bujiang of the same county. The betrothal gifts having been offered, the wedding was to take place after the betrothed came of age. Qin Zili refused to continue with his schooling when he was only twelve and left school to practice martial arts. Since Zili was the only son, his parents doted on him and let him have his way. By sixteen, he had grown to be a tall young man of strong physique, skilled in archery and the various martial arts. As the saying goes, "Like attracts like." Some good-for-nothing young men joined him in raising falcons and hawks, training dogs, riding horses, and hunting—all for their own pleasure.

After Qin Zili killed three tigers in a row one day, a yellow-robed old man with a cane appeared to him and said in praise, "You are as brave as Bian Zhuang and Li Cunxiao of old.[2] But all creatures on earth are supposed to share the same love for life and the same abhorrence of killing. The ancients said, 'If men mean no harm to tigers, tigers do not prey on men.' Why did you have to kill them? The tiger is the king of beasts and should not be killed without a good reason. Mr. Huang in the olden times[3] was skillful in subduing tigers with his precious sword, but even he was later killed by a tiger. If you indulge in killing to show off your valor, you violate the laws of heaven and will hardly be spared from misfortunes."

These words enlightened Qin Zili. There and then, he broke an arrow in a vow never to kill tigers again. One day, laden with some small game, he was on his way back from a hunting expedition all by himself when he saw, in a place called Big Tree Slope, a yellow-striped tiger in a cage-trap. It so happened that the hunter who had laid the trap was not around. At the sight of Qin Zili, the tiger kneeled down on its forelegs and, its head lowered, its ears drooping, made some guttural sounds as if in supplication. Zili said, "Listen, you beast! I have vowed not to harm tigers again, but you threw yourself into the trap. I am not to blame."

The tiger kept its eyes on Zili and continued to whimper. Zili said, "All right, I'll help you get out, but remember not to harm humans in the future." The tiger nodded. Zili smashed the trap and set the tiger free. The tiger gave a wild jump and scampered off. Zili said to himself, "Other people catch tigers to make a profit. I set one free to do a good deed. But it's not right if my good deed deprives others of their profit." So thinking, he laid the game he had with him into the trap and went home empty-handed. Truly,

> Let go when it's time to let go;
> Do good when it's right to do good.

Because of Qin Zili's aversion to proper pursuits, the Qin family circumstances began to decline. To make matters worse, being a generous and hospitable person, Qin Zili often brought his good-for-nothing friends home, where they made a nuisance of themselves, asking for wine and food. Zili's parents, out of their profound love for him, forced themselves to humor the men at first, but gradually their patience began to wear out. They said to their son, "At your age, you should be working to support the family, but you loaf about day in and day out. When will you ever change? Other people's sons of your age are engaged either in farming or in business and support their parents with whatever they make, unlike you—with nothing in, but everything out. Family circumstances are going downhill, but you continue to entertain your friends with wine and food. You have no idea how hard we try to get by on next to nothing. There are only so many clothes and jewelry items we can pawn or sell. We may even die of hunger if it comes to the worst. Now listen: next time you bring your friends home, we won't offer even a cup of tea, and don't you get mad at us!"

After this lecture from his parents, Qin Zili left home without a word. Mr. and Mrs. Qin did indeed enjoy peace for a time. However, more than a month later, their son again brought about ten hunters home to borrow a pot to cook rice with.

Mr. Qin Senior said, "Let's give it to him." Mrs. Qin refused, saying, "I don't begrudge the firewood, but I've been so happy all this time because I thought we had talked him around, and yet here he is, getting on our nerves again. If we make an exception today, where do we draw the line? He'll be coming back with demands for tea and wine again. I'm sick and tired of it all. We'd better be firm and not pamper him."

Seeing that she was adamant, Mr. Qin slipped out of sight. Mrs. Qin closed the middle door and called out from behind it, "This house is not an inn. We don't have any firewood to offer. Why don't you go somewhere else?"

The men had to leave. With a sigh, Qin Zili thought, his face burning with shame, "I have always been supported by my parents. I have never made a penny or two on my own, and their income is so limited. I must not blame them. I heard that with the turmoil in Annam Protectorate,[4] the imperial court is recruiting soldiers everywhere. By the order of the regional commander, the government of this prefecture has put up recruitment posters all over. Several of my friends have already registered for service. With my martial arts skills, I may be able to make something of myself and get to return home in glory. A man with any pride in him shouldn't hang on to six feet of land and be a pest to his parents. There's one thing, though: Father and Mother will not let me enter army service. But my career prospects are at stake. I'll have to think of a way. All right, I know what to do." Right away, he went off to the prefectural yamen to register for military service, without his parents being any the wiser. The prefect gave him a test and, upon finding that he had outstanding martial arts skills, made him a company commander and entered him in the registry books of the military council. Before many days had passed, having recruited enough men, the recruiting officer did a roll call, assigned numbers to the men, distributed provisions among them, and arranged to have armor and weapons prepared for them. On a chosen auspicious day, they fired cannons and set out for the battlefront. It was three days after his departure that Qin Zili had a county yamen bailiff whom he happened to run into send a letter to his parents to inform them about what he had done. Mr. Qin Senior opened the letter and saw that it ran as follows:

"Your unworthy son Zili has been quite a burden to you. I have entered military service and have been made a company commander. We are heading for Annam. If, by any stroke of luck, I can win honor for myself on the battlefield, I will surely return home in glory. Please don't worry."

After reading the letter, Mr. Qin was lost for words for quite a while. Mrs. Qin asked, "Where's our son? What does the letter say? Why don't you tell me?"

"I didn't tell you because I was afraid it would be too much of a blow to you. Our son is with the army and is on an expedition to Annam."

Mrs. Qin said, laughing, "What's so bad about it? Let's call him back after ten days or half a month, and that'll be that!" (*What a woman!*)

"What does a woman know! Annam is ten thousand li from here! Letters will be few and far between. What's worse, he's in military service, and swords are merciless. This looks bad to me. If he dies in battle, who'll take care of us in our old age?"

Mrs. Qin burst into wails of grief. Mr. Qin also broke down in tears. A few days later, Mr. Lin, to whose daughter Zili was betrothed, got word of the news and came over to ask if it was true. Mrs. and Mrs. Qin could not very well keep the truth from him, and told him everything, whereupon they were all overcome with sadness. After Mr. Lin went back home, the entire family grieved upon hearing his account. Truly,

> *No joy is greater than making new friends;*
> *No grief is deeper than bidding farewell.*
> *Parting with others is sorrow enough,*
> *But the pain is crushing when it's your own flesh and blood.*

Time flew like an arrow. Quite unnoticeably, three years elapsed. Nothing was heard from Qin Zili since that one letter. Mr. Lin sent messengers from time to time to ask for news about Zili, but, like golden needles dropping into the sea and silver vases falling into the well, his inquiries all came to nothing. There were several men who had joined the army with Zili, and nothing was heard from them, either. Mr. Lin's wife, Liang-shi, said to her husband, "Young Mr. Qin has been gone for three years now, and we have no idea if he's alive or not. Our daughter has come of age. We mustn't take chances with her future. Why don't you ask the Qins for a definitive answer? There may be a bond between the two families, but their son and our daughter come from different wombs. How can our girl be made a widow without ever having even seen her intended husband?"

"You're right, Mother," said Mr. Lin. (*Mr. Lin trusts everything his wife says.*) In all haste, he betook himself to the Qins' house and said to Mr. Qin, "My daughter is not getting any younger, and your son still hasn't been heard from. If he's not going to return, what's to be done? My wife worries about this day and night, and that's what I'm here to talk about."

Well aware of the purpose of this visit, Mr. Qin said, "That good-for-nothing son of mine indeed does injustice to your daughter. But things having already come to this, could you please ask your wife to give him another three years? If he doesn't come back in six years, you'll be free to marry your daughter to another family. I will not complain."

Acknowledging the good sense in what Mr. Qin said, Mr. Lin resignedly took his leave, feebly voicing his agreement. After returning home, he relayed those words to his wife. Liang-shi had never liked her prospective son-in-law because she thought him a worthless loafer. His three-year-long absence could not have suited her better. Upon hearing that they were to wait another three years, she was so upset that she wished ten days would flash by in one day's time so that the three years would quickly draw to an end, because her daughter would then be free for a better match.

Time flew like an arrow. Quite unnoticeably, another three years elapsed. Mr. Lin said, "The engagement with the Qin family is over. Let me pay them another visit to hear what they have to say."

Liang-shi said, "The ancients said, 'A word once out of the mouth can't be overtaken even by a team of four horses.' Mr. Qin has given his word. We are not to blame. We're just like travelers who take whichever road is best. Why do we have to talk with them again? We can tell them after our daughter has found a match."

"You're right, Mother," said her husband. "But even so, we should at least let our girl know about this."

"Chaoyin is a strange girl. If you say outright to her that we're going to arrange another match for her because Qin has been away for six years, she'll surely object, and we'll end up being ridiculed by old Qin. We must do thus-and-so."

"Right, Mother," said Mr. Qin again.

The next day, Liang-shi was sitting with her daughter Chaoyin when Mr. Lin came in from outside. In exaggerated agitation, he said, "Mother, have you heard? You know why Mr. Qin hasn't sent us a word? Because he died in battle three years ago! A soldier who came back from Annam yesterday said he saw it."

Chaoyin went deathly pale upon hearing these words. Fighting back her rising tears, she rushed into her own room. Her mother heaved a false-hearted sigh and said over and over again, "Oh poor thing!" A few days later, she said to her daughter, "The dead can't be brought back to life again. Now he's gone, but you are still young. I've told your father to have a matchmaker find you another match. Don't pass up on a good marriage while you're still young."

Chaoyin retorted, "You are quite mistaken, Mother. Father betrothed me to the Qin family when I was still a child. A woman should not drink tea from two different families. If Qin Junior is there, I am his wife. If he is dead, I remain a member of the Qin family. How can I do otherwise just because he is gone? I'll never do such a thing!"

Her mother said, "Don't be so stubborn, my child! You are our only child. You have no brothers. After you marry, your husband will be like half a son to us. But to stay loyal to a dead man before you even marry him will bring you nothing but empty fame. We, your parents, are alive and yet you turn your love to a dead man. You care nothing about your parents' future. Aren't you a foolish girl and an unfilial daughter?"

These harsh words reduced Chaoyin to silence. Soon there came a stream of matchmakers, male and female, to offer them marriage proposals. Unable to prevail over her parents, Chaoyin thought of a plan. She said to her parents, "I would never dream of disobeying you, but I don't have the heart to promise myself to another man the moment I hear about Mr. Qin's death. Please allow me to observe three years of mourning by way of doing my wifely duty. After the mourning period is over, I will do whatever you say. Otherwise, I would rather die than obey."

Realizing how firm she was in her determination, Mr. Lin and Liang-shi felt obliged to let her have her way, lest she do something desperate. Truly,

> *One determined mind*
> *Stops ten thousand men.*

Mr. and Mrs. Qin, in the meantime, thought Miss Lin would soon marry into another family now that the six years were up. But when they heard that she had resolved to observe three years of mourning, they were beside themselves with joy. "If our son comes back before the three years are up, she'll remain our daughter-in-law," they said. Time flew like an arrow. Quite unnoticeably, another three years went by. Believing that her intended husband had indeed died, Chaoyin had adopted a vegetarian diet and dressed herself only in white, as befits one in mourning. Even after the three years were up, she still refused to eat meat, nor would she put on any clothes of color. The moment the topic of marriage was brought up, she would threaten to kill herself.

Mr. Lin consulted his wife, saying, "She's so stubborn. It looks like another match is not going to happen. What should we do?"

"Let's secretly pick a son-in-law," said Liang-shi, "and have his family send the betrothal gifts to my older brother's house. Let's not tell her anything. On the day of the wedding, we'll just say that a cousin is getting married and has sent for her. That'll trick her into changing her clothes and getting into the sedan-chair. The drummers and the wedding procession can meet her midway. By then, she'll have to comply."

"You're right, Mother."

As planned, Mr. Lin reached agreement with his wife's older brother, Mr. Liang, and betrothed Chaoyin to the third son of a Squire Li. Everything from making the marriage proposal to giving the betrothal gifts was done in Mr. Liang's house. When going to receive the betrothal gifts, the parents told their daughter that it was an engagement ceremony for her uncle's oldest son. Chaoyin did not have the slightest suspicion. When the wedding day was soon approaching, Mr. Liang went to the Lins' house, falsely claiming that he was inviting the whole Lin family to attend his son's wedding on a certain date. Liang-shi promised him that they would all go as scheduled. When the wedding day rolled around, Uncle Liang sent over two sedan-chairs for his sister and his niece. After having arrayed herself in finery, Liang-shi had her daughter change into colored clothes and follow her. The unsuspecting Chaoyin complied. Having hardly ever ventured out of her boudoir, Chaoyin had no idea how to get anywhere. After being on the road for a while, suddenly, from a bend in the mountain path, emerged lanterns and torches amid drum music that filled the air. Members of the wedding procession had been waiting at this spot for the bridal sedan-chair. As the procession started moving forward in front of the sedan-chair, playing wind and percussion instruments, Chaoyin grew suspicious but there was nothing she could do. Oblivious to her sobs, the crowd kept urging the sedan-chair carriers to go faster. Suddenly, dark clouds gathered and a driving rain came down. Everyone dived into the woods for shelter and waited out the rain before they resumed the journey. But they had hardly gone a few paces when a sudden strong gust of wind blew out all the lanterns and torches. A yellow-striped tiger with bulging eyes and a white forehead was seen leaping down from midair. The crowd shrieked and ran pell-mell in all directions.

They thought their lives were in danger;
Their souls took flight in fear.

When the wind died down and the tiger was gone, everyone cried out, "Thank heaven!" They relit the lanterns and the torches, and as they were preparing to go on with their journey, the sedan-chair carriers exclaimed, "Oh no!" Of the two sedan-chairs, one was now empty. A look with a torch confirmed that the bride had disappeared. The door of the sedan-chair was damaged. All too clearly, the tiger had snatched her away. Liang-shi burst into sobs. Without the bride, the wedding procession lost all enthusiasm. The musicians stopped playing, and half of the lanterns and torches were put out. "What's to be done?" people asked one another. The night was too dark for them to go on a search, and they didn't have the courage to do so anyway. Afraid of running into tigers if they dispersed, they agreed to go together to Mr. Lin's house before deciding on the next course of action. This was indeed a case of "setting out in joy, returning in gloom."

Now, Mr. Lin was cleaning his house when he heard violent knocks on his door. He made haste to open it, only to see the same two sedan-chairs back at the door, and members of the wedding procession looking as forlorn as stray dogs without a home. Much taken aback, he wondered if his daughter, in her stubbornness, had been up to something in the sedan-chair. His heart racing, he asked what had happened. His wife Liang-shi in her sedan-chair burst into tears but couldn't get a word out through her sobs. It was from the others that Mr. Lin learned about the encounter with the tiger. Mr. Lin pounded his chest in agony and regret. "Had I known something like this would happen to my child, I would have let her have her way and not marry," said he. "And now, I ruined her!"

He sent messengers to Squire Li and Uncle Liang to inform them about what had happened. At the same time, he assembled his tenants and got hunting equipment ready for a search of the tiger and the girls' bones on the mountain after daybreak. Indeed,

In sorrow, he missed his daughter;
In hatred, he cursed the tiger.

Our story forks at this point. After joining the army, Qin Zili rendered worthy service in Annam. Commander-in-Chief Geshu Han [d. 757] made him his personal bodyguard and gave him his own sword. Such was his trust in Qin Zili. Three years later, the Tubo Tibetans invaded, and Qin followed Geshu Han on the expedition to wipe them out. After victory was won, the imperial court promoted Geshu Han to be the grand marshal to guard Tongguan Pass with his subordinate officers and a hundred-thousand-strong army. Having twice won distinction in his service, Qin Zili was now a battalion commander. All too unexpectedly, An Lushan rose in rebellion.⁵ When An Lushan's troops bore down on Tongguan, Geshu Han happened to be ill and, overwhelmed by the onslaught of the rebels, surrendered and yielded the strategic pass to them.

Unable to do anything without support, Qin Zili had to abandon his subordinates and flee all by himself, armed with his sword. We shall not speak of the hardships he went through on the road but come directly to the time when he arrived home. It just so happened to be the very night Mr. Lin was trying to marry his daughter off.

He got down on his knees and kowtowed to his parents, saying, "Please forgive me for being an unfilial son." Only after a close look did Mr. and Mrs. Qin realize this was their son. Though he had been big and tall when he left, he was now of much stronger physique. His beard and the traces that a rough life on the frontier left on his face gave him a decidedly changed look. Mr. and Mrs. Qin shed sad tears as bitter memories came flooding back.

"My son," said Mr. Qin. "Why have we never heard from you all these ten years? People say you died in battle. We cried our eyes out."

Mrs. Qin said, "If you had come back only one day earlier, let alone ten years, your fiancée would not have gone to another man."

"What did you say about my fiancée?"

His mother explained, "Three years after you left, your father-in-law wanted to marry her to someone else, but your father objected and finally got them to agree to a three-year grace period. Then, your fiancée heard that you had died and decided all on her own to observe mourning for three years. Now this is the tenth year after you left. She can't be blamed for having gone off as a bride earlier this evening."

At this account, Qin Zili's eyebrows knitted in an angry frown. Through his gnashed teeth, he said, "Which scoundrel has the audacity to take Qin Zili's wife? Let me give him a taste of my sword!" So saying, he stormed out of the house, sword in hand. His mother had never been able to discipline him. How could she be expected to hold him back now? She had to let him be. Breathless with fear, she waited in the hall for news. Truly,

> A green dragon and a white tiger
> Bring either joy or woe, when together.⁶

Having always known how to get to Mr. Lin's house, Qin Zili now took that route. He walked until dusk approached. A downpour of rain drenched his clothes. Remembering that this place was called Big Tree Slope, with an ancient tree hollow in the middle so big that the trunk measured about ten arm spans around, Qin

Zili went up to the tree for shelter from the rain. He then stepped into the trunk and found it quite spacious inside. The rain, though heavy, stopped in a short while. Qin Zili was about to jump out of the tree trunk when a fierce gust of wind sprang up. He thought, "Let me wait until it blows over." But then again, he thought, "There's a rank smell to that wind. How strange!" He stuck his head out for a look, and saw two red lanterns flickering off and on. The next moment, he heard a deafening sound as if the sky were falling and the earth were cracking open. An object fell in his direction from midair, giving him such a shock that he shrank back into the tree. In a trice, the wind subsided, and a moan caught his ear. By then the clouds had dispersed, the rain had left off, and a pale moon had appeared over the horizon. Qin Zili stepped forward and, by the light of the moon, saw a woman moaning. He helped her up and asked who she was. The woman took a moment or two to answer. "I am Chaoyin, daughter of the Lin family," she said.

Recalling his fiancée's name but unsure of himself, he asked, "Do you have a husband?"

"I am betrothed to Qin Zili, but, because he has never been heard from since he joined the army ten years ago, my parents wanted me to marry another man. I vowed to die rather than obey. My parents betrothed me to someone without my knowledge and tricked me into a sedan-chair, saying that my uncle had sent for me. I realized it was a trick when I was already on the road. I was about to kill myself when there came a strong gust of wind. By the light of the torches, I saw a tiger with bulging eyes and a white forehead charging through the crowd right at my sedan-chair. It picked me up with its mouth and deposited me here. It's gone now. I'm not hurt. Who might you be, sir? If you could take me back to my parents, they'll surely repay you handsomely for your kindness."

"I am none other than Qin Zili. I joined in the expeditions against Annam and then against the Tubo Tibetans. And then I followed Grand Marshal Geshu in guarding Tongguan Pass. I just returned home. I heard that your parents married you off earlier this evening, which is why I'm on my way with my sword, to cut down those who violate the moral codes of behavior. I never expected to run into you in this place! Heaven must have sent the tiger to give you back to me, so that I wouldn't have to put my sword to use. How fortunate!"

Chaoyin said, "You may very well say so, but I'm not married yet, so I've never seen my intended husband. How would I dare to believe whatever I hear? Please take me back home. If my father recognized you as his son-in-law, all the years I waited will not have been in vain."

"That old swine promised one daughter to two families. Why would I want to see such heartless people? I'm going to carry you on my back to *my* home for you to meet your parents-in-law. I will then send a messenger to your home, if only to shame that old swine." That said, he put Chaoyin on his back before she could say anything and, his left arm supporting Chaoyin on his back and his right arm holding his sword, he headed for home along the dirt road. Before long, the roars of a tiger came into hearing. On the top of the hill a long way off shone two lanterns. Peering more intently, he realized that the red lanterns were the eyes of a yellow-striped tiger with bulging eyes and a white forehead. All of a sudden, Qin Zili recalled the yellow-striped tiger with bulging eyes and a white forehead that he had set free from a trap ten years before. He said to himself, "A tiger that knows I was returning home tonight and snatched my wife from a crowd to return her to me must have magic powers." Aloud, he cried out, "Tiger! Thank you for returning my wife to me!" With a roar, the tiger gave a leap and vanished out of sight. The story about the tiger reciprocating an act of kindness became in later times a legend that inspired many poems, of which one by Hu Zeng [of the Tang dynasty] was the best:

> Tigers have always been known to harm humans;
> But here is one that pays a debt of gratitude.
> All too many men, heartless and depraved,
> Lack the loyalty that beasts possess.

Let us come back to Mr. and Mrs. Qin as they waited anxiously at home. At the first sound of footsteps, they lit a lamp and went out for a look. Who should walk in but their son, Qin Zili, carrying someone on his back! Putting the person on the floor in the hall, he exclaimed, "Father, Mother! Meet your daughter-in-law!" (*Qin Zili is as straightforward a person as the likes of Big Brother Li* [Li Kui] *in the novel* Outlaws of the Marsh.) Finding her to be a beautiful woman, Mr. and Mrs. Qin asked how he had come by her, and, upon hearing the wonderful story of a tiger paying a debt of gratitude, they raised their hands to their foreheads and cried, "How fortunate! How fortunate!" Mrs. Qin helped her daughter-in-law into an inner room and served her with porridge and soup to nurse her back to health. The next morning, they sent a messenger to the Lins to tell them the news.

Lin had begun searching the mountain with his tenants before the day even broke, but all to no avail. With a sigh, he resignedly went home. Suddenly, there came the messenger from Mr. Qin, bringing him the good news that his son had just returned and that a tiger had sent his daughter back. How was he to believe such nonsense!

"I see," said he. "The Qins heard that our daughter was carried off by a tiger and therefore came up with all this nonsense to make fun of us."

His wife Liang-shi said, "Anything can happen in this world. The other day, a spotted-feathered chicken of ours got lost, and was taken in by a neighbor. One day later, a stray cat came to our house with a chicken in its mouth. I drove away the cat and saw that the chicken was the very spotted one I was missing. What a curious coincidence! Now, the tiger is a most intelligent large beast. A story I've heard says that there was once a scholar who lived in a remote village. One night, he heard a noise outside. When he looked, he saw a tiger's paw coming in through the window, and in the paw was stuck a large bamboo splinter. The scholar understood what the tiger was asking for, and pulled out the splinter. The next evening, the tiger brought him a sheep in its mouth to thank him. Clearly, tigers can communicate with humans. Maybe heaven sent that tiger to give our girl back to the Qins out of sympathy for her determination to stay a widow. Why don't you go to the Qins' house to see if our son-in-law is back or not? We'll then know for sure."

Mr. Lin said again, "You're right, Mother."

That very day, Mr. Lin betook himself to the Qins' house. Mr. Qin went out to greet him, and they sat down as host and guest. After Mr. Qin gave an account of what had happened the previous night, Mr. Lin's face burned with shame. He apologized over and over again, adding, "May I see my good son-in-law and my daughter?" Qin Zili refused to meet his father-in-law, but his parents finally talked him around, and, out of regard for his wife, he resignedly came out, made a bow sulkily, and immediately took himself off. Mr. Qin had his wife dress the girl up and invited Mr. Lin into the room where his daughter was. Nothing could exceed the joy of the father and daughter at this all-too-unexpected, dreamlike reunion. Mr. Lin wished to take his daughter home, but Mr. and Mrs. Qin would not hear of it. On a chosen auspicious day, the wedding took place in the Qins' house. Having learned about Qin Zili's return, Squire Li raised no complaints.

Later, after grand marshals Guo Ziyi [697–781] and Li Guangbi [708–64] recovered Chang'an from the rebels, Emperor Suzong [r. 756–62] checked the records of all the civil and military officials after he assumed the throne. When still the crown prince, he had heard about Qin Zili's meritorious service in the battlefields. His name being absent from the list of rebels, the emperor awarded him for not having joined the rebels and made him marshal of the imperial guards. Qin Zili again rendered worthy service in the later suppressions of the rebels An Qingxu [d. 759; An Lushan's son] and Shi Siming [d. 761]. After he retired, Qin Zili and his wife lived together to a ripe old age. There is a poem in testimony:

> No one likes a person full of malice;
> Even tigers love acts of kindness.
> Be advised: make life easier for others,
> And be merciful whenever there's a chance.

6

Divine Foxes Lose a Book at Small Water Bay

All forms of life, high or low, are alike;
All sentient beings share a common bond.
Do not forget favors done unto you;
Even birds show gratitude with jade rings.

The above four lines are about a story set in the Han dynasty. The hero of the story, Yang Bao, a native of Huayin [in present-day Shaanxi], was a gifted young man of twenty and a most erudite scholar. On the Double Ninth Festival [ninth day of the ninth lunar month], he went on an excursion to the outskirts of the town. Tired from walking, he sat down for a rest in the woods. As he admired the lovely scenery with all the verdant foliage and the chirping birds, he heard a plump. A bird had fallen right in front of him. It kept tweeting and was frantically flapping its wings in a vain attempt to rise into the air. Yang Bao thought, "How very strange! What happened to this bird?" He stepped forward, picked it up, and saw that it was a siskin, wounded and whining in pain. Feeling saddened, Yang Bao said to himself, "Let me take it home. I'll nurse it back to health and then set it free." He was still examining the bird when a young man with a slingshot in his hand walked up from behind and said, "Scholar, this bird was shot down by me. Please give it to me."

"To give it back to you is not a problem," said Yang Bao. "But listen: birds may look different from humans, but they are living beings, no less. How can one have the heart to kill them? Also, even a hundred dead birds won't give you enough meat for one meal, and money from selling ten thousand birds won't make you a rich man. Why don't you take up some other means of livelihood? I would like to pay for this bird's redemption." So saying, he produced some money that he had on him.

"I'm not after its meat, nor do I want to sell it for profit," said the young man. "I was just trying out my shooting skills for fun. If you want the bird, I'll just give it to you."

"What has this bird done to deserve being a victim of your pleasure?"

The young man said gratefully, "I now realize I was wrong." With that, he threw away his slingshot and walked off. Yang Bao took the bird home, put it in a hatbox, and fed it daily with the pistils of chrysanthemums. Gradually it began to grow new feathers. By the hundredth day it was able to fly about, but it came back to Yang Bao every time. Yang Bao found himself tenderly attached to it. One day, it flew off again, but this time, not to return. Yang Bao felt miserable. All of a sudden, a yellow-robed young boy with refined eyebrows and narrow eyes entered the house and threw himself at Yang Bao's feet, but Yang was quick to raise him. Handing Yang Bao a pair of jade rings, the boy said, "This is a humble gift to thank you for having saved my life. With this, your descendants in successive generations will attain the three highest positions at the imperial court."

"But I haven't ever seen you before. How did I save your life?"

The boy replied with a smile, "Have you forgotten? I am none other than the one hit by a slingshot in the woods. You kept me in a box and fed me with the pistils of chrysanthemums." That said, he changed into a siskin and flew away. Thereafter, Yang Bao's wife gave birth to a son, Yang Zhen, who later became grand commandant in the court of Emperor Ming [r. 58–75]. Yang Zhen's son, Yang Bin, became grand commandant in the court of Emperor He [r. 89–105]. Yang Bin's son, Yang Ci, became prime minister in the court of Emperor An [r. 106–25], and Yang Ci's son, Yang Biao, also became prime minister, under Emperor Ling [r. 168–88]. Sure enough, the Yang clan produced four officials of the highest ranks in four successive generations. There is a poem in testimony:

> He fed the bird with flowers not to seek rewards
> But out of compassion for all living beings.
> The glory that lasted through the generations
> Showed how rewarding acts of kindness could be.

Storyteller, everyone knows that story about the siskin returning a favor with jade rings. Why even bother to tell it? Well, dear audience, I did so because I plan to move on to a story about a young man who also hit nonhuman beings with slingshot pellets. But, unlike the one who repented after having hurt the bird, this young man ruined his family's considerable fortune as a consequence of his action and became an object of ridicule. What I told about the bird with the jade rings was just a prologue story to exhort people to do good and follow Yang Bao's example, rather than emulate that young man who courted disaster. Truly,

> Hold your peace when it is right to do so;
> Take action when it is time to let go.
> If you can follow this advice of mine,
> You'll be blessed with a long and peaceful life.

What I am going to relate took place in the reign of Emperor Xuanzong [r. 712–56] of the Tang dynasty. The young man of our story, a native of Chang'an, was called Wang Chen. He had only a slight acquaintance with the classics and histories and barely knew the rudiments of writing. Instead, he was much given to drinking and swordsmanship, and was most skilled in horse riding and shooting with the slingshot. His father having died when he was a child, he lived with his mother, his wife neé Yu, and his brother, Wang Zai, who, being a master of martial arts with remarkable physical strength, served as a member of the imperial guards. Wang Zai was yet unmarried. The Wangs were living contentedly in comfortable circumstances with their many servants when An Lushan rose in rebellion and seized Tongguan Pass.[1] As the emperor retreated to the west, Wang Zai followed the imperial entourage. Believing they would not be able to hold out for long in the capital, Wang Chen abandoned the family estate, packed up all portable valuables, and set out on a south-bound journey across the Yangzi River with his mother, his wife, and the servants. They settled down in a place called Small Water Bay in Hangzhou, where they purchased some land and made a living off the property.

Later, upon hearing that the capital had been recovered and the roads were safe to travel again, Wang Chen thought of making a trip back to the capital to visit relatives and friends and put things in the old house to order in preparation for the family's return. He told his mother about his plan and packed for the journey that very day. With only a servant called Wang Fu accompanying him, he bade farewell to his mother and his wife.

On his way north, traveling by water, he stopped at the wharf in Yangzhou. Called Jiangdu at the time, Yangzhou was a transportation hub of the Jianghuai region, a vital strategic spot that linked the north and the south. The wharf was alive with boats going up and down the river. With its dense population along the banks and its crowded markets, it was a city of bustling activity and glamour.

Wang Chen left his boat and went ashore. He hired a few porters and draft animals and, dressed up as a military officer, toured one scenic spot after another, traveling by day and resting by night. A few days later, he came to a place called Fanchuan, which had once been enfeoffed to Fan Kuai [d. 189 B.C.E.] of Han dynasty, not far from the capital. The villagers having all fled afar from the ravages of war, not a single sign of human habitation was seen all along the way. Even wayfarers were few and far between. Behold:

> The hills stretched fold upon fold,
> The trees stood in dense foliage.
> The pointed peaks pierced the sky;
> The steep ridges rose to heaven.
> Silver foam spouted from slanting waterfalls;
> Colorful twigs swung from hanging wisteria.
> On the hilltops hidden in the clouds,
> Winding bird trails outnumbered wayfarers.

In the forest thick with haze,
Few locals were seen in the forlorn villages.
The mountain flowers smiled in all their charm,
The birds, names unknown, chirped with abandon.

Wang Chen was so fascinated by the scenery that as he rode along slowly on slack reins, he was unaware that the day was already far advanced. Hearing what he thought were the sounds of human talk in the dense woods, he walked up and found two wild foxes talking and laughing. Leaning upright against an ancient tree, they were discussing the book that one of them was holding in its hand. Wang Chen said to himself, "What extraordinary animals! I wonder what book they're reading. Let me hit them with my pellets." He put the reins down, took up his slingshot made of waterstone-polished horns, reached into his pocket, retrieved a pellet, placed it in the slingshot, and took aim. The bow formed the shape of a full moon and the pellet flew like a comet. "Take that!" he cried. (*If unprovoked, one should not make an enemy of anyone, not even a nonhuman being.*)

The two foxes, carried away in the heat of their discussion, were oblivious of the prying eyes behind the trees. As they looked up at the sound of the bowstring, the pellet struck the one with the book smack in its left eye. The book fell. A scream escaped the fox as it fled in pain. The other fox was about to pick the book up when another pellet from Wang Chen hit it on its left cheek. It got down on all fours and ran off, howling as it went. Wang Chen spurred his horse forward and had Wang Fu pick up the book, only to find it printed in ancient tadpole-like characters completely unknown to him. He thought, " I wonder what's written there. Let me take it to some knowledgeable scholar." So he slipped the book into his sleeve and rode out of the woods onto the road in the direction of the capital.

At that time, even though An Lushan had died, his son An Qingxu was still going strong, and Shi Siming had risen in rebellion a second time after having surrendered to the imperial court. Military commanders in the border areas were also amassing troops, biding their time to seize power. As a security measure against enemy spies, the gates of the capital were tightly guarded. Everyone leaving or entering the city was subjected to rigorous questioning, and the gates were closed as soon as dusk began to set in. By the time Wang Chen arrived, afternoon had dimmed into evening and the gates were already closed. He had to go to an inn to stay for the night. He dismounted upon reaching an inn and walked in. Impressed by his look of a military officer with his slingshot and sword, the innkeeper dared not be remiss in courtesy, and stepped forward to greet him. "Officer, please take a seat," said he. He then had a waiter serve tea. Wang Fu unloaded the luggage and carried everything indoors.

"I'd like to have one of your nicer rooms," said Wang Chen to the innkeeper.

"I have plenty of rooms. You can take your pick, sir." With that, the innkeeper lit a lantern and led Wang Chen on a tour of the rooms. Wang's luggage was then laid down in a chosen clean room, and the horses were led to the back of the house to be fed.

After everything had been put in order, the waiter came into his room and asked, "Would you like to have some wine, sir?"

"Yes, bring me two measures of good wine and one plate of sliced beef. Give the same things to the porters." The waiter went out to do as he was told. Wang Chen closed the door after him and went outside.

Carrying the wine and the meat to him, the waiter asked, "Would you like to have the wine in your room or right here?"

"Here," replied Wang Chen.

The waiter set the wine on a table. Wang Chen sat down and began to drink, with Wang Fu pouring out the wine for him. After two or three cups, the innkeeper came up to ask, "Where are you from, sir?"

"From south of the river."

"But you don't have a southern accent."

"To be honest with you, I'm actually from the capital. I took my family south of the river because the emperor went to the Sichuan region after An Lushan's rebellion. Having learned that the rebellion has been put out and the emperor is back in the capital, I'm now on my way there to put the family estate in order so that I can then bring the whole family back. I'm wearing a military officer's uniform because I was afraid it might be a dangerous journey."

"So we are from the same place! Like you, I've been staying in these rustic parts to get out of harm's way. I've been here for less than a year." Being fellow townsmen, they warmed up to each other and had much to tell about the hardships of an unsettled life. Truly,

> The rivers and mountains remain unchanged,
> But half of the town's residents are gone.

In the midst of their animated conversation, they heard a voice behind them saying loudly, "Innkeeper! Do you have vacancies?"

"Yes, I do," replied the innkeeper. "How many people?"

"There's just me."

Seeing that the man was alone with no baggage, the innkeeper said, "If there's only you, I dare not keep you."

Angrily, the man said, "Is it because you think I won't pay you?"

"No, that's not what it is. It's just because Grand Councilor Guo [Guo Ziyi, 697–781], who's taking care of the capital in the emperor's absence, has warned innkeepers all over the area against taking on suspicious strangers. Those who shelter bad people will be punished severely if found out. With Shi Siming in rebellion, the situation is even worse. Now you, sir, have no baggage with you, nor have I ever seen you before. That's why I can't keep you."

"So you don't recognize me," said the man with a smile. "I'm Hu [homophone of "fox"] Er, a guard in Grand Councilor Guo's establishment. I'm on my way back from a trip to Fanchuan on official business, here to stay at your inn because the city gate is already closed. That's why I have no baggage with me. If you don't believe me, you can go with me tomorrow morning to the city gate. Every guard there knows me."

Believing in this false presentation of an impressive background, the innkeeper said, "Please don't take offense if I didn't know you were an officer serving the great Mr. Guo. Let me show you to your room."

"Wait!" said the man. "I'm hungry. Give me some wine and food first." Then he added, "I'm on a vegetarian diet. Just vegetables and wine will do." Having said that, the man walked over to Wang Chen's table and sat down, facing him. As the waiter set out food and wine, Wang Chen looked at the man and saw that he was covering his left eye with a sleeve, as if in severe pain.

"Innkeeper," said the man. "As bad luck would have it, I ran into two fur balls today. I fell and hurt my eye."

"What did you say you ran into?" asked the innkeeper.

"I was on my way back from Fanchuan when I saw two wild foxes rolling about and howling in the forest. I went forward to catch them, but I tripped and fell. The foxes got away, and I hurt my eye when I hit the ground."

"No wonder you're covering up your eye with your sleeve," said the innkeeper.

Wang Chen chimed in, saying, "I also ran into two wild foxes earlier today when I was passing by Fanchuan."

The man hastened to ask, "Did you catch them?"

Wang Chen said, "They were reading a book in the woods. I hit one of them in the left eye with a pellet from my slingshot. It threw down the book and ran away. The other one was about to pick it up when I shot it in one cheek. It also ran for its life. So I only got the book."

The man and the innkeeper said in amazement, "How extraordinary that foxes can read!"

The man added, "What's written in that book? May I take a look?"

"It's full of strange-looking ancient characters. I can't read a single one of them," said Wang Chen as he put down his wine cup and reached into his sleeve for the book. What followed happened in less time than it takes to tell. Before his hand was deep into his sleeve, a five- or six-year-old grandson of the innkeeper's walked into the room. In his innocence, the little boy saw the man as a wild fox. Unable to call the animal by its proper name, he ran forward and said, pointing at it, "Grandpa! Why is a big wild cat sitting here? Why don't you drive it away?"

At these words, Wang Chen realized that it was none other than the fox whose left eye he had hit. Quickly he drew his sword and swung it right at the man's head. The man dodged backwards, rolled over on the floor, and, now showing its true shape as a fox, ran frantically out the door. Wang Chen gave chase, sword in hand.

After running past more than ten houses, the fox jumped over a wall and disappeared. In the darkness of the night, Wang Chen had no idea where to go further and resignedly turned back to the inn. With a lit lantern, the innkeeper and Wang Fu went out to meet him and said to him, "Why don't you just let it go and spare its life?"

Wang Chen said, "If it weren't for your grandson, that beast would have got the book back from me."

"That fur ball is a clever one," said the innkeeper. "I'm afraid it'll be back with another trick to get the book."

"I'll take anyone who brings the matter up to trick me to be that beast in disguise and hit him with my sword!" So saying, Wang Chen reentered the inn. Having heard about this extraordinary event, merchants lodging at the inn gathered around him to hear more. After talking himself quite dry in the mouth, Wang Chen ate supper and retired to his own room. Considering how the fox had tried to get the book back in spite of its pain, he thought that there must be something wonderful about the book and therefore cherished it even more than before. At about the third watch of the night, he heard violent knocks at the door. "Give me back my book this instant!" a voice shouted. "I'll make it worth your while. If you don't, you'll run into troubles aplenty! Don't regret!"

These words so enraged Wang Chen that he rose, threw some clothes over his shoulders, and picked up his sword. Afraid of disturbing the other lodgers, he tiptoed his way out of his room. (*This Wang Chen is a ruthless man.*) His hand reaching for the front gate found it closed with a padlock that the innkeeper had put on. He thought, "By the time I wake up the innkeeper and have him open the gate, that fur ball will have gone off. Why make myself unpopular when I can't get at that thing anyway? Let me swallow the humiliation for now and do what I have to do tomorrow." So thinking, he went back to his room and retired for the night.

In the full hearing of everyone at the inn, the fox went on shouting a good while longer before it took itself off. The next morning, all the lodgers came to plead with Wang Chen, saying, "Since the writing in that book doesn't make any sense to you anyway, why keep the book at all? You might just as well give it back to the fox. If something should really happen, regrets will be too late."

Had Wang Chen been wiser and heeded the advice, all would have been well. As it was, however, the headstrong Wang Chen ignored all advice and, as a consequence, was later brought to ruin by the workings of the foxes. Truly,

> One who ignores good advice
> Will end up in tears of woe.

To come back to our story, Wang Chen ate breakfast, paid the innkeeper his bill, and took his baggage. As he rode into the city on horseback, he saw houses in ruins and markets deserted, not at all the way he had remembered them. Upon reaching his old residence, he was overcome with grief when he saw nothing but a pile of debris where the house had stood. With nowhere to stay now, he had to look for lodging. After finding a place, he deposited his baggage there and went out to visit those few relatives who had stayed behind. In telling one another about their woes, they shed bitter tears. Wang Chen said, "I was hoping to settle down in my old home, but I never expected to see the house all gone. I have no roof over my head now."

His relatives said, "All too many families have been torn apart since the beginning of the fighting. The fathers may be in the south, but the sons are in the north. And people have been kidnapped, killed, or made to go through the worst ordeals. Every one of us here has had a very narrow escape from death. We've all been through a lot. Nothing has happened to your family, though, except the destruction of the house. Consider yourself immeasurably lucky. What's more, you still have some land properties here. We've been taking care of them. If you really want to settle down here again, you can still be rich enough once you have everything in proper order."

Wang Chen thanked them. He then bought a house and furniture and house-wares and regained control of the land properties piece by piece.

About two months later, he was on his way out of the house when he saw a man in hemp mourning clothes coming from the east. With a parcel on his back, he was walking at top speed, as if on wings. As the man was fast approaching, Wang Chen gave a start, for this was none other than Wang Liu'er, a family servant.

"Wang Liu'er," cried out Wang Chen in alarm. "Where did you just come from? Why are you in such clothes?"

Wang Liu'er exclaimed, "Young Master, so you are here! I've been looking all over for you until my head is in a swirl!"

"Tell me why you're in mourning."

"I brought you a letter, Young Master. You'll know why after you read it." So saying, Wang Liu'er went inside, put down his parcel, retrieved the letter from it, and gave the letter to his young master. Wang Chen opened it and recognized his mother's handwriting. The letter said:

After you went away, news came that Shi Siming had risen in arms again—news that worried me day and night and led to a grave illness that no medicine or prayers have been able to cure. I will be entering the netherworld any day now. Death for a woman in her sixties is nothing unusual, but it pains my heart that I should be rendered homeless by war in my declining years and will die in a place far away from home without you and your brother at my death bed. Being a native of the Qin region, I do not wish to be buried in alien land. Yet, given the rising power of the rebels, I'm afraid that the capital will again fall into enemy hands and is therefore not a safe place to live in. After a whole wakeful night of thinking, I have decided to relinquish what little remains of our family property in the capital to pay for my funeral expenses. After you bury my dead bones, return to Hangzhou, east of the Yangzi River, where the land is fertile and the local people honest and kind. Having gone through so many hardships when first starting a home there, you must not give up easily. Wait until the fighting is over before planning to go back to the capital. If you fail to do as I say, I swear not to see you in the netherworld, for you will only be bringing trouble upon yourself and disgrace upon your ancestors. Mark these words of mine!

After reading the letter, Wang Chen wept so bitterly that he collapsed to the floor. "I was hoping to put the family fortunes here back in order so that the whole family could come back to our home base. I never expected that mother would die of worries about me. Had I known this earlier, I wouldn't have come. But regrets are too late now!" After another fit of sobbing, he asked Wang Liu'er, "What else did Mother say before she passed away?"

"Just that the family properties here haven't been attended to for so long that even if you've started over again, you must not try to keep everything, because, with Shi Siming's rebellion still going on, the capital will fall again. She wants you to dispose of everything as soon as possible and make arrangements for her burial and, after you have her coffin buried, go back to Hangzhou again to stay out of harm's way. If you don't do so, she won't rest easy in her grave."

"How would I dare go against my mother's last wishes! The Hangzhou region east of the river does seem to be a livable place. With fighting still going on in Chang'an, it does make sense to relinquish everything here." In a hurry, he ordered some hemp clothes of mourning and set out a family shrine in honor of his mother. While preparing the grave, he sought help in selling the family land and the house.

After staying for two days, Wang Liu'er said to Wang Chen, "Building the grave may take a whole month. I will be missed at home. Please let me go back first, just to put everyone's mind at rest." (*A clever way of giving him the slip.*)

"Exactly what I've been thinking, too," said Wang Chen. Right away, he wrote up a letter to his folks in Hangzhou and took out some money for the servant's travel expenses. Wang Liu'er said on his way out, "Now that I'm leaving, you, Young Master, must also finish your business quickly and get on your way."

"How I wish I could be there this very instant! You needn't have reminded me." Thereupon, Wang Liu'er took himself off triumphantly.

Upon learning of the news, Wang Chen's relatives came to offer their condolences and to talk him into not relinquishing his family property so rashly, but Wang Chen, determined to obey his mother's orders, turned a deaf ear to them. In his haste, he sold all the fine land at half the market price. He stayed on for about twenty more days, digging the grave site and building the grave. After everything had been finished, he packed and left Chang'an posthaste for Hangzhou to make arrangements for the hearse and the burial rites, taking his servants with him. Poor thing!

Sword in hand, he took a trip to Chang'an,
But all thoughts of settling down came to nothing.
His mother gone, his filial devotion a dream,
He shed enough tears to wet the clouds in the sky.

Our story forks at this point. Having heard that Shi Siming had risen in rebellion again, Wang Chen's mother and wife were worried sick about Wang Chen. How they regretted having let him undertake the journey back to Chang'an! One day, two to three months later, a servant announced to them that Wang Fu, Wang Chen's servant, had returned from the capital with a letter from his master. They immediately summoned Wang Fu in. With a kowtow, Wang Fu handed them the letter. They noticed that Wang Fu's left eye was injured, but, without bothering to ask him about it, they tore open the letter and read:

Since I left you, Mother, all has been well with me with your blessings. I checked the old family properties in the capital and am happy to report that nothing has been damaged and I have put everything back to order. You will be even more pleased to learn that I encountered an old acquaintance, Administrative Assistant Hu the Eighth, who introduced me to Prime Minister Yuan [Yuan Zai, d. 777]. The prime minister graciously granted me a post in the Youzhou and Jizhou area.[2] I have already received the letter of appointment and must report for duty very soon. I have therefore sent Wang Fu to deliver this message, so that you, Mother, can join me before we set out together for my duty station. As soon as you receive this letter, please sell all of our family land holdings in Hangzhou and come immediately to the capital. Do not be concerned about the price. Haggling over paltry amounts will only delay the journey. Since we will be meeting soon, I will stop here. Please accept my bows.

The mother and the wife were overjoyed after reading the letter. Only then did they ask, "Wang Fu, what happened to your eye?"

Wang Fu replied, "Oh, don't even bring this up! I was dozing on horseback when I accidentally fell and hurt this eye."

"How are things in the capital, compared with before? Are all our relatives alive and well?"

"The city is mostly in ruins. It's so different from before. With so many of our relatives killed, captured, or on the road as refugees, only a few families are left. And even they have had their assets looted, their houses burned, and their land seized. Ours is the only family whose house and land remain intact."

Even more delighted, they said, "So the family property is intact and, on top of that, he gets an official post. We're ever so grateful to heaven and earth and our ancestors for their blessings! Before we set out on the journey, we must hold a prayer service to offer our thanks and to pray for a bright future and everlasting happiness." They then asked, "Who is Administrative Assistant Hu the Eighth?"

"He's an old friend of my master's."

Wang Chen's mother said, "I've never heard him mention any official named Hu among people he associates with."

Wang Chen's wife, Yu-shi, commented, "Maybe they got to know each other only recently."

Wang Fu said eagerly, "Yes, exactly!"

After a few more questions and answers, Madam Wang said, "Wang Fu, you must be tired after the journey. You may go now to have some wine and food, and then take a good rest."

The next day, Wang Fu said to Madam Wang, "You will need several days to pack, ma'am, and in the meantime, my master in the capital has no one to wait on him. May I go back to him and help him pack so that as soon as you arrive, we can all immediately set out for his duty station?" (*Again, a clever way to extricate himself.*)

"Yes, this does make sense," agreed the old lady. So she wrote a letter of reply, gave him some money for travel expenses, and sent him on his way.

After Wang Fu's departure, Madam Wang sold all the family land, houses, furniture, and housewares and kept only some portable valuables. Afraid that her son might be late in reporting for duty, she did not bother to haggle, and disposed of everything at half the market price. She then engaged some monks for a prayer service. The service over, she hired a government boat and chose a day for the family's departure. Several female neighbors on friendly terms with the Wangs went to see them off. After bidding the neighbors farewell, the Wangs boarded the boat and set off on their journey. They sailed out of Hangzhou and, after passing Jiahe, Suzhou, Changzhou, and Runzhou, found themselves on the mainstream of the Yangzi River. As they sailed ahead, the servants of the family gesticulated animatedly on the boat, forgetting themselves in their joy over their young master's new status as an official.

> How sad their life as refugees in the south!
> How sudden the advent of wealth and rank!
> The whole family rejoiced and laughed;
> Soon they would be in Chang'an in all their glory.

Let us now turn to Wang Chen, who had left the capital and was on the road, traveling posthaste. In a few days he arrived at the wharf of Yangzhou. Wang Chen deposited his baggage at an inn and dismissed the porters and their draft animals. After eating supper, he instructed Wang Fu to go to the riverbank to hire a boat, whereas he himself sat down by the door of the inn to keep an eye on the baggage and watch the boats come and go. There, for all to see, was a government boat sailing against the current. On the bow stood four or five people laughing and singing merrily. When they drew near, he saw, upon a closer look, that they were none other than servants of his family. In astonishment, he said to himself, "Why are they not working at home but here on a government boat?" Then he thought again,

"Now that mother has passed away, they must be serving another master." (*A misunderstanding that can well be put into a play.*) While he was pursuing these thoughts, a woman poked her head out of the curtain over the cabin door. Wang Chen looked more intently and saw that she was a maidservant of the family. "How very strange! How very strange!" he said to himself. He was about to ask aloud when the servants on the boat recognized him and exclaimed, "Why is our young master also here? And why is he in mourning clothes?" Immediately, they had their boatman maneuver the boat toward the shore.

Hearing the commotion, Madam Wang and Yu-shi raised the curtain and looked out. At the sight of his mother, alive and well, Wang Chen hurriedly took off his clothes of mourning, opened a parcel, and changed into regular clothes and headscarf. The servants left the boat and went ashore to greet him. After instructing them to load all his baggage onto the boat, Wang Chen boarded it to greet his mother. As he happened to catch sight of Wang Liu'er, the servant, standing on the bow, he seized the man and hit him. Madam Wang emerged from the cabin and said, "Why do you hit an innocent man?"

At the sight of his mother, Wang Chen released the servant, stepped forward, and said, bowing deeply, "That dog brought a letter to me when I was in the capital, claiming that the letter was written before you passed away. He's the one who made me do an unfilial thing: putting on mourning clothes when my mother is alive!"

Both Madam Wang and Yu-shi were startled. "He's been with us every day. How could he have delivered any letter to the capital?" they said.

Wang Chen explained, "A month ago, he brought me a letter from Mother saying thus-and-so. I kept him for a couple of days before sending him back home to assuage the grief of the family. And then I disposed of our land properties in the capital and started on my way home posthaste. Why did you say he didn't go to the capital?"

These words shocked the whole family. "How could there be such a thing?" they exclaimed. "How could there be another Wang Liu'er?"

Wang Liu'er himself burst out laughing. "I didn't go to the capital," said he. "Not even in a dream!"

The old lady said, "Show me the letter. Does the handwriting look like mine?"

Wang Chen replied, "If not, how would I have believed what the letter says?"

So saying, he opened his baggage and retrieved the letter, only to find it a blank piece of paper without the slightest trace of a character. Wang Chen was dumbfounded. As he examined the piece of paper front and back, up and down, his mother said, "Show it to me."

"How very strange!" exclaimed Wang Chen. "The letter contained a lot of characters. How could it have gone blank?"

His mother was not convinced. "Nonsense!" said she. "We haven't exchanged letters since you left home until the other day when Wang Fu brought me the letter from you, saying that you will meet us in the capital. I then wrote a note for him to deliver to you. Don't tell me there was a fake Wang Liu'er to fool you with a fake letter! And now you say the letter has turned blank. Where did you learn to tell stories like that?"

Startled upon hearing that Wang Fu had brought a letter home, Wang Chen said, "Wang Fu was with me in the capital all along before we set out together on this journey. I never told him to deliver any letter to you, mother."

Both his mother and wife cried, "Good grief! This is even more of a lie! Wang Fu came home a month ago, bearing a letter that said all our family land properties in the capital were intact, that you met an Administrative Assistant Hu the Eighth who introduced you to Prime Minister Yuan, and that you got an official post and therefore would like us to sell all of our family possessions in the south and go immediately to the capital so that we can join you in your journey to your duty station. That's why we gave up everything we owned and hired a boat to go to the capital. How can you say that Wang Fu never brought a letter back home?"

Wang Chen was flabbergasted. "This is getting more and more absurd," said he. "There's no Administrative Assistant Hu the Eighth introducing me to Prime Minister Yuan. I have no official post, nor have I written any letter asking you to meet me in the capital!"

"Could it have been a fake Wang Fu?" said the old lady. "Get Wang Fu here, quick, and ask him!"

"He's gone to hire a boat and should be here any moment now," said Wang Chen.

The servants swarmed to the bow and happened to see Wang Fu approaching from afar, wearing mourning clothes, as his master had been. As they waved their hands frantically, Wang Fu caught sight of them and recognized them to be his fellow servants. In astonishment, he thought, "Why are they in this place?" As he drew near the boat, it was obvious to everyone that he looked quite different from the last time they saw him with his left eye injured, for both his big eyes were now wide open, as if about to pop out of their sockets.

They called out, "Wang Fu, you were blind in one eye last time you came home. How come it's all right now?"

Wang Fu spit in their direction and said, "You must all be blind! When did I go back home? Why do you say I was blind? Are you cursing me?"

The men laughed. "This is indeed very strange," they said. "The old lady in the cabin asked for you. Take off your mourning clothes and go this instant to see her."

Wang Fu was struck speechless. After a pause, he asked, "The old lady is still around?"

"Of course she's around. Where else could she be?"

Unconvinced, Wang Fu stormed into the cabin without taking off his mourning clothes. Wang Chen thundered, "Dog! Go change your clothes before coming to pay your respects to the old mistress!"

Wang Fu hastily withdrew from the cabin and took off his mourning clothes before reentering to kowtow to the old lady. Madam Wang rubbed her old bleary eyes and peered more intently. "How extraordinary!" she exclaimed. "When Wang Fu returned the other day, his left eye was badly injured, but now it looks perfectly normal. So the one who came the other day was not Wang Fu." She hastened to order that the letter that had been delivered the other day be opened. It also turned out to be a blank piece of paper without the slightest trace of ink. Everyone was confused. They wondered: Who could have assumed the forms of Wang Liu'er and Wang Fu? Why all this conspiracy to fool the family into self-destructively disposing of all properties in both places? They were seized with fear at the thought that misfortune might strike them again.

After Wang Chen thought long and hard about the matter, what had been said about the fake Wang Fu's blind eye suddenly made sense to him. He burst out, "Yes! It's all that accursed beast's doing!"

"What accursed beast?" asked his mother quickly. Thereupon Wang Chen told them how he had shot two foxes and picked up a book in Fanchuan, and how one of the foxes had assumed human form to fool him, and how it had pounded on the door of the inn where he was staying. He added, "I thought the accursed beast changed into human form just to get the book back. I had no idea it was so cunning."

The servants said, shaking their heads and clicking their tongues, "What a fearsome fox spirit! It imitated human handwriting, assumed human forms, and had fun playing tricks on this family across so much distance. Had you known this earlier, you might as well have given the book back to it."

"But the impudence of that accursed beast is more than I can bear!" exclaimed Wang Chen. "Now I have all the more reason not to give the book back to it. If it comes again to bother me, I'm going to burn up that source of trouble!" (*What a stouthearted man Wang Chen is! But he will end up the loser.*)

"Now that things have already come to this," said Wang Chen's wife, Yu-shi, "let's not make comments that serve no purpose, but talk about what to do next. We are now stuck in this place in the middle of nowhere. What are we going to do?"

Wang Chen said, "Our property in the capital having been all sold off, we won't have a home even if we go there. And it's so far away. We'd better turn back to Hangzhou."

"We don't have anything left in Hangzhou, either," said his mother. "Where are we going to stay?"

"Let's rent a place before deciding what to do next," suggested Wang Chen.

And so they turned the boat around and headed back for Hangzhou. The servants who had been filled with fiery enthusiasm were now reduced to icy silence, their limbs as weak and motionless as those of puppets with broken strings. (*Fiery hotness is bound to turn into icy coldness at some point in time. Those lacking in wisdom do not understand this.*) Indeed, this is a case of setting out in all cheerfulness and returning in bitter disappointment.

After arriving at Hangzhou, Wang Chen and the servants went on shore first. They rented a house near their former residence and bought all the necessary furniture and housewares before they went to transport the baggage and escort the old lady and Yu-shi into the house. Wang Chen then counted whatever possessions he had left and found that there remained less than half of what he had when he left the capital. Exasperated, he kept himself indoors and brooded over his troubles. When neighbors came to ask why Madam Wang had gone but returned, Wang Chen told them everything, and the story, so out of the ordinary, spread from mouth to mouth throughout half of the city of Hangzhou.

One day, Wang Chen was in the main hall, supervising the servants as they were putting things in order, when there walked in a distinguished-looking man in elegant attire. Behold:

> A black gauze Tang-style headscarf,
> A green silk Daoist robe,
> Green jade rings holding the scarf in place,
> A purple satin sash around the waist,
> A pair of stockings as white as snow,
> A pair of shoes as crimson as sunset clouds.
> He had the dignified look of an immortal;
> He had the ethereal air of a divine being.
> If not a deity in heaven,
> He was surely a high official on earth.

Upon a closer look at the man who had just entered the hall, Wang Chen realized that he was Wang Zai, his very own younger brother.

"Have you been well since we parted, my brother?" asked Wang Zai as he stepped forward and took a deep bow.

Wang Chen returned the greetings and said, "My good brother, you must have had a hard time looking for us!"

"I went back to our house in the capital but found it in ruins. I thought you must all have died in the war. I was filled with grief. But then I visited relatives and friends, and they told me that our whole family had fled from the war to the south, and that you, brother, had been back in the capital to put the family possessions in order but had just left again upon learning about mother's death. So I made all the haste I could and came to Hangzhou. The neighbors told me that you have moved to this place and that mother is alive and well. So I went to my boat and changed clothes before coming here. Now where's mother? And why have you moved into such a shabby house?"

"It's a long story," said Wang Chen. "I'll tell you everything after you pay your respects to mother." He then took his brother to the inner quarters of the house.

Already informed by servants of her second son's return, Madam Wang rushed out of her room in delight and ran into them midway. Wang Zai prostrated himself on the floor. After he rose to his feet, the old lady said, "My son! I've been worried about you day and night. Have you been well?"

"Thank you, Mother, for thinking about me. After I pay my respects to my sister-in-law, I'll tell you everything that has happened to me."

After Yu-shi and all the male and female servants came to exchange greetings with the younger son, the latter grabbed Wang Chen and led him back into the main hall. Madam Wang followed. After sitting down, Wang Zai asked, "Brother, first tell me why are you all reduced to this?"

Wang Chen started off with the incident of his hitting a fox in the eye and then he went on about how the family had been tricked into selling off properties in both places. After listening to the account, Wang Zai said, "So, that's what led to these sorry circumstances! It's all your fault. The wild foxes are not to blame. They were reading their book in the woods and you were traveling on the road, each minding his own business. Why did you have to hit them and seize their book? Then, at the inn, in spite of the pain in the eye, that fox tried to trick you into giving back the book, and I believe he did so because he had absolutely no other choice. If you didn't want to give the book back, fine. Why were you so spiteful as to chase him with a sword? When he pleaded to you at night, you again flatly refused. You can't even read the characters. Why would you want to hold on to something that's useless to you? And look at what all the trickery has gotten you into! This is all of your own making!"

Madam Wang said, "That's what I think, too. Why keep a useless thing? And it has turned out to be the ruin of us all!"

Thus reproached by his own younger brother, Wang Chen seethed with resentment but said nothing.

Wang Zai continued, "How big is that book? What style is the calligraphy?"

Wang Chen replied, "It's a thin volume. I don't recognize the calligraphy style because I don't know even one character."

"May I take a look?" asked Wang Zai.

Madam Wang chimed in, "Right. Show it to your brother. He may be able to read it, for all you know."

"I don't think I can read the characters. I'd just like to see a curiosity."

Wang Chen went inside and presently reentered the hall with the book, which he then gave to Wang Zai. The book now in hand, Wang Zai flipped through it and said, "Strange characters indeed!" With that, he rose, walked to the middle of the hall, and announced to Wang Chen, "The fake Wang Liu'er was me. Now that I've got the divine book back, I won't bother you again. Rest assured." So saying, he ran toward the door.

An enraged Wang Chen gave chase, shouting, "You accursed beast! How dare you! Where do you think you're going?" With a quick movement he grabbed Wang Zai's robe. As one tried to struggle himself free and the other tightened his grip, part of the robe was torn off with a screeching sound. The fox spirit then shook off all its clothes to reveal its true form. With the speed of wind, it flew out the door. Wang Chen and the servants rushed into the street and looked in all directions, but it was gone.

Partly because the fox had brought ruin to his family and given him a lecture, and partly because he had lost the book, Wang Chen gnashed his teeth in rage and continued to look for the fox as he went along. At the sight of a Daoist priest, blind in one eye, standing under the eaves across the street, he asked, "Have you seen a wild fox?"

"Yes," said the priest, pointing east. "It went in an easterly direction." Thereupon, Wang Chen and the servants pressed ahead east. Before they had passed five or six doors further down the street, the priest called out from behind them, "Wang Chen, the fake Wang Fu was me. And the one who passed off as your brother is also here!"

Upon hearing this, the men turned around and saw two wild foxes holding the book and frolicking merrily. As the men fearlessly charged at them, the foxes got all their legs down on the ground and ran away at full gallop. When Wang Chen gained his own door, his mother cried, "Isn't it good enough that we're already rid of those pests that brought ruin to us? Why do you have to pursue them? Come in this instant!"

Swallowing his resentment, Wang Chen obeyed his mother and called the servants off the chase. Once inside the house, he picked up the fox's articles of clothing to examine them. Each article changed as soon as he touched it. What, you may ask, did they change into?

> The silk robe changed back into broken plantain leaves;
> The gauze scarf was in fact a torn lotus leaf.
> The green jade rings were made of willow twigs;
> The purple sash was no more than a vine.
> The stockings were two sheets of white paper,
> The crimson shoes, two pieces of pine bark.

Everyone was appalled. "Such magic powers!" someone commented. "I wonder where the second master is. How did the fox manage to look so exactly like him?"

As for Wang Chen, the more he thought about this, the more upset he became. His depression led to an illness that confined him to bed. His mother engaged a physician for him, but let us move on with our story.

Several days later, the servants were in the main hall when a man walked in. They saw that he was none other than Wang Zai, wearing the same gauze scarf and silk robe that the fox had worn. Believing this was again an impostor, they cried, "The demon fox is here again!" They picked up sticks and rods and went up to beat him. (*One who takes what's false to be real is bound to take what's real to be false. Wang Chen is by no means the only one with undiscerning eyes.*)

"You scoundrels!" roared Wang Zai. "The temerity! Go and let my mother know I'm here!" But they all ignored him and rained blows on him. Unable to control his temper any longer, Wang Zai seized a stick from a servant's hand and brandished it so fiercely that the servants scattered in all directions. Not daring to draw near him, they hid themselves behind doors and cursed, pointing at him, "You evil beast! You got your book back, didn't you? Why are you here again?"

Not understanding what they meant, Wang Zai angrily made for the inner section of the house. The servants ran helter-skelter before him. Madam Wang, hearing the commotion, was already hurriedly on her way out. Running into the servants, she asked, "Why are you in such panic?"

"That demon fox is fighting its way in, and it's again in the shape of the second young master!"

"How can that be!" said Madam Wang, appalled. Before the words were quite out of her mouth, Wang Zai was already standing in front of her. He threw down his stick and sank to his knees in prostration. "Mother," said he, "why did those scoundrels call me a demon fox and an evil beast and beat me up?"

"But are you really my son or not?"

"You gave me birth, Mother. How can I not be real?"

At this point, seven or eight men carrying baggage came into the house. Only then did the servants realize that this was the real Wang Zai. After they kowtowed and begged for forgiveness, Wang Zai asked what it had all been about, whereupon Madam Wang gave him a whole account of what had happened, adding, "Your older brother took it so hard that he fell ill and hasn't recovered."

Aghast, Wang Zai said, "So, the Wang Fu who went to deliver a letter to me in Sichuan was also an impostor conjured up by the fox!"

"What did the letter say?" asked his mother.

"Well, I went to Sichuan as a member of the emperor's entourage and was assigned to serve under Yan Wu, commander of the southern Sichuan region. Later, I was promoted to be an assistant general. So I didn't follow the emperor back to the capital. Two months ago, Wang Fu came with a letter from my brother, saying that all of you had fled to Hangzhou from the war, and that mother had died. I was instructed to come quickly to talk about what to do and to escort mother's coffin back to our hometown. Wang Fu said that he needed to go to the capital to get the family grave ready, and so he left the very next day. I submitted my resignation and abandoned the bulk of my possessions so that I could travel lightly with all speed. I went to the old residence and followed the neighbors' directions all the way here. After learning that Mother is well, I went back into the boat to take off my mourning clothes. I was just going to ask my brother why he gave me such false information. I never expected to hear such strange things!" (*What did Wang Zai do to deserve such punishment? The foxes were wicked enough. That's why they don't get to be reincarnated as humans, after all.*)

When he retrieved the letter from his baggage, it was also seen to be a blank piece of paper. Everyone found this both laughable and exasperating.

Wang Zai then went with his mother to greet his sister-in-law. When he told his brother in his sick bed about what had happened, Wang Chen almost fainted from rage.

Madam Wang said to her younger son, "However wicked the foxes are, at least they got you back home from Sichuan to be reunited with your mother. That's a credit that lessens their offense. Let's not hate them!" (*The old lady is quite a peacemaker.*) Wang Chen did not regain his health until two months later. They then registered as residents of Hangzhou. Henceforth, swindlers are called wild fox spirits in the Wu and Yue regions even unto this day.

> *Snakes and tigers keep to their own kind;*
> *Foxes treasure their own books divine.*
> *His family fortune ruined, the book gone,*
> *Wang Chen will be ridiculed to the end of time.*

7

Scholar Qian Is Blessed with a Wife through a Happy Mistake

The wine-laden fishing boats set out with sunrise;
The flute is played in the depths of blossoming reeds.
The wind subsides, the clouds vanish, the lake regains peace;
The water glitters like green glaze under the sky.

The above poem was written by Yang Bei of the Song dynasty when he was touring Lake Tai, located a little more than thirty li southwest of Wu Prefecture [present-day Wu County, Jiangsu]. You may ask, how large is the lake? It is two hundred li from east to west, one hundred and twenty li from north to south, five hundred li in circumference, and about two hundred forty thousand hectares in area, and along the lake sit seventy-two hills and three cities. Which three cities? Suzhou, Huzhou, and Changzhou.

Bodies of water to its south and east all flow into Lake Tai. It is also alternatively called Zhenze Lake, Juqu Lake, Lize Lake, or Lake of Five. Why Lake of Five? It converges with Song River of Changzhou in the east, Zha Creek of Wucheng in the south, Jing Creek of Yixing in the west, Lake Ge of Jinling in the north, and Jiu Creek of Jiaxing, again in the east. Hence Lake of Five. With these five bodies of water converging with it, it is therefore called Lake Tai [vastness]. In Lake Tai itself, there are again five lakes named Lake Ling, Lake You, Lake Mo, Lake Gong, and Lake Xu. And then there are three small lakes: Meiliang Lake to the east of Fujiao Hill, Jinding Lake to the west of Duqi Hill and to the east of Yucha Hill, and East Gaoli Lake to the east of Linwu Hill. The natives of the Wu region refer to them simply as Lake Tai. Of the seventy-two hills in Lake Tai, the two Dongting hills, East Dongting Hill and West Dongting Hill, are the largest, dwarfing other hills that are scattered throughout the lake, sometimes hardly visible behind the rolling waves. There is in testimony a poem by Xu Qian of the Yuan dynasty:[1]

Linked with ten thousand bodies of water,
It runs past prefectures far and near.

It stretches to the horizon in the south;
It holds mountains afloat in the west.
Separated by winding paths,
The waters surge into the sea.
Amid white-capped waves blown by the autumn wind,
The fishing boats ply calmly back and forth.

East Dongting Hill and West Dongting Hill being surrounded by water and inaccessible by horse carriage from land, those wishing to tour the two hills must take boats and place themselves at the mercy of the waves. Fan Chengda, prime minister in the Song dynasty, wrote the following poem when caught in a windstorm on the lake:[2]

White-capped waves spout high in the misty air;
The boats rise and fall like bamboo leaves.
I dare not lead an idle life,
But my heart is with the hills and rivers.

Residents on the two hills tended to be good merchants and traveled frequently in all directions on business journeys, giving rise to the sobriquet known all around the lake: Crafty Dongtingers. Of the Dongting merchants, I shall now tell of a rich man named Gao Zan, of West Dongting Hill. He started his grain business when he was quite young. After he had amassed an impressive fortune by trading in grain in Hubei and Hunan, he opened two pawnshops and hired four assistants to manage them. He himself retired to enjoy a leisurely life at home. His wife, née Jin, had given birth to a boy and a girl. The boy was named Gao Biao, and the girl, two years older, was called Qiufang. Gao Zan engaged an elderly scholar as a live-in tutor for the two children. Qiufang had a sharp intelligence. She started her education at age seven and by age twelve was well versed in the classics and the histories and was good in calligraphy and writing. At age thirteen, she stopped going to the tutor and learned to do needlework in her own room, embroidering phoenixes. By sixteen, she had grown into a ravishing beauty, as attested to by the following lyric to the tune of "Moon over West River":

Her face like the freshest peach,
Her body as fair as snow,
Her eyes sparkling, her eyebrows well marked,
Her fingers tapering like bamboo shoots.

She is just as beautiful as Xishi[3]
And no less charming than Cui Yingying.[4]
She moves lightly on tiny feet,
Her bearing as graceful as can be.

Refusing to marry such a beautiful and intelligent daughter to just any ordinary man, Gao Zan was determined that his son-in-law should be a scholar with both talent and looks. He did not mind the value of the betrothal gifts and would gladly offer more dowry instead as long as the candidate was worthy. Goodness knows how many rich and powerful families sent matchmakers to propose, but Gao Zan turned all of them down because he found the young men lacking in talent and in looks. Though Dongting was surrounded by water, it had easy access to three cities, and Gao Zan was a man of wealth. The matchmakers spread the word around, saying that Mr. and Mrs. Gao were willing to ignore the value of the betrothal gifts and offer more dowry instead, as long as they could find a dashing scholar worthy of their beautiful and intelligent daughter. Every bachelor with even a modicum of talent and looks assiduously sought the service of matchmakers. Each was made out to be as handsome as Pan An[5] and as talented as Cao Zhi,[6] but each turned out, after verification of the facts, to be nothing more than average. Exasperated by the endless jabber of the matchmakers, Gao Zan announced to them, "From now on, spare me your eloquence. If you find a really outstanding candidate, just bring him to me. If he is to my liking, I'll take him! As simple as that!" After this proclamation, the matchmakers dared not go to his house without a good candidate in tow. Truly,

> *Seeing is believing;*
> *Trust not the spoken word.*
> *With a touchstone in place,*
> *Those with fake silver shake in fear.*

Now let me start a second thread of the story and tell of a scholar named Qian Qing, courtesy name Wanxuan, who lived in Pingwang of Wujiang County, Suzhou Prefecture. He was endowed with poetic talent and well versed in the classics and the histories, and he was also a handsome man. There is in testimony the following lyric to the tune of "Moon over West River":

> *His lips red, his teeth white,*
> *His eyes bright, his brows well shaped,*
> *His elegance came not from new clothes;*
> *His grace was beyond comparison.*
>
> *He had the gift of a ready pen;*
> *His improvised writings dazzled all.*
> *His good repute spread far and wide;*
> *Everyone held him in profound respect.*

Mr. Qian came of a refined and highly cultivated family, albeit one of limited means. After his parents' death when he was still young, the family circumstances further deteriorated. Too poor to marry though he had come of age, he lived with an old family servant Qian Xing, who provided him with a meager living by working as a petty trader. Luckily, he became eligible for the county school that year. A rich cousin of his, who lived outside of North Gate in the same county, invited him to study at his home. Both Qian Qing and that cousin, Yan Jun, courtesy name Boya, were eighteen years of age. Yan being three months older, Qian addressed him as "Older Brother." Yan Jun's father had passed away, and Yan Jun, yet unbetrothed, was living with his mother.

Storyteller, Qian Qing was still a bachelor because he was poor, but why did a rich young man like Yan Jun remain unbetrothed at eighteen years of age? Well, let me explain. Yan Jun had the unfortunate habit of setting his sights too high. He had vowed not to marry unless he found a girl of unparalleled beauty, and that was not something easy to accomplish. To make things worse, Yan Jun himself was a decidedly ugly man. How do I know this? There is in testimony a lyric to the tune of "Moon over West River":

> His face as black as the bottom of a wok,
> His eyes as round as brass balls,
> His cheeks dotted with pimples and their scars,
> His hair brown and disheveled.
>
> His teeth plated with gold,
> His body as hard as iron,
> His fingers as rigid as drumsticks,
> He does injustice to his name.[7]

In spite of his unprepossessing appearance, Yan Jun devoted much attention to his clothes. He wore bright red and green and gave deep-throated laughs, believing himself to be an attractive man. Moreover, he was a man of little learning, unable to compose anything coherent on paper, and yet he was prone to making comments on history and current affairs in order to pass himself off as a scholar. Qian Qing knew that he had hardly anything in common with this cousin, but, being obliged to Yan for giving him a place to study, he humored his cousin in every way. Yan Jun was so pleased that he consulted Qian in everything, and the two got along amicably.

Not to encumber our story with unnecessary details, let me tell of what happened one day at the beginning of the tenth lunar month. Yan Jun had a distant relative called You Chen, courtesy name Shaomei. A man with considerable business acumen, he ran a fruit store in front of his house on capital borrowed from Yan Jun. On the particular day of which I speak, after returning home from a trip to Dongting Hill where he had bought several loads of oranges just in season, You Chen filled a tray with some and carried it as a gift to the Yan residence. Having heard during his trip that the Gao family was on the lookout for a son-in-law, he mentioned this to Yan Jun in passing as they chatted. It was idle gossip on his part, but Yan Jun found the information important. He thought, "I've been looking in vain for a good match. Now here's where my marriage destiny lies! With my literary talent and good looks and family wealth plus the glib tongue of a match-maker, what do I have to fear?"

After a wakeful night, he rose bright and early the next morning, hurriedly combed his hair and washed, and went to You Chen's house. You Chen happened to be opening his door when Yan Jun arrived. "Young Master," said You Chen, "why are you up so early?"

Yan Jun replied, "I have a big favor to ask of you. I'm here early because I was afraid you might go out."

"How can I be of help? Please come in and tell me."

Once in the living room, Yan Jun bowed and sat down in a guest seat.

You Chen said, "I'll surely do everything I can for you. I'm only afraid that I might not be of much help."

"I'm here to ask you, Shaomei, to make a match for me."

"I'll be only too glad to get a matchmaker's reward, but which family do you have in mind?"

"The very Gao family of West Dongting Hill you mentioned yesterday. That's a very good match for me. Please do this favor for me."

You Chen giggled. "Young Master, let me be frank with you. I would readily comply if you had picked any other family. If it's the Gao family, please give the job to someone else."

"Why don't you want the job? You gave me the information and now you're turning me away?"

"It's not that I want to turn you away, but Mr. Gao is a difficult man to talk to and is quite unpredictable. That's why I hesitate."

"He may be difficult to talk to and beat about the bush in other things, but a marriage proposal is something he would welcome. Unless his daughter doesn't want to marry, he will have to talk to matchmakers. However difficult he is, he won't be rude to a matchmaker. What do you have to fear? Or maybe you are the one being difficult and unwilling to see me happy! Well, in that case, I'll just ask someone else to make this match for me, and you can forget about coming to my wedding banquet!" With that, he abruptly rose to go.

Being in debt to Yan Jun, You Chen had always bowed and scraped to him. Now that Yan Jun was displeased, he changed his tone and said, "Young Master, don't be upset. Sit down. Let's talk about it."

"If you are willing to do it, go ahead and do it! If not, just forget about it. What's there to talk about?" However, even as he said those words, he turned around and sat down again.

You Chen said, "It's not that I'm trying to make things difficult, but that old man is indeed quite unpredictable. Other parents ask to look at candidates for a prospective *daughter*-in-law, but he wants to personally interview candidates for a prospective *son*-in-law. He will marry his daughter only to the one he picks from the interviews. With such a hurdle, I'm afraid I'll only take all the trouble for nothing. That's why I dared not do it."

"But this sounds easy. If he wants to look at me, I'll let him look his fill! I'm not a cripple. What am I afraid of?"

You Chen burst out laughing. "Young master, please don't take offense. You may not be ugly, but he has rejected those far better looking than you are. If he doesn't get to look at you, you may have a slight fraction of a chance. But if you show your face to him, the whole thing is off."

"As they say, no match is made without a lie. Why don't you embellish the facts a little? Just tell him that I exceed his expectations. If I'm destined to marry his daughter, maybe he'll be satisfied with your presentation and skip the interview."

"But what if he insists on an interview?"

"We'll think about it if he does. Now, go quickly to see him!"

"If you say so, I'll do it then."

As he rose from his seat, Yan Jun added, "Be sure to bring this match off for me! If you do, I'll give you back the receipt for your loan of twenty taels of silver, plus a reward for your matchmaking services."

"I'll try. I'll try," said You Chen.

Yan Jun departed. Soon thereafter, he had someone take half a tael of silver to You Chen so that he could rent a boat the next day. That night, Yan Jun lay awake in bed, thinking, "If he doesn't do a good job and tries to fob me off after he comes back, won't this trip be in vain? Let me send along a clever servant to go with him and listen to what he says. Good plan! Good plan!"

The next day, at first light, he called forth his servant, Xiaoyi, and told him to follow Mr. You up the hill on his matchmaking trip, and so Xiaoyi left. Yan Jun, still preoccupied with the matter, hurriedly combed his hair, washed, and went to a nearby temple of Lord Guan to ask for a divination.[8] Once in the temple, he lit some joss sticks, prostrated himself on the floor, and rose to shake the pot that contained the divination bamboo slips. With a thud, one bamboo slip fell on the ground. He picked it up and saw that it was slip number seventy-three. On it was inscribed a divination quatrain:

> *If you parted with your wife some time ago,*
> *You will not hear from her from this day on.*
> *If you foolishly want this match,*
> *All your hopes will come to naught.*

Though Yan Jun was not much of a scholar, the simple language of these lines was clear enough to him. Flying into a rage at this divination, he said, "This is not right! Not right!" And he left the temple in a huff. Once back at home, he sat down and thought, "How can this match not come off? Will they really think I'm too ugly for them? They can't value beauty in men as much as they do in women. After all, a man needs only be presentable in his appearance. They can hardly expect to have a Chen Ping or a Pan An for a son-in-law!"[9]

In the midst of these thoughts, he took a mirror and peered into it, tilting his head this way and that. His self-perception not yet distorted beyond redemption, he found his face repulsive even to himself. Putting the mirror down on the table, he sighed and sat as if in a trance. I shall not speak of how he spent the rest of the day in gloom but come to You Chen.

You Chen and Yan Jun's servant, Xiaoyi, took advantage of the windless day and rowed a three-scull fast boat to West Dongting Hill. It was early afternoon when they moored the boat in front of the Gao family's house. After Xiaoyi presented You Chen's name card, Mr. Gao came out, led them in, and asked for the purpose of the visit. When told that You Chen was there as a matchmaker with a marriage proposal for his daughter, Gao Zan asked, "Which family is it?"

You Chen replied, "It's a kinsman of mine who lives in the same county as I do. His family fortunes are quite impressive, enough to match yours. He's eighteen, and he is a fine scholar."

"How does he look? I have made it clear that I must personally look at all candidates before I can make a commitment."

Aware of Xiaoyi standing right behind his chair, You Chen felt obliged to tell a barefaced lie. He said, "His looks are even more impressive. He is tall and imposing, and impeccable in every way. And he's such a fine scholar! He came out first in the county-level civil service examinations at age fourteen. In the last few years, observation of mourning for his father's death has kept him from school, but several old scholars read his compositions and predicted that he would surely score high on the examinations. Now, I rarely make matches for people. It's just that during my frequent trips to this hill to buy fruit, I accidentally heard about your daughter's talent and beauty and about your carefulness in choosing a son-in-law. I believe that this kinsman of mine meets your standards quite well. That's why I made so bold as to come here."

Delighted at these words, Gao Zan said, "If your kinsman is truly as talented and handsome as you say, this old man will gladly oblige. But I'm afraid I won't feel easy until I see him with my own eyes. Could you bring him here for a little talk?"

"Sir, you will know in due course that I am being truthful. However, this relative of mine is a person who hardly ever goes out of his study. He may not be willing to come. If I push him into coming, it'll be well and good if everything works out. But if not, he will be too ashamed to go back. And he'll put the blame on me."

"If he's all perfection, the match will surely come off. But this old man is extremely cautious by nature. I must see him with my own eyes. If your relative wouldn't deign to come to this house, I will go to your house and you can casually bring him to me. Wouldn't that be a nice solution?"

Afraid that Gao Zan would hear about Yan Jun's unprepossessing looks once he went to Wujiang County, You Chen quickly changed his tune. "If you're so determined to meet him, I will bring him here. I won't presume to inconvenience you." With that, he said good-bye, but Mr. Gao was not about to let go of him yet. He instructed the servants to lay out wine and food. Host and guest dined for about two hours. To Mr. Gao's pleas for him to stay overnight, You Chen said, "I've got my own bedding in the boat. I'll be setting sail early tomorrow morning. So good-bye for now, until I come again with my kinsman."

Mr. Gao offered You Chen an envelope containing money for his travel expenses. You Chen said his thanks and boarded the boat.

The next morning, with a favorable wind, the boat went in full sail and arrived at Wujiang in about half a day. Yan Jun was standing immobile at the door like an idiot, waiting for news. At the sight of You Chen, he rushed forward to greet him and said, "Thank you so much for undertaking this trip. So, what did he say?"

You Chen gave a detailed account of his talk with Mr. Gao, adding, "He insists on seeing you. What are you going to do?"

Yan Jun said nothing.

You Chen continued, "Let's talk about this later." With that, he went home.

Yan Jun went inside and summoned Xiaoyi for a questioning, afraid that You Chen might not be speaking the truth. After Xiaoyi corroborated You Chen's account, Yan Jun thought for a moment, and a plan came to his mind. He again went to You Chen's house for a consultation. You may well ask, what plan did he have? Truly,

> In his fiery passion for the match,
> He cudgeled his brains through sleepless nights.
> Marriages are determined by fate,
> Not by the designs of human minds.

Yan Jun said to You Chen, "As for what you said some moments ago, I have thought of a plan that should work."

"What good plan is it?"

"My cousin Qian Qing who is doing his studies with me is better than I am in looks and in scholarship. Tomorrow, I'll ask him to go with you. You just present him as me and keep them believing so until the betrothal formalities have been gone through. By then, I'll have nothing to fear. They won't be able to back out of it."

"If they see Young Master Qian, they will certainly not reject him. I'm just afraid that Young Master Qian won't agree to do it."

"He's family, and we're great friends, too. I'm only asking him to answer to my name for a while. He will not be shortchanged! He won't turn me down." With that, You Chen bade him good-bye and went home.

That very evening, Yan Jun went to the study and had a sumptuous dinner set out for Qian Qing. In astonishment, Qian said, "I'm already imposing myself every day on your hospitality. Why go to all this trouble today and lay out such a feast?"

"Take a few cups of wine first. I have a minor favor to ask of you, my good brother. Do not turn me down."

"I'm willing to do anything for you in whatever small way I can. What is it?"

"Let me be frank with you. You Chen, owner of the fruit store across the street, is trying to make a match for me and the daughter of the Gao family on West Dongting Hill. He stretched the truth in the excitement of the moment and made me out to be a man of both good looks and talent. But as it turned out, Mr. Gao was so overjoyed that he insisted that I go to see him face to face before he would go ahead with the betrothal formalities. Yesterday, I consulted You Chen about this. If I go myself, I'm afraid I won't answer those descriptions. In that case, You Chen will be embarrassed and the match will be off. That's why I'm asking you to go with You Chen and pass yourself off as me, so as to fool Mr. Gao and bring off the match. I will be ever so grateful. I'll reward you well."

Qian Qing replied after a moment of thinking, "I'm afraid this is the only thing I'm not able to do. They may be fooled for now, but once they find out about this later on, it won't look good on either of us."

"To fool them for now is exactly what I intend to do. Once the betrothal formalities have been gone through, what do I have to fear even if they learn the truth? And they don't know who you are. They'll blame the matchmaker, if there's anyone to blame. What does that have to do with you? What's more, they live on West Dongting Hill, a hundred li from here. News won't leak out that quickly. Rest assured. Just go ahead. Don't be afraid."

Qian Qing fell silent. If he were to comply, he would be committing an ungentlemanly act. But if not, he would offend his host, and his days as a houseguest would be over. It was a difficult choice.

Observing Qian's pensive look, Yan Jun said, "My good brother, as they often say, 'Even if the sky falls down, the tall ones will hold it up for the rest of us.' With me behind you, you have nothing to worry about."

"It may very well be so, but I'm in rags. I can't pass off as you."

"I've already taken care of this."

Nothing further happened that night.

The next day, Yan Jun rose bright and early and went to his study, where he had a servant take out a leather suitcase filled with fashionable, brightly colored clothes of silk and satin emitting the fragrance of the finest perfume made of ambergris. He offered them to Qian Qing, along with a pair of white socks and silk shoes, so that he would have enough changes of outfit. But because Yan didn't have the right kind of headscarf that scholars wore, a new one was made straightaway. Handing Qian a packet of two taels of silver, he said, "This meager amount is just for you to buy paper and brush-pens with. I'll have more rewards for you later on. This outfit is a gift from me. I only ask that you keep this a secret.

I'll talk with You Chen today. The two of you will start on your way early tomorrow morning."

"As you say. I'll give the clothes back to you after I return. As for the silver, I can't take any."

"The ancients even shared horse-carriages and fur coats with friends. Even if I were not asking a favor of you, I would not have grudged giving you a few pieces of humble clothes. These few items are just an expression of my gratitude. To decline them is to humiliate me."

"All right. I'll accept your generous offer of the clothes against my inclinations, but I can't take the silver. I just can't."

"If you insist, I'll take it that you want to back out of our deal."

Only then did Qian Qing accept the silver. That very day, Yan Jun met with You Chen, who was unwilling to do this but felt obliged to take on the job for fear of offending Yan Jun. Yan Jun engaged a boat, bought food and bedding for their use on board, and dispatched two page boys, in addition to Xiaoyi, to wait on them.

Before the night was out, everything was ready for the men to set out on their journey the next morning in all pomp and circumstance. Yan also instructed Xiaoyi and the other two page boys to address Mr. Qian as Master and never to blurt out the surname "Qian."

The next morning, Yan Jun rose at first light to hurry Qian Qing up in his preparations for the journey. After combing his hair and washing, Qian Qing put on the fashionable and splendid clothes. Emitting whiffs of fragrance with every movement, he cut an even more dashing figure than usual. He was a veritable

> *Xun Yu with his lingering fragrance*
> *And Pan An smelling of fruit.*[10]

At Yan Jun's invitation, You Chen went to his house and had breakfast with Qian Qing. Xiaoyi and the other two page boys then followed them into the boat. With a favorable wind, the boat sailed smoothly to West Dongting Hill. As the hour was late by the time they arrived, they spent the night in the boat. After breakfast the next morning, at an hour when Mr. Gao Zan should have arisen, Qian Qing wrote a visiting card, calling himself modestly "Yan Jun, your humble junior." Xiaoyi took the card and delivered it to the gatekeeper of the Gao residence, saying, "Mr. You is here with Young Master Yan, to see Mr. Gao."

Recognizing Xiaoyi, the gatekeeper promptly went in to announce the visitors. At Gao Zan's order to usher the visitors in, You Chen followed the fake Yan Jun into the main hall.

Gao Zan was already three-tenths satisfied as his eyes fell upon the handsome, dignified, and well-groomed young man. After an exchange of amenities, Gao Zan asked him to take the seat of honor, but Qian declined, saying he was too junior in status to accept the offer. In the end, he took the guest seat facing east, and Mr. Gao took the host seat facing west.

Gao Zan thought joyfully, "A modest, well-mannered young man indeed."

After everyone had sat down, You Chen spoke up first, apologizing for having imposed himself on Mr. Gao's hospitality some days before.

"But I wasn't a good host," said Mr. Gao. Then he asked, "Is this Young Master Yan, your kinsman? I didn't ask for his courtesy name the other day."

"I am too junior to have a courtesy name," volunteered Qian Qing.

"His courtesy name is Boya," cut in You Chen. "Bo is the character that means 'older' and Ya is the character that means 'elegant.'"

Gao Zan commented, "Good name, and also true!"

"I don't deserve this compliment!" exclaimed Qian Qing.

To Gao's questions as to his family background, Qian gave ready answers. Impressed by his refined diction, Gao Zan said to himself, "He's quite satisfactory in appearance and style of conversation. I wonder how good a scholar he is. Let me call in the teacher and my boy to test him out."

After the second cup of tea, Mr. Gao said to the servants, "Go to the study and bring the teacher and my son here to see the guests."

Before long, a scholarly-looking man in his fifties led a boy out from the interior section of the house into the main hall. Everyone rose and bowed to them.

"This is my son's teacher, Mr. Chen, who is affiliated with the prefectural school. This is my son Gao Biao."

Looking at the boy with refined features and a graceful bearing, Qian Qing thought, "If the son is so good-looking, I can well imagine how the daughter looks. My cousin is a lucky man!"

After another cup of tea, Gao Zan said to the teacher, "This gentleman, our guest, is Yan Boya of Wujiang County, a fine scholar in spite of his youth."

The teacher took the master's hint. "Wujiang is a place that produces great scholars," said he. "People of Wujiang are more knowledgeable than average. I've heard that in your county, there are three shrines, each dedicated to a great historical figure. May I ask which three?"

"They are the shrines dedicated to Fan Li, Zhang Han, and Lu Guimeng," replied Qian.[11]

"What is so remarkable about these three men?"

Qian Qing expounded on each one of them. Then the teacher and Qian Qing asked each other questions. Unimpressed by the teacher's mediocre scholarship, Qian Qing deliberately launched into a grandiose speech about everything under the sun, past and present. The teacher was awestruck and kept saying, "What a wonderful scholar! What a wonderful scholar!"

Gao Zan almost danced for joy. He instructed servants to serve lunch, adding in a hushed voice, "Make it nice!" Thus ordered, the servants immediately laid out on the table fruits of all colors. Gao Zan himself set the chopsticks and cups. After some demurral, Qian sat down in the guest seat at the table. The next instant, the table was covered with ten dishes, three kinds of soup, and many appetizers.

You may well ask, how was such a fine spread possible in so short a time? Well, what happened was that Gao Zan's wife, Jin-shi, who doted on her daughter, had sneaked out to hide herself behind the screen upon hearing that the matchmaker had brought Young Master Yan. Peeping at the visitors, she was pleased by the young man's appearance and articulateness and was convinced that her husband would feel the same way. So she ordered preparations for lunch in advance, and that was why the meal was served almost as soon as the master gave the order. The five men, guests and hosts, wined and dined until sunset. When Qian Qing and You Chen rose to leave, Gao Zan asked them to stay for a few days, hating the thought of parting with them, but Qian turned a deaf ear to his pleas. After trying a few times to no avail, Gao felt obliged to let them go. Qian addressed Mr. Chen, the teacher, first and said, "I am grateful for having benefited from your teaching." Next, he turned to Mr. Gao and said, "I will not come again to bid you farewell before our boat sets sail tomorrow morning."

"I haven't been a good host," said Gao. "Please do not take offense."

The little boy also bowed and bade the guests farewell. Jin-shi had prepared some farewell gifts, which consisted of wine, rice, fish, meat, and a packet of cash for their travel expenses. Gao Zan pulled You Chen to a quiet place and said, "Young Master Yan's looks and talent are impeccable. If you could bring off this match, I'll consider myself an extremely lucky man."

"I will do as you wish," promised You Chen.

Gao walked them all the way to their boat before bidding them farewell. He and his wife spent the whole night talking about Young Master Yan. Truly,

> There was no need for a pestle of jade;
> A red string was already tied around their ankles.[12]

The next day, Qian Qing and You Chen set sail against an unfavorable wind and did not arrive at home until midnight. Yan Jun was still sitting by candlelight, waiting for good news, when the two men knocked at his door and entered. After listening to their account of the visit, Yan Jun was so overjoyed at the success of their mission that he quickly picked an auspicious day within one month to deliver the betrothal gifts. True to his promise, he gave back to You Chen the receipt for the loan of twenty taels of silver, thus canceling You's debt by way of showing his gratitude. The third day of the twelfth lunar month was chosen for the wedding. Being so fond of his potential son-in-law and having prepared the dowry long ago, Gao Zan did not object to the date.

The days and the nights went by and, before they knew it, the eleventh month was drawing to an end and the wedding day was approaching. People in regions south of the Yangzi River did not observe the ancient rites whereby the groom went to his parents-in-law's house to meet the bride and bring her home. Instead, the bride's parents and brother delivered the bride to the groom's house in a send-off ceremony. Gao Zan, however, in his determination to spread the news about his wonderful son-in-law, insisted that the son-in-law go to his house to meet the bride. And he made preparations for a grand feast to which all neighbors as well as relatives and friends from far and near were invited. When his messenger told You Chen about this, You Chen grew alarmed. In haste, he went to relay the message to Yan Jun.

"In that case," said Yan Jun, "I'll have to go myself."

Stamping his feet, You Chen said, "The other day when Qian Qing was there, all the family members looked their fill. I'm sure they can even draw a portrait of him from memory. Now that the son-in-law is going to look different, what shall I the matchmaker say? The match will surely be off, and I'll only bring humiliation on myself!"

Upon hearing this, Yan Jun turned the tables on the matchmaker and grumbled, "I did say that if this match was in my destiny, it would work out whatever happened. If I had gone to their house myself the first time, I would never have landed in this mess! It was you who played a trick on me and purposely made Mr. Gao out to be a man hard to deal with and had my cousin go in my place. But Mr. Gao turned out to be a most easy-going man and readily gave his consent. He didn't try to make things difficult. And that's because I'm destined to be his son-in-law, not because he thought my cousin was me! What's more, since he has accepted my betrothal gifts, his daughter is already my wife. How can they go back now? You just watch me go and see what he's going to do about me. He can't back out of the deal!"

Shaking his head, You Chen said, "This is not going to work. The bride is still with her family. What can you do? If they refuse to get her into the sedan-chair, there's nothing you can do about it."

"I'll take more men with me. If she gets into the sedan-chair, well and good. If not, we'll storm into the house and get her by force. Even if they sue me, I can produce the betrothal documents as evidence. The court will judge against them for breaching their promise of marriage. I am not at fault."

"Young Master, don't be so sure! As the proverb says, 'A mighty dragon can't defeat a snake when the snake is on its own turf.' You may bring lots of men with you, but you'll be in the Gaos' home base. They can outnumber you. If something untoward happens and they sue you, the old man can say that the groom is not the one who went to propose. The court will surely summon the matchmaker for questioning, and I'll have to come out with the truth if I'm put under the bamboo rod. This will also ruin Mr. Qian's future. This is certainly not the way to do it!"

After reflecting for a while, Yan Jun said, "In that case, I won't go. You go tomorrow to tell him that since he already met with his son-in-law the other day, he'd better go with the custom of this county and escort his daughter here instead of having me go to bring her over."

"This is an even worse idea. Mr. Gao is so pleased with his son-in-law-to-be that he's been bragging everywhere about the young man's talent and looks. His neighbors and kinsmen are looking forward to seeing the young man when he goes to meet the bride. There's no getting out of the trip."

"What's to be done, then?"

"In my humble opinion, the only way out is to have your cousin, Young Master Qian, undertake another trip. Let the deception last longer. Once the bride crosses your threshold, you are the boss. They can't snatch her from you. After the wedding ceremony is over, you'll have nothing to fear."

After a pause, Yan Jun said, "Good point. But it's my wedding, yet my cousin gets all the glory. I'm sure he'll make things difficult for me when I go beg him."

"Things being the way they are, this is the only solution. His glory will be short-lived. You are the one who gets to enjoy the marriage for the rest of your life!"

Yan Jun was both pleased and vexed by these words. Right away, he took leave of You Chen and returned to the study, where he said to Qian Qing, "My good brother, I have one more favor to ask of you."

"What is it?"

"The third day of next month is my wedding day and I'm supposed to go over one day earlier to meet the bride and bring her here. I would like you to go again."

Qian Qing said, "The trip to bring the bride home is much more important than what I did for you the other day. I can't replace you at such a major ceremony. No, this will never do!"

"You do have a point, my good brother, but since they already know you, they'll surely be suspicious when they see me, and change their mind. Not only will the wedding be called off, but they may also bring a lawsuit against me. If so, you will be implicated, too. Won't you be paying a big price for a minor concern? And you'll ruin my otherwise splendid chances. After you bring the bride home, I'll have nothing to fear about what they accuse me of. So this is only to tide me over. My good brother, this will be the last favor I ask of you. Please do not turn me down."

Qian Qing felt obliged to comply with this earnest plea.

Yan Jun hired a band of musicians, called together a group of people to make up the procession, and told everyone not to let a word about this get out. He also promised to reward them handsomely after they successfully carried out their mission. All agreed to do as instructed. Early in the morning of the second day of the twelfth month, You Chen went to Yan Jun's house to help prepare gifts for the bride's family and seal the packets of reward money. All the items Qian Qing would be using, along with his scholar's scarf, his round-collared silk gown, and his black boots, were ready, and food provisions for every boat were distributed. There were two large boats—one for the bride, and one for the matchmaker and the groom—four middle-sized boats for men of the procession, and four small boats for escort as well as for possible miscellaneous errands. The ten boats set sail on the lake amid the clang of gongs and the rhythmic chants of the boatmen.

A joyful journey it was, complete with firecrackers and fire balls swung around in wire nets. Truly,

The family was jubilant;
The son-in-law was ideal.

It was already afternoon when the boat arrived at West Dongting Hill. It moored about half a li away from the Gao residence. You Chen went to the house first, to announce their arrival and to make arrangements for the delivery of the gifts and the preparations for the bridal sedan-chair. Surrounded by hundreds of lanterns and torches, a well spruced-up Qian Qing mounted the sedan-chair, which was protected against the cold by a cotton-padded blue silk curtain and carried by four men, with another four following behind as reserves. Amid the music struck up by the band of drums and *sheng* pipes and *xiao* flutes, the procession headed straight for the Gao residence. Residents from far and near on the hill, having heard about the talent and looks of the Gao family's new son-in-law, swarmed to the house to look, like a jostling crowd gathered around a storyteller at a fair. The spectators burst out into cheers as they saw the handsome Qian Qing sitting solemnly in the sedan-chair. A woman who knew Qiufang, the bride, commented, "What a perfect match! The Gao family has been so picky about a son-in-law, and they've picked a really nice one!"

Let us leave the spectators and turn our attention to the Gao family, who had laid out a grand feast in honor of friends and relatives. Before dusk had set in, the main hall was already brightly lit by ruddy candlelight. As the music came to their ears, the gatekeeper announced, "The groom is here!"

The best man, in red and wearing flowers, rushed to the sedan-chair, bowed, recited a poem, and asked the groom to dismount. The other attendants present also bowed respectfully and led the groom into the main hall. After the gifts were presented, the groom exchanged greetings with everyone, and none did not secretly admire his handsome appearance. After tea and refreshments were served, the groom was led to the dinner table to his assigned seat. In a departure from convention, the new son-in-law was given a table all to himself and a seat facing south, with friends and relatives sitting around him, plying him with wine. The groom's attendants were entertained in another room.

Listening to all the praise of his talent and looks and of Mr. Gao's wise choice, Qian said to himself with an imperceptible smile, "They are seeing a phantom and I'm in a dream. When the one who dreams wakes up, he will see all this as a lot of nonsense. I wonder what those seeing the phantom will end up doing. Let me enjoy the moment as long as it lasts." Then he thought again, "It's under false pretenses that I get to enjoy all the pleasure today. I wonder when I can ever truly possess all this. I don't think I'll ever attain such wealth and high rank." These thoughts saddened him and he lost all interest in the wine.

Gao Zan and his son eagerly took turns offering him toasts, but Qian Qing was anxious to go, afraid that he might make a mess of his cousin's important event. Gao Zan insisted that he stay longer at the table, and so he complied. After dinner was over and the servants had also finished eating and drinking, it was already the fourth watch of the night. Xiaoyi, sitting by Qian's side, urged him to go, whereupon Qian instructed Xiaoyi to distribute the packets of gift money around. That done, he rose to go. Gao Zan guessed that it was already the predawn fifth watch and, since he had already arranged to have all the dowry items loaded onto the boat, it was time to lead the bride into the sedan-chair. At this point, the boatmen walked up to him and said, "It's too windy for the boats to set sail. We'll have to wait a while until the wind dies down." A strong wind had in fact sprung up in the middle of the night. Behold:

> Trees were uprooted amid flying dust on the hill;
> Waves surged and spouted high in the lake.

It was because of all the drum music that no one in the house was aware of the raging storm outside. As soon as the musicians stopped by Gao's order, the furious screech of wind became audible. Everyone was aghast. You Chen stamped his feet in exasperation. A displeased Gao Zan had no choice but to invite everyone back to the dinner table. At the same time, he sent a servant out to watch the weather. At daybreak, the wind gathered even greater force. Dark clouds blotted out the sky and snowflakes began swirling about. Everyone rose to look at the sky and they gathered together to consult one another. One said, "It doesn't look like the wind is going to die down any time soon." Another said, "A wind that starts in the middle of the night won't stop until the middle of the next night." Then another said, "In such snowy weather, the boats can't go even if there's no wind." Another one commented, "I'm afraid the snow's going to get heavier." Another voice added, "The wind is so high that after it subsides, the lake's going to freeze over." Another man remarked, "But the snow and the wind are more frightening than a frozen Lake Tai."

All these comments made Mr. Gao and You Chen even more anxious. Some moments later, after breakfast was over, the wind roared louder and the snowflakes fell thicker and faster. Gao Zan gave up all hope of crossing the lake that day. But after that auspicious day had passed by, there probably would be no more lucky days left throughout the rest of the winter. Moreover, the musicians had come so cheerfully. How could they all be told to leave without even going through the wedding ceremony?

In this dilemma, one of the guests, an elderly man named Zhou Quan, spoke up. An old neighbor of Gao Zan's, he was known in the neighborhood for his troubleshooting skills. Observing that Gao Zan was deep in thought and indecisive, he said, "As this stupid old man sees it, this problem can be easily solved."

"What idea do you have?" asked Gao Zan.

"Since this is the chosen day, you must not postpone the wedding. Your son-in-law is already in the house, so why not hold the wedding right here? Before the dinner table is cleared, put on the wedding candles. The wedded couple can take their time and go to the groom's house after the storm is over. Wouldn't that be nice every way you look at it?"

"Yes, that would be best!" everyone present echoed.

Gao Zan had been thinking along the same lines and was delighted that Mr. Zhou voiced his own thoughts. Right away, he instructed servants to prepare the bridal chamber and the wedding candles.[13]

Now, let us come to Qian Qing. Though physically present, he felt quite detached from the event and cared little about the windstorm. Zhou Quan's words alarmed him. He hoped Mr. Gao would reject the idea. As it turned out, Mr. Gao readily gave his consent. Qian Qing panicked and secretly cried out in dismay. He turned to You Chen, meaning to ask him to intervene, but, being a man disposed to drinking, You Chen had been downing one large vessel after another partly due to the coldness and partly due to his anxiety, and was slumped in a chair by the wall, snoring in drunken stupor.

Qian had to speak out for himself. "This once-in-a-lifetime event should not be something to rush into. It would be better to choose another day for me to come and get the bride."

Turning a deaf ear to him, Gao Zan said, "You and I are family now. Why stand on ceremony? Also, since your parents have both passed away, you are your own master." With that, Gao Zan went to the interior of the house.

Qian Qing then appealed to the guests and stated his unwillingness to hold the wedding ceremony there and then, but they were determined to please Mr. Gao and were all for going ahead with the ceremony. Left at the end of his wits, Qian Qing excused himself and went out, ostensibly to go to the outhouse. But in fact, he consulted Xiaoyi, the servant. Xiaoyi was also against the idea but, without a good plan, could only urge Mr. Qian to decline.

Qian Qing said, "I have been trying to decline over and over again, but Mr. Gao just wouldn't listen! If I go on declining, I'll only arouse his suspicions. I've submitted myself to this humiliation just to help your master out in this big event of his life. I have no ill intentions. Heaven forbid!"

As they were talking, a crowd gathered around them. Someone said, "This is a good thing! Your father-in-law is quite determined. You needn't hesitate!"

Qian Qing was speechless and allowed himself to be politely ushered back into the hall. After lunch was over, preparations for the wedding banquet got under way. The best man and bridesmaid put on red gowns and made the announcements for the ceremony. The groom and the bride ascended the dais in proper attire, took the ceremonial bows, and were announced as husband and wife. Truly,

> *A long-lasting marriage began that night;*
> *Conjugal life started from that hour.*

A victory turned into a defeat;
A schemer came up against an honest man.

That night, after the feast was over and the party broke up, Mr. and Mrs. Gao personally escorted the groom into the bridal chamber. The bridesmaid helped the bride remove the jewelry from her hair and urged the groom to go to bed, but to her surprise, Qian Qing refused. The bridesmaid resignedly left the chamber after helping the bride to bed. The maidservants closed the door and urged the new master to go to bed. His heart thumping violently, Qian Qing said feebly in response, "You go ahead and retire for the night first."

Having worked frantically all evening, the maids immediately tumbled into bed. Qian meant to sit by the lamp the whole night through, but didn't have a chance to ask for a few extra candles. When the candle burned down, he could not very well call out for more. Instead, he swallowed his mortification and lay down on his side on the edge of the bed, fully clothed, without the faintest idea where the girl's head was.

At the first light the next morning, he rose and went out to the bride's brother's study to comb his hair and wash. Mr. and Mrs. Gao thought the young man was being demure and therefore did not take it amiss. Later in the day, the snow stopped, but the wind did not subside. Gao Zan had the festivities continue. Qian Qing became very much the worse for liquor and sat around until midnight before he entered the bridal chamber. The girl again went to bed first. Unable to fight off his sleepiness, Qian also lay down, fully clothed, as before, without daring to even touch the bride's quilt. After he rose the next morning, he stated his intention to leave because the wind was slackening. However, Gao Zan insisted that he stay for three nights. Failing to win the argument, Qian Qing again spent the day drinking. When he had a chance, he secretly told You Chen about how he had slept fully clothed. You Chen mumbled something in response but did not quite believe him. Things having already come to this pass, there was nothing You Chen could do.

Meanwhile, the bride Qiufang had privately been very pleased since the first glimpse she had stolen of the handsome groom on the very first night of the wedding. But she was bewildered by the way he slept with all his clothes on for the subsequent two nights in a row. "Is he angry with me because I went to bed first, without waiting for him?"

On the third night, Qiufang said to the maids, "When he comes in, make him retire first."

Thus instructed, the maids went up to him as soon as he entered the chamber to remove his clothes and headscarf. In alarm, Qian took off his headscarf, jumped into bed, and lay down on the far side of the bed against the wall, still in all his clothes. The bride was displeased and also slept without removing her clothes. She could not bring herself to tell her parents about this.

On the fourth day, the weather cleared up. Having already prepared the boats to escort the bride to her husband's house, Gao Zan was now ready to board the boat with his wife to escort their daughter and sail across the lake. The mother and daughter rode in one boat. Gao Zan, Qian Qing, and You Chen took up another boat. It was a bustling scene with the festooned boats sailing amid sky-shaking drum music. Xiaoyi, dejected by the thought of the task his master had given him, rode in front in a fast-going small boat.

Let us pick up another thread of the story and come to Yan Jun, who had been waiting anxiously for news since sending off the procession. At midnight on the second day of the month, he panicked at the sound of the snowstorm, but his worst fear was that the boats would go too slowly in such weather, thereby missing the auspicious hour chosen for the wedding. It never even occurred to him that it would be impossible to cross the lake. Having made all the preparations for the wedding candles, he waited throughout the night in vain. Gloomily, he thought, "Actually, it would be better not to sail in such a storm. I would be worried sick if they tried to cross the lake." Then he thought, "But if they don't set sail, the chosen day will go by. My father-in-law wouldn't send his daughter over just on any day but would surely pick another lucky day. But which day will be good? Oh, how frustrating!" Then again, he thought, "If You Chen is smart enough, he should be able to push my father-in-law into sending the girl over as soon as possible. Lucky day or not, I'll get to enjoy the marriage sooner."

These thoughts made him so edgy that he kept going to the door to peep out. On the fourth day, when the storm died down, he felt confident that good news was on the way. In the afternoon, Xiaoyi arrived and announced to him, "The bride is now only about ten li away."

"The chosen day has gone by. Why is the Gao family willing to let go of her?" asked Yan Jun.

"Well, the Gaos were indeed afraid of missing the chosen day. So they insisted on holding the wedding ceremony right away. Young Master Qian has been the stand-in groom for three days now."

"Don't tell me Young Master Qian slept in the bridal chamber the last three nights!"

"Yes, he did all right, but he didn't touch her. Young Master Qian just lay there by her side. Nothing more."

"Don't give me this crap! It's impossible! What did I tell you to do? Why didn't you tell him to turn down the offer? Now look at what a filthy thing he did!"

"I did ask him to turn Mr. Gao down. But he said, 'I only want to help your master out. I haven't the least ill intentions, as the gods in heaven know!'"

In a towering rage, Yan Jun knocked Xiaoyi down with one slap across his face and stormed out the door to wait for Qian Qing and fight it out with him. The boats had pulled in to shore by this time. Being a cautious man, Qian had told You Chen to stay with Mr. Gao whereas he himself jumped on shore first. With a clear conscience, Qian Qing went confidently in big strides to the Yan residence.

At the sight of Yan Jun, he smiled and was ready to step forward, make a bow, and tell him the truth. However, Yan Jun, being a petty and spiteful man, was used to measuring honorable people with his own yardstick. As the saying goes, "Eyes widen when foes meet." Before Qian Qing had a chance to say a word, Yan Jun charged at him and cursed through his clenched teeth, "Damn you! A good time you had!" Before the words were quite out of his mouth, he grabbed Qian by his headscarf and hair and rained blows and kicks on him while cursing over and over again, "Damn you! What a double-dealer! Having a good time at another man's expense!"

He was so busy cursing and beating Qian Qing that the latter's explanations fell on deaf ears. None of the servants dared step forward and put in a placating word. Terrified under the blows, Qian began to yell, "Help! Save my life!"

Hearing the commotion, those in the boats went ashore to see what it was all about. Wondering why an ugly man was beating up the groom, they walked up to try to calm him down, but there was no stopping him.

Gao Zan asked the servants what it was all about. Knowing that they would not be able to lie their way out of this, the servants told him the truth. It would have been all right had Gao not heard, but he did, and was seized with fury. He burst into a torrent of curses against You Chen for being so deceptive in his match-making and for playing the girl false. Then he pounced on You Chen and landed blows on him. Those Gao family servants who were in the wedding procession also got indignant. They gathered around the ugly man, ready to beat him, but the Yan family's servants fought them in their master's defense. The commotion had begun with a fight between Yan Jun and Qian Qing, one on one. Then, Gao Zan and You Chen had exchanged blows. And now the servants of the two families fell into a melee. Spectators gathered around to watch, and the crowd grew so thick that the streets were blocked out. It was like

> The battle formation at Nine-Li Hills
> And the battle array at Kunyang Gate.[14]

Coincidences do occur. It so happened that the magistrate of the county was passing by North Gate in his sedan-chair, on his way back from seeing off his superior, when he heard the sky-shaking clamor and saw that it was a group fight. He had his sedan-chair carriers come to a stop and ordered the lictors to arrest the troublemakers. The crowd quickly dispersed at word that the county magistrate had issued an arrest order, but Yan Jun still had Qian Qing firmly in his grip, and Gao Zan still seized You Chen. With everybody talking at once, the magistrate could not make anything out of what was said. And so he had them brought to his tribunal, where he could question them one by one and allow no interruptions from anyone else. Gao Zan, being the most senior in age, was the first one called up to the dais.

"I live on West Dongting Hill," said Gao Zan. "My name is Gao Zan. I selected a handsome and talented candidate as son-in-law and betrothed my daughter to him. On the third day of this month, my son-in-law came to meet the bride and take her to his home, but, because of the snowstorm, I kept him and held the wedding ceremony in my house. I escorted my daughter here today but all too unexpectedly ran into this ugly man who beat my son-in-law black-and-blue. I asked why, and learned that the man had bribed the matchmaker so that he could marry my daughter under false pretenses and sent that young man, Mr. Qian, to come in his place to my house. Your Honor need only question the matchmaker to establish the facts."

"What's the name of the matchmaker?" asked the magistrate. "Is the matchmaker here?"

Gao Zan replied, "He is You Chen, and he's right here in the tribunal."

The magistrate dismissed Gao Zan and ordered You Chen to come forward. "So, you tried to palm off an imposter on the bride. How clever of you! Out with the truth now, or you will be put under torture!"

You Chen equivocated and tried to deny the allegation. The magistrate flew into a rage and ordered that the ankle-squeezers be applied to him. You Chen may have been of a lowly station in life, but he had never been subjected to torture. He saw no alternative but to tell the truth. He began with how Yan Jun had "implored me to propose marriage on his behalf," and went on to describe how picky Gao Zan was in wanting someone of outstanding talent and looks, and how Mr. Qian the scholar had visited the Gaos under a false identity. Then he finished with an account of the wedding ceremony.

"Yes, this sounds like the truth," said the magistrate with a nod. "That fellow Yan Jun went to all that trouble only to lose the game to someone else. No wonder he was so angry, but he has himself and his evil plots to blame."

The magistrate then summoned Yan Jun for a confession. Having heard You Chen's testimony and being relieved at the magistrate's mild tone, Yan Jun related everything, corroborating You Chen's account. Finally, the magistrate summoned Qian Qing. Feeling somewhat favorably disposed toward this handsome young man beaten black-and-blue, the magistrate said, "You are a scholar well read in the Confucian classics and grounded in the tradition established by the Duke of Zhou.[15] How could you compromise your integrity by posing as the groom and thus joining in the deception?"

Qian Qing replied, "I did not wish to do so. But because Yan Jun is my cousin and because I am so poor that I live in his house with free room and board, I agreed reluctantly to his repeated requests, in the hope of helping him out just this one time."

"Enough!" bellowed the magistrate. "Granted that you went for the sake of your family ties with him, you shouldn't have gone through the wedding ceremony."

"I thought my job was just to go and bring the bride home, but a windstorm came on and lasted for three days. So it was impossible to cross the lake. Mr. Gao was afraid of missing the right day chosen for the wedding. Therefore he insisted on holding the wedding ceremony there and then."

"Since you knew you were just a stand-in, you should have declined."

Yan Jun prostrated himself on the floor and said with a kowtow, "Your Honor! His consent is evidence of his evil intentions!"

The magistrate snapped, "Silence!" He then ordered the lictors to push him down off the dais.

Turning to Qian Qing, the magistrate asked, "Are you sure you had no improper thoughts when you gave your consent?"

Qian Qing replied, "Your Honor need only ask Mr. Gao. I declined over and over again, but Mr. Gao just wouldn't listen. If I were to insist, I was afraid that he would get suspicious, and I would be ruining my cousin's chances. That's why I complied. Even though I shared one bed with the bride for three nights, I slept fully clothed. I didn't touch her."

The magistrate burst out laughing and said, "Ever since ancient times, only Liuxia Hui was able to resist sexual temptation.[16] There was also the man of the state of Lu who, knowing he was no Liuxia Hui, refused to let in a woman who knocked on his door in a snowstorm. Now, you are in the prime of your youth. Don't tell me you shared a bed with a woman for three nights but didn't touch her! Whom are you trying to fool?"

"I am telling the truth. If Your Honor doesn't believe me, please have Mr. Gao verify the truth with his own daughter."

The magistrate thought, "If the girl did something inappropriate, how can I expect her to tell the truth?" But an idea came to him. He had lictors bring to him an honest midwife and told her to go to the boat and check if the bride was still a virgin or not and come back immediately to report to him. Before long, the midwife returned to say that Miss Gao indeed remained a virgin.

Upon hearing that Gao-shi remained a virgin, Yan Jun at the foot of the dais shouted, "Since she has not been violated, I am quite willing to marry her!"

"Silence!" roared the magistrate again. Turning to Gao Zan, he asked, "To whom do you wish to give your daughter?"

Gao Zan replied, "It was Scholar Qian whom I had my eye on. And the wedding ceremony was for him and my daughter. Even though Scholar Qian is impeccably honest and refrained from conjugal relations with my daughter, he is in fact her lawfully wedded husband. Picking Yan Jun would be not only against my wishes but also against her own wishes."

The magistrate said, "This is exactly what I've been thinking."

Qian Qing, however, was against the idea. "I undertook the trip not for myself," said he. "Should she marry me, all the pains I took in not removing my clothes for three nights in a row would be in vain. It's better to have her marry someone else than let me come under suspicion and be an object of gossip!"

The magistrate said, "If she marries someone else, your two trips over the lake would be construed as motivated by deceptive intentions. Such immoral behavior would jeopardize your future. If you stay in the marriage, your misbehavior would be all covered up. What's more, now that your thoughts are out in the open and the Gao family is willing, what suspicion are you talking about? Don't say no anymore. Let me write my judgment of the case." That said, he took up his brush-pen and wrote the following:

"Gao Zan is fully justified in choosing a husband for his daughter. Yan Jun's engagement of someone else to pass off as himself is something quite unheard of. The son-in-law was chosen, but the buffalo turned out to be a goat. The neighbors may make unkind remarks, but one can hardly call a deer a horse.[17] Twice he crossed the lake, not unlike Liu Yi, who delivered a message to the crystal palace.[18] For three nights, he slept with his clothes on, not unlike Guan Yu holding a candlelight vigil.[19] With the wind and the snowstorm as the matchmakers, the good man and woman became husband and wife in a happy match. The one hunting for a wife remains a bachelor through his own fault. No second ceremony is necessary for Gao-shi to be wedded to Qian Qing. Yan Jun was wrong in planning the deception and, later, resorting to physical force. However, since his attempts have come to naught, he is hereby acquitted. All the expenses he has undertaken in connection with the marriage are hereby judged to be compensation for the physical abuse to which he subjected Qian Qing. You Chen, having started all the deception with his words of enticement to both sides, is to be severely punished to serve as an example."

After announcing the judgment, the magistrate had the lictors give You Chen thirty strokes of the rod and then drive him out of the yamen but spared him from affixing his fingerprint to the confession, because the magistrate did not want the public to know that Qian Qing had been guilty of taking on a false identity. Gao Zan and Qian Qing bowed in gratitude and all those involved in the case left the yamen. With shame written all over his face, Yan Jun scurried away, keeping his resentment to himself. For several months thereafter, he dared not venture out of his house. You Chen went home to nurse his wounds, but of this, no more.

Gao Zan invited Qian Qing to his boat and thanked him profusely, saying, "If you, my good son-in-law, were not so talented and handsome as to have deeply impressed the magistrate, my little daughter would have married a villain. Now I would humbly ask you to stay at my home for some time with my daughter. May I ask what other people you still have in your family?"

"My parents have both passed away. I'm all alone."

"In that case, there's all the more reason for you to live with us. I will pay for your tuition. What do you say?"

"I will be ever so grateful for your support!"

That very night, they sailed from Wujiang and slept in the boat as it went. The next day, after they arrived on West Dongting Hill, their story spread all over the hill. Everyone admired Qian Qing for his moral rectitude. Later, Qian Qing achieved instant fame by passing the imperial civil service examinations upon the first try, and husband and wife lived together to a ripe old age. There is a poem in testimony:

> *The ugly one tried in vain to get a pretty wife;*
> *The plot ended up in his cousin's favor.*
> *How sad that the moon over Wujiang*
> *Shed its cold light on the love birds on the lake!*

8

Prefect Qiao Rearranges Matches in an Arbitrary Decision

Marriages have always been made in heaven;
Human efforts can only be futile.
If destined, a couple far apart will come together;
If not, those meeting face to face will not join in marriage.

Peach blossoms may drift on water out of fairylands;
Palace maids may write love poems on tree leaves flowing out of the ditches.
But romances are written in the books of destiny;
Matchmakers need not even open their mouths.

The above lyric to the tune of "Moon over West River" makes the point that marriages are predestined and therefore not to be forcibly brought about by human intervention. Let me now tell you a story about some marriages that took everyone by surprise. It is entitled "Prefect Qiao Rearranges Matches in an Arbitrary Decision."

In which dynasty and where does the story take place?

Well, in Hangzhou Prefecture, during the Jingyou reign period [1034–37] of the great Song dynasty, there lived a physician named Liu Bingyi and his wife, née Tan. They had a son and a daughter. The son, Liu Pu, was a handsome twenty-year-old young man betrothed to Sister Pearl, daughter of Mrs. Sun, a widow. Liu Pu began studying diligently from an early age. He was already quite an accomplished scholar by age sixteen, but his father wanted him to abandon his books and learn to be a physician. However, determined to attain high ranks as a distinguished scholar, Liu Pu refused to go into the medical profession—but let us speak no more of this for now. The daughter, Huiniang by name, was fifteen and was betrothed to the son of Mr. Pei the Ninth, owner of an herbal medicine store in the neighborhood. Huiniang was a girl of unusual beauty and charm. How do we know this? Behold:

Her arched eyebrows delicate and well-marked;
Her phoenix eyes bespeak tender love.
Her tiny waist sways like a willow in a breeze;
Her rosy cheeks like soft petals by water's edge.
As lithe as Lady Zhao Feiyan of Han,[1]
As charming as Xishi of Wu,[2]
She is a fairy sent to earth from heaven,
A goddess here in this world from the moon.

But enough of Huiniang's beauty. Now, because his son had come of age, Mr. Liu consulted his wife about the boy's wedding. They were about to ask a matchmaker to approach Mrs. Sun when another matchmaker came to them, on behalf of Mr. Pei, to talk about Mr. Pei Junior marrying Huiniang. Mr. Liu said to the matchmaker, "Please thank Mr. and Mrs. Pei but my daughter is still too young, and our preparations for the dowry have not yet been completed. We will need to wait until our son gets married before we go about our daughter's wedding. We definitely cannot comply with the request at this time."

The matchmaker duly reported back to the Pei family. Because Mr. Pei had had his son rather late in life, he cherished the boy as he would a piece of treasure. How he wished the boy could grow older with every blow of the wind, get married, and give him grandchildren as soon as possible! Mr. Liu's refusal bitterly disappointed him. He sent the matchmaker again to the Liu family with this message: "At fifteen years of age, your daughter is not too young to marry. After she joins our family, she will be treated like our very own daughter. We will never make things the least bit difficult for her. And the amount of the dowry is entirely up to you. We won't mind. We only hope that you will give your consent."

But Mr. Liu remained adamant that his son's wedding should take place before his daughter's. The matchmaker went back and forth several times but to no avail. Mr. Pei gave up and saw no other choice but to wait. Had Mr. Liu given his consent, wouldn't that have made things much easier? As it turned out, his stubborn refusal led to a story that still circulates today. Truly,

One wrong move
Cost the whole game.

After declining Mr. Pei's request, Mr. Liu sent Matchmaker Auntie Zhang the Sixth to Mrs. Sun to bring up the subject of wedding. Mrs. Sun, née Hu, had married at age sixteen. Her husband, Sun Heng, came from a distinguished family of long standing. At seventeen, she had given birth to a daughter, whom they named Sister Pearl. One year later, she gave birth to a son. He was named Sun Run, nicknamed Jade Boy. The two babies were still in their swaddling clothes when Sun Heng died. Mrs. Sun, now a widow, was a woman of honor. She took care of the two children with the help of her housekeeper and refused to remarry. All and sundry came to call her Widow Sun. As time sped by, the children grew up. Sister Pearl was betrothed to the Lius' son, and Jade Boy was betrothed to Wenge, daughter of Xu Ya, an artist. Both Sister Pearl and Jade Boy were as striking in their good looks as jade statues or dough figurines, and both were endowed with sharp intelligence. Jade Boy excelled in his studies, and Sister Pearl in needlework. In addition to their good looks and talent, they were also full of filial and sibling devotion. But let us get on with the story.

Auntie Zhang the Sixth went to see Widow Sun and told her about Mr. Liu's intention to choose an auspicious day for the wedding and to bring Sister Pearl over the Lius' threshold. Widow Sun, deeply attached to her children, would have liked to wait longer, but, conceding that a wedding was a big event in life, she felt obliged to give her consent. To Auntie Zhang she said, "Please tell Mr. and Mrs. Liu that, being a widow with two fatherless children, I am not able to come up with a lavish dowry. I'm giving my girl nothing more than some coarse cotton clothes. Please ask them not to take it amiss."

After Auntie Zhang the Sixth reported as much to Mr. Liu, the latter prepared eight boxes of food, fruit, and other gifts and delivered them to the Suns, along with his written proposal for a wedding date. After accepting the date, Widow Sun rushed into preparations for the dowry. With the wedding day drawing near, the mother and daughter dreaded the thought of having to part with each other, and wept all day long.

All too unexpectedly, Liu Pu, the groom to-be, caught a cold. His excessive sweat and other symptoms grew so severe that he went into a coma. While he was in this critical condition, all the medicinal broth he was fed failed to work and might as well have been splashed onto a rock, and all the divinations ended in dire predictions of death. Frightened out of their wits, Mr. and Mrs. Liu stayed by his bedside, stifling their sobs.

Mrs. Liu said to his wife, "Our boy is so ill. The wedding can't take place. We'd better tell the Suns that we'll have to call it off and pick another day after he gets well." (*Mr. Liu is an honest man, but his skills as a physician can't be more than mediocre.*)

Mrs. Liu said, "Old man! At your age, how can you not know what to do in such a situation? A wedding will help a critically ill patient get well because the joy of the occasion can break the bad luck. Those unbetrothed will go out of their way to seek a match. Our boy is already betrothed. How can you go the other way and call off the wedding?" (*What does a woman like her know?*)

"I think our boy's chances of getting well are slim. If a wedding brings him back to health, I need not say how happy we'll be. But if it doesn't work, won't we be ruining the girl? She'll have to remarry, and her reputation will be tarnished." (*Good point.*)

"Old man!" said his wife. "You care more about other people than you do about ourselves. You and I went to a lot of trouble before we landed this marriage deal.

How were we to know that our luckless boy would fall sick right before the wedding date? If we call off the wedding and our boy recovers, well and good. But if something happens to him, what will we have left? It would be generous of them if they returned only half of our betrothal gifts to us. Wouldn't we be losing both our boy and our money?"

"So, what would you do?"

"If I were to have my way, I'd tell Auntie Zhang not to breathe a word about our son's illness but to bring the girl over to our house and have her stay with us, just as a child daughter-in-law stays with her prospective husband's family. If our boy recovers, we'll pick a lucky day for a proper wedding. If not, and she wants to remarry, we won't let her go until we get all of our betrothal gifts back and our other expenses reimbursed. Won't that be nice every way you look at it?"

With his credulous ear, Mr. Liu took his wife's advice and hastened to tell Auntie Zhang the Sixth not to leak anything out.

As the ancients said, "If you don't want people to find out what you did, you shouldn't have done it in the first place." Mr. Liu thought the Sun family was being kept in the dark. However, his next-door neighbor, Mr. Li Rong, called "Manager Li" by all and sundry because he had once managed a pawnshop, was a most sly and cunning man much given to prying into other people's business and spreading rumors around. With the money he had acquired by devious means as manager, he had wanted to buy Mr. Liu's house, which shared a foundation with his. Mr. Liu had turned him down. Henceforth they became estranged, although, for the sake of appearances, they did not fall out publicly. Already wishing for some misfortune to befall the Liu family, Li Rong was filled with joy when he learned about Liu Pu's critical condition. Without a moment's delay, he rushed to inform the Sun family.

Upon hearing about her prospective son-in-law's grave illness, Widow Sun immediately ordered the housekeeper to bring Auntie Zhang the Sixth over for questioning, for she was afraid that her daughter's marital future would be ruined. Auntie Zhang the Sixth was caught in a dilemma. If she refused to tell, Widow Sun would put the blame on her later on if Liu Pu died, but if she told the truth, the Liu family would come down hard on her. As she hesitated and checked herself every time she found herself about to speak up, Widow Sun pressed her even harder. Knowing that she would not be let off the hook, Auntie Zhang the Sixth said, "Well, he just caught a cold. Nothing serious. He will have recovered by the wedding day."

"I heard that he's in critical condition," rejoined Widow Sun. "How can you play it down like this? This is no joke. I've had more than my share of hardships in bringing up my two children. They are my treasure. If you cheat my girl, I'm going to fight you to the death. Don't be surprised if we come to that. Now, you go and tell the Liu family: If he is indeed gravely ill, why not let him recover and postpone the wedding date? They are young. Why all this rush? Be sure to get a clear answer from them and report back to me."

Thus ordered, Auntie Zhang the Sixth turned to go, when Widow Sun called her back and said, "I know you too well to believe that you'll tell me the truth. My housekeeper will go with you. I will then get to know the truth."

Alarmed upon hearing that the housekeeper would be going with her, Auntie Zhang the Sixth said, "Oh, she needn't go! I won't fail you, ma'am!"

Turning a deaf ear to her pleas, Widow Sun gave the housekeeper some instructions and had her depart with Auntie Zhang. Unable to shake her off, Auntie Zhang could do no more than take her to the Liu residence. It so happened that Mr. Liu went out the door just as they approached. Since Widow Sun's housekeeper had never seen Mr. Liu before, Auntie Zhang said to her, "Now you wait here, young lady. I need to ask that man a question. I'll be back soon enough." Hurriedly she walked up to Mr. Liu, pulled him aside, and relayed Widow Sun's message to him, adding, "She's so worried that she sent her housekeeper along with me to get a truthful answer. What are you going to say?"

At a loss as to what to do upon hearing that Sun's housekeeper was there, Mr. Liu said grumpily, "Why didn't you stop her? How could you have brought her along!"

"I did try to stop her from coming, but they ignored me. There was nothing I could do. You'll have to let her in and make her wait while you discuss between yourselves what to say to her. Don't get me into trouble!" Before she had quite finished speaking, the housekeeper had walked up to them. Auntie Zhang said, "This is Mr. Liu."

The housekeeper bowed deeply in a curtsy. Mr. Liu bowed in return and said, "Please come in and sit, miss."

Together they entered the house and went into the main hall.

"Auntie Zhang," said Liu, "you sit here and keep the young lady company. I'll go and bring my wife out."

"Go ahead, please," said the matchmaker.

Mr. Liu rushed into the inner quarters of the house and told his wife what had happened, adding, "Their housekeeper is right there in the main hall. What are we going to say to her? If she wants to come in to see our boy, how are we going to fob her off? We'd better pick another day for the wedding."

"What a useless thing you are!" snapped his wife. "Since Mrs. Sun has accepted our betrothal gifts, her girl is a member of our family now. What do we have to fear? Don't panic. I know what to do." To her daughter, Huiniang, she said, "Go and clean up the bridal chamber and then ask that woman from the Sun family to stay for refreshments."

As Huiniang left to do her mother's bidding, Mrs. Liu went into the hall, exchanged greetings with the housekeeper, and said, "It's so kind of you to come and see us, miss. What message have you brought from your mistress?"

"My mistress heard that the young master was ill. She's so worried that she sent me here to inquire after him and also to relay this message to you, madam, and to the master: If the young master is only beginning to recover, this may not be the most opportune time for the wedding to take place. It would be better to wait until he has fully regained his health and then pick another date."

Mrs. Liu replied, "I'm much obliged to Mrs. Sun for her concern. My son is indeed slightly indisposed, but it's just a common cold rather than anything serious. Choosing another date is out of the question. Ours is a small business. We went through a lot in order to get all the wedding funds ready. If the wedding is not to take place on the day already chosen, won't we have to start all over again? What's more, a sick person needs a happy event to break the bad luck. There are often cases where people who know how to do things right would deliberately arrange a wedding for a sick person. We notified you about the wedding date quite some time ago, and we've already sent out wedding banquet invitations to our clansmen. If we suddenly change the date, they won't know that it's because the bride's family backed out of it; they will say that we can't afford to take in a daughter-in-law. If word gets spread around, won't we be laughed at? Won't our family's reputation be tarnished? Please tell your mistress not to worry. The stakes are high for this family!"

"Right you are, madam," said the housekeeper. "But where is the young master? May I go to his bedside and pay him my respects so that I can report to my mistress and put her mind at rest?"

"He just took some medicine to induce a good sweat and is fast asleep in his room. I will convey your good wishes to him. I've already told you everything there is to tell."

Auntie Zhang put in, "I did tell you that it's just a cold and not something serious. Your mistress didn't believe me and sent you along. Now you know I wasn't lying."

"All right," conceded the housekeeper. "I should be going." So saying, she rose to go.

Mrs. Liu said, "Don't go yet! We've been so busy talking that I haven't even served tea. How can you go without a cup of tea?" After she led the housekeeper inside, she said, "My room is a mess. Let's go sit in the bridal chamber."

After being led into the bridal chamber, the housekeeper saw that it had already been beautifully decorated. Mrs. Liu continued, "You can see that we've got everything ready. How can we change the date? But even after the wedding, the young master would need to stay in my room to recuperate. He won't be able to share the same room with the bride until he is fully recovered."

The sight of the well decked-out chamber convinced the housekeeper that she was being told the truth.

Mrs. Liu then had tea and refreshments served and called her daughter Huiniang out to greet the guest. Upon seeing Huiniang, Mrs. Sun's housekeeper thought, "Our Sister Pearl is already as pretty as could be, but here's another beauty!" (*Foreshadowing what is to come.*) After tea was over, she rose to go. When she and

Auntie Zhang were on the point of leaving, Mrs. Liu said to the latter over and over again, "Be sure to come back and let me know what they say."

The housekeeper returned home with Auntie Zhang the Sixth. After they told the mistress about their visit, Widow Sun felt at a loss as to what to do. She said to herself, "If I agree but my son-in-law is really gravely ill and something untoward happens, my daughter's future will be ruined. If I do not agree but my son-in-law is indeed only slightly indisposed and is recovering, we'll miss the lucky date chosen for the wedding." In this moment of indecision, she said to Auntie Zhang the Sixth, "Auntie, could you come back tomorrow morning to get my reply? I need some time to think."

"Of course, take your time, ma'am. This old woman will come back tomorrow morning." With that, Zhang took herself off.

Widow Sun then consulted her son, Jade Boy. "What's to be done?" she asked.

"I believe he's gravely ill, which was why they didn't want our housekeeper to see him. If we insist on changing the date, they'll have to agree. But then all the expenses they've gone into would be for nothing, and we would be accused of being heartless. If he gets well later on, we'll feel awkward when we meet him. But if we do as they say and something happens, we'll be caught in a dilemma, and regrets will be too late. I have an idea that can let us have it both ways. Would you like to hear my plan?"

"Yes! What is it?"

"When Auntie Zhang comes tomorrow morning, tell her that the wedding can go ahead on the date they have chosen, but the bride will take no dowry with her. On the third day after the wedding, we will bring her home. She will wait here until he recovers before returning, along with the dowry. In this way, even if something untoward happens, we won't be in their control. Isn't that a good plan that can let us have it both ways?" (*That's why Jade Boy gets to go in the girl's place.*)

"What does a child like you know!" said Widow Sun. "What if they give a false promise and then refuse to let her go on the third day after the wedding?"

"Indeed. What can be done in that case?"

After a few moments of thinking, Widow Sun said, "The only way out is to ask Auntie Zhang to go to them tomorrow to say what you proposed, but on the wedding day, I'll hide your sister and have you dressed up as the bride and go in her place. You will take a leather trunk with a Daoist robe and a pair of shoes and socks. If they let you come home on the third day, fine. If not, you wait there and see. If something happens to him, you put on the robe and come home. Who can stop you?"

"I can do anything but this!" exclaimed Jade Boy. "If others get to know about this, how am I going to show my face in public?"

Widow Sun flew into a rage at her son's objections. "If other people get to hear about this," said she, "they'll laugh, and that'll be that. What great harm can that do to you?"

Being a filial son, Jade Boy hastened to add, to pacify his mother's anger, "All right, I'll go. But I don't know how to do my hair!"

"I'll have the housekeeper go with you."

And so the decision was made. The next morning, when Auntie Zhang the Sixth came to ask for a reply, Widow Sun set out her terms, concluding, "If this can be done, my daughter will go. If not, change the wedding date."

Auntie Zhang the Sixth reported back to Mr. and Mrs. Liu and got their consent to everything. You may ask, why were they so obliging? Well, it was because Liu Pu's condition was getting worse. Afraid that the worst would happen, they felt the deal would be closed as long as the daughter-in-law was in their house. And so they accepted Widow Sun's terms without the least haggling, little knowing that Widow Sun had seen through their scheme and was sending over a piece of counterfeit merchandise. Mrs. Liu became a veritable Zhou Yu, whose self-claimed wonderful stratagem ended up in a double loss.[3]

Let us not encumber our story with idle comments but describe what happened on the wedding day. Widow Sun made up Jade Boy until he looked exactly like her daughter. Even she herself could hardly tell one from the other. Then she taught him some feminine manners. All went well except two details that might give him away. Which two?

First, his feet were too large for a woman. A woman's feet, in tiny embroidered shoes with pointed tips that show ever so discreetly from under a long skirt, move in minced steps as delicately as flower blossoms that flutter in the breeze. But Jade Boy's feet were three to four times larger than those of the average woman. Even though he was made to wear a floor-length skirt to hide them and taught to walk slowly in minced steps, he still looked awkward. But he might be able to get away with it if no one were to raise his skirt and examine his feet.

Second, the lack of earrings would give him away. Earrings are indispensable for a woman. Even a woman with simple taste would hardly do without a pair of clove-shaped earrings. A girl in a poor family that could not afford gold or silver would sport earrings made of copper or tin. And now, as a bride wearing ornaments all over his hair, how was Jade Boy to get by without earrings? His parents had had his left earlobe pierced when he was small in order to pass him off as a girl in the eyes of the gods so as to increase his chances of survival. But his right ear was not pierced and therefore could not wear an earring. Widow Sun turned her thoughts this way and that, and finally came up with an idea. You may well ask, what idea? Well, she had the housekeeper apply a small piece of plaster on his right earlobe. If asked, he was to reply that he had a festering boil in his earlobe where the hole was and therefore could not wear an earring. In the meantime, he was to leave his pierced left earlobe exposed to view.

When all the preparations for the journey were done, Sister Pearl was taken into a room to hide, in anticipation of the procession to greet the bride. When dusk fell, the bridal sedan-chair arrived at the door amid sky-shaking drum music.

Auntie Zhang, the first one to enter the house, was overjoyed at the sight of the bride, all spruced up and looking like a goddess. Noticing that Jade Boy was missing, she asked, "Where's the young master?"

Widow Sun replied, "He doesn't feel well today and is asleep in bed."

The unsuspecting Auntie Zhang the Sixth did not ask further.

Widow Sun laid out a feast by way of thanking members of the procession. The meal over, the best man recited a poem and asked the bride to mount the sedan-chair. Jade Boy put the bridal veil over his head and bade farewell to his mother. Widow Sun made a great show of grief and sobbed her way out of the house to see him off. As Jade Boy got into the sedan-chair, taking with him no dowry but only one leather trunk, Widow Sun told the housekeeper to follow behind on foot and, turning to Auntie Zhang the Sixth, said, "As I've told you before, she must be sent back home on the third day. Be sure to keep your promise!"

Auntie Zhang said, "Of course! Of course!"

Let us leave Widow Sun and follow the brightly lit bridal procession all the way to the Liu residence amid the music of the *sheng* pipes and *xiao* flutes. The best man entered the house and said, "The bride will be out of the sedan-chair any time now. Without the groom to greet her, she can't very well go through the wedding ceremony by herself, can she?"

"Oh what's to be done?" said Mr. Liu. "Let's skip the ceremony!"

Mrs. Liu said, "I know what to do. I'll just have our daughter act on behalf of the groom." (*This is the will of heaven.*)

And so Huiniang was led out to greet the bride. After the best man recited poetry, the bride was helped out of the sedan-chair. With the housekeeper and Auntie Zhang the Sixth holding his arms and Huiniang walking in front, Jade Boy the bride entered the main hall. The bride and the groom's sister bowed first to heaven and earth and then to their parents and relatives. Believing they were two girls making the wedding bows, all the servants attending the ceremony laughed in their sleeves. Lastly, the groom's sister and the fake bride bowed to each other.

At Mrs. Liu's order for the bride to go to the groom's chamber to let the joy of the occasion dispel his illness, the band struck up music and ushered the bride into the young man's room. Mrs. Liu raised the bed curtain and cried, "My son! Your bride is here to break your bad luck! Pull yourself together!" She repeated these words three or four times without drawing a response from her son. By the light of the lamp that Mr. Liu brought over, they saw that the young man was lying there unconscious, his head lolled to one side. What had happened was that Liu Pu had gotten so weak from the illness that the drum music had sent him into a coma. Frantically, his parents pinched the groove over his upper lip in an effort to revive him and forced hot water down his throat. Breaking into a cold sweat, he regained consciousness. Mrs. Liu told her husband to keep an eye on him, whereas she herself led the bride to the bridal chamber.

When Mrs. Liu lifted the bridal veil, everyone present broke into cheers at the sight of the beautiful face, but Mrs. Liu moaned to herself in anguish, "Isn't this pretty girl a perfect match for my son? If they can support me and my husband in our old age, all the pains we've taken in this life will not have been in vain. Who would have predicted that the boy would be so luckless as to fall gravely ill at this juncture! The odds are nine to ten against him. If the worst comes to the worst, my daughter-in-law will most likely remarry into another family. Wouldn't the joy of this moment mean nothing?"

Let us leave Mrs. Liu to her thoughts and turn our attention to Jade Boy. Raising his eyes, he caught sight of Huiniang, whose beauty stood out among all the kith and kin present. "What a pretty girl!" he thought. "Too bad that I, Sun Run, am already engaged. Had I known her earlier, I would surely have proposed to her."

While Jade Boy was admiring her, Huiniang was thinking, "Auntie Zhang has indeed said a lot about her beauty, but I never quite believed those words. Now I know she does deserve the praises. Too bad my brother doesn't have such luck. She'll have to sleep alone tonight. If my intended husband is as good-looking as she is, my life will not be worthless. I'm afraid I don't have such luck, either!" (*What a stupid girl! How can she compare the bride to her prospective husband?*)

Let us leave the two of them in their mutual admiration and come back to Mrs. Liu. She invited all the guests to the wedding banquet. After the banquet was over, all went their separate ways to retire for the night. The best man and the musicians were dismissed. There being no extra room to accommodate Auntie Zhang the Sixth, she also went home. In the bridal chamber, the housekeeper took off Jade Boy's jewelry and he sat holding a candle, not daring to go to sleep.

Mrs. Liu said to her husband, "How can we let our new daughter-in-law sleep by her forlorn self? Let's have our girl keep her company." (*Again, the will of Heaven.*)

Mr. Liu said, "I'm afraid that wouldn't be appropriate. Let her sleep alone."

Turning a deaf ear to him, Mrs. Liu said to Huiniang, "Go to the bridal chamber and sleep with your sister-in-law tonight, so that she won't feel lonely."

In her admiration for her sister-in-law, this order could not have suited Huiniang better.

Mrs. Liu led Huiniang into the bridal chamber and said to the bride, "Your husband is slightly indisposed and cannot share a bed with you. My daughter will keep you company tonight."

Afraid of giving himself away, Jade Boy said, "There's no need. I am shy with strangers."

"Good gracious!" exclaimed Mrs. Liu. "You two are about the same age. You could be sisters. You'll get along fine. What are you afraid of? If you don't think this is proper, just use separate quilts. That's all."

To Huiniang she said, "Go and bring your quilt over." And Huiniang went to do her mother's bidding.

Jade Boy was alarmed and delighted at the same time—delighted because he was already smitten with this beautiful girl, and this heaven-sent directive from

Mrs. Liu meant that he stood a pretty good chance of having his way with her; alarmed because if the girl rejected him and started to scream, he would be ruined. Then again, he thought, "If I miss this opportunity, I'll never have another one! This girl looks like she's old enough to know what love is. Let me think of a way to lead her on. I'm sure she'll fall into my trap."

While he was thinking these thoughts, Huiniang walked in with a maid carrying her quilt. After the maid put the quilt on the bed, Mrs. Liu rose and left with the maid. Huiniang closed the door, went up to Jade Boy, and said, all smiles, "Sister-in-law, I noticed that you didn't eat anything. Aren't you hungry?"

"No, not yet."

"Sister-in-law, if you want anything, just let me know. I'll get it for you. Don't be shy." (*This girl talks too much. This offer of hers is right up his alley.*)

Delighted at her eagerness to please, Jade Boy said, "Thank you so much for your kindness!"

Noticing the big flower-shaped snuff on top of the lampwick, Huiniang said, smiling, "Sister-in-law, that snuff is directly facing you, which means you'll soon have reason to celebrate!"

Jade Boy replied with a smile, "Don't make fun of me, Sister-in-law. The good tidings are meant for you!"

"You do know how to make fun of people, Sister-in-law!"

And so the bantering went on.

"It's getting late now," said Huiniang after a while. "Let's go to sleep."

"After you," said Jade Boy.

"You are the guest. I am the hostess. How can I go first?"

"But in this room, you are the guest." (*Only Jade Boy could say this.*)

"All right, I'll go first," said Huiniang affably. And so she took off her clothes and got into bed.

In the meantime, all this jocularity made the housekeeper realize that Jade Boy was up to some mischief. "Young Master," she whispered to him. "Behave yourself. This is no joke. If the madam knows about this, you'll get me into trouble, too."

"You need not say a thing," rejoined Jade Boy. "I know what I'm doing. You go to sleep now."

The housekeeper accordingly went to one side and lay down on a makeshift bed.

Jade Boy rose, picked up a lamp, walked up to the bed, and raised the bed curtain. By the lamplight, he saw that Huiniang was lying under her quilt on the side of the bed next to the wall.

Smiling, Huiniang said to Jade Boy with the lamp, "Sister-in-law, why do you need a lamp? Aren't you coming to bed?"

Jade Boy replied with a grin, "Yes, but first I want to check on which end of the bed you're resting your head." (*Good scene.*)

He put the lamp on the bedside table, took off his clothes, and got in under the curtain. "Sister," said he, "let's sleep head to head, so that we can talk."

"Good!" agreed Huiniang.

Jade Boy slipped under his quilt and stripped to the waist but left his underpants on. "Sister, how old are you?" asked he.

"Fifteen."

"To which family are you betrothed?"

Huiniang was too shy to answer that question. Putting his head on her pillow, Jade Boy whispered into her ear, "I'm a girl, too. You need not be shy."

"It's the Pei family, owner of an herbal medicine store."

"When is the wedding going to be?"

Huiniang replied in a subdued voice, "They've sent the matchmaker over several times lately to set the date, but my father asked them to postpone it because I'm still young."

Jade Boy said, laughing, "Aren't you upset that your father turned them down?"

Huiniang pushed his head off her pillow and said, "You are a bad one! You tricked me into telling you everything, and then you turn around and make fun of me. If I get upset over something like that, just imagine how you must be feeling tonight."

Jade Boy maneuvered his head back onto her pillow, saying, "Tell me, why should I be upset?" (*Good scene.*)

"How can you not be when the groom is absent from the wedding?"

"But the sister is here to make a couple of us. What's there to be upset about?"

"You mean you are my wife," said Huiniang, laughing.

"I am older than you are. So I am the husband." (*Gradually getting where he wants to go. And this is only to be expected.*)

"Didn't I make the wedding bows in my brother's place? So I am the husband."

"Enough of this fight! Let's be a female married couple," said Jade Boy.

All this bantering deepened their affection for each other. Believing he could get away with this, Jade Boy went on to say, "Since we're a married couple, why don't we share one quilt?" So saying, he raised Huiniang's quilt with both hands and slid over to her side. As he caressed her body, enjoying her smooth skin, he realized that she, too, had her underpants on. By this time, Huiniang was aroused by his advances. Delirious with pleasure, she let Jade Boy feel her body without the slightest resistance. Jade Boy found her protruding small breasts as soft as sponge and the lovely nipples like water lily seeds.

Huiniang also caressed Jade Boy's body. "Sister-in-law, what a soft and smooth body you have," said she. When her hand moved to his chest, she felt only two small nipples. She thought, "My sister-in-law is older than I am, but why are her breasts so much smaller than mine?"

Having caressed his fill, Jade Boy held her in his arms and kissed her, sticking his tongue into her mouth. Taking this as nothing more than some frolicking between sisters-in-law, Huiniang also embraced him and held his tongue with her lips. She then stuck her tongue into Jade Boy's mouth. He held her tongue and sucked it hard until she felt her whole body tingle and go limp. "Sister-in-law," said she. "We're not like a female couple but a real married couple."

Aware that her desires were stirring, Jade Boy said, "If you want to have some fun, why not take off your underpants as well? Won't it be nice if we could sleep in each other's arms?"

"But I'm too bashful to take them off."

"We're just going to have some fun. What's there to be bashful about?" So saying, he took off her underpants and reached for her private parts. She hastened to ward him off, saying, "Sister-in-law, don't do this!"

Turning her face toward his, Jade Boy kissed her on the mouth and said, "It's all right. You can feel mine."

When Huiniang took off his underpants and reached for his private parts, what did her hand touch but that member of his, as hard as iron! She gave a start and immediately withdrew her hand. "Who are you?" she asked. "You are an impostor pretending to be my sister-in-law!"

"I am your husband. Why bother to ask?" With that, he turned over and sat astride her. As he tried to part her thighs, Huiniang pushed him away with both her hands and said, "If you don't tell the truth, I'll have to scream. You'll be in big trouble!"

Jade Boy panicked. "Don't be so upset, young lady!" said he. "Let me explain. I am Jade Boy, your sister-in-law's brother. We heard that your brother is gravely ill, but we were not sure. My mother can't bear to let go of my sister, but she doesn't want to miss the wedding date chosen by your family, either. That's why she made me come in disguise, meaning to send my sister over later on, after your brother recovers. I never dreamed that you and I would become man and wife by the will of heaven. Now, this is a secret between you and me. Not a word is to get out!" Having said that, he mounted her again.

Huiniang had lost her heart even to one whom she believed to be a woman. Now that the one she loved turned out to be a man, Huiniang was only too delighted. Moreover, she was already so aroused by Jade Boy that she felt as if in a trance. With mixed feelings of surprise and joy, she yielded to him after some initial show of reluctance and said, "You were so deceitful!" In no mood to respond, Jade Boy held her tightly in his arms and had his way with her.

> He was a young man having his first taste;
> She was a virgin enjoying her first time.
> One said the wedding candles were meant for them;
> The other said the quilts inspired conjugal love.
> One said they were predestined for each other
> And needed no matchmaker.

The other said neither must forget the other
And vowed eternal love.
Both enjoyed themselves to the full,
To the neglect of their family ties.
Both sought only instant pleasure,
Ignoring their betrothed status.
They were two butterflies flitting among flowers
And a pair of lovebirds swimming in water.

After the game of clouds and rain was over, they went to sleep, locked in each other's arms. In the meantime, afraid that Jade Boy was up to mischief, the housekeeper had been lying on her makeshift bed on one side of the room, wide awake. Noticing the change from bantering to panting amid the creaks of the bed frame, she knew what the two of them had done and groaned inwardly in dismay.

The next morning, Huiniang went to her mother's room to wash and do her hair. The housekeeper did Jade Boy's toilette. While doing so, she said to him under her breath, "Young Master, you gave me your promise last night. But you didn't mean it. What a thing you did! If they get to know about it, what's to be done?"

"I didn't go out of my way to get her. She came to me, didn't she? I couldn't very well send her away."

"Where's your will power?"

"Sharing a bed with such a beauty would melt even a man of iron, let alone me! If you keep your mouth shut, who is to know?" (*What the eye doesn't see, the heart doesn't long for.*)

After the toilette was done, the housekeeper took him to Mrs. Liu's room to pay his respects to her.

"My child," said Mrs. Liu. "Have you forgotten your earrings?"

The housekeeper replied, "No, but there's a boil on her right earlobe, so she can't wear earrings, and she's applied a plaster over it."

"Oh, I see," said Mrs. Liu.

Jade Boy went back to the chamber. Members of the clan, male and female, all came to exchange greetings with the bride, Auntie Zhang the Sixth among them. After completing her toilette, Huiniang also entered the room and exchanged smiles with Jade Boy. That day, Mr. Liu treated members of both clans to a feast, which lasted amid loud music until late in the evening. After the party broke up, Huiniang went, as before, to share the bride's bed. That night, they were even more tender to each other in their games of clouds and rain and their vows of eternal love.

Three days went by, and the two of them remained inseparable. But the housekeeper was on pins and needles. She said to Jade Boy, "Three days have gone by. Tell Mrs. Liu that we must be on our way."

Burning with passion for Huiniang, Jade Boy was certainly not ready to go home. He said with a show of sincerity, "I can't bring myself to say I want to go home. It would be better if mother could send Auntie Zhang here to talk to them." (*Saying one thing and meaning another.*)

"Well, you've got a point," said the housekeeper. And so she went back alone.

In the meantime, Widow Sun, with her dark secret, was waiting anxiously for a report from Auntie Zhang the Sixth. At long last, the housekeeper showed up on the fourth day after the wedding. Widow Sun hastened to ask how things turned out, whereupon the housekeeper gave her a full account of how the son-in-law was gravely ill, how the sister made the wedding bows in his place, and how the sister and Jade Boy had slept together and made love. Widow Sun stamped her feet and cried out, "This was inevitable! Get me Auntie Zhang, quick!"

Before long, the housekeeper brought Auntie Zhang the Sixth to her.

"Auntie," said Widow Sun. "We had an agreement. My daughter was to be sent back on the third day. The deadline has gone by. Could you please go and ask them to send her home quickly?"

Thus instructed, Auntie Zhang the Sixth went with the housekeeper to the Liu house. It so happened that Mrs. Liu was in Jade Boy's room, chatting. As Auntie Zhang relayed Widow Sun's message, Jade Boy and Huiniang, hating to part with each other, said inwardly, "If only she could refuse!"

Amazingly enough, Mrs. Liu did refuse. "Auntie," said she, "you've been a matchmaker for so long that you should have known better. Has there ever been any rule that says a daughter-in-law must return home on the third day? Had she refused to marry into this family, there would have been nothing I could do about it. But now that she's here, she is a member of this family. She's not in her mother's control anymore! After all the pains I took getting this daughter-in-law, how can I let her go back on the third day? What a thing to say! If she can't bear to part with her daughter, why agree to marry her off in the first place? (*What a sharp tongue!*) She has a son, so she will have a daughter-in-law, too. Would she be willing to let her daughter-in-law go on the third day? I heard that she is a sensible person who knows the rules of propriety. Shame on her for even suggesting such an idea!"

Auntie Zhang the Sixth was rendered speechless. She dared not report back to Widow Sun. As for the housekeeper, afraid that someone would barge into the bridal chamber and catch them red-handed, she kept a tight watch at the door. Nor did she dare return home.

Now, after he was shocked into a cold sweat on the wedding night, Liu Pu gradually regained his health. Pleased upon hearing that his wife was in the house and that she was quite a beauty, he recovered even more quickly. A few days later, he struggled to sit up in bed, and his condition improved day by day. After he was able to comb his hair and get dressed, he asked to go to the bridal chamber and see his wife. Afraid that he was still too weak to walk alone, Mrs. Liu had a maid support him while she herself followed behind. As they slowly drew near the bridal chamber, they saw the housekeeper sitting on the threshold.

"Please let the young master enter," said the maid, whereupon the housekeeper rose and shouted at the top of her voice, "The young master is here!"

Jade Boy was holding Huiniang in his arms and flirting with her when he heard the shout. He made haste to walk away.

As Liu Pu raised the door curtain and stepped in, Huiniang said, "Brother, I'm so glad to see you all dressed and combed. But you shouldn't overtax yourself."

"That's all right," said Liu Pu. "I'm here just for a little while. I'll go back to bed soon enough." Having said that, he bowed to Jade Boy, who turned his back to him and dropped a curtsy.

"My son!" exclaimed Mrs. Liu. "Don't tire yourself out bowing!" Noticing that Jade Boy was standing with his back toward her son, she said, "Young lady, this is your husband, here to see you now that he has recovered. Why did you turn your back toward him?" Walking to her son, she said, "My son, she's a perfect match for you."

Liu Pu was so delighted with his wife's beauty that his health took another big turn for the better. Truly, as the saying goes, "A happy event cheers the spirits."

"My son," said Mrs. Liu, "go back to sleep now. Don't be too hard on yourself." The maid went to support him, as before, and Huiniang also left.

Impressed by Liu Pu's good looks in spite of his illness, Jade Boy thought, "It's not a bad deal for my sister if she gets this man for a husband." And then he thought again, "Now that he's well, he'll surely come to sleep with the bride, and we'll be found out! I'd better go home soon." In the evening, he said to Huiniang, "Your brother has recovered. I can't stay here any longer. You can urge your mother to send me home and bring my sister over. Only thus can our secret be safe. If I stay any longer, we'll be found out."

"Going home is easy enough for you, but what am I going to do about my future?" (*Why didn't she think of her future earlier?*)

"I have given this matter a lot of thought, but you and I have both been betrothed to other people, and I can't think of a way to change that fact. What's to be done?"

"If you can't think of a way to marry me, I swear that my soul will be with you always. I'll be too ashamed to serve another man!" (*It is to her credit that her tune ends on a dignified note.*) With that, she burst into sobs. Jade Boy wiped off her tears and said, "Don't worry. Give me time to think." But then as they lovingly embraced each other, they put the matter of Jade Boy's return aside.

One day, after lunch, the housekeeper went to the back of the house. Jade Boy and Huiniang closed the door and talked about what to do. They talked and talked, but no plan came up. In despair, they fell in each other's arms and wept, stifling their sobs.

Ever since her daughter-in-law's arrival, Mrs. Liu had observed that her daughter never left the girl's side, and that the two would close the door of the bridal chamber to sleep before the evening was quite advanced and would not rise until almost noontime. Mrs. Liu was quite displeased, but, believing that it was nothing more than sisterly love, she dismissed it from her mind in the beginning. But as the same pattern repeated day after day, she began to grow apprehensive, although she still attributed it to the laziness of youth. Several times she was about to speak up but checked herself because she still thought of the daughter-in-law as a pampered newcomer who hadn't yet shared her husband's bed. On that particular day, however, something was destined to happen.

When Mrs. Liu was passing by the bridal chamber, her ears caught the sound of sobbing inside. Taking a peek through a crack in the wall, she saw that her daughter-in-law and her daughter were in each other's arms, sobbing in a subdued voice. This posture aroused her suspicions. She was about to flare up when she checked herself because her son, who had just gotten well, would be upset if he learned about this. She raised the door curtain but found the door bolted.

"Open up!" she cried out.

Recognizing her voice, the two inside wiped their eyes dry and rushed over to open the door.

Stepping inside, Mrs. Liu asked, "Why were you crying in each other's arms behind closed doors in broad daylight?"

Their faces aflame, Jade Boy and Huiniang were at a loss for an answer, which further convinced Mrs. Liu of their guilt. Her limbs tingling with fury, she grabbed Huining and said, "A fine thing you did! Come here! I want to have a word with you!" So saying, she dragged the girl to an empty room at the back. The maid saw them, but with no idea what this was all about, she slipped out of sight.

Once in the room, Mrs. Liu bolted the door. The maid went to peep through a door crack and saw that Mrs. Liu picked up a wooden stick and said harshly, "You cheap little hussy! Out with the truth now and I'll spare you a beating. If you hold anything back from me, I'll break you in half!"

As Huiniang tried to deny any wrongdoing, her mother said, "You slut! Let me ask you something. She's been here for just a few days, and you've grown so attached to her that you cry in each other's arms behind closed doors. Why?"

Huiniang could not come up with an answer. The mother raised the stick as if to beat her but did not have the heart to bring it down.

Believing she would not be able to lie her way out of this, Huiniang thought, "Things having come to this pass, I'd better come out with everything, so that I can ask Father and Mother to break off the engagement with the Pei family and marry me to Jade Boy. If they refuse, I'll just kill myself, and that'll be that."

Aloud, she said, "When Mrs. Sun heard that my brother was ill, she was afraid of ruining her daughter's future and wanted to wait and see. So she asked Father and you, Mother, to postpone the wedding, but you firmly refused. That's why she disguised her son Jade Boy as the bride. Who would have known that you, Mother, made me keep the bride company! So we became husband and wife. We are deeply in love and vowed to stay true to each other to the end of our lives. Now that my brother has gotten well, Jade Boy is afraid that we would be found out and wants to go home in exchange for his sister. As I see it, a woman should not have two husbands, and so I was trying to talk Jade Boy into thinking up a plan to marry me. But no good plan came up, and we couldn't bear the thought of parting. That was when you caught us crying. Everything I said is true."

These words filled Mrs. Liu with rage. She tossed the stick aside and screamed, stamping her feet, "So, that old witch is so deceitful she tried to palm off a man on me! No wonder she wanted to have him back on the third day. Now that they have ruined my daughter, I'll have to fight it out with them! I don't care what happens to me, but let me get that young scoundrel!" She opened the door and stormed out. Alarmed that her mother was going to beat up Jade Boy, Huiniang hastened forward to hold her back, throwing all considerations of maidenly demurral to the wind. One push from her mother, and she fell on the floor. By the time she rose to her feet, her mother was already well on her way to the bridal chamber. Huiniang ran after her, followed by the maids.

To retrace our steps, Jade Boy knew from the way Mrs. Liu dragged Huiniang off that they had been found out. He was fretting in his room when the housekeeper came in to say, "Oh, horrors, Young Master! Things have gone terribly wrong! I just came from the back and heard a commotion in the room that's supposedly empty. I looked and saw that Mrs. Liu was interrogating her daughter and beating her with a big stick."

Upon hearing that Huiniang was being beaten, Jade Boy felt as if his heart was being stabbed with a knife. With tears flowing from his eyes, he was at a loss as to what to do.

The housekeeper said, "If we don't go now, we'll be in big trouble soon enough!"

Right away, Jade Boy removed his hairpins, tied up his hair into a knot, took out the Daoist robe, shoes, and socks from the trunk, put them on, walked out of the room, closed the door behind him, and fled home helter-skelter. Truly,

> The jade cage broken, the colored phoenix flew off.
> The golden lock opened, the flood dragon got free.

Both delighted and alarmed upon seeing her son returning in such a fluster, Widow Sun asked, "Why are you in such a state?"

After the housekeeper related what had happened, Widow Sun said bitterly to her son, "I sent you there just as a stopgap measure. How could you have done such an outrageous thing? If you had come back on the third day, the wicked thing you did would have been kept under wraps and you wouldn't have been found out. And then there's that hateful old hag Auntie Zhang! She hasn't come back to report to me ever since the day she left with you." Turning to the housekeeper, she continued, "Why didn't you come home earlier so that I wouldn't have to worry day and night? Now that such a thing has been done and the girl ruined, what's to be done? What good is this unworthy son?"

Thus scolded, Jade Boy felt overcome with shame.

The housekeeper said, "The young master did want to return home, but Mrs. Liu refused to let go of him. I was afraid that they would do something improper and so I watched the door all day long and dared not come home. Today, I went to the back of the house just for a little while, and Mrs. Liu barged in on them. Luckily we immediately headed home before she came upon us to do us harm. Now, the young master should hide himself for a couple of days. If the Liu family doesn't raise hell, we can consider ourselves the luckiest people there are."

Widow Sun accordingly told Jade Boy to hide himself while waiting for the Lius' next move.

Let us retrace our steps and come to the moment when Mrs. Liu rushed to the bridal chamber. Finding the door closed, she thought that Jade Boy was still inside and lashed out, "You scoundrel condemned by heaven! What do you take me for? How dare you play such a trick and ruin my daughter! Let me fight you to the death, to show you what kind of a woman you're dealing with! Come out this instant! If you don't open the door, I'll smash my way in!"

At this point, Huiniang arrived and tried to drag her mother away. "You slut!" cursed her mother. "Shouldn't you be feeling ashamed of yourself? Don't stop me!" So saying, she pushed the girl away with all her strength. Her movement was so forceful that the door gave way. Mother and daughter tumbled inside in a heap.

Mrs. Liu cursed, "Scoundrel! Tricking me like that!" She scrambled to her feet to look for him, but failing to find him anywhere, she said, "Confound him! How clever! So he fled. But I'll get him even if he fled to the sky." To her daughter, she said, "Now that you've done such a disgraceful thing, how are you going to face the world if the Pei family gets to know about this?"

Huiniang replied between sobs, "I have only myself to blame. Please have pity, mother, and talk father into calling off the engagement with the Pei family and marrying me to Jade Boy. Only thus can I redeem myself. Otherwise I'll have to kill myself." With that, she collapsed onto the floor in a fit of weeping.

"You make it sound so easy!" said Mrs. Liu. "After going through all the betrothal formalities, will anyone agree to call off the engagement without a good reason? What will you father say if they ask for a reason? He can't very well tell them that his daughter has found a lover all by herself!" (*What a mean thing to say!*)

Smarting with humiliation, Huiniang covered her face with her sleeve and burst into another fit of bitter sobs.

Being a loving mother after all, Mrs. Liu was afraid that her daughter would ruin her health by such violent weeping. Relenting, she said, "My child, actually you are not to blame. It's all because that old witch thought up that evil scheme and sent that scoundrel over in disguise. I was so unsuspecting I fell into her trap by making you keep him company. Since no one else knows about this, let's not say a word about this again so as to keep your reputation intact. That would be the right thing to do. To call off the engagement and marry that scoundrel is out of the question. (*What a "right" thing to do!*)

Huiniang cried even louder at her mother's rejection of her idea. Torn between pity and anger, Mrs. Liu did not know what to do,

In the midst of the commotion, Mr. Liu came home from a medical house call. Passing by the bridal chamber, he heard his daughter sobbing and his wife talking loudly. Wondering what all this was about, he couldn't bear the suspense and raised the door curtain. "Why are the two of you in such a state?" he asked. Whereupon Mrs. Liu told him in detail everything that had happened.

Mr. Liu was so infuriated that he stood speechless for the longest time. After thinking the matter over, he eventually spoke up and laid the blame squarely on his wife. "It's all your fault, you old hag! You ruined our daughter! When our son became gravely ill, I wanted to postpone the wedding, but you came up with all sorts of arguments and insisted on keeping the original date. Then, when the Sun family's housekeeper came with their proposal, I would have gone along, but you with your glib tongue played them false. When the boy came over, I said let the bride sleep alone, but you had to make our girl keep him company. And what fine company that was!" (*Why did he yield to her in the first place, only to regret it now? Because old man Liu is a henpecked husband.*)

Because Jade Boy was gone and she loved her daughter too much to let off steam on her, Mrs. Liu had been trying to stifle her rage. Her husband's reprimand gave her a vent for her pent-up fury. Out came a stream of angry words: "Old turtle! The way you put it, that scoundrel did right in ruining my daughter!" With that, she threw herself at him. (*So brazen even at this moment.*) Mr. Liu, also at the top of his wrath, held her and started hitting her. (*Now he's acting like a man!*) With Huiniang trying to pull them apart, the threesome got entangled in one heap. A maid ran in consternation to report to Liu Pu, saying, "Horrors! Young Master! The master and mistress are fighting in the bridal chamber!" Liu Pu rose from bed and went to the bridal chamber to try to calm them down. At the sight of their son, the old couple stopped their blows out of fear for his fragile health but continued to throw verbal insults at each other. Liu Pu talked his father into leaving the room and then asked, "Why has my sister joined the fight and where is the bride?"

Huiniang felt so overwhelmed with shame upon hearing these questions that she covered her face and broke down in a flood of tears without saying a word. Liu Pu grew impatient. "Answer me!" said he. Only then did Mrs. Liu tell him everything. Liu Pu was aghast, his face deathly pale. After a prolonged silence, he said, "A family scandal must not be leaked out to the public, or we'll become a laughing stock. Things having already come to this, we need to think about what to do."

Mrs. Liu stopped yelling and walked out the door. Huiniang tried to stay behind, but her mother pulled her along and then closed the door after them with a huge padlock. Back in her own room, Huiniang felt so ashamed of herself that she crouched in a corner and wept. Truly,

All the water of River Xiang
Could not wash the shame off her face.

In the meantime, Manager Li had been leaning against the wall, listening to the uproar next door. He was only able to deduce that something had gone wrong but could not figure out the details. The next morning, when a maid went out of the house, Manager Li beckoned her into his house and questioned her. The maid refused to say anything at first, but Manager Li offered her forty to fifty copper coins and said, "If you tell me, I'll give you these coins to buy some goodies to eat."

Her greed stirring at the sight of the coins, the maid took them, hid them on herself, and told Manager Li everything from the very beginning. Manager Li privately rejoiced. "Let me tell the Pei family about this scandal," he said to himself. "I'll urge them to come over and raise hell. The Lius will surely feel too ashamed to stay on, and their house will be mine." In all haste he went to report everything to the Pei family and he embellished the story, to further infuriate Mr. Pei the Ninth.

Mr. and Mrs. Pei were already angry at the Liu family for having turned down their proposal. This scandal involving their prospective daughter-in-law made their blood boil. Mr. Pei rushed over to the Liu house, called Mr. Liu outside, and launched into the following tirade: "When I had a matchmaker propose a wedding date, you turned us down, saying your daughter was too young to marry. Now we know that you kept her at home so that she could carry on with a lover. If we had our way, there would have been no scandal. We are a family of stainless reputation. We don't want one who would only bring disgrace to us. Give us back our betrothal gifts so that we can look for another match! Don't ruin our son's future!"

The color on Mr. Liu's face came and went. He thought, "How did they get to know so early this morning what happened only last evening? How very strange!" Not wishing to admit it, he said in denial, "Where did all this come from, my kinsmen? Why are you insulting my family in such foul language? If others get wind of this, they'll believe it to be the truth. What a loss of face for both families!"

Mr. Pei cursed, "You spineless dog! Old turtle! Who hasn't heard about the fine thing your daughter did? Imagine lying to me like this, still covering up for her!" He took a step forward, rubbed his forefinger against Mr. Liu's cheek in a gesture to shame him, and said, "Old turtle! Don't you feel ashamed? Wait until I give you a mask before you show yourself in public!"

Thus humiliated, Mr. Liu burst out, "Damn you! Why did you have to come to my house and insult me?" So saying, he charged headfirst at Mr. Pei and knocked him to the ground. As the two exchanged blows, Mrs. Liu and Liu Pu heard the fracas and came out for a look. At the sight of Mr. Pei and Mr. Liu locked in a fight, they rushed forward and pulled them apart. Mr. Pei continued to curse, his finger pointing at Mr. Liu, "Old turtle! It's a good thing you beat me up! I'll see you in the prefectural court!"

After Mr. Pei cursed his way out of the house, Liu Pu asked his father, "Why did Mr. Pei come here to make a scene so early in the morning?" After his father repeated Pei's words to him, Liu Pu said, "How strange that they heard about this so quickly!" and then he added, "Since word about it is already out, what are we going to do?"

Recalling the insults Mr. Pei had hurled at him, Mr. Liu felt rage rising in him. He stomped his feet and said, "This is all the fault of that cursed woman Sun! She is the one who brought disgrace to our family and made us suffer so much humiliation. If I don't sue her, how can I feel vindicated?"

Ignoring Liu Pu's advice to the contrary, Mr. Liu had an official complaint written and went with all speed to the prefectural yamen. It just so happened that Prefect Qiao had called his morning court session to order and was ready to take complaints. Although a native of the region west of Tong Pass [in Shaanxi], Prefect Qiao was an upright and intelligent man who appreciated talent, loved the people, and was as wise as the gods in his judgment of cases. He was therefore called Blue Sky Qiao throughout the yamen.

Now, Mr. Liu had just arrived at the yamen when he ran into Mr. Pei the Ninth. Seeing Mr. Liu with a letter of complaint in his hand, Mr. Pei thought that Liu was suing him. (*Another foul-up. Good plot.*) "Old turtle!" he yelled. "You let your daughter do that disgraceful thing and yet you turn around and sue me. Let's go to see the prefect!" So saying, he pounced on Mr. Liu and the two men again came to blows. Their written complaints fell in the tussle. The two men fought all the way into the main hall until Prefect Qiao saw them and ordered that they kneel down, one on each side of the dais.

"What are your names? Why were you fighting?"

The two men shouted their replies at the same time.

"Order!" exclaimed the prefect. "The older of the two can come up and state your case first."

Pei the Ninth ascended the dais and stated on his knees, "I am Pei the Ninth. I have a son Pei Zheng, betrothed since childhood to Huiniang, daughter of Liu Bingyi, kneeling down there. My son and his daughter are both fifteen now. Being of an advanced age, I would like my beloved son's wedding to take place as soon as possible. I repeatedly asked the matchmaker to propose a date, but Liu Bingyi declined each time, saying his daughter was still too young. In fact, he has been putting his daughter up to an adulterous affair with Sun Run and secretly got him into their house, so that they could back out of the engagement. This morning, I went to his house to reason with him, but he beat me up instead. In desperation, I came to this court, Your Honor, to seek justice, and he came too, to assault me again. Please do justice by me, Your Honor, and save my life!"

"You may withdraw now," said the prefect. He then summoned Liu Bingyi and asked, "What do you have to say?"

"I have a son and a daughter. My son, Liu Pu, is betrothed to Sister Pearl, Widow Sun's daughter. My daughter is betrothed to Pei the Ninth's son. When Pei the

Ninth proposed a wedding date, I turned him down, partly because my daughter was too young and we hadn't gotten the dowry ready, and partly because we were busy making preparations for my son's wedding. But my son suddenly fell ill when his wedding date was drawing near. Not daring to make our daughter-in-law share a bed with him, we told our daughter to keep the bride company. As it turned out, that treacherous Widow Sun had hid her daughter and sent over her son, Sun Run, disguised as the bride, and he raped my daughter. I was about to seek justice from the yamen when Pei the Ninth learned about it and went to my house to assault me. I was so mad that I yelled at him. I have no wish to break off the betrothal."

Intrigued by the story of a man disguised as a bride, Prefect Qiao said, "A man disguised as a woman will surely look different from a woman. Were you not able to tell?"

Mr. Liu replied, "In all the weddings that take place, who has ever suspected a bride of being a man? What's more, Sun Run's face is as pretty as a girl's. My wife and I were delighted to see him. We never suspected any foul play."

"Didn't the Sun family promise their daughter to you? Why would they dress their son up as a woman and send him instead? There must be a reason behind it." After a pause, Prefect Qiao said again, "Is Sun Run still in your house?"

"No, he fled back home," replied Mr. Liu.

Right away, Prefect Qiao ordered lictors to bring Widow Sun, her son, and her daughter to court, and ordered another team to bring Liu Pu and his sister Huiniang to court for questioning. Before long, they were all brought to the prefect's presence. (*What a scene of excitement in the yamen!*)

Prefect Qiao raised his head and saw that Jade Boy did bear a strong resemblance to his sister and was just as beautiful. Liu Pu was also a strikingly handsome youth, and Huiniang a rare beauty. The prefect thought in admiration, "What fine young couples they make!" As he did so, he was taken with a desire to help bring about a happy union or two. Turning to Widow Sun, he asked, "Why did you disguise your son as the bride to cheat the Liu family and ruin their daughter?"

Whereupon Widow Sun launched into an account of how her son-in-law fell gravely ill, how Liu Bingyi refused to change the wedding date, how she feared for her daughter's future, wanted to break the bad luck, and therefore sent her son in disguise, and how she told her son to return home on the third day after the wedding. She explained that hers was just a stopgap measure and that she never expected Liu Bingyi to have Huiniang keep her son company, leading to the disgrace.

"I see," said Prefect Qiao. Turning to Mr. Liu, he said, "When your son fell gravely ill, you should have postponed the wedding, but you refused to do so. Why? If you had agreed to Mrs. Sun's proposal, there would have been no scandal. You have only yourself to blame. You compromised your daughter."

"I shouldn't have listened to my wife," said Mr. Liu. "And now, regrets are too late." (*Be warned! Never listen to a woman!*)

STORY 8

"Nonsense!" said Prefect Qiao. "You are the master of the family. Why listen to your wife?" He then summoned Jade Boy and Huiniang and said, "Sun Run! You did wrong in passing yourself off as a woman, and then you seduced a virgin. Do you know what the punishment is for such offenses?"

Jade Boy kowtowed and said, "I do plead guilty, but I didn't do it on purpose. It was Mrs. Liu who told her daughter to keep me company."

"But she did so out of the best intentions without knowing that you are a man. Why didn't you decline the offer?"

"I did try, but she insisted."

"By law, I should put you under the bamboo rod. However, considering your age and the fact that it was both sets of parents who caused wrongdoing on your part, I'm going to spare you this time."

Jade Boy kowtowed and tearfully said his thanks.

Prefect Qiao then addressed Huiniang. "You did wrong, but we need not go over that again. Now, do you want to marry Mr. Pei Junior or Sun Run? Tell me the truth." (*Important question.*)

Huiniang replied, sobbing, "I compromised my chastity without going through the proper matchmaking channels. But I cannot serve another man. I am deeply attached to Sun Run and I have vowed never to marry another man. If Your Honor rules to separate me from him, I will kill myself here and now. I will be too ashamed to live on and be laughed at." With that, she burst into a fit of violent sobs.

Impressed by the depth of her emotion, Prefect Qiao felt sorry for her. He ordered her to step aside, called up Pei the Ninth, and said to him, "By rights I should rule that Huiniang marry into your family. However, she has already lost her chastity to Sun Run. If you take her on as your daughter-in-law, your family's reputation will be tarnished, and you will become a laughing stock. She, on her part, will be known as the woman with two husbands. Both sides will be losers. My ruling is for her to marry Sun Run to salvage her honor, and for Sun Run to return your betrothal gifts to you, so that your son can find another match."

Mr. Pei the Ninth said, "My daughter-in-law being involved in such a scandal, of course I'm not going to take her into my family. But by giving her to Sun Run, who wrecked a betrothal, Your Honor is doing the adulterous couple a favor. I'm not going to accept that! I would rather not take back one penny but request that Your Honor make her marry another man, so as to meet me half way."

"If you don't want her, that'll be that. Why make an enemy of her?" asked Prefect Qiao.

"Your Honor," said Mr. Liu. "Sun Run already has a fiancée. How can my daughter serve him as a concubine?"

Prefect Qiao had made his ruling without knowing that Sun Run had a fiancée. Upon this revelation, he said, "Now what's to be done?" Turning to Sun Run he said, "You were already engaged, so you had all the more reason not to compromise another girl. Do you realize what you did to her?" (*What a wise prefect!*)

Jade Boy dared not utter one word. Prefect Qiao continued, "Who is your wife? Has the wedding ceremony been held yet?" (*Good question.*)

Sun Run replied, "My intended wife is Xu Ya's daughter. The wedding ceremony hasn't taken place."

The prefect said, "Oh! Then this case is easy to solve." He shouted, "Pei the Ninth! Since Sun Run is betrothed but not yet married and I have already ruled that he marry your son's fianceé, I now rule that his intended wife marry your son, so as to let you feel vindicated."

"How would I dare contradict Your Honor's wise judgment?" said Pei. "I'm only afraid that Xu Ya may object."

"Now that I have said the word, who would dare object? Go home now and bring your son over. I will have Xu Ya and his daughter brought here. I'll announce my rulings in everyone's presence."

Mr. Pei hurried home and took his son Pei Zheng to the yamen. Xu Ya and his daughter also arrived. Prefect Qiao saw that both the young man and the young woman were good-looking and thought they would make a nice couple. He said to Xu Ya, "Sun Run having seduced Liu Bingyi's daughter, my ruling is that he marry the girl. I shall now rule that your daughter marry Pei Zheng, Pei the Ninth's son. The weddings will take place this very day. You will all report back to me. Anyone who raises objections will be severely punished."

With the prefect making the decision, how would Xu Ya dare object? Everyone agreed. Prefect Qiao took up his brush-pen and wrote the following:

A brother passed himself off as his sister at her wedding; two sisters-in-law slept together. The parents' love for their children is well within the bounds of reason. But, with one male, one female, things took an unexpected turn. When dry wood is placed near a raging fire, it will surely burst into flames. When fine jade is put next to a bright pearl, they form a perfect pair. Young Mr. Sun acquired a wife through his sister; he needed not jump over the wall for a tryst with a lover. Miss Liu got a husband disguised as a sister-in-law; she needed not flaunt her beauty in her wish to marry. Love leads to marriages; rites are based on what is right. When what normally assumes importance is lacking, flexibility is called for. (His approach can turn scandals into romances. Otherwise, there would be no end to strife and lawsuits. Therefore, a good official is one who knows how to dissolve disputes.) *My ruling is to pair Xu Ya's daughter with Pei the Ninth's son and to marry Pei Zheng's intended wife to Jade Boy Sun. By taking away the wife of one who steals another man's wife, this ruling settles the grievance between the two families. Happiness is better enjoyed in company than alone. The three couples will be as harmonious as fish in water. Even though the brides and grooms trade places, they are brides and grooms no less.*

Even though they step over different thresholds, they are the right spouses meant for each other. Love leads to love; the parents serve as matchmakers. Neither kith nor kin, I the prefect bring off the match. (A wonderful statement.) *With this ruling in place, the couples are to be ready for their weddings.*

Prefect Qiao had a clerk read the above statement aloud right there in the hall. Everyone wholeheartedly accepted the ruling and kowtowed in gratitude. Prefect Qiao took out from the prefectural treasury six lengths of red silk and had them draped over the three couples. Three bands of musicians were put together and three bridal sedan-chairs prepared for the brides. The three grooms and their parents followed the sedan-chairs on foot. This event caused quite a stir throughout the prefecture of Hangzhou. Everyone spoke well of the prefect for his kindness and for his willingness to make things easy for people. After the wedding ceremonies were held, none of the three families had any complaints.

Manager Li had planned to set Widow Sun and Pei the Ninth against Liu Bingyi so that he could stand to benefit. It turned out, to his dismay, that the prefect made a wise judgment that brought about Jade Boy Sun's happy marriage. And, to add to his chagrin, the neighbors did not think it a scandal but spread the story around in admiration.

In less than one year, Prefect Qiao selected Liu Pu and Sun Run as candidates for the imperial civil service examinations. Manager Li felt too ashamed to stay in the area any longer and took refuge in the countryside. Later, Liu Pu and Sun Run both won honors at the imperial examinations. They assumed official posts in the capital and attained high ranks. With their support, Pei Zheng also obtained an official post. All members of their clans gained wealth and position. Liu Pu rose to be a member of the Dragon Diagram Academy.[4] Manager Li's house ended up being annexed to the Liu residence. What good did that villain bring himself? A later poet had this to say, to warn people against following Manager Li's evil ways:

> *Honesty and kindness are the first essentials;*
> *Why rack your brains to do people harm?*
> *Consider how the ancients chose places to live:*
> *They'd pay any price to have good neighbors.*

Another quatrain praises Prefect Qiao for a judgment well rendered:

> *The exchange of brides and grooms was predestined,*
> *Thanks to the judgment of the wise prefect.*
> *Honor was preserved and a scandal covered up;*
> *Prefect Qiao well deserved the sobriquet "Blue Sky."*

9

Chen Duoshou and His Wife Bound in Life
and in Death

The affairs of the world are like a game of chess
Between two players locked in a fight to win.
Once the game is over and the pieces are put away,
Who, in the end, is the winner and who the loser?

The above quatrain likens the affairs of the world to a game of chess. The vicis-
situdes of life are just as transient as a game of chess between two players locked
in the kind of red-eyed, throat-burning, life-or-death battle of wits between Sun
Bin and Pang Juan.[1] Or, as in the case of Liu Bang and Xiang Yu fighting for the
throne, the rivalry will not end until one of the two dies, as Xiang Yu did by the
Wu River.[2] As soon as the game is over and the chess pieces are put away, the play-
ers dismiss it from their minds with a smile. Therefore, wise men living in hermit-
age find pleasure in spending their leisurely hours playing chess. Of the numerous
poems about this pursuit, the one written at the order of the emperor by Zeng Qi,
a *zhuangyuan* winning first honor in the imperial examinations earlier in our dynasty
[the Ming] , stands out in its excellence:

> *Two kings set up camps face-to-face,*
> *And devise strategies to wipe out the other.*
> *Their horses gallop over the battlefields;*
> *Their pawns cross the waves of the mighty river.*
> *Lady Yu sang and danced in tears at Gaixia;*
> *The Han generals' flags bore down on the Chu.[3]*
> *Their joy complete, their plots exhausted, their battle ends,*
> *Their chessboards mottled with the shadows of pines and flowers.*

Good as the poem is, its detractors find the reference to Lady Yu and Han gen-
erals too much of a cliché and the seventh line about their joy complete and their
plots exhausted too much of a damper on the spirit. A poem by imperial order and

meant for the emperor's eyes should be more majestic, they say. Another poem, ordered by Emperor Renzong in the Hongxi reign period [1425] in this dynasty, takes a far higher stand:

> *Two states vying for power deploy troops;*
> *In battle array, they're poised for victory.*
> *The horses lead the attacks, taking winding paths;*
> *The generals guard the camps against the invaders.*
> *The chariots charge in danger to take out the pawns;*
> *The cannons fire across the river at the enemy camp.*
> *Strategies are learned in hours of leisure;*
> *With victory comes the reign of peace.*

Why all this talk about chess today? Well, it's because there were once two families who became close friends through chess playing and formed a marriage alliance between their children, an alliance that led to a wonderful story. Truly,

> *Marriages are made not in this life,*
> *But were predestined five hundred years ago.*

Our story takes place in Fenyi County, Jiangxi, where two farmers, one called Chen Qing and the other Zhu Shiyuan, lived across the street from each other. Though they could hardly be considered rich, they were doing well enough with the estates inherited from their ancestors. The two families had been neighbors for generations. Chen Qing and Zhu Shiyuan, both in their forties now, shared the same tastes, and both were decent men who minded their own business and were averse to stirring up trouble. Every day, they met after their meals for a game of chess to while away their leisure time. Sometimes they took turns playing the host, but they never treated each other to anything more lavish than tea and simple, homely meals. The neighbors would go to watch the games when they had the time. Among them was a Wang Sanlao. In his sixties now, he had been in his youth quite a master player of chess, but, as he had been suffering lately from excessive internal heat, he had stopped playing for fear that the concentration of mind and the excitement might be injurious to his health. He now enjoyed spending his time watching chess games and never got tired of it.

In fact, chess players dread being watched. As the saying goes, "The spectator sees the game better than the players." If a spectator can't hold his tongue and inadvertently lets out a comment at a critical juncture, the one going to win will end up the loser, and the one going to lose will turn around and win the game. This is not something worth an outburst of anger, but the loser finds it hard not to grumble a word of complaint or two. As the ancients put it so well,

> *A silent chess-game watcher is a real gentleman,*
> *A ranting drinker is a petty rogue.*

Luckily, Wang Sanlao had the virtue of never making an undue comment before the game was over. It was only after the victor had emerged that he would analyze which move had been the brilliant one that had won the game and which one the lousy move that had lost the game. Zhu and Chen liked his comments and never took them amiss. (*Descriptions irrelevant to the story but quite interesting.*)

One day, Zhu Shiyuan was at a game in Chen Qing's house, with Wang Sanlao watching. After lunch, they were resetting the chessboard for another game when a little schoolboy walked in. How did he look?

> *His face as fair as if powdered,*
> *His lips as red as if rouged.*
> *His head all shaven clean,*
> *His hands as if made of jade,*
> *He carried himself with grace;*
> *He walked at a dignified pace.*
> *He looked more like a celestial being*
> *Than an ordinary boy of this world.*

The schoolboy was Chen Qing's son, named Duoshou. His satchel in his arms, he stepped into the living room from outside. All calm and composed, he laid down his satchel on a chair, called out a greeting to Wang Sanlao, addressing him as "Grandpa," and bowed deeply. Before Mr. Wang could return the greeting, Chen Qing held him and said, "At your age, you must not stand on ceremony. Otherwise, the undeserved respect he gets will only bring him bad luck!"

"What kind of talk is this?" Wang protested. While Chen Qing was trying to hold him down, he managed to rise a little from his seat and bow slightly by way of accepting the courtesy.

The schoolboy then greeted Zhu Shiyuan, addressing him as "Uncle," and bowed to him. Zhu bowed in return. Being on the other side of the chess table, Chen Qing could not very well stop him, so instead he bowed to Zhu in acknowledgment of the courtesy. (*Nice detail.*)

After greeting the two guests, the boy bowed to his father and said, straightening himself up, "Father, tomorrow is the Double Ninth Festival, so my teacher has dismissed the class and returned home.[4] He'll be gone for a couple of days. He told me not to play at home, and assigned me homework to do." Having said that, he picked up his satchel from the chair and went to the interior section of the house, carrying himself with dignity.

Wang Sanlao and Zhu Shiyuan were deeply impressed by the boy's poise, his articulateness, clear voice, and his correct observance of etiquette. They burst into profuse praises.

"How old is your son?" asked Wang Sanlao.

"Nine," replied Chen Qing.

"It still seems yesterday when we had the 'noodle-soup feast' for him," said Wang

Sanlao.⁵ "So it's been nine years in the twinkling of an eye. Time does fly like an arrow. We've certainly aged!"

Turning to Zhu Shiyuan, he continued, "I remember that your daughter was born in the same year."

"Yes," said Zhu. "My daughter, Duofu, is also nine years old now."

"Well, don't blame this old man for speaking out of turn," said Wang, "but as you two have been playing chess together all your lives, why don't you marry your children to each other and become in-laws? In ancient times, there was a Zhu-Chen village where there were only two clans, the Zhus and the Chens, and they intermarried for generations and generations. You happen to be a Zhu and a Chen. Isn't this the will of heaven? With such a nice boy and such a nice girl, as we can all see, isn't this a great idea?"

Having already decided that the boy was a good candidate for son-in-law, Zhu Shiyuan said before Chen Qing had a chance to speak up, "Yes! What a good idea! I'm only afraid that Brother Chen would not agree. If he could kindly accept the match, I would have nothing more to ask for!"

Chen Qing replied, "Since you don't scorn the lowliness of my family, why would I object as the father-in-law? Could we trouble Sanlao to serve as the matchmaker?"

"Tomorrow, Double Ninth, is not a lucky day," said Wang Sanlao. "I'll visit you at home the day after tomorrow, which is a most lucky date. Since both of you are sincere in wishing for this match, it's all settled then. As for me the matchmaker, a few cups of the nuptial wine will be enough for my services."

"Let me tell you a joke," said Chen Qing. "The Jade Emperor⁶ wished to form a marriage alliance with a human emperor. After considering the matter, he concluded, 'Both being imperial families, the matchmaker must also have the status of a monarch.' So he asked the Kitchen God to descend to earth and make the match. Alarmed at the sight of the Kitchen God, the human emperor said, 'Why does this matchmaker have such a dark complexion?'⁷ The Kitchen God replied, 'Have you ever seen a fair matchmaker who works for nothing?'"

Wang Sanlao and Zhu Shiyuan both burst into laughter. Zhu and Chen resumed their chess game, and they did not part company until late in the evening.

> One brief game of chess
> Led to a marriage of three lifetimes.

Nothing of note happened on the next day, the Double Ninth Festival. On the tenth day of the ninth lunar month, Wang Sanlao put on a new colored robe and went to the Zhu residence to make the marriage proposal. Zhu Shiyuan having already told his wife, Liu-shi, about the boy's good qualities, the proposal was accepted most readily. The bride's parents cared little about the amount of betrothal gifts, saying that as far as betrothal gifts and the future dowry were concerned, both sides needed only give according to their family circumstances and that neither was to raise complaints. Wang Sanlao relayed the message forthwith to Chen Qing, much to the latter's delight. Chen Qing then chose an auspicious day for the wedding and delivered the betrothal gifts by way of confirming the alliance. The Zhu family sent over the horoscope card of the girl, and the betrothal feast lasted a whole day. Henceforth, the two families addressed each other as in-laws, and the two fathers continued to play their games of chess.

Time sped by. Before they knew it, six years had elapsed. Chen Duoshou was now fifteen. Well versed in the classics, he was expected to take the civil service examinations, win honors, and bring glory to the family. However, luck ran against him. He suddenly fell ill with the vile disease of leprosy. In the beginning, it was thought to be just a case of scabies and was not taken seriously. A year later, the disease broke out in full force and changed his appearance beyond recognition.

> *His flesh withered, his skin chapped;*
> *The toxins in his body broke out in boils.*
> *He itched all over in misery, day and night.*
> *It was far worse than scabies and the same as leprosy.*
> *The handsome boy now looked like a toad;*
> *His skin was like that of an old turtle.*
> *The scratching fingers smelled of pus;*
> *The sordid body gave off a foul stench.*

Chen Qing loved his only son as dearly as his own life and was devastated by the boy's illness. He even lost his interest in chess. (*Good observation.*) He sought the services of physicians and fortune-tellers, offered incense, and redeemed his vows to Buddha. There was nothing he did not do. One whole year went by amid these frantic activities, but all the money he spent went down the drain. The boy's condition did not improve in the slightest. That he and his wife fretted in grief goes without saying.

Zhu Shiyuan was just as worried about his future son-in-law's illness. He asked after the boy's condition at all times of the day and hardly ever left the Chens' door. Three years went by without any good news. Ever since she learned about her prospective son-in-law's illness, Liu-shi had been grumbling tearfully at home to her husband, saying, "My daughter is not going to spoil like some perishable food. Why did you have to rush like that and betroth her when she was only nine? And now, what's to be done? If that toad drops dead, my girl will be set free. But he's neither dead nor alive, and our daughter is coming of age. We can't marry her, nor can we call off the engagement. We can't very well watch that leper make a virtual widow of our daughter, can we? It's all the fault of that meddling old turtle Wang Sanlao! He has ruined my daughter's life!" And so amid wails of grief she railed against that "old turtle" Wang Sanlao. Being a hen-pecked husband, Zhu Shiyuan held his tongue and let her carry on until she ran out of steam.

One day, while cleaning drawers, Liu-shi came upon her husband's chessboard and chess pieces. Flying into a rage, she launched into another tirade. "You two old scoundrels! You made the match against my daughter's interests just because you had fun playing chess with each other! Why keep this source of trouble?" (*How interesting that she calls it a source of trouble!*) As she said so, she headed for the door, tossed the chess pieces into the street, and smashed the chessboard.

A meek man by nature, Zhu Shiyuan knew that there was no way he could hold her back when she was in such a fit, and therefore he fled the scene. Their daughter, Duofu, was too bashful to come forward to calm her mother down, and so Liu-shi was left to her ranting until she grew tired. It's been said since ancient times:

> If walls have ears,
> How can windows have no eyes?

Chen Qing had not quite believed what he had heard about Liu-shi lashing out at home at the matchmaker and at her husband, but now, with the chess pieces scattered all over the street, the truth had fully sunk in. He said to his wife, Zhang-shi, "Let's put ourselves in their shoes. We have our own bad luck to blame for our son's illness, for which there seems to be no cure. It'll be a sin for us to marry that flower of a girl to a leper of a husband. The girl will feel miserable and resentful. A forced marriage will not be harmonious, and we can hardly expect her to be dutiful to us. This match was made out of the best intentions, and we didn't spend much in the first place. A good person can be good in a thousand ways, but goodness is goodness, pure and simple. Let's be good all the way so as not to turn a good relationship sour. We should look farther down the road. Let's give our daughter-in-law's horoscope card back to her family and give her the freedom to marry another man. If heaven takes pity on us and cures our boy, we will surely be able to find a wife for him. We are the cause of a fall out between Zhu and his wife with all her tears and her nagging. I feel guilty."

Having thus come to a decision, Chen Qing hurried over to the Wang residence. Wang Sanlao was chatting with several old men at his door. At the sight of Chen Qing, he rose with alacrity, bowed, and asked, "Has your son been getting better the last couple of days?"

Chen Qing replied with a shake of his head, "No. I have something to say to you. Could you follow me to my house?"

Without a moment's delay, Wang Sanlao followed Chen Qing to the latter's house and the two men sat down in the living room, one as the host, the other as the guest. After tea was served, Sanlao asked, "What is it that you want to say to me?"

Chen Qing hitched his chair closer to Sanlao and, as they sat knee to knee, he spoke his mind. He began with a description of his son's grave condition and then went on to tell Wang about the Zhu couple's complaints.

Wang Sanlao had also heard something along those lines, but, out loud, he said, trying to cover up his alarm, "I don't think this is true."

"How would I dare make irresponsible remarks?" said Chen Qing. "I'm not blaming my in-laws. I just feel uncomfortable about the marriage. I'll be glad to return the horoscope card so that the Zhu family can pick another son-in-law. This will be good for both families. I don't want to force anything on them."

"I'm afraid this won't do!" exclaimed Wang Sanlao. "This old man makes, not breaks, matches. Should you regret later on, the responsibility of it all will be too much for me to bear."

"I've talked this over time and again with my wife. We won't go back on our words. And they need not even return the humble gifts that we sent them."

"Since you're returning the horoscope card, the betrothal gifts should by rights be returned. But heaven looks after good people. Your son will get well eventually. You must think well before you act."

"Even if my son will be lucky enough to grow new skin, there's no telling when that'll happen. It'll be like searching for a needle in the river. We can't afford to ruin their daughter's chances." With that, he retrieved the horoscope card from his sleeve and handed it to Wang Sanlao. Tears fell from his eyes in spite of himself.

Also feeling saddened, Wang Sanlao said, "Since you've already made up your mind, I'll have to oblige. But I believe that your in-laws will never agree. They know the rules of propriety."

Trying to hold back his tears, Chen Qing said, "I'm doing this out of my own will, not under pressure from the Zhu family. If they hesitate, please intervene on my behalf and stress that the break-off suggestion comes from the bottom of my heart. It's not an empty gesture."

"As you wish, as you wish."

Right away, Wang Sanlao rose and went to the Zhu residence.

Zhu Shiyuan greeted him, led him in, and offered him a seat in all politeness. Before Wang had a chance to speak up, Zhu called out loudly for tea. There was a reason for his cordiality: even though Wang Sanlao might not have heard Liu-shi call him names, Zhu Shiyuan felt a twinge of conscience and was afraid that Sanlao was here to complain. Hence the exaggerated courtesy. As it turned out, Liu-shi, in her bitter resentment against Wang Sanlao, the maker of this unfortunate match, ignored her husband's calls and refused to serve tea. This shows how petty-minded a woman can be.

After sitting for a while, Wang Sanlao said, "What I'm going to say may be out of turn, so let me caution you first, Big Brother. Please don't feel offended." Being the first born, Zhu Shiyuan was called Big Brother Zhu in the neighborhood.

"Please say whatever is on your mind," said Zhu Shiyuan. "You didn't do anything wrong. Why should I be offended?"

Wang Sanlao then proceeded to tell him about Chen Qing's offer of withdrawal from the marriage commitment. "This is Mr. Chen's idea," he added. "I'm just the messenger. The decision is yours."

His wife's nagging having driven him to the limit of his patience, Zhu Shiyuan could hardly wait for a break of the marriage alliance, but he couldn't very well bring the matter up himself. Wang Sanlao's words were for him nothing less than an imperial decree of pardon. Overjoyed, he said promptly, "However kind the Chens are, I'm afraid that if they regret later on, there will be more harm than good."

"I've made the same arguments with him, but his mind is made up. Have no doubt. I've also brought back your daughter's horoscope card. Please take it."

"How can we take this back without having first returned their betrothal gifts?"

"He said that the gifts were too modest to be worth mentioning. Being the meddlesome old man that I am, I said that since he was giving back the horoscope card, the betrothal gifts should by rights be returned to him."

"Of course. We had accepted from him twelve taels of silver, all of which I will return to him, not a mace less. And then there are two silver hairpins, but they are with my daughter. I'll get them from her and return them to you. You can keep the horoscope with you for now."

"No, no. You take it back. I'm going home now. I'll be back tomorrow to pick up the betrothal gifts and then return them to the Chens." With that, he bade Zhu Shiyuan good-bye. There is this quatrain in testimony:

> The marriage bond came off;
> The matchmaker's words were all taken back.
> What a remarkable man, that Wang Sanlao!
> The same man who made, then broke the match!

Zhu Shiyuan went to the interior section of the house and relayed to his wife Wang Sanlao's message about the break-off of the engagement. Liu-shi was delighted beyond measure. She even contributed money from her private savings to make up the full amount of twelve taels. After handing it over to her husband, she went to collect the pair of silver hairpins from her daughter.

Now, even though Duofu was unlettered, she was a fiercely proud girl. Already dismayed by her mother's constant grumbling, she now guessed rightly that the demand for the hairpins meant the break-off of the betrothal. Without a word, she walked into her own bedchamber, closed the door, and burst out sobbing.

Being a wise man, Zhu Shiyuan knew from his daughter's reaction what was on her mind. He said to his wife, "Duofu must be upset because of the break-off of the betrothal. You talk gently to her. Don't rush it. If you are too hard on her, she might be driven into doing something foolish. Regrets will be too late by then!"

Mindful of her husband's advice, Liu-shi knocked at her daughter's door and called out, all humbleness, "My child, whether to return the hairpins or not is up to you. Why throw a temper tantrum? Open the door now. Tell your mother what's on your mind. I may let you have your way."

The girl ignored her at first. Only after Liu-shi called out several times did she unbolt the door. "It's open," she said as she sullenly went to sit down on a stool.

Liu-shi picked up another stool, set it next to her daughter, and sat down. (*A vivid description.*) "My child," she said. "Your father and I feel bad for having chosen the wrong husband for you. Luckily, the bridegroom's family is now willing to break off the engagement. This is something that doesn't happen even after ten thousand prayers. That leper will never get well. Won't the marriage ruin your chances? Let's give the hairpins back to them and have a clean break with them. With your good looks, you'll have no lack of good families asking for you. Now, don't be stubborn. Give the hairpins back to them."

The girl kept silently shedding tears. Liu-shi continued to talk gently to her and, observing the state she was in, said in a soothing tone, "My child, your father and I are doing what's best for you. Tell me straight whether you are willing or not. If you keep your misery to yourself, how are you going to make us feel?"

The girl said bitterly, "Doing what's best for me indeed! It's too early to ask for the hairpins back!"

"Good gracious!" exclaimed Liu-shi. "Those two hairpins put together aren't even worth two or three taels. Why worry about such trifles? If you marry into a rich family, you can have all the gold and jade hairpins you want." (*The gentleman sees what is moral; the small man sees what is profitable.*)

"Who cares about gold and jade hairpins!" shot back the girl. "Have you ever seen any good woman taking betrothal gifts from two families? Wealth, poverty, misery or happiness, are all predestined. I am a daughter-in-law of the Chen family while alive and will be a ghost of the Chen family after I die. These hairpins will be buried with me in my grave. Don't even think about giving them back!" Having said those words, she burst into another fit of sobbing.

At her wits' end, Liu-shi reported back to her husband and added, "It looks like we're stuck with this marriage."

Zhu Shiyuan, being a bosom friend of Chen Qing's, had never wanted to cancel the betrothal in the first place. He agreed to the cancellation only because he couldn't put up with his wife's nagging and his ears wanted a little peace and quiet. Pleased that his daughter turned out to be so unyielding, he said, "In that case, don't be too hard on her. Tell her that the betrothal still stands."

Liu-shi told her daughter as much. Only then did the girl hold back her tears. Truly,

> Three winters do not bend the lone pine tree;
> Ten thousand hardships won't shake the proud girl's resolve.

Nothing of note happened further that evening. The next day, without waiting for Wang Sanlao to come, Zhu Shiyuan went to tell him about his daughter's stubborn refusal to retract from the commitment, and gave him back her horoscope card.

"Such a girl is really hard to come by! Hard to come by!" said Wang Sanlao. Right away, he went off to Chen Qing and told him thus and so.

Since Chen Qing hated the thought of breaking off the alliance, he was more than pleased upon hearing that his daughter-in-law remained committed to the betrothal and had rejected his break-off offer. Bowing repeatedly to Wang Sanlao, he said, "I've given you so much trouble! However, I'm afraid that the marriage will be hardly possible if my son doesn't recover. So I may need your services again."

Waving a hand in protest, Wang Sanlao said, "I've already conveyed your message. I'm not going to do this again."

Let us skip unnecessary descriptions and turn our attention to Zhu Shiyuan. Now that his daughter refused to cancel the engagement, Zhu Shiyuan fussed about his son-in-law even more than before. He went everywhere seeking well-known physicians and provided travel money for them to come and treat Duoshou. The physicians who came all began with promises of cure. The enthusiasm even rubbed off on the patient himself as he took his medicine. But as time went by without any improvement in his condition, the enthusiasm began to wear off. Some physicians came with letters of recommendation, talked big, demanded exorbitant fees, and gave assurances, but every attempt to cure faded away after a brave beginning. (*Typical of quacks.*) The days went by, and before they knew it, more than two years elapsed. The physicians now claimed that this was an intractable disease quite beyond cure.

With a sigh, Duoshou asked his parents to come to him and said to them, his eyes misting over, "My father-in-law refuses to break off the engagement and brings famous doctors to me with their medicine, all in the hope of seeing me cured. But no medicine has worked so far. It looks like I'll never get well. Let's not ruin their daughter's chances. I am determined to break off this engagement."

Chen Qing said, "We did make that clear to them. The parents agreed, but the daughter did not. That's why the horoscope card has been returned to us."

"If she knows that it's my wish, she will surely give in."

"My child," said his mother Zhang-shi, "you should care only about your own health. Don't let yourself be bothered by these things."

"If the engagement is canceled, you'll be taking a load off my mind," said Duoshou.

"You can speak directly to your father-in-law when he's here," said his father. Before those words were quite out of his mouth, a maid announced, "Mr. Zhu is here to see his son-in-law."

After Zhang-shi removed herself from this male guest's presence, Chen Qing invited Zhu Shiyuan into the study in the inner part of the house, where Duoshou exchanged greetings with his father-in-law and thanked him profusely. The sight of Duoshou, who looked far more like a ghost than a human, depressed Zhu Shiyuan. After tea, Chen Qing rose and left on some excuse. Duoshou opened his heart to his father-in-law and voiced his determination to call off the betrothal because he would never get well enough to marry. He then took out from his sleeve a card on which was written a quatrain. Zhu Shiyuan opened it and read:

For this unlucky one tormented by illness,
A good marriage destiny goes awry.
On this day, I untie the marriage bond,
So as not to ruin a fine girl's future.

Back when he had first agreed to renounce the betrothal, Zhu Shiyuan had done so under his wife's pressure and against his own inclinations. This time, observing how sickly the boy looked and how firm his tone in the poem, Zhu found himself hardly able to resist the idea. (*Good people are often misled by second thoughts.*) Out loud, he said, "What kind of talk is this! It's more important to take care of your health." With that, he folded up the stationery, slid it into his sleeve, and bid the young man good-bye.

Chen Qing met him in the living room and said, "My son was most sincere in what he said. Please gently talk your daughter around. Here's her horoscope card."

"Since both father and son insist, let me accept it for now but give it to you again in the future."

Chen Qing walked him to the gate.

Upon returning home, Zhu Shiyuan recounted his son-in-law's words to his wife. "Since he doesn't want to get married," said Liu-shi, "it won't make any sense for our girl to wait for him. You explain the poem to her. I believe she'll come around."

Handing the poem to his daughter, Zhu Shiyuan said, "Young Master Chen's health hasn't improved. He told me personally that he is determined to break off the betrothal. This quatrain is in fact his letter of divorce. So you should be thinking of your own future. Don't be stubborn."

Without saying a word after reading the poem, Duofu returned to her room, took out a brush-pen and an ink slab, and wrote a quatrain after the one by Duoshou:

For the unlucky one tormented by illness,
A marriage bond remains a marriage bond.
A woman should serve only one man;
I care not about the flower of youth.

As an old saying goes, "Good news never leaves the house; bad news travels a thousand li." News about Young Master Chen rejecting his wife-to-be and telling so to his father-in-law's face soon spread far and wide. Auntie Zhang, Granny Li, and others who made a living out of matchmaking descended on Zhu Shiyuan's house, all equipped with lists of candidates with impressive backgrounds and offers of lavish betrothal gifts. Even though matchmakers' words were not to be trusted, Liu-shi was quite tantalized and, like Qian Yulian's mother, was eager to dump her son-in-law in favor of a richer man.[8] However, her daughter Duofu remained unshaken in her resolve. Noticing that her mother was treating matchmakers to the finest tea and wine, she knew what was afoot. Since her intended husband was unlikely to recover and her parents refused to let her preserve her chastity, she decided, after thinking long and hard, that it would be best for her to die. By lamplight in the evening, she took out Young Master Chen's poem, put it on the table, and read it over and over again. After weeping for about four hours until her parents were sound asleep, she untied her silk waistband, threw it over a beam in the ceiling, and hanged herself. Truly,

> *Everything is done with the three inches of breath;*
> *All is gone once the last breath goes out.*

It was by now the third watch of the night. Duofu was not meant to die at this time after all. In his sleep, Zhu Shiyuan felt as if he was being shaken and his daughter's sobs came to his ears. With a start, he rubbed his eyes and woke up his wife, saying, "I just heard our daughter cry. Could she be up to something? Go take a look."

His wife said, "She's sleeping in her room. All's well. You're talking nonsense. You go ahead and look if you want to. I'm going back to sleep."

Zhu Shiyuan threw some clothes over his shoulders and got up. In the darkness, he opened the bedroom door and groped his way to his daughter's room. He pushed at the door with both hands, but it did not yield. He called out her name a few times, but there was no response. He heard only the strange sound of the rattling of phlegm in the throat. Appalled, he kicked open the door with all his might and saw, by the almost-extinguished lamp on the table, his daughter's body dangling from a beam and turning round and round like a revolving lantern.

Aghast, Zhu Shiyuan pulled up the wick of the lamp and cried out, "Mother! Come here! She has hanged herself!"

Hearing this in her dream, Liu-shi felt as if she were drenched in cold rain. Without sparing a moment to put on clothes, she threw her quilt over herself and, calling out terms of endearment for her daughter, ran tearfully to the girl's room.

Being a man of some brains after all, Zhu Shiyuan had already taken the girl down. With his knees pressed firmly against her buttocks, he had slowly untied the fast knot on her neck and was gently stroking her. With the shivering Liu-shi calling out her name, Duoshou's souls began to return to her body about an hour later. As the girl started to breathe, Liu-shi thanked heaven and earth, went back to her room, put on her clothes, and went to boil some water. As she poured warm water down her daughter's throat, the girl gradually came to. Opening her eyes and seeing her parents in front of her, she burst into a fit of sobs.

"My child!" said her parents. "Even crickets and ants love life. How could you have tried to kill yourself!"

Duofu replied, "If I died, I could have preserved my good name as a chaste woman. Why did you revive me? If I don't die now, I'll die later. You might as well let me go sooner, so that you won't have to worry about me anymore. It'll be as if you've never had this daughter." With that, she broke down in a flood of tears. Zhu Shiyuan and his wife were not able to stop her, however hard they tried. As soon as it grew light enough, Zhu Shiyuan told his wife to stay with the girl as she rested in bed whereas he himself went to the temple of the city god for a divination. The lot that he drew was inscribed with this quatrain:

> *Good fortune has not yet come;*
> *Ill luck has dogged you in the last few years.*
> *The clouds will disperse to reveal the sun,*
> *Fortune and long life will unite by heaven's will.*

A careful reading of the quatrain confirmed the truth of the first two lines. The third line "The clouds will disperse to reveal the sun" meant that out of the depths of misfortune comes bliss. As for the last line, "Fortune and long life will unite by heaven's will," "fortune" being in the girl's name ["Fortune" is *fu*, as in the girl's name Duofu] and "long life" in the boy's name, ["Long life" is *shou,* as in the boy's name Duoshou], Zhu Shiyuan wondered if it meant that Young Master Chen was to get well one day and that the young couple would marry by the will of heaven, but he could not be sure.

When he returned home, his wife, still sitting in the girl's room, hastened to wave a hand at him. "Hush!" she said. "She has just cried herself to sleep."

The night before, Zhu Shiyuan had seen a card on the table when he was pulling up the lamp wick, but he hadn't had the time to read it. Now he took it out to read and found it to be a poem written by his son-in-law, followed by another quatrain in what he recognized to be his daughter's handwriting. After reading them, he said with a sigh, "What a high-minded girl! We parents should help her with the marriage rather than force her to do what is not right." Whereupon he told his wife about the lines inscribed on the lot he had drawn in the temple of the city god, adding, "That 'fortune' and 'long life' will unite is something destined by the will of heaven. Anyone trying to change that out of petty considerations won't have the blessing of heaven. What's more, since she has taken a vow in her poem to die rather than to live on, how are we going to keep her from doing that again? The slightest inattention on our part and she'll kill herself, and we'll be ridiculed for our lack of moral principles. As I see it, we'd better marry her to the Chen family, partly to show our good will and partly to fulfill her own wishes. And we won't be held responsible for anything that goes wrong. (*Good thinking.*) What do you say, mother?"

Her heart still thumping from the scare her daughter had given her, Liu-shi said, "You decide. I'm in no condition to take care of this!" (*Had Duofu not tried to take her own life, the mother would not have agreed so readily.*)

"I'll go ask Wang Sanlao to do it," said Zhu Shiyuan.

As chance would have it, Zhu Shiyuan had just gone out the door when Wang Sanlao passed by. Zhu stopped him and invited him in. After relating in detail everything that had happened, Zhu said, "I would now like to have the wedding take place. Could you please send the message to them?"

"I've said before that I make, not break, matches. What you're proposing is the right thing to do. I'll surely be of service."

"My daughter has written a poem in response to my son-in-law's poem to express her feelings. If they decline, you can show this to them."

Wang Sanlao took the poems and rose to go. As the two families lived right opposite each other, Wang Sanlao was barely out of the Zhus' house before he had already crossed the Chens' threshold.

Upon hearing that Wang Sanlao was in his house, Chen Qing hastened to come forward to greet him, believing that it was about renouncing the betrothal.

"Sanlao, you must be here to convey a message from the Zhu family," he said.

"Exactly."

"This time, it's my son wishing to break off the engagement. They should have no objections, I presume?"

"I'm here today not to break off, but to confirm the match."

"You jest, Sanlao."

Thereupon Wang Sanlao told him how the girl had tried to take her own life and how the parents had panicked, adding, "They are afraid that something might happen again if they keep their daughter at home. They would rather send her over to serve the young master. I believe this is indeed a good solution every way you look at it. The Zhus will have nothing to worry about and a good name to gain. You and your wife will get a help around the house, and your son will have someone reliable to look after him. Won't that be nice?" (*Thoroughly laying down the facts.*)

"They may have the best of intentions, but I'll have to ask my son if he agrees."

Wang Sanlao gave the card with the matching poems to Chen Qing and said, "Your daughter-in-law has written a poem to match your son's poem. She is very determined. If your son rejects her, it'll be the death of her. Won't that be terrible?"

"I'll give you an answer soon enough."

Right away, Chen Qing went for a consultation with his wife, Zhang-shi. "The girl is so determined to preserve her chastity that I believe she'll be a devoted wife and daughter-in-law," said he. "If she can come and attend to him as a wife, she will do the job better than we do as parents. If by any chance a child is born, even if our son dies, the Chen family name will be carried on. (*Getting into a further aspect of it. So this marriage has six advantages: First, a furtherance of the family relationship. Second, fulfillment of the wish to preserve chastity. Third, peace of mind on the part of the parents. Fourth, a helping hand for the bridegroom's parents. Fifth, someone to attend to the patient. Sixth, hope for a descendant.*) If the two of us make the decision, our son won't say no."

Without a moment's delay, they went to the study and told their son, Duoshou, about what had transpired. Duoshou objected at first but fell silent when the matching poem was shown to him. Construing his silence to mean approval, Chen Qing reported as much to Wang Sanlao, chose an auspicious day for the wedding, and sent over some gifts of clothing and jewelry. Upon learning that the gifts were from the Chen family in preparation for the wedding, Duofu was more than pleased. On the chosen day, the bride was brought into the Chens' house amid the music of pipes, flutes, and drums. Hearing that the leprous son of the Chen family was getting married, the neighbors spread the news around, saying, "A toad gets to eat the meat of a swan." Some unkind idlers made up a four-line song that ran as follows:

The short-lived one happens to be called "Long Life";
The sweet girl chases after the foul smell.
The union beneath the red satin quilt
Will be a battle of fragrance and stench.

Let us get on with our story. After she married into the Chen family, Duofu, now Zhu-shi, proved herself to be gentle and obliging. She looked after Young Master Chen with the utmost devotion. How do we know this?

She waited on him hand and foot;
She gave him every attention.
She brewed the medicinal broths and tried them on herself;
She rose early and retired late;
She hardly had time to undress for bed.
She stroked his aching and itching spots;
She washed and scalded his blood-and-pus stained clothes.
She was a mother caring for a child,
Short of baring her breast to feed him.
She was a devoted wife
Willing to offer her own flesh for soup.
She stayed away from games of clouds and rain;
She worked hard, day after day, year after year.
A wife she was only in name;
This pretty girl, poor thing, had more worries than joys.

Two years went by in this fashion. The bridegroom's parents were pleased at everything except one: The young couple slept apart at night, however genial they were to each other during the day. They never shared a quilt or a pillow. Zhang-shi was hoping for them to consummate the marriage but could not very well bring up the matter. One day, when noticing that the daughter-in-law was not present when she entered their room, she said to her son, "My child, your pillow is soiled. Let me wash it for you." Then she added, "Your quilt is also dirty." She gathered them up into a bundle and carried them out, leaving only one quilt and one pillow on the bed, intending all too clearly for the couple to be together and have children.

The fact was that both the husband and the wife had ideas of their own. Young Master Chen was telling himself, "I'm going to die any day now. The marriage won't last long. Why soil a virgin?"

The young wife Zhu-shi was thinking, "My husband is so ill and so weak. How will he be up to it?" (*How devoted they are to each other! They have proven themselves to be true husband and wife.*) Therefore they had always used separate quilts and separate pillows.

That night, they were left with only one quilt and one pillow, both belonging to the wife. Usually, she from the Zhu family would help her husband go to sleep first. She herself would then do some needlework by the lamp and retire for the night only after her parents-in-law had both gone to bed. That night, when Duoshou, the son, asked his mother for his quilt and pillow back, the latter said, "I've just washed and starched them. They're not dry yet. Make do by sharing one set tonight."

The young wife gave her own set to her husband. Afraid that he would soil her quilt, Duoshou slept in his clothes. Duofu didn't take off her clothes, either. They slept separately as usual.

The next day, upon learning about this, Zhang-shi seethed with resentment against her daughter-in-law for being too high and mighty to engage her son in the consummation of marriage. Construing the young woman's good will to be evil intent, she unleashed her anger on unrelated matters in a stream of harsh words that were obliquely meant for her daughter-in-law.

With her quick mind, Zhu-shi realized what was being referred to but, afraid of hurting her husband's feelings, she pretended not to understand and only shed tears furtively. (*What a good woman! Women like her are far too few!*) Young Master Chen also gained some idea of what was going on and felt deeply apologetic. Another year went by in this manner.

After Young Master Chen had contracted the disease at age fifteen, his condition had grown grave when he was sixteen. At nineteen, he proposed to cancel the engagement but was rejected, and the wedding took place when he was twenty-one. For almost a decade now, he had felt neither dead nor alive and was deeply depressed. He heard that there had newly arrived from south of the Yangzi River a blind fortune-teller called Mr. Wonderful, who was quite candid with his clients. Young Master Chen wanted to go to him to know when he was going to die. Ever since he had gotten ill, Chen Duoshou had rarely left the house because he thought himself too unsightly, but on this day, in order to have his fortune told, he spruced himself up and went to Mr. Wonderful's shop.

The fortune-teller wrote down the eight characters representing the year, month, day, and hour of his birth, matched the positions of the five planets with the five phases [metal, wood, water, fire, and earth] contained in his horoscope, and asked, "How is this person related to you, sir? Please tell me. And I'd venture to speak the truth only if you don't take offense."

Young Master Chen said, "Please tell me the truth. Don't hold back anything."

"This person's first phase in his destiny was from four to thirteen years of age. Since his childhood is already gone, I need not dwell on it. The ten-year period from fourteen to twenty-three is most unfortunate. A vile disease leaves him more dead than alive. Am I right?" (*Fortune-tellers mostly only get it half right. One can't believe everything they say.*)

"Yes, you're right," said Young Master Chen.

"In those ten years, even though the water phase is lacking, he can get by. The period from twenty-four to thirty-three is even worse. The oars and the rudder of the boat are lost among perilous waves; the reins of the horse break on the brink of a cliff. This is the horoscope of a short-lived man. Give me the eight characters of someone with a better fate. This one is not worth wasting my breath on."

The young master was struck speechless. Quickly he paid the fortune-teller and bade him good-bye. As he brooded over the fortune-teller's words, tears fell down his cheeks. He thought, "The fortune-teller was accurate about the past ten years. If the next ten years are even worse, life will be too hard for me. It's all right if I die, but my good wife, poor thing, has never had a night's pleasure with me in all the three years she waited on me. How can I make life even harder for her? But since life is no different from death for me, what good will a few more years do? I'd better die soon, so that she'll be free to find another match while she's still young and pretty."

And so the idea of suicide came to him. When passing by an herb store, he bought some arsenic and hid it on him. After returning home, he said nothing about his fortune-telling trip. When going to bed that night, he struck up a conversation with Zhu-shi and said, "When we were betrothed at nine years of age, the hope was that we would grow up to be a harmonious couple, have children, and set up a household. Who would have foreseen that I would contract this vile disease that's beyond cure? Because I was afraid I would ruin your future, I offered twice to break off the engagement. But you were too kind. You rejected my offers, and we got married. Even though it's been three years since the wedding, we are husband and wife in name only. I wouldn't dream of soiling your body. This is evidence of some decency in me. After I die, you'll still be able to keep your honor. No one will call you a 'second timer.'"

"Husband, being a wedded couple, we are by rights supposed to share both joys and sorrows. Your illness is my fate. Together we live and together we die. Pure and simple. Don't ever suggest again that I remarry."

"You are indeed a determined woman. But you and I sticking together is no solution in the long run. In all the years you've been serving me, you've done more than your share as a wife. If I can't repay you in this life, I will surely do so in the next one."

"Why are you saying such sad things? Between husband and wife, what repayment is there to speak of?"

And so they talked and did not get to sleep until midnight. Truly,

They never talked much as husband and wife,
But opened their hearts to each other that night.

The next day, Young Master Chen chatted for a long time with his parents, loathing to part with his flesh and blood now that he was determined to die. Around dusk, he said to Zhu-shi, "I'd like to have some wine."

"You don't normally drink wine for fear of itching," rejoined Zhu-shi. "Why do you want it now?"

"I don't feel well and I'd like to have some wine. Please heat a pot for me."

Although she had been somewhat suspicious at his ominous tone the night before, Zhu-shi was not thinking along those lines. She got from her mother-in-law a pot of the finest wine, heated it up until the wine was nice and warm, and set a tiny cup and two side dishes on the table.

"I don't want a tiny cup. A tea bowl will be quicker and neater."

Zhu-shi picked up a tea bowl and was about to pour wine into it when he said, "Wait! Let me do it. I don't want the side dishes. Get me some fruit to go with the wine, if you have any."

Having thus sent Zhu-shi away, he removed the lid of the pot of wine, took out the arsenic, emptied it into the pot, and quickly poured out the wine and drank it. Zhu-shi had just taken a few steps before she felt uneasy and turned her head around. Noticing that her husband looked flustered and occupied, she wondered what was wrong. As doubts assailed her mind, she promptly turned back. By this time, he had already finished one bowl and was refilling the bowl.

Finding the color of the wine not quite right, Zhu-shi held down the pot and refused to let her husband take it.

"Let me tell you the truth," confessed Young Master Chen. "There's arsenic in the wine. I want to kill myself and put an end to our suffering. I've already downed one bowlful. I'm beyond rescue. You might as well let me get drunk before I die, to save some trouble." So saying, he snatched away the pot and drank from it.

"I've said before that together we live and together we die," declared Zhu-shi. "If you take poison, I'm not going to live on alone." She seized the pot and drank up in big gulps all that was left. By this time, Young Master Chen was experiencing too much pain in the stomach to be watching her. In a trice, the couple collapsed in a heap to the floor. A poet of the time had this to say:

In his sickness, they had little pleasure;
In death was her devotion made known.
They were ready to die for love;
Such loyalty is worth more than gold.

In the meantime, having learned that her son was asking for wine, Zhang-shi filled a plate with pieces of fried sweet dough and took it personally to his room. Upon reaching the door, she heard the words "take poison." In alarm, she quickened her pace. At the sight of the couple lying on the floor, she knew something terrible had happened and cried out in panic. Chen Qing came to the scene and saw remnants of arsenic in the pot. He knew of an antidote that called for the blood of a freshly killed goat. Forcing the blood down the throat of someone who had taken arsenic would save his life.

The young husband and wife were not destined to die, after all. It so happened that in the neighborhood lived a butcher who sold goat meat. Chen Qing rushed over and asked him to slaughter a goat and get the blood. By this time, Zhu Shiyuan and his wife had also arrived. Chen Qing and his wife forced the blood down their son's throat, and Zhu Shiyuan and his wife did the same to their daughter. Fortunately, the blood induced vomiting and the young couple regained consciousness.

With the remnants of the poison still in their stomachs, their skin cracked and blood flowed out. It was after more than a month of convalescence that they resumed a normal diet. Now, the strangest thing happened: Duofu's recovery was extraordinary enough, but as for Young Master Chen, his illness had lasted for ten years, during which time he had been seen by famous physicians and had taken medicine, all to no avail. As it turned out, the poison in the wine had the all-too-unexpected effect of fighting poison with poison, as prescribed in medical books. Foul blood spurted out of the cracks in his skin. With the detoxification of his body, the lesions on his skin gradually healed. When he was fully recuperated, all the scabs had fallen off and he was his old smooth-skinned self again. Even his own parents did not recognize him when he walked up to them. Indeed, it was as if he had shed his skin, changed the bones, and found another incarnation. This couple's dedication to each other had so deeply moved heaven and earth that even poison turned benign and death turned into life. This is a case of good coming out of misfortune and laughter coming out of tears, bearing out the inscription on the divination lot at the temple of the city god: "The clouds will disperse to reveal the sun,/Fortune and long life will unite by heaven's will."

Chen Duoshou and his wife went to the temple of the city god to burn incense in gratitude. Zhu-shi donated the silver hairpins she had received as part of the betrothal gifts. Hearing about this, Wang Sanlao took some neighbors along and, carrying pots and boxes, went over to offer congratulations. The celebration feasts lasted for several days.

Twenty-four years of age now, Chen Duoshou picked up his studies of the classics and the histories. At age thirty-three, he passed the imperial examinations at the provincial level and at age thirty-four, he became a *jinshi*. Mr. Wonderful had predicted that he would die between twenty-four and thirty-three. As it turned out, the best things in his life happened within this period. Indeed, the mysteries of fate are not meant to be figured out by ordinary people.

Chen Qing and Zhu Shiyuan became even closer friends. They continued to play chess until they died in their eighties. Chen Duoshou rose to be an assistant censor. Duofu, his wife, gave birth to a son and a daughter, and the deeply loving couple lived to a ripe old age. Their clan thrives even to this day. This story is thus called "Husband and Wife Bound in Life and in Death." As the poem says,

> *What paragons of love, Zhu and Chen!*
> *A game of chess led to their marriage.*
> *For their virtues and their devotion,*
> *Heaven bound them in life and in death.*

The Liu Brothers in Brotherhood and in Marriage

One in a robe and a hat may not be a man;
One with fancy headdresses may not be a woman.
Enough strange things have happened since ancient times
To render hills into dales and seas into land.

In the Chenghua reign period [1465–87] of this dynasty [the Ming], there lived a certain Sang Mao, a native of Shandong, who was from a family of modest circumstances. When he was still a boy with rosy cheeks and smooth skin, his parents sent him on a mission one day to a relative's house in the village. On his way there, a heavy rain came down, and he went into a deserted temple for shelter. Seeing an old woman in the temple, also taking shelter from the rain, he sat down beside her.

As the raindrops fell thicker and faster, making it impossible to stick one's head out for even one instant, the old woman began to lead the pretty boy on with suggestive language. Not entirely uninitiated in matters relating to lovemaking, Sang Mao thought that the old woman was soliciting his services as a male partner. But when they went into action, the old woman revealed what was hidden between the thighs and took the boy by his "rear court." (*The fact that the boy was not alarmed shows his depravity.*) The rain had not stopped when they finished.

Being but a boy after all, Sang Mao asked, "How can a woman like you have that thing?"

"Let me be frank with you," said the old woman. "But don't let this on to anyone else. I'm not a woman. I'm a man, but my feet were bound when I was small and I learned how to dress up like a woman and speak softly. I'm also skillful at needlework. I secretly left my home village and, calling myself a widow, asked to be introduced to rich families as a teacher of needlework. The women usually admire my skills and let me stay in the house. So, with free access to the women's quarters, I get to sleep with them and have as much pleasure of them as I want. They grow quite attached to me and keep me for months on end without ever letting me out of the house. In cases of virtuous women who reject me, I apply the 'seduction drug,' which I spray onto their faces with water when they're asleep. After they pass out, I do whatever I want to them. By the time they wake up, I've already had my way with them, and they feel so ashamed that they dare not say a thing. Instead, they give me lavish gifts and send me away, telling me to keep my lips sealed. (*How abominable! This man deserves the death sentence!*) I'm now forty-seven years old. I've been to both capital cities [Beijing and Nanjing during the Ming dynasty] and nine provinces and slept with beautiful women wherever I went. I've always been well provided for. And I've never been caught."

"How wonderful!" exclaimed Sang Mao. "Will I be able to do the same?"

"A boy as pretty as you are will easily pass off as a girl. If you are willing to be my apprentice and travel with me, I'll bind your feet, teach you needlework, and introduce you to people as my niece. You'll get your chance when the time is right. I'll also pass on the formula for the 'seduction drug' to you. It'll do you a lifetime of good."

Sorely tempted, Sang Mao bowed four times in the deserted temple, honoring the old "woman" as his teacher. As soon as the rain stopped, he set out with his teacher on their journey, without completing his mission to his relative's house or going to ask for advice from his family.

And so the teacher and Sang Mao traveled together and slept together. When they were out of the borders of Shandong, the teacher parted Sang Mao's hair into three locks, the way girls' hair was done, took out a blouse from his baggage, and put it on the boy. Then he wrapped up Sang Mao's toes tightly and slipped onto his feet a pair of narrow pointed shoes. Looking quite like a girl now, Sang Mao changed his name to Second Sister Zheng.

When he was twenty-two years old, Sang Mao wanted to bid his teacher farewell and venture out on his own. His teacher gave him these words of advice: "You've got an old head on your young shoulders. You'll surely be taken good care of. But remember this: You must not stay in one place for too long, especially when things go well for you. After five days to two weeks at most, you must move on, to avoid giving yourself away. Another thing: In this line of business, you must keep to women as much as possible and stay away from men. Do not on any account engage in conversations with men. If there are men in the house, try to stay away from them. If a man sees through your disguise, your life will be in danger. (*This is a veteran criminal. Too bad nothing is told about what became of him. If he did not die a violent death in this world, he must have been punished in the netherworld.*) Mark my words!"

Thus instructed, Sang Mao bade him farewell.

Henceforth Sang Mao the imposter traveled far and wide under the name of Second Sister Zheng. Of the two capitals, he went to one, and of the provinces, he visited four. The women he defiled were too many to enumerate.

When his travels took him to a town in Jiangxi at age thirty-two, the women of a wealthy family kept him in the house so that he could impart to them his needlework skills. Loath to tear himself away from the legions of women in the establishment, Sang Mao stayed for more than twenty days and had no intention of leaving. That family had a son-in-law, a Mr. Zhao, who had acquired status as a student of the National University through monetary contributions.

One day, Student Zhao was paying his respects to his mother-in-law in her room when he accidentally ran into Second Sister Zheng. Impressed by her good looks, he told his wife to bring the woman to his own house. (*Just as the teacher had predicted.*) The unsuspecting Second Sister Zheng went there merrily.

As soon as Zheng was invited into the study, Student Zhao clasped her by her waist and demanded that she yield herself to him. Second Sister Zheng would rather die than submit and screamed. Being an uncouth man, Student Zhao was seized with a rush of rage. Recklessly, he pinned Second Sister Zheng to the bed and groped to untie the latter's pants. (*This is a moment an uncouth man can be put to some use.*) Second Sister Zheng's resistance notwithstanding, Student Zhao's hand reached inside and came upon that member of his. Realizing that this was a man disguised as a woman, he summoned his servants, trussed Sang Mao, and delivered him to the government yamen. Sang Mao was beaten at the interrogation session until he confessed his true name and all the sordid things he had done over the years. The prefectural yamen reported the case to higher authorities and all agreed that this was something never heard of before. After reporting the case to the emperor, the Ministry of Justice pronounced that a man posing as a woman violated human decency and constituted an unlawful act punishable by death and dismemberment, and ordered that the death sentence be executed without delay. So, after gaining some advantage by disguising himself as a woman for the better part of his life, that poor thing Sang Mao died at the hands of Student Zhao. Truly,

> *Weal and woe come by the will of heaven;*
> *The laws, fair and just, override emotions.*

The above story, about a man violating common decency by passing himself off as a woman, leads me to my main story, one about a woman who disguised herself as a man but, in doing so, preserved both her chastity and filial piety. Indeed,

> *Fragrant herbs and stinking weeds do not mix;*
> *King Yao and King Jie formed a sharp contrast.[1]*
> *What look alike may well be worlds apart;*
> *The benchmarks provide you with good guidance.*

This story takes place during the Xuande reign period [1426–35], also in this dynasty [the Ming]. An elderly gentleman named Liu De lived in the town of Hexiwu [in present-day Wuqing County, Hebei], located on the banks of the Grand

Canal, about two hundred li from Beijing. This being an important town on the way to and from the capital, boats moored in the canal were as numerous as ants, and carriages and horses went through the town day and night in endless streams. The hundreds of families living along the banks and the marketplaces brought the town great prosperity.

In their sixties now, Liu De and his wife had neither siblings nor children but only a house with a few rooms, dozens of *mu* of land, and a small wineshop in the front section of their house. Mr. Liu, much given to works of charity, was always ready to render assistance to those in need. He did not mind if his clients happened to be short of cash. But whenever he found that he was paid too much, he would invariably take whatever was his due and return the balance to the client without ever taking one cent that he did not deserve. People aware of this habit of his asked him, "You can very well keep and enjoy what's given to you by mistake. Why give it back?"

He replied, "I have no children, most probably because I did not do enough good deeds in my previous incarnation. I will have no one to make sacrificial offerings to my spirit after I die. With such a punishment, how can I do dishonest things again? If I gain one cent that's not destined to be mine and run into trouble or fall ill as a result, I'll only end up paying more. It's not worth it. I'd rather give back the money and enjoy peace of mind."

Out of admiration for his honesty and fair-mindedness, the people of the town called him Venerable Elder Liu.

One wintry day, amid cutting blasts of the north wind and dense masses of dark cloud, a snowstorm came on and lasted the whole day. Behold:

> It swirls its way through portieres and window curtains;
> It starts with a few flakes but soon thickens
> Until the air is filled with
> Dancing willow catkins and falling pear blossoms.
> The bamboo leaves transmit their soft swish;
> The plum branches convey their sweet fragrance.
> Soldiers up north put on armor to fend off the cold;
> Hermits in the hills wrap themselves in warm quilts.
> Young princes drink from golden vessels at the feast table;
> Beautiful maidens add beast-shaped charcoal to the burning stoves.

To keep warm in this cold weather, Mr. Liu heated a pot of wine. He and his wife then sat down facing the fire to enjoy the wine. After they drank for a while, they rose and went to the door to watch the snow. From afar there came a man, with a bundle on his back, walking with a boy in the wind and snow. As they drew near, the man suddenly fell on the snow-covered ground. As he struggled in vain to get up, the boy tried to help him but lacked the necessary strength. As they pulled at each other, both slipped. They fell in a heap and tumbled like a dumpling. When they finally rose to their feet after much crawling, Mr. Liu rubbed his age-dimmed eyes and saw that the man, about sixty years old, was wearing leggings, a pair of rope sandals, and tattered clothes. The boy had fine and delicate features and was wearing a pair of small, cotton-padded boots. (*The small boots remind one of Mulan. Intriguing.*)[2]

Beating the snow off himself, the old man said to the boy, "My child, I'm cold. I can't walk anymore in all this wind and snow. Let's buy a pot of wine from this shop to warm ourselves up before we continue."

And so they entered the shop. The man sat down at a table and laid the bundle on it. The boy sat down by his side. Mr. Liu heated up a pot of wine, cut enough slices of beef to fill up a plate, put them in a tray along with two side dishes, two cups, and two pairs of chopsticks, and carried the tray over to them. After he set it down on their table, the boy picked up the pot, filled one cup, and offered it with both hands to his father before pouring some for himself.

Impressed by the boy's observance of proper etiquette, Mr. Liu asked, "Is this your son, sir?"

"Yes, he is."

"How old is he?"

"Twelve. His pet name is Shen'er."

"What is your honorable surname, sir? Where are you going in this big snowstorm?"

"I'm Fang Yong. I'm a guard in the Beijing garrison, on my way back to my hometown, Jining of Shandong, to get my allowance.[3] I certainly didn't expect to be caught in a snowstorm. What is your honorable surname?"

"My surname is Liu. The shop sign bears my humble sobriquet Jinhe [Near the River]. Now, Jining is quite far from here. Why don't you rent a draft animal to make your journey easier?"

"How can a poor soldier like me afford a draft animal? We'll just have to make our way there little by little."

Noticing that the two were only helping themselves to the vegetables and the wine but leaving the meat untouched, Mr. Liu asked, "Officer, are you and your son vegetarians?"

"Soldiers are no vegetarians!"

"If not, why haven't you touched the meat?"

"To be honest with you, I may not have enough money to reach home even if we keep to vegetables and rice only. This plate of meat will cost us several days' worth of provisions. How are we going to get home?"

Saddened by the man's poverty, Mr. Liu said, "You need some wine as well as meat to ward off the cold in such heavy snow. Just eat your fill. It's on the house."

"Don't make fun of me! How can I eat without paying?"

"Officer, the fact is, this shop is unlike any other. I never charge those who happen to be hard up. Since you are short of traveling money, consider this my treat."

Realizing that Mr. Liu did indeed mean it, the soldier said, "Thank you so much for your kindness, but, as they say, 'Taking undeserved rewards is a sin.' I will surely repay you on my way back."

"Well, another saying goes, 'All men within the four seas are brothers.' You need not be so polite over such trifles!"

Only then did the old soldier raise his chopsticks to pick up the meat. Mr. Liu then brought over two bowls of rice, saying, "You need a full stomach to get on with your journey."

"This is too much!" exclaimed the soldier.

Both father and son being famished, they lifted the bowls of rice and wolfed down everything until they were full. Truly,

> Help those who are in distress;
> Give to those who are in need.
> The thirsty drink with more delight;
> The hungry eat with greater relish.

The meal over, Mr. Liu had his wife bring them two cups of hot tea. As the soldier took out silver to pay the bill, Liu stopped him, saying, "I just said that it was my treat. How can I take your money? If I did, it would look like I was trying to sell you that plate of meat. You keep your money. You'll need it during the rest of your journey."

The old soldier withdrew his hand and, with profuse thanks, put his bundle on his back, bade Mr. Liu farewell, and went out the door. The snowflakes were now falling so thick and fast that one couldn't have seen a person standing right in front of him. As the full force of the cold wind struck them, they staggered a few steps back. The boy said, "Father, how are we going to make it through such heavy snow?"

"We'll just have to press ahead until we see an inn."

Mr. Liu's heart ached when he saw tears falling from the boy's eyes. "Officer," he intervened. "What's the hurry? Why suffer like this in such a bad snowstorm? We've got an extra room and an extra bed. Why don't you stay here until it clears up? You'll still be in good time!"

"Yes, that would be best," said the soldier. "But we shouldn't be putting you to such inconvenience."

"Nonsense! Have you ever seen any traveler on the road carrying a house on his head? Come in, quick! Don't get wet!"

The old soldier reentered the house, with the boy in tow. Mr. Liu led them to a room, where the soldier put down his bundle and saw that there was a bed complete with a mat and a layer of straw. Afraid that they would still not be warm enough, Mr. Liu brought out another bundle of straw and spread it on the bed. The soldier opened his bundle, took out a quilt, and rolled it out over the straw.

As the hour was not yet too late, the father and son went out of their room after they had settled down. Mr. Liu had already closed the shop and was sitting with his wife by the fire. Seeing the guests coming out of their room, he cried out, "Officer Fang! If you're cold, we've got a fire going here. Come and warm yourselves up!"

"That would be nice," said the soldier. "But is it proper—in your wife's presence?"

"We're too old to be concerned about that!" rejoined Mr. Liu. Only then did the soldier and the boy walk over and sit down by the fire.

Feeling that he knew Mr. Liu well enough by now to call him by his sobriquet, the soldier said, "Jinhe, why are there just the two of you? Do your sons live elsewhere?"

"To be frank with you," replied Mr. Liu, "my wife and I are both sixty-four years old, and we've never had children. Certainly no son."

"Why didn't you adopt one? At least you would have someone to take care of you in your old age."

"I did want to," said Mr. Liu. "However, I've seen how some adopted sons not only can't be depended on but also make their parents' lives miserable. It's better to stay childless and enjoy some peace and quiet than to have such sons. Also, even if we wanted one, we wouldn't have found one to our liking if we didn't take our time looking around. That's why we gave up the idea. How nice if we could have someone like your son! But that's hardly likely."

And so they chatted. As it grew late, the soldier asked for a lamp, said goodnight to Mr. and Mrs. Liu, and retired to the guest room with his son. To the boy, he said, "My child, we are lucky to have run into such good people. If it weren't for them, we would have frozen to death. Tomorrow, let's leave early, snow or no snow. I feel bad for having put them to such trouble."

"Yes, father."

Thereupon, father and son went to bed to sleep.

As it turned out, the old soldier had caught a cold. After midnight, growing fiery hot and short of breath, he asked for some hot water, but, being in an alien place, the boy did not know where to get any.

When dawn came at last, the boy got up and went out the door. He realized that Mr. Liu and his wife had not risen. Not wishing to disturb them, he returned to the guest room, closed the door, and stood by the bed to keep watch over his father. Before long, he heard Mr. Liu cough. Immediately he rushed out the door.

"Young Master," said Mr. Liu upon seeing him. "You're up early!"

"My father started to run a fever last night, sir. He was short of breath and asked for water. That's why I'm up early."

"Good gracious! So he caught a cold yesterday! He must not drink cold water. Let me boil some water for him."

"I can't trouble you with that, sir!"

Mr. Liu asked his wife to boil a large pot of water. He then carried the hot water to the guest room. The boy helped his father sit up and drink two bowls of the water. Seeing that Mr. Liu was there, the soldier said thankfully, "You're so kind! What can I do for you in return?"

Mr. Liu went up to him and said, "Don't say that. Take it easy and keep warm. You'll be all right again if you get a good sweat."

The boy helped his father lie down. Mr. Liu tucked the old man in. As he did so, he noticed that the quilt was too thin. "That's why you caught a cold," he said. "Such a thin quilt won't get you a good sweat."

Mrs. Liu was at the door at this point. Hearing this, she went to get a large and thick cotton-padded quilt. Returning to the guest room with the quilt, she said, "Old man, I've got a quilt here for him. You tuck him in well. This cold weather is not to be taken lightly." (*This old couple do good deeds with the same heart and mind. Why are such people childless?*)

The boy took over the quilt. Mr. Liu tucked the old man in tightly before leaving the room. A short while later, after combing his hair and washing, Mr. Liu went to the guest room again and asked, "Any sweat?"

The boy replied, "I just felt him. There was no sweat at all."

"If so, this is a really bad cold. Let me get a doctor to prescribe some medicine and induce a sweat. Otherwise, the chill in him won't be gotten rid of."

"Sir, we don't have money. We can't afford a doctor and medicine."

"You don't have to worry about this," said Mr. Liu. "I'll take care of it."

The boy kowtowed and said, "I'm ever so grateful to you, sir, for trying to save my father's life. You are so kind! If I can't repay you in this life, I'll repay you as a dog or a horse in my next life."

Mr. Liu quickly raised him to his feet and said, "Don't do this. Since you're my guests, consider me your own family. How can I look on without doing anything? Now, stay by your father's side and take good care of him. I'll go get a doctor."

By this time the sky had cleared up. The storm was over. The snow that had accumulated on the ground had been trampled by carriages and horses into a muddy slush more than a foot deep. Wearing a pair of wooden sandals, Mr. Liu stepped out onto the street and turned back into the house after one brief look around. Seeing him returning, the boy thought that he had given up. Tearfully, he was about to go forward and ask when he saw Mr. Liu leading a donkey out of a shed behind the house. To the boy's relief, he mounted the donkey and went off.

Luckily, the doctor lived nearby and arrived before long, also riding a donkey. A servant followed behind, carrying a medicine box. They dismounted at the door, and Mr. Liu invited the doctor into the main hall. After tea was served, he led the doctor into the guest room. The old soldier had fallen unconscious.

The doctor took his pulse and said, "His fever is caused by repeated bouts of cold. The chill has deeply lodged under the pores. According to medical literature, fever caused by repeated bouts of cold is beyond cure, because the resulting yin and yang imbalance is a poison that can kill in seven days. This is incurable. Another doctor may tell you that there is hope. I'm an honest man. I don't lie. No medicine will work in this case."

The boy was aghast. His tears falling like rain, he prostrated himself on the floor and said, "Please take pity on my father and on me, doctor. We are travelers on the road. Please do prescribe some medicine and save his life. We'll never forget your kindness!"

The doctor raised him to his feet and said, "It's not that I'm making things difficult for you. The patient is too far gone. There's nothing I can do."

"Doctor," put in Mr. Liu. "As they say, 'Medicine can't kill, and Buddha only delivers predestined believers.' You need not stick to traditional ways. Just follow your own inclinations and be bold and decisive. Maybe he is not destined to die at this time. Maybe he'll recover, for all we know. But if he doesn't, surely we won't blame you."

"If you say so, sir, I'll give him a dose of medicine. If he breaks into a sweat after taking it, he'll have a chance. Let me know as soon as possible, and I'll prescribe some more. If he doesn't break into a sweat, there's no hope, and you need not come for me."

He had his servant open the medicine box and picked herbs from different compartments to make up a dose. Handing the package to Mr. Liu, he said, "Add ginger to it to make it work better. Go now and make the brew. There's only a minimal chance. Don't get your hopes up too high."

Mr. Liu took the medicine and, handing the doctor a package containing a hundred cash, said, "Please take this trifle just for good luck."

Refusing to take the money, the doctor departed.

Mr. Liu and his wife brewed the medicine and brought it to the guest room. With the boy's help, they raised the patient to a sitting position, fed him the soup, and covered him from head to foot with the quilt. The boy stayed by his side to keep watch over him.

Having spent the whole morning busying himself with the patient, Mr. Liu had neglected his business. Nor did he have time to cook. He didn't eat breakfast until noon. He asked the boy to join him at breakfast, but the boy was too worried about his father's critical condition to be hungry. It was after much persuasion that the boy ate half a bowl of rice. Later in the day, they felt the patient's body but did not find a drop of sweat. Even Mr. Liu panicked. When he went again to seek the services of the doctor, the latter refused to come. On exactly the seventh day, the soldier passed away. Indeed,

> *Everything is done with the three inches of breath;*
> *All is gone once the last breath goes out.*

The boy Shen'er collapsed to the floor, weeping. A pitiful sight it was. Mr. Liu and his wife, watching him cry so bitterly, also broke down in tears. They raised him to his feet and said, trying to calm him down, "Young Master Fang, the dead won't come to life again. Crying doesn't help. You have your own health to take care of."

The boy fell on both knees and said tearfully, "I lost my mother the year before last. She hasn't had a proper burial. My father and I were planning to return to our hometown to raise some money and go back for the burial. We never expected that we would run into such a heavy snowstorm and such hardships on the road. We were most fortunate to have met you, our benefactors. You offered us wine and food and kept us overnight. It's too bad that we didn't have the blessing of heaven and father fell ill. You, sir, engaged a doctor, served my father medicine, and watched over him day and night. You are kinder to us than our own flesh and blood. My father and I only hoped that we could do something for you in return after he recovered. Who would have thought that my father would never rise again? We've let you down. I have no one else to turn to in this place and I have no money. I can't afford his burial clothes and coffin. Could you, sir, make arrangements for a small burial place for my father's body? I will gladly be your servant for the rest of my life in repayment for your great kindness. Would you agree, sir?" With that, he prostrated himself on the floor.

Mr. Liu raised him and said, "Don't worry! I'll take care of the funeral. How can he be buried without a proper coffin?"

The boy again bowed and said, sobbing, "It already exceeds all my expectations that my father's bones get to be buried underground. How can I put you to additional expense! When can I ever pay you back?"

"I'm always ready to do these things. I don't expect repayment."

Right away, Mr. Liu took out some silver and went to buy burial clothes and a coffin. He then hired two gravediggers, encoffined the body, prepared sacrificial food, and burned paper coins. The boy's grief need not be described here. The coffin was then carried to the empty lot behind the house and buried. A tablet was raised over the grave with the inscription "Grave of Fang Yong, guard of the Beijing garrison."

Everything done, the boy bowed again to Mr. and Mrs. Liu in gratitude. Two days later, Mr. Liu said to him, "I had a mind to tell you to go to your hometown, visit your relatives, and then return here and escort the coffin back home. But I'm afraid you are too young to know how to get there. So you can stay with us for now. If any acquaintance of yours happens to pass by here, I'll have him take you back to your hometown. We'll then think of a way to send the coffin back. What do you say?"

The boy fell to his knees and said tearfully, "Without repaying any of the immense kindnesses you have done for me, how can I talk about returning home? You don't have children. However unworthy I am, I'll be glad to be a servant to you and wait on you day and night, to do my filial duties to you in my humble way. In the future, after you pass away, I will take care of your graves. I will then return to Beijing to bring my mother's remains back here, bury both my parents next to your graves, and live here for the rest of my life. Such is my wish."

Mr. and Mrs. Liu were immensely delighted.

"If you're willing to do this, you are the one sent by heaven to be our son," said Mr. Liu. "We would never let you be a servant. From now on, we are your parents, you are our son."

"Since you are so kind as to accept me, let me honor you as my father and mother in the proper manner right now." So saying, he moved two chairs over to the middle of the room, asked the old couple to sit down, and bowed four times to each parent. He changed his surname to Liu. However, Mr. Liu didn't have the heart to suppress the boy's own surname altogether. So he used the boy's original surname Fang as his given name and called him Liu Fang. Henceforth, the boy worked assiduously from morning to night, waiting on Mr. and Mrs. Liu as a most filial son. The old couple, on their part, treated him as if he were their very own son. There is a poem in testimony:

> Liu Fang was their son though not born to them;
> Liu De had no offspring but was now blessed with one.
> The boy served parents both dead and alive;
> The old soldier passed away but never died.

Time flew like an arrow. Before they knew it, two years had gone by since Liu Fang had settled in Mr. Liu's house. It was late autumn. After more than two weeks of high winds and a heavy rain, the water level in the canal rose about a hundred feet and the churning and chopping waves capsized many boats. One afternoon, Liu Fang was cleaning up the shop and putting things in order when he heard a commotion outside. He rushed out to see if something was on fire but instead saw a dense crowd gathered on the shore. Everyone was staring at the river. Quickly he made his way through the crowd and saw a large wind-damaged passenger boat floating downstream. Most of the passengers had fallen into the water. The remaining ones were holding on to the masts and the rudder and crying out for help.

Those on the shore did want to help, but the choppy waves were too rough for anyone to dare jump in at the risk of his own life. Watching the passengers fall into the water one by one, they cried, "Poor thing!" And that was it.

Suddenly, a gust of strong wind blew the boat to shore. The crowd exclaimed, "Good!" In a trice, more than twenty hooks were cast out. The boat was thus held in place and more than ten passengers were rescued and taken to different inns. Among the rescued was a teenage boy. Wounded by the hooks and unable to walk, he collapsed onto the ground. He had difficulty breathing, but he still held on tightly to a bamboo chest, refusing to let it go. The sight evoked in Liu Fang memories of what had happened to him that winter, and tears rolled down his cheeks before he knew it. He thought, "This young man is just as wretched as I was. If it were not for Mr. Liu, both my father and I would have died without even a burial place.

Now this young man needs help. Let me go back and tell Father and Mother about this, so that his life can be saved."

He dashed off back home and told Mr. and Mrs. Liu about what he saw, adding that he would like to bring the young man home and nurse him back to health.

"That's nice," said Mr. Liu. "It'll gain you credit in the next world. That's the right thing to do."

"Why didn't you bring him home with you?" asked Mrs. Liu.

"I didn't dare do it without first getting your approval."

"Nonsense!" said Mr. Liu. "Let me go with you."

The father and son went to the shore, where a crowd had gathered around the youth. Mr. Liu thrust his way through the crowd and exclaimed, "Young man! Hang on! Let me get you to my home so that you can recover."

The youth opened his eyes and nodded.

Mr. Liu and Liu Fang leaned forward and tried to raise him, but one being too young and the other too old, they didn't have enough strength. At this point, a sinewy young man approached them and said to Mr. Liu, "Step aside, sir. Let me do it." Effortlessly he raised the wounded youth to his feet. With the sinewy young man on the right and Mr. Liu on the left, they supported the youth under the arms and helped him along. Though incapable of speech, the young man's mental faculties remained intact and he kept pouting his lips toward the bamboo chest.

"Let me carry the chest for you," said Liu Fang. He put the chest on his shoulder and walked in front to lead the way. The crowd parted to let them through and then followed on their heels to watch.

Someone who knew Mr. Liu commented, "Mr. Liu is, after all, more compassionate than everyone else. No one was kind enough to offer shelter to that poor young out-of-towner all the while he lay there. Mr. Liu somehow got word of it and came to take him to his own home. There are all too few people like him in this world. Too bad he doesn't have a son. The gods are not fair."

Another man remarked, "It's true that no son has been born to him, but his adopted son Liu Fang is very dutiful, even more so than a birth son might be. This is something of a reward from heaven."

Those who did not know Mr. Liu thought that the youth was related to the two men helping him along and to the boy carrying his bamboo chest. But when they learned the truth from the locals, they all burst into praise for Mr. Liu's kindness. There were also some mean-spirited people who wondered whether that bamboo chest was empty or laden with riches. Indeed, people may look alike in the face but are certainly different at heart. (*If they had seen riches laden in that chest, they would have offered him their arms long ago.*) But let us get on with our story.

So Mr. Liu and the sinewy young man supported the wounded youth under the arms and went to Mr. Liu's house. After arrival, Mr. Liu sat him down in a guest room. Mr. Liu thanked the sinewy young man, and the young man took himself off. Liu Fang set the bamboo chest by the wounded youth's side. Mrs. Liu quickly had him change into dry clothes and helped him lie down in bed. Knowing that people who had fallen into water must not drink hot wine, Mr. Liu had his wife warm up some strong wine only slightly and let him drink his fill. They then covered him with Liu Fang's quilt and had Liu Fang keep him company for the night.

The next morning, when Mr. Liu went into the guest room to check on his condition, the youth was already feeling much better. Eagerly he struggled to sit up, meaning to get off the bed and say his thanks. Mr. Liu quickly stopped him and said, "Don't overtax yourself. You need to recuperate well."

The young man kowtowed, knocking his head against the pillow, and said, "Sir, you saved me when I was on the verge of death. You are a parent of my rebirth. What is your honorable name, may I ask?"

"My humble surname is Liu."

"It's the same as mine!"

"Where are you from?"

"I am Liu Qi, from Zhangqiu of Shandong. Two years ago, I followed my father to Beijing for the three-session examination for incumbent officials. We ran into bad luck and caught an epidemic. Both my parents died a few days after contracting the disease. I didn't have the means to buy coffins and take their bodies to our hometown. I had to opt for cremation." Pointing at the bamboo chest, he continued, "I was carrying their bones for a simple burial when the boat capsized. I thought I was going to die, but then heaven sent you to save my life. With all my baggage gone and nothing left on me, how am I going to repay you for your great kindness?"

"You are quite mistaken!" said Mr. Liu. "Compassion is human nature. As they say, 'Saving a human life is better than building a seven-story stupa.' If you talk about repayment, you make it look like I'm after material gains. That's certainly not the case."

Liu Qi felt even more grateful.

After two more days of rest, Liu Qi was able to get out of bed. He kowtowed to Mr. and Mrs. Liu and thanked them tearfully. Liu Qi proved to be a youth with a gentle nature and good manners. Mr. and Mrs. Liu took such a great liking to him that they treated him to good wine and food day in and day out. Overwhelmed by their hospitality, Liu Qi felt uneasy and thought of returning home, but his wounds from the hooks festered and made walking difficult, nor did he have any travel money. He had no choice but to stay on. Indeed,

> However dear to heart his native town,
> He made his home where he was shown great kindness.

Liu Fang and Liu Qi, of about the same age, found each other compatible. Upon exchanging the stories of their lives, they realized that they even shared a similar background. And so they swore brotherhood and loved each other as if they were born brothers. (*Of one heart and mind.*)

One day, Liu Qi said to Liu Fang, "My younger brother, why doesn't a nice young man like you take up the study of the classics and the histories?"

"I do wish to do so, but there's no one to teach me."

"To be frank with you, I did a lot of reading when I was a child and was quite learned about current and past events. I had my sights set on a career as a scholar-official. But I haven't had the mood to pursue my studies ever since my parents passed away. If you're interested in learning, find some books. I'll teach you."

"What a lucky person I am!" exclaimed Liu Fang. Without a moment's delay, he went to tell Mr. Liu about this. Delighted beyond measure upon hearing that Liu Qi was quite a scholar and willing to teach Liu Fang, Mr. Liu immediately went out and bought many books. Liu Qi gave his utmost in his teaching and Liu Fang proved himself to be exceedingly intelligent and understood the texts upon the first reading. During the day, he took care of business in the shop. In the evening, he studied by the lamp. In a matter of a few months, he became well versed in classic writings. (*How fast! How lovely!*)

After living for about half a year in Mr. Liu's house, where everyone respected and loved one another as if they were related by blood, Liu Qi still felt uneasy for being so well provided for without having to work for it. His wounds having long since healed, he wanted to return to his hometown. To Mr. Liu he said, "I'm ever so grateful to you and Mrs. Liu for having saved my life and letting me stay for half a year. I can never thank you enough for your kindness. But I would like to bid you good-bye for now and carry my parents' bones home for burial. I will seek ways to repay you after the three-year mourning period is over."

"How can we stop you from this filial act?" said Mr. Liu. "But when are you leaving?"

"Now that I've told you about this, I'll depart tomorrow."

"In that case, let me find you a boat that happens to be going in the direction of your hometown," said Mr. Liu.

"It's too dangerous to travel by water, and I have no travel money. It's easier to take the road."

"To take the road, you'll have to rent a draft animal. The cost can be several times higher than by water. And you'll get more tired, too."

"I don't need a draft animal. I'll walk."

"You're too weak to walk over such a long distance."

"Sir, as the saying goes, 'If you have money, enjoy. If you don't, work.' I'm poor. Why would I be afraid of tiring myself out?"

After a moment of reflection, Mr. Liu said, "That can be easily taken care of." He had his wife prepare wine and a send-off feast for Liu Qi. In the midst of the drinking, Mr. Liu said between sobs, "Since you and I met by chance half a year ago, we've been like one family. I really hate to see you go. But burying deceased parents is important for any son. I can't force you to stay. And yet, after you leave, I wonder when we will ever see you again!" With that, he broke down in a fit of sobbing. Mrs. Liu and Liu Fang also shed tears. (*This old couple do have tender feelings. That's why their affection is reciprocated by the two sons.*)

Liu Qi also wept. He said, "I have no other choice. As soon as the mourning period is over, I'll come here posthaste to serve you. Please don't feel too bad."

"We are both getting on seventy," said Mr. Liu. "Like candles flickering in the wind, we may be gone any time now. We may not be here when you return after the mourning period is over. If you don't object, could you come for a visit right after you bury your parents' bones, just for old time's sake?"

"Of course, if you say so!"

The night went by without further ado. Early the next morning, Mrs. Liu served Liu Qi wine and breakfast. Mr. Liu placed a bundle on the table, had Liu Fang lead the little donkey out from behind the house, and said to Liu Qi, "I've kept this donkey for a long time now. This old man is not going to make any long-distance journeys. You take it, so that you won't have to pay for a draft animal along the way. In the bundle there are a quilt and some cheap clothes, just for you to keep off the cold." From his sleeve he retrieved a packet of silver and, handing it to Liu Qi, he continued, "Here are three taels of silver. If you use them sparingly, they should last until you get home. But after the burial, be sure to come back for a visit. Don't go back on your word."

At the sight of so many gifts, Liu Qi kowtowed and said, weeping, "I'll never be able to repay you in this life for such kindness. Let me repay a tiny fraction of it as a dog or a horse in my next life."

"Nonsense!" said Mr. Liu.

Right away, Liu Qi loaded the bundle and the bamboo chest onto the donkey's back, said his farewell, and set out. Mr. and Mrs. Liu saw him out the door and bade him a tearful farewell. Liu Fang could not bear seeing him go and walked with him for ten li before they parted company. Truly,

> They met by chance, but they became family;
> At the parting, their tears flowed in streams.
> The farewell song over, they looked forward to dreams,
> As the distance between them grew wider.

Liu Qi traveled by day and rested by night, stopping for food and drink only when he felt the need. In a matter of days, he arrived at his hometown in Shandong. As it turned out, that severe rainstorm the year before had caused the Yellow River to overflow. The village and town of Zhangqiu had been swept away. All the people, animals, and houses had vanished without a trace. Looking into the distance, he saw no signs of human habitation over an expanse of dozens of li of land. With nowhere to go, Liu Qi had no alternative but to find lodging at an inn. He had a mind to stay on and bury the bones there, but, without a home, he would not be able to make a living. He must have his own quarters before taking the next course of action. And so he went to nearby villages and towns in search of relatives, but all to no avail. More than a month later, when the three taels of silver were about to run out, he panicked. "If the money is all gone," he thought, "I won't be able to do anything. I'd better go back to Hexiwu and ask my benefactors to give me an empty lot so that I can bury the bones and continue to live with them. That would be a better way out." He paid the innkeeper his bill, mounted the donkey, and headed for the Liu residence posthaste.

Getting off the donkey upon arrival, he saw that Liu Fang was in the shop, reading a book that he held in his hand.

"My good young brother! Have Mr. and Mrs. Liu been well?"

Liu Fang flung down his book when he saw that it was Liu Qi and rushed out to lead the donkey to the back of the house. He unloaded the baggage and then said, with a bow to Liu Qi, "Father and Mother have been thinking of you day and night. They'll be so glad to see you!"

Together they walked into the main hall. Upon seeing Liu Qi, Mr. and Mrs. Liu went delirious with joy. "Young man!" they exclaimed. "We missed you so much!"

Liu Qi walked up to them and threw himself at their feet. Mr. Liu bowed in return. After this exchange of greetings, Mr. Liu asked, "So, have you buried your parents' bones?" Tearfully Liu Qi gave a detailed account of his experience in his hometown, adding, "There's no place for me to stay in my hometown. I've brought the bones back with me and would like to ask that you give me a piece of land to bury them. I'll honor you as father and live with you and serve you every day. Would you approve?"

"I do have vacant lots. Take your pick! But I wouldn't presume to take you on as a son."

"So you don't approve because I'm unworthy?" With that, he made Mr. and Mrs. Liu take the seats of honor and, there and then, formally honored them as his parents. (*When the morally superior have sons, the whole family becomes a paragon of virtue and honor. Mr. Liu is hereby blessed with a son.*) He then buried his own parents' bones in the lot behind the house.

Henceforth the two brothers worked with one heart and mind, attending to the business, and family circumstances began to prosper. In serving their parents, they did every possible thing expected of the most filial sons. No one in the entire town did not admire the childless Mr. Liu for having thus gained two sons. This was a case of virtue getting its due.

Time sped by. Soon another year elapsed. The father and sons contentedly went about their business. However, Mr. Liu and his wife, both being old and on the decline, succumbed to illness. The two sons attended to them day and night without even taking the time to undress for bed. They prayed to the gods and engaged physicians, but all to no avail. When it looked like all hope was gone, the two sons were stricken with grief. Yet, afraid of distressing their parents, they talked to them in comforting words and wept only when their parents were out of hearing.

Knowing that he was not going to get well, Mr. Liu called his two sons to his bed and said, "Your mother and I thought we were going to die childless. We never expected that the gods in their infinite compassion would give the two of you to us. You may be adopted, but you are dearer to us than even birth sons might be. I'll have no regrets when I die. After I'm gone, the two of you must work together to keep what modest inheritance I leave you. If so, I'll rest easy under the Nine Springs."

The two sons kowtowed tearfully and promised to do as told. Two days later, Mr. and Mrs. Liu died, one after the other. The two sons burst into heart-wrenching wails of grief. How they wished they could die in their parents' stead! (*The two sons' grief was not enough to repay their parents for their kindness.*) They bought lavish burial clothes and coffins and engaged monks for nine days and nights of prayers to assist their parents' souls in passing into the other world. After the bodies were encoffined, the two brothers planned to build a large grave site so that the parents of the three families could be buried together. (*Right thing to do.*)

Liu Fang traveled to Beijing and brought back his mother's coffin. On a chosen auspicious day, they buried Mr. and Mrs. Liu in the middle grave, Liu Qi's parents' bones in the one on the left, and Liu Fang's parents' remains in the one on the right. The three grave mounds stood like a chain of pearls. (*Fulfillment of filial obligations in a triple sense. Exemplary.*) All the residents of the town came to attend the funeral out of admiration for Mr. Liu's honesty and kindness as well as for the two brothers' filial piety.

Let us not encumber our story with unnecessary details but move on. After Mr. and Mrs. Liu died, the two brothers slept together and ate their meals together, and their devotion to each other deepened. They closed the wineshop and began to deal in fabrics. Traveling merchants who passed by and bought from them spread word far and wide about the two young men's honesty and fair prices. Their reputation drew so many customers that their shop was filled to bursting. In one to two years' time, their business grew several times larger than when Mr. Liu was alive. They hired two servants, who brought their own families, as well as two page boys, and acquired elegant furniture and utensils. Impressed by the two young bachelors' prosperous circumstances, a few rich families in the town made marriage proposals through matchmakers. Liu Qi was quite interested, but Liu Fang firmly rejected all offers.

"My brother," said Liu Qi, trying to talk him around. "You're nineteen, and I'm twenty-two. This is high time for us to marry, so that we can have children to carry on the three families' lines. Why don't you want to do that?"

Liu Fang replied, "You and I should devote these best years of our youth to our business rather than waste our time on such matters. What's more, we loving brothers have always been living in peace. If wives come in and they turn out to be bad women, there will be a strain on our relationship. If this is how things will turn out, we'd better stay bachelors." (*One has been in love all this time, like the girl who was Song Yu's neighbor. The other is oblivious to the sentiment, though not the way Mr. Liuxia was.*)[4]

"I don't agree," said Liu Qi. "As the saying goes, 'A woman makes a house a home.' You and I are too busy attending to business in the shop. The inner part of the house is neglected. Also, our circle of acquaintances is expanding. If we have guests coming and there's no one to take care of dinner, we won't look too good. But that's a trivial thing. The important thing is that when our father adopted us, he said he wanted us to have children to carry on the family name and to keep watch over his grave generation after generation. If we don't marry, the family line will end with us. Won't we be going against his wishes? How are we going to face him under the Nine Springs?"

To his pleas, Liu Fang gave only evasive responses without a definite answer. In the absence of his younger brother's agreement, Liu Qi felt he could not very well go it alone and marry.

One day, when Liu Qi was visiting his good friend Big Brother Qin, the topic of marriage came up by chance in their conversation. Thereupon Liu Qi told his friend in detail about Liu Fang's refusal to marry, adding, "I wonder what my younger brother can be thinking of."

Big Brother Qin said, laughing, "This is all too obvious. The two of you jointly built up the family business, but he was the first one to arrive. You came later. If you marry first, he'll resent it. That's why he's fobbing you off." (*How petty! What does he know of a noble mind?*)

"My brother is a most kind and honest man. What you say is impossible."

"Don't tell me a handsome young man like your brother would stubbornly refuse to enjoy the pleasures of the conjugal bed. If you don't believe me, send someone to him quietly and offer him a match. I guarantee that he will agree most readily."

Half convinced by this man's words, Liu Qi took his leave and headed for home. Quite by coincidence, he ran into two matchmakers on their way to his house to make a marriage proposal on behalf of Squire Cui San, owner of a silk fabric store in the same town, whose daughter's horoscope matched that of Liu Fang.

"This is a perfect match for my brother," said Liu Qi. "But he's a little strange and he's shy in the presence of strangers. You go ahead and talk to him quietly. If you can pull this match off, I'll have nice rewards for you. I'm not going back for now. I'll be waiting in the oil store at the entrance of the lane."

The two matchmakers went off right away. Before long, they went to report to Liu Qi what had transpired. "Second Master is indeed strange," said one of them. "We talked our heads off, but he just kept saying no and lost his temper in the end. What a letdown for us!"

Only then was Liu Qi convinced that, for whatever reasons, Liu Fang meant what he said.

One day, at the sight of swallows making a nest on the house beam, Liu Qi wrote a poem on the wall in an attempt to sound Liu Fang out:

The swallows, both male, labor at making a nest,
Transporting bits of earth from morning to night.
If they seek not female companions,
Theirs will remain an empty nest.

All smiles, Liu Fang read it several times before he picked up a brush-pen and wrote a matching poem after it:

The swallows, both on the wing, make their nest;
Heaven put him and her together long ago.
If she is content with her companion,
Does the truth to him remain unknown? (The metaphor reveals what she has in mind.)

Liu Qi was flabbergasted upon reading the poem. "The poem implies that my brother is a woman," he thought. "No wonder he's so delicate and his voice so high-pitched. And he never takes off his underwear or his stockings when he goes to sleep at night, and wears two layers of clothing in the heat of summer. So, he's another Mulan!" But he still had his doubts and dared not speak lightly. Again he went to see Big Brother Qin and read the poem aloud to him.

"That settles it," declared Big Brother Qin. "Your brother is not a man. But you've been sleeping with him all these years. Can't you tell?"

Liu Qi explained that Liu Fang had never taken off his underwear. (*The older Liu is a good man but stupid. The younger Liu is a good woman and smart.*)

"That further proves it! Now, you ask him outright and listen to what he has to say in reply."

"But there's such a deep bond between us. We are like loving brothers born of the same parents. How can I bring myself to ask such a thing?"

"If she's indeed a woman, she can marry you. The bond and the love are both there. Why can't it be done?"

And so they talked on and on. Big Brother Qin brought out wine and food, and the two men sat drinking as the afternoon wore on. It was already dusk when Liu Qi returned home. Liu Fang greeted him and, seeing that he was in an inebriated state, helped him into the house and asked, "My brother, where have you been drinking for so long?"

"I had a few drinks at Brother Qin's house. I didn't realize I stayed for so long." While speaking, he peered closely at Liu Fang. When he hadn't the slightest suspicion, he never detected any signs that would give Liu Fang away. (*No suspicion, no detection. This is evidence of Liu Qi's decency as a person.*) But now, in his determination to find out his brother's true identity, the more closely he looked, the more he was convinced that Liu Fang was a woman. Though free of impure thoughts, he wanted to get to the bottom of it all, and yet he felt it would be too awkward to ask Liu Fang point-blank.

"Your matching poem on swallows is nice," said he. "It's better than mine. Could you write another one?"

Liu Fang smiled without saying anything. She took up a piece of paper and a brush-pen and wrote another poem without a single pause. The poem said,

> The swallows make their nest, softly chirping;
> Waste not your youth as the years go by.
> Pity that piece of flawless jade!
> Why did the kings of Chu not accept it?[5] (When love is there, it will
>   surely come out in a poem.)

Liu Qi took it and said, after reading, "So, my good brother, you are in fact a woman."

At these words, Liu Fang blushed deeply. (*Why should she feel ashamed for having kept her chastity for all these years?*)

Before she had time to answer, Liu Qi continued, "You and I are like flesh and blood. Why hide anything from me? But my good brother, what happened to make you put on men's clothing in the first place?"

"After my mother died, I followed my father on a journey back to our hometown, and I wore men's clothing because of fears that a girl might have awkward moments when traveling on the road. Then my father died. Because he was only buried in a shallow earth pit and I wasn't able to give him and my mother a proper burial together, I dared not change my appearance. At the time, I needed a roof over my head so that my father's remains could have a temporary place. Luckily, our adoptive father left us his business, and the remains of both my parents got to be buried properly. I did intend to tell you at that time, but then I thought that because the business was not looking good, you might have a hard time managing it alone. So I dragged my feet. (*She has a mind of her own.*) But now, with you urging me to marry, I feel I have to let you know."

"My good brother, you have gone to such great pains to accomplish what's important to you. And you've been sharing the same bed with me for years without ever giving yourself away. You preserved your chastity and performed your filial duties. You are a hero among women! Admirable! I interpret your poems as meaning you're willing to stoop and marry me. And I will absolutely not take anyone else for wife. We met by chance and lived as brothers for years. It's heaven, not human matchmakers, that is now bringing us together as husband and wife. If you agree, let's take the marriage vow. What do you say?"

"I've been thinking a lot about this. The three graves are all here. If I marry another man, I won't be able to pay my respects to my parents day in and day out. What's more, our adoptive parents treated us as if we were born to them. I don't have the heart to abandon them. If you, my brother, don't scorn my ugly looks, I will be glad to serve you and, together with you, burn incense for our three sets of parents. But it's not proper decorum to marry without the services of a match-maker. Please think about this so as to forestall gossip and leave nothing to be regret-ted." (*She knows what to do. Wise and meticulous. A real hero among women.*)

"Brilliant idea, my good brother," said Liu Qi. "I'll act on it immediately."

That night, they slept in separate rooms. The next morning, Liu Qi asked Big Brother Qin to have his wife officiate as the matchmaker. By this time, Liu Fang had changed into women's attire. Liu Qi bought clothes and jewelry and picked an auspicious day for the wedding. After making sacrificial offerings to the three graves, they held the wedding ceremony, complete with carved candles. All the neigh-bors in the area were invited to the wedding banquet. The event caused quite a sensation throughout the town of Hexiwu. None did not marvel at it. All praised the Lius for their filial piety, their sense of honor, and their chastity.

After they were married, the loving couple remained deferential to each other. Their business flourished, and five sons and two daughters were born to them. To this day, theirs remains a large clan with numerous descendants. The place where they had lived is called by all and sundry "Liu Fang's Village of Virtues." There is a poem in testimony:

> *Without love, blood relations become foes;*
> *With love, strangers become family.*
> *Their good name spreads through the Village of Virtue;*
> *Their stories go down a thousand years.*

Three Times Su Xiaomei Tests Her Groom

Bright men attain ranks and titles;
Bright women do not stand a chance.
But if allowed to take the exams,
Women outshine lords and dukes.

When the earth was first separated from heaven and the male from the female, even though the Creator was fair and impartial, the yin and the yang were given different functions. The yang moves, the yin stays still. The yang gives, the yin takes. The yang turns outward, the yin inward. Therefore, men are in charge of all matters outside the home, and women take care of everything inside.

Those in charge of matters outside the home wear hats and robes in manly manner, and there is nothing they cannot do as generals or court ministers. They are expected to know all there is to know about the past and the present and to be able to adjust their tactics to the demands of the situation.

Those who take care of things inside the home do their hair in fancy ways and wear blouses and skirts. Their daily concerns are the meals, the well, and the mortar. What matters to them the most in their whole lives is the bearing and raising of children. That is why even girls in rich families are not expected to do much with their education except to read names and keep family accounts. Ineligible for the civil service examinations, they seek no fame, and therefore literary pursuits mean little to them.

Be all this as it may, natural endowments vary from person to person. There are stupid women for whom learning to read is as difficult as a journey to reach the sky. There are also brilliant women who can recall many lines of prose or verse after a single glance and learn on their own without a teacher. Some rival Li Bai [701–62] and Du Fu [712–70] in their writing of poems, and Ban Gu [32–92] and Sima Xiangru [179–117 B.C.E.] in their composition of rhapsodies. This is because the element of refinement in nature occasionally also finds its way into women. For example, there was Cao Dagu [neé Ban Zhao], who finished her older brother Ban Gu's *History of the Han Dynasty*. There was Cai Yan [daughter of Cai Yong of Eastern Han dynasty], whose "Eighteen-Stanza Song for a Tartar Reed Pipe" has come down to posterity through the ages.

In the Jin dynasty, there was a Xie Daoyun [niece of Prime Minister Xie An, 320–85], who, when composing poems with her brothers to describe a snow scene, outshone them all by her line comparing snow to willow catkins borne in air by the wind. Shangguan Wan'er of the Tang dynasty, when told by Emperor Zhongzong [r. 705–10] to evaluate poems by officials in the court, proved herself to be a most insightful literary critic. The Song dynasty abounded in outstanding women, Li Qingzhao [1084–1151] and Zhu Shuzhen among them. Both were women poets par excellence and both deserved husbands of matching talent. As it happened, though, the god of marriage made errors in his registry book and married both of them to men of little talent or learning. Their discontent as wives shows through their writings, as the following quatrain attests:

> *Gulls, egrets, and love birds are thrown together,*
> *Though they are birds of different feathers.*
> *If the god of spring cares about flowers,*
> *Why not let them grow and bloom in pairs?*

What follows is a lyric by Li Qingzhao, entitled "The Sorrows of Autumn," to the tune of "Note after Note":

> *Seeking, searching, in solitude and sorrow,*
> *I find little peace in the capricious weather.*
> *A few cups of weak wine don't go far enough*
> *To ward off the chill of the evening wind.*
> *It pains me to see wild geese flying by,*
> *For I remember them well from the past.*
>
> *The ground is strewn with yellow flowers;*
> *Who will blithely gather these wilted petals?*
> ("Blithely gather" is a nice expression.)
> *By my forlorn self at the window,*
> *How am I to get through the night?*
> *Amid the drip-drip of rain from the paulownia leaves,*
> *My sorrow defies all descriptions by word.*

Zhu Shuzhen, sitting in boredom by the lamp while her husband was away, intoned the following quatrain as she listened to the pitter-patter of the rain outside the window:

Tears ruin my eyes; my heart is broken;
Dusk, my most-feared time of day, is here again.
With a dismal early autumn drizzle,
The night is long for me and my feeble lamp.

Later, her poems were made into a collection entitled *Gut-Wrenching Grief.*
Storyteller, why did you pick out two women with unhappy marriages? Well,
that is because I'm now going to tell of a brilliant woman who married a brilliant
man. With one intoning poems and the other improvising lines to match, they
became the stuff of which many stories were made. Indeed, stories about them

Appeal to men with a literary bent
And charm women in their boudoirs.

Our story takes place in Meizhou of Sichuan. In ancient times it was called var-
iously the Shu Prefecture, or Jiazhou, or Meishan. In the region are the Mayi and
the Emei mountains, Min River, and Huan Lake. The refinement of nature found
personification in a great scholar named Su Xun [1009–66], courtesy name
Mingyun, sobriquet Old Fountain. He was also called Old Su. He had two sons,
Big Su and Little Su. Big Su was Su Shi [1037–1101], courtesy name Zizhan and
sobriquet Eastern Slope.[1] Little Su was Su Zhe [1039–1112], courtesy name Ziyou,
sobriquet Riverside. Both sons had the ability to command civilian and military
affairs and knew all there was to know about the past and the present. They passed
the imperial civil service examinations in the same year. The court was impressed
and made both of them academicians of the Imperial Academy. All and sundry
called the two brothers the Two Sus, and the father and sons the Three Sus. But
of this, no more need be said.

The natural refinement of the mountains and the bodies of water happened to
favor this family alone, for apart from having those two distinguished sons, Su Xun
also had a daughter, Xiaomei [Little Sister], whose intelligence was second to none.
If she was taught one thing, she was able to figure out another on her own, and to
every question she had a ready answer. Her father and brothers all being brilliant
scholars, daily conversations at home centered on the histories and the classics, and
poems in all their various metrical patterns constantly rang in her ears. As the ancients
put it, "What's near cinnabar goes red; what's next to ink turns black." With her
endowments that were ten times the average, Xiaomei learned everything there was
to learn.

When she was ten years old, Xiaomei went to live in the capital with her father
and brothers. In their courtyard stood a hydrangea bush. It being spring, the bush
was covered with blossoms. Old Fountain, the father, looked at the flowers in admi-
ration and took up a brush-pen and a piece of stationery to write a poem. He had
just finished the fourth line when the gatekeeper announced a visitor. Old Fountain

laid down his brush-pen and went out. It so happened that Xiaomei wandered into her father's study at this point and saw on the table these lines:

A mound of jade exquisitely carved by nature,
It flashes on the eye in its quiet splendor.
A white cloud must have emerged from the branches;
The bright moon must have lingered over the stems.

Realizing that these were lines in praise of the hydrangea and recognizing her father's handwriting, Xiaomei wrote four lines to complete the poem, without even pausing once for reflection:

Taken apart, they are butterflies' wings;
In clusters, they form crystal balls.
With a breeze wafting its scent through the air,
Why envy the plum blossoms on the hills?

Leaving the poem on the table, Xiaomei returned to her room with unhurried steps. After seeing the guest out, Old Fountain went back to his study and was about to finish his eight-line poem when he saw that it already had eight lines. Impressed by the beauty of the lines, he guessed that they were the work of his daughter. He called her in and asked. Upon confirming that they were indeed written by her, he said with a sigh, "Too bad you're a girl. If you were a son, wouldn't you be another legend in the examinations?"

Henceforth, Old Fountain cherished his daughter all the more dearly. He let her devote all her time to her studies and no longer urged her to take up needlework. When she reached sixteen, he decided to find her a husband by screening all eligible brilliant young men over the length and breadth of the empire, but this proved to be a time-consuming endeavor.

One day, Prime Minister Wang Anshi [1021–86], courtesy name Jiefu, sent a messenger to Old Fountain to invite him to his residence for a chat.[2] Before winning honors on the examinations, this Wang Anshi had enjoyed a reputation as a man of virtue, but he seldom washed his face or changed his clothes, and his body was infested with lice. Old Fountain detested him, believing that a man who had so little regard for everyday human values would do evil if he attained a high position, and wrote an essay entitled "On Recognizing Characteristics of Evil Men" to mock him, thus incurring Wang Anshi's resentment. Later, as Big Su and Little Su passed the examinations one after the other, Wang laid aside his grudge and made up with the Sus. Old Fountain, for his part, also went out of his way to befriend Wang, who was now the prime minister, for fear of compromising his sons' careers. (*Such are the ways of the world.*) Indeed,

Men of old made friends for friendship's sake;
Men of today make friends for personal gains.

Those out to gain know not true brotherhood,
Those with friendship at heart share a deep bond.

That day, Old Fountain accepted the prime minister's invitation. As usual, their conversation ranged from historical events to current affairs. And then they poured out wine and fell to drinking. In an unguarded moment when the wine was beginning to take its effect, the prime minister said boastfully, "My son Wang Pang can recite from memory anything he has read only once."

Also in an inebriated state, Old Fountain retorted, "Whose son needs to read twice?" (*It was Wang Anshi's habitual boastfulness about his son that drew such an unkind remark from Old Fountain.*)

The prime minister replied, "I shouldn't have said that. I shouldn't have been boastful in the presence of a master."

"Not only can my sons recite from memory after one reading," said Old Fountain, "my daughter does the same."

In astonishment, Prime Minister Wang said, "I knew that your sons have great talent, but I've never heard anything about your daughter. So, all the refinement of nature in this region goes to the Su family!"

Regretting his own thoughtless remarks, Old Fountain hastened to take his leave. Wang Anshi had a page boy take out a scroll of calligraphy and, handing it over to Old Fountain, said, "This contains samples of my son's homework. I would appreciate it if you could give some comments."

Old Fountain tucked the scroll into his sleeve and respectfully mumbled something inaudible as he took his leave. After getting home, he went straight to bed. At midnight, when he woke up from his wine-induced sleep, he remembered what had happened and thought, "I shouldn't have boasted about my girl's talent. By asking me to look at his son's homework, he must be thinking of having my daughter marry his son. I don't want this marriage alliance, but what can I say to turn him down?" He gave himself up to thought until daybreak.

After he washed and combed his hair, he took up Wang Pang's scroll and read the writings. Indeed, each essay was a specimen of elegance, and each word a gem. Overwhelmed with admiration for the young man's talent, he said to himself, "I wonder if there *is* a predestined bond between him and my daughter. Let me show this scroll to her and see if she likes it or not."

He covered up the name on the scroll and said to a maidservant, "A young gentleman gave me this scroll and asked me for my comments on his writings. But I don't have the time to do that. Take it to your mistress and tell her to do it for me. As soon as she finishes, come back and report to me."

The maidservant accordingly presented her mistress with the scroll and relayed the old master's instructions. Xiaomei added drops of water to her ink slab, ground vermilion ink, and wrote comments on the scroll from beginning to end. Upon finishing the job a few moments later, she said in admiration, "What beautiful writing!

The author is a real talent. But it looks like every last bit of his talent has been exhausted, and there's more show than substance. I'm afraid this is not someone destined for a long life." She wrote the following lines on the cover by way of a final commentary:

> *Strengths: unique style and lavish prose;*
> *Weaknesses: lack of reserve and grace.*
> *Honors in exams can be had for the taking,*
> *But chances for a long life are slim and remote.*

Later, Wang Pang won first honors as a *zhuangyuan* on the civil service examinations at age nineteen but died soon thereafter, bearing out Xiaomei's prediction. Such was her insight into human character. But let us come back to our story, to the point where Xiaomei finished writing her commentary on the scroll.

Xiaomei had her maid return the scroll to her father. Old Fountain was aghast upon reading what she had written. "How am I to show Wang Anshi such comments? He'll surely take offense!" But he could hardly wipe out the ink from the cover. At this point, a messenger came from the prime minister, announcing, "I am instructed by the prime minister to take back the scroll and to relay a verbal message to Mr. Su in person."

In consternation, Old Fountain saw nothing for it but to cut off the cover that bore Xiaomei's poem. Then he replaced the cover and wrote flattering comments on it before handing it back to the messenger.

"The prime minister told me to ask if Miss Su is betrothed or not," said the messenger. "If not, the prime minister would like to make a marriage proposal on behalf of Young Master Wang."

Old Fountain replied, "I wouldn't dream of rejecting the prime minister, but I'm afraid my daughter is too ugly to deserve the honor. Please put this nicely to His Honor. It's not that I'm trying to find an excuse. He'll see for himself if he comes for a visit."

The messenger reported as much to Prime Minister Wang, who was more than a little displeased upon noticing that the cover had been replaced. Afraid that Miss Su might truly be unprepossessing in looks and therefore disappoint his son, he sent a subordinate to ask around quietly.

It so happened that Academician Su Dongpo [Eastern Slope] and his sister, Xiaomei, were much given to making fun of each other. Dongpo wore a moustache and a beard. Xiaomei had this to say in mockery of him:

> *I look and look, but fail to find his mouth;*
> *Suddenly a sound comes from amidst the bush.*

Xiaomei had a protruding forehead. Dongpo wrote in retaliation:

> *A few steps before her feet were out in the courtyard,*
> *Her forehead is already out of the painted door.*
> (One is quite the equal of the other.)

Xiaomei also had this to say about Dongpo's long chin:

A lovesick teardrop from last year
Has not yet reached his jaw.

In response, Dongpo wrote the following lines about her slightly sunken eyes:

Too deeply hidden in her face for the wiping hand,
The two fountain sources remain untouched.

Having learned about these exchanges, the prime minister's man reported to His Honor, saying, "Miss Su's talent is indeed impressive, but her looks are not."

The prime minister therefore did not bring up the matter again. However, as news about the prime minister's marriage proposal spread around, Xiaomei's prodigious talent also became known throughout the capital. Admirers who had heard about the prime minister's failed attempt swarmed to the Su residence en masse with offers of marriage. Old Fountain had all of them submit samples of their writing and made his daughter go over them. Some she dismissed outright; some she found only minimally appealing. There was only one good piece of writing. The name on the scroll said Qin Guan [1049–1100]. Xiaomei wrote the following comments:

A brilliant scholar today,
A great Academician tomorrow.
Too bad he lives in the times of the two Sus;
Otherwise he could have had no equal.

This commentary made it abundantly clear that she thought Qin Guan was equal in talent with her two brothers and that no one but the two Su brothers could measure up to him. Upon reading the quatrain, Old Fountain knew that his daughter had set her heart on this man. To the gatekeeper he said, "If Scholar Qin Guan comes here, quickly invite him in. The other suitors are all to be turned away."

As it turned out, to everyone's surprise, all those who had submitted samples of writing came to ask for a reply—with the sole exception of Qin Guan. Why? Well, Scholar Qin Guan, courtesy name Shaoyou, a native of Gaoyou, Yangzhou Prefecture, was as supercilious as he was gifted and turned up his nose at everyone except the Su bothers. Even though he flaunted his talent in his attempt to sell himself to the brilliant Miss Su whom he admired, he was afraid that he would do harm to his reputation by following the horde in seeking a reply.

Having waited for Qin Guan in vain, Old Fountain sent a messenger to the Qin residence to extend his greetings. Inwardly overjoyed, Qin Guan thought, "I've only heard about Xiaomei's talent, without ever having had a chance to test her in person. But they say she's not much to look at, with her protruding forehead and sunken eyes. I wonder how hideous that face can be. I'll have to see her to put an end to the suspense." Upon learning through inquiries that she was going on an incense-offering trip to the Temple of the Sacred Mountain, he decided to take the opportunity and go in disguise to see for himself. Indeed,

> *Seeing is believing;*
> *Hearsay doesn't count.*
> *If hearsay is to be believed,*
> *Everyone on earth will be misled.*

Now, women from distinguished families go to temples either early in the morning or late at night. Why? Early in the morning because they want to beat the crowds, and late at night because the crowds have dispersed by then.

At around the fifth watch of the night, before dawn of the first day of the third lunar month, Qin Guan rose, washed, combed his hair, and dressed himself up to look like a mendicant Daoist priest, complete with a Tang dynasty-style blue cotton headscarf, two fake cut-and-polished jade earrings, a black cotton Daoist robe with a yellow waist ribbon, and a pair of white socks and straw sandals. Around his neck hung a string of prayer beads, each as large as a thumbnail, and in his hand was an alms bowl of gold lacquer. The first gray of dawn found him already in front of the Temple of the Sacred Mountain, waiting. When the sky was beginning to brighten, Miss Su's sedan-chair arrived. Qin Guan stepped aside and watched the sedan-chair enter the temple grounds and stop in the left corridor. He then saw Xiaomei leave the sedan-chair and walk up to the main hall. She was not a beauty in a bewitching sort of way but had an unassuming and quiet refinement unadulterated by the least speck of vulgarity. "But I wonder how talented she really is," thought he.

After a while, believing that the incense-burning session should have ended, Qin Guan went up the corridor and encountered her on the left side of the main hall. Joining his palms in salutation, Qin Guan said,

> *Destined for fortune and longevity,*
> *Would the young lady kindly show mercy?*

Without missing a beat, Xiaomei replied,

> *Based on what good deeds and ability*
> *Does the priest dare ask for charity?*

With another salute, Qin Guan pressed on:

> *May the young lady be like medicinal herbs*
> *That keep a hundred illnesses at bay.*

Xiaomei replied as she kept walking,

> *You may talk until lotus flowers grow from your tongue;*
> *I have not half a penny to give away.*

Qin Guan followed her all the way to her sedan-chair and said, with one more salute:

> *The young lady had such a day of pleasure;*
> *How can I give up on this hill of treasure?*

Xiaomei rejoined with the following lines:

> *The deranged priest is so greedy in his folly;*
> *Would I walk around laden with money?*

Xiaomei was mounting the sedan-chair while delivering this retort. Qin Guan turned around and mumbled, "So the 'deranged priest' gets to match 'the young lady.' What a stroke of luck!"

Already in the sedan-chair by this time, Xiaomei did not pay him any attention, but her old servant found that remark offensive. The old servant was about to turn back and raise objections when he noticed a cute little page boy emerging from the corridor and calling out to the priest, "Young Master, come here to change your clothes!" As the page boy followed the priest, the old servant tapped the boy on the shoulder and asked in a subdued voice, "Who is that?"

"It's Young Master Qin Guan from Gaoyou," replied the page boy.

The old servant said nothing. After returning home, he told his wife about this, and soon enough, the story spread to the young mistress's quarters of the house. Upon learning that the priest begging for alms was in fact Qin Guan in disguise, Xiaomei laughed it off and told the maidservants to keep their mouths shut.

Let us pick up another thread of our story and come back to Qin Guan, who looked his fill at Xiaomei that day and found her to be far from ugly. Moreover, the way she gave her replies confirmed her brilliance. On a chosen auspicious day, Qin Guan went personally to propose marriage. Old Fountain gave his consent, and the necessary betrothal gifts were delivered to the prospective bride's house. This happened at the beginning of the second lunar month.

Qin Guan was eager to hold the wedding ceremony as soon as possible, but Xiaomei refused, for she was sure that Qin Guan, with his elegant style of prose, would pass the imperial examinations that were quickly approaching. She wanted a wedding ceremony that featured an official's ivory tablet and black gauze hat. Qin Guan felt obliged to yield to her.

The imperial civil service examinations at the national level were held on the third day of the third lunar month under the auspices of the Ministry of Rites. Qin Guan passed and won himself instant fame. He went to pay his respects to his future father-in-law and to talk about the wedding ceremony. There being no one available from his own family, he proposed that the wedding be held in the Su residence.

Old Fountain said joyfully, "Today is the day you learned about your success on the exam and gained the right to change from the white robe of a commoner to the green of an official. What day can be more auspicious? Why bother to pick another day? Won't it be nice to hold the wedding ceremony right here in this house this very evening?" Academician Su off to one side voiced his agreement. That evening, Qin Guan and Xiaomei made their nuptial bows to the bride's parents and became husband and wife. Truly,

> *A bright young lady married a bright young fellow;*
> *He passed the exams, but more tests were to follow.*

After the feast in the main hall was over on that evening of glorious moonlight, Qin Guan was about to enter the bridal chamber when he found its door tightly shut. In the courtyard stood a small table on which were laid stationery, ink, a brush-pen, an ink slab, three envelopes, and three cups—one made of jade, one of silver, and the other of baked clay.

To the maid clad in green who was standing by, Qin Guan said, "Please tell your mistress that the groom is here. Why isn't the door open?"

The maid said, "My mistress has three tests for you. She won't let you in unless you pass all of them. The tests are contained in the three envelopes."

Pointing at the three cups, he asked, "What do these mean?"

"The jade cup is for wine, the silver one is for tea, and the clay one for plain water. If you pass all three tests, you will be offered three cups of fine wine with the jade cup and invited into the bridal chamber. If you pass two tests but fail one, you'll be entitled to tea with the silver cup to allay your thirst and to take another test tomorrow evening. If you pass only one test, you'll be given only plain water with the clay cup and, as a punishment, study for three months in a separate room."

With a scornful smile, Qin Guan said, "Another scholar would have begged for easier tests, but this one has passed the imperial exams with flying colors. I can take three hundred tests like this, let alone three! What do I have to fear?"

"My mistress is no ordinary bookish examiner doing a perfunctory job. Her tests are difficult! (*Even Xiaomei's maidservant knows a thing or two!*) The first test is a riddle in the form of a quatrain. You, sir, are asked to solve the riddle, also in the form of a quatrain. The second test is another quatrain, with each line containing the name of a historical figure. You pass this test only if you get all four names right. The third test is easier. You need only write a matching line to make up a couplet. If you can come up with a good line, you pass, and you'll get to drink the fine wine and enter the bridal chamber."

"Give me the first test."

The maid opened the first envelope and showed it to the groom. On a piece of stationery with floral patterns was written a quatrain:

> *As one anneals iron in the furnace,*
> *Ants climb up the whitewashed walls;*
> *The yin and the yang contain the truth;*
> *Between heaven and earth stands the person.*

Qin Guan thought, "Any other person wouldn't be able to solve the riddle. Now, I have disguised myself as a mendicant Daoist priest to beg for alms at the Temple of the Sacred Mountain in order to see Miss Su. In the first line, 'anneals' rhymes with 'appeals.' In the second line, 'ants' rhymes with 'grants.' The third line refers to the Daoist truth. And in the fourth line, 'person' refers to me. Therefore, this quatrain contains the phrase, 'The Daoist person who appeals for grants.'" He took up the brush-pen and wrote by moonlight a matching quatrain after Xiaomei's:

> Who appeals for the advent of spring?
> The flowers bloom by the grant of nature.
> With the Daoist truth borne by the spring breeze,
> No person dares ascend the flowerbed.

After he finished his quatrain, the maid folded up the stationery twice and slipped it under the window, shouting at the top of her voice, "The groom has finished the first test!" (*Funny.*)

Xiaomei smiled almost imperceptibly when she detected the phrase "The Daoist person who appeals for grant[s]."

Qin Guan opened the second envelope and found another piece of stationery containing the following quatrain:

> The grandson had the greatest power.
> He made a hole in the wall to read by his neighbor's light.
> His clothes make the traveling son think of his mother.
> The grandfather leans against the door to look out.

Without the slightest hesitation, Qin Guan wrote down the answers. The first line was contrived from the name Sun Quan [182–252, founder of the kingdom of Wu, literally, "Grandson," "Power"]. The second line was a reference to Kongming [literally, "Hole," "Light," courtesy name of Zhuge Liang, 181–234, strategist of the kingdom of Shu]. The third line contained Zisi [literally, "Son," "Think," courtesy name of Confucius's grandson Kong Ji]. The fourth line was a reference to Grandfather Lü Wang [literally, "Look out," adviser to King Wen, who established the Zhou dynasty.]

As before, the maid slipped the stationery under the window.

Without saying anything out loud, Qin Guan thought, "So, the first two tests didn't baffle me. The third one is for me to write a matching line to make up a couplet. Well, I began learning the art of composing matching couplets when I was five or six years old. She can't beat me at this." The third envelope was opened to reveal the following line:

> I close the door and push the windows open unto the moon.

The line looked simple enough at first glance. But the more he thought about it, the more he admired the cleverness of it as a line to be matched. If his matching line was too mundane, he would not be given credit. He turned his thoughts this way and that, but could not come up with a good line. He panicked when the third watch of the night was struck on the drum tower and his mind was still a blank.

It so happened that Dongpo, not yet gone to bed, stepped out of the house to see how things were going for his brother-in-law. Lo and behold! Qin Guan was pacing around in the courtyard, intoning "I close the door and push the window open unto the moon" and holding out his right hand as if to push open a window. (*Vivid description.*)

"That must be a line by Xiaomei, and he's having a hard time trying to match it," thought Dongpo. "If I don't help him out, who's going to save this marriage?" He hunted desperately for a good line, but none came to mind.

In the courtyard stood a flower vat that happened to be filled to the brim with water. Qin Guan stopped by the vat and stared at the water. The sight gave Dongpo inspiration. "I've got it!" he thought. He was about to offer his idea to Qin, but he was afraid that his brother-in-law might lose face should Xiaomei get to know about this. So he gave a cough from where he stood, picked up a piece of brick from the ground, and tossed it into the vat. Drops of water splashed onto Qin's face, and the reflection of the moonlit sky in the water was shattered. In a flash of inspiration, Qin Guan took the brush-pen and wrote (*Qin Shaoyou was indeed brilliant.*):

I toss a stone and break the sky apart under the water.

The maid delivered the third piece of stationery. With a creak, the door of the bridal chamber opened wide. Another maid walked out with a silver flask. She filled the jade cup with wine of superior quality and offered the cup to the groom, saying, "Scholar, please drink three cups as a reward."

Radiant with his triumph, Qin Guan drained the three cups in quick succession and was escorted by the maids into the bridal chamber. The talented young couple enjoyed the night to their hearts' content. Indeed,

For those in joy, the night goes by too fast.
For those in loneliness, dawn never comes.

Henceforth, the husband and wife lived in blissful harmony, but of this, no more need be said. Later, when Qin Guan was traveling in the Zhejiang area in search of an official position and Academician Su Dongpo was in the capital, Xiaomei went to the capital to see her brother, for she missed him.

Dongpo had a Buddhist friend, Abbot Foyin, who advised Dongpo to retire when his career was still at its height.[3] One day, Abbot Foyin sent Dongpo a long poem. It was a most strange poem, consisting of one hundred and thirty pairs of duplicating characters. What, you may ask, are the characters?

Wild wild, birds birds, sing sing, often often, with with, longing longing, spring spring, air air, peach peach, blossoms blossoms, thrive thrive,

over over, branches branches, orioles orioles, sparrows sparrows,
jointly jointly, chirp chirp, songs songs, rock rock, cliffs cliffs,
flowers flowers, red red, like like, brocade brocade, screens, screens,
are are, eye-pleasing eye-pleasing, hills hills, graceful graceful,
lovely lovely, hills hills, face face, smoky smoky, mist mist,
rising rising, freshly freshly, lightly lightly, waves waves,
quicken quicken, babbling babbling, slow-moving slow-moving,
water water, scene scene, tranquil tranquil, deep deep, place place,
good good, chasing chasing, swimming swimming, by by, water water,
foams foams, like like, snow snow, pear pear, blossoms blossoms,
aglow aglow, bright bright, clear clear, delicate delicate, exquisite exquisite,
like like, falling falling, silver silver, flowers flowers, spinning spinning,
most most, blissfully blissfully, soft soft, velvety velvety, river river,
bank bank, grass grass, green green, pairs pairs, pretty pretty,
butterflies butterflies, flying flying, arrive arrive, here here, fallen fallen,
petals petals, piles piles, amidst amidst, birds birds, warble warble,
chirp chirp, without without, stop stop, to to, recall recall, spring spring,
scenes scenes, lovely lovely, weeping weeping, willows willows,
branches branches, tips tips, spring spring, colors colors, grace grace,
frequent frequent, oft-held oft-held, parties parties, drinking drinking,
spring spring, mellowed mellowed, wine wine, seemingly seemingly,
intoxicates intoxicates, idle idle, viewers viewers, of of, spring spring,
scenery scenery, gather gather, meet meet, vying vying, recount recount,
tours tours, hills hills, lakes lakes, hearts hearts, calm calm,
leisurely leisurely, return return, go go, come come, rest rest, work work.

Dongpo read the poem a few times without being able to make any sense of it. As he gave himself up to solid thinking, Xiaomei took over the stationery and understood upon the first reading. "Brother," said she, "what's so difficult about this poem? Let me read it out for you." And right away, she started reading aloud. (*Her understanding of the abbot's subtle message is alarmingly quick.*)

Wild birds sing; wild birds sing often with longing.
Often with longing, spring air [and] peach blossoms thrive.
Spring air [and] peach blossom thrive over branches.
Over branches, orioles [and] sparrows jointly chirp songs.
Orioles [and] sparrows jointly chirp songs [by] rock cliffs.
[By] rock cliffs, flowers red like brocade screens.
Flowers red like brocade screens are eye-pleasing.
Eye-pleasing hills—hills graceful [and] lovely.
Graceful [and] lovely hills face smoky mist rising.
Hills face smoky mist rising freshly [and] lightly.
Freshly [and] lightly, waves quicken babbling, slow-moving water.

Waves quicken babbling, slow-moving water—[a] scene [so] tranquil,
[A]scene tranquil [and] hidden, [a] place [so] good,
[A]hidden place [so] good [for] chasing [and] swimming,
Chasing [and] swimming by water foams,
By water foams like snow,
Like snow [and] pear blossoms aglow, bright, clear.
Pear blossoms aglow, bright, clear, delicate [and] exquisite,
Delicate [and] exquisite like fallen silver flowers spinning,
Like fallen silver flowers spinning most blissfully.
Most blissfully, soft [and] velvety riverbank grass.
Soft [and] velvety riverbank grass—green, [oh so] green.
[In] pairs [and] pairs, pretty butterflies, flying, arrive here.
Butterflies, flying, arrive here [on the] fallen petals,
[On the] fallen petals [and] trees amidst birds' warble.
Amidst [the] trees, birds warble [and] chirp without stop,
Without stop to recall spring scenes [so] lovely,
To recall spring scenes [and] lovely weeping willows,
Weeping willows [and] branches' tips—branches' tips [that]
      spring colors grace.
Spring colors grace frequent, oft-held parties [of] drinking,
Frequent, oft-held parties drinking spring-mellowed wine.
Spring-mellowed wine seemingly intoxicates,
Seemingly intoxicates idle viewers of spring scenery.
Idle viewers of spring scenery gather [and] meet,
Gather [and] meet, vying [to] recount tours [of] hills [and] lakes,
Vying [to] recount tours [of] hills [and] lakes [as] hearts calm [down].
Hearts calm, [they] leisurely, leisurely return, go, [and] come,
Return, go, [and] come, [to] rest, [or to] work, [to] rest, [to] work.

After she finished reading, Dongpo said in amazement, "You mind works so much faster than mine! If you were a man, you would win a much higher official rank than I have!" He copied Foyin's letter, wrote down Xiaomei's version of it, and sent both to Qin Guan, along with explanations of how he had failed to understand it after repeated attempts and of how Xiaomei had figured it out as soon as she laid eyes on it.

Qin Guan also failed to make any sense out of Abbot Foyin's writings. It was only after he read his wife's version that light dawned on him. Overcome with a sense of his own inadequacy, he sighed and wrote these lines by way of a response:

The abbot's song was beyond my ken—
The one with repetitive pairs of words.
Every word was a gem in fact,
Every line a string of pearls.

> *Consider how you understood it at first sight,*
> *But I read it three times and had no clue.*
> *I attach a poem and send it afar,*
> *In imitation of the same style.*
> *Read it with care,*
> *For it gives voice to my heart.*

After these lines, he wrote a poem in the same style, using every character twice in succession, and it certainly was strange in appearance:

> *I've missed her for long barred from returning*
> *quietly*   *I recall*
> *water-clock dripped away when parting*

Qin Guan's letter arrived when Dongpo and Xiaomei were by the lake, watching lotus seeds being picked. Dongpo opened the letter, read it, and handed it to his sister, saying, "Can you make anything out of this?"

Xiaomei replied, "This poem is written in imitation of Abbot Foyin's style." Out loud, she read,

> *Quietly I've missed her for long;*
> *For long barred from returning, I recall [the] parting.*
> *I recall [the] parting when away dripped [the] water-clock.*
> *Away dripped [the] water-clock quietly; I've missed her for long.*

With a sigh, Dongpo said, "My sister is truly the brightest of the bright! (*Xiaomei is so admirable that it's no surprise Mr. Qin is so smitten.*) Let's each make up a poem on the picking of lotus seeds and send them to your husband to let him know about this excursion of ours today." And so Dongpo wrote a poem, and Xiaomei did the same. Xiaomei's poem goes as follows:

> *of lotus seeds sing at Green Poplar Ford*
> *pickers*   *one*
> *sing jade as pretty as song new*

Dongpo's poem looks like this:

> *of flowers returned on horse as if on wings*
> *admirer*   *wine*
> *came nightfall awoke I weakened effect*

When read out loud, Xiaomei's poem turns out to be as follows:

> *Pickers of lotus seeds sing at Green Poplar Ford,*
> *Sing at Green Poplar Ford one new song—*
> *One new song as pretty as jade.*
> *As pretty as jade sing pickers of lotus seeds.*

Dongpo's poem, when read aloud, turns out to be:

[The] admirer of flowers returned on horse as if on wings.
On horse as if on wings, [the] wine's effect weakened.
[The] wine's effect weakened, I awoke. Nightfall came;
I awoke, nightfall came, [the] admirer of flowers returned.
>   (Fresh and pretty, with the flavor of Tang dynasty poems. A com-
>   parison of the two poems shows the one by the brother inferior to
>   the one by the sister.)

Upon receiving the poems, Qin Guan read them and was overwhelmed with admiration. He and Xiaomei composed too many matching poems back and forth for us to recite here.

Later, Qin Guan was recruited as an academician on the strength of his scholarly fame and served in the Imperial Academy together with his two brothers-in-law. Never in history had there ever been three brothers-in-law serving as academicians at the same time. Empress Xuanren [mother of Emperor Shenzong, r. 1068–85], hearing of Su Xiaomei's talent, often sent eunuchs to her, bearing gifts of silk or food and beverage, to ask for her poems. Every time the empress obtained one, it would be intoned in the palace and then spread throughout the capital. (*With an empress setting such great store by talent, Su Xiaomei was not disappointed in her aspirations.*)

Xiaomei died before Qin Guan. He missed her so much that he never married again. (*He loved her too deeply. No one was good enough to replace her.*) There is a poem in testimony:

The three Sus are giants in the history of letters;
Xiaomei had a mind superior to her husband's.
Three times she tested her groom—what a story!
Her talent had no equal all over the land.

Four Times Abbot Foyin Flirts with Qinniang

His writings move heaven to tears;
His demise spells doom for those in our calling.
In talent and success he surpassed Sima Yi;[1]
In fame and fortune he outshone Yao Chong.[2]
Refinement went with him from this world,
And the ancient styles also faded away.
Where are all the volumes of his writings?
The fire god took them to the celestial palace.

Who wrote the above eight lines? It was Liu Kezhuang [1187–1269], sobriquet Rear Village Hermit, during the reign of Emperor Lizong [r. 1225–64] of the Song dynasty.

In the court of Emperor Shenzong [r. 1068–85] of the same dynasty, there was an Academician Su Shi [1037–1101], courtesy name Zizhan and sobriquet Dongpo [Eastern Slope]. He was a native of Meishan County of Meishan Prefecture, Xichuan. Academician Su had a friend called Abbot Foyin.[3] What, you may ask, is the background of this abbot? Well, he was a native of Fuliang County of Raozhou Prefecture, Jiangxi. Xie Duanqing by name and Juelao by courtesy name, he had begun his studies of the Confucian classics from an early age and learned all there was to learn about the past and the present. He was also well versed in Buddhism and Daoism, hence his fame as a most erudite man.

One day, Xie Duanqing arrived in the capital to sit for the civil service examinations. Academician Su, having heard about his scholarship, engaged him in conversation and, through many more of such conversations, the two men came to respect and admire each other. After going together on excursions intoning poems and enjoying wine, they grew to be close friends.

During a severe drought, Emperor Shenzong approved the request of the Imperial Observatory for a ceremony to pray for rain. In the Grand State Councilor Monastery was set a vegetarian feast for one hundred and eight monks. Eminent monks were engaged to explicate the sutras and pray for rain to provide relief for the populace. Academician Su Shi was charged with the mission of drafting the prayer to heaven and officiating at the ritual. He was instructed to move into the monastery three days prior to the event to observe a Buddhist diet and sleep alone. A eunuch who came to inspect the altar announced that the emperor would be arriving in a few days. A chair was set in the abbot's cell for the emperor, and everything was done to befit the grandness of the occasion until the entire monastery was spotlessly clean and color-fully adorned. By the order of the prefectural magistrate, guards were deployed all around the monastery to block unauthorized persons from entering it, so as not to incur any displeasure from the emperor. But of this, no more need be said.

Now, Xie Duanqing heard about the upcoming event when he was visiting Academician Su in his study. "May I go with you, my brother, into the monastery to look at the emperor?" asked Xie.

Everything would have been well if Dongpo had refused him. But Dongpo did want to have Duanqing's company. "If you want to go," said he, "that can easily be done. You need only dress yourself as an acolyte and serve at the altar. That way, you can look your fill at the emperor."

Everything would have been all right had Xu Duanqing refused to pose as an acolyte. But in a moment of childish thoughtlessness, he gladly agreed to do so. He borrowed the right clothes, made himself up to look like an acolyte, and followed Dongpo into the monastery, where Dongpo had already told the abbot to summon Duanqing the acolyte the moment His Majesty arrived. In the meantime, Duanqing was free to chat with Dongpo in the latter's cell.

On the day of the ceremony, the abbot struck the bell at the fifth watch before dawn, to call everyone to assemble. Amid the curling wisps of incense smoke, the resplendent candles, the multicolored flying banners, and the resonant music, the ceremony proceeded in great pomp and circumstance. Dongpo lit some joss sticks, bowed to an image of the Buddha, and went back to sit in his own cell. As soon as breakfast was over, it was announced that the emperor would soon be arriving. Being an academician charged with drafting imperial decrees, Dongpo had daily access to the emperor and therefore the news did not excite him, but it sent Xie Duanqing's face aflame and his heart aflutter. After a few moments trying to collect himself, he finally calmed down and went to the Hall of Sakyamuni. Along with other acolytes, he replenished the joss sticks, trimmed the candles, served food, and laid out the lamps. Before long, Emperor Shenzong arrived. Dongpo and the assembly of monks stood in orderly rows and dropped to their knees in welcome. After entering the great hall, the emperor picked a few joss sticks from the bundle of the finest joss sticks held by a eunuch, and bowed three times on the clean mat prepared for him. The abbot then led His Majesty to the abbot's cell, where the emperor sat down in his seat and accepted the kowtows of the monks. Emperor Shenzong praised Academician Su for the elegance of the prayer he had written, and the academician prostrated himself on the floor repeatedly, saying, "This is too much of an honor for me!" When the abbot ordered that tea be served, it was none other than Xie Duanqing who came in with the tea tray.

What happened was that during the ceremony in the main hall, Xie Duanqing had not managed to get a good look at the emperor from his position among the crowd. So he contrived to be the one to serve tea. Stealing a glance at the emperor when he got near, Xie Duanqing was so impressed by the emperor's majestic bearing that his hair stood on end. Not daring to look his fill, he promptly withdrew, but not before the emperor noticed him. It was his distinguished looks, with his square face, large ears, bright eyes, well-marked eyebrows, and majestic figure, that set him apart from other acolytes and caught the emperor's eye. (*Good looks are important, but in this case, his looks played an unfortunate role in his career.*)

Pointing at Duanqing, the emperor said, "Who is this acolyte? How long has he been serving in this monastery?"

Not having asked for any information about Duanqing, the abbot was unable to answer, but Duanqing himself had the presence of mind to say with a kowtow, "Your humble subject's name is Xie Duanqing, a native of Raozhou Prefecture, Jiangxi. I have just recently joined the Buddhist order in this monastery. I am so happy to be in Your Majesty's presence."

Pleased at his fluency and articulateness, the emperor continued to ask, "Do you know the classics?"

"I began my studies at an early age. I also know the Buddhist scriptures well."

"Since you know the Buddhist scriptures well, we shall give you a Buddhist name Liaoyuan and a sobriquet Foyin and have you take the monk's tonsure here and now."

Being as learned as Academician Su was, Xie Duanqing had come to the capital to take the civil service examinations in hopes of winning instant fame and making his mark in the world. He had certainly no intention of becoming a monk. But an emperor's words are as good as the will of heaven, as the saying goes, and violating an imperial decree is a crime for which one deserves ten thousand deaths. The emperor having already given the order, how would he dare to say that he was an acolyte in disguise and had no plans of becoming a monk?

Dismayed beyond measure, Xie Duanqing resignedly kowtowed and thanked the emperor for his grace. Right away, the abbot took Duanqing to the main hall, where he was to bow to the image of the Buddha. That done, he was taken back into the presence of the emperor for the tonsure. The emperor then bestowed upon him a purple silk monk's robe. An official from the Ministry of Rites who was traveling with the emperor took out an ordination form, filled it out with information about Foyin's Buddhist name, birth, native place, and date of tonsure by imperial decree, and handed the document to him.

Covered all over in purple, Duanqing in his Buddhist robe looked no less than an arhat reincarnate. The ordination paper in hand, he kowtowed time and again to acknowledge his gratitude.

"Now that you are a monk," said the emperor, "We shall make you assist in the holding of this ceremony. If you can observe the Buddhist commandments strictly, you may become the abbot of this monastery. Do not bring any disgrace to the Buddhist order, or you will disappoint Us." With that, the emperor rose to go.

Dongpo and the assembly of monks went out the monastery gate and, on bended knees, saw the emperor off before they returned to their ceremony. But of this, no more.

And so Xie Duanqing forsook his name and called himself Foyin, but everyone addressed him most respectfully as Sir Yin because he had taken his tonsure by imperial grace. In the Song dynasty, taking the tonsure was a major event. An ordination paper cost a thousand strings of cash, and now Duanqing had obtained one without spending a penny. Had he been a real acolyte, wouldn't he have rejoiced jubilantly at this all-too-rare opportunity? However, as it was, what had begun in fun ended in dead earnest and, having joined the Buddhist order in an act against his own will, he suffered from quite a few bouts of depression. Later, he resignedly gave himself up to the study of the scriptures and the Buddhist doctrines in the Grand State Councilor Monastery and abandoned his aspirations for fame, fortune, and riches. Instead, he embraced the idea of quiescence and nonaction. Being a reincarnation of Abbot Mingwu of the Tang dynasty, he was endowed with such unusual intelligence that he detached himself from Confucianism and gained a thorough knowledge of Buddhism as fast as snow thawing by the furnace.

On the other hand, Academician Su Shi was a practical man bent on making his mark in this life and had quite a different outlook on the world. He said, "Xie Duanqing was here in the capital to sit for the exams. It was I who brought him to the monastery and told him to disguise himself as an acolyte in order to look at the emperor. Now that he's been made to take the tonsure, I am the one to blame! Mortifying his flesh like that in the monastery, he must be thinking hard thoughts of me. Even though he's strictly observing the commandments, I'm afraid he's only putting on an act. He can't be that unflinching deep down." So Dongpo teased him from time to time, but Foyin remained stoic at heart and unyielding in speech, without the slightest signs of wavering. However, Dongpo was still skeptical. Later, because of poems that ran afoul of Prime Minister Wang Anshi, Dongpo was demoted time and again until Emperor Zhezong reinstated him as a Hanlin Imperial Academician in the Yuanyou reign period [1086–94]. After Dongpo's rehabilitation, Abbot Foyin returned to the Grand State Council Monastery from his travels as a mendicant monk. He was not yet past the prime of his life. Upon seeing him, Dongpo recalled what had led to Foyin's taking the tonsure many years before, and made another attempt to talk him into renouncing Buddhism. He said, "If you would be willing to return to secular life and enter civil service, I would surely do my best to recommend you to a nice post." But Foyin turned a deaf ear to him. Dongpo then mocked him in these words:

No shave, no knave; no knave, no shave.
If knave, then shave; if shave, then knave.

Foyin smiled but said nothing in return. One day in the middle of spring, Academician Su was sitting idly in his house when a servant announced, "Abbot Foyin is at the gate." The academician instructed to have him shown in. A moment later, Foyin entered the main hall. After an exchange of greetings, Dongpo ordered tea. The tea over, he had servants clean up the pavilion in the rear garden and took Foyin there. Both sat down in the pavilion located near the back hall. After wine and dishes of fruit and food were set out on the table, Dongpo had a servant pour out the wine, and the two toasted each other. After three cups, Dongpo said, "The pleasure of a feast is not complete without music. Let me have a young musician in my house sing a few songs to add to our enjoyment." With that, he told a servant to relay his order to the interior section of the house. Before long, there came to Foyin's ears a beautiful singing voice.

> *The sweet and mellow voice shook dust off the carved beams;*
> *The clearly rendered notes wafted o'er the table like a breeze.*
> *Like an oriole warbling in the royal garden,*
> *Like a phoenix singing on the divine hill,*
> *It delivered lyrics refined and elegant,*
> *And a tune worthy of the clear breeze and bright moon.*

After the song ended, Abbot Foyin commented, "Wonderful! Indeed, a Han E and a Qin Qing, no less![4] If the song doesn't halt the clouds, it surely shook dust off the beams."

"Why doesn't the abbot write us a nice poem?" suggested Dongpo.

"Bring me paper and pen, please," said Foyin, whereupon the academician told the servant to bring the four treasures of the study.[5]

Without saying anything out loud, Foyin thought, "The singing couldn't have been better. I wonder what the singer looks like." He picked up the brush-pen and wrote a lyric to the tune of "Moon over West River":

> *Layers of curtains shield this narrow place;*
> *The tiny pavilion stands exposed to the wind.*
> *Behind the green window and red door under the moon,*
> *The sweet melody came into hearing.*
>
> *If the ears have such pleasure,*
> *Why aren't the eyes just as blessed?*
> *With the divine being so close by,*
> *The embroidered curtain blocks her from sight.*

As soon as Foyin finished writing, Dongpo burst out in hearty laughter. "So you regret that you don't see the singer," he said. By Dongpo's order, a servant stepped forward and rolled the curtain halfway up, enough to reveal the tiny feet of a girl. Foyin said to himself, "Though the curtain is already halfway up, I still can't get a complete view of her, and the curtain hooks are too low in the first place."

"Now that you've seen her," said Dongpo, "you wouldn't begrudge another poem?"

Thus urged, Foyin took up the brush-pen and wrote another lyric to the tune of "Pinziling":

> At the sight of the feet,
> I wonder if the waist is narrow. (This is hilarious.)
> Her singing halts the clouds;
> Is she slim enough to stand on a palm?[6]
>
> My eyes bleary with wine, I'd better return
> And force myself to mortify my flesh.
> Time and again I wished to raise the curtain,
> But I stayed my hand, for the host might take offense.

Bursting with more to say, Foyin composed another four lines:

> The clapper and the songs are within hearing,
> But the charming eyes are out of sight.
> May a kind breeze rise from the ground
> And raise the curtain above its golden hooks.

After Foyin intoned the above quatrain, Dongpo burst into another guffaw. He then had servants roll up the embroidered curtain and called forth the girl. Emerging from behind the curtain, the girl bowed deeply to Abbot Foyin. As she stood in the pavilion, prim and proper, Foyin saw that the one with such a good voice was also fair to look upon. Behold:

> Her delicate eyebrows slightly trimmed,
> Her lotus-like cheeks faintly rouged,
> She is as lithe as a divine being;
> She has a quiet grace endowed by nature.
> In colored silk clothes, she holds an ivory clapper
> Showing fingers tapering like bamboo shoots.
> On her feet shaped like golden lotus
> She wears tiny shoes with embroidered phoenixes.
> Placed by water's edge, she is another river goddess;
> Placed in the moon, she is another Goddess Chang'e,
> More beautiful than celestial maidens,
> More charming than fairies in the moon.

Dongpo told a servant to serve wine and then said to the girl, "Come here and offer a toast to the abbot." Turning to Foyin, he continued, "This is Qinniang [Lute

Girl]. She grew up in my house and is quite a musician. She plays the seven-string zither and is versatile in her music talents. Now that you've seen her, why don't you write another nice poem?"

Already more than half drunk by this time, Foyin declined, saying, "I should be going."

"Please stay, Abbot, and have a few more cups," urged Qinniang.

Complying with Dongpo's request, Foyin took up the brush-pen and wrote another lyric, to the tune of "Butterflies Lingering over Flowers":

> *The sweet girl with the clapper asks the guest to stay;*
> *She adjusts her golden hairpins*
> *With fingers slender and tapering.*
> *Her song soars to the sky, her voice halts the clouds.*
>
> *The ears get to hear her with their marriage bond;*
> *The eyes get to see her with their marriage bond.*
> *When the eyes and the ears are so destined,*
> *What else does the marriage bond cover?*
>   (This could not have been written by Foyin!)

Delighted upon reading the poem, Dongpo told Qinniang to sing these lines while plying Foyin with more wine. In his inebriated state, Foyin was quite oblivious of any impropriety in his poem. The hour being late, Dongpo had a servant help Foyin to a study and prepare him for bed.

"I've been trying for so long to talk this monk into resuming secular life and entering civil service," thought Dongpo, "but he just doesn't yield an inch. While he's being flirtatious with Qinniang today, I'd better make sure he has his way with the girl, so that he cannot but renounce his monastic life. If I can produce evidence of his misconduct and force him to return to secular life, he'll surely do as I say. Good plan! Good plan!" Right away he called Qinniang to him and said to her, "Do you know what that monk's poem means? Listen to the last two lines: 'When the eyes and the ears are so destined, What else does the marriage bond cover?' That monk is no decent sort. His poem shows he has taken a fancy to you. Go to the study tonight and sleep with him. You must let him have his way with you, and then you must bring me evidence. I'll reward you with three thousand strings of cash as your dowry. Then I'll find you a good man to marry. If you don't do that with him, I'll get the housekeeper tomorrow and have her give you twenty strokes of the bamboo rod and drive you out of this house."

Trembling with fear, Qinniang said, "I'll do as you say, sir." She left the room and, blushing furiously, went in her mincing steps to the study. By the light of the lamp on the wall, she saw Abbot Foyin lying in a drunken stupor on the couch. Without knowing what to do, she sat down by his side and shook him with her dainty hands. But it was like a dragonfly trying to topple a stone pillar or a mole cricket trying to push a hill. How was she able to wake up the thunderously snoring monk? But let us not encumber our story with unnecessary details.

It was the first watch of the night when Qinniang first tried to shake the monk. She waited and waited in vain for him to wake up. At the fifth watch, she began to panic. Tears welled in her eyes as she thought, "If I fail to do what I'm supposed to do tonight, I'll be given twenty strokes of the bamboo rod tomorrow and driven out of the house. Oh, what am I going to do?" But nothing could be done with the monk when he was in such a besotted condition. As she flicked off her tears with her hand, a few drops landed on Foyin's face. Lo and behold! Foyin woke up with a start. (*Her hands that failed to shake him awake lack the force of a few drops of tears.*)

As he woke up, his eyes happened to rest upon the lamp on the wall. By the lamplight, he became aware of a pretty young woman sitting by his side. In alarm, he asked, "Which family are you from? Why are you here at this time of the night?"

In surprise mixed with joy, Qinniang dropped a curtsy and said, blushing, "I am Qinniang, the one whom you heard sing during the day. Having detected in your poems a hint of admiration for me, I came here in the darkness of the night, unobserved, in order to play a game of clouds and rain with you, Abbot. Please do not reject me."

Flabbergasted, Foyin said, "You are quite mistaken, madam! The wine made me rant and rave last night as I was enjoying the academician's kind hospitality. There's nothing amorous in my poems. You go back this instant. If you're seen, tongues will wag even though nothing happened, and my reputation will be ruined."

As Qinniang stoutly refused to leave, Foyin said, "Yes, yes, you must have been sent by the academician to trap me! In all the years I've been practicing the Buddhist virtues, poetry and wine are as far as I go in the way of entertainment. I have no other mortal desires. Now, tell me the truth and I'll try to save you. If not, there's nothing I can do for you!"

At these words, Qinniang said, tears trickling down her cheeks, "It was indeed the academician who sent me here. If you, sir, would be willing to engage in a game of clouds and rain with me, he will reward me with three thousand strings of cash tomorrow and find a good match for me. If not, he'll have the housekeeper give me twenty strokes of the bamboo rod and drive me out. Please think of a way to help me, sir!" This said, she bowed deeply.

Foyin indulged in a roar of laughter. "Don't worry!" he exclaimed. "I'll help you." From a book bag he retrieved a scroll of paper. Noticing all four treasures of the study on the table, he picked up a brush-pen and wrote a lyric to the tune of "Sand Washed by Waves":

> My encounter with the fairy last night
> Also fulfilled a kind of marriage bond,
> In wine-induced sleep as when awake.

I woke up, believing it was a dream,
But there she was, right by my side.

What is there to say about what happened?
How would I dare have tender feelings?
Not even a string on the lute was touched.
Mark this, Academician Su!
Take back what remains entirely intact.

Feeling he had not expressed himself fully, Foyin wrote another four lines:

A word to the fair lady of Mount Wu:
Do not disturb King Xiang in his dream.[7]
My heart of a monk, like muddied catkins,
Does not flutter with the east wind of spring.

Qinniang took the poems and, once back in the Su residence, presented it to Dongpo. Greatly delighted upon reading them, he proceeded to the study, where he found Foyin sitting in a chair, his legs crossed in a lotus position.

"Virtue be praised!" exclaimed Dongpo. "You are a real monk!" He rewarded Qinniang with three hundred strings of cash and found her a good match. Henceforth, Dongpo respected Foyin even more and treated him as a bosom friend. Foyin did not even have to remove himself from the presence of Dongpo's wives. Every so often, Foyin explicated the Buddhist principles to Dongpo and gradually Dongpo began to embrace Buddhism. Dongpo's calm acceptance of the end of his life, as tradition has it, served as proof that he had attained the fruit of enlightenment. To this day, he is still called the Immortal Po, and much credit should go to Foyin's guidance. There is a poem in testimony:

Dongpo failed to talk Foyin around;
Foyin succeeded in converting him.
Had it not been for the Buddha's boundless power,
Dongpo would not have crossed the river of love.

13

The Leather Boot as Evidence against the God Erlang's Impostor

Past tender green willow branches,
In lingering chill as soft as water,
Amid a drizzle as fine as dust,
Blows a gust of east wind, bringing
Wrinkles to gauze and ripples to water.

Fairy maidens, spirits of flowers and the moon,
Play pipes and flutes to cheer the new season.
With toasts to the long life of the sovereign,
With what the Nine Clouds cups have to offer,
Comes eternal drunkenness on the scents of spring.

The above lyric, to the tune of "Green Willow Tips," was written by a scholar of the Song dynasty founded by Emperor Taizu [r. 960–76].[1] The eighth emperor who succeeded the throne, Emperor Huizong [r. 1101–25], also known as the Venerable Daoist Emperor of Xuanhe of the Jade Hall of Purity in the Highest Layer of Heaven, was in fact a reincarnation of Li Yu [937–78] from south of the Yangzi River, last king of Later Tang. What had happened was that in an interior hall of the palace one day, his father, Emperor Shenzong [r. 1068–86], came upon the portrait of King Li when viewing the portraits of emperors and kings of past dynasties. Li Yu's gracefulness and otherworldly appearance so impressed him that he let out one sigh of admiration after another. Later, he had a dream in which he saw King Li enter the palace, a dream that was soon followed by the birth of Emperor Huizong. Enfeoffed as Prince Duan in his childhood, Emperor Huizong cut a dashing and romantic figure very early on and proved himself capable in every endeavor he undertook. Upon the death of his older brother, Emperor Zhezong [r. 1086–1101], Prince Duan succeeded to the throne with the support of the court ministers. Thereafter, peace reigned throughout the land and the imperial court had little to do.

With his love of gardens, Emperor Huizong ordered a grand construction project in the first year of the Xuanhe reign period [1119–26]. A park with a pond was to be built in the northeastern corner of the city, and the site was named the Silver Hill of Longevity. Emperor Huizong put Liang Shicheng [d. 1126], the eunuch, in charge of the construction and ordered Zhu Mian [1075–1126] to collect and offer to him prized and rare flowers, trees, bamboos, and ornamental rocks from the area south of the lower reaches of the Yangzi River and the Sichuan and Liangguang regions.[2] He called the project the Organized Transportation of Flowers and Rocks.

It took several years, all the savings of the treasury, and the best craftsmen of the land to build the park, which, when completed, also came to be called Ten-Thousand-Year Hill. It was filled with exotic flowers, beautiful trees, and rare birds and animals. The grandeur of the towers and terraces defies description. There were Jade Flower Hall, Peace Preservation Hall, Jasper Forest Hall, Great Serenity Chamber, Celestial Purity Chamber, Wonders Chamber, Rolling Hills Chamber, Rosy Clouds Pavilion, Phoenix on Clouds Pavilion, and, indeed, more attractions than can be enumerated. The six court ministers, Cai Jing [1047–1126], Wang Fu [1079–1126], Gao Qiu [d. 1126], Tong Guan [1054–1126], Yang Jian [d. 1121], and Liang Shicheng, known as "the Six Villains of Xuanhe," often toured the grounds. There is a poem in testimony:

> The forest of jade buildings stood amid
> The mottled shade of bamboos and pine trees.
> Those touring the grounds by imperial grace
> Thought that they were treading on clouds.

Southwest of Peace Preservation Hall, there stood True Jade Hall in which resided Lady An, the emperor's most beloved consort, and a splendid place it was. The gate was adorned with elaborately carved golden heads of beasts that held ringed knockers in their mouths. Along with the dainty jade railings, they dazzled the eye and quickened the pulse. Cai Jing and his cohorts, as guests of the emperor at the banquet table there, had left poems on the walls, as the following lines attest:

> To Peace Hall in all its autumn splendor
> The emperor invited mortal souls.
> To the wining and dining in True Jade Hall
> Was added the pleasure of viewing Lady An.

But this is not a story about how Lady An enjoyed the special favor of the emperor. Instead, I shall tell of another imperial consort, a certain Lady Han Yuqiao. She was only fifteen when she was selected into the palace. With her jade pendants tinkling and her silk skirt swaying as she walked, she had skin as fair as glistening snow and a face as charming as a lotus blossom. However, since the emperor gave Lady An undivided attention, Lady Han never had a chance to be with the emperor.

Our story begins on a spring day when the enchanting scenery saddened our beauty, Lady Han, and gave her chills as she lay on her red mattress under her green quilt. When the moon shone on the jade terrace, her sorrow made her deaf to the notes of pipes and flutes. When insects chirped by her white walls, her grief kept her awake under her quilt embroidered with lovebirds. She grew weary of doing her morning toilette and languished from the torment of her spring desires. With one sigh after another, she became ill, as attested by the following lyric:

> She let the east wind blow her youth away,
> While the tears never ran dry on her face.
> Early or late, cold or warm, rain or shine,
> Every spring takes away some beauties' lives.
> Only drifting fallen flowers hang on to spring.
> The sweet grass confuses the dancing butterflies;
> The green willows talk to the orioles in vain.
> One has made the love potion,
> But the lover is gone.
> She finds herself in a trance,
> As if dancing in rapture,
> As if waking with a start from a dream.

She gradually wasted away like a shriveling willow or a fading flower. An imperial physician took her pulse and gave her a prescription, but the medicinal broth she took might just as well have been splashed onto a rock.

One day, Emperor Huizong summoned Marshal Yang Jian of the palace guards to a side hall and gave the marshal these instructions:[3] "Since you are the one who offered Lady Han to me, you take her to your home now and take good care of her. She can come back to the palace after she regains her health. The imperial caterers will continue to deliver her food every day, and the imperial pharmacy will provide her with medicine. Let me know as soon as her condition begins to improve."

Yang Jian kowtowed in acknowledgment of the order and immediately had palace attendants as well as his private attendants transport Lady Han's trunks, cases, household utensils, and miscellaneous items to his residence. She was then carried there in a curtained sedan-chair with an entourage that included two waiting women and two maids. The marshal went inside first to tell his wife about the matter so that she could come out and greet the guest. The residence was then divided into two sections, and the western quarters were cleaned up for Lady Han to live in. A padlock was put on the gate, through which only physicians and household servants were allowed access. The marshal and his wife went to visit Lady Han once every day. For the rest of the time, the gate remained locked. A bucket stood to one side, for the delivery of food, beverages, and messages. Truly,

> *The green grass by the steps bespeaks spring;*
> *The orioles behind the leaves sing in vain.*

In about two months, Lady Han regained the color in her cheeks, and her appetite grew slightly. In delight, the marshal and his wife laid out a feast, partly to celebrate her recovery and partly to bid her farewell.

After five rounds of wine and two courses of dishes, the marshal's wife said, "We're so glad you've regained your health. This indeed calls for celebration. Let's report to the emperor soon and pick a day for you to return to the palace. What do you say?"

Lady Han clasped her hands in a gesture of respect and said to the marshal's wife, "My ill-starred fate brought me so much sorrow that I had to be confined to my sick bed for two months. Now that I am beginning to feel better, I would like to stay here for a while longer. Please do not report to the emperor yet. But I feel bad to have to impose on your hospitality like this and put you to such inconvenience. I will surely remember to repay your kindness some day."

The marshal and his wife felt obliged to humor her.

Two months later, Lady Han set out a feast in return of the hospitality and engaged a storyteller for the occasion. One of the stories narrated was about a Lady Han in the palace of Emperor Xuanzong [r. 847–59] of the Tang dynasty. (*Another Lady Han! Indeed, without coincidences, there would be no stories.*)

Never having enjoyed any attention from the emperor either, this Lady Han, in despair, wrote a poem on a red leaf, which then floated away on water that drained from the palace ditch. The poem said,

> *Why does the water flow in such haste?*
> *There is nothing to do all day deep in the palace.*
> *Heartily I thank the red leaf*
> *On its way to the world of the mortals.*

It so happened that outside the palace, a young man called Yu You, who was in the capital to sit for the examinations, picked up the red leaf, wrote a poem in reply, and put it into the ditch again to let it float back into the palace. Later, the young man passed the examinations and won instant fame. Upon learning about what had happened, the emperor ordered that Lady Han be married to Yu You. The husband and wife lived in conjugal bliss to a ripe old age.

At this point in the storyteller's narration, a sudden thought struck Lady Han, and she heaved a sigh. Without saying anything out loud, she thought, "If I could be so lucky, I wouldn't have lived my life in vain!"

The feast over, the table was cleared, and all retired to their own quarters. At about midnight, Lady Han felt her head aching, her face hot, her limbs weak, and her body numb. Tormented by her irrepressible desires, she fell ill again. This time, her condition was worse than before. Truly,

> An all-night rain wrecks a hut already leaking;
> A head wind slows down a boat already late.

The marshal's wife came to see her in the morning and said, "Luckily, we haven't yet told the emperor that you could be taken back. While you're here, you'd better forget all cares, set your mind at rest, and recuperate well. Don't worry about returning to the palace."

Lady Han said thankfully, "I'm so grateful for your kindness. But I'm already beyond cure. If heaven is too far away, I'm certainly getting nearer to the world down below. Since I can't repay your great kindness in this life, let me do that as a dog or a horse in my next reincarnation!" With that, her breathing became weak and labored. It was a heartbreaking sight.

Feeling saddened, the marshal's wife said, "Don't say such things. Heaven looks after the virtuous. Once this bad spell in your fate is over, you'll surely recover. Now, if the medicine isn't working, I'm afraid that taking more of it will only do harm to your body. I wonder if you owe the gods any unfulfilled pledge from your days in the palace? Maybe the gods are angry with you, for all we know."

"Since I entered the palace, I've been too preoccupied by my sorrows to make any pledges to the gods. But now that I'm so ill and medicine isn't working, I'll be only too happy to go to a nearby temple and make a vow, if the god of that temple is responsive to prayers. If I can pull through, I'll fulfill my vow."

"I do have some information for you, madam," said the marshal's wife. "In this area, there is the Temple of the Immortal Master of the North Pole and the Clear Source Temple of the god Erlang. They are most responsive to prayers. Why don't you set an incense altar and pray for their protection? If you recover, I'll be glad to go with you and make sacrificial offerings of gratitude. What do you say?"

Lady Han nodded her assent, whereupon the servants brought over an incense altar. Unable to rise, Lady Han leaned against her pillow and, her hand on her forehead, prayed, "I, Han-shi, have never enjoyed the emperor's attention since I entered the palace at an early age. I am therefore ill and am staying in the Yang residence. If the gods will protect me and let me get well, I will embroider two long streamers and offer them, along with other items, to your temples to express my gratitude."

The marshal's wife also held joss sticks and prayed for Lady Han. She then bade Lady Han farewell, but we shall speak no more of this.

Strangely enough, after the vow was taken, Lady Han's condition began to improve gradually and she was fully recovered after a month of convalescence. Beside themselves with joy, the marshal and his wife again set out a feast to celebrate her recovery.

The marshal's wife remarked to Lady Han, "The gods indeed answered your prayers. This is ten thousand times better than medicine. Now you must not go back on your word and fail to honor your promise."

"I wouldn't dream of being so ungrateful. After I've finished embroidering the streamers, would you be willing to go with me to the temples to fulfill my vow?"

"Yes, of course. I'll accompany you there."

After the feast was over, Lady Han took out some money for the purchase of sacrificial items, and her embroidery project of four streamers got under way. As the ancients put it so well:

> A pig's head gets cooked tender with a fire going;
> Official business gets done with money talking.

With money, even the most bizarre and preposterous things in this world can get done. In a matter of days, the embroidery was finished and, when raised high with bamboo poles, the streamers dazzled the eyes. At the chosen auspicious hour on the chosen auspicious day, palace attendants as well as the marshal's household servants carried joss sticks and the offerings to the gods, and escorted the two ladies to the Temple of the Immortal Master of the North Pole first. Upon learning about the arrival of Marshal Yang's family, the head priest of the temple rushed out to meet them and ushered them into the main hall. There, a prayer was read aloud and the streamers were hung up. Lady Han clicked her teeth [as a token of piety] and paid homage to the god. Then they made a tour of the temple, after which the head priest served tea. The ladies had a servant offer a reward of money. They then mounted their sedan-chairs and returned home in the same grand procession as before.

The night went by without ado. The next morning, they rose and proceeded to the temple of the god Erlang. And this visit led to some mysterious events. Indeed,

> Bear this in mind: words are like fishlines and hooks;
> They pull out trouble right in front of your face.

Let us not encumber our story with unnecessary comments but come to the moment when the ladies were touring the temple after the head priest read aloud the prayer and burned the joss sticks.

When the marshal's wife was in a side hall, Lady Han stepped forward, gently lifted the gilded yellow silk curtain over the altar, and peered inside. All would have been well if she had not taken that peek, but she did, and she gave quite a start. Behold:

> On his head, a scarf with golden flowers;
> Over his body, a brown embroidered gown.
> Around his waist, a Lantian jade belt;[4]
> On his feet, black boots with designs of flying phoenixes.

Although made of clay and wood,
His was a dashing figure, with bright eyes and white teeth.
If he had breath, he would have spoken.

Lady Han's eyes glazed over and her heart galloped. Unbeknownst to herself, her innermost thought slipped out through her tongue, "If I am meant to have a bright future, I wish I could marry a husband who looks just like you. If so, my life's wish would be fulfilled."

Before the words were quite out of her mouth, the marshal's wife drew near, asking, "What were you praying for, madam?"

With alacrity, Lady Han said, "I didn't say anything!"

The marshal's wife did not press further. They continued with their tour until late in the afternoon. Then they went home and retired to their own rooms, and there we shall leave them. Indeed,

To know what lies in the depths of the heart,
Listen to what comes out of the mouth.

Back in her own room, Lady Han took off her regalia, tied up her hair, and put on casual wear. She then rested her chin on her hands and fell into a reverie, her mind filled with the image of the god Erlang. All of a sudden, an idea flashed into her mind. She told her servants to set up an incense altar in a secluded spot in the garden. She then prayed to heaven, saying, "If I am meant to have a bright future, please let me marry a husband who looks just like the god Erlang. That will be so much better than living a miserable life in the palace." With these words, tears streamed down her cheeks. She bowed and prayed and bowed again, indulging in nothing less than wild flights of fancy.

Then, the least expected thing happened: after her prayer session was over, she was preparing to go back to her room when, suddenly, a loud bang came from the depths of the flowers and a godlike figure appeared in front of her. Behold:

With his dragon-like brows, phoenix-like eyes,
White teeth and bright red lips,
He had an otherworldly grace
And possessed breathtaking looks.
He must be from the immortals' abode;
His diet must consist of rosy clouds and dew.

A closer look revealed him to bear exactly the same features as the statue of the god Erlang in the temple. He also held a slingshot in his hand in the stance of Zhang Yuanxiao, the fertility god.

Lady Han was alarmed and delighted at the same time—alarmed because there was no knowing whether the advent of a celestial god portended disaster or blessing, and delighted because the god, all smiles, began to talk.

Lady Han stepped forward, solemnly dropped a curtsy, and, opening her rouged lips and revealing her pearly teeth, said, "Since you did me the honor of descending to this place, please go into my room and let me pay my respects to you."

The god Erlang affably went with her into her room and sat down in all complacency. Her salutations completed, Lady Han stood before him, ready to be of service.

"You were good enough to make generous offerings to me, madam," said the god Erlang. "I was taking a stroll in the divine realm just now when I heard your fervent prayers. I learned that you were in fact an immortal living by the Jasper Pool. Because you had not rid yourself of the desires of the flesh, the Jade Emperor banished you temporarily to the royal palace in the mortal world, to enjoy all the wealth and glamour that the human world has to offer. When your banishment term expires, you will return to the realm of the immortals. You will know then that you are no mortal being."

Joy flooded Lady Han's heart. Again she prayed, "Honorable god, I do not wish to go back into the palace. If I am meant to have a bright future, I would like to marry a good man who looks just like you and live with him for the rest of my life. Only then would I be worthy of the spring flowers and the autumn moon. I don't care a thing about wealth and glamour."

With a smile, the god Erlang said, "That can be easily done. I'm only afraid that you may not be firm enough in your determination. If such is your marriage destiny, you will surely get to meet your intended, however great the distance." That said, he rose and jumped onto the windowsill. With a bang, he was gone.

It would have been all right had Lady Han never laid her eyes on him, but she did, and she was smitten by his looks. As if in a trance, she went to bed without even removing her clothes. Truly,

> In joy, the night goes by all too quickly;
> In loneliness, the hours drag on; dawn never comes.

She tossed and turned in bed, hardly able to suppress her amorous desires. She talked to herself one moment, thinking aloud, and fell into silence again the next moment. "When the god was here a while ago," said she, "there were such tender feelings as we looked into each other's eyes. Why did he leave all of a sudden? Maybe as a god, he has more wisdom and moral integrity than mortal beings. My passion was ill-placed!" Then she gave herself up to her thoughts again and said, "In all his grace and affability, that god looked just like a mortal being. How could my beauty not have any effect on him? Or did I let him go in a momentary lapse of attention? I should have shown him more affection, enough to melt even a man made of iron or rock. Now that I missed this chance, I may never get to see him again!"

Unable to snap out of these thoughts, she waited for dawn to come before deciding on the next course of action. But when night did give way to morning, she drifted off to sleep and did not rise from bed until just before noon. For the rest of the day, she was listless, and when the long-awaited darkness of the evening fell at last, she again set up the incense altar in the garden and prayed as before, "If I could get to see the god once again, I would consider myself most fortunate." (*An infatuated fool.*)

Even as she spoke, the god Erlang appeared before her with another loud bang. Lady Han's heart leaped for joy. All her sorrows vanished like melting ice and crumbling tiles. She advanced one step, dropped a curtsy, and said, letting her excitement get the better of her, "May I ask you, honorable god, to go into my room? I have something to say to you in confidence."

Gleefully the god Erlang took her hand and went with her into her chamber. After her salutations were over, the god Erlang sat down in the middle of the room, with Lady Han standing respectfully before him.

"You have the qualities of an immortal, madam," said he. "So you may sit."

Lady Han sat down across from him. She then had servants bring in wine and fruit. There, in her room, she and the god drank one cup after another and she confided in him her innermost feelings. As they say,

> Spring adds flavor to tea;
> Wine adds fire to lust.

Eager for intimacy, Lady Han said, "If you don't despise my unworthiness, please briefly put aside your heavenly official business and enjoy some moments of the pleasures of the human world."

The god Erlang agreed readily enough. They went to bed, hand in hand, and engaged in a game of clouds and rain. Lady Han did her part with abandon. They tarried until it was almost dawn. The god Erlang rose, told her to take good care of herself, and promised that he would visit her again. He dressed, picked up his slingshot, leaped up onto the windowsill and, with a loud bang, disappeared without a trace.

The idea that this was a god visiting the mortal world had taken full possession of Lady Han's mind, and she was in a transport of joy. Afraid that the marshal and his wife would urge her to go back to the palace, she pretended to be much more gravely ill than she was and hardly ever put on a smile. But when evening came, she radiated with joy. After the god arrived, they would drink three cups of wine before starting their amorous sport in bed, and he would leave by dawn. This went on for some time.

One day, the weather having turned colder, Emperor Huizong ordered that autumn clothes be distributed around the palace. Suddenly he thought of Lady Han, whereupon he sent a palace attendant to Marshal Yang's residence to deliver a message as well as a silk robe and a jade waistband. Lady Han set up her altar and thanked the emperor. The palace attendant said to her, "I'm so glad that you are well, my lady. His Majesty misses you so much that he sends you a silk robe and a jade waistband. If you have recovered, please return to the palace as soon as possible."

Lady Han treated the attendant to dinner and said, "I have a favor to ask of you. My illness is only half gone. Could you please relay my plea to His Majesty and ask him to give me more time? I would be ever so grateful."

"That shouldn't be a problem," said the palace attendant. "His Majesty won't mind the absence of one lady. After I go back, I'll just say that Your Ladyship hasn't fully recovered and needs to take good care of herself."

Lady Han thanked him, and the court attendant bade her farewell.

In the evening, the god Erlang said to Lady Han upon arrival, "I'm glad that the emperor still cares about you. May I see the silk robe and jade waistband he gave you?"

"How did you know about this, honorable god?"

"Nothing under heaven escapes my eyes. How can I not know about this triviality?"

At these words, Lady Han all too readily showed him the objects.

"One must not keep any treasure in the mortal world to oneself," said the god Erlang. "I happen to need a jade waistband. Should you be willing to part with it, that'll be an act of charity and gain you merit in heaven."

"All of me now belongs to you, honorable god. With such a predestined bond between us, please feel free to take the jade waistband."

The god Erlang thanked her and they made merry in bed. He rose before dawn and, slingshot and jade waistband in hand, leaped up onto the windowsill, and was gone with a loud bang. Indeed,

> If you don't want people to know what you did,
> You shouldn't have done it in the first place.

Even though Lady Han and the Yang family were living apart in two separate sections of the residence, the marshal had put her quarters under tight watch because of Lady Han's status as an imperial consort. No unauthorized persons would presumably dare venture into that well-guarded area. However, it had often been observed that lights in the west wing were on all night through, and subdued voices and movements had been heard. And Lady Han was seen to be glowing in high spirits, her face wreathed with smiles. After long and hard debates with himself, the marshal finally said to his wife, "Have you noticed anything out of the ordinary about Lady Han?"

"I did have some suspicions, but then I thought this place is so well guarded that nothing can happen. So I dismissed those suspicions of mine. Now that you bring this up, we can easily do something about it. Tonight, let's have a few of the smarter servants climb onto the roof to find out what's going on, so that we don't do her any injustice."

The marshal said, "Good idea." Right away, he summoned two able servants and told them to do thus-and-so, adding, "Do not use the door. Just put the garden ladder against the wall. When all's quiet, climb over to Lady Han's bedroom and watch what goes on there. Then come back and report to me. This is no small matter. Do be careful." Thus instructed, the two men left, and the marshal waited for their report.

In less than four hours' time, the two servants came back to report what they had witnessed. They had the marshal dismiss all other servants before they proceeded to tell him that there was a man in Lady Han's room, sitting there and drinking. "Lady Han kept addressing him as 'Honorable god,'" they said. "Well, we've been doing some thinking: The walls are high, and security is tight. Even if there's some criminal lurking around, he couldn't have gotten there without wings. That man may very well be some kind of god."

The marshal gave a start. "How extraordinary! How can there really be such a thing! You two must not lie, because this is no trifling thing."

"Everything we said is true."

"Now, this whole thing is just between you and me," said the marshal. "You must not let a word of this get out."

The two servants promised and took off. The marshal relayed the information to his wife and added, "I'll have to see with my own eyes to believe what they said. I'll go tomorrow night to see for myself what that god looks like."

The marshal waited until the next evening before he summoned the same two servants and said to them, "One of you will go with me there, and the other one will wait here. Don't tell anyone about this." Having given these instructions, the marshal and one of the servants went on their mission. They tiptoed their way to Lady Han's window and peeped into it. Sure enough, there sat in the room a god that fitted the two servants' description. The marshal was about to cry out, but, afraid that he might not be able to get himself out of an awkward situation, he swallowed his anger and returned to his own quarters after reminding the two servants not to breathe a word to anyone.

Back in his room, the marshal confided in his wife, adding, "It must be Lady Han's youthful wild desires that drew some evil god here. He's sullying an imperial consort, no less. This is surely not the work of a human being. We'll have to engage a priest to do an exorcism. You talk to her. I'll go to find a priest."

Thus instructed, the marshal's wife went to the west wing early the next morning. Lady Han greeted her and offered her a seat. After tea was served, the marshal's wife dismissed all the servants. Seated face to face with Lady Han, she said in a confidential tone, "I'd like to have a word with you. Whom do you talk to every night in your room? You've been heard, and rumor has reached my ears. This is no trifling thing. You must tell me everything. Don't hold anything back."

At these words, Lady Han blushed and said, "I haven't been talking to anyone at night in my room, although I do chat with my maidservants to while away the time. I have no visitors."

Thereupon the marshal's wife told her about what her husband had seen the night before, sparing no details. Lady Han was dumbfounded, completely at a loss as to what to do.

"Don't be alarmed," said the marshal's wife gently to comfort her. "The marshal is out looking for an exorcist. Soon enough, we'll know if he's human or a ghost. You must be careful at night. But don't be afraid." Having said that, the marshal's wife departed, leaving Lady Han sweating with fear. Darkness had barely fallen when the god Erlang appeared, his slingshot tightly in his grip.

In the meantime, the exorcist engaged by the marshal had already begun his conjuration in the front hall. He was the famous Priest Wang, disciple of Sage Lin of Lingji Palace. When report came at dusk about the god's arrival, Priest Wang threw on his robe and, sword in hand, marched majestically toward Lady Han's room.

"What evil spirit are you?" he roared as he burst into the room. "How dare you violate an imperial consort! Don't move! Try a taste of my sword!"

Quite unruffled, the god Erlang said, "The temerity!" Behold:

> His left hand as if holding up Mount Tai,
> His right hand as if carrying a baby,
> His slingshot drawn to look like the full moon,
> He sent pellets that flew like shooting stars.

One pellet hit Priest Wang right in the forehead. As blood flowed down, the priest fell backward, his precious sword cast aside. Witnesses of the scene quickly raised him and helped him into the front hall. In the meantime, the god leaped onto the windowsill and, with a loud bang, was gone. How did it all end? Indeed, when the truth was known,

> Even the sky and the earth were frightened;
> Even the gods and the ghosts were startled.

Witnessing how the god Erlang had beaten the priest, Lady Han was all the more convinced that he was a genuine god who had descended into the world of the mortals. She set all her fears to rest.

Realizing by this time that the priest was not any good, the marshal saw nothing else for it but to pay him for the trouble he had taken and send him away. Then he engaged a Priest Pan of the Five Mountains Temple, a priest who specialized in the Five Thunder Heavenly Zenith Orthodox method of exorcism. Meticulous in his work, he was also wise and resourceful. He came as soon as he learned that he was wanted by the marshal. After the marshal acquainted him with all the details of what had happened, Priest Pan said, "Have someone take me quietly to the west wing. I need to see the place he frequents to know if he's man or ghost."

"Of course," said the marshal.

Thereupon, Priest Pan took leave of the marshal and went first to look all around

Lady Han's bedroom in the west wing. Then he asked to be introduced to Lady Han. After examining her complexion, he turned to the marshal and said, "With all due respect to you, sir, judging by her complexion, I don't see any sign of evil spirits. This is all the doing of a man who knows sorcery. I know how to deal with him. I don't need magic charms or holy water, and there's no need to beat drums or ring bells. The moment he appears, this humble priest will catch him as easily as catching a turtle in a jar. My only concern is that he may have guessed what's going on and won't show up. In that case, there will be nothing I can do."

"I couldn't be happier if he doesn't show up again," said the marshal. "Please stay, sir, and let's have a chat."

Storyteller, if that brute was indeed onto what lay in store for him and had the good sense to do what was best for him under the circumstances, he should never return, like a kite with a broken string. Wouldn't it be nice for him to have enjoyed a good time without tarnishing his name and go on to try his luck elsewhere? As they say, "Do not repeat a trick that got you too good a deal. Do not go again to the place where you made undeserved gains."

To get on with our story, we do not know yet whether that god Erlang was a man or a ghost. Anyway, having tasted the joys of his conquest, he came again that night, little knowing what was good for him.

Lady Han said to him, "I had no idea what was going to happen last night, and I'm sorry for having given you offense. I'm so glad that you're not hurt. Please do not take it ill."

"I am a true god from heaven, here because I have a predestined celestial bond with you, madam. One of these days, I'll deliver you from your mortal frame and fly with you to heaven in broad daylight. That idiot be cursed! Even if he had a thousand soldiers, he couldn't have gotten near me!"

Lady Han was all the more impressed and their union of delight was doubly affectionate.

In the meantime, the marshal had received information about the visit. The marshal, in his turn, notified Priest Pan, who then asked the marshal to send a maidservant to Lady Han's room, ostensibly to wait on them, but in fact to steal the slingshot, so as to render the god Erlang helpless. After the maidservant went off, Priest Pan tightened his clothes around him and, dispensing with the usual exorcist's robe and sword, he only took up a cudgel and told two servants to guide him some distance off, holding torches to light him on his way.

"If you're afraid of his pellets, you can hide yourselves in advance," he said to them. "I will then proceed alone, to see if his pellets can even get near me."

The two men laughed in their sleeves and commented to each other, "What a talker! One of the pellets will surely get him!"

In the meantime, the maidservant had gone to Lady Han's room, ostensibly to offer services. She maneuvered to get near the god. While he was busily exchanging toasts with Lady Han, the maidservant stole his slingshot and put it away. By this time, Priest Pan had arrived at the door. The servants guiding him announced, "This is the place!" Immediately they scurried away as fast as their legs could carry them, leaving the priest there all by himself.

Priest Pan raised the door curtain and swept the room with his eyes. At the sight of that god sitting in the room all cool and poised, Priest Pan gave a shout, began wielding his cudgel, and aimed a front blow at the god Erlang. In haste, Erlang reached for his slingshot, but it was not there. "I've been had!" he cried. He quickly drew back and got onto the windowsill. In less time than it takes to narrate, Priest Pan's cudgel hit him in the back of his leg and brought down an object. With a loud bang, the god Erlang disappeared into the flower bushes.

Priest Pan picked up the fallen object and saw by lamplight that it was a black boot sewn with four pieces of leather. He took it and reported to the marshal. "This humble priest believes that he must be a sorcerer. This has nothing to do with the real god Erlang. (*Knowing that the real god Erlang had nothing to do with this made it easier to take action. If one mistake led to another, goodness knows how many innocent people would be wronged and how many criminals would go unpunished.*) Now how are we going to catch him?"

"You've worked hard enough, sir. You may go now. I'll make arrangements for an investigation." With that, he paid Priest Pan and thanked him. Of Priest Pan, we shall say no more.

The marshal went off by sedan-chair to the residence of Preceptor Cai and entered the study.⁵ He gave a whole account of the happenings and added, "We can't let things go on like this. That brute will laugh at us. What a disgrace that'll be!"

"That can be easily taken care of," said the preceptor. "I'll have Prefect Teng of Kaifeng take on this case. Give him this boot as a clue and assign a few able officers to investigate and hunt the culprit down. Then deal with him according to the law."

"Thank you for your advice," said the marshal.

"Sit here for a while," said the preceptor, who then ordered Clerk Zhang to go with all speed to bring Prefect Teng over. After an exchange of civilities upon his arrival, the servants were dismissed. The preceptor and the marshal said, "How can we allow such trespasses in the very capital of the empire? You, Prefect Teng, must give the case your utmost attention and not be negligent in any way. This is no trifling matter. And take care not to 'stir the grass and alarm the snake,' so to speak. Otherwise he'll slip away."

The prefect was so frightened that he turned deathly pale. Without delay, he said, "You can count on me."

Taking the boot with him, he said good-bye to the preceptor and the marshal and returned to his yamen. Immediately he summoned Inspector Wang, who was on duty that day, dismissed the attendants, and acquainted him with all the details of the case. "I give you three days to bring to me the one wreaking havoc in Marshal

Yang's residence. But don't make a big fuss over it. Do a thorough job, and you'll be rewarded well. If not, you'll have a lot to answer for!" And with that, he dismissed Inspector Wang.

Inspector Wang took the boot into his own office and assembled all the officers. He sighed. Behold:

His eyebrows double locked in deep furrows;
His heart laden with ten thousand worries.

Among the officers was a Ran Gui, popularly known as Big Ran, whose operations covered three major cities of the empire. A most brilliant, quick-thinking detective, he had helped Inspector Wang solve goodness knows how many baffling cases, and Inspector Wang thought the world of him. Noticing the inspector's furrowed brows and worried look, Big Ran did not press him but kept up a steady chatter about things having little to do with the case.

Seeing that none of his men appeared to take him seriously, Inspector Wang produced the boot and threw it on the table, saying, "Life is hard for us officers! How can our magistrate be so muddle-headed? A boot cannot talk, and yet he gives us three days to bring him the owner of this boot—the man who's been wreaking havoc in Marshal Yang's house. Don't you find this ridiculous?"

The officers took turns examining the boot. When it was passed to Big Ran, he took little notice of it but kept saying, "This is a tough job! A tough job! The magistrate is indeed muddle-headed. Inspector, I don't blame you for feeling frustrated!"

Surprised at such complaints from Ran, the inspector said, "Big Ran, even you are saying this is a tough job. We can't call it quits just like that, can we? You're making things harder for me. What am I going to say to the magistrate? Like everyone else, you get paid by this office, and yet you say nothing but 'it's a tough job!'"

"An ordinary case like burglary or theft would be easy to tackle," said the men. "But if it's a sorcerer we're dealing with, how are we going to get him? If it's easy to get him, that Priest Pan would have done so long ago. Even he could do nothing more than knocking a boot off him. We have only our own bad luck to blame for being assigned this mysterious case. This is hopeless."

If Inspector Wang's worries had registered five on a scale of one to ten, they went all the way up to ten after he heard these arguments, which all sounded valid to him. But, calmly, Ran Gui said, "Inspector, let's not be discouraged yet. Isn't he just a human being like us? He doesn't have three heads and six arms. If we can find some telltale signs, we will be able to track him down." He turned the boot over and over in his hands, his eyes taking in every detail.

The other men burst out laughing. "Big Ran, there you go again! There's nothing exotic about this boot. It's made of leather dyed black, sewn together with thread, and lined with blue cloth. And it has been shaped with a shoe last and stiffened with water."

Big Ran did not say a word but continued to examine the boot closely by lamp-light. There were four finely stitched seams. Noticing that one seam split open slightly at the tip of the boot, Big Ran poked his little finger at the place and as he did so, there popped two stitches, and the leather curled upward. When he looked inside the boot under the lamp, he saw a layer of blue lining. A closer look revealed a piece of white paper. He slipped two fingers in, took out the note, and read it. It would have been a different story if he had not read it, but he did, and he rejoiced as someone who had found gold or a treasure trove in the middle of the night. Inspector Wang's face also burst into a smile at this godsend. The others all went forward to look at the note. It said, "Made by Ren Yilang, the shoe-maker, on the fifth day of the third month in the third year of the Xuanhe reign period."

The inspector said to Big Ran, "This is the fourth year of the Xuanhe reign. So the boot was made just a little over a year ago. If we can get this Ren Yilang, we stand a good chance of solving the case."

"Let's not alarm him today," suggested Big Ran. "Let's wait until tomorrow morning and then send two men to him to say that the magistrate has a job for him. Once he's here, tie him up. He'll surely tell us the truth."

"I just knew you would come up with something good!" exclaimed the inspector.

They stayed awake throughout the night, drinking. None of the men dared to leave. At the crack of dawn, two men set out with the speed of the wind to get Ren Yilang. In less than four hours, the unsuspecting Ren Yilang was brought to the detective's office. As soon as Ren was in the office, the officers suddenly turned fierce and trussed him up, shouting, "A fine thing you did! How dare you!"

Trembling, Ren Yilang said, "Can't we talk nicely? What did I do to make you tie me up like this?"

Inspector Wang said, "What do you have to say for yourself? Wasn't this boot made in your shop?"

Ren Yilang took the boot and peered at it intently. "Yes, Inspector," he said. "This boot was indeed made by me. Let me explain. Ever since I opened my shop, I have kept a ledger at home. It records every order I've received from government officials and every purchase by visiting customers, complete with dates and the names of the clerks from official residences bearing the orders. Inside each boot, there's also a slip of paper with the same serial number as that entered in the ledger. (*If the story took place today, with the way people do things now, the officers wouldn't be able to find a lead.*) Sir, if you don't believe me, you need only cut open this boot and get that slip of paper to know that I'm telling the truth."

Convinced that this was indeed the truth, Inspector Wang said, "He's honest. Untie him and talk to him nicely."

Right away, they untied Ren Yilang and said, "Don't blame us, Yilang. We had to do this because our superiors so ordered."

When they showed him the slip of paper, Ren Yilang said, "Inspector, you don't have anything to worry about. Even if this boot was made four to five years ago, not to mention within the last two years, I still have the record in my ledgers at home. Please have someone go with me to get them and check the record. The truth will be out."

Thereupon two men were dispatched to follow Ren Yilang to his home. They took the ledgers and ran apace back to Inspector Wang's office, their feet hardly touching the ground. Inspector Wang personally examined the ledgers from the very first page and when he got to the fifth day of the third month of the third year of Xuanhe, he saw that the serial number exactly matched that on the slip of paper. Upon reading the rest of the entry, he gave a start and fell silent, for the boots were ordered by none other than Clerk Zhang in the employment of Preceptor Cai Jing in his residence. Without a moment's delay, Inspector Wang took Ren Yilang, the boot, and the ledger, and hurried to Prefect Teng's yamen for a report.

This being a special case which the magistrate himself had assigned them, they were immediately led into the prefect's presence. Inspector Wang related what had happened and presented the prefect with the ledger as well as the slip of paper. After checking the numbers and finding them to be identical, Prefect Teng was flabbergasted. "That explains it!" he remarked. But, still feeling skeptical, he thought for a moment before saying, "So Ren Yilang is not involved in the case. He can go now."

Ren Yilang bowed in gratitude and took off, but Prefect Teng called him back and gave him these words of admonishment: "I'm letting you go, all right, but you must not leak out a word about this. If anyone asks you, just say something noncommittal and change the subject. Mark my words!"

"Yes, sir!" said Ren Yilang. With that, he went merrily on his way.

Prefect Teng took the boot and the ledger and, along with Inspector Wang and Big Ran, went to Marshal Yang's residence in his sedan-chair. The marshal had just returned home from the day's court session with the emperor. Upon the gatekeeper's announcement of the visitors, the marshal went into the main hall to receive them. Prefect Teng said, "This is not a good place to talk." The marshal then took them to a small study in the west wing, dismissed all servants, and kept only Inspector Wang and Big Ran. The prefect related everything in due order and said in conclusion, "What's to be done now? I dare not act on my own."

The marshal was dumbfounded. For a considerable time, he sat immobile and thought, "The grand preceptor is such an important official of the empire, rich and eminent. He can't have done this. But this boot is from his residence. The culprit must be someone close to him." Turning the matter over in his mind, he thought of taking the boot to the grand preceptor's mansion and confronting him with it, but he was afraid this would mean a severe loss of face on the grand preceptor's part and he would only put himself in a difficult position if the grand preceptor took offense. Then he thought of dropping the case altogether, but it was no small matter. With the involvement of two exorcists, detectives, and Ren Yilang, the case had already gone public. If he tried to keep the lid on it, he would not be able to pretend he knew nothing once it became exposed. Should the emperor fly into a rage, he would have a lot to answer for. After thinking long and hard about different options, he dismissed Inspector Wang and Big Ran. He called for his sedan-chair, had a servant tuck the boot and the ledger safely in his seat, and went at top speed with Prefect Teng to a certain place. Truly,

> You've worn out iron shoes on a long, fruitless hunt;
> But here he is; you need not have searched.

It was to Grand Preceptor Cai's residence that the marshal and the prefect went. They waited at the gate for what seemed like ages before the grand preceptor called them into his study. After an exchange of greetings and the usual serving of tea, the grand preceptor asked, "Have you got to the bottom of the case?"

The marshal replied, "We know who the criminal is, but for your sake, we dare not make an arrest."

"This is no small matter. How can I shield him?" said the grand preceptor.

"Even if you won't shield him, you'll be in for a minor shock."

"Why don't you just tell me who it is? Why all this suspense?"

"Please dismiss all the servants before I tell you."

The grand preceptor promptly dismissed all the servants. It was only then that the marshal opened his briefcase and produced the ledger. After the preceptor examined the contents, the marshal said, "You are the only one who can make a judgment in this case, Grand Preceptor. No one else can."

"How very strange! How very strange!" said the grand preceptor.

The marshal continued, "This being a case of vital importance, please do not hold me to blame."

"I won't hold it against you. I'm only wondering where this boot came from."

"The ledger says it was ordered by Clerk Zhang of your establishment. This can't be wrong."

"Zhang Qian may very well have ordered it, but he may not have had anything more to do with it. In fact, all the formal clothes, boots, shoes, and socks in my house are taken care of by different maidservants. All the items are clearly recorded, including those made by my house staff, those received as gifts, and those sent out as gifts. Every month, they make detailed reports. Everything is done in good order. Let me have someone check the in-house ledger, and then we'll know the truth."

Straightaway, he ordered that the maidservant in charge of boots be brought forth. Presently, she came with a ledger in hand.

The grand preceptor said to her, "This is a boot from this house. How did it end up with an outsider? Check this ledger for me."

The maidservant checked item by item and found that the boot had been ordered in the third month of the previous year. Soon after the pair of boots was delivered, a student of the grand preceptor's, by the name of Yang Shi, also known as Gentleman of Mount Gui, had come to bid farewell to the grand preceptor because he had just been promoted to be magistrate of a county near the capital, and he was in the grand preceptor's good graces.[6] Being a philosopher, he was unkempt in appearance. The grand preceptor therefore gave him a round-collar robe, a silver waistband, a pair of boots, and four Sichuan fans by way of farewell presents. And this was the very boot given on that occasion. (*Those giving presents, be warned!*) The record was indeed clear. The grand preceptor showed it to the marshal and the magistrate, who immediately apologized, saying, 'So this has nothing to do with members of the grand preceptor's household. Please forgive our impertinence, but we were trying to do our duty."

The grand preceptor said affably, "You did the right thing. You are not to blame. But I doubt that Mr. Yang of Mount Gui is capable of such things. There must be more to the case than what we know so far. Since his duty station is not far from here, let me have him brought here for questioning. You can go now, but don't let a word out about this." The marshal and the prefect took leave of Grand Preceptor Cai and went their separate ways home.

Right away, the grand preceptor sent for Magistrate Yang. After two days, Magistrate Yang arrived in the capital and was brought into the grand preceptor's presence.

After tea was served, the grand preceptor said, "The magistrate of a county is supposed to be like a parent to the local people. How can you commit such a heinous crime?" He then launched into a complete account of the case.

"My respects to you, my venerable teacher," said Magistrate Yang, half rising from his seat. "Last year, after I took your generous gifts, I was suddenly afflicted with an eye ailment when I was still at home, before leaving the capital to take up my post. I was told that there is in these parts a Clear Source Temple of the god Erlang, who is wonderfully responsive to prayer. So I pledged that as soon as my eye ailment was gone, I would go to the temple to offer incense and express my gratitude. So after I got well, I kept my word and went to the temple to offer incense. There, I noticed that the statue of the god Erlang was in impeccable attire, except that his black boots were torn and looked quite out of place. So I offered my boots to the god. This is the whole truth. I have never done anything dishonorable in my life. Being a student of the classics of Confucius and Mencius, how would I stoop so low? The grand preceptor will surely give the matter your fullest consideration."

Knowing the Gentleman of Mount Gui to be a great Confucian scholar averse to acts of impropriety, the grand preceptor replied, "I know your good reputation. I asked you here just to answer some questions to convince those people." He then treated Magistrate Yang to dinner, after which the magistrate took leave of him and was about to depart when the grand preceptor reminded him not to reveal any of this to anyone. Magistrate Yang then bade him good-bye and took himself off. Truly,

> *He who has done nothing against his conscience by day*
> *Need not fear the knock on his door at night.*

The grand preceptor then invited Marshal Yang and Prefect Teng over and explained everything to them, adding, "So, you see, Magistrate Yang is not our man, either." (*Clearing Mr. Yang in a light-hearted, humorous way.*) The Kaifeng Prefecture will have to keep on trying."

There was nothing Prefect Teng could say. He took back the boot, said good-bye, and returned to the yamen. Once there, he called Inspector Wang over and said to him, "Whatever clues we had have all vanished into thin air. Take the boot back. I give you an extension of five days. Be sure to bring the criminal to me."

Thus ordered, Inspector Wang returned to the detectives' office with a heavy heart. To Big Ran he said, "Luckless me! How nice it was when you tracked down Ren Yilang! Since the grand preceptor's household is involved, I thought the case was closed because one official would cover up for another. Who would have thought that they would want to pursue this case! Where am I going to start looking? Actually, since Magistrate Yang gave the boots to the god Erlang, it may indeed have been this god who indulged in a few escapades, for all we know. But how do we get evidence to show the magistrate?"

Big Ran said, "Even if you didn't say so, I just knew that Ren Yilang and Grand Preceptor Cai and Magistrate Yang had no part in this. You say this was the work of the god Erlang, but I can hardly imagine a god doing such an unconscionable thing. It must have been the work of some sorcerer living near the temple. Let's go to the area around the temple and try to find out something. If we can catch him, don't rejoice. If not, don't be upset."

"Right," conceded the inspector. He gave the boot to Big Ran, who then filled two baskets with small general merchandise and carried them on a pole across his shoulder. Brandishing a rattle-drum called Get the Housewives Out, he headed straight for the temple of the god Erlang. Once there, he put down his load, lit a joss stick, and prayed under his breath, "God, please help me, Ran Gui, catch the one who wreaked havoc in Marshal Yang's house and, in doing so, clear your name." After he kowtowed, he drew three lots in succession and each time the divination was favorable. Big Ran thanked the god, picked up his load, and took a walk around the temple. He kept his eyes wide open, looking left and right, without closing them for an instant. (*Ran Gui was a famous detective in the Song dynasty, who often kept his eyes closed. Hence the reference to his not closing his eyes.*) Then he approached a house with a single-leaf door with a well-used speckled bamboo curtain over it and a half-window next to it. As the door was standing ajar, he heard someone cry from inside, "Peddler, over here!"

Big Ran turned around and saw a young woman. "What can I do for you, madam?"

"You buy back used items, don't you? I've got something here that I'd like to sell for a few pennies to buy candies for my boys. Will you take it?"

"My load is called 'Take 'em All.' There's nothing I don't buy. Show me what you've got."

The woman told her son to bring out the item and show it to Big Ran. What did the boy bring out? Indeed,

> *The case of the deer baffled the prime minister of Zheng;[7]*
> *The dream about a butterfly confused Zhuangzi.[8]*

What the boy brought out was a black leather boot sewn with four pieces of black leather, exactly the same as the one knocked off by Priest Pan. Showing none of the joy that flooded his heart, Big Ran said, "You've got only one, so it's not worth a lot. How much do you want for it? Don't ask for too much, though."

"I just want a few pennies to buy some candies for the boys. You name the price, but be fair."

Big Ran took out one and a half strings of cash and, handing them to her, said, "Now if this is fine with you, I'm taking it. If you don't think this is enough, the deal is off. One boot out of a pair isn't worth much, you know."

"What are a few pennies to you? Give me a couple more!"

"I can't," said Big Ran as he started to walk off with his load.

The boy burst into tears. The woman had to call Big Ran back. "Just a little more, please."

Big Ran took out twenty pennies and said, "Oh well, so be it. This is more than the thing's worth." He took the boot, tossed it into one of his baskets and set off, saying to himself in exultation, "This case is as good as half solved! But I mustn't make a fuss about this. I need to find out more about that woman before I can make my move." That evening, he deposited his load in a friend's house by Tianjin Bridge and went to the detectives' office. When Inspector Wang came to inquire, he said he had nothing new to report.

After breakfast the next day, he went again to Tianjin Bridge, picked up his load from his friend, and betook himself to the woman's house, but he found the door locked. The woman must have gone out. He knitted his brows in thought and soon hit on a plan. He put down his load and went from door to door, looking around. He saw an old man sitting on a small stool in front of a house, making a rope with straw. Big Ran asked apologetically, "Uncle, could you tell me where the young lady in the house on your left is?"

The old man stopped working and, looking up at Big Ran, said, "Why do you ask about her?"

"I'm a peddler of miscellaneous goods. Yesterday I bought an old boot from her. I didn't look carefully enough at the time. It turned out that I got shortchanged in the deal. So I'm here again to get my money back."

"My advice is to let it go at that. That woman is not one to provoke. She's the mistress of Magic Powers Sun, custodian of the temple of the god Erlang. That Magic Powers Sun is quite a sorcerer and a real holy terror! This old boot must have been taken off the statue of the god and given to her to buy candies with. She's gone to see her mother today. She's known the temple custodian for quite some time now. For some reason, they got estranged for two to three months but have recently been seeing each other again. (*Estranged because he had Lady Han. After his boot was struck off, he resumed his relationship with this woman. Meticulous attention to details of the narrative.*) If you ask her for your money back, you don't have a chance. If you upset her, she'll tell her lover, and he'll use his sorcery on you. What can you do?"

"I see. Thank you for your advice."

Big Ran took leave of the old man, picked up his load, and returned to the detectives' office, all smiles. Inspector Wang asked, "Got lucky today?"

"Yes, indeed! Show me that boot."

Inspector Wang took out the boot. Big Gui compared it with the one he had bought and saw that they were identical.

"Where did you get that one?" asked Inspector Wang eagerly.

All calm and composed, Big Ran related everything to him and added, "Didn't I say that it wasn't the doing of the god Erlang? Now we know that Magic Powers Sun is the culprit! No doubt about that!"

Inspector Wang went delirious with joy. Without losing one moment, he burned incense to ask for the gods' blessings and, offering a toast to Big Ran by way of thanking him, said, "Now, how are we going to get him? If there's a leak, that swine will give us the slip, and the game will be up."

"It's easy!" said Big Ran. "Tomorrow, let's prepare the three kinds of sacrificial offerings [pig, sheep, and ox] and go to the temple. We'll say we want to thank the god and fulfill our pledges. Once we reach the temple, the custodian will surely come out to greet us. A wine cup can be flung as a signal for action. We can then easily catch him."

"Sounds good," said the inspector. "We need to report to the prefect first, to get authorization for the arrest."

Straightaway, Inspector Wang reported to the prefect. Overcome with delight, Prefect Teng said, "You've got quite a job on your hands. Be careful. Don't make any wrong moves. I heard that sorcerers can make themselves invisible and slip away. I suggest that you bring along some antidotes like pig's blood, dog's blood, garlic, and manure. Pour those on him, and he won't be able to get away."

Thus instructed, Inspector Wang left to make the preparations. Early the next morning, they went to the temple, having first secretly ordered a few men to carry the four antidotes and wait at a distance for the signal. They would go forward for action as soon as the culprit was caught. After giving all the necessary instructions, Inspector Wang and Big Ren changed their clothes and, together with all the other officers, went into the main hall to burn incense. Magic Powers Sun, the custodian, came out to greet them and read the prayer. He was into the fourth or fifth sentence when Big Ran, who was pouring out wine next to him, flung a wine cup to the floor. The others all swarmed forward and overpowered the custodian. Truly, it was like

Black vultures pouncing on a small swallow;
Fierce tigers devouring a lamb.

The four antidotes were then poured right over his head. The custodian knew what the antidotes could do. However immense his magic powers, he lost the use of his limbs. The officers beat him with a rod every step of the way as they brought him to the Kaifeng prefectural yamen.

When word got to him that the sorcerer had been caught, Prefect Teng assumed his bench in the court and roared in anger, "You vile scoundrel! How dare you use your sorcery to violate an imperial consort and cheat her out of her precious possessions? And right in the capital of the empire, too! Now, what do you have to say for yourself?"

Magic Powers Sun tried to deny the charges, but under torture, he confessed, knowing that he would not be able to lie his way out of this. "I began to learn sorcery since childhood from gangs. Later I became a priest at the temple to the god of Erlang and bribed my way into the position of custodian. I overheard Lady Han's prayer that she wanted to marry a husband just like the god Erlang. That gave me the evil idea of pretending to be the god. I did indeed defile her and cheat her out of her jade waistband."

Prefect Teng ordered that he be put in a big cangue and thrown into jail, and also instructed the wardens to watch him closely while waiting for the emperor's decree.[9] He then put together a file on the case and brought it to Marshal Yang. Together they went to Grand Preceptor Cai's residence, where they consulted each other and wrote a memorial to the emperor.

The emperor's decree, when it came, was found to contain these words: "For the crimes of defilement of an imperial consort and acquisition of valuable property under false pretenses, the criminal is hereby sentenced to death by multiple cuts. His wife shall render unpaid services to government yamen. The jade waistband will be returned to the palace, if yet undisposed of. Lady Han, henceforth forbidden to enter the palace on account of her debauchery, is to be married off by Marshal Yang to a law-abiding commoner."

After an initial surge of fear, Lady Han later found her longing for love gratified and her wish fulfilled, for she was married off to a merchant who was a native of a distant place but ran a government-sponsored shop in the capital. Determined not to take her to his hometown, he traveled back and forth between the two places and they lived in conjugal harmony until a ripe old age. But this happened later.

The prefect of Kaifeng brought Magic Powers Sun from jail and the verdict was read out loud in court. A notice was put up listing his crimes and announcing the sentence of death by multiple cuts. He was then taken to the marketplace and executed in public. Indeed,

All the evil deeds he had done in the past
Came back to haunt him in his darkest hour.

There was a jostling crowd of spectators at the execution that day. After the supervisor of executions finished reading out his crimes, the executioners shouted, "All avenging spirits, come here!" With that, they brought their knives down on Magic Powers Sun, stirring a great commotion at the marketplace.

This story used to circulate among storytellers in the capital, but has now found its way into the unofficial history of the Song dynasty. Truly,

> Be sure to observe Confucian decorum;
> Do not violate Xiao He's penal code.[10]
> The depraved deserve violent deaths;
> Magic powers are of no avail.

The Fan Tower Restaurant as Witness to the Love of Zhou Shengxian

When peace reigns in the land, the day stretches long;
The joy of music and wine spreads hither and yon.
At word that His Majesty is arriving,
Everyone waits in eager expectation.

The above quatrain is about emperors touring scenic spots. Every place chosen to be the capital of the empire is invariably blessed with natural beauty and an abundance of talented people. The famous mountains and bodies of water add delight to the happy events. For example, the Winding Pond of the Tang dynasty and the Golden Bright Pond of the Song dynasty, both known for their scenic splendors throughout all four seasons, teemed with sightseers, among whom were scions of nobility, fair maidens, and dashing young men.[1] The emperor also toured these attractions from time to time to share the joy of the populace.

Our story takes place during the reign of Emperor Huizong [1101–25] of the great Song dynasty. By the side of Golden Bright Pond in the Eastern Capital stood a multistoried restaurant called Fan Tower.[2] A certain Big Brother Fan owned a wineshop in the tower. He had a younger brother, yet unmarried.

Our story begins on a day when spring was giving way to summer. Joining the droves of sightseers touring Golden Bright Pond, Second Brother Fan was quite impressed by the many fair maidens and dashing young men he saw. When his feet led him into a teahouse, his eyes fell upon a young lady about eighteen years of age. She was such a marvel to the eyes that he stopped to stare. Indeed,

She had captivating charm that bound men to her,
Deep in her boudoir behind roadside willows.
She had feet as dainty as lotus flowers;
She had a waist so narrow one hand could hold it.
Her soft cheeks the color of peach blossoms,

Her fragrant skin as fair as the finest jade,
Her lovely bearing enthralled wild young men;
Her allure made admirers burn with yearning.
Dreams of joy behind a drawn bed curtain—
Where and when can they be fulfilled?

The fact of the matter is, neither passion nor lust is something easily controllable. As Second Brother gazed at the young lady in the teahouse, their four eyes were locked in mutual attraction. The young lady said to herself joyfully, "How nice it would be if I could get to marry such a young man! If I pass up this chance while he's here, when will I ever get another one?" Then she went on to think, "Now, how am I going to engage him in conversation and find out if he's married or not?" Her maidservant and the nurse accompanying her knew nothing about what went on in her mind.

Wouldn't you say that coincidences do happen? At this point, the clinking of water vessels outside became audible. With a knit of her brows, the young lady came up with a plan. "Water peddler," she cried. "Give me a cup of sweet water!"

The water peddler filled a brass cup with sweetened water and offered it to her. No sooner had she accepted it and taken a sip than she tossed the cup into the air and said at the top of her voice, "A fine thing you did, trying to hurt me on the sly like that! Don't you know who I am?"

Second Brother Fan said to himself upon hearing this, "Let me listen to what she has to say."

"I am the daughter of Mr. Zhou of Cao Gate. My name is Zhou Shengxian. In all my eighteen years of life, no one has ever tried to harm me on the sly. And now here you are, trying to harm an unmarried girl like me!" (*Even bolder than the young lady of the* Story of the Western Chamber.)³

Second Brother Fan thought, "Those revelations are quite uncalled for. They're clearly for my benefit."

"Young lady," said the water peddler. "How would I dare harm you?"

"But you did try to harm me! There was a blade of grass in my cup," declared the young lady.

"That couldn't have harmed you in any way," rejoined the water peddler.

"You were trying to do harm to my throat. Too bad my father is not at home. If he were, he'd surely sue you."

Her nurse chimed in, "What a scoundrel!"

At the commotion, the waiter came over and said to the water peddler, "You'd better leave and take your load of water with you."

Second Brother Fan thought, "With that hint from her, how can I not reciprocate?" At the top of his voice, he cried, "Water peddler! I'll have a cup of sweet water, too!"

The water peddler poured him one. Fan took the cup, sipped from it, and tossed the cup in the air, shouting, "A fine thing you did! You are indeed out to get people on the sly! Who do you think I am? My older brother, Big Brother Fan, is owner of a wineshop in Fan Tower Restaurant. I'm Second Brother Fan, nineteen years of age, and no one has ever been able to harm me on the sly. I'm good at archery and the slingshot, and I'm not married."

"Are you out of your mind?" said the water peddler. "What do you mean by giving me all this information? You want me to be your matchmaker? You can go ahead and sue me. I'm here to sell drinks. How would I even dream of doing people harm?"

Second Brother Fan objected, "But you do harm people! There was a blade of grass in my cup, too!"

These words filled the young lady Shengxian's heart with joy. The waiter stepped over and pushed the peddler out. Shengxian stood up, saying, "Let's go back." Turning to the water peddler, she said, "Would you dare follow me?"

Young Mr. Fan thought, "That's an invitation for me to follow her." And this adventure was to lead to a baffling court case. Truly,

> *Do not say one word more than needed;*
> *Do not venture out if the trip can be spared.*

Believing the young lady was some distance off by now, Second Brother Fan sallied out of the teahouse and saw her far ahead of him. Transported with delight when she looked back, he followed her all the way to her house. She had barely entered the house when she turned around and raised the door curtain to look out. (*In every move, the girl comes across as doubly more romantically inclined than the young man.*) Second Brother Fan was all the more thrilled. After the young lady disappeared into the house, Fan continued to pace back and forth in front of the house like a man possessed and did not return home until dark.

After returning home, the young girl felt indisposed and declined all offers of food. Alarmed, her mother asked Ying'er, the maid, "Did the young mistress eat anything uncooked that upset her stomach?"

"No, ma'am," replied Ying'er. "She didn't."

After the young lady had lain in bed for several days in succession, her mother walked up to her bed and asked, "My child, what's bothering you?"

"I'm aching all over. My head also aches. And I cough a little."

Mrs. Zhou wanted to engage a doctor for a house call, but as her husband was away on a trip and there were no men in the house, she thought it inappropriate to do so.

Ying'er suggested, "Why don't you ask Granny Wang from two houses away to take a look at the young mistress? She's called Can-Do-Wang. She delivers babies, sews, arranges marriages, takes the pulse of the sick, and diagnoses illnesses. Every family in the neighborhood goes to her for help with everything."

So, by Mrs. Zhou's order, Ying'er brought Granny Wang over. After an exchange of greetings, Mrs. Zhou explained that her daughter had fallen ill after undertaking a trip to Golden Bright Pond.

"You need say no more," remarked Granny Wang. "Let me take the young lady's pulse, and I'll know what ails her."

"That would be wonderful," said Madam Zhou.

When Ying'er led Granny Wang into the young lady's room, they found her lying in bed. Opening her eyes, she said, "Please forgive me for the lack of courtesy."

"That's all right," said Granny Wang. "I'm here just to feel your pulse."

Shengxian thereupon stretched out her arm. After feeling her pulse, Granny Wang commented, "Your head aches, your body is sore all over, and you feel like throwing up."

"Yes!" said the patient.

"Anything more?" asked Granny Wang.

"I also cough a little."

It would have been a different story if Granny Wang had not heard this, but since she did, she thought, "How strange that she got so ill after taking a little walk!" Aloud she said to Ying'er and the nurse, "Could you please go out for a moment? I want to be alone with her and ask her a few questions."

After Ying'er and the nurse were gone, Granny Wang said to Shengxian, "I know what this is."

"How could you possibly know, Granny?"

"Yours is an affliction of the mind." (*Granny Wang must have had the same experience in her youth.*)

"How is that so?"

"Young lady, did you meet someone and take a liking to him before you fell ill? Am I right?"

The girl hung her head and said, "No."

"Tell me the truth, young lady. I'll think of a way to save your life."

Encouraged by her tone, the girl came up with an account of what had happened, adding, "He's called Second Brother Fan."

"Can it be Second Brother Fan of the wineshop in Fan Tower Restaurant?"

"Yes."

"In that case, you have nothing to worry about, young lady! I may not know other people, but I happen to know his older brother and sister, the nicest people there are! And Second Brother is such a smart young man! His brother has asked me to find a wife for him. If I propose that you marry him, would you take him?"

The girl smiled. "Oh yes! But I'm afraid my mother won't hear of it."

"Don't you worry! I know what to do!"

"If you can bring this about, I'll thank you with a nice reward, Granny."

After leaving the chamber, Granny Wang declared to Mrs. Zhou, "I know what's bothering her."

"What is it?"

"Give me three cups of wine before I tell you."

"Ying'er," cried out Mrs. Zhou. "Serve wine to Granny Wang!"

While Granny Wang was drinking the wine, Mrs. Zhou asked, "So, what is my daughter suffering from, Granny?"

After Granny Wang repeated what the girl had told her, Mrs. Zhou said, "What's to be done?"

"The only solution is to marry her to Second Brother Fan. If not, she's not likely to get well again."

"My husband is away. This can't be done in his absence."

"Madam, you can give the young lady your word now, but wait until your husband comes back before you hold the ceremony. The important thing now is to save your daughter's life."

"You're right, you're right," conceded Mrs. Zhou. "But how are we going to go about it?"

"I'll go over to the Fan family right now. I'll bring you back their response soon enough." With that, Granny Wang left the Zhou residence and headed straight for Fan Tower Restaurant. At the sight of Big Brother Fan sitting behind the counter, Granny Wang chanted a greeting. Returning the courtesy, Big Brother Fan said, "Granny Wang, you're the very person I'd like to see. I was just going to invite you over."

"What could it be about?"

"It's about my brother. After he went out for a walk a couple of days ago, he skipped supper, saying he didn't feel well. I asked him where he had been. He said, 'To Golden Bright Pond.' He's still lying in bed, too sick to take in any food or drink. I was just going to ask you to check his pulse."

Big Brother Fan's wife came out and, after greeting Granny Wang, said, "Please take a look at my brother-in-law."

Granny Wang said, "Big Brother, Big Sister, please stay out of his room. Let me ask him one on one what has led to this illness."

"All right," Big Brother agreed. "Go ahead, Granny. We'll leave you alone."

Granny Wang found Second Brother lying in bed. "Second Brother," she called out, "Granny is here!"

Opening his eyes, Second Brother Fan said, "Granny Wang, haven't seen you for a long time. I'm dying."

"What can you possibly be dying of?"

"A headache, nausea, and a little cough."

Granny Wang burst out laughing.

"How can you laugh at me when I'm so ill?"

"I'm laughing only because I know the cause of your illness. Is it because of Mr. Zhou's daughter of Cao Gate?"

Now that Granny Wang had hit him right on his sore spot, he jumped from bed and said, "How did you know?"

"The Zhou family sent me over to propose marriage."

Nothing would have happened if Second Brother Fan had not heard this, but he did, and his heart exulted. Truly,

> *Glad tidings cheer up the spirit;*
> *A good conversation warms up the heart.*

Without a moment's delay, Second Brother Fan dashed out of his room with Granny Wang to talk to his brother and sister-in-law.

"But you're ill," said his brother and sister-in-law upon seeing him. "Why are you out of your room?"

"Brother, I'm myself again!"

His brother and sister-in-law rejoiced. Granny Wang said to Big Brother Fan, "The Zhou family of Cao Gate sent me here to propose marriage to Second Brother."

Big Brother was delighted.

Let us skip unnecessary details and come forthwith to the point where agreement was reached between the two parties. They then exchanged betrothal gifts and all went well. Second Brother Fan had never been reconciled to staying at home in his spare hours, but after the betrothal, he didn't go out anymore but helped his older brother tend to business in the wineshop. As for the young lady Shengxian, she had seldom picked up the needle to sew, but after the betrothal, she willingly took up needlework. In full contentment, the two of them happily awaited Mr. Zhou's return, when the wedding ceremony would take place.

The betrothal was settled on in the third lunar month, but Mr. Zhou did not return until the eleventh month, and the first day of his arrival was devoted, as it rightly should be, to welcome parties that neighbors and relatives threw in his honor. It was the following day that his wife told him about their daughter's engagement.

"So it's been settled?" asked Mr. Zhou.

"Yes."

His eyes popping wide open, Mr. Zhou lashed out at his wife, "Stupid old woman! Who gave you authority to make the betrothal? He won't rise to be more than a wineshop owner. Our girl will have enough candidates from rich and powerful families. Why did you have to promise her to that man? Where's your pride? Aren't you afraid people will laugh at you for what you've done?" (*What a killjoy, this old man!*) He was still carrying on when they heard Ying'er scream, "Ma'am! Come help the young mistress!"

"What happened?" asked Mrs. Zhou.

"Something upset her so much that she fainted and fell on the floor behind the screen."

In terror, Mrs. Zhou rushed forward, staggering every step of the way. There the girl was, lying on the floor.

None could tell if she was dead or alive;
All her four limbs were surely immobile.

Of all the multifarious factors that cause illnesses, anger does the most damage. What had happened was that the young lady had been listening behind the screen. Upon hearing her father's tirade against her mother for promising her to Second Brother Fan, she collapsed to the floor in a seizure of anger. Her mother rushed forward to revive her, but Mr. Zhou stopped his wife, cursing, "Stupid woman! That cheap little slut who disgraces the family—let her die! Why even try to revive her?"

Seeing that Mrs. Zhou was being restrained by her husband, Ying'er went forward, but Mr. Zhou gave her a resounding slap across the face. As she staggered back to the wall, Mrs. Zhou sank to the floor from sheer indignation. After Ying'er went forward and brought her back to consciousness, Mrs. Zhou burst into loud wails of grief. Hearing her cries, the neighbors came over for a look. There were Auntie Zhang, Auntie Bao, Auntie Mao, and Auntie Diao, and they filled up the room. The truth of the matter was that Mr. Zhou did not get along with people, but his kind and gentle wife was popular in the neighborhood. To the many neighbors gathered around them, Mr. Zhou snapped, "This is a private family matter. You need not intervene."

At these words, the neighbors dispersed and went their separate ways. Mrs. Zhou felt her daughter's body and found that she was icy cold all over. The mother held the girl in her arms and broke down in a flood of tears, for the girl would not have died had someone attempted to revive her. To her husband she said, "What an evil man you are! I just knew that you'd hate to spend three to five thousand strings of cash on a dowry, and that's why you deliberately killed my girl!"

Flying into a towering rage, Mr. Zhou said, "You accuse me of begrudging three to five thousand strings of cash? How can you insult me like that?" With that, he went out in a huff.

Mrs. Zhou was overwhelmed with grief. Her daughter had been as pretty as the Bodhisattva Guanyin and was quick and clever by nature and skilled in needlework. Indeed, at the loss of such a girl, who was good in everything, how would the mother not grieve?

Mr. Zhou bought a coffin, as he was duty-bound to do, and had eight men carry it home. Mrs. Zhou wept her heart out at the sight of the coffin entering the house. Glowering at his wife, Mr. Zhou said, "You say I hate to spend three to five thousand strings of cash on a dowry. Well, all the jewelry in your daughter's room is going into that coffin!" Without losing one moment, he told the undertaker to have the body put into the coffin. He then had a message delivered to the two keepers of graves, the Zhang brothers, asking them to dig a brick-lined grave. To make a long story short, I will just tell you that the usual and obligatory prayer service for the deceased was dispensed with, and that the funeral was to be held the very next day, allowing little time for the coffin to remain in the house. Mrs.

Zhou pleaded for a few days' postponement of the funeral, but her husband would have none of it. The funeral procession left early in the morning and after the body was buried, everyone returned home.

> How sad that three feet of pitiless earth
> Covered up a young lady filled with love!

Our story branches at this point. Among those present at the funeral was a young man in his thirties, Zhu Zhen by name, who was a thief. He often served as the undertaker's assistant and doubled as a gravedigger, and he helped encoffin Miss Zhou's body and dig her grave. Upon returning home after the funeral that day, he said to his mother, "I'm in the best of luck. I'll be a rich man tomorrow!"

"What luck are you talking about, my son?" asked his mother.

"A funny thing happened: the daughter of Mr. Zhou of Cao Gate died. Her parents got into a quarrel. The wife accused the husband of having driven the girl to her death. So he defiantly put into her coffin three to five thousand strings of cash, which had been meant to be her dowry. When so much money is to be had for the taking, what am I waiting for?"

His mother said, "This is no joking matter. It's not just some petty offense against the law for which you get only eight strokes of the bamboo rod or thirteen blows with a staff.[4] And there's your father's experience to consider. When he opened the lid of a coffin in a grave robbery twenty years ago, the corpse grinned at him. Your father had such a shock that he died four or five days after he came home. My child, you must not do this. This is no joke!"

"Mother, you can't stop me." From under his bed he pulled out an object and showed it to his mother.

"Don't take it!" said his mother. "Your father put it to use and died."

"Everybody has his own fate. I've had my fortune told several times this year, and each time the fortune-teller said I'd be making my pile pretty soon. Don't stop me."

What, you may ask, did he retrieve from under the bed? It was a leather bag containing a crowbar, an ax, a lamp with a leather shade, an oilcan, and a straw cape.

"Why would you need a straw cape?" said his mother after examining the contents of the bag.

"I'll need it in the middle of the night."

It being the middle of the eleventh lunar month, a heavy snow was falling. That brute Zhu Zhen threw the cape over his shoulders and attached to the straw cape was a patch made of about ten bamboo strips. When the wearer of the cape walked in the snow, the bamboo patch trailing on the ground would wipe out all footprints. (*How remarkable!*)

At the second watch, late at night, Zhu Zhen said to his mother, "When I come back, I'll knock at the door. Be sure to open it for me."

For all the hustle and bustle of the capital city, the open country in the suburbs was quiet and deserted. Moreover, few would venture out into the snow at this time of the night. After leaving the house, Zhu Zhen looked back and saw no footprints. He then wended his way to Miss Zhou's grave. Upon arriving, he stepped over the lowest point in the fence wall, but, unfortunately for him, the grave keepers had a dog. At this point, it emerged from its straw kennel to bark at the intruding stranger. Earlier in the day, Zhu Zhen had prepared a piece of fried dough and stuffed some drug in it. He now tossed the dough to the barking dog. The dog sniffed at it and, liking the aroma, ate it up. The very next moment, the dog gave a bark and collapsed to the ground. As Zhu Zhen drew near the grave, Second Brother Zhang, one of the grave keepers, cried out, "Older brother! The dog barked once and then stopped. That's strange! Could there be something wrong? Why don't you go take a look?"

His brother said, "Why would a thief want to steal anything from us?"

"The dog gave one loud bark and stopped. Yes, there just may be a thief around. If you don't go, I will." He rose, threw some clothes over his shoulders, and went out, a spear in hand.

Hearing men's voices, Zhu Zhen quietly took off his straw cape and tiptoed his way to a willow tree with a trunk large enough to block him from view. He crouched on the ground, his wide-rimmed bamboo hat covering up his body, his straw cape by one side. From that position he saw the door open and Second Brother Zhang emerge from inside. Looking cold, Zhang cried out, "You cursed beast! What's there to bark about?" Having just risen from sleep, he shrank back from the wind-driven snow and hastened back inside. "Brother," he said, "there is indeed no one around!" With that, he quickly took off his clothes and drew up his quilt all the way over his head, saying, "Brother! It's cold out there!"

"Didn't I tell you there's no one out there?"

It was by now the third watch, around midnight. After the brothers talked for a while, all was quiet again. Zhu Zhen said to himself, "No hard work, no big money." He rose, put on his bamboo hat and his straw cape, tiptoed his way to the grave, and cleared away the snow with his crowbar. Having helped out at the site earlier in the day, he knew the layout. After prying open the stone slab, he lowered himself into the pit, gained a firm foothold, took off his hat and his cape, and put them on one side. He then retrieved two long nails from his leather bag, drove them into the space between two bricks, laid the leather-shade lamp on top, took out a bamboo tube containing a pilot spark of fire, blew it into a good flame, poured some oil from the oilcan, and lit the lamp. With his crowbar, he took out the large nail that held the coffin lid, tossed aside the lid, and cried, "Young lady, don't take offense! I would like to borrow your possessions, but I'll have sutras chanted for you!" Having said that, he removed the many pieces of jewelry from her head. Her clothes, however, were not that easy to take off. That brute, being as smart as he was, untied the sash from her waist, and put one end around her neck and the other end around his own. With the corpse thus half raised, he removed all her clothes, including her underwear, until she was stark naked. The sight of the girl's fair-skinned body stirred such desires in this scoundrel that he gave in to his lust and raped her. Amazingly enough, the girl opened her eyes and held Zhu Zhen in her arms. How did that come to pass? Truly,

> The Book of Predestination *has it right;*[5]
> *No one is master of the ups and downs of life.*

As it turned out, the young lady, with all her heart set on Second Brother Fan, had died a few days ago from a fit of rage against her father when he was lashing out at her mother. Now, however, upon the acquisition of the yang element so soon after her death, she came back to life. Zhu Zhen was flabbergasted. The girl spoke up, "Brother, who might you be?"

With his quick mind, Zhu Zhen dodged the question and said instead, "Sister, I'm here to help you."

As she sat up, the truth of what had happened dawned on her. With all her clothes piled up on one side of her and an ax and a crowbar lying on the other side, how in the world would she not know? Zhu Zhen had half a mind to make short work of her but did not have the heart to.

"Brother," said Shengxian. "Help me and take me to Second Brother Fan of the wineshop in Fan Tower Restaurant. I will have a handsome reward for you."

Zhu Zhen thought, "Such a nice girl is hard to come by, even when one goes into all the expenses of wife hunting. If I take her home, who would ever know how I got her?" Aloud, he said, "Don't worry. I'll take you home and help you meet Second Brother Fan."

"If I can get to see him, I'll go with you."

There and then, Zhu Zhen helped her get dressed, gathered her pieces of jewelry, wrapped them up with the rest of her clothes, blew out the lamp, poured the remaining oil back into the oilcan, put away his tools, picked up his bamboo hat, and helped her climb out of the pit. He himself followed her up, put the stone slab back on, and covered it with snow. He then carried the girl on his back and threw his straw cape over her. With one hand holding the leather bag and the other grabbing the package of jewelry, he managed to put the bamboo hat over his head, and wended his way home. At his knocks on the door, his mother knew that it was her son and opened the door for him. As he walked in, the old woman gave a start. "My child," said she. "Why do you have to bring the corpse back as well?"

"Be quiet, mother."

He laid down his things and took the girl into his own bedroom. Picking up a gleaming knife, he said to the girl, "I've got something to tell you. If you do as I say, I'll take you to Second Brother Fan. If not, do you see this knife? I'll cut you in half with it!"

Terror-stricken, the girl said, "Brother, what do you want me to do?"

"First, don't make a sound. Second, don't leave this room. If so, I'll talk to Second Brother Fan in a couple of days. If not, I'll kill you."

"I'll do whatever you say."

After this warning, Zhu Zhen went out to talk to his mother, but let us not digress.

As was only to be expected, the girl was made to share that brute's bed at night. After a couple of days of confinement in the room, the girl asked, "Have you seen Second Brother Fan yet?"

"Yes, I have. He's at home, sick because of you. He'll come for you after he gets well."

This happened on the twentieth day of the eleventh lunar month. The days went by, and we come now to the fifteenth day of the first month of the following year. That evening, Zhu Zhen said to his mother, "Every year I hear about the amazing turtle-shaped hills of lanterns at the Lantern Festival, but I've never seen one. I'm going out now to see them. I'll be back at daybreak." Having said those words, he went into the city to view the lanterns.

As coincidence would have it, at the first light of daybreak, Zhu Zhen's mother heard cries of "Fire!" She quickly opened the door to look. Indeed, the wineshop about four or five doors down was on fire. In panic, she hurried back into the house to pack. Having heard the commotion, the girl said to herself, "What better time than this to get away?" She stepped out of her room and invited Mrs. Zhu in to get her things. The unsuspecting Mrs. Zhu went in. The girl took advantage of the commotion and slipped out, but, not knowing which way to go, she asked passersby, "Where's Cao Gate?"

Someone told her, pointing ahead, "There it is!"

After going through the gate, she asked again, "Where's Fan Tower Restaurant?"

"Right ahead," was the reply.

She grew afraid. If she were to run into Zhu Zhen, there would have been no more story to tell. As it turned out, she found the wineshop in Fan Tower Restaurant, where a waiter was greeting patrons at the door.

When the girl dropped a deep curtsy, the waiter reciprocated, bowing and chanting a greeting. "Young lady," said he. "How can I be of help?"

"Is this Fan Tower Restaurant?"

"Yes, it is."

"May I ask if Second Brother Fan is here?"

The waiter grumbled to himself, "What a fine thing that Second Brother did, attracting his lucky star to our door!" (*Interesting choice of words.*) Aloud, he said, "He's right there inside the wineshop."

Heading for the counter, Shengxian cried out, "Greetings to you, Second Brother!"

It would have been a different story had Second Brother Fan not heard her, but he did. As he stepped down for a look, he was appalled. "Be gone! Be gone!" he cried.

"Second Brother," said the girl. "You may think I'm a ghost, but I'm not."

How was Second Brother Fan to believe her? Still crying, "Be gone! Be gone!" he kept himself from falling by holding on with one hand to a bench on which, unfortunately, stood a row of water jars. In his agitated state, he picked up one and flung it right in the girl's face. As chance would have it, it hit her on the temple. With a scream, she fell. In alarm, the waiter rushed over, only to see the girl lying on the floor. (*That scoundrel Zhu Zhen, who robbed the girl's jewelry, brought her back to life. That young man Second Brother Fan, with whom she was in love, caused her death. Nothing could be more bizarre.*) Was she dead or alive? Truly,

> *The east wind ravaged the garden last night,*
> *And scattered plum blossoms all over the ground.*

The waiter found the girl dead in a pool of blood as Second Brother Fan was still crying, "Be gone! Be gone!" Hearing the clamor of voices, Big Brother Fan rushed out to investigate. "Why did you do this?" he asked his brother, who still kept crying "Be gone! Be gone!" A good while later, after Second Brother calmed down, Big Brother asked again, "Why did you kill her?"

"Brother, she's the ghost of the daughter of Mr. Zhou, the sea-going merchant who lives by Cao Gate."

Big Brother Fan countered, "No. If she were a ghost, she shouldn't have blood. Now what are we going to do?"

At the door of the wineshop twenty to thirty spectators had gathered. The local headman came quickly on the scene to arrest Second Brother Fan. To the crowd, Big Brother Fan announced, "She's the daughter of Mr. Zhou of Cao Gate. She died in the eleventh month of last year. My brother believed she was a ghost, not a mortal being, and hit her. She fell dead. I still have no idea whether she's a human or a ghost. If you want to arrest my brother, let me first call Mr. Zhou over to identify the body."

"All right, go now and bring him here soon," the crowd agreed.

Big Brother Fan ran at top speed to Mr. Zhou's house. At the door, he saw the girl's nurse, who asked him, "Who might you be?"

"I'm Big Brother Fan of the wineshop in Fan Tower Restaurant. I have an emergency to report. Please announce me."

The nurse went immediately inside to bring the master out. Before long, Mr. Zhou emerged and exchanged greetings with Fan. Big Brother Fan then told him what had happened, adding, "If you could be so kind as to identify the body, I would be forever grateful."

Mr. Zhou did not believe what he had heard, but Big Brother Fan was not someone prone to lying. Mr. Zhou followed him to the wineshop and was also stupefied at the sight. "My daughter had already died some time ago," said he. "How could she have come back to life? How could there be such a thing?"

Over Big Brother Fan's protests, the local headman apprehended everyone involved. The next morning, they were taken under guard to the Kaifeng prefectural yamen. Prefect Bao[6] read the complaint, but, unable to make anything of it, he sent Second Brother Fan to the lockup to await trial. While the corpse was being examined by the coroner, the prefect instructed the detectives to take up the case. After the officers had some laborers dig open the grave, they saw that the coffin was empty. They questioned the grave keepers, the Zhang brothers, who replied, "One night during a snowstorm in the eleventh month of last year, we heard our dog barking. At daybreak when we opened the door to look, we found the dog lying in the snow, dead. We don't know what happened."

A written report was presented to the prefect. In a rage, the prefect ordered that the culprit be hunted down and brought to court within three days. The deadline was later extended two or three times, but to no avail.

A golden vase has vanished without a trace into a well;
An iron rod needs more work to be ground into a needle.

In the lockup, Second Brother Fan gave himself up to thought. "How very strange! If she was a human, she had already died once before. The undertaker who was present at the burial can testify to that, and the grave is also there. But if she was a ghost, she did bleed when hit, and the corpse is still there. What's more, her coffin is now empty." These thoughts kept haunting his mind. And then, another thought struck him: "Too bad she was such a beauty! If she was a ghost, well and good. But if she was not a ghost, wouldn't I have taken an innocent life?" He tossed and turned, kept awake by these thoughts, his heart full of misgivings. Recalling their first encounter in the teahouse, he said to himself, "How I was smitten that day! We gazed into each other's eyes, but I had no chance to make my move. Ghost or no ghost, I should have taken my time, rather than so impetuously doing her to death! What a sin! Now that I'm locked up and the case remains unsolved, what am I going to do? Regrets are too late now!" The remorse set off new thoughts, which, in turn, led to further remorse. After another four miserable hours, he drifted off to sleep. In his dream he saw a richly adorned Shengxian approach him.

Aghast, Second Brother Fan said, "So you're not dead, after all!"

"You missed my temple. I fainted but didn't die. I've had two brushes with death now, both times for your sake. After I learned that you were here, I came expressly to see you, to fulfill our wishes. Please do not reject me. This is all in our destiny."

Forgetting himself, Second Brother Fan engaged her in a game of clouds and rain, and the joy was boundless. After it was over, they bade each other an affectionate farewell. Upon waking up, he realized that it had all been but a dream. He plunged again into remorseful thoughts. The same thing happened the following night. On the third night, she appeared again and was even more loving than before. On the point of departure, she said, "My allotted lifespan is not over yet. I've been recruited by General Wudao of the Five Ways [a Daoist god of life and death] into his service. My mind all filled with thoughts of you, I tearfully pleaded to the General, and, out of compassion, he gave me three days' leave. The three days are up. If I try to stay longer, I will surely be reproached. I now bid you farewell. We will never meet again. I have begged General Wudao of the Five Ways to take care of you. Be patient. You will be out of all trouble in one month's time." (*General Wudao of the Five Ways has good sense.*)

Deeply saddened, Second Brother Fan burst into sobs and woke up. Recalling what he had heard in his dream, he wondered if all this had really happened. Then, exactly thirty days later, by the magistrate's order, the wardens took him to the tribunal for interrogation.

What had happened in the meantime was that a peddler by the name of Dong Gui had gone out of the city of Kaifeng with his basket of goods. By the city gate, an old woman accosted him and offered him an object. What was it? It was a string of pearls fashioned into the shape of a gardenia blossom. It had dropped to the floor after Zhu Zhen returned home from the grave that night. His mother had quietly picked it up. Knowing nothing about the value of this piece of jewelry, she was hoping she could sell it for a couple of strings of cash, to put into her private savings.

"How much do you want?" asked Dong Gui.

"Whatever you care to give."

"How about two strings of cash?"

"All right."

After paying her, Dong Gui headed straight for the detectives' office and reported to the inspector. The inspector proceeded forthwith to Cao Gate and showed the pearl gardenia blossom to Mr. and Mrs. Zhou, who recognized it as one of the pieces of jewelry put in their daughter's coffin. Without a moment's delay, the police went to apprehend the old woman.

"My son Zhu Zhen is not at home," said the old woman.

Zhu Zhen was not found at that moment because he was at a circus, watching a show at the Sang Family Entertainment Center. The police arrested him there and took him to the Kaifeng prefectural yamen, where Prefect Bao sent him to the office in charge of prisons. Under interrogation, Zhu Zhen realized he would not be able to lie his way out of it and confessed everything. When drafting the sentence, Officer Xue in charge of the case wrote that Zhu Zhen was to be put to death for grave robbery and Second Brother Fan to be banished to a labor camp with his face branded as a convicted criminal. However, before submitting his report for approval, Officer Xue saw in a dream that night a god with every resemblance to General Wudao of the Five Ways, who said to him in anger, "What wrong did Second Brother Fan do to deserve exile as a branded criminal? Set him free immediately!"

Officer Xue woke up with a start. He then changed the sentence to say that Second Brother Fan was attacking what he thought was a ghost, not a human being, and that, in such an unusual case, the accused should be acquitted. Magistrate Bao approved. Jubilantly, Second Brother Fan returned home. He later married, but, treasuring the memory of Zhou Shengxian's love, he never failed to burn paper coins and make sacrificial offerings at General Wudao of Five Ways' temple at every seasonal festival. There is a poem in testimony:

> *Devoted lovers in their passion*
> *Provide material for tales of romance.*
> *But if they are compared with heartless ingrates,*
> *It's the latter who gain all the advantages.*

In Eternal Regret, He Daqing Leaves Behind a Lovers' Silk Ribbon

Disguised in flesh, blood, and bones,
It bewitches and casts spells on men.
Mighty heroes of all times fall willing victims,
To lie in dust in humble oblivion.

The above quatrain was written in the olden times by Xingruzi as a warning to those who ruin themselves by indulging in debauchery.[1]

As a matter of fact, debauchery is of quite a different order from sensual pleasure. An ancient poem says:

One smile topples a city;
Another smile topples a state.
But city or no city, state or no state,
A beauty like this is not to be had again!

This was a poet given to sensual pleasure.

In the case of a man who cares nothing about looks but is interested only in the sheer number of conquests, he is "a bag of lime that leaves its traces everywhere," as the idiom goes. What sensual pleasure is there to speak of? This is nothing less than debauchery.

Be all this as it may, there are also distinctions to be made in the indulgence of sensual pleasure. In the case of Zhang Chang, known for his habit of painting his wife's eyebrows, or of Sima Xiangru, who enjoyed drinking with his wife, Confucian moralists may hold them to ridicule, yet their deep love for their wives is a virtue that lies at the heart of human relationships and is therefore a case of legitimate sensual pleasure.[2]

If a man possesses pretty concubines and maidservants and revels in their company wherever he goes in grand style, and if he engages female singers and dancers and keeps them for his own lavish entertainment, it may not be a one-on-one man-

and-wife relationship, but at least the entourage is like leaves to a flower, and this, therefore, is a case of partially legitimate sensual pleasure.

There are also men who frequent houses of ill repute to indulge in brief escapades for which they spare no expense. When traveling on the road, they engage in amorous excursions to relieve the boredom of the journey and to fulfill their desires. Such pursuits, favored by libertines and shunned by men of decency, cannot be called otherwise than pursuits of wicked sensual pleasure.

As for those who commit incest and degrade humanity to the level of beasts, who sneak through holes and climb over fences and resort to devious tricks for transient, illicit gratification of the flesh, they are villains to the end of time, to be punished by humans when alive and condemned by ghosts after death. These are cases of evil sensual pleasure.

Now, there are also cases that do not fall into the categories of legitimate or partially legitimate, evil, or wicked sensual pleasure. These are situations where the lust-driven set traps for their prey and bring disgrace to the family, the gods, and the Buddha. Before they are claimed by the other world, the justice of heaven will overtake them even in this world of the living. To all and sundry, a word of advice: watch your conduct! Truly,

> *For the sake of the Buddha, if not the monks,*
> *Mix no debauched thoughts in your prayers.*

Our story takes place in Xingan County of Linjiang Prefecture, Jiangxi, in the Xuande reign period [1426–35] of this dynasty [the Ming]. There was a student of the imperial college named He Yingxiang, courtesy name Daqing, who was a dashing and dissolute young man much given to sensual pleasures. He treated the courtesans' quarters and the houses of song and dance as his own home and squandered away a little less than half of his otherwise impressive family property. His wife, Lu-shi, pleaded with him to change his profligate ways, but he turned the tables on her and accused her of failing to be an understanding wife, and picked quarrels with her at every turn. Lu-shi therefore resolved to let him be. Confining herself and their three-year-old son, Xi'er, in a secluded room, she observed a vegetarian diet and chanted the sutras, leaving He Daqing to his debauchery.

One day during the Clear and Bright Festival,[3] He Daqing went alone to the outskirts of the city, dressed in finery, to enjoy the sights of spring. There is in testimony a poem by Zhang Yong of the Song dynasty:

> *Amid the crowds seeing the sights of spring,*
> *One finds maidens as lovely as flowers.*
> *In twos and threes, they stand by the blossoms;*
> *Airily they look as if ready to rise to the clouds.*

He Daqing headed only for spots with gatherings of women. He swaggered his way in front of them or behind them, showing off his dashing figure to best advantage and looking for a beauty who might have a predestined bond with him. To his disappointment, he had no such luck. In low spirits, he went to a wineshop to order a few drinks, for lack of a better thing to do. After mounting the stairs, he picked a seat by the window overlooking the street and sat down. The waiter brought him wine and food, and he poured himself one cup after another while keeping his eyes on the pedestrians down below. Before he knew it, he had eaten his fill and, in a half-tipsy state, rose and went downstairs. After paying his bill, he left the wineshop and went wherever his feet led him. It was early afternoon by this time. Soon the wine began to take its toll on him. His mouth was parched, and he craved tea to allay his thirst. Wondering where he was to find a cup of tea, suddenly he saw in the woods ahead of him some banners flapping in the wind and heard the ringing sound of the percussion instruments of a Buddhist monastery. He hurried forward in delight. Entering the woods, he saw a large monastery looming in front of him. It was surrounded by whitewashed walls. In front of the gate stood about ten weeping willow trees. In the middle, facing south, was a double-leaf gate, at the top of which was hung a horizontal board bearing the inscription "Non-Void Nunnery" in gilded characters. He nodded and said to himself, "I've often heard people say that there are pretty nuns in the Non-Void Nunnery outside the city, but I've never had a chance to come and see for myself. And now, surprise, surprise! Here I am!"

He straightened his clothes and hat and went through the gate. To the east stretched a cobblestone path flanked by elms and willows. He had not taken many steps down this tranquil and tastefully laid out path when he came upon another gate, which led to a small three-room house with a statue of the guardian god Skanda facing it. In the courtyard stood towering pine and cypress trees, with birds chirping noisily in them. Behind the statue of the Buddha lay another path parallel to the house. Daqing headed in an easterly direction and saw a house with a carved door, the two halves of which were tightly closed. Stepping forward, he tapped at it gently three or four times. With a creak, the door was opened by a little girl neatly dressed in a black nun's robe with a silk sash around her waist. Quickly she saluted the visitor, and He Daqing returned the greeting. He then stepped over the threshold and saw a three-section hall of worship. Even though the hall was not very large, the high ceiling lent it a spacious look. In the middle were three grand gilded statues of the Buddha with imposing features.

After bowing to the statues, Daqing said to the novice, "Could you please announce to your mentor that she has a visitor?"

"Please take a seat, sir. Let me go inside and announce you."

Before long, a young nun emerged and held one hand in front of her chest in a Buddhist salute to Daqing, who promptly returned the courtesy. With his half-open, half-closed, flirtatious eyes, he ogled the nun and found her to be less than twenty years old, with a complexion as fair as white jade and an innate bewitching charm that was quite out of the ordinary. His burning desire so weakened him that he could hardly raise his head again after the deep bow. Indeed, he had gone as soft as a piece of hot, sweet rice cake just out of the wok!

After the exchange of greetings, he and the nun sat down as guest and hostess. He thought, "I've been knocking around the whole day without finding anyone I fancy. Who would have guessed that such a beauty is hidden right here, of all places! Let me be patient and slowly lead her on. She'll surely fall for me."

While Daqing was planning his move, it turned out that the nun was thinking along the same lines. According to proper etiquette, visitors to the nunnery should be greeted by the elder nuns. The young nuns, just like unmarried maidens, live secluded lives and are not supposed to receive visitors other than family members or patrons whom they know well. If the older nuns happen to be away or are indisposed, visitors are turned away. Even in the case of a powerful figure determined to see a young nun, she would not come out until she had been called three or four times, and the visitor's patience had run out. So, why had this nun sallied forth so readily? Well, let me tell you why. She may have been chanting the Buddhist sutras, but, in fact, her cultivation of the spirit was all pretense. She loved romance more than seclusion and hated life in the nunnery. She had seen Daqing through the chink between the double doors and was quite impressed by the young man's looks. That was why she had sallied forth so readily.

Her eyes riveted on Daqing, like two needles attracted to a magnet, she asked smilingly, "What is your honorable name, sir? Where do you live? How can this humble nunnery help you?"

"My name is He Daqing. I live in the city. I was on a spring outing in the outskirts of the city today when my feet led me here. I have long heard about your great spiritual accomplishments. Since I'm already in the neighborhood, I decided to come in for a visit."

Gratefully, the nun replied, "Your visit to this humble dwelling is too much of an honor for someone who lives in such an out-of-the-way place and with no accomplishment or ability to speak of. But there are too many people passing by this hall. Let's go to an inner room for a cup of tea."

These last words got Daqing's hopes up. Joyfully, he rose and followed her into the inner section of the compound. After passing a few halls and through another corridor, they came to a hall with three exquisitely furnished rooms. In the courtyard surrounded by balustrades stood two parasol trees, some bamboo, and a variety of flowers that set one another off and emitted a fragrance that assailed the nostrils. In the middle room was hung a portrait of the Bodhisattva Guanyin, and wisps of incense smoke arose from the bronze brazier. Under the portrait lay a prayer mat. In the room to the left, there were four vermilion cupboards, all under lock and key, containing most probably volumes of Buddhist scripture. A screen ran around the room to the right. Inside was a long desk made of paulownia and cypress wood. To its left stood a small rattan chair, and to its right, against the wall, a speckled bamboo couch. On the wall was hung an ancient zither with cracks in it, and on the desk lay brush-pens and an ink slab, all exquisite and spotlessly clean. From the pile of Buddhist scriptures on one corner of the desk, Daqing picked up the first volume that came to his hand and flipped through the pages, which were filled with small golden characters of regular script in imitation of the style of Zhao Mengfu.[4] Beneath the line indicating the date on which the calligraphy was done, there was a line that read, "Written by Apostle Kongzhao."

"Who is Kongzhao?" asked Daqing.

"My very humble self," said the nun.

Turning the pages back and forth, Daqing showered praises on her calligraphy. They then sat down opposite each other across the table. When the young novice brought in tea, Kongzhao took a cup with both hands and offered it to Daqing before she took the other cup for herself, holding it with her lovely fair-skinned hands with pointed fingers. Daqing took a sip from his cup, and found the tea to be of truly superior quality. There is in testimony a poem by Lü Dongbin:[5]

> *Jade Pistils and Flagpoles are the best of tea leaves;*
> *Monks are masters in the art of brewing tea.*
> *Rabbit Hair in shallow cups makes fair fragrant clouds;*
> *Bubbles like shrimp eyes float in tiny waves.*
> *Tea leaves keep drowsiness away from your desk*
> *And bring fresh vigor into your body.*
> *They grow around rocks by quiet streams*
> *And refuse to be uprooted and brought to the city.*

Daqing asked, "How many are you in this nunnery?"

"There are four of us altogether, mentor and students. Our mentor is advanced in years and has been confined to her sick bed in the last few days. I'm in charge for now." Pointing at the novice, Kongzhao continued, "She's my student. Another student of mine, her junior, is in her room, intoning sutras."

"When did you join the Buddhist order?"

"When I was seven years old, upon my father's death. It's been twelve years now."

"At nineteen, you're in the prime of youth. How can you put up with such dullness?"

"Please don't mock me, sir! Life in a nunnery is many times better than life in the outside world."

"How is that so?"

"We nuns are free from the trammels of the sundry matters of daily life, nor are we tied down with children. We can devote ourselves all day long to reading the scriptures while enjoying the aroma of incense and a nice pot of tea. When drowsy, I take a nap with a paper bed-curtain around me. In leisure, I play my zither. What a peaceful and carefree life this is!"

Daqing rejoined, "But when you play the zither in leisure, you need someone appreciative to applaud. More importantly, when you take a nap with a paper bed-curtain around you, wouldn't it be frightening if you had a bad dream and there was no one to wake you up?"

Recognizing this as a bait, Kongzhao replied, all smiles, "Even if the bad dream kills me, I won't demand your life in return!"

With a laugh, Daqing countered, "Bad dreams can kill ten thousand people for all I care, but wouldn't it be too bad if a fairy like you should perish?"

And so they exchanged banter until gradually enough intimacy had grown between them for action.

"May I ask for another pot of your fine tea?" asked Daqing.

The meaning was not lost on Kongzhao. After she had sent the girl away to brew tea down the corridor, Daqing continued, "Where is the fairy maiden's bed-chamber, may I ask? And may I see for myself the kind of paper bed-curtain you use?"

Already burning with irrepressible desire, Kongzhao said demurely as she stood up, "Why would you want to do that?"

Daqing went forward, put his arms around her, and planted a kiss on her lips. As Kongzhao turned back, he followed her on her heels. Softly she pushed open the back door that led to her very bedchamber. It was even more tastefully fur-nished than the room they had just left, but Daqing was in no mood to admire the décor. The two went to bed in each other's arms and joined in a union of delight. There is in testimony a song called "The Little Nun":

> The little nun in the nunnery
> Slaps the table and laments her fate.
> From midair descends a handsome young man;
> They chat and they hit it off right away.
> Greedily they cling to each other
> And fulfill their desires on their very first date.
> They may not be lawfully wedded,
> But surely they're not any less attached.

The two were in the middle of their enjoyment when the young novice sud-denly pushed the door open and walked in on them. With alacrity they rose, but the girl set down the tea tray and left, hiding her smile with a hand. The hour being late by now, they lit a lamp. Kongzhao then put together some wine, fruit, and vegetables, and laid them out on the table. She and Daqing had hardly sat down opposite each other when Kongzhao rose again to bring the two girls over to sit at the same table, so that they would not set their tongues wagging.

"We observe a vegetarian diet in the nunnery," said Kongzhao. "Not knowing that we would have a distinguished guest today, we did not prepare any meat dishes. Please forgive us for being such poor hostesses."

"You and your students have already shown me more kindness than I deserve. Such modesty on your part will only make this young man feel uneasy."

The four of them offered one another toasts until they were all tipsy. Daqing rose to his feet, went over to Kongzhao's side, laid an arm around her neck, drank up half of his own cup of wine, and held it out to her lips. As Kongzhao leaned forward and drank it all up, the two girls rose to remove themselves from this sickening scene, but Kongzhao grabbed them and said, "Since you're already here, we are in this together!"

Unable to free themselves from her grip, the two girls covered up their faces with their sleeves. Daqing darted forward, gathered them into his arms, pushed away their hands off their faces, and kissed them. The two girls, having reached puberty by this time, were only too glad to join the fun, since their mentor was kind enough to offer them the chance. Holding one another in a tight embrace, the four of them drank until they were quite inebriated. They lay down in the same bed, nestled up against one another, embraced, and became as inseparable as lacquer and glue. He Daqing did his best to please them, and each of them, in her first taste of amorous sport, wished she could dissolve herself into him.

The next morning, Kongzhao summoned the old acolyte and, with a reward of three maces of silver, told him not to breathe a word to anyone about what had happened. She then gave him more money and instructed him to buy fish, meat, wine, and fruit. The old acolyte, with his meager provisions, normally always complained about bad eyesight, hardness of hearing, a weak constitution, and slow legs. But now, richer by three maces of silver and told to run a pleasant errand—buying wine and meat, he became keen of eye, deft of hand, and as strong as a tiger and as fast as wind. Soon his mission was accomplished, and preparations got under way for a feast in Daqing's honor, but of this, no more.

Now, Non-Void Nunnery was divided into two wings. The east wing was occupied by Kongzhao, and the west wing by another romantically inclined nun by the name of Jingzhen. This Jingzhen had under her a young novice and an old acolyte. Noticing all the shopping trips in the last couple of days, that acolyte said to Jingzhen that there must be something going on in the east wing. Guessing that Kongzhao must be up to some mischief, Jingzhen had the novice look after the premises, whereas she herself made for the east wing. At the gate, she ran straight into Kongzhao's acolyte, who had just emerged from inside, carrying a large wine flask in his left hand and a basket in his right.

"What brought you here, madam?"

"I'm here to chat with my sister."

"All right. Let me announce you first."

With one sweep of her hand, Jingzhen grabbed him and said, "I know everything. You need not alert them."

These words touched the acolyte to the quick. His face flaming red, he dared not say a word in response but meekly followed Jingzhen upon her heels, closed the gate after him, and, upon reaching the door to Kongzhao's room, cried out, "The madam of the west wing is here to see you!"

This announcement threw Kongzhao into consternation. For lack of a better plan, she told Daqing to hide himself behind the screen while she herself rose to greet the visitor.

Jingzhen walked up to her and, seizing her by her sleeve, said, "A fine thing you did! A nun ruining the reputation of a nunnery! Let me take you to the local headman!" So saying, she pulled her toward the door. In terror, Kongzhao's face became a patchwork of dyed color blotches, going red and pale by turns, and her heart went up and down, like hundreds of hammers at work. She could not get half a word out nor move half a step.

Amused by the way she looked, Jingzhen said with a chuckle, "Relax, sister! I was just teasing you! But with such an honorable guest in the house, how can you keep him for your exclusive enjoyment without letting me know about this? Now bring him to me this instant!"

These words set Kongzhao's fears to rest. Right away, she brought Daqing out to meet Jingzhen.

Impressed by the attractiveness and grace of Jingzhen, who, at twenty-five or twenty-six years of age, was older than Kongzhao but was the more charming of the two, Daqing asked, "Which nunnery are you from, madam?"

"I'm from the west wing of this very nunnery."

"I'm sorry for not having paid my respects to you earlier. Pray forgive me."

And so the conversation went on. Falling for his dashing manners and his candid speech, Jingzhen couldn't take her eyes off him and said with a sigh, "I never knew that there lives such a handsome man in this world. How lucky my sister is to have him all for herself!"

Kongzhao rejoined, "You need not be envious. If you don't take me for an outsider, I'll share the joy with you."

"If so, I'll be ever so grateful to you. Come visit me at my place this evening. Please be sure not to treat me as an outsider." With that, she rose and took leave of them. Once back in the west wing, she set about preparing wine and food for the occasion. Before long, Kongzhao and He Daqing arrived hand in hand and were greeted at the gate by the novice. As he entered the courtyard, He Daqing found the winding veranda and the flower-lined path no less charming than those in the east wing and the three rooms even more exquisite than those of Kongzhao's. Behold:

> The pavilion, the rooms, the doors, the windows,
> All have a refined aura about them.
> On the paintings, misty scenes south of Yangzi River;
> In the incense burners, fine sandalwood from Cambodia.
> The bamboo in the courtyard rustle in the wind;
> The flowers outside the curtain glow in the sun.
> The pine trees cast their warm shadows

Through the railings on the zither and the books.
The hues of the hills, transferred to the rooms,
Cool down the pillows and the bamboo mats.

Filled with delight at Daqing's arrival, Jingzhen dispensed with the exchange of greetings this time around and asked him forthwith to sit down. After tea was served, fruit, wine, and food were set out. Kongzhao made Jingzhen sit next to Daqing, whereas she herself sat facing them and pulled a novice over to sit on one side. After the foursome had sat drinking one cup after another for a good while, Daqing gathered Jingzhen onto his lap and made Kongzhao move over to his side. His arms around their necks, he showered endearments on them in a hundred ways. Even the novice sitting by one side blushed and felt her desires aroused.

They drank until evening fell. Kongzhao rose to say, "Be a good bridegroom. I'll come tomorrow morning to offer you my congratulations." Having said that, she asked for a lamp and was escorted to the gate. After she was gone, the novice told the old acolyte to close the doors and the windows before she returned inside to put the room in order and serve hot water to wash hands and feet with. Daqing carried Jingzhen to bed, undressed her, and slipped into the quilt. Their bodies tightly pressed against each other, He Daqing, exhilarated by the wine, put to good use all the skills he had acquired in his life, and brought Jingzhen to such ecstasy that her limbs went all limp and she lay sprawling in bed, helpless. They slept until almost noon.

Henceforth, both nuns bribed the acolytes into letting them have their fun by turns. His lust knowing no bounds, He Daqing abandoned himself to the pleasures and forgot all about returning home. About two months later, he felt worn out. Hardly able to keep up the necessary level of energy, he thought of going home. However, the nuns, enjoying the fun in the prime of their youth, would not hear of it. Time and time again he pleaded, "I'm more than honored that you favor me with such kindness and I really don't have the heart to leave you. But I've been here for more than two months now. My family must be worried about me because they have no idea where I am. I need to go back and comfort my wife and my son before returning to you. It will be just a matter of four or five days. Don't get suspicious."

Kongzhao said, "In that case, we'll have a proper feast this evening. You'll be free to go tomorrow morning. But you must not go back on your word like a treacherous man."

He Daqing said in a vow, "May I perish if I ever forget your kindness!"

Kongzhao went to the west wing and reported the matter to Jingzhen, who said, after a moment of reflection, "He may have taken that vow in good faith, but once he's gone, he won't come back."

"Why do you say that?" asked Kongzhao.

"Who wouldn't fall in love with such a dashing young man? He's a frequenter of houses of pleasure, of which there are quite a few, and he can't tear himself away from every one he visits. However he may wish to come back, he just won't be able to."

"In your opinion, what should be done?"

"I do have a wonderful plan that will tie him to us without ropes and make him stay with us in utter devotion."

Kongzhao hastened to ask what the plan was. Jingzhen stretched out a hand and, sticking up two fingers, explained what she had in mind. It was a plan that would

> Make him who wallowed in flower beds
> Perish under the peony blossoms.

This was what Jingzhen said: "At the send-off feast this evening, let's get him drunk and shave his head clean. Surely he won't be able to go home with his head shaven. (*Ingenious!*) What's more, he has a woman's facial features. If he's dressed up the way we are, even Bodhidharma himself won't be able to tell that he's a man.[6] This way, we get to enjoy him forever, risk-free. Wouldn't it be lovely whichever way you look at it?"

"What a brilliant idea! You're so much smarter than I am!"

When evening came, Jingzhen told her novice to look after their quarters and she herself went to the east wing. To He Daqing, she said, "Why do you want to leave when we're having so much fun? How can you be so heartless?"

"It's not that I'm heartless, but I've been away from home for so long. My wife and my child must be missing me. That's why I'd like to be gone for a few days. I'll be back soon enough. How would I even dream of staying away from you for too long and forgetting your love?"

"My sister having already given you her promise, I can't force you to stay. But you must not go back on your word, lest you lose your credibility."

"You need not worry on that score!"

A moment later, a fine spread was laid on the table, around which the four women and one man sat down. Jingzhen said, "This being a send-off banquet, let's get ourselves gloriously drunk!"

"Of course!" chimed in Kongzhao.

They plied him with wine until the third watch of the night was struck. When He Daqing was dead drunk and lost all consciousness, Jingzhen rose and removed his head-covering. Kongzhao took out a barber's razor and shaved off all his hair. The two nuns then helped him to Kongzhao's room to retire for the night before they took leave of each other.

Upon waking up at daybreak, He Daqing found Kongzhao sleeping by his side. As he turned in bed, he had a feeling that his head rolling on the pillow was hairless. Quickly he touched his head with his hand and found that, indeed, his head had been shaven clean. In horror, he sat up and cried, "What did you do to me?"

Kongzhao woke up with a start and, seeing him in such an agitated state, also sat up and said, "Don't be angry! It was all because you wanted to go home. All four of us hated to see you go, but we didn't know how to keep you. That's why we made this desperate move, to pass you off as a nun, so that we can go on having fun." So saying, she laid her head on his chest and used all her charms on him, casting such a spell on him that he was at a loss as to what to do.

"Granted that you acted out of the best intentions," he conceded, "but you did go too far! How am I going to show myself in public?"

"You can wait until your hair grows back before showing yourself in public."

He Daqing saw nothing else for it but to do her bidding. Dressed as a nun, he made the nunnery his home and indulged in pleasures of the flesh day and night. Kongzhao and Jingzhen brought in the two novices even though just between the two of them, Daqing was already fully occupied.

> Sometimes it was a union of five;
> Sometimes it was one-on-one.
> In that wing, how would the lustful ever give him up?
> In this wing, how would he, eager to please, dare not to do his best?
> Two sharp axes are too much for a piece of dead wood;
> One tired soldier is no match for four brave generals.
> When a lamp going out is lit again,
> The flame is not one to last much longer.
> When a water clock dries up but still drips,
> Do not expect the droplets to be wet and moist.
> A man of iron would have melted;
> The remaining days will be hard to get through.

Daqing received no sympathy for his illness. In the beginning, he had good days and bad days, and on the bad days, the nuns thought he was just feigning illness to shirk his duty. It was only when he began to stay under the quilt for extended periods of time that they grew alarmed. They had a good mind to send him home, but, with his head now shaven, they were afraid that if his family found out the truth and brought a lawsuit against them, the reputation of the nunnery would be ruined and they would have no place to stay. But if he were to stay on, they were afraid that if anything untoward should happen, they wouldn't know how to dispose of the corpse, and if the local headman found out about this and raised a fuss, their lives could be in danger. Nor did they dare engage a physician. Instead, they had the acolytes go to a physician, describe the symptoms to him, and bring back some medicine. But the medicinal broth might just as well have been poured onto a rock. It did not work. Kongzhao and Jingzhen dutifully brewed the medicine in water, fed Daqing the broth, and attended to him day and night, hoping he would regain his health. As it turned out, his condition grew worse. As he lay on the verge of death, Kongzhao said to Jingzhen, "There's no hope now. What are we going to do?"

Jingzhen replied after a moment of reflection, "It's all right. I'll tell the acolytes to buy several loads of lime. After he's gone, let's not ask outsiders to help dispose of the body. We'll do it ourselves. We'll first dress him up as a nun, as usual, and instead of going out to buy a coffin, we'll just put him in the one that our mentor has prepared for herself. And then, you and I and the acolytes and the girls can all pitch in and carry it to an empty spot in the backyard. We'll dig a grave, pour the lime into it, and bury him inside. Not even the gods or ghosts will be any the wiser!"

So much for the nuns' discussion. Let us come back to Daqing as he lay in Kongzhao's bed. Suddenly hit by the thought that none of his kith and kin was there with him, he burst into copious tears. Kongzhao wiped off his tears and said, trying to assuage his grief, "Don't feel sad. I'm sure you'll get better."

"Since I met the two of you by chance, I've been hoping for our love to last forever. I certainly never thought that our predestined bond would go only so far. It's so sad that I would have to part with you midway. Because you are the first one I got to know, I'd like you to deliver an important message for me. Please do not fail me on any account."

"I'll surely do whatever you tell me to do," promised Kongzhao.

From under the pillow, He Daqing retrieved a lovers' silk ribbon. Why was it called a lovers' silk ribbon? Well, half of this ribbon was parrot green, and half light yellow. Hence the name "lovers' silk ribbon," because of the two intertwining colors. Handing it to Kongzhao, Daqing said tearfully, "My family doesn't know I'm here. Now that I'm leaving this world, please deliver this ribbon to my wife, because she will recognize this keepsake, and tell her to come here quickly to see me. I'll then be able to find peace in death."

The ribbon in hand, Kongzhao had the novice bring Jingzhen over to a side room. After she showed Jingzhen the ribbon and asked what to do about it, the latter said, "By harboring a man in a nunnery, you and I have already broken the rules. Worse still, we worked him to the verge of death. If his wife comes here, she will certainly not let the matter rest. And if she raises a fuss about it, what are we going to do?"

Kongzhao, being an inexperienced young woman after all, did not have the heart to betray Daqing. But Jingzhen seized the ribbon and tossed it up into the storage space above the false ceiling. Alas, this ribbon was not to see the light of day for some time to come.

"If you toss that ribbon away, what am I going to say to him in response?"

"Just say that you've sent the acolyte to deliver the ribbon to his wife. If his wife refuses to come, he can't blame us!"

Kongzhao did as she was told. For days on end, Daqing kept asking if there was a reply from his wife. Convinced that his wife was refusing to see him out of spite, he felt even more saddened and broke down in sobs. Another few days later, his allotted span of life expired, and it was all over with him.

> One more lustful ghost in the netherworld;
> One impostor nun gone from the earth.

Watching him breathe his last, the two nuns dared not cry out loud but choked back their sobs. They washed his body with warm scented water and put new clothes on him. They then woke up the two old acolytes, fed them an ample meal, lit a lamp, and led them to a big cypress tree in the backyard, where the two acolytes dug a large grave with iron shovels, dumped in lime, carried out the coffin that the old nun had prepared for herself, and lowered it into the grave pit. When all was ready for the burial, they went into the room where the corpse was and transferred it onto one leaf of a double door. They could not have cared less whether it was an auspicious day for burial or not. With the help of the nuns and novices, the acolytes carried the corpse to the backyard and placed it in the coffin. After putting the lid on, they perfunctorily hammered in a few nails, dumped a liberal amount of lime on it, and spread earth evenly over the top, so that no trace of a grave could be detected on the flat ground. Pity that He Daqing! In a little more than three months' time from the Clear and Bright Festival, when he got entangled with that nun, he met his end without ever laying his eyes on his wife and son again. How sad that he left behind a sizable estate but was buried in a deserted backyard! There is a little song in testimony:

> The amorous one!
> Your passion was ill placed this time!
> To be entangled with that little nun
> Was the very last thing you should have done.
> That little nun is a real lustful one;
> She was too much for you to handle.
> Your scalp was all shaven clean,
> And you ceased to be in the end!
> To be buried in a weed-grown grave—
> That's what lies in store for debauched rakes!

Let us pick up another thread of the story and turn our attention to Lu-shi, He Daqing's wife. After he left home on a spring outing on the day of the Clear and Bright Festival, Lu-shi thought he must have been having fun in some brothel and did not worry even after four or five days went by. But after about ten days, she had a servant make inquiries from brothel to brothel. Upon hearing that he had not been seen ever since the day of the festival, Lu-shi panicked. After more than a month had gone by without any news about him, Lu-shi began to weep day and night. She had posters put up everywhere, but to no avail. All the members of the clan were beside themselves with anxiety.

In the wake of the rainy autumn of the previous year, several houses owned by the He family needed repair, but, the head of the family being absent, Lu-shi was in no mood to have anything done. It was not until the eleventh month of the year that she called in a few workmen for the repair jobs. One day, when Lu-shi was out on an inspection, her eyes happened to rest on a lovers' ribbon around the waist of one of the workmen. It looked just like the one in her husband's possession. She gave a start. Without a moment's delay, she had a maidservant tell the man to take it off and show it to her. The workman was called Kuai San, a skillful bricklayer and carpenter and, in fact, a well-known versatile craftsman. The He family being an important client of his, Kuai San knew everyone in that household. Hearing that the mistress wanted to have a look at it, he promptly untied the ribbon and handed it to the maidservant, who, in her turn, gave it to Lu-shi. Upon close examination, Lu-shi found that it was indeed the very ribbon that belonged to her husband. Because of this ribbon,

> The libertine's name spread far and wide,
> And the lustful nuns came to grief.

The fact was that He Daqing and his wife had bought two identical ribbons, one for each. And now the ribbon was there but the man wearing it was gone. Her face awash with tears as she looked at the ribbon, Lu-shi asked Kuai San, "Where did you get it?"

"I picked it up in a nunnery outside the city."

"What's the nunnery called? What are the names of the nuns?"

"It's the famous Non-Void Nunnery. It's divided into two wings. The east wing is occupied by a nun called Kongzhao, the west by the nun Jingzhen. There are also a couple of novices who haven't yet taken the tonsure."

"How old are the nuns?"

"They are both only about twenty. Both are very pretty."

Lu-shi thought, "My husband must be so enamored of those two nuns that he is hiding in that nunnery. Let me have some men take Kuai San there with this ribbon as evidence and search the grounds. He'll surely be found." She had just turned around when another thought struck her. "How can I be sure it has fallen off my husband? I shouldn't be unjust to the nuns. Let me ask Kuai San for more details." She called out after Kuai San and asked again, "When did you pick up the ribbon?"

"Less than half a month ago."

Lu-shi thought, "So my husband was still in the nunnery half a month ago. This sounds suspicious." Aloud, she asked, "Where did you pick it up?" (*Good attention to details.*)

"From the storage space above the false ceiling of the bedchamber of the east wing. The roof leaked after a rainstorm, so they asked me to redo the tiles. That's where I came upon it. May I ask you, madam, why so many questions about this ribbon?"

"This ribbon belongs to my husband, who hasn't been seen or heard from since spring. Now this ribbon gave me an idea; he must be where the ribbon was. I'd like to go with you to ask the nuns to give him up. After I find him and bring him back, I'll reward you well, as announced in the posters."

In astonishment, Kuai San thought, "Now what is this? Why get me involved?" Aloud, he said, "I just happened to have picked up the ribbon. I know nothing about what happened to your husband."

Lu-shi asked, "How many days did you work in the nunnery?"

"About ten days altogether. They still owe me my wages."

"Did you see my husband there?"

"I'll be perfectly honest with you. During all those days we worked there, we were allowed access everywhere, but I never even saw the shadow of Mr. He."

Lu-shi thought, "If he's not in the nunnery, the ribbon can hardly prove much." After turning her thoughts this way and that, she said to herself, "There must have been a reason why the ribbon was in the nunnery. Or my husband may be hidden somewhere else. Since Kuai San says they still owe him his wages, let me give him a tael of silver and tell him to go every so often to check the place out, ostensibly to ask for payment. There'll surely be some telltale signs. If I confront the nuns by then, I should be able to get to the bottom of it all." Thereupon she gave Kuai San detailed instructions as to what to do, adding, "I'll give you one tael of silver first. After you bring me definite news, I'll have handsome rewards for you."

Pleased at the prospect of getting one tael of silver, to be followed by handsome rewards, the bricklayer readily consented to put himself at her disposal. Lu-shi returned to her room and reemerged with a tael of silver, which she handed over to Kuai San. Thankfully Kuai San took his leave.

The next day, Kuai San waited until lunchtime was over before he started making his way to the nunnery. As he slowly approached the gate, he saw the old acolyte of the western wing sitting on the threshold, holding his clothes out against the sun and hunting for the lice in them. Kuai San walked up and greeted him. Raising his head, the old man recognized Mr. Kuai and said, "Haven't seen you for quite a few days. What brings you here? Her Reverend is about to ask you to do some minor jobs. You've come at the right time!"

This could not have suited Kuai San better. "What jobs does Her Reverend have for me?"

"Well, I have no idea. She didn't say more than what I just told you. Let's go inside and ask. We'll know soon enough." The acolyte straightened his clothes and went inside with Kuai San. After many twists and turns, they entered the chamber where Jingzhen was copying scriptures.

"Madam," said the acolyte. "Craftsman Kuai is here."

Putting down her brush-pen, Jingzhen said, "I was just going to have the acolyte bring you here for some jobs that need to be done. You've come in the nick of time."

"What are the jobs?"

"The antique altar table in front of the statue of Buddha has been here for so many years that the paint is peeling off. I've been meaning to get a new one, but no donation has come our way. The other day, Granny Qian kindly offered us some pieces of wood, with which we can make an altar like the one in the east wing.

Tomorrow is an auspicious day for the job to start, and it must be done by you. None of your assistants is any good. I'll pay you all at once after this job is done."

"All right," said Kuai San. "I'll surely be here tomorrow." As he mouthed these words, his eyes wandered all around the sparsely furnished room. Believing no one could possibly be hiding there, he left the room, glancing in all directions as he went. "Since I picked up the ribbon in the east wing, I should go there and see if I can find something more," he said to himself.

Upon leaving the gate, he said good-bye to the acolyte and repaired to the east wing, where the gate stood ajar. There being no one in sight, he noiselessly sidled his way in and tiptoed step by step into the inner quarters of the wing. When coming upon a locked door, he peeked through the chink between its two halves and found it was an empty room and all was quiet and still. As he approached the kitchen door, his ears caught ripples of laughter. He stopped in his tracks and applied his eyes to an aperture in the window. Two girls were locked in a playful tussle. In a trice, the younger one of the two fell on the floor. The older one sat astride her the way a man would do and kissed her. As the younger one started to scream, the older one said, "That hole of yours has already been stretched, so why are you screaming?" (*A good scene.*)

Kuai San was enjoying the scene when he suddenly sneezed. The two girls jumped to their feet in alarm and cried out, "Who is it?"

Drawing near, Kuai San said, "It's me. Is Her Reverend here?" As he said this, he was still thinking about what he had just witnessed, and a chuckle escaped him. Aware that they had been seen, the girls reddened and said, "Mr. Kuai, what do you have to say to her?"

"Nothing much. Just to ask for an advance on my wages."

"She's not here. Come again another day."

Thus rejected, Kuai San could not very well press on. Resignedly, he turned on his heels and walked off. Closing the door, the girls cursed, "That swine's like a thief. He sneaked up to the kitchen door without a noise. What a hateful man!"

Kuai San heard them all too clearly, but, as those words were not said to his face, he could not very well confront them. As he walked along, he turned over in his mind the line "That hole of yours has already been stretched." He thought, "What it refers to is not clear, but it certainly sounds a little suspicious. Let me come again tomorrow and try to find out more."

The next morning, he betook himself to the west wing of the nunnery, carrying his tools. As his hands were busily taking measurements with his ruler and using his ax and handsaw, his mind was preoccupied with ways to find out the whereabouts of He Daqing. In early afternoon, Jingzhen stepped out to watch him at his work. As they chatted away, it so happened that she raised her head and noticed that a wall lamp had gone out, whereupon she told the novice to go and bring a pilot fire. Before long, the girl came back with a lit lamp, which she deposited on the table. As she tried to let down the rope that held the wall lamp in place, the rope slackened and the lamp slid down fast. As chance would have it, since Jingzhen was standing right under the lamp, it fell straight on her head. With a crash, the lamp broke in half and the oil trickled from her head all the way down. (*According to folk belief, grease stains bring bad luck. How true!*)

Jingzhen flew into a rage. Ignoring the grease stains all over her, she grabbed the girl by her hair and began to rain blows and kicks on her, cursing, "You slut! Hussy! Whore! You had so much fun in bed you lost your head! You ruined my clothes!"

Kuai San put down his tools and hastened over to pull them apart. Still fuming with anger, Jingzhen headed for her bedchamber to change her clothes, cursing as she went.

Her hair all in disarray, the novice broke down in bitter sobs. Now that Jingzhen had disappeared into the inner quarters of the house, the girl mumbled, "You beat and curse me over a broken lamp. What punishment do you deserve for taking a human life?" (*Heaven put these words in her mouth.*) Intrigued upon hearing these remarks, Kuai San went over with alacrity and asked her what it was all about. Truly,

> Bear this in mind: words are like fishlines and hooks;
> They pull trouble right out of the air.

As a matter of fact, this girl, having reached puberty, was itching for the kind of pleasure that Jingzhen had enjoyed with He Daqing. However, Jingzhen was of a far more intolerant disposition than Kongzhao and was much given to jealousy. She was soft on Kongzhao only because Kongzhao was the one who had initiated the affair. When she could not have enough of the man in her own room, how would she willingly share him with anyone else even for a brief instant? The novice had therefore been nursing a grudge against her all along. And now, in a moment of anger, she came out with the truth and thus played right into Kuai San's hands.

"How did she take a human life?" he asked.

"She and those whores of the east wing took turns having fun day and night, which cost the life of a Mr. He, student of the imperial college."

"Where's the corpse?"

"It's buried under the big cypress tree in the backyard of the east wing."

Before Kuai San had a chance to ask more questions, the acolyte appeared. Both fell silent. The girl then sobbingly went inside.

Finding that this information tallied with what had been said by the novice of the east wing the day before, Kuai San knew that he had gathered almost all the facts of the case. Before the hour grew late, he put together his tools and, on the plea of a prior engagement, raced in one breath to the He residence, asked to see Mrs. He, and told her everything.

Upon hearing of her husband's death, Lu-shi burst into wails of grief. Before the night was out, she invited members of the He clan over for consultation and kept Kuai San for the night. The next morning, she assembled her servants and armed them with hoes, spades, axes, and the like, and, with her son in the care of the housekeeper, mounted a sedan-chair and led the procession of about twenty people to the nunnery three li away. Upon arrival shortly thereafter, Lu-shi dismounted and told half of her servants to keep watch at the gate. The rest of them followed her in, carrying their hoes and spades and whatnot. With Kuai San leading the way, they went straight to the east wing and knocked at the gate.

Though the gate of the nunnery was open, the nuns had just risen from bed. Hearing the knocks, the acolyte went out for a look. Seeing a crowd with a woman, he thought they were there to offer incense and went in to report to Kongzhao. In the meantime, Kuai San, who knew his way around the backyard, led the group of people straight in. On their way there, they encountered Kongzhao, who said, at the sight of Kuai San with a woman visitor, "So, you are Mr. Kuai's wife!" As she stepped forward to greet them, Kuai San and Lu-shi brushed her aside and shot off like a puff of smoke to the backyard with the rest of the group.

Wondering what this feverishness was all about, Kongzhao followed on their heels into the backyard and saw that the group headed directly for the cypress tree. Once there, they began digging busily with their hoes and spades. At this point, it dawned on Kongzhao that their secret was out. Her face drained of all color, she rushed in terror into the house and said to the novices, "We're in trouble! Our secret about Mr. He is out! Follow me! Let's run for our lives!"

The two girls were also dumbfounded. They followed Kongzhao out, empty-handed. They had hardly reached the main shrine when the acolyte came to report, "For some reason, a lot of people are blocking the main gate and they won't let me go out."

Kongzhao gave a mournful shriek and said, "Let's go to the west wing first!" With the speed of wind, the four of them dashed off to the west wing. As soon as the acolyte there opened the gate in answer to their knocks, they told him to close it after them quickly and not to open it to anyone else. When they rushed inside, they found Jingzhen's door closed, for she was still in bed. Kongzhao pounded on the door and shouted at the top of her voice. Recognizing Kongzhao's voice, Jingzhen hastened out of bed, put on her clothes, and stepped out. "Why are you in such an agitated state?" she asked.

"Our secret about Mr. He is out. I have no idea who leaked it. That cursed carpenter Kuai took a large group of people into the backyard and they are digging. I was about to flee for my life, but the acolyte says the gate is blocked. We can't get out. I'm here to ask you what to do."

Jingzhen was also appalled. "Kuai was working here yesterday. And you say he's here again today and taking a lot of people? And he knows so much, too! Someone in this nunnery must have leaked something out before that dog raised a hue and cry. Otherwise, how did they get wind of our secret?"

Hearing this conversation, the novice standing off to one side regretted having thoughtlessly blurted out everything. She was seized with fear.

The novice of the east wing put in, "Carpenter Kuai has been onto us for quite some time now. The day before yesterday, he sneaked up to our kitchen window to spy on us. We got angry and drove him away. I wonder who could have told on us."

"Let's talk about this later," said Kongzhao. "But what are we going to do now?"

"There's nothing else for it but to flee," said Jingzhen.

"The gate is blocked," Kongzhao reminded her.

"Let's take the back door then," said Jingzhen. She had the acolyte check out the back gate. When he came back, saying there was no one there, Kongzhao was overjoyed. She told the acolytes to lock up every door, whereas she herself went back to her room and took her silver, leaving everything else behind. All seven of them, including the acolytes, went out the back gate and locked it after them.

"Now, where are we going to hide?" asked Kongzhao.

"We'll surely be seen if we take the high road," said Jingzhen. "We'll have to keep to quiet alleys and take refuge in Ultimate Bliss Nunnery, which is in a sparsely populated area. No one will get to know anything about us. And Liaoyuan of that nunnery is a good friend of ours. She won't turn us away. After this thing blows over, we'll think of what to do next."

Kongzhao readily agreed. Keeping to small alleys, quite oblivious to the wretched conditions of the ground, they fled in desperation to Ultimate Bliss Nunnery for refuge, but of them, for the time being, no more.

In the meantime, Lu-shi, Kuai San, and the others were hard at work, digging under the cypress tree. After shoveling off the surface soil, they came upon a layer of lime, and they knew that the story was true. The lime mixed with water had hardened into a solid slab and did not yield easily to the hoes and spades. It was a long time before the lid of the coffin was exposed to view. Lu-shi burst into loud sobs. After the lime was all shoveled away, the lid still could not be opened. Those watching the gate were so anxious that they ran into the backyard to find out what was going on and, seeing the chaotic scene, they pitched in and dug deeper to loosen the entire coffin from the earth. Then they swung their axes high and brought them down on the lid.

When the coffin lid burst open, there, for all to see, lay a nun, not a man. Everyone was aghast. Instead of taking a closer look, they stared at one another and quickly put the lid back on.

Storyteller, let me ask you something: He Daqing hadn't been dead for a year. You don't mean to say that his wife couldn't recognize him even though all his hair was gone?

Well, dear audience, you may not have thought about this, but when he first left home, He Daqing was a handsome young man aglow with good health, but after being confined to bed in the nunnery in a protracted illness brought on by exhaustion, he was reduced to a bag of bones upon death. Had he looked into a mirror, he wouldn't have recognized himself. What's more, would anyone who suddenly sees a shaven head in a nunnery not take it to be that of a nun?

Let us resume. Lu-shi grumbled at Kuai San, saying, "Didn't I tell you to find out what really happened? Instead of getting all the facts, you came back to me with a false report. And now, look at this mess! What are we going to do?"

"The novice told me all that yesterday. How can you say I gave you a false report?"

"That is a nun all right," someone among the crowd commented, "no matter how you try to talk your way out of it!"

"We might have dug at the wrong place. Why don't we try over there?"

An elderly member of the He clan said, "No! No! The law says that anyone who opens a coffin with a corpse in it is punishable by death. Digging up a grave must also be a capital crime. We've already violated the law, and if we dig up another nun, that's two capital offenses. We'd better report to the yamen and have the novice taken there for questioning. Only then will we be let off the hook. If the nuns go to the yamen ahead of us, we'll be in a lot of trouble."

Everyone agreed. Without a moment's delay, they dropped their tools and led Lu-shi off. But not a single nun was seen as they went from the inner quarters all the way to the main gate. The elderly man spoke up again, "This looks bad! The nuns must have gone to get the local headman, or they may have got a start on us and are already at the yamen, complaining against us. Let's get out of here! Quick!"

General panic set in. Everyone was only too anxious to clear out of the place. With Lu-shi in the sedan-chair, they ran with all the speed they could gather to the Xingan County yamen to report to the authorities, but by the time they got to the city, half of the relatives had slipped away.

Let us pick up another thread of the story and turn our attention to a man known as Mao the Ruffian, a hired hand among the men brought along by Lu-shi. Hoping to find something valuable in the coffin, he had been hiding off to one side. After everyone else was gone, he emerged and opened the coffin lid. He felt under the upper garment but found nothing. As fate would have it, with a pull of his hand, the trousers slid down, revealing you-know-what. Mao the Ruffian burst out laughing. "So, this is not a nun but a monk!" he said. He put the lid back on and walked around, looking in every direction as he went. There being no one in sight, he tiptoed into a room, which happened to be Kongzhao's bedchamber. He found a few things of some value, stuffed them into the bosom of his shirt, left Non-Void Nunnery, and went as fast as his legs could carry him to the county yamen.

Arriving at a moment when the county magistrate was away paying a courtesy call and Lu-shi and her followers were waiting, Mao the Ruffian went up and said, "Don't panic yet. I felt a little uneasy, so I went back for another look. I found that although the corpse is not that of Mr. He, it's not a nun either. It's a monk."

Everyone rejoiced. "That's much better!" they exclaimed. "But from which monastery was that monk? And why was he murdered by the nuns?"

Now, coincidences do happen. While they were jabbering away, an old monk walked up to them and asked, "A monk was murdered in a nunnery? Which monk? Which nunnery? How did he look?"

"It's the east wing of Non-Void Nunnery outside the city," came the reply. "It's a tall and thin and sallow-faced young monk. It looks like he died not long ago."

"He must be my disciple."

"How come your disciple died in that place?"

"I am Jueyuan, chief monk of Wanfa Monastery. That disciple of mine was called Qufei, twenty-six years old, who behaved badly. I couldn't keep him in line. He left the monastery in the eighth month and hasn't returned. His parents are the extremely doting kind. Instead of admitting their son's faults, they accuse me of having murdered him. I'm here today to stand trial. If that corpse is him, I'm exonerated."

Mao the Ruffian said, "Reverend, if you hire me, I'll take you there."

"That would be best!" said the old monk.

They were about to go when an old man and an old woman rushed up to them. Giving the monk two slaps across the face, the old man cursed, "You bald lowlife! Where did you put my son's body after you killed him?"

"Calm down," said the monk. "Your son's body has been found."

"Where is it?"

"Your son had an affair with the nuns of Non-Void Nunnery and died, for one reason or another, and was buried in the backyard." Pointing at Mao the Ruffian, the old monk continued, "The witness is here."

As the monk pulled Mao along, the old couple followed behind. By the time they arrived at the nunnery, people living nearby had already heard the story and had all turned out, old and young, to watch the goings-on.

Mao the Ruffian took the old monk all the way to the inner quarters of the nunnery. Then they heard someone calling in a room. Mao pushed open the door and saw an old nun on the verge of death, calling from her bed, "I'm hungry. Give me something to eat!"

Ignoring her, Mao closed the door, went with the monk to the cypress tree in the backyard, and removed the coffin lid. The old couple rubbed their eyes for a good look, and, believing that the corpse bore some resemblance to their son, they burst into wails of grief. When the spectators gathered around them and asked what had happened, Mao the Ruffian launched into a detailed account enlivened by animated gestures.

Now that the couple had identified their son, the old monk, eager to clear his own name, could not care less if the couple had made a mistake or not. Gripping the old man with one swift movement of his hand, he said, "Let's go! Now that you've found your son, let's go to report to the yamen and have the officers interrogate the nuns. Hold your tears for now!"

And so the old man stopped crying. They put the lid back in its place, left the nunnery, and went with all speed to the county yamen. It so happened that upon their arrival the county magistrate had just returned. The officer charged with guarding the old monk had been looking everywhere for him and was bathed in perspiration.

At the sight of Mao the Ruffian and the old monk, those of the He clan gathered around them and asked the monk, "Is it your disciple?"

"Yes, it is!" said the monk.

"If so," said members of the He clan, "let's combine the two cases and make our report together."

The officer escorted all of them into the tribunal, where they dropped to their knees. A servant of the He family went forward first and told about the master's disappearance, the sighting of Mr. Kuai's silk ribbon, the novice's story, the opening of the coffin, and the identification of the corpse as that of a monk. Then the old monk went up and said that it was his disciple, who had disappeared from the monastery three months before and had somehow died in that nunnery. He concluded by saying that the bereaved parents had accused him wrongly, adding, "Now that the truth has been established, please set me free, since this case has nothing to do with me."

The magistrate asked the old man, "Is it indeed your son? Don't make a mistake."

"Yes, it is indeed my son. How can I be wrong?"

The magistrate forthwith summoned four officers and told them to go to the nunnery and bring the nuns for interrogation. Thus ordered, the officers raced with the speed of wind to the nunnery, which was by then filled with crowds of spectators going in and out. The nuns were nowhere in sight. The officers finally came to the room where the old nun was lying in bed, on the verge of death. One of the officers suggested, "They may be hiding in the west wing." Thereupon they hurried to the west wing but found the gate closed. As there was no response to their knocks on the gate, the officers grew impatient and climbed over the fence wall. They searched throughout the grounds and found all the doors padlocked. There was not even a trace of a human being. After each of them picked up a few objects of value, they went for the local headman and took him to the yamen, where the magistrate was waiting.

"The nuns of Non-Void Nunnery have all fled, no one knows where," said the officers. "We've brought the local headman for questioning."

"Do you know where the nuns are hiding?" the magistrate asked the local headman.

"How would I know?"

The magistrate said sharply, "It was on your watch that the nuns had affairs with a monk and committed murder, and you chose not to report on such offenses which are against the law. Now that the truth is out, you're again trying to cover up for them and pretend that you know nothing. What good are you as a local headman?" He ordered that the headman be given a beating. It was only after the headman pleaded desperately for mercy that the magistrate relented and spared him the bamboo rod but gave him three days to find the murderers and released him on bail, to await further interrogation. Two strips of paper were glued crisscross on the gate of the nunnery to close it off to the public.

Let us retrace our steps and come back to the moment when Kongzhao, Jingzhen, the novices, and the acolytes were at the gate of Ultimate Bliss Nunnery. They kept knocking on the tightly closed gate for what seemed like an eternity before the acolyte of the nunnery emerged to open it. Recklessly, they burst in and told the acolyte to close the gate instantly. The head nun, Liaoyuan, who was waiting at the entrance, surmised at the sight of all of them together and in such a state of consternation that something must have gone wrong. She invited them into the main hall, showed them to their seats, and sent the acolyte to prepare tea before she asked them the purpose of their visit.

Jingzhen pulled her to one side, told her everything that had happened, and asked to be allowed to take refuge in her nunnery. Liaoyuan was aghast. After reflecting for a few moments, she replied, "I should, by rights, keep you two here when you come to me for help. But this is no small matter. You may be safer in a place farther away. This is a small nunnery, with lots of ears and eyes. If you're seen, not only will you be unable to get free, but I will also be implicated. This is no place for you!"

Why, you may well ask, was Liaoyuan so reluctant? Well, she was also a fine nun much given to clandestine love affairs. In fact, she had been hiding the young monk Qufei of Wanfu Monastery for more than three months now in their life as man and wife, both with clean shaven heads. Although Qufei was dressed as a nun, they were in constant fear of being found out. Therefore they kept the gate tightly closed all the time. Now that Jingzhen was asking to take refuge with her for the same reasons, Liaoyuan was afraid that if Jingzhen were arrested, her own secrets would also be exposed. That was why she turned them down.

Thus rejected, Kongzhao and her companions looked at each other in dismay, at a loss as to what to do. Jingzhen, after all, was the one with the quicker mind. Knowing what a lover of money Liaoyuan was, she retrieved some pieces of silver from her sleeve, picked out two to three taels, and said to Liaoyuan, handing them to her, "What you said, my sister, may all be very true, but everything happened so quickly. We didn't even have a chance to discuss where to go. And now where are we supposed to seek refuge in this desperate hour? For the sake of our friend-ship, please let us stay for two or three days. We'll go somewhere else after the whole thing blows over. These small pieces of silver are to help you with your expenses."

Sure enough, the sight of money made Liaoyuan forget what was at stake. "If it's just two or three days, that will be fine," she promised. "But how can I take your money?"

Jingzhen rejoined, "We shouldn't be imposing ourselves on you in the first place. How can we put you to extra expense?"

After making a show of declining the offer of money, Liaoyuan took the pieces of silver and led the whole company into the house to hide.

Now, the young monk Qufei, hearing from the acolyte that the five guests were from Non-Void Nunnery and that all of them were goodly to the sight, hurried out to see for himself. As he ran into them and exchanged greetings with them, Jingzhen peered intently at him and, failing to recognize him, asked Liaoyuan, "Where is this sister from? Why have I never seen her before?"

Liaoyuan replied, lying, "She's a newcomer who has just taken the tonsure. That's why you don't know her."

Delighted that the two visiting nuns were prettier than Liaoyuan, the young monk thought, "What a lucky guy I am! I wonder why I'm so blessed. Since Heaven sent these wonderful girls here, let me take them on as well and enjoy them by turns!"

During the vegetarian meal that Liaoyuan laid out in their honor, Jingzhen and Kongzhao could scarcely sit still, their minds occupied elsewhere, their ears burning, their eyelids twitching, and they had no appetite. In midafternoon, they asked Liaoyuan to send the acolyte who was in her service to their nunnery to find out how things stood, so that they could make plans for the future. Right away, Liaoyuan did as they requested.

Being a simple-minded man knowing nothing about what was at stake, the acolyte went straight to Non-Void Nunnery and looked all around. This was the moment when the local headman was sealing off the gate with his followers by the magistrate's order. Indifferent to the fate of the dying nun inside, they spread the two strips of sealing paper crisscross over the gate. Just as they were about to turn their way back, they noticed an old man prowling about. Believing this was a spy, they went forward and roared, "Good timing! You're wanted by the yamen!" One of them picked up a noose and was on the point of throwing it over the acolyte's head when the acolyte said, paralyzed with fear, "They've taken refuge in our nunnery and sent me over here to find out how things are. I have nothing to do with this whole thing."

"We know you're here just to see what's happening. Now, tell us which nunnery it is."

"It's Ultimate Bliss Nunnery."

With this information, the men called for a few more helpers and took the acolyte to Ultimate Bliss Nunnery. With enough men to keep watch over the front as well as the back gates, they knocked at the front gate. Believing it was the acolyte, Liaoyuan rushed out and opened it, whereupon the men stormed in and apprehended Liaoyuan. They then searched high and low and arrested everyone, including the young monk hiding in terror under the bed.

Liaoyuan said to the men, "They are just taking temporary refuge in my nunnery. I had absolutely no part in what they've done. I would be happy to give all of you some money for you to buy wine with, so that you can do me a special favor and spare this nunnery."

"That won't do!" exclaimed the men. "Our county magistrate is not one to fool! If he asks us where we caught them, what are we going to say? We don't know whether you had any part in this or not. You've got to defend yourself in the tribunal."

"That can be easily done," said Liaoyuan. "But my disciple here has just taken the tonsure. Please spare her, as a special favor to me."

Enticed by the promise of silver, the men agreed. But one of them changed his mind, saying, "Can't be done! If she had no part in it, why was she so scared as to have hidden herself under the bed? There must be something fishy about her, too. Let's not get ourselves involved."

In a chorus of assent, the officers tied up all ten of them, male and female. Like a string of sweet rice dumplings eaten at Dragon Boat Festival, the procession was led out the nunnery gate in the direction of the Xingan County yamen. The gate was locked and sealed up. All along the way, Liaoyuan reproached Jingzhen for having gotten her implicated. Jingzhen dared not venture half a word in reply. Truly,

> When the old turtle's meat won't cook tender,
> Innocent mulberries are cut down to feed the fire.

As it was far on in the afternoon now and the magistrate had finished with the business of the day, the local headman brought the captured individuals to his home for the night. There, Liaoyuan whispered to the young monk, "In the tribunal tomorrow, just say that you're the new disciple here. Don't say a word too many. Let me handle this. Nothing can happen to us."

The next day, at the morning session of the tribunal, the headman marched his captives in and announced, "The nuns of Non-Void Nunnery were all hiding in Ultimate Bliss Nunnery. They are now here under arrest, as are the nuns of Ultimate Bliss Nunnery."

The magistrate ordered them to kneel on the eastern side of the dais. Then he summoned the old monk, the He family servant, Kuai San, and the young monk's parents for questioning. In an instant, everyone was brought in and ordered to kneel on the western side of the dais. Stealing a glance at them, the young monk said to himself in surprise, "Why has my mentor got himself into this case? Even my parents are here. How very strange!" But he kept his thoughts to himself, not daring to call out. Afraid that his mentor might recognize him, he hung his head and prostrated himself on the floor. (*What a dramatic trial!*)

Thrusting aside all regard for the magistrate on the dais, the old man, with his wife by his side, pointed at the nuns and tearfully lashed out at them, "Shameless whores! Why did you murder my son? If you had returned him to us, alive and well, all would have been forgiven!"

Even more surprised that his father was asking Jingzhen to give him up, Qufei the young monk thought, "But I *am* alive and well. How was I murdered?"

Believing that those were He Daqing's parents, Jingzhen and Kongzhao dared not utter a sound.

After silencing the old man with a sharp order, the magistrate called up Kongzhao and Jingzhen and asked, "Having renounced the world, how could you have violated the Buddhist laws, carried on an affair with a monk, and then murdered him? Out with the truth now, or you'll be put under torture!"

Knowing the gravity of their offense, Jingzhen and Kongzhao were so frightened that all the internal organs of their bodies were at sixes and sevens, in a complete mess. The magistrate's questions about a monk rather than He Daqing further puzzled them. Jingzhen's normal glibness of tongue vanished. It was as if her lips had been sealed with raw lacquer and fish glue. Not a single word could find its way out. (*Good depiction of Jingzhen.*) It was after the magistrate had asked four or five times that she managed to say, "I did not murder that monk."

The magistrate thundered, "You murdered Monk Qufei from Wanfa Monastery and buried him in the backyard. How dare you deny it? Apply the squeezers on her!"

The yamen runners lined up on both sides roared in acceptance of the order and moved forward, ready for action.

Realizing that the magistrate had taken the corpse to be that of Qufei and was pursuing the interrogation along these lines, Liaoyuan gave a violent start, for the charge struck her right on her sore spot. Her body involuntarily shaking, she thought, "Now, how did all this come about? They've got Mr. He's corpse. Instead of asking about that, he's focusing on what involves me. How strange!" Unable to make head or tail of this, she stole a glance at the young monk, who, knowing by now that his parents were mistaken, was also looking at her uneasily.

Being of delicate constitution and tender skin, how could Jingzhen and Kongzhao withstand torture? All but fainting away as soon as the squeezers were applied to them, they cried out, "Your Honor, please stop the torture! We confess."

The magistrate ordered the runners to stay their hands, so that he could listen to the confession.

The two nuns said in unison, "Your Honor, the one buried in our backyard is not a monk but Mr. He, student of the imperial college."

At these words, the He family servant and Kuai San both moved closer on their knees, the better to hear them.

The magistrate asked, "If it's Mr. He, why was his head shaven?"

Thereupon the nuns gave him all the details of He Daqing's visit to the nunnery as a sightseer, their illicit liaisons, the scheme to tonsure him and dress him up as a nun, his death of illness, and his burial. Finding that the confession tallied with the account of the He family servant the day before, the magistrate knew that this was the truth. He spoke up again, "So the facts about Mr. He have been established. But where is that monk hiding? Tell everything!"

The two nuns said tearfully, "That we don't know. We can't admit to any wrongdoing in that case, even if we're beaten to death."

The magistrate then called up the novices and the acolytes and interrogated them one by one. They all corroborated the nuns' words.

Realizing that the nuns indeed had no part in the case of the monk, the magistrate called up Liaoyuan and the young monk and said, "You gave safe haven to Jingzhen and Kongzhao in your nunnery, so you must be in collusion with them. Apply the squeezers on these two as well!"

Now that the other two nuns had confessed everything, clearing the young monk, Liaoyuan felt much easier. Calmly she said, "Your Honor, there's no need for torture. Please let me explain. Jingzhen and the others lied to me when they went to my nunnery the other day. They said that they had been blackmailed and therefore wanted to stay with me for a couple of days. That was why I kept them, which I shouldn't have done. I haven't the slightest knowledge about their illicit affairs." Pointing at the young monk, she continued, "This disciple of mine has just taken the Buddhist order. She has never even seen Jingzhen and the others before. Moreover, even if Your Honor hadn't uncovered such shameless acts that tarnish the reputation of Buddhist temples, I would have come forward to expose them had I heard the first thing about their doings. How would I even dream of giving these people safe haven after they had been found out? Please give my case your kindest consideration, Your Honor."

Impressed by her argument, the magistrate said affably, "Nice words. I hope you mean what you say." With that, he told her to withdraw to one side. He then ordered that Kongzhao and Jingzhen be given fifty strokes of the bamboo rod each, the two novices of the east wing thirty strokes each, and the two acolytes twenty each. They were beaten until their skin split, their flesh ripped, and blood flowed. After the beating was over, the magistrate took up his brush-pen and gave the sentences. Jingzhen and Kongzhao were sentenced to death in accordance with the law for their schemes of lecherous acts that took a life. The two novices of the east wing, in a lighter sentence, were to be flogged eighty times and sold as servants by the government. The two acolytes were also to be flogged for failure to inform on wrongful acts. Non-Void Nunnery, where the debauchery had taken place, was to be torn down and the land confiscated as government property. As for Liaoyuan and her disciple, even though they knew nothing about the wrongdoings, they gave safe haven to the criminals and were to pay a penalty in exchange for exemption from flogging. The novice of the west wing was to return to secular life. He Daqing having already died from his own sins, his case was closed. His coffin was to be buried properly by his family. All the parties were made to sign on the sentencing papers.

Now, knowing that the corpse was not that of his son, the old man seethed with greater resentment because he had wept for nothing the day before. He moved closer to the magistrate on his knees and petitioned the magistrate to make the old monk give him back his son. The old monk, in his turn, said that the young monk had stolen from the monastery and hidden the objects at home, and accused the father instead of bringing a false charge against him. As the two men exchanged heated words, even the magistrate was unable to come to a decision. If the old monk had killed the young man, there was no trace of the victim, and therefore he had no case. If the young monk had hidden the stolen goods at home, the father would hardly dare to confront the old monk and ask for his son back. After a great deal of reflection, the magistrate said, "There's no evidence to show whether your son is dead or alive. I have nothing to work on. You will be escorted out now. Come back when you've gathered sufficient evidence."

Kongzhao, Jingzhen, and the two novices were all taken to jail. Liaoyuan, the young monk Qufei, and the two acolytes were released on bail. The old monk and Qufei's parents were escorted by the very same officer who had guarded them before, to search for evidence of Qufei's whereabouts. All the others were free to return home. As most government establishments admit people through the east door and let them out through the west door, all of the parties in this case exited by the steps on the west side of the building.

Liaoyuan and the young monk were secretly overjoyed at having fooled the magistrate and avoided bringing disgrace upon themselves. Still afraid that he would be recognized, the young monk hung his head low and trailed behind everyone else. However, there was trouble in store for them. Hardly had they cleared the west door when Qufei's father grabbed the old monk and cursed, "You old bald swine! You murdered my son and tried to fob me off with another man's corpse." So saying, he rained blows on his face. Crying out in protest, the old monk was trying to dodge the blows when more than ten of his disciples, gathered there to wait for news about the trial, saw that their mentor was being beaten and, rushing forward, knocked the old man over and landed their fists on him.

In his fear for his father's safety, the young monk forgot that he was in the disguise of a nun. He walked up and said, 'Brothers, please stay your hands." Raising their heads to see who it was, the monks recognized Qufei. Letting go of the old man, they grabbed Qufei and cried, "Reverend, all's well! Qufei is right here!"

The guard escorting Qufei, not knowing the facts, said, "This is a nun from Ultimate Bliss Monastery, in my charge and out on bail. You are quite mistaken."

One monk commented, "Oh! So he's disguised as a nun and has been enjoying himself in the nunnery while his teacher suffered on his account!"

Upon realizing that they were looking at a monk, all present burst out laughing, but Liaoyuan groaned in despair. She turned deathly pale. The old monk threaded his way through the crowd, seized Qufei, and, giving him four or five slaps across his face in quick succession, cursed, "You accursed dog of a slave! You had fun but put me through so much misery! Let me take you to the magistrate!" With that outburst, he started to drag the young man along.

Seeing his son alive and well in the guise of a nun, the father knew that the young man would be in for punishment if brought before the magistrate. Kowtowing to the old monk, he pleaded, "Reverend, I'm so sorry for my rudeness. Please accept my apologies! Out of regard for your bond as teacher and pupil, please forgive my boy and don't take him to the yamen!"

Having suffered so much humiliation from him, the old monk turned a deaf ear to his pleas and dragged the young man all the way to the yamen. Liaoyuan was also brought in by the guard. Upon seeing them, the magistrate asked, "Why is the old monk dragging that nun here?"

"Your Honor," said the old monk. "This is not a nun. This is Qufei, my disciple, dressed as a nun."

The magistrate could hardly keep himself from laughing. "What a strange case this is!" he said. Sharply he ordered the young monk to confess.

Knowing he would not be able to lie his way out of it, Qufei had no choice but to confess everything. The magistrate recorded his confession, ordered to have him and the nun given forty strokes each, sentenced him to banishment in accordance with the law, and ordered that Liaoyuan be sold as a servant by the government and that Ultimate Bliss Nunnery be torn down. The old monk and Qufei's father, being innocent, were acquitted. The culprits were put in cangues and paraded through the streets with one cheek each smeared in black. The old couple, speechless over their son's unlawful acts, followed their son out of the yamen, their faces awash in tears, their hands holding on to the cangue around their son's neck. The event caused quite a sensation throughout the town. All the townspeople, male and female, old and young, turned out en masse to watch. A busybody made up the following song:

> Pity the old monk who lost his pupil;
> In fact, the nun hid him in her chamber.
> The young one is a man, no less,
> But was mistaken to be a lass.
> For the sake of a fake nun,
> Was implicated a real monk.
> A monk was hardly declared dead
> When he was caught, alive and well.
> In the yamen, the monk was beaten up;
> On the streets, the monk was stared down.
> For the sake of what hangs between the legs,
> The pretty nuns lost their precious lives.

The He family servant ran with Kuai San all the way home. Upon hearing their report, Lu-shi wept until she almost fainted. Before the night was out, she prepared the burial clothes and a coffin and, after obtaining authorization from the magistrate, broke the seal on the nunnery gate, personally went into the nunnery, and had the body exhumed and placed in the new coffin, which was then brought to the He family grave site to be buried on a chosen day. By that time, the old nun had died of hunger in her bed. The local headman reported the death to the authorities and buried the body, but of this, no more.

Due to the fact that her husband had not learned virtuous ways and had died from addiction to lust, Lu-shi applied strict discipline in her son's education. Later,

Mr. He Junior attained an official post after graduating from the imperial college and rose to be an administrative aide to the regional commander. (*All ends are neatly tied up without one omission. The work of a master.*) There is a poem in testimony:

> *He indulged in lust among wild grass and flowers;*
> *And died content like a bee and a butterfly.*
> *A famed nunnery in a fairyland dream*
> *Makes a mockery of Buddhist teachings.*

In Defiance, Lu Wuhan Refuses to Give Up the Colored Shoes

We beam with smiles when we land a good deal;
We lament to ourselves when things don't go our way.
But the will of heaven works in reverse:
A gain may turn out to be a loss in the end.

Not long ago, there lived a man with the surname Qiang [Strong], who enjoyed gaining petty advantages and bullying those weaker than himself. He was such a dread and terror to his neighbors that he came to be called Qiang the Bully. One day, he was sauntering idly down the street when he saw a stranger ahead of him pick up from the ground a money belt that looked quite heavy. Feeling sure that the money belt was well stocked, he rushed up and blocked the man's way, saying, "This money belt is mine. It fell off my waist. Give it back to me."

The stranger from out of town said, "But you were walking behind me. How could it have fallen off your waist? What an unreasonable man!"

Over the stranger's protests, Qiang the Bully reached for the money belt and seized one of the strings. As the stranger held on to the money belt and Qiang kept tugging at it, some neighbors gathered around them and asked what was going on. But, with both claiming to be the rightful owner of the belt, the spectators could not come to a judgment.

An elderly man among the crowd spoke up, "Just saying you are the owner is no good. Tell us what's in this money belt. The one who gets it right is the rightful owner."

Qiang the Bully retorted, "Who has the patience for a riddle like that? This belt belongs to me! Give it back to me and all will be well. If not, I'll fight you to the death!"

Judging by these words alone, the onlookers realized that the money belt did not belong to him. Among those who wanted to help him out of fear of him, one stepped forward and said to the stranger, "Sir, don't you know who Big Brother

Qiang is? He's a powerful man in this town. You picked up this money belt from the ground, so it most probably doesn't belong to you anyway. Why don't you just give it to him as a present by way of getting acquainted with him? That would be the right thing to do."

Yielding under the pressure, the stranger said, "You're right. This belt isn't mine. But money should be gotten through the right means, not by force. Since you mean well in your advice, let me open it and see what's inside. If there's indeed something valuable, let's divide it into three portions, one for me, one for Big Brother Qiang, and one for a few cups of wine for all of you in a wineshop as a reward." (*This traveler has good sense.*)

"That's a most sensible idea," said the old man. "Now, Big Brother Qiang, please let go of the belt. This old man will handle everything."

The old man opened the money belt and exposed to view a cloth package. Inside the package were two large ingots of snow-white silver wrapped in a few layers of paper. Each weighed about ten taels.

The sight of the silver enraptured Qiang the Bully. Cunningly, he said, "It would be a shame to break these beautiful ingots into three portions. I have with me some loose pieces of silver worth a few taels. I was going to buy a draft animal with them. Let me give them to the traveler. I'll keep the ingots." So saying, he took out three or four small packets from his waist, the contents of which did not even add up to four taels of silver, and they were supposed to cover the wine bill as well. The traveler adamantly refused to accept this offer. As the two men came to heated words again, another onlooker offered this advice to the traveler, "Big Brother Qiang is not someone to be trifled with. Just take them and be done with it!"

The old man chimed in, "Sir, take all these four taels. We give up our portion. We can enjoy a cup of wine anytime on our own. With the wine bill out of the way, you can have more to share between the two of you." Before he even finished speaking, Qiang the Bully had already snatched the two ingots from his hand.

The traveler saw nothing for it but to take the four taels.

Qiang the Bully said, "Even though I have no more loose silver with me, let's all go to that wineshop down the street. It's owned by my brother-in-law. I appreciate the time you've all taken. Let's have a few drinks there."

"In that case," said the onlookers, laughing, "the traveler should join us, so that we can get acquainted." And so, all fourteen or fifteen of them went to Zhu Sanlang's wineshop down the street and took their seats upstairs. Partly because he was elated at gaining two large ingots of silver at no expense to himself, partly because he was grateful to the onlookers for their help, and partly because he was not entirely without some qualms of conscience for having taken advantage of the traveler and denied the onlookers their due, Qiang busily ordered fine wine and food, showing off his connection with the owner of the wineshop. A hearty meal they had. Everyone ate and drank his fill, and the bill came to more than three taels of silver, which Qiang the Bully asked to be credited to his account. Then they bade adieu to each other and went their separate ways. The traveler, now richer by four taels of silver, also headed home.

Two days later, when Qiang the Bully was about to go out and buy a draft animal, someone from his brother-in-law's wineshop came to demand payment of the wine bill. There being no other pieces of silver in the house at the time, he went to a silversmith's shop and asked to have the two large snow-white ingots melted, hoping they would turn out to be of greater value. The silversmith turned the ingots over and over, examined them closely, weighed them in his hands, and asked, "Where did you get them?"

"From a transaction," replied Qiang the Bully.

"You've been had, Big Brother. The ingots are filled with lead and iron under a thin layer of silver."

Refusing to believe him, Qiang asked him to break the ingots apart.

"If I make a mess of it, don't hold me to blame, Big Brother." Having said that, the silversmith began driving a chisel into one of the ingots. As he hammered away, the layer of silver split open, exposing the lead and iron inside. Qiang the Bully still refused to accept the evidence of his eyes. He had never suffered such a loss before, but he had only himself to blame. No one else was at fault. As he sat by the counter, staring dumbfounded at the two ingots, a stream of people entered the shop to look at the fake silver. Their idle comments only added to Qiang's rage. He was about to find an excuse and flare up when two police officers came in. With a sharp command, they threw a chain around his neck before he could protest and, taking along the fake silver, marched him to a certain place.

What had happened was that the county treasury had found a few ingots of fake silver in its collection of tax payments, and the police were investigating by the magistrate's secret order. Those two ingots in the money belt from some unknown source happened to be identical to those found in the treasury. That was why the police apprehended Qiang and brought him to the county tribunal.

Upon seeing the ingots, the magistrate concluded that Qiang was the rascal who had counterfeited the silver and, without giving him a chance to explain, had him given thirty strokes of the bamboo rod, threw him in jail, and, once every three days, demanded payment to make up for the loss suffered by the treasury. Qiang the Bully had no alternative but to sell his landed property at a discount to the government. At the same time, he asked someone with connections to explain to the magistrate the circumstances under which he had come by the silver. As a courtesy to the man pleading on his behalf, the magistrate pardoned Qiang and let him go home, but not before he had spent more than a hundred taels of silver. His none-too-plentiful family fortune had thus been wiped out. A song came to be circulated in the neighborhood in derision of him:

> *Qiang the Bully, Qiang the Bully,*
> *Let me tell you about his folly:*

He gained two ingots of iron
And lost a hundred taels of silver.
The bamboo rod rained blows on him alone;
The feast in the wineshop was enjoyed by all.
If you want to stop this losing streak,
Be sure to mend your bullying ways.
Change your name from Mr. Strong to Mr. Weak,
Be known as Mr. Loser, not as Mr. Gains.
Next time you try to bully your neighbors,
I'd hate to see you tremble in terror!

The above story is titled "Greed Turns Qiang the Bully into a Loser." Indeed, a gain may turn out to be a loss.

I shall now propose to tell a story titled "In Defiance, Lu Wuhan Refuses to Give Up the Colored Shoes." It also tells of one who gained a petty advantage but brought upon himself a calamity of monstrous proportions. Truly,

Too much good food ruins the stomach;
Too much happiness leads to misery.

During the Hongzhi reign period [1488–1505] of this dynasty [the Ming], there lived in Hangzhou, Zhejiang, a young man named Zhang Jin. Born to a family that had enjoyed immense wealth for generations, he had attended school in his childhood, but, free of control after his parents' early death, he abandoned his books and devoted all of his time to associating with dissolute young men. After learning to play musical instruments and to play ball, he sharpened and showed off these skills in the courtesans' quarters. What with his dashing looks, his affectionate ways, his tactfulness, and his money, he enjoyed popularity among the girls, and they cast such a spell over him that he banished from his mind all thoughts about his family. His wife could only let him have his way, because all of her remonstrations were to no avail.

One spring day, when the peach blossoms along West Lake were in full bloom, Zhang Jin went on a boat tour with two famous courtesans, Jiaojiao and Qianqian, whom he had engaged the previous evening, along with a few of his male friends. Decked out in a crepe-silk hat of a fashionable style, a pink robe in silk produced in the Wu region, a white embroidered satin shirt, a pair of white satin stockings and vermilion shoes, and a fan bearing a painting and calligraphy, he sallied forth, followed by a pretty young boy, his favorite page boy, called Qingqin, who carried over his left arm a cape and held with his right hand a three-stringed zither and a purple *xiao* flute in covers made of Sichuan brocade. So Zhang Jin strutted with great pomp in the direction of Qiantang Gate. As he was passing through Chess Lane, he suddenly raised his eyes and saw a girl on the second floor lift the window curtain and throw away water from a washbowl. She was a bewitching beauty.

How do we know this? There is in testimony a lyric to the tune of "Stretching
Clear River":

> *Whose daughter is she?*
> *She outshines even Xishi in her charm.¹*
> *Her face as if powdered, her hair as thick as a cloud,*
> *She bewitches everyone by her side.*

Melting with desire at the sight of this girl, Zhang Jin stopped as if transfixed.
Then he forced a cough. (*How would coughing help him approach a woman? This
goes to show how flippant he is.*) After throwing away the water, the girl was about
to let down the curtain when she heard the cough. As she looked down, she saw a
handsome young man in a gaudy outfit. She also fixed her gaze on him. As the four
eyes met, the girl flashed a smile, which threw Zhang Jin into raptures. There was
only one difficulty: with one upstairs and the other down in the street, they could
hardly strike up a conversation. At this moment, a middle-aged man emerged from
the door. Zhang Jin dodged him with alacrity. By the time Zhang Jin returned to
the spot, when the man was a safe distance away, the curtain was down and the
girl had disappeared. He remained standing there for a while, but she did not
reemerge. He then told Qingqin to remember which house it was, so that he could
come again the next day to try his luck. Only then did he go away, but not with-
out turning around a few more times. Normally, the short walk to West Lake was a
delight to him, but this day, after seeing that girl, he found every step too much of
an effort, and he felt as frustrated as if taking a mountain path hundreds of li long.
After he passed through Qiantang Gate, he arrived at the spot where the boat he
had engaged was moored. The two courtesans and his group of friends were already
in the boat. Seeing Zhang Jin boarding, they all turned out to the bow to greet
him. After he stepped into the boat, Qingqin put down the cape, the zither, and
the flute, and the boatman began to punt the boat toward the middle of the lake.

It was a glorious day. The causeway was swarming with sightseers, male and
female, carrying wine and food baskets and strolling amid the blooming peach blos-
soms and the budding willow trees. There is a poem in testimony:

> *Hill beyond green hill, tower beyond tower,*
> *When will songs and dances by West Lake ever cease?*
> *Intoxicated by the warm breezes,*
> *The sightseers take Hangzhou for Bianzhou.²*

In the boat, every one of Zhang Jin's friends sang and played musical instru-
ments in a show of their artistic skills, but Zhang Jin, his mind fully occupied with
the girl, was in no such jovial mood. His chin resting on his hand, his eyes vacant,
he looked as if he were lamenting the autumn rather than enjoying the spring. His
friends commented, "Brother Zhang, you're not your usual self today. Why so sad?
There must be a reason."

Zhang Jin mumbled something noncommittal.

"Don't be sad. Cheer up and have a drink. Whatever is bothering you, we brothers will take care of it for you!" To the courtesans Jiaojiao and Qianqian, they said, "The young master must be upset at you because you do nothing for him. Come on, serve him wine!"

With alacrity, Jiaojiao and Qianqian poured out wine and offered Zhang Jin a cup to cheer him up. As they made a fuss about him, Zhang Jin forced himself to play along, but his thoughts were elsewhere, and he rose to go before evening set in. The others did not press him to stay.

After he got on shore, he passed through Qiantang Gate and took Chess Lane, as before. As he drew near the door above which the girl had appeared, he gave another cough. (*In his ten years of study, he learned nothing but to cough.*) Seeing nothing astir upstairs, he walked out of the lane, but then he turned back again. And so he went back and forth several times, to no avail. Qingqin, the page boy, suggested, "Young Master, let's come back tomorrow. If we keep going back and forth, people will get suspicious."

Following this advice, Zhang Jin resignedly went home.

The next day, he went again and asked neighbors about who lived there. One neighbor told him, "That family has quite a reputation. The man is called Pan Yong, or Holy Terror Pan. He and his wife have only a daughter, Shou'er. She's sixteen now. Holy Terror has some slight acquaintance with a government official's family and he uses that connection to extort money and get free wine and food from people in these parts. Everyone fears and hates that shameless and cunning scoundrel."

Making a mental note of these words, Zhang Jin slowly walked past the door. It just so happened that the girl lifted the window curtain at this point to look out, and the four eyes met again. With their eyes conveying their passion for each other, they felt closer than before. Henceforth, Zhang Jin came every so often to stand under her window and give a cough by way of a secret signal. Sometimes he got to see her, and sometimes he did not. Amid exchanges of significant glances, their passion grew deeper. The only regret was the lack of opportunity for him to go upstairs.

On the fifteenth day of the third month, Zhang Jin, finding it impossible to sit still at home, went out after supper into the streets in the glorious moonlight that shone as bright as day. All alone, he went to Pan Yong's door and found no one in sight except that girl gazing at the moon by her window, with the curtain rolled up high. Zhang Jin coughed softly. The girl recognized him, and they exchanged smiles. Zhang Jin then took out a red satin sash from his sleeve, folded it into the shape of two overlapping diamonds [a symbol of love], rolled it into a ball, and tossed it up. (*An object that leads to fornication.*) The girl caught it with both hands, examined it closely by the light of the moon, slipped it into her sleeve, took off a shoe, and dropped the shoe out of the window. Zhang Jin caught it with both hands and saw that the upper part of the shoe was a patchwork of pieces of colored fabric. (*Sowing the seeds of all troubles to come.*) He measured it with his hand and found that it just fitted the span from his thumb to his index finger. He tied it to a handkerchief, hid it in his sleeve, and bowed deeply. The girl returned the courtesy. Just when they were beginning to have fun, the girl's parents called out for her. With resignation, she closed the window and disappeared. Zhang Jin also returned home, satisfied with the adventure. Back in his study, he untied the shoe from his handkerchief and toyed with it by the lamp. It was indeed an exquisite lotus-petal of a shoe. How do we know this? There is, again, a lyric to the tune of "Stretching Clear River" that bears testimony:

> *A three-inch silk shoe, soft and narrow,*
> *It is prettier than a flower petal;*
> *With one more bit of thread, it will burst into blossom.*
> *Sweet and free of dirt, it's only worn in her room.*

After toying with the shoe for a while, Zhang Jin tied it up again to the handkerchief, thinking, "I need someone to deliver a message to her and work out a plan for me to go upstairs to her. If we go on like this, flirting only with our eyes, the eyes may be enjoying the feast, but the stomach is hungry. What good does that do?" Turning his thoughts this way and that, he finally came up with an idea.

The next morning, he tucked some silver in his sleeve and went to the Pan residence. Not seeing the beauty at the usual spot, he asked for a seat in a shop some distance off and sat down to keep an eye on the door. As coincidence would have it, before long, a woman peddler carrying a small bamboo basket went into the house. About two hours later, she reemerged, the bamboo basket in hand, and went off the way she had come. Zhang Jin caught up with her and saw that it was Madam Lu, peddler of beauty products to rich families. She lived right at the entrance of Chess Lane. Under the cover of selling beauty products, she was in fact a matchmaker, specializing in acting as a pimp. She was therefore quite well off. Her son, Lu Wuhan, ran a shop in the front part of their house, slaughtering pigs and selling wine. Much given to drinking and rowdy behavior, he was such a savage that he would even raise a fist against his own mother. The old woman was so afraid of his blows that she gratified every wish of his and dared not contradict him in any way. (*Foreshadowing.*)

"Madam Lu!" cried out Zhang Jin.

Turning around, Granny Lu recognized him and said, "Ah, what brings you here, Young Master Zhang? Haven't seen you for a long time!"

"I went to visit a friend but didn't find him. I'm passing through here on my way back. Why haven't you come to my home for so long? The maids are looking forward to buying from you."

"Every day I tell myself to come see your wife, but there are just too many trivial things for me to take care of."

While they talked, they reached her house. Lu Wuhan was selling meat and wine in his bustling shop.

Madam Lu said, "Have a cup of tea before you go, Young Master, although my house is not nice enough for a distinguished guest like you."

"Tea is not necessary, but I need to talk with you. Let's move on."

"Just a moment," said Madam Lu. She rushed inside, put down her bamboo basket, and hurried out again. "What is it?" she asked.

"This is no place to talk. Follow me." Having said that, he led her to a wineshop, went up the stairs, and sat down in a small booth. A waiter set the table and asked, "Are you expecting more company?"

"No. There're just the two of us," replied Zhang Jin. "Heat up two flasks of good wine for us and bring over some fresh fruit to go with it. Also, bring us about three or four fine dishes."

Thus instructed, the waiter withdrew. Before long, a fine spread was laid out on the table. After drinking a few cups of wine, Zhang Jin dismissed the waiter, closed the partition door of the booth, and said to Madam Lu, "I have a favor to ask of you. I'm only afraid that you may not be able to do it."

Madam Lu let out a chuckle. "I don't want to boast, but nothing is too difficult for this old woman. Just tell me whatever you want me to do, and I'll take care of it. You have my word."

"Wonderful!" said Zhang Jin. Resting his elbows on the table, he stuck out his neck and whispered to the old woman, "There's a girl who wants to take up with me, but, there being no one to push things along, I've got no chance yet. I know that you are on the best of terms with her family. That's why I'm asking this favor of you. Please deliver a message to her. If you can take me to her, I'll never forget your kindness. I have ten taels of silver here for you for a start. After you pull this thing off, you'll get another ten taels." So saying, he took out two large ingots of silver from his sleeve and set them on the table.

"Money is not important. Just tell me: which family's girl is it?"

"Sister Shou of the Pan family of Chess Lane. You know her very well?"

"Oh, it's that little girl. She seems to me to be decent enough. She's a virgin, and doesn't look like someone eager for an illicit affair. How did she cross paths with you?"

Zhang Jin told her everything about their chance encounter and her gift of a shoe the night before.

"This is a difficult job," said Granny Lu.

"Why difficult?"

"Her father is very strict, and they have no visitors. The three of them keep to one another and are never so much as a step apart. Also, their door is closed early in the evening and opened late in the morning and is so well guarded that there's no way you can get in. I can't do this for you."

"Ma'am, didn't you say just now that nothing is too difficult for you? How can you refuse to do this little favor for me? Are you offended by the paltriness of the payment and deliberately trying to make things difficult for me? Well, you'll just have to do this job for me, whatever happens. Let me add ten taels and two bolts of satin for you to make your burial clothes with. How does that sound?"

Her eyes already bloodshot at the sight of the two large ingots of snow-white silver, she was further tantalized by the promise of more rewards. Hating to let go of the deal, she said after a few moments of reflection, "Since you're so determined, it would be too presumptuous of me to turn you down. I'll try my best. It will all depend on whether there's a predestined bond between the two of you. If I can bring this off, you're lucky. If not, I can't force it. Don't blame me. You can keep the silver for now. I'll come to claim it after I succeed. But I need that shoe she gave you, to start the conversation going."

"If you don't take the silver, how can I set my mind to rest?"

"In that case, I'll take it. But if this thing doesn't work out, I'll return the ingots to you intact." So saying, she slipped them up her sleeve.

Zhang Jin took out his handkerchief, untied the shoe, and gave it to her. Holding it in her hand, she examined it and cheered, "Nice shoe!" And she put it away. (*A good predestined romance. Too bad it is handled by the wrong person.*)

The two of them had more wine and food before they rose and went downstairs. After paying the bill, Zhang Ji went out of the wineshop with the old woman. Before they parted company, Madam Lu said, "Young Master, this will take time. Impatience won't get you anywhere. If you set me a deadline, I won't be able to do it."

"As long as you give your mind to it, a few more days won't matter. If you have good news, please come to my house and tell me." With that they took leave of each other. Truly,

> With three cups of wine for the matchmaker,
> He brings about a predestined romance.

In the meantime, after laying her eyes on Zhang Jin, Pan Shou'er spent her days in a trance. Losing all appetite for tea and food, she said to herself, "If I could marry this man, I won't have lived in this world for nothing. I wonder where he lives and what his name is." After seeing him that moonlit night, how she wished she could grow two wings, fly down the stairs, and go away with him! The red sash now in her possession, she treated it as she would a lover and held it in her arms as she slept. (*Vivid description of an infatuated girl.*) The next morning, she slept on in her befuddled condition until her mother woke her up at high noon.

Two more days went by. After breakfast on the third day, Pan Yong left home, leaving Shou'er upstairs. While playing with the sash, she heard someone talking downstairs. Upon hearing footsteps ascending the stairs, she quickly put the sash away and went to the staircase to see who it was. Walking up the stairs with Mrs. Pan was none other than Madam Lu, seller of beauty products, bamboo basket in hand.

Once upstairs, Madam Lu said, "Sister Shou, I'm here to show you several new kinds of artificial flowers that I got yesterday." Quickly she opened her basket and took out one. "Look, Sister Shou! What do you think? Isn't it like a real flower?"

Shou'er took it and commented, "Yes, very nice!"

Offering one to Mrs. Pan, Madam Lu said, "You take a look, also, Mrs. Pan. You probably never saw such nice designs when you were young."

"That's true," Mrs. Pan agreed. "When I was young, the fake flowers we wore were crude stuff, nothing like the exquisite ones they make now."

"This is only the mediocre kind. I also have some of the superior ones. They'll make the blind see and rejuvenate the old and add years to their life." (*Making impromptu jesting remarks is the first essential requirement for a pimp.*)

"Show us everything you have," said Shou'er.

"I'm only afraid you're not a good judge of quality and can't afford the price."

"If we can't afford to buy your stuff, we can at least look at them," said Shou'er.

With an apologetic smile, Lu said, "I was joking. You didn't have to get serious, Sister Shou! How much could this stuff be worth, plus this basket of mine? Let me show them to you. I'll show you only the good ones. You can take your pick." So saying, she produced a few more, of even more lovely designs than the previous ones.

Shou'er picked a few nicer ones and said, "How much are you asking for them?"

"Good grief! Have I ever haggled over prices with you? Why do you even ask? Just name your price!" Turning to Mrs. Pan, she added, "Ma'am, I'd like to have a cup of hot tea." (*A trick to send Mrs. Pan away.*)

"I was so engrossed in admiring the flowers that I forgot all about tea. You like your tea hot, so I'll go boil some water." With that, she went downstairs.

Now that Mrs. Pan was out of the way, Madam Lu put her flowers in the basket in order, retrieved a red silk packet from her sleeve, and put it in the basket.

"What's in that packet?" Shou'er asked.

"It's an important object that you shouldn't see."

"Why shouldn't I see it? I want to see it!" So saying, she reached for the packet.

"I'll never let you look at it!" While mouthing these words, Madam Lu gave Shou'er a chance to pick it up (*Resorting to tricks to gradually lead her on.*), then she cried in alarm and made a show of reaching for the packet, but Shou'er dodged her and opened it. Upon seeing that it was the very shoe she had given to the young man the other night, she blushed.

Wresting the shoe from her, Madam Lu said, "How can you seize other people's property like that?"

"Ma'am, it's just a shoe. Why treat it as if it's something that demands respect? Why wrap it up in silk and forbid people to look at it?"

Laughing, Madam Lu said, "You may very well say that it's worthless. But a certain young gentleman believes it's as precious as his very own life and wants me to look for the other shoe to make a pair."

It dawned on Shou'er that Madam Lu was the messenger sent by the young man. Filled with delight, she went to get the other shoe and said smilingly, "Ma'am, I do have the other one here. They make a pair."

"So the shoe has been found all right, but what are you going to say to that young gentleman?"

In a subdued voice, Shou'er said, "Since you already know about this, I'm not going to hide anything from you. I might as well ask you everything I want to know. Who is he? What's his name? What kind of a man is he?"

"He's Zhang Jin, from a fabulously rich family. And he's a very affectionate person, too. He's been thinking of you day and night and forgetting all about eating and sleeping. Knowing I'm a good family friend of yours, he asked me to get a reply from you. Is there any way you can let him in?"

"You know how things are in this family. My father is so strict and guards the door so closely. After I blow out my lamp and go to sleep, he'll check my room with a lamp before going to bed. We need to think of a plan. Ma'am, do you have any idea? I'll thank you properly if you can bring us together."

After a moment's reflection, Madam Lu said, "Don't worry. I've got an idea."

"What is it?" asked Shou'er eagerly.

"You go to bed early. After your parents check your room by lamplight, get up and listen for a cough downstairs. Then tie several lengths of fabric together and drop the other end down, so that he can climb up the fabric rope and then climb down again before dawn. No one will know even if he does it for a hundred years. The two of you can have all the fun you want. Won't that be nice?"

Exhilarated upon hearing this, Shou'er said, "I'm ever so grateful to you for bringing this off for me. So when can he come?"

"It's too late today. I'll tell him tomorrow morning, and you two can make a go of it at night. But you need to give him another token of pledge, so as to show him how well this old woman gets things done."

"Give him both shoes then. He can give them back to me when he comes tomorrow night." (*The old pimp does get things done well, and the young woman is also shrewd enough.*) Before the words were quite out of her mouth, Mrs. Pan came upstairs with the tea. Hastily Madam Lu hid the shoes in her sleeve and drank two cups of tea.

"Madam Lu," said Shou'er, "I don't have money at hand today for the flowers. May I pay you another day?"

"A few days late is all right. I'm not a petty-minded one." Picking up her bamboo basket, she said good-bye and rose to go. Mrs. Pan and her daughter walked her to the middle door of the house.

"Ma'am, come for a chat tomorrow if you have time," said Shou'er.

"As you wish," said Madam Lu.

Mrs. Pan had no idea what they were referring to. Indeed,

> *The wild young man and the beauty*
> *Conveyed their passion with their eyes.*
> *However unbridled their lust,*
> *They enlisted a matchmaker's services.*
> *Knowing her job, wagging her tongue,*
> *She devised plans for clouds and rain.[3]*
> *Nothing less than a pimp she was;*
> *She brought good families to grief.*
> *Fearless of heaven and earth, deaf to idle gossip,*
> *Secretly she brought together young lovers*
> *Who were sick with longing day and night.*
> *It's fate that brings sweet foes together;*
> *Kill the pimps and feel avenged!*

Instead of returning home, Madam Lu headed straight for Zhang Jin's home. When she saw his wife, she claimed that she was there to sell them beauty products. Upon inquiry, she was told that Zhang Jin was not at home. The many women in the Zhang household snapped up every piece of her merchandise, some paying cash, others asking for credit. After the racket died down, she felt she could not wait for him any longer. She bade them good-bye and left.

At first light the next morning, she wended her way again to the Zhang residence, the shoe in her sleeve, and was told that he had not returned home the night before, his whereabouts unknown. (*The fact that she missed him twice forebodes ill.*)

Madam Lu returned home, where her son Lu Wuhan was fretting because his assistant was away at a time when he wanted to slaughter a pig. Upon his mother's return, he exclaimed, "Good timing! Help me tie up the pig."

With her fear of her son, she dared not say no. "Wait until I take off my clothes first," said she as she went into her room. Lu Wuhan followed her in. When she was taking off her outer garments, a packet wrapped in red silk fell onto the floor. Taking it to be a packet of silver, he picked it up and walked outside with it. Upon opening it and seeing a pair of colorful woman's shoes, he said in admiration, "What nice small feet! I wonder whose daughter she is." After looking at it for a while, he thought again, "A woman with such tiny feet is surely attractive enough. If I can have such a woman in my arms for one night, I won't have lived my life in vain." Then again, another thought struck him. "Why are these shoes with my mother? They are no longer new but are wrapped up with such care. There must be a reason behind this. When she looks for them, I'll say something to scare her. She'll come out with the truth." He wrapped the shoes up again and stuck the packet in his bosom.

After she took off her outer garment, Madam Lu helped her son truss up the pig and kill it. Then she washed her hands and dressed, ready to go and look for Zhang Jin again. She was about to go out the door when she checked her sleeve and realized that the shoes were gone. Quickly she turned back into the house to look for them, but not even a shadow of them was anywhere in sight. As she gave one frantic shriek after another, pleading to heaven and earth for help, Lu Wuhan watched her out of the corner of his eye. It wasn't until she sighed in despair that he spoke up, "What did you lose to upset you so much?"

"A packet that's very important, but I can't tell you what it is."

"Tell me what it looks like. Maybe your eyes are bleary with old age. Let me help you look for it. But if you can't tell me, you do it yourself. It's no business of mine."

Guessing from her son's tone that he knew something, she said, "If you found it, give it back to me. It'll bring in enough money to give a boost to your business."

His greed aroused at the mention of money, he said, "Yes, I found it all right, but I'm not giving it back to you until you tell me everything."

Madam Lu took him to the inner quarters of the house and told him everything about the lovers, sparing no detail. Elated, Lu Wushan said with a show of alarm, "I'm glad you told me. Otherwise, something bad could have happened."

"What could have happened?"

"As the ancients said, 'If you don't want anyone to find out what you've done, you shouldn't have done it in the first place.' How can such a thing be kept a secret for long? What's more, that Holy Terror Pan Yong—would you dare make an enemy of him? If the secret is out, and he knows that you made money out of it at his expense, well, not only will I get no boost for my business, but this entire shop of mine will be his, and he will still demand more!" (*Though he's playing a trick, what he says does make sense.*)

In consternation, Madam Lu said, "You do have a point, my son! Let me give the silver and the shoes back to him and tell him that the whole thing is off. I'm not going to poke my nose into their affairs anymore."

"Where's the money?" Lu Wuhan asked, smiling.

Madam Lu went to get the silver and showed the ingots to her son.

Slipping the ingots into his sleeve, he said, "Mother, leave the silver and the shoes here. If they cause a scandal in the future and get you implicated, you can produce them as evidence. If things don't come to that pass, the money will be ours to spend. Would he even dare to come and ask to get it back?"

"But what's to be done if Mr. Zhang comes to ask for a reply?"

"Just tell him that the Pans keep such strict rules in the house that he's not going to have his chance any time soon. And then say that if there is a chance, you'll let him know. After you put him off a few times, he'll surely stop bothering you."

With both the silver and the shoes in Wuhan's possession, Madam Lu had nothing to show to her client, nor did she dare demand them back from her son. Afraid of making a wrong move, she did not go to see Zhang Jin.

With the ten taels of silver, Lu Wuhan bought some expensive clothes and a crepe-silk hat. In the evening, after his mother had gone to sleep, he decked himself out in his new outfit, hid the shoes in his sleeve, padlocked the door from the outside, and went to the Pan residence. That night, the moon was bedimmed by clouds and there was not enough light to see things clearly. To his delight, it was also very quiet at this time of night. At one soft cough from Lu Wuhan as he stood against the wall, Shou'er upstairs eagerly went to the window, which creaked when she opened it. Afraid that it would wake up her parents, Shou'er picked up the teapot from the table, poured some tea on the window hinge, and the window yielded noiselessly when she opened it further. She tied the makeshift fabric rope tightly to the post and let it down. His heart flooding with joy at the sight of the fabric rope coming down, Lu Wuhan hiked up his robe, stepped forward, held the rope in a tight grip with both hands, got his feet up against the wall, and climbed up step by step. Soon he reached the ledge of the window and noiselessly crossed the windowsill into the room. Shou'er drew back the rope and closed the window. Lu Wuhan gathered her into his arms and kissed her on the mouth. She stuck her tongue into his mouth, it being too dark to tell if this was the right man. In their fiery passion, they held each other in a tight embrace. Then they undressed and went to bed. Wuhan spread her thighs apart and mounted her. Shou'er eagerly received him. In their union of delight, Lu Wuhan satisfied his lust to the fullest. Truly,

> *A budding flower in all its fragrance*
> *Was ravished by a withered vine.*
> *A tender blossom with all its pistils*
> *Was violated by pelting rain.* (How tragic! How hateful!)
> *An owl got into a lovebird's nest;*
> *A phoenix mated with a common crow.*
> *He called her honey and sugar,*
> *As if in a grocery store.*
> *She thought of him as her darling,*
> *Little knowing this was the wrong man.* (A vivid scene.)
> *The go-between acted on behalf of one,*
> *But ended up bringing in another.*
> *How sad that a fine piece of jade*
> *Was ravaged by a lowly butcher!*

It was after their passion had abated that they began to strike up a conversation. Wuhan took out the pair of shoes and mouthed sweet words of love. Shou'er also laid bare her heart. Their desires yet unfulfilled, they resumed their game of clouds and rain, this time even more lovingly than before. At about the fourth strike of the watch-drum, they rose, opened the window, and let down the fabric rope. Wuhan climbed down and ran all the way home at top speed. Shou'er drew back the rope, put it away, gently closed the window, and returned to bed. From that time on, Lu Wuhan came every night, unless it was raining or the moon was too bright.

About six months into their loving relationship, Shou'er's appearance and the way she talked began to change, unbeknownst to herself. Her parents began to have suspicions. They questioned her time and again, but she held her ground and said nothing to give herself away. One night, when Wuhan came again, she said to him, "For some reason, my parents are onto something and ask me questions every now and then. Even though I haven't said anything, these last couple of nights they've been watching me more closely than before. If we're found out, it'll be bad for all of us. Why don't you stop coming for a time? We can meet again after they let down their guard."

"You're right," said Wuhan, but in fact he thought otherwise. (*If Lu Wuhan had followed Shou'er's advice, the evil man would have gone unpunished. This is not the way divine justice works!*)

At the strike of the fourth watch, he made his exit, as usual. Earlier that night, Pan Yong had heard murmuring words upstairs when he was half asleep, and had strained his ears to listen more carefully so that he could rise and catch them in the act. But after listening for a while, he drifted off to sleep again and didn't wake up until daybreak. To his wife, he said, "That little slut has indeed been up to no good in spite of her denials. I heard voices upstairs last night. I meant to listen in and then catch them in the act, but somehow I fell asleep again."

"I'm also a little suspicious," said Mrs. Pan. "But there's no passageway that leads from her room upstairs to the outside. There can't be a god or a ghost that comes and goes without a trace?"

"Let's beat her up and make her tell the truth!"

"No, we can't do that! As they say, 'A family scandal must not be known to the public.' If we beat her, our neighbors will know. And if word spreads around, who'll be willing to marry her? Regardless of whether or not she has done what we suspect her of doing, let's tell her to move downstairs. We'll lock up her door before she goes to bed. Then nothing can go wrong. You and I will sleep upstairs in her room. If something happens at night, we'll get to know the truth." (*Mrs. Pan is most sensible.*)

"Good plan!" Pan Yong agreed.

During supper that evening, Pan Yong said to his daughter, "Beginning from tonight, you sleep in our bedroom. We'll move upstairs to yours."

The implication was not lost on Shou'er. Not daring to object, she secretly groaned in despair. That night, they exchanged rooms. After locking his daughter's door, Pan Yong said to his wife, "If a man goes upstairs tonight and we catch him, I'll treat him as a burglar and kill him to let me blow off steam." Leaving the window unlatched, he lay in wait for the man. (*He wants more than to catch the man in the act. He means to kill.*)

We shall leave Pan Yong and his wife in their consultation and turn our attention to Lu Wuhan. Although displeased that Shou'er told him not to go to her for a few days, he did manage to suppress his desires for several nights in a row, and refrained from going. One night more than ten days later, unable to control his lust, he wanted to make merry with Shou'er again. Afraid that Pan Yong might get him, he picked up a sharp knife for slaughtering pigs as a weapon of defense and padlocked his house door from the outside. Upon reaching the Pan residence, he gave his usual cough. He waited a while, but, getting no response from upstairs, he thought Shou'er had not heard him. So he coughed again twice. There was still no response. He thought that Shou'er must be asleep. He tried a few more times, but, when the fourth watch of the night [one o'clock] was struck, he knew that he did not have a chance and turned back home in resignation, thinking, "I shouldn't blame her. I haven't come for quite some time. How would she know that she should be expecting me tonight?"

He went again the following night, but, just as the night before, nothing was astir. He grew impatient and not a little irked. On the third night, he drank at home until he was half tipsy and, in the depth of the night, went to the Pan residence, carrying a ladder on his shoulder. Without giving the usual cough signal, he climbed up the ladder and gently pushed open the window. He then jumped in, pulled up the ladder, closed the window, and groped his way to the bed. Indeed,

> Dreaming of clouds and rain,
> He sneaked into the phoenix tower.

When Pan Yong and his wife first moved upstairs, they strained their ears to listen for movements and dared not sleep soundly. But more than ten nights having passed in all quietness unbroken by even the squeak of a mouse, they let down their guard, thinking that their daughter must have been innocent. As coincidence would have it, that very night, the hasp on Shou'er's door broke. As it was impossible to lock her door now, Mrs. Pan said, "Let's just lock up the front and back doors of the house and seal her door with a strip of paper. Nothing can happen tonight." Pan Yong did as she said. That night, they had a few cups of wine and, in drunken exhilaration, went to bed and engaged each other in activities of an unseemly nature. Then, tired from the exertion, they fell fast asleep in each other's arms, totally unaware that Wuhan had climbed up and opened and then closed the window.

Now, having groped his way to the bedside, Wuhan was on the point of taking off his clothes when he heard two people snoring. Seized with rage, he said to himself, "No wonder she ignored my coughs the last two nights and pretended to be asleep! So this whore has taken up with another man! That's why she came up with this story about her parents bugging her and told me to stop coming. She's obviously determined to break up with me. Why would I want such a heartless whore?" So thinking, he took out his sharp knife, found two necks with his hand, and quickly slit Mrs. Pan's throat first. Then he twisted his knife three or four times to make sure that all life was gone. He then plunged his knife into Pan Yong and killed him, too. (*The murder of Holy Terror Pan is an act of retribution that he richly deserved.*)

After wiping his bloody hands clean and putting away his knife, Lu Wuhan pushed open the window, let down his ladder, stepped over the sill, closed the window behind him, and climbed down noiselessly. Carrying his ladder on his shoulder, he raced home as fast as his legs could carry him.

As for Shou'er, after exchanging rooms with her parents the first night, she kept worrying that her lover would come again and give himself away by his coughs. But as her parents said nothing the next morning, she regained her peace of mind. After more than ten days, she thought the whole thing had blown over. After she got up that morning, she waited for her parents until midmorning, wondering why they had not come downstairs. Not daring to open her door with the strip of paper seal on it, she cried out from her room, "Father! Mother! Get up! It's late!" Getting no response after she had cried for some time, she opened her door and mounted the stairs. As she lifted the bed-curtain for a look, what should she see in bed but two dead bodies lying in a pool of blood. She fainted and collapsed onto the floor.

After she came to, she held on to the bed and burst into a fit of violent sobbing. Wondering who could have killed them, she thought, "This is serious. If I don't inform the neighbors, I'll get implicated." Without a moment's delay, she took a key and opened the house door. But feeling too shy to step out (*Why pick this time to feel shy?*), she remained inside the room and cried at the top of her voice, "Oh horrors! My good neighbors! My parents have been murdered! Please help me!"

As she cried again and again, the pedestrians and those neighbors who heard her from next door and across the street all barged into the house. As she staggered back from them, they asked, "Where were your parents sleeping?"

Between sobs, Shou'er said, "They were perfectly all right when they went upstairs last evening, and this morning, all the doors remained closed. Someone killed both of them."

Upon hearing that the bodies were on the second floor, everyone rushed up the stairs. When they raised the bed-curtain, they saw that, indeed, the old couple were lying there dead. As they began to look around the room, they found that even though there was a window overlooking the street, there were no protruding eaves and it was impossible for anyone to climb up the wall.

Shou'er added that the doors had all been locked, that she had just opened them, and that there had been no one else in the house.

"How strange!" the neighbors commented. "This is no joking matter." Forthwith they reported the killings to the local authorities. The headman came, examined the place, and took Shou'er and the neighbors to the yamen to report the case. Never having traveled anywhere, poor Shou'er now had to wear a bandanna that reached down to her eyebrows, lock up the front door, and follow the group to the Hangzhou prefectural yamen.

News about the murder caused a sensation through half of the city of Hangzhou.

As the story spread around, Lu Wuhan also got wind of it and realized that he had killed the wrong people. Stricken with remorse and deeply distraught, he raised a rumpus at home. Madam Lu, knowing what her son had been up to, had a hunch that the murder case had everything to do with him but dared not ask him. Troubled by her conscience, she dared not go out of the house, either. Indeed,

> *You go where crowds are thickest when justice is on your side;*
> *You stay behind closed doors when stung by your conscience.*

When Shou'er and the neighbors arrived at the Hangzhou prefectural yamen, the prefect happened to be sitting in the tribunal, handling cases. They went in and reported, "A Pan Yong and his wife, of Chess Lane, were both murdered last night. Their windows and doors remained closed. We're here with their daughter, Shou'er, to report the crime."

The prefect told Shou'er to approach him and asked, "Give me more details. When did your parents go to bed? Where did they sleep?"

Shou'er replied, "After supper last evening, they locked up the doors and went upstairs to sleep. As they hadn't gotten up by midmorning, I went upstairs to see if anything was wrong and found them under their quilts, murdered. The window upstairs remained closed and the doors downstairs remained locked and untouched."

"Was anything taken?" asked the prefect.

"No."

"How can a murder take place when the windows and doors remain closed? And nothing was taken, either. This is very strange." After a moment's reflection, the prefect asked again, "What other people are there in the family?"

"We were a family of three. There are no others."

"Did your father have enemies?"

"No one in particular."

"How very strange!" The prefect mused a long while before light dawned on him. He told Shou'er to raise her head. Seeing that the upper part of her face was all covered by her bandanna, he ordered the lictors to take it off. When her exceptionally attractive face was exposed, the prefect asked, "How old are you?"

"Seventeen."

"Are you betrothed?"

"No," replied Shou'er in a subdued voice.

"Where is your bedchamber?"

"Downstairs."

"Are you telling me you sleep downstairs and your parents slept upstairs?" (*This prefect is a good detective.*)

"I used to sleep upstairs. We exchanged rooms about half a month ago."

"Why did you exchange rooms?"

At a loss for a better answer, Shou'er said, "I don't know why my parents wanted to do it."

The prefect thundered, "You are responsible for the murder of your parents!"

Bursting into tears of mortification, Shou'er said, "Your Honor, how would I do such a thing to my own parents?"

"I know it wasn't you. It was your lover. Tell the court his name!"

In consternation, Shou'er said, denying, "I never even go out of the middle door of the house. How would I have a lover? If I had, the neighbors would know. Your Honor can ask them. They'll tell you what kind of a person I am."

With a smile, the prefect said, "The neighbors knew nothing even when two people were murdered. How would they know anything about a love affair? The facts of the case are: Your parents found out about the goings-on between you and your lover and therefore exchanged rooms with you to block your lover's chances. In rage, he killed them. Otherwise, tell me why they made you sleep downstairs."

As the proverb says, "A thief has a guilty conscience." The prefect's words touched a raw nerve. Shou'er's face blushed and paled by turns and the words failed on her lips as she stammered and stuttered. All the more convinced of her involvement, the prefect ordered that the finger squeezer be applied on her. The lictors sprang forward and drew out her hands. Her delicate hands, as fair as jade, could certainly not withstand the pain. The squeezer was hardly on her fingers when she broke down under the crushing pain and confessed.

"Your Honor," said she. "Yes, yes, I do have a lover!"

"What's his name?"

"Zhang Jin." (*How unjust!*)

"How did he go upstairs to you?"

"Every night, after my parents went to sleep, he would cough under the window as a signal. I would then take out a long fabric rope I made, tie one end of it to the post, and let it down. He would use the rope as a ladder to climb up, and he would go down before daybreak. This went on for about half a year. My parents sensed something wrong and questioned me several times. I denied everything and I told Zhang Jin not to come anymore, to avoid a scandal. He promised and stopped coming. Then my parents exchanged rooms with me and made me sleep downstairs, and they locked the doors. I was determined to stop doing wrong and return to a virtuous life, and I was happy to sleep downstairs so as to have a clean break with him. This is the truth. I know nothing about my parents' murder."

Now that she had confessed, the prefect ordered that the squeezer be withdrawn. He then ordered four lictors to go with all speed and bring Zhang Jin to the court for interrogation. The four men raced off with the speed of the wind. Indeed,

> You sit at home peacefully in your room,
> But disaster strikes out of the blue.

As for Zhang Jin, after he bade adieu to Madam Lu in the wineshop, he spent three nights in a brothel. Upon returning home, he learned that Madam Lu had come twice to see him. In haste, he went to her to ask for news, but she said, frightened by her son's words and unable to produce the shoes, "Sister Shou took back the shoes and told me to give you her regards. But her holy terror of a father is so strict with the house rules that there's no way you can get in. He's going on a trip very soon and will be away for about half a year. Wait until he's gone. You can then feel free to act." (*What a liar!*)

Zhang Jin believed her. Thereafter, he often went to her to find out how things stood. He saw Shou'er several times, and they smiled at each other, but both for the wrong reasons. Shou'er smiled at him because she took him to be her nocturnal visitor, and he thought that she was acting flirtatiously in order to seduce him. (*Both were dreaming.*)

The days went by but no word came. The lovesickness gradually wore Zhang Jin down, so much so that he had to take medicine to regain his health. That day, he was sitting gloomily in his study when a servant came in, announcing, "There are four yamen lictors outside. They want to ask you some questions, sir."

Quite taken aback, Zhang Jin thought, "Something must have happened in a brothel." So he went into the main hall to greet them.

When asked the purpose of their visit, the lictors replied, "It may have something to do with taxes or corveé. You'll know soon enough when you get there."

In relief, Zhang Jin changed his clothes, tipped the lictors, and went with them to the prefectural yamen, followed by a whole entourage of his servants. Along the way, he heard that Pan Shou'er had acted in collusion with her lover and murdered her own parents. Appalled, he thought, "How could that girl have done such a thing? Luckily I didn't get involved with her. So she turned out to be just another worthless piece of dirt! I almost got myself into trouble!"

Before long, the procession arrived at the yamen. Sizing up Zhang Jin with his eyes, the prefect saw that he was a handsome young man who did not look like a savage murderer. Feeling a little apprehensive, he asked, "Zhang Jin! You seduced Pan Yong's daughter and murdered her parents. Confess!"

Being a dashing young man good at nothing but indulgence in the pleasures of the flesh in houses of ill repute, Zhang Jin had never seen the inside of an awe-inspiring government establishment. He was already trembling with fear from the very moment he was brought in. And now, the accusation that he was the murderer struck him like a thunder bolt from a clear sky. The words stuck in his throat. It was with prodigious effort that he managed to say, "I did take a fancy to Pan Shou'er, but I never got together with her. I never even entered her room, let alone kill her parents."

The prefect roared, "Pan Shou'er has confessed that your illicit affair with her lasted for half a year. How dare you deny?"

Turning to Pan Shou'er, Zhang Jin said, "When did I ever have an affair with you? Why do you want to get at me like that?"

Pan Shou'er had not believed Zhang Jin to be the murderer, but now, mortified that he denied their affair, she began to suspect that he just might have done it. She burst into sobs and stuck to her story. Zhang Jin's self-defense unavailing, the prefect ordered that the ankle squeezer be applied.

With a roar, the lictors lined up on both sides of the hall swarmed forward and seized his feet. Zhang Jin had grown up wearing silk and satin, and his skin would be irritated by the slightest roughness in fabric. How would he be able to withstand such torture? The squeezer had barely been placed around his ankles when he screamed like a pig about to be slaughtered. "I confess!" he said, kowtowing over and over again.

The prefect ordered that the squeezer be laid aside and told him to write his confession.

Zhang Jin said, weeping, "I know nothing. What am I going to write?" (*Injustices like this abound in this world because the judges lack the patience to try the cases thoroughly. What a good prefect!*) To Pan Shou'er he said, "I don't know who seduced you. How can you claim it was me? But never mind now. I'll just admit to whatever you say."

"You brought all this on yourself!" retorted Shou'er. "How can you not confess? Didn't you make passes at me from the street? Didn't you toss up a sash to me? Didn't you catch my shoe?"

"Yes, that's all very true, but I never went upstairs to spend time with you."

The prefect shouted, "When one accusation is true, all the others are true! (*But even if a hundred accusations are true, there may be one that's not true. The prefect is quite mistaken.*) What more do you have to say? Write up your confession now!"

His head bent low, Zhang Jin wrote everything Pan Shou'er accused him of and all too lightly confessed to a capital crime. After he signed the written confession and showed it to the prefect, the latter sentenced him to death. Shou'er, even though she had had no part in the murders, was also sentenced to death for having caused her parents' death by her adultery. Each was given thirty strokes of the bamboo rod and put into a cangue.[4] Zhang Jin was taken under guard to the death row, and Pan Shou'er to the women's cell, and there we shall leave her for now.

Luckily for Zhang Jin, the lictors knew that he was rich and therefore had landed the tips of their rods on the floor when they beat him, so as not to hurt him too much. As he was now in jail, still protesting his innocence but with no one to turn to for help, the wardens were as delighted as if they had carried a load of silver ingots into the cell. Trying to curry favor with him, they gathered around him and asked, "Mr. Zhang, how could you have done such a thing?"

"Brothers, I'll be honest with you. I did see Sister Pan Shou a couple of times. Even though both of us took a fancy to each other, we never got to meet. Someone must have seduced her and then trumped up the charge against me. Do I look like a murderer to you?"

"But why did you confess?"

"With my frail constitution, would I be able to hold out against torture? And I've just recovered from an illness that confined me to bed for quite a few days.

This is like adding frost to snow! If I confess, I may get to live a few more days. If not, I would be dead tonight. Well, that's something determined in my previous life. I'd rather not talk about it. But Sister Pan Shou is so firm in her allegations that I believe there must be something more to it. Now, here are ten taels of silver for you to buy some wine for yourselves. Please take me to Sister Shou, so that I can question her in detail and get to the bottom of it. I'll then die in peace."

The head warden said, "Mr. Zhang, it's not difficult to see Pan Shou'er, but ten taels is not enough."

"Five taels more, then."

"That's still not enough to be shared among so many of us. Twenty taels would be the minimum."

Zhang Jin agreed to pay. With two wardens supporting him, one on each side, he went to the fence gate of the women's cell, where Pan Shou'er was weeping. The wardens escorted her out to the fence gate. At the sight of Zhang Jin, a tearful Pan Shou'er unleashed on him a stream of curses: "You ungrateful, traitorous swine! How foolish of me to have been seduced by you! What did we do to you to deserve death—all of us, my parents and I?"

Zhang Jin said, "Stop yelling. Let me explain. The first time we saw each other, you were so good as to have given me tender glances, and both of us found each other attractive. Then, one moonlit night, I gave you my sash, and you reciprocated with a shoe of colorful fabric patches. Because I didn't know how to get to meet you and I heard that Madam Lu, seller of beauty products, often visited your family, I gave her ten taels of silver and the shoe, and asked her to approach you. She then came back to me and said that you took back the shoe, but your father was strict with house rules, and that since he was going on a trip and would be away for a few months, she would make an appointment for me with you after he was gone. From then on, she made me appointments and then retracted them and went back and forth like that countless times. Half a year went by, and I still didn't get a confirmed date. And yet sometimes when I did see you, you always smiled at me, making me long for you so much that I got sick and had to stay at home and take medicine. When did I ever go to your room? And then you turned around and ruined me with false accusations. Look at the pass you got me into!"

Sobbing, Shou'er said, "You ungrateful scoundrel! You're still trying to deny your way out of it! That day, you told Madam Lu to give me back my shoe and make an appointment. The plan was to wait after my parents had gone to bed before you would give a cough under the window as a signal. Then I was to let a fabric rope down to serve as a ladder for you. The next night, you did cough down below. I let down the fabric rope to help you up. Then you produced the shoes as proof. From that time on, you came every night. It turned out that my parents sensed something and questioned me several times. I told you not to come anymore, so as not to cause a scandal and tarnish our names. I said that we could meet again after my parents let down their guard. Who would have guessed that you, heartless swine, would hate my parents so much that you somehow managed to climb upstairs and kill them! How can you still deny that? You even deny what had happened before!"

After a moment's reflection, Zhang Jin said, "Since you and I supposedly had a relationship for over half a year, you must know my looks and my voice only too well. Now look closely. Am I that man?" (*A turning point in solving the mystery.*)

"Your point is well taken," chimed in the wardens. "If it's indeed you, you're a monster. You deserve to be executed. Even dismemberment is not too much."

Shou'er hesitated for a while before she looked intently at Zhang Jin.

Zhang Jin continued, "Am I or am I not that man? Say it now! Don't hesitate!"

"The voice is quite different, and you're not as big. I never got to look closely because it was always dark. I only remember that there was a thick scar as large as a copper coin on the lower left side of your back. This will be an easy mark to identify." (*If there hadn't been a scar, how would justice ever have been done?*)

The wardens said, "That's easy enough. Mr. Zhang, take off your clothes and let everybody see. If there's no such scar, we'll report as much to the prefect tomorrow. We can be your witnesses and get you acquitted."

Jubilantly, Zhang Jin said, "Many thanks to you all!" Eagerly he took off his clothes, revealing a body as white as jade. There was not the slightest sign of a scar on his back. Shou'er was speechless.

"Young lady," said Zhang Jin. "Now you know it was not me!"

"No need to say another word," put in the wardens. "You were indeed wronged! We'll report to the yamen tomorrow on your behalf." So saying, they helped him to another room and let him sleep there for the night.

The next morning, when the prefect called the court session to order, the wardens dropped to their knees and gave him a report about the confrontation between Zhang Jin and Pan Shou'er the previous night. The prefect was flabbergasted. Without losing a moment, he ordered that both of them be brought in for further questioning. Zhang Jin was the first one ordered to go up to the dais and give his deposition. After Zhang Jin said everything he had to say, the prefect said, "So, after you gave the shoe to Madam Lu, she didn't return it to you?"

"That is correct."

When it was Shou'er's turn to approach the prefect, she also gave a detailed account of what she knew.

"So, you gave a shoe to Madam Lu and then the following night, Zhang Jin gave both shoes back to you. Is that correct?" asked the prefect.

"Yes," said Shou'er.

With a nod, the prefect concluded, "Madam Lu betrayed Zhang Jin and gave the shoes to someone else, who then pretended to be Zhang Jin and seduced you." (*A crime of passion. The will of heaven is bound to prevail over human machinations. Now that the wrongful accusations have been thrown out, the facts of the case need only be further verified. A prefect of divine wisdom.*)

Straightaway, the prefect ordered that the old woman be brought to court. Before long, she was brought in. She was immediately given forty strokes of the rod. Then the prefect asked, "Zhang Jin asked you to arrange a date with Pan Shou'er. Since you promised her to have him meet her the following night, why did you trick Zhang Jin and tell him not to go while you turned around and gave the shoes to another man so that he could go under Zhang's name and seduce her? If you tell the truth, I'll spare your life. If there's the slightest deviation from the truth, I'll have you beaten to death here and now!"

Already badly beaten, with her skin torn and blood flowing, the woman dared not say even half a word that deviated from the truth. She came up with every detail, from how she had approached the girl, ostensibly to sell her artificial flowers, to how she tried to arrange a rendezvous, how she was not able to find Zhang Jin, all the way to how, while preparing to help her son slaughter a pig, she had dropped the shoes, how her son had frightened her, and how, when Zhang Jin had asked for a reply, she had fobbed him off because she was unable to produce the shoes. She concluded by saying that she knew nothing about the fornication or the murders.

Noticing that her account tallied with those of the other two, the prefect knew for sure that it was the work of Lu Wuhan. By his order, the man was brought to court.

"Lu Wuhan," said the prefect. "You seduced a young woman of a respectable family and killed her parents. What do you have to say for yourself?"

Lu Wuhan said in denial, "Your Honor, how would a stupid commoner like me do such a thing? It was Zhang Jin who had begged my mother to be the go-between, seduced Miss Pan, and murdered her parents. Why lay the charge on me?"

Before he was able to finish, Shou'er shouted, "This is the voice of the one who seduced me! Your Honor, you need only check the lower left part of his back to see if there is a thick scar. If there is, he's the impostor!"

Then and there, the prefect ordered that the lictors take off his clothes. Lo and behold: there was indeed a thick scar on the lower left part of his back. It was only then that Lu Wuhan changed his story, saying he would gladly pay with his life. He then made a clean breast of everything he had done, from his seduction of the girl to his killing of her parents by mistake. (*Heaven used this girl to humiliate Pan Yong the Holy Terror, to take the life of Lu Wuhan the unfilial son, and to bring trouble to Zhang Jin the young rake. If heaven used a girl like this, how can people not watch their behavior?*)

The prefect ordered that Lu Wuhan be given sixty strokes of the rod and sentenced him to death. The sharp knife with which he had committed the murders was found and brought to the yamen. The death sentence on Shou'er remained unchanged. Madam Lu was sentenced to labor camp in accordance with the law for having talked an otherwise decent girl into adultery. As for Zhang Jin, even though he did not have his way, he should not have plotted to seduce Shou'er by devious means. He was the very source of the tragedy that followed and, as such, was also sentenced to a labor camp but was released on bail. There, in the court, every one of them was convicted of crime, and documents were prepared for submission to higher authorities.

Pan Shou'er thought, "I was first seduced by Lu Wuhan, and then I caused my parents' death and brought about such a scandal." Consumed with regret, she felt too ashamed to live on. She rose, charged at the stone slab steps leading to the dais, and dashed her brains out. She died instantly. (*A clean death.*)

> *How sad that a maiden as fair as a flower*
> *Was reduced to an aggrieved, bloodstained soul.*

His heart going out to Shou'er as he witnessed her death, the prefect sharply ordered that Lu Wuhan be given an additional forty strokes of the rod, to make a total of one hundred. He was then put on death row to await court papers for execution in autumn. The neighbors were instructed to carry Shou'er's corpse out, sell Pan Yong's house and other possessions, buy with the proceeds three coffins and a piece of land for their burial, and surrender the balance to government treasury. But of this, no more.

Deeply saddened at Shou'er's death by the dais, Zhang Jin thought, "It was all because of me that the whole Pan family perished." Upon returning home, he rewarded the lictors and the wardens with silver and paid for his own redemption. After he was nursed back to health, he went to a monastery to have the sutras chanted in repentance to get the souls of Pan Shou'er and her parents out of hell. He himself adopted a vegetarian diet and vowed never to seduce women again, not even to visit the houses of pleasure. And so he lived a peaceful and comfortable life at home and passed away at the age of seventy. A poet of the times made these comments:

> *Gambling leads to robbing, and lust to killing;*
> *How true the ancients' words of warning!*
> *Keep away from whoring and gambling,*
> *And you shall live a life of peace.*

Zhang Xiaoji Takes in His Brother-in-Law at Chenliu

Scholars pursue their studies, farmers till their land;
Craftsmen and merchants work hard making their fortune.
Be sure not to fritter away your time,
For idleness ruins young men's chances in life.

I have heard storytellers of older generations tell of a highly placed official—a cabinet minister, no less—who was laden with riches. Of his five sons, he told only the eldest one to pursue a scholarly career and made the other four sons a farmer, a craftsman, a traveling merchant, and a tradesman, respectively. The four younger sons were displeased, but they knew nothing about their father's reasons for doing so. Upon their request, someone asked the elderly minister, "Why don't you want your four younger sons to be scholars? Farmers, craftsmen, traveling merchants, and tradesmen have to work hard for a living, unlike upper-class gentlemen. You have more than enough money for your sons to live in comfort. Why should they turn leisure into hard work and pleasure into hardships? I'm afraid the four of them won't be able to adapt."

The minister laughed. Raising two fingers, he launched into the following lengthy speech:

Everyone applauds scholarly pursuits,
But what about those who fail in their studies?
All students aspire to official posts,
But how many attain high ranks at court?
Neither a gentleman nor a commoner,
One may end up a failure wearing a tattered gown.
Too frail to withstand cold, heat, and the winds,
Too pampered for hardships of any kind,
He is a loser in every way,
But he keeps his high and mighty airs.
He does no farm work and seeks idle pleasures,

Not knowing that idle pleasures shorten lives.
Farmers, craftsmen, merchants, and tradesmen may be lowly,
But their work and business keep them busy.
Hard work is a habit formed over time;
Those used to it build up a strong physique.
Spring breezes bring all flowers into bloom,
Be they peach blossoms or humbler varieties.
Success in life has never been easy to attain;
Idleness does not help build family fortune.
Rank and riches this old man may love,
Posts rotate on the stage of officialdom.
Rather than have my sons bullied once I lose power,
Far better if I arranged their future early on.
The fragrance of books I leave to my eldest,
Different lines of work I assign to the other sons.
Adequate food and clothing are hard to come by;
Be industrious and requite heaven's kindness.

These words of admonition from the old minister are still widely quoted even today. Their wisdom has won much admiration. Why? Well, there is no shortage of rich youths who, claiming to be occupied with scholarly pursuits, do not devote themselves to what is fundamental in life. Wearing scholars' hats and long robes, they believe themselves to be members of the upper class. They acquire flippant manners and know nothing about the hardships of a farmer's life. With their coming of age, they take up drinking and whoring and whatnot. In bad cases, they squander away their entire family fortunes and live out the rest of their lives in poverty. That is why the ancients said, 'When the five grains are not ripe, they are worth less than weeds and grass. One greedy for what can be had on credit loses what is already in hand." Indeed,

Diligence leads to a life of plenty;
Extravagance ends only in tragedy.

As the story goes, at the end of the Han dynasty, there lived in Xuchang a fabulously rich man named Guo Shan. Indeed, he owned vast tracts of land crisscrossed with footpaths, herds of oxen and horses, dozens of houses, and countless servants and page boys. For all his wealth, he remained a frugal man. He never wore new clothes or tasted a delicacy, never toured scenic spots with friends among flowers or on a moonlit night, and never prepared a banquet on festive occasions in honor of his kith and kin or his neighbors. Every day, behind closed doors, he frowningly fed himself coarse food, washing it down with inferior tea. He carried a key with him wherever he went and took out or put away everything with his own hands. On his table, there was nothing except an abacus and several account books. With his body as strong as if made of iron and copper, it seemed that he was going to live forever. Day and night, he busied himself with his calculations, always expecting his wealth to beget ten times more wealth, and he never wasted a penny. Indeed,

> *No one lives to be a hundred years old;*
> *Why make plans for a thousand years later?*

In his fifties now, Guo Shan was called the Old Master in the household. His wife had passed away, leaving him with only a son and a daughter. The son, Guo Qian, was engaged to the daughter of Mr. Fang. The daughter, Guo Shunü, was as yet unbetrothed. Pleased with his son's good looks and quick mind, Guo Shan was determined to make him a scholar but, begrudging the expense of hiring a private tutor for him at home, sent him instead to a relative's house to share a teacher with other youths.

It turned out that the son of this tight-fisted miser was a spendthrift. (*A rich father is bound to have a prodigal son. Money comes and goes, as is the way it should be.*)

The young man had several weaknesses: He treated books as enemies but women as his saviors. His hobbies included drinking, gambling, playing football and stickball, showing off his dashing looks, keeping hawks, and vying to play the chivalrous knight. He also enjoyed shadowboxing, horse riding, and brandishing spears and lances.

As the ancients said, "Like attracts like." The frivolous Guo Qian drew around him a group of dissolute youths. Still afraid of his father at this time, he left home every morning but always came back in the evening.

His mind entirely taken up by money matters, Guo Shan thought his son's days were spent in school and never bothered to check. Moreover, Guo Qian had bribed the page boy whose job it was to deliver his daily lunch, so that on the way to the school every day, the page boy ate the lunch he was supposed to deliver and kept his mouth tightly shut about the deception. How was Guo Shan to know? To the teacher, Guo Qian said that he was too busy with business at home to attend class. Once every few days, he would put in an appearance and offer the teacher small gifts. Not unaware of what was afoot, the teacher nevertheless played deaf and dumb, partly because he didn't think Guo Qian was scholarly material anyway, partly because he didn't think the father was seriously committed to making a scholar of the son, and partly because he liked the gifts. Feigning ignorance, he did not try to discipline the young man. And so Guo Qian ran wild, with his family none the wiser.

As the proverb says, "If you don't want people to know what you've done, you shouldn't have done it in the first place." Mr. Fang somehow learned about Guo Qian's behavior and had a messenger bring word to Guo Shan. Guo Shan did not believe what he heard. He thought, "If he's really loafing around like that, he needs quite a bit of money, and where does he get it? And the page boy who delivers his lunch to school every day has never said that he was truant. This can't be true."

But then again, he thought, "Mr. Fang is an honest man. He wouldn't have told me if he didn't believe it was true. I must not dismiss his words lightly."

He summoned the deliverer of his son's lunch and asked him, "The young master never goes to class. So, what have you been doing with his lunch every day?"

Being as clever as a well-trained monkey, the page boy said, "The young master does go to class every day. Who told you such a lie?"

Guo Shan believed the boy and stopped questioning further. In the evening, when Guo Qian returned home, the page boy quickly went and alerted him. Once Guo Qian was in his father's presence, his father asked him, "Why don't you go to school but loaf around every day?"

"Who said that? Bring him in and give him a few slaps across the face to warn him against lying again in the future! When was I ever truant? What a vicious lie!"

Partly because he loved his son, partly because he thought his son had no money, and partly because the young man's story corroborated the page boy's version, Guo Shan took him at his word and never brought up the matter again. Indeed,

> He had no watchful eyes behind his back;
> The warnings went in one ear and out the other.

A few days later, Mr. Fang again sent someone with this message: "Old Master Guo, why don't you discipline the young master and keep him in school? Why do you still allow him to sow his wild oats all over town?"

"I don't believe this!" said Guo Shan. He then sent a servant to the school to check if his son was there. Sure enough, he was not. In response to the servant's question, the teacher said, "He said something came up in the family. He hasn't shown up for quite a few days now."

The servant rushed home and reported to Guo Shan. Flying into a rage, Guo Shan said, "So, that little beast has been playing tricks with me!"

Right away, he had the page boy who delivered lunch beaten up. Unable to hold out, the boy said, "It's true that the young master doesn't go to school. But I have no idea where he goes for fun every day. He told me over and over again not to tell you, Old Master."

His hands and feet trembling with rage, Guo Shan only wished that this prodigal son were standing in front of him at that very moment so that he could work off his anger by whacking the young man to death with one blow of the rod. But his daughter Shunü, by his side, counseled patience. When evening finally came and Guo Qian returned home, the old man's wrath had already half subsided.

"You beast! You're up to a lot of mischief but keep me in the dark!" Before the old man could go on, Shunü cut in, "Brother, where have you been fooling around these last few days, upsetting father like that? Kneel down and ask for forgiveness!"

And so Guo Qian dropped to his knees and said, lying, "I never missed school. I only skipped these last few days because a classmate invited me to his home for a gathering to offer thanks to the gods. I was afraid you might scold me, so I told the page boy not to say anything about it. Please forgive me!"

"Don't be angry, father," said Shunü. "My brother will surely apply himself to his studies from now on, and that'll be that."

Again Guo Shan fell for his son's lies. He gave the young man a severe lecture and locked him in the house so that he could devote himself to his books.

Two days later, an offer was made to Guo Shan for the sale of several hundred *mu* of land. After the price was agreed upon and a contract was drawn up, he went to a back room to take the silver from a trunk. As soon as he opened the trunk, he gave a start. It had contained more than two thousand taels of silver, but the bulk of its contents was gone. What had happened was that Guo Qian, knowing there was silver inside, had secretly made a duplicate of the key. At night when his father and younger sister were asleep, he would rise from bed, open the trunk, and steal. Little by little, he had taken more than he could count.

Hearing her father cry in dismay, Shunü came in haste to ask what was happening. When told that a lot of silver was missing, she said, "How strange! How can anything be missing from this place? Could you be mistaken, father? Maybe there wasn't that much?"

"I'm not mistaken! That beast has been stealing from me to pay for his expenditures!" Quickly he found a rod and called Guo Qian to him.

The love of silver getting the better of the love for his son at that moment, Guo Shan pulled his son over before the young man could protest and rained blows upon him. As the young man rolled on the floor in pain, Shunü tried for all her worth to calm her father down. Even after she had managed to pull her father aside and hold down the rod, Guo Shan continued to thunder, "Beast! How did you steal it? Where did you spend the money? If you tell the truth, I might let you off easy. If there's one word of lie, I'll beat you to death!"

The pain being too much for him, Guo Qian could not do otherwise than come up with the truth and he even took the key from his waistband.

Stamping both feet in rage, Guo Shan cursed, "You beast! Why should I keep such an unworthy son? I'll only make myself a butt of ridicule! You'd be better off dead now and be done with it!" Before he could raise his rod again, all the other members of the household gathered around him and fell to their knees in supplication. Thereupon Guo Shan asked for a chain and locked the young man up in an empty room. Giving up all thought of the land transaction, he sank in desperation to the floor in a corner of the room. Having beaten up his son in a moment of towering rage, this old man was now feeling the pain in his own heart. He said to himself, "He certainly doesn't look like a bum. How could I have guessed that he would ruin me like this! What can I do to turn him around?"

While he was thinking these thoughts, little knowing what to do, Shunü, trying to cheer him up, said, "Father, since things have already come to this, it doesn't help to stay angry. It's all because he's young and has been led astray. If he does his studies at home and is not allowed to leave the house to join those friends of his, he'll surely have a change of heart."

The servants also chimed in, saying, "Locking him up is no solution in the long run, Old Master. Now that he's come of age, why don't you let him marry? With a wife by his side, he won't go out to find fun elsewhere. Won't that be a good solution every way you look at it?"

Guo Shan agreed. After two or three days, he brought his son out of confinement and, with many kindly words, exhorted him to mend his ways.

Having taken so much beating and scolding, Guo Qian stayed at home, much against his inclination, and dared not even step out the door.

Half a month later, Guo Shan chose an auspicious day and sent a matchmaker to the Fang family to propose a wedding date. Being also a man of immense wealth, Mr. Fang had prepared the dowry very early on and readily gave his consent. On the day of the wedding ceremony, the bride was brought over to the Guo residence. In keeping with Guo Shan's frugal ways, the wedding was a none-too-sumptuous affair.

As a newlywed, Guo Qian was pleased at his wife's beauty and her impressive dowry, and stayed at home day after day in her company with nary a thought of venturing out of the house. Guo Shan's heart overflowed with joy.

After some time had elapsed, Fang-shi, the wife, went back to her parents for a visit. One day, for lack of better things to do, Guo Qian slipped out of the house, quite unobserved, and joined his friends in their excursions here and there. Feeling inhibited by his lack of funds, he thought of his wife's trunks, which he believed were filled with valuables. Resorting to the same trick that had served him well in the past, he opened the trunks and helped himself freely to their contents. He spent the money so extravagantly that even his wife's clothes and jewelry were all gone in the end.

Before many days had passed, his wife came back and let out shrieks of anguish upon finding all her trunks and boxes empty. When she asked Guo Qian, he feigned ignorance. Some heated words arose between husband and wife. When Guo Shan got wind of what had happened, he was so infuriated that his hands and feet went numb and icy cold. He called his son to him, grabbed the young man by his hair, threw him to the floor, and gave him a brutal beating. This time, even Shunü was not able to stop him.

"You beast!" roared Guo Shan. "I thought you had changed your ways and I've been looking forward to the day you could turn over a new leaf. I never suspected that you would relapse to your old ways. Now what hopes are there for me? You'd better die now, to let this old man live a few more days!" Noticing a wooden club nearby, he picked it up and aimed a frontal blow at his son.

Scared out of her wits, Shunü held his arm with both her hands and cried tearfully, "Father, if you have to beat him, use some other object. You must not use this club!"

"Father-in-law," said Fang-shi, frightened at the ugly turn things had taken, "please don't be angry. I didn't have all that much to begin with. It's not that important."

Only then did Guo Shan let go of his son. Shunü helped her father to his room and pleaded, "He's your only son, father. How could you beat him so cruelly? If you accidentally kill him, who will support you in your old age?"

"That beast's not going to change into a decent human being anyway. How can I expect any help from him? Let me finish him off, to spare me a lot of gossip and ridicule!"

Shunü rejoined, "The ancients said, 'A prodigal son who returns runs the best house.' My brother is still young. He won't stay this way the rest of his life. If you kill him today in a moment of anger, you'll regret it and there'll be nothing you can do to bring him back to life!"

With his daughter taking such pains to calm him down, Guo Shan's anger subsided a little. He thought of seeking out his son's cohorts and taking them to court for punishment, but, afraid of running into expenses, he swallowed his anger. Henceforth, Guo Qian, dreading the sight of his father, hid himself in his room and dared not step out the door.

As the proverb says, "A cat that steals food will never change its nature." Guo Qian had become used to his wild ways of living. To him, a life within the confines of the home was nothing less than the life of a prisoner. How would he be able to sit still? More than a month later, he again sneaked out without his father's knowledge. His wife's repeated remonstrations with him fell on deaf ears. She had a mind to tell her father-in-law about it but, haunted by the memory of the severe beating last time, felt obliged to keep her mouth shut. (*Excessive strictness is just as unwise as excessive leniency.*)

With no money on him now, Guo Qian found no enjoyment in his lonely wanderings for days on end. Convinced that there was no way he could manage to get more money from home, he ran around town mortgaging the family's land and spent the days and nights in the courtesans' quarters, the wineshops, and the gambling houses, with never a thought of returning home. After ascertaining the facts, Fang-shi saw nothing else for it but to report to Guo Shan, for she was afraid that her husband might run into trouble. Flabbergasted, Guo Shan said, "I thought that beast was still in his room. So he's out again!" Reproachfully, he said to Fang-shi, "My daughter-in-law, why didn't you tell me when he first left the house? Why did you choose to come to me only now?"

"I didn't dare tell you because you beat him up so badly last time."

"Let me kill that unworthy son! What do I need him for?" Without losing one moment, he dispatched servants to search in all directions for his son. Shunü and Fang-shi, fearing for Guo Qian's safety, hid all the rods, clubs, and sticks from Guo Senior.

In the meantime, Guo Qian got wind of what lay in store for him. He weighed his chances and thought that if he returned home this time, he would surely be put under confinement under lock and chain and never allowed to go out. Concluding that he might just as well never return, he got himself a prostitute and took shelter at the home of one of his good-for-nothing friends. There, he continued to indulge in pleasure. As soon as word got out about his hiding place, he moved to another place. Four to five months' time went by in this manner. Even though the servants did hear some rumors, none of them dared make an enemy of the young master, and so they fobbed Guo Shan off, saying that they were not able to find him.

Even more exasperated, Guo Shan wrote a letter to the county yamen, accusing his son of the crime of filial impiety, but Guo Qian's friends bribed high and low throughout the yamen on Guo Qian's behalf, and so no arrest was made.

As the proverb says, "If water knew contentment, there would be no waves; if humans knew contentment, there would be no disputes." It was for monetary rewards that those friends of Guo Qian's bribed high and low on his behalf. If their gains had been shared equally, they would have happily kept Guo Qian's secret. As it turned out, those who had not acted quickly enough but who hated to see others raking in reward money wagged their tongues and told Mr. Guo Senior with whom Guo Qian associated, how he whored and gambled, and for how much he mortgaged the family land, adding that he was three thousand taels of silver in debt.

The old man went pale. He thought, "The audacity of that brute! The way he spends money, how long can it last? In two years, this body of mine will be someone else's property!" Aloud, he asked, "Where's that brute now?"

"He's with Wang San by Three Li Bridge outside of East Gate. The front door is never open. Take the small alley. The tiny bamboo garden in the middle of the alley leads to his back door. You'll see inside a three-section thatched hut. That's where your son is staying."

Thus informed, Guo Shan called together five or six servants and went out of East Gate. Upon arriving at Three Li Bridge, he instructed the servants to wait for him by the bridge, adding, 'Don't scare him away and don't come forward until I call you."

As if something was destined to happen that day, Guo Qian had just been talking with a friend and, before he knew it, he walked the friend out of the garden gate. After bidding his friend good-bye, he was about to turn his way back when someone roared from behind, "You beast! Where do you think you are going?"

Turning around, Guo Qian saw that it was his father. He was so terrified that his legs gave way under him and he could not budge so much as an inch. In less time than it takes to narrate, Guo Shan took a step forward and, before the young man could protest, picked up a large stone from the ground. With a grunt, he threw it right against the top of his son's head. Guo Shan heard a crash and thought that the beast was finished. Indeed,

One more unfilial ghost in the underworld;
One less prodigal son on earth.

He thought he had smashed his son's head but, in fact, the young man, being keen of eye, had ducked when he saw his father's menacing hand. The stone had hit a pile of broken bricks by his side, bringing the bricks tumbling down. Guo Qian ran for all he was worth toward the mouth of the alley, but he lunged ahead with such force that he knocked his father down. Guo Shan scrambled to his feet and yelled as he ran, "The scoundrel who tried to kill his father is on the run. Get him! Quick!"

When the servants heard him, they went forward, but by this time Guo Qian was far ahead of them. Choking with rage, Guo Shan managed to shout, "Get him! Rewards for those who catch him!"

Thus ordered, the servants ran after their young master in different directions. Panting in anger, Guo Shan sat on the bridge all by himself. About four hours went by, but no one brought word to him. As it was getting dark, he could do no more than swallow his anger and return home, dragging his feet. Judging from his angry look, Shunü had a fair idea of what had happened and went forward to ask. After Guo Shan told her everything in detail, she said, with tears in her eyes, "Father, you're in your fifties and you don't have seven sons and eight daughters. He's the only son you've got. He may be a bad son, but you can talk to him. How could you have struck so hard? Luckily he was quick to dodge and wasn't hurt. If something should have happened to him, the family line would have come to an end! Father, you must not do this ever again!"

Through gnashed teeth, Guo Shan said, "I don't mind if I have no male descendant to make offerings to my ghost after I die. I must not have mercy on that swine!"

Let us leave Shunü in her efforts to placate her father and turn our attention to Guo Qian. Having escaped death, he ran as fast as he could, keeping to small alleys. As he tore along, two men running behind with the speed of wind caught up with him, seized him, and demanded that he return home with them. Who, you may ask, were these two men? Well, they were Guo Shan's adopted grandsons Little Three and Little Four. By Guo Shan's order, they were trying to catch the young master and happened to spot him in this alley. Trying in vain to struggle himself free, Guo Qian raised a fist and furiously landed it right on Little Four's chest. Little Four cried "Oh no!" and fell backwards, silent.

Seeing his brother lying on the ground, not making a sound, Little Three thought he was dead. Screaming at the top of his voice, Little Three kept a tight grip on the young master. Things having come to this pass, Guo Qian was at a loss as to what to do. He thought, "Oh well, it's either him or me. So here goes!" With that, his fists rained blows on Little Three. Having taken lessons in the martial arts, he was quite a good fighter. (*Learning martial arts just to hit one of his own.*) Hardly able to ward off his blows, Little Three had to let go of him. Turning back, he found his brother coming to. Little Three helped him up and asked for some water from people living in the neighborhood. After Little Four drank it, they returned home and reported to the master what had happened. The other servants, who had not found Guo Qian, also came home. Guo Shan heaved one sigh after another, but of this, no more.

In the meantime, Guo Qian was pressing ahead while thinking, "Father is out to get me. He complained to the county yamen to accuse me of being a bad son. And now that I've killed Little Four, I'm adding crime to crime. I'm as good as dead! While I still have three or four taels of silver on me, I'd better run for my life and go as far as I can before I figure out what to do next." So determined, he fled that very night. Truly, he was

> As distraught as a dog that lost its home;
> As desperate as fish slipping out of a net.

After half a year had gone by without any news about Guo Qian, rumors began to float around the neighborhood, saying he had died. Those ne'er-do-well friends of his, in order to sever all ties with him, urged the creditors to demand payment from Guo Shan, in silver or in land. The creditors all being influential people, Guo Shan could not afford to give them offense but tried to placate them with polite words. However, one had hardly left before another came to the door. With the creditors coming in a never-ending stream, Guo Shan stopped seeing them altogether. Thus rejected, the creditors descended on the county yamen with their complaints, and Guo Shan was brought into the yamen for interrogation.

After reading the loan contracts, the magistrate announced to Guo Shan, "These are all debts that your son ran up. Denying them doesn't do you any good."

Guo Shan said, "That vile son of mine didn't follow my teachings but was led astray by those petty rogues and squandered away the entire family fortune. My charge against him is still on file at this yamen. It hasn't been processed only because he's still at large. What funds I have left are just enough to cover my funeral expenses. Paying off his debts is out of the question. And making the father pay off the son's debt is something quite unheard of!"

The magistrate said genially, "If you the father are unwilling to be responsible for your son's debts, how can you expect outsiders to let him freeload off them? What's more, the creditors are by no means the ones who led your son astray. How can you turn them away? In brief, don't blame other people for your son's bad conduct. As long as the father is alive, the son should not be allowed to act on his own. As for the creditors, they are hungry for exorbitant interest and they signed loan contracts directly with your son out of ill intentions. My judgment is for you to repay the principal as recorded in the contracts but not the interest. (*Good judgment.*) On the day the principal is paid up, the loan contracts will be destroyed right here in this courtroom. The middlemen will be charged with crime and punished."

How would Guo Shan dare contest the magistrate's judgment? With no alternative but to pay off the debts one by one, he hated his son with a new intensity. In fact, he relished the thought of his son's demise in some other part of the country. Miss his son he did not. Indeed,

Wild land is better than tilled land that yields no crops;
To be childless is better than having a wayward son.

But the story continues. Guo Shan's daughter, Shunnü, was filial and amicable by nature and was fair to look upon, but, at eighteen years of age now, she was yet unbetrothed. You may well ask, why had there been no offers of marriage for a girl of this age and from such a wealthy family, too? Well, Guo Shan wanted an outstanding son-in-law for his cherished daughter, but, unable to claim kinship with families of higher status and yet refusing to go lower, he turned down every one of the legions of candidates recommended to him. Hence the delay. In addition, with such an unworthy son, he set even greater store by his daughter and wanted a candidate who was not only head and shoulders above all the others, but also willing to be a live-in son-in-law to take over the family business in the future. The search was thus made more difficult.

Our story forks at this point. There lived in Guo Shan's neighborhood a man named Zhang Ren who came from a long line of scholar farmers and was quite well-to-do. He and his wife had only one son, Xiaoji [Foundation of Filial Piety], who, fair of face and tall of frame, was well versed in the histories, poetry, and the classics. At age twenty now, he was yet unengaged. A matchmaker whose services Zhang Ren was seeking spoke to Guo Shan, who had seen Xiaoji before and was impressed by his looks. Delighted that the young man's family was of a matching social status, he said, "With this young man as my son-in-law, I won't have to worry about my daughter's future."

Zhang Xiaoji being an only son, Mr. Zhang Senior could ill bear to let him live with the bride's family but, giving in to the pressure of the matchmaker acting on behalf of Guo Shan and considering the girl's fine repute, he gave his consent. As was the practice, written documents of the names and dates of birth of the prospective bride and bridegroom were exchanged, presents were offered to the bride's family, and Xiaoji went to live with the Guo family.

Even though he was now a live-in son-in-law, Xiaoji still went to see his own parents every day. His devotion to them remained unabated. He and his wife were as deferential to each other as they were to guests, and he respected Guo Shan as much as he did his own parents. Being of an unassuming and kind disposition, he was all affability to everyone, to the hearty admiration of all and sundry, high and low. Guo Shan loved him as he would his own son and gave the more challenging business problems to him, to test his ability. Xiaoji handled them efficiently and found optimal solutions to them. Guo Shan was all the more pleased. Fang-shi, however, still felt miserable. She stayed alone in her room day and night, sorely missing her husband and not knowing where he was or if he was dead or alive, for not a word had been heard from him.

Time flew like an arrow. More than two years had elapsed since Zhang Xiaoji had moved into the Guo residence, when suddenly Guo Shan took ill. Prayers to the gods were unavailing, nor did medicine make any difference. Fang-shi and Shunü served him medicine and nursed him day and night. Xiaoji moved his own bedding to the front section of the house so that he could better attend to the business, but the old man's condition kept deteriorating, and Guo Shan knew that he was not likely to get well again. So he told his daughter to prepare a banquet in honor of all the neighbors and the relatives.

To the assembly of guests, he announced, "My respects to you, everyone. By the grace of heaven, earth, and my ancestors, I have made a modest fortune in the hope of passing it on to my offspring so that it can last from generation to generation. Unfortunately, my wayward son, who is on the run from justice, squandered away much of it. I have no idea whether he is dead or alive. Luckily, I still have a daughter. She and her good husband are a comfort to me in my old age. But I have fallen gravely ill and will soon leave this world. That is why I have invited all of you here, so that you can serve as witnesses as I pass on all my possessions to my son-in-law, who will carry on the Guo family line. I drew up my will a long time ago, and ask that every one of you sign it. If that disobedient son of mine is still alive and returns home to fight for the inheritance after he hears of my death, please present this will to the authorities. They will surely know the right thing to do."

Having said that, he took out the will from under his pillow and had a servant show it to the guests. While they were debating in their mind whether the son-in-law was behind this, Zhang Xiaoji spoke up before they did. "I am very grateful to you, my father-in-law, for your kindness," he said. "However, you do have a son. It doesn't stand to reason to pass on your fortune to someone bearing a different family name while your son is alive. In your son-in-law's humble opinion, you should dispatch a messenger to search everywhere for your son and bring him back, so as to pass on the family fortune to *him* and to fulfill the love between father and son. Your daughter and I will by rights return to the Zhang clan. If my brother-in-law is unfortunately not in this world anymore, the inheritance should be passed on to his widow if she observes widowhood. And then a search can be conducted among the clan for a boy to be the designated heir. That would be the right thing to do. If I inherited the family fortune, you would be accused by outsiders of expelling your son in favor of the son-in-law, and I would also be spoken ill of for gaining possessions that are not rightfully mine. I will not presume to obey your order."

Shunü added, "My brother is on the run only because he's afraid of punishment from you, father. I believe he's alive. My husband bears a different surname. How can he be an heir?"

Moved by the husband and wife's sincerity, the guests said, "There's something in what your son-in-law and your daughter say. Why don't you search for the young master first? Wait for half a year or a year, and you can decide what to do when you hear news about him."

"What my son-in-law said will only do me a disservice," said Guo Shan.

"How would that be doing you a disservice, Old Master?" asked the guests.

"I worked my fingers to the bone all my life, but that disobedient son of mine treated my hard-earned money as so much dirt and squandered more than four thousand taels in less than half a year. With such extravagance, any amount of savings would be gone in a matter of days. After the money is gone, he will sell off land and even the family grave site. Not only will this old man's bones be without a burial place but even my ancestors' bones will be dug out and left to rot in the wilderness."

Xiaoji said, "My brother-in-law was too young and was led astray by bad people. He's older now and he has the benefit of our exhortations. He will surely turn over a new leaf rather than do what you just described."

"I don't think so! I don't think so!" said Guo Shan. "He didn't change his ways even when I was there to punish him. After I die, who will be able to keep him in line?"

The guests said, "In our humble opinion, the best way out is to divide everything in half, so that your son will have nothing to complain about after he comes back."

But Guo Shan held his ground. As Xiaoji and his wife adamantly refused to take the inheritance, Guo Shan flew into a rage. "Are you trying to imitate that scoundrel and drive me to death?"

Convinced by this outburst that he meant what he said, the guests said to Xiaoji, "Your father-in-law is determined. You'd better not insist." Thereupon they signed the will and gave it back to Mr. Guo.

Shunü said, "You're giving all of the family inheritance to me and my husband, but what about my sister-in-law?"

"I have made arrangements for her. You need not worry." So saying, he handed the will to Xiaoji. In tears, Xiaoji and his wife accepted it. Then Guo Shan took out another two pieces of paper and, holding them in his hand, called Mr. Fang to him and said, "That wild son of mine made your daughter a virtual widow. This old man is really sorry for this. It won't do for her to stay here forever. I have written a letter addressed to her. After I die, please take her home with you and find her a better husband. Should that swine come back and raise objections, you can go to court with this letter. I'm also giving her a hundred *mu* of land in compensation for the dowry that my vile son had squandered away." With that, he handed the two pieces of paper to Mr. Fang.

Mr. Fang refused to take them. He said, "My daughter is your son's wife and, as such, anything relating to her is a matter within your family and therefore no concern of mine. What's more, no daughter of my humble family is ever to marry twice. Please do not bring this up again." Having said that, he headed for the door, turning a deaf ear to Xiaoji's pleas for him to stay.

After Guo Shan called his daughter-in-law out of her room and told her about what had happened, Fang-shi said, sobbing, "I understand that a virtuous woman should remain faithful to her one and only husband until her death. A woman with any pride would not stoop to a second marriage after her husband's death. What's more, my husband is still alive. How can I do such a shameful thing?"

Guo Shan said, "So what if he's still alive? That lowlife is not worth waiting for!"

Fang-shi rejoined, "He may not be a good man, but my resolve is not to be shaken. If you want to change my mind, I'll have to die."

"It's a good thing that you're so determined. But after I die, my son-in-law will be in charge. It'll be unseemly for you to stay on."

At this point, Shunü put in, "Father, since my sister-in-law is committed to observing widowhood, the family property should all go to her, and I should join my husband's family."

Fang-shi objected, "My sister-in-law, I have no children. Why would I want to have so much? Since I'm given a hundred *mu* of land, I should return to my parents' house and live off the land for the rest of my life. Even if my husband returns, we'll still have enough to live on."

The guests all cheered the good solution.

"My daughter-in-law," said Guo Shan, "you bring me such great credit that I'll add another two hundred *mu* of land and throw in two hundred taels of silver. That should be enough to last you a lifetime."

Tearfully, Fang-shi said her thanks.

Having thus settled everything, Guo Shan had his son-in-law lead the relatives and the neighbors to the main hall for wine. The party did not break up until late at night. Already gravely ill, Guo Shan had overexerted himself by forcing himself to go through these proceedings. After he had talked himself short of breath for so long, his condition worsened that night. His daughter and daughter-in-law sat by his bedside and wept. Zhang Xiaoji, for his part, made preparations for his father-in-law's funeral and got everything ready. A few days later, Guo Shan gave up the ghost. Truly,

> Everything is done with the three inches of breath;
> All is gone once the last breath goes out.

The daughter and the daughter-in-law cried their hearts out and fainted several times. Zhang Xiaoji was also overcome by grief. The burial clothes and the coffin were nothing short of spectacular. In the middle of the forty-nine-day mourning period, monks and priests were engaged for a memorial service to ask for blessings for the deceased. On a chosen auspicious day, the body was buried in the ancestral grave site. No money was spared on any detail of the rituals. After the burial was over, Fang-shi packed and returned to her parents' house. Hating to part with each other, the two young women sobbed uncontrollably as they bade each other farewell, but of this, no more.

Zhang Xiaoji entered into the account books each and every item of his inheritance in the form of cash, grain, and the like. He also sent servants to look everywhere for Guo Qian, but nothing came of the searches. Time flew like an arrow and the months and the years went by like the flow of water. In the twinkling of an eye, five years elapsed. Zhang Xiaoji now had two sons and had added a pawnshop in the front portion of the house, with a manager tending to the business. The family fortune had increased several times more than in Guo Shan's time.

Let us not digress but come to the day when Zhang Xiaoji went to Chenliu County on business. After finding lodging at an inn, he took his servant on a sightseeing tour of the town. When they found themselves in the marketplace at the end of the tour, they saw a sickly looking beggar sitting under the eaves of a house. Occupants of that house were telling him to leave. His heart going out to the beggar, Zhang Xiaoji instructed his servant, Zhu Xin, to give him a few coins. Zhu Xin was an old servant of the Guo family, a clever man and a good mind reader. When he gave the money to the beggar, he peered into his face and gave a start. He rushed back and said to Zhang Xiaoji, "You have never stopped looking for the young master. Now, that beggar looks just like him."

Zhang Xiaoji stopped in his tracks and said, "Go take another good look. If it's really him, he'll surely recognize you. Don't tell him yet that I'm the son-in-law of the family and that I inherited everything from his father. Just say that the Guo family has been ruined and that I am your new master. Listen to what he has to say, and then bring him to me. I will know what to do."

Thus instructed, Zhu Xin went back. The beggar had slipped the coins into a belt and was tucking it around his waist, his head bent low. Zhu Xin looked intently and, this time, he had no doubts. When taking the alms, the beggar had fixed his eyes on the money and could not care less from whom it came, but this time, since he had already tucked the money away, with Zhu Xi staring at him, he raised his eyes and recognized the servant. "Zhu Xin," he cried out involuntarily. "Whom are you with?"

"Young master, why are you in such a state?"

Tearfully, Guo Qian replied, "After I fled from home, I did want to ask someone to talk to father, but on the way I ran into Little Three and Little Four. They stopped me and insisted on taking me home. I thought that to return home when father was so furious would be the death of me. In the rush of the moment, I hit Little Four with my fist. He fell and died. I was so frightened that I ran away. I walked day and night and came to this place after a few days. I stayed at an inn and was driven out after I used up all my money. The best I can do is to beg for a living. I miss home so much, but I have no one to ask for news about home. Heaven brought you to me today. Tell me, what did father say after Little Four died?"

"Little Four came back to life. He did not die. But the Old Master died five years ago."

Letting out a cry of anguish upon hearing about his father's death, Guo Qian fell onto the ground. After Zhu Xin helped him up, he choked with emotion and the sobs stuck in his throat. He whimpered almost inaudibly for quite a while before he burst into loud wails. "I've been hoping to go back home, to find someone to persuade father to take me, so that father and son can be reunited. Who would have thought that he's no longer in this world!"

The dolefulness of the tone moved Zhu Xin to tears also. After crying for a while, Guo Qian asked, "With father gone, who is in charge of the family property?"

"Before the Old Master died, all your creditors came to demand repayment of your debts. He refused to pay and was brought to court. He spent a lot of money there. And then, at the trial, the judge ordered that he pay back all of the debts, which took away the bulk of the land property. Then the young mistress married, and her dowry was another big chunk out of his savings. On his deathbed, he divided the balance among the relatives because he was angry at you for not behaving. After he passed away, there being no rightful master in the house, the servants fought over what little money was left and didn't even leave one penny behind. Only the house remained but it was sold to my new master, Mr. Zhang, in exchange for enough money for the funeral. So now, not even an inch of land is left."

Bursting into another fit of sobbing, Guo Qian said, "I thought at least the family fortune was still there, and that I could drag myself home and start a new life as a good person. I never thought that the family would be ruined like this!" Then he asked again, "Now that the family fortune is all gone, where's my wife? And whom has my sister married?"

"The young mistress lives nearby with her husband's family. But about your wife, I dare not tell the truth."

"Why?"

"The Old Master thought you had died because he hadn't heard from you for so long. So he sent her back to her parents and told her to remarry."

"Has she remarried?"

"My new master often sends me on trips to faraway places. So I don't get to stay at home very often. I didn't ask about this. I would think she has remarried."

Stroking his chest, Guo Qian said in aching grief, "This unworthy person has brought ruin to the whole family! The money now belongs to other people, and my wife has gone to someone else. I am the biggest sinner there is in this world! Why would I want to hang on to this worthless life? I'd be better off dead!" So saying, he lunged toward the stone steps in an attempt to kill himself. With a quick movement, Zhu Xin seized him and said, "Young master, even crickets and ants love life. How can you do this?"

"I swallowed my shame and hung on to life only because I thought I would return home some day. Now that I don't have a home to return to, I'd better die sooner rather than making a fool of myself here."

"As they say, a wretched life is better than an honorable death. You must not do this. My new master is a very kind person. Let me introduce you to him and ask him to take you to his home. If you can be of service to him in any way, why don't you settle down in his house, so that you can have support in your old age? If you die here, who will put away your remains? Won't you have died for nothing?"

After reflecting for a while, Guo Qian said, "What you said does make a lot of sense. But I'm too ashamed of myself to be introduced to him. If he doesn't want to keep me, it will be a loss of face for me."

"You're in no position to care about a loss of face."

"True enough, but don't tell him my real name. Just say that I'm a relative of yours."

"But I already told him. How can I change my story?"

For lack of a better choice, Guo Qian straightened his tattered clothes and followed Zhu Xin. Watching as he stood under the eaves of a house some distance off, Zhang Xiaoji gave a deep sigh as he sensed, from the way Guo Qian wept, that he was repentant.

Guo Qian walked up to Xiaoji and stood with his head bent low. Zhu Xin was the first one to speak up. "Master," said he, "this is my young master in the old days. He got stranded here as a refugee, and would like to ask you to keep him." Raising his voice, he said, "Come and greet the master!"

Taking a step forward, Guo Qian pulled at his own sleeves in preparation for a proper bow, but he had only half of a sleeve left on each arm, and a tattered half at that. However he tried, there was not enough of it to reach down to his hand or cover his arm. He could do no more than fold his arms, inserting his hands into what remained of his sleeves, and chant a greeting.

Zhang Xiaoji felt even more saddened. Out of regard for Guo Qian's status as his brother-in-law, he felt he could not accept this salute without returning the courtesy. So he bowed slightly and said, "Well! You are from a good family. Why are you in such a state? If I take you home, what am I going to do with you if you can't do anything?"

"Master," said Zhu Xin, "just keep him, please."

"Can you do gardening?" asked Zhang Xiaoji.

"I haven't done it before, but I can learn and I'll try hard."

"You were used to high living. Are you ready for hard work?"

"How would I not be, the way I am now?"

"All right. But you have to promise me three things before I can take you home. If not, I won't be able to keep you."

"What three things, may I ask?"

"First, you will stay only in the garden. I'll arrange to have food delivered to you. Do not ever leave the garden. If you do, you won't be allowed back in."

"Having brought such disgrace to my ancestors, I am too ashamed to go out and be seen. I'll be only too happy to live in the garden. I promise."

Pleased at the repentant tone, Zhang Xiaoji continued, "Second, you must rise early and retire late. Do not oversleep and be lazy and loaf on the job."

"I will get up before daybreak and stop working after it's dark. If there's good moonlight, I'll also work in the evening. I will not loaf on the job. I promise."

"You don't have to work in the evening. Not loafing on the job during the day will be good enough. Third, if you don't do a good job, you will let me punish you. Do not complain."

"Since you are taking me home, you are a parent of my rebirth. Punish me as much as you want. I won't complain even if I die."

"Since you promise, follow me now."

Without going on with his sightseeing tour, Zhang Xiaoji turned around and led Guo Qian to the inn. Guo Qian was about to enter when the innkeeper, seeing a beggar, cried out and stopped him. "Don't drive him away," said Zhang Xiaoji. "He's a member of my household."

"This beggar often works the streets around here. How is he a member of your household?" asked the innkeeper.

Zhu Xin said, "He's been stranded here. We just ran into him."

Once inside his room, Zhang Xiaoji sat down and gave these instructions: "Now that you're with me, you can't go on looking like this. Zhu Xin, ask the innkeeper to heat some water for him to take a bath. Then give him some spare clothes and bring him food."

Thereupon Zhu Xin went to ask the innkeeper to heat some water. When the water was ready, he called Guo Qian over to take a bath. In all these years living away from home, Guo Qian had not once laid eyes on warm water. As he washed, dirt and grime came off his skin and filled half the bathtub. After Zhu Xin put clothes on him and combed his hair, he looked quite a different person. Zhu Xin then brought him food and he ate to his heart's content. He had always been frail and, after having suffered many hardships, taken a bath in a windy spot, and overeaten, he fell ill that night, for a combination of all these factors was beginning to take a toll on him. Zhang Xiaoji engaged a physician for him. He did not recover until more than a month later.

His business over, Zhang Xiaoji paid the innkeeper his bill, packed, hired another draft animal and a porter for Guo Qian, and set out on his return journey. As all four of them traveled on the highway, Zhang Xiaoji said, "Guo Qian, you are from an old distinguished family. I don't feel comfortable calling you by your name. From this day on, I'll call you Xiaoyi [a common name for servants]." Addressing Zhu Xin, he continued, "You will all call him Brother Xiaoyi. This is more appropriate for everyone."

"All right," said Zhu Xin.

"Xiaoyi," said Zhang Xiaoji, "since we don't have anything better to do on the road, why don't you tell me some of the exciting things you did in the past, just to while away the time?"

"Master," said Guo Qian, "don't remind me of the past! I'll be ashamed to death!"

"You were a dashing man about town," rejoined Zhang Xiaoji. "What's there to be ashamed of? Come on!"

Guo Qian gave in to the pressure and told about his extravagances in the past.

"So you really lived it up in the old days," said Xiaoji. "And then you were reduced to such misery begging in the streets. Don't you feel bad about it?"

"I was young and ignorant, and I was led astray. That's why I was reduced to such a state. Regrets are too late now!"

"I shouldn't be surprised if you go back to your old ways as soon as you lay your hands on some silver," said Zhang Xiaoji.

"I'm lucky enough that I'm still alive. How would I do such a thing? I wouldn't dare even if you kill me!" (*Zhang Xiaoji's strategy is working.*)

To Zhu Xin, Zhang Xiaoji said, "You were an old servant of the Guo family. Do you know if your old master had lived it up like that?"

Zhu Xin replied, "Bless his poor soul, his only thoughts were on how to save money. He never spent one penny that he didn't think was necessary."

"Tell me how frugal he was," said Xiaoji.

Counting the old master's virtues on his fingers, Zhu Xin related how hard-working Mr. Guo Senior had been and what pains he had taken to build up his family fortune, going all the way back to his youth, and added at the end, "Who would have known that Brother Xiaoyi would treat the family fortune like dirt and bring ruin to the family!"

Listening to him, Guo Qian melted in tears.

"Tears are too late now," said Zhang Xiaoji. "But if you turn over a new leaf, you may still have a future."

All along the journey, Zhang Xiaoji and Zhu Xin worked as a team, making comments that tugged at Guo Qian's heartstrings. Gradually, bitter remorse seized hold of him. Truly, it is too late

> *To rein in the horse when already on the cliff,*
> *And to fix the boat when already in midstream.*

After traveling for several days, they arrived in Xuchang. Zhang Xiaoji had Zhu Xin carry the luggage home and report to Shunü, whereas he himself took Guo Qian to his own parents' home and told them about what had happened. After he introduced Guo Qian to his parents, he led Guo Qian to the back garden, cleaned up a hut, and gave him his bedding. After telling him to retire for the night, he instructed Guo Qian in these words: "Do not go out and walk around. If I find out, you'll be in for punishment."

Over and over again, Guo Qian said, "I wouldn't dare! I wouldn't dare!"

Xiaoji took leave of his parents, went home, and quietly told his wife about the whole thing, much to her gratitude.

Now let us come back to Guo Qian after he retired for the night. He rose bright and early the next morning and carried tools to hoe the weeds. It was a large garden surrounded on all sides by bamboo fences. Mr. Zhang Senior was also a frugal man. He grew no flowers and trees but filled his garden with vegetables. He had more than one gardener. Having just started out, Guo Qian did a poor job, but he kept on and hoed away with might and main. Several days later, he began to realize with delight that his skills had improved. Every day, he carried loads of water, irrigated the fields, weeded, and hoed from dawn to dusk without stopping or talking to anyone. In foul weather when the wind howled and heavy rain came down, he would miss his father and burst into stifled sobs. He wanted to kowtow to his father's grave but, remembering the restriction on his movements, dared not leave the garden. Having heard that his sister was married and living nearby, he wished to see her, but he had no idea exactly where she was. And then he thought, "Being in such a lowly position, I'm too ashamed to see her anyway. Even if she doesn't look down on me, her husband and in-laws would, and if so, won't I be bringing disgrace on myself?" And so he banished the idea from his mind altogether.

In the meantime, Zhang Xiaoji dispatched someone to spy on him every day. His diligence filled Zhang Xiaoji with joy. Then Xiaoji sent a servant to talk to him and sound him out. The servant said, "Brother Xiaoyi, why do you work so hard from morning to night? Why don't you take some time off and go out with me for some fun? I'll treat you to a few cups of wine."

Guo Qian said hotly, "You are already wrong to want to loaf on the job, and you try to drag me along, too! If you say this again, I'll surely report you to the master!"

One day, Zhang Xiaoji came to inspect the garden. He deliberately found fault with Guo Qian's work, lectured him severely, and threatened to beat him. Prostrating himself on the ground, Guo Qian said, "I am indeed at fault. I deserve punishment."

After a few more reproachful words, Zhang Xiaoji said, "You're new on this job, so I forgive you this time. If you do these things wrong again, I won't let you off easy!"

Guo Qian kowtowed and respectfully mumbled assent. Henceforth he worked even harder.

About half a year later, as he showed no signs of fatigue and never took so much as one step out of the garden, Zhang Xiaoji was convinced that his resolve to repent was firm. One day, he went to the garden again, accompanied by a servant carrying a suit of clothes, a headscarf, and shoes and stockings, and said to Guo Qian, "I'm impressed by your diligence and prudence. I can use your services. I need someone to help out in the treasury. You can fill that vacancy. Now, put on the headscarf and clothes and follow me."

"I never even expected that you would keep me as a gardener. How would I dream of being a treasury clerk?"

"Don't decline. If you work hard on the job, it'll be to your credit."

Thereupon Guo Qian put on the headscarf and the clothes, looking quite a different man now. He followed Zhang Xiaoji to the main hall and bade Mr. Zhang Senior farewell before leaving the house. Feeling too ashamed to look people in the eye, he kept his head bent low as he walked along. Before long, he saw the gate of the Guo residence. The sight so saddened him that he shed furtive tears. Upon reaching the gate, he saw servants whom he knew lined up on both sides, their hands joined respectfully in front of their chests, letting Zhang Xiaoji pass through.

"How come our family's servants are now all working for him?" he thought. "They must have been sold with the house."

Not daring to call out to them, he kept walking, his head lowered. The servants all followed him into the house. Once in the main hall, everyone stopped. The sight of the tables, chairs, and other furniture, so familiar to him, saddened him even more.

"Follow me," said Zhang Xiaoji. "Let me take you to someone."

Wondering who it could be, Guo Qian followed in his footsteps and turned left from the main hall onto a path that Guo Qian recognized as one that led to the family shrine. As they drew near the site, Xiaoji said, pointing at it, "There's someone inside. Why don't you go in?"

Eagerly Guo Qian went in. As he raised his head, what should he see but his father's portrait! He prostrated himself on the floor and said sobbingly, "Your unworthy son succumbed to evil and brought disgrace to the family. While you were alive, I was not there to tend to you in your sick bed. When you passed away, I was not there to bury your bones either. Such offenses are more than I can redeem, even if my bones are smashed!" As he spoke, he knocked his head against the floor until blood trickled down all over his face. As he was weeping, he heard someone approaching him from behind, crying between wails of grief, "Brother! You stayed away from home all these years without ever giving a thought to father!"

Raising his head, Guo Qian saw that it was his younger sister. Grabbing her, he said, "Sister! I thought I would never get to see you in this life. Imagine seeing you again!" The brother and sister fell on each other's shoulders and dissolved in tears.

> His erstwhile vagrant life was heart-rending;
> This reunion today is gut-wrenching.
> If it were not for a bone-chilling spell,
> The plum blossoms would not be so sweet-smelling.

After weeping for a while with his sister, Guo Qian bowed gratefully to Zhang Xiaoji and said, "If you, my brother-in-law, had not saved my life, I would have ended up a ghost in an alien land. How can I ever repay your kindness to me?"

Raising him up, Zhang Xiaoji said, "We are flesh and blood. Why say such a thing? To turn over a new leaf and comfort your father's soul in heaven would be better than repaying me."

Guo Qian said tearfully, "I will continue to abide by the rules you laid down for me. If I make a mistake, please still go ahead and punish me."

Zhang Xiaoji laughed. "That was just a temporary measure before you had been told the truth. Now that you know everything, how can we go back to that way of doing things? Self-discipline will be enough." Having said that, Zhang Xiaoji called together all the servants so that they could greet the young master. The greetings over, Shunü set out wine and food in her room in honor of her brother.

Guo Qian asked, "About my wife, whom has she married?"

"Brother, how can you say such a thing! You do her such injustice! When father was gravely ill, he told my sister-in-law to remarry, but she firmly refused." After giving a whole account of what had happened to Fang-shi, Shunü continued, "She's now living with her parents. How can you say she has remarried?"

When Guo Qian heard that his wife remained loyal to him, tears sprang to his eyes again. "How was I to know?" he said. "That was Zhu Xin's story."

Zhang Xiaoji put in, "He said that just to fob you off for the moment. After some time, I'll go with you to your parents-in-law's house and bring Sister-in-law back."

"I'm in no hurry to do that, but I do want to visit father's grave."

"That's no problem," said Zhang Xiaoji.

The next morning, they prepared some sacrificial offerings and went together to the grave. In tears, Guo Qian bowed and said, "This unworthy son deserves to die ten thousand times for having disobeyed you, father. I'm now determined to turn over a new leaf to redeem my sins. Please watch me well." With that, he burst into another fit of sobbing, but Zhang Xiaoji calmed him down with comforting words.

Once back in the Zhang residence, Zhang Xiaoji counted the money in the treasury and entrusted all of it to Guo Qian. Even though he had now taken over responsibility for the treasury, Guo Qian still rose early and retired late, just as he had done when working in the garden, sparing no pain to acquit himself well. He was so fair and meticulous in the business transactions that none of his clients was not gratified. He treated Zhang Xiaoji and his sister like parents and sought their counsel whenever difficulties arose. He took up his quarters right there in the shop, never reverting for a moment to his old ways. (*This was achievable when he was working as a gardener, but now, knowing that Zhang Xiaoji was his brother-in-law and the family fortune and the treasury had all been the Guo family property, he still felt no stirrings of greed and remained as assiduous as before. None but a man of superior moral caliber is capable of that.*) By this time, all the relatives had learned about his return and had come to see him, but they did little more than exchange greetings with him, for they did not deem it appropriate to engage him in serious conversation. About two or three months later, Zhang Xiaoji, still afraid that he might be tempted easily, again sent someone to sound him out.

"Young master," said that man, "you used to love having a good time, and you borrowed money everywhere. Now, with so much silver around you, how can you just sit tight and keep watch over it? I know a place where they've just taken in a most beautiful girl. Shall we go together for a cup of tea?"

Guo Qian shot back, "You scoundrel! It was precisely because I had been led astray that I ruined my family and almost died. I can't hate those rascals enough, and now here you are, trying to do the same thing to me!" So saying, he seized that man and tried to drag him to see Zhang Xiaoji. It was not until the man apologized that Guo Qian let go of him. Zhang Xiaoji was beside himself with joy when he heard the report.

Time sped by. Quite unnoticeably, another six months elapsed. After closely examining the account books without finding the slightest error in them, Zhang Xiaoji said to Guo Qian, "Of the three offenses against filial piety, being childless is the most serious. When you first returned, I had a mind to report to your parents-in-law and bring about a reunion between you and sister-in-law. But I was afraid that they would still take you to be a prodigal son and therefore might not agree to accept you, so I dropped the idea. Now that everyone knows you've repented, they won't reject you if you go to bring Sister-in-law home. I can go with you right now."

Guo Qian agreed. He changed into the new clothes that Shunü had taken out for him and went with his brother-in-law to the Fang residence. To Mr. Fang, who came out to greet them, Guo Qian said, prostrating himself on the ground, "This unworthy son-in-law has let my father-in-law and my good wife down! But I have mended my ways and would like to be reunited with your daughter."

Raising him to his feet, Mr. Fang said, "There is no need to prostrate yourself. I know all about how you're doing. Since my daughter belongs to you, I'll surely send her to you."

Zhang Xiaoji asked, "When are you going to do that, sir?"

"How about tomorrow?" said Mr. Fang.

"Could you also come, sir?" said Zhang Xiaoji. "I will have some announcements."

Mr. Fang agreed. Guo Qian and Zhang Xiaoji took leave of him and returned home. Zhang Xiaoji then invited all their relatives and neighbors to a celebration banquet the next day. Fang-shi arrived before noon the next day. Guo Qian and his sister went out to greet her. Joy and sorrow mingled at the reunion. Fang-shi also went to bow her thanks to Zhang Xiaoji. Soon, all the guests arrived. After an exchange of greetings, everyone praised Xiaoji and his wife for having made all this possible. They also praised Guo Qian for having mended his ways and Fang-shi for her loyalty. Before long, the banquet was ready. Zhang Xiaoji assigned the seating in the order of seniority, and everyone sat down.

After several rounds of wine and three courses of dishes, Zhang Xiaoji rose and excused himself from the hall, only to reemerge with a servant carrying a box, which was then placed on the banquet table. Zhang Xiaoji filled a large cup with warm wine and handed it to Guo Qian, saying, "My brother-in-law, please drink it up."

Not daring to refuse what Xiaoji was respectfully offering to him, Guo Qian accepted the cup with both hands and said, "I should be the one offering you a toast. Now you're going the other way around!"

"Please drink it up, my brother-in-law. I have something to say after you do."

After Guo Qian drank up the wine in one gulp, Zhang Xiaoji opened the box with a key, took out about ten account books, and said, handing them over to Guo Qian, "Please accept these account books."

Guo Qian took them and asked, "My brother-in-law, what accounts are these?"

"Take them before I explain in detail." Turning to the guests, Zhang Xiaoji continued, "My respects to you, honorable elders! I have something to announce."

The guests stood up and said, "We old men will be glad to hear whatever you have to say to us." As they listened with attention, Xiaoji raised two fingers and delivered a speech that won everyone's admiration. Indeed,

> He treated money as nothing more than dung and dirt;
> To him, kindness was worth a ton of gold.
> He remembered the dying man's words,
> And remained loyal, whether rich or poor.

This was what Zhang Xiaoji said: "My father-in-law passed on the family inheritance to me because my brother-in-law was prone to prodigal ways. All my repeated refusals were of no avail. My father-in-law being ill at the time, I was afraid that if I incurred his anger, I would be guilty of an act of disrespect. Therefore I agreed, much against my will. But you venerable elders were all witnesses to that event, so I need not go into details. After my father-in-law passed away, I sent people to search everywhere for my brother-in-law, but no trace of him was found in four to five years' time. By heaven's will, I ran into him in Chenliu. I intended to tell him everything and give the inheritance back to him. However, I thought that if he reverted to his old free-spending ways, I wouldn't be doing justice to my father-in-law's kindness. So I hid the truth from him. I made him work in the garden and set rules for him, so as to test both his mind and body. At the same time, I offered him many kindly words of advice and gave him admonitions in roundabout ways in the hope that he would turn over a new leaf. Fortunately, he repented more and more deeply his misdeeds of the past and completely changed his ways. Since he took charge of the treasury several months ago, he has been fair and prudent in the business transactions and most meticulous in his work. Afraid that he might still waver in his resolve, I sent people to test him several times, but his determination proved to be as firm as a rock and he remained impervious to temptation. He has become a man of impeccable integrity. That is why I invited all of you here, so that you can witness this event. I am returning to my brother-in-law everything that my father-in-law had passed on to me, plus the income accrued over the last few years in the form of grains, fabric, silk, and silver. I entered every item into the account books without ever daring to spend any of the money for any unwarranted purposes. Today, I give them back to my brother-in-law, and, tomorrow, I will move back to my parents' home with my wife." (*It is not difficult to refrain from coveting other people's money, but it is difficult to go out of your way to bring about other people's happiness. Xiaoji is one in a million.*)

From the box he took out a document and, handing it to Guo Qian, continued, "This is my father-in-law's will, which I'm also giving back to my brother-in-law. The toast I offered was meant to advise my brother-in-law to conscientiously practice frugality and industry, so as to live up to my deceased father-in-law's expectations. Do remember to guard against complacency and a return of the wrong ideas. Be on the alert!"

By this time, the guests were fully convinced of Zhang Xiaoji's sincerity in turning down Mr. Guo Senior's offer years before. As they broke into praises, Guo Qian prostrated himself on the floor and said tearfully, "When I violated the Way of Heaven and was reduced to a vagabond's life, I thought I was going to die on the streets and never get to return to home. To have the family inheritance was something unthinkable. Luckily, my brother-in-law saved my life, brought me home, and taught me untiringly to become a better person. He reestablished my ties with my father and reunited me and my wife for the continuation of the clan. Indeed, my parents gave me life, but my brother-in-law made me a real person. Kindness of such a magnitude is more than I can ever repay, not even with my death. I don't even deserve to be his servant. How would I dream of entertaining other desires? What's more, having disobeyed my father all my life, I am guilty of more sins than I can ever redeem. It was my father's wish to pass on the family inheritance to my brother-in-law. If it is given to me, wouldn't that be against my father's will and adding to my sins?"

Zhang Xiaoji raised him to his feet and said, "You're quite mistaken! My father-in-law worked hard all his life in order to pass on his possessions to his descendants from generation to generation. He picked me only because you were leading a wandering life and he had no other son to pass the family fortune on to. He did this as a last resort. It was by no means his original intention. Now that you have mended your ways and are able to keep the inheritance, just as your father had wished, he will be smiling contentedly in heaven. How would that add to your sins?"

Again Guo Qian objected. As they strenuously resisted each other's offer, the guests were at a loss as to what to do. Finally, Mr. Fang spoke up. To Zhang Xiaoji he said, "My son-in-law is obligated not to let you down in your great kindness to him. But how could he feel at ease if everything goes to him? In the humble opinion of this old man, the inheritance should be split in half between the two of you. That way, he won't feel overwhelmed."

The others exclaimed in agreement, "Good idea! These old men also made this proposal before, but Master Guo rejected it, and so we dropped the idea. We never anticipated that the idea would be revived today. This goes to show that mature minds think alike."

Addressing Mr. Fang, Zhang Xiaoji said in objection, "Sir, it's only right for a son to inherit his father's estate. Why should he feel ill at ease? If it's to be split in half, that won't be much different from not returning it at all. That will never do."

Mr. Fang came up with another proposal. "If you don't want any share of it, you can continue to live here and manage the estate together with him. In the future, you can pass on your share to your children. How does that sound?"

Zhang Xiaoji replied, "My family has its own estate, albeit modest. My children should by no means take the Guo family's property."

He was so adamant in his refusal that the guests all turned to Guo Qian and advised him to take the offer, but Guo held his ground. Guo then ran to the inner quarters of the house and saw his sister enjoying a cup of wine with Fang-shi. Between sobs, he told them about what had happened and asked his sister to persuade Zhang Xiaoji to accept half of the estate. To his dismay, Shunü only repeated her husband's argument. Both Guo Qian and Fang-shi knelt down and begged her, but she did not relent.

Unable to turn down the offer, Guo Qian finally bowed and accepted. The guests said in admiration, "Mr. Zhang's selflessness is unrivaled in all history!"

Luo Yin [833–910] of the Tang dynasty had this to say in praise of Xiaoyi:

> One who begets a son may not give him wealth;
> One who gives his son wealth may not teach him well.
> In this case, the one who died regained life;
> The one without a penny acquired wealth;
> The petty rogue became a gentleman.
> Glory to Xiaoji, teacher of all time! (Good eulogy.)

The banquet lasted until late into the evening. The next day, Zhang Xiaoji had his wife pack for their return to the Zhang residence. Guo Qian pleaded with them to stay, saying, "You already declined any share of the inheritance. Why don't you go on living here with us so that we can still be together? How can you have the heart to leave?"

"My home is not far from here," said Zhang Xiaoji. "We'll be able to see you daily. It'll be just as if we were living here."

Knowing he would not be able to keep them, Guo Qian said, "In that case, please let me prepare a send-off feast for you before you leave the day after tomorrow. All right?"

Xiaoji agreed.

The next day, Guo Qian set out a grand feast to which he invited many relatives and neighbors, male and female, as well as Zhang Xiaoji's parents. Mrs. Zhang declined the invitation, preferring to stay at home to look after the house. Mr. Zhang Senior was offered the seat of honor at the head of the table, and the rest of the guests took their seats in the order of seniority. The female guests sat with Fang-shi and Shunü in the inner quarters of the house, and there we shall leave them.

It was a sumptuous feast, complete with delicacies of the sea and land. The guests thoroughly enjoyed themselves before the party broke up. After all the guests had left, Zhang Xiaoji remarked to Guo Qian, "My brother-in-law, your father never went into such expense. Be frugal in the future. Don't do this again."

Guo Qian respectfully mumbled his assent.

The next day, Zhang Xiaoji and his wife bade farewell and departed, taking along only their two sons and Shunü's toilette articles. Nothing else was touched. Guo Qian, his wife, and the servants went with them all the way to the Zhang residence, where they were treated to wine before they turned their way home. Henceforth, Guo Qian set even higher demands for himself and became known throughout the area as a man of moral integrity. Because he had suffered so many hardships, he gradually grew to be as tightfisted as his father had been. (*Going too far is just as bad as not going far enough.*) Later, a son was born to him, and he named the boy Guo Shijian [Practicing Frugality]. To prevent his son from repeating his errors, Guo Qian gave his son rigorous training in virtuous behavior. But we will not go into what happened later.

Now, out of admiration for Zhang Xiaoji's virtues, the elders in the neighborhood reported the matter to the county government, which, in turn, reported to the imperial court, which had just been usurped by Cao Pi.[1] In an attempt to win the hearts and minds of the populace, Cao Pi issued Zhang Xiaoji a letter of appointment. However, loathing Cao Pi, the usurper of the throne of the house of Han, Zhang Xiaoji regarded a career in such a court as an insult to his honor, and turned down the offer on the plea that he needed to take care of his aging parents. (*Even more remarkable.*) Later, after his parents passed away, his grief reduced him to a mere shadow of his former self. He took great pains giving them a proper burial, and his fame spread even wider. The prefectural yamen recommended him for an official position on the strength of his filial piety and moral character, but he declined all five appointments to official positions that came his way, pleading illness. When asked why, he smiled without answering. And so he lived a quiet life in his village, taking pleasure in doing farm work and educating his two sons, Zhang Ji and Zhang Shao. Both of them were filial sons with moral integrity and wide learning. Of the many candidates who sought marriage with his sons, he chose two from families with high moral standing for generations back.

One day when he was in his fifties, Zhang Xiaoji had a dream in which the Lord on High summoned him, whereupon both he and his wife fell ill. Their two sons served them medicine and tended to their needs day and night without even bothering to take off their clothes to sleep. Upon hearing about this, Guo Qian went over, along with his son, Guo Shijian, and the two of them nursed Xiaoji as if they were his sons. Thankfully, Xiaoji tried to stop them, but Guo Qian said, "Out of gratitude for your kindness to me, how I wish I could trade places with you! What little I'm doing for you is not worth mentioning."

A few days later, Zhang Xiaoji and his wife passed away at the same time. An exotic fragrance filled their bedchamber at the hour of their death. The neighbors heard the sound of music and the rumbling of a horse-chariot crossing the sky in an easterly direction. We need hardly say that the two sons were overcome with grief. Guo Qian wept until he fainted, and, after coming to, he spit blood. He undertook all the expenses for the funeral, turning a deaf ear to Zhang Xiaoji's two sons' tearful pleas to let them defray the expenses.

One month later, friends who came back from a trip to Luoyang went to the Zhang residence to offer their condolences and said to the two sons, "We were touring Mount Song when we suddenly saw a procession of chariots complete with banners, canopies, and footmen. We hid ourselves behind the trees for a good look and saw a man sitting in a chariot majestically like a king, wearing a crimson robe and a jade belt. On both sides of him were guards wearing brocade uniforms and fancy headgear. We looked carefully and recognized him to be your deceased father. It was such a pleasant surprise that we went out of the woods to pay our respects to him. He dismounted the chariot and greeted us. We asked him, 'When did you accept the appointment to such an eminent position?' Your father replied, 'I am an official not of the mortal world but of the netherworld. The Lord on High assigned me the job of guarding this mountain because of what I did in returning the inheritance to the rightful heir. Please convey a message to my sons and tell them not to feel too sad.' With that, he suddenly disappeared, which made us realize that your father is now a god."

The two sons were overcome with emotion upon hearing this. When the story went around the area, none did not marvel at it and all vied with one another in doing good works. The area thus became known as the Village that Inspires Virtue. During the reign of Emperor Wudi [r. 265–90] of the Jin dynasty, the prefectural yamen recommended the two sons of the Zhang family for official positions on account of their filial piety and moral character. Both of them rose to high ranks. Guo Qian lived to his eighties. Both clans multiplied and formed marital ties from generation to generation.

> The return of the estate was a good deed to his credit;
> The Village that Inspires Virtue enjoys eternal fame.
> All those fighting over family inheritance
> Should feel ashamed when confronting Mount Song.

18

Shi Fu Encounters a Friend at Tanque

One gave back a belt and changed the course of his fate;
One returned gold and carried on the family name.
Good works never fail to turn luck in your favor;
Every thought, mark my words, is known to ghosts and gods.

The above quatrain contains two stories, each about a man in the olden times who did a good deed that earned him moral credit in the netherworld.

The first line, "One gave back a belt and changed the course of his fate," is about Pei Du [765–839], Duke of Jin in the Tang dynasty. Before rising to prominence, Pei Du did not have a penny to his name. All chances of gaining fame and fortune were against him. He went to a fortune-teller to know what lay in store for him, so he could act accordingly. The fortune-teller said, "Better not ask about fame or fortune yet. Promise me you won't be offended before I say what I have to say."

"I'm here to ask for ways to get out of my sorry plight. How would I presume to take offense?"

"You have two vertical lines, called flying snake lines, that extend from both sides of your nose down to your mouth, which means that you will die of hunger in a ditch within a few years' time."

The fortune-teller was not even willing to accept payment for his service.

Being a man quite reconciled to the dictates of fate, Pei Du did not take this dire prediction to heart. (*This theory about vertical lines was proven true in the cases of Deng Tong and Zhou Yafu, but not Duke Pei, which goes to show that man can change his heaven-ordained destiny.*)[1]

One day, he was idly touring Fragrant Hill Temple [in Luoyang] when a shining object on the altar table caught his eye. He went up to the table and saw that it was a jeweled belt. He picked it up and said to himself, "How did such a jeweled belt find its way into this quiet temple?" After he examined the belt for a while, he thought again, "Maybe some highly placed person was here to pay homage to the Buddha, and his servants, when helping him change his clothes, misplaced it in a lapse of attention. They'll surely be back to claim it." And so he sat in the veranda to wait. Before long, a woman in an agitated state entered the temple and walked straight to the altar. After looking the table over, she groaned in despair and sank to the floor in a fit of sobs. Pei Du approached her and asked, "Young lady, why do you cry?"

"My father was sentenced to death on a framed-up charge. I did not know how to appeal, so I came here to pray for the Buddha's blessings. The other day, my father was granted a reprieve and allowed to buy back his freedom. But I had no money to pay for the redemption. So I went from door to door, asking for help from rich families. Yesterday, a highly placed person gave me a jeweled belt out of sympathy. Believing this was the work of the Buddha, I brought the belt here to put it before the statue of the Buddha and offer my thanks. But in my eagerness to redeem my father, I left in a hurry and forgot to take the belt. I didn't realize this until I had already gone a good part of the way. I hastened back to get it, but it appears that someone has already taken it. Without this belt, my father won't be let out of prison." So saying, she broke down in another fit of weeping.

"Don't grieve so, young lady," said Pei Du. "I am the one who picked up the belt, and I've been here waiting." As he handed the belt to the woman, she blinked back her tears and said in gratitude, "May I ask your name, so that my father can come to thank you?"

"I'm sorry that I'm too poor to be of more help to you when such an injustice has been done to your family. To return lost objects to the rightful owner is nothing out of the ordinary. Why thank me?" And so he left without telling her his name.

A few days later, he ran into the fortune-teller again. In amazement, the fortune teller said, "What good deeds have you done?"

"I haven't done any good deeds."

"Your physiognomy has completely changed from the other day. Your moral credit lines [lines under the eyes] are prominently visible now. You will certainly rise to the highest official rank and live to a ripe old age. You will enjoy more riches and honor than I could ever describe in words."

Pei Du thought the fortune-teller was jesting. But sure enough, he did rise to high ranks in the imperial court and served four emperors. He was enfeoffed as Duke of Jin and lived to a ripe old age. There is a poem in testimony:

> The vertical lines over his mouth spelled his doom;
> He returned the belt on Fragrant Hill and changed his fate.
> In Huaixi he won honor by wiping out the rebels;
> For thirty years, on him rested the peace of the land.

The second line of the quatrain, "One returned gold and carried on the family name," is an allusion to the story about Dou Yujun of the Five Dynasties [907–60].

Dou Yujun, a native of Jizhou [present-day Jixian, Hebei], titled Grand Master of Remonstration, was still childless when he was thirty years of age. In a dream one night, he saw his grandfather, who said to him, "You are destined to be childless, and your allotted life span expires next year. But if you make haste and do good works, things may change."

Yujun meekly voiced his agreement. Being already a kindly natured person, he grew all the more devoted to doing good deeds after this dream. Early one evening, he picked up thirty taels of gold and two hundred taels of silver at the side of Yanqing Temple. The next morning, he rose bright and early and went to wait in front of the temple for the owner to return and claim it. Before long, he saw a young man in tears coming in his direction. Yujun approached him and asked him why he was crying. The young man replied, "My father is in jail for a grave crime. I asked all my relatives and acquaintances for money and borrowed two hundred taels of silver and thirty taels of gold. I went yesterday to redeem my father, but the treasury manager was not there, so I had to return home. A relative kept me for dinner and wine. I had a drop too much and somehow lost the money. Now I have nothing with which to redeem my father!"

Noticing that the young man gave the right figure, Mr. Dou retrieved the gold and silver from his sleeve and gave them back to him, saying, "Don't worry! I picked them up at this spot, and I've been waiting for you."

The young man took the package, opened it, and found that the money was intact. He kowtowed and tearfully thanked Mr. Dou. Mr. Dou raised him to his feet and gave him some more money before taking leave of him. Dou Yujun also did other good deeds, which were too many to be enumerated here.

One night, Dou Yujun again saw his grandfather in a dream. "You were destined to have a short and childless life," said his grandfather. "However, because of your many good deeds, including the return of the gold, your name has been submitted to heaven, and you've been granted an extra thirty-six years of life plus five illustrious sons." Henceforth, Mr. Dou became even more of a performer of good works. Later, five sons were born to him in succession. Named Dou Yi, Dou Yan, Dou Kan, Dou Cheng, and Dou Xi, they all rose high in officialdom, serving in the court of the Song dynasty. Mr. Dou himself lived to be eighty-two. One day, after he took a bath, he died while chatting pleasantly with relatives, bidding them farewell. Feng Dao [882–954], with the sobriquet the Contented Old Man, wrote this poem in his honor:

> Mr. Dou of the Yan Mountains
> Followed the right way in teaching his sons.
> The magic toon tree enjoyed a long life;
> The red cassia sported five blossom-laden twigs.

Storyteller, why do you tell these two stories? Well, because the story proper that I am coming to is also about a man who returned lost property to its rightful owner. Though he did not rise to prominence, as did the two men of the prologue stories, he did manage to be spared major calamities and amass a considerable family fortune. Indeed,

> *As you sow, so shall you reap;*
> *As you brew, so shall you drink.*

Our story takes place in a town called Shengze, seventy li from the seat of Wujiang County, Suzhou Prefecture. It was a densely populated town where the people, of an unsophisticated nature, were all engaged in raising silkworms and weaving silk. The men and the women worked hard, and the sound of weaving looms echoed in the air day and night. Silk shops flanking the river numbered in the hundreds. Bolts of silk woven in villages far and near were transported there to be sold at the markets, and the roads were filled to bursting with merchants who had traveled there from all directions to purchase silk products. It was indeed a town that produced the finest silk and satin, and was the very best of the legions of sericultural centers along the lower reaches of the Yangzi River. The following song bears witness:

> *In the warm wind in the second month south of the river,*
> *Everyone is busy raising silkworms.*
> *Keep the worms warm and the mulberry leaves dry,*
> *And the silk will shine like jade fine and bright.*
> *Ten thousand filaments are reeled into yarn;*
> *By the spoolers stand baskets large and small.*
> *The beauties reel the silk and wet their fingers*
> *As they weave the warp and woof on the looms.*
> *Amid the music of the creaking shuttles,*
> *The floral patterned fabric rolls into bolts.*
> *Worry not about the supply of food!*
> *Tomorrow, more merchants will come to town.*

During the Jiajing reign period [1522–66], there lived in this town a man named Shi Fu and his wife, née Yu. They had no children. They raised several baskets of silkworms every year and, with the wife reeling silk yarn and the husband weaving at the family loom, they led a comfortable life. All the other families in this town were quite well off. They usually saved their bolts of silk until they had about ten, or at least five or six, before they went to the markets to sell. Large families with bigger productions did not go to the markets but stayed at home and waited for middlemen to bring clients to them. Being a small producer with limited capital, Shi Fu went to the market every time he had accumulated three or four bolts.

One day, having four bolts in stock, he folded them up nicely, placed them in a cloth bag, and went to the market, which was abuzz with people and activities. Shi Fu headed for a shop he was familiar with, and saw a crowd of sellers gathered at the door and three or four buyers sitting inside. The shopkeeper was behind the counter, examining the bolts of silk and calling out the prices. Shi Fu threaded his way through the crowd and gave the shopkeeper his silk. The shopkeeper took the cloth bag, opened it, examined the bolts one by one, weighed them on his scales, chanted the prices, and gave them to a merchant, saying, "This Mr. Shi is an honest man. You'll have no trouble. Give him your finest silver."

And indeed, the buyer picked silver of the finest quality and paid Shi Fu. Shi Fu took out a small steelyard that he had brought with him and weighed the silver. Believing he was slightly shortchanged, he asked for one or two maces more, and the deal was closed. He then asked for a piece of paper, wrapped up the silver with it, stuffed the packet in his money belt, put away his steelyard and his cloth bag, and, joining his hands in a salute to the shopkeeper, thanked him, and started on his way back.

Before he was a stone's throw from the shop, he caught sight of a small blue cloth parcel at the edge of the sidewalk in front of a shop. He walked up to it, picked it up, slipped it into his sleeve, and went to an open space so that he could stop and look at it. As he untied the parcel, there came into view two ingots plus three or four small pieces of silver and a copper coin. He weighed them in his hands and found them to be more than six taels. In delight, he thought, "Today's my lucky day! This can be a boost to my business." Quickly he wrapped them up, stuffed the parcel into his money belt, and headed home. As he walked, he thought, "The loom we already have at home is enough for our daily needs. With this silver, I can buy another loom, which will bring in extra income every month. We'll save the extra money and not use it, just as if we don't have it. After one year, we will have saved up a tidy sum. Then the year after that, we'll buy another loom, which will bring in even more extra profit. In ten years, we'll have a thousand taels of silver. By that time, we'll be able to build a larger house and buy more land."

As he happily did his calculations, he was soon approaching home. Suddenly, he started on a new train of thought: "If it was a rich man who lost this parcel of silver, it's like an ox shedding one hair. It won't make any difference to him. There's no reason why I can't enjoy it. But what if it was a traveling merchant? He made the money through hard work, leaving his wife and children at home and putting up with the hardships of a life on the road. He must be upset about the loss. If it was someone with a large business, he wouldn't mind the loss too much because he can always make up for the loss in other ways. But if it was a petty trader with no more money for capital than this, or if it was someone like me, working hard for a living, he must have gotten the money by selling his silk, and these two ingots could very well be what he needs for survival. If he lost them, it would be as if his last breath were gone. His good and kind family members will blame one another for the loss of their means of living, and may have to sell off themselves or the children. If they are bad-tempered, they may even get carried away with anger and die. (*One who thinks such thoughts is among the top category of good people.*) Even though it won't be too much of a sin for me to keep what I found, I'll think about it too often and I won't have peace of mind when I spend it. And this silver may not exactly help me strike it rich. Haven't I been living all right all these years without this parcel of silver? I'd better go back to the spot where I found it and wait for the owner to come and claim it. If I can return it, I'll be able to breathe easier." So thinking, he turned around and retraced his steps. Indeed:

> Evil thoughts may turn into kind ones;
> Kind thoughts may turn into evil ones.
> Be advised: do everything that is good;
> Stay away from everything that is bad.

So Shi Fu went back to the spot where he had found the parcel. He waited for the longest time by the counter of the shop, but no one came to claim it. He had left home without eating, and now he began to feel hungry. He had a mind to go home for lunch before returning, but, afraid that the one who had lost the money would be back during his absence, he felt obliged to continue waiting in spite of the pangs of hunger. Before long, a young man looking like a farmer ran up in a sweat and barged into the shop. "Shopkeeper," he said at the top of his voice, "I left my silver on your counter. Did you see it?"

"What a horrible man!" said the shopkeeper. "I gave you the silver this morning, and now you come back to ask me for it! If you left something on the counter, someone would have taken it, whatever the amount."

Stamping his feet, the young man said, "That money was to be used on my farm. And now it's gone! What am I going to do?"

Shi Fu asked, "How much did you have?"

"Six taels and two maces of fine silver, the amount I got here from selling my silk."

"What did you wrap it in?" asked Shi Fu. "How many pieces were there?"

"There were two large ingots and three or four small pieces. I wrapped them up in a piece of blue cloth."

"In that case, you have nothing to worry about. I picked up the parcel. I've been waiting here for you for quite some time now." So saying, he took the parcel from his money belt and gave it to the young man. The young man thanked him profusely and, upon opening the parcel, found the silver intact.

Passersby gathered around them as if to watch an intriguing show. "Where did you find the silver?" they asked.

Shi Fu replied, pointing, "At the edge of the sidewalk."

The young man said, "Such a kind-hearted man is hard to come by. He even waited here for me to show up. Another man wouldn't have done this. Now it's as if *I* have found money. I'll be glad to share it with you, brother, half and half."

"If I wanted it, why didn't I take all of it? Why would I want to take half of it from you?"

"Well, how about one tael as a reward, just for you to buy sweets with?"

Shi Fu said, laughing, "What a blockhead! I turned down the money, all six taels of it. Why would I take one tael now?"

"If you don't want money, what can I thank you with?"

The bystanders put in, "This man looks like a kind person. Since he doesn't want a reward, why don't you take him to a wineshop and treat him to a few cups of wine, just to show your gratitude?"

"Right!" the young man agreed and invited Shi Fu to go with him to a wineshop.

"You don't have to do this," objected Shi Fu. "I have work to do at home. I mustn't stay any longer." With that, he turned to go, ignoring the young man's pleas.

"What a lucky man you are," the bystanders commented to the young man. "You got your lost money back without even having to give a reward."

"Yes," said the shopkeeper. "I had no idea there was such a good man in this world."

The young man put away his parcel, thanked the shopkeeper, and walked down the steps. The onlookers also went their separate ways, commenting as they went. One said, "That Shi Fu is an idiot, waiting like that for the owner instead of pocketing what he found." One said, "That man accumulated credit in the netherworld. He'll surely be rewarded in the future." Let us say no more of the onlookers but follow Shi Fu home.

When Shi Fu arrived at home, his wife asked, "What took you so long?"

"Oh, you have no idea! I was almost home when I turned back because of something that had happened. That was what took me so long."

"What was it?"

After Shi Fu told her about his returning money he had found, his wife said, "You did well. As the ancients said, 'A windfall doesn't make a poor man rich.' If we kept something that we weren't destined to have, it would probably bring us bad luck, for all we know."

"That's exactly why I gave it back," said Shi Fu.

Neither the husband nor the wife believed that pocketing lost money was something to rejoice over. Instead, they found peace of mind in returning the money. There is no lack of upper-class gentlemen who tend to forget what is right at the mere sight of money. How surprising that a man and a woman of humble status had such good sense!

> Wedded couples must act with one heart and mind;
> He sings, she follows; these two live virtuous lives.
> To them, ten thousand taels of silver is so much dirt,
> But one little act of kindness is worth a ton of gold.

Henceforth, Shi Fu's sericultural business yielded considerably more annual profit than before, and family circumstances began to improve. (*Heaven compensates the kind-hearted.*)

In sericulture, there are ten things to watch for.[2] When and how much to feed the silkworms is determined by the two different shades of color their bodies assume. There are also eight rules to observe.[3] There are three situations in which the silkworms need to be put far apart from one another, and five places that must be spacious.[4] Of first importance is breed selection. If the breed is good, the cocoons are small, shiny, thick, firm, and narrow, and the silk is best for reeling into silk yarn. Inferior breeds of silkworm are only good for silk floss and the profit is just a fraction of what can be made from fine silk. Then there is luck. Lucky silkworm growers can make silk out of inferior breeds. Those without luck get nothing more than silk floss out of the best breeds of silkworms. In the north, silkworms molt three times, whereas those in the south molt four times. They all need to be fed as soon as they emerge from their pupal state. In addition, silkworms are sensitive to heat and cold. A mild temperature is best, but because the hours of the day are, for them, comparable to the four seasons—with morning and late afternoon being equivalent to spring and autumn, noon to summer, and night to winter—it is most difficult to make sure that the temperature is right. Along the lower reaches of the Yangzi River, there is a song that goes:

> The fourth month is the hardest month of all;
> The silkworms like it mild; the wheat likes it cold.
> The rice seedlings need the sun; the hemp needs rain;
> The girls picking mulberry leaves want them nice and dry.

Partly because Shi Fu picked better breeds of silkworms and partly because he was lucky, none of his silkworms turned out to be the silk floss kind. The silk filaments he harvested were fine, round, tight, even, spotless, and sparkling. Not one filament was knotty or of uneven width. And his silkworms per tray produced much more silk than average. The silk fabrics he wove the usual way were so dazzlingly shiny that clients snapped them up, paying him more than he asked for and thus adding to the profit he made out of each bolt. With things going so well for him, he bought three or four more looms within several years. His family circumstances thrived, and in the neighborhood he came to be called Shi Runze [Shiny Silk]. When a son was born to him, he honored the Bodhisattva Guanyin as the child's guardian and named him Guanbao [Protected by Guanyin]. At two years old, the child had grown to be a fine boy with well-formed eyebrows and bright eyes.

Let us skip irrelevant details and come to the year when mulberry leaves were in short supply throughout the town after the silkworms had just molted a third time. Shi Fu also had only enough mulberry leaves to last for two days. He grew alarmed because he had no idea where to buy them. Usually, at this time of the silkworm-raising season, the weather is chilly and humid, and the leaves fed to the silkworms are wet with cold dew. In such conditions, about half of the silkworms die off, leaving enough mulberry leaves for the ones that survive. But in the year of which we speak, the weather was warm and the silkworms in every household did well, hence the shortage of leaves.

While Shi Fu fretted and wondered where to buy mulberry leaves, he heard the neighbors say that there was an ample supply of leftover mulberry leaves on Dongting Hill and that about ten families were planning to cross the lake on a purchasing trip. Shi Fu equipped himself with some silver and, carrying along his bedding in a bundle, joined the group of buyers in their boat. The scull was set in motion in early afternoon. They left the town, went past Pingwang, and came to a village called Tanque located on the side of Tai Lake, forty li from the town of Shengze. As it was by now too late in the day to cross the lake, they moved the boat into a small harbor, tied it to its mooring place, and laid down the oars. When they set about making preparations for supper, they realized that they had forgotten to bring a flint stone. Someone asked, "Who would be willing to go ashore and get something to start a fire with?"

As if prodded on by supernatural beings, Shi Fu said, "I'll go." (*No supernatural being prodded him at this point. It was all thanks to his act of returning lost gold to its rightful owner.*) Picking up a bundle of hemp stalks, he jumped on shore. All he saw was one closed door after another. You may well ask, why were the doors all closed when it was not yet dark? Well, the truth of the matter is, what silkworm raisers dread most is to have strangers come to their door in the forty days from the hatching to the spinning of the cocoons. During this period, all the families close their doors tightly and refrain from mutual visits, whatever happens. After walking past several doors, Shi Fu said to himself in surprise, "Are these people afraid that some ghosts are here to drag them off? Imagine closing the door when the sun is still up!" Then suddenly he remembered: "Phooey! I'm an old hand at raising silkworms. How can I forget that silkworm raisers are in greatest fear of strangers coming to ask for a torch. What am I doing? Now where shall I go to get a fire?" He was about to turn back when he thought again, "It would have been all right if I hadn't promised. If I go back empty-handed and someone else goes out and gets a fire, I won't look so good. Maybe there is a house or two without silkworms. Who knows?" So he walked on.

At the sight of a door standing ajar, he ran recklessly up to the house. Not daring to barge in, he stood under the eaves and, craning his neck, called out, "Anybody home?"

A woman emerged from inside, asking, "Who is it?"

With an apologetic smile, Shi Fu said, "Madam, could you light a fire for me?"

"At this time of the year, other families won't do this for you, but this household has no such taboos. I'll light one for you."

"Thank you so much!" said Shi Fu as he handed his bundle of hemp stalks to her. The woman took it, went in, and reemerged with one end of the bundle alight. Shi Fu took it, thanked her, gave his apologies for having put her to inconvenience, and turned to go back. Before he had passed two doors, a voice called out from behind, "Come back, you who came for fire! You dropped something!"

"What did I drop?" said Shi Fu to himself as he went back.

"You dropped your money belt here," said the woman as she handed it back to him.

Thankfully, Shi Fu said, "Such a kind-hearted person like you is hard to come by, madam."

"Why thank me? Some years ago, my husband was selling silk in Shengze when he dropped more than six taels of silver. A kind man found it and waited at the spot until my husband went back to look for it. That man returned the packet of silver intact to my husband without taking even a drop of wine that my husband offered to him. Now, that's a kind-hearted person for you!"

Surprised that what the woman had described was exactly what had happened to him years before, he asked, "When did that happen?"

Counting on her fingers, the woman said, "It's been six years."

"To be frank with you, madam, I'm also a Shengze native. I also found more than six taels of silver and waited for the owner until he came back to claim it. He was a silk seller. He invited me to a wineshop, but I declined. Might he be your husband?"

"You don't say!" exclaimed the woman. "Let me bring my husband out, and you'll know if it was him."

Worried that his boat companions might grow anxious, Shi Fu was going to say no, but his bundle of hemp stalks was burning up. So he said, "Madam, that can wait. I would be more than grateful if you could light a piece of touch-paper for me so that I can go back and start a fire."

Without answering, the woman disappeared into the house. In a trice, she reemerged with a young man. Even though six years had passed, both men easily recognized each other, and the young man saw that the visitor was indeed the good man who had returned his money to him. Truly,

> Like a duckweed floating on the vast sea,
> You never know whom you may meet one day.

The young man said with a deep bow, "I often think of you, but I had no idea where to find you and pay my respects to you. I never dreamed that heaven would bring you here today."

Shi Fu hastened to return the courtesy. After the two men's exchange of greetings, the woman also saluted Shi Fu.

"You were so kind to me," said the young man. "But in the rush of the moment, I forgot to ask for your name and address. Later I did go several times to your town to sell silk. I asked the shopkeepers, but they didn't know you, and I searched all around the town for you but also in vain. I never expected to see you here! Please sit inside!"

"You're too kind, but some friends of mine are waiting in the boat for me to bring back fire to cook supper with. I have to go."

"Why don't you bring all of them here?" asked the young man.

"That is preposterous!" Shi Fu objected.

"Well, at least you can come back here after you deliver the fire to them," said the young man, whereupon he told his wife to bring another torch. After his wife hurried into the inner section of the house, he turned to Shi Fu and asked, "What is your honorable name and courtesy name? Where are you heading?"

"My name is Shi Fu, my sobriquet Runze. My friends and I are on our way to Dongting Hill to buy mulberry leaves."

"There are plenty of mulberry leaves in my yard. You can stay in this humble house tonight and let the others go their way. I'll escort you back to your home by boat tomorrow. What do you say?" (*Virtue pays.*)

Delighted that there were mulberry leaves to be had right at the house, Shi Fu said, "If so, I need not cross the lake. But let me go and take leave of my friends first."

At this point, the woman brought fire. The young man took it and said, "I'll go together with you, my brother." He then told his wife to prepare dinner. Right away, the two men went to the boat and passed the fire to those in the boat.

The men in the boat who had worn their eyes out looking for Shi Fu to return grumbled, "Weren't you just out to get a fire? What could have taken you so long?"

"Oh, you have no idea! People in these parts all raise silkworms. So I wasn't able to get a fire. Then I met this friend of mine and stopped for a little chat. That's why I was late. Please don't be angry." Then he continued, "This friend of mine happens to have some mulberry leaves at home. I've already bought them, so I won't go with you across the lake. My baggage is in the boat. Could you give it to me?"

His boat companions found his baggage and held it out for him. The young man took it, saying, "Let me carry it!" Thereupon Shi Fu said at the top of his voice, "Good-bye for now, everyone! I'll see you after I return home!"

Having thus bid farewell to his fellow townsmen, he joined the young man and asked, "Everything happened so quickly just now that I forgot to ask your name."

"I'm Zhu En, courtesy name Deyi."

"How old are you?"

"Twenty-eight."

"So I'm eight years older than you are. Do you live with your parents?"

"My father passed away many years ago. I live with my mother. She's sixty-eight now. She's a vegetarian."

They chatted as they walked along and before they knew it, they were already at Zhu En's door. Zhu En pushed the door open and invited Shi Fu into the main room, where a lamp on the table had already been lit. Zhu En put down the baggage and called out, "Wife! Bring in tea!" Before the words were quite out of his mouth, his wife appeared by the door curtain and held out two cups of tea for Zhu En, who took them and handed one cup to Shi Fu, keeping the other one for himself. He asked again, "Wife, have you slaughtered a chicken?"

"I've been waiting for you to help me do it," replied his wife.

Quickly, Zhu En put down the tea and jumped up to pick a chicken from the coop against the left wall of the room. Shi Fu stepped forward and said, stopping him, "Since we're friends, the most simple food will be enough to show your hospitality. Why take a life? What's more, the chickens must already be asleep by this time. How would I have the heart to kill one?"

Knowing him to be a straightforward man, Zhu En complied and sat down. "All right, I'll kill one tomorrow and serve it for dinner," he said. Then he called out to his wife, "Let's not kill a chicken today. Bring over whatever food you have in the kitchen. Don't keep the guest hungry. Be sure the wine is nice and warm!"

"I shouldn't be troubling you like this at such a busy time. Luckily you don't have any taboos in this house."

"To tell you the truth," said Zhu En, "this house used to have the most taboos in this neighborhood, but now, this is the only house without any taboo."

"Why?"

"After you returned my money to me that year, I came to understand that everything is determined by fate, not by whether one does or doesn't follow taboos. From that time on, I cared nothing about the taboos, and I still made good profit year after year, which goes to show that taboos don't mean a thing. It's we human beings who are frightening ourselves with our imaginations of the doings of ghosts and gods. It's human beings who dream up demons and believe in them."

"You are a wise man," said Shi Fu. "There's so much truth in what you said."

"There's another remarkable thing: We always raised ten trays of silkworms every year, and we always had to buy mulberry leaves in addition to the supply from the trees in our own yard. This year, we've got fifteen trays of silkworms and we still have the same number of mulberry trees in the yard. And yet, we not only have enough leaves for ourselves but also a lot of surplus, enough to help you out. These leaves seem to have grown just for you. Isn't this fate?"

"You do have a point. Our meeting today is also predestined. We got to see each other the first time because you lost something. And we meet again today because I lost something, and then your wife returned it to me and brought up what had happened years ago."

"It looks like it's all because there's a predestined bond between the two of us. Shall we take a vow of brotherhood? What do you say?"

"I have no brother. If you don't think I'm unworthy, I would be only too glad to take the vow."

There and then, the two of them took eight bows and became sworn brothers. At Shi Fu's request, Zhu En brought his mother out to accept Shi Fu's bows. Zhu En then called his wife out to exchange greetings with his newly acquired brother. In the exuberance of the joy that permeated the house, wine and the usual fare of fish and meat were laid on the table. As the two men toasted each other, Zhu En asked, "How many sons do you have, my brother?"

"Only one. He's two years old. How many do you have?"

"I have only a daughter, also two years old." He had his wife bring the baby over for Shi Fu to see.

"Brother," said Zhu En again, "shall we form a marriage alliance between our two families?"

"That would be best. I'm just afraid that my family is too poor to claim such a kinship with yours," Shi Fu demurred.

"What a thing to say, my brother!"

Right away, they agreed on the marriage alliance. Feeling even closer to each other, they drank until midnight. Zhu En laid a door panel across two benches against the right wall of the main room and spread a straw mat on the makeshift bed. Shi Fu opened his baggage, took out his quilt, and shook it well before laying it in bed. After bidding him good night, Zhu En closed the door that separated the main room from the inner section of the house and went inside. Shi Fu blew out the lamp and lay down. As he tossed and turned, unable to fall asleep, he heard the chickens cackle nonstop in the coop. "Why are the chickens so noisy?" he thought. About two hours later, the chickens suddenly made terrible noises, as if they had been bitten. Thinking that there must be a yellow weasel preying on them, Shi Fu leaped up from bed, threw some clothes over his shoulders, and rushed over to the coop. What followed happened in less time than it takes to tell: he had just taken three or four steps before something fell on his makeshift bed with a deafening crash. Shi Fu was so frightened that he stood transfixed.

Zhu En was feeding the silkworms with his mother and his wife when they heard the chickens cackling. Also believing that a yellow weasel was around, he quickly lit a lamp and went to look. He had barely taken one step before the crashing sound burst on his ears. Stamping his feet, he cried out, "Good grief! I killed my brother! What am I going to do?" As he dashed off, his mother and his wife, also appalled, exclaimed, "Oh no!" And they followed on his heels.

Zhu En had just opened the middle door and gotten a foot inside when he saw Shi Fu standing in the middle of the room. In happy astonishment, Zhu En said, "My brother, I was almost scared to death! Luckily you got up in time and were spared."

"If the chickens had not made so much noise, I wouldn't have gotten up to look, and would have been smashed to a pulp. But what was it that fell?"

"It must have been the axle that was lying on the rafter. I wonder why it fell." By the light of the lamp, they saw that the door panel had been smashed to smithereens, and both benches had been knocked down. The axle, as thick as a water bucket, had rolled over to rest against the wall. Shi Fu was so frightened that he stuck out his tongue and it was some time before he remembered to retract it. Zhu En's mother and wife went inside, relieved that Shi Fu had emerged unscathed. The chickens had also quieted down.

"My brother," said Zhu Fu, "you asked us not to slaughter any of the chickens, and what do you know, they saved your life!"

The two of them forthwith vowed never to kill living beings again. There is a poem in testimony:

> *A siskin did a good turn to Yang Bao of old;*[5]
> *A few chickens repay a debt to Shi Fu of today.*
> *If animals have such good sense,*
> *Why do humans kill one another?*

Zhu En lit another lamp, rolled up Shi Fu's bedding, spread a layer of straw on the floor, and made another makeshift bed for Shi Fu. When they arose the next morning, it was raining outside. After breakfast, Shi Fu wanted to return home, but Zhu En said, "This is such a special occasion. You must stay for one more day. I'll escort you home tomorrow morning."

"You and I are in a busy season. One more day would make both of us feel uneasy. I'd better go now. When we have time, we can chat for days on end without having to worry about anything."

"But there is nothing to worry about. You would have gone to Dongding Hill anyway. Stay, and let's spend another day chatting."

Zhu En's mother also came out to press him to stay. So he had to oblige them. Sometime before noon, a severe windstorm sprang up, blowing sand and felling trees. It was followed by a downpour of rain. Zhu En said, "Heaven sent you to me, my brother. Luckily you didn't go. Those crossing the lake today are in danger."

"You're right. I didn't know there would be such a strong wind. It's really scary!"

The wind did not die down until evening. The rain also stopped. Shi Fu spent another night there. By the time he arose the next morning, Zhu En had already finished picking the mulberry leaves for him and gotten the family boat ready. After breakfast, they packed in preparation for their journey. Shi Fu wanted to pay Zhu En for the mulberry leaves but, believing that he would reject his offer, said, "My good brother, I don't think you'll be willing to take money for the leaves, so I'm not going to insist. But you're needed in the house. Accompanying me home will take you two days. Won't it be good for both of us if I hire a boatman?"

"I would like to know where you live, so that I can come to see you in the future. Why don't you want me to go with you? They don't need me at home at this time."

Finding it difficult to turn him down when he was so determined, Shi Fu bade farewell to Zhu En's mother and wife and boarded the boat. Zhu En set his scull in motion and the boat got under way.

They arrived in Shengze a little after lunchtime. Shi Fu moored the boat and the two of them carried the mulberry leaves ashore. The neighbors, worried about the fate of those out on the lake in the storm of the day before, were waiting at their own doors for news. Upon seeing Shi Fu, they exclaimed in unison, "Hooray! They're back!" Eagerly they approached him and asked, "Where are the others? How many leaves did you all buy?"

Shi Fu replied, "I ran into a relative at Tanque and he gave me leaves that he had in surplus. I didn't cross the lake with the rest of the group."

"Lucky you!" they said. "Do you know if they had a hard time crossing the lake?"

"They should be all right," Shi Fu assured them.

"That's good to know," they said.

Shi Fu asked a few of his good friends to help him carry the leaves to his home. After he said his thanks to them, they went their separate ways. His wife came out and, seeing him, said, "I was worried about you. How did you manage to cross the lake in such a windstorm yesterday?"

"Come and greet Brother Zhu first. I'll tell you everything later."

Zhu En stepped forward and bowed deeply. Yu-shi returned the greeting. Shi Fu said, "Take a seat, my good brother. Wife, serve tea and bring our son over to pay respects to his future father-in-law."

Never having seen Zhu En before, Yu-shi wondered why he called the visitor his brother and his son's future father-in-law. Quickly she poured out two cups of tea and led her son out.

Shi Fu took the tea and offered one cup to Zhu En. Then he put his own cup aside, gathered his son into his arms, and carried him over for Zhu En to look at. The boy's refined features delighted Zhu En. He put down his cup of tea and took the boy into his arms. The boy smiled, as if he knew the man, and was not the least shy, as was his wont with strangers.

Shi Fu said to his wife, "Mr. Zhu is the very person who lost his silver years ago. He lives in Tanque."

"Oh I see. How did you two meet?"

Shi Fu related how he had inadvertently dropped his money belt when asking for a fire the other evening, how he learned from the ensuing conversation who his host was, how he was kept in the Zhu residence and swore brotherhood with Zhu, how they agreed to form a marriage alliance between their children, how they refrained from killing a chicken, how the chickens warned him against the falling of the axle, why he did not cross the lake, and how he had come home with the leaves. Yu-shi was overcome by amazement and delight, and her heart swelled with gratitude. Without a moment's delay, she set about preparing wine and dinner.

They were in the midst of drinking when loud wails in neighboring houses came to their ears. Wondering what was afoot, Shi Fu went out to inquire. What had happened was that the boat carrying those back from their leaf-buying mission had capsized in the lake the day before. All on board, about ten in total, drowned— except one, who was the bearer of the news. He had floated on a broken piece of the boat and a fisherman had rescued him. Shi Fu was flabbergasted. He went back into the house and told Zhu En and his wife. Joining his palms, he said thanks to heaven and continued to say, "If my good brother hadn't made me stay, I would have died!"

Zhu En said, "This is because of all the good deeds you have done. It has nothing to do with me." (*Heaven goes out of its way to protect people of virtue as well as to help those who wish to repay their benefactors. Do not say that heaven knows nothing.*)

Shi Fu kept Zhu En for the night. After breakfast the next morning, Shi Fu said, 'I would like to ask you to stay for a few more days, but, knowing how busy you are at home, I wouldn't presume to keep you. I'll invite you again after the busy season is over."

"We can easily travel back and forth. There's no need for invitations."

Shi Fu offered him two boxes of gifts bought specially for the occasion, gifts that Zhu En did not decline. After bidding farewell to Yu-shi, he untied the ropes and got the boat under way. Shi Fu accompanied him all the way out of the town border before taking leave of him. Truly,

> *Their friendship started from the return of silver;*
> *Their brotherly bond grew too deep for today's parting.*

That year, having made several times more profit than he had done in previous years, Shi Fu planned to buy another loom, but his house was not big enough to accommodate it. Generally speaking, when fortune favors someone, everything will go his way. Shi Fu was raking his mind for a way to accommodate a new loom when it so happened that a neighboring family was all eagerness to sell its two small rooms, attributing its losses in the silkworm business for years on end to the bad feng shui of the house. This offer could not have suited Shi Fu better. The neighbor had started out volunteering a reduction in price when there were no buyers. When Shi Fu came along and made an offer, the seller turned around and, claiming that the feng shui was superior, asked for more than the original price, deliberately making things difficult for Shi Fu. Only after the seller squeezed maximum advantage from the deal did he vacate the premises in contentment, leaving the house a shambles. Shi Fu engaged workers to renovate the house and, in the meantime, picked an auspicious day for the placing of the loom.

As he was hoeing the ground to make a pit where he could place the loom, Shi Fu turned up a large square tile when he had dug about a foot deep. Removing the tile, he saw underneath it a round jar brimming over with rotten rice.

"How wasteful that a jar of rice was buried underground!' said Shi Fu to himself. But then he thought, "The top layer is all rotten, but the middle part may still be good." He threw down his hoe and scraped away the top layer with his hands. Before he had gotten one inch deep, he caught sight of something as white as snow. A closer examination revealed it to be an ingot of the finest silver, narrow in the middle and turning upward at both ends. Shi Fu was about to dig further down when he thought better of it, because he was afraid the workmen might stumble upon him and spread the word around. In haste, he covered up the spot with the earth he had removed and went to tell his wife about it. In the evening, after the workmen left, husband and wife began to act and, to their immense joy, found about a thousand taels of silver.

Having escaped two calamities and gained this windfall, Shi Fu became all the more devoted to good works. He did his utmost whenever he could but did not force himself to seek the impossible. (*If everyone were like him, this world would be nothing less than a paradise.*) Thus he began to gain respect in the neighborhood as a venerable elder. He and his wife continued to live a frugal life while working hard to build up the family business. Within ten years, their family wealth grew to thousands of taels of silver. They bought a grand mansion nearby, acquired thirty to forty looms, and engaged a good number of servants and page boys, until there was nothing more they could ask for in their impressive estate. They also engaged a live-in tutor for their son, Guanbao, who had now been given the school name of Deyin. They then sent betrothal gifts over to the Zhu residence for the engagement of their son with Zhu En's daughter. As the proverb puts it so well, "All those within the six degrees of kinship share the same fate." Zhu En's family circumstances also began to prosper. The two men saw a great deal of each other's company and were as devoted to each other as brothers born of the same parents.

Let us get on with our story. In Shi Fu's newly bought house, every room was now in good condition except the main hall, which was on the point of falling apart and therefore needed a good renovation job. Being of humble background and accustomed to hard work, Shi Fu joined the workmen, in spite of his status as a rich man, in carrying the bricks and tiles, fetching water, and applying plaster. Not knowing that he did this out of a frugal and industrious nature, the men thought that he was there to oversee their work and, as a consequence, everyone put his best foot forward.

About half a month later, the pillars of the house were driven into the ground and the beams were ready to be hoisted onto them on a chosen auspicious day. While the workmen were away at the feast to pray for good luck, Shi Fu, left all alone by himself, checked the base of each pillar and shimmed those that were not perfectly level with the ground. Noticing that the base of the middle pillar on the left side of the room was uneven, he tried to slip a brick underneath, but, strangely enough, however he tried, inserting the brick from the left and from the right, the pedestal remained unsteady. He thought he might as well dig open the ground around it and see what was wrong. As he dug, he saw a triangular sandstone with the pointed top pressed against the bottom of the pedestal. "What a lousy job they did!" he said to himself. "How could they have left this stone here, right under the pedestal?" As he tried to lift the stone, it readily gave way, revealing, to his surprise, a large pile of snow-white silver ingots of all sizes. The ones on top, each of the same size and tied in the middle by a red cotton yarn, dazzled the eye with their sharp contrast of colors. He was filled with joy and amazement—joy at the windfall and amazement at the bright colors of the ingots and the red yarn, even though the silver must have been stored there for a good many years.

In the excitement of the moment, he stuffed his clothes with ingots of silver, put the stone back in its place, dashed off to his room, and poured the ingots onto the bed. Yu-shi hastened to ask, "Where did you get them?"

Before he found time to answer her, Shi Fu saw that their son was also in the room and cried out, "Guanbao, follow me!" With that, he raced off again. Yu-shi immediately caught on to what was happening.

And so father and son went to the spot. With the son keeping watch, Shi Fu transported the silver in several trips while the workmen were still away at the feast. It was after his job was completed that he told his wife everything. Husband, wife, and son were beside themselves with joy. They closed the door and put the silver away. There were more than two thousand taels in all, of which only eight ingots, each exactly three taels, had red yarn around them. After the room was put back in order, Shi Fu wanted to bow to heaven and earth. So he put on a scarf, a hat, and a gown, and walked out the door. At this point, the workmen came back to work. When they began busily installing the beams and putting up the pillars, they noticed the mess around the base of one pillar. "Who made this mess?" they said. "We'll have to do this spot all over again."

Shi Fu said, "That's because you did a poor job. You'd better fix it." Realizing this was the doing of the master of the house, the workmen dared not say another word but set about cleaning up the mess, knowing nothing of the secret.

Looking up at the sky, Shi Fu said, "It's going to be broad daylight soon. Get the job done quickly!"

At these words, the workers picked up speed. Soon, all the pillars and the beams were ready. A large plate filled with steamed buns was brought out for the workmen to throw down from the beams in a ritual celebrating the installation of the beams. The neighbors also came with offers of fruit and wine to congratulate Shi Fu. Having found a trove of treasure, Shi Fu was all the more jubilant and drank until he was half tipsy. Indeed,

> A happy event cheers one's spirit;
> A midautumn moon shines with brighter light.

After sending off the neighbors, Shi Fu took off his scarf, hat, and gown and, in his short jacket and trousers, joined the workmen in their labor. He was outside the house a little before noon when he saw an old man in his sixties with gray eyebrows and white hair approaching the door. After looking around for a while, the old man asked, "Is this the Shi residence?"

"Yes," replied Shi Fu. "Whom are you looking for?"

"The master of the house. I have a question for him."

"I am the master of the house. What question do you have for me, sir? Please come and sit down inside."

The old man looked him up and down and said, "Are you really the master of the house?"

Shi Fu said, laughing, "The master of the house is but a commoner. Why would I lie?"

Raising a hand, the old man said, "All right, I won't stand on ceremony with you. Let's step aside. I want to have a word with you." He pulled Shi Fu to one side and asked, "Were the beams of the house put on earlier today before broad daylight?"

"Yes."

"Did you find money under the middle pillar on the left side of the room?"

Shi Fu was startled at this question. "How did he know?" he wondered. "Can he be a supernatural being?" Not daring to hide anything, since the old man already knew his secret, he said, "Yes, I did find some."

"Are there eight ingots with red yarn on each one?"

All the more surprised, Shi Fu said, "Yes, but how come you know so much?"

"These eight ingots of silver belong to this old man. That's why I know."

"If they're yours, why were they under a pillar in my house?"

"Let me tell you why. My name is Bo Youshou. I live in a town called Huangjiangjing. My wife and I have no children. The front portion of our house is a shop where we sell snacks like cakes and steamed buns. Every time we saved three taels' worth of loose pieces of silver from our daily expenditures, we had them melted and made into an ingot. My wife, in her childishness, tied a red yarn around each of them in the middle. It's just a gesture to show how much store she sets by them. Because we live in a humble house, she made a point of stuffing them into a pillow and then sewing it up, so that they wouldn't be seen by outsiders. We thought we were perfectly safe. Throughout the years, we've saved eight ingots, which we thought would be enough for our burial expenses after we die.

"Now, something entirely unexpected happened. At the fifth strike of the watch-drum this morning before daybreak, I saw in my dream that there walked out of my pillow eight little boys wearing white robes, each with a red ribbon around his waist. They gathered by my bedside to consult one another. One said, 'At the first light this morning, pillars and beams will be installed in Mr. Shi's house in Shengze. All those relatives of ours who should be at his house by now are already there. It's time we join them.' Another one asked, 'Where in the house are they?' One replied, 'They're all under the middle pillar on the left side of the main hall.' And then they started going off. One said, 'We've been living here for so long that we'll be too heartless if we go without saying good-bye.' (*Yes, it would be heartless indeed. These eight ingots are the more loving kind.*) So they turned back and said to me, 'We're ever so grateful to you for having taken care of us for so long. Now that we're leaving you, please don't take offense!'

"At that point in my dream, I still had no idea who those eight boys were or where they had come from. I asked, 'When did the eight of you come? Why don't I know you?' One of them replied, 'We only got to see you once after we came to your house. You immediately put us under your head and dismissed us from your thoughts. That's why we know you but you don't know us.' (*Money is like a foun-tain. It takes joy in flowing away, not to return.*) Pointing at the red ribbon around his waist, he said, 'You gave me this the first time we met. Remember?'

"I couldn't remember when I gave that to him. Without a son of my own, I liked their fresh-faced looks so much that I wanted to adopt them. So I said to them, 'Since you're already here, why don't you stay on as my sons and help me out? Why go elsewhere?'

"All eight of them burst out laughing and said, 'You want to adopt us just so that we can take care of your burial expenses, but we're destined for a more pros-perous place. Too bad you are not meant to enjoy us.' And so they all went out. While I felt that I was still lying in bed, somehow my body was at the door trying to keep them. But however hard I tried, they never even took a look back. I only heard them say, 'We'll be late. Quick!' And they ran off. I ran after them but tripped over some grass roots and woke up in alarm. Then I told my wife about it. We wondered if something strange had happened to the eight ingots. So at the crack of dawn we opened the pillow for a look and found them all gone. I came here just to check if that dream of mine was true or not. Now I know it's true."

Shi Fu was aghast. "How remarkable!" he exclaimed. "Don't feel bad, sir. Follow me in and sit for a while."

"Now that I've confirmed what I dreamed of, I should be going."

"You've come such a long way. You must be hungry by now. We've got refresh-ments in the house. Please have some!"

Mr. Bo did not decline the offer of refreshments and followed him in. What met his eyes were three spacious new rooms with high ceilings and magnificent woodwork. The air resonated with the hammering of the workmen as they put in even more effort than usual. Why, you may ask, were they working so hard? Well, on the day of the completion of the house, tradition has it that there should be a feast to thank the workmen, at which there would also be offers of cash rewards. Looking forward to the feast and the cash rewards, the workmen made a show of diligence at the sight of the master of the house. Watching the busy scene, Mr. Bo sighed inwardly and said to himself, "No wonder those little fellows said I was not meant to enjoy them and wanted to go to a prosperous place. Now this is a pros-perous place, if ever there was one! So, money itself is also snobbish!"

Soon he was brought into a small lounge, where Shi Fu offered him a seat. Then Shi Fu dashed off inside and told his wife about what had happened. Also much taken aback, Yu-shi said, "Since the silver is meant for their burial expenses, why don't we give the money back to them? That would be a nice thing to do."

"I was thinking the same thoughts," said Shi Fu. "That's why I'm here to con-sult you."

Yu-shi took out the eight ingots and wrapped them up in a piece of cloth. Shi Fu slipped the packet into his sleeve and instructed that wine and food be brought out to Mr. Bo.

Back in the lounge, Shi Fu retrieved the packet and said, "Look! Are these the eight ingots you were talking about?"

Mr. Bo took the packet, opened it, and found them to be indeed his. "Yes, these are indeed the eight strange little fellows," he said. After he examined them, turning them left and right, he continued, addressing them, "Wasn't the pillow sewn up tightly? How did you get out? This place is ten li from our town. Even humans can't cover all this distance on foot and need a boat. You don't even have legs. How did you manage to be here in so little time?" Even as he spoke, he thought how easy it was to lose what one had gained through painstaking efforts, and tears coursed down his cheeks.

Shi Fu said, "Don't feel sad, sir. I'll be glad to give them back to you for your future use."

"You are very kind, but such good fortune is just not in my stars. That's why they left me. If I take them back, they're bound to leave me again. Why bring so much worry on myself?"

"But you're getting them from *me*. This should be all right."

Mr. Bo kept waving his hand in refusal. "No, I don't want them! This old man knows the will of heaven. Anything done forcibly won't work."

Thus firmly rejected by Mr. Bo, Shi Fu went inside to consult his wife. Yu-shi said, "He may not want it, but this will weigh heavily on our conscience. If he thinks eight ingots are too much for him, one or two ingots should be all right."

"He's determined not to take even one."

"I have an idea. Let's stuff two ingots in two steamed buns, one in each, and give the buns to him. When he sees the silver after he gets home, he'll let the matter drop. He can't very well come back here and return them to us."

"Wonderful idea!" said Shi Fu.

Yu-shi went to the main hall to lay food and wine on the table. Mr. Bo took the guest seat and Shi Fu sat opposite him as host.

"I'm so sorry for putting you to so much trouble!" said Mr. Bo.

"We didn't go out of our way to buy the wine and the food. Don't mention it!"

After a few cups, Mr. Bo, who didn't have much capacity for wine, began to feel the effect of the wine. Shi Fu asked for rice and offered it to him. The dinner over, Mr. Bo was about to rise and say his thanks when a servant presented him with two steamed buns. Shi Fu said, "This will make a simple snack for you to eat on the road."

"I'm so filled up with the wine and food that I'll go without supper this evening. Why would I need a snack on the road?"

"Even if there's no need, won't you just take the buns home?"

"No! No! I'm in this line of business. I make buns every day. You keep them for other people."

Shi Fu pushed the buns into Mr. Bo's sleeve and said, "The filling of these buns is very good and tastes different from yours. Try them, and you'll know."

Finding it hard to turn down such hospitality, the old man said, "I came here for something unimportant, and I ended up being treated to wine and food and I even take some away! This is too much of an honor! Too much of an honor!" Folding his hands respectfully across his chest, he continued, "I'm ever so grateful to you!" With that, he turned to go. As Shi Fu walked him to the door, the old man mumbled to himself, "There was no problem when I came here, but I wonder if I can get a boat on my way back."

Seeing that the old man was drunk and afraid that he would lose the two buns, Shi Fu said, "That's all right, sir. I have a boat. I'll have someone take you home."

Nodding, the old man said, "Such a kind man like you is hard to come by. That's why you are so blessed."

Shi Fu summoned a servant and told him, "Take this gentleman home on the family boat. Be sure to escort him home and remember the address so that I can go to visit him in the future." The servant promised to do as told.

Mr. Bo took leave of Shi Fu and boarded the boat. As the boat sailed in the direction of Mr. Bo's hometown, the old man, exhilarated by the wine, asked about this and that and kept up a steady chatter. Before long, they arrived. The servant moored the boat and helped the old man ashore and into his house. Mrs. Bo greeted them and asked, "Old man, is all that true?"

"Yes, it's all very true." So saying, the old man retrieved the two buns from his sleeve and said, handing them to Shi Fu's servant, "I have too many things to attend to, so I'm not going to keep you for tea. Please take these buns instead."

The servant objected, "But my master gave them to you. How can I take them?"

"I'm grateful to your master for giving them to me. Now I transfer them to you as a token of my good will. Don't decline."

Unable to fend him off, the servant had to take the buns. He took leave of Mr. Bo and rowed the boat back home. After tying the boat to its mooring place, he went ashore, the buns in hand. It so happened that Shi Fu went out of the house at this point. His eyes falling on the buns, he asked, "I gave the buns to Mr. Bo. Why did you take them?"

"He gave them to me, saying it was because he couldn't keep me for tea. I wasn't able to turn him down, so I had to take them."

Shi Fu was privately amused. "So, that old man doesn't even get to enjoy those two ingots of silver and gives them away," he thought. "Well, maybe the servant is in luck. Who knows?" Aloud, he said to the servant, "These two buns have a special flavor. Don't give them away to anyone else."

The servant said, "Of course." He then went to look for his wife and gave her the buns. Before he had a chance to tell her where they were from, some friends called him away to join them for a drink outside. His two children being ill with stomach complaints, his wife thought as she took the buns, "If the two little ones see the buns and eat them on the quiet, their stomachs will be acting up again. I'd better go to the mistress and trade the buns for something else for them to eat."

So she went to see Mrs. Shi and said, "Ma'am, I have no idea where my husband got these two buns, but our two little ones are both ill with stomach trouble. If they see the buns and eat them without my knowing it, they'll get even worse. Could you trade the buns for some other snacks that won't hurt the stomach?" So saying, she set the buns down on the table.

The unsuspecting Yu-shi picked a few food items, gave them to her, and put the buns away. A moment later, Shi Fu came in and told her that Mr. Bo had given the buns away, adding, "The servant is in luck."

Yu-shi realized that those were the very two buns she had just received. "So, that's what happened!" she exclaimed. "How remarkable!" She brought the buns over and said, handing them to Shi Fu, "Open them and see for yourself."

Little knowing what she meant, Shi Fu broke open a bun with his hands. At the sound of a clatter as the silver fell on the table, Shi Fu saw that it was an ingot of silver with a red yarn around the middle. "Why did you take back the buns?" he asked.

After Yu-shi described to him how the woman had come to trade the buns for something else to eat, husband and wife were overcome with emotion. They came to realize that when you are in luck, money follows you, however hard you try to drive it away. But if you are not destined to have money, it won't come to you, however hard you pursue it.

Out of sympathy for Mr. Bo, Shi Fu often sent over money and rice to him, and the two families saw as much of each other as if they were kith and kin. After Mr. and Mrs. Bo died, Shi Fu bought a grave site for them. After Shi Deyin came of age, Zhu En's daughter was brought over as his bride and the young couple remained devoted to Shi Fu and his wife. Shi Fu became the richest man in town. Both he and his wife lived into their eighties and died peacefully of natural causes. The Shi clan, forming marriage alliances with the Zhu clan of Tanque, thrives unto this day. There is a poem in testimony:

> However trivial the return of lost money,
> Heaven acknowledges the good deed.
> At the chance meeting at Tanque, good was returned for good;
> Virtue pays in the end, when all is said and done.

Bai Yuniang Endures Hardships and Brings about Her Husband's Success

The eyes observe the injustices of the world, old and new;
The heart burns with wrath at all wrongs, past and present.
Where the grand Sui palace and garden used to be,
Now stands a ferry crossing, forlorn in the setting sun.

In a burst of emotion, one intones a hundred poems;
In a drunken moment, one comments on all history.
Gods and demons are but illusions;
Only the three guides and five virtues last forever.[1]

The above lyric to the tune of "Moon over West River" exhorts people to be committed to benevolence, righteousness, and the three cardinal guides and five constant virtues. Wealth, rank, glory, and splendor are transient, as has been proven since time immemorial. Only loyal officials, filial sons, devoted husbands, and chaste wives acquire undying fame. The mere mention of their names inspires awe even in a humble laborer. Consider devoted husbands and chaste wives such as Song Hong, who did not abandon his wife of humble background, and Luo Fu, who rejected the advances of an admirer.[2] Do you not agree that they espoused the cardinal guides and the constant virtues? As for Huang Yun, who drove away his wife in order to marry his superior's niece, and Zhu Maichen's wife, who abandoned him before he rose to power, do you not agree that they violated the guides and the virtues?[3] Truly, human hearts can be as different as the clear Jing River is from the muddy Wei River. There is a poem in testimony:

Huang Yun drove out his wife and ruined his own name;
Maichen, sadly, was abandoned by his wife.
Married couples should be like mandarin ducks:
Some perch on branches, some fly together.

Toward the end of the Song dynasty, there lived a man named Cheng Wanli, courtesy name Pengju. He was a native of Pengcheng [present-day Xuzhou, Jiangsu]. His father, Cheng Wenye, was director of a government ministry. Both his parents died when he was sixteen years old. At nineteen, he entered the imperial academy as the son of a former official. He was tall and powerfully built, and he set his marks high. He was much given to literary pursuits as well as archery and horsemanship. Deeply troubled by the growing power of the Mongol army, he offered advice to the imperial court on the strategic options of counterattack, passive defense, and truce. However, his frankness ran afoul of the powers that be. Afraid of punishment, he abandoned his servants and left the capital city on the quiet, all alone. Not daring to return to his hometown, he headed for Jiangling Prefecture to enter into the service of Ma Guangzu, military commissioner of the Jinghu region [present-day Hubei]. Before he reached Hankou, word came that the crack Mongol troops of Grand Marshal Uriyangkhadai had pushed triumphantly deep into the country. Appalled at the news, Cheng Wanli dared not press on. As he hesitated, evening set in. Behold:

> *Rosy clouds greet the setting sun;*
> *Weary birds return to their nests.*

Cheng Wanli thought, "Let me find an inn and learn how things are before deciding what to do next." That night, he heard nothing but the hurried footsteps of a ceaseless flow of refugees from the north and their heart-rending sobs. Realizing that the Mongol troops must have been closely in pursuit, Cheng Wanli rose before the night was out and joined the crowds. It was daybreak when he remembered that he had left his baggage in the inn. Having gone thus far, he could not very well go back to claim it. Penniless and hungry, he had no choice but to beg for food in a village before pushing on. About half a li later, a group of soldiers charged from the side into the crowd. Cheng Wanli dashed off into the nearby woods for shelter. Those were, in fact, stray soldiers under Zhang Meng, brigade commander subordinate to Grand Marshal Uriyangkhadai of the Yuan court. When the scouts caught sight of a stalwart man without baggage diving into the woods, they thought he must be a spy. So they rode into the woods and, without allowing a word of protest, trussed Cheng Wanli up and took him to Commander Zhang's camp. There, Cheng Wanli explained that he was not a spy but a commoner seeking refuge from the troops. Commander Zhang liked his imposing looks and kept him on as a servant. For lack of a better alternative, Cheng Wanli complied. His heart ached as he witnessed how the Yuan troops wreaked havoc in the land every day, like gusts of wind blowing dead leaves before them. Truly,

> *Far better to be a dog in days of peace*
> *Than to be a human in times of war.*

Now this Commander Zhang, a native of Xingyuan Prefecture [present-day Hanzhong, Shaanxi], was a master of martial arts with enough muscular strength to raise a thousand-catty object. He used to be a bully, tyrannizing his neighborhood. Then the regional military commander heard about him and made him an aide-de-camp. Later, when Mongol troops invaded the region, Zhang killed the regional commander, turned traitor, and joined the Yuan army. The Yuan sovereign promoted him to regional commander as a reward for having surrendered the city. As the vanguard for Uriyangkhadai, he rendered distinguished service in battle after battle. Now, having been on the road for so long, he missed his family and wrote a letter to them. He filled a wagon with his loot and divided the men and women he had captured into two groups. He then had two officers escort the wagon and the captives to his home. Poor Cheng Wanli was among the captives, and he wept his way to Xingyuan Prefecture, far away from his hometown.

Once in Commander Zhang's house, the officers handed over the letter and the loot, and made the captives kowtow to Mrs. Zhang. Being a woman of good sense, Mrs. Zhang assigned rooms to the captives and kept them for daily household service. After getting a letter of reply, the officers went back to their camp to report to the commander.

After Cheng Wanli had lived in Xingyuan for more than a year, the Song and Yuan courts reached a peace agreement. The hostilities ceased, and the officers and soldiers returned home, Commander Zhang among them. After greeting his wife, he accepted kowtows from all the servants. Cheng Wanli felt obliged to do as the others did. A few days later, Commander Zhang picked a few strongly built men and told them to stay on, whereas the rest of the captives were to be sold off. He summoned the men he was keeping and said to them, "Unfortunately, you live in a time of war and have to suffer such misery. Your parents and wives most probably have perished in the chaos. You are lucky to have met me. Otherwise you would have died long ago. Now, even though you are away from home, since we live in the same house as master and servants, we are one family. This evening, I'll give each of you a wife. So, set your mind at ease and do not have any traitorous thoughts. In the future, I'll take you to the army, so that you can have a chance to distinguish yourselves in battle and win just as much wealth and status as I have. If you get other ideas and do something to defy me, I will not let you off easy."

In tears, the men kowtowed and said, "We would be only too grateful to you, master, for giving us a new lease on life. How would we dare get other ideas!"

That very evening, Commander Zhang picked several women from among the female captives, and Mrs. Zhang gave them some clothes. With Commander Zhang and his wife leading the way, the women went into the brightly lit main hall, where the men were standing respectfully in two lines on both sides. Commander Zhang then matched the men and women, one couple at a time. Everyone kowtowed in gratitude and the men took their wives into their respective rooms.

Cheng Wanli also was matched with a woman. Back in his own room, he closed the door and exchanged greetings with his new wife. He looked closely at her and found her to be a beautiful girl of fifteen or sixteen, with none of the looks of a lowly servant. How do we know this? There is in testimony a lyric to the tune of "Moon over West River":

> Her eyebrows curved like crescent moons,
> Her eyes sparkling as if with ripples,
> Her hair coiled up like a spiral shell,
> Her rosy cheeks delicate and soft.
>
> She was the very image of Chang'e, the moon goddess,
> And of the Weaving Maiden resting on an autumn night.[4]
> In the painted hall lit by wedding candles,
> She bashfully stopped in her tracks amid the cheers.

Pleased that he was given such a beautiful girl, Cheng Wanli asked, "What is your name, young lady? Did you grow up in this establishment?"

Before she started to answer, tears coursed down her cheeks. Cheng Wanli wiped her eyes dry with his sleeve and asked further, "Why do you cry?"

"I am a native of Chongqing. My name is Bai Yuniang. My father, Bai Zhong, was a military commander. Yu Jie, the regional commander of Sichuan, transferred my father to Jiading Prefecture [in Sichuan]. Then Commander Yu died unexpectedly. The Yuan grand marshal Uriyangkhadai took advantage of the situation and launched an attack. The Song army defended the city until they ran out of provisions and the soldiers were too exhausted to hold out. My father was captured on the day the city fell. He refused to surrender and died. Out of anger against my father for having defended the city against him, Uriyangkhadai killed my entire family. I was spared because Commander Zhang took pity on me, as I was young. He brought me home to be a maidservant for his wife. I never thought he would make this match for me. Where are you from? Were you also one of the captives?"

This account of her background as a fellow captive struck a chord in Cheng Wanli's heart. Unbeknownst to himself, tears also rolled down his cheeks as he told of his native place, his name, and the circumstances of his capture. Both were deeply grieved. At the second strike of the night watch-drum, they undressed and lay down in bed. After spending a blissful night, they rose the next morning, combed their hair, washed, and went together to thank Commander Zhang, after which Yuniang went as usual to the inner section of the house. Out of gratitude for Commander Zhang, Cheng Wanli performed his duties with double the usual care and found favor with the commander. (*This works to his advantage.*)

On the third night after the wedding, Cheng Wanli was sitting alone in his room when he was suddenly struck by the thought that, his pursuit of fame and honor unavailing, he had brought disgrace to his ancestors by working as a lowly servant in an alien land, failing in both loyalty and filial piety. He wanted to escape but saw no chance. With a deep, long-drawn sigh, he felt the tears falling thick and fast. While he was thus lamenting his fate, Yuniang emerged from the inner section of the house. In haste, Wanli wiped off his tears and greeted her, his face still sad and tear-stained. Yuniang was a smart woman and a good mind reader. She lit a lamp, sat down by his side, and asked him why he looked so miserable. Being a cautious man, Wanli was not going to lay his heart bare in the rush of the moment. As the ancients said,

> Be sparing of words even between man and wife;
> Say not everything that lies in your mind.

Forcing a smile, he said in response, "It's nothing!"

Though convinced that he had something to hide, Yuniang refrained from pressing him. It was not until they had closed the door, blown out the lamp, and gone to bed that she whispered softly (*Yuniang is even more cautious.*), "Husband, I have something to say to you. I wanted to say it to you during the day, but I didn't dare. Just now I noticed that you looked sad. In fact, I have a fairly good idea of what you're thinking. You need not hide anything from me."

"No, I haven't been thinking of anything. Don't be suspicious."

"As far as I can observe, you have the ability to rise above a subordinate position. Why don't you escape at the first opportunity and seek ways to bring honor to your ancestors? If you are content with staying here as a servant, how are you going to make your way up in the world?"

These words astonished Cheng Wanli. He thought, "How can a woman think so much like a man? Those words hit me right on my sore spot. What's more, husbands and wives would normally hate to part, but in our case, this is only the third day into our marriage. Our love is only beginning. How can she turn around and advise me to go back to my hometown? Could Commander Zhang have put her up to it, to sound me out?" Aloud, he said, "What nonsense is this? I was captured by stray soldiers. I thought I was going to die for sure. Luckily, the master set me free, kept me on as a personal guard, and gave me a wife. Such kindness is as immense as heaven and earth. I haven't repaid any of it. How can I betray him? Not a word more!"

Yuniang fell silent, which convinced Cheng Wanli that Commander Zhang had put her up to it. After getting up the next morning, he thought, "Since Commander Zhang made her sound me out, let me report her to him and put a stop to his suspicions, so that I can get away in the future when he's not watching."

As soon as he had combed his hair and washed, he went to ask Commander Zhang to go to the main hall. After the latter sat down there, he said, "Master, last night my wife suddenly advised me to escape. But here's what I think: When I was captured by stray soldiers, you saved my life and kept me on as a personal guard, and now you've given me a wife. I haven't yet repaid the slightest fraction of your kindness to me. What's more, my parents have died, and I have no relatives. This is my home. Where can I escape to? I already told her off last night. I'm reporting this to you because, knowing she's in the wrong, she may come to you and tell tales about me."

Commander Zhang seethed with rage. Without a moment's delay he summoned Yuniang and lashed out at her, "You slave! Because your father resisted the heavenly army, Grand Marshal Uriyangkhadai wanted to kill your entire family, but I spared your life because you were small and I took pity on you. And then, afraid that you might be killed in the chaos, I brought you home, raised you with kindness, and gave you a husband. Instead of returning the favor, you told your husband to betray me. Why would I want to keep you?" Turning to his servants, he said, "Get the family whip of discipline! Hang her up and give her a hundred lashes with it!"

Her face awash in tears, Yuniang remained silent. Promptly the servants got ropes and the family's whip of discipline, and trussed her up. Verily,

> She pointed out the right path for him,
> But he thought her kind advice meant ill.

Witnessing how Commander Zhang flew into a rage and ordered that his wife be hung up and beaten, Cheng Wanli was seized with remorse. He thought, "So she really meant what she said. I did her an injustice!" But he could not very well step forward and plead for mercy on her behalf. At this critical juncture, Mrs. Zhang, having heard that her husband had angrily ordered that Yuniang be beaten, rushed out to offer protection for her. The fact of the matter was that, after joining the Zhang household, Yuniang had proved herself to be a girl with such a gentle nature, graceful deportment, and unsurpassed skills in needlework that Mrs. Zhang took a great liking to her. Even though she was officially a servant, Mrs. Zhang treated her as if she were a daughter and had been determined to find her a good husband. She had picked Cheng Wanli because Cheng's distinguished looks bespoke a better future. So as soon as she heard that the girl was to be beaten, she rushed out, wondering why.

Just when the servants were about to act, Mrs. Zhang stopped them and, stepping forward, asked her husband, "Why do you want to do this to Yuniang?"

After Commander Zhang told her everything he had heard from Cheng Wanli, she called Yuniang to her and said, "I always favored you because you are young and bright, and I went out of my way to pick a good husband for you. How could you have advised your husband to escape? We shouldn't have saved you in the first place. Considering this is the first time you do wrong, I'll talk to the master and beg for mercy. But don't do this ever again!"

Yuniang said nothing in response but kept shedding tears. To the commander, Mrs. Zhang said, "Husband, Yuniang is too young to know what's right. For my sake, please forgive her this time for having said the wrong thing."

"Since you say so, I'll let her off this time. But if she does this again, she'll be punished for both offenses."

Yuniang kowtowed thankfully and left with tears in her eyes.

Commander Zhang called Cheng Wanli over to him and said, "For your loyalty, I'll treat you differently from the others."

Cheng Wanli thanked the commander profusely. When he went outside, he thought again, "He's still laying a trap to get me, after all. Otherwise, why did he so quickly take back his order to give her a hundred lashings as soon as his wife began pleading? Hadn't he been boiling with rage? Also, how did his wife so quickly hear about it and rush out to shield her? Luckily I didn't say too much last night."

By night, when Yuniang came into their room, he saw that she looked sad but not at all resentful. (*Even more proof of Yuniang's strength of character. Truly a woman of heroic spirit.*)

"So, this is even more proof that she had been sounding me out," thought Cheng Wanli. He grew even more discreet in his speech.

Another three days went by. On the sixth night, Yuniang looked her husband up and down as if she wanted to say something, but hesitated. After she had thus checked herself three or four times, the urge to speak finally got the better of her. "I said those things to you from the bottom of my heart," she spoke up. "How could you inform against me? I almost got beaten up! Luckily Mrs. Zhang came to my rescue. Now, judging from your ability and your looks, I'm convinced that you'll make your mark someday. Why don't you think of a plan to leave this place? If you hang on here, you won't amount to anything more than a servant!"

Listening to his wife bringing up the subject of escape again, Cheng Wanli was assailed by even greater doubts. He said to himself, "Here she goes again! The tongue-lashing the other day didn't intimidate her. Commander Zhang must have told her to test me and see if my resolve is firm enough or not." Without a word of reply, he got his bedding ready and lay down to sleep. The next morning, he again went to Commander Zhang and informed against Yuniang.

In a transport of rage, Commander Zhang yelled, "Bring that abominable slave here and beat her to death!" Not daring to lose one moment, the servants dashed into the inner quarters of the house to summon her.

Knowing that something ominous must have come up again, Mrs. Zhang refused to let Yuniang go, which further enraged Commander Zhang. However, out of regard for his wife, he could not very well push further. Privately, he thought, "Since that slave is determined to go, why not just let her go? Should the love between the husband and wife deepen with the passage of time, even a good man like him will be won over by that slave and have a change of heart." To Cheng Wanli he said, "The way that slave tried to talk you into leaving me, she must be having traitorous thoughts, which is not good for you. You'll surely be the worse for it later on. I'll wait until she comes out tonight, and then I'll have her sold off first thing tomorrow morning. I'll pick a nicer girl to be your wife."

Upon hearing that his wife was to be sold, Cheng Wanli realized that she had been all sincerity. A surge of remorse swept over him for having informed against her. (*No two people are closer to each other than husband and wife. Even so, one did not believe the other's good advice. One must watch what one says.*) Aloud, he said, "Now that you, master, have warned her twice, I don't think she'll do this again. Even if she does, I'll turn a deaf ear. If you sell her, I'm afraid I'll be accused of being a heartless man who sells his wife after only six days of marriage."

Commander Zhang said, "The decision is mine. Who would dare speak ill of you?" With that, he headed straight for the inner quarters of the house.

Noticing the angry look on her husband's face, Mrs. Zhang thought he was there to punish Yuniang again. Quickly she told Yuniang to hide. She herself rose and greeted her husband but refrained from bringing up the subject. Nor did Commander Zhang say a word about Yuniang, for he was afraid that his wife would be loath to part with her.

Now that Cheng Wanli had observed how determined Commander Zhang was to sell Yuniang, the very thought of it pained his heart. He sat in his room and wept. In the evening, after emerging from the inner quarters of the house, Yuniang said tearfully to her husband, "I offered you wifely advice out of the bottom of my heart. I never expected that you would inform the master against me and accuse me of having traitorous thoughts. The master is a hot-tempered man. He'll surely hate me and I'll die I know not where! But my life or death is nothing. My only regret is that, with your imposing looks, you're content with a servant's life and don't make plans to escape!" (*A woman of heroic caliber.*)

At these words, Cheng Wanli burst into a flood of tears and said, "My good wife, your words of advice are most enlightening. I hate myself for having suspected you of trying to sound me out on behalf of the master. That's why I informed him. And now I brought you to such a pass!"

"If you would follow my advice, I'd die without regrets."

Touched by his wife's sincerity and saddened by the thought that she would be taken away the next day, Cheng Wanli burst into abundant tears. Feeling he couldn't very well tell her about what lay in store for her, he went to bed in tears and wept until the fourth strike of the night watch-drum.

Believing that there must have been a reason for his ceaseless weeping, Yuniang asked, "Is it because the master is going to do something to me that you're so sad? Why don't you tell me?"

Knowing he would not be able to hide it from her, Cheng Wanli told the truth. "I hate myself for being so unworthy of you. Tomorrow, the master is going to sell you off. Nothing can stop him now. That's why I grieve so!"

Yuniang broke into a flood of bitter tears. In each other's embrace, they choked back their sobs, not daring to give way to their grief and cry freely. (*How sad!*) They rose before daybreak to comb their hair and wash. Yuniang gave one embroidered shoe to her husband in exchange for an old shoe of his and said, "If we ever get to see each other again, these shoes will serve as evidence. If we never meet again, I will die with this shoe in my arms. It'll be as if you and I were in the same grave."

(Such an excellent plot! Too bad the pedantic village schoolmaster who penned Story of the Shoes *did it injustice and made it dull.)* With that, they fell into each other's arms again, awash in tears, and the shoes were put away.

After daybreak, Commander Zhang sat down in the middle hall and summoned Yuniang. Fighting back his tears, Cheng Wanli joined her.

"You slave!" thundered Commander Zhang. "I raised you. What wrong did I do to you that you had to repeatedly urge your husband to betray me? I should have cut you down with one strike of my sword. Out of regard for my wife, I spare you your life. Go to a better master now!" He summoned two servants and said to them, "Take her to a middlewoman. Never mind the price as long as she's matched up with someone of a lowly status, so that this girl who doesn't know what's good for her can be tormented to death!"

Yuniang asked to be allowed to say farewell to Mrs. Zhang, but the commander turned a deaf ear. Yuniang bowed twice to him, rose, and said to her husband, "Take good care of yourself!" In tears, she followed the two servants and was gone. (*What a sad moment!*) His heart aching as if stabbed by a knife, Cheng Wanli could do no more than walk her out the gate and return, alone. Truly,

> *Of the ten thousand sad events in this life,*
> *None is sadder than parting for the last time.*

By the time Mrs. Zhang learned of what had happened, Yuniang was already gone. Knowing Commander Zhang's temperament, Mrs. Zhang had been worried about Yuniang's life. Now that the girl was safely out of the reach of the tiger's jaws, so to speak, Mrs. Zhang did not raise objections.

Let us now follow the two servants as they escorted Yuniang to a middlewoman's house. It so happened that a small businessman in town was there, looking for a maidservant. Delighted at Yuniang's good looks and cheap price, he promptly paid the servants and took her home. But of her, no more for the moment.

Let us turn our attention to Cheng Wanli. Since his wife's departure, the more he thought about it, the more remorseful he was. Every night as he entered his room, he was overwhelmed with grief. He would take out her shoe and his, toy with them by the lamplight, and sob for the longest time before going to bed. (*His remorse is genuine.*) Later, when he learned that she had been sold to someone living nearby in the town, several times he wanted to go on the quiet to see her, but, afraid that he would be seen and reported to Commander Zhang, he dared not go, for that would only ruin his big plan. Commander Zhang, however, gave full credence to Cheng Wanli because he had rejected his wife's advice, and entrusted him with everything with never a doubt. Cheng Wanli, on his part, feigned diligence even as he grew more cautious. The commander felt so favorably disposed toward him that he offered Cheng another woman for wife. Cheng refused, saying, "There's no rush. Let me wait until I follow you to the battlefield and prove myself worthy before I find a wife from a good family, to bring credit to you."

Time sped by. Another year elapsed. On the occasion of the fiftieth birthday of Uriyangkhadai, who was stationed in the garrison of Ezhou at the time, Commander Zhang, as a former adjutant of his, put together a great number of valuable items as gifts for the grand marshal. He had been looking for an able person to deliver them, but so far without success. Cheng Wanli got word of it and thought that this would be a good opportunity to escape. Immediately he went to see Commander Zhang and said, "I heard that you, master, are looking for a messenger to deliver birthday presents to Grand Marshal Uriyangkhadai. In fact, everyone else is occupied except me. I have little to do in the house. I would be glad to take on this mission."

"Yes, you're the best man for the job. But the hardships of the journey may be too much for you."

"It's exactly because my life here has been too easy that I need to go through some hardships of a life on the road. Otherwise I'm afraid I won't be ready to go to the battlefield with you."

Convinced by this impeccable logic, the unsuspecting Commander Zhang gave his consent. He wrote a letter of greeting, drew up a list of the gifts, and gave Cheng Wanli a travel document in case he was stopped for questioning on the road. After all the preparations were completed, a day was chosen for his departure. Cheng Wanli packed and hid Yuniang's shoe in his baggage. On the day of departure, Commander Zhang handed over everything to him, gave him all the necessary instructions, assigned a servant called Zhang Jin as his travel companion, and gave him ten taels of silver for travel expenses. Cheng Wanli was upset that he was to have a travel companion, but he couldn't refuse for fear of incurring the commander's suspicions. He would just have to play it by ear and make his move when the right time came. So he took leave of Commander Zhang, loaded the gifts onto the pack animal, left Xingyuan, and headed for Ezhou. There were no delays along the road, and government courier stations took care of their room and board.

A few days later, they arrived in Ezhou and found an inn to stay at that night. Early the next morning, they took along the letter and the gifts and went to the grand marshal's mansion, where they took a number and waited in line. Grand Marshal Uriyangkhadai being an important official at the Yuan court guarding a major border town, there were countless gift-bearing visitors from everywhere. It was quite a lively scene at the gate. After three flourishes of the bugles, the gate opened and the grand marshal was ready to grant audiences. After he had received many officers and other subordinates, his adjutant ushered in the messengers bearing letters and gifts. Grand Marshal Uriyangkhadai read the letters, checked the gifts, and told them all to wait in their respective lodgings for his letters of reply. Thus instructed, the messengers left the grand marshal's residence, but so much for this.

Now, after delivering the birthday gifts, Cheng Wanli thought this was the time to go. However, being always in the company of Zhang Jin and sharing the same room with him, Cheng Wanli could not come up with a plan to extricate himself. And yet, heaven sent him an opportunity, for his destined time had come. What with the exhaustion of the journey and the cold, Zhang Jin fell ill at the inn. Cheng Wanli said to himself, rejoicing, "This couldn't suit me better!" He was about to go when he thought again, "A man of honor should carry a job through before moving on." So he went to the grand marshal's residence and obtained the letter of reply. (*Not unlike the heroes described in* Outlaws of the Marsh.) Back at the inn, where Zhang Jin was lying unconscious, Cheng Wanli wrote a letter and put both letters in Zhang Jin's bag. As for the ten taels of silver, because Zhang Jin had asked for a share of the money, Cheng Wanli had insisted that they be kept in Zhang's bag so as not to arouse Zhang's suspicions, and promised that they would buy gifts for friends after they arrived in Ezhou. Now that Zhang Jin was in bed, sick, Cheng Wanli took out the ten taels of silver and put them into his own bedding, along with the travel document. (*He had deliberately yielded what he would later take back. Wanli was a good strategist.*)

His baggage thus ready, he called over the innkeeper and said, "The two of us were sent by Commander Zhang of Xingyuan to deliver birthday gifts to Grand Marshal Uriyangkhadai. We'll be going next to Prime Minister Shi [Shi Tianze, 1202–75] of Shandong. But my colleague has fallen ill from the hardships along the journey and can't move now. If I wait until he gets well, I'm afraid our mission will be delayed. So I'll go alone while he stays here for a few days until he recovers. After I accomplish the mission, I'll come back here and go home with him." Handing five maces of silver to the innkeeper, he said, "This is just a small token of my gratitude. Please take good care of him. After he recovers, I'll have better rewards for you."

The unsuspecting innkeeper took the money and promised, "I'll surely take good care of him, morning and night. You have nothing to worry about. But please come back as soon as possible."

"Of course," said Cheng Wanli. He asked for more food, ate his fill, swung his baggage over his shoulder, bade the innkeeper adieu, and set out in large strides. Verily,

> *The sea turtle freed itself from the golden hook,*
> *Shook its head, flicked its tail, and vanished for good.*

He left Ezhou and headed in the direction of Jiankang [present-day Nanjing]. Equipped with the travel document, he easily passed through all the checkpoints and encountered no obstacles. By this time, the regions east of the Huai River had all fallen to Mongol Yuan troops. Deeply saddened, Wanli pressed on until he was on Song territory again and made his way straight to Lin'an [present-day Hangzhou]. The ministers of the Song court had all been replaced, but he did find Zhou Han, a former student of his father's and now vice director of the Military Privy Council, and stayed with him. It so happened that Emperor Duzong [r. 1265–74] was at this time recruiting descendants of former officials of the Song court. Thanks to Zhou Han's recommendation, Cheng Wanli was appointed as marshal of Fuqing County in Fujian. With a servant, to whom he gave the name Cheng Hui, he set out on a chosen day on his journey to assume his post, but of him, no more for the time being.

Now, back to the inn. Zhang Jin did not regain consciousness until several days later. Failing to see Cheng Wanli, he asked the innkeeper, "Where's Mr. Cheng?"

The innkeeper replied, "Mr. Cheng said ten days ago that he needed to go on a mission to Prime Minister Shi of Shandong. Because you were ill, he went alone. He'll be back to return home with you."

Zhang Jin was aghast. "There is no mission to Shandong! That swine took advantage of my condition and gave me the slip!"

In alarm, the innkeeper asked, "Didn't you come together? Why would he want to escape?"

After Zhang Jin told him that Cheng Wanli had been a captive, the innkeeper was seized with regret. Afraid that Cheng might have taken his clothes, Zhang Jin had the innkeeper immediately check the baggage. There were a letter from Cheng Wanli and a letter of reply from Grand Marshal Uriyangkhadai. None of the articles of clothing was missing, but the travel document and the money were gone.

"That savage, cunning wolf!" cursed Zhang Jin. "The commander treated him so well, but his heart is still with the south. No wonder even his wife meant nothing to him." He rested for another few days before he was able to walk and move about. He then informed Grand Marshal Uriyangkhadai about the matter and asked for money and a travel document. At the same time, an order was issued to arrest Cheng Wanli. After settling his bill with the innkeeper, Zhang Jin bade him farewell and set out posthaste for home. Upon arrival, he presented Grand Marshal Uriyangkhadai's letter to Commander Zhang and told him about Cheng Wanli's escape. When Commander Zhang opened Cheng's letter, this was what he read:

> To my master and benefactor, from Cheng Wanli, your humble servant:
> I am ever so grateful to you for having kept me as a trusted servant rather than taking my life. Unlike grass and trees, all humans know gratitude. However, I hear that migrant birds from the south build their nests on branches pointing south and foxes turn their heads in the direction of their lair when they die. My kith and kin being all buried in the south under the Song dynasty rule, I miss them so much that I have even lost all appetite for food. I did intend to ask for a leave of absence so that I can pay a visit to my hometown, but, out of fear that you would not grant me permission, I made bold to act on my own. You, my benefactor, have so many servants that one fewer will not make any difference. To let me return to my hometown is not unlike releasing a mere pigeon. Thoughts of repaying my debt of gratitude to you are never absent from my mind. I will do whatever it takes to return your kindness, in life and in death.

Stamping his feet, Commander Zhang roared, "That scoundrel tricked me and gave me the slip! If I get him some day, I'll cut him into ten thousand pieces!" Commander Zhang was later impeached because of his excessive avarice. All of his property was confiscated and both he and his wife died of mortification. But this happened later.

In his new post, Cheng Wanli missed Yuniang so much that he refused to take another wife out of regard for Yuniang's devotion but, the north and the south being at war, he could not go out on a search for her. Time flowed like water. More than twenty years went by quite unnoticeably. On account of his integrity and competence as an official, Cheng Wanli rose to be commissioner of central Fujian. By that time, the Song dynasty was already doomed. The troops of Kublai Khan, the first emperor of Yuan, swept south all the way to the lower reaches of the Yangzi River, as if moving through a no-man's land. The last emperor of Song had to flee to Yashan Island of Guangdong. Only the entire province of Fujian, with its eight wards, had been spared the ravages of war thus far. However, it was hardly possible for such a small region to fend off the advancing enemies. Hating to see the people suffer, the local officials consulted one another and wrote a memorandum to the Yuan emperor, offering archives and maps of the area, whereupon the Yuan emperor gave every official throughout the province a promotion that skipped two grades. Cheng Wanli thus became assistant administrator of Shaanxi and went to his duty station to take up his post. Since Xingyuan was within his jurisdiction, he gave his servant, Cheng Hui, the embroidered shoe that Yuniang had given him, as well as his own shoe, and sent him on a mission to Xingyuan to make inquiries about his wife. Of this, more later.

Now let us retrace our steps and tell of what had happened to Yuniang. The man who took Yuniang home was Gu Dalang, owner of a wineshop in town, whose family was quite well off. He and his wife, He-shi, were approaching forty but remained childless. He-shi had often advised her husband to take on a maidservant so that she could give him children. In the beginning, Gu Dalang thought this would be inviting trouble and was reluctant, but his wife told a middlewoman to look for a candidate. Upon hearing that Commander Zhang was offering a girl for sale, the matchmaker enthusiastically recommended her to He-shi. Upon Yuniang's arrival, He-shi was delighted to find her a pretty and gentle girl. She put a makeshift bed in the bedroom and, by evening, set out supper in the same room. Yuniang guessed what was afoot but, feigning ignorance, went to sit in the kitchen. He-shi walked over to her and said, "Supper is in the bedroom. Why are you here?"

"Madam, you go ahead. I'll eat my supper here."

"Ours is a small household with none of the rules observed in a large establishment. We're frugal and unpretentious. Let's just call each other Sister."

"I am but a lowly servant. I'm happy enough not to be scolded when I don't do things right. How would I dare sit at the same table with you, madam!"

"Don't worry. I'm not a jealous one. It's my idea that you marry him. It's because he's middle-aged but still childless that I told him to take a concubine. If you can give him a boy or a girl, you'll have the same status as I do. Don't be shy. Come sit with us and have a cup of wine in celebration."

"It's not that I'm not grateful to you for elevating my status, but I'm one born to suffer. My husband jilted me, and I vowed never to marry again. If I have to break the vow, I'd rather die." (*Her heart as firm as iron and stone, her words harsh and uncompromising.*)

He-shi was displeased. "If you're determined to be a servant," said she, "I'm afraid you may not like the hard work!"

"I'm in your hands, madam. If I don't satisfy you, please punish me in whatever way you see fit."

"All right. I need your service in the bedroom now!"

And so Yuniang followed her into the bedroom. The husband and wife sat across from each other and drank while Yuniang poured the wine for them. He-shi went out of her way to make things difficult for Yuniang. They drank until after midnight. In a besotted condition, Gu Dalang went to bed without bothering to take off his clothes. Yuniang cleared away the table, ate a perfunctory supper in the kitchen, and went to her makeshift bed to sleep, fully clothed. The next morning, He-shi made her work at the loom the whole day. Without raising her head even once, Yuniang finished her assignment before evening fell. As she handed in what she had woven, He-shi was privately quite impressed, but she gave her another assignment for the night. Yuniang did not object. She worked at the loom until daybreak. Several days and nights went by in the same manner, but Yuniang showed not the slightest sign of fatigue.

Observing how she refrained from warming up to him and spent her days and nights at the loom, Gu Dalang thought it was all because his wife was jealous. (*It was a good thing he was mistaken.*) He was displeased, but he could not very well confront his wife. Several times he tried to flirt with Yuniang when his wife was not looking, but Yuniang sternly rejected his advances. Gu Dalang dared not say a word for fear that his wife would laugh at him. Several days later, his patience ran out. To his wife he said, "You got this girl for me out of the best intentions, but why do you make her work all day and all night without letting her get near me?"

"It's not my fault," said He-shi. "It's just that she put on such high and mighty airs the first night and refused to do what I asked of her. So I've been making her life miserable on purpose. Why do you turn around and blame me?"

Gu Dalang was not convinced. "Don't make her work tonight," he said. "Tell her to go to bed early and then see what happens."

"That's easy," said He-shi. In the evening, when Yuniang handed in her assignment, He-shi said, "You've been working for very long. You can rest tonight and continue tomorrow."

Having gone without sleep for about ten nights, Yuniang was indeed exhausted.

These words could not have pleased her more. After supper was over and the house was put in order, they all went to bed. Having been deprived of sleep for so long, Yuniang fell fast asleep as soon as her head hit the pillow. Gu Dalang stole up to her makeshift bed, noiselessly raised her quilt, and got in. As he laid a hand on her and found that she had not taken off her clothes, he set about undressing her, but she had tied all the ribbons on her clothes into fast knots. In his impatience, Gu Dalang began to pull at the ribbons. He had just torn off one ribbon when Yuniang woke up with a start. As she jumped up, Gu Dalang pounced on her and held her tightly in his arms. Yuniang screamed, "Murder!" Gu Dalang said, "You are in my house. Screaming won't help you. You'll have to do as I say!"

He-shi pretended to be asleep in bed and made not a sound.

While trying unsuccessfully to struggle herself free, Yuniang hit upon an idea. "Master," she said, "if you have your way with me tonight, I'll kill myself tomorrow. Commander Zhang's wife likes me very much. If she knows I killed myself, she'll make you pay for this. Your family will be destroyed, your business ruined, and even your life will be in danger. Regrets will be too late by that time!" (*So unyielding, so inviolable!*)

Gu Dalang did indeed take fright. He let go of her and returned to his own bed. Yuniang sat through the night without a wink of sleep. Realizing now that it was impossible to bend such a strong will, He-shi gave up and adopted her as a daughter instead. Only then did Yuniang set her mind at rest. At night she slept without undressing, and during the day she worked diligently at the loom until late in the evening.

In about a year, estimating that the bolts of fabric she had woven must be worth twice the price for which she had been bought, Yuniang offered them to Mr. and Mrs. Gu in exchange for permission to become a nun. Convinced of her sincerity, He-shi did not press her to stay but told her to offer most of the fabric to the nunnery. (*He-shi is also a good woman.*) She prepared some gifts appropriate for Buddhists and, together with her husband, escorted Yuniang to Tanhua Nunnery to the south of the city. Being as intelligent as she was, within three months Yuniang had learned by heart all the Buddhist sutras taught to her, but her husband was still constantly in her thoughts, and she wondered if he had been able to escape. She made a bag for the two shoes and hid the bag on her. Whenever the reverend mother was out, she would take out the shoes and look at them tearfully. Later, she asked the reverend mother to make inquiries about Cheng Wanli. Upon learning that he had indeed escaped, she was filled with joy. Day and night, she intoned sutras and said prayers for him, as well as for Mr. and Mrs. Gu, out of gratitude for their kindness to her. When she learned that all of Commander Zhang's property had been confiscated and that the commander and his wife had died, Yuniang recalled their kindness in raising her and broke down in a flood of passionate weeping. A memorial service was then held in their honor. As the poem says,

Grateful for their kindness in raising her years before,
She recited the sutras in a service in their honor.
Those honest and kind in their dealings with people
Are most endearing, even without ties of blood.

Let us turn our attention back to Cheng Hui. Carrying out his master Cheng Wanli's order, he traveled posthaste to Xingyuan and stayed for the night at an inn. The next day, he went to the market and found his way to Gu Dalang's house. By this time, Mr. and Mrs. Gu were in their hoary late sixties. They had closed their shop. They now observed a vegetarian diet and spent their time at home chanting the Buddha's name. Mr. Gu had come to be called by all and sundry Monk Gu. When Cheng Hui approached the door, the old man was sweeping the ground. With a bow, Cheng Hui said, "Grandpa, may I ask something?"

Mr. Gu returned the courtesy. Detecting an unfamiliar accent, Mr. Gu asked, "Do you need directions, traveler?"

"No. I want to ask if Mrs. Cheng who left Commander Zhang's household many years ago is with your family?"

"Where are you from, traveler? Why do you ask this?"

"I'm a relative of hers. We parted in the chaos of war when she was small. I'm now looking for her."

"Oh, don't even get me started! Years ago, I wanted to take her on as a concubine because I was childless. But after she came to this house, she slept without ever undressing. I tried several times to have my way with her, but she firmly refused. I was so impressed by her chastity and determination that I dared not offend her again and adopted her as a daughter. She came to be as close to my wife as a birth daughter. And she worked hard at the loom, sometimes until daybreak. In less than a year, she redeemed herself with the fabric she had woven and wanted to become a nun. My wife and I couldn't very well keep her against her will, so we let her offer the bolts of fabric to the nunnery. Then we prepared some gifts that would be appropriate for a temple, and took her to Tanhua Nunnery to the south of the city, to be a nun. It's been more than twenty years now. She hasn't taken a step out of the nunnery. My wife and I often go to see her. We're like family. I heard the reverend mother say that she still sleeps without undressing. I wonder why. I haven't been well these last few days, so I haven't been there to see her. Since you're a relative of hers, why don't you go there directly? It's not far from here. When you see her, please give her my regards."

Having thus learned the truth, Cheng Hui took leave of Mr. Gu and wended his way to Tanhua Nunnery. Before long, he arrived. The nunnery did not seem to be a large one to Cheng Hui. He went through the gate and, turning left, saw a three-section hall of worship in which sat a nun intoning sutras. She was a middle-aged woman but still quite pleasant-looking. Cheng Hui thought, "So this must be her." Instead of going in to make inquiries, he sat down on the threshold and took out the two shoes from his sleeve. Toying with them, he said aloud, addressing no one in particular, "What nice shoes! Too bad they are not in pairs!" (*Wise move.*)

The nun engrossed in intoning sutras was none other than Yuniang. Upon suddenly hearing a man's voice, she looked up and saw a man sitting on the threshold toying with two shoes that looked exactly like those in her possession, but the man was not her husband. Mystified, she quickly put away her book and went to greet the man. Cheng Hui laid the shoes on the threshold and eagerly returned the courtesy.

"May I look at the shoes, sir?" she asked.

Cheng Hui picked them up and handed them over to her. The nun examined them and spoke up again, "Where did you get them, sir?"

"From my master. He sent me here to look for a lady."

"What is your master's name? Where is he from?"

"He is Cheng Wanli, a native of Pengcheng. He's now assistant administrator of Shaanxi."

Immediately the nun took out two shoes from a bag she was carrying on her. The four shoes formed two pairs. (*Grief and joy mingle.*) The nun broke down in copious tears. (*Recalling the pain now that the pain is over.*) Cheng Hui fell to his knees and said, bowing, "My master sent me to look for you, Mrs. Cheng. It was Mr. Gu who gave me directions. Luckily I got to see you, madam."

"How did your master rise so high?"

Cheng Hui gave her an account of how his master had started his official career in Fujian, how the region had been surrendered to the Yuan court, and how he had been promoted and transferred to this place. He added, "Master said that if I find you, madam, I should take you to his duty station to be reunited with him. Could you please pack while I go to rent a horse carriage?"

"I had given up hope for a reunion in this life. Now that I see the shoes, my wish has been fulfilled. I have no other wish. Please take the shoes to your master and his wife and relay this message to him: Be a good official worthy of the trust of the imperial court and kind to the people. I have been in the Buddhist order for more than twenty years now. I have long since given up the mortal world. Tell him not to think of me in the future." (*Free from the conventions of this world.*)

Cheng Hui said, "My master vowed never to remarry, out of gratitude to your devotion. (*Right thing to do.*) Please do not refuse."

Turning a deaf ear, the nun went inside. Cheng Hui begged the reverend mother to talk to her, but Yuniang never came out again. (*She is no longer of this mundane world.*)

Cheng Hui did not want to press too hard. Taking along the two pairs of shoes, he returned to the inn, picked up his baggage, and went back to the yamen of Shaanxi before the night was out. He presented the shoes to his master, acquainted him with all the details of his encounter with Mr. Gu, and related how Yuniang had recognized the shoes but refused to follow him. Assistant Administrator Cheng's heart sank. He put away the shoes and wrote a memorandum about the matter to the provincial governor, who had served in Fujian with him and had a good collegial bond with him. Amazed upon reading the memorandum, the provincial governor immediately instructed the officials of Xingyuan prefecture to prepare gifts and go to the nunnery to bring Yuniang to the provincial seat. Not daring to be remiss in his mission, the prefect of Xingyuan prepared clothes, other gifts, and an elegant carriage and, along with his subordinates and two maidservants for the nun, went to Tanhua Nunnery in a grand procession, complete with a band of musicians. As the news spread throughout the town, people of all ages came in droves to watch.

Upon reaching the nunnery, the prefect and his subordinates dismounted their horses and, telling their attendants to stand back, entered the nunnery. When the reverend mother came out to greet them, the prefect explained to her the purpose of the visit and asked that Mrs. Cheng mount the carriage. The reverend mother went inside to relay the message. Knowing that she would not be able to turn away the prefect and his entourage of officials, Yuniang resignedly went out to greet them.

The prefect announced, "By the order of Assistant Administrator Cheng of Shaanxi, my superiors at the provincial level instructed us to bring gifts to you, madam, and invite you to mount the carriage and go to Shaanxi for a reunion. Please change your attire and mount the carriage that is ready outside." Having said that, he told the maidservants to present to her the gifts and the clothes.

Not daring to refuse the offer, Yuniang had the reverend mother accept the gifts. After expressing her thanks to the officials, she gave half of the gifts to the reverend mother for her subsistence in her old age, and instructed that the local officials use the other half for a proper reburial of Commander Zhang and his wife, as a token of her gratitude to them for their kindness in raising her. (*Bai Yuniang hates Uriyangkhadai but not Commander Zhang. Another proof of her fair-mindedness.*) She also left instructions for a salvation rite for seven days and nights in memory of members of her own clan. After all this was done, the maidservants presented her with the clothes they had brought, whereupon Bai Yuniang changed her clothes, bowed four times to the statue of the Buddha, bade the reverend mother farewell, went out of the nunnery, and mounted the carriage. The prefectural and county officials followed behind. She then announced that she would like to go to the marketplace to say good-bye to Mr. and Mrs. Gu. Amid the music struck up by the band, the procession wended its way to the Gu residence. As she dismounted, Mr. and Mrs. Gu came out to greet and congratulate her. Yuniang went inside, bade them farewell, and offered them gifts by way of thanking them for their kindness in years gone by. (*She forgets old grievances but remembers to repay kindnesses, acts that only the honorable are capable of.*) The elderly couple tearfully accepted the gifts. They walked her to the gate, loath to part with her. Bai Yuniang was also heartbroken. With moist eyes, she mounted the carriage. The officials escorted her until they came to a wayside pavilion ten li from town. After bidding her adieu, the prefect instructed a subordinate, Li Kefu, to lead three hundred foot soldiers to escort the carriage. All along the way, local officials who had heard about the event turned out to offer gifts. When approaching the provincial seat of Shaanxi, an array of civilian and military officials went ten li outside the city with gongs, drums, and banners to welcome her. (*A grand occasion.*) Assistant Administrator Cheng himself went a long way outside the city to greet her. Amid the resounding beats of the gongs and drums and the earthshaking music of *sheng* pipes and *xiao* flutes, the townspeople welcomed the approaching procession with fragrant flowers and brightly lit lamps along streets decorated with festoons.

After Yuniang dismounted at the back gate of the yamen that led to Administrator Cheng's private living quarters, the administrator told his subordinates that he would see them the next day. After he closed the gate and went into his private quarters, he and his wife bowed to each other four times before they stood up and fell tearfully into each other's arms. After apprising each other of everything that had happened to them after their parting, they dissolved in abundant tears again. Then all the servants came to kowtow to the mistress. A celebration feast was set out, and they drank until the second strike of the night watch-drum before going to bed. How sad that their marriage had lasted only six days but the separation had been more than twenty years! Their reunion that night was just like a dream. The next day, when Administrator Cheng went to his office, his subordinates offered him congratulations and gifts. He, in his turn, set out a banquet for them, a banquet that lasted three days amid loud music. Subordinates stationed in other towns also sent messengers to offer congratulations, but of this, no more.

Lady Bai managed the household so well that she won admiration from all and sundry. She herself being too old to bear children, she searched far and wide for concubines for her husband. (What a virtuous wife! And how the assistant administrator's blessings in life changed from paltry to abundant!) Two sons were born in quick succession to Administrator Cheng, and he himself rose to be administrator of the grand secretariat. He was enfeoffed as Duke of Tang, and Bai Yuniang as a Lady of the First Grade. The two sons also rose high in officialdom. A poet of later times had this to say:

> Married for six days but separated for twenty years,
> To each other the husband and wife remained true.
> The shoes, taken apart, now joined as two pairs,
> Leaving behind a story to last through the ages.

Zhang Tingxiu Escapes from Death and Saves His Father

Follow divine will, seek not the impossible;
You need not take pains to hatch clever plots.
Be content with three square meals a day;
Take in your sails after a good ride in the boat.
If you stir up trouble, more trouble will haunt you;
Harm set, harm get, and so the cycle goes on.
Better lose an enemy than make one;
Look over your shoulder and check what is behind.

Our story takes place during the reign of Emperor Wanli [r. 1573–1620], the thirteenth emperor on the throne since Emperor Hongwu founded this dynasty [the Ming]. Under the rule of Emperor Wanli, with his divinely inspired knowledge of military and civilian affairs, his sagacity, benevolence, and observance of filial piety, every court official was deserving of his post, and every worthy man was in the service of the empire.

Of all those worthy men, let me tell of one named Zhang Quan of Jinxian County, Nanchang Prefecture, Jiangxi. The Zhang family used to be rich and had therefore been put in charge of collecting farm tax in the form of grain and delivering it to government-assigned granaries. But then their family circumstances declined and their landed estates were gradually sold off. By the time Zhang Quan's father was head of the household, the last inch of land was gone, but the tax-collecting duty was still his to perform. Next to the Zhang residence was a shop run by a carpenter from Huizhou [in southern Anhui]. As a child, Zhang Quan had often watched the carpenter at work and had taken up tools and tried his hand at carpentry just for amusement. However, as it turned out, his poverty-stricken parents later decided to make him pursue this line of work for a living, for lack of other means of livelihood. After his parents died and the carpenter returned to Huizhou to retire, Zhang Quan took over the shop. Being an honest man, he had no lack of clients, and he married after a few years' hard work. He and his wife, née

Chen, made just enough money to get by, but the burden of the tax-collecting duty still weighed heavily on them. After consulting each other, they relocated to Suzhou and opened a shop next to Huanghua Pavilion outside Chang Gate. Zhang Quan gave himself the sobriquet of Yangting [Rely on the Pavilion] and, on the whitewashed wall of the shop, painted in two rows these large characters: "Finest furniture by Zhang Yangting of Jiangxi/Customers first."

After Zhang Quan moved to Suzhou, his business went well and afforded him a comfortable life, and two sons, one year apart, were born to him. As the saying goes, "Worry only that you may not have children; worry not that they will not grow." The two boys grew apace. When they were seven and eight years old respectively, Zhang Quan sent them to a tuition-free school run by a neighbor. The older boy was given the school name of Tingxiu, and the younger one Wenxiu. Of the ten or so children in the school, they were the only two who needed to be taught everything only once. Within a few years, they knew the classics by heart. Tingxiu was now thirteen, and Wenxiu twelve, both strikingly good-looking. When their teacher began to teach them writing, they easily mastered the art of composition and rhetoric. Even though Zhang Quan himself worked with his hands, he was pleased at the way the two boys applied themselves in their studies, and he placed high hopes on their future.

As it turned out, there was no rainfall throughout the autumn of that year. Nothing grew in the fields. In the drought, wealthy families hoarded grain for speculation purposes, but the poor and lowly, especially the old and young among them, died of hunger in large numbers. Acting out of sympathy for the plight of the people, the government opened the public granaries to provide relief, but only three or four catties of grain out of ten were actually delivered to the needy. The rest ended up fattening corrupt petty officials and clerks. The government distributed rice to monasteries and temples so that the monks could cook porridge for the needy, but much of the rice was embezzled. The porridge was so watery that only a few grains of rice could be found in each bowl. There were also cases where chaff and even sawdust were mixed into the porridge. Those who ate such porridge vomited and, in many cases, died more quickly. Government authorities thought they were doing the people good, little knowing that those abusing power had rendered government aid something that existed only in name. Indeed,

> The higher officials may be as pure as water,
> But minor clerks are as slick as oil.

In this drought, Zhang Quan was obliged to withdraw the boys from school and teach them the skills of carpentry. Being as brilliant as they were, they learned the skills in a few days. In fact, they became even more sophisticated in their craftsmanship than experienced carpenters. Zhang Quan's face was wreathed in smiles. The skills of carpentry had been acquired all right, but the pieces of furniture the father and sons made and displayed at the door had no buyers. Soon, what little savings there were in the house were exhausted. Even clothes were pawned to buy food to fill stomachs. Zhang Quan anxiously consulted his wife, Chen-shi, and concluded that he should try to find temporary work elsewhere and decide what to do next after the drought was over. And so he went out in search of work but found none. The best he could do was continue as before, making furniture in his shop and hoping desperately for buyers.

After lunch one day, a man in his fifties, wearing silk from head to foot, walked leisurely down the street, followed by a page boy. Noticing the exquisite pieces of furniture on display at Zhang Quan's door, he stopped to look. Seeing him, Zhang Quan put down the work at hand and went to greet him. "How can I help you, sir? Please step inside and look around."

Walking up the steps, the man asked, "Did you make all these yourself?"

"Yes, I made them with my own hands. The wood is drier and thicker and the workmanship better than elsewhere. If you can help me out, I'll give you a one-tenth discount."

"I'm not buying now. I just want to know if you would be willing to come to my home and make a few things?"

"Yes, that would be fine. Where do you live, sir? And what do you want me to make?"

"I live opposite the imperial treasury in Zhuanzhu Lane. I'm Wang, owner of a well-known jadeware shop. I need a set of furniture as a dowry for my daughter. I've got plenty of timber. What I'm looking for is sturdiness and fine workmanship. After the dowry is done, I'll also need you to make some other pieces of furniture such as tables, chairs, and bookshelves. If you're willing to take on this job, please also bring a couple of able assistants."

This was exactly the kind of job Zhang Quan had been looking for. Wasn't this a godsend? He replied, "Thank you, sir, but when do I start?"

"Why not tomorrow if you can?"

"All right. I'll be there tomorrow morning." After Zhang Quan made that promise, the man took leave of him and went off.

You may well ask, who was that man? Well, he was Wang Xian, who came from an old and wealthy family. After inheriting a family fortune that numbered in the hundreds of thousands of taels of silver, he opened a jadeware shop and grew even richer. He was called Squire Wang by all and sundry on account of his wealth. In spite of all his money, he was a modest and a kindhearted man, much given to works of charity. There was only one thing bothering him: he was in his fifties now but still without a male heir. He and his wife, Xu-shi, had only two daughters. The older one, Sister Rui, had married two years earlier, and her husband, Zhao Ang, had moved into the Wang residence. The younger daughter, Sister Yu, fourteen years old now, was yet unbetrothed. She was both intelligent and pretty. Squire Wang and his wife loved her more than they did her older sister.

Zhao Ang was from an old family of distinguished lineage. His father and Squire

Wang had been good family friends. It was out of regard for his deceased parents that Squire Wang made Zhao Ang a live-in son-in-law. Squire Wang also bought Zhao Ang a place in the imperial academy, hoping he would apply himself to his studies and amount to something. However, once he got into the imperial academy, Zhao Ang began to act high and mighty. His books all tossed aside, he spent his time swaggering up and down the streets, sporting his finery. He was also wicked and malicious by nature. Since Squire Wang did not have a son, Zhao was convinced that, as a live-in son-in-law, he was the indisputable sole heir beyond the shadow of a doubt. It so happened that his wife didn't know any better, either. A vile woman, she was entirely on her husband's side. Jealous of her sister, whom her parents favored over her, she was afraid that she would have a live-in brother-in-law to share the inheritance with her husband. A poem on live-in sons-in-law put it well:

> He is a fool who has live-in sons-in-law;
> An alien branch can't be grafted onto your own.
> From the couple expect no devotion to you;
> They're too busy making designs on your wealth.
> They fret themselves sick lest you have a son;
> They think cruel thoughts in jealousy of your other daughter.
> "Half a son" though in name, he fills you with rage;
> Far better if you stay childless and accept your fate.

Our story forks at this point. Zhang Quan had just been worrying where his next meal was to come from when this windfall came right into his lap. Joy flooded his heart. Early the next morning, he stocked up some firewood and rice, told his wife to look after the house, and left with his two sons, carrying axes, chisels, and saws. They went past Chang Gate and, approaching the imperial treasury, saw a large jadeware shop. Believing this was the Wang residence, Zhang Quan stopped and was about to make inquiries when Squire Wang emerged from inside. Eagerly Zhang Quan went up to greet him.

"How many assistants did you bring?" asked Squire Wang.

"Only two," answered Zhang Quan, whereupon he told his sons to come up and greet Squire Wang. So they handed the tools to their father, stepped forward, and bowed deeply. Squire Wang bowed slightly in return. Finding them to be mere boys, he said, "I gave the job to you because I want it done properly. Why do you bring two little boys?"

Before Zhang Quan had time to speak up, Tingxiu, the older son, said, "Sir, it has been said since ancient times, 'Hold the young in awe.' We may be young, but we can do great things. Try us out! Don't look down on us." (*He showed his potential the moment he opened his lips.*)

Impressed by the two boys' refined looks and Tingxiu's ready tongue, Squire Wang asked Zhang Quan, "How are they related to you?"

"They're my sons."

"Good for you!"

"I wouldn't say that. They've got nothing to eat."

"With such nice boys, what do you have to worry about? Follow me inside."

Father and sons followed Squire Wang into the main hall. Squire Wang then had Wang Jin, a servant, prepare a workroom. The timber was brought out and the styles and specifications of the furniture were given to Zhang Quan. The father and sons measured, drew sketches, and set their tools to work. Busily they worked until evening set in. After supper, they asked for a few lamps and worked until midnight before going to bed. Five days later, they asked Squire Wang to look at the finished pieces. Squire Wang examined them one by one and exclaimed, "What fine craftsmanship!" After examining these finished pieces, he turned to watch Zhang Quan's two sons, who, totally absorbed in their work, did not even look up once. (*Material for great accomplishments in life.*) Involuntarily, his thoughts began to dwell on the fact that he had no son of his own. Sadly, he went in silence to the inner section of the house and sat down in a corner of his bedroom, his eyebrows contracted in a frown, his lips shooting out in a pout. His wife Xu-shi asked him what was wrong, but he remained silent. She repeated her question several times, but to no avail. Anxiously she went out and asked with whom the squire was angry. Everyone said that the squire had just been examining the new pieces of furniture and had not been angry with anyone. So Xu-shi went back inside, only to find her husband still sitting in the same position, the very picture of dejection.

"Squire," she said, "we have all the food and clothes we'll ever need. We may not be fabulously rich, but we're doing quite all right. We're in our fifties now. Even if we live to be eighty, spending freely every day, we won't have more than thirty years ahead of us. What can have happened to make you so upset?"

"Mother," said Squire Wang, "I'm upset precisely because we don't have that much time ahead of us. Just think, after working so hard for half our lives and having saved a tidy sum, we don't have a son to whom we can pass on the family fortune. We do have two daughters, but even if we support them for a hundred years, they are still other people's daughters-in-law and have no obligation toward us. (*Sober words.*) Let's look at Sister Rui. Since she got married, all she thinks about is her husband. You and I don't mean anything to her anymore. Does she care the least bit about how we are? Now, Mr. Zhang the carpenter is better off than we are, even though he's just someone who works with his hands. He looks about ten years younger than I am, but he has two wonderful sons, both good-looking, smart, and diligent. The three of them are deeply attached to one another, and the boys behave well without having to be disciplined. The pieces of furniture the boys made are just exquisite. Even experienced old carpenters don't measure up to them. Too bad they were born into such a family and ended up working as carpenters. If I had such sons, I would have hired a teacher for them. They'd surely pass the civil service examinations and bring glory to our ancestors."

Trying to assuage her husband's anguish, Xu-shi said, "What's so difficult about that, squire? The proverb says,

> *Flowers wilt when given too much care;*
> *Willows flourish when left unattended.*

Since Carpenter Zhang's sons are so smart and good-looking, why don't you talk him into letting us adopt one, so that we can have a son, too?"

Squire Wang was elated. "Well said, mother!" he cried. "But I wonder if he'd be willing." The night passed without further ado.

After breakfast the next day, when Squire Wang appeared in the main hall, Zhang Quan went up to him and said, "Squire, I need to go home tonight to check if everything's all right. Could you give me an advance payment so that I can buy some firewood and rice for my wife? I'll be back tomorrow morning."

"That's no problem, but I have a question for you."

"What is it, Squire?"

"How old are your two boys? What are their names?"

"The older one is Tingxiu, fourteen. The younger one is Wenxiu, twelve."

"Can they read?"

"They've had a few years of schooling, but then I pulled them out of school because I couldn't afford it anymore. So they are literate."

"I would like to adopt your older son. We can be relatives and see each other often. Would you be willing?"

"Don't make fun of me, sir! I'm but a craftsman. How would I dare aspire to such an honor? My boys are not so destined, either."

"How can you say such a thing? Poverty or wealth is not something that comes with your bones. If you're willing, let's pick a lucky day for the adoption ceremony. I'll engage a teacher for him. What little family fortune I have will all be his."

Realizing that Squire Wang was serious about wishing to adopt his son, Zhang Quan said, his face breaking into a happy smile, "If you're so determined to raise my son's status, I won't object, but let me first go home with them together and tell my wife about it. You can then pick a day for the ceremony, sir."

"You are right," Squire Wang agreed. He went back inside, told his wife about it, and took one tael of silver for Zhang Quan as an advance payment for the work.

That evening, Zhang Quan took his two sons back home. As Chen-shi came out to greet them, Zhang Quan told her about Squire Wang's offer to adopt their son. The husband and wife were beside themselves with joy. Tingxiu himself was delighted at the prospect of taking lessons from a private teacher.

Let us not encumber our story with unnecessary details but come to the auspicious day Squire Wang had chosen. Zhang Quan put on Tingxiu the new clothes that Squire Wang had sent over. Indeed, clothes make the man, just as gilt makes a fine statue of the Buddha. Clad in these elegant clothes, Tingxiu was even more strikingly handsome than before, with none of the looks of a poor man's son. As he took leave of his mother and his brother, Chen-shi gave him many words of advice, reminding him to be obedient, loving, modest, respectful, and humble. With eager deference, Tingxiu promised to do as told. Even though he was not leaving for good, mother and son could not help but shed tears. Zhang Quan personally escorted Tingxiu to the Wang residence. A grand banquet had been laid out in the main hall, which was already filled with relatives and friends. At the announcement that the boy had arrived, the guests all turned out to greet him. After he bowed to them, he was led to the family shrine to pay homage to the ancestors, after which Squire Wang and his wife sat down in the main hall. Tingxiu bowed four times to each of them and exchanged bows with Zhao Ang and his wife. He then went to the inner quarters of the house to greet Sister Yu. After he had greeted every one of the relatives, male and female, he sat down at the banquet table for a cup of wine. His name was now changed to Wang Tingxiu. Being two months younger than Sister Yu, he was considered the third child of the family and became, therefore, "Number Three."

At the banquet table, Tingxiu's polite and respectful manners won praises from everyone present except Zhao and his wife, who were quite displeased. The banquet lasted until midnight amid the resounding music of wind instruments, gongs, and drums.

The next day, Zhang Quan and his younger son went to thank Squire Wang before going as usual to the main hall to continue with their work. Within a few days, Squire Wang engaged a teacher and said to Zhang Quan, "Your second son is such a fine young man. His talent shouldn't go to waste. Why don't you tell him to study with Tingxiu and take his meals with us?"

"But I can't put you to so much trouble!" Zhang Quan demurred.

"We are family now. Why say such a thing!" said Squire Wang.

Henceforth Wenxiu also took his lessons at the Wang residence. Zhang Quan hired other helpers with the work, but we will not go into this. Now, having only recently abandoned their studies, Tingxiu and his brother still remembered what they had learned. Impressed by the brilliance of the two boys, the teacher made every effort to teach them well. Within one year, they were able to pass all three sessions of the civil service examinations. By this time, all the work that needed to be done at the Wang residence had been completed. In addition to the wages, Squire Wang gave Zhang Quan an extra amount of money, and Zhang Quan returned home to resume his business.

> *He could not measure up to some,*
> *But he did better than others.*

Squire Wang's second daughter, Sister Yu, was now fifteen years old. Still unbetrothed, she had no lack of offers from a never-ending stream of matchmakers. Because she was his beloved daughter, Squire Wang was determined to pick a son-in-law with outstanding talent and looks. None of the legions of candidates proposed to him was to his liking. Impressed by Tingxiu's diligence in his studies, Squire Wang had a good mind to make the young man his son-in-law. Unsure if the young man would come up in the world in the future, he secretly asked the teacher, who profusely praised the two young men for their writings and assured him that they would go far. Squire Wang thought he was exaggerating and dismissed the praise as flattery. In order to set his fears to rest, Squire Wang obtained a few samples of their writing from the teacher and showed them to an elderly scholar he knew. The scholar confirmed the teacher's words. Overjoyed, Squire Wang consulted his wife. Xu-shi was also much taken with Tingxiu's exceptional ability, good looks, and diligence in his studies, and strongly urged her husband to bring about the marriage.

His mind thus made up, Squire Wang asked his cousin, Third Uncle Wang, to talk to the Zhang family. Accordingly, Third Uncle Wang went straight to the Zhang residence and relayed to Zhang Quan Squire Wang's proposal to have Tingxiu as a live-in son-in-law. Zhang Quan declined the offer, pleading the mismatch in family status. Third Uncle Wang said, "My cousin made this proposal because he's impressed with your son's talent and looks and he believes the young man will go far. *He* is begging *you*, not the other way around. Why turn him down?"

Only then did Zhang Quan give his consent. Third Uncle Wang reported back to Squire Wang, who then set about choosing an auspicious day for the delivery of betrothal gifts. Of this, more later.

Zhao Ang and his wife were already displeased that Squire Wang had adopted Zhang Tingxiu as son and engaged a private teacher for him, but they could not stop the squire from doing so. Now that Sister Yu was to marry the young man, they grew even more jealous. After consulting his wife about ways to block the marriage, Zhao Ang went to see Squire Wang.

"There's something that's probably not for me to say," said Zhao to his father-in-law. "But since I am a member of the family and this concerns me as well, I feel obliged to say it. And yet, I'm afraid you will take offense if I do. So I dare not speak up."

"If I did something wrong, it's only right that you should correct me. Why would I take offense?"

"Well, it's about my sister-in-law's marriage. You turned down numerous offers from rich and eminent families. Why do you now offer her to Number Three? He's of humble family background. You adopted him, but that's still what he is—adopted. Nobody said anything about the adoption because it's not a formal arrangement. But if you take him on as a son-in-law, won't you become a laughing stock?" (*Clever words.*)

Squire Wang replied with a smile, "My good son-in-law, this is not something for you to worry about. I know what I'm doing. As they say, 'A good marriage is a marriage to the person; a bad marriage is a marriage to the house.' Goodness knows how many young men I've looked at. None of them satisfies me. Tingxiu may be of humble family background, but he has a dignified appearance and outstanding ability. What's more, he's a diligent student. Everybody praises his writing and says he'll surely pass the examinations. Why would I forsake the one right at hand and search among all those good-for-nothing wine pots and rice bags? (*Bravo! Zhao Ang is not even aware that these epithets were meant for him.*) If I pick a good one, the marriage may turn out well. But if, in a foolish moment, I settle on a stupid one with a questionable character and not quite right in the head, wouldn't I be ruining my daughter's future? If I get laughed at now, it'll just be for a short while. Later, when he becomes successful, people will admire me for my foresight."

Zhao Ang gave a guffaw. "When it comes to looks, you may be right to a certain extent. If you say that everyone praises his writing, you've certainly got it wrong! Let's not talk about other places, but in Suzhou alone, there are any number of learned scholars who have labored at their studies from morning to night, but all the pains they've taken haven't gotten them anywhere. He has just started out in his education. After just one year of schooling, is he likely to pass the imperial examinations with flying colors? My father-in-law, just think: each nationwide examination produces only three hundred *jinshi*. That's a tough selection process, you know. You talk as if it's so easy! Those who praise his writing fooled you because you didn't know better. You were so serious that they didn't have the heart to dampen your spirit, and so they said those things to humor you. How can you take them at their word?"

Before the squire could respond, Sister Rui walked up to him and said, "Father, with our family circumstances and my sister's looks, how can you worry that there're no candidates from a well-matching family background? Why do you have to give her to a carpenter's son? Aren't you bringing disgrace to the family and inviting ridicule? As I see it, axes and saws are just right for him. What does he know about writing? What good does marrying a craftsman do to my sister? How are we going to associate with them?"

A wave of rage swept over Squire Wang. "If he's my son-in-law and I pass on my money to him, he'll have more than he needs for the rest of his life, even if he doesn't pass the examinations. I don't see why you can't associate with a carpenter. As I see it, he may be poor now, but in the future, he'll be way ahead of you! Who needs your meddling anyway? You've been talking nothing but nonsense!" So saying, he headed for the inner quarters of the house.

Their faces aflame with humiliation, Zhao Ang and his wife called after him, "What do we care? We offered you advice only because you'll lose face. Where does this outburst of anger come from? We're only afraid you'll regret it in the future, and it'll be too late when you recall what we said today!"

Turning a deaf ear to them, Squire Wang stormed into his own room, his rage unabated. Upon seeing him in such a state, Xu-shi asked, "What makes you so angry?"

After hearing her husband's account of what had happened, Xu-shi was also upset.

Stung by Zhao Ang's disparaging remarks about Tingxiu, Squire Wang set his heart on helping Tingxiu make a good showing, and the betrothal receded to the back of his mind. He put five hundred taels of silver in a gift box, which he then had a trusted servant carry, and quietly offered the box to Zhang Quan, so that he could buy a house, give up carpentry, and open a new shop. A day would then be chosen for the presentation of betrothal gifts. Zhang Quan and his wife were overwhelmed with gratitude for Squire Wang's generosity.

As the ancients said, "Without coincidences, there would be no stories." Zhang Quan was about to look for a larger house when a big neighboring fabric shop offered to sell the shop as well as the house. Wouldn't this purchase serve two purposes at the same time? Allured by the convenience of the deal, Zhang Quan bought the shop in spite of the steep price and opened it for business. He also engaged a maid and a servant who came with his family. The house was furnished beautifully. Squire Wang then chose a day for the presentation of betrothal gifts and laid out a grand banquet to which many relatives and friends were invited. Even though Tingxiu was the prospective groom, he was not allowed to return home. Zhao Ang, feeling unwanted, went out so as not to attend the banquet. Sister Rui stayed in her room, refusing to join the celebration. Because this was a case of the son-in-law entering the bride's household, Squire Wang was the one presenting the betrothal gifts, and Zhang Quan the one offering gifts in return. Everyone in the neighborhood cheered the abundance of the gifts. Henceforth, Zhang Quan's business boomed. His shop became so crowded that he had to hire another helper. Most people are snobbish. With Zhang Quan doing so well in his business, everyone began to call him Zhang Yangting instead of Carpenter Zhang. Indeed,

> When one's luck runs out, even gold glitters no more;
> When one's time comes, even iron takes on luster.

Let us pick up another thread of the story and turn our attention to Zhao Ang, who, after being reproached by Squire Wang that day, directed all his anger at Zhang Quan and his sons. Believing that his father-in-law must have secretly provided the funds for Zhang Quan's new house and new shop, he hated them with a new intensity. It was a hatred nothing could dissolve. The idea of murdering the Zhang father and sons and keeping all of Squire Wang's wealth to himself began to take possession of his mind. Wondering how to make his move, he went to consult his wife.

"Nothing easier!" said the woman. "I have a wonderful plan that'll make them perish in prison, whatever they say in their own defense!"

Elated, Zhao Ang asked what plan she had, and the woman launched into the following explanations: "Who doesn't know that Zhang Quan is a poor carpenter? All of a sudden, he bought a house and opened a large store. Only you and I know that he bought them with money from that old thing, but the neighbors don't know that. They must be wondering to themselves. Now, that old thing is going to escort a shipment of grain to the capital. After he's gone, let's bribe the police with several tens of taels of silver and make some criminals confess that the Zhangs had joined them in robbery and had hidden their loot at home. When the neighbors are brought to court to testify, they'll say truthfully that the Zhangs had indeed been poor and had somehow suddenly struck it rich, which would bear out the criminals' allegation. That's a capital crime. They won't be able to get away with it. Their house and property will surely be confiscated by the government and sold off. They are not from here and have no relatives in these parts. So, in the absence of that old thing, who will take care of them? There's no way they'll live through all this. After Carpenter Zhang dies, let us slowly poison the old thing's mind against Zhang Tingxiu until he drives him away. Then we'll set a trap for Sister Yu and accuse her of having illicit love affairs. That old thing is a simple-minded sort. When he hears of such a scandal, he'll surely get rid of her. With that root of trouble gone, who will be there to share our inheritance with us?"

"Wonderful! Wonderful!" exclaimed Zhang Ang. And so they waited for Squire Wang to depart on his mission before making their move.

Because he was a large landowner, Squire Wang was assigned the duty of supervising a shipment of tax grain to the capital. He had a mind to hire someone to perform the duty in his place, but, afraid that the job might not be done well, he felt obligated to do it himself. (*Without a son, he became encumbered by his wealth. It was also foolish of him to personally supervise the shipment of grain. That boastful Zhao Ang, being a son-in-law, was duty-bound to help him out. If Zhao Ang had done a good job of it, Squire Zhang stood to gain. If not, Zhao Ang would have had to shut his mouth.*) Squire Wang also planned to take some jadeware along for sale in the capital, thus accomplishing two purposes at the same time. After making arrangements for household affairs during his absence, he was ready to set out on his journey. He reminded Tingxiu to apply himself to his studies and told his wife to take good care of the young man. Generally speaking, those who associate with the rich have a precious lot of social obligations to fulfill. For an occasion like Squire Wang's departure on a long journey, the relatives could hardly avoid giving farewell feasts. And the wining and dining lasted quite a few days. It goes without saying that, as a major recipient of the squire's largesse and as father of the new son-in-law, Zhang Quan had all the more reason to host a lavish dinner in Squire Wang's honor, and so he did. On the day of the squire's departure, the Zhang father and sons saw him as far as his boat before bidding him good-bye.

After the long-awaited departure of his father-in-law, Zhao Ang began to wonder who among his acquaintances could help him bribe the police into framing Zhang Quan. Suddenly he recalled that he had a childhood schoolmate, Yang Hong, who he had heard was now a police officer. Why not ask him for help? But he had no idea where this Yang Hong lived. "Let me go to the yamen and make inquiries," he said to himself. "Someone will know where he lives." Right away, he asked for fifty taels of silver from his wife, wrapped them up, equipped himself with an additional few loose pieces of silver, and went to the yamen with all the haste he could muster. In front of the yamen, he saw groups of officers here and there. His mind preoccupied, he was in no mood to watch this lively scene. Raising a hand, he asked an elderly officer, "Sir, do you know where Officer Yang Hong lives?"

"Oh, Yang the Greedy One? He lives on Black Magpie Bridge Lane. I just saw him go into the chief's office."

"Thank you," said Zhao Ang. With the speed of wind, he raced off to the police chief's office and saw Yang Hong emerge from inside. Blocking Yang Hong's way, he said, his fists joined in salutation, "I have a favor to ask of you, my brother. Let's find a place to talk."

"What is it about? We can talk here,' said Yang Hong.

"No, this is no place to talk."

Zhao Ang held Yang Hong's arm and took him out of the gate of the yamen into a wineshop, where they sat down in a quiet corner. After they exchanged amenities, a waiter brought them wine, fruit, and a few dishes. While eating, Zhao Ang said in a subdued voice, "I have a favor to ask of you. I have an enemy. Please make a criminal accuse him of complicity in a crime, so that he can be sentenced to death, and I can breathe easier." So saying, he put his parcel of silver on the table, untied the knot, and added, "These fifty taels of silver are yours. After the job is done, I'll give you another fifty taels, to make a hundred in total. Please don't turn me down."

As the ancients said, "An officer seeing money is like a fly seeing blood." How would the sight of such a large pile of snowy ingots of silver not stir up Yang Hong's greed? He exclaimed, "Put it away for now! If we're seen, we won't look too good!"

Zhao Ang wrapped up the silver and laid the parcel aside.

"Now tell me, who's your enemy? What's his name? How much money does he have? If I arrest him, will there be another male adult in the family to press charges against me?"

"His name is Zhang Quan. He used to be a humble carpenter from Jiangxi and now lives by Huanghua Pavilion at Chang Gate. He used to be poor, but recently he got a windfall of questionable origin and bought a large house and opened a fabric store. He has only two sons, both still too young. There's no one else. So don't worry."

"That doesn't sound too bad. We just arrested five men who robbed Magistrate Pang. Because Mr. Hou, our chief, is out on a mission, they haven't been brought to trial. I'll tell them to accuse your enemy of being an accomplice. I can guarantee that he'll get a death sentence. And then to make short work of him in the prison will be as easy as turning over a hand."

Bowing deeply, Zhao Ang said, "I'm counting on you, my brother! In addition to the one hundred taels, I'll also have other rewards for you."

"We're childhood friends. Why stand on such ceremony with me?" So saying, Yang Hong slipped the silver into his sleeve and the two men indulged themselves in wine. After paying the bill, Zhao Ang again brought up the subject when they were about to leave the wineshop, reminding Yang Hong to do a good job. Yang Hong said, "You need not say another word. I won't fail you." Joining his hands in a salute, he returned to the yamen. Zhao Ang went home and told his wife everything. The couple kept their delight to themselves.

Without telling any colleagues about the gift of silver, Yang Hong finished some business in the yamen, went back to his home, and told his wife to put the silver away. Then he went out, bought some fish and meat, cooked them, bought a large flask of wine, heated it until it was nice and hot, and cooked a large pot of rice. After everything was ready, he closed the middle door, went to the back, and opened the jail gate with his key. Thinking he was going to beat them again, the five robbers frantically begged for mercy. Yang Hong laughed. "I'm not going to beat you!" he said. "I did beat you last time because my colleagues might think I had secret ties with you if I didn't. So I had to do what they wanted. Actually, it pained me to see you suffer these last couple of days. While my colleagues are away today, I've bought you some wine and meat, so that you can have a good time before you go to court tomorrow."

Overjoyed that they were not only spared a beating but also offered wine and meat, the robbers thanked him heartily. Soon, the wine and food were brought into the cell and a fine spread they made on the table. Everyone was given a bowl of meat, a bowl of fish, a large bowl of wine, and two large bowls of rice.

Yang Hong unlocked the iron chain on one of the robbers and let him help himself to his meal. Having been deprived of wine and meat and having gone through a great deal of pain in the last couple of days, the man pounced on the food like a hungry tiger on a lamb and polished everything off in the twinkling of an eye. After he was locked up in his chain again, another one was set free. Those waiting for their turn watered profusely at the mouth. Soon, each had his fill. Yang Hong cleared away the table and then entered the cell again. "Have you stolen from Zhang Quan the carpenter, who is now owner of a fabric store by Chang Gate?"

"No," they replied in unison.

"If not, why did he send word time and again, after he heard about your arrest, asking us to kill you off as soon as possible? Does he have any grudges against you? Think hard!"

The robbers did indeed give themselves up to fanciful thought. One said, "Yes! Yes! Three months ago, I was buying fabric in a fabric store by Chang Gate when I got into an argument with the shopkeeper over a payment. I called him every name I could think of. He must be seeking revenge and wants us killed."

Feeding the flames of the hostility, Yang Hong said, "That's a trivial thing not even worth mentioning. Why would he want so many of you dead just for a trifle like that? What a horrible man!"

The robbers gnashed their teeth in indignation.

"But you can easily take revenge on him," said Yang Hong. "In court tomorrow, you can say that he's an accomplice and that your spoils are all hidden in his house. What's more, he became rich very suddenly. If you stick to your story, he won't be able to talk himself out of it. So he'll have to share your sufferings. With all his money, he can very well afford some bribery." Then he added, "Don't name him too readily. All of you name him together when the investigation is almost over. That would be more convincing."

In delight, the robbers said, "Uncle Yang is the wisest one, after all."

Yang Hong went on to tell them about Zhang Quan's background and other information about him, and then reminded them not to let any of this on to his colleagues. "They've all been bribed into working in collusion with him," he added. The robbers kept everything he said in mind. Pleased at the way things were going, Yang Hong locked up the cell door as before and went to the yamen to ask what was new. Learning that Deputy Magistrate Hou would be returning to the yamen that night, he went to notify the other officers to take the detainees to court the next day. There is a poem in testimony:

> *Police are dispatched to hunt down criminals;*
> *Alas! The police turned out to be even worse.*
> *For making criminals accuse the innocent,*
> *He will be punished by heaven, if not by law.*

The next morning, the police officers went to Yang Hong's home, wrote up an order to take the accused to court, took the spoils, and brought the gang of robbers to the police chief's office to await summons for trial. Soon, Magistrate Hou assumed his bench.

Yang Hong and the other officers brought the robbers into the hall and made them kneel before the magistrate. Presenting the document, Yang Hong said, "We arrested these five robbers at Pingwang a few days ago. These are the very ones who robbed Magistrate Pang. The spoils are also here."

Magistrate Hou read the document, which contained the robbers' names. They were Ji Wen, Ji Shi, Yuan Liang, Duan Wen, and Tao Sanhu. After a roll call of their names, the magistrate checked the goods one by one, which did not amount to much value. Turning to the officers, Magistrate Hou said, "I heard that Magistrate Pang is very greedy and corrupt and that the robbers took all of his many possessions. Why are there just these few worthless items? Where are the rest of them?"

"These items were all that we found," replied the officers. "There was nothing else. Maybe they're still hidden somewhere. You will know soon enough if you ask them, Your Honor."

Magistrate Hou called the robbers up to the dais and asked, "How many of you are there in your gang? How many years have you been at it? How many people have you robbed? Where have you hidden the spoils? Out with the truth if you want to be spared torture!"

The robbers said, "There are just the five of us. We've spent all the money we robbed. This is all that's left. We're not hiding anything anywhere."

In a towering rage, Magistrate Hou ordered that the ankle squeezers be applied. Hardly had the squeezers been put on them when they cried out, "Yes, there are a few others in our gang. They've all escaped except one, Zhang Quan, the carpenter from Jiangxi. He lives by Chang Gate. All the silver we robbed is stored in his house. He's now the owner of a fabric shop."

Since they all sang the same tune, Magistrate Hou believed them. Straightaway, he wrote an order for Yang Hong and the others to bring along two of the robbers to arrest Zhang Quan and seize the spoils. The other three were to be chained to the posts in the hall and await further interrogation when Zhang Quan was brought in. In the meantime, Magistrate Hou was to attend to other business.

Yang Hong and the other officers took the two robbers all the way to Chang Gate. Zhao Ang had been making inquiries at the yamen. At the sight of Yang Hong, Zhao Ang knew that everything had worked out according to his plan. He slipped out of sight but sent a servant to follow the officers and watch what was going to happen. Arriving at Zhang Quan's shop, Yang Hong stopped and said, "This is it." While Zhang Quan was busily attending to the customers who filled his shop, Yang Hong pushed his way through the crowd to the counter and threw a chain over Zhang Quan's neck.

"Good gracious!" exclaimed Zhang Quan. "What is this?"

Giving him two slaps across the face, Yang Hong roared, "You robber! How dare you even ask? You live it up with your stolen money and put us to hard work as we try to meet the deadlines!"

Zhang Quan cried out in anguish. "Where does this come from?" he exclaimed. Before he could say anything in his own defense, the officers went inside with the robbers. Afraid that his colleagues would pocket the best stuff, Yang Hong quickly locked the chain around Zhang Quan with an iron padlock and joined the other officers, ostensibly to find the spoils. The members of the Zhang household were scared out of their wits, but there was no place for them to hide. Some customers got their money back from the shop assistant and went to buy from other stores, but those who stayed to watch still filled the room to bursting. The officers ransacked the house for things of value, pocketing pieces of silver and jewelry as they did so. They then wrapped up everything else, including the bolts of fabric in the shop, into several large bundles. Zhang Quan and his wife cried on each other's shoulders, saying, "What a bolt from the blue!" As they clung to each other, the officers yanked them apart and dragged Zhang Quan off.

Those neighbors who didn't know better believed the officers. One said, "I was wondering why someone in his straitened circumstances could suddenly afford to buy a house and open such a big shop. And he got his son betrothed, too! I thought he had dug up a trove of treasure. But in fact he's in that line of work and therefore so rich."

Some, who had better sense, defended him, saying, "He's a good man! It was Squire Wang, his son's father-in-law, who supported him. This must be a frame-up." But these words fell on deaf ears. The neighbors followed the procession to the yamen, making comments, some favorable, some unfavorable, all along the way.

When Yang Hong and the others took Zhang Quan into the yamen, Magistrate Hou was in the courtroom, waiting for them. The officers marched Zhang Quan into the room, made him kneel down, and piled up the bundles.

"Zhang Quan is here!" said Yang Hong.

Magistrate Hou ordered that the three robbers be freed from the posts to stand trial together. After the magistrate checked the confiscated items one by one, Zhang Quan pleaded tearfully, "Your Honor, I am innocent. I've never seen these people, let alone committed robbery with them. This is a frame-up! Please do right by me!"

Magistrate Hou thundered, "If you haven't committed robbery with them, where did you get these spoils?"

"These are not spoils. I earned them through hard work." Turning to the robbers, he said, "I don't know you. What have I done to you to make you ruin me like this?"

"We didn't intend to name you, but we couldn't stand the torture, so we confessed. Why don't you also confess, so as to be spared the pain?"

"You scoundrels deserve to die by a thousand cuts!" Zhang Quan cried at the top of his voice. "Who gave you money to make you falsely charge me?"

"Zhang Quan!" said the robbers. "In all conscience, you were the one who came up with the idea of robbing Magistrate Pang. It's true you didn't join us every time, but all the stuff we got is stored in your shop for you to sell. How can you deny that?"

"Your Honor," said Zhang Quan, "I've been living here for almost twenty years now. I've never even gotten into an argument with anyone. How would I dare commit such offenses against the law? If I had done such things, I would have moved to a quiet place. How would I dare to run a shop in a busy marketplace? If you don't believe me, Your Honor, please bring my neighbors here and ask them. They know what kind of person I am."

Seeing that he was so firm in his denial, the magistrate said to the robbers, "You must be protecting a real accomplice and falsely accusing this man." With that, he ordered that the squeezers be applied to them.

As the lictors swarmed forward to apply the squeezers, all five of the robbers screamed like pigs about to be slaughtered but they stuck to their story that Zhang Quan was an accomplice, adding, "Your Honor, he's but a carpenter. Who doesn't know that he used to be poor? How did he suddenly get to buy a house and open such a large fabric shop? It's obvious enough."

"That makes sense," said Magistrate Hou. Turning to Zhang Quan, he continued, "You were but a poor carpenter. How did you suddenly strike it rich? You can't explain this away, can you?" He ordered that squeezers also be applied to Zhang

Quan. Zhang Quan explained that Squire Wang, his son's father-in-law, had provided him with the funds, but his words fell on deaf ears. Poor Zhang Quan! He had never been put under torture. And today, the ankle-squeezer plus one hundred strokes of the rod put him through several rounds of fainting and reviving. Unable to hold out any longer, he pleaded guilty. Magistrate Hou ordered that the ankle-squeezer be released and that all of the accused be given forty strokes of the bamboo rod. Based on the confessions, the magistrate sentenced all of them to death in accordance with the law. The spoils were carried into the yamen treasury, and Zhang Quan's house and other possessions were all sold cheaply and became government property. After all six men signed their confessions, they were brought in shackles and handcuffs to prison. Before the night was out, the magistrate wrote a report to his superiors. Truly,

> *As you sit at home behind closed doors,*
> *Disaster strikes out of the blue.*

Let us pick up another thread of the story. Watching her husband being taken away by the police, Chen-shi cried until she fainted and collapsed onto the ground. Luckily, the maidservant revived her. She then had a servant and the shop assistant go to the yamen to find out how things would turn out. At the same time, she sent a messenger to her two sons.

Tingxiu and his brother were reading in the classroom when the messenger came with the news that their father had been named an accomplice by a gang of robbers. Frightened out of their wits, they flung down their books and dashed out, staggering as they ran. The teacher also followed behind. Hearing the commotion from inside, Xu-shi sent a few servants with them to make inquiries. By the time they arrived at the yamen, Zhang Quan had already been taken inside, so they stood at the gate, keeping their eyes and ears open. They listened to him defending himself and, upon hearing that he was being put under torture, they grew frantic and wanted to go inside to speak to the magistrate. Quickly their teacher held them back, saying, "If you go in, you'll be stuck there. Who's going to run around and ask for help so that justice can be done?"

There being much sense in what the teacher said, the two brothers stopped. When their father's cries of pain came to their ears, they called out, "Injustice!" But the gatekeeper drove them away. A short while later, they saw two men help their father out, his eyes closed, looking more dead than alive. Upon hearing that he had been sentenced to death, they went forward, held him in their arms, and burst into bitter sobs, hardly able to get a word out.

Recognizing his sons' voices, Zhang Quan opened his eyes. As soon as he did so, tears fell thick and fast down his cheeks. He was about to say something to them when Yang Hong came up, pushed Tingxiu away with one hand, and shoved Zhang Quan along with all speed to prison, where Zhang Quan was transferred to the custody of the wardens. The wardens opened the gate and helped Zhang Quan in.

Tingxiu and his brother wanted to join him, but the wardens would not hear of it. Quickly they closed the gate. The poor young men cried so passionately that they sank to the ground. Their teacher, the shop assistant, and the servants soon arrived. Raising Tingxiu to his feet, they said, "Things having already come to this pass, crying won't help. Let's go home now before deciding on what to do next."

Seeing no other way, the two young men held back their tears and respectfully asked the wardens to take good care of their grievously wronged father, promising them a handsome reward.

"Young men," said a warden, "as the proverb says, 'Live on the mountain, live off the mountain; live by the water, live off the water.' For us who work for the yamen, eight hundred cash in hand is better than a thousand on credit. It's none of our business whether he is wronged or not, nor do we expect handsome rewards. If you have anything, give it to us today and we'll take good care of him. If not, it's all right. No one will press you for anything. But don't give us promises that you can't deliver right now. We can't wait that long."

Tingxiu said, "We don't have anything on us right now. We'll come back tomorrow morning."

"All right, go home now. Don't worry. We know what to do."

The Zhang brothers, followed by the others, did not go to Squire Wang's house but headed straight for Chang Gate to see their mother. Upon arrival, they saw that two sealing strips had been laid crisscross over the gate by Magistrate Hou's order, and their mother Chen-shi and the maidservant were weeping by the gate. When her sons drew near, Chen-shi fell into their arms in tears. Indeed, to pain was added more acute pain; to grief was added more aching grief. None of the bystanders did not shed tears and lament the injustice. In such a state of affairs, the shop assistant and the servants did not offer to stay with them but went their separate ways to look for jobs elsewhere. The mother and sons decided that, without a place to go to for shelter, they had to take up temporary quarters in Squire Wang's house before weighing the next course of action. On arriving at Squire Wang's house, Tingxiu went in first to announce them, whereupon Xu-shi and her daughter came out to greet the visitors. After an exchange of greetings, the guests were taken into the inner quarters of the house. Zhao Ang being in Yang Hong's home to find out how things stood, Sister Rui went to greet them. As Tingxiu and his mother gave a tearful account of what had happened, Xu-shi was also heartbroken, and Sister Yu tried to hide her tears. Sister Rui, however, was jubilant but she false-heartedly mouthed comforting words. That night, Chen-shi partook nothing of the wine and food Xu-shi set out in their honor but kept shedding bitter tears, and Xu-shi patiently tried to calm her down.

The next day, Tingxiu told his mother that he wanted to go to the prison to see his father but added, "Yesterday I promised the wardens I would have something for them. But in fact I have absolutely nothing. What's to be done?"

At this point in their despair, Xu-shi came over. Upon hearing about their plight, she took out ten taels of silver and gave them to Tingxiu, saying, "Take them. If you need more, let me know. After your father-in-law comes back, everything will be easier."

Thankfully Chen-shi said, "We haven't been able to repay any of the great kindnesses you've done to us. And now, here we go again, taking your money! If we can't repay you in this life, we'll do it from the netherworld!"

"What kind of talk is this! Your husband is in such misery and my husband is away, unable to be of any help. Why thank me for such a trifle?"

Tingxiu and his brother kept eight taels of the silver, wrapped up the remaining two taels, and asked their teacher to go with them to offer the money to the wardens. The wardens considered the amount too little. Only when one more tael was added did they agree to let the Zhang brothers in. While the teacher waited outside, the wardens took the Zhang brothers to the prison cell at the back, where Zhang Quan was lying on a pile of straw in a corner, on the verge of death, his legs lacerated, his hands and feet tightly shackled. Their hearts aching as if hit by ten thousand arrows, the two sons broke into loud wails and ran to him, crying, "Father! We're here!"

As they raised him up, Zhang Quan opened his eyes. At the sight of his sons, he said through sobs, "My boys, could this be a bad dream?"

"No, it's not a dream, father!" said Tingxiu. "Imagine being hit by such a sudden misfortune! With things in such a state, what are we going to do?"

Stroking his two sons, Zhang Quan said, "My boys, I've been good all my life. I never thought heaven would punish me with death in prison. My death hardly matters, but I haven't been able to repay Squire Wang's kindness. I won't rest easy even in death. If you come up in the world some day, do not forget him."

Tingxiu said, "Put your mind at rest, father, and recuperate well. We will do our best to appeal for justice to higher government authorities and get you out."

Waving a hand, Zhang Quan said, "Don't do that! Those criminals testified in court against me, and I have no idea who's behind the false charges. So whom are you going to accuse when you appeal? What's more, Deputy Magistrate Hou is in charge here. Even if higher authorities accept the case, officials always shield each other. They won't overturn the verdict, and I'll only be put through more suffering. Also, you two are so young. What means do you have to undertake such a big job? I've been put under so much torture that I don't have much longer to live. I don't have many instructions for you, except to serve your mother well, just as you served me. Study hard. You will be successful one day and bring honor to me." With that, father and sons burst into another fit of sobbing.

> The tale of woe of one unjustly sentenced
> Would grieve even a man of iron and stone.

To one side of them, there was a man called Zhong Yi, also on death row. He had killed a man a year earlier when he had seen that man bullying another. Feeling saddened by the father and sons' sobs, he said, "Now, don't cry. I am Zhong Yi. I killed a man out of my lifelong commitment to helping the weak and bullied. When I saw you come in yesterday, I thought you were a robber and so I didn't pay you any attention. I didn't know such an injustice has been done to you. How can I sit by and do nothing! (*That Zhang Quan gets a new lease on life when on the verge of death testifies to heaven's reward for his virtues.*) The two young masters can feel free to go back to your studies. From now on, I'll take care of your father's food and beverage. You need not send any. At this moment, the wounds look bad but they shouldn't be life threatening. With me here, the wardens won't dare demand money from you for all the expenses in prison. When the new imperial inspector comes to this region, go appeal to him. Your father's death sentence will surely be overturned."

As soon as they heard him out, Tingxiu and his brother eagerly kowtowed and said, "You are so kind! If justice can be done, we will surely return the favor!"

Zhong Yi raised them to their feet, saying, "There's no need to thank me. Now help your father to my room to rest."

And so the brothers bent forward to help Zhang Quan up, but his legs were in too much pain and the two brothers were too young and weak to raise him. Unable to bear the sight, Zhong Yi rolled up his sleeves and helped Zhang Quan to his feet. Slowly he led Zhang Quan to his own room and made him lie down in his own bed. Then he applied healing plasters to Zhang Quan's wounds.

Now that there was someone to take care of his father, Tingxiu felt slightly relieved. He offered two taels of silver to Zhong Yi for the various expenses. In the beginning, Zhong Yi refused to take them. It was only at the Zhang brothers' insistence that he accepted the money. The father and sons couldn't bear to part from each other, but the hour was late and the wardens were urging the brothers to leave. Tearfully, the two brothers bade their father adieu, went out the prison gate, found their teacher, and wended their way home. As they went, the brothers consulted each other about where their mother was to stay, because they didn't think it proper to have her stay with the Wang family. They finally decided to rent a house near the prison so that she could often see her husband and take care of him. Their minds thus made up, they went to tell their mother about their decision. The next day, with the rest of the money they had, they rented a two-room house and bought a few pieces of furniture.

To his mother-in-law, Xu-shi, Tingxiu said, "My mother is moving out to her own place." Xu-shi and Sister Yu pleaded with her to stay, but to no avail. In resignation, they sent servants to escort her to her place and gave her some money, rice, and other gifts. With her two sons and her maidservant, Chen-shi moved into the rented house. We need hardly describe the heart-breaking scene when she saw her husband on her first visit to the prison. The two brothers stayed for three or four days with their mother before they returned to the Wang residence to pursue their studies. However, preoccupied with thoughts about their father, they paid him constant visits, to the neglect of their studies.

Let us now turn our attention from Tingxiu to Zhao Ang. After he succeeded in his scheme to land Zhang Quan in prison, he consulted his wife again on a plan to drive Tingxiu out. That woman said, "To drive him out is easy. You just have to spend a few more taels of silver."

"What good plan do you have? Tell me. I'll be happy to spend the money."

"You'll need to bribe everyone in the house, so that after father comes back, everyone will tell him that Tingxiu has been stealing from us and whoring and gambling in town. If everyone sings the same tune, he'll surely be at least half convinced. You and I can then add a few stinging remarks to him to further infuriate him. I'm sure he'll drive Tingxiu out of the house. After Tingxiu's gone, our next target will be Sister Yu."

Following his wife's advice, Zhao Ang bribed all the servants in the household, male and female. What did those mean wretches know about decency and honor? At the sight of money, they all agreed to do Zhao Ang's bidding.

Before many days had passed, Squire Wang came back from Beijing, his mission to escort the shipment of grain accomplished. Everyone in the house, old and young, went to greet him, except Tingxiu, who had gone to visit his mother in her illness. Wenxiu had already moved out of the Wang residence to take care of his mother, but he was not of much concern to Squire Wang anyway. So Squire Wang asked, "Why don't I see Number Three?"

Everyone feigned ignorance, whereupon Xu-shi spoke up and acquainted him with all the details of the frame-up against Zhang Quan, adding, "He must be visiting his father."

Squire Wang was appalled. Soon, Tingxiu returned and came to see the squire. Upon Squire Wang's inquiry as to the details of his father's case, Tingxiu gave a tearful account of what had happened and pleaded that Squire Wang help him.

"You go back to your studies," said Squire Wang. "I'll come and talk with you about this after I settle down."

Tingxiu bowed his thanks and returned to the study. The next morning, worried about his mother's condition, he went out again to visit her, without first notifying his teacher. It so happened that Squire Wang went to see the teacher first thing in the morning and again he failed to find Tingxiu. He asked the teacher where Tingxiu was, and the teacher replied that he had gone out early in the morning. Squire Wang was more than a little displeased. After chatting with the teacher for a while, Squire Wang began to check Tingxiu's writings but found very few of them. Afraid that the master would be upset, the teacher explained, "Since his father was unjustly thrown into prison, he has been visiting his father so often that he hasn't been spending much time on his studies."

Squire Wang was even more displeased upon hearing that Tingxiu had been neglecting his studies. He took leave of the teacher and went outside. Encountering Tingxiu's page boy, who was on his way into the study, Squire Wang asked, "Do you know where Number Three is?"

Having been bribed by Zhao Ang, the page boy answered in these words: "Number Three has been whoring and gambling and often stays out for several nights in a row."

Not quite believing what he heard, Squire Wang harshly ordered him to get out of the way, but deep down, he was assailed by doubts. When he asked other servants in the household, he got the same story. As the ancients said, "If everybody joins in the slander, even the hardest metal will be worn away." However favorably disposed he had been to Tingxiu, Squire Wang gave credence to those slanderous words on everyone's lips. Beginning to regret what he had done for Tingxiu, he thought, "I did all this because I hoped he would become a scholar and amount to something. I never thought that his father would be convicted of crime and sent to prison. Whether it's a frame-up or not remains to be seen. And instead of applying himself to his studies, he goes out whoring and gambling. Won't my daughter's future be ruined? Zhao Ang and Sister Rui did warn me against him years ago, but my wits were so clouded at that time that I told them off. And now, they've been proven right. What am I going to do?"

At a loss as to what to do, he paced up and down the hall. In the meantime, the servants had told Zhao Ang that the master had been asking questions. Zhao Ang was overjoyed because that meant that his plot was well on its way to success, so he went out of his room to investigate further and happened to run into his father-in-law. Before the latter had time to speak up, Zhao Ang said, "I have one more thing to say to you, my father-in-law, but I don't quite dare say it because you may again take offense."

"Don't remind me of what happened in the past! Just say what's on your mind! What is it?"

"After you left, Carpenter Zhang joined a criminal gang. He's now in prison on a death sentence. At first I thought he had been wronged, but, according to his neighbors, he did do those things. As for Number Three, he took advantage of your absence and went out every day to whore and gamble, all on the excuse of visiting his father. The neighbors are all talking about this. You got yourself a good-for-nothing son-in-law whose father is a criminal. Even I feel too ashamed to show myself in public. If you had listened to my advice, all this would not have happened."

Squire Wang had already been quite displeased. These remarks so exasperated him that the words stuck in his throat. It was after a considerable while that he was able to find his tongue again. "I was foolish and did you an injustice," said he. "And now it's too late to repent my folly."

Zhao Ang said, "No, as I see it, you still have a chance to save the situation."

"Tell me how!"

"If the wedding ceremony had been held, there would have been nothing you could do. Luckily, they're not yet officially married. You can give Tingxiu a good lecture when he comes back and drive him out. In the meantime, quickly have a matchmaker find a family of matching status and marry Sister Yu off. Tingxiu's young and doesn't have any kinsmen to stand up for him. If he sues you, Sister Yu will have married by that time, and the authorities surely won't give her back to him. Also, since he's the son of a criminal, the authorities won't take him seriously. Only if you do this will no one laugh at you. Otherwise, if you don't follow my advice, Sister Yu may do something disgraceful if she's left without a marriage to look forward to. Won't regrets be too late by that time?"

If Squire Wang had a mind of his own, he would have asked elsewhere to get at the truth and wouldn't have ended up being known as a man who changed his heart all too quickly. However, being of a straightforward nature, he did not have second thoughts but believed in Zhao Ang and said, nodding, "Yes, you're right." Knowing his wife was well disposed towards Tingxiu, he did not go inside to consult her, for fear that she would stop him. Together with Zhao Ang, he remained sitting in the main hall, waiting for Tingxiu to return, and there we shall leave him for now.

After visiting his mother, Tingxiu hurriedly went back, believing that his father-in-law must be looking for him. When he saw his father-in-law sitting in the hall, talking with Zhao Ang, he went up to them and bowed. Without returning the courtesy, Wang Xian said sternly, "Why do you loaf around instead of applying yourself to your studies?"

Alarmed at the harsh tone, Tingxiu said, "My mother's ill. I went to see her."

"I'll let that pass," said Squire Wang. "But let me ask you something: Since I left, how much homework have you done? Show me."

"Because of my father's case, I've been running around all day long. I haven't had much time to study, so I've done very little homework."

In a rage, Squire Wang said, "I had been hoping that you would succeed as a scholar. That's why I didn't care about your humble status and adopted you as a son and then a son-in-law. It turns out that your father is in fact a bad one. He did things that disgrace my family. And you, you swine, instead of learning good ways of behavior, you take advantage of my absence and spend your days loafing around and whoring and gambling. People laugh at you. My daughter has always been given the very best in this house. What future does she have with a bum like you? This is no place for you. If you get out this instant, I'll spare you a beating. If you drag your feet, I'll have you beaten up."

Hearing this harangue from the master, the servants all dispersed, afraid that they would be called to give testimony.

His father-in-law's sudden hostility racked Tingxiu's heart. Prostrating himself on the floor, he said through his tears, "You are a father to me. I do hope I can repay your immense kindness to me, but this misfortune struck. I've been eagerly awaiting your return so that you can help him. Someone must have been speaking ill of me and driving a wedge between father and son. If I have done anything wrong, you can punish me however you want, and I'll die without regrets. But if you want me to leave, I won't do it!" As he spoke, he broke down in a flood of passionate weeping that was heart-rending to see.

At this point, afraid that his father-in-law would change his mind again, Zhao Ang chimed in, "Number Three, you shouldn't have misbehaved like that. It's too late to cry now."

"How did I misbehave? You're making things up!"

"You're all the more in the wrong now," said Zhao Ang. "Who would hate you so much as to badmouth you? Father-in-law is not one who listens to lies. You must have been seen once or twice wherever you were, and father-in-law is upset because he has found out the truth. How can you shift the blame onto someone else?"

"Who saw me and where? Let him show his face here and say it to me!"

"You swine!" lashed out Squire Wang. "If you don't want to be found out, you shouldn't have done anything wrong in the first place. Who doesn't know your wild acts all over town? How can you deny it?" He grabbed a stick and swung it at Tingxiu, saying, "Swine! Get out of my sight this instant!"

Instead of recoiling, Tingxiu stepped forward and held Squire Wang in his arms, saying between bitter sobs, "Father, I won't go even if you beat me to death!"

With alacrity, Zhao Ang pulled them apart and said, "Number Three! Father-in-law is not one who changes his mind easily. Do as he says and leave. After he calms down, he'll surely miss you. Won't you still be a son-in-law to him? But now he's at the height of his anger. He won't listen to you even if you cry yourself to death."

Tingxiu gathered from his father-in-law's fierceness and Zhao Ang's insidious remarks that Zhao Ang was the one conspiring against him. Realizing that he would not be able to stay on in that place, he said, "If things have come to this, let me say good-bye to my mother-in-law before I go." But Squire Wang turned a deaf ear and would not even let him see the teacher. Zhao Ang pushed Tingxiu out, saying, "Number Three, how can you be so stupid? Why even ask to see your mother-in-law?" And so he pushed Tingxiu all the way out the gate. Verily,

> Would that feelings on first acquaintance remain unchanged,
> So that no rancor could ever raise its ugly head!

In the meantime, Xu-shi, in the inner section of the house, heard the commotion and the crying in the main hall but she thought it was Squire Wang beating up the page boys. She had no inkling that this was all about Tingxiu. So she did not pay attention, nor did any of the servants breathe a word about it to her. By afternoon, upon hearing that the teacher had been sent away, she grew a little apprehensive. She asked the servants, but all professed ignorance. It was not until late in the evening when Squire Wang entered their bedchamber that she learned, upon inquiry, that Tingxiu had been spoken ill of and had been driven out. Xu-shi defended Tingxiu as best she could and advised her husband to take him back. However, his mind poisoned by all those vicious words, Squire Wang stoutly refused and accused Xu-shi of covering up Tingxiu's wrongdoings. Sister Yu felt as if she had been stabbed through the heart, but, not daring to speak up in her parents' presence, she could only shed furtive tears.

Unable to put her mind at ease, Xu-shi acted on her own initiative and told the servants to bring Tingxiu back to see her, but the servants, in collusion with Zhao Ang, fobbed her off, saying they were not able to find him.

Let us turn our attention from Xu-shi and her daughter back to Tingxiu after he left the Wang residence. Distraught with grief, he staggered and stumbled his way to his mother's house. Wenxiu, who happened to be at the door, asked, "Why are you back so soon, brother?"

Choking with mortification, Tingxiu could hardly get a word out.

"What could have maddened you like this?" asked Wenxiu again.

It was a while later that Tingxiu was able to acquaint him with the facts.

"There's nothing surprising about the snobbish ways of the world," said Wenxiu.

"It's just that Squire Wang has always gone out of his way to shower us with kindnesses, and yet he did this almost as soon as he got home. Zhao Ang, with his inflammatory speech, must be behind all this. Now, don't tell mother any of this. It'll only add to her worries."

"You're right, my good brother," said Tingxiu.

The next day, Tingxiu went to the prison to see his father. By this time, Zhang Quan's wounds had healed, thanks to Zhong Yi, and he had regained his health. After hearing Tingxiu's tearful account, Zhang Quan sighed in lament over Squire Wang's lack of consistency.

"Come to think of it, maybe Zhao Ang is also behind the plot against you," suggested Zhong Yi.

"There's never been any grudge between him and me," said Zhang Quan. "It can't be him."

Tingxiu put in, "When I was betrothed, I did hear that he and his wife tried to talk my father-in-law out of the idea because of our carpenter background. My father-in-law didn't listen to them and gave them a tongue-lashing. Maybe that was the cause of it all."

"So it must be him," concluded Zhong Yi. Addressing Tingxiu, he continued, "Whether it's indeed him or not, you can have someone write a complaint and submit it to the yamen, because the new imperial inspector will soon be in Zhenjiang. Just say that Zhao Ang bribed the police and a gang of criminals, and made up a case to frame your father. And then let the authorities find out the truth. If it was him and torture is applied, someone in the know is bound to confess. If it wasn't him, little harm can be done."

Zhang Quan and his son readily agreed. After parting with them and leaving the prison, Tingxiu consulted his brother, had an official complaint written up, and began preparing for a journey to Zhenjiang to file the complaint. As the saying goes, "If a secret is not tightly kept, disaster strikes before you know it." Such things can only be discussed in whispers, but Zhang Quan was an honest man unfamiliar with the ways of the world, and Zhong Yi was an uncultured and straightforward man who never watched what he said. They were overheard by a warden who happened to be a cousin of Yang Hong's. With the speed of wind, he raced off to report to Yang Hong. Yang Hong was aghast. Losing no time, he rushed to Squire Wang's residence to see Zhao Ang, but, not daring to go straight in, he asked a page boy who happened to be entering the house to relay a message, just to say that a man named Yang at the gate wished to speak to Young Master Zhao.

Believing it must be Yang Hong, Zhao Ang immediately went out to greet him. "What is it, Brother Yang?" he asked.

Yang Hong pulled him to a quiet and secluded spot and said, "Zhang Tingxiu already knows that you and I are the ones plotting against them. He's going to see the imperial inspector and file a complaint. If the case is accepted and we're put under interrogation, we might confess under torture and end up being punished. Won't we be bringing trouble on ourselves? Luckily my cousin overheard them and told me about it. That's why I'm here."

Zhao Ang was struck speechless. After a good while, he said, "What are we going to do?"

"Well, since we've started something, we might as well finish it off," said Yang Hong. "With your money and my work, let's do away with those two boys and be done with it. As the idiom goes, when killing weeds, dig up the roots."

"Money is not a problem," said Zhao Ang. "But we don't have a good plan."

"I've got one. They are too poor to hire a private boat. They'll most probably try to get a free ride. I'll get the police boat ready and have my brother and two assistants moor at Chang Gate. I'll ask my cousin to find out when they're leaving. We will then secretly follow them out of the city and invite them to take our boat. I'll go to Zhenjiang first to wait for them. Those two boys won't know where they are, so I'll row them to the middle of the river and toss them into the water. Won't that be a good way out?"

Zhao Ang was delighted. He told Yang Hong to wait awhile and went to take out thirty taels of silver. Handing them to Yang Hong, he said, "Please do a clean job and 'dig up the roots,' as you said! When the job is done, I'll have a more handsome reward for you." Yang Hong took the silver and went his way.

Equipped with the official complaint, Tingxiu was now ready to go to Zhenjiang, to which city the imperial inspector, so he heard, would soon be traveling. By this time, his mother, Chen-shi, had recovered from her illness and had learned about how Squire Wang had driven her son out, but there was nothing she could do. Hearing that Tingxiu was going to lodge a complaint with the authorities, she said to him, "You've never traveled before. I'll worry too much if you go alone. You must go with your brother, so that you have someone to talk to if something comes up."

"Of course it would be better if my brother could join me, but there would be no one to take care of you."

"You'll be away for just a few days, and I have the company of the maidservant. So don't worry about me."

Tingxiu listened to his mother and packed for the journey. The brothers went first to the prison to bid adieu to their father. Then, their baggage on their backs, they went out Chang Gate to find a boat. When they were at Ferrying Monks Bridge, they heard a voice behind them crying, "Where would you two young gentlemen like to go?"

"To Zhenjiang," replied Tingxiu.

"We're going to Zhenjiang. We can give you a ride. It's fast and safe."

Hearing the offer of a ride, Tingxiu stopped in his tracks and said to Wenxiu, "A private boat is better than a crowded ferryboat."

"Whatever you say, brother."

To the boatman, Tingxiu said, "Where's your boat? Are you leaving right now?"

"The crime section of the prefectural yamen hired us on a mission. We'd like to give a ride to a couple of passengers to make enough extra money for a cup of wine along the way, but it's all right if we don't get anyone. Yes, we are leaving right now."

"In that case, please take us," said Tingxiu.

The boatman led them to the boat and offered them seats at the stern. A moment later, a man with baggage on his back walked up. The boatman greeted him and let him board the boat.

"Who are these two boys?" asked the newcomer.

"They're also going to Zhenjiang. Please allow us to take them, so that we can make enough extra money for a cup of wine along the way. Please do us this favor."

"All right, but just these two. Not one more."

"We met these two by chance," said the boatman. "We won't dare take more." With that, he set the boat in motion.

Who, you may ask, was that newcomer? He was Yang Jiang, Yang Hong's brother. The boatman was an assistant.

"What are your names? Where do you live? And why are you going to Zhenjiang?" asked Yang Jiang.

Tingxiu told him their names, where they lived, how their father had been framed, and that they were now on their way to lodge a complaint with the inspector.

"So you're from a good family," said Yang Jiang. "You poor things! If you don't like the stern, you can use the cabin."

"Thank you so much!" said Tingxiu. So the two brothers moved their bedding to the cabin. Yang Jiang made a great show of attention towards them along the way, sharing his wine and meat with them and promising them that he would look after their father. The two young men's hearts overflowed with gratitude.

The boat was a police clipper. After sailing all night with a favorable wind, they arrived in Zhenjiang at dusk the following day. The boatman took payment from Tingxiu and false-heartedly urged them to go ashore. Tingxiu picked up their baggage and was about to go when Yang Jiang said, "Hey, boatman, you're so inconsiderate! These two young gentlemen have never traveled before. It's getting late now. Where do you suppose they can find lodging?" Turning to Tingxiu, he said, "Just ignore him! You stay in this boat tonight. I'll go ashore with you tomorrow morning. After you find lodging, you can then go to the inspectorate to ask when the inspector is arriving. Won't you have saved one night's lodging expenses?"

Believing that he was a good man, the brothers thanked him profusely and laid down their baggage. Yang Jiang took out some money and told the boatman to buy some wine and meat and to moor the boat at a quiet spot. The boatman said yes. He moved the boat out of West Floodgate and moored where the river was wide. After the boatman brought wine and meat into the cabin, Yang Jiang strenuously plied wine on the Zhang brothers until they lay down in the cabin in drunken stupor. At this point, Yang Hong, who had been waiting for the boat, came on board as soon as the boatman gave a whistle. The boatman then untied the ropes and quietly rowed the boat out of the mouth of the river down the current into the Yangzi. After passing Jiao Hill, they reached a point where the river was wide. There, the men took out ropes and trussed up the two brothers until they looked like two wontons. Waking up in pain from their wine-induced sleep, they found themselves unable to move. Before they had time to cry out, Yang Hong and Yang Jiang raised them and tossed them with a splash into the river. They were to die any moment now.

> How sad that such talented young men
> Were to become ghosts under the waves!

Just imagine the surging waves of the Yangzi River! The river sweeps majestically down to Zhenjiang all the way from Sichuan, Huguang, and Jiangxi and plunges into the sea at Zhenjiang. Even a rock would be swept down the current, but Tingxiu and his brother floated against the current. In surprise, Yang Hong and Yang Jiang turned their boat around. As the boat went upstream, each of them threw a boat pole at the Zhang brothers. In less time than it takes to narrate, the poles were less than one foot from hitting them when three or four waves surged forward and bore the Zhang brothers away. The boat almost capsized and the poles missed their targets. Convinced that the Zhang brothers could not possibly survive, Yang Jiang sailed back to moor the boat at the same place as the day before. The next morning, they returned to Suzhou and reported to Zhao Ang. Immensely delighted, Zhao Ang gave them another thirty taels of silver. Offended by the paltriness of the amount, Yang Hong got into an argument with him and they parted in a huff, each flushed with anger, but of this, no more for now.

In Henan Prefecture there lived a man called Chu Wei. In his sixties, he was much given to works of charity. He and his wife, both vegetarians for many years, had no children. He made a living as a merchant of fabric, traveling in regions south of the lower reaches of Yangzi River. One day he set sail from Zhenjiang on a large boat laden with fabric and headed north to Henan. After the boat had gone less than thirty li, evening began to set in and, with the wind against him and the waves too high, he resignedly moored the boat, as others had done. In the middle of the night, he heard in his sleep something bumping against his boat, but he ignored it. He was about to go back to sleep when he felt as if someone were pushing him. The thumps against the boat grew louder, and a human voice was faintly audible. Intrigued, he rose and opened the window to look. There, on the surface of the water, floated a man making faint sounds in his throat. Quickly, Chu Wei woke up the crew and had them bring the man into the boat. By lamplight, Chu Wei saw that he was in fact a fifteen- or sixteen-year-old boy with refined looks. All trussed up, he hardly had any breath left in him.

After the ropes were taken down and some heated water was forced down his throat, he gradually came to and threw up a lot of water. Chu Wei gave him a change of dry clothes and asked what had happened to him. The boy said, sobbing, "My name is Zhang Wenxiu. Because my father is in prison on false charges, my older brother Tingxiu and I set out for Zhenjiang to file a complaint with the imperial inspector. A man who claimed to be an employee of the crime section of the Suzhou yamen gave us a ride in his boat. He was very attentive to us along the way, but it was just a show. Last evening when we arrived at Zhenjiang, he kept us on the boat and then he got us drunk, tied us up, and threw us into the water. We have no idea who he is or why he wanted to kill us. Fortunately you saved me. What is your honorable name? Where are we? How far are we from Zhenjiang? If you could somehow take me home, I'd never forget your kindness!"

Being a man given to acts of kindness, Chu Wei felt deeply for this young man in his distress. At first he did intend to escort him home, but then a thought suddenly struck him: How did the boy get here from Zhenjiang against the current? Could it be that the boy was destined for greatness later in life and therefore had the protection and blessing of the gods and ghosts? I don't have a son. Why don't I keep him and adopt him as a son? Won't that be nice?

Guilefully he said, "I'm Chu Wei of Henan. I'm on my way home after a trip selling fabric. We are more than a thousand li from Zhenjiang, too far from there to take you home. What's more, the one who tried to kill you last night must be a trusted follower of an enemy of yours. That's why he did such violence to you. If you go home, they'll surely try again to get you in some other way. I have no son of my own. If you don't think it's beneath you, let me adopt you as a son and take you to my home. Next year, I'll take you down to Zhenjiang to look for the man who did this to you last night. After we find him, we'll then bring a lawsuit against him and save your father. All right?"

However eager he was to see his parents, Wenxiu could do no more than agree.

Chu Wei adopted him as a son, changed his name to Chu Simao [Prosperous Offspring], and took him upriver to Henan, and there we shall leave them for now.

As for Zhang Tingxiu, he thought he was going to die when he was thrown into the river, all trussed up. As it turned out, he sank but rose and stayed afloat until huge waves bore him to a patch of reeds by a sandbar. After daybreak, he saw a good many boats plying up and down the river, but they were all too far from the shore for anyone to hear his cries. In the afternoon, at the sight of a boat coming along the shore toward the sandbar, Tingxiu cried out for help. The boat pulled in to the sandbar. He was then taken into the boat, cut free from his ropes, and made to sit up. Luckily, he was not hurt in any way. He looked up and saw in the boat two middle-aged men and about ten sixteen or seventeen-year-old boys. You may well ask, who were these people? Well, they were entertainers employed by Secretary Sun of Shaoxing Prefecture, Zhejiang. Of the two middle-aged men, one was the mentor Pan Zhong, and the other a servant in charge of the trunks containing costumes and stage props. They were on their way to Nanjing for a performance when they passed the place and saved Tingxiu. They had Tingxiu change into dry clothes and asked him what had happened, whereupon Tingxiu tearfully told them that his father had been framed, that he was on his way to the inspectorate to seek justice, and that he was victim of a murder attempt. "Thank you so much for having saved my life," he added. "If you could take me to my home, I'd surely repay your kindness."

It so happened that Pan Zhong was searching for a replacement for an actor who had lost his voice. Impressed by Tingxiu's good looks and ringing voice and glad that Tingxiu was of about the right age for that male role, Pan Zhong thought, "If properly trained, this young man will fit that role well." With this selfish design on Tingxiu, Pan Zhong would probably not have let him go home even if Suzhou *were* on their way.

"We are entertainers in the employment of Secretary Sun of Shaoxing," said Pan Zhong. "We're on our way to Nanjing on business. We don't have time to turn back and take you home. We'll soon be arriving in Nanjing. Why don't you join us and stay there for a while? We can then take our time looking for someone who happens to come this way to take you home. If you don't want to do that, we'll just have to drop you on the sandbar where we found you. You can wait for another boat to take you home."

Alarmed at this tone, Tingxiu hastened to say, "Since my home is out of your way, I'll be glad to go with you to Nanjing."

"All right," said Pan Zhong.

Although he himself survived the murder attempt, Tingxiu shed copious tears at the thought that his brother must have perished. With a favorable wind, they arrived in Nanjing that very night. The next morning, they went into the city and found lodging at an inn. As a matter of fact, the entertainers of the Sun establishment were quite famous and received invitations to perform as soon as they arrived in Nanjing. Tingxiu followed them wherever they went. A few days later, Pan Zhong said to him, "We are all working for enough money to support our families. No one is willing to have you as a freeloader. Also, if you find someone to take you home, where's the travel money to come from? You'd better learn some skills as an entertainer and earn your keep, to get yourself ready for going home."

Tingxiu already felt unworthy of their kindness in first rescuing him and then providing for him. These words of Pan Zhong's added to his sense of shame. He thought, "I had been hoping for a day when I could win academic honor and bring glory to my ancestors. I certainly never dreamt that such disasters would befall us. Our family is broken up, my brother is dead, my father is in the south, and I'm stranded in the north! If I learn the skills of a lowly entertainer, what future will there be for me? But if I don't obey him, I won't be able to stay on." Then he started on a new train of thought, "In ancient times, Qizi had been a slave and Wu Zixu had been a beggar.[1] Even such great men had to be flexible when hard times hit. In my position, I can't afford to think of my dignity. Let me scratch out a living first and then think about what to do next."

So he did as Pan Zhong told him to do and began to learn the male role. With his natural endowment, he quickly learned to sing the arias that were taught to him just a few times. In a few days, he was good enough to go on stage. His performance exceeded expectations and appealed to both refined and popular tastes. After working every day for more than half a year in Nanjing, he thought that he had saved enough money to go home. To his dismay, Pan Zhong had anticipated what he would be thinking of and had quietly hid the silver due to him, so that Tingxiu remained empty-handed and unable to leave. Afraid that the young man would still give him the slip, Pan Zhong made a point of being with Tingxiu at all times of the day, walking or sitting. Without a chance to leave, Tingxiu had to stay on, for lack of a better choice. Truly,

> Knowing these were not his right companions,
> He stayed with them in his desperate straits.

Let us pick up another thread of the story and come back to Chen-shi. After she sent her sons off, she worried that they were too young and might therefore say the wrong things in the intimidating yamen. She never thought there would be a murder attempt against them. After ten days, at the slightest rustle of grass in the wind, she would hasten to the door to see if her sons were back. Ten days stretched to half a month and then to twenty days. She began to sit by the door all day, eagerly on the lookout for them. At this point, she still thought that her sons were waiting in Zhenjiang for the arrival of the inspector. After learning that the inspector had finished his work in Zhenjiang and was moving on to another place, she grew as frantic as an ant crawling on a hot frying pan. She went in all haste to the prison to tell her husband about it and asked people to put up posters everywhere and look for them, but all to no avail. She and her husband wept bitterly in regret, saying, "Had we known this, we wouldn't have let them go. And now, we've lost our boys before justice is done. Whom are we going to turn to for help in our old age?" The more they thought about it, the more grief-stricken they became. In the beginning, they still hoped against hope that the boys would return home. After more than a year went by, they gave them up for dead and began to offer sacrifices to their spirits. Their tears never ran dry. Then the maidservant died of illness, leaving Chen-shi all to herself in greater misery. Verily,

> *An all-night rain wrecks a hut already leaking;*
> *A strong headwind thwarts a boat already late.*

After driving Tingxiu out at the instigation of Zhao Ang, Squire Wang wanted to find another husband for Sister Yu, but, out of fear for Tingxiu's complaint and other people's gossip, he dared not do anything yet. Later, upon hearing that Tingxiu and his brother were going to the inspectorate in Zhenjiang to lodge an official complaint, he panicked because he thought it was about his breach of the engagement. Without saying anything openly, he secretly sent servants to make inquiries. Little by little, word came that the Zhang brothers were gone and that no one knew whether they were now dead or alive. In the exuberance of his joy at the news, he immediately engaged the services of a matchmaker, who spread the word around among those of the same profession. Within a matter of days, several tens of families proposed, coveting the wealth of a family without a male heir, even though Squire Wang already had a prospective son-in-law.

When Tingxiu was first expelled from the house, Sister Yu took it extremely hard, but she still hoped that her father would bring him back. If not, at least she could join the Zhang household after the wedding. When bad news came to her ears, she remained dubious. Now, witnessing her father interviewing a never-ending stream of matchmakers, trying to find another match for her, she thought that Tingxiu must have been confirmed dead. Casting all her scruples aside, she gave way to her grief and burst into loud wails as she climbed up the stairs to her room. Squire Wang's house, you see, was a two-storied one. The old couple's bedchamber was on the first floor and Sister Yu's was upstairs. And there, in her room, she kept weeping, declining all offers of tea and food. She thought, "I may not have married yet, but I've been engaged since childhood. Unfortunately my intended one has died. How can I hang on to life at the expense of my chastity? I will only be spurned by the public while I'm alive, and I will be too ashamed to face him after I die. I'd rather die in dignity than live on in shame, partly to bring credit to my husband and partly to show my devotion to him. Mother is the only one I worry about, but things having come to this, I can't afford to be concerned about her." With these thoughts, she burst into another fit of weeping.

As she choked over her sobs, Xu-shi, who cherished her as she would a lustrous pearl in her palm, grew frantic. Without any idea as to what to do, she said over and over again, "Don't cry. Tell me, why do you cry like this?" As Xu-shi spoke, she herself also broke down in tears. When Sister Yu told her the truth, she said, to cheer her up, "My child, let's ignore that old fool! I have the final say. I'll send someone tomorrow to find out what has happened to Number Three. If something unfortunate did happen, you will be given half of the family estate so that you can observe widowhood. If that old fool insists on marrying you off, I'll fight him to the death!" Turning to a maid, she said, "Get the squire here. I'll talk to him." Then she added, "If he's with someone, be sure not to say anything else."

The maid dashed off to see the squire. As it turned out, Squire Wang was with a matchmaker sent by a young scholar who had just passed the imperial examinations at the county level. Delighted upon hearing that the young man was as talented as he was handsome and from a distinguished old family, too, the squire had kept the matchmaker for a meal. The maid arrived at a moment when the conversation was at its liveliest and everyone was well warmed with wine. "Her ladyship asks for your presence," said the maid, but as far as the squire was concerned, the announcement went in one ear and out the other. He showed no sign that he was about to rise. The maid remained standing until her legs ached and her feet went numb. Eventually she saw nothing for it but to go back and report to her mistress.

Xu-shi continued to try desperately to calm Sister Yu down. The girl had just stopped crying when Zhao Ang's wife stormed upstairs, and the wails of grief started all over again. Why? Well, having gotten rid of Zhang Quan and Tingxiu, Zhao Ang was now aiming to drive Sister Yu to death so that he could be the sole heir to the family fortune. He had not yet made a move only because no opportunity had presented itself. Now that Squire Wang was searching for another candidate, he felt let down and had been conferring with his wife in their room about a plan to block the marriage. Hearing that Sister Yu was averse to her father's idea and was crying upstairs, he felt that his chance had come.

So Sister Rui approached her sister and said purposely, "Sister, how can you be so unappreciative? Father matched you with a carpenter's son in a moment of foolishness and brought disgrace to our family. With that one gone now, consider yourself lucky that you'll be married off to someone with a matching family background. What's there to cry about? Don't tell me that you think being the daughter-in-law of a criminal and the wife of a carpenter is better than marrying into a decent family!"

Blushing hotly at these remarks, Sister Yu burst into another flood of tears. Xu-shi was displeased.

Lacking the good judgment to know when to stop, Sister Rui pulled her mother to one side and said in a subdued voice, "Mother, could my sister and that little scoundrel have been secretly up to some mischief? Is that why she misses him so much?"

Xu-shi was so enraged that her eyes flashed fire, and she spit right into Sister

Rui's face. But, afraid of exasperating Sister Yu, she dared not speak her mind plainly and said only, "You are her blood sister. How can you harbor such evil thoughts? I had just calmed her down and you had to come here and make her start crying again. And what a filthy thing you said! What if she's the daughter-in-law of a criminal and wife of a carpenter? What's it to you to make your tongue run away with you like that?"

Overcome with mortification by this heated lecture, Sister Rui quickly went down the stairs, saying as she went, "How you cover up her faults! I'm afraid you won't see a more shameless girl in the whole wide world! She loves her man so much before she even marries him. If she had given him a child, she would want to be buried in his coffin. She's so thick-skinned she has no sense of shame!" And so she jabbered away as she went along, obviously determined to drive Sister Yu to suicide.

Xu-shi did not want a fight and therefore feigned deafness to Sister Rui's raving and ranting. Sister Yu had cried herself into a stupor and was oblivious to what was being said. By evening, a gloriously drunk Squire Wang came into the room with the support of a page boy and went directly to bed, little knowing what his daughter had gone through. Xu-shi sat with Sister Yu until midnight. Succumbing to irresistible drowsiness, her eyes heavy with sleep, she said to Sister Yu, "My child, don't feel so bad. I'll have a definite answer for you tomorrow. It's late now. Go to sleep." She pushed her daughter to bed, removed the girl's hairpins, tucked her in under her quilt without undressing her, and let down the bed-curtain. Then she told the maids to keep a good watch on the candles. Most maids in the employment of wealthy families are lazy and tend to oversleep. Of every ten of them, you would barely find one who is hardworking. Xu-shi had seven or eight maids, three of whom tended to Sister Yu and slept upstairs. That night, having stayed up so late, they were all slouching every which way, only too eager to lie down to sleep. Now that Xu-shi had tucked Sister Yu in, they scattered to clear things up and waited for Xu-shi to go downstairs, so that they could close the door above the staircase and go to sleep. After descending the stairs, Xu-shi saw that Squire Wang was deep in his wine-induced sleep. Without disturbing him, she checked everywhere with her lamp and undressed for bed, and there we shall leave her.

Sister Yu brooded over her situation as she lay in bed and plunged into deeper grief. She thought, "Mother may be on my side, but father may not think the same way. So, mother's advice may not work out." Then again, she thought, "The way mother suddenly lashed out at sister, she must have been angry at some unkind thing that sister had said about me. I'm spotlessly chaste. Why submit myself to ridicule and humiliation? I'd better die and be done with it!" After weeping for another two hours, she rose amid the snores of the maids. Having ascertained that all was still downstairs, she tearfully picked up a kerchief, carried a stool to the middle of the room, stepped onto it, tossed the kerchief over the beam, made a noose, slipped her neck into it, and kicked over the stool. Alas! Indeed,

Unable to tell anyone else her tale of woe,
She turned to her husband in the netherworld.

However, Sister Yu was not destined to die at this point after all. She had just kicked over the stool when a maid appeared. During the day, because Sister Yu had gone without lunch, the maid who cleared away the table had gorged herself on the food without the knowledge of the other two maids. Sister Yu's supper went the same way. And now, in the middle of the night, the maid felt bloated and her belly ached. She rose to relieve herself but couldn't find the chamber pot. She gave one groan after another because, in her eagerness to go to sleep, she had forgotten to put the chamber pot in its usual place and now she urgently needed to go. In her naked state, she went to look for it. Her eyes blurry with sleep, in the flickering candlelight she did not see Sister Yu's body hanging from the beam. In her haste, she bumped into the body. With a loud thump, the maid fell onto the floor, knocking over the stool. Xu-shi and the maids downstairs all woke up in alarm. Squire Wang also woke up with a start from his drunken slumber. "What was that noise?" he asked.

The maid's belly had hit the stool when she fell, expelling a stream of urine and feces onto the floor. In the middle of the mess, she raised her eyes and cried out in terror, "Oh no! Sister Yu has hanged herself!"

Hearing the cry, Squire Wang was so frightened that the last drop of wine in his body vanished. He jumped from bed and, fumbling for his clothes, asked, "But why?"

Between sobs and cries of "My baby, my darling," Xu-shi cursed her husband, "You old swine! You killed her! And you have the temerity to ask!"

Not bothering to ask again, Squire Wang frantically grabbed whatever came first to his fumbling hands. It was a jacket belonging to Xu-shi, but he couldn't care less. Throwing it over his shoulders, he began to look for his shoes, but, failing to find them, he ran barefoot up the stairs. Xu-shi groped around and found her skirt but not her blouse. Wrapping herself in the bedsheet, she slipped her feet into her husband's shoes backwards and staggered tearfully upstairs. In his frantic state, the old man lost his footing and tumbled down the staircase, bumping into his wife as he did so. The two of them rolled all the way down in one heap. Ignoring the aches all over their bodies, they scrambled to their feet and charged up the stairs again.

The door above the staircase remained closed. As the squire's fists pounded it as if beating a drum, the maids upstairs and downstairs, all up by now, groped for their clothes. Some found their skirts but not their blouses. Some found their blouses but not their pants. One got both feet into one trouser leg; one threw her blouse the wrong way over her shoulders and couldn't find the sleeves. And so they pulled and dragged and tugged at one another's clothes in a confused hubbub of shouts and screams. The maid who had made a mess was so busily occupied wiping herself clean and looking for her clothes that she did not answer the door. As Squire Wang's pounding on the door grew more frantic, all three upstairs maids picked up their clothes and rushed over to open it. When the old couple burst into the room, the sight of her daughter's body filled Xu-shi with aching grief. She burst into loud wails, but Squire Wang had the presence of mind befitting a man to hold back his tears. He rushed forward to feel his daughter's body with his hand. Finding the body still warm and hearing a rattle in her throat, he cried out, "Mother! Don't cry! There's still hope!" Holding his daughter's body, he told a maid to get up on the stool and release her from the noose, and ordered another maid to boil some water.

Hearing that there was hope, Xu-shi stopped crying and lit a lamp to take a good look. The maid picking up the wooden stool got her hand into the filth. As a stench assailed her nostrils, she screamed, "How come this stool is so filthy?" As Xu-shi happened to be at this spot with her lamp, she saw a pool of feces and urine on the floor. Unbeknownst to himself, Squire Wang was standing right in the middle of the pool. Believing all this had come from her daughter, Xu-shi lowered the lamp and said, "What hope is there when she's already in such a state?" And she started wailing again. The fact is, those who hang themselves are beyond rescue if their feces and urine have come out.

"Never mind!" said Squire Wang. "Let her down first!" Her hands all smeared with filth, the maid stepped onto the wooden stool to untie the noose, but her hands trembled in her agitation. Losing patience, Squire Wang had a maid bring him a knife. He cut the kerchief down, carried his daughter to her bed, gently untied the fast knot around her throat, and had Xu-shi give her mouth-to-mouth resuscitation. After more than ten attempts, Sister Yu's breath came back and her hands and feet stirred. They then forced a few mouthfuls of the boiled water down her throat. Gradually she regained consciousness and began sobbing. Xu-shi said, also weeping, "After what I said to you, how could you have done this to yourself?"

"I'm born to suffer," said Sister Yu tearfully. "Why hang on to life? I'd be better off dead!"

Turning to Xu-shi, Squire Wang said, "You said some moments ago that I killed her. Explain that to me."

After Xu-shi told him how Sister Yu refused to marry another man, Squire Wang said to his daughter, "How can you be so stupid? I made that betrothal for you in a moment of foolishness. I could have ruined your future. With that scoundrel gone goodness knows where, I'm looking for a good candidate for you out of the best intentions. How could you have done such a thing! You almost scared me to death!"

Sister Yu said nothing but kept weeping.

"You old fool! What do you know?" snapped Xu-shi. "You were full of praise for Tingxiu and adopted him as a son and then as a son-in-law, all by your own decisions. No one talked you into it. And then when he was in our house behaving as well as he had always been without doing anything improper, you believed the lies of some confounded rascal and drove him out as soon as you returned home. And now we have no idea what has happened to him. If he has indeed died, we should at least wait for a couple of years and see what our girl wants to do before making the next move. But before we even know for sure whether he's dead or alive, you're already making a big splash and searching for another son-in-law, and you keep me in the dark, too! Of course she's mad at you! Luckily she's been brought back to life. If she had died, what would you have done? Now, call off that search and send people out to ask about what has happened to Tingxiu. If he's fine, I need not say what should be done. But if there's bad news, give Sister Yu half of the family property so that she can observe widowhood and keep her chastity. If you don't listen to me but drive her to something desperate again, I'm not going to let you off easy!"

Now that he had witnessed how stubborn his daughter could be, Squire Wang resignedly mumbled something in assent. After he went downstairs, Xu-shi said to Sister Yu, "My child, I've laid everything out to him. He will listen. Now don't cry anymore. Your clothes are soiled. Take them off and go to sleep for a good rest." Without asking if Sister Yu was willing or not, she pulled hard at her ribbons, trying to undress her. Unable to fend her off, Sister Yu had to undress and go to bed amid the commotion that lasted until daybreak. When Sister Yu saw in the daylight that her clothes were spotlessly clean, the maid who was responsible for the mess felt obliged to admit the truth, to the great mirth of all the other maids.

Henceforth, Sister Yu confined herself to her room without ever stepping downstairs, like one in religious training. Even though Squire Wang did not make inquiries about Tingxiu's whereabouts, he at least called off the search for a candidate. Afraid that her daughter would be up to some mischief again, Xu-shi slept by her side and was never so much as one inch apart from her. Her husband being in no hurry to make inquiries about Tingxiu, she gave a servant money out of her own private savings and told him to do his own investigations and to go to Tingxiu's mother for information. (*The mistress of the house has to bribe servants into doing errands for her. Such are the ways of the world.*) Truly,

> *If only he could appear when called!*
> *That moment would be worth more than a ton of gold.*

Let us retrace our steps and go back to the moment when Zhao Ang's wife went downstairs after receiving a tongue-lashing from her mother. She unburdened herself of a string of abominable words as she went down the stairs to her own room. After telling her husband about what had happened, she added, "Now that the bad blood is out in the open, let me put my tongue to good use morning and night and send that girl on her way."

The next morning, inwardly pleased upon hearing that Sister Yu had tried to hang herself, she went up and offered insincere words of solace. But when she was with her father alone, she said many a malicious thing to poison his mind. Secretly she bribed Sister Yu's maids and told them that if Sister Yu was to try to hang herself again, they should let her die and not make a fuss. Hearing that Xu-shi had sent someone to make inquiries about Tingxiu, she paid the man generously and made him declare that nothing had come of his inquiries.

In the meantime, Zhao Ang made every show of deference toward his father-in-law, trimming his sails to the wind and insinuating himself into his father-in-law's good graces in every way possible. As for Squire Wang, Sister Yu's determination to wait for Tingxiu having incurred his displeasure, he felt kindly towards Zhao Ang and his wife for their attentions to him and enjoyed their lively company. In every matter, he followed their advice. It goes without saying that Zhao Ang glowed with triumph. There was only one little thing that preyed on his mind. You may well ask what it was. It was the problem of Yang Hong. Having accomplished two major missions for him, Yang Hong came every so often to him to demand payment. In the beginning, Zhao Ang did pay up. Then he grew tired of Yang Hong, but there was no good excuse to put him off. And every time, Yang Hong complained about the paltriness of the sum. After Zhao Ang fell behind in his payments three or four times, Yang Hong grew resentful and began to grumble. Afraid that word would leak out to his father-in-law, Zhao Ang swallowed his anger and continued with the payments. Detecting Zhao Ang's fear, Yang Hong applied even greater pressure on him. At his wits' end, Zhao Ang came up with the idea of taking a trip somewhere to steer clear of the man.

It so happened that Squire Wang was again assigned to escort a shipment of tax grain to the capital. Taking advantage of this opportunity, Zhao Ang conferred with his father-in-law and proposed that, since he had a mind to go to the capital to seek an appointment to an official post in his status as a student of the National University, he could escort the shipment of grain in his father-in-law's place, thus doing two things at once. Squire Wang was pleased that his son-in-law was going to the capital to seek an appointment to office and, in addition, that he could be relieved of this tiring assignment. Of course he did not object. Zhao Ang then asked for a thousand taels of silver from his father-in-law so as to pull a few strings in the government. After send-off feasts given by friends and relatives, Zhao Ang paid Yang Hong once more before departing.

Let us follow another thread of the story and tell of Zhang Tingxiu, who had been working as a stage performer in Nanjing for about a year without ever having a chance to return home. One day, he and the other members of his group were called to perform in the residence of an official of the ministry of rites, Shao Cheng'en by name. A native of Ninghai County, Taizhou Prefecture of Zhejiang, he was a *jinshi*, serving at this time in the ministry of rites as a bureau director. His wife, Zhu-shi, had given birth to several children, but only a daughter survived. Fifteen years old now, she was skilled in needlework, pretty, kind, and virtuous. That day being Mr. Shao's sixtieth birthday, his colleagues went to his home to offer their congratulations and he laid out a feast in their honor. Tingxiu's performance was so true to life that everyone applauded. Mr. Shao, well versed in the art of physiognomy, was impressed by Tingxiu's facial features, which he believed bespoke a bright future. But, just to make sure that he was not mistaken, he called Tingxiu up to him about halfway through the performance. After a close examination of his face, Mr. Shao concluded that this young man, for all his current lamentably low status, was destined to be a highly placed court official in the future. He asked for Tingxiu's name and made a mental note of it. After the feast was over and the guests had departed, Mr. Shao sent the performers on their way but said that he wanted the one playing the leading male role to stay behind to entertain his wife and that he would have a servant escort the actor back the next day.

Afraid that Tingxiu would take the opportunity to get away, Pan Zhong was reluctant, but, not daring to disobey a government official, he emphatically gave his consent and led the others out.

Tingxiu followed Mr. Shao into the back hall, which was flooded with candlelight. Tables and wine vessels had been laid out. As Mrs. Shao and her daughter stepped forward to greet Mr. Shao, the male servants stood at a respectful distance and Tingxiu also stood off to one side. Those walking about the hall rendering services were all maidservants. After the young lady offered birthday congratulations to her father, Mrs. Shao raised her wine cup and offered a toast. Mr. Shao returned her toast before sitting down. He then called Tingxiu over to greet his wife and sing an aria. After Tingxiu finished singing, Mr. Shao said, "Zhang Tingxiu, with your imposing appearance, you certainly don't look like someone of a lowly status. Tell me the truth. Where are you from? How old are you? Why did you have to learn such lowly skills? Tell me everything. I may do something for you."

Tingxiu went up to him and told him the whole story, adding, "I am eighteen years old. I'm in the acting profession out of necessity rather than choice."

Mr. Shao sighed deeply. It was a long time before he said, "So you are the victim of a major miscarriage of justice. If you stay in this profession, when will you ever make your way in the world? Since you've had some education, you should be able to write poetry. Make a poem for me and let me judge." Forthwith he ordered that the four treasures of the scholar's study be brought in and set on the table next to him.[2] Tingxiu picked up the brush-pen and, without pausing for reflection, composed a poem on the spur of the moment and presented it to Mr. Shao, who saw that it was a birthday poem entitled "A Thousand Years":

> From a jade terrace on jasper grass,
> A black crane soars high into the clouds.
> At the feast, amid music and singing,
> The one from the divine realm and blessed isles
> Good-humoredly finds this world too small.
> Amid claps of hands in unison,

Songs are sung to eternal youth and spring.
The dragon flags shine over the palace;
The South Pole Star sheds its auspicious light;
Another year is added to your life.
The Blue Bird comes with a note in its beak,
To announce the advent of the fairies.
Would that your life were as long as Mount Song!
May your life last ten thousand years!

Exhilarated upon reading the poem, Mr. Shao was profuse in his praise. "Milady," he said, addressing his wife, "this talented and handsome young man is surely destined for a distinguished career. I have a mind to adopt him as a son. What do you say?"

His wife replied, "Yes, by all means. That would be very nice."

Turning to Tingxiu, Mr. Shao said, "I'm already sixty, and I still don't have a male heir. Should you be willing, I'll engage a teacher for you. That'll be better than making a fool of yourself in public, the way you do now."

"You, sir, are the father of my rebirth by raising my status like this. But I'm from a humble family. I'm afraid that, if adopted as a son, I'll only besmirch your good name."

"What a thing to say!" exclaimed Mr. Shao.

Then and there, Tingxiu bowed four times each to Mr. and Mrs. Shao, honoring them as his adoptive parents. He bowed also to the young lady, now his sister, before sitting down in a chair by their side. His name was changed to Shao Yiming. Director Shao instructed all the servants to call him young master. Anyone failing to show him proper respect was to be severely punished. Of this, we need say no more.

Now, as for Pan Zhong, after spending a wakeful night without a wink of sleep, he went first thing in the morning to stand at the gate of the Shao residence and wait for Tingxiu to appear. By noon, when he still didn't see Tingxiu, he humbly asked the gatekeeper to relay his message to Mr. Shao. Mr. Shao summoned him in and said to him, "Zhang Tingxiu is from a good decent family. After an attempt was made on his life, you kindly saved him and kept him as an entertainer. He's now a member of this household. You can go ahead and hire someone else to replace him." With that, he instructed a servant to reward Pan Zhong with five taels of silver.

When Pan Zhong heard that Tingxiu was now a member of Director Shao's household, his jaw dropped and he stood there stupefied for a good while, mouth agape. Finally he resigned himself to the situation, kowtowed, thanked the director, and took his leave.

That very day, Mr. Shao engaged a teacher and had a study cleaned up and prepared for Tingxiu. Even though he had gotten rusty, Tingxiu was, after all, a diligent student. From morning to night, he applied himself assiduously to his studies. After more than two months, his writing gained such beauty and elegance that Mr. Shao was filled with joy. As the triennial provincial-level civil service examination was coming up later in the year, he enrolled Tingxiu in the National University. In autumn, Tingxiu sat for the examination and came out fifth. Mr. Shao's face was wreathed in smiles. After thanking the chief examiner, Tingxiu told Mr. Shao that he wished to go to Suzhou to help exonerate his father.

"Not so fast!" said Mr. Shao. "A better course of action is for you to take the next level of exams in the capital. If you get the *jinshi* degree, you can request to be assigned to an office in the town where your father is, so that you can track down the culprit and have justice done to him. Won't that be more satisfying? If you don't pass the exams, you can send people to investigate and identify the culprit and then I'll go with you to inform the local officials, so as to bring him to justice. If you go now, you would only alert him prematurely. He'll surely go into hiding, and all of your efforts will come to nothing, and you'll miss the examinations, too."

Convinced by his logic, Tingxiu felt obliged to comply. Mr. Shao was so taken with Tingxiu that he wished to marry his daughter to the young man but, since he had already adopted him as son, he could hardly raise the matter for fear of incurring gossip. He therefore had a matchmaker drop Tingxiu a hint. Partly because his father's wrongs had not yet been redressed and partly because he did not know how Sister Yu would take it, Tingxiu refused to breach his existing betrothal. He explained the situation to Mr. Shao and put a stop to the attempt. Then he packed and went to the capital for the examinations at the next level. Truly,

> *Before he avenged his father and tracked down his foe,*
> *He went to win honors in the exams.*

Let us follow another thread of the story and turn our attention to Zhang Wenxiu, now called Chu Simao since he settled down in Henan. The kindly Mr. and Mrs. Chu cherished him dearly and engaged a teacher for him, but his thoughts were all with his parents and his brother day and night. Even though he was in Henan, his heart was in Suzhou, and books had lost their appeal for him. He could hardly wait to join Mr. Chu on his fabric-selling trip to the lower reaches of Yangzi River, so that he could have a chance to return home. However, Mr. Chu being advanced in years and the family fortunes quite ample, Mrs. Chu advised him to give up his travels and confine his business to home. Upon hearing this, Wenxiu was so dejected that he fell ill. Mr. Chu engaged a physician for him and consoled him with kind words. About a year later, the examinations at the local level came around. Wenxiu took the examinations in spite of his illness and he passed.

As the proverb says, "Luck brings wisdom." After passing the examinations, Wenxiu pushed the thought of returning home to the back of his mind. He thought, "Now that there *is* a chance I can make my mark some day, let me go sit for the provincial-level exams. If, by a stroke of luck, I get the *jinshi* degree, saving father and avenging him will be as easy as turning over a hand." Heaven hardly ever fails to grant the wish of one with such a determination. Sure enough, he passed all three sessions of the examinations and his name was posted on the list of successful candidates. After taking part in the banquet held by the chief examiner in honor of the successful candidates, he went home to pay his respects to his parents. Mr. and Mrs. Chu went delirious with delight. Relatives and neighbors came to offer their congratulations, filling the house to bursting and praising Wenxiu in glowing terms. Goodness knows how many rich families offered lavish gifts of betrothal for Wenxiu, but, thoughts of his father having taken full possession of his mind, he turned a deaf ear to all the marriage proposals. Eagerly, he asked two other successful examinees to join him, packed, and, taking along a servant, went to Beijing for the national level of the examinations. Mr. and Mrs. Chu accompanied them for ten li before taking leave of them.

They traveled by day and rested by night. After quite a few days, they arrived in the capital and found lodging at an inn. By the will of heaven, Tingxiu and Wenxiu stayed next door to each other in the very same inn and were thus able to see each other frequently, but they did not recognize each other because by this time their places of residence and style of life had changed their manners and altered their appearance. Neither of them was his haggard and emaciated old self, although their figures remained the same and reminded them of each other. However, one was Young Master Shao Yiming of the eminent Shao family of Zhejiang and the other was Chu Simao, son of a wealthy family of Henan. The thought that they could be brothers born to the same parents did not occur to them even in a dream.

A few days later, after all three sessions of the examinations were over, some candidates staying at the same inn waiting for the results of the examinations went together to seek pleasure in the courtesans' quarters, but Shao and Chu firmly refused to join them. Chu Simao bought some wine and invited Shao Yiming over for a chat to while away the time. As they sat talking, they felt even more drawn to each other.

"Mr. Shao," asked Simao, "why did you choose not to go to the courtesans' quarters? Is it because your parents are strict with you?"

With tears flowing, Yiming replied, "My heart is too heavy. I sat for the examinations only because I had to. I'm in no mood to seek pleasure. But why didn't you join them? You've got a wise head on young shoulders. There are far too few people like you!"

With a long-drawn sigh, Simao said, "In fact, my heart is doubly heavier than yours. I hope you'll win high honors in the exams so that you can avenge me."

Feeling deeper affinity with him at these words, Yiming said, "You and I passed the provincial exams in the same year, though in different provinces. Now that we've met in this place far from home, we should be brothers to each other. Your enemy is my enemy. Why don't you tell me the truth?"

Simao looked pensive for a moment. It was after Yiming pressed him time and again that he came out with the truth. Before he had said many words, Yiming burst out, "So you are my brother Wenxiu! I'm your older brother Zhang Tingxiu!"

They fell on each other's shoulders and wept. Each told the other how he had changed his name. They rejoiced that they had both passed the provincial examinations and gotten to meet each other in the capital, but the joy was mingled with grief.

> It was like a sweet rain after a long drought;
> It was better than meeting an old friend in alien land.
> Don't ask yet about wedding festivities;
> Wait first for the list of successful examinees.

When the list of those who had passed the spring examinations was posted, it was seen that Shao Yiming and Chu Simao were both among the best one hundred candidates who had passed. After the palace examinations presided over by the emperor, the brothers were rated as second-class *jinshi*. When the period of internship was over, Yiming was assigned to be judicial supervisor of Changzhou Prefecture in the Southern Metropolitan Area, and Simao was selected into the Imperial Academy. In his eagerness to help his father, Simao asked for a leave of absence and went together with Yiming to Suzhou. In the meantime, he sent the servants back to Henan and told them to escort Mr. and Mrs. Chu to Suzhou to meet him before going to the capital. Of this, more later.

After leaving Beijing, the brothers went south by land. Upon arrival in Nanjing, Tingxiu first went to see Mr. Shao. Mr. and Mrs. Shao were overcome with delight. Tingxiu then said, "My brother Wenxiu was rescued from the river by Mr. Chu of Henan. His name has been changed to Chu Simao. He also passed the national exams and is now with the Imperial Academy. He came with me and wishes to pay his respects to you, father."

Mr. Shao gave a start. "How extraordinary! Bring him in, and be quick about it!"

The servants promptly brought him in. Once in the hall, Wenxiu pulled a chair over to the middle of the hall and asked Mr. Shao to sit in it, so that he could greet the old man with proper decorum. Mr. Shao adamantly declined the honor, saying, "This just isn't right! You are a distinguished guest. How can I be so presumptuous?"

Wenxiu said, "Since my older brother is your adopted son, I am a nephew to you. It's only right that I should pay homage to you." After both of them tried to yield the seat of honor to each other, Mr. Shao finally relented but rose slightly from his seat in acknowledgment of the honor. Wenxiu then asked Mrs. Shao to come out and accept his greetings. Mr. Shao had a celebration banquet laid out, and the dinner lasted until midnight. The next day, fellow officials in the yamen came to visit Tingxiu upon hearing about his appointment. The two brothers returned the greetings to every one of them.

Between sips of wine during lunch, Mr. Shao asked Wenxiu, "Did you marry in Suzhou or in Henan?"

"I haven't married because of the misfortune that struck my family."

"So you're not married. This presumptuous old man has only one daughter, sixteen now. She may not be a beauty or a paragon of virtue, but she is quite skillful in needlework. If you don't find her beneath you, I would gladly offer her to you as wife."

"I am ever so grateful to you, sir, for being so kind to me. I wouldn't dream of disobeying you, but I wouldn't dare act on my own without my parents' permission."

Tingxiu put in at this point, "Since Father has made this kind offer, let's tell our parents about it when we're in Suzhou before going ahead with the formalities."

Mr. Shao said in agreement, "That makes sense."

In the midst of their conversation, they heard a commotion outside. Mr. Shao sent a servant out to ask what it was all about and was told that messengers were at the gate, announcing that Mr. Shao had just been promoted to be assistant education commissioner of Fujian. His face bursting into a smile, Mr. Shao instructed servants to tip the messengers. As Tingxiu and his brother rose to offer him toasts, he said, "So we'll be going in the same direction. Shall we set out together in a few days?"

Tingxiu said, "May my brother and I depart first and wait for you in Suzhou?"

Mr. Shao agreed. The next day, they hired a boat, took leave of Mr. Shao, and, followed by a few servants, left Nanjing. Traveling downstream, they arrived in Zhenjiang in just one day. Tingxiu told the boatman not to reveal his identity as the judicial supervisor of Changzhou. The boatman scrupulously kept his promise. They passed Zhenjiang and Danyang and sailed downstream before the wind and arrived in Suzhou just two days later. After mooring the boat at the Xu Gate Pier, the two brothers equipped themselves with some silver, told the servants not to follow them, and went ashore in their commoners' clothes. Quietly they headed for home, which was near the prison. Tears sprang to their eyes as their house came into view. Upon entering, they saw that their mother was seated on a stool making hemp ropes, her face awash in tears. They went up to her and cried, "Mother! We're back!" So saying, they threw themselves at her feet and burst into sobs.

Chen-shi wiped her eyes dry, looked at them, and said, "My boys! Where have you been all these years? I missed you so much I almost died!" Mother and sons fell into one another's arms. They gave way to their emotions and wept with abandon. The two sons told her about the murder attempt against them and about how they had each been rescued. Tingxiu added softly, "Both of us are now *jinshi*. I've been assigned as judicial supervisor of Changzhou, and Wenxiu is now a member of the Imperial Academy. We haven't gone to take up our posts yet because we wanted to see you first. How is father's health?"

Joy flooded her heart when she heard that both sons were now government officials. Her melancholy all gone, she said, "Thanks to Zhong Yi, your father has been well. His case is now under review in Changshu. So he's been taken there and will be back either tomorrow or the day after tomorrow. Now that you are officials, is there any way you can get him out of prison?"

"Getting him out of prison is easy," said Tingxiu. "But we have yet to find those who brought harm to us father and sons, so as to feel vindicated."

Wenxiu said, "Let's get father out first before moving on to the next course of action."

"Has Squire Wang ever sent anyone to ask after me?" said Tingxiu. "Is my fiancée still single or has she married?"

Chen-shi replied, "After you left, not even a page boy came to visit. I cried day in and day out and was in no mood for asking after her. Third Uncle Wang did mention when he was passing by our house that Squire Wang wanted her to marry another man, but she refused and hanged herself; however, she was rescued and brought back to life. More than a year has gone by. I don't know if she is still unmarried. There were a few times when I did want to go, but first, my maid-servant died and there was no one to go with me, and secondly, since the squire had broken off with us, I would only be asking for humiliation if I went. That's why I never went. Now, you would do well to remember only his kindnesses and to forget about his harshness to you. Even if she has married, you should still go tomorrow to thank him."

Tingxiu felt even more saddened by these words. The two sons said in unison, "You're right, mother."

Turning to his brother, Tingxiu said, "Since father is not here, could you go get a sedan-chair and take mother to the boat?" Thereupon, Wenxiu went to hire a boat. Chen-shi put a few articles of clothing together and, leaving behind everything else, mounted the sedan-chair and went to the mouth of the river, where all three of them boarded the boat. How sad that the mother and sons had been separated for so many years! It was only after the sons had escaped from the jaws of death and now returned in glory that they were able to reunite. Truly,

> The brothers passed the exams in the same year,
> Adding flowers to the brocade.
> They reunited with their mother,
> Sending charcoal in snowy weather.

The next morning, the two brothers put on their official robes and, each in a sedan-chair carried by four men, went to the prefectural yamen. The prefect was not yet in the office, so they went first to see judicial supervisor Zhu, a native of Shandong, the fourth in command in the yamen. It turned out that his father had passed the examinations in the same year as Mr. Shao had, and the conversation went pleasantly.

"Why didn't the government courier station send someone to announce your arrival?" asked Supervisor Zhu.

Tingxiu replied, "We came by a small boat. We didn't want to put people in the courier station to inconvenience. So they don't know."

"Where did you moor your boat?"

"We sent the boat away. We are staying in Mr. Wang's jadeware store in Zhuanzhu Lane."

"When are you assuming office?" Mr. Zhu asked Tingxiu.

"I need your help in redressing a wrong here in Suzhou first. So I haven't decided on a date for assuming office."

"What wrong has been done to you?" asked Mr. Zhu.

Tingxiu had Mr. Zhu dismiss his attendants before he launched into a detailed account of his father's case.

Appalled, Mr. Zhu said, "So the two of you are brothers! And you were victims of such an injustice! As soon as your father is brought back from Changshu, I'll have guards take him back home and track down the culprit for punishment."

The brothers thanked him. After taking leave of Mr. Zhu, they went to see the prefect and also acquainted him with the details of their father's case. As the saying goes, "Officials look out for one another." With two *jinshi* brothers claiming to be victims of injustice, other officials could hardly stand by without doing something for them, even if they were guilty; imagine to what length the fellow officials would go when the parties involved were innocent! The prefect's reaction was the same as that of Supervisor Zhu. Thankfully, Tingxiu and his brother took leave of him and returned to their boat.

Tingxiu said to his brother, "Let me make myself look like a poor man and go to Zhuanzhu Lane to find out how things are with Squire Wang. You can take your time dressing properly and then join me there." After they drew up their plan, Tingxiu put on a tattered blue cloth gown and a hat and went off straight to Squire Wang's house. (*He was an entertainer for a time, after all, and had a flair for drama.*)

Back to Zhao Ang. When in the capital two years before, escorting the shipment of tax grain, Zhao Ang had won permission to be deputy magistrate of Hongtong County, Pingyang Prefecture of Shanxi, whenever the post became vacant. This was one of the most coveted lucrative sinecures, and was always filled as soon as it became vacant. Zhao Ang had gone to a great deal of expense before obtaining the candidacy for this post. The incumbent's term of office having just expired after Zhao Ang had waited at home for more than a year, an auspicious day had been chosen for Zhao Ang to set out on his journey to assume the post. That day when Tingxiu went to find out how things stood, Zhao Ang was at home, hosting a farewell banquet, complete with entertainment by hired actors.

Hearing the clang of cymbals and the beating of drums that came from the house, Tingxiu thought, "What's the grand occasion? Could it be my fiancée's wedding?" His heart full of misgivings, he thought again, "Let me go straight in and see what's going on."

As he marched into the house, he ran straight into Wang Jin, the servant. "Wang Jin!" he shouted. "Where are you off to?"

Recognizing him, Wang Jin said in astonishment, "It's you, Number Three! Where have you been all these years?"

"I've been having fun in a faraway place. I came back only yesterday. Let me ask you something: What's all this excitement about? Is Sister Yu marrying another man?"

In the rush of the moment, Wang Jin came out with the truth. "Good grief!" he exclaimed. "Sister Yu tried to kill herself for your sake and almost died. How could you say such a thing!"

Feeling a surge of relief, Tingxiu said, "You go ahead and get on with your errand."

After Wang Jin left, Tingxiu went straight in. Upon reaching the main hall, which was filled with guests and servants, Tingxiu pushed his way through the crowd to take a better look. There Zhao Ang was, at his table, brimming with smugness and watching the play *Thornwood Hairpins* about Wang Shipeng.[3] Tingxiu thought, "When my father-in-law was trying to drive me out of the house, Zhao Ang said malicious things to help things along. While he's at the height of his enjoyment, let me put him to shame."

After maneuvering his way to the middle of the hall, he said, saluting the guests around the hall with folded hands, "My respects to all of you, my kinsmen!" He was not yet twenty years old when he left the house. Being much taller now and wearing a hat, he was not recognizable to the relatives. Bowing to Squire Wang, he continued, "Father, please accept this bow from me!"

Being one who used to see Tingxiu on a daily basis, Squire Wang recognized him. Appalled, he thought, "Didn't they say he's dead? Why is he here?" Noticing his tattered clothes and woebegone look, he said, "Where have you been all these years? What do you intend to do?"

"Your son has been traveling around as an entertainer. Having learned about brother-in-law Zhao's appointment to office, I've come here expressly to offer my congratulations and to put on a show for him."

Because his daughter had stubbornly refused to marry another man, Squire Wang had half a mind to keep him upon first seeing him and therefore had asked him those questions in a kindly tone. At Tingxiu's announcement that he was an entertainer, Squire Wang's face went purple red. Collapsing into his chair, he cursed, "You beast! I'm no father of yours! Get out this instant!"

"If you don't want me to call you father, would you like it better if I called you father-in-law?"

"I'm no father-in-law of yours, either!" thundered Squire Wang.

"Father you are not, but father-in-law you are!" said Tingxiu. "Why can't I call you that?"

Zhao Ang was so frightened upon seeing Tingxiu that he turned deathly pale.

He thought, "Didn't that little rascal die in the river? How did he get away unscathed? Could Yang Hong have been bribed into setting him free and then lied to me?" Having heard Tingxiu call him brother-in-law, he snapped, "Zhang Tingxiu! Who is your brother-in-law? You're full of nonsense! If you don't make yourself scarce, I'll have your beggar's legs beaten up!"

"Zhao Ang!" exclaimed Tingxiu. "Men with wealth and rank don't throw their weight around in their own neighborhood. But look at you, as gleeful as that when the post you've landed is so petty! My offer to put on an act for you is made out of the best intentions. How can you be so rude!"

Enraged at the way Tingxiu had called out his name, Zhao Ang ordered his servants to lock up this pauper.

Third Uncle Wang, also present, put in, "Be quiet, everyone! Whether he's a member of the family or not can be discussed at another time. But now, since he's an actor and he offers you congratulations out of good intentions, why don't you let him put on a show like a hired entertainer, just for the fun of it? Why all this anger?" Pushing Tingxiu from behind, he continued, "Go and make yourself up for the role. Don't listen to them."

The other kinsmen present applauded and said, "Third Uncle is right!"

Thus pushed all the way into the dressing room, Tingxiu put on an official's robe and gauze hat. He performed for the audience the scene where Wang Shipeng held a memorial service by the river.[4] Recalling what he had just heard about Sister Yu's suicide attempt and identifying her with Yulian in the play, he put all his heart in his singing and acting, as if he were none other than Wang Shipeng himself. Moved to tears and sniffles, the audience cheered heartily, but Squire Wang and Zhao Ang were deeply mortified.

While the show was still going on, a servant came to announce that the prefect was here to see judicial supervisor Shao of Changzhou Prefecture and Imperial Academician Chu. The guests and the entertainers were so unnerved that they could hardly stay still. The play was brought to a halt. (*Good plot.*) Squire Wang and Zhao Ang darted outside and said to the messenger, "There are no Mr. Shao and Mr. Chu staying in this house."

The messenger rejoined, "Mr. Shao said himself this morning that he would be staying in this house. How can you say he's not here?" Tossing them a visiting card, he continued, "You go and tell that to the prefect." And off he went.

In consternation, Squire Wang and Zhao Ang said, "Where can we get a smooth talker to speak to the prefect?"

Tingxiu came over and said, "Father, let me do the talking on your behalf."

Only too happy to have someone act on his behalf, Squire Wang said to Tingxiu, his anger evaporating, "Yes, it would be nice if you could go." Noticing that Tingxiu was still wearing a gauze hat and a round-necked official's robe, he added, "If you're going, you'd better change your clothes, and be quick about it."

"I'll just go in these clothes. Who has the patience to change?"

Zhao Ang said, "You mustn't be so flippant with government officials."

With a smile, Tingxiu replied, "That's all right. I'll take responsibility for everything. You won't get blamed."

"Are you out of your mind?" said Squire Wang.

Tingxiu gave another smile. "Even if I am, still let me go. You need not concern yourself about this."

With a loud bang of the cymbals from the messenger from the courier station, the prefect arrived. Frantically, Squire Wang and Zhao Ang abandoned Tingxiu and dashed back into the house.

The prefect dismounted his sedan-chair just as Tingxiu went out the gate. The two of them bowed to each other as they went into the main hall, where they sat down to chat. They drank two cups of tea and had a long, drawn-out conversation. Then the prefect took leave of Tingxiu and went his way. There is a poem in testimony:

> *Who would have guessed that Mr. Shao of Changzhou*
> *Was Wang Shipeng on the stage?*
> *The prefect came, the guests dispersed,*
> *And the guilty party was appalled.*

Sister Yu had been spending her days and nights with her mother without ever taking a step downstairs. Her sister had been flaunting Zhao Ang's appointment to office to her, but she was not impressed. That day, she rejected Sister Rui's invitation to the show at the banquet outside. Since she didn't want to go, Xu-shi also refused to watch the show. A short while later, when Tingxiu threw the main hall into an uproar, Sister Rui among the audience was also startled. When Tingxiu began singing, she hurried inside and cried out, 'Good news! Good news! Your sorely missed husband is back! He's singing and acting outside."

Believing this was said in jest to mock her, Sister Yu reddened but said nothing in response. Xu-shi also thought it was a lie and ignored her. Being thus snubbed, Sister Rui said, giggling, "Well, I'm going back to watch my brother-in-law acting." With that, she went downstairs.

Before long, maidservants came in to report the same thing. The unbelieving Xu-shi went to the main hall and peeked from behind the screen. Finding that it was indeed Tingxiu, she was overwhelmed with happy astonishment but lamented to herself, "How did he get himself into such a state?"

"Mother," said Sister Rui, "was I lying?"

Ignoring her, Xu-shi returned to Sister Yu's room upstairs and told her about what she had seen. Sister Yu remained silent as tears fell from her cheeks. Xu-shi said, trying to cheer her up, "My child, don't feel bad. You can start a happy life with your husband now." After spending some time with Sister Yu, she went out again to take a look around, afraid that Squire Wang would again kick Tingxiu out of the house. Whom should she see but Zhao Ang and Sister Rui, followed by

Squire Wang, running frantically toward the inner section of the house! You may well ask, what had happened? Well, after Squire Wang, Zhao Ang, and the guests had fled the main hall upon the prefect's arrival, a servant came to say, "Number Three is sitting there, chatting with the prefect." None of them believed this report. Everyone went up to the screen and peeked from behind it. Indeed, there they were in the hall, chatting away.

Squire Wang thought, "So, that cursed one is now an official, in this disguise just to trick me. I shouldn't have listened to bad advice and driven him out. Luckily the girl had the pride not to remarry, which makes it easier for me to talk to him. Otherwise, I wouldn't have stood a chance! But I just said a few more things offensive to him. I'm too ashamed to see him. Let me get mother out to talk to him first." That was why he was running so frantically to the inner quarters.

As the old saying goes, "A thief is troubled by his conscience." As for Zhao Ang, because of what he had done to Tingxiu in the past, his fear was of a different order from the squire's. He was beside himself with terror. He told his wife about what had just happened and dashed off to his room to gather his things and his bedding together, so that he could set out on his journey the very next day, to steer clear of that nemesis of his. He didn't even want to go back to announce to the guests that the banquet was over. Truly,

> Had he known things would come to this,
> He wouldn't have done it in the first place!

So, running into Xu-shi, Squire Wang exclaimed, "Mother! Our little son-in-law is back!"

"What if he is?" said Xu-shi. "Why such a fuss?"

"Oh, you have no idea!" And then he launched into an account of what had just happened. "I'm too ashamed to see him. I ran back here just to ask you to talk to him and make peace with him."

At this all-too-unexpected piece of good news, Xu-shi said in exhilaration, "How extraordinary!" After telling a maid to go upstairs and report everything to Sister Yu, she went with her husband to the main hall, at the moment when Tingxiu had just returned after seeing the prefect off. As the clansmen swarmed over to greet him, Xu-shi said, "Number Three! I missed you so much! Where have you been? We couldn't find you anywhere."

At this point, Tingxiu went forward, asked the elderly couple to sit down, and kowtowed to them. Stopping him with a hand, Squire Wang said, "My good son-in-law, I have wronged you badly. I wouldn't dream of having you kowtow to me."

Tingxiu said, "I am indeed unworthy of your expectations of me. Why say that you wronged me?" After his kowtows, he exchanged greetings with the other clansmen. Then he said, "I don't see my brother-in-law Zhao here. Please invite him over, so that I can greet him." A page boy immediately went in.

Zhao Ang didn't want to see him but, afraid that Tingxiu would be suspicious if he didn't go, forced himself to go out and said, "I gave you offense a few moments ago. Please do not bear me ill will."

"I am indeed unworthy and brought the humiliation on myself. How would I dare blame you, my brother-in-law?"

Shame flooded Zhao Ang.

Detecting a sarcastic tone in Tingxiu's remarks, Squire Wang said, "My good son-in-law, I believed some malicious words against you and wronged you. Please don't hold this against me."

Xu-shi asked, "Where have you been all these years? How did you become an official?"

Tingxiu told them about the murder attempt against him and how he had risen to be an official, but held back information about his brother's status as an official. None of the clansmen present did not marvel. They said, "What enemy of yours could have borne you such malice? Do you know who he is?"

"I wish I knew!" said Tingxiu.

As Tingxiu was talking, Zhao Ang was devoured by anxiety, blushing and growing pale by turns. Only when he heard this last remark did Zhao Ang set his fears to rest.

"Enough talking," said Third Uncle Wang. "Please sit and let me offer you a toast by way of congratulations, presenting Buddha with borrowed flowers, so to speak." The clansmen insisted that Tingxiu take the seat of honor. Tingxiu would not hear of it, but, his demurrals unavailing, he had to comply in the end. Still in the robe and hat he had worn on stage, he sat down facing the door. The entertainers entered the hall again and put on their show. The clansmen were all obsequiousness to Tingxiu. Xu-shi returned upstairs and there we shall leave her for now.

In the meantime, Zhang Quan returned from his trip to Changshu for a review of his case. Those escorting him were none other than Yang Hong and his cohorts. As a rule, whenever a case was up for review, the prisoner was to be escorted by the very guards who had arrested him. Their presence was indispensable because if an injustice had been done, the guards would also be put under questioning. Before setting out on the journey, Yang Hong had gotten money from Zhao Ang. He and his brother Yang Jiang went together. After returning, they put Zhang Quan back in his prison cell and went to Zhao Ang's house again, ostensibly to report to him but, in fact, to extort more money. As they went down Zhuanzhu Lane, they heard the residents say that the prefect had just paid a visit to the Wang family. The Yang brothers were puzzled because Zhao Ang was but a student who had just landed a post, and that post was not within the prefect's jurisdiction, either.

Upon reaching the gate of the Wang residence, they heard the sounds of a stage performance inside, but there was no one at the gate. So they sat down on the stone steps to wait for someone to emerge and announce them. They had barely sat down when they saw a sedan-chair, carried by four men, stopping at the gate. At the sight of a young official alighting, the two of them quickly rose to their feet. Who was that official? None other than Imperial Academician Zhang Wenxiu. (*Wenxiu's appearance on the scene makes this an even better story.*) Stepping over the threshold, Wenxiu raised his eyes and gave a start when seeing the two men, whom he recognized to be Yang Hong and the yamen runner who had tried to kill him. He thought, "So the two of them were in collusion! I wonder why they are sitting here." Without saying a word that might reveal his identity, he went straight into the house.

Yang Hong did not recognize him but commented to Yang Jiang, "What rank can Zhao Ang have that such a highly placed official would want to visit him?"

You may well ask, why did Yang Hong fail to recognize Wenxiu? Well, Wenxiu was but a boy at the time of the murder attempt and now, in his official's outfit, with an air of dignity, he was far beyond recognition. Wenxiu, however, recognized the Yang brothers upon the first glance because the bitter memory had never left him.

Now, a servant who had spotted Wenxiu dashed off to report, "Here comes another official!" Before the words were quite out of his mouth, Wenxiu was already in the hall. The clansmen and the entertainers again ran helter-skelter in all directions, leaving Tingxiu alone.

Peeking from behind the screen, Squire Wang observed that Tingxiu behaved differently with this official than with the prefect. Instead of saluting him with folded hands, Tingxiu simply stood up and said, "So here you are!"

"Why did they all scurry away when they saw me?" asked the official.

Tingxiu couldn't suppress a giggle.

"Don't laugh!" said Wenxiu. "I have an important thing to tell you." Then he whispered into Tingxiu's ear, "The government runner and Yang Hong who tried to kill us are now sitting outside."

"What!" exclaimed Tingxiu in astonishment. "Why would they be sitting here indeed? This looks suspicious. Get hold of them quickly before they get away." While Tingxiu asked for his official's hat and waistband and took off his stage costume to change into proper attire, Wenxiu dispatched servants to apprehend the Yang brothers.

The servants rushed out, overpowered Yang Hong and his brother, and dragged them into the hall. Believing Zhao Ang was behind this, Yang Hong cursed, "You ungrateful scoundrel! I did so many big jobs for you. How can you turn around and beat me up?"

In the commotion, a servant announced, "Judicial Supervisor Zhu is here!"

The servants pushed the Yang brothers to one side. Tingxiu and his brother went out to greet Mr. Zhu and brought him into the hall. After sitting down, Tingxiu said, hardly able to contain his excitement, "Mr. Zhu, there's no greater joy than this: the criminals who tried to kill me and my brother have shown up, courting death. They've already been seized."

"Where are they?" asked Supervisor Zhu.

Tingxiu had the servants push the two men toward him. As the brothers fell on their knees, Tingxiu asked, "Do the two of you recognize me?"

Yang Hong replied, "No, we don't."

"You don't recognize those who took your boat on their trip to Zhenjiang to lodge a complaint, and whom you tied up and dumped into the water?"

Realizing they were the Zhang brothers, the two men cowered in fear.

"Let me ask you," said Mr. Zhu. "What grudge do you bear against them? What made you conspire against that family?"

"We bear them no grudge."

"If not, why did you try to kill them?"

Knowing that they were as good as dead, they thought they might as well name Zhao Ang, who was so miserly in his payments. They said, "It had nothing to do with us. It was Zhao Ang who begged us to do this. He had a grudge against the father and sons and plotted against them."

Tingxiu and his brother were aghast. "So it *was* that scoundrel, after all! Why did he want to get rid of us?"

"Who is Zhao Ang?" asked Mr. Zhu. "Where does he live?

"He's a student who bought his way into the National University. He lives in this house," replied Tingxiu.

"Seize him, quick!" exclaimed Supervisor Zhu.

Thus ordered, his attendants stormed into the inner quarters of the house and brought Zhao Ang out. As the children cried in shock and confusion, the clansmen all slipped away through the back door. The entertainers also left in the commotion.

The moment his eyes laid on Yang Hong and his brothers, Zhao Ang knew that his conspiracies had come to light, but he said not a word. Mr. Zhu immediately went back to the yamen and sent lictors to the prison to set Zhang Quan free and escort him in a sedan-chair to the Wang residence. Then he set about interrogating Zhao Ang, who initially denied involvement in the case. Only after he was put under the rod did he come clean. Yang Hong also named the two helpers on the boat, who were soon brought in. Zhao Ang, Yang Hong, and Yang Jiang were each given sixty strokes of the rod and sentenced to death by decapitation in accordance with the law. The two helpers were each given forty strokes and sentenced to death by strangulation. All were sent to jail. Judicial Supervisor Zhu then wrote a report about the case to the provincial governor and the provincial chief justice and later, in the names of all three, to the Ministry of Justice. But of this, no more.

After seeing off Judicial Supervisor Zhu, Tingxiu and his brother returned inside and changed into casual clothes. By that time, Squire Wang had learned that the visiting official was Zhang Wenxiu. He and his wife went out to greet him. To their question why Supervisor Zhu had arrested Zhao Ang, Tingxiu gave them an account of the truth. Squire Wang said through gnashed teeth, "So it was all that evil swine's doing!"

As they were talking, a maidservant came to report, "Sister Rui has hanged herself and she's dead!" What had happened was that, upon learning about the exposure of their conspiracy and the arrest of her husband, Sister Rui knew that her husband was as good as dead and that she wouldn't be able to live down the shame. So she chose to end her life. (*Sister Yu also hanged herself but didn't die. Sister Rui died. Heaven never misses the mark.*) Resenting her and her husband for their murderous plots, Squire Wang and Xu-shi felt no pain. How they set about buying a coffin and preparing for the burial is no part of our story. Squire Wang gave orders for another banquet and sent servants to the boat to bring Chen-shi, the Zhang brothers' mother. Before long, a servant announced, "Master Zhang is here, escorted by Mr. Zhu's guard!" Tingxiu, Wenxiu, and Squire Wang went out together to greet him. It so happened that the sedan-chair carrying Chen-shi also arrived at this point. At this reunion of husband and wife and parents and sons, they fell on one another's shoulders and cried their hearts out. Verily,

> As in a dream, their misery turned to joy;
> Their new lease on life threw them into raptures.
> Flesh and blood joined in reunion;
> Zhao Ang would be scorned for a thousand years.

Zhang Quan said, "I thought I would never get to see you again. Who would have thought that father and sons would be reunited!" He wept every step of the way into the hall, where he first thanked Squire Wang and Xu-shi. Squire Wang apologized over and over again. Then the two sons kowtowed to their father and acquainted him with all the facts. When they got to the heartbreaking details, the father and sons broke down in tears again. In their lamentation, they forgot about the man Mr. Zhu had sent to escort Zhang Quan home. The man asked the servants to remind the Zhangs about him, whereupon Tingxiu wrote a letter to thank Mr. Zhu and tipped the man three maces of silver before sending him on his way. Xu-shi invited Chen-shi to her room in the back, and Sister Yu went downstairs to greet her mother-in-law, and another sad scene it was. Soon, preparations for the banquet were completed and two tables were laid out, one in the main hall and one in the inner quarters of the house. The celebration lasted until the middle of the night.

The next day, Tingxiu and Wenxiu went to the yamen and thanked Judicial Supervisor Zhu. They dismissed their boat and took up quarters in Squire Wang's house. While waiting for Mr. Shao to come so that Wenxiu could settle his marital future and go to assume his post, Tingxiu told his parents about Mr. Shao's offer to take Wenxiu on as a son-in-law. Preparations for betrothal gifts went under way, so that the formalities could proceed as soon as Mr. Shao arrived. Half a month later, Mr. Shao arrived, followed by Mr. and Mrs. Chu of Henan, as well as clerks from Changzhou sent to take Tingxiu to his new office, turning the Wang residence into a hive of activity. Following Tingxiu's suggestion, Third Uncle Wang served as the matchmaker, and the betrothal gifts were duly sent to Miss Shao. An auspicious day was then chosen for both brothers' wedding ceremonies. When that day came around, Squire Wang set out a magnificent banquet. To make an impression on his clansmen, he invited legions of guests to the event. Amid the resounding notes of the wind instruments of *sheng* pipes and *xiao* flutes and drums, by the light of the carved bridal candles, stood the two pairs of newlyweds and four sets of parents in all pomp and circumstance—the grooms in their black gauze officials' hats and crimson robes, and the brides in their phoenix coronets and embroidered, tasseled capes. There is a poem in testimony:

> *All four families possessed wealth and rank;*
> *Two couples enjoyed double happiness.*
> *In bed, they poured out their tales of woe;*
> *Their blood and tears stained their embroidered nets.*

Officials in the prefectural and county yamen who heard about the event all came to offer their congratulations.

After three days, the couples set out separately for their journeys. Zhang Quan and his wife followed their elder son Tingxiu to his duty station in Changzhou. Mr. and Mrs. Chu went with Wenxiu to the capital, and Mr. Shao went to Fujian. With his large estate to take care of, Squire Wang could not very well go anywhere. So he and his wife stayed at home to enjoy their wealth. In a few days, an imperial decree came, granting permission to execute Zhao Ang, Yang Hong, and Yang Jiang. The chief justice authorized Tingxiu to oversee the execution. On the day of the execution, people who turned out en masse to watch all said that Zhao Ang had brought this on himself. None of his clansmen had any sympathy for him. Even his father-in-law, Squire Wang, didn't go to the execution ground. Truly,

> *Good and evil, each gets its due;*
> *It is just a matter of time.*
> *Be advised: do nothing evil;*
> *Heaven is not to be defied.*

Out of gratitude to Zhong Yi, Tingxiu asked Judicial Supervisor Zhu to have him acquitted. Because of his father's experience in a framed case, Tingxiu performed his duties with meticulous care and convicted criminals only after all the facts had been well established. With his fine reputation, he was promoted to be a supervising secretary in the imperial court in Beijing. As for Wenxiu, after three years of study in the Imperial Academy, he was appointed as the censorial inspector of Shanxi. Because his ancestral graves were in Jiangxi, Zhang Quan returned to his native town, took up his old line of business, and built a house for himself. Later, when Mr. Shao and Mr. Chu passed away, Tingxiu and Wenxiu each took a leave of absence and attended to the funerals. After three years had gone by, they wrote to their superiors asking to resume their original surname. The request was granted. Tingxiu had three sons. He had his second son assume Squire Wang's surname and the third son assume Mr. Shao's surname by way of thanking them for their kindness to him. Wenxiu also had two sons, the second of whom became heir to Mr. Chu. Zhang Quan and his wife lived into their nineties and died of natural causes. Squire Wang and his wife also lived to a ripe old age. Tingxiu and his brother rose to the highest rank in court and their descendants have, to this day, won honors in the civil service examinations from generation to generation. As the poem says,

> Commoners can rise to be ministers;
> Wealth or poverty of the moment does not count.
> In everything, remember the will of heaven;
> Be content and luck will fall into your lap.

With Her Wisdom Zhang Shu'er Helps
Mr. Yang Escape

Money has always been a cause for ruin;
Wisdom never fails to shield one from harm.
The vile monks laid murderous hands on the scholars;
The fair maiden put her faith in the learned man.
Luckily he escaped from the tightly-knit net;
His success came in his darkest moment.
Once he gained high rank, he redressed wrongs, returned favors,
And showed himself to be a true man of honor.

Our story takes place during the Zhengde reign period [1506–21]. There was a man called Yang Yanhe, courtesy name Yuanli, who had passed the civil service examinations at the provincial level. His ancestors having moved from their native town of Chengdu in Sichuan to Yangzhou Prefecture in the Southern Metropolitan Area, he was now a resident of Jiangdu County, Yangzhou Prefecture. His skin as white as snow, his lips as red as if rouged, his face as well-shaped as if carved out of the finest jade, he outshone by far the likes of Pei Kai and Wang Yan.[1] He was refinement itself. In addition, he was richly endowed with literary talent and had acquired considerable knowledge early in life. When he was reading an antique book, his fingers would keep turning the pages, making a rustling sound, and he would finish a book in less time than it takes to drink a cup of tea. People thought he was counting the pages, but, in fact, with each turn of the page, he had thoroughly committed the lines to memory. Every time he wrote, with a scroll spread out in front of him, he would dip the tip of his brush-pen in the well-ground ink and wield it without a pause until the entire scroll was filled with characters amid the rustling of the paper, as if pelting rain had splashed onto the scroll, and every word was a gem. Verily,

The brush-pen called up wind and rain;
The writing moved ghosts and gods to tears.
By no means of the common run,
The scroll deserved a place in a sacred shrine.

At seven years of age, he had been able to write large characters in his calligraphy exercises. At eight, he could compose ancient-style poems. At nine, he mastered the skills of writing essays in the format prescribed for the civil service examinations. At ten, he was enrolled in the prefectural school, and the very next year, having tested first place, he won a government stipend. Then his parents died, one immediately after the other, and he observed a six-year mourning period. Orphaned at such a young age, he remained unbetrothed.

Thanks to his diligence, he came out second in the civil service examinations at the provincial level at the age of nineteen, but he was displeased that he had not won first place. With a sigh, he said to himself, "No one in the world recognizes my ability." He felt disinclined to go to Beijing for the examinations at the national level. His relatives and friends all advised him to set out on his journey as soon as possible, and six other people who had passed the examinations in the same year that he had urged him repeatedly to join them in their journey. He said he didn't want to go only because he was angry at not having won first place, but, in fact, he was all eagerness to achieve worldly success. One day, yielding to the pressure from his fellow examinees, he set about packing in high spirits. His deceased father had managed the family financial matters well and had left him real estate and land property. He sold off a couple of places to get enough money for his trip to the capital and set out with his six companions on their journey to Beijing. Who were the six? They were Jiao Shiji, courtesy name Zizhou; Wang Yuanhui, courtesy name Jingzhao; Zhang Xian, courtesy name Taobo; Han Fanxi, courtesy name Kanghou; Jiang Yi, courtesy name Lisheng; and Liu Shan, courtesy name Quzhi. Of the six, Liu and Jiang were of humbler family circumstances. The other four were all quite well-to-do. Wang Yuanhui, from a family whose wealth numbered in the millions, was known locally as Little Wang Kai.[2] In fact, his family fortune had an ever-so-subtle bearing on his status as a *juren* [one who had passed the exams at the provincial level]. And so, having recently passed the examinations, this group of friends, followed by five or six servants, set out on their journey jauntily in an impressive procession. How do we know this? Behold:

With delicate brows and well-shaped eyes,
They looked dashing in their exquisite attire.
The bamboo hats on their backs fluttered in the wind,
Their colorful rain capes shone in the sun.
Their jade-reined horses' neighs

Pierced the mist on willow-flanked dykes;
Their green-curtained chariots
Crushed fallen pine twigs and snow on the hills.
Their carved arrows were an awe-inspiring sight;
Their silk quivers a fine display of might.
When they raised their whips and urged the horses on,
No wayfarer dared to be in their way.
When their procession swept through villages and towns,
Everyone stood and stared in awe.
Truly, horses can rest wherever there are green willows,
But men go to Chang'an whenever there is a chance.

For all the bows and swords that the entourage sported, none of the men in this procession was a master of martial arts. In most situations, discretion is the first essential for travelers on the road, who should be watchful in everything they do. (*Good advice. Everyone undertaking a journey, be warned!*) The last thing they should do is go after vainglory. At the pier of Yanzhou Prefecture of Shandong, their servants exchanged silver for copper coins, with which they filled their leather trunks. The sheer weight of the coins wore the horses and the carriers out. Everyone who laid eyes on the trunks along the way thought they were filled with silver, little knowing that there were nothing but copper coins. When they found themselves in a desolate place about seventy to eighty li from the seat of Qing County, Hejian Prefecture,[3] they heard the ringing sound of bells. Raising their eyes, they saw a large monastery:

Embowered by dark pines and ancient cypresses
That coiled in the shape of crouching dragons,
It was flanked by tall cliffs that pierced the sky,
And surrounded by a hundred misty waterfalls.
The carved dragon heads on the roof soared high;
The decorations on the eaves hung low.
It stood half-hidden among the clouds,
Giving off light like an abode of the immortals.

The horizontal board above the gate bore the inscription "Baohua Monastery" in gold characters. Tired after days of traveling, our group of men were delighted upon seeing such a magnificent monastery. They got down from their horses and went in on a tour. Along shaded winding paths, old stone stelae lay scattered about. From the blurred inscriptions on them, the young men concluded that the stelae must have been erected during the Kaiyuan reign period [713–41] of the Tang dynasty. While they were examining the stelae, a young monk dashed inside to report. Soon, a middle-aged slick-looking monk sallied forth. At the sight of this group of well-dressed visitors strolling in, he bowed and led them into the main hall. After he exchanged greetings with them, showed them to their seats, and asked their names and where they were from, the young monk brought in tea. After drinking the tea, the visitors asked the middle-aged monk, "Reverend, what is your Buddhist name?"

"My Buddhist name is Wushi. What brought you gentlemen to this humble monastery?"

"We are on our way to the capital to sit for the examinations. We were impressed by your monastery and came in to look around."

"Forgive me for not having gone out to greet you!" After this exchange of amenities, Monk Wushi went out and instructed an acolyte to serve more tea, along with fruit and refreshments. Then he walked up to the gate and saw that the pieces of luggage looked sumptuous and that the servants were all dressed up in finery. With a knit of his brows, he hit upon a plan and said to himself in secret delight, "If only we could get to enjoy what's in all those pieces of luggage! If they chose to stop at this deserted place, they were sent by the will of heaven. One who lets go of what's to be had for the taking will never see it again. Why don't I keep them for the night before deciding on the next thing to do?"

He turned back and said to the travelers, "My respects to you all. I have a word of advice for you. Please don't take offense."

"Let's hear it!"

"Strange to say, I had a most unusual dream last night: A large star fell smack into the backyard of this humble monastery and changed into a green rock. I said to myself in delight, 'An eminent man will be coming to this monastery.' And indeed, you gentlemen came today. Of the seven of you, one will surely place first in the exams. I wouldn't otherwise presume to ask distinguished gentlemen like you to stay in such a deserted place, but because of that dream, I would like to keep you for the night. If you don't think it beneath you, please stay here for one night, to bear out the good omen. But please don't take it amiss if we serve only vegetables produced in these hills."

Pleased by the description of the dream, all the travelers except Yang Yuanli were eager to accept the offer. Skeptically, Yang Yuanli said to his friends under his breath, "This place is too deserted. This monk is nice enough, but it's hard to know one's heart. There must be a reason behind his insistence that we stay."

"Mr. Yang, you are too cautious!" said his friends. "There are more than forty of us, servants included. Why should we be afraid of a few monks in the wilderness? If your luggage is stolen, the rest of us will compensate you."

Yang Yuanli said, "It's only thirty to forty li before we reach the place where we plan to stay. We should make haste and go there."

Zhang Taobo and Liu Quzhi, in their exhilaration, were determined to stay. They said to Yuanli, "For one thing, it's already too late in the day for us to make it to the village inn, and something might happen on the way there. Don't you see the nice rooms in this monastery? Let's enjoy tonight and resume our journey tomorrow morning. No harm can be done. If you must make it to the village inn tonight, please feel free to go. We won't keep you."

Observing that the travelers were talking in subdued voices and that Yang Yuanli was insisting on leaving, Monk Wushi said to Yuanli, "Sir, about ten li away, there's a place called Yellow Mud Plain, which is infested with robbers, and it's getting dark now. I can't guarantee your safety if you take to the road. You gentlemen's lives are too precious. Please stay here tonight and depart early tomorrow morning. You may have covered less distance, but it's much safer." (*In most cases, clever arguments easily convince people. That's why evil men all too often have the ear of monarchs.*)

While his friends were applying pressure on him and the monk was exhibiting nothing but cordiality, Yang Yuanli's servants were also unwilling to resume the journey now that they were being offered hot tea and hot water. (*There is a price to pay for monks' hot tea and hot water.*) The servants said to their master, "Didn't His Reverence say that Yellow Mud Plain is not safe at night? Why don't we spend the night here?"

Since their words did make sense, Yuanli relented. His friends began to instruct the servants to carry the luggage into the monastery and said that they would be leaving the next morning.

Secretly rejoicing that his plan was working, the monk eagerly set about preparing for dinner. He instructed the acolytes to slaughter chickens and geese and cook fish and turtles, and in a trice, a fine spread of dishes was ready. How was it possible to buy these things in such a place? Well, the monks of this monastery certainly knew how to live well. They raised all kinds of fowl in the monastery and were thus able to slaughter them right there on the spot. (*What kind of monks are they? This alone shows that they are not the decent sort.*)

A winding veranda led from the main hall to an exquisitely furnished three-section hall. Seven tables were laid for the guests and one table at the lower end for the host. An impressive sight it was. As the host, Wushi the monk raised his cup and the guests took their seats in the order of their age. After a few rounds of wine, Zhang Taobo proposed to his fellow travelers, "Why don't we play a wager game for more fun?"

Turning to the host, Liu Quzhi asked, "Reverend, do you have a dice board?"

"Yes, yes," said the monk. He had an acolyte bring out a dice board and offer a large cup brimming with wine to Mr. Jiao, who was to make the first throw of the dice. Without demurring, Jiao Zizhou drank the wine and cast the dice. As they took turns casting the dice, the one getting a die with a red spot was to be the official thrower. After the thrower cast the next dice, the number of dots on the dice would determine which man, in the order of the seating arrangement, was to drink. The visitors found the wine delicious and drained their cups to the last drop. In fact, this was no ordinary wine. The rice had been soaked in wine and spices, and sleeping drugs had been added to the yeast until the color of the wine turned as dark as amber and the taste was sweet and delicious. After drinking it, one would feel groggy and weak in the limbs. The travelers, having drunk all along the journey nothing but inferior, watery wine and wine that tasted as bitter as medicine and as stinking as urine, were doubly excited after downing this strong brew. (*Words that please the ear may not be sound advice. Wine that pleases the palate may not be a good beverage. May everyone think twice when things seem to be going well!*)

Playing finger-guessing and wager games, they finished one cup after another. Monk Wushi had the young monk drink with the servants in an outer room and had an acolyte drink with the sedan-chair carriers and the grooms until everyone drank himself into a stupor, except Yang Yuanli. When he first began to feel drowsy as he imbibed the fragrant and mellow wine, he thought, "What good wine for such a place! But this drowsiness isn't right. There must be something going on." There and then, he hit on a plan. He feigned a stomachache and stopped drinking. Knowing nothing of what was going through his mind, his friends said, "You must have caught some kind of a cold along the way. Hot wine is exactly what you need to take out the chill. Why stop drinking?" As they were talking to him, the monk chimed in, saying, "Mr. Yang, this wine has been stored for three years by my bed, and I've never touched it. I opened it today expressly to offer it to you. Your stomachache must have been caused by the chill in your body. Ten large cups of this wine in quick succession will take out the chill."

Growing even more suspicious at the way the monk tried to force wine on him, Yang Yuanli held his ground.

"Must you be such a killjoy?" said his friends. "Let the rest of us drink to our hearts' content and not disappoint His Reverence."

Monk Wushi plied them with large cups of wine, but he felt uneasy about Yuanli, thinking to himself, "Why did he stop drinking? But even if he's sober and doesn't fall into the trap, he'll be the only one. I should have nothing to fear." As he offered a large cup of wine to Yuanli, the latter said, "Thank you so much, but I really can't take another drop." So the monk turned away to work assiduously on the others.

The lower-ranking monks brought the travelers' luggage inside. After the servants picked clean rooms and spread out the bedding, the drunken scholars, flatteringly calling each other *zhuangyuan* and *huiyuan,*[4] stumbled their way into their rooms and, without bothering to wash their faces or take off their clothes, climbed into bed and, as soon as their heads hit the pillows, began to snore thunderously. The monks and acolytes forced large bowls of wine on the servants, and they, too, drank recklessly until their eyes glazed over, their jaws dropped open, their hands and feet went limp, and they fell in a senseless heap on the floor.

Well, Monk Wushi was also drinking away at the table. Why wasn't he any the worse for it? The fact was, he had instructed the young monks to pour him wine from another flask. The color and the flavor were the same, but it was not drugged. When he occasionally had to drink from the vessel meant for the visitors, in response to their invitation, he had no choice but to swallow the wine, but then he went to his own room to drink a potion to dispel its effect. That was how he managed to stay sober.

With the visitors fast asleep, those vile monks rubbed their hands, eager for action. Wushi said, "We need to strike now. We don't have a moment to lose. If the effect of the wine is gone, we won't be able to do anything." By his order, the monks tiptoed to the scholars' rooms, each carrying a sharp knife. As they listened at the door, ready to break in, a monk from Sichuan, named Juekong, whispered to Wushi, "To make short work of those bookworms is easy. We'd better finish the servants first. As they say, when you kill the weeds, you'd better dig up the roots, so as to stamp out all sources of trouble once and for all."

"Well said," Wushi agreed. Immediately they turned to the servants' quarters, burst in, and cut off every head they saw. Those besotted men were slashed like vegetables, and their blood flowed all over the floor. How tragic!

As for Yang Yuanli, he went to bed without undressing, his heart full of misgivings. He tossed and turned in bed, unable to go to sleep, straining his ears for sounds outside. He was not destined to die at this time, after all. Having heard no voices in the quietness after dinner, he wondered, "Living in these hilly parts, the monks should be helping themselves to the leftovers, or they should at least be clearing away everything. Why are they so quiet?" A few moments later, his ears caught stealthy footsteps outside the window and what sounded like human voices. He grew even more apprehensive. After another few moments, he heard cries of alarm, mumbled words, and thumping sounds. Aghast, he jumped up. "Oh no!" he said. "We've fallen into the scoundrels' trap!" As he heard the faint sound of footsteps approaching, he frantically pushed his drunken friends, but nothing could wake them up. Some, like logs of wood, made no response. Some mumbled a few incoherent words. As he kept pushing, he heard a creak as the door opened. Yuanli couldn't afford to be concerned with the others now. In this desperate moment, he had a sudden flash of inspiration. He jumped out the back window. Seeing a large tree in the yard, he climbed up the trunk with all the speed he could muster and peeked into the room where he had been. Lo and behold, a group of monks and laymen, armed with sharp knives, stormed in and cut off every head they saw.

Yuanli was so shaken at the sight that he gave a mighty leap over the fence wall, little knowing if land or water was on the other side. In fact, it was a grove of brambles. He was about to crouch down and hide himself there when it occurred to him that he had forgotten to close the back window. The evil monks would surely chase him, so this was not a safe place. With all his strength, he parted the brambles and struggled his way through them. Soon, with blood trickling down his face, he found himself in open wilderness. He hobbled along for two or three li. There were gusts of ominous wind under a sky darkened by black clouds. He had no idea where he was. All he saw were abandoned graves and deserted earth mounds. Making a turn, he came upon a solitary, forlorn-looking house, with light leaking through the chink between the double doors. He said to himself, "I'm too tired to move another step. While there's still light in this house, let me ask to be put up for the night before I decide what to do next." Truly,

> *A green dragon and a white tiger*
> *Bring either joy or woe, when together.*[5]

Yuanli gently knocked on the door. A woman about fifty years old came to answer the door, bearing a lamp. Upon seeing Yuanli, she asked, "Why knock on my door at this time of the night?"

"I'm really sorry for doing this, but I'm in a desperate situation. Please do me a favor and let me stay here for the rest of the night."

"There are no men in this house. I can't keep you. You have no baggage, no servants, and you speak a different dialect. Without knowing anything about you, I can't oblige."

Yuanli thought, "Things having come to this, I'll have to tell her the truth." Aloud, he said, "Madam, my surname is Yang. I'm a native of Yangzhou Prefecture. I'm on my way to the capital to sit for the examinations. Monks at Baohua Monastery urged me and my companions to stay there, and so we did. Who would have guessed that they had evil designs on us! They got all six of my companions drunk and killed every one of them. I was the only one who stayed sober and escaped."

"My goodness! Amitabha Buddha! I don't believe this!"

"If you don't believe me, please look at the bloodstains on my face. I climbed up a big tree in the backyard and jumped into a grove of brambles. My face is all lacerated."

The old woman opened her eyes wide and saw that his face was indeed lacerated. "So you are indeed in trouble," said she. "All right, I'll have to take you in. If you pass the examinations, be sure to take care of me, and we'll be even."

"Thank you so much for your kindness, madam! As the ancients said, 'To save a life is better than to build a seven-story stupa.' I'll close the door after me. You can go to sleep. I'll just take a nap here at this table. I'll go as soon as it's light."

"Do as you please. I can tend to the door. Don't worry. It's so seldom that a scholar taking the exams comes to this house. As they say, 'After an important person visits your home, you'll have firewood and rice aplenty.' I have an auntie who sells wine in the next village. I'll go there and get a flask of wine to calm your nerves. Otherwise, without any bedding, you'll be too cold sleeping here."

In pleasant surprise, Yuanli said, believing his bad luck was behind him, "It's already too kind of you to keep me for the night. And now, you go out of your way to get me wine. How shall I ever repay you? If I pass the exams, I will never forget your great kindness."

"You sit here for a while. My daughter will keep you company while I'm away. Daughter! Come and greet the young gentleman. Close the door for now. I'll be back soon with wine." After leaving a few words of instructions with her daughter, the old woman picked up a flask and went out.

The girl examined Yuanli's face and looked as if she found something lamentable.

"May I ask how old you are, sister?"

"I'm thirteen."

"Why do you stare at me like this?"

"I stare at you because I'm wondering why someone with your good looks should be hit with such a disaster. Too bad you know nothing about the ways of the world in spite of all the books you've read."

In alarm, Yuanli asked, "Why do you say this? What you just said gives me a bad feeling."

"Do you know why my mother refused to take you in at first?"

"Because there are no men in the house and it was the middle of the night."

"After you told her what had happened to you, why did she change her mind?"

"Because I aroused her compassion."

"You are like 'a swallow that nests in a hall, unaware of the spreading fire.'"

Even more alarmed, Yuanli asked, "Don't tell me your mother is also plotting against my life? I have nothing on me. What good would my death do to her? Sister, you are not trying to scare an already frightened man, are you?"

"Do you have any idea to whom this house belongs and who supports us?"

"What strange questions! How would I know what goes on in your family?"

"My surname is Zhang. I have an older brother, Zhang Xiaoyi. He's adopted. He runs a small business away from home and the money for his business comes from Monk Wushi of Baohua Monastery. This thatched hut was also put up by those in the monastery. My brother came home last evening and went today to the monastery to hand in his profits. Luckily he's not here. If he had seen you, he wouldn't have let you off easy."

Yuanli thought, "I did see laymen mixed with the monks in the killings. Zhang Xiaoyi must have been one of them." Aloud, he asked, "Since your mother is in cahoots with the monks, why did she go to buy wine for me?"

"She didn't go to buy wine. She's using that pretext to report to the monks. They'll be here any moment now. You're doomed! I can tell by your graceful appearance that you're destined for greatness. That's why I'm telling you all this, so that you can make your escape."

A cold sweat broke out all over Yuanli. As he turned to go, the girl laid a detaining hand on him and said, "It's all very well for you to go, but my mother has the sharpest mind. If she doesn't see you after she comes back, she'll know that I gave the secret away. How will I be able to stand the punishment?"

"If you really want to save me, you'll have to put up with the punishment. I'll never forget to repay you."

"I've got an idea. Tie me to a post before you go, quick! I'll cry out for my mother. When she comes back, I'll tell her that you were going to rape me and tied me here but my screams frightened you. And you were also afraid that my mother would be back soon. So you ran away. That's the only way to spare me from punishment." (*This girl is full of wisdom. How worthy of respect!*) Quickly she took out from a trunk an ingot of silver and, handing it to Yuanli, said, "This is a loan from the monks. If mother asks about it, I know what to say."

Yuanli demurred at first, but, at the thought that he had absolutely no money for his journey, he felt obliged to take it. As he tied the girl up, he thought, "This girl is as wise as she is kind. I must not forget her great kindness in saving my life. I might as well make a marriage proposal to her and come back later to get her." Aloud, he said, "My name is Yang Yanhe, courtesy name Yuanli. I'm nineteen and a native of Jiangdu County, Yangzhou Prefecture, of the South Metropolitan Area. I'm not yet engaged because my parents died early. Out of gratitude for your kindness in saving my life, I'd like you to be my wife. I'll come back later to get you and marry you. I won't go back on my word. What do you say?"

"My pet name is Shu'er. I'm thirteen. If you don't think I'm unworthy of you, I'd be willing to marry you. I won't ever regret it. There's one thing, though. My mother went to report to the monks only because she has received many favors from them and doesn't want to betray them. Please don't hold this against her in the future. Now it's getting more and more dangerous. Don't stay a moment longer." (*She sets Yuanli free without forgetting to exonerate her mother first. The thoroughness of an outstanding woman of spirit.*)

No sooner had Yuanli heard her answer than he turned to go. He was barely out of the door when he looked back and saw a group of torch-bearing men flocking to the house. Horror smote him to the heart. Losing his senses altogether, he staggered forward, not daring to take another look back.

Let us pick up another thread of our story. With the old woman leading the club-bearing Juekong, the monk from Sichuan, followed immediately by Wushi, the group of twenty-odd men, including Zhang Xiaoyi, angrily stormed into the house. Hearing footsteps approaching, the girl burst into wails at the top of her voice.

Upon entering the room and finding her daughter tied up, with the man named Yang nowhere in sight, the old woman said in alarm, "Why are you in such a state?"

The girl said tearfully, "After you were gone, mother, that man wanted to rape me. I rejected him, and he found a rope and tied me up. I cried out madly, so he ran away. Then he turned back and asked me for money. I refused. He searched the trunk and took something before he went off."

The old woman was struck dumb and looked as woebegone as a drowned chicken. Quickly she went to check the trunk and realized that an ingot of silver was missing. "Oh horrors!" she cried. "He stole the loan from His Reverence!"

With Yang Yuanli gone, the monks could not afford to waste time. Frantically they raced off, but, little knowing which way he had gone, they soon returned to the monastery with a sigh. Stamping their feet in regret, they said, "One who strikes at a snake but doesn't kill it on the spot will surely bring trouble upon himself." Things having already come to this pass, there was nothing more they could do than bury the many corpses in the backyard. The trunks, cases, and bedding rolls of the deceased were found to be filled mostly with copper coins, but there were also eight or nine hundred taels of silver, which was good enough. Monk Wushi shared them with Juekong, the monks, and the acolytes, and gave some to Zhang Xiaoyi, much to everyone's joy and gratitude. He also gave some to the old woman, partly as hush money and partly to compensate her for her loss, but it was still a loan, as before.

In the meantime, after fleeing the scene, Yang Yuanli ran about in the darkness, but, in fact, he had been going in circles and had never left the area. Utterly worn out, he saw nothing else for it but to stay in a deserted shrine for the night. He rose at the crack of dawn and pressed ahead. Upon reaching Qing County, he was about to go through the city gate when he ran into an old man, who cried out to him, "My nephew! I heard that you passed the examinations at the provincial level. Congratulations! But shouldn't you be on your way to the capital for the next level of exams? Why are you here alone without a servant?"

Who, you may ask, was that old man? He was Yuanli's uncle, Yang Xiaofeng, who ran a business in Beijing and was passing Hejian Prefecture on his way to Shandong to sell his goods. What was his delight when he ran into his nephew who had just passed the examinations!

Encountering his uncle in this desperate moment, Yuanli poured out his tale of woe, beginning from the events at Baohua Monastery and ending with his escape from the old woman's house. Appalled, Yang Xiaofeng took his hand and dragged him to a restaurant, where he treated Yuanli to a meal, gave Yuanli his own servant, Asan, lent him about one hundred and thirty taels of silver, and hired a mule and a sedan-chair for his journey to the capital. Indeed,

> *Without experiencing bone-chilling cold,*
> *How would the plum blossoms smell so sweet?*

After bidding Xiaofeng farewell, Yuanli went to the capital to take the examinations. He came out second. "I'm just not that good, after all!" he lamented. "But I did pass, so I can keep my promises and also see that justice is done."

At the palace examinations where the emperor himself was the examiner, he won third place and therefore entered the Imperial Academy. He had a friend called

Shu Youqing, who had also just passed the national examinations. Shu Youqing's father, Shu Ting, was an imperial inspector currently on duty in Shandong. So Yuanli gave Shu Youqing a detailed account of the murders of his six friends and the servants. Youqing reported the case to his father. All the monks of the monastery were then brought under guard to the county yamen. Wushi and Juekong, the ringleaders, were put under torture during the interrogation. They confessed. They were then taken to the backyard of the monastery, where the corpses were dug up and identified. All the monks were then thrown into jail. Zhang Xiaoyi had died of illness by this time. Shu Ting forthwith wrote a memorial, requesting permission to destroy the monastery, execute the monks, and erect a monument on the site. The local population applauded the decision. Later, when returning to the place on a leave of absence from his post, Yuanli visited the site where the monastery had stood and composed a poem in memory of his six friends, but of this, no more.

Being a trusted friend of the monks, the old woman wanted to flee as soon as she heard that the monastery had been destroyed and the monks put to death. The girl said to herself, "If I follow mother, how will Scholar Yang be able to find me?" She was in the middle of these thoughts when an old man entered the house and asked, "Is this Mrs. Zhang's house?"

"Yes, my deceased husband's surname is Zhang," replied the old woman.

"Is your daughter called Shu'er?"

"How do you know my daughter's name?"

"I am Yang Xiaofeng of Yangzhou. My nephew Yang Yanhe passed the provincial exams and was here on his way to the capital for the national exams when the monks of Baohua Monastery did an evil thing and killed the six scholars and the many servants traveling with him. My nephew escaped and has just won third place on the palace exams. Out of gratitude for your daughter for having saved his life and given him an ingot of silver, he asked me to come here and propose marriage."

The old woman was so shocked that she was lost for words for a good while. Observing how consternated her mother was, the girl pulled her into another room and said, "That night, I thought he would go far some day, judging by his impressive looks, and it would be too bad if he were to die. So I gave him money and told him to escape. He proposed marriage then and there. I said, 'My mother has received many kindnesses from the monks. Even if she has indeed gone to report to them, it's because she doesn't want to owe them anything. You must not bear a grudge against her.' He gave his promise. So you have nothing to fear."

Thereupon, Yang Xiaofeng took Shu'er and her mother to Yangzhou and rented a house for them. A wedding ceremony was held as soon as Yuanli returned in glory. The old woman dared not go into the presence of Yuanli. It was only after her daughter strenuously asked Yuanli for forgiveness on her part that the two finally managed to meet. She prostrated herself on the floor, but Yuanli raised her to her feet and said not a word about what had happened earlier. Later, Shu'er and Yuanli had a son, who grew up to be a scholar and became a zhuangyuan in the year of Xinwei [1571], and the Yang clan prospered from generation to generation. Had Yuanli not fled under cover of night, how would this marriage have been possible? Indeed, marriages are predestined, and the bonds are made at gatherings of the immortals. There is a quatrain that bears witness:

> *He ran into bandits on his way to the exams;*
> *The heroine saved him in his distress.*
> *Leave yourself a way out in everything you do,*
> *So that you won't regret having done what you did.*

With His Flying Sword Lü Dongbin Attempts to Kill the Yellow Dragon

> At night I sleep among verdant wutong trees;
> At dawn I roam around Penglai Island;[1]
> Chanting poems, I fly over Dongting Lake.
> Tipsy from a drinking bout on Yueyang Tower,
> I drop off to blissful slumber,
> With Jade Mountain as my pillow.
> In my wild, untrammeled ways,
> I leave no traces wherever I go;
> I keep no timetable in my travels.
> My basket and sword I carry with me;
> If I look like a peddler, I sell clouds and mist.
> I drifted for many years in the human world;
> I was guest at the grand feast of Lord Donghua.[2]
> I toppled a jade tower to plant my wonder tree;
> I drained the Yellow River to plant my golden lotus.
> I smashed the corals, flew to the North Sea,
> And bowed to the Daoist God on his throne.
> Nothing can ever stop me.
> I aim to perform eight hundred feats
> And three thousand exploits.

The above lyric to the tune of "Spring in the Qin Garden" was written by an immortal who lived both in heaven and on earth. Who was this immortal? He was Lü Yan, courtesy name Dongbin, Daoist name Chunyangzi.[3] After he found the Daoist truth in a "yellow millet" dream,[4] he followed his mentor Zhongli and spent his days learning the Dao in the Zhongnan Mountains.

One day, Dongbin said to his mentor, "Sir, I'm ever so indebted to you for having delivered me from the cycles of life and death and taught me the wonderful formula of immortality. But is there an end to the Daoist transmigrations?"

"How can there be no end to them?" replied his mentor. "From the time the earth was first separated from heaven, a small kalpa, one hundred twenty-nine thousand and six hundred years long, will see the world become one, and there will be no more sages. A large kalpa, two hundred fifty nine thousand and two hundred years long, will see Confucianism come to an end. An Asura kalpa, three hundred eighty-eight thousand and eight hundred years long, will witness the demise of our Daoism. A Samvara kalpa [the kalpa of destruction], seven hundred seventy-seven thousand and seven hundred years long, will bring Buddhism to an end. Such is destiny."

Dongbin asked again, "What about the human world, sir? Is there an end to its height, length, and width in all four directions—north, south, east, and west?"

"How can there be no end to them? Let's begin with the Central Plains: They consist of four hundred military regions, three thousand counties, and seven hundred border areas under the sun and the moon from the point where the sun rises in the east to where the sun sets in the west, and from the southern regions to the northern Yan."

"If I want to tour the Central Plains, where should I start and where should I end?"

"Single digits multiplied by nine make up numbers carrying the yang element. So you may start with the nine prefectures in front of the Mountain [possibly the Qinling Mountains] and the nine behind, the twenty-seven (three times nine) military regions of North and South Huai, the thirty-six (four times nine) military regions of Hebei, the forty-five (five times nine) military regions west of Tong Pass, the fifty-four (six times nine) military regions of Xichuan, the sixty-three (seven times nine) military regions of Jinghu, the eighty-one (nine times nine) military regions south of the Yangzi River, and the four prefectures of Chaoyang that stretch into the sea. They add up to four hundred military regions in total."

"What's the population of the four hundred military regions?"

"Of this world, three-tenths is mountains, six-tenths is water, and one-tenth is people."

"How long has it been since you acquired the Dao, sir?"

"Well, the Han dynasty lasted four hundred and seven years, the Jin one hundred and fifty-seven years, the Tang two hundred and eighty-eight years, the Song three hundred and seventeen years. So it's been more than one thousand and one hundred years in total."

"In those more than one thousand and one hundred years, how many people have you delivered from suffering?"

"Only you."

"Why only me? Is it because Daoists are not compassionate enough to deliver everyone? If you give me three years, I will be able to deliver more than three thousand people in the Central Plains only, to invigorate the Daoist school."

His mentor broke into hearty laughter. "Enough!" said he. "This world abounds in treacherous and unfilial people. How can those lacking in virtue and honor be allowed to gain immortality? I'll give you three years all right. If you can find me even one, I'll give you credit for it."

"So I bid you farewell this very day, sir. Off I go to the world of the mortals!"

"Not so fast! You're not ready to go yet. I have here a magic weapon that I haven't yet passed on to you." Turning to his page boy, he said, "Bring me the Tai'e divine-light demon-subjugating sword."

After the page boy brought it to him, Mr. Zhongli continued, "I pass on to you the sword that my mentor, Lord Donghua, gave me."

Dropping to his knees, Dongbin said, "At your behest, sir."

"This sword can fly on its own to slash off a head. After you tell it someone's location and name and finish chanting the incantation, it will change into a green dragon, fly to cut off the man's head, and come back with the head in its mouth. (*If only this sword could be used to cut down all the villains of this world! Oh, the joy of it!*) Such is its magic power. Let me pass on to you the incantations to make it go as well as to make it come back."

Dongbin kowtowed and learned the incantations. Hanging the sword over his shoulder, he said, "I bid you farewell today, sir. I'm going down these mountains."

"No! You're still not ready to go. You must first promise me three things."

"What three things, sir?"

"First, once you are in the Central Plains, do not pick fights with Buddhist monks. (*Let snakes and tigers go their own separate ways. That is how the Dao can serve public interests.*) Do you promise?"

"I promise."

"Second, be sure to bring back my sword and not lose it. Do you promise?"

"I promise."

"Third, you have exactly three years. Do not tarry. If you don't come back in three years, you will be executed and your human form destroyed. Do you promise?"

"I promise."

In delight, Mr. Zhongli said, "All right, go then and godspeed!"

"You, sir, were so kind as to teach the Dao to me. I now know everything about the kalpas, geography, and the incantations for the magic sword. Let me intone a poem in gratitude to you before I go down these mountains to deliver people from their sufferings." The poem goes as follows:

> When purity reigns in all twenty-four parts of the body,[5]
> The three thousand exploits will be complete.
> With clouds and mist around the earth's axis,
> With the stars and the moon brightening the sky,
> Why bother to sow the seeds of jade
> And till the land of golden cinnabar?

With knowledge of the wondrous formula,
Who will fail to achieve longevity?

After Dongbin finished intoning the poem, Mr. Zhongli laughed boisterously and said, "Remember to come back in three years, whether you succeed in delivering people or not. Do not miss the deadline, do not lose the magic sword, and do not pick fights with Buddhist monks. Go quickly and come back in time!"

Thereupon, Dongbin took leave of his mentor and went down the mountain. Would he be able to deliver people? Truly,

Bear this in mind: words are like fishlines and hooks;
They pull trouble right out of the air.

And so Dongbin went down the mountain. He brought his cloud to land in the mortal world and set about seeking out people predestined to acquire the Dao. A whole year went by, but he found no trace of even one such person. There is a quatrain in testimony:

Countless years have gone by since I joined the Daoist order;
Several times seas have changed to dust.
The formula for longevity now in my knowledge,
I cannot pass it on lightly to just any person.

Dongbin traveled for a whole year without finding a good candidate. What was he to do? With a knit of his eyebrows, a plan came to his mind. When in the mountains, he had heard his mentor say that if he were to look out from the top of the universe, he would find powerful overlords where purple vapor hovered, and monsters of the mountains and rivers where there was black vapor, whereas blue vapor bespoke the presence of people destined for immortality and the acquisition of the Dao. He betook himself to a deserted place and called out, "Rise!" Immediately he ascended on a cloud and rose all the way up to the top of the universe. Looking left and right, he saw in the distance a streak of blue vapor rising straight to the sky. "Good!" he cried out. "I've got a candidate there!" With a favorable wind blowing most of the way, Dongbin, in his eagerness, rode on a cloud and arrived at the place with the blue vapor, about a thousand li away.

Wondering what place it was, Dongbin called out, "Where's the local god?"

A wind sprang up. As it blew past, the local tutelary god materialized. How did he look?

He was short in stature,
With a scarf around his enormous head,
A dragon-headed cane in his hand,
And a black tiger's tail around his waist.

"Your Honor," said the local god, chanting a greeting. "How can this humble one be of service to you?"

"What is this place? Who lives where the blue vapor is? A man or a woman?"

"This is the western capital in Henan Prefecture [present-day Luoyang]. At the mouth of Copper Camel Lane lives a woman, a Miss Yin, more than thirty years old but still unmarried. Hers has been a family that has pursued the Dao for generations and has accumulated much credit in the netherworld. In fact, she is a descendant of Yin Kaishan of the Tang dynasty and has been a woman for the last seven incarnations. That's why there's a blue vapor."

"You may go now," said Dongbin.

With another gust of wind, the local god vanished. Dongbin alit from the cloud and, in the disguise of a shabbily clad priest, went into the city. At the entrance to Copper Camel Lane, he saw a board bearing the inscription: "The Yin Family Candle Shop—We make the finest candles with long-lasting clear wax." In the shop stood a woman in Daoist attire, wearing a hat adorned with fish bones. The hint of a blue vapor between her eyebrows so excited Dongbin that he gave a cheer, quite forgetting himself. Truly,

> Iron boots are worn out in the long, fruitless search;
> And now you find what you need without a stroke of work.

"Greetings!" called out Dongbin. Engaged in a conversation with the candle-maker, the woman turned around and said, "Please wait, sir."

Lü Dongbin went forward for a look. Detecting too much anger in her disposition, he exclaimed, "Too bad!" From his sleeve he drew out a piece of paper on which was written a quatrain:

> I vowed to deliver three thousand people,
> But found none so destined throughout my search.
> With high hopes I made this special journey,
> But Miss Yin lacks an immortal's qualities.

After the quatrain were a few characters that read "By the Immortal with Double Mouths." Noticing a sheet of paper fluttering down from the priest's sleeve, the woman had someone pick it up and show it to her. Realizing that the priest was none other than Patriarch Lü in disguise, the character Lü being composed of two characters for "mouth," she ordered the man to run after him, but the priest vanished with a refreshing breeze. Miss Yin was seized with remorse. Indeed, those without a predestined bond will not meet even if brought face to face! That quatrain preyed on the woman's mind for twelve years until she died while sitting in the lotus position.

Before he knew it, another year went by, and Lü Dongbin still had not found a worthy candidate. Again he ascended to the top of the universe. There, he saw a horse galloping toward him. The horse stopped right before him, and the messenger on it dismounted and, retrieving a letter of invitation from the scroll bag on his back, announced, "Your Honor, Wang Weishan, an official who is a Daoist believer and lives on Maxing Street of Kaifeng, the eastern capital, is going to hold a prayer service and a feast for three hundred and sixty people in his house on the fourteenth day of this month to celebrate your birthday. He has also engaged two thousand priests for the occasion. I am here to deliver the invitation."

"Oh yes, I forgot that tomorrow is my birthday. Thank you so much for taking all this trouble and coming over such a distance!"

"I went first to the Zhongnan Mountains, where the old master told me that you were in the Central Plains. So I came all the way here to see you, sir."

Lü Dongbin took a celestial fruit from his basket and offered it to the messenger, who ate it, bowed in gratitude, mounted his horse, and went off.

Dongbin rode on a cloud and flew to a deserted place in the eastern capital, where he alit from the cloud. Afraid of being recognized, he shook his head and cried out, "Change!" Presto! he changed himself into a shabbily clad mangy priest. Upon arriving at Maxing Street in the city, he saw banners and flags being put up for a prayer service and invitations being chanted for the immortal to join the celebration. Dongbin had arrived just in time. Indeed, if there is a wish, heaven will grant it. Now let us watch to see if the host of these festivities was predestined for immortality or not.

Dongbin went to the altar and saw that the host was the grand marshal of the imperial court, a eunuch, who was much given to works of charity and was a devoted Daoist with a hint of a blue vapor between his eyebrows. Dongbin thought, "This man is not yet ready, but let me use some magic power on him. He may not have a change of heart in the beginning, but later on, he will attain the fruit of enlightenment."

After partaking of the feast, instead of paying his share of five hundred copper coins and five piculs of rice, Dongbin said, "This poor priest is good at ink-wash painting. A bowl of water is enough. I don't need a brush-pen. Just give me a scroll of silk and I'll produce a landscape painting by way of thanking you for the meal."

This request was passed on to the grand marshal and a scroll of silk was brought to Dongbin. He ground an ink stick in water and splashed the water onto the scroll, ruining it. Witnessing the scene, the grand marshal said, "The audacity! How dare that brute make a fool of me! Bring him up here!"

Observing the grand marshal's flare of anger, Dongbin turned to go. As the attendants ran after him, he vanished in a refreshing breeze, leaving behind a scroll of white paper that hung in midair. When the scroll was brought to him, the grand marshal spread it open and saw that it bore this quatrain:

> The host of the event seeks immortality,
> But fails to know my identity.
> To know the name of this humble priest,
> Look at the painting on the silk scroll.

The grand marshal had the ruined silk scroll picked up and spread out again for another look. He would have felt all right had he not looked, but, having seen it, he sank to his knees and kowtowed. What did he see? Truly,

> *Immortals who conceal their identities*
> *Ruin the chances of mortal beings.*

It was a portrait of Lü Dongbin. Only then did Grand Marshal Wang realize that the priest was no less than an immortal. Regrets were too late now. He had this portrait of the immortal taken into the inner quarters of the palace, where the empress dowager had it mounted and put in the imperial storehouse. After submitting a memorial to the emperor, Grand Marshal Wang returned his house and landed properties to the imperial court, dismissed all the servants, and went to the Wudang Mountains to join the Daoist order. When picking medicinal herbs in the mountains one day, he encountered Lü Dongbin and gained immortality through the latter's initiation. (*According to this account, Patriarch Lü had actually delivered two individuals.*) But this happened later.

The three-year deadline was soon approaching, but Lü Dongbin had not yet delivered even one person. What was to be done? In low spirits, he rose again to the top of the universe to look for blue vapor. There in the south hovered a streak of blue vapor. Promptly he rode on a cloud and headed in that direction. When drawing near the blue vapor about four hours later, he said, "Stop!" Then he called out, "Where is the local mountain god?"

As a gust of wind swept by, the local mountain god appeared before him. Wearing a gold helmet, gold armor, a brocade robe, and carrying a hatchet, he bowed in greeting and said, "Your Honor, how can I be of service?"

"What kind of a family lives down there where the blue vapor is?"

"At the foot of Yellow Dragon Hill in Huangzhou in the Jiangxi region, there lives an old man with the surname of Fu and Buddhist name of Yongshan [forever kind]. He has accumulated much credit in the netherworld, and his ancestors have been doing good deeds for generations. That explains the presence of the blue vapor."

"You may go now," said Dongbin.

When the vital forces gather, they assume human form. When they disperse, they vanish into the air, as did the local mountain god. Dongbin alit from the cloud and went straight to the Fu residence at the foot of Yellow Dragon Hill. It just so happened that Mr. Fu was hosting a feast in honor of some Buddhist monks. Lü Dongbin went into the main hall and greeted Mr. Fu.

"I'm here to form a bond with you for more blessings and to awaken you to the Daoist truth," said Dongbin.

"Don't be offended by what I'm going to say," responded Mr. Fu. "In this house, we honor Buddhist monks but not Daoist priests."

"Sir, Confucianism, Buddhism, and Daoism have always been one family," rejoined Dongbin.

"I am no worshiper of Daoism! You Daoists lie too much."

"How is that so?"

"You fooled even the First Emperor of Qin and Emperor Wu of Han, not to speak of folks like us!"

"Tell me from the beginning: how did we Daoists fool the Emperor of Qin and Emperor Wu of Han?"

"You must know Bai Juyi's satirical poem.[6] It says,

> In the depths of the cloud-like snowy waves
> Of the vast bottomless and boundless ocean,
> Stand three divine hills, or so they say.
> The hills abound in herbs of immortality
> That turn mortals into divine beings.
> The Qin and Han emperors believed the claims;
> Alchemists go there for herbs year after year.
> Penglai Island has been much heard of,
> But where is it amid the misty water?
> On the vast seas, braving the roaring winds,
> All wear their eyes out but fail to see Penglai.
> Refusing to go back without seeing it,
> Boys and girls grow old right there in the boat. (How does he know that?)
> Xu Fu the magician's claim to find fairyland was a lie.
> Prayers to the god Taiyi serve no purpose.[7]
> Turn your eyes to Mount Li and Mount Mao![8]
> What do you see but weeds blown by sad winds?
> The Daode jing of the grand patriarch
> Says not a word about medicinal herbs,
> Or immortals, or ascensions to heaven."

After Mr. Fu finished speaking, Lü Dongbin said, "If we Daoists lie, I beg to be enlightened on the eminent virtues of the Buddhists."

"I will not talk about Sakyamuni of Holy Vulture Peak.[9] I will speak only of Abbot Huinan of Yellow Dragon Monastery on Yellow Dragon Hill in our area. He explains the sutras, teaches Buddhism in easy terms to the public, delivers people from the sufferings of this world, and leads them onto the path of enlightenment. He has given numerous lectures on the scriptures and delivered more individuals than can ever be counted. The thousands upon thousands of people who listen every day to his lectures find immense delight in them. I have hardly ever seen Daoists explain Daoism to the populace and deliver people from their sufferings. All you do is cure your own illnesses. (*True enough.*) That's why I have no respect for Daoists."

It would have been a different story had Mr. Lü not heard this, but he did, and he burned with rage. "Is that monk giving a lecture today?" he asked.

"He never takes a break, all year round. Today is no exception."

Without bothering to say good-bye to Mr. Fu, Lü Dongbin went straight off to Yellow Dragon Hill, his sword in hand, to challenge Abbot Huinan and see who was holier. Who would turn out to be the winner and who the loser? Indeed,

> *For the vain glory of the snails' horns[10]*
> *And profits the size of a fly's head,*
> *Why lead such a hurly-burly life?*
> *Everything is predetermined by fate.*
> *Why care about who is strong and who is weak?*
> *Seize all moments of leisure ere old age sets in,*
> *And enjoy yourself in an untrammeled life.*
> *A hundred years means thirty-six thousand bouts of drinking.*
> *Just think, how many days do you have left?*
> *Why let sorrows and hardships take up half of them?*
> *Happily, in the clear breeze, under the bright moon,*
> *Spread out the mat, raise high the curtains.*
> *Enjoy life south of the Yangzi river*
> *With fine wine and songs to the flowers.*

As we were saying, without saying good-bye, Dongbin went straight to Yellow Dragon Hill to seek out Abbot Huinan. The abbot, having beaten the monastery drums and struck the gongs, was about to start his lecture in the hall when a gust of wind swept right to his seat, bringing with it a streak of blue vapor. Upon closer inspection, the abbot inwardly let out a groan, "Here comes an obstacle from the devil!" His ruler in hand, he announced to the audience from his podium, "This old monk is not going to talk about the dharma, nor about the scriptures. I am only going to intone to you a poem with a Buddhist message and see if any of you can provide a response to it." Before the words were quite out of his mouth, Lü Dongbin emerged from the crowd and said, "Monk! Out with your poem!"

The abbot intoned the following quatrain:

> *This old monk grew bold this year,*
> *And pitched camp on Yellow Dragon Hill.*
> *From my sleeve I draw my golden hammer,*
> *And smash the universe to smithereens.*

Dongbin burst out laughing. "Monk!" he said. "So you didn't grow bold last year or the year before last, and you won't grow bold next year, but only grew bold this year? Say that again!"

> *This old monk grew bold this year.*

"Stop!" Dongbin shouted,

> *This poor priest has always been bold,*
> *And good at attacking camps by surprise.*

I seize the golden hammer from your sleeve,
And leave the universe intact.

The audience burst into cheers. It was as if a gust of wind had broken a thousand bamboo stems and a flood had swamped the camps of a million soldiers in the middle of the night. They cried out, "What a priest! What a good response!"

The abbot held up his ruler and the audience quieted down.

"Monk!" said Dongbin. "Those four lines are but a prelude, not something by which to decide who's the winner. I also have a poem with a Daoist message. Let's not bet money but use this poem to decide who is the better of the two." Having said that, he drew his magic sword from the sheath on his back, drove it into the crack between two bricks on the ground, and continued to say, patting the sword with both hands, "Listen, everyone! If the monk wins, he will kill me. If I win, I will kill Yellow Dragon." This announcement came as such a shock that everyone turned pale with fright. The abbot said, "Out with it, quick!"

The following was what Lü Dongbin intoned:

> *An iron ox tilling the land planted gold coins;*
> *A child on a stone carving put on woven fabric.*
> *A world is hidden in one grain of millet;*
> *Mountains and rivers are cooked in one tiny pan.*
> *The hoary Laozi's eyebrows droop to the ground;*
> *The green-eyed foreign monk's hand points to the sky.*
> *Say not that there is more to the mystery;*
> *Inside this mystery there is nothing more.*

Having intoned the poem, Lü Dongbin asked the monk, "Can you come up with a matching poem?"

The abbot of Yellow Dragon Monastery said, "Repeat yours for me."

Dongbin agreed and started over again,

> *An iron ox tilling the land planted gold coins*

Before he could go on, the abbot said, "Stop!" And the following was what the abbot intoned:

> *I have a furnace with raging flames that makes jade coins;*
> *I had not a stitch on when I was a child.*
> *One grain can change the whole wide universe;*
> *The vast seas take in a hundred rivers.*
> *The furnace of summer spews leaping flames;*
> *The riverbed of winter contains a cool sky.*
> *None knows the wonders of the Buddhist truth;*
> *For the truth begets more truth in an endless cycle.*

Lü Dongbin said, "Monk! You lost! One grain cannot change the whole wide universe."

"What did you say? Come here! This old monk is hard of hearing!"

The unsuspecting Dongbin went up to the monk's podium. With one swift movement, the monk of Yellow Dragon Monastery grabbed him and said, "Let me ask you something: if one grain can't change the universe, why can the world be hidden in one grain of millet? Answer me! Also, if mountains and rivers are cooked in one tiny pan, what is there outside the tiny pan?" (*Argumentative people always end up finding themselves cornered.*)

Dongbin could not come up with an answer.

The monk continued, "My message means more than it appears to. Your message means less than it appears to. I should have killed you, but Buddhists don't kill. So I'll let you off this time!" So saying, he whacked at Dongbin's head so hard with his ruler that a lump appeared. (*The Buddhist patriarch wasn't this competitive. The monk should not have applied his ruler.*) Dongbin reddened. As the audience broke into cheers, Dongbin felt deeply humiliated. With his eyes fixed on the abbot, he laughed loudly three times, shook his head three times, clapped his hands three times, slipped his sword back into the sheath, and went off. The audience cried out, "Hey! Weren't you the loser?"

Raising his ruler to quiet down the audience, the abbot of Yellow Dragon Monastery said, "Everyone! This old monk is doomed today. I wonder what tomorrow will bring. There is a Buddhist hymn that says,

> *Repeat five times the five-beat rhythm,*
> *And learn to beat the He Mountain drum.*
> *Watch a wrestling game under Yellow Dragon Hill*
> *Rather than try to win a bet in this place.*
> *The melons in the fields are sweet in every bite,*
> *But those not yet ripe taste bitter with their stalks.*

Everyone! Do you know why he clapped his hands three times, shook his head three times, and laughed three times? Yee! The finest cream has turned into poison. After the third watch of tonight, a flying sword will come to cut off my head."

After the abbot finished speaking, the audience dispersed. The abbot left the podium and went into his cell, where he called the monks together and said to them, "This old monk has something to tell you. At the third watch tonight, Lü Dongbin's flying sword will come to get my head. I will be able to survive if my magic power serves me well. If my magic power is not strong enough, your heads will also be gone. Take good care of yourselves." The monks fell to their knees, joining their palms, and said, "Please save us in your mercy!"

Abbot Yellow Dragon nodded. Raising two fingers, he said a few words that saved all the monks of the monastery. Verily,

Be advised: Do not make enemies for yourselves;
Deep feuds can hardly ever be dissolved.
An enemy made in one day
Will remain an enemy for a thousand days.
An act of kindness to a foe
Is like hot water poured on snow.
Repaying injury with injury
Is to set the wolf against the scorpion.
All those sowing seeds of feud
Fall victims to its torments.

Abbot Yellow Dragon said to the monks, "Remember, everyone, to close every door tightly and not to light lamps and candles. Also, wrap your heads with scarves or put on hats to keep yourselves out of harm's way. I'll see you all tomorrow morning."

After leaving the abbot's cell, the monks mumbled to themselves, "He gives lectures day after day on the Buddhist doctrine and, in the end, lands us all in such a spot! All three hundred of us monks in this monastery will have our heads cut off like so many watermelons!" The more intrepid monks stayed in the monastery and the timid ones fled before the night was out.

The abbot called the gatekeeper to him. As the gatekeeper went up to him, chanting a greeting, the abbot told him to draw near and then whispered something into his ear. Thus instructed, the gatekeeper went off. Evening fell. After such a raucous scene, Yellow Dragon Monastery was to enjoy no peace and quiet throughout the night.

Sitting on a rock in the mountains, Lü Dongbin said to himself, "The deadline is coming up soon, but I still haven't delivered even one person. My teacher has indeed warned me against picking fights with Buddhist monks. But how can I call it quits after he hit me so hard with his ruler? It's either that monk or me! I'll impress everyone if I kill that abbot with my flying sword. But if I don't kill him, what am I going to say when I go back to see my teacher?" Raising his head, he noticed that the stars had changed their positions in the sky and the third watch of the night had just begun. He took out his sword and said to it, "By order of my mentor, I carry you with me for protection. Do not let me down. Go now to Yellow Dragon Monastery on Yellow Dragon Hill. When you see Abbot Huinan, whatever he is doing—walking, sitting, or lying, act quickly and bring me his head." After saying an incantation, he shouted, "Quick!" With a resounding clang, the sword changed into a green dragon and flew in the direction of Yellow Dragon Monastery. Dongbin gave a cheer.

He waited for about two hours, until it was already the fourth watch. The sword was like a stone that had sunk into the sea or a kite whose string had broken. Frantically he intoned the incantation for it to come back. Three thousand times he repeated the incantation, but nothing happened. Panic seized him. "If this sword is lost, I'll be decapitated and my human form destroyed." So thinking, he rose onto a cloud and flew to Yellow Dragon Monastery. Alighting from the cloud, he saw that all the doors of the monastery stood wide open. As a matter of fact, it was the gatekeeper who had left them open by the abbot's order.

Lü Dongbin said to himself, "Too bad I didn't know that that monk was not on guard. Otherwise, I would have gone directly into his cell and cut him in half." When approaching the abbot's cell, he saw that the room was brightly lit by two large red candles. On the couch, amid swirling wisps of fine incense, sat Abbot Yellow Dragon.

"The one with double mouths!" cried out the abbot. "So you are coming for your sword. It's right here. Come in and take it."

Mr. Lü raised the door curtain and walked in, saying, "Monk! Give me back my sword!"

The abbot pointed at the sword. It was half buried in the ground.

Lü Dongbin thought, "If I go and try to pull it out, I may fall into his trap. What am I going to do?" Aloud, he said, "Oh well, give me back my sword, and we'll call it quits."

"Double mouth! This old monk is not going to stoop to your level. I wanted to make short work of you, but I thought better of it out of deference for your teacher."

"What a sharp tongue!" thought Dongbin. "Let me pull the sword out and cut the brute down!" In big strides, he went forward and laid both hands on the sword. He pulled at it with all his might, but the sword did not budge, as if it were an iron rod weighing tens of thousands of catties and had taken root in the ground.

Laughing out loud, the abbot said, "Double mouth! As the ancients said, 'If men mean no harm to tigers, tigers don't make men their prey.' I was going to return the sword to you and let you go back to your teacher, but you wanted to pull out the sword and cut me down! I'm not going to offer it to you. If you have the strength, pull it out and take it with you."

Dongbin thought, "He is using his magic to fix it to the ground. How will I be able to pull it out with sheer strength?" So thinking, he intoned an incantation to release it, but the incantation only stuck it faster to the ground. Seeing no chance of drawing the sword out of the ground, Dongbin said, "Monk! Give me back the sword and be done with it!"

The abbot said, "I have here a quatrain. If you get its meaning, I'll give the sword back to you."

"Read it to me!"

The monk retrieved from his bosom a piece of paper on which was drawn a circle with a dot in the middle of it. The quatrain underneath the circle read:

> The cinnabar is in the sharp point of the sword;
> The sword is in the heart of the cinnabar.

The one who understands the reason
Will transcend the wheel of life and death.

Dongbin could make nothing of the quatrain.

"Double mouth!" said the abbot. "Do you understand its meaning?"

Dongbin was at a loss for words.

"Where's the guardian god of the dharma?" said Abbot Yellow Dragon.

As a gust of wind blew past, the guardian god of the dharma appeared in the air. What did he wear?

A golden and dark purple helmet
With red tassels hanging down like hair
And gold armor all over his body.
In his hand, at all times,
A demon-subjugating magic staff.
And he had the rosy complexion of a child.

The guardian god stepped forward and asked, "What orders do you have for me, sir?"

"Guardian god, take this Lü to Demon-Detaining Hill. Bring him back to me only after he sees the Buddhist truth. Give him one steamed bun every day from the celestial kitchen."

"Yes, sir!" said the guardian god. Turning to Lü Dongbin, he said, "Please come with me, sir!"

"Where am I going?"

"Just come with me!" said the guardian god. "If you don't, you'll get a taste of my magic staff! For your information, I am the guardian god Skanda. This staff weighs eighty four thousand catties. If you refuse to go, it'll drive you into the ground!"

Recalling his mentor's warning against picking fights with Buddhist monks, he resignedly followed the guardian god of the dharma to Demon-Detaining Hill to do his meditations, and there we shall leave him for now.

At the fifth watch, when the day broke, the monks of Yellow Dragon Monastery went to the abbot's cell to see how the abbot was doing.

"I scared you last night," said the abbot.

The monks replied, "Thanks to your immense power, nothing happened."

"You say this because you slept through it all. In fact, there was quite a commotion here last night."

"Do you have proof?"

Following the abbot's pointing finger, the monks saw the sword. They felt as if

The eight pieces of their skulls opened up
And half a bucket of ice and snow poured in.

Everyone bowed in admiration of the abbot's immense spiritual power. Countless men, women, monks, and nuns from all around the hills and the city swarmed to the abbot's cell to look at the sword, turning Yellow Dragon Hill and Huangzhou prefecture into hives of activity.

In the meantime, Lü Dongbin heard a clamor of voices as he sat in a cave on Demon-Detaining Hill, and called out for the local god of the hill. As the god appeared and chanted a greeting to him, he asked, "Why is there all that excitement in the monastery?"

"Sir, people from all over have come to see the magic sword and no one has been able to pull it out of the ground. Hence all the excitement."

"You may go now," said Dongbin.

After the local god of the hill withdrew, Dongbin thought, "What shall I say in defense of myself if my teacher learns what a mess I made here in Huangzhou? I'd better confess and ask for forgiveness."

Skanda the guardian god not being there, Dongbin walked out of the cave and rose on a cloud.

Upon returning to Demon-Detaining Hill but failing to see Lü Dongbin, Skanda went to the abbot's cell to report to Abbot Yellow Dragon. "Mr. Lü is gone," said he. "Do you want me to give chase, sir?"

"Guardian god, I don't want you to tire yourself out. You may return to the celestial palace now."

Thereupon, Skanda changed into a refreshing breeze and vanished.

In the meantime, Lü Dongbin flew all the way to the Zhongnan Mountains on his cloud and stopped to stand at the entrance to the cave. Upon seeing a page boy, he stepped forward and bowed, and the page boy returned the greeting.

"Is my mentor in?" asked Dongbin.

"No, he's picking medicinal herbs in the mountains."

And so Dongbin climbed up the mountains. When he found his mentor, he fell to his knees and prostrated himself on the ground. Knowing what had happened, Mr. Zhongli laughed heartily and said, "Have you brought back disciples? How many people have you delivered? But give the sword back to me first."

Dongbin apologized for his mistakes and added, "Please help me, sir!"

"I told you time and again not to provoke Buddhist monks. The lump on your head hasn't gone down. Aren't you ashamed to see me? How can you challenge people when you don't yet have enough spiritual powers? Instead of bringing back disciples, you did such dishonor to Daoism! I forgive you this time because this is your first offense. Now go and bring the sword back."

"Sir, please forgive me, but he has cast a spell on the sword. I won't be able to get it."

"I've written a letter to the abbot, my fellow student, who is in fact Pratyeka Buddha. He will surely give the sword back to you. Be careful with the letter. Don't damage the seal." Having said that, he produced the letter from his basket.

Dongbin said with a deep bow at the sight of the letter, "So, you know everything about the past and the future, sir."

Equipped with the letter, he wended his way to Yellow Dragon Monastery and alit from his cloud. A guardian announced to the abbot, "Mr. Lü is outside the cell, waiting for instructions."

"Bring him in," said Abbot Yellow Dragon.

The guardian said to Dongbin, "Sir, you're invited in."

After entering the cell, Dongbin joined his palms and prostrated himself, pressing his head against the abbot's feet in a Buddhist salute, and said, "I brought with me a letter from my mentor."

Already knowing this, the abbot asked for the letter. After Dongbin presented it to him with both hands, the abbot opened it and read the prophetic quatrain that was written underneath a circle with a dot above it:

> *Cinnabar is but a sword;*
> *A sword is but cinnabar.*
> *Get the sword and understand cinnabar.*
> *Get the cinnabar and understand the sword.*

The abbot said, "Out of deference for your teacher, I'll let you go with the sword."

Dongbin stepped forward, and this time he pulled out the sword easily. "Thank you, sir," he said. "May I ask what is the meaning of having the dot in the circle, the way you, sir, had it, and having the dot above it, the way my mentor had it?"

"If you honor me as your teacher, I'll impart my knowledge to you."

"I will gladly be your disciple, sir."

After making nine bows in total—three toward the front, three toward the back, and three to the statue of Buddha, Dongbin joined his palms, sank to his knees, and listened respectfully as the abbot said, "You said that 'The world is hidden in one grain of millet.' The small contains the large. Therefore, a dot above the circle. I replied, 'One grain can change the whole wide universe.' The large contains the small. Hence, a dot inside the circle. This is Dao, and I impart the knowledge to you."

Lü Dongbin was fully awakened to the truth. Such was the force of the enlightenment that it was as if the bottom of a fully loaded bucket suddenly fell out.

"Thank you, sir. I shall now return to the Zhongnan Mountains to thank my teacher."

"Remember, I taught the truth to you. In the future, do not claim that you learned it yourself. Now, write me a poem as testimony."

The four treasures of the scholar's study were then brought in. Lü Dongbin ground the ink stick in water, dipped the brush-pen in the ink, and composed the following poem:

> *I smashed the bottle-gourd and my zither;*
> *I was born to join the Daoist order.*

> *Today I acquired Yellow Dragon's art,*
> *After all these years of futile learning.*

After writing the poem, he bade farewell to Abbot Yellow Dragon and returned to the Zhongnan Mountains, where he gave the sword back to his mentor. Henceforth, he devoted himself in all serenity to the perfection of his inner nature and refrained from taking a single trip down the mountains for several hundred years. After he attained perfection in his accomplishments, he became an immortal right on earth. Truly,

> *At dawn he rode a white deer over the three isles;*
> *By dusk he rose to heaven astride a blue bird.*

Later, people saw on the wall of Tianqing Daoist Temple in Fengxiang Prefecture a poem in characters that looked like dragons and snakes. At the end of the poem was written "By the Double-Mouthed Daoist." Upon inquiries, they learned that the author was Patriarch Lü Dongbin. The poem said,

> *In the eight hundred years since I acquired the Dao,*
> *I did not take a head with my flying sword.*
> *Without a summons from the Jade Emperor,*
> *I hang on to life under the sun.*

Prince Hailing of Jin Dies from Indulgence in Lust

Orioles yesterday and cicadas today,
And the better part of each day is spent in bed.
With the sun flying in the chariot drawn by six dragons,
Why do harm to oneself when life is already short?

The above quatrain, written by Sikong Tu of the Tang dynasty, makes the point that, life being short and the passage of time relentless, one would do well not to hasten one's death by wallowing in pleasures of the flesh. But this seems to be an admonition for ordinary folks, who, however lustful, can in fact hardly go beyond the confines of the home. However they may want to indulge in debauchery, they lack the means to do so. But in the case of a monarch whose possessions include everything within the four seas, what command from him would not be obeyed and what desire of his would not be fulfilled? Cases in point: King Zhou of the Shang dynasty, who was enamored of Daji; King You of the Zhou dynasty, who showered favors on Baosi; Emperor Cheng of the Han dynasty, who doted on Zhao Feiyan; and Emperor Xuanzong of the Tang dynasty, who pampered Consort Yang. Even they who fixed their affections on *one* woman ended up plunging their empires into chaos and their people into misery and, in the worst cases, bringing death to themselves and demise to their empires. How much more severe the consequences when a sovereign is never satiated—even with an endless supply of women—and indulges in unbridled debauchery against all sense of decency and ethical norms! If such a man goes unpunished, who will ever believe that heaven rewards the virtuous and punishes the evil?

Our story is about Prince Hailing of the great state of Jin.[1] For all his intelligence, he was a dissipated and depraved man with a contempt for decorum and a propensity to violate principles guiding human relationships. In the twelve years he sat on the throne as emperor, he changed his reign title twice. The first reign period, Tiande, lasted three years. The second, Zhenyuan, also lasted three years, and the last one, Zhenglong, lasted six years. In the last year of the Zhenglong reign period [1161], he mounted a massive attack against the Song dynasty and was killed at Guazhou. His successor to the throne, Emperor Shizong of Jin, with the reign title of Dading, demoted him posthumously to Prince of Hailing. A story was later written on the basis of historical accounts of the circumstances leading to his posthumous dethronement, as a warning to generations to come. Indeed,

> *Later generations should learn from their forefathers,*
> *So that the dead will not scorn their offspring.*

Here begins our story. Prince of Hailing, emperor of Jin but later demoted, was the second son of Wanyan Zonggan, Prince of Liao. Called Wanyan Digu at first, and then Wanyan Liang courtesy name Yuangong, Hailing was deceitful, impetuous, suspicious, cruel, and crafty. At eighteen years of age, he became a *fengguo* general as a member of the royal clan and entered the service of Wanyan Zongbi, Prince of Liang, who made him a brigade commander. He then rose to be supreme cavalry general and, before long, supreme general of the imperial guards. Through successive promotions, he came to be assistant director of the department of state affairs in Bianjing, the southern capital, with power to act on behalf of the Jin court. Later he was made prime minister. Emperor Xizong [r. 1135–49] had succeeded the throne as a grandson of Emperor Taizu [r. 1115–23], but Hailing thought that since his father, Prince of Liao, was Emperor Taizu's eldest son, he was just as much a grandson as Xizong was and therefore had the same entitlement to the land. Coveting the throne, he did everything he could to establish his might to coerce people into submission. Later, he went so far as to kill Emperor Xizong and usurp the throne. Afraid that the sons of Emperor Taizong [r. 1123–35] would pose future threats to him, he consulted imperial librarian, Xiao Yu, on a plan to exterminate them. Based on the accusations of treason that the insidious Xiao Yu fabricated against Zongben, Bingde, and other sons of Emperor Taizong, Hailing killed Zongben and arranged to put to death Bingde, Zongyi, and seventy other sons and grandsons of Emperor Taizong, and more than thirty sons and grandsons of Zonghan, Prince of Qin. (*How diabolical!*) After Zongben's death, Xiao Yu, the imperial librarian, made a follower of Zongben, named Xiao Yu [different character for "Yu"], write up a denunciation against his master, accusing the latter of treason. The letter of denunciation was then circulated throughout the land and aroused much indignation from the public. As a reward for his services, Xiao Yu, the imperial librarian, was promoted to be assistant director of the department of state affairs and the deputy director of the same department and, concurrently, of the imperial secretariat. Because of his rampant abuses of power, he was later ordered to commit suicide on a charge of treason.

When he first took up the post of prime minister, Hailing feigned a simple lifestyle and had no more than three concubines. After he assumed the throne, he yielded to his lust and surrounded himself with women who, apart from the empress Tushan-shi, included the beautiful Da-shi, Xiao-shi, and Yelü-shi. He summoned into his harem all the women with whom he had had relations and granted each the title of "royal consort." At the same time, he searched for more beauties far and wide. He did not care whether they were of the same surname as he was, or about their status, or whether they were married or not. As long as they took his fancy, he collected them by every possible means to satisfy his lust, and made many of them royal consorts. There were twelve royal consorts in all, including nine Ladies of Zhaoyi and Ladies of Chongyuan, one Lady of Jieyu, one Lady of Meiren, one Lady of Cairen, and numerous other titled ladies of lower ranks. He ordered extensive construction in the palace complex to accommodate his concubines, spending as much as twenty million on one log of timber and employing as many as five hundred men for one shipment of construction materials. The halls in the palace were all gilded and decorated in bright colors. During construction, gold shavings flew in the air like flakes of snow. Expenditures on one hall could run into millions upon millions. Completed projects would be destroyed and rebuilt in a bid for the greatest lavishness. But we will not go into details about this.

Let us focus our attention now on Royal Consort Alihu, née Pucha, daughter of Meiliye, an imperial in-law. She was a bewitchingly beautiful and dissolute woman and an enthusiastic drinker. Before she married, she had seen her father concoct various kinds of aphrodisiacs, such as "Moaning Beauty," "Golden Spear," "Sulphur Ring," and "As-You-Wish Ribbon." (*How can one let children see such things?*) Wondering what they were for, she secretly asked Axiliuke, the maidservant, "What are these? What are they for? Why is father working so hard to make them?"

Axiliuke replied, "These are aphrodisiacs. When men can't keep up their game of copulation with women, they use this stuff for more enjoyment."

"What is copulation?"

"Well, people copulate, just as chicken and dogs do."

"What's so good about copulation that humans also do it?"

"Those doing it for the first time may not like it very much, but pleasure comes with practice."

Alihu burst into giggles. Her desires stirring, she asked, "Where did you learn all this?"

The maid replied with a grin, "I've had a taste of it."

Soon thereafter, Alihu married Ahu Die, a descendant of the royal clan, and gave birth to a daughter, whom they named Chongjie. Ahu Die was executed when Chongjie was seven years old. Without observing the mourning period, Alihu married Nanjia, another member of the royal clan, bringing along Chongjie. Nanjia was a lustful man. Helped by aphrodisiacs that she concocted from her father's recipes, Alihu and Nanjia indulged in carnal pleasures day and night, and Alihu let her daughter watch her antics. (*Alihu had, in fact, learned from her father, and Chongjie from her mother. One can never be too cautious!*) Nanjia later died of exhaustion. His father, Tuge Su, grand marshal in Bianjing, southern capital of Jin, had known that Alihu was a debauched woman but had not found a way to stop her.

After Nanjia's death, he took Alihu to Bianjing and locked her up in a room, forbidding her to see anyone.

Alihu had long heard about Hailing's skills in bed and his love of beautiful women, and she lamented the immense distance between them. While fretting dejectedly over her lack of a chance to cavort with him, she heard that he was then also in Bianjing, whereupon she drew a portrait of herself and wrote a poem on the scroll:

> *Alihu, Alihu,*
> *Xishi and Mao Qiang can't measure up to me.*[2]
> *Since I came here after my husband died,*
> *I've been a victim of his father's advances.* (*What venomous slander!*)
> *If only someone could release me from this cage*
> *And rid me of all misery, past and future!*

She then sealed up the scroll and, bribing the warden with ten taels of silver and a gold hairpin she had taken from her head, told him to deliver it to Hailing. Hailing had long heard about Alihu's beauty without quite believing it. At the sight of the portrait, he danced for joy and itched to see her. He sent a messenger to Tuge Su to say that he wanted to marry her, but Tuge Su would not hear of it. Hailing then spread rumors that Tuge Su was having illicit relations with his daughter-in-law, hoping that Tuge Su would set her free so that his name would not be tarnished. Knowing Hailing's intentions all too well, Tuge held his ground. (*Good for him!*)

Three days after usurping the throne, Hailing issued an imperial decree, ordering Alihu to return to her parents' home. Then, with proper etiquette, he had her brought into the palace. She gave herself up to drinking and pleasures of the flesh with greater abandon, and Hailing was so smitten that he regretted not having met her earlier. Several months later, she was granted, on an exceptional basis, the title of Lady of Xian, and then Lady of Zhao.

One day, Chongjie went to the palace for a visit. Since her now-deceased father, Ahu Die, had been a cousin of Hailing's and Alihu was her mother, she was kept in the palace for the night. Suddenly, Hailing saw her and his heart was inflamed by her youthful charms that set her quite apart from his other women. Determined to seduce her but afraid that Alihu would stand in the way (*His desires were insatiable.*), he concocted aphrodisiacs and chased Alihu and the ladies-in-waiting around, all naked, in Alihu's brightly lit room in order to arouse Chongjie's desires. Hearing the ripples of laughter, Chongjie quietly rose from bed to listen and peek through a chink in the door. Seized with irrepressible excitement, more than once she almost tried to burst into the room, but her shyness got the better of her each time. The racket did not stop until the night watch-drum struck four times. In the dead silence, after all the other women had blown out the candles and gone to sleep, Chongjie bit her fingers, caressed her chest, and fidgeted so much that she never sat in her chair long enough for it to get warm. Finally, with a sigh of resignation, she lay down under her quilt, fully clothed. All of a sudden, she heard noises coming from her mother's bed next door. She wanted to get up for a look, but her head was so dizzy that she lay down again to lean against her pillow and listen. There came a knock at her door. She ignored it, but the knocks grew louder. Chongjie asked who it was. Hailing feigned a female voice, claiming to be a maidservant here to get a lamp, to trick Chongjie into opening the door. (*So unscrupulous in his lust! This is no way for a monarch to behave!*) Chongjie forced herself to rise. Barely had she unbolted the door when Hailing burst in, gathered her in his arms, and planted a kiss on her lips. Chongjie attempted to struggle herself free, but Hailing forced her to her bed. As his groping hand found that she was wearing no pants but only a skirt, he began caressing her soft and smooth upper thighs. Her desires aroused, Chongjie covered her face with her sleeves and let him have his pleasure of her, little knowing how much he would hurt her. In his lustful frenzy, he brought spots of blood to her skirt with that mighty member of his. Her eyebrows knitted, her teeth gnashing, Chongjie let out cries of pain. Time and again, in sheer agony, she begged him to stop. And so, like a dragonfly skimming the surface of the water one moment, and a bee or butterfly hungry for a flower the next, Hailing stopped and resumed and spent the rest of the night sporting with the girl.

After about ten days without seeing him, Alihu burned with lust. In her obsession with her desires, she forgot that Chongjie was still in the palace. (*Such forgetfulness before old age sets in is a consequence of her lust.*) When she told the ladies-in-waiting to find out where Hailing was, one of them said, "With his newfound girl, His Majesty has forgotten about his old love."

"Who is the new one?" Alihu asked in alarm. "When was she brought into the palace?"

"His Majesty is with Ahu Chongjie in Zhaohua Hall. How can you not know, my lady?"

Alihu's face went crimson. In a boiling rage, she thumped her chest, stamped her feet, and heaped curses on Chongjie.

"My lady," said a lady-in-waiting, "I'm afraid you'll be laughed at if you fight with her for His Majesty's affection. What's more, His Majesty has a short temper. Anything could happen."

Alihu snapped back, "Her father is dead, and I have remarried. Her ties with me have long been cut. I'm not afraid of being laughed at. I swear I will kill either myself or that whore! (*Who gave birth to that whore?*) What can His Majesty do to me?"

The lady-in-waiting rejoined, "Chongjie is so young and attractive that His Majesty cherishes her more than he does heaps of pearls. You, my lady, are not getting any younger. (*Sowing the seeds of hatred.*) You would do well to yield to her. (*Raising Alihu's hackles.*) Why get so angry?"

Even more enraged at this reproachful tone, Alihu said, "His Majesty swore never to leave me when he first got to know me. (*How stupid of her to believe that!*) But now here comes along this whore to take away my livelihood." (*How deep the hatred!*)

She rushed off to Zhaohua Hall, where she saw Chongjie at her toilette, with a maid standing to one side holding her phoenix hairpin. Alihu went up to Chongjie, slapped her across the face (*How impetuous!*), and lashed out, "That old man is already bad enough, indulging in lust like that without any regard for me. But you play up to him, and you so young and my very own daughter, too! Don't you have any sense of decency? Don't you have a heart?"

Chongjie also flew into a rage. "You old crone!" she cursed. "What sense of decency do you know? How shameless can you be? You and your maids were merrily fighting over a man, all naked, in your brightly lit room when I, as a visitor, got trapped in this web of debauchery. I want to live, but what a life! I want to die, but I can't. I was just cursing you, old crone, for thinking only of yourself as you harm others and do no end of evil. (*Right!*) And now you turn around and accuse me!"

From exchanging heated words back and forth, the two of them came to blows. As they were thus locked in fight, the many ladies-in-waiting intervened and pulled them apart. After Alihu returned to her quarters in a huff, Chongjie broke down in a fit of sobs and sat brooding. Before long, Hailing came. Noticing the mournful look on her tearstained face, he went up to her and, pressing his face against hers, asked, "What's bothering you?"

Chongjie did not answer, but a lady-in-waiting said, "The Lady of Zhao slapped the Lady of Guiren across the face and said nasty things about Your Majesty. That's why Her Ladyship is upset."

Hailing exploded with wrath. To Chongjie, he said, "Don't let this bother you. I'll do something about it."

After Alihu returned to her quarters that day, she drank with greater abandon and spouted streams of vile epithets against Hailing, who then sent a messenger to reprimand her. Recklessly, she had articles of her clothing sent on the sly to the son of Nanjia, her second deceased husband. Upon learning of this, Hailing said indignantly, "She belongs to me now, and yet her ties with Tuge Su remain uncut!" Henceforth he ignored her.

Hailing had made it a rule for the maids serving the royal consorts to dress like men. They were thus called "fake page boys." (*Strange outfits.*) One of Alihu's personal maids, Shengge, who was as strongly built as a man, judged from Alihu's listlessness, indisposition, and insomnia that she was consumed with carnal desires. Thereupon, Shengge asked a eunuch in the palace to buy from the market a device known as "Mr. Horn" and presented it to Alihu, who then had Shengge try it on. If the device was lacking in some ways, it was satisfying in other ways. (*A means with which to amuse herself.*) From then on, Alihu and Shengge stayed together day and night, with never a moment apart. A kitchen maid called Sanniang, ignorant of what was truly afoot, secretly informed Hailing, saying, "Shengge is in fact a man in a woman's disguise and is having improper relations with Lady of Zhao."

Having sported with Shengge before, Hailing knew her to be a woman and did not take the information seriously. He only sent someone to warn Alihu against punishing Sanniang. Blazing with anger at Sanniang for having informed against her, Alihu had her beaten to death.

Hearing word of a death in Alihu's quarters, Hailing thought, "It must be Sanniang. If it's true, I'll kill Alihu." Inquiries into the case proved him right. However, his son, crown prince Guangying, having just been born, Hailing had vowed secretly not to a take a life during that month. Moreover, Empress Tushan led many ladies of the court in asking for mercy on Alihu's behalf. So Hailing refrained from killing her. (*The empress is a good woman.*) Dreading punishment, Shengge took poison and died. Hearing that Hailing had wanted to kill her, and shaken at Shengge's death, Alihu declined all offers of food and prayed at the altar for heaven to release her from this life. (*Retribution for her lust.*) After a month, when she had become too weak to feel anything, Hailing had her strangled to death and had the maids who had beaten Sanniang also put to death. Henceforth he did not visit Chongjie's quarters again, dismissed her from the palace, and made her marry a commoner. (*Hailing the lecher was too unkind. His orders to kill or to keep were all for the wrong reasons.*) But later, he resumed summoning Chongjie frequently into the palace and granted her the title Lady of Zhao.

There was a Lady of Rou, called Mile, who was of the Yelü clan. She was such a marvel to the eyes upon birth that she impressed all the members of the clan. By age ten, she had grown into even more of a beauty, to everyone's greater amazement. Knowing that she was in a class all by herself, she came to be conceited and boastful. Her mother and a neighboring woman, being good friends, often visited each other. The neighbor's son, twelve-year-old Hamidulu, a well-shaped boy, and Mile often played together and teased each other, so much so that they began to do things that overstepped the bounds of propriety.

Storyteller, what do a twelve-year-old boy and a ten-year-old girl know? These two were just playing. Why pass such harsh judgment on them? Well, dear audience, you may not know that in the north, children reach puberty early. In addition, adult Tartars don't hide their acts from their children. Thus, having watched often enough, they begin to misbehave, young as they are.

Time flies. More than a year went by. One day, as if something had been destined to happen, Mile was bathing in her room, having forgotten to bolt her door first. Hamidulu walked right in on her. Mile was quick to tell him to go back, saying, "My mother will be here any moment now to add water for me." Enraptured at the sight of Mile's snowy white body that looked like a jade column in the washing basin, Hamidulu insisted on joining her in her bath. Mile tried desperately to keep him out. In the midst of the racket, Mile's mother came onto the scene. After Hamidulu slipped away, Mile's mother gave her a good beating and a severe lecture, and put her under strict watch, forbidding her to play with Hamidulu ever again.

In the second year of the Tiande reign period, when Mile had reached fifteen,

Hailing got word of her beauty and ordered Dinian'abu, secretary of the Ministry of Rites, to bring her to Bianjing, the capital. Dinian'abu, or Xiao Gong in Chinese, was the husband of Zetelan, Mile's older sister. A romantically inclined handsome young man, he was spellbound by Mile's beauty, but his fear of Hailing kept him from making any unseemly move. As it turned out, having been separated from Hamidulu for so long, Mile was burning with desire and was quite taken with this handsome man. However, as they traveled in different boats, she had no means of conveying her feelings to him. Then, an idea struck her. She screamed throughout the night, claiming that she was haunted by ghosts. (*A wicked plan.*) Her maid-servants had no choice but to ask Dinian'abu to take her into his boat and, sure enough, all was quiet again, but the maidservants had no inkling of her real motives.

And so, exchanging significant glances, the two of them could hardly contain their fiery passion. Every evening, they ate at the same table and flirted in every way possible. Dinian'abu refrained from going further only because, taking Mile to be a virgin, he feared reprisal from Hailing if he violated her virginity. One night, after the boat was tied to the bank in a driving rain, the two of them were about to retire for the night when a song burst upon their ears. Afraid that there might be robbers around, Dinian'abu sat up to listen. It was the night watchman singing a folk song:

> *In the rain that blocks out the sky,*
> *The bird flies to the painted hall.*
> *The nestless swallow sleeps on the beam;*
> *The girl lies with her brother-in-law.* (The song, matching the thoughts
>   in their minds, serves as a go-between.)

Having heard the song, Dinian'abu said with a sigh, "The writer of this song is obviously mocking me, little knowing that I did no such thing. Indeed, I didn't get to eat the mutton but ended up with the odor all over my body, so to speak." In the midst of his lament, he heard the sound of footsteps. He looked intently and whom should he see but Mile, walking all alone toward his bed.

"Did Your Ladyship see something?" he asked in alarm. "Why are you here?"

"The song led me here. Are you so old and hard of hearing that you didn't hear it?"

"I did, but the song bothered me, and I didn't know how to put my thoughts into words. But why haven't you retired for the night?"

"I didn't understand the song," said Mile. "Please explain it to me."

As Dinian'abu explained the song to her, line by line, she reddened and said, cuddling up to him, "So, that's what it is! But are you not so inclined?"

Kneeling by the bed, Dinian'abu said, "I'm not made of wood or stone. How can I have no feelings? But I'll be in for big trouble if word gets to His Majesty's ears."

Holding him in her arms and raising him to his feet, Mile said, "Because you and I are related, our case is different. I know what to say to His Majesty. You have nothing to fear." (*Beauty arouses desire, and desire confuses the mind. They should be cautious because what they are doing will bring them instant destruction.*) Carried away by their wild passion, they engaged each other in a game of clouds and rain right there in the boat.

> *As the bee busily buzzed about,*
> *The flower clung to it, tender and soft.*
> *Moist with the many beads of dew,*
> *The flower let out bewitching groans.*
> *He was an old hand in the game;*
> *She had tried it some time before.*
> *He applied all his skills;* ▬
> *She at last found fulfillment of her desires.*
> *To her, he was so much better than the boy;*
> *To him, this sister-in-law outshone his wife.*
> *She thought nothing of her loss of virginity;*
> *He forgot all about his sovereign's strict orders.*
> *The lovebirds' hundred-year bond led to this union,*
> *Their lust-driven audacity was as boundless as the sky.*

They made merry with each other day and night throughout the rest of the journey. After much dilly-dallying, they arrived in Yanjing. One look at Mile convinced Dinian'abu's father, Xiao Zhonggong, Regent of Yanjing, that she was not a virgin. With a sigh, he said to himself, "His Majesty will be so suspicious he'll surely kill my boy!" Little did he know that his son was indeed guilty.

Once in the palace, Mile was seized with fear that what she had done would be found out. Her face awash in tears, she trembled in the presence of Hailiang and dared not step forward to greet him. (*Nervous because of her fear of being found out.*) Giving a free rein to his lust, Hailing had two rows of candles set out and ordered the ladies-in-waiting to undress her for him. Not knowing how to cover up her secret, Mile gave herself up to him. Realizing she was not a virgin, Hailing said in an outburst of rage, "Did Dinian'abu dare take your virginity? What a scoundrel!" He called in eunuchs to tie up Mile and put her under interrogation. Tearfully, Mile said, "Hamidulu had his way with me when I was thirteen. And this is the way I've been since then. Dinian'abu has nothing to do with it."

"Where is Hamidulu now?" thundered Hailing.

"He died a long time ago."

"How old was he when he died?"

"Sixteen."

"How could a sixteen-year old boy have hurt you like this?" Hailing said angrily.

Between her sobs, Mile said, "I've committed a capital crime. But Dinian'abu does indeed have nothing to do with it."

Hailing laughed. "I know now. You lost your virginity to Hamidulu and Dinian'abu took advantage of the situation."

Mile kowtowed silently. That very day, she was expelled from the palace and Dinian'abu was put to death. A few months later, Hailing yearned for Mile again. He summoned her and granted her a title as Lady of Chongyuan. Her mother, Zhang-shi, received the title of Lady of Huaguo in the name of Mile, and her aunt, Xiao-shi, Madam Lanling, was made Lady of Gongguo. Some time later, in the name of Mile, Hailing cunningly summoned Dinian'abu's widow, Zetelan, into the palace and had his way with her, saying gleefully, "Dinian'abu knew how to fish in troubled waters. It's my turn now to retaliate by having some fun with his widow." (*He killed the man and violates his widow. How can he justify such behavior?*) He then named Mile Lady of Rou, gave Mile's original title to Zetelan, and cavorted with them every so often.

There was a Dingge, née Tanghuo, wife of Wudai, regional commander of Chongyi, whose sparkling eyes were like those of Chang'e the moon goddess and whose well-shaped eyebrows were like those of a Jade Maiden of the Jasper Pool in heaven.[3] There are just not enough ways to count her charms. When still in Bianjing, before his assumption of the throne, Hailing caught a glimpse of her under a raised curtain and was so captivated by her beauty that he stood in dumb amazement for a good while. "How can there be such a beauty in this world?" he thought. "Wouldn't it be too bad if she belonged to someone else?"

Quietly he had an attendant find out whose wife she was. Upon coming back from his mission, the attendant reported, "She is wife of Wudai, the regional commander. She's a most enchanting woman, but no one can get near her. There are legions of maidservants in the house. Her favorite one is Guige, who is always with her. That Guige is not unattractive, either."

Hailing thought up a plan. He had a servant bring to his home a woman hairdresser who frequented Wudai's residence. (*A hairdresser who doubles as a go-between, as is usually the case. Beware of such people!*) He had this woman do his hair and rewarded her with ten taels of silver. Knowing him to be a distrustful and mean person with awe-inspiring power, the woman strenuously rejected the payment. Hailing said, "I pay you because I will need more of your services in other ways. Do not turn down my payment."

"Sir, I will do anything for you as best I can, but I wouldn't dream of taking such a lavish reward."

"If you don't take my money," said Hailing with a smile, "that means you won't do things for me as best you can. If you are willing to work for me, I'll do you a good turn in the future."

"But what can I do for you, sir?"

"Does Regional Commander Wudai live in the tall building at the southern end of the street?"

"Yes."

"I heard that you often go there to offer your services."

"Yes, I do the hair of his wife and the maidservants."

"Do you know a maid called Guige in that house?"

"She's the lady's favorite maid and also a close friend of mine. She often gives me things secretly and does me favors."

"What's the lady of the house like?"

"She's stern and reserved. But, for some reason, she likes Guige. However angry she is, as soon as Guige goes up to her and talks to her, the worst crisis will just go away. That's why everyone in the house, up and down, is afraid of Guige."

"Since you and Guige are good friends, please convey a message from me to her."

"Is Guige related to you, sir, in any way?"

"No."

"Are you related to one of the women in the house and therefore got to know her?"

"No."

"Has she worked here for you before?"

"No."

"Since there's no connection between you and Guige, what do you want me to say to her?"

"I have here a pair of rings and a pair of hairpins inlaid with pearls. Please give them to Guige and tell her that they're from me. Would you do this?"

"Yes, I'll do that, but since there's no connection between you in any way, and you've never even seen each other before, she'll ask me why you would want to give her such nice gifts out of the blue. What am I going to say in reply?"

"You've got a point. I shouldn't keep her guessing. All right, let me tell you, but you must put your mind to this job and not let me down."

"If you tell me everything, I'll know what to do."

"The other day I saw the lady of the house standing under a raised curtain and was very impressed by her loveliness. But I don't have a chance to get to meet her. I've asked around and learned that you are the only one with easy access to the house and that the lady favors Guige. That's why I'm paying you and asking you to deliver these things to Guige, so that she can convey the message to her mistress and admit me into the house for a night of fun with the lady."

"To have an adulterous affair is no easy thing. What's more, the lady is a little eccentric. I can't do this for you."

Hailing said harshly, "Old crone, would you dare to say three times that you refuse to go? If so, I'll kill you this very moment, you old sow!"

The woman was so frightened that her hair stood on end. Shivering all over, she said, "All right, I won't say that, but this is not something to be rushed into. Don't get angry."

"I won't get angry with you again, but you must get me there within a month. Don't drag your feet."

The woman accepted the order with eager deference. Back at her home, she scoured her mind for a plan, but no good idea came to her. She rose early the next morning and, after doing her toilette, she took along the rings and the hairpins and went straight to the Wudai residence. At the very gate she ran into Guige.

"What brings you here so early today?" asked Guige.

"I have a relative who's had a brush with the law and told me to sell a couple of nice items of jewelry. That's why I came so early."

"Where are they? Would they suit me?"

"Yes! It would be so nice if you could buy them."

"How many strings of cash? Show them to me first."

"I'll show you when we get inside."

So Guige led the woman into her own room, took some snacks from the kitchen, and asked the woman for the items of jewelry. The woman put the pair of rings on the table. Inlaid with four emerald jewels, they glittered with a brilliance rarely ever seen in this world. With joy flooding her heart, Guige asked, "What's the price?"

"Two thousand taels of silver for one, four thousand for the pair."

Guige bit her tongue in surprise and said, "I can afford something worth a few strings. But this is too expensive. Even my mistress can't come up with so much money on such short notice, let alone me! I'll just be content with looking at them." Then she said, "But let me show them to her, just for her to know that there is such nice jewelry in this world."

"Wait! Let me tell you something before you go ahead and show them to her."

"Say whatever's on your mind. Don't hide anything."

"I'm ever so grateful to you for all your kindnesses to me. I'm going to say something quite out of turn. Don't get angry and find it offensive."

"Have you taken leave of your senses today? You've been visiting this house for so many years and you've said so many things. Why would I get mad at you today for something you're going to say now? Go ahead and tell me!"

"This pair of rings is in fact a gift that someone wants me to transmit to you. There's also a pair of hairpins inlaid with pearls." (*Doing things methodically.*) Eagerly she retrieved the pair of hairpins from her waist and laid them on the table.

Guige said, giggling, "You've really gone out of your mind! I've been living in this house since I was child. I've never left the house nor made any friends. Why would anyone want to send me gifts worth several thousands of taels of silver? Maybe someone is looking for an official post and you dropped my master's name and wheedled the jewelry from him. But then you were found out and so, afraid that word would get to my master, you came here first thing in the morning to give me this story!"

"If so, I'll be as good as dead! Come over here. Let me whisper something in your ear."

"There are no eavesdroppers here. It'll be enough just to lower your voice a little bit."

"These items of jewelry are from none other than the second son of the Prince of Liao. He's Wanyan Digu, now assistant director of the department of state affairs and deputy director of the imperial secretariat. It's he who asked me to give them to you."

"Is Master Wanyan the beardless handsome one with fair skin?" (*Good beginning.*)

"Yes, that's him."

"How strange! He does associate with my master, but just as an ordinary acquaintance. He's neither a member of the clan nor an intimate family friend, and he's never been invited to dinner. And as for me, he's never even seen me. Why would he be so generous to me?"

"It's indeed a remarkable and funny story. If I don't tell you, I will be remiss in my duty to him. But if I tell you, and in a low voice, too, you'll be just as shocked as I was." (*Out she comes with it. This old woman does have some nerve.*)

"What is it?" asked Guige, grinning. "Tell me!"

The woman took a deep breath and whispered into Guige's ear, "A few days ago, Director Wanyan was walking down the street when he caught a glimpse of your mistress standing under a raised curtain. He wanted to meet her, but there just wasn't a chance. He asked around and heard that you are the only one who has the lady's ear. So he begged me to give these things to you, so that you can bring him and the lady together. Isn't this the strangest request? Don't you find this ridiculous?"

"A toad in a sewer is craving for a swan's flesh. He's dreaming! (*Yes, he's dreaming.*) My lady doesn't like to socialize, and none of us maids dares to contradict her. She will even turn away her husband of so many years, if she's not in the right mood, let alone a stranger! How could Director Wanyan be daydreaming like that?"

"The way you put it, he doesn't stand a chance. Let me give the jewelry back to him and be done with him, so that he won't bother us anymore."

While mouthing those words of refusal, Guige, in fact, coveted those splendid pieces of jewelry and could ill bear to let the woman take them back. So she said to her, "You're an experienced go-between, not some young thing who has seen nothing of the world. This is not something new to you. Why all this rush? In everything one does, one must take time to think well before going into action. You can't dig a well by removing just one shovelful of earth."

"I'm not trying to rush things. It's just that the way you put it, there is no hope at all. What kind of a reply is that for me to relay to the director? I'd better give him back the jewelry and enjoy some peace of mind."

"Well, what I said is true all right, but you can leave these things with me for now. Let me take my time and give you a reply at the first opportunity. If there's the slightest chance, I'll transmit them to her. How about asking the director to give me two pieces as well?"

"Of course, but be sure to try hard. Don't lose time, and don't forget about it. I'll come in two or three days to check with you, so that I can have a reply for the director." With that, she took leave of Guige, who then put the jewelry in her own trunk and set about racking her brains for a plan.

She dared not breach the subject to Dingge, her mistress, until one clear, moonlit night, when she saw Dingge sitting alone by the balustrades of the veranda, admiring the moon. Guige walked up to her and stood there peering intently into her face. Indeed, her beauty was so astonishing that it would make fish sink, geese fall from the sky, the moon hide, and flowers blush for shame. But there was a hint of unhappiness in her face. With a fair idea of what was preying on her mistress's mind, Guige said offhandedly, "Aren't you lonely, madam, looking at the moon all by yourself? Why don't you have the master join you and view the moon over a cup of wine? Wouldn't that be more fun?" (*When her mistress is saddened by moonlight and fresh breezes, that roguish girl seizes the moment to put her tongue to work.*)

Dingge replied, frowning, "As the ancients said, 'The beauty under the moon— a picture of serenity.' I may look lonely sitting all by myself under the moon, but at least I don't do injustice to the glorious moon. If that filthy thing comes here and raises his cup to the moon, won't Chang'e the moon goddess laugh at me as well because of his uncouthness?"

"With all due respect to you for your kindness to me, I beg to be enlightened: What marks refinement from uncouthness?"

With a smile, Dingge said, "I don't blame you for not knowing this. Let me tell you. Don't marry until you find someone refined and understanding. Otherwise, it would be better to stay unmarried all your life than be sullied by an uncouth boor." (*Her heart is laid bare.*)

"Pray continue, madam."

"A man who is fresh-faced, handsome, dashing, graceful, well-educated, and understanding is a man of refinement. A man who is ugly, vulgar, coarse, stupid, detestable, and filthy is an uncouth boor. I didn't do enough good deeds in my previous life, which is why I'm married to exactly such an uncouth boor in this life. He's not even worthy of a glance out of the corner of my eye. It gives me more pleasure to look at the moon all alone."

"Forgive my ignorance, madam, but let me make so bold as to ask this: if I married an uncouth boor by a stroke of bad luck, would it be all right if I looked for another husband, a man of refinement?" (*What a clever tongue! There's sharp wit hidden under her dumb appearance, fire under her coldness, and force under her softness.*)

Dingge let out a chuckle. "What an interesting thing to say! A woman can only marry one man. How can she have two husbands? To have two men would be committing adultery, and that's not right."

"I've often heard people talk about committing adultery. So, adultery means a relationship with someone other than one's husband?"

"Yes. Don't do that after you marry."

"If you can guarantee that I marry a good husband," said Guige, smiling, "why would I commit adultery? But if I marry someone like your husband and suffer as you do, I would go ahead and find myself a refined and understanding man and carry on a secret affair with him, so as not to miss out on the pleasures of life. You have only one life to live, you know, just as grass lasts for only one season. How can you muddle through life like this? Whatever gives you the idea that those who do the right thing and refrain from adultery necessarily gain eternal fame for their chastity?"

Dingge remained silent for a good while before she said eventually, "Enough of your nonsense! It'll be awkward if you're heard."

Guige continued, nonetheless, "Your husband is the master of the house, and you are the mistress. No one else has any claim to authority. The master is often away. Who would dare say no to you if you do cheat a little? Well, this is all just empty talk. There's nothing to it."

Dingge heaved a sigh as she looked up to the moon. She was about to say something but checked herself.

"Am I not your confidante?" Guige pressed on. "If there's anything you want to say from the bottom of your heart, don't hide it from me."

"I'm not ignorant of what you said just now. But I'm like a bird in a cage. Even if I'm so inclined, there's no one who strikes my fancy. I'll only be yearning in vain. And even if someone does strike my fancy, there's no messenger to bring him over here."

"If there is someone you like, I'll act as a go-between and a messenger. How can you say you have no messenger?"

Dingge gave another chuckle in an absent-minded way and fell silent. (*There is a tacit understanding between those who know each other's hearts.*)

As Guige turned on her heels and made as if to go, Dingge stopped her and said, "Where do you think you're going? Are you panicking because I turned you down? It's not that I turn you down. It's just that what you said was so out of line and so laughable!"

"I picked up a couple of precious things this morning and hid them in my room. Let me bring them here and show them to you."

"What precious things? Where did you find them? But I'm no judge of prices."

Without bothering to answer her, Guige dashed off to her own room, took the rings and hairpins, and rushed back to show them to Dingge. "Madam," said she, as she handed them to her mistress, "would they be good enough as betrothal gifts?"

As she examined them, Dingge said, "Where did you get them? They are indeed wonderful. Only a royal family can afford to offer such good jewelry as betrothal gifts. How did a little rascal like you come by them? Tell me the truth!"

"I won't hide anything from you, madam. A man begged our hairdresser to act as a go-between and these are betrothal gifts from him."

Dingge burst out laughing. "Have you taken leave of your senses, you little rascal? I don't have children, nor do I have in-laws of marriageable age, male or female. What betrothal is the hairdresser talking about? Betrothal with whom?"

"He's only interested in the one right here."

"Don't tell me the hairdresser is making a match for you?"

"How would I be worthy of such precious rings and hairpins?"

"Could it be a match for one of the maidservants? They should be even less worthy."

"They are out of the question! Only fairy maidens in heaven, or women like you, can do justice to them."

"The way you put it," said Dingge, smiling, "I should start all over again and ask the hairdresser to make a match for me as a new bride, with you as the bridal maid."

Dropping to her knees, Guige said, "If you could oblige the hairdresser, I'd be only too glad to be your bridal maid."

With a chuckle, Dingge gave Guige a playful slap and said, "I've always liked you, but you've gone quite mad today. What crazy things you are saying! If you're overheard, I'll lose face, too!"

"I wasn't talking nonsense. I'm serious. These are indeed gifts for you, transmitted by the hairdresser."

Her willow-leaf-shaped eyebrows knit in an angry frown, her starry eyes wide open, Dingge said in a blaze of wrath, "I'm a lady of second class, not some widow of a poor family! How can she look down on me like that and make such fun of me? Tell the master about this tomorrow and have that woman brought here and beaten up to vindicate me!"

"Don't get angry, madam. Let me first tell you everything quietly, just for your amusement. As the idiom goes, 'If there's nothing to tell, there's nothing to laugh about. If there's no beating, there's no screaming.' I believe that after I tell you the whole story, you'll laugh and scream at the same time." (*The artful lady puts on many acts. The sly maid wags a clever tongue.*)

Guige had always been her mistress's favorite and had never failed to calm her down every time she threw a temper tantrum. This time, her outburst being quite unwarranted, Dingge was ready to reconcile with the girl. And so she said in response, her wrath evaporating, "All right, tell me the whole story."

"A few days ago, the deputy director of the imperial secretariat went by our gate and saw you standing under a raised curtain, looking as beautiful as Mao Qiang and Zhao Feiyan.[4] His soul flew out of his body to you, madam. After he returned home, he spent the next two days in a daze, doing nothing but thinking of you. But without a chance to see you again, he asked the hairdresser to give you these pieces of jewelry so that he could get to meet you. If you are willing, you can see him under that very same raised curtain, and the jewelry will be yours to keep. In fact, the director is none other than Wanyan Digu, the handsome one, and an official richly blessed by fate, too. In fact, you should have seen him before, ma'am."

Her anger turning to joy, Dingge said, "Oh, is he the young official who often comes to see your master? He's handsome and graceful all right, but his heart is not in the right place." (*How does she know his heart is not in the right place? What remarkable physiognomy!*)

Laughing boisterously, Guige said, "All physiognomists need to sit down and look at a person for a long time, from head to foot. The hands need to be looked at, and the waist examined. Even so, they know only the exterior but not the heart. You took only a quick glance at him and you know where his heart is. Doesn't this mean that there is a heart-to-heart bond between the two of you?"

"Not so loud, little rascal! Let me ask you: What exactly did the hairdresser say to you? And what did you say in reply?"

"She's an old hand. She's afraid of saying anything that might get her into trouble. So she hemmed and hawed and went in circles and beat about the bush until I said, 'Hey, old woman! You need not say another word! Some man must have taken a fancy to my mistress, and you want to be a go-between. Why go to all this trouble instead of coming right to the point?' (*Clever repartee.*) She laughed and clapped her hands wildly, and said, 'What a smart girl! Someone must have bored a smartness hole in you. You guessed right on the first try!' I spat right into her face (*Clever words again, this time to exonerate herself.*) and cursed her, 'Old procuress! Old whore! Where's your sense of shame? Thousands of men must have bored smartness holes in you before you learned how to do people's hair! I was born smart. I pick up the slightest hints, and no joke!' Then she said, 'Good girl, don't get mad at me. I was just teasing you. You're a girl with a mind of your own. You won't take on a lover.' I said, 'Now you're talking! I'll let you off easy this time, but stop pestering me!' Then she said, 'I'm here for your mistress's sake. How can you dismiss me after tearing me to pieces like that? (*Slowly getting around to what she is only too eager to reveal.*) Now tell me what kind of a person your mistress is. I can tell her fortune by her face, her voice, and her bones, and I know the methods of Master Hemp Robe and Master Bodhidharma.[5] I'll be able to guess right away what's on her mind.' So I said, 'I have absolutely no idea about what you want to know, but let me tell you this about my mistress: she's stern in her management of the household and never gives us so much as a smile. None of us would dare even turn sideways in her presence!' She said, 'If that's how she is, a word of congratulations is due! My mission as a go-between is as good as accomplished.' (*How remarkable!*) So I said, 'Your tongue is running away with you! You're inviting a thrashing with the rod!' She said, 'This is what I learned from a fortune-telling manual.' I asked, 'What fortune-telling manual would say a thing like that?' She said, 'As they say, those who laugh readily aren't the right ones to approach; those who look stern are the most eager to fool around.'" (*Where did she pick up such rubbish?*)

At this point, a chuckle escaped Dingge, and the tea in her mouth spurted all over her face. "That old crone does have a way with words! Bring her here tomorrow and slap her a few times across the face before I forgive her."

By this time, the incense in the burner had given out. The Weaving Maiden Star had changed its position, and the night watch-drum struck twice. After helping her mistress retire for the night in her room, Guige asked, "Where should I put these precious pieces of jewelry?" (*Sounding her out again.*)

Dingge replied, "Put them in my jewelry box for now, under lock and key." Guige did as she was told and, of this, more later.

Eight or nine parts reassured by this reaction from Dingge, Guige had a good night's sleep. The next morning, while helping Dingge with her toilette at her dressing table, Guige noticed that she was in a more jovial frame of mind than usual. Trying to help things along, Guige commented, "Why don't you send for that old thing and have her beaten up?" (*Cleverly leading her on.*)

"Take it easy!" said Dingge with a smile. "She'll come of her own accord."

"It's not that I'm impatient, but she really gets my back up."

"Fiery heat should be brought slowly down by water. (*A trick in an amorous relationship.*) Don't lose patience."

In a subdued voice Guige spoke up again, "In most situations, it takes a push to complete a job. Long delays always mean trouble. He's so good-looking. If someone else gets him, it'll be too late!"

"Why should his good looks have anything to do with me?"

"Well, I shouldn't be shooting off my mouth like this, but my master is often away, leaving you all alone. I go to the outhouse too often to keep your feet warm. If that handsome one can be here to hold your feet, it'll be better than using a hot-water bottle in winter or a cool bamboo pillow in summer."

"What a lot of nonsense! Don't you tell me how to behave!"

"Madam, I care so much about you because you are kind to me. How can you say I'm telling you how to behave?"

Ignoring her remarks, Dingge took out a ten-tael ingot of silver from her purse and, giving it to Guige, said, "This is a reward for you. Have a silversmith make a pair of bracelets out of it and wear them on your wrists. It's a token of my gratitude for your service. Don't breathe a word of this to anyone."

Guige kowtowed, took the silver, and said, "Once a commitment is made, there is to be no change of mind. Since you've rewarded this go-between, I'll send for the hairdresser and have her bring the man here tonight."

Giggling with a hand over her mouth, Dingge said, "An unmarried girl is posing as a go-between! She can't even take care of herself! Has there ever been an unmarried go-between in this world?"

"Isn't a go-between also a woman? Why can't I be a go-between?"

"You do talk funny," said Dingge, amused. "But it's so embarrassing to make an appointment with someone I hardly know."

"You may very well feel bashful about other things, but this is known only to me and the hairdresser. What's so embarrassing about it? As they say, 'Feel shy, get a slap on the face. Feel shy again, get slapped again. Go on feeling shy, go on getting slapped. Stop feeling shy, stop being slapped.' (*Anyone with such a maid-servant will surely be led astray.*)

"What a girl!" exclaimed Dingge. "Where did you pick up such colorful language?"

And so they bantered back and forth until the toilette was done. Guige then went to the main hall and said to the messenger on duty, "Bring the hairdresser here. Her Ladyship wants to have her hair done and her facial hair removed."[6]

"Her Ladyship is not going out to an incense-offering event or a banquet," said the man. "Why would she want to have her facial hair removed?"

"How can her facial hair be allowed to grow long?" retorted Guige. "Don't ask about what doesn't concern you!"

"All right. When the hairdresser is here, be sure to have her remove your facial hair as well, before it reaches the ground."

Guige spat at him and went inside. (*A comic scene.*) Before long, the hairdresser arrived. After an exchange of greetings with her, Dingge took her to the dressing table and ordered that while her hair was being combed, none of the maidservants was to come in except Guige. The hairdresser opened her bag and set out on the table a whole array of items, eleven in all: a large comb, an all-purpose comb, a hair-brush, four fine-toothed combs, a pick, a small brush, and a pair of hairpins. She let down Dingge's hair and patted and pinched it all over, front and back, left and right, before giving it a comb or two. As Guige pouted her lips by way of a signal, the hairdresser took the hint and spoke up. "The color of your scalp is an omen that a happy event is coming up."

Guige chimed in, "When will the happy event be?"

"Any time now, and it's an unusually happy one."

Dingge rejoined, "The imperial court has not been giving out favors, nor have I asked for any titles. What event can be so unusually happy?"

"It's an event that will bring you a living treasure."

Guige put in, "Giant pearls from the West and bells from Burma are treasures, but only human beings are living treasures. As far as human beings go, this house is full of them, too many for Her Ladyship to need one more. So, what living treasure are you talking about?"

The hairdresser continued, "Just as there are different classes of people, there are different grades of goods and treasures. And there's a ranking to the different ways of living, too! The way you shoot off your mouth and talk big in front of Her Ladyship! What rare living treasures have you ever seen?"

For all the eagerness in her heart, Dingge could not bring herself to come to the point.

Guige asked the hairdresser again, "Are you here to do Her Ladyship's hair or to present a treasure?"

"Don't listen to that girl with her big mouth!" said Dingge, giving the hairdresser a playful push.

"Living treasures I have galore," said the hairdresser as Guige winked at her. "I just doubt if Her Ladyship has any use for them."

"Yes, she does," said Guige. (*It's like guessing a riddle.*)

"Cut it out!" snapped Dingge. "Say no more!"

"I just can't stop making comments, standing here. Let me stay a distance from you." With that, Guige strutted off to one side.

"Let me ask you something," said Dingge to the hairdresser. "When did that man see me? What did he say to you? Some nerve you've got, laying a trap for me on his behalf!" (*Protesting her innocence.*)

"Please don't hold me to blame, madam! Let me tell you everything. One day some time ago, you were standing under a raised curtain, looking at the pedestrians on the street, when that man passed by your door and saw you. He said with a sigh, 'Too bad such a beauty is married to someone else! What a luckless man I am!'"

Affably, Dingge commented, "No, he's not the luckless one."

Guige walked over and said, breaking into the conversation again, "If he's not the luckless one, who is?"

"It's me," said the hairdresser.

"Why is it you?" asked Guige.

"If Her Ladyship hadn't married, I would have made a match and got a hundred taels of silver from that man for my services!" said the hairdresser.

"Maybe Her Ladyship would be willing to see you richer by a hundred taels, but he may not be lucky enough to enjoy Her Ladyship."

Dingge said, "He's such a highly placed official. As an assistant director of the department of state affairs, he has no lack of women at his service. He's not the luckless one. I am."

"You are a nice judge of character, madam," said the hairdresser. "But he's no flippant sort. He doesn't easily fancy just anyone. How can you say you're luckless?"

All this time, the woman did not stop combing Dingge's hair. In the exuberance of the conversation, the three of them cast all scruples to the wind. Merrily, Dingge took out a nice outfit from a trunk and ten taels of fine silver and said to the hairdresser, handing her these objects, "This is payment for the good job you did on my hair. I'll have better rewards for you later on."

With profuse thanks, the hairdresser put the objects away and whispered into Dingge's ear, "Madam, shall I get him here today or tomorrow?"

Her face flaming red, Dingge could not bring herself to give an answer. (*Being obsessed by the devil, how could she not blush with shame?*)

Guige put in, "This old woman does things in the wrong order! What a ridiculous thing you said! It's a lucky day today. Everything will go well. What's more, that man has been waiting for your reply for quite a few days now. He must be in a frenzy of impatience. Why don't you go quietly now and tell him to come here this evening? He needs only wait until the sun is down and the moon is up. Why tomorrow?" (*This little rascal does know how to push things.*)

"Silly girl!" said Dingge, laughing. "How long have you been with that man to be able to read his mind?"

"I may not have spent any time with him, but I am a mind reader all right."

With a snort, Dingge lowered her head and toyed with her skirt ribbon.

"So I'm leaving now to talk to him," said the hairdresser. "What would you give me as a token of this pledge?"

Guige gave her a phoenix gold hairpin of Dingge's. What were the good qualities of that hairpin?

> *Its gold leaf was made in a foreign land;*
> *Its color a superior fiery red.*
> *Its filigrees were in the shape of two phoenixes,*
> *As true-to-life as if alive.*
> *Inlaid on top was a cat's eye*
> *That illuminated the sky.*
> *From the diamonds in the beaks of the phoenixes*
> *Hung two flowing pearly strings that ended in a knot.*
> *Nestling in hair, it looked like*
> *A red dragon above dark clouds;*
> *Now in a sleeve, it was no less*
> *Than a token of a royal decree.*
> *The hairdresser, with this object,*
> *Was none other than a bodhisattva*
> *Who wiped out evil and helped the distressed*
> *And a veritable fairy to save the lovesick.*

Handing the hairpin to the hairdresser, Guige said, "This can serve as a token of the pledge."

With a chuckle, Dingge said, "How dare you be so generous with my jewelry!"

"This is the first time I've done this. Please forgive me, madam!"

"All right, I forgive you!"

Beside herself with joy, the hairdresser took the hairpin and ran all the way to Hailing's residence. Entering the study where Hailing was sitting, she said, "Congratulations, sir!"

"This is already the seventh or eighth day since I gave you that job. I've been thinking hard thoughts of you. What's there to congratulate?"

"I'm not a hairdresser anymore. I'm Han Xin, who wiped out three former Qin generals and helped Liu Bang found the Han dynasty. I'm Wu Zixu, who showed my might at Lintong in support of the house of Zhou. I'm the great Prince Wuji of Wei, carrying the commander's tally to rescue the besieged.[7] How can you be thinking hard thoughts of me?"

Joyfully Hailing said, "I didn't know you'd done it. I did you an injustice!"

After acquainting him with all the details, the hairdresser retrieved the phoenix hairpin with the two pearly strings that ended in a knot, and, handing it to him, said, "This is proof of the order from the king and the tally of the commander. You are supposed to leave this very instant. No delay is allowed."

Hailing was so delighted that he fidgeted as if bitten by bugs and fleas all over, as if his skin had gone dry and his bones weightless." Thank you so much," he said. "But when would be a good time for me to go? Which path to take?"

"At dusk, wrap up your head with a kerchief and put on a black robe. Just say that you're a nun whom Her Ladyship asked me to invite over to read the scriptures, and enter through the door in the left corner of the house. Nothing can go wrong."

Hailing said, amused, "You're indeed smarter than Sun Wu and Wu Qi and more cunning than Lu Jia.[8] Even I won't be able to get free from such a trap!" With that, he quickly rewarded her with twenty taels of silver.

The hairdresser said, "Guige gave the mistress the precious rings and hairpins you told me to give Guige. So you need to give Guige another two items this evening."

"I still have two more pairs of rings and hairpins. They are even better than the ones I gave you. I meant to keep them for Her Ladyship. But since she already took those two pairs, I'll take the other two pairs with me this evening and give them to Guige. You'd better confirm with Her Ladyship, so that we can meet regularly in the future."

Thus instructed, the hairdresser went to see Dingge and repeated Hailing's words to her. Her face wreathing with smiles, she had Guige see the hairdresser to the gate and said, "Come again soon."

As she headed for the door, the hairdresser said furtively to Guige, "Mr. Wanyan said thanks to you over and over again. He'll have another two pairs of rings and hairpins for you, and they're even better than the ones I brought to you. You must be nice to him. Don't make Her Ladyship do all the work."

"Tut-tut! What a meddlesome go-between!" said Guige before they went their separate ways.

As the evening was well advanced, Dingge instructed that the front and back doors be closed and that everyone, male and female, retire for the night. All the maidservants were told to go back to their rooms at once and not to walk about. Guige was the only one allowed to wait on Dingge in her room. (*Orders were strict that night.*) Soon the night watch-drum struck and the bell of the faraway monastery rang. Unbeknownst to his wife, Hailing sneaked out of the house all by himself, without taking even one servant, and wended his way to the hairdresser's house. "Is the madam in?" he called out as he knocked at the door.

The hairdresser came to answer the door, a small lantern in hand. Seeing Hailing standing there all alone in the darkness, she said, "Come on in and sit for a while before you go there."

"It's too late. I can't sit with you."

"She doesn't put on airs with me. Why should you? What's the rush?"

With a chuckle, Hailing took her by hand and pulled her along.

"Behave yourself!" exclaimed the hairdresser. "Don't tease this old woman!"

With the small lantern, the two of them went stealthily all the way to the gate at the corner of the Wudai residence. At their soft, cautious tap, a maid came out, a small gauze lantern in hand, and beckoned them inside. No sooner had Hailing entered the gate than the maid quickly bolted it. Tugging at Hailing, the hairdresser said, "Mr. Wanyan, this is Sister Guige."

Thus informed, Hailing bowed over and over again to Guige in gratitude. Taking out from his sleeve a pair of rings and a pair of hairpins, he said, "Thank you, sister, for having gone to so much trouble. These are a token of my gratitude. I hope you won't despise them."

Trying to push things along, the hairdresser said, "Look carefully, sir! Such a pretty girl is well worthy of your betrothal gifts."

With a grin, Hailing said, "I dared take such liberties exactly because Sister Guige is so kind to me. In fact, I'm unworthy of her!"

"Don't be so modest, sir," said the hairdresser. Turning to Guige, she continued, "And don't be afraid, sister. Why don't the two of you drink a cup of nuptial wine first?"

"Good idea!" said Hailing. "But where's the wine? Where are the cups?"

Pushing their heads together, the hairdresser said, "How can you be so stupid, sir? The cups are on your lips, and the good wine is in your mouths. A nice, sweet kiss is a drink of nuptial wine, no less!"

"I was indeed stupid. I never thought of that," said Hailing as he put his arms around Guige and tried to kiss her. Guige dodged but Hailing held her by the waist and sought her mouth as she turned her head left and right. Finally she gave in. Hailing planted a kiss full on her lips and, applying his prolongation skills, sucked and bit them for the longest time. The hairdresser spoke up, amused, "My good sister, drink a little less wine. Don't overdo it. You'll be making a scene if you get yourself drunk." (*Good words of derision.*)

Giving the hairdresser a playful tap on the shoulder, Hailing said, "This old woman talks nonsense instead of attending to proper business."

As they bantered, they went into Dingge's room, which was resplendent with candlelight. A fine spread of delicacies, including seafood, had been laid out. It was like a betrothal ceremony where all were dressed in their best finery, and a celebration banquet with a colorful display of fine food. Hailing walked up to Dingge and dropped to his knees. After Dingge quickly returned the greeting, they sat down, one as hostess, one as guest.

The hairdresser said, "You should be sitting on the edge of the bed at this stage of the wedding ceremony, to take blessings from well-wishers. Why sit face to face as if you were parents-in-law?" (*Acting the go-between all the way.*) So saying, she pulled Dingge over and made her sit by Hailing's side.

Guige said, grinning, "The go-between doubles as a personal attendant."

Hailing commented, "This is a case of 'One does the work of two, so that all have less to do.'"

And so Hailing and Dingge sat down shoulder to shoulder at the table. They offered each other one toast after another with honeyed words of love. The hairdresser sat off to one side, plying them with wine. Guige stood behind them, wine vessel in hand. As she watched them flirting with each other, she blushed and grew pale by turns. When they were well warmed with wine, the hairdresser said, "A night of joy goes by quickly; a night of loneliness never ends. Don't miss your chance to tie up the lovers' knot!" With that, she cleared the table, closed the door, and left with Guige to retire for the night. Hailing and Dingge went to bed in each other's arms for a union of delight behind the silk curtains. They undressed and caressed each other in a tight embrace, sending each other into wild transports of joy. Truly,

> Their passion kept them in bed, attracting
> Butterflies that smelled lusty spring.

They cavorted with each other for about four hours as if glued to each other and did not close their eyes to sleep until they were totally spent. While the hairdresser was snoring, Guige was sleepless. She listened to the lovemaking for a while and got up and furtively watched them for a while. What she saw and heard made her feel so listless that she tossed and turned in her bed in dejection throughout a wakeful night. (*Not unlike Hongniang in* Story of the Western Chamber.)[9] As the night watch-drum struck dawn, the water clock dripped dry, and the military bugles sounded, Guige felt obliged to go up to her mistress's bed and awake them. She called out, "The roosters will be crowing soon. Please get up quickly and arrange to meet again."

Waking up from his dreams, Hailing scrambled to his feet, threw on his clothes, and set off. Dingge also threw some clothes on herself, ready to accompany him on his way out, but Hailing told her to go back to her sleep and not to get out of bed.

"Escort him out," Dingge said to Guige. "And come back immediately."

A lamp in hand, Guige quietly opened one door after another for Hailing. Noticing an empty room on one side, Hailing gathered Guige in his arms and asked for sexual favors. Guige said, "My lady easily gets suspicious. If I'm late going back, she'll be upset."

"You've done her good service. She should be rewarding you. She won't get jealous." So saying, he carried Guige into the side-room, where he had his way with her on an old couch that happened to be standing against the wall. As a matter of fact, Wudai, Dingge's husband, had long had his eye on Guige, now at age fifteen or sixteen. Several times he had tried to seduce her but held back out of fear for his wife. Now Guige joyfully submitted herself to Hailing because she had witnessed how Dingge and Hailing had enjoyed each other. To her surprise, she felt stabbing pain and begged Hailing to let go of her. With a soft spot in his heart for Guige, Hailing curbed his urge to give full rein to his desire. But unwilling to let go immediately, he caressed her at considerable length before departing through the gate at the corner.

Growing suspicious at the prolonged absence of Guige after she left to see Hailing off, Dingge noiselessly went out and stood by the gate to wait for her. At the sight of the girl slowly returning to the gate, Dingge dived into a shadow to listen to what she might say. When closing the gate, Guige mumbled to herself, "What's so delightful about that thing? What's all the fuss about? How laughable!" As she giggled her way to her room, believing that she was unheard, little did she know that Dingge was furtively following her. Once in her room, she turned back to close the door. Only then did she see Dingge standing outside the door. She was so frightened that she collapsed to the floor in acute embarrassment.

Raising her to her feet, Dingge said, "A fine thing you did with him! I saw everything."

"I didn't do anything!" protested Guige.

"You think you can lie your way out of it? If it were anyone else, I wouldn't be so forgiving. But you are the one who brought him here, and he's indeed so much better than that pig of a husband of mine. I'm ready for more fun with him. You're by no means unneeded. Just be sure that you don't get ahead of me in the future." (*So she's still jealous, after all.*)

"How would I dare do that! Please forgive me!"

Cheerfully, they went on talking until dawn, but of this, no more.

Henceforth, Hailing regularly visited Dingge and made merry with her all night through. Guige and Dingge became as close as sisters and were not jealous of each other. Gradually, all the maidservants learned what was afoot, but they dared not meddle in what did not concern them. Wudai, the husband, was the only one kept in the dark.

Time flew like an arrow. After several months went by in this fashion, Hailing, always on the lookout for prey, moved on to other women. During his prolonged absence, Dingge felt so lonely and miserable that she even lost interest in trying on new outfits and spent her days tearfully grumbling in dejection. She had Guige ask the hairdresser to write a note to Hailing and urge him to resume his visits, but the hairdresser was confined to bed by an illness and could not move around. Fighting a losing battle against her yearnings, Dingge found every day as long as a year. The sight of her husband, Wudai, who was nothing less than a thorn in her flesh, irritated her even more, but there was nothing she could do.

Among the male servants was a Yan Qi'er, a good-looking and spirited youth barely twenty years old. Dingge took a fancy to him but, afraid of objections from Guige, dared not speak her mind. One day, while Guige was out visiting her parents, Dingge went all by herself in her mincing steps to a hall and called Yan Qi'er out, ostensibly to give him a few words of instructions, and began an affair with him. What was so delightful about the affair?

> *She had been missing the pleasures of the flesh;*
> *He was with a woman for the first time.*
> *One was a hungry tiger chasing a lamb;*
> *One was an eagle pursuing a hare.*
> *On the pillows are scattered silk stockings;*
> *Under the quilt, her hair came loose.*
> *Dingge's desires were brought to fruition;*
> *Qi'er's stamina now found an outlet.*
> *Would that the love last forever,*
> *Day after day and night after night.*

And so the affair went on. One day, upon her return and seeing none of the melancholy on her mistress's face, Guige asked, "When did he start coming back?"

"He didn't come. He either took on other women or moved upon order to another duty station. I missed you, but I also thought hard thoughts of you. Why didn't you come back earlier?"

"Why did you miss me, and why did you think hard thoughts of me?"

"You brought him to me. So I missed you. He doesn't come anymore. So I think hard thoughts of you."

Guige was quite perplexed by these words, but she dared not ask further. A few moments later, Dingge called Guige to her room and was about to speak up when she caught herself, blushing. Guige stood a while and finally felt obliged to ask, "There must be something you want to say to me. Why don't you speak up?"

With a sigh, Dingge said, "While you were away, something happened to me. I'd like to talk to you about it. That's why I called for you. Now that you're here, I can't bring myself to say it."

"You never held back anything from me, madam. Why so evasive and anxious?"

"I just can't bring myself to say it. I've been taken advantage of."

"If you can forgive whoever took advantage of you, everything is all right. If not, you can have the servant on duty take him to the police and have him beaten up and put under a heavy cangue for two or three months. You'll feel avenged that way."

"No, you don't know whom I'm talking about. I called you here precisely because I need to discuss it with you."

"Who is it?"

"It's Yan Qi'er, the servant."

"If it's Yan Qi'er who offended you, punishment is even easier. If you don't want to beat him yourself, you need not send him to the police. Just wait until the master is home and have the master give him a few hundred strokes of the rod and drive him out of the house, and that'll be that. What's there to discuss?"

Whispering into Guige's ear, Dingge said, "It's not that. Several days ago, Yan

Qi'er raped me. I can't tell anyone else about it, so I've been waiting for you to return, so as to discuss this with you."

Guige said, smiling, "According to the house rules, no man is allowed into the inner quarters without permission. Even when that one was here, he had to be introduced by the hairdresser and led in by me. How could that dog have dared barge into your chamber and rape you? You were indeed taken advantage of. How could that dog have dared do such a thing? Did he barge in during the day or at night?"

Her color coming and going, Dingge replied, deeply embarrassed, "To tell you the truth, he came under cover of night."

Dissolving in giggles, Guige said, "So it was an affair, not a rape. Qi'er is guilty of crime all right, but so are you, madam!"

"I was asleep in bed. I have no idea how he managed to slip in and seduce me."

"That dog is more like a woodpecker," said Guige, laughing. (*This smart maidservant knows how to come up with vivid images.*)

"Why is he like a woodpecker?" asked Dingge, amused.

"I've heard that a woodpecker draws a few lines on the tree with its beak, shakes it a few times, and the worms inside will come out on their own to offer themselves to the bird. Your door is tightly bolted up and you have maidservants keeping you company in the room. And somehow, that scoundrel drew a few lines on the door, shook it a few times, and the door opened of its own accord. Wasn't he a woodpecker?"

"Rascal! You're laughing at me again!" cursed Dingge, laughing. "Let me be honest with you. That one hasn't been here for so long that I grew really resentful. And you were away, too. There being no one who knew my heart, I felt so lonely that I made the best of the situation and took Qi'er. Now that you're back, I'll break up with him and never let him in again."

"According to the law laid down by Xiao He,[10] a consensual adulterous affair is also punishable by flogging. What you said just now is punishable. You do whatever you think is right. But I doubt that the worm wants to hide. It may be eager to come out and offer itself to the bird!"

As they were talking, the janitor came to announce that Wudai had returned home. They went pale with alarm and rushed out to greet the master. Of this, no more.

In spite of what she had told Guige, Dingge in fact could not bear to break up with Qi'er. Furtively she carried on the affair as before when there was a chance, but stopped the all-night revelries. Guige knew all too well about the goings on but feigned ignorance and refrained from confronting her.

Among the maidservants there was a Xiaodiyaoshinu. One day, she happened to see Dingge and Qi'er talking on the veranda, and went to inform Guige about it. Guige told her not to concern herself about the matter so as not to invite punishment from Her Ladyship. And so the maid did not breathe a word about this to anyone.

Qi'er often tried to flirt with Guige so as to make her join the merrymaking, but Guige ignored him. One day, his eyes wide open, Qi'er carelessly held Guige with one sweep of his arm and sought her mouth. Guige snapped, "You dog! You've committed a crime punishable by death from a thousand cuts! And yet you have the nerve to seduce me. If I tell, you'll die without even a burial place!"

Thus scolded, Qi'er quietly told Dingge about this, after which he gave up the idea and never dared take liberties with Guige again.

Later, after Hailing assumed the throne, Wudai remained regional commander of Chongyi. To celebrate New Year's Day as well as the emperor's birthday, Wudai dispatched a servant, Gelugewen, to the court to present gifts. Dingge also sent Guige to inquire after the two empress dowagers' health. The sight of Guige awakened in Hailing his fond memories of days gone by. So he had Guige convey to her mistress the following message: "There have been emperors with two empresses. If you could kill your husband and come to me, I'd make you the second empress."

When Guige relayed the message to her mistress, the latter said, smiling, "The whole ugly affair was shameful enough when I was younger. Now that my children have grown up, how can I do such a thing to shame them?" (*Words righteous enough to partially offset her past wrongdoings.*) But, in fact, she loathed the thought of having to part with Qi'er. Upon learning of Dingge's response, Hailing again sent a messenger to Dingge with these words: "If you don't have the heart to kill your husband, I shall destroy your whole family." In terror, Dingge replied by saying that she did not have a chance to do his bidding because her son Wudabu never left his father's side. Immediately, Hailing summoned Wudabu to the court and made him keeper of the royal seals. Dingge consulted Guige and came to the conclusion that there was nothing for her to do but comply. When Wudai was intoxicated with wine, she had Gelugewen, the servant, strangle him to death. (*How terrible!*) It was the seventh month of the third year of the Tiande reign period. Putting on a show of sorrow at Wudai's death, Hailing ordered a lavish funeral. He then had the maid Xiaodiyaoshinu relay his royal decree to Dingge, announcing his proposal of marriage. When Dingge was about to depart, with Guige as her personal maid, Xiaodiyaoshinu said in jest, "After you're gone, what's Yan Qi'er going to do?"

Afraid that she would inform against her to Hailing, Dingge put eighteen maidservants under her command as a bribe and told her to keep her mouth shut about her affair with Yan Qi'er.

After Dingge entered the palace, Hailing made her a royal consort. In the first year of the Zhenyuan reign period, he granted her the title of Lady of Gui and, showering favors on her, promised to make her empress and granted her male servant, Sun Mei, the *jinshi* degree. Whenever Hailing went around the palace lake in the same chariot with Dingge, all the other royal consorts followed behind on foot. As an old servant of Dingge's, Yan Qi'er was brought into the palace as an attendant.

Later, as Hailing acquired more and more royal consorts, Dingge rarely got to see him. One day, Dingge was alone by herself when Hailing and another royal consort passed by in a chariot under her window. She called out to him, asked to leave the palace, and cursed him in abominable words. Hailing pretended not to have heard her and went off. Feeling even more bored, Dingge wanted to resume her relationship with Qi'er. She sent a nun to ask Qi'er for an article of clothing she had left with him. Knowing this was an attempt to seduce him, Qi'er said with a grin, "So the royal consort has forgotten me in her exalted status now."

Dingge wanted to bring Qi'er into her wing of the palace but, afraid that the gatekeeper would get suspicious, she first told a servant to fill a large basket with her underwear and have it delivered into her wing of the palace. The gatekeeper demanded to inspect the contents of the basket but, upon finding nothing but underwear, he regretted having done this and grew afraid. Dingge then had someone reprimand the gatekeeper, saying, "Those are underwear for a royal consort's body. What a thing you did, feasting your eyes on them! I will report you to the emperor." (*Is the woman trying to imitate the clever Yang Dezu?*)[11] Terror-stricken, the man asked for forgiveness, saying he would fain die than repeat the offense. And so Dingge had the nun hide Qi'er in a similar large basket and smuggle him into the palace. Sure enough, the gatekeeper dared not ask to inspect the basket. For more than ten days after Qi'er was thus brought in, Dingge indulged in pleasure to her heart's content, for this good fortune exceeded her wildest hopes. But the joy was not to last. For lack of a better choice, she put him in woman's clothes and made him follow a motley crowd of maidservants out of the palace under the cover of evening. Upon hearing of this, Guige informed Hailing, who then had Dingge strangled and sought out Qi'er and the nun and killed them both. Guige was granted the title of Lady of Cuiguo. Xiaodiyaoshinu was given fifty strokes of the rod for having concealed information about Dingge's adultery and was later ordered to kill herself.

Shige, Consort of Li, Dingge's younger sister, was married to Wen, director of the palace library. Hailing had an affair with her and wished to bring her into the palace. He asked Andugua, concubine of Wen's father, to approach Wen, adding, "He must give up his wife. Otherwise, I'll have to do something about it."

When Wen looked indecisive upon being told of Hailing's message, Andugua said, "By 'doing something about it,' he meant killing you. How can you let yourself be killed because of your wife? You shouldn't be as stupid as that!" In resignation, Wen held his wife in his arms and wept bitterly before bidding her farewell. As Hailing was in Yanjing at that time, he made Shige a royal consort in his palace there.

One day, seated in a lounge with Shige, Hailing summoned Wen to him and asked him, pointing at Shige, "Do you still miss this woman?"

Wen replied, "As the poem goes, 'Once she entered the depths of the mansion, / He became nothing more than a stranger.' How would this humble subject of yours harbor any improper thoughts?"

Hailing was overjoyed. "Now this is an honorable man," he said, whereupon he gave him Zetelan, Dinian'abu's widow, for wife. Upon Dingge's death, Hailing expelled Shige from the palace but, after a few days, called her back and promoted her to be Lady of Zhaoyi and then Lady of Rou in the first year of the Zhenglong reign, and Lady of Li the following year.

There was a Yelü Chaba who used to be married to Xiao Tanggudai of the Xi tribe. Upon hearing of her beauty, Hailing took her by force and granted her the title of Lady of Zhaoyuan. He then made Xiao Tanggudai an imperial guard. Observing how many royal consorts Hailing had and how he kept favoring new consorts over old ones, Chaba forced herself to please him but, deep down, she remained in love with Tanggudai. One day, she had a maidservant give her a few gold-traced satin bags embroidered with quails and wrote on them a poem for Xiao Tanggudai. The poem said,

> In idleness in the depths of the palace,
> I let tears stain my face, thinking of you.
> Though the wedding knot is not to be maintained,
> Let me reclimb the hill to await my husband.

Upon receiving the poem, Tanggudai requested a leave of absence, out of fear of the possible consequences. Soon after he left for the Hejian courier station, the matter came to light. When Hailing questioned him, he spoke the truth. Hailing said, "You committed no offense. The one thinking of you is the culprit. I will form a marriage between the two of you in your next lives." Having said that, he ascended Baochang Tower and stabbed Chaba with a knife. She fell from the tower to her death. Royal consorts witnessing the scene trembled in fear and dared not raise their eyes. The maidservant who had delivered the satin bags was also put to death.

After killing male members of the imperial family, Hailing picked the more attractive of the women and wanted to keep them in his harem. To his prime minister he sent this message: "I don't have many sons. Among these women, there are some remotely related to me. What do you say if I bring them into the palace?"

Tushan Zhen [Hailing's brother-in-law] relayed the message to Xiao Yu, the prime minister, who said, "Many objections have been raised by the public, both domestic and foreign, against the recent killings of members of the royal clan. Why does he also have to take their women?"

When Tushan Zhen reported back to Hailing, Hailing said, "I just knew that Xiao Yu would not agree." Thereupon he ordered Tushan Zhen to talk Xiao Yu into complying and make it sound as if it was Tushan's own idea. Dispensing with the pretense, Tushan Zhen said to Xiao Yu, "His Majesty has already made up his mind. If you want to stop him, you'll only be inviting trouble upon yourself."

"If he's so firmly determined, he can only take one."

Tushan Zhen said, "You must tell him so yourself."

Now knowing that Hailing was not to be stopped, Xiao Yu wrote a memorandum to him accordingly. Thereafter, Hailing took as consorts Gao-shi, wife of Bingde's brother Zhali; the wife of Shalula, son of Zongben; and the wives of Zong Gu's sons Hulila and Hushilai. He also brought into the palace Alan, wife of Zong Min, prince of Shucao, and in the first year of the Zhenyuan reign period granted her the title of Lady of Zhao. A court minister wrote a memorandum advising Hailing against doing so, citing Zong Min's seniority in the generational hierarchy. So Hailing released Alan and granted Gao-shi the title of Xiuyi and made her father, Gao Xieluwa, state-defending upper general, and her mother, Wanyan-shi, Lady of Miguo. Shigu, princess of Shouning and daughter of Zong Wang, prince of Song; Pula, princess of Jingle and daughter of Zong Bi, Prince of Liang; and Shigu'er, daughter of Zong Jun, were all Hailing's cousins. Shali Guzhen and her younger sister Yudu were both daughters of Zong Ben, the grand mentor, and therefore Hailing's cousins twice removed. Nailahu was wife of his cousin Zhang Ding'an, and Lady of Li's younger sister, Puluhuzhi, was also married. Shigu was a widow. Without the slightest scruple or sense of shame, Hailing conveyed a message to all of them via Gaoshigu, Neige, and Agu, to recruit them into his harem. Of them all, Shali Guzhen was the best looking and the most dissolute. Gaoshigu said to her, "You know how His Majesty is attracted to women. Would he give up someone as beautiful as you are? You were his cousin twice removed, but once you married, the kinship between you came to an end. You are no longer blood relatives. Why don't you enter the palace and serve him so as to win his favor?" Shali Guzhen smiled and took her advice. She went into the palace to see Hailing, who did his very best to win a smile from her. (*Wonderful.*) The very next day, he assigned her husband Sasu to night duty at the office of the imperial guards and said to him, "Your wife is young. When you're on night duty, she must not stay at home. She must come into the palace and take the place of a royal consort."

Sasu dared not say a word in response. Every time Guzhen was summoned into the palace, Hailing unfailingly stood waiting for her on the veranda. When tired from standing, he would sit down in Gaoshigu's lap and continue to wait. Gaoshigu said, "You are the emperor. You have royal consorts aplenty. Why wear yourself out like this?"

Hailing replied affably, "I have always believed that to be an emperor is easier than to have such a rendezvous."

As soon as Shali Guzhen arrived, he would make a fuss over her and stop at nothing to gratify her, lest she be displeased. Outside of the palace, Guzhen wallowed in dissipation and debauchery and, emboldened by her liaison with the emperor, gave her husband severe thrashings. There was nothing her husband could do to keep her in check. She solicited high-ranking officials, talented scholars, and handsome men skilled in the art of lovemaking, and made merry with them without the slightest sense of shame. Upon hearing this, Hailing boiled with rage and yelled at her, "So you love high-ranking officials, but who outranks the emperor?

You love talented men, but is there any man more talented than I am in both the military and civil arts? You love fun, but who is better endowed than I am?" As his rage choked him, Shali Guzhen replied nonchalantly with a grin, "I find your incompetence amusing."

In a blaze of anger, Hailing expelled her from the palace. Later, he had second thoughts and resumed summoning her every so often. (*Why is Shali Guzhen able to play fast and loose with the ruthless Hailing and get away with it? Is it her talent? Her beauty? Maybe heaven was partial to her.*)

Her sister Yudu was Paiyinsonggula's wife. After having had his pleasure of Yudu, Hailing commented, "You may not be a beauty, but your skin is much smoother, fairer, and lovelier than Shali Guzhen's."

In resentment, Yudu said, "If she's that much of a beauty, why don't you, sire, trade her skin with mine to make her perfect?"

"I'm not King Yama of the underworld. How can I change someone's skin?"

"From now on, I wouldn't dare serve you, sire."

Hailing said, consoling her, "I was just teasing you. Don't take my words too seriously and grow resentful." He granted her the title Princess of Shouyang and gave her royal consort status.

He also had Neige bring Shigu into the palace and gave her the title of Lady of Zhao. Shigu was the wife of General Walahami, a powerfully built man over nine feet tall. Strong enough to lift a cauldron and eat an ox, he needed to have relations with two or three women each night or he would feel so uneasy that he had to lift heavy objects to find an outlet for his energy. Every time he was intimate with Shigu, she was so shattered as to want to die. After Walahami died in battle, Shigu found it so hard to live all by herself that she started a clandestine relationship with a young servant, but was not gratified. The young man began to take aphrodisiacs and was able to stay tireless throughout the night. Shigu said with a chuckle, "You can pass." Those who heard about the comment later referred to the young man derisively as "the one who passes."

Upon hearing of Shigu's skills in the art of copulation, Hailing had Neige convey this message to her: "You're such an alluring beauty and yet you get involved with a subordinate. Won't you have lived your life in vain without meeting the prince of love? His Majesty is powerfully endowed. Why don't you go and share some of the fun?"

Shigu replied, smiling, "I don't think His Majesty's endowment, however powerful, amounts to even half of Walahami's. Also, he has so many court ladies. Why would he need me?"

"His Majesty has long had his eye on you. If you don't go, I'm afraid there's no telling what he'll do if he gets angry."

Shigu had to go into the palace. Before she arrived, Hailing had a small room prepared for her and a lute put in it. After the exchange of greetings, Hailing took her hand, sat her in his lap, and plucked at the lute to please her. He then made her Princess of Zhaoning. Leafing through a volume of *A Guide to the Pleasures of Bedchamber,* he said jovially, "Let's try all these twenty-four postures one by one tonight."

Shigu replied, giggling, "If Your Majesty challenges me to battle, how would I dare not to accept the challenge?"

Hailing had barely tried half of the twenty-four postures when he wanted to take a short break. Clinging to him, Shigu said, "Your Majesty is a skillful fighter all right, but your endowment is not all that impressive."

Feeling humbled, Hailing asked, "How was Walahami's endowment?"

"Of a different order from yours."

Hailing was displeased. "You are old and your beauty is fading. You're lucky that I didn't give you the cold shoulder. What a thing to say!"

Shigu bitterly regretted her words. After she left the palace the next day, she secretly told her young servant about the experience, adding, "I did learn something from His Majesty. It was worthwhile."

The indiscreet young man told someone else about it. The man said to him, laughing, "So, His Majesty has been 'the one who passes.'"

Nailahu, Puzhihalachi's daughter, with her beauty and fair complexion, was a marvel to the eyes. When she came of age, she married Regional Commander Zhang Ding'an. Ding'an being Hailing's cousin, a young Hailing had often played at his home. While there, Hailing had shared the same mat with Nailahu, chatted jovially with her all day long, and made merry with her. When Zhang Ding'an went to Song dynasty territory on mission by order of Emperor Xizong, Hailing and Nailahu sported night after night like a wedded couple. Even the maidservants were not spared. All too unexpectedly, Emperor Xizong ordered Hailing to be military aide to the Prince of Liang, whereupon Hailing had no choice but to bid Nailahu farewell, and he did not see her again until he assumed the throne and made her Lady of Rou.

And then there was a maidservant called Pilan. While her husband was away, Hailing wanted intimacy with her. He made her princess and summoned her into the palace. Detesting her protruding belly, for she was pregnant, he ordered musk soup, forced it down her throat, and rubbed her belly. Pilan said plaintively, wishing to save the fetus, "After I give birth, I won't take care of the baby but come to serve Your Majesty."

"If I wait until after you give birth, your vagina will be too wide to be of any use." What did he do but continue to rub her belly until the baby was aborted! A few days later when they copulated, Hailing's member was stained. Smiling at the sight, Hailing came up with the following lines:

> *This gourd, all bare and bald,*
> *Is suddenly covered with blood.*
> *Dyed all over in red today,*
> *It'll go into the field again.*

Pilan laughed and chanted in response:

> *This brook, all shallow and flat,*
> *Lets a catfish swim at will.*
> *Water overflows the shallow ditch,*
> *And the fish goes red and away.*

Hailing continued,

> *Water flows gently by the black pine woods;*
> *Into the stream petals of flowers fall.*
> *The fish swimming in the spring waves*
> *Breaks through the mist atop the pine trees.*

Pilan replied,

> *A monk in front of the ancient temple*
> *Wears a cassock half dyed in red.*
> *Henceforth he forsakes the path to bodhi,*
> *So as not to knock at the moonlit gate again.*

Hailing said, laughing, "You are good at coming up with matching lines!"

Chacha, daughter of Pucha Ahudie and Princess Qingyi, Hailing's older sister, had been raised since her earliest years in the residence of Zongwo, Prince of Liao. Upon coming of age, she married Bingde's younger brother, Teli. When Bingde was executed, Chacha was exempted from punishment only because the empress dowager had Wutong plead to Hailing for mercy. Hailing then stated to the empress dowager his wish to take Chacha on as a concubine. The empress dowager said, "When this girl was born, the late emperor carried her in his arms and told our family to raise her. And so we did until she came of age. You are therefore more like her father than her uncle. How can you do such an indecent thing?"

In submission to his mother, Hailing gave up the idea.

Chacha was of a dissolute nature. Not content with being alone, she started an illicit relationship with Wanyan Shoucheng. Shoucheng, originally named Elilai, was a fair-complexioned and sociable youth. Chacha fell head over heels in love with him. The empress dowager, upon getting wind of it, married her off to Yibula, son of Andahai of the royal clan, but Yibula was not able to gratify her. Every day she had terrible scenes with him. Not knowing why the couple did not get along, Hailing repeatedly sent messages to Yibula, urging him to divorce her. And then Hailing took her on as a concubine. The empress dowager did not know any of this in the beginning.

Her thoughts still with Shoucheng, Chacha wore a constant frown on her face. She put on a cheerful countenance every time she had to serve Hailing, but afterward she would curse him. When informed about this, Hailing said angrily, "So I don't measure up to Wanyan Shoucheng?" Thereupon he had Shoucheng beaten to death. He was about to kill Chacha when the empress dowager interceded on her behalf. So he just released her from the palace. Soon, Chacha's household servants informed Hailing that Chacha, mourning Shoucheng's death, cursed Hailing day and night in the most vicious words. Hailing went personally to berate her, saying, "So you cursed me over Shoucheng's death? You can't see him, can you? I'll now send you on your way to be with him!" So saying, he killed Chacha and dismembered her corpse.

Then there was Pusuwan, younger sister of the empress and wife of Alihu, the official in charge of affairs of the royal clan. She had prepossessing looks as well as moral rectitude. She was kept in the palace for the night when she was there visiting the empress. In the evening, Hailing insisted that she share his dinner table, but Pusuwan sternly rejected his invitation and went to eat with the empress behind the curtain. She tied up all the ribbons in her clothes tightly and, instead of lying down at bedtime, remained seated to guard against Hailing's possible advances. Sure enough, when the night watch-drum struck, the military bugles sounded, the candles in the silver candleholders flickered feebly, and Pusuwan was half asleep, Hailing was suddenly upon her and, forcibly taking her into his arms, demanded that she submit to him. Pusuwan adamantly refused. As Hailing continued trying to overpower her, she resisted fiercely until Hailing used all his force and pinned her down. In a thundering rage, roaring like a baby tiger, he ordered the maidservants to hold her in place and cut all the ribbons in her clothes, inside and out. Exhausted, Pusuwan could not hold out any longer. Without the strength to cry out her boundless grievances, she resignedly closed her eyes tightly, spread out her arms, and let Hailing scornfully have his way with her. It was just as if she had breathed her last and lost all consciousness. After doing whatever he pleased to her body without getting a response from her, Hailing lost interest and went off.

The empress asked Pusuwan later in the day, "Sister, don't you normally enjoy the act? How did you manage to do that today?"

"Sister, are you a human being? Ehuang and her sister Nüying of high antiquity were single when their father King Yao married them to King Shun. I am a married woman. If I share a husband with you, wouldn't we be laughed at? And you won't be able to face the world, either."

"Things having already come to this pass, there's nothing I can do. As the saying goes, 'Do what the locals do, wherever you are.' I don't care if people laugh at me!"

"What a thing to say, sister!" objected Pusuwan. "I'll just pretend you never said this. No peace can last for a hundred generations; no emperor can live a thousand years. How would you take the humiliation if it were you?"

Looking saddened, the empress could not get a word out. The night passed without ado. The next morning, Pusuwan left the palace for home, never to return. When Hailing summoned her again under one pretext or another, she pleaded illness, saying, "I will be dying any day now. I will not be able to see the empress ever again." Hailing had to give up. (*It would thus appear that all the other women were willing victims. So one shouldn't blame everything on Hailing.*)

Zhang Zhongke, childhood name Niu'er, was a vagabond who went around the streets telling stories of romance and making comic remarks. His tongue was so long and pointed that its tip could reach his nose. Hailing had listened to him for amusement. After assuming the throne, Hailing made him director of the grand secretariat and a resident of the palace. Whenever he learned of something worth commenting on, Zhang Zhongke would seize the moment and make obscene remarks without the slightest scruples. There were times when Hailing had the bed curtains taken off when frolicking with his concubines, so that Zhongke could add to the excitement by making ribald remarks. Sometimes Hailing would make Zhongke bend over to serve as a cushion for the woman's back, or rub aphrodisiacs on his member. On some occasions, he would stand between two lines of women, with everyone naked, and have Zhongke tie up his member with a string and lead him past the lines of women. He would then copulate with the woman Zhongke led him to, and Zhongke would assiduously push his behind as he went into the woman. Therefore Zhongke had seen all the royal consorts' private parts.

There was one young beautiful virgin who had a quick mind and a ready tongue. Hailing was fond of her. Whenever he copulated with other women, he would point at this girl and say to Zhongke, "This girl is too weak and small to bear me. So I'll wait. I don't have the heart to see her in pain." And Zhongke would break into cheers. One day, while Hailing was bent over a table in a wine-induced nap, Zhongke took a rest under the eaves. Afraid that Hailing might catch a cold, the girl covered his shoulders with a robe. Upon waking up with a start and seeing the girl with his wine-sodden eyes, Hailing gathered her into his arms and began to have his way with her, forgetting all about her fragile constitution and her tender age. Sure enough, the pain was too much for her. As she broke down in tears, Hailing quickly withdrew, and a stream of blood flowed out from the girl. Feeling sorry for her, Hailing told Zhongke to lick the blood with his tongue. Saying that he would be committing a capital crime, Zhongke dared not even look up. Over and over again, Hailing forced him to lick the blood, but as the girl rose to her feet in mortification, the bleeding stopped. Hailing said to Zhongke, "You're also a man with a sexual organ. Do you get an erection when you watch me and the royal consorts make merry? Take off your pants and let me look at it."

Zhongke objected, "In Your Majesty's august presence and in this solemn palace, how would this lowly subject dare commit an offense by baring myself?"

"I want to look at that member of yours. You're not committing an offense. I won't punish you."

As Zhongke kowtowed and asked to be let off, Hailing ordered a eunuch to remove all his clothes. Zhongke bent over in his kneeling position, his hands covering his private parts. Hailing then had the eunuch tie Zhongke up on a bench, face up. Zhongke's organ stood up, large and tall, about two-thirds of Hailing's in size. All the royal consorts present covered up their faces and giggled. Hailing said, "Don't laugh. Isn't he also a man? Won't he also give a virgin pain?" The women burst out laughing again. Zhongke was not freed from the ropes until his member shrank after a long while.

Hailing had also gathered his male courtiers together in one hall and made all of them bare themselves and compare their endowments. Those with the largest members ranked in the first category and were each awarded a plate bearing the inscription "Marquis of Yang" (*Marquis of Yang—a new title.*) and the right to violate a palace maid unwanted by Hailing. Those in the second category were each awarded a hundred ingots of silver and a plate bearing the inscription "Count of Yang." Those ranking below them were declared unworthy of awards. With the exception of court sessions held in the main hall and major festive occasions when seating was arranged in accordance with official ranks, at all other gatherings such as drinking parties in the inner halls and night-duty sleepovers, participants were lined up in accordance with their plates, regardless of their official ranks, by way of amusing themselves. (*What kind of a world is that!*) Even Tushan Zhen [Hailing's brother-in-law] was not exempt. Of the one hundred men, the one whose endowment was closest to Hailing's won first place. One slightly inferior to Hailing in that department placed second. None was superior to Hailing. There came into circulation at the time the following song:

> *The court follows the yang in everything it does;*
> *Promotions and appointments follow separate rules.*
> *Competence and talent go to waste;*
> *What counts is the object below the waist.*
> (The last two lines are wickedly acrimonious.)

The song was not lost on Hailing's ears, but he feigned ignorance and continued with his debauchery. On top of the royal consorts, Hailing also included in his harem women who were married to various officials. He assigned the husbands to night duty by turns, so that he could sport with the wives. But he wanted to have them whenever he wanted and so, not content with the arrangement and finding the rotation of night duty too much of a bother, he simply sent all those husbands to Shangjing [present-day Baicheng in Jilin] and kept the women in the palace. Whenever he wanted to perform the act, he ordered that the bed curtains be taken down and a music band play by the bed until the act was over and that they resume the next time he started. He cavorted with several women each time and always enjoyed himself to the full without gratifying the women, as a consequence of which every one of them was full of complaints. When dealing with a virgin, he would give mighty thrusts, mindless of the woman's pain. In the case of one who resisted him, he would have other women pin down her hands and feet so that she could not move. When seated with his women, he would throw something on the floor and make a male attendant look for it. He who took a glance sideways would be killed. Hailing had also warned male attendants in the court that he who ogled a royal consort would have his eyes gouged out. And the servants were not allowed to walk alone. He who wanted to take a trip to the outhouse must be accompanied by three other men. The official in charge would keep watch on them, sword in hand, and those who disobeyed were put to death. Those who walked as far as the foot of the dais after sundown were also executed. Informers were rewarded with hundreds of thousands of cash. If a man and a woman touched each other inadvertently in a moment of hurry, the one who spoke up first would be rewarded with a third-grade official post. The one slower in speaking was to die. Those who spoke up at the same time would be set free.

There was a Liang Chong who used to be a slave in Dagao's residence before he followed the empress into the palace and became a eunuch to serve Hailing. He was a sycophant eager to pander to his master. Hailing was so partial to him that he always followed the eunuch's advice. Liang Chong sought everywhere for magic formulas of longevity and exotic ingredients to foster the yang element so as to concoct aphrodisiacs for him. After trying what he offered and finding them effective, Hailing grew even more unbridled in his debauchery. With almost ten thousand women at his disposal, he still regretted the lack of ravishing beauties to satisfy him. Thereupon Liang Chong spoke to him in profuse praise of the unrivalled beauty of Consort Liu of the Song court.

"Describe her looks and manners to me," said Hailing.

"She has soft, lustrous, and abundant hair. She has a slim but full figure. Her complexion is as fair as snow and her face lovelier than the prettiest flower. She is radiant when viewed from afar, and her deportment is as charming and graceful as can be. She has an exceedingly sharp mind and she's also an outstanding singer and dancer."

Immensely delighted, Hailing decided then and there to attack the Song in the south. Before he set off on the expedition, he ordered Gaoshigu to put together purple silk bed curtains, a marble bed, partridge pillows, a mattress made of rhinoceros hair, embroidered silk quilts, a green net, and fine cloth towels. The bed curtains—light, thin, and transparent—warded off chilly winds in winter but brought in cool air in summer. Their color was of such a subdued tone that one could hardly tell their presence. The light marble bed was a gift from the Huns. The pillows were in the shape of partridges made of seven kinds of gems. The brightly colored mattress, exceedingly smooth and soft and made of rhinoceros hair, was from Korea. On the quilts were embroidered three thousand mandarin ducks amid exotic flowers and leaves, topped by multicolored lustrous pearls as large as berries. The green net, forty feet wide and one hundred feet long, was light, transparent, and thin. There was nothing like it. When fully spread out in the air, it looked as if it were made of green threads with pearls strewn in between. It did not leak in the heaviest rain because borneo camphor had been applied to it. As for the towels, they were as white as glittering snow and as soft as silk floss, and they would not soak through, nor would they get soiled after years of use. They were from Guigu, the far-off land north of the Kunlun Mountains, and Hailing planned to put them to use after he captured Consort Liu. (*Making plans when there is no guarantee of success.*) He also took along a nine-color jade hairpin, an anger-dissolving ball made of rhinoceros horn, a jade scepter for good fortune, a dragon silk robe, and a dragon-beard purple whisk. The hairpin was in the shape of nine phoenixes, each of a different color. Bearing the inscription "White Jade," it was so exquisitely made that one wondered if more than human hands had been involved. The ball, when worn on the body, could dissolve anger. The piece of jade was in the shape of a peach with seven holes, said to symbolize paths toward enlightenment. The robe was less than one or two taels in weight and could be easily balled up and held in one hand. The brightly purple whisk could stretch out three feet long. With a crystal handle and a red-jade ring, it would shine as if in wrath when dipped in water or waved on a rainy day. When placed in the middle of a room, it kept away flies and insects during the day and mosquitoes and gnats at night. When flicked, it gave off a sound that frightened chickens and dogs into fleeing. When dipped into a pond, all creatures in the water would swim toward it. When it splashed water into the air, the drops of water would turn into cascades. When the meat of swallows was being cooked, the whisk could conjure up dragon-shaped wisps of curling smoke and vapor.[12] It was said to have come from Dongting Lake. This was another object that Hailing planned to give to Consort Liu. After he had finished all the packing, a messenger came to announce that Consort Liu had passed away. Hailing was deeply saddened. Quickly he ordered that the corpse be brought to him for a look after he wiped out the Song, so that his desire for her could be laid to rest. Truly,

> *No lovers' knot was tied while alive;*
> *Li Shaojun worked in vain after her death.*[13]

Emperor Shizong was at the time magistrate of Jinan.[14] His wife, Wulinda-shi, with skin as fair as jade, a lithe and sweet-smelling body, and graceful manners, was beauty itself. Hailing coveted her, but Wulinda-shi's behavior was so impeccable that no opportunity presented itself to Hailing. One day, he issued a royal decree to summon her. Her husband angrily rejected the decree and refused to let her go. In tears she said to him, "My body is yours. I am determined not to serve another man. How would I ever consent to be sullied by His Majesty? But if I ignore the decree, I would be guilty of defying the emperor. If you ignore the decree, you would be guilty of being a disobedient subject. If His Majesty wants to put you to death on this score, what can you say in your own defense? I will try my best not to get you implicated." (*What a surprise to see such an honorable woman in such a vile world! Believe it or not, whatever moral rectitude there is that vibrates in the air between heaven and earth originates from human hearts.*) As her husband wept, hating the thought of parting with her, she resolutely took to the road. All along the way, she was weighed down with grief. At a place called Liangxiang, she sewed up tightly the clothes all over her body, wrote a poem on the front of the outermost layer of her clothes, and killed herself. The poem said,

> The ways of the world change all too quickly;
> The monarch is more ruthless than the wolf.
> In his fierce pursuit of debauchery,
> He violates all norms of ethics.
> Here I die, my body unsoiled,
> My husband not dishonored, my name unsullied.
> To the messenger I humbly say,
> Take my blood to His Majesty.

When the messenger brought news of Wulinda-shi's death, Hailing ordered, with a show of grief, that her body be sent in a coffin back to her husband. When opening the coffin, her husband saw that her face looked as if she was still alive but her neck, where she had cut herself, was covered with blood. In crushing agony, he gave her a solemn burial. Later, after he assumed the throne, out of respect for Wulinda-shi's death he never had another empress during all the twenty-nine years of his rule. (*Virtue and honor.*) But this happened later.

Let us come back to Hailing's major offensive against the south. He built warships, using wood from razed houses and fuel from the fat of dead bodies. He spent money as if it were so much mud and sand, and treated human lives as if they were nothing but straw. While he was out in the south with his troops, the ministers of his court, in response to the people's grievances, put Wulu, Duke of Caoguo, on the throne in Liaoyang [in 1161]. He changed his name to Wanyan Yong and the reign title to Dading [Great Peace]. Hailing was demoted to prince. Upon hearing word of the coup, Hailing said with a sigh, "I had been meaning to conquer the region south of the Yangzi River and then change the reign title to Great Peace. Isn't all this a manifestation of Heaven's will?" So saying, he showed to his subjects a scroll on which he had written the line "Once I put on my armor, I bring great peace to the land." (*How extraordinary!*) He called his generals together and led the army on its way back north. When they reached Guazhou, Yelü Yuanyi, regional commander of Western Zhejiang, plotted with others to assassinate Hailing. When an arrow flew into his tent, Hailing thought the Song troops had caught up with him but, upon an inspection of the arrow, said, "This is from my own army." He was on the point of picking up his bow to shoot back when a second arrow hit him and he fell. Nahewolubu, vice magistrate of Yan'an Prefecture, stabbed him with a knife. As his limbs were still moving, they strangled him to death. Dozens of his concubines were also killed. Later, in view of all his evil doings, Emperor Shizong did not think he deserved entitlement to land or a place in the grave sites for members of the royal clan. Shizong therefore demoted him posthumously to Prince of Hailing and again to the status of a commoner and had his corpse reburied in a spot forty li southwest of the city. A later poet had this to say:

> *What man in this world does not fall for beauty,*
> *But none went to such extremes as did Hailing.*
> *Before he had a chance to conquer the south,*
> *The reign title was changed, to his chagrin.*
> *In vain he lamented;*
> *He became a man without a home or a country.*
> *He died alone in alien land, a sad sight to the beauties;*
> *In infamy his name goes down through the ages.*

Emperor Yang of the Sui Dynasty Is Punished for His Life of Extravagance

While "Jade Tree" was sung and dancers waved their sleeves,[1]
Swords lay in wait throughout Jingyang Palace.
The morning stars took over the sky,
To the lament of the king and his ladies.

The above quatrain is a reference to the demise of the Chen dynasty. Emperor Wen of the Sui dynasty seized the power of the Northern Zhou house, wiped out the Chen dynasty, and assumed the throne. Peace and order reigned throughout the land. Indeed, no family needed to bolt the door and no one picked up and pocketed anything lost on the road. Emperor Wen designated Yang Yong as the crown prince, but the empress Dugu-shi was displeased. As a matter of fact, the empress was a most jealous woman, whom Emperor Wen feared but loved. He often said, "The earlier dynasties were plagued by fratricides that arose from jealousy between sons born of wives and sons born of concubines. Now my five sons are all born of the same mother. I have no other sons. This is a guarantee of peace. There will be no trouble in the future."

As it turned out, however, Crown Prince Yong neglected his wife, Yuan-shi, and gave his undivided attention to Yun Dingxing's daughter,[2] in consequence of which Yuan-shi died of a broken heart and all of the crown prince's children were born of the concubine. In resentfulness, Empress Dugu often spoke ill of Prince Yong in the emperor's presence. Being a henpecked husband, Emperor Wen gave her credence and gradually distanced himself from the crown prince.

Emperor Wen's second son, Yang Guang, Prince of Jin and chief commander of Yangzhou, was born with a prepossessing exterior and a brilliant mind. At age ten he was already an avid reader of books, ancient and contemporary, and knew all there was to know about medicine, astrology, geography, and the various arts. However, he was scheming, crafty, treacherous, much given to spying out interpersonal relationships, and able to endure humiliation and keep up pretenses. When he found out that Crown Prince Yong had lost favor with the empress, he racked his brains day and night for a plan to drive the wedge between them deeper. He spent his days with his wife, Consort Xiao, only. None of the ladies in his harem was able to be near him. Every time a messenger came from Emperor Wen and Empress Dugu, Yang Guang went to the gate with Consort Xiao to welcome him and to wine and dine him, treating him like a friend. Before the messenger took leave of them, Yang Guang would slip some money into his sleeve. Therefore, all and sundry unanimously praised Yang Guang in front of the empress, extolling him for his kindness, filial piety, and intelligence, which was more than they could say about the crown prince, who was lacking in benevolence and manners and made so much of Yun-shi as to have ended up with so many little beasts. Empress Dugu was very much of the same mind. Day and night she vilified the crown prince to her husband, saying that Yang Yong was not worthy of succession to the throne. Later, Yang Guang, Prince of Jin, heavily bribed Yang Su, Duke of Yue, with gold, pearls, and other precious items, and urged him to propose deposition of the crown prince. Yang Su being one who had done the most meritorious service to Emperor Wen, the emperor acted on his advice in everything. With the empress and Yang Su working together, one from within and one from without, Emperor Wen, whose anger against Yong had been accumulating over time, finally deposed the crown prince and put him under house arrest as a commoner in one of the palace halls. Guang was then made the crown prince. On the day the edict was announced, even the earth shook. All those with good judgment saw through the conspiracy. The ruthless Yang Su triumphantly boasted, "I am the one who made all this possible for the new crown prince." His power inspired awe throughout the land. The court officials, one and all, feared and venerated him at the same time.

After Empress Dugu's death, the royal concubines began to receive summonses from the emperor. Of them, there was a Chen-shi, Lady of Xuanhua, who was the daughter of King Xuan of Chen, assigned to be a royal consort when the house of Sui annexed the state of Chen. With intelligence and beauty none could excel, she was promoted to Lady of Gui after the death of the empress. The emperor gave her his undivided attention. None of the other royal consorts stood a chance. When Emperor Wen fell ill and lay confined to his bed in the Hall of Benevolence and Longevity, both Lady Chen and Crown Prince Guang attended to him. One morning when Lady Chen went out for a change of clothes, the crown prince made advances to her. She rejected him and, her hair disheveled, returned in a fluster to the emperor's room. Surprised at her agitated state, the emperor asked her what had happened. Bursting into tears, she replied, "The crown prince insulted me."

In rage, the emperor said, "How can I let that swine succeed to the throne? Dugu did me a disservice!" He was referring to the late empress. He then called to him Liu Shu, secretary of Ministry of Defense, Yuan Yan, director of the chancellery, and Yang Su, minister of works and Duke of Yue, and said to them, "Bring my son to me!"

Liu Shu and the others were about to get Guang the crown prince when the emperor said, "Get me Yong!"

Yang Su declared, "I dare not carry out your order, because a crown prince can't be changed back and forth."

The emperor choked with wrath. He turned his head to face the wall and remained silent. Yang Su went out and said to Guang, the crown prince, "Things have taken an ugly turn and we don't have much time."

Bowing to Yang Su, the crown prince said, "My future is in your hands, sir."

Before long, attendants came to report to Yang Su, "The emperor does not respond to voices calling him, and there's a rattle in his throat."

Yang Su rushed in again and saw that the emperor had already passed away. Lady Chen and the other royal consorts looked at one another in despair and broke down in sobs. Late in the afternoon, Guang the crown prince sent a messenger to Lady Chen and presented to her a golden sealed box with a strip of paper on which he had written words specifying that it was a gift for her. Believing it contained poisonous wine, she was so frightened that she refused to open it. At the urging of the messenger, she finally opened it and saw in the middle of the box several lovers' knots. The attendants congratulated her, saying, "You're not going to die, after all!" But Lady Chen indignantly refused to sit down and say a word of gratitude. It was only at the insistence of all the attendants that she bowed to the messenger. The crown prince entered her room at night and had his way with her, in violation of the proper family hierarchical relationship.

The next morning, after the emperor's death was announced, Prince Guang had the former crown prince Yong murdered, and assumed the throne. As attendants helped Prince Guang up to the dais, his feet somehow went limp and he staggered a few times. Yang Su dismissed the attendants and helped the prince up to the dais with his own hands, to the awe of every official present.

After returning home, Yang Su said to members of his family, "Now that I've made that younger son an emperor, I wonder if he'll be up to the job." Emboldened by the meritorious service he had rendered to the new emperor, he addressed the latter mostly as "Your Highness" only. Every so often, he would have his meals in the inner quarters of the palace. Once, when a palace attendant accidentally spilled wine on his clothes, Yang Su sharply ordered that the attendant be taken down the steps and beaten. The emperor was indignant but swallowed the humiliation and refrained from unleashing his temper.

One day, the emperor and Yang Su were fishing by the pond in the palace garden, sitting side by side under umbrellas held up by attendants to block the sun. The emperor rose to go to relieve himself. After coming back to the spot, he was so struck by Yang Su's distinguished looks and imposing air that he was seized with jealousy. Every time he stated a wish to do something, Yang Su would overrule him, thus further infuriating him. When Yang Su was on his deathbed, the emperor vowed, "I will kill all those who try to keep Yang Su alive, along with members of their clans to the ninth degree of kinship."

Prior to this, Yang Su had been on his way to the court one day when he saw the late emperor Wen, who was threatening him with a golden ax, crying, "Scoundrel! You disobeyed me when I wanted to have Yong succeed to the throne. Today you die!" Horrified, Yang Su ran into a room and summoned two of his followers, to whom he said, "I'm going to die. I just saw Emperor Wen." Soon he gave up the ghost.

After Yang Su's death, the emperor wallowed even more recklessly in the pleasures of the flesh. One day, he commented to a personal attendant of his, "While enjoying the fat of the land, a ruler should also indulge in other pleasures while he's still in his prime. And now the empire is rich and peaceful, with no disturbances on either side of the border. What better time than this for me to enjoy the pleasures of life? My palace is grand and spacious all right, but there are no secret rooms, small cozy dens, or dainty balustrades. If I could have those, I'd be content with spending my old age there."

Gao Chang, a personal attendant of the emperor's, said, "I have a friend called Xiang Sheng. He's a native of Zhejiang. He claims to be able to build palaces."

The next day, the emperor summoned Xiang Sheng and asked him what he could do. Xiang Sheng said, "I will present you with a sketch first." Two days later, he presented the emperor with a blueprint. Upon examining it, the emperor was immensely delighted. That very day, he ordered that officials find timber and other materials and recruit tens of thousands of laborers. It took several years to finish the construction. The new palace was now complete with belvederes, verandas, secluded rooms, and jade vermillion balustrades that ran continuously all around the compound. With numerous gates linking the halls together, the palace glittered in its dazzling resplendence. With carved golden dragons lying under the beams and jade animals crouching by the gates, the walls glowed and the carved windows glistened in the sunlight. The excellence of the workmanship was unrivalled since time immemorial. The expenditure that went into the construction wiped out the imperial treasury. Those who happened to enter the new palace by mistake would spend a whole day there in a futile attempt to find their way out. The emperor went for a visit and was overjoyed. Looking at his attendants, he said, "Even fairies who tour this place will find it quite a labyrinth. Let's call it 'the Labyrinth Compound.'" Thereupon he granted Xiang Sheng a fifth-grade official post and an abundance of gold ingots and bolts of silk. He then issued an imperial decree for the selection of thousands of young women from good families. Those selected were housed in the new palace. Every visit from the emperor lasted several months.

One day, court minister He Chou offered the emperor a small wheelchair that could accommodate only one woman. On the chair was a device that could be used to bind the woman's hands and feet, if she happened to be a virgin, so that she could not make the slightest move. (*What joy is there for him if not even the slightest movement is possible?*) The emperor tried the device out with a virgin and was thrown into raptures. He called He Chou to him and said, "What a wonderful device you came up with!" Whereupon he rewarded He Chou with a thousand taels of silver. Then He Chou offered him another wheelchair, one that could go up a staircase as smoothly as if gliding on flat land. When he was sporting with a woman, the chair would move and shake on its own. The emperor was even more pleased. "What's the name of this chair?" he asked.

He Chou replied, "I made it without a fixed plan. So it doesn't have a name. Would Your Majesty kindly give it a nice name?"

"You came up with the ingenious design for me to enjoy to my heart's content. I'll name it 'Heart's Content Chair.'"

The emperor then ordered artists to do dozens of paintings of men and women copulating and had the paintings hung up in a hall.

Later that year, Shangguan Shi, who returned to the court from beyond the Yangzi River on rotation of duty, made dozens of bronze mirrors, each five feet tall and three feet wide. They could stand in a circle in the bedchamber. He offered them to the emperor, who put them in the Labyrinth Compound. Immensely delighted upon seeing in the screen of mirrors every movement in his sexual encounters with women, the emperor said, "Paintings can only capture images. With reflections of real people, these mirrors are far superior to paintings."

Day and night, the emperor wallowed in pleasures of the flesh in Labyrinth Compound and wore himself out. He then marked out two hundred li of land for a garden and press-ganged a million laborers to build sixteen compounds replete with exquisite rockeries and artificial lakes. An imperial decree was issued for specimens of every kind of bird, animal, and plant throughout the land to be transported to the capital via government courier stations. By imperial order, the sixteen compounds of the west garden were named Clear View, Welcoming Sunlight, Perching Phoenix, Morning Light, Bright Sunset Clouds, Verdant Splendor, Serenity, Precious Jewels, Mottled Shades, Graceful Phoenixes, Benevolence and Wisdom, Quiet Cultivation of the Spirit, Treasure Trove, Peaceful Brightness, Beautiful Moon, and Red Sun.

Only outstanding beauties among the court ladies were selected to inhabit the compounds, and those most favored by the emperor were made the matrons of the compounds. Eunuchs were assigned to them to take care of purchases at the market. Five lakes were dug, each ten li in diameter. The one in the east was named Emerald Light Lake, the one in the south Greeting the Sun Lake, the one in the west Golden Beams Lake, the one in the north Clean Water Lake, and the one in the middle Vast Brightness Lake. In each lake stood a hill of piled-up rocks, and in each lake was built a pavilion and winding verandas magnificent to the last degree. Then another large lake named North Sea was dug. With a circumference of forty li, it boasted three islands in imitation of the legendary Penglai, Fangzhang, and Yingzhou islands respectively, with pavilions and verandas all over them. The water was dozens of feet deep. Boats in the shape of dragons and phoenixes navigated the five lakes and North Sea, which were all linked together. In his many tours of the east lake, the emperor composed eight poems to which he gave the title "Songs on the Lake: Viewing Scenery South of the River." The poems are as follows:

The first one:

> The moon on the lake favors fairies' abodes.
> With bamboo mats spread over the chilly water,
> With golden snakes wriggling over the shaking waves,
> What better moment to ride a floating boat?
> A slanting rainbow adds to the splendor;
> Cold dew gathers on the shadow of the moon.
> The west wind blows cassia flowers off the branches;
> At the banquet, thoughts run on the vast and the boundless.

The second one:

> Willows on the lake tremble in the mist;
> The morning fog opens their charming lids;
> The east wind shakes their fine narrow waists;
> They look best when shrouded in misty rain.
> Over the curving shores span painted bridges in shadows.
> When breezes fan wayfarers in the spring evenings,
> When willow catkins fly like snowflakes on warm days,
> The tranquility is at its deepest.

The third one:

> Wind-driven snowflakes fall thick and fast on the lake,
> Sometimes tapping gently the bamboo window frames.
> In their quiet beauty they vanish into the waves,
> Piling like shavings of jade outside the window.
> The lake blends into the sky at the horizon.
> Ignore the "Ode to the King of Liang's Garden,"[3]
> But listen in the morning to the beauties' songs,
> Intoxicating in their charm.

The fourth one:

> The green grass by the lake ripples like waves;
> Dancers' feet do little harm to the long blades.
> In their abundance they serve as carpets,
> But hardly as linings for the fragrant quilts.
> Their rainwashed color as fresh as ever,
> They grow far and wide in the traveler's absence.

> *The beauty's thoughts of spring wander afar,*
> *Defying expression in empty words.*

The fifth one:

> *Flowers by the lake are nourished by heavenly dew.*
> *Their pistils spread jade powder at the water's edge;*
> *Their buds glow under rosy clouds—*
> *A sight seen only in fairies' abodes.*
> *In full blossom, they adorn the hair;*
> *In the chill of spring, they are coldly elegant.*
> *The glow of the jade railings brings warmth to the scene;*
> *Thoughts fill the mind in quiet admiration.*

The sixth one:

> *The girls on the lake, chosen for their grace,*
> *Regret having left the golden palace.*
> *They meet none but lotus pickers,*
> *Singing in clear, dulcet voices.*
> *From the verandas, they merrily enter the ponds.*
> *Notes of the flutes and zithers echo through the night;*
> *As games are played on the green grass,*
> *The emperor joins in the frolic.*

The seventh one:

> *Wine on the lake adds to the daily pleasures;*
> *Silvery nails pluck the strings, with clappers beating time.*
> *As foam floats on the surface of the fragrant wine,*
> *Blurry eyes steal glances at each other.*
> *In the halls of spring, beauties holding trays;*
> *On the lake, how lovely the scenery!*
> *In the vast land of wine-induced slumber,*
> *The emperor enjoys peace and quiet.*

The eighth one:

> *As water of the lakes flows around the royal garden,*
> *The setting sun warms the rippling green waves,*
> *The falling petals dye the ripples red,*
> *And fresh breezes arise from the duckweeds.*
> *Far ahead, fish leap over lotus leaves.*
> *As the oars sweep gently and steadily,*
> *The shadows encroach upon the divine palace,*
> *Pushing it even further away.*

In his frequent tours of the lakes, the emperor often made the royal consorts sing these poems. By the sixth year of the Daye reign period [605–18], the flora and fauna in the imperial gardens were thriving and the peach trees and willows overarched the meandering paths. Herds of golden monkeys and black deer moved about. A trail was blazed from the palace into the west garden, flanked by tall pine trees and willows. The emperor mostly slept in the gardens and visited them at all times of the day. The royal attendants often slept by the paths while the emperor cavorted with his consorts in the middle of the night.

Daozhou [in Hunan] offered the emperor a midget called Wang Yi. With thick eyebrows and well-shaped eyes, Wang Yi had a clever tongue and won the heart of the emperor. He was often made to accompany the emperor on his travels but never allowed into the palace. He was told that he was not fit for service in the palace, whereupon he left the emperor's presence and castrated himself, in order to gain admission into palace grounds as a eunuch. (*Shudiao has a follower.*)[4] The emperor therefore loved him even more and granted him access to the royal chamber, where he mostly slept by the emperor's bed.

The emperor was in the habit of sleeping in one of the sixteen compounds after a tour of the lakes. One hot summer evening, he went quietly to Perching Phoenix. Qing'er, the consort occupying the compound, was lying behind a bed-curtain. In the bright light of the crescent moon, Qing'er was seen wildly screaming in a nightmare, looking as if she were going to die. Telling Wang Yi to call out her name, the emperor personally went and raised her to a sitting position. When she woke up a considerable while later, the emperor asked, "What dream could have terrified you like this?"

Qing'er replied, "I dreamed that Your Majesty was taking me by my arm, touring the compounds as usual. When we got to the tenth compound, Your Majesty went in and sat in the hall. Suddenly a fire broke out. As I ran away, I turned back for a look and saw Your Majesty sitting in raging flames. I kept screaming for people to come and rescue Your Majesty, and then I drifted off to sleep."

The emperor said, resorting to sophistry, "Death occurring in a dream is an omen for survival. Fire inspires awe. By sitting squarely in the middle of a fire, I acquire its awe-inspiring qualities." Later, he was assassinated during a visit to Jiangdu [present-day Yangzhou]. The dream of him sitting in a fire in the tenth compound was, in fact, an omen that portended his death.

One day, the emperor stared at a wall-painting of Guangling [another name for Jiangdu] for the longest time, unable to move away from it. Empress Xiao by his side said, "What kind of painting is it that so attracts Your Majesty?"

"I'm not attracted to the painting itself but to the place that I've visited before." With his left arm on Empress Xiao's shoulder and his right hand pointing at the scenery, the villages, and the temples depicted vividly in the painting, he said to the empress, "I toured the place when I was fighting against the King of Chen. As it turned out, after I won the throne, I've been so swamped with official duties that

I haven't been able to enjoy that place again." With these words, sadness clouded his face.

Empress Xiao said, "If Your Majesty likes Guangling so much, why don't you take a trip there?"

The emperor readily agreed. That very day, he summoned the court officials and told them that he wished to go on a pleasure trip to Guangling, adding that he would be going on a very large boat from the Luo River to the Yellow River and from there to the sea, then to the Huai River, and to the final destination of Guangling. All the court officials objected, saying, "That would be too long a journey. Moreover, the water at the Mengjin Ferry Crossing is too turbulent and the sea is likely to be too rough for Your Majesty's boat. Something untoward might happen."

Xiao Huaijing, the empress's younger brother and grand master of remonstration, said, "To my knowledge, during the reign of the First Emperor of Qin, an aura bespeaking the presence of a future sovereign arose in Jinling. So, by the order of the First Emperor, the main hill in the gorges was cut down, and the kingly aura vanished. There is again such an aura in Suiyang. Your Majesty likes the southeast region, but the Mengjin Ferry Crossing is too dangerous. Now, there being a dried-up riverbed northwest of Daliang [present-day Kaifeng] that the First Emperor of Qin had ordered Wang Ben to inundate by digging a canal and drawing water from the Yellow River, I propose that Your Majesty recruit laborers on a large scale and dig a canal, starting at Daliang, and make the canal run from Heyin in the west to bring in water from Mengjin Ferry Crossing, and ending at Huaiyin in the east to let the Mengjin water out. The total length of the canal will not exceed a thousand li. In addition, since the canal will be running through Suiyang, it will have the double advantage of reaching Guangling as well as puncturing the kingly aura in Suiyang."

Immensely delighted, the emperor ordered that all who dared to oppose the canal project be executed. He then appointed Ma Shumou, marshal of the north expeditionary force, as the director of the canal construction project and Li Yuan, commander of troops suppressing banditry, as the deputy director.[5] Li Yuan turned down the offer, pleading illness, whereupon Linghu Da, general of the garrison, filled the post. An imperial decree was then issued for the recruitment of all male laborers throughout the land who were over fifteen and under fifty. Those who shirked the corvée duties were to be executed, along with members of their clans to the third degree of kinship. The five million four hundred and thirty thousand laborers worked frantically day and night. Another decree followed, ordering the prefectures in the Yangzi and Huai river valleys to build five hundred large ships, and envoys were sent to urge compliance. Every family that was assigned the duty of building a ship was ruined. Unable to come up with enough money even after they sold off everything they owned, the heads of households were given thrashings on the back and made to wear cangues until they were left with no choice but to sell their children in order to make up the amount they owed the government. When the canal was near completion, the ships were also ready. [6] Exultantly, the emperor prepared to go to Jiangdu. Yang Tong, King of Yue [Yang Guang's grandson], was ordered to guard Luoyang, the eastern capital. Half of the court ladies did not join the emperor on his journey. Tearfully they vied to stop the emperor from going, saying, "That tiny state of Liao is not worthy of an expedition by Your Majesty in person. A general will suffice." The emperor, however, was not planning to return. He wrote a poem in farewell to his courtiers:

> Yangzhou appeals to me in my dreams;
> To conquer Liao is of lesser concern.
> If the landscape remains unchanged,
> This is my farewell to you, once and for all.

A million people followed the emperor. Ten days into the journey, a fifteen-year-old girl named Yuan Bao'er was brought to him from Chang'an. With her narrow waist, her naiveté, and her natural charms, she won special favors from the emperor. At this time, a messenger from Luoyang presented to him some flowers with twin blossoms on the same stalk, saying, "No one knows the name of this flower, which grows in the valley of Mount Song. Those who picked them marveled at them and wanted to present them to the emperor." Because the emperor was in his chariot at this point, the flower was thus named "Greet the Chariot Flower." The emperor had Bao'er hold them and called her "The Flower Girl."

While Yu Shinan was drafting the imperial decree on the expedition against Liao, Bao'er, who was standing off to one side, holding the flowers, kept her eyes on him.[7] To Yu Shinan the emperor said, "It has always been said that Zhao Feiyan could dance on a palm, but I've never taken this as more than some scholar's exaggeration, because I didn't think it possible for any human being to do so.[8] But now that I see Bao'er, I know better. And yet she is so naive. While she's staring at you like that, why don't you write a poem to mock her, as talented as you are?"

Complying with the emperor's order, Yu Shinan wrote a quatrain that said,

> She tries her hand at makeup but stops midway;
> Her sleeves drooping, she slouches in awkward ways.
> Yet for this she wins the emperor's heart,
> And holds flowers as she follows the chariot.

The emperor was overjoyed. Upon arriving in Bianjing, the emperor boarded a dragon-shaped boat, and Empress Xiao boarded a phoenix-shaped one. The Wu-Yue region offered five hundred girls, all fifteen to sixteen years old and called "palace-towing girls." Each boat, whether in the shape of a dragon or a phoenix, was tied to ten colorful ropes, each pulled by ten "palace-towing girls" in tandem with ten young goats. As it was the height of summer, Yu Shiji [Yu Shinan's older brother], a Hanlin academician, offered this proposal: "Plant weeping willows along the cause-ways of Bian Canal, first because the roots will take hold and protect the cause-ways, secondly because the foliage will provide shade for people who tow the ships, and thirdly because the goats towing the ships can feed on the leaves."

The emperor was immensely pleased. He ordered that a bolt of silk be given as a reward for each willow tree offered by the populace. As a result, people fought to offer willow trees. The emperor personally planted one. The court ministers fol-lowed suit before the people planted them on a large scale. A song began to go around: "The son of heaven planted first; the populace planted later." "Plant" being a homophone of "be hit by disaster," this song was an ill omen of what was to come.

After the planting project was completed, the emperor took up his brush-pen and bestowed on the willow his very own surname "Yang." Henceforth, willows [*liu*] became known as *yangliu*.

From Daliang all the way to Huaikou, the thousand-li canal was filled with boats in unbroken lines. Whenever a fancy boat with brocade sails went past, the fragrance would travel several li. One day, when about to board his dragon-shaped boat, the emperor leaned against the shoulder of a palace-towing girl, Wu Jiangxian, for help, and was so smitten by her unusual attractiveness that he stood transfixed. Wu Jiangxian was skillful in painting eyebrows. Unable to control his desires, the emperor summoned her after he returned to the chariot and offered her the title of Lady of Jieyu. Being a jealous woman, Empress Xiao was displeased. After ris-ing from bed, gratified, the emperor called the girl "Lady of Kongtong Hill" and promoted her to the position of first oarswoman on the dragon boat. Henceforth all the towing women outdid one another in painting their eyebrows long, the way Wu Jiangxian did. The official in charge of supplies provided them each day with five piculs of dark-green eyebrow paint imported from Persia. Each pellet of the paint was worth ten taels of silver. Later, as military taxes ran short, it was replaced by eyebrow paint of a less superior quality. Wu Jiangxian was the only one with a never-ending supply of the Persian kind. Every so often, the emperor would lean against the window curtain and feast his eyes on Jiangxian, unable to take his eyes off her. Once he commented to the eunuch in charge of transmitting orders, "The ancients said, 'Beauty is a feast to the eye.' A girl like Jiangxian can indeed stave off hunger." He went on to chant a poem which he titled "At the Oar":

> An old song sang of a peach leaf,[9]
> The new rouge puts plum blossoms to shame.
> Had I not leaned against the softly swishing oar,
> I wouldn't have known we were crossing the river.

He then issued a decree for all of the towing women to sing the lyrics.

When the Yuexi region offered a tribute of satin with shiny veins, the emperor transferred the gifts to the "Flower Girl" and Jiangxian exclusively, much to the indignation of Empress Xiao. Henceforth the two girls gradually lost their access to the emperor. The emperor often climbed up towers to recall memories of them. He wrote two poems under the title of "Southeast Pillars":

> Gloomily, sorrow pierces my bones;
> Slowly, I fall prey to illness.
> White hair, you see, grows mostly
> On the heads of those longing for love.

The second one:

> As I languish in memories of love,
> White hair grows on my temples.
> Idly I lean by the threshold,
> To look out with eyes filled with tenderness.

After the towing maidens arrived in Guangling, they were all told to make preparations for the emperor's Moon-Viewing Hall. Jiangxian and other girls were not allowed to serve the emperor in his bedchamber. When a military commander back from a mission to Guazhou offered a kind of twin fruit, the emperor had a young eunuch send it to Jiangxian posthaste on horseback. The stem connecting the twin fruit was broken as the horse jolted up and down. Jiangxian bowed in gratitude upon receiving the gift but she wrote the following quatrain on a small piece of red stationery paper to be delivered back to the emperor:

> The messenger on horseback sent the twin fruit,
> Along with the emperor's tender thoughts.
> But I'd rather bid farewell to my lord;
> Once apart, the twins will never rejoin.

The emperor was displeased upon reading it. To the young eunuch he said, "Why is Jiangxian so resentful?"

The eunuch bowed and replied, "The horse jolted so much that when I arrived at Moon-Viewing Hall, the fruit had already been shaken apart. The stem was no longer joined."

The emperor then commented, "Jiangxian is not only pretty but also writes good poetry. She's a really talented woman poet, and not any less so than Consort Zuo."[10]

On a visit to the imperial harem one day in a state of inebriation, the emperor was quite taken with a maidservant called Luoluo and demanded intimacy, but, out of fear of the empress, Luoluo dared not comply. On a plea of being inconvenienced by menstruation, she asked to be exempted. The emperor intoned a quatrain to mock her:

> This girl holds ripples of water to blame,
> The one with painted brows and a high forehead.

She'd do well to keep me with her in her dreams;
Why turn me abruptly out of her bed?

After arrival in Guangling, the emperor plunged into a life of dissolution and debauchery and often encountered evil spirits. When touring Wugong Terrace [in present-day Jiangdu County], he thought in a trance-like moment that he had encountered the late king of Chen. In his childhood, he had been friendly with the king. He now rose to greet him, forgetting that the king was a dead man. Wearing a blue gauze hat, a long blue robe with wide sleeves, and square green brocade shoes with purple patterns, the king addressed Yang Guang as "Your Highness." Of the dozens of dancing girls around the king, there was one of exceptional beauty. As the emperor cast frequent glances at her, the king of Chen said, "Doesn't Your Majesty know her? She's Royal Consort Zhang Lihua. I often recall how I rode with her in a battleship north from Peach-Leaf Hill.[11] At the time, Lihua, in mortification, sat by her window and, wielding her brush-pen made of the finest rabbit hair, wrote on a piece of smooth red silk her response to Prime Minister Jiang Zong's poem. She was in the middle of the line that started with 'The moon of jade' when Han Qinhu on his fine horse charged at us with his ten thousand armored cavalrymen, dispensing with all proper etiquette.[12] That was how we got here." (*An elegant description of a violent event. Wonderful skills typical of the Tang dynasty writing style.*) So saying, he took up a small wine cup with green patterns, filled it with red sorghum wine, and offered it to the emperor. Exhilarated by the liquor, the emperor asked Lihua to dance to the tune of "Jade Tree and Rear Court Flowers," written by the king of Chen. After telling the king about it, Lihua declined the request, saying that after she left her hiding place in the well, she had gained too much weight around her waist and that her figure was not what it used to be. (*Words spoken in a dream.*) But the emperor was so pressing that she complied and danced until the tune came to an end.

"How does Empress Xiao compare to her?" asked the king.

The emperor replied, "Orchids of spring and chrysanthemums of autumn are lovely in different ways."

The king then went on to recite more than ten poems. The emperor didn't remember them all but liked most the one entitled "Small Window" and the one entitled "To Green Jade the Maidservant." The one entitled "Small Window" is as follows:

I rose from a wine-induced afternoon nap;
No one was around; my dream woke me up,
When the setting sun, as if by design,
Leaned against my small, bright window.

The one entitled "To Green Jade" says,

Our parting brought me gut-wrenching grief;
The pangs of love wore down my bones.

If my mournful soul has not come apart,
One beckon will put it back together again.

To Lihua's request for a poem, the emperor replied that he was not able to comply. Lihua said, smiling, "I've heard the saying, 'If I'm rejected in this place, there will be others to take me in.' How can you say you are not able to?"

Much against his inclinations, the emperor took up a brush-pen and quickly composed the following quatrain:

Though never having met you before,
I have long heard of your fame.
Born with a hundred charms,
You are a good one to be acquainted with.

Holding the poem in her hand, Lihua reddened in displeasure.

The king asked the emperor, "Are you enjoying your tours in the dragon boat? I thought that Your Highness would be a better ruler than even the sage kings Yao and Shun of high antiquity. But here you are, out on a pleasure trip. Since you also love the pursuit of pleasure, as does everyone else, why did you denounce me so harshly years ago? Your thirty-six letters of denunciation against me upset me even to this day."[13]

All of a sudden, the emperor remembered that the king of Chen was a dead man. Angrily he said, "Why do you still address me only as 'Your Highness'? And why did you have to bring up the past?"

Even after the king and his royal consort faded from view, the emperor did not regain his peace of mind until a considerable while later.

Later, when taking another trip on his dragon boat, the emperor heard a mournful song:

My brother joined the expedition to Liao
And died of hunger under the green hills.
Here I tow the dragon boat today,
And find myself stranded by the Sui causeway.
With famine spreading throughout the empire,
There is hardly any food left for me.
On this three-thousand-li journey,
How can I be sure of my safety?
As my cold bones lie in deserted sands
And my ghost weeps on misty grassland,
My wife is overwhelmed with grief,
My parents wear their eyes out, looking for me.
May a righteous man lend a helping hand!
Put this abandoned corpse to fire
And take the forlorn soul back to its home,

> *Carrying these white bones on his shoulders.*
> (Sad enough to bring tears to the eyes.)

After hearing the song, the emperor ordered that the singer be brought to him. The search lasted until morning, but none was found. The emperor spent the whole sleepless night in agony, knowing that he had fallen out of divine favor. He wanted to make a trip to Yongjia, but none of the court officials was willing to join him. When he held a court session in Yangzhou, no tribute-bearing messenger came from anywhere. Those messengers who did show up had their tributary gifts robbed on the way by the troops. After consulting the court officials, the emperor issued a decree for all thirteen regions to put their troops to use and to kill those who refused to send in tributes.

Being well versed in astrology, the emperor often rose during the night to observe the stars. He summoned Yuan Chong, grand astrologer, and asked him, "What astrological signs do you see?"

Prostrating himself on the ground, Yuan Chong said tearfully, "The omens are very bad. An evil star is pushing aggressively against the emperor star. Disaster is likely to strike any moment now. May Your Majesty practice virtue so as to conquer it!"

Displeased, the emperor rose and went into a side room, where he ordered wine and sang the following song for his own amusement:

> *Swallows fly in the dense shade of the palace trees;*
> *Rises or falls make up sad tales of history.*
> *The Labyrinth Compound is a memory of joy*
> *Where flowers bloomed in their spellbinding charm.*

After he finished singing, he succumbed to uncontrollable grief. A personal attendant said, "We have no idea why Your Majesty sang in such sorrow for no apparent reason."

"Don't ask!" he snapped. "You will know soon enough." After a prolonged silence, his head bent down, he summoned the midget Wang Yi. "Do you know that there will be chaos throughout the land?" he asked.

Wang Yi replied, sobbing, "This useless person from a remote place is deeply indebted to Your Majesty for having taken me into the depths of the palace. And I castrated myself in my eagerness to be near Your Majesty. As for chaos throughout the land, this is not something that just started brewing today. When you tread on frost, you know that ice cannot be far off. Chaos has long been in the making. As I see it, major calamity will strike, and it will be one beyond redemption."

The emperor said, "Why didn't you tell me so earlier?"

Wang Yi replied, "If I had, I would have died along ago."

With tears dripping down onto his clothes, the emperor said, "Explain to me what has led to this sorry state of affairs. I would like to know the causes."

The next day, Wang Yi presented this letter:

"This humble subject from a poverty-stricken area in southern Chu voluntarily entered the service of the wise emperor at the expense of my physical integrity. A midget with inferior mental faculties, I have, in the years I have served Your Majesty, won favors that far exceeded my hopes and have been able to move about freely in the palace compounds, with attendants and vehicles at my disposal. Though of humble background, I have a passion for the study of the classics and have gained a fairly good knowledge of the root causes of good and evil and of rises and falls. In my frequent contacts with the populace, I have learned what should be of concern to all. I dare to make this statement only because Your Majesty was kind enough to seek my views.

"Since assuming power by divine will, Your Majesty has been making arbitrary decisions over objections and protests, building the extravagant west garden and undertaking two expeditions against the Liao. Dragon boats number in the thousands and palaces are constructed everywhere for your sojourns. Army draftees number one million, but civilians live in dire poverty. Of the soldiers joining the attacks against Liao, less than one-tenth survived. Of the dead, less than one-tenth were buried. The imperial treasury is empty, the price of grain is soaring, yet Your Majesty continues to take pleasure trips everywhere and at all times. Guards and attendants often watch over an empty palace. All are disappointed, and the empire has gone to ruin. Most villages throughout the land are deserted. Young men have died in military expeditions, and the old and weak languish in the wilderness. The corpses of soldiers pile up like hills, and the corpses of those who died from hunger fill the fields. Dogs and boars have grown tired of human flesh; vultures and fish have fed on too many corpses. The stench spreads all over the land, and bones cover the plateaus. Ill winds sweep through deserted dwellings; ghosts cry under chilly grass. No smoke rises from kitchen chimneys for thousands of li as far as the eye can see. Thousands have lost their homes and face imminent death. Fathers leave behind young children and wives mourn their deceased husbands. Misery is widespread; famine is rampant. After the breaking up of families, death follows. Had the sovereign loved the people, things would not have come to this pass.

"Your Majesty being of a fiery temper, who would have dared to protest? Those who did were ordered to be executed. Looking at one another in dismay, court officials decided to hold their tongues in order to stay alive. Even if Guan Longfeng had come back to life, he would not have dared to remonstrate.[14] Ministers close to Your Majesty are all obsequious and reject good advice in their attempts to please you, for only by so doing can they attain wealth and rank. From where can Your Majesty learn about your wrongdoings? After another failed expedition against the Liao, Your Majesty stays on in Yangzhou while the empire is more precarious than the thawing snow of spring and war spreads in all four directions. People live in such dire misery, yet no official dares to speak up. Your Majesty would do well to ask yourself, what is to be done? If Your Majesty wishes to mobilize the army again, the officers and soldiers will disobey. If your Majesty wishes to go on another pleasure trip, the guards and attendants will not follow. By then, what can be done? Your Majesty may resolve to practice virtues and do good works for the people, but, for all the good intentions, the empire is already lost. The game is over. The opportune moment will not present itself again. When a big mansion is falling apart, one pillar is of no avail. When the river overflows, one handful of earth makes no difference. Being an uncouth person from a remote region, I have no fears. How can I not speak out when calamity is imminent? If I don't die now, I will die later in the ravages of war. As I present Your Majesty with this letter, I stretch out my neck, awaiting the sword."

After reading the letter, the emperor said, "Has there ever been a state that does not perish, or a sovereign who does not die?"

Wang Yi rejoined, "So Your Majesty is again trying to defend your errors. Your Majesty often says, 'I will surpass the three sage sovereigns and five virtuous kings,[15] outshine the kings of the Shang and Zhou dynasties, and leave in the dust all the sovereigns of ten thousand generations to come.' How has Your Majesty been faring so far? Is Your Majesty ready to return to the palace and rule?"

As the emperor heaved one sigh after another, Wang Yi continued, "I didn't speak up earlier because I loved life. Now that I have already written such a letter, I will be glad to die as an expression of my gratitude. Chaos has just begun throughout the land. Take care of yourself, Your Majesty." With that, he took himself off. Before long, word came that Wang Yi had committed suicide. (*If he was so willing to die, why didn't he offer remonstrations earlier?*) Overcome with grief, the emperor ordered that Wang Yi be buried in a lavish funeral.

Pei Qiantong, chief of the royal bedchamber guards; Sima Dekan, chief of the imperial guards; and General Yuwen Huaji of the garrison plotted a rebellion. They asked that the imperial guards be replaced by former slaves who had been recruited into the army. The emperor granted their request and issued the following decree:

> *Winter and summer change places, relieving each other in the cycle of seasons. The sun and the moon also change positions, alternating work with rest. Hence students need relief from their studies, just as farmers need periods of hiatus. The imperial guards have been assiduously carrying out their duties with never a lapse of attention, letting dust accumulate in their hair and fleas grow in their helmets. We feel for them in their hard life. They will henceforth be able to rotate their duties in order to have some time for recreation. We need no Dongfang Shuo to submit pleas on behalf of the guards.[16] Our kindness to the imperial guards is profound. The aforementioned is to be put into effect forthwith.*

A few days later, upon hearing noise in the middle of the night, the emperor rose hurriedly from bed, got dressed, and went to an inner hall. Soon after he sat down, the soldiers lying in ambush all around him charged forward. As Sima Dekan charged at the emperor, drawn sword in hand, the emperor cried out angrily, "We have been paying you well all these years. We have never ill-treated you. How can you betray Us like this?"

Zhu Gui'er, the emperor's favorite consort, now standing by his side, said to Dekan, "Three days ago, out of concern for the imperial guards as autumn weather turned chilly, His Majesty had palace tailors make warm cotton-padded coats for them. His Majesty personally supervised the project, and thousands of coats were completed within two days and were distributed just the other day. How can you not know that? How dare you threaten His Majesty like this?" As she lashed out at him, Dekan cut her down with his sword, splashing blood onto the emperor's robe. Dekan then stepped forward and recounted the emperor's crimes, adding, "Let your subject tell Your Majesty the truth: Rebellion has spread throughout the empire. The two capitals are both in the rebels' control. All hope is lost for Your Majesty, nor do I myself stand much of a chance of survival. Since I have already irreversibly violated the code of behavior for a court minister, I would like to offer your head to the public!" So saying, he raised his sword against the emperor.

The emperor said in another outburst of rage, "Don't you know that a three-year-long severe drought will follow the bloody assassination of a prince, let alone an emperor? There are other ways to die." He asked for poisonous wine, but there was none to be had. A silk scarf was then brought to him. He was forced into his bedchamber, where he hanged himself. Empress Xiao led palace maids in taking headboards off their beds to make a coffin. A simple funeral was then held at the foot of Wugong Terrace, where the emperor had encountered the king of Chen in a dream.

When alive, the emperor had never liked his third son, Prince Jian of Qi. In fact, the sight of the prince was enough to make him gnash his teeth. Every time he undertook a trip, he would bring the prince along under armed guard. When the coup just began, he asked Empress Xiao, "Is Ahai behind this?" Ahai was the pet name of Prince Jian of Qi. After killing the emperor, Sima Dekan and the others dispatched cavalrymen to arrest Prince Jian of Qi in his own home. His head bare, his feet unshod, he was driven into the street. The prince said, "If the emperor wants me dead, at least let me be properly attired." He thought it was the emperor who was seeking his death. How sad that both the father and the son died believing the other had ordered his death!

Later, when entering the capital with his army, Emperor Taizong of the Tang dynasty commented with a sigh as he laid his eyes on the Labyrinth Compound,[17] "This is nothing but the people's blood and sweat!" He ordered that the palace women be set free and the palace be burned down. The fire lasted for months. The song and the poem circulating among the populace had been borne out, proving that the emperor's death was not just a matter of destiny. A later poet had this to say:

> Once the thousand-li canal was complete,
> Waves to swamp the Sui house rolled from the ninth heaven.
> Before the brocade sails furled, battle cries arose;
> Sadly, the dragon boats never returned.

Mr. Dugu Has the Strangest Dream on His Journey Home

With butterflies aflutter in the east garden,[1]
With fragrant flowers abloom on Luofu Hill,[2]
All for what purpose—the dreams long and short?
Do not hold on to your pillows and tarry!

There was once a newly wedded young couple as inseparable from each other as lacquer and glue, and as fish and water. But on the third day after their wedding, the husband was summoned by the government yamen for an urgent assignment and ordered to escort a shipment of grain for the army. His name having already been inscribed in the government document, he was ordered to start on his journey right away without so much as a look back, for any delay in delivery was punishable by military law. He was allowed only to send an oral message home. Truly, one on official duty is no longer a free man. As he pushed on in haste, he thought only of his wife. Since he could hardly confide in anyone, he kept his sorrows to himself. On his first day on the road, his thoughts went back to his wife ten thousand times. That night, as he slept in his room at an inn, he dreamed that he was together with his wife again and doing what wedded couples do. Henceforth, no night went by without such a dream. One month later, he dreamed that his wife was pregnant. Upon waking up, he dismissed the dream with a smile. Luckily, he delivered the grain and money on schedule and, all safe and sound, started posthaste on the homeward journey. After submitting the receipts to the government office, he returned home and reunited with his wife in boundless joy after a three-month absence. As the saying goes, "The joy of reunion with one returning from afar exceeds that of the newlyweds." That he and his wife fulfilled their love that night goes without saying. His wife told him how she had missed him and described to him the dreams that had come to her every night. They tallied with his dreams in every detail. And, indeed, she was by this time three months pregnant. If the husband had told of his dreams first, there might have been reason to suspect her of lying, but she was the one who described them first. Clearly, their souls met in their dreams, and their devotion to each other was thus able to lead to a pregnancy. Let me now tell a story that is also about dreams—dreams made possible by the devotion of a wedded couple living apart. Truly,

> *Your dreams at night may not be unreal;*
> *Your daytime adventures may not be real.*

As the story goes, in the Zhenyuan reign period under the rule of Emperor Dezong [r. 780–804] of the Tang dynasty, there lived on Chongxian Lane in the eastern section of Luoyang a man by the name of Dugu Xiashu, who later became a *jinshi*. With outstanding innate intelligence, he was able to compose essays when he was ten. By age fifteen, he was well versed in the classics and the histories and could write essays of thousands of words without a pause for reflection. His father, Dugu Ji, director of the Bureau of Noble Titles and Inheritance Claims, engaged his son to Juanjuan, daughter of Bai Xingjian who had passed the imperial examinations in the same year he had and was now a director in the Department of Revenue.[3]

Juanjuan, apart from being as pretty as a flower and as lovely as the moon, was skillful at needlework and was well educated and good at writing poems. Had she been allowed to sit for the civil service examinations, she would have easily won first honors. The parents arranged this betrothal because they thought that Juanjuan and Xiashu would make a perfect like-minded couple. However, all too unexpectedly, Xiashu's parents died one after the other and both his prospective parents-in-law also passed away. Before he had gained worldly success, his family circumstances went on the decline and all the servants left him. All that remained were a few rooms.

Bai Changji, Bai Xingjian's son, was a heartless man and a snob. Now that Xiashu had fallen on hard times, Bai Changji wanted to back out of the engagement and marry his younger sister into a rich family in Anling. Luckily, Juanjuan was a young woman of honor with a mind of her own. She cut off her hair and vowed not to betray her betrothed. Failing to talk her around to the idea, Bai Changji resignedly married her to Xiashu but gave her no dowry. All she was allowed to take with her were the clothes and the jewelry items she was wearing, as well as Cuiqiao, the maid who had served her ever since she was a child.

After she moved into Xiashu's house, Bai-shi accepted the destitute life contentedly, without the slightest resentment. She kept herself busy from morning to night, cooking and making hemp threads, so that Xiashu could continue with his studies. And Xiashu admired her resoluteness, her literary talent, and her beauty. Indeed, they were a couple as happy in their union as fish in water. Xiashu, a scholar whose time had not come, was held in high esteem by all members of the Bai clan except Bai Changji, the snob, who said that his sister, born to be a pauper, had made him lose face by throwing in her lot with a starving man. Indeed,

Xiashu was a thorn in his flesh and a sting in his eye. On Xiashu's part, in spite of his poverty, he was not one to bow and scrape, and so the two men refused to visit each other.

The fifteenth year of the Zhenyuan reign period being a year for civil service examinations, the imperial court announced that in the third month of the year, all eligible candidates were to go to Chang'an, the capital, for the examinations. Xiashu took leave of his wife, Bai-shi, and went to Chang'an, believing that, with his literary talent, his name would surely appear at the top of the list of successful candidates to be posted later in the spring. Well, the examiner Zheng Yuqing, cosecretary of the Ministry of Rites, did give Xiashu's paper the highest grade, but Xiashu's essay contained the following sentence: "The unfortunate incident of Fengtian happened because Lu Qi, the evil minister, usurped power, which enabled Yao Lingyan, regional commander of Jingyuan [in present-day Ningxia Autonomous Region], and Marshal Zhu Ci to incite the troops to loot the government treasury.[4] It thus appears that even though there may be many noble-minded men working to maintain peace, one villain is enough to wreak havoc throughout the land. Conclusion: the sovereign cannot be too careful in the selection of officials." (*This serves to prove that he is indeed not one to bow and scrape.*)

It so happened that Emperor Dezong was a man with a most suspicious and jealous mind. Accusing Xiashu of "criticizing the court and mocking government policies," he tossed this essay aside, even though it had been given the highest grade, and rejected Xiashu out of hand. Two members of the Bai clan, one called Bai Juyi, the other Bai Minzhong, were given high honors, although they did not measure up to Xiashu in literary talent.[5] Being the only one in his group who failed the examinations, a dejected Xiashu packed that very night for his journey home. Hearing word about his imminent departure, Bai Juyi and Bai Minzhong went to offer him a farewell dinner and walked with him to the wayside pavilion ten li from the city. In low spirits during his journey, Xiashu wrote the following poem:

> *I went west in my youth for the exams;*
> *At age twenty, I find myself a failure.*
> *Not meant to gain favor with the emperor,*
> *This humble scholar took the trip in vain.*

After many days on the road, Xiashu arrived at his home in the eastern capital, Luoyang, and was overcome with shame upon seeing his wife. Henceforth he confined himself in his study and devoted all of his time to his books. Every time he recalled his failure at the examinations, tears would trickle down his cheeks. His wife, Bai-shi, consoled him by saying, "A man of worth will surely win recognition some day. Why torment yourself like this?"

Xiashu replied gratefully, "Thank you so much for your kindness and your words of comfort, but we're so poor we run short of food and clothing. Even if I strike it rich some day, there's nothing to relieve our poverty now. What's to be done?"

Bai-shi said, "As they say, 'Even if nine pleas for help out of ten are in vain, at least you get enough to keep hunger away.' As I see it, in all the thirty years of my father-in-law's career, he should have had a few students or friends who are incumbent officials. With all the time you have on your hands, why don't you go to them and ask for help? You may even get enough money to pay for your studies for three years."

His wife's advice made him see the light. He replied, "You do have a point, but I've been so absorbed in my studies ever since childhood that I've never been introduced to my father's acquaintances. I know none of my father's students and friends except Wei Gao, courtesy name Zhongxiang, who is a native of Chang'an. When he was driven out by his father-in-law, Zhang Yanshang, he came to father for help, and father recommended him to an official post, for which he was very grateful.[6] He's now regional commander of Xichuan. If I go to him, he'll surely help me out. But it's such a long journey from the eastern capital to Xichuan that a round trip may take years. During my absence, where are you going to get money for household expenses? I can't leave you."

Bai-shi rejoined, "Since you do know someone, I should by rights help you pack and send you off on your journey. I'll take care of the house. If I need anything, I can always borrow from relatives. Don't worry."

Joyfully Xiashu said, "If so, you've taken a great weight off my mind. I'll go."

"But there will be many hardships on the road. We have no servant to travel with you. What's to be done?"

"That's true, but we don't have that much money anyway. It's all right."

On a chosen auspicious day, Bai-shi and Xiashu, along with Cuiqiao the maid, carried his winter and summer clothes and went to Kaiyang Gate, where they bid each other farewell with a cup of wine. As the husband and wife clung to each other, unable to tear themselves apart, a rainstorm suddenly came on and they dashed for shelter into a deserted monastery by the roadside. It was called Longhua Monastery, built by the Prince of Guangling [Tuoba Yu] during the Northern Wei dynasty. It used to be a magnificent monastery with prized flowers and exotic fruits planted all around it. It also had a bell tower with a bell that, when struck, could be heard fifty li away. But the bell was later moved into the palace by Empress Dowager Hu.[7] During the reign of Emperor Taizong of the Tang dynasty, a foreign monk made another bell for the tower, one that, when struck, could be heard more than twenty li away. By the time of Emperor Xuanzong of Tang, there were five hundred monks in the monastery and a never-ending stream of worshipers offering incense. Later, when Shi Siming [d. 761], cohort of the rebel An Lushan [703–57], seized Luoyang, all the monks were slaughtered, the bell was melted and made into weapons, and the plants were cut down for use as firewood. The monastery was thus reduced to ruins. As he looked around with his wife at what remained of the monastery, Xiashu said with a sigh, "How can there be no kind-hearted people to renovate such a grand monastery?" To the statue of the Buddha he vowed, "If I make a name for myself by blessings from the unseen world, I will use my salary to renovate this monastery." After the rain stopped, the couple bade each other farewell and went their separate ways. Truly,

> For petty profits, merchants take to the road;
> Over tiger-infested paths wayfarers go.

Let us turn our attention from Bai-shi on her way home and follow Xiashu on his journey. Traveling by day and resting by night, he arrived after one whole month at Jingzhou, where he boarded a boat. His journey from that point on was to be by water up the river. Sails were unfurled only when there was a strong favorable wind. If the wind was light, the boat was towed with a kind of rope special to the Sichuan region. More than one thousand feet long, the rope was made of hemp glued with raw lacquer to bamboo slips more than one inch in width, and was coiled up around the winch placed on the stem of the boat. A drum was beaten in the boat as a signal for the laborers on the shore to begin towing. As he witnessed the scene, Xiashu recalled these lines by Du Fu:[8] "Towing boats with Sichuan ropes" and "Who is beating the drum to launch the boat?" Now he had firsthand knowledge of what those lines referred to.

Yellow Ox Gorge did not come into view until after the boat had traveled for about another ten days. The ox-shaped hill by the gorge was visible from thirty or forty li away, but the water was so rapid that reaching the hill by a boat going upstream could take more time than one would think. A ditty popular in the area said, "The ox is seen at dawn; the ox is seen at dusk; the ox never budges from dawn to dusk."

After traveling for about another ten days, Xiashu came upon Qutang Gorge, where the current was even swifter. In the middle of the river stood a rock hill called Yanyudui. At higher water levels in the fourth and fifth months of the year, only the tip of the hill was visible above the surface of the water. It posed such a peril to boats going downstream that if they were too slow in dodging it, they could be smashed to smithereens. In the face of such danger, Xiashu said to himself with a sigh, "How will my wife know that I have to go through all these perils on a long journey that may or may not end with the help I set out to seek?"

There are three gorges, one immediately after the other, in the eastern Ba region. The first one is Qutang Gorge, the second one Guangyang Gorge, and the third one Wu Gorge. Of the three gorges, Wu Gorge is the longest. It is flanked on both sides by high and steep mountains overgrown with ancient leafy trees that cast their shadows over the water. Only a narrow strip of the sky was visible between the hills. Light came through only when the sun or the moon was directly over the gorge. There was no sign of human habitation along the banks for several hundred li. The only sound that broke the silence was the crying of apes, day and night. Hence the saying:

Of the three East Ba gorges, Wu is the longest;
The apes' cries bring travelers gut-wrenching grief.

Soaring above Wu Gorge is Mount Wu with its twelve peaks. On Mount Wu stood Gaotang Temple, where King Xiang of Chu was said to have dreamed one night of a beauty who offered to keep him company in his sleep. Before she departed, she told him that she was Emperor Fu Xi's beloved daughter Yaoji, and that she had died before she ever married but was now the goddess of Mount Wu.⁹ At dawn she conjured up clouds and at dusk she made rain. From dawn to dusk she busied herself at the terrace. His thoughts still with the divine maiden after he woke up from his dream, King Xiang asked Grand Master Song Yu [ca. 290–ca. 223 B.C.E.] to compose a rhapsody, entitled "Gaotang fu," to describe her ravishing charms. Later, a temple dedicated to the divine maiden was erected on the mountain.

In midstream, Xiashu scooped up a handful of water and poured it into the river again by way of offering a libation and, his eyes fixed on the temple, prayed silently to the divine maiden, "With your magic powers in the dreamland, please tell my wife Bai-shi in her dream that I am fine, so that she won't worry about me. I will surely compose a poem to express my gratitude to you. Far be it from me to come up with lewd comments to sully your good name, as did Grand Master Song. Please grant this wish of mine." (*Only people in desperate straits would go to burn incense and offer vows in every temple they see. But it is much to Xiashu's credit that he intends to clear the divine maiden of her name.*) The ancients put it well, "Heaven blesses the deserving person." Since he had said his prayers and promised in all devoutness to write a poem in her honor, the divine maiden would surely do something more magical than conjuring up clouds and rain. His prayer was bound to be answered. Truly,

He prayed for a message via a dream to his wife,
Just to say that he was safe and sound on the road.

After passing through Wu Gorge into a wider expanse of the river, Xiashu traveled for more than a month through the middle and western parts of the Ba region [in present-day Sichuan] before he arrived in Chengdu which borders on the Dijin [Rinsing Brocade] River. Why, you may ask, is it called Rinsing Brocade River? Well, it's because Chengdu produces fine brocade, known to the imperial court as "Shu brocade." The woven fabric must be rinsed in the river to brighten its colors. Hence the name "Rinsing Brocade River." When taking refuge from An Lushan's rebellion, Emperor Xuanzong of the Tang dynasty had lived temporarily in Chengdu and called it the southern capital. It was also where the regional commandery of Xichuan was first set up. Indeed, with thousands of li of fertile land and a thriving population, it was a place as beautiful as the finest brocade.

In no mood for sightseeing, Xiashu went directly into the city and all the way to the residence of the regional commander to make inquiries about Wei Gao. To his disappointment, the commander had left with his troops for Yunnan several months earlier to put down an armed tribal rebellion there, and would not return home until peace was restored. Now, won't you agree that warfare doesn't follow a fixed time schedule? Xiashu was so disappointed that, not knowing whether to go or to stay, he said with a sigh, "As the proverb goes, 'Birds fly into the forest for survival; people travel afar to seek help.' But fate is against me. I've traveled over ten thousand li to seek help, but there's none to be had. What's more, all my travel money is gone, and I have no relatives or acquaintances in this place. I've made it here all right, but how am I going to make my way back? Good heavens! I'm done for!"

As the ancients said, "Heaven looks after the virtuous." As Xiashu was lamenting his fate at the gate of the regional commander's residence, a Daoist priest suddenly appeared before him and asked, "Why do you sigh, sir?"

Xiashu replied, "I am Dugu Xiashu from the eastern capital, here to see an old acquaintance, Wei Zhongxiang, to ask him to help me out in my reduced circumstances. But as bad luck would have it, he is out on a military expedition. If I wait for him, there's no way of knowing when he'll come back victorious, and I can hardly stay long. But if I turn back home now, I've used up the last penny of my travel money and therefore can't undertake the journey. I can't stay, nor can I go. That's why I sigh."

The priest said, "Being a Daoist, I make it my business to help people. My temple is not far from here. Since you're in such a plight, why don't you stay in my temple while you wait for the commander, if you don't object to the humble food? That way, you won't have taken this long journey in vain."

Xiashu was profuse in his thanks. "If so, I'll be ever so grateful to you! But won't I be imposing on you?" So saying, he followed the priest to the temple. Isn't it a wonder that the priest, who knew nothing about Xiashu, offered to accommodate him? If no one had appeared to offer him help that day, wouldn't he have got stranded in that place without knowing when to return? Wasn't this a stroke of good luck for Xiashu in his distress?

So Xiashu and the priest left the gate of the regional commander's residence. Before they had covered two li, there loomed before them a wide curving road, flanked by verdant pines and cypresses, leading to a temple which bore the inscription in three golden characters, each the size of a winnowing pan, "Blue Sky Temple." It was a temple built during the Han dynasty by Liu Bei for Priest Li Ji.[10] During the reign of Emperor Xuanzong [r. 712–56], a man named Xu Zuoqing, who had acquired the Dao, renovated it. Indeed, it was like an abode of the fairies without a speck of dust from the mortal world. After entering the temple, Xiashu paid homage to the statues before the priest took him into a room, where they exchanged amenities anew and sat down as host and guest. Looking around the room, Xiashu was impressed by its cleanliness and air of refinement. On the wall hung a scroll of poetry. Which ancient poet's writing was it? Well, in fact, it was a poem written by Xiashu's father, Director Dugu, on the occasion of Xu Zuoqing's return to the Shu region. The poem said,

> *The priest is about to leave amid strains of music;*
> *Friends ply him with wine at the send-off feast.*
> *Memories of the green dragon gate linger,*
> *As he stays on White Crane Hill, never to return.*

What had happened was that, upon hearing about Xu Zuoqing's fame as one who had acquired the Dao, Emperor Xuanzong had offered him a post in the imperial court and had him brought to the palace in a small chariot with wheels wrapped up in cattail leaves so as to ensure a smoother ride. But as Zuoqing refused to pursue a career in officialdom, the emperor allowed him to use government means of transportation on his way back to the hills, whereupon officials of the court wrote poems in his honor, but none of the poems measured up to the one by Dugu. Thus it was kept in the temple and cherished like a priceless piece of jade.

At the sight of his father's handwriting, Xiashu was so overwhelmed by emotion that tears coursed down his cheeks.

"What makes you cry upon reading this poem?" asked the priest.

"To be candid with you, I feel sad because this is my father's handwriting."

Now knowing that Xiashu was Dugu Ji's son, the priest attended to his daily needs with great respect. Time sped by. All too soon, half a year elapsed. Wei Gao pacified the tribes of Yunnan and returned to his residence. Losing no time, Xiashu prepared gifts and went for a visit, partly to offer congratulations upon the commander's victorious return and partly to acquaint the commander with his impoverished circumstances and state the purpose of his long journey. Indeed,

> *Friends from the rich man's past expect his largesse,*
> *But few rich men ever show them much sympathy.*

Wei Gao treated Xiashu to a sumptuous feast and was going to invite him to stay for a few more days for a good chat when news came that the *tsampo* [king] of the Tubo Tibetans, who often made intrusions into the Shu region using Yunnan tribesmen as guides, was making trouble again. Having heard that Wei Gao had put down the rebellion by Yunnan tribes and thus cut off his wings, so to speak, the *tsampo* led a three-hundred-thousand-strong army and swept over the boundary to challenge Wei Gao. In this emergency, Wei Gao wrote a memorial to the court and assembled his troops and his officers in preparation for taking on the enemy. Xiashu said to himself mournfully, "I got to see him after having waited here for half a year. And now he's again suddenly called away to the border. Isn't this fate?"

To Xiashu's request to leave, the regional commander replied, "With the Tubo troops all over the area, how will you be able to make your way home? I've told the priest to take good care of you. Wait until the enemy troops have been driven out and the roads have regained peace. I will then give you a decent farewell dinner." (*You are your own boss at home, but, once outside, you're at other people's beck and call. This is the kind of misery all travelers have to go through. Those who haven't had the experience can hardly understand.*) For lack of a better choice, Xiashu agreed and continued to stay in Blue Sky Temple, and there we shall leave him for now.

Wei Gao and his mighty army marched out of Chengdu to Jiameng Pass [south of present-day Guangyuan County, Sichuan], where they encountered the Tubo troops. Through an interpreter, Wei Gao said to the *tsampo*, "When our court married a princess to your king to form a familial tie, you agreed never to invade our land.[11] Why have you gone back on your word and repeatedly encroached upon the Shu region?"

The *tsampo* replied, "The Yunnan tribes are our subjects, but you had the audacity to lead your army across the border. Give Yunnan back to me nicely, and I'll go home. If not, you won't even be able to keep Xichuan."

Wei Gao said, "Tell me, which place under the sun does not belong to the great Tang dynasty? If you want a fight, let's fight. You will never have Yunnan."

Without Yunnan tribesmen as their guides, the Tubo troops knew little about the terrain. Wei Gao had flags put up throughout the deep woods and valleys to make it look like there were Tang troops in ambush in those places, and ordered foot soldiers to crawl ahead and wave shields over their own heads while hacking with their swords at the legs of the enemies' horses. At the signal of a cannon shot, the drums were struck and the bugles were blown, and all the men in the Tang army charged forward. The Tubo troops, thrown into confusion, were put to rout and driven over the border all the way to Mobo, the new capital that the *tsampo* had built, until the city of Mobo fell. The ground was strewn with corpses and blood flowed in streams. A fierce battle it was, but a great service was done to the imperial court. With the Tubo troops retreating far into the distance, Wei Gao ordered his army to start on the way back home and sent a messenger to deliver the good news to the court at top speed. All along the way back,

> Cheerfully they rapped their stirrups with whips;
> Joyfully they returned, singing songs of triumph.

Let us turn our attention back to Dugu Xiashu in his prolonged stay in Blue Sky Temple. In low spirits, he took walks around the temple to divert his mind. In one of his walks, he came upon a bridge called Where Immortals Rose to Heaven. Back in the Han dynasty, Sima Xiangru,[12] suffering humiliation because of his poverty after eloping with Zhuo Wenjun from Linqiong County and returning to Chengdu, had written two rows of large characters on the post of this very bridge: "This man of honor will not cross this bridge unless in a grand four-horse chariot." After he became commander of the imperial guards, he returned to his hometown in glory on his way to open up a direct route to Yunnan by imperial order, thus fulfilling his vow. Pacing to and fro on the bridge, Xiashu looked east and said with emotion, "I'm not any less talented than Sima, and my wife not any less beautiful than Wenjun.

When are we ever going to get our grand four-horse chariot?" After leaving the bridge, he was about to return to the temple when, it being late spring, he heard a cuckoo in the woods cry over and over again, 'Better go home! Better go home!"

Even more saddened, Xiashu said with another sigh, "When I said good-bye to my wife, I thought I would be away for a year at most. Little did I know that I would be stranded here all this time, unable to return. Alas! I dare not hope for much generosity from Wei Gao. I only hope that he will drive back the Tubo troops as soon as possible and send me home, so that my wife won't have to wait for me anxiously at home day and night."

Spring went, summer came, and more than a year elapsed before Wei Gao returned in victory. The messenger bearing good news having preceded him, Emperor Dezong was immensely pleased that Wei Gao had done the court great service by pushing back the Tubo troops. With his personal brush-pen, he wrote a decree granting Wei Gao the post of secretary of the Ministry of Defense and Grand Guardian of the Heir Apparent on top of his current post of regional commander of Xichuan.

On the day Wei Gao returned to his residence, all court officials, military and civilian, went to offer him toasts of congratulations. After the commander's official activities began to wind down, Xiashu also went to his residence to offer congratulations. Being in an alien place without the means to buy a gift, he composed a poem and entitled it "Easy Is the Road to Shu." Why, you may ask, was it called "Easy Is the Road to Shu?" Well, during An Lushan's rebellion in the last year of the Tianbao reign period [742–56] under Emperor Xuanzong, Yan Wu, Duke of Zheng, was the regional commander of Xichuan. There was a Remonstrator Du Fu [712–70] who had come to Xichuan to seek safety and also a Mr. Fang Wan [697–763], former prime minister, who had been demoted to be an adjutant in the regional commander's office. Because Yan Wu was a ruthless man with a suspicious mind, Academician Li Bai [701–62] had written a poem entitled "Formidable Is the Road to Shu," of which two lines toward the end read:

> *The Brocade City may be filled with pleasures,*
> *The best course is to head for home.*[13]

This was a friendly warning to Fang Wan and Du Fu. Now Xiashu changed the format into a ballad and the word "formidable" into "easy," partly to say that Wei Gao's merit far exceeded that of Yan Wu and partly to say that he, Xiashu, a sojourner in the Brocade City, was luckier than Fang and Du because he had met someone who recognized his talent. This was the subtle way in which he hoped to gain the commander's favor. The poem said:

> *Alas! The road to Shu, since ancient times,*
> *Has been a formidable climb.*
> *The pioneers founded the kingdom of Shu,*

With its verdant hills and winding rivers.
The gold ox path was blazed in the Qin dynasty;
Tall ladders and rock trails link up the peaks.
Overhead, the vast expanse of blue sky;
Down below, the surging torrents of cascades.
Even nimble apes cannot go across,
Let alone humans, with their sad laments.
Commander Wei, guarding the Pass,
Subdued foes in the west and the south.
War over, people's lives prosper;
Merchants from everywhere swarm to the markets.
They climb the hills and ford the streams,
Which to them are as smooth as mats.
With taro to stay the pangs of hunger,
And homespun fabric to ward off the cold,
This land of plenty abounds in divine blessings.
Travelers should rejoice at the good tidings.
With so many delights in the Brocade City,
Why entertain thoughts of going back home?

In his admiration for the poem, Wei Gao said to Xiashu, "When Li Bai wrote 'Formidable Is the Road to Shu,' He Zhizhang, Advisor to the Heir Apparent, called him an immortal banished from heaven. Now, your talent is not any less remarkable than Li Bai's. I happen to have a vacant post for a scribe in the secretariat of this commandery. Let me ask the emperor for approval for me to hire you as a counselor of the Ministry of Rites and concurrently director of the secretariat of the Xichuan regional commandery. I can then benefit from your talent at all times of the day. Would you be kind enough to accept the post?"

Xiashu replied, "The imperial court attaches the greatest importance to the civil service examinations. Those who did not pass the exams may rise to be high officials, but in the end, they get browbeaten. (*It has always been so. How lamentable! Though Guo Ziyi* [697–781]*, Li Guangbi* [708–64] *and others* [Illegible].) I have failed the examinations three times, but I remain undaunted. I'm not going to give up so easily on my chances at the examinations. I've stayed in this town for over a year now without ever receiving a word from my wife, Bai-shi. I just can't dismiss her from my thoughts for even one moment. I was looking forward to your return so that I could bid you farewell. Please understand my situation and don't blame me for disobeying you."

Wei Gao said, "I wouldn't impose my wish on you if you're not willing, but it being the end of the year, there is too much snow and ice on the roads to travel. It would be better to wait until spring so that I may prepare some clothes for you and send you off on the road. It won't be too late, will it?"

Partly because of the sincerity of Wei Gao's offer and partly because the weather was indeed too cold to be out on the road, Xiashu saw nothing for it but to stay.

After what remained of the last lunar month finally went by, New Year's Day rolled around, followed by the Lantern Festival. With its fertile land and dense population, Chengdu was a major metropolitan area in the southwest. Since Emperor Xuanzong had established temporary residence there, tribute-bearing envoys from all directions converged in Chengdu, lending it the aura of a capital. In addition, Yan Wu, Duke of Zheng and regional commander of the Ba and Shu regions, vigorously pursued a policy of peace, as a result of which the populace lived a life of plenty and the government coffers were full. And now the successor, Wei Gao, in his fame for having subdued the Yunnan tribal rebels and pushed back the five-hundred-thousand-strong Tubo troops, was pleased to see stability throughout the region and the people's happy acceptance of his command. Prior to the Lantern Festival, he ordered in his ebullient way that all residents inside and outside of the city display fancy lanterns in a joint celebration of the festival. Who would refuse such an order? For five nights, from the thirteenth through the seventeenth of the first month, frames were put up at every door for the display of lanterns of novel designs, which, together with fancy fireworks, lit up the city as bright as day. Lion dances, masked barbarian king dances, and acrobatic shows lasted throughout the night amid the music of drums, *sheng* pipes, and *xiao* flutes.

Every evening, Wei Gao set out a banquet at the Strewing Flowers Tower and invited Xiashu there to share the joy. On the day the lanterns were removed, Xiashu went to bid Wei Gao farewell. His attempts to keep Xiashu unavailing, Wei Gao said, "If you're so determined, I can't very well force you to stay. But I'll have a send-off dinner and some small gifts for you. Let's meet east of Wanli [Ten Thousand Li] Bridge for the occasion. Please don't turn me down." Right away, he ordered that a boat be prepared for Xiashu's journey home and sent to Wanli Bridge to wait there for Xiashu the next day. He also assigned a soldier to escort Xiashu throughout the journey. The next morning, at the farewell banquet by Wanli Bridge, Wei Gao raised his golden cup and said, "This is an ancient bridge. When Zhuge Liang [181–234] saw Fei Wei off on a mission to the state of Wu, he said, 'A ten-thousand-li journey starts from this bridge.' Hence the name of this bridge. It is also the starting point of your brilliant career. I hope you will take good care of yourself. In my humble position, I will be eagerly awaiting good news from you about your success at the examinations so that I can offer you my congratulations."

After plying him with three cups of wine in succession, Wei Gao finally took out an embroidered bag and said, "I owe my career to your father's recommendation. My official duties have kept me from repaying you my debt of gratitude. I sweat with shame when I think about how I've let you down after you've undertaken such a long journey. However, with banditry on the rise, it's not safe for you to carry too much money on you. I have here three hundred taels of silver for your travel expenses. I have also prepared ten thousand taels of gold and a thousand bolts of Shu brocade to be delivered to you after the roads become safer. Now don't take me for a senseless ingrate." (*In the olden times, such was the stuff of which friendship was made.*) He then called the soldier to him and said, "Take good care of Mr. Dugu along the way. Don't ever be remiss in your duty."

The soldier kowtowed in acknowledgment of the order. Xiashu bowed time and again in gratitude, saying, "This generosity is already far beyond my expectations. I wouldn't dream of having more!"

Carrying the embroidered bag, Xiashu boarded the boat, followed by the soldier. Wei Gao stayed on the bridge and did not return home until the boat was out of sight. Of this, no more.

After bidding Wei Gao farewell, Xiashu sailed east. The boat went downstream as fast as an arrow. Within three days, he found himself at Wu Gorge. Looking at the Divine Maiden Temple of Mount Wu from afar, he thought, "When I was passing this spot last time, I prayed silently to the divine maiden for a dream to my wife and I promised to compose a poem by way of showing my gratitude. I wonder if my wish has been granted or not. If it has been granted, I must not break my promise." Thereupon he intoned a poem in fulfillment of his vow:

> A narrow strip of sky breaks through ancient trees;
> The twelve peaks of Wu lock in cold vapors.
> King Xiang's dream of romance was all his own;
> Blame it not on the Divine Maiden of clouds and rain.[14]

After finishing the poem, he bowed in gratitude toward the temple atop the mountain. After passing the Three Gorges, he arrived in Jingzhou. All too unexpectedly, the escorting soldier fell ill and Xiashu had to take care of him in a reversal of roles. After another few days, they reached Hankou. They would then travel by land from Runing to Luoyang. Though the soldier had recovered from his illness, a bumpy ride on horseback would have been too much for him. Xiashu wrote a letter, gave him some travel money, and told him to go back on the same boat. Xiashu then took his own luggage and went ashore. In a wise move, he bought a horse and went in the direction of Luoyang. He arrived in Luoyang about a month later. Dusk had set in when he was only about thirty li from Kaiyang Gate. In his eagerness to get home, he spurred on the horse and had covered about another ten li when the moon rose. In moonlight he went about another ten li and, upon hearing the faint sounds of bells and drums, said to himself, "So the city gate is closed. Even if I make it to the gate, I won't be able to enter the city. Here's the ancient Longhua Monastery. Both the horse and I are exhausted. Why don't I take a rest here?" He untied his luggage, dismounted, and went into the monastery. As it turned out, that very night,

> He met his wife in his dream,
> And heard her song under the stars.

Let us now pick up another thread of the story and tell of what happened to Bai-shi after she parted with her husband Xiashu in front of Longhua Monastery. Although in hard straits with little means of livelihood, she was, luckily, most skillful in needlework and she wrote beautifully. Moreover, the Bai clan being a large one in the eastern capital, there was no lack of cousins who took lessons from her in needlework and the writing of poetry, and they paid her in kind, enough to let her get by. But her husband's parting words were never absent from her mind. Didn't he say he would be back in one year? Why wasn't he home now that three years had gone by? To make matters worse, she heard that the road to Xichuan was difficult of access. There were the "Narrow Strip of Sky," the "Man in the Jar," the "Snakes' Horror," the "Devils' Bane," and other inaccessible spots. Hence the saying, "No road is as hard of access as the one to Shu." She thought, "My husband must have experienced many a shock on his way there. I haven't received a word from him since he left. I wonder if he's well. Oh, I'm so worried about him! How I wish to go to Xichuan and look for him, but, being a woman confined to the home, what can I do? May I meet him in a dream, so I know how he is doing!" Day and night, her thoughts were all with him. One day, feeling drowsy and listless in her boredom, she wrote a poem in her room:

> Between Western Shu and the Eastern Capital,
> No letters have traveled back and forth.
> Thinking of him in vain behind closed doors,
> I'm weighed down with worries, away from the hills.

Her husband never absent from her thoughts, Bai-shi kept wishing for a dream in which to see him, but three years went by without one. On one Clear and Bright Festival, her cousins came to ask her to join them in their spring outing, but, being in no mood for frolic, she turned them down. In the evening, she sat by a solitary lamp and plunged into mournful reveries. After sitting like this for the longest time, she turned her head and saw that Cuiqiao the maid was sound asleep. Feeling listless, she also went to bed. Tossing and turning, wide awake, she thought, "I'm one luckless woman. I don't even get to see my husband in a dream." Then she thought, "But even if I do see him in a dream, a dream is a dream. It's not for real. Oh well, I'll have to go to the Shu region and find him before I can stop worrying." Then again, she said to herself, "How will my cousins let me go if they hear about this? I'd better slip away first thing tomorrow morning. They'll be none the wiser." As she was thinking along these lines, she heard roosters crowing, and the sky was turning light. In haste, she rose, did her hair, dressed herself like a village woman, took some pieces of silver for travel expenses, and packed a few articles of clothing. As Cuiqiao was fast asleep, she opened the doors, one after another, and went out without waking her.

In a trice, she was out of Chongxian Lane, past Kaiyang Gate and Longhua Monastery. Before she knew it, she was at Sending-Brocade Pavilion in Xiangyang.

Back in the former Qin times [350–94], there was an Annamese general, Dou Tao by name, who took his favorite concubine, Zhao Yangtai, to his post as garrison commander of Xiangyang, leaving behind his wife, Su-shi. Su Hui by name and Ruolan by courtesy name, she was as beautiful as she was talented. She wove a palindrome poem into a piece of brocade eight inches long by eight inches wide. With five different colors to mark out the different sections, the palindrome poem contained in total eight hundred forty one characters that could be read backward and forward to make three thousand seven hundred fifty-two poems. (*Introducing a story that has much relevance.*) Upon reading the poem delivered by a messenger, Dou Tao immediately sent Yangtai back in exchange for Su-shi, and the love between the husband and wife grew deeper than before. People of later times built a pavilion in this spot in commemoration of the event.

Bai-shi entered the pavilion and looked into the distance for a considerable while before she said to herself in lament, "I may not be as talented as Ruolan was, but I do have a rudimentary knowledge of the art of poetry. Even if I weave a palindrome poem into a scroll of brocade, who will deliver it for me, so that my husband can return early to live with me in conjugal bliss?" Thereupon she intoned a palindrome poem and wrote it on a post of the pavilion:

> *Warm spring and charming melody,*
> *Beautiful brocade and praiseworthy poem.*
> *Sadly she wove, love in heart;*
> *Sorrowfully they parted, pining and aching.*
> *Green phoenixes of remaining fragrance,*
> *Blue birds of dreaming dawn.*

When read backwards, it becomes another good poem:

> *Dawn dreaming of birds blue;*
> *Fragrance remaining of phoenixes green.*
> *Aching and pining, parted they sorrowfully;*
> *Heart in love, wove she sadly.*
> *Poem praiseworthy and brocade beautiful,*
> *Melody charming and spring warm.*

After she finished writing the palindrome poem, Bai-shi left Sending-Brocade Pavilion and, before she knew it, she had passed Jingzhou and was in Kui Prefecture. As the hour was late, she went into a temple to spend the night. Raising her eyes and seeing a board bearing the inscription "Gaotang Temple" in large gold characters, she knew it was the temple dedicated to the divine maiden of Mount Wu. Picking up a pinch of earth at the altar for lack of incense, she prayed, "I, Bai-shi, Juanjuan by pet name, am a resident of the eastern capital Luoyang. Since my husband, Dugu Xiashu, left three years ago to Xichuan to see Wei Gao, the regional commander, no word has come from him. That is why I'm out on this arduous ten-thousand-li journey to look for him. During my stay tonight in this palace of yours, I make bold to pour out my heart to you. Since you, divine maiden, were able to meet the king of Chu in his dream, please also give a dream to me, a woman like you. (*So she believes the divine maiden did meet the King of Chu in a dream. She contradicts Xiashu on this point. A dream within a dream. Remarkable.*) Please manifest your magic power and give me a dream. I shall be forever devoted to you." Having said this prayer, she went to sleep.

In a dream, she indeed saw the divine maiden, who said to her, "Xiashu had been staying in Xichuan all this time, safe and sound, but he has already left the place and is traveling east on his way home. How will you be able to see him if you continue pressing ahead? Go back home quickly and beware of false alarms along the way. Take care!"

Bai-shi woke up with a start and saw that it was already broad daylight. Recalling the divine maiden's words that remained fresh in her memory, she was confident that it was not just a fanciful spring dream. She rose and, after thanking the divine maiden, left the temple and turned back the way she had come, in the direction of Luoyang.

Traveling by day and resting by night, she wended her way east. It being late spring, she feasted her eyes, as she went along, on the pink peach blossoms and green willow branches amidst which swallows danced and orioles chirped. Evening came upon her before she was aware of it. Finding herself more than twenty li from Kaiyang Gate, she quickened her pace under the moon. Suddenly, she saw ahead of her a group of people talking and laughing boisterously as they gradually approached her. Who were they? They were a group of frivolous young men about town. Bringing zithers, wind instruments, blue wine vessels, and green tents with them, they all too frequently went about in groups to ogle women and show off their dashing figures.

Feeling threatened by this oncoming group of unsavory characters, Bai-shi tried to get out of their way, but, her beauty doubly striking in the moonlight, these young men had already seen her. Closing in on her in a circle, they said to her, "We are on a spring outing and have gone as far as this place to enjoy the moon. But enjoyment of the moon is not complete without wine, and enjoyment of wine is not complete without women. Let's do justice to the wonderful evening! Would you, young lady, be so kind as to join us in some fun in Longhua Monastery nearby, where the peaches and plums are in full bloom?"

A surge of wrath rose from the soles of her feet to the roots of her ears. Her face flaming red, she cursed, "You must be thugs under that rebel Shi Siming! In these times of peace, who would dare take liberties with a decent woman? What's more, I'm no commoner! I'm Director Bai's daughter, Director Dugu's daughter-in-law, and wife of Dugu Xiashu, a scholar with a *jinshi* degree![15] I'm not one to be trifled with!"

However, these young ruffians had no regard for officials or family status. Bai-shi could have screamed herself hoarse for all they cared. They pushed and shoved and hustled her into Longhua Monastery to view the flowers. As the saying goes, "The worst that can happen to iron is to fall into the furnace; the worst that can happen to a person is to fall into a trap." Truly,

> A lady of the finest family
> Becomes a singing girl in a wineshop.

To retrace our steps, Xiashu had to spend the night in Longhua Monastery because the city gate was already closed. Wondering how his wife Bai-shi was doing in the three years that had elapsed since his departure, he intoned two lines from a poem by Meng Haoran [689–740] of Xiangyang:

> My anxiety grows as I draw nearer home;
> I dare not ask the one who approaches.[16]

After intoning the lines several times, he felt tears coming down his cheeks. Still awake in the depth of the night, he suddenly heard a hubbub of voices nearing the monastery from outside the walls. "These are human voices all right," thought he. "They're not ghosts. But in this stillness of the night, could they be runners from a government yamen?"

As he was wondering, he saw about ten people with brooms and dustpans sweeping the hall. Soon after they left, about a hundred people appeared. Some spread out mats, some laid wine and food on the tables, some carried in lamps and candles, some held musical instruments in their arms. Coming in an endless stream, they worked until the hall was tidy and clean. Xiashu thought, "Oh I know. Today is the Clear and Bright Festival, so they must be some rich young men on a tour out of the city, here to admire the bright moon and the spectacular peach and plum blossoms in the yard. If they see me, they'll surely drive me out. I'd better hide myself under the altar behind the screen at the back and go to sleep after their feast is over. What a luckless man I am! I can't even get a good night's sleep in an old temple!" So thinking, he rose and hid himself behind the screen in the rear of the hall, not daring to make the slightest sound.

After a while, he saw six or seven young men in clothes of assorted styles push a young woman to the feast table in the hall. The woman was offered the seat of honor at the head of the table, facing east. The young men sat around the table, fixing their eyes on her.

"So I'm right in guessing that they are rich young men on a spring outing. The woman is either a licensed courtesan or an underground one. But why are they so obsequious? Or could she be a woman of a decent family willing to drink with them in this place? Could she have been seized by force or abducted?" He noticed that the woman, sitting sideways, wore a deep and angry frown. His eyes riveting on her from his hiding place, he realized with a start that she bore a strong resemblance to his wife, Bai-shi. Feeling as if he had been dumped into an ice bucket, he shivered all over with cold but thought again, "Pshaw! What a fool am I! My wife is an honorable woman. She spends all her time in the house and hardly ever even sees her relatives. How would she willingly follow these men? There are all too many people who look alike in the whole wide world. Why should I assume that she is my wife?"

Although his thoughts ran along these lines, he still felt uneasy. Quietly, he took one step forward after another in the shadow for a closer look and, sure enough, the voice and the demeanor were unmistakably his wife's. Then again, he thought, "My eyes must be playing tricks on me." So he rubbed his eyes until they were nice and bright and looked again. It was her all right. Again he thought, "Could I be asleep and she's in my dream?" He blinked and stomped his feet. He was wide awake. (*Vivid descriptions.*) "How very strange! She had the honor to cut her hair and take a vow before she was married, but now she's abasing herself like this! Could she have compromised her chastity because I've been in Xichuan for so long and she thinks I won't ever return? When Su Qin returned home after he failed the examinations, he was angry at his wife for not even bothering to leave her loom to greet him.[17] After he became prime minister, of course he refused to keep her. I wonder how she will bring herself to face me when I return home tomorrow morning."

Consumed with rage, he rubbed his hands and clenched his fists as if ready to charge forward and pick a fight, but, with one against so many of them, wouldn't he be plucking a tiger's whiskers? So he swallowed his anger and decided to wait and see how it was all going to end.

A young man with a long beard addressed Bai-shi, raising his cup, "As the ancients said, 'When one faces the corner weeping, all around the table find no joy.' This may be the first time we meet you, young lady, but we meet by a predestined bond. Such beautiful scenery and glorious weather are hard to come by. Why look so woebegone? Please let yourself go and happily drink a cup of wine. Please also sing a song for us, to add to the enjoyment."

Hating them for having forced her to this place, Bai-shi didn't want to sing but then she thought, "This is a bunch of young ruffians and I'm all alone in this place. If they get angry and become violent, wouldn't I be bringing insult on myself?" In resignation, she wiped her eyes dry, took off her golden hairpin, and, beating time with it, sang the following song:

> *Now or another time? To live or not to live?*
> *My husband is away, at the end of the earth.*
> *In grief, the tree in the garden blooms three times.*

As the ancients said, "Poems must be sung by beautiful women." As she sang the song she made up about what preyed on her mind, her charming voice, her mournful tone, the sweet melody, and the appealing inflections could have stopped birds in their flight and inspired fish to dance in the water. Amid the profuse applauses around the table, the long-bearded one said over and over again, "Thank you! Thank you!" And he drained his cup.

From his hiding place in the darkness, Xiashu observed how his wife had pulled out her hairpin to beat the time as she sang, and recognized it as a betrothal gift he had given her. In his teeth-gnashing rage, he didn't pay attention to the meaning of the lyrics but again was seized with the impulse to charge forward and make a scene. However, his fear of being hopelessly outnumbered and losing out to the group kept him transfixed to the same spot. He decided to continue watching.

A yellow-robed stout man, raising his cup to Bai-shi when it was his turn to offer a toast, said, "Listening to your beautiful voice, a man drunken for days on end will wake up and find all his vulgar thoughts gone. May I venture to ask for another song? Please do not turn me down."

Bai-shi was upset. Her face all crimson, she said, "You don't know when to stop! Isn't one song enough? Why do I have to sing again?"

Picking up a giant wine vessel, the long-bearded one said, "Let me set a rule. One who refuses to sing will be penalized by drinking up this giant vessel. One who doesn't finish the wine or wears a displeased look, or sings the same old song, will pay the same forfeit."

Bai-shi took fright at the ferocious look of the long-bearded one and saw no alternative but to sing another song:

> How sad the withering grass!
> How mournful the cries of the grasshopper!
> My husband is gone, never to return;
> Here I sit, my temples white with worry.

Amid the cheers, the yellow-robed one finished his cup of wine and said, "Thank you!"

Watching his wife sing another song, Xiashu was seized with even greater wrath, and looked as if fire would shoot out from his eyes to burn the whole monastery down.

A fair-complexioned young man, when it was his turn to offer a toast, said, "It was a good song all right, but such a melancholy tone is at great odds with the lively atmosphere around the table. Sing us a more cheerful song!"

The other men agreed, saying, "Good point! Sing something different to help our wine go down!"

Resignedly Bai-shi sang again:

> Have a cup of wine! Do not turn me down!
> The falling petals linger in vain on the stems;
> The water flows on, never to return.
> Do not expect your youth to last long;
> All too quickly it will be gone!

Before she had finished, the fair-complexioned one cried out, "Didn't I tell her to come up with a more cheerful song? And yet she purposefully sang a sad one! Penalize her with a large vessel!"

The long-bearded one was about to administer the penalty when a purple-robed youth stood up and said, "Hold the penalty!"

"Why?" asked the fair-complexioned one.

"In the courtesans' quarters, everybody contributes to the fun. If we get too strict with the forfeits, we'll be the vulgar ones spoiling the fun. Now keep the penalty in mind but let her sing another one. Won't that be better?"

"Well said!" said the long-bearded one.

The large vessel was put down, and it was now the turn of the purple-robed one to toast. Knowing she would not be able to get out of it, Bai-shi forced herself to sing another song, her tears flowing.

> As I bemoan my empty boudoir, waiting,
> The autumn sun refuses to set.
> My husband sends me not a word;
> Letting messenger geese fly, unburdened.

After she finished, the white-robed one said, laughing, "Again, nothing but laments without the slightest hint of romance!"

The purple-robed one said, "Maybe she was trained in that school of singing. Don't be overly critical." So saying, he finished his cup.

A Tartar in a black hat, cup in hand, when it was his turn to offer a toast, said, "I don't know much about music. Sing us anything you want, young lady, to help this cup of wine go down my throat. Just don't leave us in the cold." (*This dream, with all the roles and props, can very well be made into a stage play.*)

Short of breath after singing those songs in succession, Bai-shi was beginning to lose patience. Hearing another request for her to sing, she turned aside her head and paid no attention. At this signal of refusal, the long-bearded one cried out, "You must not refuse!" As he said so, he pushed over a giant vessel of wine. Being in no position to resist, Bai-shi had to choke back her sobs. She drank this vessel of penalty wine and sang:

> As the evening wind sweeps past in haste,
> The dew moistens the grass in the yard.
> My husband is gone, never to return,
> Little knowing how I weep in my room!

After the Tartar in the black hat drank up his wine, a green-robed youth, raising his cup in his turn, said, "The night may be deep by now, but our party is still in full swing. Please sing some more and let us make a night of it!"

Bai-shi's voice was already broken and overly strained when she sang the last song. At this request from the green-robed one, her tears fell thick and fast, to the amusement of the men around the table. They said, "With such gorgeous flowers, bright moon, fine wine, and beautiful songs, this is a happy moment. How can you be so miserable and such a joy killer? Pay forfeit!"

Fearing another vessel of wine, Bai-shi started singing again, tearfully:

> *Fireflies wing their way among the poplars;*
> *Gusts of doleful wind stir the weeds.*
> *Could I be walking in a dream?*
> *The path to my home is shrouded in grief.*

Like the plaintive cries of a cuckoo or a gibbon, this song with its broken notes saddened everyone around the table. After the green-robed one drank up his wine, the long-bearded one said with a grin, "I don't have much of a voice, but it's not polite not to do something in return. Let me improvise a song by way of a response. Don't laugh at me!"

"When did you ever learn this art? Go ahead and sing!" said his companions. Letting go of himself, the long-bearded one began to sing:

> *I met you by the side of the flowers*
> *And I sent you off at the same spot.*
> *Why say anything about dreams?*
> *Is not life itself a dream?*

His voice was like that of a panting toad or a sick old cat. His companions all doubled over with laughter and their lips got all twisted out of shape. (*Comic.*) They commented, "We just knew you couldn't sing! Imagine fooling us like that!"

The long-bearded man was a cheeky one. However boisterously the others laughed, he kept his composure and went on singing until he finished the song. Only then did he say, "Stop laughing! I paid good money to learn this song. You would do well to learn to sing those few lines I just did."

His companions burst into another peal of laughter. Ignoring them, the long-bearded one filled a cup with wine, offered it to Bai-shi, and did not sit down until the cup was finished.

When he first watched his wife drinking with this group of men, Xiashu was so filled with rage that had it not been for the ventilation through his two nostrils, he would have exploded. But by this time, judging from the way the men made her sing and the way she wept in resentment, it began to dawn on him that she had been taken here by force, and his rage subsided a little. But then he thought, "Shouldn't she have been staying at home? How did she get to be abducted by these swine to this deserted place?" His mind full of misgivings, he decided to go on watching and see what would happen next.

Again, it was the fair-complexioned one's turn to drink. Raising his golden cup, he said to Bai-shi, "All you sang were sad songs that made even men like us shed tears, spoiling the pleasure. You must sing one about romance. We'll be all ears. Don't say no."

Xiashu said to himself, "These swine abducted a decent woman and made her sing, and they are picky, too!"

Having sung so many songs, her mouth parched, her strength depleted, Bai-shi was already upset. How would she agree to sing more? She hung her head and said nothing. The long-bearded one shouted, "You're violating the rules!" With that, he pushed over another giant vessel of wine. At this point, Xiashu's patience gave out. Quietly he picked up two large broken pieces of brick from the floor and, throwing the first one, hit the long-bearded man right in the head. The second piece hit Bai-shi on the forehead. Pandemonium broke out in the hall. "Burglars! Burglars!" they cried as they ran helter-skelter in all directions. In a trice, everyone vanished. Xiashu walked into the hall and looked around but found no one in sight. Not even the wine vessels and tableware were anywhere to be seen. How very strange! He grew so frightened that his eyelids quivered, his heart thumped, and his tongue stuck out. It was some time before he remembered to retract it.

After a few moments of reflection, Xiashu said to himself with a sigh, "I know. My wife must have died. It was her soul I saw just now. My bricks scared her off." He was unable to sleep the rest of the night. Before the roosters started crowing, he straightened his clothes and set out on the road, and arrived at the city gate of Luoyang before daybreak. After going through Kaiyang Gate, he headed for Chongxian Lane with tears in his eyes. When his house loomed in sight with no signs of mourning, his heart began to pound violently, as if there were fifteen clanging buckets going up and down in the same well.

After going through the gate, he walked up into the hall, where he ran into Cuiqiao, the maid. "Is the mistress all right?" he asked, breathless with fear, lest she say something ominous.

Cuiqiao replied without a sign of anything amiss, "The mistress is in bed in her room, complaining of a headache this morning. So she hasn't gotten up to wash or do her hair."

Upon hearing that his wife was fine, Xiashu felt a surge of relief, the kind that a woman in labor feels when the baby comes out with a plop. But, wondering about the episode last night, he rushed into the bedchamber and asked, "What kept you from sleeping well last night and from getting up this morning?"

Bai-shi replied, "I had such nightmares last night! Because you were away for three years without ever sending a word to say when you'd be back, I missed you so much that I had a dream last night in which I wanted to go to Xichuan myself to look for you. I went all the way to Mount Wu and took a rest in the Divine Maiden Temple. The divine maiden appeared to me in a dream, saying that you had already left the Ba and Shu regions and would be home soon, and that if I missed you by going in the opposite direction, all the pains I had taken would be to no avail. So I turned back. At about twenty li from Kaiyang Gate, I was heading for the gate in the moonlight when I suddenly ran into a group of young men, who took me by force to Longhua Monastery to view the moon and the flowers. While drinking wine, they asked me to sing. I sang six songs in total, and a man with a long beard made me drink wine several times in penalty. Then all of a sudden, two bricks fell from midair. One broke the head of the long-bearded one and the other hit my forehead. At that very moment, I woke up with a headache. That's why I'm still in bed."

"How strange!" cried Xiashu. "How can that be?"

To Bai-shi's question about what was so strange, Xiashu replied by giving her an account of how he had stayed overnight in the monastery and what he had witnessed, sparing no detail.

Bai-shi was also mystified. "So, what I dreamed about last night was real?" she said. "But who are those young ruffians?"

"They were just part of the dream," said Xiashu. "We need not pursue this further."

Storyteller, let me tell you something: This world abounds in liars, but the average liar would hardly exceed the bounds of plausibility. We've never met a grand master like you, capable of such monstrous lies. Bai-shi couldn't have been in bed, dreaming about singing in Longhua Monastery. Had she not physically been there, how could Xiashu have seen her? Even a three-year-old child won't believe such barefaced lies, let alone us!

Well, dear audience, you may not know this, but in most situations, dreams arise from thoughts, which, in turn, have their causes. When there is a cause, there are thoughts, and thoughts give rise to dreams. Her husband was never absent from her thoughts, whatever she was doing. The spirits transcended bodily limits and entered dreams. Xiashu missed his wife so much that his soul entered his wife's dream, even when he was wide awake. This is a case of two souls in communion with each other. Isn't this obvious enough? How can I be guilty of lying? (*Brilliant reasoning!*) Indeed,

> They missed each other so much after they parted
> That their spirits quietly entered their dreams.

Bai-shi said, "All right, let's not talk anymore about the dream in which we saw the same things, but let me ask you: I never received any word from you all the time you were away. I dreamed that I was praying at Mount Wu Temple for a dream, and then the divine maiden appeared to me and said you had a safe journey and that everything went well. The road to Shu being so difficult, I was wondering how you made it to Chengdu. After you arrived there, did you get to see Wei Gao? And after you saw Wei Gao, did he give you anything?"

Xiashu said in astonishment, "When I was passing Wu Gorge, I secretly prayed to the divine maiden of Mount Wu because she's said to have magic powers. I prayed that she send you a message to say I was fine. So she did indeed relay the message to you. She does have magic powers! Well, after I got to Chengdu, it so happened that Wei Gao had to go on two expeditions. So I stayed in Blue Sky Temple for two whole years, and the journey took half a year. That's why I broke my promise to you. Luckily, Wei Gao is a man who values friendship and treated me very well.

If I had not insisted on leaving, he would have kept me from returning." As he told her everything about his arduous journey, the hardships of a life on the road, and Wei Gao's hospitality, gift of silver, and generosity in providing transportation and escort for him, both husband and wife were overcome with emotion.

With the three hundred taels of silver going toward daily household expenses, Xiashu devoted all his time to his studies, literally burying his head in his books. After more than half a year, two officers sent by Wei Gao arrived, bringing a letter, ten thousand taels of gold, and one thousand bolts of Shu brocade. With alacrity, Xiashu wrote a thank-you letter and treated the messengers to a sumptuous meal before they left. To Bai-shi, he said, "My father was a government official for more than thirty years, but he never had such wealth. Being a descendant of a family of stainless reputation and also a Confucian scholar with a simple lifestyle, I think Wei Gao's first gifts are enough for us to live on. Why would we need so much? Let's seal these up and put them away. After I pass the examinations, I'll have a use for them." Bai-shi did as her husband said and put the gifts away. Of this, more later.

Now, during the Tang dynasty, the palace examinations were held once every three years. After failing the examinations in the fifteenth year of the Zhenyuan reign period, Xiashu undertook his journey to the Ba and Shu regions and therefore missed the one held in the eighteenth year of the same reign period. When the twenty-first year came around, he packed, took leave of his wife, and went to the capital for that year's round of examinations. The examiner, Cui Qun, assistant director of the grand secretariat, had long heard of Xiashu's talent. He made a point of picking Xiashu's paper out for first honors. (*Secret searches make sure that talent does not go unrecognized.*) He presented Xiashu's paper to Emperor Dezong, who personally wrote the inscriptions awarding him the *zhuangyuan* degree. Xiashu's fame having been established long before, everyone accepted the justice of the choice when the list of successful candidates was publicized. In keeping with tradition, those who had passed the examinations were led through the streets on horseback for three days, treated to a grand banquet at Qujiang Pavilion, and taken to Great Wild Goose Tower to inscribe their names on the wall. The emperor made Xiashu a historiographer of the Hanlin Academy and a drafter of imperial decrees. After thanking the emperor, Xiashu wrote a letter home and sent an attendant to bring his wife, Bai-shi, to the capital to share his wealth and eminent status.

In the meantime, Bai-shi was at home, counting the days on her fingers. The day of the examination over, she eagerly awaited good news. One day, she was in her bedchamber when she heard a commotion in front of the house. Quickly she told Cuiqiao to go and find out what it was all about. Indeed, a messenger from the capital was there, announcing the good news. Upon asking for details and learning that her husband had come out first in the examinations, Bai-shi clapped her hand to her forehead in a gesture of joy and bowed in gratitude to heaven. She then prepared wine and food in honor of the messenger. In an instant, the news spread all over town. All members of the Bai clan came to offer their congratulations. Bai Changji, who had been so dismissive of Xiashu, now had the cheek to come to offer congratulations, laden with gifts. Being a virtuous woman who remembered people for their kindnesses rather than their insults to her, Bai-shi put the past behind her, for he was after all a brother born of the same parents, and she was beside herself with joy upon seeing him. Now that he had insinuated himself into her good graces again, Bai Changji did not let one day go by without coming to dance attendance on her. Even some relatives who had never associated with her and had been quite distant and aloof now descended on her house to wait on her hand and foot. In fact, they only made her busier as she played the hostess. The attendant sent by Xiashu, who had been traveling posthaste to Luoyang, now arrived and, with a deep bow, presented the letter to Bai-shi. Bai-shi opened it and saw a poem at the end of the letter. The poem said:

> *Yours truly in the magnificent capital*
> *Has been awarded glittering robes of silver.*
> *A word to the poor woman at the loom:*
> *You may now look up at Su Qin with pride.*[18]

When she finished reading, Bai-shi said with a smile, "So he wants me to go to the capital." She told the bearer of the letter to stay and chose an auspicious day to start on the journey. The prefectural government assigned a boatman to her and, on the day of departure, all kith and kin came for a send-off feast in her honor. Bai Changji personally escorted his sister to the capital. Xiashu led them into his official residence in the yamen. In the exuberance of their joy as the husband and wife met, Bai Changji stepped forward and apologized. Xiashu, with his magnanimous mind, did not bear the slightest grudge against his brother-in-law. A family banquet was set out, but of this, no more.

As it turned out, Emperor Dezong passed away that year. With the support of officials of the court, Emperor Shunzong succeeded to the throne. In less than half a year, Emperor Shunzong also passed away. Emperor Xianzong assumed the throne and changed the reign title to Yuanhe. In the fourth month of the first year of the new reign period, Xiashu became a Hanlin academician while retaining his position as drafter of imperial edicts. You may well wonder why he was promoted so rapidly. Well, the imperial edicts left behind by the deceased emperors and the edicts by the succeeding emperor—four edicts in total— were all composed by Xiashu. These being major pieces of writing from the imperial court, Xiashu was thus eligible for promotion on an exceptional basis. In the fifth month of the year, the emperor issued a decree of general amnesty throughout the land. Xiashu took this opportunity and asked to be the announcer of the amnesty. He and his wife thus had a chance to return to Luoyang in all their glory. Their relatives went to a spot ten li from the city to greet them. Prefectural and county officials also went out of the city gate to welcome them.

Once back at home, Xiashu burned yellow sacrificial papers and paid homage at the ancestral grave site, slaughtered a pig and a sheep, and held a celebration banquet to which he invited all relatives and neighbors. In the midst of the drinking, he recalled his vow at Longhua Monastery and donated Wei Gao's gift of ten thousand taels of gold and a thousand bolts of Shu brocade to the monastery for renovation of the various halls. An auspicious day was then chosen for the groundbreaking ceremony of the construction project. Bai Minzhong resigned from his post as director of the grand secretariat and returned to Luoyang, his hometown. Bai Juyi, having been newly appointed as prefect of Hangzhou, was also in Luoyang on his way to his new duty station. Both of them went to congratulate Xiashu and both gave generously to the project. Prefectural and county officials, eager to curry favor with Xiashu, all came to offer their help with the construction. Soon the project was completed and Longhua Monastery stood in greater grandeur than ever before. Behold:

> The grand monastery towers against the sky;
> The imposing gate dwarfs the jambu trees.

Having served for so many years as the garrison commander of the Shu region, Wei Gao grew afraid that, since he was getting on in years, he might not be able to cope with any insurgencies of the southwestern tribes and might thus compromise his reputation. Therefore he wrote a memorandum to the court, stating his intention to retire and recommending Xiashu as his successor. Consequently, an imperial decree was issued, saying, "After long years of distinguished service as garrison commander of the Shu region, Wei Gao is hereby awarded the title of Guanglu Grand Master,[19] assistant prime minister, grand councilor, and Duke of Xiang, and is to report to this court. Dugu Xiashu, having served the emperor well in his capacity as drafter of imperial edicts and having won general praises for his versatile talents, is hereby granted the position of secretary of the minister of defense as well as regional commander of Xichuan. He is to assume the post without delay."

The scroll of decree in hand, Xiashu immediately set out on the journey with his wife, so as not to be late in reporting for duty. Before they had covered half of the distance, they encountered the officers Wei Gao had dispatched to greet them and take them to Kui prefecture for the handover ceremony. The Temple of the Divine Maiden of Mount Wu being right by the seat of Kui Prefecture, Xiashu and Bai-shi proceeded first to the temple, which lay on the way, to offer incense in gratitude to the divine maiden for the dreams. Then Xiashu went to see Wei Gao. After exchanging the usual amenities, Wei Gao handed over the official seal to him and briefed him on all of the items of military administrative business. Mr. Wei then hosted a feast paid for by the government. Later that day, Xiashu treated Wei Gao to a meal in return. The next morning, he assembled a cavalcade for Wei Gao for his journey to the capital.

After assuming office, Xiashu applied himself assiduously to his duties maintaining order in the region. With the army and the civilians enjoying peace, his fame spread even wider. The imperial court repeatedly commended and awarded him, granting him the titles of grand guardian, grand secretary of the Ministry of Personnel as well as the Ministry of Defense, and Duke of Weiguo. Bai-shi was granted the title of Lady of Weiguo. The husband and wife lived together to a ripe old age and their descendants thrived. There is a poem in testimony:

> *Dreams arise from what occurs in the day;*
> *Dreams are real when the heart is sincere.*
> *Mock not the dreamer for taking flights of fancy;*
> *Those who do are in fact bigger fools.*

Magistrate Xue Proves His Divinity through a Fish

> *What made the white dragon acquire fish scales?*
> *Isn't a vast river its rightful home?*
> *When it loses its power to command rain and clouds,*
> *It may well be trapped in a puddle.*
> *To attain divinity in one's mind,*
> *And be able to change shape at will,*
> *One must learn about the impermanent void.*
> *Not that joy is a benighted state:*
> *Just as Zhuangzi dreamed of a butterfly,*
> *Xue Wei changed into a fish.*[1]

As the story goes, during the Qianyuan reign period [758–59] under Emperor Suzong of the Tang dynasty, there lived a man named Xue Wei, a native of Wu County and a *jinshi* who had passed the civil service examinations at the national level in the last year of the Tianbao reign period [742–56]. After he acquired fame in his first official position as marshal of Fufeng County, he rose to be assistant magistrate of Qingcheng County in the Shu region [approximately present-day Sichuan]. His wife, Gu-shi, came from the most eminent clan in the Wu region. She was not only fair to look upon and graceful in her bearing, but also sweet and gentle in her temperament. The husband and wife were deeply attached to each other and held each other in great respect.

All too quickly, three years had elapsed since Xue Wei had assumed his post as assistant magistrate. When the magistrate received a promotion and vacated his post, the superiors, impressed by Xue Wei's integrity and ability, handed over the county seal to him. Qingcheng County being located in a remote hilly region with infertile land, the crop failures over the previous few years had further impoverished the local people, and robbers and thieves ran amok. After he took over the county seal, Xue Wei established mutual security units in the villages, which pooled their efforts in bringing the criminals to justice. He also set up schools to provide tuition-free education and opened the public granary for the benefit of orphans and widows. In spring, he went from village to village, inspecting the work of the farmers in the sowing season and, with many kindly words, exhorting them to honest ways of living. As a result, crops did well throughout the county and robbers and thieves mended their ways. Indeed, under Xue Wei's governance, there was no need to bolt the door at night, for burglary was nonexistent, and no one picked up and pocketed anything lost on the road. In their gratitude, the local people made up a song in praise of Xue Wei's virtues:

> *In autumn, harvest; in spring, plough and till.*
> *Tax collectors need not press for payment;*
> *Doors need not be bolted day or night;*
> *The people live and work in contentment;*
> *Schools thrive in pursuit of the civil arts;*
> *To Mr. Xue is owed life and enlightenment.*
> *Of the children named after him,*
> *Some are called Xue'er [Son], some Xuesun [Grandson].*

Assistant Magistrate Xue loved the people as he would his own children. He was not only full of integrity, prudence, benevolence, and kindness but was also modest, respectful, and generous in his associations with his colleagues in the county government—the director and two county marshals. The director, Zou Pang, was a good friend of his and also a *jinshi* who had passed the examinations in the same year he had. The two county marshals, Lei Ji and Pei Kuan, like the director, were officials of absolute integrity. Sharing the same views and interests, the three of them often got together in their spare time to talk about poetry or play chess or enjoy a cup of wine by a flowerbed or a bamboo fence. They saw a great deal of each other's company and were the best of friends.

One evening, Assistant Magistrate Xue enjoyed a fine dinner with his wife in his official residence in celebration of the seventh evening of the seventh moon.[2] This is a time when every family, rich or poor, prepares wine and fruit for a feast to pray for skills in needlework. Why pray for skills in needlework? Well, the god of heaven has a daughter, called the Weaving Maiden Star, who kept herself busy at her loom day and night. Out of love for her industriousness, the god of heaven married her to the Herdboy Star. To her father's dismay, once married, Weaving Maiden gave herself up to the pleasures of the conjugal life and spent her time at her dressing table rather than at the loom. The god of heaven fumed with anger. As punishment, he ordered that she live east of the Heavenly River [the Milky Way] and the Herdboy Star live west of the river. They are allowed to meet only once a year on the seventh day of the seventh lunar month. On that day, by order of the god of heaven, magpies form a bridge over the river to let them cross. At the hour of the crossing, humans down on earth try to make colored threads go through needles' eyes by the light of the moon and the stars. Those able to do so will be inspired in their needlework.

Those who fail will not be as inspired. This is how the occasion is used to predict one's luck in needlework in the next year. Now, come to think of it, after eagerly looking forward throughout the year to this roughly eight-hour reunion, wouldn't Herdboy and Weaving Maiden be too busy talking about how they missed each other to bless human beings with needlework skills? The absurdity of it all!

And so Magistrate Xue and his wife spent that evening toasting each other in the courtyard. Before they knew it, the night had deepened, and they went to bed. As it turned out, Magistrate Xue caught a cold. Hot from head to foot as if burned by charcoal, he found himself awash in sweat. Gradually he lost all appetite for the three meals of the day, and his spirits sagged. He kept saying, "I can't get through one more moment. Why do you keep me here? Why don't you just let me go?"

Now, won't you agree that it is not a good sign if a patient says such things? Gu-shi was frightened out of her wits. She could not very well watch him die, could she? Naturally, she engaged physicians, consulted fortune-tellers, prayed, and made pledges to gods.

In the county there was a Qingcheng Hill, which was the fifth dwelling of Daoist immortals. The temple atop the hill, with a statue of the supreme patriarch Laozi, was most responsive to prayers, whether they were for sunny days or for rain, for a boy or for a girl. The temple had therefore the largest crowd of worshipers making offerings. So Gu-shi wrote a prayer and sent a servant to the temple with it. Having heard that divination by drawing bamboo slips was most accurate, she told the servant to draw a divination slip in addition to praying for continued blessings for her husband and an end to ill luck. Upon hearing about this, the assistant magistrate's three colleagues also climbed up the hill to offer incense, wearing white robes and belts with decorations made of rhinoceros horn. They were willing to shorten their own life spans in exchange for prolongation of the magistrate's life. They had barely left the temple when large numbers of villagers led by the elders throughout the county arrived and dropped to their knees in supplication. Clearly, Magistrate Xue's good service to the people had won their hearts and minds. The bamboo slip drawn was numbered thirty-two. On it were inscribed these lines:

> A hundred clear springs flow into the river;
> The water chills the soul of the dreamer.
> Why bother to go to Dragon Gate?
> There is a divine fish three feet long.

The servant copied the inscription and returned to the Xue residence to show it to Gu-shi. Quite baffled by these lines, she thought, "They say that these divinations are all as accurate as if the gods were face to face with the one whose fate is being asked. But this divination talks about some fish that's totally unrelated to my husband's illness. There's no way of knowing if this portends good or evil." Feeling as if on pins and needles, she sank into deeper gloom. Then she thought, "Well, since the divination didn't work out, let me engage a physician. That would be the more proper thing to do." Right away, she sent someone to find a good physician. As it turned out, there was in Chengdu Prefecture a Daoist priest called Li Eight Hundred, who claimed that he was the best student of Sage Sun, from whom he had inherited eight hundred secret prescriptions from the Dragon Palace.[3] That was how he came to be called by all and sundry "Li Eight Hundred." According to his patients, he was so divinely inspired that one touch of his hand was enough to cure them. On his door he posted a couplet that said,

My herbs, as were Han Kang's, are fixed in price;[4]
Like Dong Feng, I plant a thousand apricot trees.[5]

He rarely accepted invitations for house calls. If he did, the patient stood a good chance of survival. The kind of payment he asked for also marked him out from other physicians. In some cases, he demanded several hundred taels of silver before he even opened his medicine box. In other cases, even after the patients recovered, he asked for nothing but a few drinks until he succumbed to the influence of the liquor. There were cases where he would go as soon as he was invited, and cases where he would refuse to go, however pressing the invitation. Thus he was quite unpredictable. But in general, he was willing to go on a house call if the patient sincerely believed in him.

Upon hearing of Li Eight Hundred, Gu-shi immediately sent a messenger, along with gifts, to bring him over posthaste. Being a resident in the same prefecture, Mr. Li arrived soon enough, to Gu-shi's slight relief. However, no sooner had he entered the house than he said, without even taking the patient's pulse, "He may look like he's going to die, but he won't. Why bring me over?"

Gu-shi told him the circumstances in which her husband had fallen ill and the divination from the temple of Laozi, and asked him for a prescription. Li Eight Hundred snorted and said, "This is an illness that has never found its way into a medical book, nor do I have a prescription for it. The only thing you can do is to feel his chest every now and then after he dies. As long as his chest does not turn cold, do not put him in a coffin. In about half a month or twenty days, he will want some intake of food. And then he'll gradually wake up. The divination from the temple will turn out to be accurate, but it'll only be proven so later on. It's not something anyone can guess correctly at this point." Still refusing to prescribe medicine, he abruptly took himself off. There was no way of knowing whether the magistrate would indeed pull through without medicine or whether this was the physician's pretext because the patient was already too far gone for any medicine to work. Indeed,

A green dragon and a white tiger
Bring either joy or luck, when together.[6]

With Li Eight Hundred gone, Gu-shi said in lament, "Even such a famous doctor refuses to prescribe medicine. Would there be anyone else who dares to do so?

This can only mean that the illness is too far advanced. There's nothing to do except wait for death."

The magistrate's fever lasted for seven days and nights, and his condition went from bad to worse. All of a sudden, he fell into a coma. His eyes closed; he did not wake up however loudly his name was called. Sobbingly, Gu-shi sent a servant to enlist the help of his three colleagues in making preparations for the funeral. It just so happened that they were on their way at that very moment to inquire after his health. At the news of his death, they all broke down in tears. They hastened into the Xue residence and wept by the corpse. They then went to see Gu-shi and tried to assuage her grief. As the autumn season had just begun, the weather was still warm, so they went at once separately to make preparations for funeral clothes and the coffin. On the third day, when everything was ready for the body to be laid into the coffin, Gu-shi found, when weeping by the corpse, that the chest was indeed still slightly warm. Therefore she gave full credence to Priest Li's words and insisted that the body be left in the bed.

The servants said, "A dead person's chest does remain warm for three or four days after death. It doesn't turn cold as soon as the breathing stops. This means nothing. And the weather is still hot in this seventh month of the year. If it thunders, the corpse will become too bloated to fit into the coffin."

Gu-shi rejoined, "Priest Li said that the body must not be put into the coffin as long as the chest doesn't turn cold. Since his chest is still warm, even if we don't believe Priest Li, we should still wait for half a month or twenty days. How can we have the heart to put him in a coffin in less than three days when he's still warm? Since the coffin is ready, let me wait here alone by his body. There'll be enough time to put him in the coffin as soon as his chest turns cold. Oh heavens! May Priest Li be proven right about my husband's revival! Saving my husband's life will mean saving my life as well!"

To everyone's exhortation to the contrary, Gu-shi turned a deaf ear. Failing to win the argument, they had to give in to her wish. Magistrate Xue's body was left in bed for her to keep watch over, and there we shall leave her for now.

Let us retrace our steps. On the seventh day after he fell ill, Xue felt so hot that, unable to endure another moment of such misery, he wished with all his heart to go to a cool place to reduce his body heat, so that he might still stand a chance of recovery. Quietly, he picked up a bamboo cane and sneaked out of the room without asking for a servant to follow him. His wife and his colleagues were none the wiser. In a trice, he was out of the city gate. As happy as a bird out of the cage and a fish out of the net, he forgot all about his illness.

You may well ask, being an official, how was he able to leave the yamen premises without anyone's knowledge? Well, he was so desperate in his wishes that a dream had come to him. While his soul was having these sensations in the dream, his body remained in his bed without budging. As his wife kept vigil and wept day and night, hoping for his revival from death, he, the dreamer, was floating in air, free from all cares in a moment of joy amid misery. (*Zhuangzi said, how do I know if the dead don't regret their death and start praying for life again? Those who are enlightened transcend life and death and are thus free from misery and joy.*)

After leaving South Gate, Magistrate Xue headed for the mountains and stopped on a hill called Long'an [Dragon Peace] Hill on top of which stood a pavilion built by Emperor Wen of the Sui dynasty on the occasion of granting his son Yang Xiu the title of King of Shu. Named "Summer Retreat Pavilion," it was surrounded on all sides by dense woods and tall bamboo and fanned continuously by breezes from all four directions but unlit by the slightest ray of the sun. Therefore, every summer, the king of Shu took his guests here for relief from the heat. Upon reaching this cool spot, Assistant Magistrate Xue instantly felt refreshed. "If I hadn't gone out of the city, how would I ever have known there was such a nice spot in the mountains? If I haven't ever been here before in all the years I've been living in Qingcheng County, I don't think my three colleagues know about this place, either. How I wish to meet them here and bring a jar of wine for a feast celebrating the relief from the heat! Too bad they are not here to share the joy with me!" Inspired by the delightful scenery, he wrote a poem:

> *In a stolen moment of leisure,*
> *I climb up the steep ladder and tall cliff.*
> *Though the gates of heaven are close at hand,*
> *Do not let me be borne away by the wind.*

After sitting for a while in the pavilion, he pressed on. The mountain path was unrelieved by any shade from the sun and there was none of the cool pleasant air of the pavilion. And so, the longer he walked, the more suffocated he felt. After walking for more than ten li, he saw a big river looming ahead. What river was it? Well, the great Yu of high antiquity dredged the Min River out of Mount Min as one of his projects of water control and, after passing Maozhou and Weizhou [in present-day Sichuan], dredged this river, called the Tuo River. To this day, giant iron chains can be seen hanging from the banks, and they go all the way to the bottom of the river. Goodness knows how long they are. This is where the great Yu locked up the winged dragon. When working on his water-control projects, Yu called for the winged dragon's service wherever the watercourse was blocked. With one shake of its tail, any high mountain or giant rock hundreds of li in circumference would instantly split apart. That is why the great Yu is also known to all and sundry as "the Divine Yu." If he had not been able to enlist the service of this dragon, he would not have brought the floods under control within eight years. To this day, an iron chain can also be seen in the Si River, locking up the monkey-shaped water god, just as the winged dragon is chained in the Tuo River. Both had rendered service in the water-control projects but are now under chains so that they will not come out to wreak havoc. Aren't these nothing less than holy sites?

While he was feeling suffocated, walking on the mountain path in his feverish condition, Assistant Magistrate Xue suddenly saw the Tuo River down below. Indeed, the vast expanse of autumn water joined the sky at the horizon. Instantly, he had a cool sensation that went straight into his bones. Taking what would be the space of three regular steps in one, he ran forward with the speed of a windmill, little knowing that even though the river appeared near enough when viewed from above, it was in fact far, as he realized when he was down on level ground. There lay between him and the river a large East Pond with water as clear as a mirror, so clear that the bottom was visible even at places where the water was deep, and the bamboo and trees around the pond were reflected in the water. It was indeed a charming autumn scene. The magistrate took off his clothes and plunged into the pond for a bath. Being a native of the Wu region, which abounds in rivers and lakes, he had learned to swim in early childhood but had not had a chance to swim after attaining adulthood. He was overjoyed that a long-cherished wish to play in water was now fulfilled. Suddenly, he said with a sigh, "Human beings can't swim as well as fish. How I wish I could borrow some fish scales, so that I could swim everywhere! Oh, the joy of it!" (*Strange thoughts, to be followed by strange events.*)

A little fish nearby said, looking at him, "To change into a fish is nothing hard to do. Why borrow scales? Let me speak to the river god on your behalf." Before it had quite gotten the words out, it disappeared. In astonishment, the magistrate thought, "I didn't know that the pond was inhabited by goblins. I must not swim all by myself in it. I'd better leave this place, and the sooner, the better!"

As it turned out, once the magistrate entertained the notion of being a fish, he became obligated to clear some karmic encumbrances. Indeed,

> He shed his clothes for relief from fatigue;
> Fish scales soon grew over him in the water.

Xue was thinking about putting his clothes on and turning back when, suddenly, the little fish appeared to report, "Congratulations! The river god has already issued a decree." In the meantime, a man with a fish head came up, riding on a large fish amid a procession of numerous small fish, and this was the decree the fish-headed man read out:

> *Those who inhabit the cities are of quite a different order from those who live in water. If humans were not fond of eating fish, the paths of humans and fish would never cross. You, Xue Wei, a native of Wu, in your sinecure as assistant magistrate of Qingcheng County, took delight in the vast clear river and swam freely in it. In your disgust of the hustle and bustle of the human world, you shed your clothes and bade farewell to it. You are hereby granted scales so that you can lead a temporary, rather than permanent, existence as a red carp in East Pond. Alas! If you wander too far and forget to return, you will be subject to punishment by divine will. If you swallow bait and get caught by fishhooks, you will*

perish under the kitchen knife. Do not put us to shame and let yourself be caught! Mark my words!

After listening to the decree, Xue looked down and saw that he had become a carp with golden scales. Although appalled at the sight, he thought, "Since things have come to this, let me have some fun first and enjoy what an aquatic life has to offer." From that time on, he swam at his own sweet will in any river and lake that took his fancy. However, since the decree of the river god specified that he was to be a red carp of East Pond, he returned to East Pond to rest after each excursion, as if East Pond were his home. ([Illegible.] *live beings* [Illegible.] *will have karmic encumbrances. Therefore the Buddhist doctrine is wisest.*) This alone made him feel slightly dissatisfied.

A few days later, the little fish came again and said to Xue, "Haven't you heard that in Pingyang Prefecture of Shanxi, there is a Dragon Gate Hill made when the Great Yu was bringing floods under control? The Yellow River is right under that hill. Because the water at the top of that hill joins the heavenly river and plunges down to be the source of the Yellow River, the spot is called River Joint. It being the eighth month now, the autumn rains will soon be upon us after the thunder stops. Every carp everywhere will want to go there and try to jump over Dragon Gate.[7] Why don't you ask the river god for permission to join the procession to Dragon Gate? If you succeed, you'll be a dragon. Won't that be better than being a carp?"

Assistant Magistrate Xue had, in fact, grown restless in his life in East Pond and his heart leaped for joy at this news. Right away, he took leave of the little fish and headed straight for the river god's palace. Behold! In the palace, the pillars were made of coral and the beams of hawksbill turtle shells. Indeed, the treasures of the water palace were of a different order from those of the human world. From all the bodies of water under the rule of the river god—Min River, Tuo River, Ba River, Yu River, Fu River, Qian River, Pingqiang River, Shehong River, Zhuojin River, Jialing River, Qingyi River, Wu Stream, Lu Creek, Seven Gate Beach, and the Three Qutang Gorges—came carp to inform the river god about their wish to jump over Dragon Gate.

Being the only carp with golden scales, Xue was elected by all as the leader in the river god's audience with all of them. According to the rules of the palace, there was to be a grand banquet, just like the banquet in honor of candidates for the civil service examination prior to their departure. After partaking of the banquet and thanking the river god for his kindness, Xue and the carp from all over went together for an attempt at jumping over Dragon Gate. To their disappointment, they failed and returned home, each with a red dot on its forehead. Why a red dot on the forehead? Because when a carp is trying to go up against the stream and jump clear of Dragon Gate, all its blood and energy go up to its head and leave a mark on its forehead, as if from a vermilion brush-pen. That is why one who fails the civil service examinations is said to have a red dot on his fore-head. Truly,

> *The surging waves defy attempts to jump over Dragon Gate Hill;*
> *A red dot shows on the forehead—a reminder of one's failure.*

Now, in Qingcheng County there lived a fisherman, Zhao Gan by name. He and his wife made a living by catching fish in the Tuo River with a net. To their dismay, a giant soft-shelled turtle got into their net. It swam off with the net and almost dragged Zhao Gan into the river. His wife grumbled, "This net is our only means of livelihood. Now that it's gone, our business goes with it. We have no money to buy another net. And the county officials come every so often to collect fish. What are you going to give them?" And so she went on throughout the night.

Unable to hold out any longer against her nagging, Zhao Gan equipped him-self with a fishing rod in preparation for a fishing trip to East Pond. Why did he prefer a pond to a big river? Well, the water of the Tuo River was too rapid for a fishing rod, now that he had lost his net. That was why he thought of moving to East Pond. Once there, he fixed a large piece of fragrant oily dough onto the fish-ing hook and dipped the line into the water.

In the meantime, after returning from Dragon Gate with a red dot on his fore-head, Xue gloomily hid himself in East Pond for several days in a row without ven-turing out to look for food, and was ravenously hungry. When Zhao Gan's fishing boat approached, he couldn't help but swim along the boat to see what was up. As he swam along, he felt tempted by the good smell of the bait. He was on the point of biting into the bait when a thought struck him: "I should know all too well that there is a hook behind the bait. If I swallow the bait, won't I be caught? I am a fish only temporarily just for the fun of it. Can't I go to other places for food? Why do I have to take that bait?" (*Fragrant bait entices fish just as fame and riches entice humans.*)

As he made another circle around the boat, he found himself unable to resist the intense aroma that assailed his nostrils. Hunger got the better of him. He thought, "I'm a human being. How can this little hook bear my weight? Even if I'm caught, how can he, fisherman Zhao Gan, not know that I'm the third-most-important official in the county? He'll surely take me to the county yamen. What harm can there be if I eat the bait?" So thinking, he took a bite at the bait. Before he had time to swallow it, Zhao Gan pulled him up. This is a case of "He sees the danger but yields to hunger."

Having caught a three-foot-long carp with golden scales, Zhao Gan clapped a hand to his forehead and cried, "This is my lucky day! If I can catch a few more fish like this one, I'll have enough money to buy another net!"

"Zhao Gan!" shouted Xue. "You're a fisherman in my county. Take me to the county yamen, quick!"

Instead of answering, Zhao Gan passed a straw rope through the gills of the fish and laid it in the cabin.

His wife said, "With messengers from the county government coming so often to collect fish, if one of them sees such a big fish, how much do you think they'll pay us at the official rate? We'd better hide it among the reeds and sell it to some fishmonger who comes here. That way, we'll be able to make a few more pennies."

"Good point!" said Zhao Gan. He hid the fish in the reeds and covered the spot with a tattered straw poncho. Then he returned and said to his wife, "If we can get a better price for it, I'll buy some wine and have a good drink with you. Let's pray for good luck tonight. Maybe I'll catch two more tomorrow!"

Soon after Zhao Gan hid the fish and returned to his boat, a county lictor called Zhang Bi came and said to him, "Marshal Pei wants a big fish to poach in spicy sauce. I went to look for you this morning along the bank of the Tuo River, but you've moved here! I've been running all around looking for you until I'm all sweaty and short of breath. Now pick a big one for me and go with me to the yamen."

"I'm sorry I put you to so much trouble. It's not that I want to move over here. It's just that I lost my net the other day and have no money to buy another one. So I had no choice but to come here and angle a few fish to sell. But I didn't get any big ones. I only have three to four catties of small fish here. You can take them all."

"Mr. Pei wants a big fish. I can't go back to him with small ones."

With a plop Zhang Bi jumped down into the cabin and raised the lid of the hold. Indeed, the fish there were all small. He was about to take them to Marshal Pei, fifth in command, when he thought, "This is such a large pond. Can there really be no large fish? This fellow must have craftily hidden them somewhere." He got on shore and looked around but still found nothing. But then, among the reeds, he saw a tattered straw poncho flopping up and down. Believing that there must be fish underneath, he rushed forward and lifted the poncho. What should he see but a three-foot-long carp with golden scales!

Zhao Gan and his wife cried out in anguish. Ignoring their protest, Zhang Bi set off with the fish. As he walked along, he turned back his head and said to Zhao Gan, "A fine job you did, trying to fool me! Let me report to Mr. Pei and have you beaten up!"

Assistant Magistrate Xue shouted at the top of his voice, "Zhang Bi! Zhang Bi! Don't you recognize me? I went swimming in East Pond and changed into a fish just to have a good time. Why do you not bow to me but carry me in your hand?"

Xue's words fell on unhearing ears. Fish in hand, Zhang Bi strode all the way to the county yamen, followed by Zhao Gan. All the while, Assistant Magistrate Xue kept up a stream of curses. When they reached the city gate, a guard, Hu Jian, said to Zhang Bi, "What a big fish! Mr. Pei is hosting a dinner and is waiting for a fish to make spicy poached fish out of it. You were gone for so long that he tossed out another bamboo slip to remind you of your job. Make haste!"

Raising his head, Xue saw that he was at the south gate, Yingxun Gate, through which he had so recently left the city. He shouted at the guard of the gate, "Hu

Jian! Hu Jian! When I left this gate the other day, I said to you, 'I'm going out for a walk. Don't report to my colleagues and don't send anyone to bring me back.' It's been less than a month and you already forgot that? Now is the time for you to report to my colleagues and make arrangements for someone to greet me. How can you turn up your nose at me like this? The audacity!"

To his exasperation, again his words fell on unhearing ears. Fish in hand, Zhang Bi strode right into the yamen compound. While still ranting and raving, Assistant Magistrate Xue saw inside the gate a treasury clerk and a law enforcement clerk playing chess, one facing east and the other facing west.

The clerk of the treasury office said, "How frightening! Such a giant fish! It should weigh more than ten catties."

The clerk of the law enforcement office commented, "What a lively golden carp! It should be kept in the Green Ripple Pond in the backyard for viewers' enjoyment. How can anyone have the heart to serve it on the dinner table?"

Assistant Magistrate Xue cried out again, "Hey, the two of you who work for me every day in the tribunal! Even though I've changed into a fish, you should still recognize me! (*Since he's a fish now, how can he expect anyone to recognize him? Stupid! Stupid!*) Why don't you stand up in my presence and announce me to your superiors?"

The two clerks went on playing chess, for they heard nothing. Xue thought, "As the saying goes, 'Fear not just any official. Fear only those who officiate over you!' Is it because there's nothing I can do to them that they're not afraid of me? Was my post abolished during my absence? But even if it was, I haven't left my duty station. I'm still their supervisor. Let me tell my colleagues about them and have them put to the rod!" Dear audience, please remember what he said and listen to what unfolds in the next installment.

Now, after keeping vigil for more than twenty days over her husband's corpse, Gu-shi found no sign of any change for the worse all over his body. In fact, his chest felt warmer than before to the touch of her hand. Gradually, the warmth extended to his throat in one direction and to his belly in the other. Recalling Priest Li's words, which had now been proven to some degree, she pricked her fingers until blood came out and wrote a prayer with her blood. She then engaged several well-known priests and had them hold a service in the temple of Laozi on Qingcheng Hill to pray for a divine formula for her husband's revival. She also pledged to have the temple renovated and the statues gilded. On the day the prayer was read aloud, Xue's three colleagues and all the clerks and the people throughout the county burned incense and said their own prayers, just as they had done before. As I recall, the ancients had a saying, "Heaven looks after the virtuous." With officials and the people of the whole county praying for him, Heaven could hardly ignore an official as good as Assistant Magistrate Xue. There was only one difficulty in reviving a man who had been dead for more than twenty days: Although promises made in the temple of Laozi are never unfulfilled, the king of the netherworld never sends back to the mortal world a dead person who has already registered with him! Indeed,

> *Be advised that good deeds must be repaid in kind;*
> *Say not that divine power doesn't work.*

That evening, the priest set out on the prayer table seven brightly lit lamps in the shape of the Big Dipper. The seventh star of the Big Dipper, at the tip of the handle, points east in spring, south in summer, west in autumn, and north in winter. The only star of the dipper that does not move around in the sky is the fourth one, called Heavenly Hub. Therefore the lamp placed in the position of the Heavenly Hub Star was assigned as the one representing the fate of Assistant Magistrate Xue. If that lamp remained bright, he would pull through. If it darkened, that meant his condition had turned critical. If it went out, he was beyond hope of recovery. Ritual implements in hand, the priest intoned the incantations and devoutly prayed for the end of Xue's illness. Then he bent over the table for a nap while his soul left his body and flew to the gods of the stars to ask them to let Xue's soul return to the mortal world. When the priest rose from his nap to check the seven lamps, they were seen to be shining brightly, especially the one representing Magistrate Xue, which served to show that he was not meant to die at that time. The priest said, congratulating Gu-shi, "The lamp representing Magistrate Xue being as bright as it is, he will surely come back to life any time now. Do not break down in excessive grief, for it will only disturb his spirits and hinder his return."

With tears in her eyes, she said gratefully, "If he can come back to life, this prayer service will not have been in vain, and the day-and-night vigil will not have been for nothing." Feeling slightly relieved by the priest's words, she involuntarily drifted off to sleep and had a dream in which she saw her husband entering the room in haste, with blood all over his naked body. Covering his neck with both hands, he cried out, "Bad luck! Bad luck! I was riding in a boat down the river, feeling lighthearted, when suddenly, a blast of wind whipped up high waves and capsized the boat. I fell into the water. Luckily I encountered the river god. Considering that my allowed span of life is not yet up, he gave me gold armor and took me out of the water. I was looking for the road into the city when I ran into a bandit who killed me with one swing of his sword in order to have my gold armor. If you still have any regard for your husband, please keep good vigil over my spirits and take me back."

At these words, Gu-shi burst into loud wails of grief and woke up. She thought, "Didn't the priest say that he was not going to die? Why this nightmare? I remember this line from a book about dreams: 'A death in a dream is a life regained.' Perhaps he has broken free from all calamity and troubles, which explains why he was stark naked. Let me just keep good vigil over his body."

The next day, she divided up the offerings on the altar table into three portions and gave them to her husband's three colleagues in an event called "distributing the good luck." Later that day, County Marshal Pei hosted a dinner to which he invited his colleagues. It was an event called "drinking for good luck." That was why Marshal Pei had sent Zhang Bi to the fisherman to buy a big fish to poach in spicy sauce, to go with the wine. Overcome with emotion at the thought of his friendship with Assistant Magistrate Xue, Director Zou, second in command, said in lament, "This dinner is different from any other dinner. We are praying for Mr. Xue's revival, and offerings on the altar make up half of the spread on this table. With Mr. Xue's life or death still hanging in the balance, how can we swallow any of this food?"

Marshal Pei said, "The ancients forbade heaving sighs at the dinner table. You can't be the only one missing your friend who passed the exams the same year you did. Don't we also miss him as a colleague? The priest said he was to come back to life either last night or today. Let's enjoy the fish with the wine. We can wait for news about him as we drink to our hearts' content. Why can't we have it both ways?"

It was already early afternoon when Zhang Bi brought the fish into the yamen and stopped at the dais in the main hall. Marshal Pei, being the host of the dinner, had suspended the drinking to wait for the fish. He was eating a peach and watching Director Zou and Marshal Lei, fourth in command, playing *shuanglu* checkers when suddenly he turned around and saw Zhang Bi. Flying into a rage, he said, "I told you to get fish. What took you so long? If I hadn't issued an order to urge you, you probably wouldn't have come, right?"

Busily kowtowing, Zhang Bi gave a detailed account of how Zhao Gan the fisherman had hidden a big fish, whereupon Marshal Pei had the lictors throw Zhao Gan to the floor and give him fifty lashes with a leather whip. Zhao Gan was beaten until his skin ripped open and blood spurted out. Why, you may ask, hadn't Zhao Gan just made himself scarce earlier? Why did he have to follow Zhang Bi to the county yamen and practically ask for this beating? In fact, he came to get what little payment he could for the fish, but instead, he ended up getting fifty lashes. Of payment he received none. Wasn't he just like the golden carp that had taken his bait? Indeed,

> All are driven by profits in life and in death;
> Hopes are not given up until the last moment.

Marshal Pei drove Zhao Gan out before he looked at what Zhang Bi had brought. Finding it to be a golden carp more than three feet in length, he cried out in delight. "What a nice fish! We can have the cook make us spicy poached fish now!"

Xue shouted at the top of his voice, "I'm no fish! I'm your colleague! How can you not recognize me? I was just going to tell you about all the humiliation I've suffered from so many people so that you can avenge me. But you also take me for a fish and even tell the cook to poach me! Wouldn't I die an unjust death? How can you have no regard for me after we've worked together for all these years?"

His colleagues did not pay him the slightest attention. In desperation, Xue cried out again, "Mr. Zou! The two of us became *jinshi* in the last year of the Tianbao reign period. We were the best of friends during our stay in the capital before we became colleagues in this place. So you are not like the rest of them. How can you say nothing and let me die?"

Director Zou said to Marshal Pei, "The way I see it, this fish shouldn't be served on our table. In front of the temple of Laozi on Qingcheng Hill, there is a large pond where people set free fish, turtles, snails, and clams that they have bought. Since what we're having for today's feast comes from the altar in honor of Magistrate Xue, why don't we put the fish into that Set-Free Pond? It'll be a token of our fellowship with him and the start of future operations of karma."

Marshal Lei chimed in, "Freeing the fish is a good idea! One must believe in the operations of karma. What's more, don't we have enough good wine and food? Why do we need spicy poached fish?"

Having heard these comments, Assistant Magistrate Xue, at his position at the foot of the dais, gave a groan and said, "Mr. Zou my friend should have known better! If he wants to save me, why not just take me home? Why take me all the way up the hill? Won't I get too thirsty? But even so, this will be better than dying by the cook's knife. After I'm put into Set-Free Pond, I'll change back to my true form, put on my official's robe, and run the business of the yamen as before. By that time, how would they, let alone vile characters like Zhao Gan, ever have the nerve to see me?"

While he was thinking these thoughts, Marshal Pei said, "I defer to Mr. Lei's age and the immense kindness of his heart in wanting to free the fish. But the prayer service for Mr. Xue is in the Daoist, not the Buddhist, tradition. This is not the right occasion to care for the operations of karma. Now, all animals are created to nourish human beings. Let's take fish, for example. If fish were not eaten by humans, they would proliferate all over the world and clog up the rivers and block traffic. In practicing virtues, the heart and the mind are more important than the mouth. (*Fallacy!*) As the proverb goes, 'Buddha sits on the heart; wine and meat go through the gut.' Another proverb says, 'To go strictly by the Buddha's laws, refrain from drinking even cold water.' Am I to understand that by eating this fish, we destroy our collegiality with Mr. Xue? Why set such a big fish free for no good reason when it can very well be made into spicy poached fish? How do you know an otter won't eat it if we don't? If it's going to die anyway, it's better that we eat it."

Xue shouted again, "Both your guests want to set me free. Why do you as the host insist on eating me? You're such a stubborn man! You don't even respect your guests, let alone love a colleague."

In fact, Marshal Lei was a man without a mind of his own. With Marshal Pei insisting on eating the fish, Marshal Lei said to Director Zou, "Since Mr. Pei doesn't believe in the operations of karma, it looks like this fish is not going to live. And he's the host today. If he wants to serve it to us guests, we can't very well resist. It's not that we are relentlessly determined to kill it. It's just that its number is up today, and there's no way we can save it."

Xue shouted again, "Mr. Lei! You don't have a mind of your own! How can you argue for both sides like this? If he doesn't listen to your advice to set me free, you should go on talking to him instead of turning around to advise Mr. Zou not to save me. Have you had so little to eat these days and gone without fish for so long that you're looking forward to gorging yourself on the spicy poached fish he promised?"

Then he called out to Magistrate Zou, "My friend! Could you have been just putting on a show of compassion? After saying those few words like a hypocrite, you think you've acquitted yourself and need not say another word. As it is said so well, 'A moment of life or death is a true test of friendship.' If I were not the one about to die and you not the one alive and well, I would never have known what a false-hearted wretch you are! If I'm set free, I'll change back to my former self and write on my door that line by Marshal Zhai, just to show you![8] And by that time, my friend, your regrets will be too late!"

However frantically he shouted, the host and the guests acted as if they had heard nothing. Marshal Pei summoned Wang Shiliang, a master chef who made the best spicy poached fish, and said to him, handing him the fish, "Do a good job, and be quick about it! Otherwise, you'll also get fifty lashes, just as Zhao Gan did!"

While voicing acknowledgment of the order, Wang Shiliang took over the fish.

Assistant Magistrate Xue grew so frantic that his three souls escaped through the top of his head and his seven spirits fled through the soles of his feet. Wailing loudly, he said, "I have been as close to you all as brothers, but why are you so bent on killing me in spite of all my desperate pleas? Ah, I know. You bear me such malice because you are jealous of me in my position as the keeper of the seal. (*So he wouldn't have known this had he not entered the pond and changed into a fish.*) Don't you know that it was those higher up who entrusted the seal to me? I didn't go out of my way to seek it. If you let me go home, I'll immediately give up the seal. What's so hard about that?" He then broke down in a fit of sobbing and, after the sobs subsided, resumed his pleas, but his colleagues remained impervious. Wang Shiliang carried the fish all the way into the kitchen and laid it on a chopping board. Raising his eyes, Magistrate Xue recognized him to be the one who had always cooked for him. "Wang Shiliang," he cried out. "Don't you recognize me, Assistant Magistrate Xue, third in command? If I had not passed on to you those recipes from the Wu region, what would you have cooked to please those colleagues of mine? Out of gratitude for my kindness to you, go quickly to tell my colleagues about this and take me home with due respect. Why put me on a chopping board? What are you going to do?"

To his dismay, Wang Shiliang picked up a knife with his right hand and, oblivious to Xue's tirade, pressed the knife against the fish head.

Seized with rage, Xue lashed out, "You dog! You wait hand and foot on Marshal Pei, but you have no fear of me. Don't you know that I also have power over you?" With an effort, he leaped up and whipped his tail against Wang Shiliang's face, as if slapping him with a hand.

His ears droning, his eyes blurry, Wang Shiliang raised his hands to cover his face. In his panic, he dropped the knife onto the floor. As he picked up the knife, he said with a malicious grin, "Fish! If you're so full of life, let me put you in boiling water in a moment. You can have fun swimming there!"

In preparing spicy poached fish, you need first and foremost a sharp knife with which to cut the fish into slices as thin as snowflakes. Then, you stir the slices quickly in boiling water, dredge them up, and add spices and sesame oil. Thus prepared, the fish can't be other than fluffy, crisp, and delicious. So Wang Shiliang set about grinding his knife.

Getting no response from the chef however frantically he screamed, Xue said with a sigh, "After he comes back with his knife all sharpened, it'll be all over with me. When I was gravely ill at home, I could in fact put up with the misery. But I sneaked out of the house, only to go through such sufferings! How I wish I hadn't seen that East Pond! Even if I saw the pond, I shouldn't have gone in for a bath. Even if I had taken a bath in it, I shouldn't have entertained the thought of changing into a fish. Even if I did think of turning into a fish, I shouldn't have accepted the river god's edict and I wouldn't have landed myself in such a pass. But before I changed into a fish, there was that little fish egging me on. After I changed into a fish, there was that Zhao Gan enticing me with bait. Everything is in my fate. I brought all this on myself. How can I blame it on others? How sad that my wife at home has no children to support her. I wish I could send her a message so that I could die in peace." As he was wailing, Wang Shiliang cut off the fish head with one single hack of his sharpened knife. Indeed, when still breathing, who would resign himself to being a loser? When death strikes, everything disappears as a spring dream. (*Thought-provoking words.*) This time, it looks like Magistrate Xue is indeed going to breathe his last.

> Before we know whether he will revive,
> We see the fish perish under the knife.

The very instant Wang Shiliang cut off the fish head, Assistant Magistrate Xue in his residence abruptly sat up in his bed. (*The Buddhist karma is infallible.*) Being a woman, Gu-shi was almost frightened out of her wits, but even all the men keeping vigil there were also appalled. Shaking their heads and clicking their tongues, they exclaimed, "How very strange! We've been keeping tight watch here. No cat has jumped over his body. How come the corpse suddenly sat up?"[9]

Xue heaved a sigh and asked, "How many days has it been since I lost consciousness?"

"Don't frighten me like this!" exclaimed his wife. "You've been dead for twenty-five days. I was afraid you might not come to."

"I didn't die! I only had a dream. But I had no idea the dream lasted for so many days!" Turning to a servant, he said, "Go to my three colleagues. They are now in the main hall of the yamen, about to eat spicy poached fish. Tell them to put down their chopsticks and come here immediately. I have something to say to them."

Sure enough, the servant found his master's three colleagues drinking wine in the main hall. Spicy poached fish had just been set on the table. They were about to raise their chopsticks when the servant said, "Magistrate Xue has come back to life. Please do not eat the fish yet. Please go to Magistrate Xue's residence now. He wants to talk to you."

The three men jumped in astonishment. "So, Physician Li Eight Hundred's diagnosis and the lamps in the temple of Laozi have been proven right!" they cried. They dashed off to Xue's residential quarters and said, "Congratulations! Congratulations!"

Xue said, "Do all three of you know that I was that very golden carp of which the spicy poached fish was made? If Wang Shiliang had not brought down his knife on me, there'd be no telling when I would have woken up from my dream." (*It thus appears that not all forms are real. Only nature is real.*)

Quite mystified, the three officials said, "Has anyone ever heard of such a thing under the sun? Pray tell us what happened. We're all ears!"

Xue said, "When Zhang Bi came with the fish, Director Zou and Marshal Lei were playing *shuanglu* checkers and Marshal Pei was eating a peach off to one side. Zhang Bi reported that Zhao Gan the fisherman had hidden the big fish and tried to fob him off with small fish. Marshal Pei flew into a rage and ordered that Zhao Gan be given fifty lashes of the whip. Am I right?"

"Yes, you're right," said the three of them. "But how could you have known all these details?"

Xue continued, "Summon Zhao Gan, Zhang Bi, Hu Jian the guard at Yingxun Gate, the treasury clerk, the law enforcement office clerk, and Wang Shiliang the cook. Let me question them."

Soon all of them were brought into the main hall.

"Zhao Gan," said Xue. "When you were fishing in East Pond, you caught a three-foot-long carp with golden scales. Your wife told you to hide it among the reeds and cover it with a tattered straw poncho. When Zhang Bi came for fish, you said you had no big ones, but Zhang Bi found it and carried it to Yingxun Gate. Hu Jian the guard said, 'Mr. Pei tossed out another bamboo slip to remind you of your job. Make haste!' When you got to the gate of the county yamen, you saw two clerks playing checkers inside the gate, one facing east and the other facing west. One said, 'How frightening! Such a giant fish! It'll taste delicious if poached and spiced.' The other said, 'What a lovely fish! It should be kept alive in the backyard pond. It shouldn't be cooked.' When Wang Shiliang pressed the fish on the chopping board, the fish leaped up and whipped its tail against his face. Then he sharpened his knife and killed it. Am I right?"

Zhao Gan and the others were aghast. "Yes, all this did happen. But how did you know?"

"I was that fish. After I was caught, I kept crying out for you to take me home. But none of you listened to me. What were you thinking?"

Zhao Gan and the others said as they kowtowed, "We didn't hear you, sir. If we had heard you, how would we have dared not escort you home?"

Turning to Marshal Pei, Xue said, "When you ordered that the fish be poached and spiced, Mr. Zou advised you time and again to set the fish free, and Marshal Lei also tried to talk you out of the idea, but you turned a deaf ear and told Wang Shiliang to take the fish away. I burst out crying and said, 'We've been colleagues all this time for nothing, because you're so determined to take my life. This is by no means what a kind-hearted person would do!' Not only did Marshal Pei ignore me, but Mr. Zou and Marshal Lei said nothing, either. Why?"

Eying each other, they said, "We didn't hear a thing!" In unison, they rose and asked for forgiveness.

Xue said affably, "If that fish had not died, I would not have come back to life. All this is behind us now. Let's not mention any of this again." He then dismissed Zhao Gan and the other witnesses. His colleagues also took leave of him and went home. They dumped the poached fish into water and vowed never to eat fish again.

Although the lips of the fish were indeed seen to be moving, Assistant Magistrate Xue's cries and wails did not make a sound, which was why his three colleagues and Zhao Gan and the others had not heard him.

Now, back to Gu-shi. Recalling the divination drawn at the temple of Laozi, which had been proven right to the last character, she told her husband everything about the divination and the prayer service, sparing no details, and stated her wish to fulfill her votive vow. Magistrate Xue said in astonishment, "In all the time I've lived here, I've indeed heard about that temple on Qingcheng Hill with its crowds of worshipers, but I had no idea it had such magic powers."

He forthwith started a seven-day vegetarian diet and prepared candles and incense sticks of superior quality for a trip to the temple to fulfill Gu-shi's votive pledge. At the same time, he asked for estimates of the amount of timber needed and the cost of having statues gilded as well as the cost of labor, so that he could put together his family savings and his salary for the project. An auspicious day could then be chosen for the construction to start.

In the morning of the seventh day, he dismissed other servants and took only a twelve- or thirteen-year-old page boy with him as he set out on his trip to the temple. After leaving his residence, he prostrated himself every step of the way in the direction of Qingcheng Hill. When he was lying prostrate on the ground halfway up the hill, he suddenly heard a voice calling, "Magistrate Xue, have you understood?"

Xue gave a start. Raising his head, he saw a young herdboy wearing a bamboo hat, sitting sideways on the back of a black water buffalo. A flute in hand, he had just emerged from the side of the slope.

"What do you want me to understand?" asked Xue.

"You must know that among the immortals, there is a Qin Gao who had risen to heaven on a red carp. When he was in the presence of the Queen Mother of the West, he took a furtive glance at Lady Tian Sifei, player of the zither, and was seized with the desires of a mortal being. For this, both he and the lady were banished to earth. Now, you were Qin Gao and your wife, Gu-shi, was Tian Sifei. Since you assumed your current post, you have been enamored of the mortal world and, unable to detach yourself from it, you were changed into a red carp of East Pond to go through all manner of sufferings, so that you can come back to heaven. Why do you still fail to understand? Are you still dreaming?"

"So you are saying that I'm a divine being gone astray, and that I need a mentor to awaken me to the truth."

"The one to awaken you to the truth may seem to be far away but is in fact close at hand. Isn't Li Eight Hundred, Daoist priest in Chengdu Prefecture, a divine being? In the Han dynasty, he went by the name of Han Kang.[10] He sold medicinal herbs at a Chang'an marketplace and never haggled over price. Later, a woman recognized him for who he really was. So he changed his name to Li Eight Hundred, which is commonly believed to have derived from the eight hundred prescriptions that Sage Sun had imparted to him. In fact, he is more than Sage Sun's equal in the mastery of the Daoist arts. He is now more than eight hundred years old, and I'm not exaggerating. You and your wife will soon be due for delivery from banishment and return to the heavenly realms. Why don't you ask Li Eight Hundred for advice and have him remove the encumbrances on your way out of the mortal world?"

His wife having told him only about the divination but nothing about Li Eight Hundred's diagnosis, the herdboy's mention of Li Eight Hundred failed to ring a bell in Xue's mind. He thought, "What does a herdboy in the hills know? How can I believe such absurd nonsense? I'll go on prostrating myself every step of the way and fulfill my wife's votive vow." To his surprise, the moment he turned back his head for a look, the herdboy and the water buffalo changed into a column of purple vapor and rose to the sky. Indeed,

> He does not know an immortal when he sees one,
> Let alone what happened in a previous life!

Already perplexed by his experience as a fish, he was more puzzled when he witnessed how the herdboy had vanished with a gust of wind. He stopped in his tracks and said, "Could I have seen that herdboy in another dream?" He could not come to a conclusion. Before long, he reached the top of the hill. He kowtowed to Laozi's statue, expressed his gratitude for his revival under divine protection, and promised to fulfill the vow on a chosen auspicious day. Upon rising to his feet, he noticed that the facial features on Laozi's statue were identical to those of the herdboy and that the statue of the water buffalo close by was just like the one the herdboy had been riding. Only then did light dawn on him. "That herdboy," he thought, "was none other than the supreme Laozi himself, showing me the way back to the heavenly realms. I have eyes that don't see! How could I have failed to recognize him when we were face to face?" Again he threw himself on the floor and asked for forgiveness.

After he returned home and repeated the herdboy's words to his wife, she said, "When you were critically ill, I engaged Li Eight Hundred, priest of Chengdu Prefecture, to take your pulse. He said, 'He may look like he's going to die, but he won't. He'll gradually come back to life after half a month or twenty days. There's no need for a prescription.' Before he left, he added, 'The divination from the temple will turn out to be most accurate, but it'll only be proven so after the fish is seen.' If he knew what had happened in the past and what was going to happen in the future, he must have been a divine being. Now we know that Laozi himself has appeared in another form to guide you back. Even if Li Eight Hundred were not a divine being, you should still go to thank him for having taken the trouble to see you and for such a divinely accurate diagnosis."

Xue said, "So, that's what happened. Of course I should go to thank him." After another seven days of a vegetarian diet, he went on foot to Chengdu to visit Li Eight Hundred, the priest. Li Eight Hundred happened to be in his herb store that day. As soon as he laid eyes on the magistrate, he asked, "So you have waked up from your dream?"

With a plop, Assistant Magistrate Xue prostrated himself on the floor and answered, "Yes, your disciple is wide awake now. Please teach me how to depart from this mortal world and understand the great Dao."

Smiling, Li replied, "You are not some novice making elixir at the furnace. You are a banished divine being, as the supreme Laozi has already told you in the clearest terms. But you still have no idea who you are and find it necessary to ask other people for verification. May I presume that you identify yourself only with the assistant magistrate of Qingcheng County?"

In that instant, revelation dawned on Magistrate Xue. Gratefully he said, "Your disciple has now truly woken up. But I haven't fulfilled the vow taken in the temple of Laozi. Let me do that first. I will then resign from my official post and, together with my wife, join the Daoist order with you and regain my place among the immortals. I should still be in good time." He took leave of Li Eight Hundred and rushed back to Qingcheng County. After he repeated Li's words to his wife, she also came to the realization that she had been Tian Sifei, player of the zither for Queen Mother of the West, banished from the divine realms because she had entertained thoughts of a mortal being. That very night, she and her husband retired to separate rooms, where they burned incense and sat in meditation over past events.

The next day, Assistant Magistrate Xue handed the seal to Director Zou and submitted a memorandum to his superiors. He pushed for the completion of the construction project, and, indeed, a splendid temple was erected, with magnificent gilded statues inside. On the day the construction finished, Director Zou, fulfilling his vow of helping with the financing of the project, went with the two county marshals to Xue's residence to inform the assistant magistrate about his intention. Believing that the master and mistress were still meditating, a servant went inside to announce the visitors, only to see a poem left on a table. Mr. and Mrs. Xue had gone none knew whither. The servant brought the poem to Director Zou, who saw that it was a quatrain bidding farewell to his colleagues:

> *All turned out well with the dreamer of fish;*
> *Had the fish been real, death would have been real.*
> *Where there is life, there is death after all;*
> *To transcend life and death, leave the mortal world.*

Overcome with emotions after reading the poem, Zou said, "Mr. Xue should have said good-bye to us before he left to join the Daoist order. I feel bad about this, but he shouldn't have gone far." Right away he sent people to look for Xue and his wife high and low. To his surprise, no trace of them was found. Marshal Pei said with a smile, "How can the two of you be so benighted? He must have missed the pleasure of swimming and changed into a carp again to have a good time. Let's just go to East Pond and get him."

Let us leave his colleagues in their wild speculations and follow Assistant Magistrate Xue and his wife. Where else did they go but Li Eight Hundred's place! Li said to the magistrate, smiling, "You were Qin Gao in your previous life. Your red carp has been waiting for you at East Pond, as instructed, because the spot where you rose to heaven is not far from there. Today, you will again rise to heaven on the back of your red carp. What do you say?" Turning to Gu-shi, Li said, "After you were banished, Dong Shuangcheng took your place as the zither player for the Queen Mother of the West. Now it's time you resume that role."

Immortals, with their tacit understanding of the Dao, need no oral formulae or tricks. A smile suffices in their communication with one another.

Gu-shi said to Li Eight Hundred, "You have delivered numerous people from suffering through your medical practice and sales of medicinal herbs. With such distinguished service, why would you want to stay any longer in the mortal world?"

Li replied, "I'm predestined to rise to heaven with you at this hour. That's why I'm waiting here for you."

In a trice, amid curling wisps of auspicious clouds and mist came the clear strains of celestial music. With phoenixes and cranes flying above them, celestial boys and maidens carrying banners, streamers, and canopies approached them to escort them back to heaven. Xue, his wife, and Li Eight Hundred rose to heaven together, with Xue on a red carp, Gu-shi on a purple cloud, and Li on a white crane. Everyone throughout Chengdu, old and young, witnessed the ascension. All bowed to heaven and marveled in admiration. The Rising Immortals Bridge of the site remains to this day. The poem says,

> *In this vast universe, strange things happen;*
> *A man becomes a fish, a fish becomes a man.*
> *Forms may change, but nature remains the same.*
> *Ignore form, cultivate nature, and be divine.*

27

Li Yuying Appeals for Justice from Jail

That they be together till a ripe old age,
That their sons and daughters be well and marry,
That they live to see their grandchildren learn to walk—
These wishes of all married couples, if fulfilled,
Bring peace to them even after death.
Would that nothing untoward happen to the wife!
With a heart more venomous than snakes and scorpions,
The stepmother poisons the husband's mind at the pillow.
Her own children she loves like treasure;
The deceased wife's children she treats like dirt.
Regular meals and tea she serves them not.
Hair disheveled, faces grimy, they weep to no avail.
Remember how Shun had sobbed every night at Mount Li,[1]
And how Min Ziqian had worn reed catkins in winter?[2]

The above lines make the point that, however ruthless in heart, stepmothers tend to love their own sons and daughters more than they do the most precious pearl. But this is only human nature and should not raise an eyebrow. What infuriates one is the way they cruelly abuse their stepchildren, looking upon them as so much dirt and muck. Those stepchildren already fifteen or sixteen years old do not fare the worst. However badly they are treated, they will soon grow into adulthood. Most pitiable are small children under ten years of age. But they can again be divided into three categories. Which three?

Children of the first category are from rich families. They are raised from birth by wet nurses and maidservants and sent to school at five or six years of age. Moreover, with the watchful eyes and ears of the multitudes of clan members and servants around the house, stepmothers who are fearful of gossip have to refrain from abusing the children, if only for appearances' sake. But if these women come to have children of their own and want no share of the inheritance to go to the stepchildren, they may choose to destroy the roots of trouble once and for all. There is a poem in testimony:

> Sadly, Shun's stepmother plotted against his life;[3]
> Shensheng was slandered; Boqi was expelled.[4]
> The world abounds in stepmothers up to mischief;
> Few husbands ever rise to do the right thing.

The second category consists of children from fairly respectable middle-income families. However, they may not have wet nurses or servants and are thus put under the care of the stepmother. Abuse is practically inevitable. If the father has a mind of his own, he will fight the wife and protect the children against her abuses. There are also stepmothers who bully the children behind the backs of their husbands out of fear of them. But if the woman happens to be a shrew who fears neither heaven nor earth, neither shame nor death, and only gathers strength from fighting, she will threaten at every turn to kill herself, wielding a knife or running off to a well or a river, just to frighten her husband. But oftentimes what begins as a bluff may end up in tragedy, and even the family property may be wiped out. As the proverb puts it so well, "No medicine can cure an unfilial son or an evil wife." If you happen to be stuck with such a wife, you would hardly want to have terrible scenes with her day after day. After a few violent scenes with her without winning, you have no other choice but to play deaf and dumb and put up with the misery. (*A thorough indictment against good-for-nothing wives.*) Some men put the children up for adoption; some send them to Buddhist monasteries and Daoist temples, and some put them under the care of their uncles and cousins. These are men of courage and moral rectitude.

Now there is also another kind of man. Heartless, cruel, and ungrateful, he may shower his wife and children with love, but after the wife dies, he marries another either out of designs for her rich dowry or out of lust for her beauty. And she may be much younger than he is in his middle age. In his infatuation with the new wife, he banishes from his mind all memory of his love for his deceased wife and begins to look on his children as thorns in his flesh and stings in his eye. When his children are yelled at and beaten, he adds his voice and his fists instead of interceding on the children's behalf, to ingratiate himself with his new wife. Oftentimes, the second wife's children have all married, but the son of the deceased wife remains unbetrothed. To pacify public opinion, the couple will perfunctorily marry the young man to the first candidate available. The stepmother will then go out of her way to put a curse on the young man's marriage. If the curse does not work, she will beat the son, scold the daughter-in-law, and urge her husband to report the young couple's unfilial behavior to the authorities and kick them out of the house.

Of the children, girls suffer more than boys. After being beaten, a boy can either devote himself to his studies or play with neighboring children to get his mind off his troubles. A girl, however, never gets to leave the house and has to stay with that yaksha of a woman to be ordered about with never a moment of rest.[5] Every day, she has to finish a certain amount of needlework. If she fails to fulfill the quota, she is naturally in for punishment. If she does fulfill the quota, the stepmother will find fault with her work and not let her off the hook anyway. If the stepmother gives birth to a baby, it becomes the bounden duty of the girl, as if by contract, to carry the baby from morning to night. According to the stepmother, if the baby cries, it is because the girl loathes the job and torments the baby. If the baby gets sick, it is because she must have given it a shock. If the baby has a mosquito bite, she must have put the mosquito on the baby. There's more: In freezing cold weather, the girl has to do laundry in the river in a hole in the ice and then she is chided for not having washed the clothes clean enough. When she finally reaches fifteen or sixteen and comes of age, her stepmother's abuse turns even more ugly. She is accused either of fancying a man or of being obsessed with thoughts of marriage. Pity the girl who, without a place to pour out her woes, has to suppress her sobs furtively! If she is heard, she will again be accused of putting on a show to win sympathy. Untold numbers of such girls, crushed by the humiliation and bullying, have taken their own lives. The following poem bears testimony:

> A henpecked husband forfeits his authority
> And lets his second wife have her own way.
> He allows his own children to be abused;
> His heart aches, but he dares not say a word.

In the third category, the parents are people who have to work hard with their hands for their daily subsistence. Even when their birth mother was alive, the children were only barely able to ward off hunger and cold. Ample food and clothing they probably had not. When they finally reach ten years of age, they are expected to learn to make a living and help out, however modestly, with family expenses. A ferocious stepmother only adds to their misery. Not knowing where their next meal is to come from, they have to learn to endure the pangs of hunger. Even if they want a drop of hot water to drink, they have to ask for permission and dare not act on their own. What they wear is nothing but tattered pieces of clothing that hardly protect them against the cold, but they dare not complain of the cold in her presence. (*Poor things!*) Their hair scarcely ever encounters a comb throughout the year. They tie up their hair perfunctorily into knots, but more often than not, strands of hair come loose and hang over their faces. Their feet are bare, with no shoes or socks. Straw sandals are to them as luxurious as black boots with white soles. It is their job to chop firewood, make fire, and carry water. If the stepmother is the slightest bit unsatisfied, fists and feet will land on them and, worse still, sticks and rods will rain down on them. Verbal abuse is so frequent that they take it as entertainment. By the time they are tall enough to carry loads over their shoulders, they are ordered to make a certain amount of money every day. If they are one penny short, they are pummeled until they are more dead than alive. A stepmother who tries to talk her husband into selling off the children as servants is actually doing them a favor and getting herself some credit in the underworld. In poor families with stepmothers, nine out of ten of the children are tormented to death, as evidenced by the following poem:

> *Children of poor families lead hard lives;*
> *The stepmothers' ire adds to their trials.*
> *Beaten, sworn at, hungry, and cold,*
> *In public, they call her mother, nonetheless.*

Storyteller, why go on and on about the many vices of stepmothers? Well, it's because yours truly is going to tell a story about a stepmother who plotted to murder her stepchildren but was overtaken by divine justice and punished in accordance with the law of the land, as a warning to all stepmothers of the world. That is why I made those opening remarks by way of a prologue. Now, the story I'm going to tell will

> *Sadden the heart of a man of iron*
> *And bring tears to a statue of stone.*

When does the story take place? It takes place during the Zhengde reign period [1506–21] of this very dynasty [the Ming]. In the office of the imperial standard-bearer guards of Beijing, there was a Li Xiong, a lieutenant, who had inherited his rank from his forefathers. Though a military officer, he had at an early age developed an aptitude for learning and a propensity for studying the classics. Upon coming of age, he was big of frame, strong of arm, and skillful in swordsmanship and archery. He was indeed an officer accomplished in both the military and the civil arts. For the distinguished service he rendered in conquering Prince of Anhua of Shaanxi in the expedition led by Zhang Yong, the eunuch, he was promoted to be a battalion commander of the imperial bodyguards.[6] He had three daughters and a son by his wife, He-shi, whom he loved deeply. The son was named Chengzu, the eldest daughter Yuying, the second daughter Taoying, and the third daughter Yueying. Yuying was the eldest of the four and Chengzu the son was the second. As it turned out, after giving birth to Yueying, He-shi succumbed to illness brought on by physical exhaustion and passed away in less than half a year. How pitiable!

> *Though pieces of fine brocade remain with him,*
> *Gut-wrenching grief seizes him from time to time.*

When their mother died, Yuying was only six years old, Chengzu five, Taoying three, and Yueying only five or six months. Though they were under the care of a maidservant and a wet nurse, they were like little chicks without the protection of the hen and kept crying in terror. Pained by the misery of the children, Li Xiong felt obliged to stay at home day after day to be with them. He must either abandon his official duties and stay at home to take care of his family or attend to official business and ignore the children. Indeed, he could not have it both ways. After a few months went by slowly in this manner, he began to think that things could not go on like this. The idea of remarrying took possession of his mind, and he sought the services of a matchmaker. Being someone who regularly did her rounds in thousands of households, the matchmaker quickly spread the news. Upon hearing that Li Xiong was only about thirty years of age and that, at his rank, his wife was to be addressed as "Your Ladyship" as soon as she stepped over the threshold, who would not jump at the chance? Before three days were gone, the matchmaker presented Li Xiong with a pile of papers from candidates, specifying their dates of birth and their horoscopes, so that he could take his pick.

As the saying goes, "Marriage bonds are predestined and not to be changed by humans of this life." After weighing his choices carefully, Li Xiong finally settled on a sixteen-year-old Miss Jiao. Her parents having both died, her older brother and sister-in-law made all the decisions for her. The brother, Jiao Rong, was a slick, unsavory character who spent his time cultivating friends in the various offices of the county yamen. In a moment of foolishness, Li Xiong chose this woman. After presenting betrothal gifts to her family and going through the usual formalities, he brought the bride home a few days later and held the wedding ceremony, complete with carved bridal candles. Jiao-shi was quite an attractive woman and was skilled in needlework. Her one drawback was that she had a streak of maliciousness in her. The sight of the four young children aroused her jealousy. The very fact that her husband cherished them and often reminded her to take good care of them only intensified her hatred. She thought, "If there hadn't been this litter of pigs, my children would get to be the only heirs to my husband's title and the family properties. Now, with this whole brood sticking around, however large the family fortune will be in the future, the better part of it will go to them. If the family possessions don't grow and stay at this level, hardly anything will be left for my children. Won't I have lived my life with him in vain, working as hard as I do? I must play up to him and then, with clever words, drive a wedge between him and the little rascals, and torment them until two or three of them drop dead. I can then easily deal with the remaining one or two."

Now, won't you agree that nothing can be more ridiculous than these thoughts? She's only sixteen years old. Little knowing how long she's going to live and whether she will have children, she's already thinking decades ahead and ruthlessly plotting against the lives of her stepchildren. How lamentable! There is a poem that bears testimony:

> Men marry in order to have children,
> But stepchildren are treated as enemies.
> It's not that women are heartless,
> But that men lack long-term plans.

Henceforth, Jiao-shi assiduously cultivated her husband's favor. In addition, being in the prime of her youth, she dolled herself up until she looked as pretty as a flower and went out of her way to please him in their unions of delight. Not surprisingly, happiness flooded Li Xiong's heart and he yielded to her in everything except one. What is it? Whenever the subject of the children came up, he would say, "Have pity on them. They lost their mother when they were so young, and they were quite coddled. If they misbehave, talk to them gently. Don't be too hard on them."

After several failed attempts to poison her husband's mind against the children, Jiao-shi could not contain herself any longer. One day, while her husband was away, she picked on Li Chengzu and gave him a brutal beating while calling him the worst names. The boy's scalp being tender, large bumps appeared instantly all over his head, like buns rising in the steamer. Wishing for a hole to vanish into, the boy wailed at the top of his lungs. However hard they tried, the maidservant and the wet nurse could not calm him down.

Yuying, as young as she was, had a sharp and quick mind. Observing how ruthlessly her brother was beaten, she realized that her stepmother was by no means a kind-hearted woman. As tears of anguish fell down her cheeks, she found herself unable to stomach anymore of the abuse. Stepping forward, she said, "Mother, please forgive my brother. He's too young to know better."

"Little cheap harlot!" snapped Jiao-shi. "Who asked you for advice? Are you saying I'm not supposed to spank him? You're in for some spanking yourself! You're in no position to ask for forgiveness on someone else's behalf!"

These words further pained Yuying's heart. While Jiao-shi was still raining blows on the boy, Li Xiong came home. The boy threw his arms around his father and wailed with abandon. The sight of the boy in such a sorry state so enraged Li Xiong that he made a terrible scene. The woman threw all considerations of appearances to the winds and stoutly defied him, going so far as to threaten to kill herself. Someone quickly went to inform Jiao Rong, her brother, and he rushed to the scene to offer pacifying words.

Li Xiong said to him, "I married your sister so that she could provide care for the children, not put them under abuse, as if they need any! And I keep telling her to pity them because they lost their mother when they were still so young and they were quite coddled. Since she's the mother now, she should make the best of the situation. But she deliberately goes the other way and beat the boy up so badly!"

After saying a few false-hearted words of reproach to his sister and offering an apology to Li Xiong, Jiao Rong continued, "My sister is too young to know much about the ways of the world. Besides, she has also been pampered since childhood and has always had her way at home. Don't get angry with her, my brother-in-law. If you feel awkward, let her go home with me and stay there for a few days. I'll talk to her and tell her to stop behaving like this." With that, he took leave of Li Xiong and went off. Some moments later, he returned with a hired sedan-chair and a maid-servant, and took Jiao-shi home.

Jiao-shi had barely crossed the threshold when she started grumbling at Jiao Rong, saying, "Brother, however unworthy I am, you should have found me a good husband for the sake of our parents. How could you have gotten me such a rotten deal? You ruined my future!"

Jiao Rong rejoined, all smiles, "Marrying a battalion commander of the imperial guards is no rotten deal. How can you blame others when you yourself don't know better?"

"Why do you say that?"

"Since my brother-in-law loves his children, you should play along and be nice to them."

"They're not my children! I don't want to go out of my way to be nice to them!"

Laughing, Jiao Rong said, "That's why I say you don't know better. As the ancients said, 'Give, in order to take.' The more you loathe them, the nicer you should be to them."

"How I wish to do away with all of them right now for my peace of mind! Why should I go the other way and be nice to them?"

"Little children like them haven't done anything wrong. What's more, the servants have been with the family all these years and haven't gotten to establish loyalty to you. If you punish the children in any way, the servants will inform their master against you. They'll exaggerate things and accuse you of cruel abuse. My brother-in-law will thus be put on guard against you. How will you ever have a chance to get rid of them? If he gets to be suspicious of you, even if he comes down with some illness and dies, his suspicion of you won't die with him. Won't that be an injustice to you when you haven't done anything? So, try to tolerate them and make a virtue of necessity. After they grow up, they'll naturally be filial to you for having raised them."

Vigorously shaking her head, Jiao-shi said, "Out of the question!"

"If you really can't tolerate them, listen carefully and do as I say. In the future, treat them as if they're your own children. Give the maidservants some small favors to win their loyalty. Then find out quietly if there are any disloyal and gossipy ones. If so, kick them out. After a year or two, my brother-in-law will believe you're sincere and the maidservants will all be loyal to you. By that time, you'll have your own child, who will take away a share of your husband's love for the children. Then you can watch for the right moment to get rid of Li Chengzu. No one will suspect it's your doing. The girls will have grown up by that time. You can tell the servants to join the maids in accusing them of having affairs. Out of fear of derision, your husband in his position as an officer will surely force them to take their own lives. In this roundabout way, won't you have been spared some unpleasantness at this time? And you'll be perceived as a kind person, too." (*Jiao Rong is even more malicious. Like brother, like sister.*)

Exultant upon hearing this advice, Jiao-shi said, "My brother, this is such a good idea! I was wrong to blame you. After I go back, I'll do as you say. I'll come for more advice before making important moves."

Enough about the conversation between Jiao Rong and his sister. Let us come back to Li Xiong in his vexation over his wife's ill treatment of his children. He thought, "I married her because I expected her to take care of them, but I ended up with a holy terror on my hands. We have a whole lifetime ahead of us. How are the little ones going to get by?" Turning his thoughts this way and that, he came up with a plan. What was that plan? Well, he had one room made into a study and engaged an old scholar to teach Yuying and Chengzu there. Every day, tea and meals were delivered to the study and the class was not dismissed until evening set in, so that the children could stay away from their stepmother and be spared verbal and physical abuses. (*Li Xiong is not a heartless man. However, jealousy being one of the seven offenses that constitute grounds for divorce, why doesn't he take action?*) Taoying and Yueying, under the care of the wet nurse, should be able to stay out of harm's way, so he thought.

As they say, quarrels and fights don't drive husband and wife apart. After several days, Li Xiong felt obliged to have Jiao-shi brought back from her brother's house. Jiao Rong prepared some gifts and escorted her back.

Upon learning that a teacher had been engaged, Jiao-shi did not make any comment, although she knew all too well why that had been done. In drastic contrast with before, she was now all smiles and affability to the children. In fact, she was affection itself and treated them even better than she would her own children. She did not even whisper a harsh word, let alone beat or yell at them. She was most generous and forgiving to all the servants as well, tipping them from time to time. In most situations servants are so petty-minded that, at the smallest gain, they will break into ear-deafening cheers and profuse praises of their employer.

In the beginning, Li Xiong was mystified. He thought that she might have been faking the cordiality out of fear of his protests, and might not have been consistent in her behavior behind his back. Quietly he asked around and observed her with a watchful eye but found nothing amiss. More than a year later, she grew even more affectionate with the children. Wild with joy, he thought, "I wonder what my brother-in-law said to her to make her mend her ways so thoroughly. This goes to show that it's not so hard to become a good person. A change of mind is all it takes." Then and there he let down his guard, and the love between the husband and the wife grew deeper. Jiao-shi could hardly wait to have a son of her own. Anxious that she was still not pregnant in the second year into their marriage, she went to one temple after another, burning incense and taking votive vows. Buddha was indeed responsive to her prayers. Many joss sticks and votive vows later, she found herself pregnant. Upon full term, she gave birth to a son, to whom she gave the pet name Yanu ["lower than a servant"]. You may very well ask, why such a name? Well, it is the local custom for parents who worry about their children's growth to give them humble names, which, they believe, will make it easier for them to grow healthily. Hence the legions of names like "Little Ox" and "Little Dog." In her anxiety for the well-being of her child, Jiao-shi followed the same practice. Forgoing the more familiar names, she picked Yanu, thinking that a name indicating a status lower than that of a servant should be just as humble as Little Ox or Little Dog.

Believing that Jiao-shi was sincere in her affection for his children, Li Xiong also made much of the baby. Needless to say, he invited family and friends to a celebration banquet when the baby was three days old and again when he was one month old.

As the saying goes, "Worry only that you may not have children. Worry not that they do not grow." In the twinkling of an eye, Yanu was one year old. By this time, Yuying was already a ten-year old girl as pretty as a picture. Endowed with a brilliant mind, she was able to recite many lines of prose and verse after a single glance and was good at writing poetry. As for such skills as embroidery, she acquired them without being taught. Her brother, Li Chengzu, although also a smart boy, could not measure up to her. The following is what she wrote about green plum blossoms:

> They are a prized variety of plum blossoms,
> But they grow on jade-green stems.
> They boast not the usual charming red;
> They laugh at the common plain white.
> When they bloom, they puzzle the orioles;
> In their fragrance, they disorient the butterflies.
> The notes of a Qiang flute echo on the Longshan Hills,
> Where the blossoms are taken for sweet green grass.

Li Xiong was doubly fond of her because of her talent. He even sent Taoying and Yueying to take classes in the study. To Jiao-shi he said, "Yuying is such a talented girl that I can't bear to see her marry into another household. Why don't we find a fine scholar and make him a live-in son-in-law? Wouldn't that be a good match?"

In spite of all her honeyed words, Jiao-shi was seized with greater jealousy and began to get ready to make her move.

It turned out, in a way no one would have expected, that in that very year, the fourteenth year of the Zhengde reign period [1519], a Yang Jiu'er led a rebellion on the Gaolan Hills in Shaanxi and inflicted on the government troops one defeat after another. As the local officials asked for emergency help, the imperial court dispatched an expeditionary force led by Zhao Zhong, commander of the imperial guards. Upon learning of Li Xiong's wisdom and courage, Zhao Zhong recommended him for appointment as the vanguard. Now, won't you agree that a war situation demands immediate action, just as a fire does? There was no time to lose. Within half a month, the troops set out on a chosen day. Li Xiong put together some articles of clothing and weapons, and led his household guards in preparing for the journey. On the point of departure, he again reminded Jiao-shi to take good care of the children.

"You need not remind me," rejoined Jiao-shi. "I only wish that the gods will protect you in the battlefield, so that you can win speedy victory and bring honor to your wife and children."

As he was bidding farewell to his wife and children, a messenger came announcing, "Commander Zhao would like to see you on the drill ground." Tearfully, Li Xiong left his residence, hurriedly mounted his horse, and went to the martial arts practice hall at the drill ground. After he finished exchanging greetings with the other officers, an official from the ministry of defense arrived to offer them bounties by imperial order. The soldiers expressed their gratitude by chanting "Long live the emperor!" three times in the direction of the palace. Commander Zhao then ordered that Li Xiong lead the advance party and set out first, whereupon Li Xiong had three cannon shots fired in acknowledgment of the order. With a loud cheer in unison, soldiers of the advance party left the drill ground amid drumbeats and began to march toward Shaanxi, holding themselves very erect and their shining weapons tightly in hand. An impressive sight it was. As they marched along, they cut paths through mountains and built bridges over rivers and, in a matter of days, reached Shaanxi. They pitched camps and waited for the main forces to arrive before marching together with them to the battlefield.

After several battles in succession with the rebel troops, winning a few times and losing a few times, Commander Zhao ordered Li Xiong to take on the enemies' challenge to battle on the fourteenth day of the seventh lunar month. Leading a group of crack troops, Li Xiong fiercely charged into the enemy ranks. Failing to fend them off, the enemy ran pell-mell in defeat. Li Xiong and his men pushed on in victory and chased them for several li. Suddenly, enemy soldiers in ambush charged forward from all directions and surrounded them.

Li Xiong and his men charged left and right, trying in vain to break through the ring of encirclement. As the reinforcement troops could not get through the encirclement either, Li Xiong and his men, however valiant, were vastly outnumbered. Valiantly they fought on, but by nightfall all of them perished. How sad that Li Xiong the peerless hero died, marking the end of a life that had been but a dream! Verily,

> His moral courage filled the universe;
> His forlorn soul lives on in the cold realm.

Let us leave Zhao Zhong's expedition for the moment and come back to Jiaoshi. She was about to make her move when her husband happened to be called away to the battlefield. Wasn't this a chance that heaven offered her? After Li Xiong had been gone for several days, she rode in a sedan-chair to her brother's house and consulted him.

"As I see it, you'd better wait a while longer," said Jiao Rong.

"Why?"

"Since my brother-in-law is away, he'll get suspicious if the girl dies. You should take even better care of her, so that my brother-in-law will have greater faith in you after he returns home. By that time, you can make your move when they least expect it. No one will suspect you. Won't that be wonderful?"

Following Jiao Rong's advice, Jiao-shi indeed took even better care of Yuying and her siblings and looked forward day and night to Li Xiong's victorious return. As it turned out, however, at the beginning of the eighth month, news finally came from Shaanxi to the capital that in a battle on the fourteenth day of the seventh month, Li Xiong, commander of the vanguard, charged courageously into enemy ranks, victoriously at first, but then the tide of the battle changed, and he died with all of his men in defeat. Jiao Rong, being a man who spent much of his time going around the various yamen offices, learned the news quickly enough. Appalled, he ran posthaste to tell his sister about it. Upon hearing that her husband had died in battle, Jiao-shi burst into wails of grief. Yuying and her siblings, even more pitiable, cried so bitterly that they fainted away but were then revived.

After consulting Jiao Rong, Jiao-shi dismissed the teacher. Every member of the family put on mourning white. A shrine was set up and a prayer service held to call back the spirit of the deceased, and relatives and friends came to offer their condolences. Pulling a long face, Jiao-shi beat and cursed the children at every turn. After more than a month, Jiao-shi said to her brother, "With my husband dead, there's nothing to hold me back. Let me strike now!"

Jiao Rong said, "I've got an ingenious plan. You need not strike. I'll make them die in faraway places and you won't be held responsible."

"What is the plan?" asked Jiao-shi eagerly.

"There's no word about where my brother-in-law's remains are. Wait for two more months. When the weather turns bitterly cold, send a trusted servant to take Chengzu to Shaanxi to look for the remains. That child has never experienced any hardships of traveling. He will fall ill in the changed environment and climate and drop dead on the road. (*What a wicked plan!*) Even if he survives the hardships of the journey and arrives at the destination, have the servant leave him there and quietly come back alone. So, without money, he won't be able to do anything. He'll die of either cold or hunger. As for the girls, you can spare their lives and sell them off as concubines or maidservants, and you'll get a tidy sum, too. Won't you be able to have it both ways?" (*One with such an evil mind should be consigned to The Avici Hell.*[7])

Jiao-shi was duly impressed by the ingeniousness of the plan. When the last month of the year rolled around at long last, Jiao-shi called Li Chengzu to her and said, "After a lifetime of hard work, your father unfortunately died in battle without even a burial place. How is he to rest easy under the Nine Springs?[8] I heard your uncle say yesterday that Commander Zhao had won a series of victories. The rebel troops have withdrawn a thousand li, and the roads are safe again. I would like to go to Shaanxi myself to look for your father's remains and bring them back for burial, as a wife is duty-bound to do. But being a young widow, I'm afraid there'll be gossip if I show myself in public. So I have no other choice than to tell Miao Quan the servant to take you on the trip. If you can bring the remains home, it'll be an act of filial love on your part. The packing has already been done. You may depart tomorrow morning."

Tearfully Chengzu said, "You're right, Mother. I'll leave tomorrow morning."

Yuying, however, was alarmed. Detecting ill intentions behind the idea, she said, "Mother, my father having died a violent death on the battlefield, it does stand to reason that my brother should go to find his remains. But he's so young and he has never undertaken a long journey. If anything untoward should happen, won't he die needlessly? It shouldn't make any difference if you send another servant, instead of my brother, to go with Miao Quan."

Jiao-shi flew into a rage. "What an ungrateful brat you are! When your father was alive, he cherished the four of you as treasures. Now that he's dead and gone, you turn your back on him and don't even want to see his remains. In all the years you applied yourself to the books, haven't you read about Mulan joining the army in her father's name and Tiying offering to take her father's punishment?[9] They were young girls just like you, and yet they were such filial daughters. Instead of drawing inspiration from them and going to look for your father's remains, you turn around and try to keep your brother from going. Now, Chengzu is a man, and he has a servant to attend to his needs along the journey. It's not as if he's going to the battlefield, as Mulan did, to face life-threatening dangers. How would anything untoward happen to cause a needless death? What good is an unfilial daughter like you?" (*Those who know nothing of morality are the very ones most eloquently preaching morality.*)

At this outburst, Yuying blushed deeply in mortification and said tearfully, "Far be it from me to forget about father's kindness and refuse to find his remains for burial. It's just that my brother is too young for the hardships of such a journey. Let me go in his place."

"You may want to have a good time touring the mountains and scenic spots, but I'm not going to let you do that."

That night, Yuying and her siblings huddled together, bidding each other farewell, and wept until deep into the night.

"Sister," said Li Chengzu, "It won't do to let father's remains lie in the open fields. Let me find them and bring them home, so as to put mother's mind at ease. You need not worry."

The next morning, with Jiao-shi urging Chengzu to be on his way, the girls tearfully bade their brother farewell. Jiao-shi said, "If you don't find your father's remains, don't come back to see me."

Li Chengzu said between his sobs, "If I don't find father's remains, I'll be too ashamed to come back and see you, Mother."

Miao Quan helped him mount the pack animal and they set out on their journey out of the capital. Who, you may wonder, was that Miao Quan? He was Jiao-shi's most trusted servant, who had come with her to the Li family as part of her dowry. He had secretly taken orders from the mistress but kept quiet about it.

Chengzu and the servant left the capital and headed in the direction of Shaanxi. The bitterly cold wind of midwinter pierced the skin like arrows. The snow accumulated on the ground being three to four feet deep, pack animals walked as if through piles of cotton. Having grown up in easy circumstances, Li Chengzu, not yet ten years old, was ill prepared for such misery. Shivering uncontrollably as he rode on the back of the pack animal, he tumbled into the snow from time to time. After more than ten days on the road, traveling by day and resting by night, he ate less and less and fell ill. To Miao Quan he said, "I don't feel well. I'd like to rest for a couple of days before continuing with the journey."

"My young master," said Miao Quan, "your mother didn't give me a whole lot of money for travel expenses. Even if we get there as fast as we can, we may still run short of money for the return trip. If we stop here and stay for a couple of days, we'll have even less money on the way back. Make an effort and get to our destination first. You can rest and recuperate for a few days there."

"How far is it to our destination?"

Miao Quan replied with a smile, "We've still got a long way to go. Twenty days at top speed."

In resignation, Li Chengzu forced himself to press on despite his illness, his eyes brimming with tears. There is a poem in testimony:

> How sad that such a child had to leave home
> On horseback, to a distant place.
> Where, pray, was the battlefield far away?
> Under dead grass, swirling clouds, and the setting sun.

After they traveled for another two days, Li Chengzu's condition worsened. He could hardly remain astride the animal, but Miao Quan refused to pause or to hire a porter. Instead, he purposely made Chengzu continue with the journey on foot, supporting the boy as they went along, all too clearly determined to do him to death. Hours later, upon reaching a place called Bao'an Village, Li Chengzu said, "Miao Quan, I can't take another step. Find an inn, quick, and let's take a rest."

Miao Quan thought, "It looks like his number is up. If I take him to an inn, I can hardly give him the slip. I might just as well turn back home now and leave him here." Aloud, he said, "Young master, there's no inn anywhere nearby. If you can't walk any further, why don't you sit down and stay here for now? I'll go find an inn first, so that I can deposit the luggage. I'll then come back here and carry you on my back all the way to the inn. What do you say?"

"Sounds good," said Li Chengzu. And so, Miao Quan helped him to the door of a house and sat him down at the curb. Then Miao Quan walked ahead in large strides, turned into a small lane, bought some food, ate it, hired a pack animal, and headed for home. Of him, no more for the moment.

Li Chengzu sat on the curb, waiting in vain for Miao Quan to return. Feeling uncomfortable in his sitting position, he lay down and fell asleep. Now, in that one-room house lived an old woman. She was sitting by the door, weaving, when she saw a man helping a little boy sit down at her door. She didn't think anything of it at the time, but when she was on her way out to fetch water at dusk, bucket in hand, she saw the boy lying fast asleep, blocking her door. "Young man," she cried out loud. "Get up! Quick! Let me go out to fetch water!"

Waking up from a dream, Li Chengzu thought that Miao Quan had come back. As he opened his eyes and saw that it was an old woman, obviously an occupant of the house, he struggled up and said, "Granny, what is it?"

Detecting a nonlocal accent, the old woman asked, "Where are you from? Why were you sleeping here?"

"I'm from the capital. I was sitting here because I'm too ill to walk on. I'll be leaving as soon as my servant is back."

"Where is your servant?"

"He said he was going to find an inn to deposit our luggage, and then he'll come and carry me on his back to the inn."

"Good heavens! I saw him when he left in the morning. It's almost evening now. He can't be still on the way. Maybe he deserted you and ran away with the money and the luggage."

Having just woken up, Chengzu found his head still in a swirl and he had not noticed what time of the day it was. He thought Miao Quan had left just a short while earlier. At the old woman's words, he quickly looked around and saw that the sun had indeed set in the west. He gave a start, thinking, "That dog must have fled because he hates to take care of me in my worsening condition. Now I'm stuck. What am I going to do?" Before he knew it, tears welled up in his eyes and he burst into a fit of wails so loud that several neighbors walked over to see what was going on. Feeling saddened by his heart-rending sobs, the old woman put down her water bucket and asked, "Young man, who are your parents? What emergency came up to make you travel on foot with a servant in such cold weather? And what's your destination?"

Tearfully, Li Chengzu replied, "Granny, to tell you the truth, my father was a battalion commander of the imperial guards. He followed Commander Zhao to Shaanxi to fight the rebels and died in battle. My mother told me and Miao Quan the servant to go to the battlefield to find father's remains and bring them back for burial. But I fell ill on the way. That dog abandoned me and ran off. I'll most likely end up as a ghost in an alien land!" With that, he broke down in another fit of sobs. Everyone around him sighed upon hearing this account.

"Poor thing! Poor thing!" lamented the old woman. "So you're from a good family. There are far too few young boys like you with such filial devotion! Being ill, you must not sleep on a cold stone curb. You'll only get worse. Now get up and sleep in my bed. Your servant may yet show up, for all we know."

"Thank you for your kindness, Granny, but I can't impose myself on you like this."

"Nonsense!" said the old woman. "Who doesn't have to go through a difficult period in life?" So saying, she helped him into the house, and the neighbors went their separate ways home.

As he crossed the threshold, Chengzu saw, on one side of the room, a heated brick bed with a mat spread over it. After putting him to bed, the old woman went in all haste to fetch water. She then boiled some of it and made Chengzu drink it. At midnight, she reached out her hand to feel him and found him as hot as burning charcoal. At daybreak, realizing that he had fallen into a coma, the old woman asked someone to bring a physician. After the physician came and took his pulse, the old woman paid for the herbs, fed him the medicine, and waited on him day and night. The neighbors, upon hearing that Li Chengzu was quite far gone in his illness, laughed at the old woman behind her back for going to such trouble over a hopeless case. The old woman caught wind of such comments but feigned ignorance and went on taking care of the boy without the slightest lapse of attention. Indeed, Li Chengzu had met such a kind-hearted person because he was not predestined to die at this time. There is a poem in testimony:

> His stepmother was his worst enemy;
> A stranger turned out to be all kindness to him.
> Those born good or evil are worlds apart;
> Strangers turn out to be better than kith and kin.

Li Chengzu did not recover from this grave illness until the middle of the second month of the following year. Lying in bed, he thanked the old woman, saying, "I'm ever so grateful to you, Granny, for your kindness in saving my life. You are a parent to me in my rebirth. If I can make my way home, I'll surely repay this debt of gratitude."

"How can you say such things? I kept you out of pity for your misery. You don't owe me any debt of gratitude. Repayment is quite uncalled for."

Time flew. In a trice, the third month went by and the fourth month rolled around. By that time, Chengzu had fully recovered. In robust health now, he told the old woman that he wanted to leave her and continue his journey to find his father's remains.

"Young man," said the old woman. "Having just recovered, you shouldn't overtax yourself. What's more, you have no idea how long the journey is going to be. You can't go like this, all alone and without money. You'd better stay here while I ask around in the neighborhood if there's anyone going to the capital, so that you can send a message home. It'll be much better if someone from your family can join you on your journey."

"Thank you, Granny, for being so considerate, but no one in my family can join me. Also, I feel uneasy staying on here, imposing on your hospitality. And thirdly, this is the right weather for me to be on the road. If I stay longer, it'll turn hot, which will only make the journey more difficult. I feel perfectly fine now. I should be all right. And I'll keep to the highway, where there'll be lots of travelers. I'll beg for food along the way. After I find my father's remains, I'll come back here to see you again."

"Even if you find your father's remains, you don't have money to have them sent back home. Won't you have gone through all the trouble for nothing?"

"There should be a government office there. I'll go and plead to them. Maybe they'll take pity on me and help me send his remains home. He died for the country, after all."

Failing to talk him into staying, the old woman scraped together a few loose pieces of silver that came to nothing more than a fraction of a tael, and gave them to him. As deeply attached to each other as real mother and son, they hated the thought of parting. As they bade each other farewell, the old woman said tearfully, "You must come to see me on your way back. Don't just pass by without stopping!"

Choking with emotion, Li Chengzu couldn't get a word out. He nodded and sobbingly turned to go. The old woman stood by the door, watching him as he turned back to look at her after every two steps. She did not return to her room, weeping, until he disappeared from view. The neighbors laughed at her, calling her a foolish old woman, saying, "She went into so much expense for a little boy stranded here from somewhere faraway. She had just nursed him back to health before he went off in all haste. What good did all this do her? And she's crying so hard, too! Where do all those tears come from?" And they spread around the story as a piece of entertainment.

Dear audience, won't you agree that this impoverished old widow did the right thing? She kept a sick little boy whom she had never seen before, nursed him back to health, and gave him money before his departure, hating to see him go. Those neighbors who spoke ill of her were all men. Instead of doing good deeds, as was expected of good men, they turned around and set their tongues wagging against her. Clearly, though human faces may look alike, human hearts can be vastly different. But enough idle comments.

Without a pack animal and having no idea where the roads led, Li Chengzu kept to the highway and asked for directions as he went along. Whenever he felt tired, he asked for lodging at temples, monasteries, towns, or villages. Thanks to what little money the old woman had given him, he bought himself enough food to keep his stomach half full until he reached Lintao Prefecture, a place deserted and sparsely populated as a result of the war. Chengzu asked for the location of the erstwhile battlefield and was directed to Mount Gaolan. When he was approaching the battlefield, he was seized with a longing to offer sacrifices to his father. With only about ten pennies left, he bought no more than a string of paper coins. Then he asked for something that could serve as a pilot flame and, thus equipped, ran all the way toward the battlefield, which appeared to him from afar to be a vast stretch of wilderness without a single human being anywhere in sight. He began to take fright and stopped in his tracks, not daring to take another step forward.

But then again, he thought, "It took me so much pain to get here. If fear stops me, how am I going to find father's remains? I must go ahead even if it costs me my life." Mustering up courage, he ran with the speed of wind to the battlefield. What met his eyes when he got there was indeed a desolate scene. Behold:

> The vast wasteland is overgrown with weeds.
> Covered with thistles and thorns all entangled,
> The expanse of yellow sand is boundless.
> Sadly, in open air lie skeletons
> Of mighty warriors of bygone days.
> Only scattered bones are left of heroes of the past.
> Amid sinister winds, eerie howls fill the ears;
> In the cold mist, foxes and rabbits meet the eyes.
> Under the moon, gut-wrenching cries of apes;
> In autumn clouds, heartbreaking calls of geese.

Li Chengzu blew the pilot flame into a fire, burned up the paper coins, and tearfully bowed to the sky on his knees. After he rose to his feet, he walked around, looking for signs of his father's remains, but all he saw were piles of bones. Not one whole body was to be found. What had happened was that after defeating the rebels, Commander Zhao had been so saddened by the sight of all the dead bodies that he had made sacrificial offerings to the war dead right there in the battlefield and had had the remains cremated, leaving no whole bodies. Worn out after searching for the longest time, Li Chengzu sat down amid the weeds for a rest. Suddenly, he was struck by this thought, "A battlefield is wherever troops happen to encounter their enemies and fight. This shouldn't be the only one. I wonder in which battlefield father died. Am I not a fool searching only in this place?" But then again, another thought occurred to him: "How could I be such an idiot? Father has been dead for so long that his body must have decomposed. Even if his bones are still here, I won't be able to identify them. If so, won't I have taken all these pains for nothing?" Mournfully he prayed, looking up at the sky, "Father! Your spirits shouldn't have gone far yet. Li Chengzu, your son, has undertaken this journey of a thousand li to search for your remains, but there's no way I can tell which bones are yours. Father, having laid down your life for your country, you must have achieved divine status now. Please show me where your bones are. I will carry them home for a proper burial, so that they will not lie exposed in the wildness, like those of a ghost that gets no sacrificial offerings." Having said this prayer, he burst into loud sobs. Then he resumed his search among the piles of bones.

When daylight faded to dusk, he took to the road to look for a place where he could spend the night. Before he had covered one li, a monk walked out of the woods on one side of the road. Looking Li Chengzu up and down, the monk said, "What a reckless child! Don't you know what place this is? How can you walk here all by yourself?"

Li Chengzu said, his eyes misting over, "I'm from the capital. My father followed Commander Zhao on an expedition and died in battle. I'm here to look for his remains and take them home for burial. But I've found nothing. As it's getting dark, I need to find a place when I can spend the night. If Your Reverence can kindly let me stay in your temple for one night, it'll be a work of great merit."

The monk said, "A child with such filial devotion is indeed hard to come by. But the bodies have been cremated. There's no way you can find your father's remains."

At these words, Chengzu sank to the ground in a flood of tears. The monk raised him to his feet and said, "Young man, crying won't help. Spend the night with me and go back home tomorrow."

Li Chengzu saw nothing for it but to follow the monk. After walking for more than two li, they came upon a small village that appeared to have only five or six households. The monk took Chengzu into a small thatched hut, got a fire going, prepared some food, and served Chengzu a meal. "Young master," he asked, "in which commandery did your father serve? Under which commander? And what's his name?"

"My father, Li Xiong, was a battalion commander of the imperial guards."

The monk gave a start. "So you're Commander Li's son!"

"Your Reverence, how do you know my father?"

"To tell you the truth, I used to be a soldier in the palace guard cavalry. My name used to be Zeng Hu'er. When I joined the expedition last year, I was put under your father's command. He was so impressed with my outstanding bravery and strength that he made me his personal guard and treated me with special favor. He promised me a promotion to officer status when we won victory. As it turned out, on the fourteenth day of the seventh month, I followed your father into battle and, after we killed hundreds of enemies, the rest of the enemy troops withdrew. In a show of valor, we chased them for more than ten li, deep into dangerous grounds. The enemies charged out of their ambush and surrounded us on all sides. Our reinforcement troops were blocked by the ring of encirclement and all of our men died except your father and me, though we were badly wounded. The two of us hid ourselves among the dead bodies. When I got up in the middle of the night to escape, I found your father dead. I saw an earthen wall some distance off. So I carried him there on my back, pushed the wall over, and buried him. With the rebel troops blocking the way, I couldn't go back to the camp. So I fled to a valley, where I met an old monk. He took me into his temple and took care of me until my wounds healed. He talked to me day and night, urging me to join the Buddhist order. I thought, having just narrowly escaped death, I might just as well take life easy. So I did as he said and took the tonsure. In spring of this year, the old monk passed away. His two disciples said I did not qualify as a monk and refused to let me stay on. I thought, since I had already joined the Buddhist order, I shouldn't get into a fight with anyone. So I gave in to them and decided to go far away as a mendicant monk. I was passing by this place when I noticed that this hut was empty. I made it my home and I eke out a living by begging for food in villages nearby. And now heaven sent you here to me."

Upon learning that his father's corpse remained whole, Li Chengzu threw himself on the floor in a bow of gratitude. The monk hastened to stop him. "You're so young and weak," said the monk. "Why didn't you bring along a servant but travel all alone?

After telling him all the details about his illness, Miao Quan's desertion, and the old woman's help, Li Chengzu added, "I had already decided to kill myself on the battlefield if I couldn't find my father's remains. And then, luckily for both father and son, I met Your Reverence here by the will of heaven!"

"This is an act of providence, made possible by the spirits of your father the hero and your touching filial devotion. But you are all alone and you're penniless. How are you going to carry the remains home?"

"I've been thinking of asking the local government for assistance. Do you think they'll be willing to help me?"

The monk laughed. "You're quite mistaken, young master! As the saying goes, 'The sympathy of officials is paper thin,' They may be your best friends when you're alive, but once you're dead and gone, it's another story. And your father didn't even know the local officials. You're dreaming!"

"In that case, what's to be done?"

The monk thought for a while before saying, "Don't worry! I've got an idea. Tomorrow, let's put the remains in a container. I'll carry it on my back. The two of us can then slowly make it back to the capital, begging for food along the way. What do you say?"

"Your Reverence is so kind! I'll be forever in your debt, dead or alive!"

"I'm just trying to repay a fraction of the debt of gratitude I owe your father for his recognition of my ability. What little I'll be doing is not even worth mentioning."

The next day, the monk got from a neighbor a battered old bamboo hamper and two ropes, borrowed a hoe, and bought a few strings of paper coins. Then he locked up the door of his hut and led Li Chengzu out onto the road. A few li later, they came upon an even more deserted village. After the hamper was put down by an earthen wall, Li Chengzu broke down in sobs. The monk burned the paper coins, said prayers, and, hoe in hand, dug open the earth, exposing to view a pile of white bones. They picked up the bones, moving from the feet up, laid them in the hamper, put the lid on, and bound the hamper tightly with the ropes. With the hamper on the monk's back and the hoe in Li Chengzu's hand, they returned to the thatched hut. The monk put together his mantle, alms bowl, and his bedding, gathered them into a bundle, and found a bamboo pole so that he could carry the bundle and the hamper on each end of it. Shouldering the load, he left his hut, returned the hoe, bade farewell to the neighbors, and asked them to keep an eye on the hut.

And so the monk and Chengzu set out on their journey. They begged all along the way and got more than enough money for their travel needs. A few days later, they arrived at Bao'an Village. Recalling the old woman's kindness to him, Li Chengzu went to her house to offer his thanks and bid her farewell. As it turned out, however, after he had left, the old woman had missed him so much that she had fallen ill and passed away. (*Heaven had extended the old woman's life just so that she could take care of Li Chengzu. Births and deaths do not happen by chance.*) A few relatives had long ago made funeral arrangements and cremated her remains out in the wilderness. Upon learning all this from the neighbors, Li Chengzu bowed toward the sky and cried his fill before resuming the journey.

More than three months later, when they were about ten li from the capital, the monk said, noticing a wineshop by the road, "Let's take a rest there, young master." After entering the shop and placing the bamboo hamper on the table, he continued, "I should escort you all the way to your home and kowtow to your father's shrine. However, even though I'm a monk now, I was a soldier. If someone recognizes me and arrests me as an army deserter, I won't be able to get away. I'll have to say good-bye to you now. I'll try to see you again in the future."

With tears in his eyes, Li Chengzu said, "Your Reverence does have a point, but I may be able to repay some of my debt to you if you can follow me home. I have nothing to offer you in this place. Oh what am I going to do?"

"What kind of talk is this?" said the monk. "I undertook this journey partly out of gratitude for your father's kindness to me, and partly because you were in desperate straits. Who covets your money?"

While they were talking, a waiter brought them wine and food. The monk offered libation, laid everything out in front of the bamboo hamper, and kowtowed four or five times before he rose to bid Li Chengzu farewell. Both shed many a tear. After drinking a few cups, the monk paid the bill and hired a pack animal for Li Chengzu and a porter to carry the hamper. Then he put his own bundle on his back, walked out of the wineshop with Chengzu, and bade him a tearful farewell. There is a poem in testimony:

> He went through thick and thin to find his father's bones;
> He covered a thousand li, sick and alone.
> The old woman and the monk lent him helping hands;
> Heaven does not let down a filial son.

Let us follow another thread of the story and turn our attention to Miao Quan, the servant. After abandoning Li Chengzu, he hired a pack animal and rushed back home. To everyone else he said that he had been to the battlefield, but that the remains were nowhere to be found, and that the young master had died of illness and had been buried on the road because there was no travel money left. To Jiao-shi, however, he secretly reported the truth.

Yuying and her sisters were in dire misery partly because they missed their father and partly because Jiao-shi beat them and yelled at them all the time. Miao Quan's words plunged them into deeper despair. Jiao-shi shed a few false-hearted tears. With both the master and the young master dead and gone, the servants went to seek employment with luckier families, leaving only Miao Quan and his wife and two maidservants behind in the now-deserted household. How Jiao-shi wished that her son Yanu would grow quickly into an adult to inherit his father's post and bring prosperity to the house again! When news came that the secretary of the office of defense had written to the emperor to ask for pension for the families of the war dead and that the matter was under review in the ministry of defense by imperial order, Jiao-shi gave her brother Jiao Rong a good deal of gold and silver for him to bribe high and low in the ministry, so that her late husband could be posthumously promoted to commander.

Jiao Rong was a man used to gaining petty advantages in his dealings with people. He was not going to make an exception in his sister's case. One day, he went to his sister for a report with an eye to getting a reward. Jiao-shi laid out for him a fine spread of wine and food. Both of them had a large capacity for wine and had never been any the worse for drinking. That day, they drank from early afternoon to dusk. After finishing all the wine in the house and longing for more, they told Miao Quan to go out and buy some more. Wine jar in hand, Miao Quan was on the point of going down the steps when he saw in the distance a pack animal on which sat a little boy who was none other than Young Master Li Chengzu. He was aghast. "So, this cursed boy is still alive," he said to himself as he spun around and ran inside. After he whispered the news to Jiao-shi, the latter immediately consulted Jiao Rong and told Miao Quan to exit the house from the back door and buy arsenic. The two of them remained in their seats, drinking and waiting for Li Chengzu to come in.

Upon reaching the door of the house, Li Chengzu jumped down from the pack animal. The porter, carrying the hamper on his back, followed Chengzu into the house and all the way into the main hall. Seeing no one around amid the silence, Chengzu thought mournfully, "So this is what the family has been reduced to after father's death!" He had the porter place the bamboo hamper on the shrine before dismissing him. Chengzu then kowtowed to the shrine. Overwhelmed by memory of all the misery he had gone through, he burst into loud sobs and bent over the shrine in a flood of tears.

When the crying reached her ears, Jiao-shi feigned concern and sent a maid out to the main hall to see what was going on. At the sight of Li Chengzu, the maid was frightened out of her wits. She staggered back to her mistress's room and said, "Madam, the young master's ghost is here!"

Spitting right into her face, Jiao-shi snapped, "You're daydreaming and talking nonsense!"

"He's crying in front of the shrine. If you don't believe me, ma'am, go with me and see for yourself."

Jiao Rong put in, feigning disbelief, "How can that be?"

Together, they went into the main hall. Upon seeing them, Li Chengzu went forward and tearfully bowed low in greeting. Jiao Rong stopped him, saying, "You've had a hard journey. You need not bow."

Forcing a few drops of tears, Jiao-shi said, "Miao Quan brought back bad news about you. You've never been absent from my thoughts. How I regret having sent you on that trip! Now that you're back, safe and sound, I can't be happier! But did you find your father's remains?"

Pointing at the bamboo hamper, Chengzu said, "There they are." Whereupon Jiao-shi put her arms around the hamper and began to wail.

In happy astonishment at word that Li Chengzu had returned unscathed, Yuying and her sisters scampered to the main hall. The four children fell on one another's shoulders and wept. Yuying said when the weeping stopped, "Miao Quan said you were dead. How did you come back to life?"

After Li Chengzu gave an account of his illness, Miao Quan's refusal to stop and rest, and his encounter with the monk who had escorted him home, Jiao Rong said in an outburst of rage, "That slave Miao Quan is so evil! Let me take him to the government yamen and have him beaten to death to avenge you, my good nephew."

"It's so nice to have you stand by me, Uncle!"

Jiao-shi said, "You must be tired after the journey. Go inside for some wine and food and then take a good rest."

Thereupon everyone went inside. Jiao Rong sat Li Chengzu down while Yuying and the other girls stood unobtrusively to one side. After telling a maid to heat the wine, Jiao-shi went to the back door, where Miao Quan was already waiting. Jiao-shi took the arsenic from him and instructed him to wait a while longer before entering the house. She then went into the kitchen, dismissed the maid, poured the arsenic into the wine pot, and went back to the room where the children were.

Before long, the maid brought the well-heated wine pot to the table. Jiao Rong took a teacup, filled it with wine from the pot and, handing the cup to Chengzu, said, "My good nephew, let me present Buddha with borrowed flowers, so to speak, and offer you this toast to welcome you back from the journey."

"Thank you so much, Uncle!" said Chengzu as he took the cup. Then he laid it down and was about to fill another cup and offer a toast to his uncle in return when Jiao Rong raised the cup again and held it to Chengzu's lips, saying, "We've drunk so much that there's only a little left in the pot. Now drink it up while it's still nice and warm."

The unsuspecting Li Chengzu finished the wine, taking one gulp after another. Jiao Rong filled the cup again and said, "Young man, you must drink another cup to make an even number." Again he held out the cup against Chengzu's lips. Thinking it would be too presumptuous for him to turn down an elder, Chengzu drained the second cup as well. When Jiao Rong again tried to fill the cup a third time, there was only enough wine to fill less than half of it, which gave Jiao Rong all the more reason to make Li Chengzu drink it up. It would have been all right if Chengzu had not drunk the wine, but as soon as the wine reached his stomach, he began to complain of a stomachache. Jiao-shi said, "You must have come in contact with some kind of poisonous air somewhere on the road."

"No, I didn't," said Chengzu.

"You say this because you may not have felt anything at the time," insisted Jiao-shi.

In an instant, the poison began to take effect. Feeling as if he was being stabbed by steel spears and burned by a raging fire, he cried out in excruciating pain, "The pain is killing me!" With that, he collapsed onto the floor.

Jiao Rong said with a show of alarm, "Wasn't he perfectly all right just a moment ago? What could be giving him so much pain?"

Jiao-shi said, "It must be cholera." Quickly she had the maid help him lie in Yuying's bed. As Chengzu tossed about, moaning in pain, Yuying and the girls, in a flurry of panic, tried futilely to hold him still. In less than an hour, his five internal organs burst and blood flowed out from the seven apertures in his head.[10] With a loud cry, he died. Standing around him, Yuying and the other girls cried their hearts out while Jiao-shi rejoiced, although she managed a few wails of grief.

Jiao Rong commented, "It looks like he has offended the gods and some avenging spirit got him. At least he was lucky enough to have returned home. But we'll inconvenience Yuying if we leave the body in her room. Let's encoffin him tonight, to spare the girls from fear." Whereupon Jiao-shi went to take out some silver. By that time, Miao Quan had sneaked in to find out how things were. Upon hearing the bitter cries inside, he surmised that it was all over with the boy and went straight in. Seeing him, Jiao-shi gave him the silver for him to buy a coffin and two pots of wine. After accomplishing his mission, he finished the wine, placed the coffin in a side room and, rolling up his sleeves, entered Yuying's room. Telling the girls to go away, he turned the corpse in the bed and raised the body without bothering to wipe off the blood and change the clothes. Partly because he was strong, partly because he was under the emboldening influence of the wine, and partly because Chengzu was only about ten years of age and shouldn't have weighed much, he carried the body effortlessly in his arms and went to the side room to lower it into the coffin. Yuying and her sisters followed behind, weeping. As it turned out, Miao Quan had kept a part of the money for himself and bought a coffin that was five or six inches too short. The legs stuck out of the coffin. When the legs were tucked in, the lid would not close. As Miao Quan pulled and pushed unavailingly, the girls, witnessing the scene, cried even more bitterly. Jiao-shi thought for a while and an idea came to her. She drove the girls and the maidservants out, closed the door, and had Miao Quan drag the body onto the floor and cut the shanks off with an ax. The shanks were then stuffed under the head to make a pillow. She did not open the door until everything had been done and the lid nailed back on. Jiao Rong returned to his own home.

Seeing that the lid had been nailed back on, Yuying thought, "Wasn't the coffin too small just a moment ago? How did they manage to put the lid back on after they drove us out of the room? Could they have used some magic and enlarged the coffin and shrunk the corpse?" And so she wondered without finding an answer.

Two days later, Jiao-shi prepared burial clothes and a coffin for her late husband's remains and, on a chosen day, buried the coffin in the ancestral grave site. It so happened that the final decision on pension for the war dead was announced at this time: Li Xiong was to be named posthumously a General of Loyalty and Bravery but not a commander. All of Jiao-shi's money spent on bribes had gone down the drain.

On the day of the burial, relatives and neighbors also came to pay their respects to the departed. Li Chengzu was buried next to his father's grave. When asked, Jiao-shi replied that the boy had fallen ill on the road and had died as soon as he had gotten home. This being a matter that did not concern them, none of the relatives bothered to get to the bottom of it. How sad that Li Chengzu survived the hardships of the journey to the battlefield only to perish at his own home! Truly,

> Strangers turned out to be his friends;
> His kith and kin proved to be his foes.
> Everything is ordained by fate;
> Nothing is up to human effort.

As the saying goes, "Be sure to draw lessons from a painful experience." When Li Chengzu was dying, Yuying was too frightened to think. After his burial, suspicions began to enter her mind: "How come he died right after he arrived home, not a moment sooner or a moment later? I don't believe this could have happened by chance. What's more, he bled through the nose and the mouth. And they didn't even take the time to consult the calendar for a burial date, or to clean up the place. When they found the coffin too small, they didn't change it for a larger one but got us out of the room and somehow managed to fit him in. There was talk of taking Miao Quan to the government yamen, but nothing is said about this anymore, and Miao Quan seems to be even closer to them than before. He was obviously acting on mother's orders. All of these are signs of something suspicious about my brother's death." ([Illegible.] *suspicious* [Illegible.]) For all her suspicions, she could do no more than shed tears.

As for Jiao-shi, after murdering Li Chengzu, she thought, "That little rascal is out of the way, but then there are those little sluts. I've been tormenting them all right, but I'm still too easy on them. I need to really come down hard on them, so that they won't dare take me lightly." Henceforth she went out of her way to find fault with them and, at every turn, lashed them with her leather whip until their skin ripped open all over. And she didn't allow them to cry out loud. If she heard even one sob, down came her whip again. Every day, she gave them only two meals consisting of nothing more than watery porridge. If they fell short of the quota she set for their needlework, apart from the inevitable curses and beatings, she would even deny them the watery porridge. Their more decent clothes were also forcibly taken off in exchange for the old and worn clothes of the maidservants. In the depths of winter, each one of them wore no more than three or four layers of unlined clothing plus a piece of old cotton wadding over their shoulders. At night, they shared a straw mat and a tattered quilt cover that were such poor protection against the cold that they clung to one another like worms. Their misery defies description. Several times they thought of death to get out of their suffering, but hopes for better days to come kept them alive as they tried to console one another. Indeed, it was too painful to live on but too early to die.

Soon, another year rolled around. Yuying was now twelve years old. In the second lunar month of that year [1521], Emperor Zhengde passed away and Emperor Jiajing took over the throne. An imperial decree was issued for the selection of royal consorts from all over the land. Government yamens ordered every family to report if there were eligible candidates in the neighborhood. Those withholding information would be punished, along with their neighbors. Jiao-shi's neighbors, impressed by Yuying's talent and beauty, reported her name to the prefectural yamen. A yellow poster was then put on Jiao-shi's door, notifying the family of the upcoming interview.

Coveting kinship with the emperor, Jiao-shi turned around and danced attendance on Yuying, dressing her up in silk and satin and feeding her the finest food to build up her health. She also gave Jiao Rong money to bribe officials in the Ministry of Rites. Even though she had been put through a great deal of tribulation, Yuying remained a beauty. After several days of recuperation, she regained the rosy color of her cheeks. Dressed in resplendent clothes now, she looked like a figure in a painting. Of the numerous young women interviewed at the prefectural yamen, Yuying came out first and was sent, along with her file, to the Ministry of Rites for the next round of selection. The officials of the Ministry of Rites were quite impressed by Yuying's beauty and deportment but thought her too young to serve the emperor. So they sent her back home. Regretting the piles of money she had paid in vain, Jiao-shi was so upset that her face fell again. She took away the fine clothes she had given Yuying, stopped the supply of good food, and grew even more ruthless in her verbal and physical abuse of Yuying.

As the proverb puts it so well, "One who sits idle will eat away a mountain of fortune; one who stands idle will eat his way into the ground." Li Xiong's family fortune was not impressive to begin with. After his death, Jiao-shi was too preoccupied with tormenting the children to think about ways to generate income. With so many mouths to feed, how long do you think the family fortune could last? And substantial amounts of money had gone down the drain to pay for an official title for the deceased and for royal consort status for Yuying. As the days went by, the family savings were exhausted. Even the two maidservants were sold off to pay for food. As a last resort, the house was sold off.

Now that the family had fallen on hard times, that villain Miao Quan thought that he could not afford to wait until the young master Yanu was old enough to inherit the official title. Coveting the money that Jiao-shi had just been paid for the house, he sneaked into her bedchamber at night, stole the silver, and slipped out of the house with his wife to some faraway place to live a good life. Jiao-shi did not learn about his betrayal until the next morning. Venting her spleen on Yuying and the other girls, she yelled, "Why didn't you wake up to stop that thief?" None of the girls was spared a thrashing with the whip. In the meantime, she had Jiao Rong ask the authorities to issue a search warrant. Two months went by, but the search turned up nothing. With the buyer of the house urging her to vacate the premises, Jiao-shi saw nothing for it but to consult her brother about selling Yuying off.

Jiao Rong said, "This pretty girl will fetch a handsome amount of money if you take your time and find a good buyer. But if you're in too much haste, you'll get shortchanged. It would be better to sell off a younger one first, to tide you over for now."

Following his advice, Jiao-shi sold Taoying to a rich family as a housemaid. The sisters were overcome with grief as they bade each other farewell. Jiao-shi rented a small house and chose a day for the relocation.

Yuying was deeply saddened at the thought that the ancestral home now belonged to someone else. As she walked out of the house and happened to see swallows repair their old nest on the beam while building a new one next to it, she said to herself with emotion, "A swallow leaves its nest in autumn but gets to return each spring. I, Li Yuying, will never be able to return here after I leave." In sorrow, she expressed her feelings through a poem about the scene. Entitled "Farewell to the Swallows," the poem said,

> The old nest is crooked, the new one not quite ready;
> It's too late to draw the thin curtains over the dust.
> In sorrow I bid the swallows farewell;
> The painted hall remains, but the owner is gone.

In order to be near her brother, Jiao-shi moved to a small lane within a stone's throw of his house. Next to Jiao-shi's house was a garden that belonged to a wealthy family. It being a house of only two rooms, everything was inconvenient and water had to be fetched from outside, which was something Jiao-shi would not condescend to do, for she was used to much easier circumstances. The job fell naturally to Yuying and Yueying, who had no choice but to swallow the humiliation and show themselves in public, doing the errands. Before long, the money from selling Taoying also gave out.

One evening, when standing idly with her son Yanu by the door, Jiao-shi saw a beggar girl, more than ten years old, crying pitifully in the street for handouts. An old woman in a neighboring house said to her, "Who will give you anything at this time? You'd better go home now."

The beggar girl said tearfully, "Granny, you have no idea what I have to go through! The old one at home orders that I bring back fifty pennies every day. One penny short and I'll be beaten half dead and denied supper. And I have to make up for the shortfall the next day. I'm still six or seven pennies short. How dare I return?"

Touched by the sad story, the old woman gave her two pennies. Others present followed suit, and, in the excitement of the moment, more than ten pennies exchanged hands. Profuse with thanks, the beggar girl turned back and went off.

Jiao-shi's greed stirred as she witnessed the scene. She thought, "That little beggar went away with quite a tidy sum. That lowlife Yueying won't fetch a lot of money with her mediocre looks. Why don't I make her take up that line of business? There's nothing to lose but everything to gain." In the midst of her thoughts, she saw Yueying coming back, carrying water.

"Little cheap hussy!" called out Jiao-shi. "Did you see that girl begging in the streets? She's younger than you are, but she makes fifty cents a day. Have you found a way to make a few cents?"

Yueying rejoined, "She's a beggar. She gets the money by begging people for mercy. How can I be compared with her?"

Jiao-shi thundered, "Don't tell me you're not as capable as she is! Starting tomorrow, go out and make fifty cents a day. One penny short and I'll beat your legs off!" (*Anyone observing Jiao-shi's behavior will not dare remarry. What a holy terror! But those without children from a previous marriage need not fear.*)

Upon hearing that Jiao-shi wanted Yueying to beg for a living, both girls were appalled. Looking at each other in consternation, they fell to their knees in unison and pleaded, their faces awash in tears, "Mother, we come from a long line of officials. Many people know us. We must keep our dignity. If we were reduced to begging, wouldn't we bring disgrace to the family and become laughingstocks?"

"Without knowing where your next meal is to come from, why are you still so concerned about dignity and becoming laughingstocks?"

Yueying said, "I'm not going, even if you beat me to death."

"You lowlife! You defy me! Let me beat you up right now and give you a taste of what you're in for later!" So saying, Jiao-shi found a piece of firewood and, seizing Yueying, rained blows on her head. Unable to take the pain, Yueying screamed, "Have mercy, mother! I'll go tomorrow!"

Jiao-shi let go of Yueying and, turning to Yuying, said, "You should be grateful that I didn't make you go. And yet you turned around and came up with all that shit!" She flung Yuying to the floor and beat her up as well with the piece of firewood. The next morning, she drove Yueying out to the streets to beg. Resignedly, Yueying swallowed the humiliation and followed her bidding. Henceforth, she begged in the streets day in and day out. If she made fifty cents at the end of the day, Jiao-shi would say nothing. If not, Yueying would be beaten half dead.

Time flew like an arrow. Before anyone knew it, Yuying was already sixteen years old. One day toward the end of the third month, Jiao-shi took Yanu to Jiao

Rong's house to offer congratulations on his fiftieth birthday. With Yueying begging in the streets, Yuying was the only one left behind to look after the house. After Jiao-shi left, Yuying closed the door, went inside, and, as her hands were engaged in needlework, she thought, "Father cherished us like pearls in his palm and never had one harsh word for us. But this stepmother abuses us in every possible way. She murdered my brother, sold off one of my sisters as a servant, made the other one a beggar, squandered away the family fortune, and got us into such a sorry condition. I wonder how we will all end up. It's better to die sooner than live on like this. While she's not here, why don't I take my own life, to spare myself from more abuse?" But then again, she thought, "I'm already sixteen now. Let me hold on until I marry. Maybe my life will change for the better. Why end this life needlessly?" Recalling the miseries she had been put through, she broke down in tears and then her thoughts again went back over her sufferings. She wept until she felt exhausted. In low spirits, she put down her needlework, walked into the yard, and looked out into the neighbor's garden, where swallows flitted by and orioles chirped amid the riot of colors, the sweeping willow branches, the quivering gossamer, and the elm pods on the ground. The scene pulled at her heartstrings and she intoned a poem, which she titled "Sending Spring on Its Way":

> The lonely wicket gate locks in the last vestiges of spring;
> Coin-shaped elm pods strew the ground but don't relieve the poor.
> My hair and clothes are half covered with mud;
> Why do the wild flowers bring so much delight?

After intoning the poem, Yuying thought again, "Since father died, my stepmother has put me through so much torment day after day that I've been in no mood to make poems. I wrote 'Farewell to Swallows' when moving into this place, but that was already more than a year ago. How time flies!" After heaving a few rueful sighs, she rushed back into the house, afraid that she would fall behind in her needlework. Upon seeing on the table a letter from Jiao Rong inviting his sister to his birthday banquet, Yuying cut off a portion of it, found a brush-pen and an ink slab, and wrote down the two poems. After reading them back and forth, she said to herself with another sigh, "Since ancient times, any number of brilliant women have gained eternal fame for themselves by writing poems either with their sisters or their husbands. But I, luckless Li Yuying, am consigned to oblivion. What a pity, and how deplorable!" In her grief, she felt even more listless, and absent-mindedly folded the piece of paper into the shape of two overlapping diamonds. She hid it by her pillow but forgot to put the brush-pen and ink slab back. With all the haste she could muster, she finished her needlework before the onset of evening. Yueying returned home first, followed closely by Jiao-shi. Noticing Yuying's tear-stained cheeks, Jiao-shi said, "Who gave you a hard time? Why put on another disgusting act?"

Not daring to reply, Yuying showed Jiao-shi the needlework she had accomplished. Yueying also surrendered to Jiao-shi what money she had made that day. After eating some porridge, Yuying went on with her needlework and did not go to bed until midnight.

The next day, noticing the brush-pen and the ink slab on the table, Jiao-shi picked up the letter and saw that a portion of the stationery had been cut off. Suspecting Yuying of having written complaints against her, she asked, "What did you write about yesterday? Show it to me this instant!"

"It's just a little poem. Nothing much to it."

Raising her voice, Jiao-shi said, "Is it a love note to arrange a date with some man? Was that why you ruined the invitation letter to me?"

Yuying reddened to the roots of her hair. The blushing convinced Jiao-shi that the girl had a clandestine love affair to hide and she forced her to produce her writing. At the sight of the folded diamonds [a symbol of love], she was even more convinced of Yuying's guilt. She picked up a rod and said, pointing at Yuying, "Whore! How dare you take advantage of my brief absence to write a love note to some man? Out with the truth now! Who is he and how long has this relationship been going on?"

Yuying burst out sobbing. "Where does all this come from? You're sullying my name with a nonexistent scandal. You do me injustice!"

In a rage, Jiao-shi said, "With the evidence here, how can you be so brazen?" She raised the rod and relentlessly rained blows on Yuying. Trying desperately to dodge the blows, Yuying finally struggled free and ran toward the door.

"Are you going to get your man so that he can help you beat me up?" cried Jiao-shi as she gave chase. But she tripped and fell, knocking her head against a brick. With blood all over her face, she screamed, "A fine job you did, beating me like this! Just you wait!"

Yueying went up and raised Jiao-shi to her feet. Jiao-shi was about to run after Yuying again when Yanu held her in a tight grip and said, "Mother, let sister off."

Afraid that she might hurt her own son, the woman felt obliged to stop and contented herself with unleashing a string of vile epithets. Yuying ran to the door and stood there, weeping. The neighbors were no strangers to the sounds of Jiao-shi abusing the two girls day in and day out, but this time, hearing a commotion that was worse than usual, they gathered at the door, talking. At this point, Jiao Rong appeared on the scene. As he pushed open the door and went in, Jiao-shi cried out, "It's a good thing you're here! That hussy Yuying has a secret lover. Look how badly she beat me up!"

Seeing blood all over her face, Jiao Rong believed her story and, without bothering to verify the facts, grabbed the rod from Jiao-shi's hands, rushed over, seized Yuying, and flailed her with it. The neighbors intervened at this point in defense of Yuying. Walking over, they said, "She's a fifteen- or sixteen-year-old girl now. She has just been badly beaten. Instead of pacifying things, you also beat her. You may be her uncle, but you still have no right to beat her."

Discountenanced by the reproach, Jiao Rong threw down the rod and took himself off. The neighbors continued, "We've never seen another family like this, with the mother abusing the two daughters day in and day out. And now even the uncle joins in the fun. It looks like the two girls won't have long to live."

Another one said, "If they die, we'll report to the authorities. The Jiaos will have to pay with their own lives!"

At this outburst from the neighbors, Jiao-shi could do no more than shut her mouth. She sharply ordered Yueying to close the door and she herself wiped off the blood. As before, she made Yueying go out to make her rounds on the streets.

After weeping for a while, Yuying went back inside in spite of her pain, to resume her needlework. Jiao-shi kept up a stream of curses. Late at night, Yuying thought, choking back her sobs, "All human beings, even if they live to be a hundred years old, will die some day. Why put up with such humiliation and abuse?" She waited until Jiao-shi was fast asleep before she quietly rose, took off her foot bindings, and tossed them over the beam. However, she was not destined to die at this time, and it was all thanks to her stepmother. Her stepmother took so little care of her that she was wearing nothing but tatters, and the fabric of the foot-bindings, having been in use for goodness knows how many years, had disintegrated to the point where with one stretch, it snapped. Yuying had barely put her neck into the noose when she fell onto the floor with a thump. Yueying woke up in alarm. Realizing that her sister was not by her side, she guessed what Yuying must have been up to. "Oh no!" she cried. She jumped up from bed and revived her sister. The two girls wept bitterly. Upon learning about what had happened, Jiao-shi said viciously, without even bothering to get up from bed, "Lousy slave! Imagine threatening me with suicide! I'll deal with her tomorrow."

The next morning, Jiao-shi told Yueying to stay at home and look after the house whereas she herself and Yanu went to Jiao Rong's house. After telling him all about what the neighbors had said the day before as well as about Yuying's suicide attempt, she added, "If she dies, you'll be implicated. The best thing to do is to take her to the government yamen and get rid of this source of trouble once and for all."

Jiao Rong said, "To get rid of her is easy. I've done a lot of things for the office of the imperial guards. I've got friends there. And yours is a military family. If you send her to the yamen, who would dare let out a peep?"

Exultantly, Jiao-shi had her brother ask someone to write up an official complaint, accusing Yuying of debauchery and unfilial behavior, and sent her, along with the two poems as evidence, to the office of the imperial guards in the yamen. Jiao Rong, being friends with the yamen lictors, went in first for explanations. Before long, the court session was called to order. Jiao-shi's letter of complaint was accepted. Four marshals were dispatched to bring Yuying to court.

Having heard only one side of the story, the interrogator ordered torture for Yuying, without bothering to find out the facts. To Yuying's arguments in defense of herself, he turned a deaf ear. Breaking down under the torture, poor Yuying admitted to everything she was accused of. The crime being punishable by death, she was taken to jail. As two guards escorted her out of the yamen, they ran into Yueying. What had happened was that, shocked at the sight of the marshals apprehending her sister, Yueying had quickly locked the door and followed behind, to see how things would develop. Upon seeing guards escorting her sister out, she ran up, held her sister in her arms, and let out wails of grief. Jiao-shi approached and pulled the two girls apart, saying to Yueying, "You lowlife! You are supposed to look after the house. Why are you here?"

Jiao-shi being to her as a cat is to a mouse, Yueying trembled with fear and dared not refuse to follow her home. Once back at home, Jiao-shi gave her another severe beating, saying, "If you sneak out again to see that whore, I'll have you thrown into the same place as soon as I find out!"

Yueying promised not to see Yuying again. However, being Yuying's blood sister, she could not bear the separation. Two or three days later, having begged harder and saved up dozens of extra pennies, she sneaked out again to the jailhouse to see if she could find out anything. (*Poor thing!*) But of her, more later.

Let us come back to Yuying. Once she was put in jail, the head warden took a fancy to this pretty girl. In a show of kindness, he put her in a nicer cell and brought her good, nourishing food. Believing him to be a good-hearted man, Yuying was overcome with gratitude and told him, "My sister Yueying will surely come to look around. Please do let her come in and see me."

The head warden remembered these words well. In the afternoon of the fourth day, when Yueying appeared at the gate of the jailhouse and gave her name, the head warden opened the gate with alacrity and led her to Yuying. That the two sisters wept in grief goes without saying, but they had to part when evening set in. From then on, Yueying often went to see her sister, but of this, no more need be said.

Now, coveting Yuying's beauty, even in his dreams the head warden thought of ways to have his pleasure of her. But there were too many eyes around for him to make a move. Also, he was afraid that Yuying might not submit herself to him. Should she scream, his chances would be ruined. Therefore he availed himself of every opportunity to strike up a conversation with her and to stir up her desires with suggestive remarks. Being as smart as she was, Yuying found these remarks offensive and realized that this was an unsavory character she needed to guard against. And so she did not readily make responses.

One day, Yuying was sitting gloomily on the threshold when the head warden walked in quietly and said smilingly in a soft voice, "Young lady, do you know why I've been taking such good care of you?"

Well aware of what he was there for, Yuying rose promptly and said, "I have no idea."

The warden continued, smiling, "You are a smart one. How can you not know?" So saying, he leaned forward to gather her into his arms.

Mortified, Yuying screamed, "Murder!"

Seeing that things were going the wrong way, the warden turned to go, saying, "So you resist me? I'll teach you a lesson tonight!"

At this threat, Yuying thumped her chest, stamped her feet, and cried so loudly that other wardens rushed over to see what was happening. After Yuying told them that the head warden had taken liberties with her, several of them, rising to her defense, called the head warden over and said to him, "Raping a female prisoner is a serious crime. If you continue to take good care of her as before, well and good. If not, we will jointly lodge a complaint against you. It's all up to you." (*She resisted the man's advances and the wardens are going to jointly accuse him of raping. They may even redress the wrongs done to her. Yee! How many people under the sun are ready to do such good deeds?*)

Knowing he was in the wrong, the head warden was profusely apologetic. "I will never bother her again," said he. Indeed,

> *The mutton bun escaped his lips;*
> *He had nothing but the foul smell all over him.*

After Yuying spent another two months in jail, the sixth month of the year rolled around. Every summer, the imperial court assigned eunuchs to government yamens to review pending cases. Those who believed they were wronged were allowed to lodge complaints. Upon hearing about the news at the beginning of the sixth month, Yuying thought that if she did not act to protest the wrong done by Jiao-shi to every one of her siblings, she would never have another chance. (*Jiao-shi is evil all right, but Jiao Rong is even worse.*) So she composed a memorandum to the emperor in which she gave a detailed account of the wrongs done to her and her siblings. Then she gave the memorandum to Yueying for her to deliver. An abbreviated version of the memorandum is as follows:

> *Your subject understands that in the words of the sages, lack of filial piety calls for the most severe form of the five punishments and that the lack of honor is most despised by proponents of the four virtues.*[11] *The Dou sisters threw themselves down a cliff, and Yunhua plunged into a well in defense of ethical norms and, in doing so, acquired undying fame.*[12]
>
> *Your subject's father, Li Xiong, battalion commander of the imperial guards, had by his first wife three daughters, including your subject, and a son, Li Chengzu, my younger brother. Unfortunately, our mother died when we were still at a tender age. Out of pity for us, our father married Jiao-shi, so that she could take care of us. On the fourteenth day of the seventh month of the fourteenth year of the Zhengde reign period, our father died in a battle against the rebels of Shaanxi, marking the beginning of a series of calamities that befell us. At age sixteen, your subject remains unbetrothed and my sisters are also in forlorn and wretched circumstances. The plums are ripe, but there are no red*

leaves to serve as messengers.[13] *I have written a poem entitled "Farewell to Spring" and another one entitled "Farewell to Swallows," both composed when overcome with despair. Alas! My stepmother, oblivious to my feelings, accused me of having an illicit love relationship and forced my uncle, Jiao Rong, to take me to the yamen on charges of debauchery and lack of filial piety. The interrogator in charge of the case failed to establish the truth and sentenced me to death. Being a woman, I stand a poor chance of successfully defending myself and therefore had to bow in submission, so as not to be accused of defying my stepmother's wishes and thus being doubly unfilial.*

By Your Majesty's grace, cases unjustly handled are under review and parties involved are allowed to state their cases. Complying with the imperial decree, I hereby state my case in the hope of being exempted from death.

My father, albeit a military officer, was well versed in the classics. Your subject, albeit female, was lucky enough to have benefited from his teaching. He passed away when my stepmother was twenty years of age and her son, Yanu, only one year old. In her impatience to have her own son inherit the official title, my stepmother made my younger brother, Li Chengzu, ten years old at the time, go to the battlefield to find my father's remains, in an attempt to drive Chengzu to death for her own gains. Fortunately, my brother brought my father's remains home, thanks to heaven's blessings on my father's spirits. Having thus failed in her first attempt, my stepmother then poisoned my brother to death and dismembered his body before burying him. Next, she sold my younger sister, Li Taoying, off to be a maidservant and deprived my other younger sister, Li Yueying, of food and clothes and made her beg for a living on the streets. She then framed a case against me, as stated above. Had I been guilty of any wrongdoing, my neighbors would have detected it and reported to the authorities. Without ever having caught anyone, my stepmother accused me of crime on the basis of two poems, evidence that is as unsubstantiated as a shadow and a puff of wind. I may be reconciled to my death, but my ten-year-old brother was not guilty of any crimes, nor are my sisters, at their tender age. I will not presume to denounce my stepmother for her offenses but should reproach myself, as advocated in the Book of Songs.[14] *My death is of little consequence. I am only afraid that all future stepmothers will be free from restraints in their oppression of their stepchildren. Humbly I ask for Your Majesty's understanding of my feelings in the hope that my case will be referred to the competent bureau, so that I can be executed without delay to gratify my stepmother. My poems can then be analyzed to determine if I was guilty in any way. I need not go into details about my stepmother's motives.* (Graceful and magnanimous. The style of a talented writer.) *Your subject will then be exonerated and my father will be grateful in the netherworld.*

The emperor personally read this statement and, convinced that the author was a victim of miscarriage of justice, issued a decree for the three judicial offices [the censorate, the ministry of justice, and the court of judicial review] to rigorously review the case. Not daring to be remiss in their duty, the officials of the three judicial offices summoned everyone involved in the case, including Taoying, and cross-examined all of them. In the beginning Jiao-shi and Jiao Rong denied everything. It was only after they were put under torture that they confessed. All the details bore out Yuying's account. Jiao-shi was convicted of the crimes of betraying her husband and murdering her stepson in violation of the law and ethical norms. Hers being a case far more serious than ordinary cases of infanticide, the judgment was for a severe sentence as a warning to all stepmothers. Jiao Rong was also to pay with his life for his part in the murder conspiracy. Yuying, Yueying, and Yanu were to return home. Jiao Rong's family possessions were to be sold off to redeem Taoying. The officials then reported to the emperor for approval.

Angry at the ferocity of the offenders, the Son of Heaven ordered that even Yanu was to be executed without delay. Again, Yuying submitted a memorandum, in which she pleaded, "Being hardly out of his swaddling clothes, Yanu is innocent and he is the only male heir left in the Li family. Please forgive him." (*Good. She keeps the larger picture in mind.*)

The emperor approved her request and ordered the ministry of justice to execute Jiao Rong and Jiao-shi only. That very day, the two of them were trussed up in ropes, taken to the execution ground, and put to death. (*Those hatching evil plans, be warned!*) Yanu was forbidden to inherit his father's official title. A son of another branch of the Li clan was to inherit Li Xiong's title. Yuying, Yueying, and Taoying all married scholars. Li Yuying's memorandum in defense of herself is contained in *Biographies of Virtuous Women*, along with these lines in praise of her:

> *Li Yuying, after her father's death and the disintegration of her family, wrote "Farewell to Spring" and "Farewell to Swallow," which incurred her stepmother's suspicions of an illicit love affair. She was thrown into jail and sentenced to death. It was her memorandum to the emperor stating her case that led to redress for the injustice inflicted on her.*

A poet of later times had this to say in lament:

> *The heartless stepmother, in her devious ways,*
> *Hatched evil plots for her own son's sake.*
> *Even if she had as much blood as water in the West River,*
> *It would not be enough to clear her of shame in death.*

28

Young Master Wu Goes to a Tryst in the Next Boat

Those who never miss a trick to seduce women
Ruin their own health and their credit record in the netherworld.
Be advised: refrain from debauchery!
The first Buddhist commandment is to guard against lust.

During the Southern Song dynasty, there lived in Jiangzhou a scholar named Pan Yu. His father, Pan Lang, had retired from his post as the prefect of Changsha [in Hunan]. After coming out first in the imperial civil service examinations at the provincial level, Pan Yu planned to bid farewell to his father, and rented a boat for his journey to Lin'an [present-day Hangzhou] for the national level of the examinations. The night before his departure, his father saw in a dream a group of drummers and musicians and a procession bearing colorful banners and a horizontal board on which was inscribed the name of the one who had come out first in the nationwide round of the examinations. It was none other than Pan Yu. The next morning, he called his son in and told him about the dream, to the latter's great delight. Convinced of his success at the spring examinations, Pan Yu set out on his journey in high spirits, singing and drinking with abandon all along the way.

Upon arriving in Lin'an some days later, he stepped into a small inn. The elderly innkeeper greeted him and asked, "Might you be Mr. Pan?"

"Yes," replied Pan Yu. "How did you know?"

"The local guardian god appeared to me last night in my dream, saying, 'Mr. Pan, the one who will come out first in the examinations will be arriving here at noon tomorrow. Take good care of him.' You, sir, are the very one. If you don't think this place too humble for you, please consider staying here."

"All right. If what you said turns out to be true, I'll surely pay you double." Right away, Pan Yu told his servant to carry his luggage into the inn.

The innkeeper had a daughter, an attractive girl of sixteen. Upon overhearing her father tell of his dream about Mr. Pan winning first honor in the examinations, she took a peek at Pan Yu through the window and was impressed by his dashing looks. To her regret, she could not think of a way to communicate her feelings to him.

One day, Mr. Pan personally went to the kitchen to get water for his ink slab because his page boy happened to be away. There, he ran into the innkeeper's daughter. She gave him a smile before removing herself from this male presence. Mr. Pan was so smitten that he handed over two gold rings and a jade hairpin to his page boy and told him to find an opportune moment to convey his sentiments to the young lady and ask for a tryst.

The young lady joyfully accepted the gifts and in return gave the page boy the embroidered sachet that she always carried around her waist, promising to go to Mr. Pan's study during her father's absence. For several days in succession, Mr. Pan wore his eyes out looking in vain for her to come.

Upon completion of the examinations, the innkeeper treated Pan Yu to dinner, and they drank until the innkeeper got gloriously drunk. Pan Yu was about to retire for the night when suddenly his ears caught a gentle tap on his door. He opened it and saw that it was the young lady. Without sparing a moment to exchange a few words with her, he led her into the study and engaged her in a game of clouds and rain. In the ecstasy, he promised that after he made his mark in the world, he would take her on as a concubine.

That night, Mr. Pan Senior again had a dream, in which the drummers and musicians and the bearers of banners and a board with the name of the Number One successful candidate went past his door. Pan Lang cried out, "These banners and the board are for this family!"

"No," answered those bearing the board.

Pan Lang ran after them to take a closer look at the board. Indeed, it bore a different name this time. One of the men carrying the board said, "Your son Pan Yu had been meant to place first as the *zhuangyuan*, but because he committed an improper act, the lord of heaven ordered that his career be taken away from him in favor of someone else."

Pan Lang woke up with a start, not knowing whether to believe in the dream or not. Soon the results of the examinations were posted. Pan Lang went to check the list of successful candidates and saw that, sure enough, the *zhuangyuan* was the very one whose name was inscribed on the board in his second dream. His son had failed.

Upon Pan Yu's return, his father asked him what he had done. Unable to fend off the questions, Pan Yu resignedly came out with the truth. Father and son sighed prodigiously. After more than a year elapsed, Pan Yu still missed the girl, but when he sent a matchmaker to her, bearing lavish betrothal gifts, he learned to his deep regret that she had already married. He sat for the examinations a few more times but failed each time and later died in dejection.

> *For a brief moment of delight,*
> *He ruined the chance of a lifetime.*

Storyteller, isn't it true that since ancient times there have been beautiful stories about talented scholars and pretty maidens starting out as clandestine lovers before the men rise to eminence and thus raise their wives' status as well? How could the grand scheme of heaven have gone wrong in this case?

Well, dear audience, listen to this: he who engages in debauchery and thereby ruins his own lifelong reputation commits a major offense. But if a man and a woman were destined five hundred years ago to marry, the Old Man under the Moon would not fail to tie up their feet with a red thread.[1] Whether they meet in trysts or in the proper way through the mediation of a matchmaker, there is a predestined bond between them and whatever they do does not count as an offense.

Now let me tell you another story, which took place during the reign of Emperor Shenzong [r. 1068–85], also in the Song dynasty. There was a man named Wu Du, a native of Bianjing. As a *jinshi*, he had been appointed controller of Changsha. At the time our story unfolds, his son Wu Yan, by his wife Lin-shi, was a dashing sixteen-year-old young man. He had been applying to his studies from an early age and was well versed in the classics, the histories, and the art of composing poems in a variety of styles. There was another thing remarkable about him. What was it? Well, this refined-looking young man had an enormous appetite. Every day, apart from what he ate between meals, he consumed three liters of rice, more than two catties of meat, and more than ten catties of wine. And these were amounts fixed by his father as a compromise, so that he would not overeat and ruin his health. Even with such a liberal diet, he still felt half starved and far from gratified.

In the third month of the year in which our story takes place, Controller Wu's term of office expired and he was promoted to be magistrate of Yangzhou. A few clerks and yamen runners from Yangzhou came in a government boat all the way to Changsha to greet Magistrate Wu and his family and take them to Yangzhou. That very day, Wu Du packed, bade farewell to his colleagues and friends, and set out on the journey in the government boat. All along the way, the boat sailed before the wind downstream. In a matter of days, they reached Jiangzhou, the very place mentioned in the line from Bai Juyi's poem entitled "Song of a *Pipa* Player" dedicated to the wife of a merchant:

Jiangzhou's vice commander finds his robe stained by tears.[2]

Magistrate Wu's boat was going smoothly midstream at full sail when, all of a sudden, a strong wind sprang up, whipping up surging waves that almost capsized the boat. Even the helmsman and the boatmen were horrified, let alone the magistrate and his wife. The sail was furled and the boat pulled in toward shore, which was only about four or five li away, but it was a maneuver that took four hours to accomplish. All the boats up and down the river were thrown into frenzy, with everyone praying to the gods and making votive vows. Those who managed to make it to the shore were profuse in their thanks to heaven. When Magistrate Wu's boat reached shore, cast anchor, and was tied to the post, another government boat was already moored nearby, about a hundred feet away. Under the half-raised door curtain stood a middle-aged woman, a beautiful young lady, and three or four maidservants behind them. From behind the curtain of his cabin door, Young Master Wu peeked at the charming young lady. How do we know she was charming? Here is a poem that bears witness:

> Her eyes like sparkling autumn water, her bones like jade,
> Her face a lotus blossom, her eyebrows willow leaves,
> She was no less than a fairy in the moon,
> Too beauteous for this world of mortals.

Stirred to the depths of his soul, Young Master Wu itched to fly to her side and hold her in his arms. The distance being still too far for him to see her as clearly as he wanted, he thought of a plan and said to Magistrate Wu, "Father, why don't you tell the boatmen to pull up by that boat? That looks like a safer spot." Magistrate Wu instructed the boatmen accordingly. Not daring to be remiss in their duty, the boatmen raised anchor, untied the ropes, and moved toward the other boat. Young Master Wu was hoping to look his fill once he had drawn near. As it turned out, however, the Wu boat had hardly pulled up to the other boat when someone closed the cabin door on the other boat, putting a damper on Young Master Wu's enthusiasm.

You may ask, who was the official in the other boat? What was his name? Well, that official was He Zhang, a native of Jiankang [present-day Nanjing], also a *jinshi*. He was formerly marshal of Qiantang County and had just been appointed revenue manager of Jingzhou. He was on his way with his family to his duty station to take up his post and was moored at this spot to take shelter from the windstorm. The third-ranking official of Jiangzhou Prefecture being a *jinshi* who had passed the examinations the same year he had, He Zhang had taken this opportunity to go into the city to visit his friend. So his wife and daughter had opened the cabin door to look out and amuse themselves. The middle-aged woman was his wife, Jin-shi, and the beautiful girl was his daughter, Xiu'e. Manager He had no son. Xiu'e, now fifteen, was his only child. Indeed, her beauty could make fish sink and wild geese fall from the sky, outshine the moon, and put flowers to shame. She was also adept in skills of needlework that she had acquired on her own. From early on in her childhood, she had learned to read and write under a tutor her father had engaged for her, and her compositions were quite impressive. Manager He and his wife loved this only daughter more than they would any prized possession. They were looking for a son-in-law who would live with them but had not yet found a satisfactory candidate. The mother and daughter were watching the feverish activities on the various boats when Magistrate Wu's boat approached. Jin-shi immediately told a maidservant to let down the door curtain and close the door. She and her daughter went back into the cabin.

Being an official himself, Magistrate Wu sent a servant to ask which official occupied the next boat. Soon the servant came back to say, "It's He Zhang, revenue manager of Jingzhou, on his way to take up his post."

Magistrate Wu said to his wife, "I met him at the examinations in the capital some years ago. He used to be marshal of Qiantang County. So he's been promoted. Since our paths have crossed, I should give him a courtesy call." He had a servant present his name card to the next boat but the servant came back and said, "Mr. He is in the city, visiting a friend." But even as he spoke, someone in the bow announced, "Mr. He is back."

Magistrate Wu had his servants take out his official robe, and, after he was properly attired, he saw from his cabin Manager He approaching in a sedan-chair carried by four men, followed by a large retinue. The fact of the matter was that Manager He's friend in the city had left a few days earlier to observe mourning for a deceased parent. That was why He Zhang had so quickly returned to his boat. When he alit from the sedan chair by the side of the boat, he wondered at the sight of another government boat next to it, "Who could be in that boat?"

Once in his cabin, he was about to ask the servants, when Magistrate Wu's visiting card was presented to him. As soon as he finished reading it, he issued an invitation. The two cabin doors being right opposite each other, Magistrate Wu needed only walk over. After an exchange of greetings, they had a lighthearted round of conversation to bring each other up to date on what had happened to them since they last met. After finishing two cups of tea, Magistrate Wu stood up to go. Before long, Manager He paid a return visit. Magistrate Wu kept him for a drink and called his son out to greet the guest. As Young Master Wu sat off to one side at his father's bidding, Manager He, without a son of his own, took quite a liking to the young man, with his outstanding looks and gentle manners. To each question about contemporary books and the classics, the young man provided a ready answer. Manager He was even more impressed. As he broke out in enthusiastic praises for Young Master Wu, he thought to himself, "This young man's looks and learning are quite remarkable. He would be a good candidate as a son-in-law. But he lives in Bianjing, and we live in Jiankang. The two cities are too far apart. Too bad this match won't work out." (*This foreshadows heaven's blessing for this union.*) But these were private thoughts that Manager He could hardly voice in the open.

Magistrate Wu asked, "How many sons do you have, sir?"

"I have only one daughter. I don't have a male heir yet."

Young Master Wu thought, "So, that pretty girl must be his daughter. She seems to be of the same age as I am. If I could have her for wife, I'll be content the rest of my life. But she's his only child. He won't let her marry into a family that lives so far away. It's no use trying to raise the subject." Then again, he thought, "I won't even be able to see her again, let alone marry her. What a wild thought I had!"

Upon hearing that Manager He had no son, Magistrate Wu said, "So, you have no son yet. Well, one can hardly do without a son. You need to get yourself more concubines so as to give yourself more chances."

"Thank you for the advice. I will consider that."

They talked until the night deepened. Before they parted company, Magistrate Wu said, "If the wind dies down during the night, we'll be on our way early tomorrow morning. So I'm afraid I won't have time to come over again to say good-bye to you."

Manager He said, "But we haven't seen each other for so long, and who knows when we'll ever meet again? Please stay for another day so that we can chat some more." Having spoken these words, he returned to his own boat, where his wife and daughter were still up, waiting with lit candles for his return.

Half tipsy, Manager He told his wife about how profoundly kind Magistrate Wu was to him and praised Young Master Wu for his looks, his learning, and his many other attributes that would certainly serve him well in a brilliant career, adding that they should set out a feast the next day for the father and son. Because his daughter was present, Manager He held back from stating his intention to have the young man as his son-in-law. (*He is doing nothing less than laying out his daughter's future in front of her.*) As it turned out, his words inspired his daughter's admiration for Young Master Wu.

The next day, the windstorm grew more severe. The surface of the river was shrouded in mist. The waves leaped twenty to thirty feet high with thunderous roars. Not a single boat was sailing for Magistrate Wu to follow. No alternative was left him but to stay put. Early in the morning, Manager He delivered an invitation card, inviting the Wu father and son to dinner. As for Young Master Wu, thoughts about Miss He had kept him awake throughout the night. The invitation could not have suited him better. He could hardly wait to go to the next boat for another look at the young lady. To his dismay, his father turned out to be a killjoy. Saying that it would be discourteous for both father and son to inconvenience the manager, Magistrate Wu went all by himself in the afternoon, bringing along a letter on behalf of his son, declining the invitation with thanks. Hardly able to raise objections, Young Master Wu seethed with silent rage. Luckily, Manager He turned a deaf ear to Magistrate's plea and sent a servant over time and again to invite the young master, but Wu Yan did not dare act on his own initiative. It was only after he got his father's permission that he changed his clothes and went over to the other boat, where he greeted the host and sat down for a cup of wine.

Upon hearing about Young Master Wu's arrival, Miss He quietly went up to the screen door and peeked from behind it. Dressed up in finery, Young Master Wu cut an even more dashing figure than usual. How do we know this? There is another poem in testimony:

> As fair in complexion as He Yan,[3]
> As well-perfumed as Xun Yu,[4]
> If he goes down the street with Pan Yue,[5]
> At whom will women throw their fruit?

Miss He found her desires stirring at the sight of such a handsome youth. She thought, "Mr. Wu Junior is indeed as handsome as father said. If I could marry such a man, I'd have nothing more to ask for. But how am I going to bring this up with my parents? If only the Wu family could approach them first with a marriage proposal! Now, how is Young Master Wu going to know what I'm thinking of? If I arrange a date with him, my parents will be in the way and there will be too many eyes and ears on both boats for us to be alone. This can't be done. I'll have to drop the idea." While telling herself to drop the idea, she still kept her eyes fixed on Young Master Wu.

Generally speaking, someone who is in love sees beauty even in the ugliest creature. Young Master Wu being a handsome young man with graceful manners, she was all the more smitten. She thought, "If I pass up on this man, even if I marry into a wealthy official's family in the future, I won't get someone with such a combination of good looks and talent." She racked her brains, but for the life of her she could not come up with a plan to have a rendezvous with him. In her vexation, she went to sit down, but before the seat cushion was warm, her feet led her again to the screen, as if there were someone pushing her. After looking out from behind the screen for another few moments, she went back to her seat, and, in less time than it takes to drink a cup of tea, she was back at her position behind the screen. Like a revolving lantern, she kept going back and forth, wishing she could be with Young Master Wu in a few strides to pour words of love into his ear.

Storyteller, let me ask you something: Miss He couldn't have been the only one in the cabin. Where were her mother and the maidservants? How could her obsession with the young man have failed to catch their attention? Dear audience, let me explain. Her mother had the habit of taking a nap at noontime. She was therefore asleep at the time and oblivious to the goings-on in the boat. As for the maidservants, they were only too happy that their mistress and the young lady did not need them for the moment, and so they took advantage of the respite to slip out and enjoy themselves rather than meddle in something that did not concern them. That was why no one sensed anything out of the ordinary. Before long, Mrs. He woke up, whereupon Xiu'e held back her feet and sank into her chair to indulge in gloomy reveries. Indeed,

> *When will she see again the one in her thoughts?*
> *Her feelings at this moment are hard to contain.*

As for Young Master Wu seated at the table, his heart was with the one in the rear of the cabin. From time to time he stole glances in that direction, but the screen door remained closed with nothing astir anywhere near it. He lamented to himself, "Miss He, I came here for the express purpose of seeing you, but things don't work out. Why is there so little destined bond between us?" In his dejection, he did not even care for wine. The afternoon was far advanced when the feast was over. Once back in his own cabin, Young Master Wu flopped listlessly into bed, fully clothed.

After walking Magistrate Wu and his son to their boat, Manager He asked his wife and daughter to the middle cabin for supper. Her thoughts all preoccupied with Young Master Wu, Xiu'e sat off to one side, silent, looking as if in a trance. She did not take one drop of the wine, nor even touch the chopsticks. (*Though in different places, they are of the same heart. Heaven will take pity on them.*) Noticing the state her daughter was in, Mrs. He hastened to ask, "My child, why are you sitting motionless like that without taking even one bite of anything?" She repeated her question a few times before Xiu'e replied, "I don't feel well. I have no appetite."

Her father said, "If you don't feel well, you may go to bed now."

Mrs. He rose and, with a maid lighting the way with a lamp, helped Xiu'er to bed. After a brief absence, Mrs. He came back to take another look at her daughter. She then told the maid to eat supper and go back to sleep in a makeshift bed in Xiu'e's room to keep her company.

Behind the bed curtain, Xiu'e tossed and turned, wide awake. Suddenly she heard someone intoning a poem outside. Straining her ears, she recognized the voice of Young Master Wu. The poem went,

> Dreams come to us, however far apart we are;
> There must be a bond between us if we're thus thrown together.
> Say not that our joy lasts but a moment;
> The vows of love are to be firmly kept.

Xiu'e was overwhelmed with delight as she listened to those lines. She said to herself, "I've cudgeled my brains for a whole day without coming up with a plan to see him privately. Now, with him intoning poetry outside, isn't this an opportunity sent by heaven? What better time than this to see him when all is quiet in the depth of the night? No one will be any the wiser." Afraid that the maids had not yet gone to sleep, she called out for them a few times. Getting no answer, she thought they must have fallen fast asleep. So she rose, threw some clothes on, turned up the wick of the lamp, and gently pushed open the cabin window. It was as if Young Master Wu had been waiting at the window all along. To her pleasant surprise, no sooner had the window been opened than he squeezed in and gathered her into his arms. Before they had time to tell each other how they had missed each other during the day, they clung tightly to each other without even bothering to close the cabin window. They then took off their clothes and conjured up a storm of clouds and rain. At the height of their ecstasy, a maidservant who was up to relieve herself screamed, "Oh no! The window is open! Burglar!" Everyone in the boat woke up at the commotion and rushed to the cabin window to look in. Mr. and Mrs. He pushed the door wide open, entered the cabin, and told the maidservants to light lamps for a search.

Cowering in panic, Young Master Wu said, "What are we going to do, Miss?"

"Don't panic. You stay in bed. They won't search the bed. Let me send them away. I'll then walk you to your boat." She had hardly got off the bed when a maid caught sight of the young man's shoes and said, "The burglar's shoes are here. He must be hiding here in the bed!"

As her parents rushed over to search, Xiu'e tried to stop them, exclaiming, "He's not here!" Turning a deaf ear to her, they found Young Master Wu. As Xiu'e groaned in despair, Manager He said, "You brute! How dare you bring disgrace to my family!"

His wife suggested, "Hang him up and beat him."

"Let's not beat him. Let's simply throw him into the river." Having said that, Mr. He instructed two boatmen to carry the young man by his head and his feet out of the cabin. As Young Master Wu pleaded for mercy, Xiu'e grabbed her parents and said, "Father, mother, it was all my fault! He is not to blame!" Ignoring her, Manager He pushed her away. With a splash, the young man was tossed into the river.

Throwing all sense of shame to the wind, Xiu'e stomped her feet, thumped her chest, and cried out between her sobs, "Young Master Wu, I'm sorry for having brought you to this!" Then she thought, "Since he died for my sake, how can I live on alone?" Whereupon she dashed out of the cabin door and jumped into the river.

> How sad that the sweet and lovely girl
> Is to perish in the surging waves!

Xiu'er had no sooner jumped into the river than she woke up with a start from the nightmare and realized that she remained lying in bed. As the maidservants cried, "Wake up, Miss," Xiu'e opened her eyes. It was already broad daylight. The maids were all up and about, and the storm was still raging.

"What did you see in your dream, Miss?" asked a maid. "You cried so hard we couldn't wake you up."

Xiu'e mumbled something evasive while thinking, "Is it because there's no pre-destined bond of marriage between me and Young Master Wu that I'm given such ill omens?" Then again, she told herself, "If I could indeed get to experience such joy, I'd be content, even if I died." Now that the details of the dream came back to her, she indulged in even more absurd flights of fancy. Since sleeping did not help her feel better, she pushed away her pillow and rose from the bed. The maids having left her cabin, she closed the door and said to herself, staring at the window, "He came through this very window last night and carried me to bed. It was all too vivid to be just a dream." Then she thought, "I can't believe that I'm not meant for the kind of happiness I had in that dream." In the midst of these thoughts, she absent-mindedly pushed open the window and looked out. There, by the wide-open cabin window of Magistrate Wu's boat sat Young Master Wu as if in a trance, staring at her window.

As a matter of fact, both Mr. Wu Junior and Miss He slept in the rear cabins of their boats, which were only five or six feet apart. If the window lattices were taken down, they might as well have been in the same room. Young Master Wu had also been tormented by dreams throughout an uneasy night of sleep and had risen early to stare at Manager He's boat through the open window and indulge in wishful thinking, like a toad craving a swan's flesh. Amazingly enough, there being indeed a predestined bond between them, something was bound to happen. When Miss He opened her cabin window, their four eyes met in happy astonishment. They smiled at each other as if they were old acquaintances. Xiu'e wanted to speak to him and arrange a tryst, but, afraid of being overheard, she took a piece of stationery paper with floral patterns, rubbed her ink stick against the ink slab until the ink was ready, dipped her brush-pen heavily into the ink, and wrote a poem. Then she folded the stationery into the shape of two overlapping diamonds, retrieved an embroidered handkerchief from her sleeve, wrapped it around the folded paper, and tossed the package into the other boat. Young Master Wu caught it with both hands and bowed deeply. After Xiu'e bowed in return, the young man opened the package to read:

> The stationery bears these lines of verse;
> The handkerchief carries my tender feelings.
> King Xiang should not have dreamed in vain;[6]
> For the clouds have moved on right to this place.

A line of smaller characters at the end of the poem read, "Tonight I shall stay up late and wait for you. The clicking sound of scissors will be the signal. Please do not fail me."

Young Master Wu was thrown into raptures. He thought, "I didn't expect her to have such literary talent as well. She's a rare find!" In admiration of Miss He, he took a piece of stationery with golden dots, wrote a poem on it, untied a brocade sash from his waist, wrapped it around the piece of stationery, and tossed the package over. Xiu'e caught it and saw that it was exactly the poem that she had heard him intone in her dream. Amazed, she said to herself, "How come I heard in my dream last night the very poem he wrote just now? It looks like the two of us are meant for each other, after all, which is why my dream was so true to life." At the end of the poem was also a line of smaller characters that read, "Since you deign to favor me with such kindness, I will readily comply." After she finished reading everything, she slipped the stationery and the sash into her sleeve. While she was delirious with joy, a maidservant bringing water for her to wash her face knocked at the door. Softly Xiu'e closed the window and let the maid in through the door. Her mother also came to check on her and felt relieved upon seeing that she was up and about.

That day, Magistrate Wu hosted a feast in return. Manager He went before noon. While Mrs. He was having her usual afternoon nap, Xiu'e took out the poem and read it over and over again, her heart filled with joy. Eagerly she waited for evening to come. Strangely enough, the days usually passed by quickly for her, but this day there seemed to be a rope tying the sun to its place, sending Xiu'e into a frenzy of impatience. Ever so slowly, dusk began to set in. Suddenly it occurred to her that the two maids would be in the way, unless she did something about it. At supper, she gave her two personal maids a large pot of wine and two extra bowls of vegetables. Like thirsty dragons at the sight of water, the two maids polished off everything.

Before long, Manager He returned to his boat from the feast. His inebriated state made Xiu'er worry whether Young Master Wu had also been drinking and was too tipsy to make the appointment. She returned to the rear cabin, closed the door, and told the maids to light incense to scent her quilt and pillow, adding, "I have some needlework to do. You two go to bed first."

The wine had begun to take its toll on the two maids. Their faces red, their ears warm, their legs giving way under them, their heads dizzy, they had been thinking of going to bed early but couldn't very well make the request. The young mistress's exhortation could not have suited them better. Eagerly they prepared for bed. No sooner had their heads hit their pillows than they began to snore, making sounds like a pair of bellows at work.

Having sat for about two hours until all was quiet on the two boats, Xiu'e believed the coast was clear and knocked a pair of scissors against the table, a sound that Young Master Wu recognized as the signal.

Remembering the appointment, Young Master Wu had refrained from drinking too much wine at the feast. After Manager He had left, Young Master Wu had returned to his cabin and listened with strained ears. After waiting for about two hours without detecting any signal, he was having misgivings when, all of a sudden, the clicking sound of scissors in the other boat fell on his ears. In a transport of joy, he quickly rose, noiselessly opened the window, climbed out, pushed the window back in place, and jumped onto the other boat. At his three gentle taps on the window, Xiu'e opened it and let him into the cabin. After Xiu'e closed the window, the two of them exchanged greetings. By the light of the lamp, Young Master Wu peered closely at Miss He and was even more impressed by her charms than before. In their fiery passion, they had no time for words. Young Master Wu gathered Miss He into his arms. Then, with buttons undone and clothes removed, they lay down in bed and pressed tightly against each other. A union of joy it was. Behold:

> *The little window opens at the gentle tap;*
> *She wonders if this is again a dream.*
> *Ten thousand joys do not suffice;*
> *The maids are asleep; wake them not.*

After the clouds and rain were over, both of them poured out their love to each other in tender words. After Xiu'e told him that she had heard in a dream the very same poem he had written to her, Young Master Wu said in amazement, "What a thing to happen! The dream I had last night tallies with yours in every detail. I was sitting sadly, lost in thought about the remarkable dream, when heaven made you open your window for a look out. We were thus able to be together. The way our dreams occurred before we meet, there is most likely a predestined bond between us. Tomorrow, I will ask my father to propose, so that you and I will get to spend the rest of our lives together."

"Exactly what I've been thinking," said Xiu'e.

They resumed their intimacy in the excitement of their conversation, and their love grew deeper. And then, before they knew it, they had fallen asleep.

As it turned out, the storm died down at midnight. All the moored boats set sail at dawn, at the fifth strike of the night watch-drum. On the He and Wu boats, the sails were also unfurled and the ropes untied in preparation for departure. The boatmen's rhythmic chants as they were hard at work awoke Young Master Wu and Miss He. They heard a boatman saying, "With such a favorable wind, we'll be in Qizhou soon enough!"

Wu groaned to himself in dismay. "What are we going to do?" said he.

"Keep your voice down," admonished Miss He. "If the maids hear you, we'll be in big trouble. Things having already come to this, panicking won't help. You stay here. We'll think of a way." (*If he had gone right after the clandestine union and both boats had set sail, nothing would have happened. There would have been no marriage but a blemish in their record of moral behavior. The fact that the wind died down and the boats got under way bespoke heaven's will in bringing off this match.*)

"I hope our dreams won't be borne out," said Young Master Wu.

This remark gave Miss He an idea. Because the disaster in her dream started when the maid spotted his shoes, she picked up his silk shoes and hid them. After much solid thinking, she came up with a plan. "I've got a plan," said she.

"What is it?"

"During daytime, you will hide under the bed. I'll pretend to be ill, so that I won't have to go out and eat with mother. They'll send the food into this cabin. After we get to Jingzhou, I'll give you some money. You can slip out in the commotion of the moment of arrival and take a boat that can carry you to Yangzhou. Then have your father send my parents a written marriage proposal. If they agree, well and good. If they don't, they'll have to be told the truth. My parents dote on me. So I believe they'll have to agree when they realize what things have come to. Won't we be husband and wife again?"

"I do hope this plan will work out!" said Young Master Wu.

At the first light of day, after the maids had risen and gone out of the cabin, the two of them also got out of bed. Young Master Wu quickly dived under the bed and stayed there, making himself as small as possible. On either side of him by the bed stood trunks and suitcases. In front of him hung the bed curtain, and Miss He sat tight on the edge of the bed, never taking so much as a step from this position. After she washed her face and rinsed her mouth, she deliberately slouched across the table without combing her hair. Her mother said upon entering the cabin, "Good gracious! Why are you bent over the table like this without even doing your hair?"

"I'm not well. I don't feel like doing my hair."

"You must have gotten up too early and caught a cold. Why don't you go right back to bed?"

"I couldn't sleep well. That's why I chose to sit."

"If you want to sit, put on one more layer of clothes. If you catch another cold, you'll only make things worse." So saying, she told a maid to find a cape and put it on her. After Mrs. He sat for a while, the maids announced that breakfast was ready.

"My child," said she, "you must not eat rice in your condition. Have the maids cook you some nice porridge. It'll help you recover."

"I don't like porridge. Rice is better. But I can't walk. Tell them to bring it in here."

"All right. I'll keep you company."

"The maids won't do their job properly if you don't keep an eye on them, mother. You'd better eat outside."

"You've got a point there," said her mother. So she turned away and instructed the maids to set the breakfast on Xiu'e's table.

After breakfast was set on the table, Xiu'e said to the maids, "You can leave now. Don't come in again unless I call you."

After thus dismissing the maids, she bolted the door and told Young Master Wu to come out from under the bed to have breakfast. The young man crawled out, stood up, stretched himself, and saw that on the table stood two bowls of meat, one bowl of vegetables, and two bowls of rice. Miss He's appetite being limited, no more than two bowls of rice were served at each meal. Now, for someone who could eat three liters of rice at one go, how would two bowls of rice fill his stomach? With an ever so slight smile, he picked up the chopsticks and finished everything in two or three gulps. Thinking it improper to complain, he dived again under the bed in spite of his hunger. Xiu'e opened the door, called in the maids, and told them to refill the two empty bowls with rice. The maids mumbled to each other, "She never eats more than two bowls. She says she's ill today, but she eats twice as much as usual. Isn't this strange?"

Mrs. He overheard them. She entered the cabin and said, "My child, why do you need so much rice when you're not feeling well?"

"It's all right. I'm not full yet."

The same thing happened with the other two meals of that day. Mr. and Mrs. He attributed the increase in appetite to their daughter's growth into adulthood, little knowing that in her cabin there was someone who was eating her food and, even so, was still weak from hunger. Truly,

> *A plan of gross deception*
> *Covers up their clandestine union.*

After supper that evening, Miss He told Young Master Wu to go to bed first. She then undressed and joined him. Upon seeing her in bed when dropping in to see how she was, her mother asked how she was feeling and went off. The maids closed the door and also retired for the night.

Unable to fight off the pangs of hunger, Young Master Wu said to Miss He, "Everything's going well except for one thing."

"What is it?"

"To tell you the truth, I have a large appetite. The three meals served today don't add up to one meal as far as I'm concerned. If I go hungry like this, I won't be able to make it to Jingzhou."

"Why didn't you say so earlier? I'll just ask for more rice tomorrow."

"If you ask for too much, you'll arouse suspicions."

"That's all right. I know what to do. But how much will be enough?"

"I don't expect to eat to my heart's content. I can get by with ten bowls for every meal."

The next morning, Young Master Wu hid himself under the bed as before, whereas Miss He feigned illness and lay in bed, moaning. Mrs. He was so worried that she wanted to engage a physician, but since they were in the middle of the river, nothing could be done. Xiu'e did not want medical help but kept complaining of being hungry. Her mother had one bowl of rice after another sent in, but each time, Xiu'e complained that it was not enough. Altogether more than ten bowls were brought in. Horrified, her mother advised her to eat less, but she threw a tantrum, saying, "All right! Take them away! I'll just stop eating! Let me die of hunger!"

Being a doting mother, Mrs. He gave an apologetic smile at this outburst and said, "My child, I meant well. Don't be upset. If you have the appetite, go ahead and eat to your heart's content. Just don't force yourself to eat more than you can." So saying, she picked up the bowl and the chopsticks and put them in her daughter's hands.

"I can't eat with you watching me, mother. I want to be alone and eat slowly. I may not be able to finish it after all."

Her mother did her bidding and took the maidservants out as well. Xiu'e drew some clothes on, got off the bed, and closed the door. In a trice, Young Master Wu emerged from under the bed. He was so ravenously hungry that at the sight of the bowls of rice, he fell to without a word of demurral. He ate more than ten bowls in rapid succession like a meteor shooting across the sky, without raising his head even once, and did not stop until he finished all but the last bowl. Miss He stared at him, spellbound. Softly she asked, "Do you need more?"

"That'll do for now. If I go on eating, I'll only be making a fool of myself." He poured himself a cup of tea, rinsed his mouth, and, with one swift movement, inserted himself under the bed again. (*Young Master Wu has the patience of a meditating monk.*)

Miss He finished what was left, opened the door, and lay down in bed. The maids had been waiting for the door to open. They now rushed in, only to see that all the rice and the dishes had been finished. As they cleared away the table, they commented, giggling, "So our young mistress is sick with an eating disorder."

At their report, Mrs. He shook her head and said, "How could she have eaten so much? What a strange illness!" Immediately she sent for her husband. After acquainting him with what had happened, she asked him to engage a physician and a fortune-teller. Her husband didn't believe what he heard. He instructed her to ignore Xiu'e's demands for lunch because treatment would be difficult if her internal organs were damaged by overeating. To their dismay, Xiu'e began to complain of hunger before it was lunchtime. When her mother tried to talk to her gently, Xiu'e began to cry. For lack of a better choice, her mother again let her have her way. The same thing happened at suppertime. Mr. and Mrs. He were seized with fear, for they thought their daughter had succumbed to some mysterious disease.

Upon arriving at Qizhou that evening, they told the boatmen not to set sail the next day. Early the next morning, they sent a servant into the city to find a doctor of good reputation, pray to the gods, and draw a divination. Before long, a well-dressed and dignified-looking physician was brought to the boat. Manager He led him into the main cabin, exchanged greetings with him, and showed him to a seat. Knowing this was an official, the physician was all politeness. After drinking two cups of tea, he asked about the patient's condition, and proceeded to the rear cabin to take the patient's pulse. That done, he returned to the main cabin and sat down.

"Doctor," said Manager He, "what is it that ails our daughter?"

The physician gave a cough before answering, "Your daughter is suffering from infantile dyspepsia."

"You're mistaken, sir!" exclaimed Mr. He. "My daughter is fifteen. How can she suffer from an infantile disease?"

The physician smiled. "Sir, you have only a partial understanding of the term. You say she's fifteen, but we're not yet out of the spring season. So she is in fact only fourteen.[7] If she was born in winter, she would be not yet even fourteen. Now, won't you agree, sir, that a thirteen-year-old girl is no more than an infant? This is an ailment that is in most cases caused by an imbalanced diet. Her case is complicated by the lack of acclimatization. So, food that stays undigested in her stomach gives rise to internal heat which, when reaching her chest, makes her feel hungry. The intake of food and beverage only intensifies the internal heat, which is why her condition worsens from day to day. If it goes without treatment for a month, she'll be beyond cure."

Believing there was a measure of truth in the explanation, Manager He said, "Your explanation makes perfect sense, sir. But how are you going to treat her?"

"First, I'm going to eliminate the undigested mass and the internal heat. Her intake of food will surely gradually decrease until it goes back to normal."

"If the treatment can work such wonders, I'll surely have a handsome reward for you," said Mr. He.

As the physician stood up to go, Manager He handed him a sealed envelope containing payment for the medicine, and sent a servant to go with the physician for the herbs. As soon as the herbs were delivered, they were put into a pot to be brewed. When ready, the medicine was served to Xiu'e.

Xiu'e was wishing with all her heart that they would reach Jingzhou soon. What could the medicine do for her? Back when she heard that her parents were going to engage a physician, she tried to stop them, but to no avail, nor could she very well come out with the truth. And so she had to let them worry. Privately amused upon learning about the physician's diagnosis, she sent the maids out of her cabin and dumped the medicine into her chamber pot.

As for the divinations, one said that the stars were against her and that she had offended the god of the crane and therefore must engage a priest to do an exorcism in order for her to recover. Another said that she must have encountered some forlorn hungry ghosts in the wilderness and could be cured by a prayer service. Mr. and Mrs. He did everything they were told to do. Observing that the medicine did not work and the girl's appetite remained unabated, Mr. and Mrs. He again engaged a physician, who came in grand style in a sedan-chair, with a retinue of three or four servants. After exchanging greetings with them, the physician delivered himself of a grandiose speech before asking what had led to the illness and taking the patient's pulse. Then he said, addressing Mr. He, "Have you engaged physicians before, sir?"

"Yes. One came just the other day."

"What was his diagnosis?"

"He said it was a case of infantile dyspepsia."

The physician burst out laughing. "No!" he exclaimed. "This is consumption, not indigestion!"

"My daughter is so young. How could she have contracted consumption?"

"This is a case of consumption caused not by the exhaustion of emotions but by her frail constitution. This is a case of children's consumption."

"But why does she have such a large appetite?"

"She easily becomes hungry because in the alternate attacks of coldness and heat, the excessive internal heat of her body goes up."

Mrs. He, listening behind the screen door, sent a servant in to say that the young lady was not running a fever. The physician said in response, "This is a case of internal heat concurrent with external coldness and ailment of the bones. That is why the patient does not feel the heat." He then asked for the prescription of the physician who had been there before him and said after reading it, "Using such powerful medicine will only damage the patient's vital energy. A few more doses of this and she will be beyond cure. Let me give you my prescription, a brew of which will dissipate the excessive heat, bring her internal organs into harmony, and limit her appetite. When that has been accomplished, I will then prescribe pills to nourish the yin, reduce the internal heat, boost her blood level and her vital energy, and slowly help her recuperate until she regains her health."

"We will be ever so grateful for your divine skills," said Manager He.

Soon after the physician took his leave, a servant brought in another physician, an old man with hoary hair and beard and faltering steps. He had hardly sat down before he began to boast of his ability to recognize the most elusive and strange diseases, claiming that he had saved the lives of eminent officials with his wonderful prescriptions. It was after a long speech of self-promotion that he began to inquire after the patient's condition and diet and to check her pulse. Impressed by his rhetoric, Manager He thought this physician would be the one to work wonders. He thought, "As they say, trust old physicians and young diviners. Maybe this doctor is indeed a good one. Who knows?"

After taking the patient's pulse, the physician said to Manager He, "You are lucky to have me on the case. Anyone else would not know what ails your daughter." (*The author is certainly a physician basher. But such characters do abound.*)

"What is it?"

"There's a special term for it: diaphragm blockage."

"It's diaphragm blockage if a patient can't swallow," objected Manager He. "But she's eating several times more than usual. How can it be diaphragm blockage?"

"There are different kinds of diaphragm blockages. In your daughter's case, it's popularly called rodent diaphragm blockage. Sufferers of this ailment stuff themselves as much as possible behind people's backs but, when watched, find even the smallest bite hard to swallow. Later, the undigested food will expand and cause stomach distension, complicating the case and making it hard to effect a cure. Luckily, she is still in an early stage of the ailment. It doesn't look too bad yet. You can count on me. I'll cure her completely." With that promise, he rose to go. Manager He walked him to the stem of the boat before bidding him adieu. Everybody believed in the theory about the rodent diaphragm blockage and nervously went about asking for advice from fortune-tellers and other physicians, little knowing that Miss He, smiling scornfully behind their backs, had dumped all the medicine into her chamber pot.

After spending several days in Qizhou, Manager He thought that things could not go on like this. He consulted his wife and asked for a prescription from the old physician, so that they could buy enough medicine for their daughter until they reached Jingzhou, where they would look for other physicians. The old man charged steeply for the prescription, reveling in his good luck. There is a poem in testimony:

> *Physicians may not know how to cure illnesses,*
> *But they do know how to take advantage of people.*
> *Naming ailments when there was none,*
> *They cheated Mr. He out of his money.*

As the saying goes, "Young men and young women are equally filled with passion." When engaged in the game of clouds and rain for the first time ever, Miss He had flinched and shied away from him. For his part, Young Master Wu was fearful and timid and dared not let himself go. So they did not find the experience to their full satisfaction. But after two or three days, they gradually entered the state of bliss and began to enjoy themselves so much that they threw all caution to the winds.

One night, when waking up in the middle of the night, a maid heard murmuring voices as the bed made creaking noises. After a while, she caught the sound of heavy panting. Feeling intrigued, she reported thus to Mrs. He the next morning. Mrs. He had been wondering why her daughter's cheeks were aglow with health, with none of the look of a patient. This report confirmed her suspicions. Without telling her husband any of this, she went to her daughter's cabin to see for herself but found nothing irregular. When examining Xiu'e's face, she found her doubly radiant. Thinking it awkward to question the girl, she was at a loss as to what to do and went out after sitting for a while. After breakfast, she went again to check on Xiu'e, still feeling uneasy, and asked probing questions.

Disliking the hints in her mother's questions, Xiu'e did not bother to answer her. All of a sudden, the sound of snoring rang out in the air. What had happened was that Young Master Wu's nocturnal activities had deprived him of sleep, and now, with a full stomach, he was fast asleep under the bed. Xiu'e was not quick enough in her attempt to drown out the snores, so her mother heard them loud and clear. Mrs. He dismissed the maids, bolted the door, and looked under the bed. Lo and behold! A boy was curled up against the wall, soundly asleep. Groaning inwardly in dismay, Mrs. He said to Xiu'e, "So this is what you've been up to! The way you claimed to be ill, you scared me and your father to death! And now, with such a scandal, how are you going to hold up your head again? And where does this cursed one come from?"

Her face crimson with embarrassment, Xiu'e said, "Yes, I have done wrong. Please cover up for me, mother! He is not just anyone. He's Magistrate Wu's son."

Flabbergasted, her mother said, "Young Master Wu has never met you before. When your father was in their boat as a guest, he was there at the table, keeping your father company. The feast wasn't over until late at night, and the boats set sail at the fourth strike of the night watch-drum. How did he manage to show up here?'

Xiu'e thereupon gave an account of how her father's praises of the young man had drawn her attention, how she had peeped at him the next day from behind the screen door, what dream she had had at night, how she had opened the window and made the appointment, and how the boat had set sail while they were asleep. She added, "In a moment of passion, your unfilial daughter lost her chastity and good name and brought disgrace to the family. This is indeed an inexcusable offense. But he and I live so far apart, and yet a windstorm brought us together. This proves that there is a predestined marriage bond between us. Heaven is behind this match, not human intervention. Young Master Wu and I have vowed to live together until death do us apart, a vow we will never break. Please talk to father nicely to get his approval for our marriage, so that my error can be redeemed. If father has other ideas, I will kill myself immediately rather than live in humiliation. So this is the whole of my shameful story. The decision is yours, mother." With that, she broke down in a flood of tears.

While mother and daughter were talking, Young Master Wu's snores grew thunderous. Mrs. He chafed with rage and vexation. She had a mind to lash out at her daughter but, partly because she didn't have the heart to do this to her pampered girl and partly because the maids would make the girl their laughing stock if they got wind of this, she swallowed her anger, pulled open the door, and went off.

As soon as her mother was gone, Xiu'e got off the bed, bolted the door, and woke up Young Master Wu. "Why did you have to snore so loudly?" she grumbled. "My mother heard you. Our secret is out."

Young Master Wu was so frightened that he broke into a cold sweat. With his teeth clattering, he was unable to get even one word out.

"Don't panic!" said Xiu'e. "I've told mother everything. If father agrees to our marriage, fine. If not, the ending of that dream is the worst that can happen. I will not let you suffer all the consequences alone." At this point, tears welled up in her eyes.

Mrs. He promptly brought her husband into their cabin and dismissed the maids. Before she spoke up, tears fell down her cheeks thick and fast. Believing she was distressed over their daughter's illness, Mr. He said in an attempt to console her, "The doctor said the medicine would work in a few days. Don't worry."

"That old thing was full of nonsense! Rodent diaphragm blockage indeed! Such a doctor can't tell what's wrong with a patient in a thousand years, let alone finding a cure in a few days!"

"What are you talking about?" said Mr. He.

When his wife told him everything, he almost fainted from sheer rage. He said, "Oh well, oh well, why would I keep an unworthy daughter who does such a scandalous thing and brings such disgrace to the family? They'd better die before the night is out, so as to be cleared of the bad name."

These words gave his wife such a shock that she turned deathly pale and said, trying to calm him down, "You and I have reached middle age, and she's our only child. If she's gone, whom do we have left? In fact, Young Master Wu is from a good family and is good-looking and talented. If we have him as son-in-law, it'll be a good match in social status. He should have made a marriage proposal rather than doing such a thing on the sly. But things having already come to this, it's too late to dwell on that. Let's make the best of the situation and quietly have a servant escort him back. We'll write to Magistrate Wu and ask him to present us with a marriage proposal. We will then hold a wedding ceremony. That will be good for everyone. If we make a fuss about it now, we'll only be advertising the scandal."

Manager He thought for a while, but, without a better alternative, he yielded to his wife. He left the cabin and asked a boatman, "Where are we?"

"We'll be in Wuchang Prefecture in a moment," was the reply.

Manager He told the men to stop the boat at Wuchang for a brief moment, so that he could send a servant home. Then he wrote a letter and gave it to a trusted servant, along with instructions as to what to do. Soon they arrived in Wuchang. The servant went ashore, hired a boat, and moored it next to the He family's boat. When Mr. and Mrs. He entered the rear cabin, Xiu'e felt so ashamed upon seeing her father that she hid her face in her quilt. Her father said only, "A fine thing you did!" Then he bent down and called Young Master Wu out.

Upon seeing Mr. and Mrs. He, the young man crawled out in trepidation, with no inkling as to their intentions. As he prostrated himself on the floor, saying he deserved to die for the offense, Manager He said reproachfully in a subdued voice, "I thought that a learned young man like you would go far. It never occurred to me that you would do such a thing and bring disgrace to our family. I should have thrown you into the river to vent my anger. But out of respect for your father, I'm going to spare your life and have a servant escort you home. If you can make your mark in the world someday, I'll marry my unfilial daughter to you. If you don't have the pride to make something of yourself, you can forget about having my daughter."

Young Master Wu busily kowtowed and promised to do as he was told. By Manager He's order, he resumed his position under the bed and waited until the servant came in the stillness of the night to take him to the other boat. Not even the maids got to see him. As he said good-bye to Xiu'e, both were full of gloomy forebodings and were overcome with grief, but they dared not cry out loud. Xiu'e pulled her mother to one corner and said, "I have no idea what father means by sending him away. Please make sure that the servant brings me back a letter from Young Master Wu, so that I can breathe easier."

Her mother instructed the servant accordingly. Early the next morning, the boat carrying Young Master Wu set sail. Manager He's boat also got under way in the direction of Jingzhou. Afraid that something untoward might happen to Young Master Wu on his journey, Miss He literally worried herself sick. Indeed,

> They were cold as ice when parting,
> But ablaze with fire once apart.
> Of all three hundred and sixty ailments,
> Missing the loved one inflicts the most pain.

Let us retrace our steps and come back to Magistrate Wu on the day his boat left Jiangzhou before dawn. At breakfast time, after covering several tens of li, he wondered why his son had not shown up and concluded that the young man must still be in bed with a hangover from the previous night's drinking. When lunchtime came with no sign of his son anywhere around, he was mystified. His wife went and called out at the young man's door, but no answer came from inside. In panic, Magistrate Wu had the servants force open the door. The cabin was empty. Mr. and Mrs. Wu were scared out of their wits. They burst into wails of grief, without an inkling as to what could have happened. Everyone in the boat was puzzled. "How strange!" they commented. "If he's not in this boat, where can he be? Unless he has fallen into the river!"

Acting on this conjecture, Magistrate Wu ordered the boat to be moored and sought help to search for the body in the water. The entire one-hundred-li section of the river from Jiangzhou all the way to the boat's mooring spot was searched, but no corpse was found. At the prayer service to call back the young man's spirits, Mrs. Wu cried until she fainted. Magistrate Wu was so devastated by the loss of his son that he said he didn't want his official post anymore. It was at the servants' insistence that he continued with the journey to his duty station to take up his post.

A few days after he assumed office, Manager He's servant arrived with Young Master Wu. Father and son were overwhelmed with happy astonishment at their reunion. After learning all the facts from the letter, Magistrate Wu gave his son a severe lecture. He then invited Manager He's servant to stay for a few days to enjoy his hospitality. In the meantime, he set about preparing betrothal gifts, wrote a letter of reply, and sent a servant of his own to go with Mr. He's servant to present the marriage proposal. Young Master Wu wrote a private letter for Miss He. Laden with the gifts, the two servants took leave of Magistrate Wu and went to Jingzhou. Manager He accepted the betrothal gifts, wrote a letter of reply, and sent Magistrate Wu's servant on his way.

After reading Young Master Wu's letter, Miss He gradually regained her health. Young Master Wu applied himself assiduously to his studies at home day and night. When the time for the examinations came around, he went to the capital to sit for them and passed upon the first try. It so happened that with his *jinshi* degree, he was assigned to Jingzhou Prefecture, of all places, to be the magistrate of Xiangtan County. As for Magistrate Wu, his son having won fame and rank, he resigned from his post and went with his son to Jingzhou, where the young man took office. On a chosen auspicious day, a wedding ceremony was held, and Miss He was brought into the Wu residence. Young Master Wu's colleagues also came to offer their congratulations.

> By the wedding candles, the new bride and groom;
> Under the brocade quilt, two old acquaintances.

After joining the Wu clan, Xiu'e gained a fine reputation for her devotion to her parents-in-law and the conjugal harmony she enjoyed with her husband. Later, wishing to be with his daughter, Manager He also moved to Bianjing, where he lived out the rest of his life. Wu Yan rose to be an imperial academician. His two sons also passed the civil service examinations. This story is entitled "Young Master Wu Goes to a Tryst in the Next Boat." As the poem says,

> The young couple were well matched in their looks;
> With two quatrains they secretly formed their union.
> A long-lasting marriage began from under a bed;
> The story of their love goes down through the ages.

With His Passion for Poetry and Wine, Scholar Lu Scorns Dukes and Earls

On Mount Fuqiu on the east bank of the River Wei
Stands amidst the clouds a bamboo hut with a hidden phoenix.
With a writing style that awes Dong and Jia,[1]
With a fame that overshadows Liu and Cao,[2]
The poet roams the green hilltops in autumn
And wields his rabbit-hair brush in spring.
When drunk, he leans against his sword, and whistles
As the wind sweeps ten thousand li and cleaves the waves.

The above lines were written by a gifted scholar in the Jiajing reign period [1522–66] of this dynasty [the Ming]. Who was that gifted scholar? He was Lu Nan, courtesy names Shaopian and Zichi, a native of Jun County, Daming Prefecture. He had a prepossessing exterior, graceful manners, and a dignified, ethereal air. He began to compose essays at age eight and poems at age ten. He could write thousands of words at one go in a matter of moments. All and sundry called him a reincarnation of Li Qinglian and Cao Zijian.[3] With a passion for wine and acts of chivalry in his unrestrained style of life, he had nothing but scorn for worldly conventions. Truly, his fame spread far and wide and his talent was second to none. He associated only with scions of the nobility. Being a descendant of a long line of officials laden with riches, he lived like a prince. In his magnificent, towering mansion located at the foot of Mount Fuqiu outside the city, he kept a bevy of beautiful women singers. He also chose several good-looking young page boys and taught them to play musical instruments for his daily entertainment. As for ordinary servants and page boys, there were too many of them to count. Behind the house, he had a garden built on a two-to-three-hundred *mu* lot, where a pond was dug and rocks were piled up in the shape of hills in an exquisite layout. He named the place the "Whistle of Delight Garden."

Since most flowers thrive in warmer climates, prized species of flowers are found

exclusively in the south. As for the northern regions, most of the flowers trans-
planted there from the south cannot survive the harsh winter, which accounts for
the rarity of flora in the north. What few flowers and plants are transported there
are invariably the possessions of the wealthy and influential, not to be easily acquired
by those outside the circle. Jun County being less accessible than the capital, the
gardens of the local rich were in fact not much to look at. Lu Nan, however, in his
determination to outdo others, went to a great deal of expense and hired people
to search everywhere for exotic flowers and unique rocks. His garden, therefore,
was unsurpassed in its beauty throughout the region. Behold:

> Amid quiet and enchanting courtyards
> Stand tall towers and belvederes.
> Porous rocks form hills of the strangest shapes;
> Flowers in their beds are of the rarest species.
> Waterside gazebos lead to bamboo cottages;
> Verandas run past windows embowered with pines.
> Winding ponds with their railings sparkle like green glaze;
> Tiered hills in their verdant grandeur seem paved with jade.
> Pairs of peacocks perch on the tree peonies by the pavilions;
> Cranes dance amidst the herbaceous peonies by the fences.
> The meandering pine-flanked trails
> Lead to small bridges in the depths of the woods.
> From among twisting stems of bright red flowers,
> Tall trees soar to the sky.
> A faint mist hovers over the foliage;
> The rain adds a rich dye to the green hills.
> Boats float on water strewn with lotus petals;
> Swings fly back and forth in the shade of willows.
> Behind vermilion-painted balustrades
> Hang bamboo screens and embroidered curtains.

Day in and day out, Lu Nan spent his time merrily roaming among the flow-
ers and the birds and writing poetry in their praise. A prince of the south could
not have lived in greater pleasure. He made a point of treating every visitor to wine
until everyone was thoroughly drunk. If it was a true friend with whom he shared
common interests, he would make that friend stay for days or even months on end
and was loath to let him go. Those in trouble who went to him for help never failed
to be amply supplied with money or gifts. None would be turned away empty-
handed, wherefore people attracted by his fame descended on his residence from
all directions in never-ending streams. Truly,

> His house was always full of visitors;
> His wine vessels never ran out of wine.

With his literary talent and wide learning, Lu Nan thought that obtaining an official post was as easy as picking up a needle or a blade of grass. Little did he know that he was not born to splendid chances in a career as a government official. However brilliant his essays, they did not please the examiners. After several failed attempts, he concluded that since no one recognized his talent anyway, he might as well give up on the examinations and stop trying to advance his prospects in officialdom. Instead, calling himself "the hermit of Fuqiu," he spent all his time conversing with poets, swordsmen, eminent priests, and monks on Buddhist doctrines and on swordsmanship, playing gambling games, drinking wine, and enjoying the beauty of nature. As an ancient poem says,

> As if on wings taking him to the sky,
> In long strides bringing him to heaven's gate,
> He trod the fragrant paths, his robe hitched high,
> Before winds that whipped up waves of the sea.
> He tied his horse to the celestial trees;
> For breakfast he feasted on ambrosia.
> He enjoyed the divine sights to his heart's content;
> Softly he whistled in tune with the phoenixes.
> None of the mud of the mortal world
> Could soil the one that flew high in the sky.

Our story forks at this point. The magistrate of Jun County was a certain Wang Cen. He had already passed the civil service examinations in spite of his youth. A rapaciously greedy man full of malice and suspicion of other people, he also had a weakness for wine. With a wine cup in hand, he could drink without stopping all through the night. Since coming to Jun County, he had not yet met a man who was his match in drinking. Upon hearing that Lu Nan was a respected fine scholar with many friends, that the splendor of his garden was second to none, and that he had an unrivaled capacity for wine, Magistrate Wang was taken with a desire to get acquainted with the man, and so he sent a messenger to bring Lu Nan to him. Don't you find this laughable? The average scholar would be only too eager to befriend a magistrate and would seize every opportunity to be introduced to him and to honor him as a mentor. At every festival, the scholar would send him gifts, hoping for larger favors in return. If the magistrate issued him an invitation, he would feel as honored as if summoned by the imperial court and would post the invitation card on the wall to impress his relatives and friends. Granted that this is the behavior of despicable people rather than those with moral integrity, an invitation by a magistrate is not something to be rejected out of hand.

Lu Nan, however, was in a class all by himself. The magistrate sent over five or six invitation cards in succession, but he paid them no attention, saying that he had never seen the inside of an official's residence and was not going to. Why did he behave in such a way? Well, with his nonpareil talent, he turned up his nose at everyone. With his high opinion of himself, he held worldly success and position in disdain. Even if a prince or a duke or an official of the imperial court were to ask him to pay a visit without coming to call on him first, he would also flatly refuse to go. What chance did a mere county magistrate stand with him? Indeed, he was pride itself, someone whose services the emperor would seek in vain and whose friendship a dignitary would want to cultivate but to no avail.

So Lu Nan was eccentric enough, but this time he ran up against a man who was also quite out of the common run, for Magistrate Wang had infinite patience. Another man would have given up the idea if the invitee had refused to accept an invitation offered four or five times, but not Magistrate Wang. He kept up the pressure. When he finally realized that nothing would make Lu Nan come to him, he decided to go in all modesty to Lu Nan instead. Afraid that Lu Nan might be away, he sent a messenger to Lu with a visiting card to set up an appointment. Bearing orders from the magistrate, the messenger went to the Lu residence and, handing the visiting card to the gatekeeper, said, "I'm sent here by the county magistrate with an important message to your master. Please show me in." Not daring to be remiss in his duty, the gatekeeper led him into the garden to see the master.

Following the gatekeeper into the garden, the messenger saw sparkling water around well-spaced bamboo groves and trees standing in all their luxuriance against a background of verdant hills. The twittering of the birds pleased the ears. Never having been exposed to such sights and sounds, the messenger felt as if he were in a fairyland. In a burst of joy, he thought, "No wonder His Honor wishes to tour this place. And what a wonderful place this is indeed! I'm a lucky man to be able to see it. My life hasn't been lived in vain." And so he feasted his eyes on the scenery as he walked along. (*An imprudent man.*) Following the twists and turns of the flower-lined paths, passing several gazebos and terraces, he came upon an octagonal pavilion with a vermilion roof, green tiles, and carved and painted beams and rafters, surrounded by a profusion of snowy white plum blossoms that emitted a refreshing fragrance. Under a horizontal board bearing the inscription "Jade Radiance Pavilion" sat the host with three or four guests, viewing the flowers and drinking wine. Off to one side were five or six pretty maidservants playing musical instruments and singing. There is in evidence the "Ode to Plum Blossoms" by Historian Gao:[4]

> They belong in the jasper terrace of heaven.
> Who planted them everywhere south of the Yangzi?
> Hermits sleep in the snow-covered mountains;
> Beauties walk in the moonlit forest trails.
> In winter they bloom by the bamboo groves;
> In spring their remnant fragrance lingers on the moss.

667

With the fishermen gone, their time is over;
The lonesome east wind sadly asks, "When again?"

The gatekeeper and the messenger stood waiting outside until the song was finished. After the gatekeeper presented the visiting card, the messenger stepped forward and said, "His Honor instructed me to pay his respects to you, sir, saying that since you consider it beneath your dignity to go to the county yamen, he will come to visit you. But afraid that he might not find you at home and therefore make the trip in vain, he sent me here to fix a date on which he can come to pay his respects to you. In addition, having heard about the beauty of your garden, His Honor also wishes to tour the grounds."

Persistence pays in most situations. Impressed by the way the magistrate humbly yielded to him instead of taking offense at his rejection of the invitations, Lu Nan began to have second thoughts: "He may be a greedy and despicable man, but being magistrate of the county, he is considered as no less than a parent to the local people. It's not bad at all for him to show such humility out of respect for someone worthier. If I still refuse, people will take me for a petty, intolerant man." Then again, he thought, "He's just a low-level official with little knowledge about the art of writing. The rules of prosody also must be too difficult for him. As for ancient books and records, he's too young. He should be glad enough that the *jin-shi* degree just fell into his lap in his sleep. He has probably never even made the acquaintance of such books. The Confucian school of the Principle and the Chan [Zen] school of Buddhism are even further out of his range. But apart from these topics, what is there to talk about? I'd better not bring this on myself." But then he thought it would be too heartless of him to reject such good will. While he was thus debating with himself, a page boy served him wine. The sight of the wine gave him an idea. He thought, "If he can drink, I'll forgive him his vulgarity."

"Does the magistrate drink?" he asked the messenger.

"Wine is as dear to His Honor as his life. Of course he drinks."

"How much wine can he hold?"

"I've seen him drink a whole night away, cup in hand, not stopping until he's quite inebriated. I don't know exactly how many drinks he can carry."

Lu Nan was delighted. He thought, "So, that vulgar thing can drink. All right, that does it!" He told a page boy to bring him a visiting card bearing his own name and, giving it to the messenger, said, "Since the magistrate wishes to tour this place, how about tomorrow, when the plum blossoms will still be in bloom? I'll be waiting for him here with wine and food."

Given this promise, the messenger went out with the gatekeeper. Once back in the county yamen, the messenger gave the visiting card to the magistrate, to the latter's great joy. However, just as he was looking forward to the visit to Lu Nan's residence to view the plum blossoms the next day, a messenger came in the evening to announce that the new prefect had just arrived to take up office. Magistrate Wang therefore had to travel to the prefectural seat before the night was out. In disappointment, he sent a messenger to Lu Nan to decline the invitation. He then went to the prefectural yamen, greeted the new prefect, and took him to a temple for the requisite incense-burning service before returning to his county yamen. The journey to and from the prefectural seat took several days. By this time,

> The jade petals of the plum blossoms had fallen,
> And floated around the painted railings.

Annoyed at having had to cancel the appointment to view the plum blossoms, Magistrate Wang hoped that Lu Nan would invite him again. However, having issued the invitation reluctantly in the first place, Lu Nan dismissed the matter from his mind. Far be it from him to issue another invitation!

Soon it was midspring. Again Magistrate Wang longed for a spring outing to Lu Nan's garden. His messenger bearing his message of greetings went to the Lu residence and found the garden in a riot of color. The grass along the causeway was as soft as a carpet. The orioles warbled, the swallows chirped, and the butterflies and the bees flitted about. It was a charming scene. The next moment, the messenger turned onto a path lined with peach trees with blossoms as resplendent as rosy clouds. There is a poem in evidence:

> Peach blossoms burst all over the branches,
> Dazzling the eye with their splendor.
> Charming and sincere in their radiant smiles,
> They succumb to wind at the break of day.

Lu Nan and his guests were beating a drum and passing flower blossoms from hand to hand under the peach trees in a game where the person in whose hand the blossoms happened to be the moment the drum-beating stopped must sing a song or drink a cup of wine. When the messenger approached him with the magistrate's letter, Lu Nan said in wine-induced exhilaration, "Go quickly back to tell the magistrate that he can come right now if he pleases. There's no need to make another appointment." (*Frivolous!*)

The guests objected: "That won't do! We are having such a good time. If he comes, we'll have to stand on ceremony. How will we be able to enjoy ourselves to the full? Make it another day!"

Lu Nan agreed, "You're right. Tomorrow, then!" So saying, he took an appointment card and gave it to the messenger for him to transmit to the magistrate.

Now, there could not have been a worse case of ill timing, for the next day, just when Magistrate Wang was on the point of leaving for his spring excursion, his five-months-pregnant wife had a miscarriage. She fainted and collapsed to the floor in a pool of blood. The magistrate was frightened out of his wits. In no mood to enjoy a feast, he was obliged to send a messenger to Lu Nan to again cancel the appointment. (*The second time.*) His wife did not recover until late in the third lunar month. By that time, tree peonies were in full bloom in Lu Nan's garden. They were the best peonies in the entire county, as evidenced by the following poem entitled "Ode to Peonies":

> *The Luoyang peonies forever vie for beauty;*
> *Praises abound for their elegance and color.*
> *Since Li Bai's peony poem spread far and wide,[5]*
> *Odes to the flower queen are written to this day.*

Preoccupied for the better part of a month with his wife's indisposition, Magistrate Wang drowned his sorrows in wine, to the neglect of his official duties. When he heard about the gorgeous peonies in the Lu residence, he very much wanted to see them, but, feeling awkward for having failed to keep the previous two appointments, he sent a messenger with an offer of three taels of silver for Lu Nan to buy books with, by way of reminding Lu of his wish to view the flowers. Lu Nan set a date for his visit but refused to take the monetary gift. The money went back and forth a few times. His repeated objections unavailing, Lu Nan finally accepted it in resignation.

On the day of the appointment, and a bright and sunny day it was, Magistrate Wang planned to finish his work early at the office and go to the Lu residence. (*The third time.*) As it turned out, he had barely left his residential quarters when an attendant came to announce, "Mr. So-and-so, supervising secretary of the personnel bureau, is passing here on his way to his hometown to visit his parents." The supervising secretary being an important person, how would the magistrate dare not to greet him? With alacrity he went out of the city gate to meet the supervising secretary and treated him to a feast. (*He wants to fulfill his social obligations and to enjoy a life of leisure at the same time. How can he expect to have it both ways?*) He thought the visitor would stay for just one or two days, leaving him enough time to view the peonies. To his dismay, the supervising secretary was a man who enjoyed sightseeing. In the magistrate's company, he toured the scenic spots of the county and lingered for seven or eight days before departing. After he was gone, the magistrate again sent a messenger to make an appointment with Lu Nan, but the peonies had all wilted. His himself had left two days earlier on an excursion to another place.

Quite unnoticed, spring came to an end and summer rolled around. In the snap of a finger, it was the middle of the sixth lunar month. Upon inquires, Magistrate Wang learned that Lu Nan had returned and was staying at home, keeping cool in the hot weather. Again the magistrate sent a messenger to say that he wished to see the lotus blossoms. The messenger forthwith hastened to the Lu residence and handed the gatekeeper the magistrate's visiting card. The gatekeeper went in and, before long, reemerged to say, "My master has something to say directly to you." Thereupon the messenger followed the gatekeeper all the way to a lotus pond that covered an area of about ten *mu*. The abundant foliage of the locust trees and willows along the causeway blotted out the sun. On the surface of the water stood red lotus blossoms and green leaves in all their charms. There is a poem in evidence:

> The lotus blossoms, fairy maidens of the ripples,
> Show off their new clothes in a contest of beauty;
> The lotus roots, through their holes and the hollow chamber,
> Emit a most beguiling fragrance.
> The flower spirits, in contrast, are too unkind,
> Tantalizing viewers only with colors.

That pond had a name—"Green Ripples Pond." In the middle of the pond stood a pavilion called "Brocade Clouds Pavilion." No bridge was built to lead to it across the water. Instead, boats used by lotus pickers served as ferries to carry people to Lu Nan's shelter from the heat. The gatekeeper and the messenger got down on one of those boats and, rowing the painted oars, soon reached the pavilion. They tied the boat to a post and went ashore. Raising his eyes, the messenger saw that vermilion railings ran all around the pavilion, which was shielded by green awnings over gauze windows. The air, stirred by gentle breezes, was filled with the fragrance of the lotus blossoms. In the water, golden carp played with water plants. At the top of the pavilion, young swallows flitted from beam to beam, looking for places to build their nests. Egrets fought one another for spots under the lotus leaves, and mandarin ducks bathed by the banks.

Once in the pavilion, the messenger saw a rattan bed, a spotted bamboo basket, a stone couch, and a bamboo side table. In a vase stood a "Thousand-Leaf" water lily; in the incense burner were lit prized "Hundred Harmonies" joss sticks. His hair disheveled, his feet bare, Lu Nan was lolling on the stone couch, with a pile of ancient books in front of him and a wine cup in hand. On the tray by his side were iced gold-colored peaches, snowy white lotus roots, plums, and melons. There was also a display of hors d'oeuvres to go with wine. With one page boy holding a wine flask and another one fanning him, Lu Nan drank one cupful after reading every few lines, thoroughly enjoying himself. (*He'd better enjoy life while he still can!*)

Not daring to step forward, the messenger stood there, thinking, "Aren't we all human beings born of parents? Why should he get to live so well? The magistrate is a *jinshi*, no less, but has to work hard all day, not at all as carefree as this man is."

Happening to raise his head at this point, Lu Nan saw the messenger and asked, "So you are the messenger from the yamen?"

"Yes, I am," said the messenger.

"This magistrate of yours is impossible! He made several appointments but didn't keep a single one. And here he goes again, saying he wishes to see the lotus blossoms. How did a man who can't make up his mind manage to enter the civil service? I can't afford the time to haggle with him. He can come any time the fancy seizes him. I don't have the patience to set up another appointment with him." (*Shockingly haughty* [Illegible.].)

"The magistrate has the utmost respect for you, sir," said the messenger. "He says he has such admiration for your great talent that he is as eager to see you and learn from you as a thirsty man is to drink water. He failed to keep the previous appointments because of situations out of his control. Please give him another chance, so that I can acquit myself."

Impressed by the man's glib tongue, Lu Nan relented and said, "All right. Let's make it the day after tomorrow."

Given this promise, the messenger asked for a written reply. After he got the reply, he boarded the boat again with the gatekeeper and they rowed back to the willow-lined causeway. The messenger then went back to report to the magistrate.

On the appointed day, Magistrate Wang left the yamen for Lu Nan's home at the lunch hour, after his morning court session was over. It being the height of summer, Magistrate Wang had already been somewhat indisposed from the unusually hot weather of the previous few days. And now, under the blazing noontime sun, he felt as if his eyes were ready to spit fire and his throat to belch smoke. He had only gone part of the way when the sky and the earth changed places on him. He fell from his sedan-chair to the ground and almost died from suffocation. (*The fourth time.*) Losing no time, his attendants revived him and carried him back to his residential quarters in the yamen, where he gradually regained consciousness. He then sent a messenger to cancel the appointment with Lu Nan and engaged a physician for treatment. He did not resume his official duties until more than a month later, but no more need be said about this.

One day, when in his study, taking stock of the gifts he had received, Lu Nan came upon the money gift Magistrate Wang had given him to buy books. He thought, "How can I take money from him when he and I have never even met? I should put this money to good use before I can have any peace of mind." When the middle of the eighth month was approaching, he sent a servant to Magistrate Wang, inviting him to view the moon on the night of the Mid-Autumn Moon Festival [the fifteenth day of the eighth lunar month]. The magistrate, being already so inclined, was delighted at the invitation. Giving a written reply to the servant, he said, "Tell your master that I will surely be there."

As the first-ranking official of the county, Magistrate Wang could hardly have received only one invitation on the occasion of the Mid-Autumn Moon Festival. Naturally the rich local families and his yamen colleagues invited him to dinner, beginning from the tenth day of the month. With his passion for wine, would he decline the offers? Without fail, he kept every one of those appointments. But on the fourteenth day, he turned down invitations for that particular evening, had dinner at home with his wife, and spent the rest of the evening with her in their courtyard, admiring the moon.

That night, the moon shone with greater brilliance than usual. There is a poem in evidence:

> Under the vast, softly lit sky,
> Golden waves flow on throughout the night.
> How sad that whether full or not,
> The moon witnesses sorrows, old and new.
> The wind reveals the moon in all its loneliness;
> The hills and rivers share the grandeur of autumn.
> The notes of a flute somewhere
> Send one to wine-induced sleep in the south tower.

The husband and wife did not go to bed until they were quite inebriated. Partly because he had not yet recovered from his recent illness, partly because he had been indulging himself in wine for the past few days and could hardly refrain from overtaxing himself with those activities that one is often prone to in wine-induced excitement, and partly because he stayed up too late into the night and caught a cold, Magistrate Wang again fell ill. The appointment with Lu Nan was missed once again. (*The fifth time.*) It took several days for him to regain his health.

For want of something interesting to do in the yamen, Magistrate Wang had a mind to amuse himself by viewing the cassia blossoms that must be in full bloom in Lu Nan's garden. It just so happened that a visitor from south of the Yangzi River came to the yamen to solicit a contribution from the magistrate, bringing with him two large vats of wine brewed with water from Huishan Spring.[6] Magistrate Wang had servants send one vat to Lu Nan.

Upon hearing that the wine was of superior quality, Lu Nan was immensely delighted, for no gift could have been more to his liking. He thought, "I shouldn't be picky about the way he does his administrative work or about his style of writing. This vat of wine alone shows that he is a man of taste." Straightaway he wrote an invitation for Magistrate Wang to come in two days to view the cassia blossoms. There is a poem in testimony:

> The curtain that filters moonlight casts a cool shade;
> Gusts of autumn wind blow from the divine palace.
> The Prince of Huainan need not have called for hermits;[7]
> His cassia trees alone are inviting enough.

The ancients said, "Every act of drinking and eating is predestined." Wasn't it extraordinary for a county magistrate, a parent-like official, to humbly ask to visit a common scholar? And yet, without a predestined bond between them, something was bound to happen to prevent them from meeting. With his request to view Lu Nan's cassia trees, Magistrate Wang was hoping with all his heart to fully enjoy himself and satisfy his long-held wish. However, on the appointed day, he was still in bed when the wooden board at the yamen entrance was struck, as was

673

the wont when an emergency situation arose. A messenger came in to announce, "Mr. Zhao, director of the judicial bureau of Shanxi, is passing through on his way to the capital to take up his new post, and has already moored his boat by the shore."

Mr. Zhao was the very examiner who had read Magistrate Wang's essays at the provincial level of the civil service examinations and recommended him to the chief examiner. How would the magistrate not want to be a good host? (*The sixth time.*) With alacrity he rose, combed his hair, washed, dashed out of the yamen, mounted his sedan-chair, and went to greet Mr. Zhao. A feast was then laid out in honor of the visitor. Now, won't you agree that a mentor and his favorite student would want to spend some time together? Naturally, Mr. Zhao stayed for a few days before continuing with his journey. By that time, the cassia blossoms were already

> *Dancing in the wind like golden millet,*
> *And strewing the ground in their divine fragrance.*

Being a forthright man of bold spirit, Lu Nan was prone to holding in equal disdain those above him as well as those below him in status. Impressed by Magistrate Wang's humbleness in trying to cultivate the friendship of a worthy man such as himself, he had a mind to condescendingly accept the association. It being the end of the ninth month, his garden was aglow with chrysanthemums. Of the many varieties of chrysanthemums, three are the most precious. Which three?

Crane Plumes, Fine Floss, and Xishi the Beauty.[8]

Each of the above kinds boasts several different colors, precious because the blossoms are large and dazzlingly gorgeous. There is in evidence a poem entitled "Ode to Chrysanthemums":

> *Aloof from the contest for beauties in the spring wind,*
> *They keep to the fences and defy autumn frost.*
> *When the garden is a scene of desolation,*
> *A few blossoms here and there still emit fragrance.*

Considering how Magistrate Wang wished to see his garden but was unable to do so each time, Lu Nan thought of inviting him while the chrysanthemums were in bloom, so as not to disappoint the magistrate in the latter's admiration for him. He wrote a letter of invitation and sent a servant to invite the magistrate to view his chrysanthemums the very next day. Bearing the letter, the servant went to the county yamen, where the magistrate was handling documents in the tribunal. The servant went straight into the tribunal and, kneeling down, presented the letter to him, saying, "My master respectfully invites you, sir, to view the chrysanthemums in his garden tomorrow."

Magistrate Wang had been meaning to see the chrysanthemums. Having failed several times to keep the appointments, he felt too awkward to bring up the subject. This invitation could not have pleased him more. After reading the letter, he said, "Tell your master that I will go with all respect early tomorrow."

The servant went home and said to his master, "Mr. Wang says that he will come first thing tomorrow morning."

Now, the magistrate said "early tomorrow" offhandedly, without really meaning it. The servant changed the phrase to "first thing tomorrow morning" by an unintended mistake. As it later turned out, as a consequence of this change, Lu Nan offended the magistrate and lost his immense wealth and almost his life. Indeed,

The tongue is the source of all gains and losses;
The mouth is the gate to fortunes good or ill.

Lu Nan thought, "That magistrate is truly a funny one. What dinner guest would arrive first thing in the morning?" Then he thought, "Maybe he wants to spend the whole day in my garden that he admires so much." To his kitchen staff he said, "The magistrate will be coming first thing tomorrow morning. So, get the feast ready early." Hearing that the magistrate would be there early the next morning, the kitchen staff set about making preparations in a frantic rush that very evening, afraid that they might be too pressed for time the next morning.

When morning came, Lu Nan told the gatekeeper, "Turn away all other visitors. You need not even announce them." He then sent a servant to the magistrate, bearing an invitation card. Before breakfast time, the feast was ready and set out in Swallow Bliss Hall in the garden. There were only one table for the host, facing north, and one for the guest, facing south, with no seats for other guests. (*This is by no means a usual seating arrangement.*)[9] A sumptuous feast it was. Truly,

A feast in a rich man's house is enough
To feed a poor man for half a year.

After accepting files of complaints that morning, the magistrate wanted to go to his appointment without even bothering to formally announce dismissal of the court session. However, observing that it was too early in the day for a feast to be ready, he picked one file and began to read it. It was a case about a group of bandits, just arrested, who had been robbing traveling merchants along the Wei River. They gave themselves away when spending one night in a brothel and were arrested by yamen detectives and taken to the yamen. The magistrate had them brought into the tribunal for interrogation. All confessed. One of them, a Brother Shi Xue, named another accomplice, a Butcher Wang, owner of a butcher shop in the same county. By the magistrate's order, the butcher was brought forthwith to the tribunal.

"Butcher Wang," said the magistrate, "Brother Shi Xue named you as an accomplice. The spoils are all hidden in your house. Confess, or you'll be put under the rod!"

"Your Honor," said Butcher Wang, "I am a good law-abiding person, with a butcher's shop under Your Honor's jurisdiction. I don't even walk about much in the marketplace. How can I do the things I'm accused of? I've never even seen these bandits, let alone been their accomplice. If you don't believe me, Your Honor, please bring my neighbors here and ask them about my character. The truth will be known soon enough."

Turning to Brother Shi Xue, the magistrate said, "Do not falsely accuse an innocent person. If I find out that he's been wronged, I'll have you beaten to death immediately, you lowlife!"

"I'm not falsely accusing him. He is indeed an accomplice!"

Butcher Wang cried out, "I don't even know you. How can I be an accomplice?"

Brother Shi Xue said, "Butcher Wang! We've been working as partners for so long. How can you pretend not to know me? I meant to cover up for you today, but I couldn't hold out against the torture, so your name slipped out of my mouth. Don't blame me!"

Butcher Wang cried out, protesting his innocence. "Where does all this come from?" he lamented.

By the magistrate's order, ankle squeezers were put to both of them. Poor Butcher Wang fainted away. After he was revived, he still refused to admit to any wrongdoing. That bandit Brother Shi Xue stuck to his story, but Butcher Wang would rather die than admit guilt. The torture had begun before noon. With both sides holding their ground, no judgment on the case could be made. When the sun began to set, the magistrate, preoccupied with thoughts about the invitation, grew impatient. He gave credence to the bandit's testimony and perfunctorily sentenced Butcher Wang to death. All of Butcher Wang's possessions were to be treated as spoils and confiscated by the government. After the papers were duly signed by the guilty parties, all were taken to death row. This done, the magistrate mounted his sedan-chair and proceeded to Lu Nan's residence for dinner. But more of this later.

You may well ask, why did that bandit stick to his story that Butcher Wang was an accomplice? Well, Brother Shi Xue used to own a small business, but then he caught a contagious disease and used up all his money, going as far as selling what worn-out pieces of furniture he had in exchange for food. After he recovered, he had no money left for starting his business again. The only thing he had was a clay cooking pot, which he thought could be sold for several tens of pennies to tide him over. But it was cracked at one spot. An idea struck him. He mixed up coal dust with clay, applied the mixture to the broken spot, made a straw tab marking the pot for sale, and carried it out to seek a buyer. He went up and down the streets for the longest time but no one wanted to buy a cracked pot.

Finally, when he was at the door of the rice shop opposite Mr. Wang's butchery, Tian Dalang, the owner, called out to him and offered to buy it. Tian Dalang was near-sighted. Detecting nothing broken, he offered eighty pennies for it, an offer that Brother Shi Xue accepted. When Brother Shi Xue was counting the money Tian Dalang had given him, Butcher Wang, witnessing the deal from across the street, shouted, "Dalang! Look closely! Don't buy anything broken!" This was said in jest, to mock Dalang's near-sightedness. But Tian Dalang indeed examined the pot again, and saw the broken spot. (*No good comes out of playfulness.* [Illegible.] *What begins as a jest can lead to enmity. Take warning!*) Dalang said to Butcher Wang, "Thanks for reminding me. Otherwise I would have been taken in. It is indeed broken." He was quick to ask for his money back and return the pot to Brother Shi Xue.

Brother Shi Xue had been filled with joy when he thought he had a deal. After Mr. Tian took his money back, Brother Shi Xue hated Butcher Wang so bitterly that he wished he could fight him to the death. But his merchandise was indeed broken and he was therefore bereft of a valid argument in his own defense, so he swallowed his rage and turned to go, pot in hand. Before he departed, he glowered at Butcher Wang, hoping the latter would talk to him, giving him a reason to start making a scene. But, having made his remarks in utter innocence, Butcher Wang did not even cast a glance in his direction. Without any provocation, Brother Shi Xue had no choice but to leave. He was so upset that, in a lapse of attention, he tripped and fell. His pot was smashed to smithereens. He hated Butcher Wang to the marrow of his bones. Now that he had nothing to live on, he thought of making a suicide attempt to frighten Butcher Wang, but he didn't want to die. Left without a choice, he took to stealing. It turned out to be an easy profession. With each swipe of his hand, he became a richer man. After more than a year of life as a petty thief, he began to find his gains too modest. So he joined a group of bandits who made their rounds along the Wei River. While enjoying his new life, with wine served in large bowls and meat in large chunks, he thought of Butcher Wang with gratitude, saying, "If Butcher Wang had not made that remark, I would have sold that pot and used the money to start up a small business. I wouldn't have been able to live it up as I do now!" And he went on living his crime-ridden life until he was arrested and brought to the yamen. Now that he was going to die, because he knew a death sentence would be fully justified in his case, he recalled what had happened years earlier, thinking, "If that butcher hadn't made that remark, I would have sold the pot for tens of pennies, with which I could have started a small business for a living, and I wouldn't have come to this!" Therefore he named Butcher Wang as an accomplice and stuck to his story. He didn't change his line even when death was upon him. ([Illegible.]) That was why he knew Butcher Wang, but Butcher Wang did not recognize him.

Autumn, the season for the execution of criminals, arrived. When Brother Shi Xue and Butcher Wang were both in the execution ground, all trussed up, Butcher Wang asked, "Since we're going to die anyway, tell me, why do you hate me so much that you have to see me end like this? Tell me, so that at least I know the truth when I die."

It was only then that Brother Shi Xue told him the truth. Butcher Wang cried out his grievances and demanded that justice be done. Now, won't you agree that no one would lend him a sympathetic ear by this time? He died a victim of a false charge. Truly,

A remark made in jest
Cost the man his life.

Let us get on with our story. After waiting in vain for the magistrate from morning until almost noon, Lu Nan sent a servant to investigate. Upon learning that the magistrate was handling a case, Lu Nan was more than a little displeased. He thought, "Since he promised to come here first thing in the morning, why is he still attending to official business at this hour?" After waiting for another good while in vain, he again sent a servant to find out how things stood. The servant came back and said, "The interrogation is still going on." Lu Nan grew more displeased. He thought, "I picked the wrong time. Let me be patient and wait a bit longer."

As the saying goes, "Waiting exasperates." After a few moments, Lu Nan again sent a servant to make inquiries. Before that servant was even out of the range of an arrow, he sent another one out. In the twinkling of an eye, he dispatched five or six servants. Before long, all of them came back together to report, "He's applying torture in the tribunal. It looks like the interrogation is going to take a while."

Lu Nan's displeasure was now complete. "So, that vulgar thing doesn't even have one single redeeming virtue," he said to himself, furious. "He does nothing but pester me. I almost mistook him for a decent person. Luckily, it's not too late." Right away he ordered the servants to clear away the table that had been set for the guest. Sitting down in the middle, facing the door, he shouted, "Heat up a large vessel of wine for me, so that I can wash my insides clean of vulgarity!"

The servants protested, saying, "What if His Honor arrives?"

Opening his eyes wide, Lu Nan snapped, "Pshaw! 'His Honor' indeed! My wine is not meant for a filthy thing like him!"

Not daring to venture another word at this outburst from their master, the servants filled a large vessel with wine and brought dishes in from the kitchen. The musicians struck up music right there in the hall. After finishing several vessels, Lu Nan asked for a large bowl and drank more than ten bowlfuls in succession. In the excitement of the moment, he shed his scarf and robe and sat down cross-legged in his chair, his feet bare, his hair unkempt, and ordered that all the dishes be cleared away. With nothing but fruit and some tidbits left on the table, he downed another ten bowls of wine or so. Then he gave the fruit and tidbits to the musicians and drank another few bowls, with nothing to go with the wine.

However large his capacity for wine, he was not able to hold that much wine gulped down all at once. After having drunk tens of bowls of wine in his rage, he bent over the table and fell asleep in a drunken stupor. Not daring to disturb him, the servants stood on two sides in neat rows, waiting.

Little knowing that Lu Nan was in a besotted condition inside, the gatekeeper rushed in when he saw the magistrate's procession coming from afar. Aghast at the sight of his master in an inebriated state in the hall, he said, "His Honor is here. Why is the master already drunk?"

Upon hearing that the magistrate was there, the servants looked at each other in dismay, at a loss as to what to do. They said, "The food and wine for the guest are untouched, but the master is asleep. What's to be done?"

The gatekeeper said, "Wake him up! Even if he's drunk, having him keep the guest company for a while would be better than turning away someone he went out of his way to invite."

For lack of a better way out, the servants went up and called out Lu Nan's name. Even though they cried themselves hoarse, he did not wake up. As voices gradually came to their ears, they realized that the magistrate was already approaching. Horrified, they dispersed in all directions, leaving Lu Nan alone. As a consequence of this event, a host and a guest became worst enemies; the good scenery and prized flowers vanished as in a spring dream. Indeed,

> *Heaven dictates the vicissitudes of life;*
> *Humans bring weal or woe upon themselves.*

Let us retrace our steps and come to the point when Magistrate Wang had left the yamen and arrived at the gate of the Lu residence. Without seeing Lu Nan or any servant there to greet them, the magistrate's attendants exclaimed, "Anyone there? Announce to the master that the magistrate is here! And be quick about it!"

Without getting a word of response, Magistrate Wang thought that the gatekeeper must have gone in to announce him. "Stop yelling," he said to the attendants and walked straight in. Over the gate was hung a white horizontal board with the characters "Whistle of Delight Garden" inscribed on it in green. He went in and took a path flanked by cypress trees. Turning around a corner, he came upon another gate bearing the inscription "Away from the Mortal World." He went through the gateway and down a path flanked by pine trees. After he was clear of the pine trees, he saw in front of him undulating hills, towers and terraces embowered with the foliage of trees and bushes, and bamboo fences ablaze with flowers. Delighted at the exquisite layout and the enchanting peace and quiet of the place, the magistrate thought, "A man of taste is indeed out of the common run."

Puzzled that there were no human voices within hearing and that Lu Nan was nowhere in sight, Magistrate Wang thought it was because there were too many crisscrossing paths in the garden. He said to himself, "He must have taken another path and therefore missed me." And so he and his retinue of attendants went about freely in search of the host. (*Funny.*) Then they came upon a three-section hall around which bloomed hundreds of bedazzling chrysanthemums amid maple trees with foliage as glorious as rosy clouds, and orange and tangerine trees with fruit that glittered like gold. The rim of the pond was dotted with hundreds of lotus blossoms in different shades of red. On the surface of the green water and under the red blossoms swam mandarin ducks and other fowl. Magistrate Wang thought, "Since he invited me to see the chrysanthemum flowers, he must be in this hall."

The magistrate dismounted his sedan-chair in front of the hall and went in. Instead of a feast, he saw a man with disheveled hair and bare feet, occupying the seat in the center of the hall, bent over the table and snoring, his head toward the door. Not even the shadow of another human being was anywhere in sight. The magistrate's attendants dashed forward, exclaiming, "His Honor is here! Get up!"

Judging by the color and style of the man's clothes, Magistrate Wang concluded that he was no servant. But noticing also the ko-hemp scarf and the commoner's gown that lay by his side, the magistrate instructed his men to stop trying to wake up the man but find out his identity first. The messenger who had been here often enough came up for a close look. Recognizing him to be Lu Nan, the messenger said, "This drunken man is none other than Mr. Lu himself."

At these words, Magistrate Wang's face went purplish crimson. Boiling with rage, he said to himself, "What impudence! So this brute deliberately set a trap for me, just to humiliate me!" He wanted to have the men smash up the flowers and the plants, but, thinking it would not be proper behavior for an official, he swallowed his rage, hurried back into his sedan-chair, and told his men to return to the county yamen. The sedan-chair carriers went the same way they had come. As before, they saw no one all the way back to the exit of the garden. The magistrate's followers all shook their heads in disbelief and commented, "He's just a National University student. How can he hold a government official in such contempt? This is quite unusual."

Overhearing these comments from inside the sedan-chair, the magistrate felt deeply mortified. In mounting anger, he thought, "Whatever his talent, he's under my jurisdiction. I invited him several times in vain. Then I offered to go to him and sent over wine and money, going out of my way to show respect to a worthy person. But he turned out to be so impudent to me. Even an acquaintance of his own social class doesn't deserve such rudeness, let alone a county official like me!" His wrath unabated after he got back to the yamen, he immediately retired into his private quarters in the same building, and there we shall leave him for now.

Lu Nan's servants and page boys did not reemerge until after the magistrate was gone. When gathered in the hall to check on their master, they saw that he was still fast asleep. When he finally woke up late in the evening, the servants said, "His Honor the magistrate came soon after you fell asleep. He left when he saw you in your condition."

"Did he say anything?" asked Lu Nan.

"We were afraid that we wouldn't know what to say. So we hid ourselves and didn't see him."

"The right thing to do!" said Lu Nan approvingly. Then he said in regret, "I was in such a rush I forgot to tell the gatekeeper to close the gate. Otherwise, that filthy thing wouldn't have gotten in all the way here and messed up my place." Turning to a gardener, he said, "Tomorrow morning, get enough water to wash clean the paths he had used." Then he had a servant seek out the messenger who had been to the Lu residence a few times to return all the magistrate's letters and the vat of wine to him. Not daring to do other than what he was told, the servant carried out his mission without delay, but no more need be said about this.

After Magistrate Wang returned to his residential quarters in the yamen, his wife asked, observing his angry looks, "Didn't you go to a dinner? Why are you so upset?"

After he told her what had happened, she said, "You brought this on yourself. Why blame him? You are the highest-ranking official in the county. Wherever you go, people wait hand and foot on you. Why did you have to abase yourself and go to pay respects to someone under your jurisdiction? Whatever talent he has, what good is it to you? And now, having gotten such rude treatment, you should know better!"

This lecture from his wife added fuel to his anger. After he sat in silent fury in his armchair, his wife spoke up again, "There's no need to be angry. As the ancients said, 'A county magistrate can ruin a family.'" This remark woke up Magistrate Wang as if from a dream. His respect for the talented scholar immediately gave way to the desire to do him harm. Without saying anything out loud, he racked his brains for a plot against Mr. Lu. "I will not feel avenged until I do him to death," he vowed. That night passed without further ado.

The next day, after his morning court session was over, Magistrate Wang told a trusted clerk to come to his office for a consultation. That clerk, Tan Zun, was a capable man and an experienced corrupt government clerk who often handled bribes for the magistrate. After giving an account of how Lu Nan had offended him, the magistrate went on to confide in the clerk his intention to find an excuse to prosecute the scholar and avenge himself.

"Your Honor must not make a rash move against that Lu Nan. To finish him off, it will take a heinous crime for which he won't have a chance for leniency. Prosecution may not do it. Actually, it may even work against you."

"Why?"

"Lu Nan and I used to live in the same neighborhood. I know that he associates a lot with highly placed officials, and he's immensely rich. He may live an unrestrained style of life out of pride for his own talent, but he hasn't done anything against the law. If you arrest him, he'll use his higher-up connections to make your superiors redress the injustice done to him. You definitely won't be able to put him to death. If you end up being accused of trying to avenge yourself of a personal grudge, won't you be suffering consequences of your own making?"

"You do have a point," conceded the magistrate. "But with his impudence, he must have crossed a few lines. You go ahead and make inquiries. I'll deal with what you find out."

Tan Zun gave his promise. When leaving the office, Tan Zun ran right into the messenger who was bringing in the letters and the wine the magistrate had sent Lu Nan. Feeling humiliated, the magistrate vented his anger on the messenger and said, "You shouldn't have brought these things back!" He put the messenger to twenty strokes of the bamboo rod but then gave the silver and the wine to him. Indeed,

> *Be advised: do nothing to hurt others' feelings;*
> *The world abounds in spiteful people.*

Our story forks at this point. At the foot of Fuqiu Hill lived a farm laborer called Niu Cheng. He and his wife, Jin-shi, were poor but, because they were not reputable characters, no one was willing to hire them to work in the fields. They had been eking out a living as long-term hired hands for Lu Nan. Two years earlier, when they had had a son, the other hired hands and a few of Lu Nan's servants had jointly offered him congratulatory gifts. A man as poor as Niu Cheng should, by rights, have declined the offer. If he indeed could not bring himself to disappoint them in their good will and had to accept the gifts, he should have contented himself with treating them to just a few cups of wine in return, on account of his poverty. Instead, he went in for a great deal of pomp and ceremony without being able to afford the expenses. He indentured himself to Lu Cai, a servant in Lu Nan's employment, for two taels of silver, which he used to pay for a grand banquet. And he sent noodle soup to all the neighbors, as was the wont upon the birth of a child. It might as well have been a bustling scene of celebration in a rich man's house. While the wining and dining was in full swing, the baby died from the fright a cat had given it the day before, putting such a damper on everyone's spirits that the party broke up before the guests had fully enjoyed themselves.

Lu Cai had been willing to lend Niu Cheng money only because he had evil designs. What designs? Well, Niu Cheng's wife was not bad-looking. Lu Cai was hoping to seduce her, with the loan of the money as a bait. To his disappointment, there was little predestined bond between them. That woman would rather do business with other men free of charge than succumb to Lu Cai, and she complained to her husband, accusing Lu Cai of trying to take liberties with her. Taking his wife to be a chaste woman, Niu Cheng hated Lu Cai to the marrow of his bones and resolved not to pay back the money.

After more than a year went by with the woman putting on demure airs, Lu Cai realized that his seduction attempts were not working. So he gave up the idea and began persistently to demand his money back. The two men quarreled quite a few times, their faces flaming red, but Niu Cheng had no money to give. Someone gave Lu Cai this idea: "Since he works for the Lu family year after year, why don't you wait until payday to deduct from his wages all the money he owes you? Won't that be a nice way out?"

Lu Cai took the advice and stopped pressing Niu Cheng for payment. When it was the middle of the last month of the year, he asked which day would be payday for the laborers and waited eagerly for that day to arrive.

Lu Nan was a large landowner. Apart from his household servants, he also hired hundreds of farm laborers, and in the middle of the last lunar month of the year, he paid the laborers in advance for the work to be done the following year. When the payday of that year arrived, all the hired laborers went into the hall to receive their wages. Afraid that his servants might cheat and shortchange the laborers, Lu Nan personally chanted out the figures and handed them the money. He then treated them to dinner. After eating and drinking their fill, they bowed in gratitude and left the hall.

Niu Cheng had just reached the gate when Lu Cai grabbed him with one swipe of his hand and demanded payment. Because he hated to part with his money and also because he bore Lu Cai a grudge for having taken liberties with his wife, Niu Cheng began to make a scene in his state of drunken excitement. Tucking the silver into his money belt, he cursed, "You dog of a servant, kicking me around over a few miserable pieces of silver! Let me fight you to the death!" So saying, he ran headlong into Lu Cai. Caught off guard, Lu Cai staggered back more than ten paces and almost fell. In a moment of blinding rage, Lu Cai charged forward and rained blows on Niu Cheng. Niu Cheng's epithet for Lu Cai having enraged all the other servants as well, they said, "What a brute! Even if justice were on your side, you're still just a hired hand in this household. You should yield to us a little. How can a debtor turn around and get violent? Beat up this dog!" They all surged forward and gave Niu Cheng a brutal beating. As the saying goes, "Two fists are no match for four hands." Vastly outnumbered, Niu Cheng was beaten black and blue. Catching sight of the money belt that contained Niu's wages, Lu Cai broke the string and snatched away the belt. The other hired laborers pleaded on Niu Cheng's behalf until the servants stopped their blows. Niu Cheng was then pushed back home.

In the meantime, the commotion at the gate became faintly audible to Lu Nan in his study. He summoned the gatekeeper for questioning. Domestic discipline in the Lu household being strict, the gatekeeper told him the truth, afraid of being implicated in any way. Lu Nan then summoned Lu Cai and said to him, "I've announced before that no servant in this household is allowed to give private loans to laborers and take advantage of them. If this rule is violated, the original receipt of the loan will be surrendered to me and the culprit will be severely punished and expelled from this house. Why did you deliberately violate this rule? And you robbed him of his wages and beat him, too! What impudence! You disgust me!" Forthwith he made Lu Cai surrender the silver as well as the receipt of the loan, put him to twenty strokes of the rod, and expelled him from the house, never to be employed again. To the gatekeeper, Lu Nan said, "When Niu Cheng is here, tell him to see me. I'll give him the money and the loan receipt." The gatekeeper eagerly promised to see this done and left the hall. Of this, no more need be said.

Back to Niu Cheng now. After that onslaught of punches and kicks and the loss of his silver when he had just had a good meal, he brooded with mounting anger over his humiliation. At midnight, he became feverish and felt suffocated.

The next morning, feeling too ill to get up from bed, he said to his wife, "I don't feel well. Can I be dying? Get my brother here, quick! I need to talk to him."

As the ancients said, "No coincidences, no stories." Niu Cheng had an older brother, Niu Wen, born of the same parents, who had been sold as an indentured servant to Tan Zun. Having been to the Tan residence a few times, Niu Cheng's wife, Jin-shi, knew quite well how to get there, which was why Niu Cheng told her to get his brother. Panic-stricken upon hearing him say he was going to die, Jin-shi closed the door behind her and, braving the wind and the cold, went to the county yamen to look for Niu Wen.

Tan Zun had been hunting high and low in vain for evidence of any wrong-doing by Lu Nan. With Magistrate Wang constantly reminding him of what he was supposed to do, he found himself in quite a dilemma. That day, he was sitting in his office when a woman in an agitated state walked in. Upon a closer look, he saw that it was the sister-in-law of his servant, Niu Wen.

After dropping a curtsy, Jin-shi said, "Sir, is my brother-in-law in?"

"He's buying food at the market in front of the yamen. He should be back in a moment. Why are you in such a panic?"

"To tell you the truth, sir, my husband quarreled with Lu Cai, servant of Scholar Lu yesterday, and fell ill at night. His condition is very bad now. I'm here to look for my brother-in-law and take him home to talk about it."

Delighted upon hearing this, Tan Zun asked eagerly, "What was the quarrel about?"

After Jin-shi gave a detailed account of the loan of money from Lu Cai and what had led to the fight, Tan Zun said, "I see. If your husband recovers, all's well and good. If something happens to him, let me know immediately. You can count on me. I'll avenge you and get a fortune out of them for you to enjoy the rest of your life."

"How nice if you would stand by me, sir!"

At this point, Niu Wen came back. After Jin-shi told him everything, they set out together. Before they left the yamen, Tan Zun reminded them, "If something happens, let me know as soon as possible." Niu Wen promised that he would. Upon arriving at Niu Cheng's house in less than two hours, they pushed open the door and went in. All was quiet. When they got to the bed, both were appalled. Niu Cheng was lying there stiff, apparently having been dead for quite some time. Jin-shi burst into loud wails of grief. Indeed,

> Husband and wife are birds in the same woods;
> When the destined hour comes, they fly their separate ways.

The neighbors, drawn by the cries to see what was happening, commented, "Such a healthy and strong young man was beaten to death. Poor thing! Poor thing!"

Niu Wen said to Jin-shi, "Stop crying. Go with me to report to my master now before we do anything else."

Following his advice, Jin-shi locked the gate, asked the neighbors to keep an eye on the house, and went off with Niu Wen. The neighbors said to one another, "They must have gone to file a complaint with the yamen. The yamen takes seriously all cases involving human lives. We must also go and make a report, so as not to get ourselves implicated later on." And so they also went to the county yamen to make a report.

The neighbors far and near in the village having all learned about Niu Cheng's death, some of them went to tell Lu Nan about it. Being a careless man, Lu Nan had forgotten all about the matter because Niu Cheng had not shown up to claim the silver in two days. Upon hearing the information, he immediately sent for Lu Cai, intending to take him to the authorities, little knowing that Lu Cai had fled as soon as he learned about Niu Cheng's death because he knew this would not be the end of the matter.

Niu Wen and Jin-shi ran in one breath to the county yamen to report to Tan Zun. In great delight, Tan Zun quietly went to report to the magistrate. He then reemerged to explain the situation to the two of them and told them what to say. In a trice, a written complaint was ready, accusing Lu Nan of having Niu Cheng beaten to death after a failed attempt to lay violent hands on his wife, Jin-shi. Tan Zun then told the two of them to beat the drum in front of the yamen and cry out their grievances. Following his master's instructions, Niu Wen went with Jin-shi to the entrance of the yamen and, with a piece of firewood, struck the drum frantically while crying, "Murder!" The runners on duty, having already received instructions from Tan Zun, did nothing to stop them.

Upon hearing the drumbeats, Magistrate Wang quickly opened a court session and told Niu Wen and Jin-shi to approach the bench. He had just begun to read their complaint when the local headman and the neighbors arrived. Magistrate Wang was so obsessed with thoughts about Lu Nan that he did not even read the neighbors' report. He just asked a few perfunctory questions and, instead of following the standard procedure and referring the case to the right office, issued the order to have runners bring Lu Nan to court immediately. One runner, who had received instructions from Tan Zun, told those about to leave on their mission, "His honor is very angry with Lu Nan. Be sure to bring everyone in the Lu residence except women and children."

The runners already knew about the bad blood between the magistrate and Scholar Lu. The Lu household being a populous one, the runners were afraid that they might not be able to make their way in if they were outnumbered. And so they gathered together forty to fifty men. Indeed, they were nothing less than a streak of ferocious tigers.

Daytime being short in the depths of winter, it was dusk by this time, and it was cold, with a freezing north wind blowing under a sky overcast with dark, menacing clouds. In an attempt to ingratiate himself with the magistrate, Tan Zun laid out wine and other drinks for the runners to fortify themselves for the mission.

Torches in hand, they ran with all speed to the Lu residence and, with a loud cry, stormed into the house, arresting everyone they saw. Without the slightest idea what had happened, the servants ran helter-skelter in terror amid the screams of the children. Lu Nan's wife and her maidservants were gathered around a stove in her room when, suddenly, the babble of voices burst upon their ears. Mrs. Lu quickly told the maids to go out and see if there was a fire. Before they had time to do so, a servant appeared at her door to announce, "Madam, horrors! Numerous men carrying torches have stormed in!"

Believing they were robbers, Lu Nan's wife was so frightened that her two rows of thirty-six teeth clattered against each other. She hastened to tell the maids to close the door. Before she had quite got the words out, some of the men were already in her room, illuminating the room with the glare of their torches. The maids ran for their lives, crying, "Don't kill us, great chieftains!"

The runners shouted, "What chieftains? We are here by His Honor the magistrate's order to arrest Lu Nan!"

Upon hearing this, Mrs. Lu realized that the magistrate was seeking revenge on one excuse or another for having been slighted by her husband. She said, "If you're from the government, how can you not know the law? Even if the county yamen has a case against us, it can't be more than a dispute about land or some household affairs of the servants. It can't be high treason! You could have come during the day. Why did you have to come in such a large group with torches and storm into the house, looting as you go? Let's lay it all out tomorrow in court. You'll be held responsible!"

The runners said, "You can state your case in court. We just want Lu Nan." They searched the room thoroughly and took as many items of jewelry and household utensils as they wanted before departing. Then they stormed into other rooms, frightening the concubines into diving under their beds. Having searched every room without finding Lu Nan, they swept into the garden, believing he must have been there.

Lu Nan was drinking with four or five guests in a heated two-storied pavilion, with entertainers playing music and singing on both sides of the room. The servant who had been sent to bring Lu Cai to him was there, reporting on the failed mission. At this point, two servants ran up the stairs, screaming, "Master! Trouble!"

Half tipsy, Lu Nan asked, "What trouble?"

"Many men are raiding the house, for whatever reason, and are looting and arresting everyone they see. They are now in your room."

The guests were shocked into sobriety. "But why?" they asked. "Let's go for a look!"

As they rose to go, Lu Nan stopped them, saying, as nonchalantly as ever, "Let them loot. We'll go on drinking. Don't let this spoil our fun! Bring us some warm wine!"

The servants protested, stamping their feet, "Master, how can you go on drinking when all hell has broken loose?"

Even as they spoke, their eyes were dazzled by the glare of torches. As the runners stormed up the stairs, the entertainers were so terrified that they dashed about, looking in vain for places to hide. Furiously, Lu Nan roared, "Who are you? How dare you! I'll have you arrested!"

The runners replied, "You're wanted by His Honor the magistrate! We're afraid you can't have us arrested!" Throwing a noose over his neck, they continued, "Go!"

"What have I done to deserve such rudeness?" said Lu Nan. "I'm not going."

The runners replied, "Frankly, you turned down polite invitations, didn't you? So we're here now to take you by force." With one leading him by the rope and others pushing from the back and tugging in front, they went downstairs. Having taken fourteen or fifteen servants, they wanted to take even the guests, but some of them recognized the guests to be from influential families, with well-known scholars among them. So they gave up the idea and left the Lu residence. In a great clamor, they returned to the county yamen. The guests, worried about Lu Nan, followed them to see what was going to happen. Those servants who had hidden themselves and thus been spared now rushed to the yamen by order of their mistress, to bribe their way into the yamen and acquire information. Of this, more later.

In the meantime, Magistrate Wang had been waiting in the tribunal, which was lit as bright as day by lanterns and torches. Amid the solemn silence that shrouded the tribunal, the runners arrived with Lu Nan and the servants and took them all the way to the foot of the dais. The magistrate, with a murderous look on his face, was the very image of the king of the netherworld. The lictors lined up on both sides were no different from the oxheads and the yakshas of hell.[10] The servants all trembled with fear.

The runners announced, "Lu Nan and his cohorts have been brought here." So saying, they brought the accused up the steps and ordered them to kneel down. Niu Wen and Jin-shi knelt on the other side. Lu Nan, in the middle, was the only one standing. Noticing a man who remained standing, Magistrate Wang peered closely at him and said with a scornful smile, "A local despot! Someone who shows such impudence in the presence of an official will surely stop at nothing to break the law. I'm not going to argue with you now. I will only invite you to sit for a while in jail."

Lu Nan took three or four steps forward and said, throwing back his shoulders, "I don't mind sitting in prison, but enlighten me as to what wrong I did to deserve that search of my house late at night!"

"You had Niu Cheng beaten to death after a failed attempt to lay violent hands on his wife. This is no small crime!"

With a contemptuous smile, Lu Nan said, "I thought I had been accused of something much more heinous than this thing about Niu Cheng. So you want me to pay for his life. Why all this fuss? However, Niu Cheng, a former hired laborer in my employment, died after a fight with my servant, Lu Cai. His death had nothing to do with me. Even if he had been beaten to death by me, I as the master don't deserve the death sentence. If you try to pin the blame on me and accuse me of something I haven't done in order to settle a personal grudge, I may submit under force, but public opinion will be hard to suppress!" (*Those bent on doing people harm do not fear public opinion. How lamentable!*)

Magistrate Wang said in a towering rage, "There were witnesses when you beat that innocent man to death. And yet you falsely accuse a servant to be the culprit. You also humiliate this official and refuse to kneel. A man so impudent in a court of law surely has no scruples in his behavior in everyday life. This is all so clear there's no need for questioning. I'll leave aside the case of homicide for now and punish you only for your defiance of a county official." With that, he ordered that Lu Nan be taken down and put to the rod.

As the lictors stepped forward with a shout and threw him to the floor, Lu Nan exclaimed, "A scholar may be killed but not humiliated. I, Lu Nan, in all my dignity, do not fear death. Why put me to torture? I can admit to any crime you accuse me of. There's no need for such punishment!"

Turning a deaf ear to his protests, the lictors kept him pinned on the floor and gave him thirty strokes of the rod. The magistrate then ordered them to stop and take Lu Nan as well as the servants to jail. The local headman was told to buy a coffin for Niu Cheng's corpse before sending it to the coroner. Niu Wen, Jin-shi, and other witnesses were released on bail to await further notification.

His body lacerated, Lu Nan went out of the gate of the yamen, supported by two servants. He kept laughing out loud as he went along. His friends went forward to greet him, but the servants stood at a distance, afraid of being apprehended.

"What is it all about? Why did they beat you?" asked his friends.

"It's just that Magistrate Wang is using his power to punish me for a personal grudge. He's attributing to me the murder that was supposedly committed by my servant, Lu Cai, and wants to put me to death by way of a small punishment."

His friends were appalled. "How can there be such injustice?" they exclaimed.

One of them said, "It's all right. Let me tell my father. Tomorrow, he'll call together all the landed gentlemen and scholars of the county and talk to the magistrate. The magistrate will surely yield to public opinion and acquit you."

"Don't worry about me! He can do whatever he likes to me. There's only one important thing: tell my family to send to jail an ample supply of wine."

"You should cut down on wine," advised his friends.

Lu Nan replied, laughing, "To live comfortably is of first importance in life. Poverty, wealth, honor, and humiliation are of little concern to me. Don't tell me that I can't drink just because he's out to get me! Wine is something I can't do without, not even for a moment!"

While they were talking, a warden spoke up, pushing Lu Nan from behind, "Go quickly into your cell. You can talk with them later." That warden, Cai Xian by name, was also one of Magistrate Wang's trusted subordinates.

Opening his eyes wide, Lu Nan said angrily, "Tsk! What an abominable man! I was talking with my friends. What business is it of yours?"

Cai Xian shot back impatiently, "Hey! You are a jailbird! No more of your rich man's high and mighty manners! You don't need them anymore!"

In a rage, Lu Nan retorted, "Jailbird indeed! I'm not going there! What are you going to do?"

Cai Xian was about to answer back when a few older and wiser lictors pushed him aside and managed to coax Lu Nan into the jail. His friends went their separate ways home, and Lu Nan's servants went home to report to their mistress, but enough of this.

When Lu Nan was on his way from the yamen to jail, Tan Zun followed closely behind him to keep watch on him, and heard everything that was said. Tan Zun then went back into the yamen to inform the magistrate.

The next morning, Magistrate Wang did not go to his office, pleading illness. When the influential local gentlemen came, the gatekeeper did not even accept their visiting cards. In the afternoon, Magistrate Wang suddenly called the court to session and summoned Jin-shi, the witnesses, and the coroner. Lu Nan and his servants were brought in from the jail. The coroner was then sent to examine Niu Cheng's corpse. Well aware of the magistrate's intentions, the coroner greatly exaggerated the condition of the wounds. The local headman and the neighbors had also caught on to the magistrate's determination to get at Lu Nan and said firmly that Lu Nan had indeed beaten Niu Cheng to death. The magistrate then inveigled out of Lu Nan the contract between him and Niu Cheng, the laborer, and, claiming that it was fake, tore it to pieces. Under severe torture, Lu Nan was convicted of a capital crime and put to twenty more strokes of the rod. He was then taken to death row with a long cangue around his neck and shackles around his joined wrists. His servants were each given thirty strokes and sentenced to three-year banishment but were put on bail to await further orders. Jin-shi, Niu Wen, and the witnesses were sent back home. The corpse and the coffin were to be disposed of upon further instructions. The magistrate then made a file of the papers of the case, including descriptions of details such as Lu Nan's refusal to kneel down, and submitted the file to his superiors. However hard the influential gentlemen of the county tried to defend Lu Nan, Magistrate Wang turned a deaf ear to them. There is a poem in testimony:

> County magistrates can destroy families;
> Gongyi Chang in his innocence would have lamented.[11]
> A great man was thrown into jail;
> No one was there to tend to the fine garden.

Being a man used to a life of luxury, Lu Nan would engage a physician for even the smallest running sore. How was he able to hold out against such severe beatings? After arriving in prison, he fell into a coma. Luckily, all those in the prison knew he was a rich man. Trying to curry favor with him, they eagerly offered him plasters and myrrh for his wounds. His wife also engaged a physician for him. With medicine for external as well as oral use, he recuperated and was his old self again in less than a month. His relatives and friends came in an endless stream to visit him in his cell. The wardens, happily bribed, let them come and go freely without ever trying to stop them. Cai Xian, the magistrate's trusted man, reported to the magistrate as soon as he found out about the situation. Magistrate Wang made an unannounced visit to the prison and found five or six visitors. All of them turned out to be well-known scholars. Hardly able to do anything to them, the magistrate just had them escorted out. Lu Nan was given twenty strokes of the rod, and four or five wardens were also severely punished. Knowing all too well that it was the work of Cai Xian, the wardens gnashed their teeth in their hatred of the man, but who would dare do anything to the magistrate's favorite?

Lu Nan was used to living in spacious rooms, wearing soft silk, eating the finest food, enjoying bamboo, trees, and flowers, and listening to the sweet notes of music. At night, he had the company of beautiful concubines in their colorful attire. Indeed, his was the easy life of an immortal in paradise. But now, he was in a dilapidated cell so small that he could hardly squeeze in. What met his eyes were other convicts on death row with their coarse speech and the ferocious looks of demons and monsters. What fell on his ears were the sounds of chains and shackles around ankles and wrists. At night, the wardens struck bells, did roll calls, struck wooden clappers and gongs, and sang songs. What a depressing life! However proud of spirit he was, he could not help but feel dejected in these surroundings. How he wished that two wings would instantly grow from his armpits so that he could fly out of prison! He could then break the prison gate with an ax and set everyone free.

Recalling all the insults he had suffered, he said to himself in wrath, his hair standing on end, "I, Lu Nan, have lived all my life in dignity, but here I am, a victim of that scoundrel's malice! When will I ever make it out of this place? But even if I do, I'll be too ashamed to show myself in public. Why would I want to hang on to life? I'd better kill myself and be done with it!" Then again, he thought, "No, I must not do that! In the olden days, Chengtang and King Wen had been imprisoned at Xiatai and Youli.[12] Sun Bin and Sima Qian had suffered humiliation. One had his feet cut and the other was castrated.[13] They were all saintly men who swallowed the humiliation and bided their time. How can I, Lu Nan, kill myself?" But then, another thought struck him: "I have friends everywhere. And a good number of them are highly placed officials. How can they passively look on when I'm in such desperate straits? Or maybe they don't know I'm being so grievously wronged. I should write letters to them and ask them to approach that scoundrel's superiors, to redress the wrong done to me." So thinking, he wrote several letters and had his servants deliver them. Those acquaintances of his, some incumbent officials, some retired, were all aghast upon reading his letters. Some approached Magistrate Wang directly and asked him to forgive Lu Nan; some went to his superiors, who, knowing Lu Nan to be a leading talented scholar of the time, were determined to help him. All of them rejected Magistrate Wang's report and remanded it back to the magistrate. In their replies to Lu Nan, they dropped hints for the servants to go to their offices to lodge complaints. The case would then be transferred to another yamen, so that justice could be done. Inwardly overjoyed upon receiving the replies, Lu Nan had his servants lodge complaints with Magistrate Wang's superiors. Sure enough, all of them referred the case to the prefectural bureau of justice and alerted the director of the bureau accordingly. Of this, more later.

Within a few days, Magistrate Wang received tens of letters, all pleading on Lu Nan's behalf. He was debating with himself about what to do when copies of his report to his superiors were all returned to him. None of his submissions had been approved. A few days later, an order from the prefectural bureau of justice came, instructing him to submit the file and to send the accused to the bureau for interrogation. It was all too clear that his superiors wished to set the man free. Magistrate Wang was seized with fear. He thought, "That swine is indeed resourceful. He sits in prison but doesn't miss one link in his plan. If he is let off the hook this time, how will he show mercy to me later? Well, having started this thing, I'd better finish it off. If I don't stamp out this source of trouble, I'll only be hurting myself in the future." That very night, he sent Tan Zun to the prison to see warden Cai Xian. By his order, Cai Xian took Lu Nan to a secluded place and beat him with a whip until he was more dead than live. Cai Xian then knocked him to the ground, bound up his feet and his hands, and blocked his mouth and his nose with a bag filled with earth. He would surely die within two hours. How sad that such a fine scholar should die so unjustly in prison! Truly,

> After heroes die in eternal sorrow,
> Their souls linger among wind-blown trees and cold mists.

Let us introduce another character into our story. In Jun County, there was a county marshal, Dong Shen, who was in charge of police affairs. A *gongshi*,[14] he was a capable official and fair in his application of the law. He felt strongly that Magistrate Wang had unjustly sentenced Lu Nan to death, but, being a low-ranking official, he could not very well speak up. Every time he went to the prison to make the rounds, he would engage Lu Nan in conversation, and the two of them became friends. That night, he happened to be on his usual inspection tour of the prison. Without seeing Lu Nan anywhere, he asked the wardens where he was, but none of them was willing to say a word. In fury, he yelled that he would put them to the rod. Only then did a warden say in a subdued voice, "His Honor sent Clerk Tan to order that he be put to death. He's now in the back."

Aghast, Marshal Dong said, "His Honor is as good as a parent of all the people of the county. How would he do such a thing? It must be you lowlifes who blackmailed Lu Nan for money and then killed him because you didn't get anything from him. Take me there. I want to find him."

Not daring to disobey him, the wardens took him to a narrow passageway in the back, where they ran into Tan Zun and Cai Xian. The marshal ordered that they be apprehended. Rushing forward to look, Marshal Dong saw that Lu Nan was lying on the ground, face up, his hands and feet bound. A bag filled with earth was sitting on his face. Marshal Dong had the wardens remove the bag. As he called out Lu Nan's name at the top of his voice, Lu Nan gradually came to. He was not predestined to die at this time, after all. The ropes were taken off and he was helped into his cell. They fed him some warm soup before he was able to speak. After he gave an account of how Tan Zun had instructed Cai Xian and how they had beaten, insulted, and tried to murder him, Marshal Dong calmed him down with consoling words and had the wardens put him to bed. Then he had Tan Zun and Cai Xian taken into the main hall. He thought, "Now that the secret is out, the magistrate may not dare to admit that the whole thing was his idea." He wanted to put Tan Zun under interrogation but then he thought, "He's the magistrate's trusted man. If the magistrate says I acted without any regard for him, it won't look good." So he called Cai Xian over and told him to confess that he had tried, together with Tan Zun, to murder Lu Nan after failed attempts to extort money from him.

In the beginning, Cai Xian refused to confess, saying only that he had acted by the magistrate's order. Marshal Dong thundered in indignation, "Apply the ankle squeezer on him!"

The wardens bore a grudge against Cai Xian because he had brought the magistrate to inspect the prison and put them to the rod. They found an extremely short and tight squeezer. The moment it was put on him, he screamed, "I confess!"

Marshal Dong told the wardens to stop, but, still seething with resentment, they pretended not to have heard the order and tightened the squeezer until Cai Xian called out for his parents and even his ancestors seventeen or eighteen generations back. They did not let go of him until Marshal Dong repeated his order over and over again. When given paper and a brush-pen for him to write his confession, Cai Xian had no alternative but to confess to what Marshal Dong was accusing him of.

Putting the signed confession in his sleeve, Marshal Dong said to the wardens, "Do not release these two men without my authorization. Let me see His Honor before coming back for them." With that, he rose, left the prison, and returned to the county yamen, where he prepared a file on the case.

The next morning, when Magistrate Wang's tribunal was in session, Marshal Dong went and presented the file. Magistrate Wang was wondering why Tan Zun had not come back for a report. As Marshal Dong brought up this matter, he was inwardly startled. Hating the marshal for having broken through the net, so to speak, but unable to do anything to him, the magistrate shook his head after reading the file and said, "I don't think this is true."

"I saw it with my own eyes. How can this not be true? If you don't believe me, sir, just summon those two men and verify with them. If Tan Zun can be excused, that Cai Xian cannot. He was so impudent he even slandered you, sir. He should be punished as a warning to others."

These words touched a raw nerve. The magistrate reddened. Afraid that his reputation would be ruined if this story got around, he resignedly fired Cai Xian and convicted him of crime. Henceforth he hated Marshal Dong and reported to the superiors against the marshal, accusing him of having illicit love affairs. Marshal Dong was stripped of his office and let go. But this happened later.

His plan having failed, Magistrate Wang wrote memorandums to his superiors and had messengers send copies to the capital to distribute among highly placed officials. The memorandums basically made the charge that Lu Nan, emboldened by his immense wealth, rode roughshod over the area, formed alliances with local influential people, beat a commoner to death, defied the official interrogating the case, and pulled strings in an attempt to get himself acquitted. The magistrate greatly exaggerated the details so that this case could gain too much publicity for anyone to dare come to Lu Nan's assistance. He also instructed Tan Zun to write a complaint in Jin-shi's name that very night and post copies of it everywhere. Having made all these arrangements, he ordered that the accused be taken to the prefectural yamen, along with all the documents. The prefectural judge was a faint-hearted one. The magistrate's memorandum and Jin-shi's statement of complaint scared him. Not wishing to bring trouble upon himself, he thought it prudent not to overturn the original sentence but referred the case to his superiors. In most situations, no one would go out of his way to change the verdict on those cases already reviewed by the prefectural yamen. Lu Nan's attempts to get himself out of prison ended up confirming the death sentence on him. He was to remain in Jun County Prison. He then hoped for the magistrate to leave, so that he could make another attempt to have justice done. To his dismay, higher-up officials in the capital praised Magistrate Wang for his integrity in having subdued a well-known rich man. Having thus won a good reputation for himself, Magistrate Wang was transferred to the capital and promoted to be a supervising censor. With him in such a powerful position, no one dared try to reverse the verdict on Lu Nan, however resourceful Lu Nan might be.

There was an imperial inspector Fan who, believing Lu Nan was unjustly sentenced, reversed the verdict on him and acquitted him. Upon learning this, Censor Wang immediately asked his colleagues to bring a charge against Inspector Fan, saying he had been bribed into acquitting a criminal guilty of serious crimes. Inspector Fan was dismissed from office, and the prefectural yamen sent Lu Nan back to prison. As a consequence, even though some higher-up officials knew that Lu Nan had been wronged, they dared not exonerate Lu Nan at the risk of their own careers.

Time sped by. Lu Nan stayed in prison for more than ten years, during which two more county magistrates came and went. Jin-shi and Niu Wen had died of illnesses, but Censor Wang had risen to be director of a central government agency. As powerful as Mr. Wang was, Lu Nan gave up hope of leaving prison. As it turned out, however, his ill luck was to run out. That year, a new county magistrate came. Because of him,

The blotted-out sun shone again;
The dewdrops did not change into frost.

The new magistrate of Jun County, Lu Guangzu, was a native of Pinghu County of Jiaxing Prefecture, Zhejiang. A man of consummate wisdom, he had the ability to run the affairs of the empire and bring prosperity to the land and a better life to the people. Before he left the capital for Jun County, Censor Wang had given him to understand the situation about Lu Nan. Feeling puzzled, he thought, "This is a case that came up when he was the magistrate. After so many years, why is he still so concerned? Why does he still find it necessary to give me all these instructions? There must be a reason behind this."

After he took up his post, he paid visits to the important landed gentlemen of the county. They all said that Lu Nan was sentenced unjustly and told him how Lu Nan had offended Magistrate Wang. Mr. Lu did not believe everything he heard, for he suspected that Lu Nan the rich man had bribed them into saying these things. Discreetly he made inquiries everywhere, but got the same answers. He thought, "How can a government official falsely charge someone of crime out of a personal grudge and condemn him to death?" He had a mind to appeal to his superiors for justice to be done, but then he thought, "If I write to my superiors, they will surely start a whole process of verification and review. No quick decision will be made. I'd better acquit him first and report later. (*Thanks to his sagacity and moral integrity, Mr. Lu's clan prospered and many of his descendants won honors on the civil service examinations.*) He took out the case file on Lu Nan and read it carefully, but did not find the slightest loophole in the reports. However, after reading it several times, he thought, "How can this case be closed without the testimony of Lu Cai?" He announced a reward of one hundred taels of silver for information about Lu Cai and set a deadline for the police to capture him. Within one month's time, Lu Cai was brought to him. Lu Cai confessed under the rod and the truth came out. Mr. Lu wrote these comments on the confession:

"The following facts have been established: Niu Cheng, upon receiving his wages from Lu Nan, got into a fight with Lu Cai, who demanded payment of a loan. That Niu Cheng was a laborer in Lu Nan's employment is beyond a doubt. There is no law stipulating that the master should pay with his life for the death of a hired laborer. In addition, Lu Cai being the one who lent money to Niu Cheng, demanded payment, and assaulted Niu Cheng, why should Lu Cai be spared but Lu Nan be convicted of a crime? How was the law applied in this case? Lu Cai fled from justice and implicated his master. Even death cannot exonerate him from his crime. A death sentence on Lu Cai is therefore justified. Lu Nan, having unfortunately served a long prison sentence, should be released," and so on and so forth.

That very day, Lu Nan was taken out of prison. Right there in the tribunal, his cangue and shackles were removed and he was set free, to the amazement of everyone in the yamen and to Lu Nan himself. Magistrate Lu wrote a report stating everything that had led to Lu Cai's fight with Niu Cheng as well as all the details involved in the injustice done to Lu Nan. He personally took the report to the prefectural yamen and handed it to the surveillance commissioner.

After reading the report, the commissioner asked, suspecting him of ulterior motives in acquitting the prisoner without authorization, "As far as I know, Lu Nan is a very wealthy man. Aren't you afraid that your motives may be questioned?"

"As a county magistrate, my first concern is to uphold the law rather than to worry about people's perceptions of my motives. My concern is whether the accused is a victim of a miscarriage of justice, not whether he is rich or not. If he is accused rightly, even if he were Boyi or Shuqi, he has to be put to the death sentence.[15] If he is unjustly accused, even if he were Fan Li, he should not die.[16] (*In the case of an unjustly accused rich man, no one makes an effort to get him released; in the case of an unjustly accused official, his colleagues dare not help him, either, for fear of accusations that they shielded him. Such are the ways in today's world.*)

Impressed by his impeccable logic, the surveillance commissioner did not ask more questions but said, "In ancient times, when Zhang Shizhi was the chief minister for law enforcement, no prisoner was unjustly charged with crime.[17] You're going in that direction. How would I hold you back?"

Magistrate Lu thanked him and left. Of this, no more need be said.

Upon Lu Nan's return home, the entire family rejoiced. Relatives and friends swarmed to his house to offer their congratulations. After a few days, Lu Nan learned upon inquiries that Magistrate Lu had returned to the county yamen. Wishing to visit him and express his gratitude, Lu Nan changed into a commoner's blue gown and small hat. His wife said, "You should offer some gifts to Mr. Lu, who has done so much for you."

"Judging from what Mr. Lu did," rejoined Lu Nan, "I believe he's a man of bold spirit, with none of the baseness of those greedy petty officials. Offering him gifts would be insulting him."

"Why would that be an insult?"

"In the more than ten years I was in prison, none of the higher-placed officials I know took on my case, for fear of being implicated. Mr. Lu, in his new position, looked into my case, established my innocence, and released me without hesitation. It takes a man with extraordinary wisdom, courage, and insightfulness to do this. If I reward him with gifts, it'll be a case of 'He understands me, but I understand not him.' I can't do that." Having said that, he took off, taking nothing with him.

Looking on Lu Nan as a distinguished scholar not to be slighted, Magistrate Lu invited him into the private quarters in the rear of the yamen. Upon seeing the magistrate, Lu Nan folded his hands in greeting but did not make a bow. Marveling inwardly at this violation of proper etiquette, Magistrate Lu returned the greeting and asked his attendants to offer the visitor a seat. An attendant pulled up a chair and set it off to one side. Dear audience, don't you find this strange? Being an exconvict and having served a long sentence, Lu Nan was released from prison thanks to Magistrate Lu. To such a benefactor who had given him a new lease on life, he should have kowtowed, even if he broke his forehead on the floor in doing so. But he just folded his hands in greeting. Another official would have been displeased at such temerity, but Magistrate Lu not only did not mind but also offered him a seat. This was clear evidence of his magnanimous mind and his worthy qualities. In fact, Lu Nan turned out to be the one displeased, because he was not given a seat in the center of the room. He said, "Sir, I, Lu Nan, can be sentenced to death, but cannot take a seat that is placed off to one side." (*A vivid description of his innate, inviolable haughtiness.*)

At these words, Magistrate Lu walked down the dais, exchanged greetings with him anew, and said, "This student is at fault." So saying, he offered Lu Nan the seat of honor. They fell into a conversation about events current and past, regretting that they had not met each other earlier, and they became the best of friends. There is a poem in evidence:

> *Of old, Ji An folded his hands but did not bow.[18]*
> *Today, Lu Nan is the one repeating the act.*
> *In a cangue yesterday, a guest of honor today;*
> *His proud spirit soared high above the clouds.*

Let us pick up another thread of the story. Stung by the news that Magistrate Lu had set Lu Nan free, Censor Wang told his trusted men to bring a charge against Lu as well as against the surveillance commissioner. But the commissioner in return wrote a report to the imperial court, detailing how Mr. Wang, as county magistrate, had framed up an innocent man for a personal grudge. The emperor issued a decree, stripping Censor Wang of his office and sending him home. The surveillance commissioner stayed in his post, and Magistrate Lu remained unscathed. By that time, Tan Zun had retired, and spent his time writing official complaints for people. After verifying the facts, Magistrate Lu obtained approval from his superiors and threw Tan Zun into jail before banishing him to a remote area for penal servitude. As for Lu Nan, with no wish for a career for the rest of his life, he indulged with greater abandon in poetry and wine. His family fortunes went on the decline, but he could not care less. As for Magistrate Lu, he loved the people as he did his own children, never taking even one undue penny. Moreover, he exposed evildoers, eliminated latent sources of trouble, and made a clear distinction between right and wrong. As a result, miscreants lay low in fear, and robbers and thieves stopped plaguing the people. All and sundry throughout the county looked up to him as to a divine being, and his prestige impressed officials in the capital. Because he did not ingratiate himself with the powers that be, he was only promoted to be a director in the ministry of rites in Nanjing. On the day of his departure, people of the county turned out en masse to see him off, some hanging on to his sedan-chair, some lying across the road to block his way. Sobbing and weeping, they accompanied him for a hundred li before turning back. Lu Nan accompanied him for five hundred li, until they bade each other a tearful farewell, hating the thought of parting. Later, Mr. Lu rose up the official echelon and became secretary of the ministry of personnel in Nanjing. Lu Nan, reduced to poverty, went south to Nanjing to live off Secretary Lu's largesse. Secretary Lu treated him as a guest of honor, providing him with one thousand cash per day to pay for his wine bills and his travel expenses. He toured the mountains and the rivers, and the poems he left wherever he stopped came to be widely intoned and spread from mouth to mouth.

One day, when he was touring the shrine of Academician Li Bai at Caishi, he encountered a barefoot Daoist priest of an unearthly appearance. Lu Nan invited him for a drink. In return, the priest poured out the finest wine from his gourd bottle and offered it to Lu Nan. Liking the extraordinary delicious taste, Lu Nan asked, "Where did this wine come from?"

"I made it myself," replied the priest. "I live in a hut at the foot of Five Old Men Peak of the Lushan Mountains. If you go with me, you can drink as much as you want."

"If there's such fine wine to be had, why don't I?" With that, Lu Nan immediately entered the shrine, where he wrote a letter of thanks to Secretary Lu. Carrying no personal belongings, he followed the barefoot Daoist priest and was gone. (*As carefree as the ancients.*)

Upon reading the letter, Secretary Lu said with a sigh, "He comes and goes in unconventional ways. He takes the universe as his room and his life as that of an ant. A real free spirit!" Several times he had attendants make inquiries about Lu Nan at the foot of Five Old Men Peak of the Lushan Mountains, but the searches turned up nothing.

Ten years later, Secretary Lu retired from his post and returned to his ancestral home in the countryside. After an official of the imperial court went to inquire after his health, he sent his second son to the capital to express his gratitude. Once there, Mr. Lu Junior's servants ran into Lu Nan, who asked them to convey his greetings to Secretary Lu. Someone said that Lu Nan had encountered an immortal and achieved the Dao. A later poet had this to say:

> *The luckless hero found himself confined;*
> *He valued poems and wine more than dukes and earls.*
> *With no worldly possessions, he floated away;*
> *His fine repute remains in eternity.*

Another later poet had this to say to caution against emulating Lu Nan's arrogance, for it will only land one in trouble:

> *A haughty maniac for poetry and wine,*
> *A free spirit who disgusts the common man.*
> *Be advised: do not do as Lu Nan did;*
> *In everything, be prudent and be modest.*

In a Humble Inn, Mr. Li Mian Meets a Knight-Errant

The affairs of the world are like a game of chess;
The wins and the losses are hard to guess.
But your conscience and sense of justice
Will tell you for sure what is wrong and what is right.

The story goes that during the Tianbao reign period [742–56] under Emperor Xuanzong of the Tang dynasty, there lived in Chang'an a scholar named Fang De. With a broad face and big ears, he had a towering build. Over thirty years of age, he lived in straitened circumstances. His wife, Bei-shi, provided the only income of the family by weaving at her loom. It was late autumn, but he had only a tattered scarf to cover his head and a worn-out, rough ko-hemp robe so threadbare and porous that it was more like a straw rain cape. He thought, "With winter just around the corner, how can I show myself like this in public?" Knowing that his wife had two extra bolts of fabric, he asked her to make him a robe. However, his wife, from a humble family background, happened to be a most narrow-minded person with a ruthless heart and a clever tongue that was sharper than a knife and always ready to outtalk others in whatever subject. Her eloquence could make the dead come to life and the living give up the ghost. In short, she was a woman with the gift of the gab. Resenting the fact that Fang De had no means of livelihood and had to depend on her for a meager living, she bullied him at every turn. Not having won recognition for his talent, he felt that his words did not carry weight and therefore let her have her way in everything. Gradually he became a henpecked husband. (*Just like Zhu Maichen, who was forsaken by his wife, and Jizi, who was snubbed by his sister-in-law.*[1] Men who are down on their luck are truly pathetic.)

When Fang De asked her for clothes, Bei-shi had just been thinking, "With my husband in such a sorry condition, when will I ever get to live a good life?" And she blamed her parents for having married her off to the wrong man and ruining her life. Caught in such a foul mood, she shot back, "A big man like you can't find work but depends on a woman for a living, and even has to ask her for clothes. Aren't you ashamed of yourself?"

Stung by these words, Fang De reddened in mortification. For lack of a better choice, he forced himself to say in all humility, "Wife, I'm ever so grateful to you for your help over the years. I may be down and out now, but I will succeed some day. Just consider the fabric a loan to me. When I make my mark in the world, I'll move heaven and earth to repay you."

Bei-shi said, waving a hand in dismissal, "I've heard too many of those honeyed words of yours over the years. I don't believe you. I need those two bolts of fabric for my own winter clothes. You can forget about them."

Very much put out by the rejection and the humiliation, Fang De wanted to unleash his fury on her, but, afraid that it would make him look even worse if the neighbors heard his wife's loud voice and her vicious words, he stormed out of the door in silent rage, hoping to seek help elsewhere.

He walked about for the longest time without meeting anyone. And just to make matters worse, the weather was also against him. A driving rain came down. Shivering with cold as his old ko-hemp robe rustled in the wind like falling tree-leaves, he braved the rainstorm and ran for shelter into an old monastery called Yunhua Monastery. On his way in, he saw a man of big frame sitting on the railing of the left corridor. An old monk was intoning the sutras in the hall. Fang De sat down on the railing of the right corridor and stared blankly at the sky. As the rain gradually let up, Fang De said to himself, "I'd better go now before the rain starts pouring again." He was about to go when he turned and saw a bird painted on the wall. The feathers, the wings, the feet, and the tail were all there, except the head. He stopped to examine the painting. Now wasn't he an imbecile to be criticizing a painting when he was so hungry and cold? (*He had absolutely nothing better to do.*)

He thought, "I've often heard that one should start with the head when drawing a bird. Why is this bird drawn differently? Why is it left incomplete?" While thinking these thoughts, he continued examining the painting, and the more he looked at it, the more he liked it. "I'm not much of an artist," he thought, "but a bird's head shouldn't be too difficult to draw. Why don't I complete this painting?" So thinking, he went into the hall, borrowed a brush-pen from a monk, dipped it heavily into ink, and came back to draw the head. The result did not look too bad. In delight, he thought, "If I had learned to paint, I would have made something of myself."

As he was painting, the man on the left came over to watch. After scrutinizing Fang De from head down, he went up and said, all smiles, "Scholar, could you follow me to a place where we can talk?"

"Who might you be? What is it you want to talk about?"

"You need not ask, scholar. Just follow me. You'll have something to gain."

As poor as he was, Fang De was delighted to hear that he had something to gain. He returned the brush-pen to the monk, straightened his tattered robe, and followed the man.

Though the storm had died down, the ground was still muddy, but Fang De could not care less. They left Yunhua Monastery, went out Shengping Gate, and stopped at a forlorn-looking house in the southern suburbs called Leyouyuan. The man knocked three times on a small corner gate. After a while, another husky fellow opened it. Looking pleased as he saw Fang De, the man stepped forward and chanted a greeting. Fang De grew apprehensive. "Who are these two men? Why did that one invite me here? What will I gain?" he asked himself.

"Whose house is this?" he asked aloud.

"Scholar, you'll know soon enough once you follow us in."

After Fang De stepped over the threshold, the two men bolted the door after them and led him into a deserted garden overgrown with weeds and bushes. After many twists and turns, they came to a tumbledown pavilion, from which emerged fourteen or fifteen strong-armed, large-fisted men with hideous facial features. At the sight of Fang De, they all broke into ingratiating smiles and said, "Please go in, scholar."

Concealing his astonishment, Fang De told himself, "These men look suspicious. But let me hear what they've got to say to me."

The men ushered him into the pavilion, where they exchanged greetings with him and politely asked him to sit down on a bench. Then they asked him, "What is your honorable name, scholar?"

"My family name is Fang. What is it you wish to say to me?"

The man who had taken him there said, "To tell you the truth, we brothers are heroes of the road, doing business that needs no capital. But because we've got more courage than brains, we almost got ourselves into trouble the other day. So we prayed to heaven for a man with a brilliant mind to lead us. That headless bird on the monastery wall was drawn when we brothers were praying to heaven and making a pledge. It meant that everything was ready except the head. We prayed that if we were destined to prosper, heaven would send us a hero to complete the painting and be our head. We waited for several days in vain. Luckily, heaven granted our wish and sent you, scholar, to us today. With your imposing looks, you must have both courage and brains. You are our heaven-sent leader. We will follow your orders and live happily in peace the rest of our lives. Won't that be wonderful?" Turning to the others, he said, "Go quickly to slaughter the animals to make offerings to heaven and earth." Whereupon three or four of them ran apace toward the back.

Having heard the man out, Fang De thought, "So, this is a gang of bandits! I'm a law-abiding man. How can I join them?" Aloud, he said, "Mighty heroes, I will gladly do whatever else you ask me to do, except this one thing."

"Why?"

"I am a scholar. I look forward to passing the examinations. How can I do things that break the law?"

"You are quite mistaken, scholar. With Yang Guozhong as the prime minister, official posts and titles are all up for sale.[2] Anyone with money can be a high official. Those without money don't stand a chance. Even Li Bai, with his prodigious talent, was humiliated by Yang Guozhong and failed the examinations. If Li Bai hadn't translated that letter from a foreign country, he would most likely have remained a commoner.³ Forgive us if we offend you, scholar, but judging from your clothes, we don't think you are well off. How can you expect to have a career as an official? You'll be better off if you join us. We drink wine in large bowls, eat meat in large chunks, wear clothing in matching suits, and divide up gold with scales. And you'll be the leader! What a happy, carefree life! If business is good, we can take over a mountain fortress and make you king."

While Fang De was pensively silent, the man spoke up again, "If you refuse, we won't force it on you, scholar. But you won't get out of here alive. We'll have to kill you if you turn down the offer. Don't hold us to blame!"

With one swift movement, every one of them withdrew a knife from his boot. Scared out of his wits, Fang De staggered back more than ten steps and said, "Don't do this! Let's talk!"

"Simply say if you agree or not. What's there to talk about?"

Fang De thought, "This is quite a deserted place. If I don't obey, I'll die needlessly. No one will be any the wiser. Let me humor them for now. Tomorrow I'll try to get free from them and give myself up to the police." His mind thus made up, he said, "I thank you, mighty heroes, for your confidence in me, but I've always been a cowardly man. I'm afraid I can't do this."

"That's all right," they assured him. "Everybody starts out feeling afraid, but after a few times, you'll get used to it." (*Real gentlemen.*)

"In that case, I defer to you."

In delight, the men put their knives back into their boots and said, "Now that we are one family, let's call each other brothers. Let's give Big Brother some clothes for the ceremony." So saying, they went in and reemerged with a robe of brocade, a fashionable new headscarf, and a pair of new boots. After putting them on, Fang De looked so majestic that the men broke into cheers and said, "With your looks, Big Brother, you could be an emperor, let alone leader of this group!"

As the ancients said, "What you don't see doesn't tempt you." Fang De had been a poor man. Never having worn such splendid clothes before, he was thrilled at having suddenly taken on this new look. Involuntarily, his mind went over what the men had been saying. After pondering over their arguments, he began to be convinced of their logic. "Yes, with Yang Guozhong as the prime minister, bribery is the order of the day. Goodness knows how many great talents have been wasted. Can a mediocre scholar like me really land a post? If not, I'll be condemned to poverty all my life, which is worse than a life of ease and comfort with these fellows." Then he thought, "A moment ago, I was still wearing such tattered clothes in late autumn weather and couldn't even get some fabric from my wife to make clothes with. When I approach relatives and friends, none of them is willing to help. These men here are more generous. They are strangers to me, but they give me such nice clothes and make me their leader. Why don't I give in to them and join them in their transgressions of the law? I'll get to live in style the rest of my life." Then another thought struck him, "No! No! I'll be dead if I'm caught!"

While these troubled thoughts kept him confused and indecisive, the men busily set out an altar table, carried over a pig and a goat, and laid them out in the open air. All eighteen stalwart men, including Fang De, knelt down in unison. Joss sticks in hand, they took their vow and, smearing the animals' blood on their mouths, swore loyalty to each other. After their bows to heaven and earth, they bowed eight times to each other, swearing brotherhood with Fang De, and told him their names.

Soon, wine and food were served. Fang De was given the seat of first honor at the feast. He ate and drank to his heart's content. Normally, he could afford only the simplest diet and not enough of it. When occasionally he did manage to lay hands on some wine and meat, there was not enough to gratify him. So this feast exceeded his wildest expectations. Moreover, the men took turns offering him toasts, addressing him as Big Brother and currying favor with him. In the exuberance of his delight, his initial reluctance gave way to a determination to devote himself to this profession. He thought, "Maybe I was destined to meet these brothers and, with their help, make my mark in the world. Who knows? If this is profitable, I'll just do it two or three times, and stop after I've saved up something. Nobody will know. And then I'll buy off Yang Guozhong and land an official post for myself. Wouldn't that be nice? (*Those who bribed Yang Guozhong were all characters of this sort.*) If I get caught, I will have enjoyed more than my share of life's pleasures anyway. I'll be content to be put to death. That'll be better than to go through life hungry and cold." There is a poem in testimony:

> *In the coldness of the windy and rainy night,*
> *The small boat was rowed in haste up dangerous shoals.*
> *He knew the perils of the waves ahead,*
> *But fear of hunger and cold drove him on.*

Offering one another toasts, the men drank until evening set in. One said, "Since today is the day we met Big Brother, why don't we do a job, just for the good luck of the occasion?"

"Good idea!" the others cried in unison. "Which house shall we pick?"

Fang De said, "Old man Moneybags Wang outside of Yanping Gate is the richest man in the capital. What's more, there's no police patrol outside the city gates, and I know the area well. This one trip will be worth more than ten. What do you say?"

In delight, the men replied, "To be frank with you, Big Brother, we've had this old man in mind for a long time now. We haven't acted just because we haven't had the chance to do so. Your idea tallies exactly with ours. This goes to show that we're of one heart and mind."

Right away they cleared the table and took out sulfur, niter, torches, and weapons, and bound them together. Behold:

> Their heads wrapped up in white cloth,
> Their feet in cotton-padded high boots,
> Their faces smeared black and red,
> Their hands carrying swords and axes,
> Their pants reaching just below their knees,
> Their girdles tight around their waists,
> Their vests reaching their stomachs,
> Their shoulder bags tied well in place,
> A group of demons descended on the world;
> A pack of tigers and leopards entered the woods.

After they got ready, they waited until evening fell before they left the gate and locked it from outside. With the speed of a tempest, they swept on to Yanping Gate, about six or seven li from Leyouyuan, and soon arrived.

Moneybags Wang was a cousin of Wang Hong, the mayor of the capital. With enough wealth to rival the imperial treasury, Moneybags Wang was known throughout the land and had been summoned into the presence of Emperor Xuanzong. His residence having been burglarized three days earlier, he had told Wang Hong to assign a police team to the case and thirty soldiers to guard the house. Luckless Fang De and his men threw themselves right into the net.

So the bandits lit their torches with a pilot flame and, wielding their swords and axes, slashed their way through the gate into the house, lighting up the surroundings as if it were daytime. The soldiers and the servants woke up from their sleep. Beating gongs and shouting at the top of their voices, they swarmed up to seize the burglars, sticks and clubs in hand. The neighbors, hearing the commotion, also came to help. Terror-stricken by the sheer numbers of the oncoming crowd, the bandits set fire and began to run away. While half of the servants were putting out the fire, the other half gave chase and encircled the intruders. The robbers fought for all they were worth and wounded a few tenants of the Wang estate, but they were outnumbered, after all. Several of them were knocked down to the ground, Fang De among them. The others ran for dear life and got away. All of the captives were tied together and were taken under guard to the mayor's office after daybreak. Mayor Wang Hong then assigned the marshal of the capital to handle the case.

Li Mian by name, Xuanqing by courtesy name, the marshal was a member of the royal clan. Honorable and righteous by nature, he had the ability to rule the land and the aspiration to bring prosperity to the empire and a better life to the people. It was because Li Linfu [d. 752] and Yang Guozhong, successive prime ministers who brought great suffering to the land, were jealous of capable people that Li Mian was not able to put his talent to good use. However, even though marshal of the capital was a low-ranking post, he was in charge of all matters relating to law enforcement. It was his job to interrogate all suspects and recommend sentences to his superiors. Therefore everyone occupying this post had been the ruthless kind, such as Zhou Xing, Lai Junchen, and Suo Yuanli, who invented different kinds of torture with fancy names.[4] What fancy names? There is in testimony a lyric to the tune of "Moon over West River":

> "A calf hanging from a cart" is a fearful sight;
> "A donkey pulling a stake" brings sheer agony.
> "A phoenix drying its wings" takes away your life;
> "A child meditating" crushes your soul.
>
> "A Jade Maiden climbing stairs" is most appalling;
> "A fairy offering fruit" does the worst injury.
> If "A monkey in fire" doesn't make you confess,
> They switch to "A yaksha looking at the sea."[5]

Partly to inspire awe through torture and partly to please higher-up officials who left instructions with them, these cruel and ruthless officials never bothered to find out the truth but fervently applied torture to get confessions and to convict on false charges. The bravest man with an iron-cast constitution would tremble in terror. Untold numbers of loyal ministers and honorable men perished at their hands. However, Li Mian was different. He valued only peaceful means and never resorted to any instrument of torture. In every case he investigated, he went out of his way to establish the truth. As a result, there were no unjust convictions on his watch.

On the morning of which we speak, Li Mian was in his office when Mayor Wang referred this case to him. The bandits—about ten in total—and the five or six wounded tenants were brought into his tribunal and made to kneel down. The swords and axes used in the assault lay in a pile at the foot of the dais. Li Mian looked around and noticed Fang De. Impressed by his imposing build and graceful bearing, Li Mian thought, "Why would such a decent-looking man choose to be a bandit?" His compassion aroused, he called to him the patrolmen and the tenants of the Wang establishment and questioned them as to the details of the burglary. Then he turned to the bandits, asked their names one by one, and learned after careful inquiries that they had been caught in the act. They all confessed and also provided information about the location of their den. No torture was applied. Without a moment's delay, Li Mian dispatched runners there to arrest the remaining bandits.

When it was Fang De's turn to answer questions, he crawled up to Marshal Li's desk and said with tears in his eyes, "I have been applying myself to my books ever since childhood. I am no bandit. My family is so poor that I went out yesterday to ask for loans from relatives and took shelter from the rain in Yunhua Monastery. It was there that the bandits tricked me and forced me to join them. I complied for lack of an alternative." He went on and gave a detailed account of how he had painted the bird's head and how he had joined the group.

Already impressed with the man's looks, Li Mian was further moved to sympathy by this statement. He had a good mind to set the man free, but then he thought, "If I let one man go when actually they are all guilty in this act, public opinion will be against me. Also, this is a case given by my superior. What am I going to say to him? Unless I can do thus and so." In a deliberately exaggerated severe tone, he ordered that Fang De withdraw and instructed that he be taken to the lockup in a cangue and shackles and stay there until further interrogation after the remaining gang members were brought in. The wounded tenants were sent back home to recuperate. The patrolmen were rewarded in recognition of their service. After everyone had been dismissed, Li Mian summoned Wang Tai, a prison warden. Now this Wang Tai had inadvertently offended Li Mian's predecessor and therefore had been unjustly sentenced to death. It was Li Mian who had established the truth and restored him to his former position in the yamen. Out of gratitude to him, Wang Tai did his utmost to accomplish every task given by Marshal Li, and was therefore made chief warden.

To him Li Mian said, "Among the bandits there's a Fang De who looks dignified and is very articulate. He looks to me like a hero whose time hasn't come. (*A hero indeed! Mr. Li is quite mistaken. That is why saintly wise men always take the trouble to verify every claim.*) I would like to set him free, but with so many people watching, I can't very well release him right there in the tribunal. You do it for me. Let him escape when there's a chance." He produced a sealed package of three taels of silver for Fang De's travel expenses and also asked Wang Tai to tell him to flee to a faraway place so that he would not be caught again.

"I wouldn't ever dream of disobeying you, sir, but how can I avoid implicating the other wardens?"

"After you set him free, bring your wife and children and hide in my place. The documents will all be under your name. The others won't be involved. You can serve me as a personal attendant. Won't that be better than working as a petty prison warden?"

"Of course I'd be only too happy if you would take me on as a personal attendant." So saying, Wang Tai slipped the silver into his sleeve and rushed out of the yamen into the lockup. To a young warden he said, "Those new arrivals haven't been put to the rod. So don't keep them together, to avoid trouble."

The young warden accordingly separated them. Wang Tai led Fang De to a quiet spot, told him about the marshal's good will, and gave him the money.

Overwhelmed with gratitude, Fang De said, "Please convey my thanks to the marshal. If I can't repay him in this life, I will do so in my next life, as a dog or a horse."

"The marshal is doing this out of a genuine wish to help you, not to seek repayment. May you turn over a new leaf, so that the marshal will not have saved your life in vain!"

"Thank you, chief warden, for this reminder. I will surely do as you say."

When night finally fell, Wang Tai and the other wardens began to lock the inmates to their beds, starting with Fang De. Seizing a moment when the other wardens were busily occupied, Wang Tai helped Fang De up, unlocked the shackles and the cangue, put his own old clothes and hat on Fang De, and led him to the gate of the lockup. Luckily, no one was anywhere in sight. Wang Tai quickly opened the gate and let him out.

In big strides, Fang De took to the road harum-scarum. Not daring to go home, he went all the way out of the city gate under cover of night, thinking, "I'm so grateful to the marshal for having saved my life. Now to whom should I go to for help? Isn't An Lushan, the emperor's favorite, recruiting worthy men into his service?[6] Why don't I go to him?" And so he made his way to Fanyang, where he happened to see an old acquaintance, Yan Zhuang. Being the regional commander of Fanyang, Yan Zhuang introduced him to An Lushan. In his long-harbored ambition to rise in rebellion, An Lushan had been recruiting fugitives and rebels into his ranks. Impressed by Fang De's distinguished appearance and finding him quite agreeable in their conversation, An Lushan took him on as a subordinate. After living there for some time, Fang De secretly sent for his wife and children, but of this, no more for now. Indeed,

> He broke through the dragnet of the police
> And left the town that gave him such sorrows.
> In conceit, he celebrated his new life
> As he looked back on his own past.

Let us retrace our steps and come back to the night Wang Tai let Fang De escape. Claiming that he had to return home to attend to some family matters, Wang Tai told the other wardens to keep a tight watch over the inmates, gave them the keys, left all the necessary instructions, and went out the gate all the way home. He then packed the family belongings and took his wife and children quietly to Li Mian's quarters in the yamen before the night was out.

The next morning, when letting the inmates go to the outhouse, the wardens came to Fang De's bed but found only the discarded cangue and shackles. The man was gone. The wardens were so frightened that they turned ashen. Crying out in dismay, they said, "The shackles and the cangue were tightly locked on him. How did he manage to break free and escape? And we'll be the ones to be punished by the law! But how did he make the escape?" They checked the four walls but found nothing amiss. No brick or tile had fallen to the ground, nor was there even the slightest bit of loose earth. They said, "That convict on death row lied to the marshal yesterday, saying he was a first-time offender. Now we know he's a master of the game with years of experience!"

One said, "Let me go tell Chief Warden Wang and have him report to the yamen and issue an emergency arrest warrant." That man ran in one breath to Wang Tai's home, only to see the door closed. He pounded on the door frantically, but there was no answer. A neighbor walked over and said, "There was quite a commotion in this house last night. It lasted for about four hours. They must have moved."

"No one heard Mr. Wang say anything about moving. That's impossible."

The neighbor rejoined, "Then why don't they answer the door? This one room is all they have. They can't be sleeping so soundly that they don't hear a thing."

Convinced by the argument, the warden forced the door open with all his might and found that the door had been bolted from inside by a wooden stick. In the room were only a few bulky items of furniture. No one was there.

"How very strange!" said the warden. "Why did he also leave? Could he have taken the prisoner's money and set him free? Well, before we know if it was him or not, let's just say for now that he did it." He closed the door and, instead of returning to the prison, headed directly for the marshal's yamen.

It so happened that Li Mian was working in his office at that time. At the warden's report, Li Mian said in feigned astonishment, "I've always thought of Wang Tai as a prudent man. I never knew he could be so reckless as to set free a prisoner on death row! He should still be in the neighborhood. You and the other wardens can spread out on a search and bring him to me. I'll have a reward for whoever catches him."

After the warden kowtowed and left, Li Mian wrote a report to the mayor. Mayor Wang Hong subsequently reported to the emperor against Li Mian, accusing him of negligence and dereliction of duty. Li Mian was thus stripped of his official post. In the meantime, the mayor had posters put up for the capture of Fang De and Wang Tai. Without delay, Li Mian surrendered his original letter of appointment from the emperor and packed for his journey back home, hiding Wang Tai among the women of his family.

> He gladly helped a poor man in desperate straits
> And hid another fleeing from justice.

Li Mian had always been of limited means. Determined to be an upright and incorrupt official, he never took an undue penny, which was why he remained a poor man upon his dismissal from office. Back in his home village, he led the servants in tilling the fields and growing their own food. After more than two years, his family circumstances deteriorated. He bade his wife adieu and, taking along Wang Tai and two household servants, went on an eastbound journey to seek out old acquaintances. When reaching Hebei, he heard that his old friend Yan Gaoqing had just been appointed prefect of Changshan, so he went to pay a visit.[7] When passing through Baixiang County, some two hundred li from Changshan, Li Mian saw a group of guards of honor carrying white clubs approach him, clearing the way and shouting, "The county magistrate is here! Get off your horses!"

Li Mian shrank back to make way for the procession. Wang Tai saw that the magistrate in the distance, riding a white horse under a canopy, was a handsome man with a dignified bearing. Upon a closer look, Wang Tai recognized him to be none other than Fang De, whom he had set free years before. "You need not yield the way to him, sir," he said, addressing Li Mian. "He is none other than Fang De."

Li Mian was overjoyed. "Didn't I say this man was a hero whose time had not come? I've been proven right! But I wonder how he became an official." He was about to go forward and ask when he thought better of it. "If I do, he'll think that we are here to demand a return of the favor because we know he's an official in this place. I'd better not ask." He told Wang Tai not to say a word and he turned around to let Fang De's procession go past.

Fang De, however, when approaching them, immediately recognized Li Mian and Wang Tai, even though Li Mian had his back toward him. In happy astonishment, Fang De called a halt to the procession, dismounted his horse, and, going up to Li Mian, said with a bow, "Why didn't you call out for me when you saw me, my benefactor? Why did you turn your back on me instead? I almost went by without seeing you."

Returning the greeting, Li Mian said, "I was afraid I might hold you from your official duties. So I dared not call you."

"What kind of talk is this! This is such a rare occasion! You must come to my home for a little talk!"

Li Mian was tired from the journey, but as Fang De was so sincere, he replied, "Since you are so kind as to invite me, I'll be happy to go with you for a little talk." And so he mounted his horse again and rode abreast with Fang De. Wang Tai followed behind.

Soon they arrived at the county yamen and dismounted right at the entrance to the main hall. Fang De took Li Mian into the residential quarters in the back and then to a cottage, which served as a study, on the left side of the compound. He told the members of the procession not to follow them in and kept only a trusted attendant, Chen Yan, at the door to await further instructions. He then ordered that a fine feast be prepared and that Li Mian's four draft animals be taken to the manger in the back. Wang Tai and the others were told to carry the pieces of baggage in.

A message was then sent to Fang De's two personal servants, Lu Xin and Zhi Cheng, telling them to come and wait on the guests. Both servants had been bought by Fang De when he was the county marshal. Now, why didn't Fang De want his retinue there? Because he had been falsely claiming to be a descendant of Fang Xuanling [579–648], an ex-prime minister. His colleagues, with no knowledge about his past, believed in his stories about his impressive family background and held him in high esteem. With Li Mian here, he was afraid that Li would bring up his brush with the law in the hearing of members of the procession. If they spread the story around, he would become a laughing stock and his career would be in jeopardy. That was why he purposefully turned them away.

So Li Mian entered Fang De's residential quarters and was shown in to the study.

This three-section cottage with southern exposure was flanked on each side by an anteroom. The study was quite spacious, with well-lit windows. In the middle of the wall facing the door hung a landscape painting by a famous artist. A bronze incense burner was emitting wisps of fragrant incense. On the left stood a speck-led bamboo couch, on the right a bookcase filled with books. Against the windows was a table displaying the four treasures of the scholar's study.[8] In the courtyard outside grew an abundance of flowers and trees in a tasteful layout. This was where the magistrate spent his leisure time, hence the elegance in the decoration.

Having shown Li Mian into the study, Fang De hastened to pull a chair to the center of the room for Li Mian to sit down. He then bent down to kowtow. Quickly Li Main stopped him, saying, "Why all this ceremony?"

Fang De said, "I was a prisoner on death row. I was able to rise to where I am only because you, my benefactor, set me free, gave me travel money, and enabled me to flee to this place and rise as high as I have. You are no less than a parent of my rebirth. How can you not accept even one kowtow from me?"

Being a straightforward man, Li Mian accepted two kowtows from him, think-ing that what he said did make sense. After rising to his feet, Fang De also thanked Wang Tai and took him and the two servants to sit in one of the anterooms. He told them, "If yamen lictors ask you about me, don't mention anything from my past."

"You don't have to remind me. I understand," said Wang Tai.

Upon returning to the study, Fang De pulled over a chair and sat down by Li Mian's side. "I have been thinking day and night about how to repay my debt of gratitude to you," said Fang De. "But I never expected that we would meet here by heaven's will."

Li Mian said, "You were just in the wrong place at the wrong time. I only gave matters a little push within my power. Why all this talk about gratitude? I should be thanking you for thinking about me so often."

After tea was served, Fang De said, "May I ask what promotion you have received? You must be passing by our humble town on your way to your new duty station?"

"Well, because I set you free, the mayor of the capital accused me of derelic-tion of duty. I was removed from office and I returned to my home village. For lack of anything better to do at home, I am out on a tour of the mountains and rivers for relaxation. I was passing this place on my way to Changshan to visit my old friend Prefect Yan. It's such a delight to meet you and to see that you are an official now."

"So you lost your career because of me. And I've been undeservedly drawing an official's salary here all this time! How shameful of me!"

"In ancient times, people laid down their lives for one another out of personal loyalty. I just lost a lowly post. It's not worth mentioning. Now, where did you go after we parted, and how did you manage to be magistrate of this county?"

"I fled from the lockup to Fanyang, where I met an old friend, who introduced me to Regional Commander An. Commander An kept me on as a subordinate and treated me most generously. After half a year, I was appointed as county marshal. Upon the recent death of the county magistrate, I took over the post through the recommendation of Regional Commander An. I feel ashamed that my ability to serve the community is so limited. I need your advice."

Although no longer serving as an official, Li Mian had long heard about An Lushan's rebellious intentions. Upon hearing that Fang De had acquired his position through An Lushan's recommendation, he began to fear that Fang De might join in An's rebellion later on. Since his advice was sought, he launched into a lecture: "Serving as an official isn't all that difficult. What you need to do is live up to the expectations of the imperial court and do no harm to the people. When it comes to important matters that involve life or death, you must uphold your integrity even at the risk of your life. Do not on any account be misled by villains or be enticed by minor personal gains and compromise your moral character. You may get away with wrongdoing for a time by a stroke of good luck, but in fact you make yourself an object of ridicule for generations to come. If you are so resolved, you will be well qualified for the job of a prime minister, let alone a county magistrate." (*Wise words that can well serve as a motto.*)

Gratefully, Fang De said, "I will forever remember these precious words of advice."

And so the conversation went on, with each man feeling well attuned to the other. After a while, Lu Xin, the servant, came to announce, "Dinner is ready. Please go and be seated."

Fang De rose and showed Li Mian into the back hall, where two tables had been laid out, one for the host, one for the guest. Fang De immediately told the servants to move the host's table over to the left side of the guest's. Realizing that Fang De was trying to sit by his side, Li Mian said in protest, "I would feel uncomfortable if you did that. Please put the table back."

"In your presence, my benefactor, it would be presumptuous of me even to sit on one side in attendance. I wouldn't dream of breaching proper etiquette."

"But we've become good friends now. Don't be too modest!"

The table was then restored to its previous position, opposite the table of the guest of honor. As the servants brought over cups and chopsticks, Fang De sat down as the host. A band of musicians spread out in one row and struck up music. It was a lavish feast with fine dishes galore.

> Though there were no phoenixes or dragons,
> There were delicacies from the hills and the seas.

The host and the guest drank heartily until late in the evening, while Wang Tai and the other two servants enjoyed their dinner in another room. Feeling even more warmly disposed to each other by this time, Fang De and Li Mian went back to the study, arm in arm. At Fang De's order, Lu Xin brought over bedding reserved for Fang De's superiors. Fang De then spread out the quilt and set the chamber pot with his own hands. Li Mian detained him with a hand, saying, "This is a servant's job. Why go to all this trouble yourself?"

"I owe you such a debt of gratitude that I can't repay a tiny fraction of it even if I work for you as a servant from reincarnation to reincarnation. I'm doing this just as a small token of my feelings. This is no trouble." (*Fang De does have a sense of propriety in the beginning.*)

After the bed was ready, Fang De had the servants set a couch on one side for himself. Touched by the sincerity of Fang De's words, Li Mian took him to be a man of loyalty and righteousness and held him in even greater esteem. They sat down facing each other by the lamp and had a heart-to-heart talk, confiding their aspirations to each other. Finding much in common, they became the best of friends, regretting that they had not met earlier. They did not go to sleep until midnight. The next day, Fang De's colleagues heard about this and came to visit the guest. When introducing Li Mian, Fang De said simply, "This is my benefactor. He had recommended me to a post back in the old days." In their attempts to curry favor with the magistrate, those officials also set out feasts in Li Mian's honor.

But let us not digress. After Li Mian's arrival, Fang De spent all of his time drinking and chatting with Li Mian, to the neglect of his official duties. He did not even go to his office. Even a most filial son would not have served his parents with greater devotion. But by dancing attendance so assiduously on Li Mian and abandoning all other activities, he only made Li Mian feel uneasy. After about ten days, Li Mian said he was ready to leave, but Fang De would not hear of it. He said, "What better opportunity than this for me to spend time with my benefactor? How can you leave so soon? You must stay for a few more months. I'll send a groom to escort you on horseback all the way to Changshan."

"I wouldn't have had the heart to say good-bye to you since you've been so kind to me, but you are the head of a county. I have kept you from your official duties. If your superiors hear about this, it won't reflect well on you. What's more, I'm determined to go. It'll be awkward if I have to stay on against my inclination." Now realizing that he would not be able to keep Li Mian, Fang De said, "If you are so determined to go, I shouldn't make you stay. But there's no way of knowing when we'll ever meet again. So please let me prepare a farewell dinner for you tomorrow by way of bringing these days of happiness to a conclusion. And you can depart early in the morning the day after tomorrow. How does that sound to you?"

"If you so kindly wish, I will have to comply and stay for one more day."

Having thus obtained Li Mian's promise to stay for another day, Fang De returned to his residence in the yamen, taking Lu Xin with him, to pack some gifts for Li. As a consequence, Marshal Li almost perished. Indeed,

> Good fortune lies within bad,
> Bad fortune lurks within good.

Those with few desires,
Scheme not and stay contented.

Let us pick up another thread of our story and turn our attention to Fang De's wife, Bei-shi. She was so used to making all the decisions in Fang De's humbler days that after he rose to power, she still thought she had the final say in everything. Her husband having summoned two servants and stayed out for more than ten days without returning to the yamen even once, she thought he must have been up to some mischief and seethed with resentment. That day, upon seeing her husband back at the yamen, she was about to unleash her temper on him when it occurred to her that she should sound him out first. So, flashing an ingratiating smile (*This woman wears masks.*), she asked, "What was it that kept you from home?"

"Oh, you have no idea! My big benefactor came. I almost missed him when we were face to face. Luckily I have keen eyes and spotted him. I invited him to stay. That's why I haven't been back home these last few days. I'm back now to consult you about what gifts we should give him."

"What big benefactor?"

"Good grief! How could you have forgotten? It's Marshal Li! He saved my life! And because he set me free, he lost his job. He was passing here on his way to Changshan to visit Prefect Yan. That prison warden, Wang Tai, is with him."

"Oh, him. How much are you going to give him?"

"He's like a parent of my rebirth. I should pay him handsomely."

"Would ten bolts of silk be too little?"

Fang De burst out laughing. "Surely you jest, madam! He did so much for me. Ten bolts of silk are not enough even for his servant!"

"Nonsense! You are a county magistrate and your servants don't make that much. That man is here to hit you up for money. Why does his servant deserve so much? I want to take care of my pennies. Nobody takes advantage of me. I'll grant him ten more bolts. Send him on his way as soon as possible."

"How can you be so stingy? He saved my life, he gave me money, and he was dismissed from office because of me. Twenty bolts of silk won't do!"

Bei-shi had always been a miserly woman. She would normally be loath to part with that much silk. It was only because Li Mian had saved her husband's life that she offered twenty bolts, which was to her already a preposterously generous gesture. Upset that Fang De dismissed twenty bolts as too paltry a gift, she said purposely, "How about one hundred bolts?"

"One hundred bolts will be enough for Wang Tai only."

That remark raised her ire because that meant many more would be needed for Li Mian. She said, "One hundred for Wang Tai would mean five hundred at least for the marshal, right?"

"Five hundred won't do, either."

Bei-shi was incensed. "How about one thousand?"

"That sounds about right." (*Far be it from Li Mian to want repayment! Fang De is using the yardsticks of a small man like himself to measure the mind of a gentleman. Even if he did give a thousand bolts, he still wouldn't qualify as a true friend.*)

At this remark, Bei-shi spat right into his face and said, "You must have lost your mind! How much have you given me since you became an official? What gives you the right to throw money around? You wouldn't get half of it even if you sold me! Where are you going to get so many bolts to give away?"

At this outburst, Fang De said, "Can't we talk about it nicely? Don't get mad!"

"What's there to talk about?" she yelled. "If you've got them, you go ahead and deliver them to him. Don't come to me."

"But we don't have all that much. I'll have to take from the county treasury."

"Tsk! The audacity! The county treasury belongs to the imperial court. How dare you use it for personal purposes? If your superiors find out, what are you going to say?"

In annoyance, Fang De said, "You do have a point, but my benefactor is leaving in such a hurry. With so little time, what am I going to do?" He sat down, fretting.

As it turned out, her husband's insistence on offering lavish gifts gave Bei-shi such gut-wrenching pain that she felt it was worse than a knife actually cutting into her flesh. An evil idea sprang to her mind. She said, "What kind of a man are you, anyway? If you can't make up your mind on such trivial things, how are you going to rise high? I've got a shortcut here to solve the problem once and for all."

Believing she had a good idea to offer, Fang De asked eagerly, "What shortcut?"

"As the ancients said, 'Too great a kindness goes unrequited.' Why don't you pick a right moment tonight and kill him? Won't that be a nice way out?"

Fang De reddened to the roots of his hair. He bellowed, "You evil woman! It was all because you refused to give me some fabric to make me clothes that I went out to ask for help from friends and got myself tricked into joining that gang. I almost died! If it hadn't been for this benefactor, who lost his job because he had set me free, how would I have been reunited with you? Instead of giving me good advice, you tell me to kill my benefactor. Do you have a heart?" (*Well said!*)

To her irate husband Bei-shi said, all smiles, "Why wasn't that good advice? What makes you so angry? If I'm right, go ahead and do it. If I'm wrong, just ignore what I said. Why make all this fuss?"

"Tell me, what can be right about your idea?"

"Do you still hate me because I refused to give you the fabric? Now, just think: Ever since I married you at seventeen, haven't I been the provider of all the daily necessities? Did I really begrudge those two bolts of fabric? I heard that in ancient times there was a Su Qin whose whole family pretended to treat him badly when he was down-and-out. Thanks to their pushing, he became prime minister of six states.[9] I was imitating his family members, hoping to push you to success. But you were not in luck. You ran into those robbers. Nor did you have Su Qin's pride. You joined them in breaking the law and got yourself into trouble. You brought this on yourself. I had nothing to do with it. Did Li Mian really set you free out of true fellowship?"

"He couldn't have done it false-heartedly?"

Smiling, Bei-shi said, "Your smartness doesn't help you much. You don't see the truth. Most officials in law enforcement are greedy and ruthless. They don't even look out for their own kith and kin who happen to be in trouble with the law. You were a total stranger to him, and you were indeed guilty as charged. Why would he risk losing his own job to set free one who had been convicted of a serious crime? The only possible reason is that he thought a ringleader like you must have a pile of spoils hidden somewhere. So he hoped you would offer him contributions discreetly after you got free. He would then use part of the money to bribe high and low. That way, he would get to keep the rest for himself without risking his career. Otherwise, why did he pick you out of the whole gang? He never expected that you were a first-time offender and would vanish like a puff of smoke. And then he got kicked out of office. As soon as he found out that you're an official, presto! here he came!"

Shaking his head, Fang De said, "No, it's not like that. He let me go out of the goodness of his heart. There were absolutely no other motives. And now he's just passing here, on his way to Changshan. We met entirely by accident. He was afraid of keeping me from my official duties, so he turned his back toward me and didn't want to see me. He didn't make a special trip to see me. Don't attribute bad motives to people."

With a sigh, Bei-shi said, "He was lying when he said he was heading for Changshan. How can you take him at his word? Never mind other things that might give him away. Just the fact that he took along Wang Tai is enough to reveal his true intentions." (*A sharp tongue pleases the ear; clever talk sows doubts in the mind.*)

"All right, so he took Wang Tai along. What of it?"

"How can you be so dumb? Li Mian and Prefect Yan are acquaintances. It makes sense for Li Mian to visit Yan, but Wang Tai, as a prison warden of the capital, can't be an old friend of Prefect Yan's. Why should he be included in this trip? As for Li's turning around and not accosting you, well, he was observing you with a watchful eye, to see if you would take the initiative and go up to him. That was a trick, not a proof of good intentions. If he really wants to go to Changshan, how would he willingly stay here for so long?"

"No, he wasn't willing. I did my best to keep him."

"That also shows how scheming he is. He was trying to test your sincerity."

Fang De was a man without a mind of his own to begin with. With his wife's tongue a-wagging, he began to grow suspicious. As he remained silent, lost in thought, Bei-shi continued, "So, in short, you must not repay this debt of gratitude."

"Why not?"

"Well, if you don't give him enough, he'll turn against you and tell everything. When that happens, you'll not only be through with your career but also be arrested as a jail breaker. You'll be dead in no time. But if you pay him well, he'll set that as a standard and come every so often to demand more. If you satisfy him, fine. If not, he'll bring up the past again. You're not going to be off the hook anyway. Why don't you put an end to this whole business once and for all? It's always been said since ancient times: 'He who strikes first gets the upper hand.' If you don't do as I say, regrets will be too late when things get that far!"

At this point, Fang De nodded almost imperceptibly. He was having second thoughts. After another few moments of reflection, he said, "But I was the one wanting to repay him. He never said a word about that. I'm afraid he's not thinking along those lines."

Bei-shi rejoined with a smile, "He's not saying anything because he hasn't seen your offer. He'll surely speak up at the right moment. Also, even if nothing else happens, your future is already in jeopardy."

"Why is that?" asked Fang De.

"You showed Li Mian so much affection that yamen lictors will surely ask his servants questions. Will they cover up for you? Of course not. They'll blab out the truth. (*She does seem to talk sense.*) You know how merciless yamen lictors are in the things they say. If they learn that the magistrate started out as a bandit, they'll surely spread the story around. If your colleagues hear about that, they may not laugh at you to your face, but they'll gossip behind your back, and that can hurt badly. You'll be so ashamed you will want to leave. But that's not the worst. Li Mian and Prefect Yan being good friends, will Li Mian keep your secret from the prefect once he's there? Of course the prefect will learn every detail. I heard that the old man is most eccentric, and you are his subordinate. If the story makes the rounds all over Hebei, it'll catch up with you even if you escape before the night is out. Won't you be as poor as before? How are you going to live out the rest of your life? Act now, so that you don't make yourself look too bad to Prefect Yan!"

Fang De had quietly told Wang Tai not to let Li Mian's two servants leak anything out. His wife's analysis struck him right on his sore spot. Casting all thoughts about repayment into the east ocean, he eagerly conceded, "Yes, you've got it right. I would be bringing ruin to myself if I do otherwise. But everyone in the yamen saw him when he came. If he disappears tomorrow, won't people have suspicions? And the corpse will be hard to dispose of."

"What's so hard about that? When you leave the yamen in a moment, take only a few trusted men with you. Dismiss everyone else. Then you get Li and his servants drunk, and send someone deep in the night to stab them to death and burn down the cottage. Tomorrow, dig out their remains, make a show of weeping, and have them encoffined in their burial clothes. People will think they died from the fire. No one will suspect anything."

"Ingenious!" said Fang De in delight. Immediately he stood up to go. Knowing her husband to be an indecisive man, she was afraid that if he and Li Mian sat talking for any extended period of time and enjoyed the conversation, he was liable to change his mind. So she said, "It's still early. Stay for a while longer before you go." Doing her bidding, Fang De stayed. There is a poem in testimony:

> The fangs in the mouth of a fierce tiger,
> The spike in the tail of a snake,
> Neither of the above is as lethal
> As the heart of a woman.

As the old proverb goes, "Walls have ears; windows have eyes." When Fang De and his wife were talking in their room, the woman was so obsessed with the silk and so carried away in her lecture to her husband on how to do a man to death that she was not on guard against any eavesdroppers. In addition, they were in their residential quarters of the yamen, where there should be no intruders, and therefore she felt free to jabber away.

As it turned out, however, their servant, Lu Xin, upon hearing Bei-shi raise her voice in anger in the beginning, pressed himself against the partition wall and listened from the point where they bargained over the gifts all the way to their discussion about murder and arson. Every word fell full upon his ears. In horror, he thought, "So my master used to be a bandit. That gentleman saved his life, but he's now returning evil for good. Heaven forbid! If he can treat such a benefactor like this, what are we servants to him? If I make a mistake, I'm a dead man. What good does it do me to work for such ruthless people?" (*With such a servant, the master and mistress should die of shame.*) Then he thought, "As the saying goes, 'To save a life is better than to build a seven-story stupa.' Why don't I save those four men? That'll be a good deed to my credit in the next world." But then another thought struck him: "If I let them go, he will be after me. I might as well go with them." So thinking, he took out some pieces of silver, hid them on himself, and, when no one was looking, slipped out of the residential quarters of the yamen to the cottage. There, he saw Zhi Cheng sitting on the threshold of one of the anterooms, taking a nap, a fan in hand, while tea was brewing. Without waking him up, Lu Xin sneaked right into the study. Wang Tai and the two servants were not there. Li Mian alone was sitting bolt upright at the table, leafing through a book. Approaching the table, Lu Xin said under his breath, "Sir, there's trouble for you! Go now, quickly! What are you waiting for?"

Giving a violent start, Li Mian asked, "Trouble? What trouble?"

Lu Xin pulled him aside and told him everything he had heard, adding, "I tell you this because I can't bear to see an innocent man murdered. If you don't go this instant, you're done for."

Li Mian shivered as if he had fallen into an ice bucket. Bowing deeply to Lu Xin, he said, "If you hadn't had a sense of justice and come to save me, I would have died. I will repay this heavy debt of gratitude. I will never do what that ingrate does."

Frantically, Lu Xin bowed in return and said, "Keep your voice down, sir. If Zhi Cheng hears us and informs against us, both of us will be done for!"

"But after I'm gone, you'll be implicated. How can I let that happen?"

"I'm not married. After you're gone, I'll also go to a faraway place. Don't worry about me."

"If so, why don't you go with me to Changshan?"

"If you are willing to take me on, I'd be glad to serve you."

"You are my savior. How can you say such a thing?" He then called out more than ten times for Wang Tai, but no answer came. Stamping his feet, he groaned and said, "Where have they gone?"

Lu Xin said, "Let me go find them."

"But the horses are at the stable in the back. What's to be done?"

Lu Xin said, "I'll try to get the horses out one way or another." He rushed out of the study and looked in Zhi Cheng's direction, but he was no longer taking a nap on the threshold. Lu Xin went into the anteroom, but he was not there either. In fact, Zhi Cheng was in the outhouse. Thinking that Zhi Cheng must have overheard everything and had gone to report to Fang De, Lu Xin panicked and dashed back to say to Li Mian, "Sir, this looks bad! Zhi Cheng must have overheard us and is off to report to the master. (*A happy mistake.*) Go quickly! Don't wait for them!"

Li Mian was so shocked that words failed him. Abandoning his luggage, he staggered his way, empty-handed, out of the cottage with Lu Xin. Seeing Li Mian, those yamen employees who had been sitting stood up respectfully. In big strides, Li Mian rushed out of the inner gate of the yamen compound. There, they saw three horses tied to the posts. These were horses for the use of the magistrate, the assistant magistrate, and the county marshal. An idea struck Lu Xin. (*Lu Xin is a resourceful man.*) To the groom he said, "Mr. Li is going to West Gate to see a friend. Bring over the horses, quick!"

Knowing Li Mian to be an important guest of the magistrate, the groom was quick to obey the order of the magistrate's personal attendant and led two of the horses over. Li Mian had barely mounted the one offered to him when Wang Tai bumped right into the horse. Carrying in his hand a pair of hemp shoes, he asked, "Where are you off to, sir?"

Lu Xin answered for Li Mian, "Mr. Li is going to West Gate to see a friend. Where have you all been?"

Wang Tai said, "Our hemp shoes were worn out. We went to the marketplace to buy new ones. Which friend is my master going to see?"

Lu Xin said, "Just follow us. Why bother to ask?" He told the groom to bring over the other horse for Wang Tai. As they rode out of the main gate of the yamen compound, Lu Xin said to the groom who followed behind, "We'll be back shortly. You need not follow." And so the groom stopped.

Having cleared the yamen compound, Li Mian whipped his horse. As the horses galloped ahead with the speed of wind, Wang Tai wondered which friend his master was so eager to see. Before they were out of an arrow's range, the two servants appeared, hemp shoes in hand. Upon seeing their master, they withdrew to one side of the road and asked, "Where are you going, sir?"

Li Mian replied, "Don't ask. Just follow us! Quick!" Before the words were quite out of his mouth, the horses had swept past the two servants. They ran for dear life but how could they possibly catch up?

When West Gate loomed into view, two men on horseback rode out from a lane. Lu Xin peered intently and saw that they were Office Manager Chen Yan and an office clerk. Recognizing Li Mian, the two men dismounted and chanted a greeting. This sudden turn of events gave Lu Xin an inspiration. "Mr. Li," he said, "the servants need horses. Why don't we ask Mr. Chen for a loan of the horses?"

Similarly inclined, Li Mian reined in his horse and said, "Good idea."

Addressing Chen Yan, Lu Xin said, "Mr. Li is on his way to visit a friend and would like to borrow your horses for his servants. They'll be back soon enough."

These two men were only too eager to ingratiate themselves with Li Mian so that he could put in a few good words for them to the magistrate. Was there any reason they would turn down the request? Enthusiastically they said, "Yes! Please take them, sir! Just take them!"

Everyone waited until the two servants staggered their way up, out of breath and in a terrible sweat. After Chen Yan and the clerk handed them the horsewhips and the reins, they mounted the horses and followed Li Mian out of the city gate. On long reins, the horses raced along the highway in the direction of Changshan, their twenty hooves going up and down in the air like so many sticks beating a gong. Verily,

> The colored phoenix flew out of the jade cage;
> The flood dragon broke free from the golden lock.

Let us pick up another thread of the story. After he returned from his trip to the outhouse and finished brewing the tea, Zhi Cheng carried the tea into the study, but Li Mian was not there. Thinking he must be strolling among the flowers and the trees, Zhi Cheng went on a search in the garden, but to no avail. He said to himself, "I know. He has been sitting in this room for so long that he must be feeling bored and has gone out to amuse himself." After about two hours had elapsed and there was still no sign of Li Mian, he went out of the cottage to look. At the gate, he ran right into his master. It so happened that, upon his wife's advice, Fang De had sat around for a considerable while before rising to leave the yamen. At the sight of Zhi Cheng, he asked, "Have you seen Lu Xin?"

"No, he must be with Mr. Li, out on a walk."

Growing apprehensive, Fang De was about to send Zhi Cheng on a search when Chen Yan appeared.

"Have you seen Mr. Li?" asked Fang De.

"I saw him just a moment ago at West Gate. Lu Xin said that Mr. Li was on his way to see a friend there and borrowed my horses for Mr. Li's servants. All five horses went as fast as a cloud, as if there was an emergency."

Realizing that Lu Xin must have overheard him and leaked out the information, Fang De gave an inward groan. Without another word, he turned back home to tell his wife. That woman was astounded upon hearing that Li Mian was gone. "Well, well! The disaster will strike all the sooner!" said she.

Now that his wife also looked consternated, Fang De was seized with such fear that he was at a loss as to what to do. He grumbled, "I never saw him do any mischief. Now look at what you've done with all your clever talk!"

"Don't panic!" said Bei-shi. "As the saying goes, 'Once you've started something, you'd better finish it off.' Things having come to this pass, complaining won't help. He shouldn't have gone too far. Have a few trusted yamen lictors give chase before the night is out. Tell them to disguise themselves as bandits and kill all of them, and make a clean job of it." (*Things that she is capable of.*)

Fang De immediately summoned Chen Yan for a consultation. "This won't do," admonished Chen Yan. "First, the lictors can only run errands. They've never killed people. Second, if they're taken by people who rescue Li Mian, they'll be the ones to die instead. Now, I've got an idea. You don't have to drag in a lot of people, but neither Li Mian nor any of his men can get away."

Overjoyed, Fang De asked, "What is this wonderful plan?"

"An extraordinary man moved next door to me a month ago. He won't say what his name is or what he does for a living. Every day he goes out and doesn't return until he's roaring drunk. Feeling intrigued by his mysterious background and his comings and goings, I kept a close watch on him. One day, a distinguished-looking man in a blue brocade robe came on horseback with a retinue of several attendants to see him and stayed drinking for three days before leaving. Quietly I asked the attendants the names of the host and the guest. They were not willing to tell me, but one of them whispered to me, 'Your neighbor is a knight-errant able to get a human head just by tossing his sword in the air. He can also fly. He covers one hundred li in the twinkling of an eye. And he's a very upright and loyal man. He killed a man in broad daylight in a marketplace in Chang'an to avenge someone. That's why he has gone into hiding in this place.' Now, why don't you go to see him and take along some gifts? Just say that Li Mian framed you and you want his help in avenging you. If he agrees to do it, consider the job done. How about that?"

"This is a good plan all right, but what if he refuses?"

"If the magistrate of this county deigns to enlist his help, surely he will not refuse. But he may not accept the gifts."

Overhearing the conversation from behind the screen, Bei-shi said, "This is a wonderful plan. Go quickly and ask for his help!"

"How much should I offer to him by way of a reward?" asked Fang De.

"He's a man of honor who puts friendship above material concerns. Three hundred taels of silver will suffice."

With Bei-shi's enthusiastic encouragement, Fang De prepared three hundred taels of silver.

When the day was drawing to a close, Fang De changed into the clothes of a commoner. Followed by Chen Yan and Zhi Cheng, he walked quietly on foot to Chen Yan's house, located in a secluded lane with only four or five other houses. Chen Yan led Fang De in, lit a lamp, and peeked through a chink in the wall. That man had not returned. Chen Yan then went out the door to wait for him. After a while, the man was seen approaching, swaying to and fro in an inebriated state. After he tumbled headlong into his house, Chen Yan rushed back to report to Fang De. As Fang De rose to go, Chen Yan said, "You must watch what you say, sir. Be sure to show him a lot of respect if you want this deal to work out."

Fang De said, nodding, "I will." Together they went next door and gently tapped twice on the door. The man opened the door and asked, "Who are you?"

Humbly, Chen Yan said, "This is the magistrate of this county, here to visit you, honorable knight."

The man replied in a voice heavy with wine, "No such person lives here!" With that, he wanted to close the door.

"No, don't close the door yet," said Chen Yan. "We need to talk!"

"I need to go to sleep. Who has the patience to talk with you? Come again tomorrow if you want to talk!"

Fang De put in, "Just a few words. We'll be off soon enough."

"All right, come on in."

The three men stepped over the threshold, closed the door, and entered a small, brightly lit sitting room. Dropping to his knees, Fang De said with a kowtow, "I didn't know earlier that you, honorable knight, graced this county with your presence, or I would have welcomed you in more appropriate style. I feel so blessed to get acquainted with you."

The man stopped Fang De from getting on his knees and said, "You are the magistrate of this county. How can you kowtow to me? This is against all decorum. What's more, I'm no honorable knight. You've come to the wrong man."

"You are the very one this humble official wishes to see. I can't be mistaken."

After telling Chen Yan and Zhi Cheng to present him with the gift, Fang De continued to say, "Honorable knight, this humble gift is for you to buy wine with. Please do not decline."

The man said, laughing, "I'm just a common vagrant with no skill. How would I presume to be an honorable knight? And I have no use for this gift, either. Please take it back."

With another bow, Fang De Said, "The gift may be humble, but the sentiment can't be more sincere. Please do not decline it so harshly."

"You kowtowed so unexpectedly to a commoner and presented such a lavish gift. Why?"

"You must accept it before I tell you."

"However poor and humble I am, I've vowed never to take anything without a good reason. If you don't tell me, I will never take it."

Sobbing in mock grief, Fang De prostrated himself on the floor and said, "An immense injustice has been done to me, but I am unable to avenge myself. I heard that you are a man of honor with the skills of Nie Zheng and Jing Ke.[10] That is why I make bold to come to pay my respects to you. Please put your skills to use and kill that villain to redress the wrong done to me. I will never forget your kindness in life or in death!"

The man said, waving a hand, "Didn't I say you came to the wrong man? I can't even take care of myself. How can I do anything so momentous for others? To kill a person is no small matter. If you are overheard, you'll get me in trouble also. Please go back now." Having said that, he turned away and headed for the door. Fang De hurried forward and held the man in his grip, saying, "I heard that, out of a sense of justice worthy of the ancients, you make it your business to wipe out the evil and help the poor and the injured. Now with this enormous injustice done to me, you show no sympathy. Oh, I will never be avenged!" With that, he made a great show of grief and burst into another fit of sobbing.

Observing him with a watchful eye, the man believed him and asked, "You were really wronged?"

"If I were not grievously wronged, how would I dare come to seek your help?"

"All right, sit down then and tell me everything about how you were wronged, your enemy's name, and where he is. I will do something if I can."

They sat down face to face, with Chen Yan and Zhi Cheng standing off to one side. Lying through his teeth, Fang De said, "Years ago, Li Mian falsely charged me with robbery (*So now he brings up the subject himself.*) and put me through all kinds of torture. Several times he sent Warden Wang Tai to murder me, but each time he failed because the plot was found out. Luckily, his successor established the truth and set me free. Then I gained this post. He and Wang Tai are now here to blackmail me. Not satisfied after getting a thousand taels of silver from me, they acted in collusion with a household servant of mine to assassinate me. The plot fell through. They then took this servant and went in haste to Changshan to talk Prefect Yan into dealing with me."

After hearing this sensational story, the man said in wrath, "How can I do nothing about such injustice! You may return to the yamen now. You can count on me. I will go to Changshan right now to seek that scoundrel out and avenge you. I'll be in your residence at midnight to report back to you."

"Thank you for being such a champion of justice! I will stay up for you by the lamp. And I will give you a handsome reward after the job is done."

The man's face fell. "I've never hesitated to draw my sword to help a victim of injustice wherever I see one. Who covets a handsome reward? I'm not taking this gift, either." Before he had quite got the words out, he had sailed out of the door like a gust of wind and was out of sight in a trice. Their eyes unblinking, their mouths hanging open, Fang De and the others managed to say, "What an extraordinary man!" Fang De took back the gift, ready to offer it again when the man came back after the mission was accomplished. There is a poem in evidence:

> *He wielded his sword to avenge the injured;*
> *He valued justice and scorned riches.*
> *Who would have imagined that a villain's tongue*
> *Would have misled the man of honor?*

Now is the time for us to follow another thread of the story. Wang Tai and the two servants blindly followed their master out of the city gate without knowing why they did not stop to visit any friend. After they had covered more than thirty li without a break, daylight faded to dusk, but still they did not pause to look for lodging. It being the thirteenth day of the lunar month, a bright moon had risen in the sky. They continued to press ahead by the light of the moon for all they were worth, notwithstanding the poor condition of the road. Afraid that they might be pursued, they did not exchange a single word as they tore straight ahead. At about the second watch of the night, after traveling for more than sixty li, thirsty and hungry they came upon a small town in Jingjing County. The horses were also too tired to go on. Lu Xin said, "We've covered a lot of ground. We should be out of danger. Let's find lodging and start on the road again early tomorrow morning."

Li Mian followed his advice and stopped at an inn. To their disappointment, every inn they came to was closed at that time of the night. It was at the other end of the town that they saw an inn with its door ajar. People inside were still busily putting things in order. They dismounted their horses together and went in, took the saddles off their horses, and led them to the stable to feed. Lu Xin said, "Innkeeper, please pick us a few clean rooms. We would like to stay here."

The innkeeper replied, "In fact, all my rooms are clean, sir. But I've only got one vacant room at this point." He had a clerk carry a lamp and show the guests to the room.

As Li Mian sat down on a bench, panting for breath, Wang Tai couldn't bear the suspense anymore. "Sir," he said, "Magistrate Fang urged you to stay and is going to assign a groom and horses to escort you the day after tomorrow. What's so bad about making the trip in greater leisure? Why leave all the luggage behind and race all night like refugees on the run? Why give yourself such a hard time? And why is Mr. Lu with us?"

Li Mian said with a sigh, "You have no idea! If it were not for Mr. Lu, you and I would have died without even a burial place! Now that we've gotten out of the tiger's mouth, we should be giving our thanks to heaven. And yet you talk about luggage and giving myself a hard time!"

In alarm, Wang Tai asked for more details. Li Mian was about to tell him when the innkeeper, getting suspicious of five horsemen asking for lodging deep in the night without any luggage, walked in to question them. "Gentlemen," he said, "what business are you in? Where are you from? And why are you here at this hour?"

Eager to unburden himself of his tale of woe, Li Mian answered, "It's a long story. Please sit down and let me tell you everything." Thereupon he launched into a detailed account of how Fang De had committed an act of robbery; how he himself had secretly instructed Wang Tai to release Fang De out of admiration for his literary learning and distinguished looks; how he had been removed from office because of that; how he had encountered Fang De on his journey; how Fang De had kept him for a stay and showered him with hospitality; how Fang De had returned home early that afternoon, believed his wife' wicked words, and plotted to kill him; how Lu Xin had informed him; and how they had fled. Wang Tai cursed over and over again, "What an ungrateful swine!" The innkeeper also sighed prodigiously.

Lu Xin said, addressing the innkeeper, "Sir, Mr. Li has had a hard time on the road. Please bring over some wine and food. We'll be on the road again after a good night's sleep." The innkeeper left, promising to do so.

All of a sudden, there emerged from under the bed a powerfully built man in the attire of a kung fu master. A dagger in hand, a murderous look on his face, he inspired a shiver of awe. Li Mian and his servants dropped to their knees in horror and said, "Mighty hero, please spare our lives!"

The man raised Li Mian to his feet and said, "Fear not! Listen! I am a champion of justice, always ready to defend the wronged and the injured and wipe out all heartless villains. (*A real champion of justice now!*) Just some moments ago, Fang De fabricated a story, falsely accusing you, sir, of having framed him and sought to murder him. He begged me to assassinate you. I had no idea he was such a ruthless and ungrateful scoundrel! Luckily you told everything. Otherwise I would have killed a good man."

Li Mian hastened to say with a kowtow, "Thank you so much for saving my life!"

The man stopped him, saying, "Don't thank me. I'll be back soon." With that, he went out into the yard, flew to the roof of the inn like a bird, and disappeared from view. Li Mian and the other men hung out their tongues in awe and wondered what he meant by saying he would be back. With this worry preying on their mind, they dared not go to sleep, nor did they have any appetite for wine or food. There is a poem in testimony:

> They rode over a long distance, out of breath;
> Suddenly, a dagger from under the bed.
> A tale of woe told in all truthfulness
> Awoke the mystery man from his dream.

Now, back to Fang De's wife. Upon her husband's return, she was overjoyed that the big job had been done and that the gift of silver remained sealed and intact. Her face wreathed with smiles, she eagerly prepared a feast, set it out in the main hall, and both husband and wife waited by the candles. Chen Yan also stayed with them to offer his services. At about the third watch of the night, as the birds in the yard suddenly cried out in alarm and tree leaves rustled and fell, a man appeared in the hall. Fang De saw that it was that very champion of justice, dressed like a divine being, looking much more distinguished than before. In happy astonishment, Fang De walked up to greet him.

Without a word of demurral, the man angrily headed for the center of the room in big strides and sat down in the seat of honor. Fang De and his wife kowtowed and said their thanks. Before they had a chance to ask how everything went, the man, wearing a glower on his face, drew out his dagger and, pointing it at Fang De, burst into this tirade: "You ungrateful scoundrel! Marshal Li saved your life. Instead of paying your debt of gratitude, you listened to the words of that woman and turned against your benefactor and tried to murder him. Since your plot failed and he escaped, you should have repented, but instead you fabricated all those lies to dupe me into assassinating him. Had he not told everything, I would have been an accomplice in a hideous crime. Only if you die by ten thousand cuts will my anger be worked off!"

Before Fang De could protest, his head already rolled to the floor. Bei-shi cowered in fear. Her gift of the gab lost in this moment of terror, she was unable to get a word out, as if her tongue were glued in her mouth. The honorable champion of justice turned to her and cursed, "You evil woman! Instead of advising your husband to do good, you put him up to evil acts. Let me see what kind of stuff you're made of!" So saying, he leaped up and, with a kick of his foot, knocked her to the floor. With his left foot on her hair and his right knee pinning her legs, the woman screamed, "Have mercy, mighty hero! I will never dare to do this again!"

The mighty hero said, "You evil woman! If I let you go, I'm afraid you won't be as kind to other people!" With his dagger, he cut open her chest. Holding the dagger in his mouth, he tore open her chest and took out her vital organs. He then went to the lamp for a better look at the blood-dripping organs in his hand and said, "I thought this evil one's lungs and liver would be different from other people's, but apparently not. How could she have been so vicious?" He tossed them down and cut off her head. He then tied the two heads together, put them in a leather bag, wiped his hands clean, hid his dagger, went out of the yard, jumped over the wall, and was gone, the leather bag in hand.

> His righteousness moved heaven and earth;
> His valor touched the gods and ghosts.

In the meantime, Li Mian and the other men waited in the inn. At about the fifth watch, at dawn, a ray of golden light flew in from the yard. They jumped up in consternation and saw that it was the knight-errant. Putting down his leather bag, he said, "I took out the organs of one of the scoundrels, and I've got both their heads here." So saying, he retrieved the two heads from his bag.

In happy astonishment, Li Mian dropped to his knees and said in prostration, 'You are indeed a champion of justice second to none in all history. Please tell me your name, so that I can repay you later for your kindness."

The man said, laughing, "I've never had a name, nor do I need repayments. Since I appeared to you from under the bed, just call me 'the knight-errant under the bed' if we ever meet again." With that, he took out a packet of powder from his bosom, picked up some with his little finger, and flicked the powder onto the wounds of the two heads. He then folded his hands respectfully across his chest and flew to the roof before anyone could try to hold him back. In a trice, he was gone none knew whither.

Terrified at the sight of the two heads, Li Mian was about to do something about them when—how uncanny—the heads shrank until they melted into a pool of clear water, much to Li Mian's relief. He sat until daybreak. After Lu Xin paid the innkeeper, they got their horses ready and took to the road.

Storyteller, didn't you say that Li Mian traveled for more than sixty li before he came to the inn? That knight-errant had no horse. How did he manage to travel back and forth between the two places with the speed of wind before the night was out ? Well, I did say that he was able to fly over a hundred li in the twinkling of an eye. This is not unusual for a knight-errant. It was dusk when he gave Fang De his promise. When he was giving chase, Li Mian was still on horseback. He got to the inn before Li Mian did and lay under the bed in waiting. He came and went like a puff of the wind without leaving the slightest trace, which was why none of the people in the inn had any idea there was a person under the bed. That's one of the wonderful things knights-errant are capable of.

Back to Li Mian. The rest of the night passed without further ado. As said before, he took to the road the next day. After traveling for two more days, he arrived in Changshan. He went directly to the prefectural yamen and saw Prefect Yan. The two old friends' reunion was filled with joy. The prefect asked him to stay, but was surprised when he saw no luggage and asked why. Li Mian gave an account of everything that had happened, much to the prefect's amazement. Two days later, the Baixiang County yamen presented a report to Prefect Yan about the murder of the county magistrate and his wife. What had happened was that Chen Yan, Zhi Cheng, and several servants had fled every which way that night when witnessing the knight-errant in action, and only left their respective hiding places the next morning. They saw two headless corpses lying in pools of blood, with internal organs on one side, but the heads were gone. As for the household furnishings, not even one piece was missing. Crying out mournfully, they reported the news to the assistant magistrate and the county marshal, who came over in alarm to see for themselves. Upon their inquiry, Chen Yan had no choice but to come clean about how Fang De had begged a knight-errant to assassinate Li Mian. Right away, the assistant magistrate and the marshal summoned several lictors, who, weapons in hand, took Chen Yan as a witness to arrest the assassin. All the people of the county turned out to watch. When the lictors arrived at the house next to Chen Yan's and broke in, they found only a few empty rooms. Not even the shadow of a man was seen.

When consulting each other about how to draft the report to the prefect, the assistant magistrate and the marshal thought that, since Li Mian and Prefect Yan were good friends, they could not very well bring Li Mian's name into the report, nor did they feel comfortable with exposing the magistrate's ruthlessness. So they circumvented the truth and said no more in the report than that burglars had broken into the magistrate's residence at midnight, killed the magistrate and his wife, and went off with their heads, and that the assassin was still at large. And so they closed the file on the case. In the meantime, they made arrangements to buy two coffins for the funeral. Prefect Yan approved of their report and forwarded it to his superior. At the time, An Lushan was in power in the Hebei region. Fang De's death deprived An Lushan of a trusted subordinate. He ordered in response to the report that the assassin be hunted down and captured.

Afraid that he would be implicated upon hearing the news, Li Mian took leave of the prefect and returned to his hometown in Chang'an. It so happened that Wang Hong had been imprisoned on a charge, and therefore all officials whom he had dismissed from office were rehabilitated and received appointments. Li Mian resumed his post as marshal of the capital. In less than a year, he rose to be an investigating censor.

One day, when he was walking down a street in Chang'an, he saw a man in a yellow robe alight from a white horse. Then, followed by two Tartar servants, he strode right into Li Mian's procession of guards, ignoring the attendants' orders for him to stand back. Upon a closer look, Li Mian saw that he was none other than "the knight-errant under the bed." Dismounting his horse, Li Mian bowed and said, "Have you been well since we parted, honorable knight?"

The man replied, smiling, "It's nice that you still recognize me."

"You are in my thoughts day and night. How can I not recognize you? Please come to my yamen for a little talk."

"I'll come another day to pay my respects to you, sir, but not today. If you don't think it beneath you, would you please come to my humble house for a visit?"

Readily Li Mian agreed and rode abreast with him. When reaching Qingyuan Lane, they entered a small postern gate. After they went through a few more gates, suddenly there loomed into view an imposing, multi-storied mansion that teemed with hundreds of servants. Li Mian nodded imperceptibly and said to himself, "What an extraordinary man!" Once in the main hall, they exchanged greetings anew and sat down as host and guest. In a trice, a banquet more sumptuous than a king's was laid out. The family musicians summoned to play music in the courtyard were all unrivaled beauties with sparkling eyes and pearly teeth.

"This is just a simple everyday meal," said the knight-errant, "not good enough for an eminent person like you. Please don't take offense."

Li Mian was profuse with thanks. During the dinner, they talked about heroes past and present and did not take leave of each other until late in the evening. The next day, when Li Mian went there again, bearing gifts, he saw only an empty house. Everyone who had been in the house the previous evening was gone. He returned, overcome with emotion. Later, Li Mian rose to be vice director of the department of state affairs with the title of Duke of Qianguo. Wang Tai and Lu Xin also became minor officials. As the poem says,

> Be sure to know whom to love or to hate;
> Returning evil for good is the worst sin.
> May "the knight-errant under the bed"
> Wipe out all villains in the world!

Regional Commander Zheng Renders Distinguished Service with His Divine-Arm Bow

Mad Maitreya went to Mingzhou,
His cloth bag dangling from his pole.[1]
Zillions of incarnations he may have,
Each one with its own tales of woe.

As the story goes, in Bianliang, the eastern capital, Kaifeng Prefecture, there lived an immensely rich Squire Zhang Junqing, who was the first-born son in his family. He used red brocade bed canopies in winter and green gauze nets in summer. Wherever he went, he was ushered by two rows of well-decked-out maids and supported by two beautiful women, one on each side. His treasure house boasted gold and silver of the finest quality, speckled hawksbill turtle shells, the most perfectly shaped pearls, rhinoceros horns, and elephant tusks. On one side of his front door was his jewelry shop and on the other, his pawnshop. His father, Old Squire Zhang, had died not long ago. His mother was living with him. For his philanthropic generosity, he was called Zhang the Bodhisattva. One day, when watching the street at his door, he saw a monk in very unusual attire. Behold:

His eyebrows bushy and snowy white,
His eyes sparkling like blue waves,
He wore a red cape patched from seven pieces of silk;
He held a demon-subduing staff with nine tin rings.
If not one with the halo of nirvana,
Surely he was a monk of the greatest merit.

The monk walked up to him and said, "Greetings to you, squire." After Squire Zhang returned the greeting, the monk retrieved from his sleeve a subscription book, on the cover of which was written "Donation of five hundred logs of *nanmu* wood for Bamboo Grove Monastery." Without saying anything out loud, Squire Zhang thought, "I've heard about Bamboo Grove Monastery ever since childhood, but who knows if it really exists? What's more, my father had pledged to use what *nanmu* wood we have to build a Praiseworthy Serenity Hall on the Eastern Peak of Mount Tai, and that pledge hasn't been fulfilled." So he said to the monk, "My deceased father had pledged to use our *nanmu* logs for another purpose, so I dare not touch them. If Your Reverence wishes to have other things, please just say the word."

The monk said, "If you begrudge the logs, this poor monk will have to send someone to take them this evening." With that, he turned to go.

"This monk is out of his mind!" exclaimed the squire.

After afternoon gave way to evening, Squire Zhang drank a few cups of wine and was about to retire to his bedchamber when the servant on guard duty came to announce, "Squire, bad news! A fire broke out in the backyard!" In horror, the squire hurried to the backyard, where flames were burning high. Amid the glare of the fire, about a hundred men, all seven to eight feet tall in shapes that did not quite look human, were carrying the logs off at the order of the monk. When the squire ran after them for a closer look, the fire instantly went out and the monk and the men all vanished. Upon returning to the backyard, the squire realized that his five hundred logs of *nanmu* wood were all gone. There was not even a trace of burned ashes. How very strange! "Now what am I going to do about father's pledge?" he said to himself. He did not get a wink of sleep all night. Behold:

> *Amid the last drips of the jade water-clock,*
> *Rays of sunlight brighten the shadows.*
> *The roosters nearby crow three times,*
> *Reminding the ladies to do their toilette.*
> *The prized horses give neigh after neigh,*
> *Urging the travelers to fight for fame and gain.*
> *A few morning clouds fly over sea cliffs;*
> *The red sun rises over the mulberry trees.*

Squire Zhang rose, washed, rinsed his mouth, and burned incense at the family shrine. Then he went to see his mother. After telling her about what had happened the previous night, he added, "We are supposed to go to the eastern peak of Mount Tai on the twenty-eighth of the third month to fulfill father's pledge. What are we going to do now?"

His mother said, "Don't worry, son. We'll think of something when that day comes."

Thus assured, the squire took leave of his mother and went to the jewelry shop to tend to the business there. It was the middle of the second lunar month, a season when

> *Horses with golden reins neigh in the green meadows;*
> *Almond bushes bloom amid the joy of wine on jade towers.*

Suddenly, the sound of gongs burst upon his ears. A young military officer and a teashop waiter came with a note inviting him to a club get-together. What had happened was that Old Squire Zhang had organized a club when he was alive. Of the ten members of the club, a few had died recently, and therefore the club had ceased to exist. Now the sons had organized another club of ten in the tradition of the older generation and were planning for an excursion, even though it was only the middle of the second month.

"I won't be able to make it," said Squire Zhang. "I lost all my wood. I have nothing to fulfill my father's pledge with. How can I go?"

"If you don't go, sir, you'll be breaking up the club," said the officer.

Unable to make up his mind, Squire Zhang went to his mother and said, "My friends invited me to a club meeting. But, with the loss of the wood, I have nothing with which to fulfill father's pledge. I can't go."

His mother took out a brocade bag and said, "I have here a priceless treasure that your father brought back from a trip abroad. You can use this instead of the wood to fulfill your father's pledge."

Squire Zhang retrieved a red paper package from the brocade bag, opened it, and saw a chain of jade rings. He thanked his mother, kept the invitation letter, promised the club he would join the excursion, and made arrangements for the trip, which was, in fact, to the temple on Mount Tai. The other nine members of the club also packed and assigned servants to go with them. We need not be concerned with them but let us take a look at Squire Zhang, all dressed up now in the style of a military officer:

> A square cap with large zigzag designs,
> A pair of animal-shaped gold rings,
> A robe made of Xichuan brocade,
> A broad crimson belt around his waist,
> A dagger with a jade hilt,
> And a pair of cotton-padded boots on his feet.

In the company of his friends in the club, Squire Zhang left home and started on the journey. Eating and drinking when necessary, they traveled by day and rested at night. In a few days, they arrived at Mount Tai and found lodging at an inn. On the appointed day, all ten club members went to offer incense at the temple, each to fulfill a votive vow. Squire Zhang donated the chain of jade rings to the shrine of God Bingling of Mount Tai by way of fulfilling his father's pledge. With nothing else to do, he stayed on the porch of the temple to watch the festivities. Then the group of young men went in high spirits on a tour of the mountain, with Squire Zhang following behind at an unhurried pace. Behold:

> Over green mountains and clear waters,
> Under soft breezes and leisurely clouds,

> *The peaks form a screen in their verdant splendor;*
> *The pines and bamboos could well be in a painting.*
> *Amid the thin wisps of a floating mist,*
> *The birds chirp and the flowers shed their petals.*
> *The gentle rays of the glorious sun*
> *Caress the willows and the sweet green grass.*

Feeling tired, Squire Zhang told his friends to go ahead without him. He then went to a pavilion to take a rest. Once there, his ears caught the clatter of axes and hammers. When he looked around, he saw a construction site surrounded by bamboo fences. Stalwart men seven to eight feet tall were working inside. All of a sudden, a piece of split wood flew out. Squire Zhang picked it up and saw that it was from a *nanmu* log taken from his yard, bearing his father's seal. When he was wondering to himself, an acolyte opened the fence gate, walked up to him, and said with a bow, "Sir, the abbot would like to invite you in for tea."

After he went through the gate, Squire Zhang felt that he was in the moon palace of a fairyland. Behold:

> *The temple gate stands tall and imposing;*
> *The temple compound serene and charming.*
> *The gate bears a board bestowed by the emperor;*
> *Two fierce warrior statues guard the entrance.*
> *The Bodhisattva's shrine abuts the land-water mass altar;*
> *Under a canopy stands the Goddess of Children.*

Once the squire was inside the temple, a monk came out and greeted him with a bow, saying, "The other day, you kindly made a donation to this temple. I am so glad you are here today. Please come into my cell for a cup of tea."

From a distance, Squire Zhang was not able to tell who it was, but upon drawing near, he saw that the abbot was none other than the very monk who had asked him for his *nanmu* wood. For lack of a better response, he said, "I thank Your Reverence for your visit the other day, but I wasn't a good host."

The monk took him into his cell and they sat down as host and guest. When they finished drinking tea, a guardian warrior in a yellow turban came up before they had a chance to start a conversation and said in a thundering voice, "Your Reverence, God Bingling is here to see you."

Squire Zhang froze with terror. Without saying anything out loud, he thought, "How can the god of Mount Tai come to this place to see this monk?"

The monk said to Squire Zhang, "Please wait for me behind the screen. I'll come back to talk with you after I'm finished."

Thus instructed, Squire Zhang quickly slipped behind the screen. From there, he saw that more than ten yellow-turbaned guardian warriors ushered in a god. Behold:

With well-marked eyebrows and narrow eyes,
He is handsome with a refined air.
A red brocade robe with royal dragon patterns,
A white Lantian jade belt around his waist,
A gold-traced hat on his head,
A pair of silk shoes on his feet.

Upon a closer look, Squire Zhang found him to be the very image of the statue of the god Bingling in the temple on Mount Tai. The monk stepped down off the dais, bowed, and asked, "How did you acquit yourself last night in that mission?"

God Bingling replied, "He adamantly refused to be just a duke and insisted on being an emperor for three years."

"He's such a difficult one to deal with," said the monk. "Bring him to me."

Several yellow-turbaned guardian warriors brought into the cell an eight-foot-tall man with tattoos all over his body. The monk asked, "Why can't you just be a duke? The way you insist on contending for the throne, you're asking for a beating!" (*Why isn't God Bingling as powerful as the monk?*)

Before the monk had quite finished, the guardian warriors threw the man to the floor and gave him a thrashing. The man said with a sigh, "Oh well, if you refuse to let me be emperor for three years, I suppose I'll have to make do with duke."

A guardian warrior placed a document in front of him and made him sign it. After the man was released, God Bingling rose and said, "Thank you so much, Your Reverence, for what you've taken the trouble to do." He took leave of the monk and went off, whereupon the monk asked Squire Zhang to come out and resume his seat.

"There being little to offer you in this temple, I have prepared only a few cups of watery wine. Let's have a little chat."

"Thank you for being so kind to me," said Zhang. Soon wine was served. After they drank a few cups, the monk ordered the wine cups and utensils cleared away and said to the squire, "Let's go for a walk on the mountain."

"As you say, Your Reverence."

And so the two men went on a tour on the mountain. Behold:

Strange-shaped peaks soar in their verdant splendor;
Majestic trees cast mottled shadows.
The craggy rocks attract leisurely clouds;
A cascade falls like a white ribbon.
Ten thousand hills spread across the blue void,
One tall peak pierces the crimson clouds.

Beside himself with joy when viewing the scenery, Squire Zhang commented to the monk, "What dangerously steep cliffs these are!"

"They are not all that dangerous," said the monk. "Please look at the water."

While Squire Zhang was staring down at the water, the monk pushed him over the cliff.

The squire gave a violent start and realized that he had dozed off in the pavilion. "How strange!" he mumbled to himself. If it had been a dream, there was the taste of wine in his mouth. If it had not been a dream, nothing seen in the dream had left a trace. While he was marveling, his friends came up, saying, "Why didn't you join us, squire? So, you've been taking a nap here, all alone!"

"I don't feel well. I'm so sorry I didn't join you." He did not say a word about his dream.

Having seen the sights, the young men did the usual thing—buy gifts and souvenirs. Then they packed and returned home.

Upon Squire Zhang's return, his relatives and neighbors went out to meet him when he was still quite a distance from home and treated him to a welcome dinner. Joy flooded his heart when he saw his mother again. Behold:

> Scenes of the four seasons race by like a shuttle;
> One year's time rolls past in the snap of a finger.

When the last month of the year came around, snowflakes began to swirl down from the sky amid blasts of a bitterly cold north wind. There is in testimony a lyric to the tune of "Partridge Sky":

> The mist freezes in the bitterly cold air;
> Auspicious snowflakes spin down from the sky.
> In a trice, the fields all around look the same;
> Soon the hills and rivers vanish without a trace.
>
> A silvery world, a jade universe,
> Blurring even the Kunlun Mountains.
> Should the snowfall last until early dawn,
> It will bury the gate of the divine palace.

Noticing how heavy the snow was, Squire Zhang told his servants to open his granary and offer rice and money to the poor.

Let us turn our attention to an inn, where the inn clerk was grumbling at a lodger, saying, "For a man as tall and big as you are, you should know better than to spend all your time sleeping! You haven't paid rent for two months now. You'd better clear out of this place."

The man said with a deep sigh, "How wretched I am! Don't scold me, brother. I can't help it."

"Squire Zhang in the next lane is giving out food and money to the poor today. Why don't you get some hot water, wash your face, and go ask for money? You can keep what you get for your travel expenses. I don't expect you to pay us anyway."

"I'm much obliged to you!" said the man. He put on his dirty threadbare head-scarf, his tattered outer layer of clothes, and left the inn barelegged and barefoot. Leaning into the wind, he walked up to the Zhang residence. As it turned out, he was a little too late. Everyone was gone. After chanting a greeting to the gatekeeper, he said, "I heard that the squire is giving out food and money to the poor today."

The gatekeeper said, "Why didn't you come earlier? It's already over."

The man gave a groan and fell to the ground.

Witnessing the scene from behind his window, Squire Zhang immediately had a servant help the man up. Before long, his three souls and seven spirits returned to his body. Upon a closer look, the squire was shocked when he realized that this was the man he had seen in his dream in the pavilion. But why was he in such a sorry state?

"Where are you from?" asked Squire Zhang. "What is your name? Where do you live?"

Folding his hands respectfully across his chest, the man replied, "Sir, I am from a rich family in Taining of Zhengzhou. My parents having died early, I have been wandering about and got stranded here. I am now staying at Granny Wang's inn in the next lane. My name is Zheng Xin."

Straight away, the squire asked for a few used articles of clothing for him and fed him a meal.

"What skills do you have?" asked Squire Zhang.

"I can write and do arithmetic."

Thereupon the squire gave him some money so that he could settle his bill with the inn, and kept him on in the residence. Because he was able to write and do arithmetic and because he looked just like the man he had seen in his dream, the squire made him general manager of the household. The man turned out to be quick and clever and tended to his duties assiduously. The squire held him in high regard and put deep trust in him.

Time went by with the speed of an arrow. The sun and moon raced back and forth like shuttles. Before anyone noticed it, the middle of the second month had rolled around. The squire's friends again invited him to join them in an excursion to the outskirts of the city, partly as a club get-together and partly to view the sights of spring. Having engaged courtesans the previous day, each of them took along his favorite one. Knowing that Squire Zhang was still in mourning and therefore would refuse to take one along, they engaged a favorite courtesan of his without his knowledge. The unsuspecting Squire Zhang went into the appointed garden for the get-together and greeted the women. From among the group of women emerged one called Wang Qian, the number-one courtesan and entertainer of poets and fun-seekers in the two capitals,[2] and she was none other than Squire Zhang's favorite. As soon as he laid eyes on her, Squire Zhang turned to go. Wang Qian stopped him with her hand and said, "Squire, I haven't seen you in a long time. I've been neglectful of you."

"Thank you for kindly saying that, sister. My father passed away. I'm still wearing mourning clothes. If we're seen in public, I would be accused of being an unfilial son." Turning around, he said to his friends, "I'm grateful to you all for your kindness to me, but I don't feel well. I can't stay. Good-bye for now."

However, at the insistence of his friends and Wang Qian, he sat down next to Courtesan Wang against his own inclinations. With one woman next to every man, they set to drinking. When everyone was well warmed with wine, a man came in. What was he wearing?

> *A blue headscarf with a pair of golden rings,*
> *A white silk shirt, a red floss waistband.*
> *A pair of hemp shoes with multiple loops,*
> *And a basket in his hand.*

The man walked up to them, put down his basket, and, folding his hands across his chest, chanted three times in greeting.

"What do you have to say?" asked the squires.

The man produced a butcher's knife from his basket, asked for a plate, took out a chunk of beef, sliced it, put the slices on the plate, and said to the company, "I heard that you gentlemen are having a drink here. So I came to offer you something to go with the wine." Having said that, he put the plate before them, chanted another greeting, and withdrew.

Squire Zhang let out a groan under his breath. "This brute has ripped me off quite a few times already," he thought.

That brute, you see, was a ne'er-do-well who was a resident of the eastern capital. Xia De by name, he was better known by his nickname "The Buffoon." His younger sister had been married to Old Squire Zhang. In a moment of rage, she had hanged herself and died. Henceforth, Xia De repeatedly extorted money from Old Squire Zhang on account of her death and had done the same thing to young Squire Zhang a few times.

"Don't worry," said Squire Zhang's friends. "He's just trying to get a tip. Let's get on with our drinking."

In a trice, the brute went up to them again and said, "I, Xia De, am in luck today, to be able to see so many of you gentlemen at once."

"Let's each give him two taels of silver," said the men.

When Xia De stopped before Squire Zhang, the latter said, "Two taels from me, as from everybody else."

Looking Squire Zhang in the eye, the brute said, "You can't do what everybody else does. They may give me two taels each, but you have to give two hundred."

"Even if I double the amount that everyone else gives, it's just four taels. Why two hundred?"

"Because I have nothing against them, but you know what there is between the two of us. You don't want me to say it outright, do you? It won't reflect well on you!"

Squire Zhang had to promise twenty taels to the blackmailer. The others said, "All right, that's good enough."

"Out of respect for you all, I'll call it quits. But I want the money now."

"I don't have twenty taels with me. I'll write you a note. You can take the note to my treasury to get the money."

Equipped with the note, Xia the Buffoon chanted good-bye, left the garden, and went all the way to Squire Zhang's treasury. He raised the blue cotton door curtain, went in, and called out a greeting to everyone inside. After they all returned the greeting, Zheng Xin, the one whose time for eminence had not yet come, asked, "Do you want to redeem a pawned article or to break an ingot of silver into smaller pieces?"

"Neither. The squire wrote me a note for twenty taels of silver."

"What did he buy from you? This is a lot of money!"

"He bought beef from me."

"He couldn't have eaten so much beef!"

"Why ask? Just do what the squire says in the note and cough up the money!"

And so the two men argued, one shouting louder than the other. Still refusing to pay, Zheng Xin said, holding twenty taels of silver in his hand, "Xia the Buffoon, let me tell you: Silver I do have, but let's go together to the garden to see the squire. If he tells me to my face to pay you, I'll give it to you." (*Why would a great hero like Zheng Xin begrudge a mere twenty taels of silver that aren't even his? Because he is outraged by the scoundrel's blackmailing.*)

Xia the Buffoon cursed, "This hired hand needs a good beating! The squire himself is giving me the silver. What business is it of yours? Why should you make things difficult for me? Let's go see the squire. This note is not a fake!"

Zheng Xin and Xia the Buffoon went to the garden, where the members of the club were drinking in the pavilion. As both men went forward and chanted their greeting, Squire Zhang asked, addressing Zheng Xin, "Is something up, manager?"

"Sir, it's about the note regarding payment of twenty taels of silver. I'm here to verify that such is your wish."

"Just give the money to that shameless good-for-nothing and be done with it."

As Xia the Buffoon tried to snatch away the silver from Zheng Xin's hand, Zheng Xin refused to let go. He said, "The money is here, and the squire does tell me to give it to you, but I refuse to do it. You are able to extort money from people in the eastern capital only because they know you to be a shameless good-for-nothing. They may fear you, but I do not. Let me fight it out with you in front of all the gentlemen here. If you win, I'll give you the money. If not, you lose your long-standing reputation."

"Luckless me, to be bullied by a hired hand!" said Xu the Buffoon.

"Don't say that you're better and I'm just trickier. There's a lot of space here. Let's fight it out fair and square!"

As Zheng Xin took off his upper garment, everyone gave a cheer. This handsome man had tattoos all over his body. On his left arm, three fairies with swords;

on his right arm, five demons catching a dragon; on his chest, a palace screen; on his back, a dragon emerging from water in the Ba Mountains. Xia the Buffoon also shed his upper garment, revealing tattoos of stick-and-ladder patterns, a doll, and the character "*ren*" [endurance].

And so the two men fought in the garden to see who would come out the winner. Zheng Xin raised his fist and, with a single lunge, hit Xia on the temple. Xia the Buffoon fell to the ground with a thud and died instantly. All the squire's friends and the women fled in horror. Soon, officers from the yamen arrived and closed in on Zheng Xin.

Clapping his hands, Zheng Xin said, "I'm a native of Taining, Zhengzhou, now working as a general manager for Squire Zhang. Xia the Buffoon extorted money from my master. My fist hit too hard and killed him. No one else is involved. You can tie me up with a rope now and take me away."

The officers said, "Brave man! He rid the eastern capital of a pest! He shouldn't pay with his life." So saying, they took him to the prefectural yamen of Kaifeng, as it was their duty to do, and kept the corpse for the coroner's examination.

Zheng Xin pleaded guilty and was put in the lockup to await sentencing. Squire Zhang bribed the wardens into taking good care of him, hoping for a transfer or a deferral until the next imperial amnesty. But there we shall leave him for now.

One day, the prefect of Kaifeng went out of the city to visit a temple. In his sedan-chair, he saw a column of black vapor rising high from an ancient well by the roadside. The prefect told his sedan-chair carriers to stop. Upon taking a good look, he exclaimed, "How very strange!" He then went on to the temple and offered incense. After returning to the prefectural yamen, instead of going to his residential quarters, he summoned all the yamen officials. After all the officials arrived and exchanged greetings with one another, tea was served. Then the prefect said, "When I went out of the city to the temple today, I saw black vapor coming out of an ancient well by the roadside. I wonder if there is some demon in it."

None of the officials dared to answer. Only the assistant prefect rose and said, "In my humble view, in order to know the mystery of the well, you might ask for permission by the imperial court to send prisoners on death row to go down into the well to check. We will then be able to know everything."

Following this advice, the prefect wrote a memorial to the imperial court and instructed the prison wardens to pick a prisoner awaiting execution and put him into the well for a closer look. The prefect and the officers all went to the spot. A prisoner on death row was put into a basket, which was then lowered on a winch. At the sound of a bell, they pulled the basket up, but only a pile of bones remained. Another man was let down, and he died, too. Several tens of prisoners died in this way. Square Zhang having asked the wardens to take good care of Zheng Xin, they withheld Zheng Xin. (*Good detail.*) However, the prefect ordered that every one of the prisoners on death row be brought over. The wardens had no choice but to bring Zheng Xin to the well.

When told by the prefect to go into the well, Zheng Xin said, "I will do so, but I would like to ask for five things." (*A man of wisdom does stand out from others.*)

"What five things?" asked the prefect.

"A helmet with armor and boots, a sword, a pot of wine, two catties of meat, and some pancakes."

Forthwith, the prefect gave him everything he asked for. Zheng Xin chanted his thanks, drank the wine, ate the meat and the pancakes, put on the armor and helmet, and held the sword under his arm. Everyone present gave a cheer. Behold:

> *He had on his head a snowy white helmet;*
> *He wore on his body a silvery armor.*
> *On his feet, a pair of black boots,*
> *In his hand, a seven-star precious sword.*

Thus attired, Zheng Xin sat in the basket, which was let down by means of the winch. When the bell rang, the basket was raised again, but Zheng Xin was not in it, and the black vapor had also vanished. At the prefect's order, the basket was again lowered to get him, but to no avail. He had disappeared like a stone into the ocean or a kite freed from its string. The prefect and the other officials waited for a considerable time before going back into the yamen.

Let us retrace our steps and come back to the moment when Zheng Xin, future regional commander in the service of the imperial court, was lowered to the bottom of the well. He got out of the basket and, sword in hand, stood in one corner of the well. After his eyes got used to the darkness, he looked down and saw a hole on one side large enough to admit a person. He crawled in. After a few steps, he raised his head and saw

> *Undulating hills, curling wisps of mist,*
> *Lush tender grass, sweet blossoms on the rocks,*
> *Verdant pine trees standing on the cliffs,*
> *Small brooklets flowing in the ravines.*

Zheng Xin pressed ahead gloomily, with no idea what this deserted place was. Around noontime, he saw, through openings among the pines and bamboo, a mansion with upturned eaves, green tiles, and multiple windows. Believing this was the abode of some hermit, he sought a path that would lead to the mansion in spite of all the perils along the way. Following the gurgling of water and the soughing of pine trees, he gradually came to the foot of a range of wooded hills. Behold:

> *The winding brooks and streams run deep;*
> *The air is still, the clouds motionless.*
> *Verdant pines embower green tiles and red roofs;*
> *Tall bamboo brush against carved eaves and jade bricks.*

With tall towers and spacious courtyards,
It is either a royal palace or a divine abode.

Zheng Xin stood in front of the palace for the longest time without seeing anyone coming out and going in. As he raised his head, he saw a vermilion board over the gate, bearing the inscription "Hall of Rosy Clouds." As there was no sign of a human being, Zheng Xin entered the gate, sword in hand, and walked into the main hall, where a naked woman was sound asleep with an object under her head as a pillow. Behold:

The orchid droops, the willow is drowsy;
The jade softens, the flower turns shy.
Like Consort Yang going to bed after a bath,[3]
Like Xi Shi lying down with a chest pain,[4]
She keeps her fine eyebrows in a frown,
As her cheeks glow like peach blossoms.
A peony by the red railings of West Garden,
A meditating Guanyin Bodhisattva of the South Seas.

Upon seeing this woman, Zheng Xin knew that she was the demon of the well. Gently he held the woman's head with one hand and drew out the object serving as a pillow. Slowly he put down the woman's head and went out. He saw that the object was a dark red leather bag. Not knowing what it was for, he dug a hole with his sword under a flowering bush and buried it. Sword in hand, he returned to the hall and shouted at the woman with all his might: "Rise!"

Opening her enchanting eyes, the woman, with her ten thousand bewitching ways, cowered in fear and said, turning her head toward him, "My dear man Zheng! You've come at last! I've been waiting for you here for so long by my forlorn self! You and I were destined five hundred years ago to be man and wife, but this is the first time we've been able to meet."

The woman had meant to show her true form at first, but, Zheng Xin having stolen her magic charm, she had to make the best of the situation. If she had not been so pretty, Zheng Xin would have cut her down with one swing of his sword. But, his heart aflutter in the presence of such a beauty, he asked, "What is your name?"

"Husband, put down your sword and take off your armor. Let's chat and make love." Behold:

The evening clouds enwrap the royal gazebo;
An ethereal mist envelops the pond.
Pairs of butterflies rest among the flowers;
Orioles, two by two, perch on the willows.
The room with painted beams peaceful and quiet,
The beaded curtain goes down; the swallows return.

The small courtyard is shrouded in darkness;
The embroidered fragrant quilt lulls one to sleep.
The wind is still; the cuckoos cry on the jade trees;
The moon moves; the flowers cast their shadows on the gauze windows.

The woman asked a maidservant to serve wine. In an instant, wine was brought in, along with an abundance of delicacies. Half tipsy after a few cups, the woman said, "By heaven's grace, I got to meet my husband today. Let's go on drinking until we are thoroughly drunk."

As Zheng Xin refused, she continued, "My dear Zheng, you and I were destined five hundred years ago to be man and wife. How can you turn me down?" After they drank for a considerable while longer, she had the maidservant clear away the table and went into her bedchamber with Zheng Xin, hand in hand. Truly,

The embroidered curtain was let down,
The silk quilt was spread out.
In their union of joy, they vowed eternal love;
In their affection, they played games of clouds and rain.
Above the thin clouds soared the phoenixes;
Into the dark water dived the lovebirds.
They pledged never to part from each other;
They swore to be wedded again in their next lives.

At daybreak, the woman rose and said, "Husband, thank you for being so loving last night."

Zheng Xin said, "I am grateful to you for your love, but who are you? If I see you again in the future, I will surely return the kindness."

The woman replied, "I am the fairy of the rosy clouds. My husband, you and I will be together forever. Why think of leaving?"

Henceforth the couple spent all their time together, walking or sitting, and enjoyed themselves day and night.

One day, the woman said to Zheng Xin, "Husband, you stay here. I need to go out, but I'll be back soon."

"Where are you going?"

"To the longevity peach banquet in heaven. The maidservants will stay behind to keep you company. Wine and food can be had at a moment's notice. But there's one thing I need to tell you. Do not go to the hall in the back for amusement. If you do, you will be in for big trouble."

After these instructions, the woman bade him adieu, leaving the two maidservants to tend to him. Without anything better to do to relieve his loneliness, Zheng Xin asked for a few cups of wine. As he drank to while away the time, he thought, "My living here is like a spring dream. My wife just told me not to go to the hall in the back. There must be sights there that she doesn't want me to see. Let me try that place out." He went out of the door and headed for the hall in the back. What he saw was another mansion with a gate. He passed the gate and saw inside a grand hall bearing a board with the inscription "Hall of Moonlight." As he stood looking, he heard footsteps, the click of shoes, and voices talking and laughing. There came into view a divine maiden ushered by a group of maidservants. She was

> *A lovely maiden with a plum blossom painted on her forehead;*
> *Her mouth a cherry, her brows willow leaves,*
> *Her hair a black cloud, her skin white as snow.*
> *Like a water lily or a lotus flower,*
> *She is unstained by a speck of dust*
> *In her captivating charm.*

Zheng Xin was sent into a transport of joy. The woman exclaimed, "Hurrah! I've been looking everywhere for my husband, but here he is!" Before Zheng Xin had a chance to say a word, the group of women gathered around him and pushed him forward.

"Husband," the divine maiden cried out, "You've come at last! I've been waiting in loneliness for you for a long time now!"

"You are mistaken, madam. I am married. My wife and I live in the hall in front of this one."

Ignoring his protests, the women pushed him into the hall, and the divine maiden ordered that wine be served. After drinking a few cups, she and Zheng Xin went into her bedchamber, hand in hand, and consummated their marriage behind bed curtains. Soon, after the clouds and rain abated, they straightened their clothes and rose from the bed. At this point, a maid came in to announce, "Madam Rosy Clouds of the front hall is here to see you."

Before the woman had time to hide Zheng Xin, the Fairy of Rosy Clouds walked up to him and said, "Husband! What are you doing here?" She grabbed him by the arm and returned with him to the front hall.

Her willowleaf-like eyebrows flying up, her starry eyes wide open, the Fairy of Moonlight shouted, "You married him, but what about me?" So saying, she led several tens of maids and ran all the way to the front hall, where she shouted, "Older Sister, he's my husband. How can you take him away from me?"

The Fairy of Rosy Clouds shot back, "Younger sister, he is my husband. What are you talking about?" Each tried to scream louder than the other.

Zheng Xin having been hidden by the Fairy of Rosy Clouds, there was no way the younger sister could find him. The two women came to blows. After they were locked in fight for a good while, the Fairy of Moonlight felt she was losing. Shouting, "Rise!" she leaped into midair and changed into her true form. The Fairy of Rosy Clouds also wanted to change, but, Zheng Xin having buried her magic object, she could not manage the transformation and therefore lost the fight.

In mortification she went over to Zheng Xin and said with tears coursing down her cheeks, "Husband, you didn't believe what I said, and brought me to this pass. Because you buried my magic object, I couldn't transform myself. If I am to defeat her, you must return it to me."

Yielding to her pleas, Zheng Xin saw nothing for it but to dig out the object from under the flowering bush outside. The Fairy of Rosy Clouds challenged her sister to another fight, but lost again. Upon her return, Zheng Xin said, "Why did you lose again?"

"I couldn't beat that slut because I'm pregnant. Now I have something to tell you."

"What is it, wife?"

The Fairy of Rosy Clouds told a maid to get what she wanted. Before long, a bow and an arrow were brought to her.

"Husband," she said. "This is not something found in the mortal world. It is called 'the divine-arm bow.' It never misses a target. (*All these twists and turns of the plot are for one purpose only: to bring out this divine-arm bow.*) I'm going to change into my true form in midair. While I fight that slut, you can help me by shooting an arrow at the white object you see."

"All right," promised Zheng Xin. "Set your mind at rest."

Hardly were these words out of his mouth when the Fairy of Moonlight came again. The two women rose to the clouds, changed into their true forms, and began to fight. Zheng Xin looked up and saw two spiders, instead of two beautiful fairy maidens, fighting in midair. One was red, the other white. "So, that's what they are!" exclaimed Zheng Xin.

As the red one lost and fled, the white one gave chase. Zheng Xin drew the bow and, taking good aim, released the arrow, crying, "Take that!" The white spider fell. In sharp pain, the Fairy of Moonlight cursed, "Zheng Xin, you ungrateful swine! You tricked me!" With that, she headed for her own hall, and there we shall leave her.

The Fairy of Rosy Clouds changed back from her true form. A ravishing beauty again, she said to Zheng Xin as she looked him in the eye, "Husband, thank you so much for rescuing me. I can now fulfill my wish of being with you forever."

Henceforth, their affection for each other grew deeper. They walked shoulder to shoulder and sat thigh to thigh. There was never a moment when they were apart. Indeed,

> *In balmy spring, they admired flowers, hand in hand;*
> *In hot summer, they stayed cool under the flowers.*
> *In clear autumn, they viewed the moon in their blissful union.*
> *In cold winter, they enjoyed each other's warmth.*
> *They took endless pleasure in unworldly pursuits;*
> *They reveled in the boundless delights of this world.*

All too quickly, three years elapsed. They had a son and a daughter. Zheng Xin thought, "Life here is pleasant all right, but how am I going to make my mark in the world?" Aloud, he said to his wife, "I am ever so grateful to you for keeping me here. It's been three years now, and we have a son and a daughter. But my wish is to make my mark in the world to return your kindness."

The Fairy of Rosy Clouds burst into a flood of tears. "Husband," said she. "What am I going to do after you leave? And what about the children?"

"If I can land an official post, I'll come to get you."

"Where are you going?"

"To Taiyuan, to join the army."

"I have one thing for you. If you go into the army with it, you'll surely make a name for yourself." She had a maidservant bring over the divine-arm enemy-vanquishing bow, which is, in fact, known in our present day as the "foot-operated crossbow." She said, "Take this to the army. You will win distinction in battle and will surely rise to be at least a fifth-grade duke. I will take care of the children. After twelve years, I'll have someone send them to you."

"If I can make something of myself, I'll come back to get you and the children."

"You and I met to fulfill a predestined bond. The three-year term has expired. An immortal and a mortal are worlds apart. We may never get to see each other again!" With that, she broke down in tears.

Zheng Xin had been eager to go, but, upon hearing that they might never see each other again, he also shed tears and offered to stay longer. The fairy said, "Now that our marriage bond has come to an end, it is only right that we should say good-bye to each other. I dare not keep you. If I jeopardize your future career, heaven will punish me." Thereupon she had the maidservants set out wine for a farewell dinner.

After a few cups of wine, the fairy said, "Husband, I'll keep the sword and armor that you brought with you and produce them as a proof when the children join you."

"As you say, my good wife."

The fairy plied three more cups of wine on him and gave him a large package of jewelry. She walked him out of the gate until, several li later, a highway came into view. "Husband," said the fairy, "that's the highway. You have a long way to go and a bright future in store for you. Take care!"

Zheng Xin was about to offer to stay when a strong gust of wind sprang up from under his feet. After the wind swept past, the fairy was nowhere in sight. Behold:

> Blue clouds hid the palace from view;
> A thin fog enshrouded the winding veranda.
> He listened but heard not a sound;
> He looked back but saw no hills or peaks.
> The palace of rosy clouds must have returned to the sea;
> The divine maiden must have gone back to Penglai.[5]

What he had seen seemed but a Zhang Sengzhou landscape;[6]
The painting had been rolled up and taken away.

The divine-arm bow in his arms, Zheng Xin stood there stupefied for a long time before he started to move forward resignedly toward the road. It was the Fenzhou highway, which took him to Taiyuan Prefecture of Hedong, not too far away. The prefect of Taiyuan, Chong Shidao, had just put up posters to recruit soldiers.[7] Zheng Xin went up to the gate of the yamen to join the army and presented his divine-arm bow. In immense delight, Prefect Chong had workmen reproduce thousands of identical bows and made Zheng Xin commander of the army. Later, thanks to the bow, Zheng Xin rendered distinguished service in battles to repel forces that invaded the empire. In more than ten years' time, he rose to be regional commander of Dongchuan and Xichuan.[8] Out of devotion to the Fairy of Rosy Clouds, he never married again.

Let us retrace our steps and come back to Squire Zhang Junqing. After Zheng Xin disappeared into the well, he missed Zheng Xin so much that on every anniversary of the event, he had his new manager prepare sacrificial meats of pig, goat, and ox for him to offer to Zheng Xin at the well. In his dedication to his friend, he never missed this annual memorial service for several years in succession.

One day, upon returning from a memorial service at the well, he felt tired and took a rest in his room. Soon he drifted off to sleep. In a dream he saw glorious multi-colored clouds in the sky. Suddenly a red-robed fairy maiden appeared out of the clouds. Carrying a boy in her left arm and a girl in her right arm, she shouted, "Zhang Junqing, these are Zheng Xin's children. I give them to you now. Raise them well. After Zheng Xin makes his mark in the world, send them to Jianmen. Do not fail me." Having said that, she tossed the children down from midair. Unable to catch them quickly enough, Squire Zhang broke into a cold sweat and woke up with a start. "How strange!" he said. Before he even had time to turn, the gate-keeper came to announce, "An old man with a white beard is here to offer a boy and a girl to you, sir. He said, 'I'm fulfilling the squire's wishes as expressed at the old well.' He also gave you this package and this sword, saying they are souvenirs of the regional commander of Dongchuan and Xichuan. He wants you to open the package with your own hands.' Without knowing what to make of this, I came to report to you, sir."

This being exactly what he had dreamt about, Squire Zhang opened the package and saw that it was a set of armor. After putting away the armor and the sword, he went out the gate to look, but the white-bearded old man was gone. The boy and the girl were there, both most adorable, one about three years old and the other about four. When asked where they were from, they answered, "Our mother, Princess of Rosy Clouds, told us to find Mr. Zheng, our father." When pressed further, neither could come up with anything more.

Squire Zhang thought, "Zheng Xin never came out of the well. How can he have children? Could it be someone of the same name?" Then he recalled his dream at the temple on Mount Tai, according to which the man was clearly destined to be a fifth-grade duke. Unable to come to a definite conclusion, he kept the children and took good care of them. At the same time, he made inquiries about what had happened to Zheng Xin.

Time flew like an arrow. The children grew apace. Squire Zhang treated them as his own children and named the boy Zheng Wu and the girl Cainiang. His own son, of a similar age, was called Zhang Wen. Wu and Wen were like twins and studied at the same school. Cainiang kept to her own room, learning needlework. Another few years went by without any news of Zheng Xin.

One day, when Squire Zhang was stepping out of the hall, the gatekeeper approached to announce, "An official sent by the regional commander of Dong-chuan and Xichuang has asked his way here, bearing a note with your name and address on it. He is on his way to present a memorial to the emperor, and he wants to see you."

Wondering who this could be, Squire Zhang instructed to have the man brought in. Behold:

> He wore a braided coir hat,
> A pair of white-soled black boots,
> A Shu [Sichuan] brocade narrow-sleeved jacket,
> And a pure silver-iron belt around his waist.
> His physique was awe-inspiring,
> But his face showed exhaustion from the journey.
> He had an attendant with him,
> Leading a big horse, following behind.

Squire Zhang went down the steps to greet the official. After an exchange of greetings, the official took out a gift package and a letter, saying, "These are from Mr. Zheng, the regional commander."

Upon opening the letter, Squire Zhang recognized Zheng Xin's handwriting. The letter said,

> I am profoundly grateful to you, my benefactor, for your kindness to me and for having taken such good care of me while I was in prison. When I was let down into the ancient well, I thought I was meeting my end. As it turned out, I encountered the Fairy of Rosy Clouds. After three years of blissful marriage, she provided me with funds and saw me off on my way to Fenzhou to join the army. As a result of my meritorious service in battle after battle, I have now been appointed to be regional commander of the Shu region. I apologize for not having written to you before, but now that a messenger is traveling to the capital to present a memorial to the emperor, I have asked him to bring to you thirty taels of gold and ten bolts of Shu brocade as a small token of my gratitude. If you do not fear the hardships of a journey to the Shu

region and would deign to pay me a visit, I would consider it my greatest fortune and would eagerly look forward to it.

Clapping a hand over his forehead in joy, Squire Zhang said, "Mr. Zheng has indeed made his mark in the world! And, not forgetting his old friend, he sends me gifts from afar. He is truly a man of honor!" After he told the messenger about his dream, the messenger was also amazed. Later that day, he treated the messenger to a feast. Even though he was a military officer of exalted status, the messenger bore instructions from the regional commander to bring Squire Zhang to the Shu region and was therefore all humility. Squire Zhang kept him in the residence and treated him to fine meals every day, but let us digress no more.

After about ten days, the messenger finished his official business and urged the squire to be on his way. Squire Zhang consulted his wife about whether to return the children to Regional Commander Zheng or not. But, because it would be awkward to bring a girl along on the journey, he took only Zheng Wu, leaving the girl at home. With luggage plus four servants and the messenger, the seven-horse procession left the capital and set out for Jianmen.

After several days, they arrived at the regional commander's yamen. The messenger went in first to report. Immediately, Zheng Xin instructed that the company be brought into his private quarters, where he exchanged greetings with the squire as servants would do. The squire had Zheng Wu greet his father before telling Zheng Xin about how a white-bearded old man had brought the children to him, along with the armor and the sword. He then went on to describe his two strange dreams. Recalling his marriage with the Fairy of Rosy Clouds, Zheng Xin was overcome with grief. It had been exactly twelve years since they parted, and the children were now twelve years older. What the fairy had said before they parted had been borne out. A grand feast was laid out, with Squire Zhang as the guest of honor. During the feast, Zheng Xin betrothed his daughter, Cainiang, to the squire's son, Zhang Wen, and the two men addressed each other as in-laws. It was an act of returning kindness with kindness.

Cherishing the memory of the Fairy of Rosy Clouds, Zheng Xin built a magnificent Rosy Clouds Hall on the bank of the Jin River and made annual visits there to offer incense.

After staying for more than three months with Zheng Xin, Squire Zhang missed his own home. Thinking it would be presumptuous of him to keep the squire any longer, Zheng Xin engaged horses and chariots for him and rode with him as far as a wayside pavilion ten li out of the city. The lavishness of the gifts goes without saying. He also provided the squire with a hundred taels of gold to donate to the temple on Mount Tai for the building of a hall dedicated to the God Bingling. Later, when Wuzhu of Jin invaded the empire, the emperor recruited soldiers from all across the land.[9] Zheng Xin led his son, Zheng Wu, in inflicting one defeat after another on the Jurchen troops. Thereafter, when he went to Bianjing for a reunion with Zhang Junqing, he got to know his son-in-law Zhang Wen and his daughter Cainiang.

Zheng Xin lived into his fifties. One day, he saw in broad daylight the chariot of the Fairy of Rosy Clouds, there to take him back, and he died in peace, without any illnesses. His son, Zheng Wu, thanks to his father's position, rose to be a pacification commissioner. To repel the Jurchen troops that kept invading the empire, divine-arm bows were reproduced throughout the counties and prefectures and took many enemy lives. After Emperors Huizong and Qinzong were captured and taken to the north, the Prince of Kang was crossing the river, pursued by Jurchen troops, when suddenly a golden-armored god appeared in midair.[10] Leading a group of celestial soldiers, the god shot at the Jurchens with his divine-arm bow until the Jurchens retreated. Noticing the character "Zheng" on the god's banner, the Prince of Kang asked the court ministers with him who he was. One minister replied, "Zheng Xin, former regional commander of Dongchuan and Xichuan, offered to the army his divine-arm, enemy-vanquishing bow. That must have been him, now a god, to protect you, Your Highness." After assuming the throne, the Prince of Kang, now emperor, granted Zheng Xin the posthumous title of the Prince of Bright Spirit and Manifest Benevolence and erected by the riverside a temple dedicated to him. The temple stands to this day. As the poem says,

> Before Zheng Xin made his mark in the world,
> Squire Zhang had learned about his future in a dream.
> One's destined hour will come, no matter what;
> Complain not about the timing, early or late.

Scholar Huang Is Blessed with Divine Aid through His Jade-Horse Pendant

In a dustless room with clean tables and bright windows,
He keeps company with books all day long.
By chance, the subject of romance came up in a chat;
Romantic affairs lead too many people astray.

As the story goes, during the Qianfu reign period [874–79] of the Tang dynasty, there lived in Yangzhou a scholar named Huang Sun, courtesy name Yizhi. At twenty-one years of age, he was of prepossessing exterior with erudite learning and outstanding literary talent to match, and his peers looked up to him as a fine scholar. He was from an illustrious family that had rendered the empire distinguished service. However, his parents having passed away early, family circumstances were not what they used to be. His father had left him a piece of precious white jade carved into the shape of a horse. Called the jade-horse pendant, it had a soft luster and was smooth and exquisitely carved. Its small size notwithstanding, it was second to none in value. Scholar Huang Sun had cherished it ever since he was a child and wore it at all times of the day without ever parting with it for the briefest moment. (*If love for a jade-horse pendant is requited, how much more so would love for people of talent be?*) One day, when taking a stroll in the marketplace, he saw an old man. How did the old man look?

He had on a bamboo hat, a patchwork robe,
A yellow silk waistband, and a fan in his hand.
With his ruddy complexion and white hair,
And square pupils in his green eyes,
He was either an immortal from Penglai,[1]
Or a Daoist priest of high esteem.

At the sight of Huang Sun, the old man gave a slight smile. His quaintly graceful air inspired such respect in Huang Sun that the young man invited him to a teahouse for a chat over a cup of tea. The old man's talk about the maxims of neo-Confucian philosophy and the wonderful essence of mystical Daoism filled Huang Sun with admiration. In the excitement of the conversation, Huang Sun happened to raise his arm. Catching sight of the jade-horse pendant, the old man asked, "May I have a look at it?" Mr. Huang immediately took it down and gave it to the old man with both hands.

While examining it closely, the old man praised it profusely and asked, "How much is this pendant worth? Would you let me buy it?"

"This is a family heirloom. If you like it, I'll just give it to you as a gift. Don't pay me." (*Such a generous person well deserves an encounter with a supernatural being.*)

"If you are so generous, I wouldn't presume to reject the offer. I will return this kindness some day." So saying, he attached the pendant to his yellow waistband, waved a hand in bidding Huang Sun farewell, and went off with the speed of wind. Agape with astonishment, Huang Sun thought, "He must be a supernatural being. I should have asked his name." But we will not pursue this thread of the story for the moment.

Now, there was a Liu Shoudao, regional commander of the Jingzhou-Xiangyang region, who, out of admiration for Huang Sun the renowned scholar, wrote a letter in his own hand, asking Huang to be his aide, and dispatched a messenger to deliver the letter, along with a gift of some silver. What was an aide supposed to do? Well, an aide was someone whom the commander would consult on all military and civilian matters within his jurisdiction and someone who would draft all the reports and correspondence of the office. Only able and wise men qualified for the job. The post carried with it good emolument and a great deal of respect. An aide could also be called a secretary or administrative assistant for someone with prior experience in another official post.

Scholar Huang Sun, being as poor as he was, readily accepted Regional Commander Liu's kind offer. He wrote a reply in which he also notified the regional commander of the date he would be reporting for duty in Jingzhou, and gave it to the messenger. After the messenger was gone, he packed, bade farewell to his relatives and friends, and set out on his journey by boat.

Upon reaching Jiangzhou, he saw moored by the shore an exceptionally large boat with exquisite windows, trim vermilion railings, and oilcloth curtains. Scholar Huang thought, "If I could get into that boat, I wouldn't have to worry about rough waves." It just so happened that a boatman left that boat to go ashore to buy wine. Scholar Huang followed him and asked, "Where is the boat from? Where is it heading?"

The boatman replied, "My client is a Mr. Han from Huizhou, on his way to the Shu region to visit a friend."

"You will need to take the Jing River to go there, and I'm on my way to Jingzhou. Would you take me on board?"

"The boat is large enough to accommodate you, but Mr. Han has his family in the boat. I don't know if he'd be willing to take you."

Scholar Huang produced three hundred copper coins for him to buy wine with and asked him to put the question to Mr. Han. The boatman replied, "Wait here for just one moment, sir. I will go ask for Mr. Han's permission. If he says yes, I'll come back to bring you on board."

Upon the boatman's return from the wineshop a few moments later, Scholar Huang reminded him of his request. The boatman gave his promise. Before long, he beckoned to Scholar Huang from the boat. With alacrity, Scholar Huang boarded. The boatman said, "The master has the greatest respect for scholars. He didn't refuse when he heard that it's a scholar traveling alone. But the front cabin is filled with goods. You can only sit at the stem and sleep in the back cabin at night. The master and his family are in the middle cabin. Be careful. Don't disturb them." With that, he led Scholar Huang to greet Mr. Han. In their conversation, Mr. Han was quite impressed by the young man. That evening, Scholar Huang sat for a while in the back cabin. Just as he was removing his clothes in preparation for bed, the mournful notes of a zither from the middle cabin fell upon his ears. He put his clothes back on and sat up to listen.

> *Now majestic, now gentle,*
> *Now deep-toned, now floating,*
> *Now like geese crying in the sky,*
> *Now like cranes singing in the wilderness.*
> *Now like a clear stream flowing to a ravine,*
> *Now like wild raindrops beating on the window,*
> *Now it was "Song to Consort Ming" of the Han Palace;*
> *Now it was "Rain on Bells," a new tune of the Tang.*

In those times in the Tang dynasty, the best *pipa* player was Kang Kunlun, and the best zither player, Hao Shansu. Xue Qiongqiong, a courtesan in Yangzhou, was the only one who had fully acquired Hao Shansu's techniques, and Qiongqiong was on the best of terms with Scholar Huang. When Emperor Xizong [r. 874–88] recruited women musicians from all over the land, the prefect of Yangzhou selected Qiongqiong. Scholar Huang missed her so sorely that he stopped listening to zither music because it pained his heart. Now, this zither player sounded so much like Qiongqiong that he marveled inwardly. In the still of the night, with everyone else in the boat asleep, Scholar Huang pushed open the window and took a peek. He saw a young girl in her early teens. In apricot-pink soft silk clothes, her hair half let down, she was a ravishing beauty. She added fragrant oil to the lamp, lit the incense burner, and began to play her zither again with her slender fingers. After she finished, the lamp dimmed, the incense burned out, and the air was as still as before. As if in a trance, Scholar Huang felt that he was in the presence of a divine maiden to whom the likes of Xue Qiongqiong could hardly compare. As he tossed and turned in his cabin without a wink of sleep, he intoned a short lyric:

I have no other wish from life
Than to be a zither playing music,
To stay near the beauty's slender fingers,
To make sweet notes on her silk skirt.
That wish fulfilled, I can die in glory. (Good poem.)

After a sleepless night, he got up at the long-awaited daybreak and wrote that lyric on a piece of floral stationery. He then added "Huang Sun of Weiyang [Yangzhou]," folded the paper in the shape of two overlapping diamonds, and hid it in his sleeve. After combing his hair and washing, he cast frequent glances at the middle cabin, but there was nothing astir. Before long, Mr. Han came to the back cabin to pay him a return visit and invited him for tea in the front cabin. Facing Mr. Han but thinking of the girl, Scholar Huang felt bad for giving irrelevant answers to questions Mr. Han directed at him, but Mr. Han was not aware of anything amiss.

Suddenly, Scholar Huang heard the clicking of a golden basin in the middle cabin. Guessing that the girl must be washing her face and rinsing her mouth, he quickly rose and went along the side of the boat to take a peek at the middle cabin through the window lattice. He was not able to get a clear view of her, but the perfume she wore assailed his nostrils, sending him into raptures. Melting with desire, he hurriedly retrieved his poem from his sleeve and tossed it through the lattice into the cabin. Afraid of being seen, he moved away from the window to stand off to one side but kept his eyes glued on the window.

Upon finishing her toilette, the girl suddenly heard a rustling sound at the window. She picked up the folded piece of stationery and opened it, only to see a short lyric. After reading it with admiration, she folded the paper back as before and hid it in the brocade purse attached to her skirt sash, knowing very well that it was the work of the scholar traveling with them after he had heard her play last night. Pleased with the sentiment as well as the words, she wondered if his looks matched his talent, whereupon she opened the window slightly and looked out. There he was, standing very still all by himself, as if lost in thought. He was so strikingly handsome that even Pan An or Wei Jie did not measure up to him.[2] She thought, "Having grown up in a merchant's family, I think it would be a disgrace if I married another merchant. If I could marry this man, what more would I want from life?" She wanted to take another look but, wary of the many eyes and ears in the boat, she felt obliged to close the window. Scholar Huang also withdrew. But upon returning to the back cabin, his longing grew more acute. The boat being still in its mooring place, Scholar Huang took one trip after another to and from the shore, each time passing the window on his way. Each time she heard footsteps outside the window, the girl opened it to show her face. Their eyes conveyed their love, but they were not at liberty to talk. Truly,

Both had a great deal on their minds;
Neither could openly speak out.

In the afternoon, an acquaintance in a neighboring boat invited Mr. Han to a restaurant on the shore. In his absence, the boatmen began to put the sail and the oars in order in preparation for getting under way early the next morning. While Scholar Huang was staring at the window, the girl pushed it open for a look outside and whom did she see but the young man abruptly stepping back abashedly, as if to dodge her! A moment later, she beckoned to him with her hand. In a burst of joy, Scholar Huang approached the window. Leaning against the sill, the girl said in a subdued voice, "Don't go to sleep tonight until I come to talk to you." (*She could hardly contain herself in her admiration for his talent and his looks.*) Before Scholar Huang had a chance to open his mouth, the girl had closed the window and disappeared from view. Wild with joy, Scholar Huang wished he could knock down the sun with one swing of his fist and spread the Monkey King's sleep bugs[3] all over the boat so that everyone would fall fast asleep, giving the two of them the chance to talk to their hearts' content. Indeed,

> Those not in love do not find the night too short;
> Those awaiting a tryst fret that the day is too long.

Mr. Han did not return until evening. In an inebriated state, he went to bed as soon as he reached his cabin. When night was well advanced and all the boatmen had gone to sleep, Huang Sun's ears caught the faint sound of three gentle taps of a finger against the partition wall. With alacrity he straightened his hat and rose to look. In the soft light of the new moon, against a gentle breeze, the girl was standing against the door that stood ajar. Scholar Huang went to the side of the boat and bowed. As soon as the girl returned the greeting, he moved toward her, ready to step into the cabin. But the girl did not let him. She said, "Out of admiration for your talent, I just wanted to have a heart-to-heart talk with you. Please don't push me too hard."

Not daring to make an undue move, Scholar Huang sat down at the window.

"Where are you from?" asked the girl. "Are you married?"

"I'm from Yangzhou. Having passed the exams at the local level, I'm a *xiucai*. I'm poor and unmarried."

"My mother was also a native of Yangzhou. Her maiden name was Pei. My father is from Huizhou, but he's been living in this boat in Shu. He took my mother on as a concubine on a trip to Yangzhou. I am their only child. My mother passed away when I was twelve. Having finished observing the three years of mourning, my father is taking me back to Shu."

"So you and I are fellow natives of the same town. How can we not feel drawn to each other? Please tell me your name, so that I can wear it on my heart."

"My name is Yu'e. My mother started teaching me to read and write when I was small, so I am quite literate. The poem you wrote is so beautiful and original. What fine sentiments you have! If you and I could be a loving married couple like Liang Hong and Meng Guang, I would have nothing more to wish for."[4]

"Since you are so inclined, I am not a piece of unfeeling wood or rock either. I will do my utmost to bring about our marriage. If I fail, I will never marry, so as to requite your kindness."

"Out of admiration for your talent, I shamelessly acted as my own matchmaker. If you gain wealth and position, please do not abandon me."

"In return for your kindness, I vow to the gods of the river that if I betray you, heaven and earth will not forgive me. But you are your father's beloved daughter and I am but a poor scholar who happens to be traveling with you. Your father may not agree even if we go through the proper channels and approach him through a matchmaker. After the boat sets sail and we take leave of each other, when will we ever meet again? Do you have any wonderful plans that can help me fulfill my vow?"

"We've been talking for too long. It's getting late. My father is very strict. He may wake up from his wine-induced sleep any time now. I don't have the time to say all I want to say. My father and I will surely have arrived in Fuzhou [present-day Fuling in Sichuan] in three months' time. On the third day of every tenth month, the river god's birthday, my father always goes to the ceremony to make sacrificial offerings. All the boatmen go with him. If you come to this boat on that day to see me, we can settle on a plan for us to marry. Please be sure to come. Don't make me wear my eyes out watching for you."

"I will definitely keep the appointment," promised Huang. Having said that, he reached out for the girl's arm. At that point, Mr. Han woke up and called out for tea. The girl quickly closed the window. Reluctantly, Scholar Huang went to his cabin to retire for the night, struck by a sense of loss. From that point on, he would see the girl every time he closed his eyes and could not get her off his mind even for the briefest moment, but the girl did not open the window to see him again. (*Quite a challenge not to open the window.*) The boat traveled for more than a month before reaching the Jing River. Eager to press on while the wind was favorable, the boatmen urged Scholar Huang to go ashore. However reluctant he was, he could hardly refuse. After paying the boatmen a tip, he took leave of Mr. Han and went ashore with his luggage. As he stood gazing at the middle cabin, on the verge of tears, the girl opened the window ever so slightly and saw him off with her eyes. All too soon, the boat set sail as if on wings. Scholar Huang stood there for the longest time, staring in the direction of the boat. Tears fell from his eyes when the boat disappeared from view. When passersby asked him why he was in such distress, he could not get a word out through his sobs. Indeed,

> *Of all the troubles that prey on one's mind,*
> *Only a fraction can be told.*

Scholar Huang remained standing in stupefaction on the shore until dusk fell. Finally, he went in resignation to an inn. The next morning, he asked his way to the regional commander's office and submitted his name card. Regional Commander Liu readily received him and told the young man how he admired his talent. At the feast that day in his honor, Scholar Huang missed Yu'e so much that he could hardly swallow anything. Judging by his distracted look, Mr. Liu believed there must have been something on his mind, but when he asked over and over again what was bothering him, Scholar Huang said only, his eyes awash in tears, "I haven't recovered from an illness I contracted during the journey." Mr. Liu consoled him with kind words. In the evening, Mr. Liu personally took him into the lavishly furnished study designated for his use. His heart being elsewhere, he remained in low spirits.

Several days later, afraid of missing the appointment Yu'e had made with him, he asked for permission to go to a neighboring prefecture to visit a friend, saying he would be back in a little over a month. Mr. Liu said, "I need your advice on pressing military matters. I will grant your request only when I can afford to spare you."

After another few days went by, Scholar Huang spoke up again, but since Mr. Liu did not relent, the young man could not very well insist. And he could hardly leave without authorization, because the compound was locked at night and tightly guarded at all times. He fretted for three days and nights but still could not come up with a good plan.

One day, he asked the page boy of the study, "Is there any place nearby where I can relax?"

"Beyond the wall is the master's garden with gazebos and trees. You can relax there."

Scholar Huang had the page boy lead him from the study into the back garden, where he took a stroll around before asking, "What is there beyond the garden?"

"It's a patrolled street. Patrolmen strike the bamboo clappers during the day and the watch-drums at night. The master has the strictest rules!"

Scholar Huang made a mental note of the information and began to think of a plan. That night, he went to bed without removing his clothes. Sleep just would not come to him. When the fifth watch had finally been struck and all was still, he thought that, since the night watchman must be tired after a whole night's work, this was the best time to go. He climbed up the pomegranate tree by the fence. With one mighty leap, he cleared the white fence wall outside the study. (*This act of leaping down a wall is more interesting than Mr. Zhang's feat.*)[5] Having landed in a large, quiet garden with a hedge of brambles atop its wall, Scholar Huang hit upon an idea. He put a few rocks at the foot of the wall, stepped on the pile of rocks, swept aside the brambles, and climbed over the wall. He was out of the regional commander's residence without anyone being any the wiser. Under cover of the predawn darkness, he tore along as desperate as a dog that had lost its home or a fish slipping through the net. There is a poem in evidence:

> *He had already entered another man's service;*
> *Why did he escape by climbing over a wall?*

Unlike Song Yu, he stole glances through the wall;[6]
Like Xiao He, he gave chase under the moon.[7]

The next morning, the page boy rose early to begin his duties of the day. "How strange!" he exclaimed. "The door and the windows are closed, but Scholar Huang is not in the room!" He rushed to report to Mr. Liu. In astonishment, Mr. Liu went to see for himself. After checking the study, he went into the garden, where he noticed a gap in the brambles atop the wall and deduced that the deceitful scholar had left in a rush. Right away, he had the bamboo clappers struck to announce a session of interrogation. All the patrolmen who were brought to him professed no knowledge of the escape. Mr. Liu gave them a severe scolding. Recalling that Scholar Huang had asked to visit a friend in a neighboring prefecture, he ordered a county-by-county search in Xiangyang, Dengzhou, and other prefectures, but the search turned up nothing. With a sigh, he gave up the effort.

Let us pick up another thread of the story. After leaving the commander's residence and going out the city gate, Scholar Huang ran as fast as his legs could carry him, afraid that he might be pursued. He asked everyone he saw for directions and went toward Fuzhou, traveling by day and resting by night. As the ancients said, "No coincidence, no story." It so happened that he arrived in Fuzhou on the third of the lunar month, the very day of the appointment.

You may wonder how he was able to make it. After all, he had been held up at Commander Liu's residence for many days. Well, Mr. Han's boat was a large and heavy one, and it was going upstream. It sailed when there was a favorable wind and stopped when the wind died down. Scholar Huang, in the meantime, took shortcuts on land and was undaunted by wind or rain. That was why he made it. As he searched for Mr. Han's boat along the shore, he saw only rows upon rows of tall masts and large boats moored one against another like so many fish scales, but Mr. Han's boat was not among them. He was mortified. "I must have missed it in my haste," he thought. "Let me go back and check again." He was about to turn back when he saw, ahead of him within a stone's throw, a single boat moored by several withered willows against the shore. He walked up for a closer look but saw no one on the boat except a girl in the cabin, leaning against the window all alone, as if waiting for someone. She was none other than Yu'e. Afraid that she might not be able to meet Mr. Huang on the appointed day with so many eyes and ears all around them, she had suggested to her father that the boat be moored in that quiet and charming spot under the willow trees. In his love for his daughter, Mr. Han indulged in every wish of hers. Scholar Huang's heart leaped for joy.

It was not yet time for wedding;
But joyfully old friends met in alien land.

Yu'e also saw Scholar Huang. Her face broke into a radiant smile. As the boat was some distance from the shore, Scholar Huang was about to jump when Yu'e stopped him, saying, "The water is rapid. You must hold on to the rope as you come over." Following her advice, he reached out for the rope. As something was destined to happen, the wind and the waves had slackened the rope tied to a willow tree stump. As soon as Scholar Huang laid his hand on the rope, the tie came loose. Won't you agree that surging waves would lend a large boat immense power? Being a scholar, Huang Sun was not a man of muscle. How would he be able to hold the rope in place with one hand? In less time than it takes to narrate, as Huang Sun let out a cry, the boat went downstream with the speed of lightning. Now seen, now hidden, it covered many li in the twinkling of an eye. Scholar Huang cried out at the top of his lungs as he ran along the shore.

The boatmen nearby had gone to the temple of the river god for the ceremony. The boatmen of the few boats that passed by were too preoccupied with their own safety to concern themselves with other people, because the section of the Yangzi River at Fuzhou, being near the Chuanjiang section of the river, was different from its lower sections. The rapid currents of the Three Gorges of Qutang poured into it as if from the sky. Scholar Huang ran frantically for about twenty li until the boat vanished from view at a wide bend of the river. He walked for another twenty li or so, but, believing he did not stand a chance of finding her, he wanted to go back and report to Mr. Han. However, afraid of bringing trouble on himself ([Illegible.]), he gave way to his grief and, facing the river, cried with abandon. He was all alone in this whole wide world now and too ashamed to face Mr. Liu. With so little money on him, he thought himself a man without a home or country to call his own. "I'd better throw myself into the river," he said to himself. "I may get to meet her soul. At least she'll know that I am not a heartless sort. Oh well, so be it!"

> Death befalls every mortal being,
> Leaving behind stories of romance.

Scholar Huang was about to throw himself into the river when someone behind him shouted, "No! No!" Scholar Huang turned to look and saw that it was none other than the old man who had obtained the jade-horse pendant from him at a marketplace in Yangzhou. Feeling a surge of shame and bitter mortification, Scholar Huang dissolved in tears.

"What grieves you so?" asked the old man. "Tell this old man. I maybe able to offer some help."

"Things having come to this pass, I have to tell you." After he gave a detailed account about the appointment by the Fu River and the boat slipping away after the rope came loose, the old man gave a guffaw. "So, that's what happened. Why lose a life over such a trivial thing?"

"You are not an involved party, sir. You think this is a trivial thing. But to me, it is much more momentous than the sky and the earth."

Counting on his fingers, the old man said, "I am a pretty good fortune-teller. Having counted the years, I assure you that she is not destined to die at this time.

You will get to see her. About one li from here, you'll see a thatched hut. It belongs to a fellow Buddhist. You can stay there for the night and tell him your situation. He will certainly help you. But I won't be able to take you there."

"If you don't go, he may not believe me and may not let me stay."

"I have on me the jade-horse pendant that you kindly gave me. My friend has often seen it. You can take it with you to prove who you are." So saying, he took the pendant down from his yellow silk waistband and handed it to Scholar Huang. As soon as the pendant was in Huang Sun's hands, the old man took himself off in light, airy steps. Preoccupied with his worries, Scholar Huang again forgot to ask the old man's name. Regret was too late now.

As the hour was late, Scholar Huang went ahead. About one li later, sure enough, he saw in the wilderness a lonely thatched hut, with its door standing ajar. He slipped in. In the Buddhist shrine was a colored glaze lamp that made a dim, flickering light in the room. An elderly foreign-looking monk, the very image of the statue of an arhat of the West, was sitting in a lotus position on a prayer mat in the middle of the room. His eyes tightly closed, he looked as if he were in meditation. Not daring to disturb him, Mr. Huang dropped to his knees in front of the monk. After about two hours, the foreign monk opened his eyes and, seeing the young man, said harshly, "Who is this layman, intruding on my meditation like this?"

With a deep bow, Scholar Huang presented him with the jade-horse pendant and relayed greetings from the old man, adding, "May I stay here tonight?"

"One night is not a problem. But with so many uncertainties on the roads lying ahead in this mortal world, where will your journey lead?"

"I, Huang Sun, do have one wish. I need your guidance, Your Holiness." He gave an account of his appointment with Yu'e, kowtowed, and asked for guidance.

"I am a monk. My heart is as dead as ashes. I am not one to offer advice about matters relating to romance."

At Scholar Huang's desperate pleas for help, the monk said, "You do have enough earnestness to move the gods. But, to me, you look like someone destined to be a highly-placed official. The guiding principle for a man of worth is to succeed in his career to bring honor to his ancestors and glory to his name. What you wish for is to be realized only after you attain fame."

Prostrating himself again, Scholar Huang said, "I have no one to turn to for help, nor do I have enough to live on. How could I entertain any ambition for fame and success? Had that old gentleman not saved me, I would have already been a ghost in the river."

"Under the pedestal of the statue of the Buddha, there are ten taels of silver that you can use for your travel expenses. You may go to Chang'an first. When the destined moment comes, your wish will be fulfilled." Having said that, he closed his eyes and went back into meditation.

Succumbing to drowsiness, Scholar Huang pillowed his head on his arm by the side of the prayer mat and dozed off. It was dawn when he woke up. What should he see all around him but the remains of a dilapidated temple! There were no walls, nor the slightest trace of a meditating foreign monk. The statue of the Buddha was also in a sorry condition. But sticking out from under the pedestal of the statue was a large shiny ingot of silver on which were chiseled two characters: "Huang Sun." "My goodness!" exclaimed Scholar Huang, now realizing that he had met a holy monk the previous night. After praying in prostration at the foot of the Buddha's statue, he set off for Chang'an, with enough silver to pay for his travel expenses. Truly, humans may violate divine will, but heaven always leaves a door open for humans.

> Nothing is determined by human plots;
> Everything is arranged by destiny.

Let us retrace our steps and come back to the moment when Mr. Han and his boatmen returned from the festivities. Failing to find his boat, Mr. Han anxiously asked around. Those who had witnessed what happened from their boats said, "The rope broke. The boat was washed away by the current. We were not able to do anything about it."

Mr. Han was appalled. He searched all along the shore but heard the same story from witnesses. After two or three days went by without any news, he set off for home, crying his heart out, but of this, no more.

Now let us turn our attention to Courtesan Xue Qiongqiong of Yangzhou. The procuress, Madam Xue, had offered her up to the imperial court two years earlier on account of her skill as a zither player. Since business was slow after the girl was gone, Madam Xue rented a boat to go to Chang'an to visit her and to ask for favors from the emperor. When she was at the Han River, she saw a capsized boat rushing downstream toward her boat. It being too late for her to dodge, the boat slammed into the stem of hers and stopped. Thinking there must be money and goods in the capsized boat, the boatmen led it to shore and cut it open with an ax, only to see a young woman inside. Upon hearing this, Madam Xue immediately told them to bring her out. The young woman was already on the verge of death.

In fact, anyone fallen into such cold water on a wintry day would have died. But, because she was in the covered middle cabin and the bottom of the boat had kept the warmth from leaking out, she was still breathing. Everything in the boat had floated away. Whatever objects remained were picked up by the boatmen and shared among them.

Madam Xue had been hoping for a substitute for Xue Qiongqiong. Delighted upon seeing such a pretty girl, she quickly took off her wet clothes, put her under a cotton quilt, and hugged the girl to warm her. (*Madam Xue's intentions are all too clear. If Yu'e had no higher aspirations, she would have become another Qiongqiong.*) Having thus gained some warmth, the girl slowly came to. Then Madam Xue gently fed her ginger soup and porridge and comforted her with kind words. The girl gradually regained speech and asked for her brocade bag that was hidden in her wet clothes. When asked who she was, she replied, "I am Han Yu'e. I was with my father on our way to the Shu region. When we reached Fuzhou, my father and the boatmen went to join festivities to worship the river god. I was alone in the boat. The rope tying the boat to shore came loose, and I was carried away by the water."

"Are you betrothed?"

"Yes, to Scholar Huang Sun of Yangzhou. What I have in my brocade bag is a poem that he wrote for me."

"Scholar Huang is my daughter Qiongqiong's friend. With his talent and good looks, he's the very man for you. Don't worry. Go with me to Chang'an. Scholar Huang will surely be in Chang'an for next year's exams. By that time, I'll find him and marry you to him. Won't that be wonderful?"

"If that works out, you will be the mother of my rebirth."

There and then, Yu'e honored Madam Xue as her godmother. Madam Xue also treated the girl as her own daughter. Indeed,

> She followed the madam in a desperate moment,
> And she was treated as her kith and kin.

After a few days, they arrived in Chang'an. Madam Xue rented a small house for Yu'e and herself. At the time, Qiongqiong was very much in the good graces of the emperor. After she heard that the one she called mother was in town, she sent messengers to her with gifts every so often, but she could not very well ask for permission to see her. As for Yu'e, she spent her time behind closed doors, doing needlework as before, to help out with the daily expenses. So Madam Xue had more than enough to live on. Time sped by like an arrow. Before anyone knew it, the year came to an end and spring rolled around, as evidenced by the following poem:

> The year ends amid the noise of firecrackers;
> Spring breezes warm up New Year's tusu wine.
> On every door on the bright sunny day,
> New peachwood charms are put up to replace the old.

On New Year's eve, Yu'e shed furtive tears as she kept thinking about her misery, with her mother dead, her father separated from her, and her lover's whereabouts unknown. In bed that night, she saw in a dream the gate to heaven opening wide and an arhat appearing in midair. She prostrated herself on the ground and poured out her heart to the arhat, who then tossed a scroll of yellow paper to the ground. On the scroll was written "Good news from Huang Sun of Yangzhou." In delight, Yu'e was about to open it to read the contents when a deafening thunderbolt woke her up. It was in fact the firecrackers set off by a neighbor upon opening the door for the first time on New Year's Day. Yu'e gave herself up to thought, feeling dejected. It being New Year's Day, she forced herself to rise and do her toilette. Madam Xue having gone to pay New Year's calls on neighbors, she let down the bamboo door curtain and watched the pedestrians on the street, thinking, "This is an examination year. I wonder if Mr. Huang has come to Chang'an. If he passes by and sees me, that will bear out the dream I had last night and I won't have survived my brush with death for nothing." She had just started on this train of thought when a foreign-looking monk appeared outside the bamboo curtain and cried at the top of his voice, "Donations from those with predestined bond with the Buddhist order!"

Taking a closer look from behind the curtain, Yu'e found him to be the very arhat she had seen in her dream. A wave of awe surged through her. Being a young woman alone in the house, she could not very well invite him in. While she was debating with herself, the monk raised the bamboo curtain and came in. Yu'e took a few steps back to stand off to one side. The monk went to the middle of the room and sat down in a lotus position, with shafts of light illuminating his forehead. Flabbergasted, Yu'e dropped to her knees. With one bow after another, she said, "Your disciple has fallen into an abyss of suffering. I have a wish that remains unfulfilled. Please point out the direction for me, arhat, and deliver me from misery."

"You do have a sincere wish to join the Buddhist order, but your bond with the mortal world is not yet over. Let me give you an object. Keep it hidden on you. Do not breathe a word about it to anyone. When you reunite with your husband, you will see what wonders it will work." So saying, he took out a precious object and gave it to Yu'e. It was none other than the jade-horse pendant. As soon as Yu'e took it, the monk vanished in a ray of golden light that soared into the sky. Realizing that it was a manifestation of the holy monk, she bowed gratefully toward the sky before tying the pendant tightly to her waistband. After Madam Xue returned, Yu'e said nothing about what had happened.

> She had no one with whom to share what weighed on her mind;
> She lit incense in her mind to thank the holy monk.

In the meantime, equipped with the monk's gift of money, Scholar Huang traveled to Chang'an to sit for the civil service examinations. However, once there, instead of reviewing the classics and the histories and conserving his energy, he missed Yu'e so much that he spent his days walking up and down the streets and lanes, hoping to meet the holy monk again. He left his lodging early in the morning and returned late in the evening, looking woebegone and glum all day long. On the day of the examinations, he felt obliged to go to the examination grounds in observance of the rules. There, he flourished his brush-pen without even thinking about what he wrote. In no mood to weigh his diction with care, he meant only to muddle through. The fact of the matter is that it is precisely those trying to muddle through who get to pass the examinations. Truly,

> Wish not that your essay would outshine all others;
> Wish only that your essay would please the grader.

When the results of the examinations were posted, Huang Sun's name appeared high on the list of successful candidates. He was assigned to be director of a bureau.

At that time, Lü Yongzhi was abusing power, employing despicable scoundrels to poison people's minds with heresies, and incurring resentment domestically and from abroad. However, nobody dared to speak up against him out of fear for his power and influence. Huang Sun was the only one who wrote to the emperor a memorial that exposed Lü's evil deeds, citing well-substantiated evidence in support of each charge. The Son of Heaven gave credence to Huang Sun and dismissed Lü Yongzhi from office. Having won high honors on the examinations and written this memorial that brought the greatest joy to people throughout the land, Huang Sun became a celebrity. None did not admire him. Members of the royal clan in Chang'an, learning that he was yet unbetrothed, begged matchmakers to approach him with marriage proposals. True to his vow of loyalty to Yu'e, he rejected all offers. Madam Xue, having heard about Huang Sun's rise to prominence, also had a mind to visit him, but Yu'e stopped her, saying, "Not so fast! As they say, men of high status make many friends; men of great wealth change wives. That's only human nature. Who knows what kind of a man Mr. Huang is, deep down?" (*Because the rich and powerful shower him with marriage proposals, Yu'e wishes to take her time watching what kind of a man he is.*) This says something about her prudence.

Now, to Lü Yongzhi. Spending his days at home working on "inner alchemy," trying to obtain the yin element from women, he sent messengers on a search everywhere for beautiful women to serve him as maids or concubines. When someone recommended to him Madam Xue's adopted daughter, Yu'e, who was strikingly beautiful but rarely showed herself in public, Lü Yongzhi said, "I'm only worried that I can't find what I want. What do I have to fear if what I want is there but hard to get?" Right away he dispatched several tens of servants, who, taking with them five hundred taels of silver as a betrothal gift, barged into Madam Xue's house without even announcing their identity and snatched Yu'e from her bedchamber. Ignoring all protests, they put her into the well-decked-out sedan-chair with padded curtains and dashed off in the direction of the Lü Mansion. Madam Xue cowered in fear, wondering what could have led to this. Later, when she learned that Yu'e had been taken to Lü Yongzhi, she dared not even let out a peep. She thought of complaining to Huang Sun, but, afraid that she might get nothing out of it other than some harsh words of reproach, she felt she would rather swallow the humiliation. But of this, no more for now.

When Yu'e was brought into the Lü residence, Lü Yongzhi himself raised the curtain of the sedan-chair for a look. Beside himself with joy upon seeing her nonpareil beauty, he had maidservants usher her into her bedchamber and let her pick from trunkfuls of fine clothes and fancy jewelry. Yu'e threw the jewelry onto the floor, weeping, and refused to try on even one outfit. At the maidservants' report, Mr. Lü said only, "Don't make things difficult for her. Just talk to her nicely."

Thus instructed, the maidservants talked their heads off, one and all, trying to make her submit, but she turned a deaf ear to them. Indeed,

He wielded power over everything;
She was unmoved by all the finery.
Marriage bonds have always been predestined;
How laughable the arrogant man who schemed in vain!

Mr. Lü's disciples and former subordinates all came to offer their congratulations on his acquisition of a new concubine. As was usual on such occasions, a feast was set out. A little before midnight, when the drinking was still going on, a groom from the manger in the back ran into the hall, panting for breath. He said, "A ten-foot-long white horse from goodness-knows-where just burst into the manger and bit our horses. As I ran after it with a stick, it charged into the inner section of the house."

In alarm, Lü Yongzhi said, "This is unbelievable!" He ordered a few able servants to carry torches and join the groom on a search through all the rooms. When they came back to report to him, not having even so much as smelled the stench of a horse fart, Mr. Lü had a hunch that this was a bad omen, but, refusing to admit it, he scolded the groom for lying, put him to forty strokes of the rod, and dismissed him. The guests dispersed in disappointment. In his wine-induced excitement, Lü Yongzhi went right into the bridal chamber, where Yu'e was weeping. Lü had a way with women. He said, "My wealth is unrivaled. If you submit to me, I will make you my head wife tomorrow. You'll have more money than you can ever spend."

"I may be just a woman, but I have a pretty good idea what honor is. I am betrothed to another man. A good woman does not marry two men. What's more, you have so many women in this house. Why would I make any difference? Please have mercy and let me keep my chastity."

Turning a deaf ear to her pleas, Lü Yongzhi threw himself on her and pinned her down in the bed with all the strength he could muster. As he tried to undress her, she held him off with both hands, cursing him as she did so, but her strength was failing her. At this critical juncture, a ten-foot-long white horse emerged from the bed, pounced on Lü, and bit him left and right. In panic, Lü Yongzhi had to let go of her. (*A human inferior to a horse.*) He ordered the maids to go up to the horse, but it pranced about the room and bit everyone who approached it, inflicting wounds on almost all the maids. Lü Yongzhi fled in terror. As soon as he was out of the room, the white horse also vanished. Knowing now for sure that it was a supernatural being, Lü Yongzhi secretly dispatched servants in every direction in search of a good exorcist.

The next day, a foreign-looking monk came to the gate, saying, "I can read omens from vapors in the air. I see a great deal of evil astir in the air above your residence, so I'm here to exorcise the evil." (*No one has more compassion than a Buddhist.*)

At the gatekeeper's announcement, Lü Yongzhi eagerly invited the exorcist in. After an exchange of greetings, the monk said, "There is a great deal of evil astir in the air above your residence, sir. This forebodes a major disaster."

"Where does the evil air come from?"

"Possibly from one of the rooms. I need to check carefully."

Lü Yongzhi personally led the monk on a search throughout the house. When they were approaching Yu'e's room, the monk said in alarm, "This is the very spot! How is the person in this room related to you, sir?"

"She's my new concubine, but the wedding ceremony hasn't been held."

"Congratulations, sir! How lucky you are to have met this old monk! If the wedding ceremony had been held, you would surely be a dead man! This girl is the spirit of the Lord-on-High's jade horse, here in the mortal world to wreak havoc. Now that she's in your home, if you don't get rid of her as soon as possible, disaster will surely strike."

Impressed by his mention of a jade horse, Lü Yongzhi broke into cheers, calling him a god and said, "What's to be done?"

"Quickly dump her on someone else and let disaster hit that man. You will be off the hook." (*This monk's glib tongue is much more effective than the hard work of Officer Gu and Xu Jun.*)[8]

However lascivious Lü Yongzhi was, he loved life more. How would he not be seized with fear when the situation was presented to him in such graphic terms? He asked again, "To whom should I give her?"

"To your number-one enemy!" replied the monk. "Within one month, that man will be hit by a horrible disaster. You can then sit back and relax, sir."

Huang Sun being the one whose impeachment of him had led to his dismissal from office, he hated Huang Sun more than he hated anyone else. His mind thus made up, he said with a bow, "I thank you for your advice." With that, he instructed servants to prepare a vegetarian dinner for the monk, along with a lavish gift of money. The monk said, "You are the luckiest person under the sun. I'm here expressly to save you. How would I even dream of taking a reward!" Without stopping to partake of the vegetarian dinner, he took off with a flick of his sleeves.

> *All of the monk's nonsense*
> *Was taken as an exorcist's words of wisdom.*

Lü Yongzhi immediately sent servants to bring Madam Xue to him. Madam Xue dared not refuse. Lü Yongzhi said to her, "Your daughter is too young. She knows nothing about decorum. I can't keep her. I heard that Huang Sun, the new *jinshi*, is single. There is bad blood between him and me. So I would like to give him this girl by way of reconciliation. You must escort her there personally, to talk him into taking her."

Madam Xue said with a kowtow, "I would not dare disobey your order!"

"All the things in the trunks and the baskets are her dowry," added Lü Yongzhi. "You can go now to pack and have them carried off. I need not even see your daughter before she goes."

This order could not have suited Madam Xue better. From the main hall she was led into Yu'e's chamber. Believing that Lü Yongzhi had sent Madam Xue to her to talk her into submission, Yu'e felt her heart beginning to pound violently. Whispering into her daughter's ear, Madam Xue said, "Your troubles are over. Mr. Lü doesn't want you anymore and told me to give you to a more romantic one."

"I came to this place, swallowing all the humiliation and hanging on to life only because I hoped to get to see Mr. Huang for a moment. If I'm palmed off on some-one else, wouldn't it be the same as ending up here? I'd rather die than be a piece of duckweed that floats with any wave or a willow catkin that flies with any wind."

"The more romantic one is none other than Mr. Huang. The clothes and jew-elry in the trunks and baskets of the room are all yours now. Let's get out of here quickly before he changes his mind."

"Oh, I see," said Yu'e. Forthwith, mother and daughter hurriedly packed, told the maidservants to convey their thanks to the master, called for porters, and were gone like a puff of smoke.

> *The sea turtle freed itself from the golden hook,*
> *Shook its head, flicked its tail, and vanished for good.*

While Huang Sun was sitting idly in his room in the yamen, the gatekeeper came to announce, "Madam Xue of Yangzhou is here to see you." Eagerly Scholar Huang asked her in. As soon as she laid eyes on him, Madam Xue said, "Congratulations!"

"What is there to congratulate me on?"

"I've been in Chang'an for more than half a year, but I wouldn't presume to disturb you for no good reason. Today I'm here to offer you a bride by order of an eminent official."

"And who is that eminent official, pray?"

"That newly deposed Mr. Lü."

In a rush of anger, Scholar Huang said, "How dare that villain use a woman to trick me! If it were not for old times' sake, I would give you a good lecture!"

"Don't get angry! The bride is none other than my daughter, who is associated with you in some way." (*Getting there step by step. Brilliant.*)

His anger subsiding, he asked with composure, "Your daughter Qiongqiong has long since been serving the emperor in the palace. Who else is there? And how is she associated with me?"

"She is my newly adopted daughter, Han Yu'e."

Scholar Huang gave a violent start. "Where did you meet her?"

Thereupon Madam Xue told him how Yu'e had been rescued at the Han River, adding, "She was recently forcibly seized by Mr. Lü, but she threatened to kill her-self rather than submit to him. I don't know why, but he told me to offer her to you, as a gesture to make it up with you."

Shaking his head, Scholar Huang said, "If that brute seized her, she must have been sullied. Otherwise, why would he let go of her without having had his way with her? And why does he pick me?"

"Just ask my daughter and you'll know."

"Maybe your daughter is not the Han Yu'e of Yangzhou?"

"Here is the little poem from you as proof." From her sleeve she retrieved a piece of paper, which, having been soaked in water, was all crumpled. Reminded of what had happened at Fuzhou, Scholar Huang burst into bitter tears. Straight away he called for a sedan-chair and a few attendants and told them to go with Madam Xue and bring Yu'e over. When they met in the yamen, they fell on each other's shoulders and broke down in tears. After they had their cry, they poured their hearts out to each other. Raising the jade-horse pendant, Yu'e said, "If it were not for this pendant, I would have been sullied by that scoundrel. If so, I would have killed myself and would never have seen you again."

Taken aback at the sight of the pendant, Scholar Huang said, "This is my family heirloom. I gave it to a foreign monk last year in Fuzhou. How did you get it?"

"I had a dream on last New Year's eve. Then on New Year's Day, I met a foreign monk who looked just like the monk I had seen in the dream. He gave me this pendant and said that it would lead to our reunion. I hid it on me. That night, when that scoundrel Lü was forcing himself on me, a white horse suddenly emerged from the bed and tried to bite him. He fled in terror. Later, I heard that a foreign monk told him, 'The white horse is a demon that will bring ruin on you.' That was why he dumped me on you, to shift the disaster onto you."

"So, it's that monk who brought about our reunion. He's really a divine being and this jade-horse pendant is nothing less than a divine object. We should give our thanks in proper ceremony today." He ordered to have an incense altar set out. With the jade pendant placed on the altar, and wine and dried fruit laid out, they got down on their knees and kowtowed. Madam Xue also kowtowed from a position off to one side. Suddenly a ten-foot-long white horse leaped from the altar and rose into midair. They rushed out of the door and saw that on a cloud stood a man whose features were still visible at that distance. Who was he?

> They first met at a Yangzhou marketplace;
> They met again at the Fuzhou ferry.
> Only when he showed himself on a cloud
> Did they learn that he was owner of the jade horse.

He was none other than the old man who had met Huang Sun at a marketplace in Yangzhou at the beginning of our story, the one who had asked for the jade-horse pendant. The old man mounted the white horse and, in a trice, vanished into curling strands of cloud. Recalling how the old man had saved his life by the river, Huang Sun bowed toward the sky again and again. When they checked the altar, they realized that the jade-horse pendant was not there anymore.

That night, Huang Sun and Yu'e became husband and wife. They supported Madam Xue until the end of her life. Huang Sun also sent a messenger to Shu with a letter and brought Mr. Han, Yu'e's father, to the capital to provide for him. Every year Huang Sun had shrines put up for the old man and the foreign monk, burned incense, and paid homage to them. (*We still don't know who the foreign monk and the old man were.*) Later, Huang Sun rose to be assistant imperial inspector. Yu'e gave birth to three sons, who all had successful careers as officials later in their lives. The husband and wife lived together in blissful marriage to a ripe old age. There is a poem in praise of them:

> *The notes of the zither on the river*
> *Joined the soul mates in marriage.*
> *Death, life, parting, and reuniting are all predestined;*
> *Seek not a marriage that is not in your fate.*

Over Fifteen Strings of Cash, a Jest Leads
to Dire Disasters

A smart and clever mind comes with birth;
The benighted state may not be for real.
Jealousy is often caused by a narrow mind;
Wars may arise from light-hearted banter.
Like the Yellow River with its nine bends, the mind is devious;
Under the layers of armor, the face is fearsome.
Wine and lust ruin families and countries;
Poems and books never harm the virtuous.

This poem laments the perils of life. The paths of the world are narrow, and the human heart is hard to fathom. Since the great Dao is not easy to attain, human nature manifests itself in multifarious ways. In swarming multitudes, people go in pursuit of profit and gain. In mindless folly, they land themselves in trouble and disaster. To protect themselves and their families, they need to navigate through the vicissitudes of life. Therefore, the ancients said, "Know when to frown and when to laugh." Indeed, one must exercise the greatest caution as to when to frown and when to laugh.

This story is about a man whose jesting remarks after a bout of drinking led to his own death, the destruction of his family, and the loss of several other lives. But let me begin with a prologue story first.

Back in the Song dynasty, there lived a young scholar, Wei Pengju by name and Chongxiao by courtesy name. He married at eighteen years of age a young lady who was as pretty as a flower and as fair as jade. In less than one year, Scholar Wei packed for his journey to the capital to sit for the spring examinations at the national level and took leave of his wife. Before he departed, his wife said to him, "Come back as soon as possible, whether you win an official post or not. Do not abandon your loving wife."

He replied, "Scholarly honors and official rank are what lie first and foremost in my future. You shouldn't worry." So he set off on his journey and went to the capital. Sure enough, he passed the examinations on the first try and won second place. Enjoying his moment of glory in the capital, he wrote a letter to his wife and sent a servant to bring her over, as was only to be expected. After some necessary words of greeting and the announcement about his eligibility for an official post, the letter went on to say, "There being no one to look after me here, I've gotten myself a second little wife. I await your arrival in the capital to share the wealth and honor with me." (*He is actually sounding her out. This is not entirely said in jest.*)

The servant put the letter in his luggage and went back home. After congratulating the mistress, he presented her with the letter. Upon reading it, she said to the servant, "Your master is such an ingrate! The moment he becomes eligible for an official post, he gets himself a concubine."

The servant said, "I didn't know he had a concubine when I was in the capital. My master must be joking. You will know soon enough when you get there, ma'am. Don't worry about it."

"If so, I'll let the matter drop." However, a boat for the journey was not to be had on such short notice. Therefore, while packing, she looked for someone who happened to be going to the capital to deliver a letter for her to her husband. Once in the capital, the messenger asked his way to the lodgings of Scholar Wei who had just won second place in the examinations, delivered the letter, and was treated to wine and a meal before he went his way. But of this, no more.

Now, Scholar Wei opened the letter, only to see that it contained one simple statement: "While you took a second little wife in the capital, I also got myself a second little husband at home. I will go with him to the capital sooner or later." (*They must be in the habit of teasing each other.*) Dismissing this as a joke, Scholar Wei did not put the letter away immediately. (*Too lazy and careless.*)

At this point, the janitor announced, "You've got a visitor!"

The visitor went straight into Scholar Wei's room and sat down, partly because accommodations at an inn are less spacious than in one's home, partly because he was a good friend who had also just passed the examinations, and partly because he knew Mr. Wei's wife was not with him. After an exchange of amenities, Scholar Wei rose to go to the outhouse. In his absence, his friend read the letter on the table. Amused, he purposely read it aloud upon Wei's return. (*How unkind of him!*) Caught off guard, Wei said, his face flaming red, "She doesn't mean it. I teased her, so she wrote that in retaliation."

The friend said, laughing, "But this is not something to joke about." He said good-bye and took himself off. [(Illegible.)]

Being a young man prone to gossip, that friend quickly spread the story about the letter all around the inns of the capital where the examination candidates were staying. Those who were jealous of Scholar Wei for having won such high honors in such youth put this rumor in a memorial to the emperor (*Rumors mostly do people injustice. A gentleman of moral uprightness should refrain from spreading them.*), claiming that Mr. Wei, in his youthful indiscretion, was fit not for important posts in the imperial court but only for lower positions outside of the capital. Scholar Wei was seized with remorse. Later, he never managed to rise higher. All too frivolously, he had forfeited a bright future. A joke had cost him a career.

Let me move on to our story proper, in which a man, as a result of a jest after a bout of drinking, lost his own life and implicated a few others, who all died unjustly. What was it all about? There is a poem in testimony:

> The rugged roads of life sadden the heart
> While some flippantly joke and laugh.
> A white cloud is innocent and means no harm,
> But wild winds draw it out to wreak havoc.

In the Southern Song dynasty, to the left of Arrow Bridge in Lin'an, the capital [present-day Hangzhou, Zhejiang], which was not any less prosperous and affluent than Bianjing, the former capital [present-day Kaifeng, Henan], there lived a man named Liu Gui, courtesy name Junjian. The Liu family used to be quite well off, but, after Liu Gui took over the family fortune, luck began to run against him. He applied himself to the books at first, but, seeing that he was not making a success of it, he tried his hand at business. Lacking training in this line of profession, like someone who turned Buddhist late in life, he felt even more inadequate. After losing even his capital, he had to sell his house and rent a smaller one with only two or three rooms. He and his wife, Wang-shi, had married young and were a loving couple. Later, because they had no son, Liu Gui took a concubine née Chen, daughter of Chen the cake peddler. They came to call her Second Sister. But this happened before they had fallen on hard times. The three of them were the only occupants of the house. The neighbors liked Liu Junjian for his friendliness. Calling him Master Liu, they said to him, "You are in this sorry condition only because you're not in luck for the time being. Everything will go well after a while." That was easily enough said. What good did it do him? As before, he stayed at home, feeling miserable and at his wits' end.

One day, as he was sitting idly at home, his father-in-law's servant, Old Wang, approaching seventy years of age, came and said to him, "It's the master's birthday. He sent me here to invite you and the mistress over."

Liu said, "I've been so down in the mouth that I forgot it's my father-in-law's birthday today!" He and his wife began to pack a few articles of clothing into a bundle, which they then gave to Old Wang to carry. Turning to Second Sister, Liu said, "Keep good watch over the house. We won't be able to return tonight, but we'll surely be back by tomorrow evening." With that, they set out.

After arriving at Squire Wang's house, more than twenty li from the city, he exchanged greetings with his father-in-law, but, in the presence of the many other guests in the house, he could not very well discuss his wretched circumstances with his father-in-law. After the guests departed, he and his wife were put up for the night in a guest room. At daybreak, his father-in-law came to talk with him. "My son-in-law," he began, "you must not go on like this. As they say, he who sits idle will eat away a mountain of a fortune. He who stands idle will eat his way into a deep hole in the ground. The gullet is as deep as the sea, and the sun and the moon shoot back and forth as fast as shuttles on a loom. You'll have to come up with a long-term plan. My daughter married you in the hope of being well provided for. You can't let things go on like this!"

With a sigh, Master Liu said, "Yes, father-in-law, you're right. But, as they say, it's easier to go up the mountain and catch a tiger than to ask for money. The ways of the world being what they are, who cares about me as you do, sir? I'll just have to put up with the poverty. Begging for help won't get me anywhere."

"I don't blame you for saying that. But this old man can't stomach anymore of this. Let me give you some money so that you can do something like open a general store and make enough money to live on. Wouldn't that be nice?"

"Of course that would be nice," said Master Liu. "Thank you so much for your kindness, sir."

After lunch, Squire Wang took out fifteen strings of cash and, giving them to Master Liu, said, "My son-in-law, take this and open up a store. After preparations for the store are ready, I'll give you another ten strings. Your wife may stay here for a few days. When you've got a date for the store to open, I'll take her to you myself and offer you my congratulations. What do you say?"

With profuse thanks, Master Liu swung the bag of money over his shoulder and went off. After arriving in Lin'an late in the afternoon, he happened to pass the house of an acquaintance who wanted to go into business. So he thought he might as well call on him for a little talk. As he knocked on the door, he heard an answering cry from inside and out came his friend. With a greeting, the man asked, "Is there anything I can do for you?"

When Liu told him about what he had in mind, the man said, "I have nothing to do at present anyway. I'll surely come to help you if you need me."

"That would be good," said Liu.

After they talked about business matters for a while, the man treated Master Liu to what wine and food he had in the house. Without much capacity for wine, Master Liu soon began to feel the effect of the drinks. He rose to go, saying, "Sorry for having imposed on your hospitality. Please come to my house tomorrow morning. We'll talk some more about the business."

The man saw Liu to the street corner, took leave of him, and returned home. So much for this man.

If this storyteller had been born in the same year as Mr. Liu and had grown up with him shoulder to shoulder, I would have held him by the waist and dragged him away by his arms, so that he would not have been struck by such misfortune. But it turned out that Mr. Liu died a death more horrible than that of

*Li Cunxiao, as recorded in History of the Five Dynasties,[1]
And Peng Yue, as recorded in History of the [Western] Han dynasty.[2]*

Carrying the strings of cash on his back, Mr. Liu slowly made his way home. It was already lamp-lighting time when he knocked on his door. Second Sister was home alone, without anything to occupy herself with. In the growing darkness, she had closed the door and dozed off by the lamp. It was some time before she heard Liu's raps on the door. Crying out, "Coming," she rose and opened the door to let him in. She then took the strings of cash from him and, placing them on the table, asked, "Husband, where did you get all this money? And what are you going to do with it?"

In his wine-induced excitement and his resentment at her for having taken so long to open the door, Liu decided to be playful and give her a scare. (*It's all right if he chooses not to explain. He should not go too far with his joke.*)

"You won't like it if I tell you. But if I don't tell you now, you'll have to know later on anyway. It's just that in a moment of desperation, for lack of a better way out, I pawned you off to a man, but only for fifteen strings of cash because I don't want you to be gone for good. If my circumstances improve, I'll redeem you with interest. But if I go on being as poor as I am, I'll just have to forget it."

The young woman found this hard to believe, but the fifteen strings of cash were there to prove his story. She wondered how he could be so heartless. After all, he had never had a harsh word for her before, and she and Mrs. Liu got along perfectly well. Not knowing what to make of it, she spoke up again, "If so, you should have notified my parents."

"If I had notified your parents, they wouldn't have let me go ahead with it. (*This is beginning to look real.*) After you go to that man's house tomorrow, I'll ask someone to talk to your parents in due course. They won't blame me."

"Where were you drinking today?"

"At the house of the man to whom I pawned you, after we signed the papers."

"Why isn't Elder Sister back?"

"She hates to see you go. She'll come back after you're gone tomorrow. I did this because I had no other way out, and I must keep my word." Barely able to suppress a furtive giggle after saying that, he went to bed without removing his clothes and soon fell asleep.

Her mind in turmoil, the young woman thought, "I wonder what kind of man he sold me off to. I must tell my parents first. If the man comes to get me tomorrow, he'll have to go to my parents' house to close the deal." After a few more moments of reflection, she put the fifteen strings of cash in a pile by Mr. Liu's feet and, while he was in a besotted state, she quietly put together a few articles of clothing, slowly opened the door, and went out. After pulling the door closed behind her, she turned left, to the house of Old Zhu San and his wife, neighbors whom she knew well. She asked Mrs. Zhu to put her up for the night, adding, "For no reason at all, my husband sold me today. I must tell my parents about this first. Could you please tell my husband tomorrow to go with the buyer to my parents' house, to talk it all out and close the deal?"

Mrs. Zhu said, "You're right. You go ahead. I'll relay your message to him."

After spending the night there, the young lady took herself off to her parents' home. Of this, no more for now. Truly,

> *The sea turtle freed itself from the golden hook,*
> *Shook its head, flicked its tail, and vanished for good.*

Now, back to Master Liu. Upon waking up at the third watch of the night, he found the lamp on the table still lit but Second Sister no longer there. Believing she was cleaning in the kitchen, he called out for tea. Getting no answer after he called quite a few times, he tried to struggle up, but, not having yet slept off the wine, he dozed off again.

As it turned out, an unsavory character happened to be at Master Liu's door at this time. He was out to steal under the cover of night to make up for the gambling losses he had incurred earlier in the day. Second Sister having only pulled the door to without locking it, the burglar gave it a gentle push, and the door swung open. Unobserved, he tiptoed his way inside. As he drew near the bed, he looked around by the light of the lamp and found nothing worth stealing. Groping his way to the bed, he saw a man sleeping with his face toward the wall. At his feet was a pile of copper coins. As he helped himself to a few strings, the burglar's movements woke up Master Liu. Sitting up, he said severely, "You good-for-nothing! I borrowed these few strings of cash from my father-in-law to make a living with. If you steal them, what am I going to do?"

Without saying a word in reply, the burglar struck Liu right in the face with his fist. (*This scoundrel says nothing but acts insolently enough.*) Liu dodged and got out of bed to fight him. Intimidated by Master Liu's quick moves, the man took to his heels. Liu gave chase and ran out of the room into the kitchen, ready to cry out so that the neighbors could join him in catching the thief. Growing frantic, the man caught sight of a shining firewood ax right by his hand. As the saying goes, a desperate moment drives one to act. He picked up the ax and swung it smack into Liu's face. As Liu fell, the burglar swung the ax one more time and cut him down. Master Liu died. Bless his soul! The burglar said, "As they say, once you start something, you'd better finish it off. It was you who ran after me, not the other way around." Having gotten thus far, he thought he might as well get the money. He turned back into the room and, after wrapping up the fifteen strings of cash with a bed-sheet and binding up the parcel tightly, he pulled the door to and went off. Of this, no more.

The next morning, the neighbors noticed that Master Liu's door was closed and no sound came from within. "Master Liu, you've overslept!" they cried out.

Without getting a response, they made their way in, surprised to find the door unbolted. Once inside, they saw that Master Liu was lying on the floor, dead from ax wounds. The neighbors said, "Mrs. Liu went to her parents' home two days ago, but where's Second Sister?"

In the midst of the uproar, Zhu San, the old man who had put Second Sister up the night before, said, "She came to our house last evening and said that Master Liu had sold her for no reason at all. She then went to her parents' home. She wanted me to tell Master Liu to go with the buyer to her parents' house to talk it all out and close the deal. If we send someone to bring her back, we'll be able to get to the bottom of this. In the meantime, let's also bring Mrs. Liu back before doing anything further."

"You're right," the other neighbors agreed.

So they first had someone report the terrible news to Squire Wang. Squire Wang and his daughter burst into wails of grief. "He left here yesterday perfectly all right," said Squire Wang. "I gave him fifteen strings of cash for him to set up a business. How did he come to be murdered?"

The messenger said, "Sir, madam, Master Liu returned home at dusk yesterday in a half-drunken state. Well, actually, we didn't know whether he had money with him or what time he returned. What happened was that this morning, when we saw his door ajar, we pushed it open and went in, only to see him dead on the floor, murdered. We didn't see even one penny of the fifteen strings of cash that were supposed to be in the house, nor was Second Sister there. So we cried out. Mr. Zhu San from the house on the left came and said that she had stayed at his house last night. According to her, Master Liu had sold her for no reason and she wanted to tell her parents about it, so she left this morning. We decided to report to Mrs. Liu and you, sir, and we've sent people to bring the young lady back. If they don't catch up with her on the road, they'll go to her parents' house. Whatever happens, we'll make sure that she is brought back to answer questions. You, sir, and Mrs. Liu must also go there so that you can avenge Master Liu."

In haste, Squire Wang and his daughter got ready for the trip, treated the messenger to wine and a meal, and hurried into the city. Of this, more later.

Now, back to Second Sister. After leaving the neighbor's house early in the morning, she took to the road. Before she had gone two li, her feet began to ache so terribly that she could not walk another step. As she sat by the roadside, she saw a young man wearing a headscarf with zigzag patterns, a straight loose gown, and a pair of silk shoes and white socks, and carrying a shoulder bag filled with copper coins. He was coming in her direction. When he drew near her, he threw her a glance. Though she was not a ravishing beauty, she was quite attractive, with her well-marked eyebrows, white teeth, rosy cheeks, and sparkling eyes. Truly,

> *Wild flowers are more eye-catching;*
> *Village wine is more intoxicating.*

The young man put down his shoulder bag and said with a deep bow, "Young lady, where are you going, all by yourself?" (*Mr. Liu died from wine; this young man is going to die from lust.*)

With a curtsey, she answered, "I'm going to my parents' home. I'm taking a rest here because I'm tired. Where have you come from, brother, and where are you going?"

Respectfully keeping his hands folded across his chest, the young man said, "I'm from the country. I just sold some silk bed-nets in the city and got some money. I'm going in the direction of Chujiatang."

"My parents live near Chujiatang. It would be nice if you could take me along."

"Of course. I'd be glad to go with you."

The two of them set off. Before they had gone three li, two men were seen running behind them as fast as their legs could carry them. All sweaty and out of breath, with the fronts of their outer garments open, they cried, "Young lady, stop! We have something to say to you!"

Mystified, Second Sister and the young man came to a halt. When the two men ran up to them, one grabbed Second Sister and the other grabbed the young man before they could protest. "A fine thing you did!" they said. "Where do you think you're going?"

Startled, Second Sister saw that they were neighbors, one of whom was the very man in whose house she had stayed the previous night. "I told you last night that my husband had sold me for no reason and that I was going home to tell my parents about it. Why have you run all the way here?"

Old Zhu San said, "I don't usually poke my nose into other people's business, but there's been a murder in your family. You must go back to answer questions."

"My husband has sold me and yesterday he carried home the money he got for the sale. What murder are you talking about? I'm not going."

Zhu San said, "You are a wayward one, aren't you? If you really don't go, we'll tell the local headman and have you arrested as a murderer. Otherwise we'll all be implicated, and he's not going to have any peace, either."

Seeing that things had taken an ominous turn, the young man said to the young lady, "In this case, you go with them. I'll go on by myself."

The two neighbors cried out, "It would be all right if you were not here, but since you are traveling with her and you stopped at the same time she did, you can't go!"

"Ridiculous! I met her on the road and just happened to walk with her for a while. I have nothing to do with all this. Why make me go with you?"

Old Zhu San said, "There's been a murder in her family. If we let you go, a party in this case will be missing." He turned a deaf ear to the protests of Second Sister and the young man. As more people gathered around to watch, some said, "Young man, you can't leave. As they say, if you didn't do anything against your conscience during the day, you shouldn't fear when there comes a knock on your door at night. Why don't you go with them? There's no harm in that!"

The neighbor who had come with Old Zhu San said, "If you don't go, it means you have a guilty conscience, and we won't call it quits." (*Not being eloquent, they don't give good reasons.*) And so the two neighbors hustled the two of them off, making a group of four.

There was a bustling scene of excitement at Master Liu's door. Upon entering, Second Sister saw that Liu was lying on the floor, dead from ax wounds. Not a penny of the fifteen strings of cash was left on the bed. Her jaw dropped open; her tongue hung out. The young man was also appalled. He said, "Luckless me! I walked with the young lady for a while in all innocence and now I've got myself involved in a murder case!"

In the midst of the commotion, with everybody talking at once, Old Squire Wang, trembling every step of the way, came with his daughter. At the sight of his son-in-law's corpse, he burst into a fit of sobbing and said to Second Sister, "How could you have killed your husband and fled with the fifteen strings of cash? Now that the truth is out by the will of heaven, what do you have to say for yourself?"

"There were indeed fifteen strings of cash," replied Second Sister. "My husband came home last night and said that for lack of a better choice, he had pawned me to another man for fifteen strings of cash. He said that I was supposed to go to that man's home today. Without knowing what kind of a man he had pawned me to, I wanted to tell my parents first. So while he was sleeping, I piled up the fifteen strings by his feet, closed the door, and spent the night at Mr. Zhu's house, and this morning I set off for my parents' house. Before I left, I asked Mr. Zhu to tell my husband to go with the buyer to my parents' house to close the deal. I have no idea why he was killed."

Mrs. Liu said, "What are you talking about? My father gave him those fifteen strings of cash yesterday so that he could set up a business and support us. How could he have told you that he got the money from pawning you? You must have had an affair the last couple of days when you were alone. And you couldn't stand the poverty of the family. Then, tempted by the sight of fifteen strings of cash, you killed him and stole the money. Then in your clever way, you spent the night at a neighbor's house and plotted with your lover to run away together. Now that you've been caught traveling with him, you're not going to lie your way out of this!"

"Mrs. Liu has got it right," commented the spectators. To the young man, they said, "Young man, didn't you plot with the young lady to murder her husband and secretly arrange to meet at a quiet spot and then run away? What exactly were your plans?"

The young man said, "My name is Cui Ning. I've never seen this young lady before. I went into the city last evening and sold some silk. The money is still with me here. I saw her on the road and asked her where she was going all by herself. Because she was going in the same direction I was, we went together. I knew nothing about what had happened."

Turning a deaf ear to his explanations, they searched his shoulder bag and found there fifteen strings of cash, not a penny more, not a penny less. (*The young man is wronged.*) Everyone cried out. One said, "As the saying goes, 'The net of heaven is of large mesh, but it lets nothing through.' You and the young woman committed a murder. You took the money and the woman and tried to flee this place with her, dragging us all into a case in which the guilty parties couldn't be found."

With Mrs. Liu holding Second Sister, Squire Wang holding Cui Ning, and the neighbors as witnesses, the whole crowd marched noisily to the Lin'an prefectural yamen. Upon hearing of a murder, the prefect immediately called a court session to order and had the parties involved brought in for statements on the case.

Squire Wang was the first one to make a deposition. He said, "Your Honor, I am from a village of this prefecture. I'm approaching sixty years of age. My only daughter has been married for some years to Liu Gui, who lived in the city. Being childless, Liu Gui took on Chen-shi as a concubine and called her Second Sister. The three of them lived together with never a harsh word for one another. The day before yesterday was my birthday, so I sent for my daughter and my son-in-law and kept them in my house for the night. The next day, because my son-in-law had no means of a livelihood and was quite unable to provide for the family, I gave him fifteen strings of cash, so that he could set up a store and make a living. Second Sister stayed at home to look after the house. After my son-in-law went home last evening, he was hacked to death, for some reason. Second Sister then fled with a young man called Cui Ning. They've been caught and brought back. Please take pity on us, Your Honor. My son-in-law died a tragic death. The adulterous couple and the stolen money are all here. Please use your wise judgment."

Having heard him out, the prefect called Chen-shi to the bench and asked, "How did you collude with your lover, kill your husband, steal the money, and run away? What do you have to say for yourself?"

Second Sister pleaded, "Although I was but a concubine to Liu Gui, he treated me well. Mrs. Liu is also a nice and kind woman. Why would I do such an evil thing? Last evening, when my husband returned home, drunk and carrying fifteen strings of cash, I asked how he had come by the money. He replied that because he could not support the family, he had pawned me to a man in exchange for fifteen strings of cash. Without informing my parents, he wanted me to go to the buyer's house the very next day. I took fright and left later that night, first to a neighbor's house to spend the night. This morning, before I left for my parents' house, I told the neighbors to say to my husband that since he had already sold me, he could go with the buyer to my parents' house to close the deal. I was on the road when the neighbor in whose house I stayed last night caught up with me and brought me back. I have no idea why my husband has been murdered."

The prefect thundered, "Nonsense! These fifteen strings of cash were all too clearly given to him by his father-in-law. Yet you say he got the money by pawning you. This is a blatant lie. Also, why would a woman walk alone in the middle of the night? You were obviously trying to escape. You are not capable of doing all this on your own. You must have had your lover help you murder your husband in order to get his money. Confess!"

The young woman was about to protest her innocence again when the neighbors fell to their knees and said to the prefect, "Your Honor, what you said is indeed the truth. She did spend the night at the second house to the left of her house and she departed this morning. When we saw that her husband had been murdered, we sent two of the neighbors to give chase. They caught up with her. Both she and the young man with her firmly refused to come back. The two neighbors had to bring them back by force. In the meantime, we sent for Mrs. Liu and her father. When they arrived, the father-in-law said that he had given fifteen strings of cash to his son-in-law the day before, so that he could start a business. And now his son-in-law is dead and the money is gone. When we questioned her time and again, the concubine said she had put the money in a pile on the bed. We searched the young man and found fifteen strings of cash on him, not a penny less. Isn't it obvious that the two of them are an adulterous couple and they plotted the murder together? With the money as evidence, how can they lie their way out of it?"

Quite convinced, the prefect called up the young man and said to him, "How can such atrocities be allowed here in this capital of the empire! You abducted Mr. Liu's concubine, took the fifteen strings of cash, and murdered Mr. Liu. How did you do that? Where were you going with her? Out with the truth!"

"I am Cui Ning, from the country. I sold some silk in the city yesterday, for which I got these fifteen strings of cash. I happened to see this young lady on the road this morning. I didn't even know her name. How would I know anything about a murder in her family?"

In a blaze of wrath, the prefect roared, "Nonsense! There can't be such a coincidence! Fifteen strings of cash disappeared from their house, and you made fifteen strings of cash from selling silk. This is all too clearly a lie! Also, as the saying goes, 'Do not covet another man's wife; do not ride another man's horse.' If you had nothing to do with her, why were you traveling with her and staying at the same inn? A brazen scoundrel like you will never confess unless you're put to the rod!"

There and then, Cui Ning and Second Sister were beaten until they were more dead than alive. With Squire Wang, Mrs. Liu, and the neighbors clamoring that those two were the culprits, the prefect could hardly wait to close the case. Unable to hold out against the torture, poor Cui Ning and the young lady confessed to the false charges. The young lady said, "Tempted by the sight of the money, I killed my husband, took the fifteen strings of cash, and fled with my lover, and this is the truth."

After each of the neighbors drew a cross with his finger on the confession by way of signature, the two accused were put in large cangues and sent to death row. The fifteen strings of cash were returned to Squire Wang, but they turned out not to be enough even for tipping the yamen lictors.

After the imperial court reviewed the file put together by the prefect, the emperor issued a decree, saying, "Cui Ning is to be executed in accordance with the law for the crimes of adultery, murder, and robbery. Chen-shi is to die by death by dismemberment in public for the heinous crime of murdering her husband in collusion with her lover."

After the confessions were read out, the two convicted were brought out of prison and taken to the marketplace, where the sentences were carried out in public. Even if they had had mouths all over their bodies, they would not have been able to defend themselves. Truly,

> *A mute tasting bitter cork-tree bark*
> *Cannot tell his disgust through words.*

Dear audience, if the young lady and Cui Ning had indeed murdered for money, they would have fled that very night. Why should she have spent the night in a neighbor's house and left for her parents' home the next morning, only to allow herself to be caught? A careful examination of the case would have identified the truth. The prefect was a fool too eager to close the case. Under torture, who would not confess to any charge? The evil things one does are all recorded in the unseen netherworld, to haunt one or one's offspring later. Those two aggrieved souls would not let go of the prefect who had inflicted such unjust deaths on them. Therefore, officials must not judge cases arbitrarily and apply torture indiscriminately. (*A motto for all officials.*) Every effort must be made to seek justice and fairness, for the dead cannot come back to life, just as a broken object cannot be made whole again. How lamentable!

Let us not encumber our story with more of such idle comments but turn our attention to Mrs. Liu, who set up a shrine to her late husband at home in observance of the period of mourning. To her father's exhortations that she remarry, she said, "I should wait at least for one year, if not the required three years." Her father agreed and left. Time sped by. After Mrs. Liu had borne the hardships of her life for nearly a year, her father thought that widowhood was too much for her. He told Old Wang the servant to bring her over, saying to him, "Tell her to pack and come back home. She can remarry after the first anniversary of Master Liu's death."

For lack of a better choice, Mrs. Liu accepted her father's advice after some solid thinking. She packed, gave her luggage to Old Wang to carry, and took leave of her neighbors, saying she would be coming back soon. After she and Old Wang were out of the city, they were caught in one of those severe rainstorms of autumn. They had to leave the road and find shelter in the woods, but they took the wrong path. Truly,

> *Like pigs and sheep on their way to the slaughterhouse,*
> *With each step they drew nearer to their deaths.*

When they were in the woods, they heard a loud cry from behind: "Stand and deliver! The king of the Jing Mountains is here!" As Mrs. Liu and Old Wang stood petrified, a man leaped out.

> A dark red scarf over his face,
> An old warrior's robe on his body,
> A red silk band around his waist,
> A pair of black boots on his feet,
> A wood-hilted sword in his hand.

As the man approached them, brandishing his sword, Old Wang, who was destined to die at this hour, said, "You bandit! I know your kind! Let this old man fight you to the death!" With that, he charged at the bandit, head down. The man dodged. Having lunged ahead with all his force, Old Wang lost his balance and fell flat on the ground. "You impudent old swine!" said the man in a rage. With a few quick plunges of his sword, blood flowed over the ground. Old Wang gave up the ghost.

Witnessing this savage act, Mrs. Liu knew she would not be spared, either, but hitting on a plan to save her own skin, she clapped her hands and exclaimed, "Good job!"

The man stopped and, popping wide his devilish eyes, roared, "Who was he to you?"

Mrs. Liu replied, feigning honesty, "When my husband died on me unfortunately, a matchmaker tricked me into marrying this old man, who was good at nothing but eating. Now you've gotten rid of a pest for me, sir."

Impressed by her cautiousness and her above-average looks, the man asked, "Would you be willing to marry me?"

She saw nothing for it but to say, "Yes, I would be glad to serve you, sir."

His anger turning to joy, the man sheathed his sword and dumped Old Wang's corpse into a ravine. He then took Mrs. Liu to a sprawling manor. He picked up a few clods of earth and tossed them at the roof. Immediately the gate was opened. Once in the main hall, the man ordered a sheep slaughtered and wine prepared for a wedding ceremony. The couple got along well together. Truly,

> Knowing full well he was not the right man,
> She submitted in a desperate moment.

In less than half a year after he married Mrs. Liu, the bandit got several windfalls in a row and was now a rich man. Mrs. Liu, with her good sense, kept advising him, "As the ancients said, 'An earthen jar used for drawing water from the well will break by the well; a general fighting battles will die in a battle.' You and I now have enough to live on for the rest of our lives. You'll come to no good end if you go on doing things that defy the will of heaven. As they say, the Liang Garden may be good, but it's nothing like home.[3] You'd do well to change your ways. A small business will give us enough income."

Under her pressure day and night, the bandit indeed had a change of heart and gave up his line of work. He rented a house in the city and opened a general store. On days of leisure, he went to temples to chant the Buddha's name and observe a vegetarian diet. (*He has a bad conscience.*)

One day, when sitting idly in the house, he remarked to his wife, "I may have been a bandit, but I know that for every injustice, there is a perpetrator; for every debt, there is a debtor. Every day, I robbed and stole in order to make a living. And then after I got you, I've had some plain-sailing days, and I've now turned over a new leaf. With all this time on my hands now, I often look back on the past. I've killed two men unjustly and ruined two other people. They are constantly in my thoughts. I'd like to hold a prayer service to them. This is something I've never told you before."

"You killed two men unjustly? What do you mean?"

"One of them was your husband. When he charged at me in the woods, I killed him. Actually I had nothing against that old man. And then I married his wife. He would never rest easy in his grave."

"But how else could we have gotten together? What's gone is gone. Don't bring it up again. Who was the other one?"

"Well, that was even more of a violation against divine will. And two other innocent people also died as a result. It was one year ago. I lost at gambling one day. Without a penny left, I went out at night to steal. When I passed by a door that was unbolted, I pushed it open and went in. There was no one around. When I groped my way into the inner room, I saw a man lying drunk in bed with a pile of copper coins at his feet. I stole a few strings and was about to leave when that man woke up and said, 'My father-in-law gave me this money for me to start a business. If you steal it, this whole family will starve to death.' Then he ran after me out of the room and was about to cry out for help. When I saw that things were going badly for me, I noticed a firewood ax right by my feet. This was indeed a case of 'A desperate moment drives one to act.' I picked up the ax and shouted, 'It's either you or me!' With two blows, I cut him down. Then I went back into the room and took all fifteen strings of cash. Later, I heard that his concubine and a young man called Cui Ning were accused of murder and robbery and that both were executed. In all the time I was a bandit, these two cases were the only ones that neither heaven nor humans will ever forgive. (*By knowing that he will not be forgiven by humans, this bandit at least has some sense of what divine will is.*) I should offer a prayer service for them."

Mrs. Liu groaned inwardly and thought, "So, this brute killed my husband and caused the unjust deaths of Second Sister and that young man. It was in fact all because I was the witness demanding that they pay with their lives. The two of them in the netherworld will never forgive me."

But in the bandit's presence she gave every appearance of joy, and the night passed without ado. The next day, she slipped out at the first opportunity and went straight to the Lin'an prefectural yamen. At the gate, she cried out, "Injustice! Injustice!"

It so happened that the new prefect who had been in this post for only half a month was about to call his court session to order. The lictors brought in the woman shouting "Injustice!" At the foot of the dais, Mrs. Liu burst into sobs before she launched into an account of how the bandit had killed her husband, Liu Gui, adding, "The prefect handling the case did not investigate thoroughly. He perfunctorily closed the case and unjustly sentenced Second Sister and Cui Ning to death. Later the bandit killed Old Wang and took possession of me. Now divine justice has caught up with him. He confessed everything to me. Your Honor, please redress the wrong in your wisdom." With that, she broke down again in a flood of tears.

Touched by her words, the prefect dispatched lictors to bring the "king of the Jing Mountains" to court. Under torture, he confessed. The confession tallied with Mrs. Liu's statement in every detail. There and then he was convicted of crimes punishable by death and the file was submitted to the emperor. Upon the expiration of the required sixty-day waiting period, the emperor issued a decree, saying, "It has been found that the king of the Jing Mountains committed murder for money and implicated innocent people. He is to be executed immediately rather than in the coming autumn [the season for executions], as stipulated by the law governing cases in which the accused is responsible for the killing of three or more members of one family for offenses, if any, that are not punishable by death. The prefect who handled the case is hereby stripped of all official ranks for the miscarriage of justice. Cui Ning and Chen-shi having died tragic and unjust deaths, the authorities are to visit their families and give them compensation. Since Wang-shi married the bandit under coercion and was able to bring the murderer of her husband to justice, half of the criminal's possessions will be given to her to support her for the rest of her life. The other half will be confiscated by the government."

Mrs. Liu went to the execution ground to watch the beheading of the king of the Jing Mountains. She then brought his head to the altars of her deceased husband, Second Sister, and Cui Ning for a prayer service, at which she cried with abandon. She donated to a nunnery her half of the criminal's possessions and spent her days reading the sutras and chanting Buddha's name in memory of the dead souls, until she died of old age. There is a poem in testimony:

> The good and the evil alike met their end;
> A simple jest led to disaster.
> Be advised: speak only in good faith;
> The tongue has always been a source of trouble.

For One Penny, a Small Grudge Ends in Stark Tragedies

Few in this mortal world take this advice:
Do not go in pursuit of fame and wealth.
In leisure, I fill my wine cup to the brim;
In delight, I chant a hundred poems.
I take the mists and clouds as companions;
I enjoy the sun and moon in my wine pot.
Where do I go after I complete my mission?
To heaven in a chariot of clouds.

The above eight-line poem was written by Daoist Hui. Who was he? He was Lü Yan, sobriquet Dongbin, a native of Hedong of Yuezhou. [1] After passing the civil service examinations at the national level in the Xiantong reign period [860–73] of the Tang dynasty, he was in a wineshop in Chang'an when he met Mr. Zhongli, Patriarch Zhengyang, who pointed out to him the meaninglessness of his pursuit. [2] Now convinced that a career in officialdom was not a worthy undertaking, he asked to be enlightened on ways to redeem people of the world. Not certain if his conviction was firm, Zhongli tested him ten times before deciding that he was sincere. Mr. Zhongli then felt ready to impart to him a secret formula of alchemy, so that he could turn stone into gold for the prosperity of the world until the completion of his life's mission.

Dongbin asked, "After I turn stone into gold, will the gold undergo changes again?"

"It will change back to stone after three thousand years."

Displeased, Dongbin rejoined, "My momentary wish will be gratified all right, but those who encounter the gold after three thousand years will be disappointed. (*The average person doesn't even care about tomorrow, let alone people three thousand years from now.*) This disciple doesn't want such a formula."

Mr. Zhongli burst into hearty laughter. "With such a compassionate heart, your mission in life is as good as accomplished. Sage Bitter Bamboo had long ago told me, 'In your travels in the mortal world, you will find a true disciple in a man with two mouths.' I have traveled all through this world, but I have never met anyone with two mouths. Now, your surname being the character *lü* [呂] with two mouths, one over the other, you are that very person."

There and then, he imparted to Dongbin the secrets of merging yin and yang.

After he became accomplished in the art of alchemy, Dongbin vowed to deliver all humans from suffering before he himself would rise to heaven. Henceforth he went everywhere, calling himself Daoist Hui, the character *hui* [回] also consisting of two mouths, one inside the other.

When in Changsha, he held in his hand a small porcelain beggar's can and exclaimed, "I have a secret formula for longevity, but I will only impart it to one who donates enough money to fill this can!"

In disbelief, onlookers rivaled one another in tossing coins into the can but, to the amazement of one and all, however many coins they tossed in, the can did not fill up. Suddenly a monk approached them from the eastern end of the market, pushing a cart that was filled with money. Playfully he said to Dongbin, "There are a thousand strings of cash in this cart. Will your little can take that much?"

Dongbin said, all affability, "It can swallow up your cart, let alone the coins in it."

The monk was not convinced. He thought, "How is it possible for that can to swallow a cart? He is lying."

Watching him lost in thought, Dongbin said, "Maybe you are not willing to give. If you are, my can will certainly accommodate this cart."

Everyone in the expanding crowd of spectators being a mortal, none believed Dongbin. As they all urged the monk to take on the challenge, the monk said, confident that Dongbin was talking nonsense, "Why would I be unwilling? Let's see what you can do!"

Dongbin turned the can on its side and, holding it with its opening toward the cart, which was about three paces away, said to the monk, "Would you dare say the word 'willing' three times?"

The monk cried, "Willing! Willing! Willing!" Each time he said the word, the cart moved nearer the can. When the word was said the third time, the cart flew right into the can, as if there were someone in the can pulling at it. In a blur of vision, the onlookers realized that the cart was gone. "How very strange!" they exclaimed in chorus. Going up to look into the can, they saw only a black hole.

Resentfully, the monk asked, "Are you a divine being or a black magician?"

Dongbin the Daoist intoned the following eight lines:

> *"Neither a divine being,*
> *Nor a black magician.*
> *Everything between heaven and earth will end;*

> *Mulberry fields will change into seas.*
> *This body does not belong to me;*
> *Why should I hang on to money?*
> *Come, follow me in my travels;*
> *Ride a whale and rise to heaven!"*

Suspecting him of being a sorcerer, the monk wanted the onlookers to join him in taking Dongbin to the authorities.

"Is it because you regret having lost a cartful of money?" asked Dongbin. "I'll give it back to you and be done with it." He asked for a brush-pen and a piece of paper, drew a magic charm, and tossed it into the can. "Come out! Come out!" he cried. The hundreds of eyes of the onlookers were riveted on the can, but nothing happened.

"This can is too greedy," said Dongbin. "It doesn't want to give up the money. Let this poor Daoist go and get it for you." Before the words were quite out of his mouth, he jumped into the can and vanished without a trace, as if he had fallen into a deep abyss. (*He can't have died?*)

"Come out, Daoist!" cried the monk over and over again, but not a sound came out of the can. In a burst of rage, the monk picked up the can and flung it onto the ground, smashing it to smithereens, but neither the Daoist nor the cart, nor even a coin donated by the crowd was anywhere in sight. There was only a scroll of writing. They picked it up and saw a quatrain that said,

> *A seeker of truth should know it when he sees it;*
> *This one knows not what is before his eyes.*
> *With one smile, we shall meet again;*
> *To East Peace Road I push the cart.*

Even as the onlookers were passing the scroll around and reading it, the characters gradually faded. Soon the white scroll also vanished into thin air. Only then did everyone believe that they had encountered a divine being. The crowd quickly dispersed. Only the monk remained, looking woebegone over his loss of a cartful of money. Suddenly recalling the last two lines of the quatrain, he anxiously set off on his return trip, and, sure enough, on East Peace Road, there stood his cart with all the money intact. The Daoist, standing by the cart, said smilingly, raising a hand, "I've been waiting here for quite some time now. Please take back your money and your cart." Then he added with a sigh, "Even a monk loves money so much. How can there be anyone who doesn't?" (*Actually, monks love money much more than lay people do.*) There is no one for me to deliver throughout this world. How sad! How lamentable!" With that, he rose on a cloud and was gone. The monk was dumbfounded. After he recovered a considerable while later, he noticed that each of the two wheels of the cart bore the character for mouth [口]. It dawned on him that the Daoist was none other than Lü Dongbin, but regrets were too late now. Truly,

It is easier to meet a divine being
Than to see a generous donor in this world.

The above story is about how, for the love of a cartful of money, a monk missed
the chance to be delivered by a divine being in mortal disguise. Someone com-
mented, "A cartful of coins is a lot of money. You can't blame that monk. There
are in this world people who begrudge even one penny." Well, as I see it, a cartful
of money is just an extension of one penny. One who begrudges a cartful of money
starts from begrudging one penny. The amount of money makes little difference.
(*Valid point.*)

Now please listen on as I tell you a story about one little penny. Dear audience,
be admonished: Suppress feelings of anger, control your desires, and do not han-
ker after immortality and attainment of the Dao. This is the best way to ensure
peace for yourself as well as for your family. As the poem says,

Keep away from greed and anger;
Be generous and be friendly.
Without money, the mind is rid of worries;
Without worries, yours is the life of the divine.

Our story takes place in the town of Jingdezhen in Fuliang County of Raozhou
Prefecture, Jiangxi. It is a port where people make a living by firing porcelain. In
a lucrative trade, merchants come from all directions to ship their products to
Suzhou, Hangzhou, and other places. Of the people in this town, there was one
man called Qiu Yida, a master hand at a porcelain kiln. His wife, Yang-shi, was
good at drawing. With Yida making unglazed porcelain biscuits and his wife paint-
ing flowers and human figures on them, they had a pretty decent income. They
lived in a quiet and secluded lane and had, in fact, more money than they needed
for their daily expenses. At thirty-six years of age, Yang-shi was something of a
beauty and quite ready to have an affair or two. Out of fear of her husband's stern-
ness, she did this only once in a while, behind his back, without ever coming into
the open. They had a son whom they called Qiu Chang'er, now fourteen. He was
none too bright. Not yet able to work in the kiln, he spent his days running and
bouncing about the house.

One day, Yang-shi had a stomachache. Craving tea brewed with prickly ash seeds,
she gave Chang'er one penny and told him to buy some prickly ash seeds at the
market. With the penny on him, Chang'er had just walked out the door when he
ran into Zaiwang, son of Liu Sanwang, who lived in the next house east of theirs,
also a maker of unglazed porcelain biscuits. At thirteen years of age, Zaiwang was
smarter than Chang'er. His favorite game was gambling on tossing coins. How was
the game played? The bet could be on either heads or tails six or eight times in a
row, or on one head and one tail alternately five or seven times in a row. When they
had money, Zaiwang and Chang'er often went to a street corner to play this game.

That day when they met in the lane, they walked together to the spot where they often played their game. As Zaiwang proposed playing one game, Chang'er said, "I don't have money on me."

"Where are you going?" asked Zaiwang.

"My mother has a stomachache. She wants me to buy some prickly ash seeds to make tea with."

"Then you must have money on you."

"I've got only one penny."

"One penny is good enough for a game. I'll add one of mine and bet on two tails. If both fall tails up, whoever tosses wins and takes both pennies. Two heads up means losing. If one head, one tail, we'll be even."

"I'm supposed to buy prickly ash seeds with this one penny. If I lose it to you, how am I going to buy them?"

"That's all right. If you win, you're lucky. If you lose, I'll lend one to you. Just remember to pay me back next time." (*It is said that gambling leads to robbery and adultery leads to killing. As it turns out, however, gambling can also lead to killing.*)

Lacking good sense, Chang'er flung his penny onto the ground. Zaiwang also took out a coin from his pocket and flung it down. Chang'er's penny turned tail up. Zaiwang's turned head up. According to the rules of this game, the one whose penny turns tail up should be the first one to make the next move. So Chang'er picked up both coins, laid them on his index finger, pressed them with his thumb, bent slightly over, and cried "Tails!" With that, he flung the coins down. Sure enough, both turned tails up. Chang'er won. He picked up one and left the other one on the ground. Zaiwang took out another penny from his pocket, picked up the one on the ground, laid them on his index finger, pressed them with his thumb, bent over slightly, and cried, "Tails!" He flung them onto the ground, but both turned heads up. Zaiwang lost again.

Chang'er put away both coins. Now he had three pennies, including the one his mother had given him. These easy wins woke up the gambler in him. He asked Zaiwang, "Have you got more coins?"

"Yes, I've got plenty of them, but you may not be lucky enough to win them." So saying, he fished out about ten clean and bright coins from his waistband and, holding them in his hand, said with exaggerated enthusiasm, "Good coins! Good coins!" Addressing Chang'er, he continued, "Do you dare play some more?" With that, he flung down another penny. The third time around, Chang'er again got two tails up. The fourth time, Zaiwang lost again, with two heads up. And so they played about ten times. Chang'er won each time. In all, he got twelve pennies, which were nothing less than a windfall to him. His face wreathed in smiles, he pocketed the coins and turned to go. But Zaiwang was not about to let him. Blocking his way, Zaiwang said, "You've won a lot of money from me. Where do you think you are going?"

"My mother has a stomachache and is waiting for prickly ash seeds to make tea with. I have to go now. I'll come again later."

"I've got more money on me. If you win again, I'll give all of it to you."

As Chang'er insisted on going, Zaiwang grew desperate. He said, "If you refuse to play some more, give me back my money. You tricked me out of so much with your one penny. How can you go off just like that?"

"I won them fair and square. I didn't rob you!"

Zaiwang produced outright all the pennies he had, all twenty to thirty of them, and piled them up on the ground, saying, "I'll let you go when I lose all of them."

Being a young boy who didn't know better, Chang'er was tempted by the sight of the money, and Zaiwang was pestering him at that. So he tossed one more time.

A favorable wind does not last forever; a victorious army does not stay victorious. This time, Zaiwang won. They went on playing as many as twenty games. Though each had a few wins and a few losses, Zaiwang won more than Chang'er did. In the end, he won back all twelve pennies, leaving Chang'er with his mother's one penny.

As the ancients said, "Gambling is all a matter of the state of mind." In the beginning, after winning one or two pennies, Chang'er grew bolder and won one game after another. When they began anew the second time around, he was tossing the coins against his inclinations, and, with greed raising its ugly head, he lost some of his assuredness. After he lost one coin after another, hating every loss, stinginess began to creep in, and the will to win was gone. (*These are comments on a trivial matter, but they can very well apply to larger situations.*) Zaiwang, however, was in a state of indignation and, being the more audacious of the two, naturally ended up the winner.

Generally speaking, it is not bad to be consistently rich or consistently poor. To fall from wealth to poverty is the worst. For Chang'er, who had started out with a penny, winning one or two pennies should have been enough. After winning twelve coins, which were more than he could hold in one fist, he was as delighted as if he had built up a family fortune from nothing. Instead of looking on the money as something extra, he treated the money as rightfully belonging to him and chafed at losing it. Then he foolishly hoped he could win it back, thinking, "Even if I lose, he promised he would lend me a penny. Why not try again?" Believing he would win the next time, he yielded to the urge and, trying to calm down, tossed once more. Again he got two heads up. In mortification, he reached for one of the two coins, but Zaiwang was quicker and had already thrown both coins into his own waistband.

"I had one penny to buy prickly ash seeds with," said Chang'er. "You promised you would lend me a penny. Why did you take all of them?"

Bearing a grudge against Chang'er for having turned to go after winning twelve pennies from him, Zaiwang seized this opportunity to vent his spleen. As the saying goes, "For a gentleman, revenge can take three years. For a petty man, there's not a moment to lose." How would he be willing to lend a penny to Chang'er? He pushed away Chang'er's hands and danced his way triumphantly back into the lane. In desperation, Chang'er burst into tears. Shouting after Zaiwang, he also turned back into the lane and grabbed Zaiwang, demanding his penny back. The two came to blows.

> *In a battle of wits between Sun and Pang, who will win?[3]*
> *In the fight between Chu and Han, which side will lose?[4]*

In the meantime, Yang-shi was waiting for prickly ash seeds to make tea with. After she waited for what seemed an eternity without seeing Chang'er return, her stomachache subsided, so she went out the door for a look. At the sight of Chang'er and Zaiwang locked in a fight, she cried out, "Little rascal! I told you to buy prickly ash seeds! Why are you here, making a scene? Let go of him, now!"

At this outburst, the two boys let go of each other. Zaiwang stood off to one side.

"Where are my prickly ash seeds?" Yang-shi asked her son.

With tears in his eyes, Chang'er replied, "Zaiwang took my penny."

Zaiwang said, "We played at tossing coins. He lost."

Yang-shi should have scolded only her own son for playing at tossing coins rather than putting the blame on someone else. Moreover, why make a big fuss out of one penny? Since her son had lost it in a gambling game, she should have called it quits. (*If so,* [Illegible.]) Yang-shi's stupidity led to major tragedies that took one life after another as they developed. Indeed,

> *Acting without thinking thrice will lead to regret;*
> *Those who take things as they come live peaceful lives.*

So Yang-shi was full of pent-up anger from waiting in vain for Chang'er to return. Without an object on which to vent her spleen, she exploded upon hearing that Zaiwang had taken a penny from her son in a gambling game. "You goddamn bastard!" she cursed. "If you want money, why don't you tell your mother to get herself a lover? Why cheat my boy out of his money?" While unburdening herself of a torrent of abominable words, she seized Zaiwang by his waistband and gave him a couple of raps on the head with her knuckles. The boy struggled desperately to break free from her, but, as he did so, the strings of his waistband snapped. The waistband fell with a clatter. The coins in it scattered and rolled all over the ground.

"I just want my penny back," said Yang-shi.

Emboldened by his mother's words, Chang'er scooped up a handful of the coins and ran home. As Zaiwang cried out in protest, Yang-shi rushed into the house and sharply ordered her son to return the money to Zaiwang. Unable to fend off his mother, Chang'er tossed the coins far out into the street. Zaiwang picked them up while cursing between his sobs. After he found all of them, he realized that he was six or seven pennies short. Believing Chang'er had kept them, he went up to

Chang'er's door and bawled out a string of curses. Yang-shi slammed the door shut while saying, "That goddamn bastard! Acting up like that!" She then went in.

After pounding the door and cursing for a few more moments, Zaiwang wept his way home. His mother, Madam Sun, was getting a kitchen fire going. When she asked what the matter was, Zaiwang said sobbingly, "Chang'er robbed me of my money. His mother didn't scold him but called me 'goddamn bastard.' And she said, 'If you want money, why don't you tell your mother to get herself a lover?'"

Everything would have been all right if Madam Sun had not heard these vile words, but she did, and she fumed with rage.

The fact of the matter was that Madam Sun doted on her son and shielded all his faults. With her fiery temper and her sharp tongue, she was a trouble-making holy terror. When she got into a quarrel, she could pour out torrents of abuse for ten days or so without getting thirsty. She won herself the nickname "Toothy Washboard." Her house being only three or four doors away from the Qiu residence, she was well aware of Yang-shi's clandestine affairs, but, because the two families had never exchanged a harsh word before, she had refrained from making her knowledge public. Zaiwang's report raised her ire. Planting herself in the street, she yelled, "Bitch! Slut! You get yourself lovers behind your husband's back. Isn't it good enough that I've kept my mouth shut? And now you turn around and accuse me! I may not be all that pretty, but I bring no disgrace to my husband. No nun comes in our front door; no monk slips in through the back door. I am squeaky clean, unlike you, hussy! What have you got under that bold front of yours? Aren't you ashamed that you make a cuckold of your husband? And you had the nerve to call people names in public! This is too much even for a whore like you! My son is too young and small for you. Don't you try to lead him on! When in heat, go back to those men of yours. Make a few more trips and make a few more bastard babies, so that after they grow up, they can go out and steal for you!" And so she went on, calling Yang-shi every foul name she could think of, until pedestrians shunned the street.

Being afraid of her husband, Yang-shi dared not respond to the taunts. Blowing off her steam on Chang'er, she said, "This is all your fault, you little swine! It was your antics that set her tongue wagging." She picked up a piece of firewood and rained blows on his head until blood flowed out. As the boy wailed at the top of his lungs, Qiu Yida returned from the kiln. On his way home, he had heard Madam Sun's screams and stopped to listen. Without missing even one word, he wondered to himself, "Who is that shameless woman who makes a cuckold of her husband and provokes that Toothy Washboard?" Upon entering the house, he asked why Chang'er was crying and realized that the commotion had originated from his own house. Being a tough man who dreaded being a laughing stock, Qiu Yida sulkily sat down without a word. The curses out in the street did not stop until evening fell.

Qiu Yida drank a few bowls of wine. When all was still in the depths of the night, he called his wife to him and asked, "You cheap hussy! What did you do behind my back? Who are your many lovers? What are their names? Out with the truth! Let me deal with them!" (*Qiu Yida is justified in his self-righteousness, but he should have been more circumspect.*)

This outburst from her husband whom she feared was to her like a thunderbolt from midair. Trembling all over, she dared not get a word out.

"Cheap slut! If you know how to get yourself lovers, why can't you tell the truth? If you don't want others to know what you've done, you shouldn't have done it in the first place. You can keep it back from me, but not from the neighbors. How am I going to show my face in public in the future? Tell me! Quick! Let me know what's been going on."

"What do you want me to tell when I've done no such thing?"

"No? Are you sure?"

"No."

"If so, why did she say those things? And why did you let her go on without a peep? You obviously have a guilty conscience and can't afford to talk back. If you're innocent and she made those things up, you go ahead and hang yourself on her door tonight to show your innocence and clear my name. I'll deal with her tomorrow."

How would she be willing to do that? As she was shedding tears, Qiu Yida slapped her across the face two or three times and threw her out the door. Then, tossing out a hemp rope, he yelled, "Go kill yourself and be quick about it! If you don't, that's an admission of having lovers." With that, he closed the door and went inside. Chang'er wanted to open the door to let his mother in, but Yida rapped his head with his knuckles until the boy gave up and went to bed, wailing. Groggy from wine, Yida also retired for the night.

Yang-shi outside the door was grief-stricken, unable to think of a way to get herself out of this fix. Believing she had only herself to blame, she thought there was no better solution than death. After spending a great deal of time in self-reproach and self-pity, she grew afraid that daybreak would soon be upon her. In a flurry of panic, she picked up the hemp rope and went in search of Madam Sun's house. In this last moment of her life, she was confused. The Lius occupied the third house to the east but she headed west. After passing six doors, she stopped at the seventh house, which looked to her like the Liu residence. In haste she put a few bricks in a pile, threw the rope over the eave, and hanged herself. How tragic that such a smart woman died as a result of a moment of anger over a penny! ([Illegible.]) Truly,

> One more aggrieved soul in the netherworld;
> One fewer painter of flowers on earth.

Now, the seventh house to the west belonged to a blacksmith. Known by his nickname, White Iron, the blacksmith rose every day before dawn to work in his shop. At this point in our narration, he opened the door to go to the outhouse. As a gust of chilly wind sent cold shivers down his spine, he looked intently and gave a violent start.

It was either a clown in a puppet show,
Or a lady playing on a swing.

Under the eaves hung an object that looked quite frightening. Wondering where it had come from and if his eyes were playing tricks on him, he turned back inside and took a lamp. By the lamplight, he saw that it was a woman who had just hanged herself, looking as if she was dead and beyond rescue. If he did nothing, wouldn't he be involved in a court case when the police saw the corpse after daybreak? Wouldn't it be a disaster out of the blue if he could not prove his innocence? A plan came to him. "If I move her elsewhere, I'll have nothing to do with the case," he thought. Trying to overcome his fear, he went up and untied the rope. White Iron was a strong man. Gently he let down the body and carried it out into the street. In his nervousness, he left the body in front of a door without bothering to find out whose house it was. Then he rushed back home without another look back. With one shiver after another, he was too frightened to start his work of the day but went back to bed. Of him, more later.

Now, back to Qiu Yida. He rose before daybreak and opened the door to find out what had happened to his wife. He walked up to Liu Sanwang's door, but nothing was out of the ordinary. From there he went to the mouth of the lane, but found no trace of her there, either. He returned home and sat down, thinking, "Can that slut have fled somewhere? But she rarely goes out. How did she manage to go far in this darkness?" Then he thought, "If she's alive, the rope must still be there." When he went again to the door to check, he saw that the rope was gone. "She must have died at the door of the Liu residence. They found her, hid the corpse, and are determined to deny everything." Then again, he thought, "Liu Sanwang didn't go home last night. Toothy Washboard and the boy don't have the strength to move a corpse around. But you never know. Even a bug has feet. They may have had someone help them. After they open the door and come out, I'll watch the way they behave, and I will know."

When the door of the Lius' house finally opened, Zaiwang emerged to go to the marketplace to buy steamed buns and other snacks. He did not look shaken in the slightest. Full of misgivings, Qiu Yida strolled up and down the lane watchfully, but found nothing amiss. Back at home, incensed at the way Chang'er was still snoring in bed, he raised the quilt and gave the boy four or five slaps on his legs. As the boy jumped up from his dream, Yida snapped, "The Liu family has driven your mother to death. You should be asking them to give her back, but here you are, still sleeping!" This was all too clearly an attempt to have Chang'er make a scene, so that he could judge how the situation was.

Upon hearing that his mother was dead, Chang'er burst into sobs. Hurriedly he threw some clothes on and tearfully dashed off to Liu Sanwang's door. "Bitch! Whore!" he yelled. "Give my mother back to me!"

Toothy Washboard Madam Sun was surely not going to take this insult from

Chang'er lying down. Rushing out of the house, she screamed, "Bastard, how dare you come to my house to bully me?" Seizing Chang'er by his hair, she was about to hit him when she saw Qiu Yida coming over. So she let go of the boy, who then hopped all over the lane, crying, cursing, and demanding to have his mother back. Qiu Yida's patience gave out. He also broke into curses. Toothy Washboard was not one to give in. With Zaiwang helping her out by her side, she yelled back until the neighbors came out and separated the two parties.

Qiu Yida told Chang'er to look after the house, whereas he himself went out, had someone write an official complaint for him, and dashed off to the Fuliang county yamen to accuse Liu Sanwang and his wife Sun-shi of homicide. The magistrate accepted the case and had the accused and the neighbors brought to court for questioning.

With her vicious tongue and her propensity to giving offense, Toothy Washboard was not a popular figure in the neighborhood. Therefore, in their depositions, the neighbors could scarcely avoid being somewhat partial to Qiu Yida. By exaggerating the malice of her verbal abuse of Yang-shi, they in fact insinuated that she was responsible for Yang-shi's death. As the neighbors were all telling the same story, the magistrate gave credence to them and believed that Liu Sanwang was hiding the corpse at home to elude the punishment of the law. Their house was searched. Even the ground was dug up, but the search turned up nothing, and thus a conviction was hardly possible. Without ordering torture, the magistrate put Toothy Washboard in detention while he sent lictors to arrest Liu Sanwang and find out what had happened to Yang-shi. Qiu Yida was set free on bail. This was a case for which no easy solution was to be found. Indeed,

> *Toothy Washboard's vicious ravings*
> *Cost the porcelain maker his living.*

Let us retrace our steps and come back to the moment when White Iron dumped the corpse at a door. It was a wineshop owned by a Mr. Wang, some sixty years old. He and his wife made a living selling wine. Around the predawn fifth watch of the night, Mr. Wang heard in his sleep a thump on the door. When he woke up, all was still again, but the moment he closed his eyes, the thumps resumed. In astonishment, he threw some clothes over his shoulders and woke up the shop assistant. Together they opened the door, only to see an object blocking the way. Believing it was a drunken man, Mr. Wang said to the assistant, "Take a good look and see if he's a neighbor or from other parts. If he's a neighbor, go wake up his family and have him taken back home."

The assistant bent down for a closer look, but, being against the starlight, he was unable to see clearly. Taking the hemp rope by the neck to be a horsewhip, he said, "He's not from these parts. I think he's a groom."

"How do you know he's a groom?"

"Because there's a horsewhip by his side."

"If he's not from here, let's leave him alone."

Being a greedy one, the assistant coveted the horsewhip. But when he tried to pick it up, he realized he couldn't, so he gave it a mighty pull, believing the rest of the whip was under the groom. As he did so, the corpse rose to a sitting position. In horror, he shrieked, "Aya!" As he quickly let go of the rope, the corpse fell back to the ground with a thud. Also startled, Mr. Wang asked, "What happened?"

"I thought it was a whip. I was trying to take it, but it turns out to be a rope around the neck of someone strangled to death."

Mr. Wang was horrified. He thought that if he called the local headman, he would be involved in a baffling murder case, but if he did not report it, he might not be able to prove his innocence later on. As he consulted his assistant, the young man said, "Don't worry. Let's get the corpse out of here, and we'll be all right."

"Good idea. But where shall we take it?"

"Let's dump it into the river," said the assistant. Right away, the two of them carried the body to the river. As there were people approaching from afar along the shore, carrying a lantern, they recklessly threw the corpse at the water's edge before the oncoming party could see them, and raced off back home. Of these two, no more for the time being.

Who, you may ask, were those with a lantern walking along the shore? The leader was a rich man of this town, called Zhu Chang. He was a crafty man full of insidious ideas and given to initiating lawsuits. In a fight for land with a Zhao family of a neighboring county, he and about ten servants, armed with many shoulder poles, ropes, and sickles, were on their way to the rice fields to reap rice. With the one carrying the lantern walking in front, they were about to board a boat when they saw someone lying on the ground right by the water's edge. Also taking it to be a drunken man, the one with the lantern said, "This damn fool got himself drunk like this! If he turns over, he'll roll into the river and drown." One of the servants, Bu Cai, Zhu Chang's number-one henchman, crouched and reached out for the waistband of what he thought was a drunkard, believing there should be some money there. The icy coldness of the body gave him such a shock that he swiftly withdrew his hands and cried out, "This is a dead body!"

When Zhu Chang heard this, an evil idea came to his mind. "Quiet!" he ordered. "Bring the lantern over here. Let's see if it was an old man or a young man."

Upon a closer look by the lantern, they saw that it was a woman strangled to death.

"Untie the rope around her neck," said Zhu Chang. "Then carry her to the stern of the boat and hide her."

"Sir, this woman must have been murdered. Why should we get ourselves into trouble?"

"Leave this to me! I will put this corpse to good use."

The servants had to do his bidding. They untied the rope, woke up the boatman, carried the corpse into the boat, hid it in the stern, and covered it up.

"Bu Cai," said Zhu Chang. "You go back and bring five or six women over."

"Why would we need so many people for just twenty or thirty *mu* of rice?" asked Bu Cai.

"You just go get them. I know what I am doing."

Without any idea as to what was on his master's mind, Bu Cai returned home, lantern in hand. Before long, he brought back enough people to fill the boat. The ropes tying the boat to shore were loosened and the boat got under way. With two of the men rowing the oars, the boat left the town.

"What use do you have for that thing, sir?" the men asked.

Zhu Chang replied, "The Zhao family will surely come to stop us from reaping the rice and there'll surely be a good fight until we report to the authorities. Now this corpse is a gift from heaven, to spare me the trouble of going to the authorities. And it'll come in handy in many other wonderful ways, too!"

"And why is that?"

Zhu Chang explained to them what they were to do with the corpse, adding, "Won't that spare me the trouble of going to court? You'll get money out of this, too. If they don't know what's good for them and go to the authorities, we'll still be the winners. Won't that be wonderful?"

The men said in delight, "Ingenious! We would never have thought of that!" Truly,

> He hatched evil schemes and applauded himself;
> He set a trap to bring ruin on others.

Being rustic villagers, these men lacked good sense. Upon hearing the master say that there was money to be had for the taking, they were elated and couldn't wait for the Zhao family to kick up a row right there by the boat. In their eagerness to lay their hands on some silver, they worked the oars furiously. As if on seven or eight wings, the boat got to their destination in no time. The sky had begun to brighten by this time. Zhu Chang ordered that the boat be moored in a deserted open space within an arrow's range of the rice fields. After they all got on shore, they found a rotten straw rope and used it to tie the boat to a bush. One man stayed behind to keep an eye on the boat, whereas all the other men and women went to the fields to reap and thresh the rice. Zhu Chang stood at a distance on the shore, to see how things would develop.

This was a place called Carp Bridge, only a little more than ten li from Jingdezhen. Another li away was Taibai Village, under the jurisdiction of Wuyuan County, Huizhou Prefecture, of the Southern Metropolitan Area. This being the border between two provinces, some residents lived on land that belonged to the other province. The man involved in a land dispute with Zhu Chang was Zhao Wan, also a man of considerable wealth. A resident of Fuliang County, he lived in Wuyuan County and owned land in both counties. Under dispute were the more than thirty *mu* that had belonged to Zhao Wan's cousin, Zhao Ning. He had mortgaged the land to Zhu Chang for a loan but then sold it to Zhao Wan. Afraid that his clandestine dealings would come to light, he rented the land out for cultivation. After hiding the facts from both sides for three or four years, he had recently died suddenly. Hence the fight between the Zhaos and the Zhus. The rice had been planted by Zhao Ning.

Storyteller, the fields being near Zhao Wan's residence, why didn't he reap and thresh the rice first but instead let Zhu Chang get a head start on him? Dear audience, let me tell you, this Zhao Wan was also a bully. Proud of his large fortune, he felt quite secure because he had bought the land from his cousin with all the proper legal procedures and, the land being close to his residence, he thought that Zhu Chang, a resident of another province, would not dare come for the rice. Little did he know that Zhu Chang was one who made it his business to build nests on tigers' heads and to risk death if he had something to gain. And so here Zhu Chang was, challenging the Zhaos.

While Zhu Chang's servants were working in the fields, Zhao Wan's men reported the situation to their master. Zhao Wan said, "That brute has the nerve to taunt me. He's courting death!"

His son, Zhao Shou, said, "Father, as the ancients said, 'The one who comes is fearless. The one who is afraid does not come.' Don't dismiss him lightly."

Zhao Wan asked the one reporting to him, "How many are they?"

"About ten men and six or seven women."

"In that case, we'll send some women there as well. Our men will take on their men and our women will take on their women. Bring them here and break their legs. And pull their boat ashore. They will then know whom they're dealing with." Forthwith he assembled more than twenty strongly built men and about ten women. Sleeves rolled up, fists clenched, they went with the speed of a storm. Zhao Wen and his son followed behind. When the rice fields came into view in the distance, they cried, "Thieves stealing rice, don't move!"

Zhu Chang's servants and their wives stopped what they were doing as soon as they saw the oncoming crowd and ran toward the river. Zhu Chang shouted, "Take off your clothes!" His men removed their clothes, stacked them up into a pile, had one of the women keep an eye on it, and turned back. "Come on!" they exclaimed. "If we lose to you, we won't call ourselves true men!"

Zhao Wan had a tenant farmer called Tian Niu'er. Proud of his own strength, he charged at them before everyone else did. Seeing how fierce he was, Zhu Chang's men quickly dodged off to both sides. When Tian Niu'er had run into their ranks, all the men and women gathered around him, laying siege. "Good!" exclaimed Tian Niu'er as he raised his huge fist and swung it at the face of an able-bodied young man, hoping that if he could knock down a strong one, the others could then be easily crushed like dry weeds and rotten wood. To his surprise, that man happened to be quite a master of martial arts. When the fist was about to land on his face, he turned his head sideways. When the fist came down, missing its target, the man easily grabbed it. Unable to struggle his fist free, Tian Niu'er frantically tried to use his left fist, but before it even got up in the air, another man seized it. With both men holding his fists, one on each side, there was little Tian Niu'er could do. The other men did not beat him but pushed and pulled him so that his feet did not even touch the ground. As if carrying a sedan-chair, they brought him all the way to the boat. The rotten straw rope that tied the boat to shore snapped as soon as they boarded, but the man at the stern had acted in advance and was holding the boat in place by pushing a punt-pole against the shore. In the cabin, the men fell upon Tian Niu'er and rained blows on him.

Seeing that Tian Niu'er had been taken into the boat, the men from the Zhao family flocked to the boat to get him back. The women of the Zhu family quickly dispersed to let them board. In less time than it takes to narrate, as soon as the men and women of the Zhu family were all on the boat, the man holding the punt-pole against the shore abruptly swung the pole around. Then, with one mighty shove with the pole, he turned the boat away from the shore, and the boat went toward the middle of the river with the speed of an arrow. There being too many people on board, the boat swayed from side to side a few times and capsized. All forty men and women from both families fell into the water. As the women struggled to get ashore, the men came to blows in the water, throwing up columns of water that then fell like driving rain. The bedazzled onlookers shouted from the shore, "Stop! If you've got something to say, come up on shore and talk it out!"

In the midst of the fight, Bu Cai took advantage of the confusion to carry over the woman's corpse. "We need the local headman!" he yelled. "The Zhao family has beaten one of us to death!" With Zhu Chang and the six or seven women picking up the cry on the shore, the clamor shook heaven and earth. Upon hearing that there was a death, the women of the Zhao family who were wringing their clothes dry fled, their hair and clothes still wet. Those in the water were frightened out of their wits. Wondering who could have done this, they were only too eager to make themselves scarce, and therefore got themselves badly beaten when the men from the Zhu family pressed their advantage and gave chase. As soon as they struggled ashore, they ran for dear life, each hating his parents for having given him only two legs.

Zhu's servants wanted to run after them, but Zhu Chang stopped them, saying, "The fight is over. Carry the corpse to their house before we do anything further."

After the corpse was pulled ashore, Bu Cai made a show of grief, claiming that the dead one was his wife. Zhu Chang then told them to pick up the poles and the oars and deposit them with a tenant farmer. To the onlookers he announced, "Neighbors, you all witnessed what happened. They beat one of us to death. I'm not falsely charging Zhao Wan. Please be so kind as to serve as witnesses in court. You need only tell the truth." Those last two phrases were said to enlist the help of a mediator. If someone among the crowd whose words carried weight had advised Zhu Chang not to carry the corpse to the Zhao residence and had instead helped bring about a settlement out of court, this whole business would not have led to the loss of so many lives later on. However, Zhao Wan and his son were not easy to talk to as a rule. If they rejected the advice, the mediator would only have been courting humiliation. Moreover, no one had any idea what Zhu Chang had in mind. Therefore, no one offered to mediate. Getting no response, Zhu Chang had his men put their clothes back on, roll up the corpse with a reed mat, and tie the bundle with strings. As four men carried it to the Zhao residence, the onlookers followed behind to see how the two families would settle the matter.

> *A copper pot clashed with an iron broom;*
> *One villain was harassed by another.*

Zhao Wan and his son had been filled with delight when they were trailing behind and watching from afar their servants chasing Zhu Chang's followers. As they drew near, however, they saw their women running helter-skelter in all directions, as wet as drowned chickens. In astonishment, Zhao Wan said, "We outnumber them. Why were our people driven into the river?" As he hastened forward, his servants saw him and cried out, "Sir, big trouble! Go back at once!"

Zhao Shou snapped, "What a useless bunch you are! How did you get yourselves beaten up like this?"

"To get beaten up is not a big deal. The problem is, one of their people died. What's to be done now?"

Upon hearing that he had a death on his hands, Zhao Wan was so horrified that half of his body went limp. He could not move another step, as if his feet had been nailed to the ground. With Zhao Shou and Tian Niu'er supporting him, one on each side, he managed to return home. A good while after he sat down, he found his tongue again and asked, "How did this happen?"

The men related how they had come to blows and how the boat had capsized, adding, "We didn't hit any women. We have no idea how that woman died. She must have drowned."

Not knowing what to do, Zhao Wan cried, "Now, what's to be done?"

All the members of the family, old and young, gathered in the room, terrified. While they were talking, the janitor came and announced, "The Zhu family's men are here with the corpse." This announcement gave Zhao Wan one more shock. He froze and sat motionless, like a monk in meditation.

As the old saying goes, "When things reach one extreme, they turn back toward the other. A man in desperation will have a flash of inspiration." Zhao Shou suddenly had an idea. "Father, don't panic," he said. "I've got a plan." To the servants he said, "You hide yourselves outside. After they come in, listen for a signal from me. As soon as I hit a gong, you all come in and seize them, but several of you keep watch at the door. Seize every one of them, take them all to the authorities, and accuse them of robbery in broad daylight. That way, the homicide case against us will be dealt with more leniently."

Thus instructed, the men turned to go. Afraid that they would beat more people to death, Zhao Wan ordered, "Just seize them. Don't beat them."

The men acknowledged the order and went out like a gust of wind. Zhao Shou kept behind Zhao Yilang, his adopted grandson, whom he trusted, saying, "You stay here." Then he told the wives and children to withdraw and not to come out.

To his son, Zhao Wan said, "We may very well accuse them of robbery, but I'm afraid robbery won't set off the crime of homicide they accuse us of."

Zhao Shou walked up to him and whispered his plan in his father's ear. Zhao Wan was so delighted upon hearing it that he regained all his vigor. "There is not a moment to lose," he said. "Act quickly and have the whole thing over and done with."

After closing every door, Zhao Shou found an ax, a wooden club, and two door panels. When everything was ready, he sent Zhao Yilang into the kitchen to summon an old man called Ding Wen. In his sixties, he was Zhao Wan's cousin on the maternal side. Suffering from hepatitis, he could eat all right but was unable to do much work. Being childless, he was made to work in the kitchen to attend to the kitchen fire for a living. Knowing nothing about what was happening, he drew near and asked, "What do you have to say, cousin?" Before Zhao Wan had time to answer, Zhao Shou lunged forward and hit him on the temple with the club. Crying "Aya!" the old man collapsed on the floor. Zhao Shou stepped forward and finished him off with another blow.

Zhao Shou thought he was unobserved, but Tian Niu'er's mother, who lived right behind the Zhao residence, saw him. Having heard about a death, she was afraid that her son might have been responsible. Anxiously she came to find out what was going on and happened to see Zhao Shou in action. She was so appalled that she sank to the floor. Too terrified to get up, she said, "Amitabha Buddha! How can anyone do such a thing, and in broad daylight, too!"

Zhao Wan heard her. He turned his head, took a glance at the woman, and signaled to his son with his eyes. Zhao Shou understood. He charged forward and hit the woman's forehead with one strike of his club. As her brains dashed out and blood flowed, he kicked her three or four times in the chest to make sure that she was dead. It was all over with her. That one penny had taken another two lives. Truly,

> *Patience does one good;*
> *Willfulness brings one disaster.*

Zhao Yilang had no inkling as to Zhao Shou's intentions when he went to summon the old man. This act of murder so shocked him that he cringed and hid himself in a corner. Old man Ding had just died when old woman Tian burst on the scene. With two deaths now, Yilang was afraid he would be the third one to go. He wanted to sneak off, but in his frenzy of panic his feet just would not budge, as if they had been held down by rocks weighing a thousand catties. In this moment of despair, he heard Zhao Wan call him, "Yilang, come here at once and help us out!"

Relieved to hear that his help was needed, Yilang struggled to his feet and helped Zhao Shou drag the two corpses into the main hall. They put the corpses behind the standing screen that blocked from view the back door leading to the courtyard, put two door panels over them, and loosened the panels of the screen from their grooves. To Zhao Yilang, Zhao Wan said, "You must not tell anyone about this. After this whole thing blows over, I'll give you a portion of the family property."

"I owe everything to you, sir. How would I dream of telling anyone about this?"

They had just gotten everything ready when a clamor of voices came to their ears. Zhu Chang and his followers were there. Zhao Wan, his son, and Yilang withdrew into a side room, closed the door, leaving a crack, and peeped out from behind it.

Zhu Chang and his servants and their wives carried the corpse to the Zhao residence. Barging right into the main hall, smashing everything they saw, they found that the doors and the windows on all sides were tightly closed. Not a shadow of a man was in sight. Zhu Chang said, "Put the corpse in the middle of the room and then let's march on to the inner section of the house, bring out that old turtle Zhao Wan, and chain him to the feet of the corpse."

They went into action. As they banged away at the screen, which had already been loosened from the grooves, the panels readily gave way and fell on the corpses. Little knowing that there were bodies on the other side of the screen, Zhu Chang and his followers charged forward.

Seeing that the screen panels had been knocked down, Zhao Shou sounded the gong, whereupon those waiting outside gave a cry and swarmed in. Hearing the gong, Zhu Chang thought that Zhao's people were there to snatch away the corpse he had brought in. Quickly he led his group back into the main hall. As the two groups of people came to blows, some rolling on the floor in one heap, Zhao Wan bellowed from the side room, "Tian Niu'er! Your mother has been beaten to death! Don't let any of them get away!"

Tian Niu'er rushed over and asked, "Why was my mother here and how did she die?"

Zhao Wan replied, "She came with Old Man Ding to ask me what was happening. Then they knocked down the screen and killed her. I ran off quickly and was spared. If I had taken a moment longer, I would have died, too!"

When Tian Niu'er and Zhao Yilang moved the screen panels away, two corpses were exposed to view. Upon seeing his mother's mangled head, Tian Niu'er burst into wails. Zhu Chang thought he was faking it, but, turning around to look, he saw that, indeed, there were two corpses. Panic-stricken, he scampered off toward the door. With the master showing a clean pair of heels, his followers, men and women, all took flight, all the while exchanging blows with the pursuers.

To their dismay, the door was closely guarded. Every one of them was captured.

Thanks to Zhao Wan, who kept shouting, "Do not hurt them!" Zhu Chang and the others were not badly beaten. Zhao Shou took out chains and ropes and tied the men and the women together in the hall.

After crying bitterly for a while, Tian Niu'er jumped up in fury and said, "Let me beat that dog Zhu Chang to death, the way he did my mother to death!"

Blocking his way, Zhao Wan said, "No! No! We'll go to the authorities. Don't beat him!" And he had some men drag Tian Niu'er to one side.

By this time, news had spread throughout the neighborhood and beyond. As the neighbors descended on the house to watch the goings-on, Zhao Wan went to the inner section of the house to prepare a feast for them and then asked them to write a deposition testifying to the "burglary and acts of homicide committed in broad daylight." Being Zhao Wan's relatives, tenant farmers, and hired laborers, they all complied. Before the night was out, Zhao Wan prepared four or five barges to carry the neighbors and the witnesses and stuffed Zhu Chang and his followers, all chained and trussed up, in two of the barges. After traveling the whole night, they arrived in Wuyuan County the next morning.

When the county magistrate called his morning court session to order, the local headman and the witnesses presented their report to him. After reading it and asking for more details, the magistrate dispatched lictors to escort the headman and Zhao Wan, Tian Niu'er, and Bu Cai, relatives of the dead, back to the Zhao residence to encoffin the three corpses and bring them to the yamen for the coroner's examination. Zhu Chang and his followers were taken to the lockup to await further instructions. Some tenant farmers went to Zhu Chang's house to report, and his son, Zhu Tai, came posthaste to see him, but we need not dwell on that.

As a proverb puts it so well, "Official wheels grind slowly." The coffins duly arrived, but the magistrate could hardly be expected to attend to the case right away. It was more than half a month later that he issued the order for the local headman to make preparations for the examination. Zhu Chang and the others were taken out of the lockup to the mortuary. After examining the corpses one by one, the coroner reported, "Ding Wen died of a wound in his temple. The wound is more than two inches long and the adjacent bones were smashed to pieces. Mrs. Tian's skull is broken. No brains remain, and three of her ribs are broken from kicking. These two individuals were indeed beaten to death. As for Bu Cai's wife, there are marks of strangulation by rope around her neck, but no signs of injury elsewhere. She died of strangulation."

The magistrate was taken aback. He thought, "The report says she drowned when the boat capsized. How could she have been strangled to death?"

At this point, Zhu Chang said, "We've got witnesses. How could she have been strangled? All too obviously, the coroner has been bribed by Zhao Wan into lying to Your Honor."

Suspecting Zhao Wan of having switched corpses, the magistrate summoned Bu Cai and asked, "Go up to take a look at the corpse. Is it your wife?"

Bu Cai went up for a look and came back to say, "Yes."

"Did she die right away on the spot that day?"

"Yes," said Bu Cai.

Having asked these questions, the magistrate went down the dais, examined the three corpses himself, and found the coroner's conclusions correct. "How strange!" he said to himself. Aloud, he ordered that the coffins be covered and sealed and brought to the county yamen, where he would be trying the case. While riding in his sedan-chair, he gave his mind to the mystery and worked out a theory.

Back in his courtroom, he sat down and ordered that the parties involved in the case all kneel down outside of the inner gate of the yamen compound. He summoned Zhu Chang and said, "Zhu Chang, you not only killed two people of the Zhao family, but also murdered that woman. Out with the truth now!"

"That woman was the wife of my servant, Bu Cai. She did indeed drown after Zhao Wen's people pushed her into the river. Local residents witnessed it. How could I have murdered her? If you don't believe me, Your Honor, just ask Bu Cai, and you'll know the truth."

"Nonsense!" roared the magistrate. "Bu Cai is your man! You think I don't know that? How dare you lie to me? Apply the ankle-squeezer on him!"

With a cry, the lictors went forward, took off Zhu Chang's shoes and socks, and applied the squeezer on him. He shrieked in pain. Being a rich man, he had never been put to such pain, although he was no stranger to the courtroom in his passion for lawsuits. He saw nothing for it but to come out with the truth. "We found that corpse by the river at Fuliang," he said. "I have no idea who had abandoned it there."

The magistrate recorded the confession, told him to kneel at the foot of the dais, and summoned Bu Cai.

"Was the dead woman your wife?"

"Yes, Your Honor."

"If so, why did you murder her and frame Zhao Wan?"

"Your Honor, she drowned when Zhao Wan's people pushed her into the river that day. There were witnesses."

The magistrate slapped the table with the "silencer"[5] seven or eight times and roared, "You scoundrel! Whose wife was she? You falsely claimed that she was your wife in order to frame another man, didn't you? Your master has already confessed. It was you who murdered her. How dare you tell such lies? Apply the squeezer on him at once!"

With the magistrate yelling and striking the table with the silencer in the manner of a Daoist priest with his magic tablet, Bu Cai was so terrified that his soul took flight. Upon hearing that his master had confessed, he said resignedly, "It was the master who told me to say she was my wife. I had no part in that." (*What kind of man is he?*)

"I want the details!" ordered the magistrate.

Bu Cai related how they had come upon the corpse on their way to the boat and how plans had been drawn up to frame Zhao Wan. His account tallied with Zhu Chang's deposition in every detail.

Knowing they had told the truth, the magistrate continued, "Even though you didn't murder this woman, you shouldn't have claimed she was your wife and framed an innocent man. But Ding Wen and Mrs. Tian were beaten to death by you and your master. There's no denying that fact."

"Your Honor, I didn't do it. Even if I die from the squeezer, I won't confess to that."

The magistrate told him to kneel down at the foot of the dais and called in Zhao Wan and the local headman. Both insisted that Zhu Chang had carried the corpse into the Zhao Residence and taken advantage of the commotion to beat those two to death. Having established the facts about Zhu Chang's attempts to frame Zhao Wan, the magistrate thought that Zhu Chang must have been lying about those two deaths as well. Again he had the ankle-squeezer applied to Zhu Chang. The pain was too much for him. He admitted to the false charge. The magistrate ordered forty strokes of the bamboo each for Zhu Chang and Bu Cai, sentenced them to death, and sent them to death row. The other ten people were given twenty strokes each. Three were to be deported to a remote area for penal service, and seven were sentenced to labor camps. All were taken to jail for the time being. The six women were flogged and sent back to their hometowns. The rice fields were given back to Zhao Wan, who, on behalf of Zhao Ning, returned the money borrowed from Zhu Chang. The magistrate then wrote a note to the authorities of Fuliang County, asking them to conduct investigations on the female corpse.

Zhu Chang had hoped that with the corpse he could bluff Zhao Wan because, for fear of a lawsuit involving a murder, Zhao Wan would surely have had a mediator arrange a private settlement. Not only would the more than thirty *mu* of land all be his, but he could also have made Zhao Wan pay through the nose. Such was the purpose of all his machinations. He never foresaw that Zhao Shou would be driven to such horrendous acts in retaliation and that he would fall into the latter's trap instead. In jail, he was overcome with regret, thinking, "If we hadn't seen that corpse that morning, things wouldn't have come to this pass." Truly,

> Had he known that he would be beaten at his game,
> He would not have racked his brain in the first place.

Believing that it would be virtually impossible to reverse the verdict in this county yamen, Zhu Chang told his son, "Those three coffins, with their thin boards and few nails, will surely begin to rot when spring comes around. Now, you go talk to people in the records office and make sure the documents of this case are not sent elsewhere. After you go back home, tell the women to keep their mouths shut about that strangled corpse. In the meantime, appeal to the higher authorities of our own province and, in the fourth or fifth month of next year, urge them to review the case. By that time, the neck with its rope marks will have decomposed, so we'll have a chance to deny the charge. If one charge can't be substantiated, the whole case will fall apart. I'm confident the death sentence can be overturned." And so Zhu Tai went to do his father's bidding. Of this, more later.

Let us come back to the assistant in Mr. Wang's wineshop in Jingdezhen. After helping with getting rid of the corpse, he looked forward to payment from Mr. Wang, but two or three days went by without a sign of anything coming his way. He dropped a few hints but still failed to get a response from Mr. Wang. After several more days, his patience ran out. To Mr. Wang's face he said, not mincing his words, "Sir, you're lucky that I got rid of you-know-what that night. If I had not been there, the local headman would have notified the authorities after daybreak, and the police would have been out investigating. They'll make allowances for someone like you whose money doesn't come all that easily, but even if they don't ask to be treated to wine, they'll ask for tea. What's worse, you may talk yourself out of saliva but still won't be able to get yourself out of trouble. I've saved you lots of money. Why don't you even thank me?"

Generally speaking, petty rogues like him are most narrow-minded. On those rare occasions when they do someone a good turn, they blow it out of all proportion and demand a handsome reward. If not satisfied, they turn around and bring ruin on the man. Those who ask the wrong people for help will suffer for it. In the case of that assistant, he did nothing but carry a heavy object for a brief moment, and yet he expected to be paid. If Mr. Wang had had better sense, he would have given the young man some money, whatever the amount, and that would have been that. As it turned out, however, old Mr. Wang was a miser who hung on to every penny. Asking money from him was like demanding flesh from his body, and he would redden to the roots of his hair.

Now that the assistant was asking to be paid, old Mr. Wang flew into a rage. "You are so unreasonable!" he lashed out. "You are a black-hearted one! I feed you. I pay you wages. How can you ask for extra payment for such a trivial thing? Didn't you just walk a few steps?"

At this outburst, the assistant yelled, "What are you talking about? It's not a big deal if you don't give me anything. Why get so mad? You feed me and pay me wages because you need me. You're not paying me for nothing. But let me make this clear: The wages are for working in the shop. They don't cover dragging corpses."

At this point, Mrs. Wang came over and said, "What a savage you are! And a cunning one, too! As the ancients said, 'Even an eggplant yields to the old.' How can you raise your voice at an old man like that? Where's your respect?"

"Ma'am, I did him a service. Instead of paying me for it, he carries on like that. How can I not raise my voice?"

"What?" shot back Mr. Wang. "Did I murder her? Are you blackmailing me?"

"No, you didn't commit the murder, but moving a corpse without authorization must also be a crime."

"All right, go ahead and report me to the authorities."

"That's no problem, but you may not be ready for it."

Mr. Wang stepped forward and said, "Go ahead and report! I'm not afraid." With that, he pushed the young man out by his neck. Caught off guard, the young man lost his balance and tumbled out the door. He fell on the back of his head and blood flowed out. Infuriated by this fall, he cursed, "Old turtle! You short-changed me, and turned around and beat me!" From the ground he picked up a brick and threw it at Mr. Wang. As fate would have it, the brick hit Mr. Wang smack in the temple. He fell and made not another sound. His wife frantically went to raise him, but, his mouth open, his eyes glazed over, he ceased to be. Mrs. Wang stamped her feet and cried to heaven and earth. That one little penny took another life.

> Lives are lost over the love of money,
> For money and life are rolled into one.

Realizing that old Mr. Wang was dead, the assistant scrambled to his feet and ran. Mrs. Wang called the neighbors for help and they caught up with him, brought him back, and chained him to Mr. Wang's feet. "What happened?" they asked Mrs. Wang, whereupon Mrs. Wang told them everything through her sobs, adding, "Please stand up for this old woman!"

The neighbors said, "We had no idea this fellow was such a scoundrel! Let's make him suffer a little before taking him to the authorities." Three or four neighbors walked up and kicked and punched him until he was more dead than alive. Then they told Mrs. Wang to close her door and go with them to the county yamen to lodge a complaint against the assistant. By this time, the story had spread around. People came from far and near to watch.

In the meantime, Qiu Yida had been searching in vain for his wife's corpse, feeling low because, without the corpse, his case could not be closed. That day, upon hearing about what had led to the assistant's killing of old Mr. Wang, he thought, "Could it be my wife's corpse?" Eagerly he went to ask. It was the very moment when Mrs. Wang was locking her door in preparation for going to complain to the authorities. Qiu Yida asked her in detail and, after counting the days, concluded that it was the very night his wife had disappeared. He said, "No wonder my wife's corpse disappeared that very night. So you disposed of it. Now that I've got a witness, Toothy Washboard won't be able to deny her way out of it. Let me go with you to the yamen."

And so the assistant was taken to the county yamen. The next morning, when the magistrate called his court session to order, the assistant was brought under guard into the courtroom. The local headman gave a report and the magistrate questioned Mrs. Wang on the details. Knowing he would not be able to deny the facts, the assistant confessed before torture was applied. He was given thirty strokes of the rod, sentenced to death, and taken to jail. Qiu Yida then stated that his wife had been murdered by Liu Sanwang on exactly the same night and that therefore the corpse must have been left at the wineshop by Liu. Now that the evidence was conclusive, he asked for a closure of the case. But the document from Wuyuan County had not arrived yet, and the magistrate could not bring the case to a close without a corpse. So he ordered another search for the corpse.

As for the assistant, he had already suffered injuries from the neighbors' fists and feet. The strokes of the bamboo rod in the courtroom were also severe enough. In jail, without anything to bribe the wardens with, he was again beaten up. In three days, he died of hemorrhage. That penny took another life.

> It was all for the love of white silver
> That each of them went to Yellow Springs.[6]

On his way home from the county yamen, Qiu Yida was passing by White Iron's shop when he heard heart-rending cries inside. What had happened was that White Iron had caught a cold when he was disposing of the corpse that night in fear. As soon as he got home and lay down in bed, he began to run a fever. After about ten days with unabated symptoms, he breathed his last, and his wife was now wailing in grief. Because of that one penny, another life was gone.

> The netherworld gained a terrified ghost;
> The mortal world lost a skilled ironsmith.

After learning upon inquiry of the blacksmith's death, Qiu Yida said with a sigh, "He was such a good man. He's just had a few days of a good life, and now he's gone. Clearly we mortal beings are all too vulnerable." Back at home, the only company he had was his son, who cowered in a corner. There was not even a drop of warm water to be had in the house. Saddened by these wretched circumstances, he began to regret his stupidity in driving his wife to her death. And now, having landed himself in such a fix, he was eaten with vexation. In no mood to attend to his work, he spent his days looking everywhere for the corpse, but to no avail.

The remainder of the year passed slowly. By the time the middle of the fifth month rolled around, the inspectorate had already accepted the appeal of Zhu Tai, Zhu Chang's son, and referred the case to Fuliang County for review. (*The strangled corpse was from Fuliang County, but the case is now referred back to Fuliang County. This is not a wise decision.*) The Fuliang County yamen accordingly asked that the prisoners and the coffins be brought from Wuyuan County for trial. Zhu Tai dragged his feet at first, but when the fifth month came around, he believed the corpse should have decomposed and therefore sent a lavish gift to the records office of Wuyuan County, so that proceedings on the case could get under way. As for Zhao Wan and his son, believing themselves off the hook because Wuyuan County had closed the case, they went to court confidently, their file in hand.

Lictors of both counties took the prisoners and the three corpses to Fuliang County and handed over their charge to the magistrate, who, in his turn, put the prisoners in jail, had the coffins taken to the county mortuary, and sent a reply to Wuyuan County, but this needs no more narration.

A few days later, the magistrate ordered that the prisoners be brought before him for trial. Zhu Tai, in his determination to defeat Zhao Wan in this case, had by this time bribed everyone in the yamen.

After the magistrate sat down in the mortuary, Zhao Wan presented him with Wuyuan County's file on the case. After reading the file, the magistrate said to Zhu Chang, "The case about your borrowing a corpse to frame another man and beating two individuals to death has already been closed. Why are you bringing it up again?"

Zhu Chang said, "Your Honor, there were many witnesses to Yu-shi's death. She drowned after Zhao Wan's people pushed her into the river. But he bribed the local headman and the coroner into falsely claiming that the woman had died from strangulation. As for Ding Wen and Mrs. Tian, Zhao Wan killed them to cover up his other act of murder, and then he accused me of beating those two to death. I don't even have to present other arguments. Just consider this, Your Honor: I and all my servants were captured at the same time by Zhao Wan's men. That very fact alone proves Zhao Wan's immense power. How would I even manage to kill two of his people? What's more, both were in their seventies. Would I have known enough about his people to pick out only those approaching death? I trust that in view of the above, Your Honor will certainly establish the truth."

"If so," said the magistrate, "why did you confess?"

"Zhao Wan had bribed the yamen into putting me to torture. If I had not confessed under coercion, I wouldn't have survived."

Zhao Wan stated, "On that day, because they had that corpse, Zhu Chang and his men hit whomever they saw. Everyone in my family fled from them, except Ding Wen and Mrs. Tian, who were too old to run fast enough and therefore died at their hands. The marks of strangulation on the corpse's neck were verified by the magistrate of Wuyuan County himself. How could this have been the coroner's fabrication? Now that so much time has gone by, the corpse must have decomposed, and that's exactly why he is trying to dupe you with those lies, Your Honor, to try to slip through the net of the law and turn the case against us. Your Honor will surely get the truth upon a careful reading of the file."

"I can't go by what you say," said the magistrate. Forthwith he ordered that the coffins be opened for an examination.

Now, won't you agree that what happened next was the strangest thing in the world? Everyone thought that the corpses should have decomposed by this time. As it turned out, however, they were so well preserved that they looked as if still alive. As for the rope marks on Yang-shi's neck, they were, if anything, more clearly visible than before. The coroner did not know what to do. Why? Because he had received bribes from Zhu Chang. If the corpse had decomposed, he could have maneuvered for Zhu Chang's acquittal and incriminated Zhao Wan. But with the marks still intact, if he lied, the magistrate might want to check again himself. If he told the truth, how would he get to keep Zhu Chang's money? While he was debating with himself, the magistrate guessed what was afoot and went down the steps to see for himself. With the magistrate keeping a watchful eye on him, the coroner dared not hide anything and made a factual report. Zhu Chang let out an inward groan.

After checking the wounds against the coroner's report as well as the record on file and finding not one slightest discrepancy, the magistrate said to Zhu Chang, "Your crimes have already been established. Why did you again file a false complaint?"

As Zhu Chang desperately pleaded his case, the magistrate snapped angrily, "Preposterous! Apply the squeezer on him! Confess! Where did you get that strangled woman's corpse?"

Under torture, Zhu Chang had to confess. "I came upon that corpse early that morning by the river. I have no idea who left her there."

With his capacious memory, the magistrate suddenly remembered. He thought, "Last year, Qiu Yida reported that he couldn't find his wife's corpse. Later, Mrs. Wang of the wineshop accused the assistant of beating her husband to death. She said that they fought because they had carried a corpse to the river and dumped it by the riverside. And the whereabouts of the corpse remain a mystery. Could this corpse be that very same one?" He made a mental note of the information. Right away, he ordered that Zhu Chang and Bu Cai be given thirty strokes of the rod each and taken to death row, as before. He commuted the other servants' sentences and released them on bail. Zhao Wan was allowed to return home. So much for this.

Upon returning to his office in the county yamen, the magistrate took out Qiu Yida's deposition as well as the file on the wineshop assistant. Sure enough, the dates were identical and the place where the shop assistant dumped the corpse was exactly where Zhu Chang had found it. Left with no doubt in his mind, he had the same lictors who were on Zhu Chang's case bring Qiu Yida, Liu Sanwang, and other witnesses and take Toothy Washboard Sun-shi from jail to the mortuary to identify the corpse.

It being the fifth month, a contagious disease was going around the jailhouse. Sun-shi had just recovered from a bout of the sickness and could hardly walk. Liu Sanwang and their son, Zaiwang, helped her along all the way to the mortuary. When the coroner removed the lid of the coffin, Qiu Yida recognized his wife's corpse. As he wailed in grief, he shouted over and over again, "Yes, this is my wife!"

The neighbors serving as witnesses also said, "This is indeed Yang-shi."

When the magistrate questioned them on the cause of the death, Qiu Yida held to his story, saying, "Liu Sanwang and his wife came to my house and beat and cursed at my wife. She couldn't take the humiliation and hanged herself as a result."

Liu Sanwang and Sun-shi tried desperately to protest their innocence. The local headman and the neighbors all explained that Sun-shi was the one who had pro-voked Yang-shi and that Liu Sanwang had nothing to do with the case. The mag-istrate ordered that the ankle-squeezer be applied on Sun-shi. Having just recovered from an illness, Sun-shi was still weak. In addition, after all the exertion of walk-ing to the mortuary and talking in defense of herself, she was already looking ghastly. The pain from the ankle-squeezer gave her such a shock that her breathing stopped. With a flop, she fell and died. That one little penny took one more life. Truly,

> One more gossiper in the netherworld;
> One fewer voice in future quarrels.

At this point, the magistrate ordered that the ankle-squeezer be removed. Liu Sanwang stepped forward and called Sun-shi's name until he was hoarse, but to no avail. With Zaiwang weeping bitterly on one side, the prefect said to Qiu Yida in sympathy, "Your wife died after a quarrel with Sun-shi, not from Liu Sanwang's fists. Now that Sun-shi is also dead, you are even. From now on, the two families should be reconciled with each other. Both families can take the corpses home for burial. Neither is allowed to bring the matter to court again. Anyone who violates this order will be severely punished."

Everyone kowtowed and accepted the order. The corpses were taken home for burial, but no more of this need be said.

Having spent so much money only to be beaten in court, Zhu Chang and Bu Cai in prison were so upset that they fell ill. And the contagious disease also got to them. Succumbing to two illnesses at the same time, both of them died a few days later. Another two lives were lost on account of that one penny.

> Before they were able to frame others,
> They brought ruin first on themselves.

Storyteller, let me say something: Granted that Zhu Chang died a tragic death and his family was destroyed because of his maliciousness—but Zhao Wan and his son brutally killed two innocent people and falsely charged two others of crime, and yet they slipped through the net of justice and got to live in peace and afflu-ence. This goes to show that the arm of divine justice is not long enough.

Dear audience, have you heard this old saying?

> Good is returned with good;
> Evil is returned with evil.
> It is not that retribution is lacking,
> But you must wait for the right timing.

Heaven remembers everything. Since time immemorial, has Heaven ever missed a mark? Zhao Wan and his son slipped through the net of justice and enjoyed peace and affluence partly because their destined years of good fortune were not up, partly because the right time had not arrived, and also because this poor storyteller has only one mouth and one tongue. When I tell of what happened on this side, I can't attend to what happened on that side, can I? I will have to take up the retributions one by one. But enough of such idle comments.

Now, having defeated Zhu Chang once again, Zhao Wan and his son returned home. Relatives and neighbors all came to offer their congratulations. A celebration feast lasted several days. After another few days, when news came that Zhu Chang and Bu Cai had both died, they were all the more jubilant. Tian Niu'er took his mother's corpse back to his hometown for burial, so that the body would not lie exposed too long, but of him, more later.

Time sped by. Before anyone noticed it, more than one year had elapsed. In spite of his advanced years, Zhao Wan remained a lustful man. He had a concubine named Aida'er, who was something of a beauty. With her coquettish ways, she was in the prime of her youth. For all his lust, Zhao Wan was getting on in years, after all, and could only muddle through the motions without gratifying her. The old man's adopted grandson, Zhao Yilang, however, was a strongly built and clever young man, yet unbetrothed. And Aida'er cast eyes of affection on him. Every so often she went to the kitchen, where she rubbed shoulders with him and led him on with flirtatious words.

Now, won't you agree that there are all too few men like Liuxia Hui and the Man of Lu in this world?[7] If a woman takes the initiative and tries to seduce a man, will that man ever reject her? After furtively exchanging significant glances for a few days, they went ahead and did you-know-what. Both being young, they were like a couple of hungry tigers. When would they ever be satiated? The woman sneaked into Zhao Yilang's room at every opportunity for a stolen moment of pleasure. Knowing a trick or two, Zhao Yilang sent the woman into transports of joy. How she wished she could be in this bodily union with him at all times of the day and night!

About half a year into this clandestine relationship, Aida'er said to Zhao Yilang one day, "You and I have been enjoying each other for quite some time now, but with so many eyes and ears around us, we are always in such haste that we don't get to enjoy ourselves to the full. We'd better slip away and go to some faraway place to be a regular wedded couple."

"If you really want to be with me, we can be husband and wife right here. Why go far?"

"You are the man of my heart. Do you doubt me? How can we become husband and wife right here?"

"Remember old Mr. Ding and Mrs. Tian? It was my grandfather and the young master who killed them and then accused the Zhu family of doing it. At the time, I helped them carry the corpses. I was promised that after the thing blew over, I would be given a portion of the family property. That wooden club is still in my possession. This is something I haven't told you since we fell in love. But if you want to marry me, I can ask Grandpa for my portion of the property and find a place to live. Then I'll ask a matchmaker to tell him I want to marry you. He will have to agree. If he doesn't want to give you up, you can slip away. Will he say no? If he doesn't know better, I'll tell Tian Niu'er the truth and go with him to the authorities. Grandpa's life will be in jeopardy."

Aida'er was beside herself with joy. "There is not a moment to lose," she said. "Get this done as soon as possible." With that, she sneaked out of his room.

The next day, learning that Zhao Wan was sitting idly by himself in the hall, Zhao Yilang went up to him and said, "Grandpa, you promised me that after that business was over, you would give me a portion of the family property. Now, the business with the Zhu family has long been settled. Please give me my share, so that I can do whatever I want with it."

Zhao Wan said, "I heard you."

The next day, Zhao Yilang went to the inner quarters of the house, where he met Aida'er, and gave her a note that said, "I've talked to Grandpa. Keep your eyes and ears open and see if he's willing." Aida'er nodded in understanding. Both then went their separate ways. Of this, no more for now.

Zhao Wan took Zhao Shou into a side room, closed the door, and, in a subdued voice, repeated Zhao Yilang's words to his son, adding, "I gave that promise in a moment of clouded wits. What's to be done now?"

"Those sweet words were said just to fool him. How can he really count on them?"

"Well, the promise was given, which was wrong, but now, if we don't give him anything, he's not going to give up."

Zhao Shou thought for a while and then another evil idea came to him. "If we indulge him, he'll come for money every month, and there'll be no end to the extortions. Since he's the only one onto this, let's do away with him, to remove a source of all future trouble."

If the old man had a kind heart and had told his son to give up the idea and fobbed Yilang off with some small gifts, he might have averted disaster. Instead, he did what he should never have done. He said, "I've been thinking along the same lines, but I don't have a plan."

"What's so difficult about that? Let's buy some arsenic tomorrow, put it in his wine, and make him drink it in the evening. And that'll be that. Outsiders know that we've always treated him well. No one will suspect anything."

Delighted, Zhao Wan thought they had the perfect stratagem, believing that his talk with his son was unbeknownst to gods and humans. But in fact, Aida'er had seen them enter the room. Suspecting that they would be talking about this matter, she tiptoed after them and pressed herself against the partition wall to listen. She did catch a phrase or two, but she was not able to make out every word.

Afraid that she would bump into them on their way out, she quickly returned to her own room. She wanted to inform Zhao Yilang about it, but, not having heard clearly, she felt she couldn't very well exaggerate what might have just been a minor thing. Then an idea occurred to her. At night, she plied the old man with wine until he was very much the worse for drink. In bed, she put her arms around the old man and used her charms on him until the old man was so enraptured that, in his wine-induced excitability, he got himself started in the game. In the midst of the joy, Aida'er said, "I have something to tell you. I haven't brought it up until now because I was afraid you would take it too hard. But not telling you really bothers me."

The old man was happily panting, but, upon hearing this, he stopped and said, "Who made you so upset?"

"It's that brute Yilang. He tried to seduce me this morning. When I wanted to take him to you, he said, 'The lives of Grandpa and the young master are in my hands. They won't make things difficult for me.' I have no idea why he boasted like that. If he says the same thing to outsiders, people will think that our family has done wicked things. Won't that tarnish the family name? We'd better think of a way to bump off that scoundrel and remove a source of all future trouble."

"The impudence of that swine! But it's all right. It'll be done tomorrow evening."

"What will be done tomorrow evening?"

That old man was destined to die at this time anyway. He told her everything about the plan to poison Yilang.

Having learned all she needed to know, the woman went to report to Zhao Yilang first thing in the morning. Zhao Yilang was flabbergasted. He thought, "They are so ruthless that they even want me to die. How can I let him off?" He took out that wooden club, locked his door, and went in all haste to see Tian Niu'er and told him everything. Tian Niu'er was so outraged that he wanted to denounce the old man to his face. Zhao Yilang stopped him, saying, "If you raise it in the open, you'll only alert them, and they'll get prepared. Let's go directly to the yamen and see them in court."

"Good idea. But which county should we go to?"

"This whole case started from Wuyuan County. The magistrate is still there. Let's go to him."

Taibai Village being little more than forty li from Wuyuan County, the two of them hurried in big strides all the way to the county yamen. It so happened that the magistrate's morning court was still in session. As they cried out at the top of their lungs, the magistrate summoned them in and made them kneel in the hall. As they brought no written complaint, they made only verbal depositions. Tian Niu'er began by tearfully describing the situation. Zhao Yilang followed by giving a detailed account of how Zhao Shou had killed Ding Wan and Mrs. Tian and falsely accused Zhu Chang and Bu Cai. Finally, he presented the magistrate with the wooden club with which Zhao Shou had committed the murder.

Finding the bloodstains still clearly visible, the magistrate said, "If that was the case, why didn't you turn them in at the time?"

Zhao Yilang said, "I didn't have the heart to turn them in out of regard for our bond as masters and servant. But now, they're afraid that I would tell, so the father and son planned yesterday to poison me this evening. That's why I have no other choice but to come here, so that I get to live."

"How did you learn what the father and son were talking about?" (*The magistrate is sharp enough.*)

In his haste, Zhao Yilang let out the truth. "My master's concubine, Aida'er, told me."

"Why would your master's concubine tip you off? Is she having an affair with you?"

That remark hit a raw nerve. Zhao Yilang's face changed color. As he stoutly denied having an affair, the magistrate said, "The facts are all too clear. It's useless to deny." Right away, the magistrate dispatched lictors to bring Zhao Wan and his son as well as Aida'er to him for interrogation. When they arrived in Taibai Village, evening had set in. Tian Niu'er took the lictors to his own home, and there we shall leave them for the night.

Zhao Shou had bought arsenic early that morning; failing to see Zhao Yilang, he asked everyone in the house, but none knew where he was. The father and son grew a little apprehensive, but who would have suspected Aida'er? At the crack of dawn, the lictors arrived, tied them up, and took them to the county yamen. Seeing that Aida'er was also taken, Zhao Wan thought that she was involved because she had resisted Zhao Yilang's advances. It was not until Zhao Yilang told about the plot to poison him that he realized there had long been an adulterous relationship between the two and regretted his own indiscretion in revealing the plan to her. The plaintiff and the accused exchanged heated words, and the Zhaos denied the charge. However, under the pain of torture, they confessed everything.

These being major offenses involving four deaths, the magistrate ordered sixty strokes of the rod each for Zhao Wan and his son and sentenced them to death in accordance with the law. Zhao Yilang, for his seduction of his master's concubine and ungratefulness to his master, was given forty strokes. Aida'er, for her adultery and her role in plotting against her husband, was also given forty strokes. Both were sentenced to death. All four were taken to jail. Tian Niu'er was allowed to go home. The magistrate then prepared a report and submitted it to his superiors for approval. After a few days, the ministry of justice issued an order approved by the emperor, which was duly read aloud. All four were to be sentenced to death, as requested, and executed after the advent of autumn. The penny cost another four lives. Even though every injustice has its perpetrator and every debt its debtor, how would Yang-shi have died if there had been no fight over that penny? Without Yang-shi's corpse, Zhu Chang would not have tried his blackmail ruse. That one little penny led to thirteen deaths in all. The point of this story, entitled "For One Penny, A Small Grudge Ends in Stark Tragedies," is to advise people not to begrudge their money and to control their tempers. There is a poem in testimony:

> *The fight was over one penny only;*
> *A small grudge led to a series of tragedies.*
> *Begrudge not your money and control your temper;*
> *Only thus will you enjoy a life of peace.*

In Righteous Wrath, Old Servant Xu Builds Up a Family Fortune

Even dogs and horses love their masters,
Let alone humans working as servants.
One day's work in servitude is enough
To establish a bond with the master
And breed love as between father and son,
In a relationship as between subject and king.
He who ill treats a servant flouts the moral code;
He who cheats his master violates norms of decency.
A good servant who stays true through times good and ill
Lives on in the annals of history.

As the story goes, during the reign of Emperor Xuanzong [r. 712–56] of the Tang dynasty, there lived a gentleman called Xiao Yingshi [717–59], courtesy name Maoting. A native of Lanling, he was endowed with intelligence and developed an aptitude for learning at an early age. He gained a thorough knowledge of the three teachings and the nine schools of thought, as well as the various theories of the masters from pre-Qin to early Han times.[1] And he knew everything there was to know about every subject, from astronomy to geography. The books he had read would fill five wagons. The essays he wrote were to enjoy eternal fame. At the age of nineteen, he placed high in the civil service examinations, and his reputation as an erudite scholar spread throughout the land.

Xiao Yingshi had a servant called Du Liang, who had waited on him in his study since his early childhood. Du Liang went about every mission dauntlessly, whatever the difficulties, and never saved even half a penny for himself. When Xiao Yingshi was reading, Du Liang would do everything he could, without being told, to prepare snacks and beverages for his young master. Sometimes he brewed a pot of tea to help his master straighten out his thinking; sometimes he warmed up a cup of wine to reward him for his hard work. He would wait on the young master all night until daybreak without dozing off even once. Whenever Xiao Yingshi grew thrilled in his reading, Du Liang, off to one side, would also be filled with joy.

Xiao Yingshi was praiseworthy in every way except two. What were his two imperfections? First, he was so proud of his own talent that he looked down on everyone else. Right after he was appointed to an official post, he ran afoul of the incumbent prime minister. A more magnanimous prime minister would have forgiven him, but this prime minister was Li Linfu [d. 752], who was most jealous of talented people. Nicknamed Li the Cat, he had ruined goodness knows how many court ministers. He harmed people by underhanded means, like a butcher capable of killing without spilling a drop of blood. Would he lightly let go of Xiao Yingshi for having provoked him? A minor ruse of his was enough to have done Xiao Yingshi nearly to death. Thanks to his mentor's intervention, Xiao Yingshi was only stripped of his official post and was sent back home.

His second imperfection was his fiery temper. When anything said in a conversation displeased him, he would explode with rage, and sparks of fire would fly out from his temples. Whenever the servants made the slightest mistake, he would beat them, and his way of beating was different from that of others. How different? Well, in punishing servants, other people would consider the nature of the offense before having another servant take a rod and do the beating. The number of strokes, ten or twenty, would be commensurate with the severity of the offense. But Xiao Yingshi would burst into curses whenever something triggered his temper, regardless of the severity of the offense. Dispensing with rods or a proxy to administer the punishment for him, he would jump up, personally seize the offending servant, throw him to the floor, pick up the first household utensil that came to hand, and hit the servant full in the face. No one was able to talk him into stopping. He would continue until he had worked off the last bit of his anger. If he was still not satisfied, he would bite the offender a few times before quitting. The servants stood in such awe of this holy terror that they gave him the slip, one after another, leaving only Du Liang.

Now, you would think that, with this only servant left to him, he should have become easier to get along with, but no! His temper had come with his birth. He remained every bit as prone to outbursts of anger as before, and his fists still itched to strike. When there were many servants, they rotated in taking the beatings. Du Liang was now the only one left and was therefore subjected to even more abuse than before.

You would think that, with such a difficult master, Du Liang should also have taken flight, as everyone else had, but no! He never budged so much as an inch from his master's side and took the beatings in all submissiveness. Often his skin split, his flesh ripped, and blood flowed from his head, but he had no regrets, nor a word of complaint. After he was beaten, he would straighten his clothes and, in spite of the pain, resume his position off to one side and attend to his master's needs.

Storyteller, the way you put it, a servant like Du Liang is one in a thousand. In fact, another one like him is not to be found in the whole wide world. But Xiao Yingshi was not some benighted imbecile. For someone who had placed high in the civil service examinations, gained a post in the imperial court, and read ten thousand books until the pages were well thumbed, he should have been a sensible man. Would he be prone to such indiscriminate physical abuse without any compassion or any remorse in his heart?

Dear audience, let me tell you. As the proverb says, "It's easy to change rivers and mountains but not a person's temperament." Xiao Yingshi was, in fact, fond of Du Liang for his carefulness and docility. After he beat Du Liang, he would say to himself in deep remorse, "This servant has been with me for so many years. He doesn't make bad mistakes. Why did I beat him black and blue? I must not do this again!" Yet when his temper rose, before he knew it, his fists and his feet would all too eagerly land on Du Liang again. But let us not put all the blame on Xiao Yingshi's fiery temper, because as soon as Du Liang heard the first word of a reprimand, he would sink to his knees like a little demon at the sight of Zhong Kui the demon-buster.[2] Being a person given to physical assault in the first place, Xiao Yingshi could hardly refrain from obliging him, since he had already assumed the stance of one ready for a beating.

Du Liang had a distant cousin called Du Ming, who lived next door to the Xiao residence. Infuriated at the way Du Liang was battered, he said to Du Liang, prodding him, "Servants choose this line of work because they are too poor to stand on their own feet. They live in their masters' homes partly for the free room, board, and clothes, and partly in the hope that the master will one day rise higher in the world, so that some of the glory will rub off on them and they will get a share of the riches. Then they can build up a small family fortune of their own to live on for the rest of their lives. Now, you work hard from morning to night for that bookworm of yours, but what good do you get from him? On the contrary, he abuses you all the time. There's no future for you if you hang on to a man who doesn't recognize a good servant. Many people can't stand him and have run away. Why don't you also leave him and find another job? Any number of people not as good as you are have found employment in important officials' homes. They get to enjoy good food and good clothes and make some extra money, too. When they leave the residential quarters of the yamen, who doesn't fawn on them? One calls you, 'Uncle, may I ask you a favor?' Before there's time to answer, another one over there says, 'Uncle, I also have a favor to ask of you.' They can't even attend to all the requests at the same time. What airs they can put on! With your brains, your writing skills, your kindness, and your discretion, you'll surely be given an important position in a family with power and influence. As for that bookworm of yours, he may be a *jinshi*, but he set himself against Prime Minister Li the moment he got started in his career and, as a result, he now sits at home, doing nothing. It doesn't look likely that he'll ever rise again. What makes you want to hang on to him?"

Du Liang said, "I know only too well what you say. But if I had wanted to, I would have left years ago. Why would I wait until you tell me to? As the old saying goes, 'A good minister chooses the right king to serve; a good bird chooses the right branch to perch on.' Servants may be lowly, but we should choose good masters. My master may be hot-tempered, but, except for this, he's the best master there is."

"There are any number of officials, members of the royal family, and powerful families in the country. Are you saying they are not as good as that poverty-stricken official of yours?"

"Rank and money are all they have."

"Aren't rank and money all that matter? What more do you want?"

"Rank is just an illusion. Money is filth. What do I care about them? My master's talent and learning are far superior. He can write a ten-thousand-word essay as fast as his brush can go without having to work out a draft first, and the writing is really up there in the clouds and spectacular. That's the only reason why I'd hate to leave him."

Upon hearing that he loved the master for his talent and learning, Du Ming burst into hearty laughter. "My brother," said he. "If you love his talent and learning so much, will they fill your stomach when you're hungry or give you warmth when you're cold?"

"There you go again with your jokes! Talent and learning are in his mind. How can they protect me from hunger and cold?"

"So they do nothing to protect you from hunger and cold. What's the good of loving them? Those holding high ranks now all play up to the powerful. None of them values talent and learning. Lowly servants like you and me need only be concerned about having adequate food and clothing and some savings for our families. How can you be so high-sounding and impractical? For the love of his talent and learning, you're willing to take all that abuse. Aren't you a fool?" (*Those holding high ranks put no value on talent and learning. A lowly servant does. This is enough to make talented scholars weep.*)

Cheerfully, Du Liang said, "I didn't come into this world with gold and silver. So I never expected to have much money. I'll just be the way I've always been."

"Maybe you haven't had enough abuse and you look forward to more."

"I thank you, my good brother, for your kindness and your concern for me. But my master is such an erudite scholar that I'm quite content to serve him even if he beats me to death." And so he rejected Du Ming's advice and continued to stay with Xiao Yingshi.

As it turned out, with punches of the fists one day and strikes of the rod the next day, in a few years Du Liang gradually developed aches throughout his body.

He coughed up blood and suffered from symptoms of consumption. He forced himself to work in the beginning, but later the pain became more than he could bear. He had to lie down for part of the day. And then he became bedridden all the time.

Noticing that Du Liang was coughing up blood, Xiao Yingshi knew he was to blame and was seized with remorse. Hoping for Du Liang's recovery, Xiao Yingshi engaged a physician for treatment and personally brewed medicine for him and served it to him. After lingering for two months, Du Liang ceased to be.

Recalling all the things Du Liang had done for him, Xiao Yingshi shed copious tears and made preparations for Du Liang's burial clothes, the coffin, and the burial. Accustomed to having everything done by Du Liang, Xiao felt acutely the inconvenience of not having Du Liang with him, and asked middlemen to look high and low for a replacement. However, as notorious as he was for his physical assaults of servants, no one took the offer. Even if there were candidates willing to fill the position, Xiao Yingshi found them inadequate. Sometimes when he got carried away in his excitement over something in his reading, he would raise his head to look for Du Liang, thinking he was still there. Not finding Du Liang, he would close the book and burst into tears.

Later, upon learning that Du Liang had ignored Du Ming's advice, Xiao Yingshi almost choked and, his face awash in tears, he cried, "Du Liang! In all the years I applied myself to my studies, I met no one who valued my talent, and I remain poor and destitute. I had no idea you appreciated me so much. I have eyes that see not. I drove you to your death. What a sinner I am!"

Even as he spoke, blood spurted from his mouth. He too succumbed to consumption. He burned all his books and kept calling Du Liang's name. He lay sick for several months before he also gave up the ghost, leaving instructions that he be buried with Du Liang. (*To be buried together with one so appreciative of his talent, he should be content under the Nine Springs.*) There is a poem in testimony:

> *Those keen on taking bribes and seeking power*
> *Put no value on the talents of the land.*
> *If those in power were all like Du Liang,*
> *No talent would have sadly gone to waste.*

Storyteller, Du Liang's love for his master's talent is indeed a rare case, but still, there was something addle-headed about him that makes him less than perfect. If you have a more fascinating and enthralling story, we'll be all ears.

Dear audience, pray sit still. Do not be so impatient. That was just a little prologue story. I have not yet moved on to the story proper, which is also about a servant, but of quite a different order from Du Liang. This is a servant who built an impressive family fortune through his own efforts for his master's widow and her children. He also married off her three daughters and got wives for her two sons. As for himself, he did not have a penny of his own all his life. His name still has a place in the annals of history. Let me take my time in telling you about it. I advise all servants to learn from him, make every effort to help your masters, and win good reputations for yourselves. Do not emulate those ungrateful ones who bite the hand that feeds them and become the tail that wags the dog. Such people will only invite cursing and spitting.

In which dynasty and where does this story take place? It takes place in the reign of Emperor Jiajing [r. 1522–66] of this dynasty [the Ming], in Chun'an County, Yanzhou Prefecture of Zhejiang. Several li from the county seat, there was a village called Brocade Sand Village, in which there lived a Xu family in a farmstead. There were three brothers in the family. The oldest, Xu Yan, and the second, Xu Zhao, each had a son. The third, Xu Zhe, had two sons and three daughters by his wife, Yan-shi. Under the order of their now-deceased father, the three brothers ate out of the same pot and tilled the land together. They saved up enough money to buy an ox and a horse. They had an old servant called Aji, in his fifties at the time our story begins. He and his wife had a son, who was only about ten. Aji was a native of the same village. He had sold himself to the Xu family when his parents died and he could not afford the funeral expenses. An honest and discreet man, he was early to rise and late to go to bed, and worked hard in the fields.

Mr. Xu Senior had benefited greatly from his help and showered favors on him. After the sons came into their inheritance, they began to loathe him, as he was getting old. Not being the kind of person who trims his sails to the wind, Aji offered them words of admonition whenever the brothers were not doing things properly. Xu Zhe was willing to take some of his advice for good behavior. (*He does have a bond with Xu Zhe from the beginning.*) But Xu Yan and Xu Zhao, in their willfulness, found him meddlesome and yelled at him, sometimes even giving him a taste of their fists.

Aji's wife tried to talk some sense into him, saying, "At your age, you'd do well to hold your tongue. This is a young people's world, a world that's constantly changing. Let them have their way. Why do you have to shoot off your mouth like that and bring such abuse on yourself?"

"I say what I say out of gratitude for my old master and my sense of duty to him."

"But since they turn a deaf ear to you, you are no longer responsible for what they do."

Henceforth, Aji followed his wife's advice and held his tongue. As he no longer intervened in their affairs, he saved himself a lot of humiliation, bearing out an old saying:

> *If you keep your mouth shut and hide well your tongue;*
> *Peace will be with you wherever you go.*

Soon thereafter, Xu Zhe suddenly caught a severe cold and died on the seventh day. Yan-shi and her children cried their eyes out. Two months after the burial and the prayer service, Xu Yan consulted Xu Zhao, saying, "You and I have only one son each, but Number Three had two sons and three daughters. Their share of the family property is equal to ours put together. Even when he was alive and worked with us in the fields, we were already shortchanged. And now, with him dead and gone, we work our fingers to the bone only to feed that brood of freeloaders. It's not so bad now, but after our sons grow up and marry, we'll have to arrange for his children's marriages as well. Won't they take away four more shares of the family fortune? (*A petty mind that fails to see the larger picture.*) So I'm thinking of dividing the family inheritance into three equal portions, so that we can have a clean break with those sponges. Whether they have anything to eat or not won't be our concern. But the old man said in his will that we three should not divide up the inheritance. If we go against his will, people will gossip. What's to be done?"

If Xu Zhao had had a kind heart, he would have advised Xu Yan to give up the idea. However, since he had long been thinking along the same lines, his older brother's words could not have pleased him more. He replied, "The old man may have said so, but he's dead. And his words are not an inviolable imperial decree. (*What an unfilial son!*) What's more, this is a private family matter. What outsider would have the nerve to gossip about it?"

Xu Yan could not agree more. There and then they secretly divided up all the land and household possessions, giving their nephews and nieces only the least desirable items. Xu Yan asked, "What are we going to do about the ox and the horse?"

After reflecting for a while, Xu Zhao said, "That's easy. Aji and his wife are getting old and weaker. While they're alive, we've got three extra mouths to feed, and after the two old ones die, we'll have to buy two coffins for them. Let's make Aji's family a part of the inheritance and give them to Number Three's widow, so that we no longer have anything to do with Aji. Won't that be nice?"

And so the plan was drawn up. The next day, they prepared a feast to which they invited a few relatives and neighbors as well as Yan-shi and the two nephews. The older boy, only seven, was called Fu'er, and the younger one, five, Shou'er. They followed their mother to the main hall. Yan-shi had no inkling of why she had been summoned.

Xu Yan and his brother rose to their feet. "Greetings to you all," began Xu Yan. "We have something to tell you. Our departed father did not leave us much. Thanks to the hard work of us brothers, we have saved up a modest family fortune, hoping that we could keep it until we got old and leave it to the next generation to be divided up among them. Unfortunately our third brother passed away recently and our sister-in-law, being a woman, has no knowledge about the size of the family fortune. What's more, a family's fortunes may change. If we make more later on so that our nephews can have more, all will be well and good. But should the family fortunes decline, we will be accused of cheating the orphans and the widow for selfish gains, and that would hurt the bond of flesh and blood among us. So we two brothers consulted each other about the matter and propose that while everything is going well, we divide the family property into three portions. Members of each branch of the family will be free to manage their portion as they see fit, so as to avoid future disputes. We have therefore invited you all to serve as witnesses."

Having delivered himself of this speech, Xu Yan retrieved from his sleeve three documents on the division of the family property and continued, "The division is done in all fairness and justice. Please do us the favor of signing the papers."

Upon hearing that she was to live apart, Yan-shi said tearfully, "My two brothers-in-law, I am a widow and the children are small. Like a footless crab, I can't even stand on my own feet. How am I going to support my family? My father-in-law instructed us not to divide up the family property and live apart. Could you two uncles still manage the household as before until my children have grown up? By that time, we'll be content with whatever you give us. We wouldn't even dream of haggling over the size of our share."

Xu Zhao replied in these words: "My sister-in-law, no feast doesn't come to an end. Even if we live under one roof for a thousand years, we'll have to divide up the property one day eventually. Our father is no longer with us. We can't go by his words. Yesterday my brother said he wanted to give you the ox and the horse, but, as I see it, my nephews are too young to take care of them. So Aji will be helping you instead. He may be old, but he's still hale and hearty. Actually, he beats a young man in farm work. His wife can weave, so she won't be a freeloader. And their son should be able to work in the fields in just a couple of years. You have nothing to worry about." (*Putting on a show of fairness to hide his selfish motives. A petty man's words have no credibility.*)

Having heard the brothers out, Yan-shi knew she did not stand a chance of reversing a decision that had already been made. There was nothing she could do but weep.

After reading the documents, the guests realized that the division was unfair, but none of them wanted to be the first one to say anything offensive to their hosts. And so they signed the papers and gently talked Yan-shi into accepting the deal. They then sat down at the feast table. There is a poem in testimony:

> *The division papers claimed ever so calmly*
> *That humans and animals were divided fairly.*
> *The old servant, worth less than an ox or a horse,*
> *Was to weep with the widow in the west wind.*

That morning Aji had been made busy running errands and delivering invitation cards, little knowing what was afoot in the house. When he returned home after delivering an invitation to a relative in South Village, the division of the family property had already been duly settled. At the door, he ran into his wife. Afraid that he would again speak out of turn once he learned about it, she pulled him to one side and said, "Number-One Master just divided up the family property. Don't you go poke your nose into their business and ask for a scolding!"

Much taken aback, Aji said, "The master left instructions in his will that the family property should not be divided up. With Third Master gone, how can the widow and the orphans be abandoned and left to their own devices? If I don't say anything, who will?" With that, he turned to go.

Again his wife seized him and said, "Even the wisest judge can't settle a family dispute. None of the many relatives and neighbors said anything. You are a servant, not an elder in the clan. What right do you have to speak up?"

"You do have a point. I won't speak up if the division is fair. If not, they'll have some explaining to do, even if I have to die for it." Then he asked, "Do you know where we are supposed to go?"

"I have no idea."

Upon arriving at the main hall, Aji saw that the party was in full swing. Thinking that he could not very well raise the matter at such a moment, he went to stand off to one side. A neighbor who happened to raise his head saw him and said, "Old Xu, you've been given to the third branch of the family. The widow and the orphans need all the help you can give them."

Aji said offhandedly, "I'm too old to be able to do much now." While mouthing those words, he thought, "So, they gave me to the third branch. They must have kicked me out because they think I'm useless now. Well, it just so happens that I resolve to bring some credit to myself. I'll help the widow build up a family fortune, so that no one can mock me." Without asking for more details about the division, he went straight to Yan-shi's room. At the door, he heard sobs inside and he stopped to listen. Yan-shi was saying between her sobs, "Oh Heaven! I thought he and I would live together to a ripe old age. Who would have known that he would abandon me halfway and leave me with so many helpless children? I was hoping that the two uncles could raise them, but before his corpse had gone cold, they had already divided up the family property. Now, with no one to turn to for help, what am I going to do?" Then she continued, "And even in the division of land, they know all the ins and outs, but I'm in the dark. They are the ones doing the division. What do I know? One instance alone shows how ruthless they are. The ox can plow the land and the horse can be hired out. So they took the two animals that can bring them profit and dumped Aji and his wife on me, who'll only be costing me money on food and clothes."

At this point, the old man abruptly raised the door curtain and exclaimed, "Third Mistress! Are you saying this old man will only be costing you money on food and clothes and is not as good as the horse and the ox?"

Caught off guard, Yan-shi blinked back her tears and asked, "So, what do you have to say?"

"The ox and the horse bring only a small profit every year, and you have to hire someone to feed and take care of them. I may be old, but I'm as energetic as ever. I can travel. I can take hardships. Even though I've never tried my hand at business, I know how to go about it. If you could quickly put together some money for me to use as capital, I'll go out to do some trading. After a few trips a year, the profit will be several times more than what an ox and a horse can bring in. My wife works hard at weaving. She can also help out with the daily expenses. As for the land, never mind whether it's good or not. Just rent it out and get back a few piculs of grain, so that you at least have something on hand. You, Third Mistress, and the girls can also do some needlework to make a living. Do not touch what cash you have. After several years, we'll surely build up a decent family fortune. Don't worry!"

Impressed by his words, Yan-shi said, "If you could help me out, of course that'll be good. But you're getting on in years. You can't take such hardships."

"To tell you the truth, ma'am, I may be old, but I'm in good health. I can go to bed late and rise early. Even a young man can't keep up with me. You don't have to worry on that score."

"What business are you thinking of?"

"In business, you can do more with a large capital and less with a small capital. I'll have to go out to see what will be good for us. I'll pick whatever I think will turn a profit. This is not something that can be fixed at home."

"Yes, what you say does make sense. Let me think about it."

Then Aji asked to see the division document. He checked every item allotted to Yan-shi and put everything together before going to the main hall to wait on the guests. The party did not break up until late at night.

The next day, Xu Yan called in a carpenter to build a partition wall in the house, and told Yan-shi and her family to use a separate door. While putting things to order, as she was bound to, Yan-shi also furtively instructed Aji to sell her jewelry and some clothes and ornaments. They fetched twelve taels of silver. Giving the money to Aji, she said, "This may not be much, but it's all I have. Our whole family depends on it. Take it. I don't expect windfalls. Small profits will be good enough. Use your good judgment and take care on the road. Do not have a brave start but end up with nothing and make my brothers-in-law laugh at us." So saying, she could not help shedding a tear.

"Don't worry," Aji assured her. "I know a thing or two. I won't fail you."

"When are you leaving?"

"Now that I've got the money, I can start tomorrow morning."

"Don't you want to pick a lucky day?"

"Any day I go out to do business is a lucky day. Why do I need to pick and choose?" (*An old man with such guts can make a success of anything.*) He put the silver in his waist bag and went to his own room. "I'm leaving tomorrow morning to do business," he said to his wife. "Help me put together some old clothes."

Aji had only talked with the mistress about his plan. His wife had no knowledge of it. Surprised at this announcement, she said, "Where are you going? What business is it?"

After he acquainted her with his plan, she said, "Good grief! This is madness!

You may be long in the tooth, but you've never had a hand in business. How could you have bragged about what you could do and offered to take on this job? A widow's mite is hard-earned money. If you make a mess of things, she'll have nothing to live on. Won't she complain about you the rest of her life? Do as I say and quickly give the money back to Third Mistress. It would be better just to work harder, rise early and go to bed late, bear more hardships, and work in the fields as before. If we help her that way, both sides will feel more comfortable."

Aji shot back, "What do you know, old woman? You're talking nonsense! How do you know I will fail in business and make a mess of things? I don't need you to predict rain when there isn't even a sign of a wind!" Turning a deaf ear to his wife, he went to pack his clothes and bedding. In the absence of a large bag, he had to wrap everything into a bundle. He also made himself a money belt and prepared some dry provisions. Then he went to the market, where he bought an umbrella and a pair of hemp shoes. After everything was ready, he went to see Xu Yan and Xu Zhao the next morning and said, "I will be going on a long trip to do some trading. There'll be no one to look after the family. Even though you now live apart, please keep an eye on that part of the house."

Suppressing a furtive laugh, the two brothers said, "You don't have to remind us of that. But after you bring home the silver, be sure to give us some gifts."

"Of course," promised Aji. After returning home and eating breakfast, he bade the mistress farewell, put on his hemp shoes, slung over his shoulder the bundle and the umbrella, and said to his wife, "Take care." When he was on the point of leaving, Yan-shi gave him a few more instructions. He nodded in assent and went off in big strides.

As soon as Aji had taken leave of them, Xu Yan and his brother burst out laughing. "How ridiculous," said Xu Yan. "That woman has no sense! If she has enough money to start a business, she should consult the two of us rather than listen to that old thing. Has he ever tried his hand at business in his whole life? He's cheating the widow out of her money so that he can live it up! The money is as good as gone."

Xu Zhao said, "You're right. she didn't produce the money when the three families were together. And now, as soon as she gets out, she tells Aji to go out and do business. She didn't bring much dowry. The money must have been secretly pocketed by Number Three from the collective account when the old man was alive and has been hoarded until now. (*He uses his own yardstick to measure another man's mind.*) In brief, Sister-in-law's been doing things behind our backs. But if we reproach her, she'll say we're jealous. Let's wait until Aji loses everything and comes back. We will then go to laugh at her." Truly,

> *From atop a cloud let us watch the fight;*
> *In the end, who will win and who will lose?*
> *As distance tests a horse's stamina,*
> *So time reveals a person's heart.*

After leaving home, Aji thought as he went along, "What business should I get into?" Suddenly, an idea struck him. "I've heard that the lacquer business is quite lucrative, and I need not travel far, either. Why don't I give it a try?" His mind thus made up, he went straight to Qingyun Mountain, where lacquer was produced, and there were middlemen for traders in lacquer. Aji found lodging near a middleman's shop. As the many traders in lacquer waited in long lines for their turns, Aji thought, "To wait like this can take days and costs money, too." An idea came to him. At the first opportunity that presented itself, he dragged the middleman to a village tavern and treated him to a few cups of wine. "I'm a small peddler," said he. "With so little money on me, I can't afford to wait. Since we're from the same place, please think of a way to let me go first. Next time I'm here, I'll treat you to a feast."

As fate would have it, the middleman had a passion for wine. Feeling he could not very well turn Aji down after being wined and dined, he readily agreed. That very evening, the middleman collected enough lacquer from the villages and packed the merchandise in containers. Afraid that other traders would complain, he deposited the lacquer in a neighbor's house. At the pre-dawn fifth watch of the night, he rose and sent Aji off.

Overjoyed that he was off to such a good start, Aji had porters carry the merchandise to the mouth of New Peace River. Then he thought, "Hangzhou is not far from here. If I go there, I won't be able to fetch a good price." So he hired a boat and went all the way to Suzhou instead, where lacquer happened to be in short supply. Clients pounced on his merchandise as if they saw some great treasure. Within three days, it was sold out. All the payments were made in silver. No one bought on credit. After he deducted his expenses, he realized that he had made more than one hundred percent profit. Inwardly he gave thanks to heaven and earth and promptly packed for his return journey.

But then he thought, "Even though I have no goods to carry, I'll be traveling by boat anyway on my way home. And all this money on me is a headache. Why don't I buy some other goods for re-sale on the way back? A little more profit will certainly help." Upon inquiry, he learned that at Maple Bridge, there was such a surfeit of long-grain rice that the price per unit had fallen a few pennies. He said to himself, "I suppose I won't be shortchanged if I trade in rice."

So he bought more than sixty piculs of long-grain rice and transported them to Hangzhou for sale. It was the middle of the seventh month and it hadn't rained in Hangzhou for a month. With rice seedlings all dried up, the price of rice soared. Selling his rice at this moment when each load sold for two maces more, he made more than ten taels of silver. He said to himself, "I'm so glad that business has been quite plain-sailing. Third Mistress is in luck." But then again, he thought, "While I'm here in Hangzhou, why don't I go ask the price of lacquer? If the price here is not too much lower than in Suzhou, I'll be able to save quite a bit of travel expenses." Upon careful inquiry, he learned that the price was actually more favorable than in Suzhou. Why? Because lacquer traders all went to places further away, assuming that Hangzhou was too near for them to get a good price. So, lacquer was, in fact, often in short supply in Hangzhou. As the saying goes, "Scarcity is what gives value to anything, great or small." That was why Hangzhou turned out to be the right place to sell lacquer. Beside himself with joy upon learning the information, Aji went to Qingyun Mountain again before the night was out. He gave the middleman some small gifts he had prepared and treated him again to a few cups of wine. His face wreathed in smiles upon receiving these small favors, the middleman again surreptitiously sold the merchandise to him. Within a matter of two to three days of his return to Hangzhou, his lacquer was sold out. When he did the calculations, he found that he had made a few more taels than the last lacquer transaction. However, because he had done business in Hangzhou this time, there was not much of a return trip and therefore no extra profit to be made on the way back, as had been the case when he returned from Suzhou with a shipment of rice. So he told himself, "I should go farther out next time."

After he settled his accounts with an agent, he packed for his journey back to Brocade Sand Village, thinking, "I've been away for so long that Third Mistress must be worried. Let me go back and report to her to put her mind at ease." Then he thought, "I need to wait for a couple of days anyway for the middleman to collect the next shipment of lacquer. Why don't I turn back to the mountain first, pay the middleman in advance, and go home while he collects the lacquer? Won't I be able to have it both ways?" His mind thus made up, he went to the mountain and paid the middleman before rushing back home. Truly,

> He sold lacquer twice for a good profit;
> He won victory on his first try ever.

In the meantime, after Aji was gone, Yan-shi had been worried day and night lest he lost all the capital. With this matter preying on her mind, she grew even more vexed when word came to her that Xu Yan and his brother had been making fun of her behind her back.

One day, she was sitting gloomily in her room when her two sons burst in, crying, "Aji is back!"

Quickly Yan-shi went out the door. There Aji was, right in front of her, followed by his wife. As Aji bowed deeply, Yan-shi felt as if she had been punched in the chest. Her heart jumping violently, she asked, fearing the worst, "What kind of business did you do? Any profit?"

His hands respectfully folded across his chest, Aji said unhurriedly, "First, thanks to the blessings of heaven and earth, second, thanks to your luck, madam, I dealt in lacquer and made a five-to sixfold profit." Then he launched into details, adding at the end, "I was afraid you might be worried, ma'am. That's why I'm back to report to you."

Her heart flooding with joy at this unexpected piece of good news, Yan-shi asked, "So where's the silver?"

"I left the money with the middleman. He's collecting the next shipment of lacquer. I'm leaving again tomorrow morning."

The whole family rejoiced. Aji stayed for one night only. He rose bright and early the next morning, took leave of Yan-shi, and headed for Qingyun Mountain again.

Xu Yan and his brother had gotten themselves drunk in a neighbor's house for the autumn worship service to the village god, and therefore knew nothing at the time about Aji's return. The next day, they approached their sister-in-law and asked, "So Aji's back from his business trip. How much did he make?"

"He has been trading in lacquer and has made a five- to sixfold profit."

"What good luck!" said Xu Yan. "If he keeps making money at this rate, you'll be rich in a few years."

"Don't laugh at us, my brothers-in-law. I'll be content as long as we don't go hungry and cold."

"Where is he now?" asked Xu Zhao. "Why didn't he come to see us after such a long absence? Where are his manners?"

"He left this morning."

"Why did he leave so soon?" asked Xu Zhao.

"Did you see the silver?" asked Xu Yan.

"He said he left the money with the middleman to buy more goods. He didn't take the money back with him."

Xu Yan laughed. "I thought he had brought back the money. So he was just saying it. His eyes had a feast, but his stomach remains hungry. You've fallen for all his sweet talk. Without knowing where the capital has gone and where the profit is, you take him at his word. A businessman's left hand doesn't trust his right hand. How can any businessman go home and leave his money with an outsider? The way I see it, most probably he lost the capital and is fooling you with all this rubbish." (*The Xu brothers are talking common sense, but it doesn't apply to Aji.*)

Xu Zhao added, "My sister-in-law, we shouldn't shoot off our mouths about your private family matters, but you are just a woman who knows nothing about the outside world. If you have money, you should consult the two of us and buy a few *mu* of land. Now, that's a long-term plan. Aji doesn't have a head for business. How could you have given him money behind our backs and let him make a mess of things? The money must either have been your dowry or Number Three's private savings. It can't have been stolen. Why did you treat it so lightly?"

With the two of them teaming up, one as a soloist, the other as the accompanist, Yan-shi fell silent. She also began to grow apprehensive. Her immense joy turned to deep worries again. But we will come back to her later.

In the meantime, old man Aji hurried to Qingyun Mountain. Having finished collecting the lacquer for him, the middleman handed over the merchandise to him. This time, Aji did not repeat his route to Suzhou and Hangzhou but went to Xinghua, where the profit was even better than in those two places. After selling out all the lacquer, he found out that the price of rice at Xinghua was one tael of silver for three piculs and that the measuring pans were larger than the standard ones. He recalled the current shortage of rice in Hangzhou and that he had made money last time by reselling rice that he had bought at the regular market price. Now that he was in a rice-producing area, he would most likely double or even triple his profit. So, with a large load of rice, he went to Hangzhou. He sold it at one tael and two maces per picul. The extra rice in the measuring pans alone was enough for his travel expenses. This time around, it was as a big customer that he returned to the mountain to collect lacquer. The middleman fawned on him. Partly because Yan-shi was predestined to become rich at this time of her life and partly thanks to Aji's business acumen, he made a good profit on everything he traded in. After several transactions in a row, he cleared a profit of more than two thousand taels of silver.

With the year soon coming to an end, he thought, "An old man traveling alone shouldn't be carrying so much money around. If something happens, all my work will have been for nothing. New Year will soon be upon us. They must be worried about me at home. I'd better go back. I'll talk with the mistress about buying some land, since land is the first essential. I can then go out and do something with what's left over."

By this time, he was equipped with all the right paraphernalia. He put the ingots of silver into the proper wrappers one by one and stuffed them into a money belt. By boat and by horse, he traveled cautiously, setting out late and retiring early for the night.

Upon arriving at home after a few days, he carried all his baggage into the house. His wife immediately went to announce her husband's return to the mistress. Yan-shi was seized with a mixture of joy and fear: joy because Aji had returned; fear because she had no idea how he had done in his business dealings. Xu Yan and his brother having scoffed at her, she was more anxious now than the last time Aji returned. Taking what would be the space for three ordinary steps in two, she hurried outside. She felt a surge of relief at the sight of the pile of luggage, for a bankrupt man would not have hauled back so much, but she was still unsure. Unable to bear the suspense, she asked, "How has business been? Have you brought back any money?"

Aji stepped forward and said with a bow, "Take it easy, Ma'am. Let me tell you everything in a while." But first, after telling his wife to bolt the middle door of the house, he carried all his luggage to Yan-shi's room, opened every piece, and handed the silver to Yan-shi, packet by packet.

The good fortune exceeded Yan-shi's wildest hopes. Eagerly she opened her trunks to store the silver. Only then did Aiji tell her about his business dealings. Afraid of stirring up trouble, Yan-shi made no mention of what the Xu brothers had said. Instead, she said over and over again, "You've worked so hard. Go take a rest now." (*Yan-shi watches what she says and can swallow humiliation. She has the qualities of a good manager of family wealth.*) She then added, "If my brothers-in-law come to ask, don't tell them the truth."

"I understand," said Aji.

At this point, there came raps on the door. Xu Yan and his brother, having heard about Aji's return, were there to find out how things were.

After Aji bowed twice to them, Xu Yan said, "I heard the other day that your business was booming. So you must have made more profit this time?"

"Thanks to blessings from you, this old servant made a net profit of forty to fifty taels of silver."

"Good grief!" said Xu Zhao. "Last time I understood that you turned a five-to sixfold profit. Much time has passed since then. How come the profit went down?"

Xu Yan said, "Never mind how much profit you made. I'd just like to know if you've brought back any silver this time."

"Yes. I gave the silver to Third Mistress."

The two brothers fell silent and went off.

After Aji suggested to Yan-shi that she buy land, they quietly asked someone to look for a deal. Generally speaking, every rich man has a prodigal son. (*"Every rich man has a prodigal son." Why? This is a question for all rich men to ponder.*) In Brocade Sand Village, there was a rich Yan family. With all his fabulous wealth and large possessions of land, Mr. Yan had only one son, whom he named Shibao [literally, "Generation Preserve"], hoping his offspring would preserve the family fortune from generation to generation. But Yan Shibao turned out to be such an expert at whoring and gambling that, one fine day, the old man dropped dead from sheer rage. The prodigal son came to be known throughout the village as "Xian Shibao [literally, "This World Retribution," meaning he was an embodiment of heaven's retribution in this, not the next, life]. Together with a gang of good-for-nothings, Xian Shibao wallowed in pleasure day and night and, after spending all the family's cash, began to sell off its land property. Saying that piecemeal sales wouldn't give him enough cash to spend, he offered to sell one thousand *mu* of land for more than three thousand taels of silver, to be paid in full in one payment. The village was not without its share of rich men, but none of them was able to put together so much money in one payment. So there were no takers. By the end of the year, Xian Shibao became so hard up that he was willing to add a country house to the deal and cut the price in half.

Upon accidentally hearing this news, Aji found a middleman and asked for a detailed record of the property. Afraid that another buyer might act before he did, Aji asked to close the transaction the very next day. Xian Shibao was overjoyed that he now had a buyer. Normally, he didn't stay at home most of the time, but that day he dared not take one step out the door, and waited in all patience for the middleman to take him to the buyer.

Believing that Xian Shibao loved to eat, Aji bought nice food and fine wine early in the morning and engaged a chef to prepare the dishes. To Yan-shi he said,

"Today's transaction is no small deal. You are a woman, ma'am, the two young masters are too young, and I'm but a servant. I can only speak out to support you. I can't stand up to the seller as an equal. You'll have to ask your brothers-in-law to be witnesses. That's the only right way to go about it." (*Another example of Aji's good sense.*)

"All right," Yan-shi agreed. "You go over and ask them."

Accordingly, Aji went to Xu Yan's door at a moment when the two brothers were talking. Aji said, "Third Mistress is buying a few *mu* of land today. She invites you two brothers-in-law to help her."

Though they mouthed words of assent, the two brothers were displeased that Yan-shi had not consulted them. Xu Yan said, "If she wanted to buy land, why didn't she ask us to do it for her? Again she gave the job to Aji and didn't tell us until the deal was closed. But in this village, there are no small pieces of land up for sale."

Xu Zhao said, "We need not take guesses. We'll know soon enough."

The two of them sat down by their door. A little before noon, they saw Xian Shibao, with several middlemen and two page boys carrying gift boxes, merrily gesticulating as he went along. The group entered the door on the other side of the partition wall. The Xu brothers were startled. "Yee! How strange!" they exclaimed. "It's said that Xian Shibao is selling a thousand *mu* of land worth more than three thousand taels of silver. She can't have that much silver. Could it be that Xian Shibao is also selling just ten or twenty *mu*?" As they were wondering to themselves, they followed the group in.

After an exchange of greetings, all sat down as hosts and guests. Aji stepped forward and said, "Mr. Yan, the price for the land was fixed yesterday. We will not give you one penny less, but on your part, I trust you will not complicate matters and have second thoughts."

Xian Shibao said stoutly, "A gentleman's words can't be taken back even by a team of four horses. If I change the price, I'm not a human being!"

"In that case," said Aji, "please draw up the contract before we pay."

Paper, ink, brush-pen, and ink slab being all ready, they were promptly brought to Xian Shibao, who picked up the brush-pen and pompously wrote a contract, pledging never to renege. Then he added, "I can sign it right now, so as to put your mind at ease. What do you say?"

Aji replied, "That would be even better."

The Xu Yan brothers threw a glance at the contract. Indeed, sold to their sister-in-law were one thousand *mu* of land plus a country house, for one thousand and five hundred taels in total. Agape with astonishment, they looked at each other, their tongues hanging out, and it was some time before they remembered to draw them back. They thought, "Aji can't have made so much profit. Could he have turned a bandit and gotten all this money by robbery? Or has he dug up a treasure trove?" They were quite mystified.

After the middlemen had all signed, Aji took the contract and brought it to Yan-shi in her room. Having borrowed in advance a scale along with all the weights, Aji set it on the table in the main hall and then brought the silver out from Yan-shi.

As the silver of the highest grade was being weighed, the Xu brothers' eyes blazed fire, and smoke arose from their throats. How they wished they could push away everyone else, snatch all the silver, and run home! Before long, the weighing was finished and a fine spread of wine and food was laid out on the table. The feast lasted until deep into the night.

The next day, Aji spoke to Yan-shi again, "That country house is quite spacious. Why don't you move there? You can take better care of the harvested rice from there."

Well aware of the Xu brothers' jealousy, Yan-shi was only too eager to keep them at a distance. Accepting Aji's advice, she chose the sixth day of the first lunar month to move into the large house. Once there, Aji engaged a teacher for the two young masters. The older one now had the school name of Xu Kuan, and the younger one, Xu Hong. The house came to be furnished magnificently.

Now that Yan-shi had purchased one thousand *mu* of land, rumors went around the village, saying that she had come upon a treasure trove with more silver than could ever be counted, and that even the latrine pit was made of silver. All tried to ingratiate themselves with her.

After everything at home was put in order, Aji again went out on a business trip, this time to trade not just in lacquer but in everything that could turn a profit. The grains harvested from the fields were also sold off to add to the capital. In ten years, Yan-shi became fabulously rich. Xian Shibao's land property now all belonged to her. Her house became a bustling scene of activity, her land swarmed with cattle and horses, and her servants, maids, and hired laborers numbered a hundred. What prosperity! Truly,

> Riches do not grow from roots;
> They come with diligent work.
> Take a look at lazy people:
> Their faces tell of hunger and cold.

Yan-shi's three daughters all married rich men. Xu Kuan and Xu Hong also married. Aji took care of all the betrothal gifts without bothering Yan-shi about any of the details. With heavy corvée duties to fill now that Yan-shi owned so much land property, Aji made contributions to the government in exchange for the status of "tribute student" for both Xu Kuan and his brother, and obtained approval for exemption from the corvée duties. Yan-shi took care of the wedding of Aji's son. Now that Aji was well advanced in years, Yan-shi told him to stay at home and run the house, and refused to let him travel anymore. She also gave him a horse for his personal use.

Ever since he began to engage in business, the old man had never kept any good food for himself to enjoy on the sly, nor had any nice clothes made for himself without Yan-shi's authorization. He sought her permission for every little bit of silk and fabric he would use. Observing the strictest etiquette, he stood up whenever he saw a member of the clan, old or young, and if he encountered them on the road, he would dismount from his horse, stand off to one side, and continue on his way only when they had gone past. Therefore, no relative or neighbor did not hold him in high esteem. Yan-shi and her children also looked on him as a respected elder of the family.

Xu Yan and Xu Zhao, for all the land property they had come to own, were as far apart from Yan-shi as sky and earth in terms of wealth. Knowing how consumed they were with jealousy, the old man advised Yan-shi to give them each a gift of a hundred taels of silver. He also had a new grave site built, to which even Xu Zhe's parents' remains were moved.

Old man Aji lived to be eighty years old. When he fell ill, Yan-shi wanted to engage a physician, but he said, "At eighty years of age, death is only to be expected. Why waste money?" He adamantly refused to take medicine. Yan-shi and her sons constantly went to his sick bed to see how he was. In the meantime, they made preparations for his burial clothes and his coffin. Several days later, as his condition deteriorated, he asked Yan-shi and her sons to sit down in his room, and said to them, "Having done my utmost in the service of the family, I die without regrets. But there's one thing in which I overstepped my bounds. Please don't hold me to blame."

Tearfully Yan-shi said, "My sons and I got as far as we have all thanks to you. If there's anything you want us to do, just say the word. We will certainly do it."

From his pillow he retrieved two documents. Handing them over to Yan-shi, he said, "The two young masters have come of age. In the future, they'll be bound to live apart. Should they disagree on the division of the inheritance, they'll be hurting the bond between brothers. So I have long ago prepared documents on an equal division of the family fortune. I give them to the two young masters now for them to manage." Then he added, "A good servant is hard to come by. You must check everything yourself. Do not entrust servants with important things."

Yan-shi and her sons tearfully gave their promise. To his wife and son who were weeping by his bed, Aji also gave a few words of instruction. Then suddenly he added, "I will regret it if I don't bid farewell to First and Second Masters face-to-face. Please invite them over for me."

When the servant sent by Yan-shi told them of Aji's wish to see them, Xu Yan and Xu Zhao said, "He didn't help us when he was well, and thinks of us only when he's going to die. What kind of nonsense is that? We're not going!"

The servant had to turn back, but, at this point, Xu Hong himself ran over to invite them. Finding it hard to disregard their nephew's feelings, they forced themselves to go. By this time, speech was already beyond the old man. He looked at them, nodded, and passed away. That his wife, son, and daughter-in-law wept goes without saying, but Yan-shi and her sons also cried with abandon. Recalling his kindnesses, everyone in the household, old or young, male or female, shed tears. Only Xu Yan and Xu Zhao looked gleeful. That poor old man:

> He worked as hard as a silkworm spinning a cocoon.
> When the silk is ready, the silkworm dies.
> Like a bee collecting pollen to make honey,
> To others he offers the sweetness.

After crying for a while, Yan-shi and her sons set about making arrangements for the funeral. At the sight of the magnificent coffin and the burial clothes, Xu Yan and Xu Zhao pulled Xu Kuan and his brother to one side and said, "He was just a servant of the family. A simple funeral will do. Why all this pomp and circumstance? Even your grandfather and your father didn't get to be buried in such grand style!"

Xu Kuan said, "He was the one who built up our family fortune. If we bury him shabbily, we won't be able to rest with that on our conscience."

Xu Zhao said, laughing, "You are an adult now, but you are still such an imbecile! You got all the wealth because your mother and you are destined for it. It was not thanks to him! Also, he has been in business for so many years. He must have fattened his own pocket. Why would you think he didn't leave anything? Why did you have to dip your hands deep into your own pockets to pay for his funeral?"

"Don't do him wrong!" exclaimed Xu Hong. "I've seen him give every penny to mother. I don't think he has any private savings."

Xu Zhao said, "Would he have shown you where he had stacked away his private savings? If you don't believe me, let's search his room. There should be at least a thousand taels of silver."

"Even if he had money, he worked hard for it. How can we take what's rightfully his?"

"You don't have to take it, but it would be good just to know."

Confused by the two uncles' words, Xu Kuan and Xu Hong gave in. Without informing Yan-shi, they went together to Aji's room, drove the maidservants out with some excuse, closed the door, and ransacked through the trunks and baskets. A search throughout the room turned up only some old clothes. Not even a penny was found. (*Old Aji knew this would happen.*)

Xu Zhao said, "He must have hidden them in his son's room. Let's go search there!"

There, they found a packet of silver worth less than two taels. In the packet was also a record. Xu Kuan read it closely and saw that the silver was the remainder of the three taels of silver that Yan-shi had given him for his son's wedding.

Xu Hong said, "I told you he didn't have private savings, but you insisted on searching. Let's put everything back in order at once. If we're seen, people will say we're petty."

Feeling humbled, the two uncles slunk off without saying good-bye to Yan-shi. ([Illegible.])

When Xu Kuan told his mother about this, they felt all the more grieved. She told all the members of the household to dress in mourning white and started the mourning ritual. Many prayer services were held in Aji's memory. After the forty-nine-day mourning period was over, he was buried by the side of the new family grave site. The burial was a grand affair. By Yan-shi's decision, a share of the family possession was given to Aji's son so that he could build up his own family fortune and support his mother. Yan-shi also told her sons to call him uncle, which goes to show her gratitude for Aji. The villagers reported Aji's virtues to the county and prefectural authorities, requesting that a memorial arch be built in his honor to exhort future generations to good conduct. After verifying the facts, the authorities reported to their supervisors, who composed memorials to the imperial court. A memorial arch was duly built in the neighborhood. The Xu clan thrives to this day and is the wealthiest clan in Chun'an. As the poem says,

> Old and weak, he was worth less than an ox and a horse;
> He built immense wealth and stood out above fellowmen.
> He proved worthy of his old master's trust;
> He put to shame that slave who became a duke.[3]

36

Enduring Humiliation, Cai Ruihong Seeks Revenge

Wine refines your sentiments and your mind;
It relieves your boredom and drowns your sorrows.
Three or five cups bring you delight;
But too much of it can shorten your life.

A discreet, honest man will turn ferocious;
A smart, sharp mind will become delirious.
Yu stayed away from Yidi with reason,[1]
For that maddening brew can drive one to vice.

The above lyric to the tune of "Moon over West River" exhorts people to be moderate in their drinking. Our story today is about an official whose weakness for wine brought great calamity upon himself.

During the Xuande reign period [1426–35], in Huai'an Commandery, Huai'an Prefecture of the Southern Metropolitan Area, there lived a Captain Cai Wu, a rich man with a legion of servants and maids. His one and only passion in life was drinking. Wine being something that meant more to him than his life, he was called by all and sundry "Cai the Drunkard." And wine had cost him his career. Dismissed from office, he stayed at home. He was not the only drinker in the family. His wife, Tian-shi, also had a thirst for wine. They were more like drinking mates than husband and wife. Strangely enough, their three children did not touch even one drop of wine.

Their oldest son, Cai Tao, and the younger son, Cai Lüe, were both still young. Their daughter, the oldest of the three, was now fifteen. Because a colorful rainbow appeared right over their house when she was born, Cai Wu named her Ruihong [Auspicious Rainbow], believing that it was a good omen. She was a ravishing beauty and skilled in the art of embroidery. She was not only adept in needlework but also smart and capable, so much so that she was the one who ran the house. Every so often, she would give her parents a piece of advice when she saw them the worse for drink, but Commander Cai turned a deaf ear to her.

Let us pick up another thread of the story and tell of a certain Zhao Gui, minister of defense. Before his rise to power, he had lived next door to the Cai family in Huai'an Commandery. In straitened circumstances, he had applied himself assiduously to his studies, staying up every night until the roosters crowed. Cai Wu's father, Captain Cai Senior, impressed by his diligence, had often sent him firewood, rice, and other daily necessities. Later, he passed the civil service examinations and climbed the official ladder until he became minister of defense. Recalling the many kindnesses of Captain Cai Senior, he promoted Cai Wu to the enviable position of mobile corps commander of the Jingzhou-Xiangyang area in Huguang. After his messenger delivered the letter of appointment, a delighted Cai Wu consulted his wife about making preparations for his journey to assume his post and choosing an auspicious day for his departure.

Ruihong said, "Father, as I see it, you'd better not take that offer."

"Why not?" asked Cai Wu.

"Those who take up official posts are willing to undertake ten-thousand-li journeys because they are after fame and gain. You, father, spend your days at home doing nothing but drinking. If you go on like this after you take up that post, who will give you money to supplement your salary? Won't you have spent all the travel money and gone through all the hardships on the road for nothing? And there are all the worries and fears along the journey. Lacking sources of income is not that bad. There are more serious matters at stake."

"What matters, pray?" asked Cai Wu.

"Father, you must have seen all too many of such cases when you were an official. How can you not know? A mobile corps commander is an enviable post in military circles. But in the eyes of a civilian superior, a mobile corps commander is just a guardian of the yamen, who goes everywhere greeting and escorting people, rising early in the morning and retiring late at night. You've been leading a free and easy life at home, doing nothing but drinking. If you continue to do the same on your job, won't your superiors punish you? And that's not the worst. If there are bandits in the garrison area and you're ordered to hunt them down, or if some emergency arises in another place and you're deployed there, you'll have to either ride a horse or travel by boat, in full armor with weapons in hand. In such a moment of life and death, if you drink as you do now, won't you be risking your life? It would be better if you remained at home and enjoyed your leisurely life. Why bring trouble on yourself?"

Cai Wu countered, "As the saying goes, 'Wine and work don't shut each other out.' Are you saying I can't attend to business properly when I drink? It's just because you're running everything in this house that I get to enjoy myself. After I start on my job, when you're not there to cover me, I'll surely be alert. You need not worry. What's more, such a nice position is out of the reach of other people even if they offer bribes for it. Now, when the secretary of defense has sent the offer to my door out of the best intentions, I would be disappointing him if I turned him down. I know what I'm doing. Don't you stop me!"

Seeing her father so determined to go, Ruihong said, "If you must go, father, please first give up drinking. Only then will my fears be set to rest."

"You know all too well that wine is my life. How can I give it up entirely? I'll just drink less." He then intoned these lines:

> *Wine is the stuff of which my life is made;*
> *I'd rather starve than go without the brew.*
> *But I'll follow your kind advice,*
> *And cut down on my intake.*
> *Instead of the usual ten times a day,*
> *I will cut back to one plus nine.*
> *Instead of the daily ten liters,*
> *I will go for one decaliter.*
> *Instead of downing one cup in one breath,*
> *I will finish it in two smaller gulps.*
> *Instead of imbibing in my bed,*
> *I will enjoy it as I walk around.*
> *Instead of drinking till the third watch of the night,*
> *I will stop after the second watch.*
> *If you want a greater reduction,*
> *You're asking for nothing less than my life.*

The next day, Cai Wu told Cai Yong, a servant, to book at the port a boat reserved for government officials, and instructed him to bring along all the portable valuables of the house. Bulkier items were sealed up and left behind, to be watched over by a servant and his family. All the other servants were to follow him to his duty station. He also bought a liberal quantity of wine for the journey. On a chosen auspicious day, a pig and a goat were offered to the river god in a sacrificial ceremony. The family bade farewell to their kith and kin and boarded the boat. The helmsman unfurled the sail and set out for Yangzhou.

What kind of man was that helmsman? Called Little Four Chen, he was also a native of Huai'an Prefecture. In his thirties, he had in his employment seven boatmen: Jam-Packed Bai, Scabby Li, Iron Jar Shen, Little One Qin, Savage Second He, Toady Yu, and Crooked Mouth Ling. They were a fiendish gang who plundered every traveling merchant who fell into their hands. Cai Wu was the unlucky one that day.

When the many pieces of luggage were first loaded onto the boat, Little Four Chen's eyes flashed fire. Then, as the members of the family boarded the boat, he caught sight of Ruihong. Smitten by her beauty, he thought, "Let me wait until we're further down the river. If we act when we're still near the town, we'll be easily seen."

After a few days, when they were approaching Huangzhou, he thought, "Now is the time to act. Let me tell my brothers." At the helm, he announced to the boatmen, "We've got a fat cat right there in the cabin. We must not pass up this opportunity. Let's make our move tonight."

The others said, laughing, "We've had our eyes on him for days now. You didn't say anything, big brother, so we thought you were going to let go of him because you're natives of the same place."

Chen said, "No! I let him live for a few extra days simply because I haven't had a chance along the way."

"He's a military officer and he has so many servants with him. We need to be extra careful."

Chen rejoined, "He's the famous Cai the Drunkard. What good is he? Let's make our move in a little while, when he's deep into his drinking. But don't do anything to the girl. I want to make her my wife."

And so they agreed on their plan. Shortly thereafter, they moored the boat at the mouth of the river at Huangzhou. The boatmen bought some wine and meat, laid them out, and fell to heartily. Then they unfurled the sail and the boat raced ahead like an arrow.

That day being the fifteenth day of the month, the moon shone in all its brilliance when it was barely dusk. Upon reaching an open and spacious section of the river, Little Four Chen said, "Brothers, let's do it now! We need not go further." In a trice, they took down the sail and cast anchor. As they bore down on the front cabin, weapons in hand, a servant happened to run into them. Horrified, he cried out, "Master! Danger!"

In less time than it takes to narrate, these words were still ringing in the air when the blow of an ax right on the servant's head cut him down. The other servants, trembling all over, could not move a step. One by one, all of them succumbed to the swords and axes.

In the first few days he had been in the boat, Cai Wu had cut back on wine, but later, feeling bored, he and his wife resumed their drinking habit with a vengeance, ignoring Ruihong's attempts to stop them. That fatal evening, he and his wife were in the midst of their drinking, more than half tipsy, when the commotion in the front cabin came to their ears. Ruihong immediately had a maid go out and see what was going on. The maid came back and, paralyzed with fear, said, "Master, they're killing people in the front cabin."

Scared out of her wits, Mrs. Cai rose to her feet, but at this point, the thugs burst into their cabin. Opening his wine-sodden eyes, Cai Wu bellowed, "I am the master here! Who dares make a move?" One quick swing of Iron Jar Shen's ax brought Cai Wu to the floor. The other men and women all knelt down and pleaded, "Take all the money but spare our lives!"

The thugs said, "We want both!"

Chen cut in, "All right, since he and I are from the same place, let's not cut off his head. We'll keep his corpse whole." So saying, he asked for a rope. Two of his men ran to the stern and brought back a rope, with which they tied Cai Wu, his wife, and their two sons together, sparing only Ruihong. In tears, Cai Wu said to Ruihong, "This is all because I didn't listen to you." Before he had quite gotten the words out, they were all thrown into the river. The rest of the maids and the servants, one and all, were hacked to death. There is a poem in testimony:

> *The commander with the golden seal loved to drink;*
> *The thugs of the greenwoods were full of spunk.*
> *The ruthless waves rose high unto the sky;*
> *Could the act have raised Wu Zixu's ire?*[2]

Being the only one of her family who had been spared, Ruihong concluded that the boatmen were surely coming to violate her. She ran out of the cabin door. When she was on the point of jumping into the river, Little Four Chen put down his ax and seized her with both arms, saying, "Young lady! Don't be alarmed! You will get to enjoy life as before!"

In a seizure of rage, Ruihong screamed, "You scoundrels! You killed my whole family and now you have the audacity to rape me! Let go of me, so that I can kill myself!"

"How would I have the heart to let such a beauty kill herself?" So saying, Little Four Chen carried her into the back cabin.

As Ruihong kept up a stream of curses at him, she enraged the other thugs. "Big brother," they said, "If you want a wife, you can have your pick anywhere. Why take all that crap from this woman?"

As they rushed over to kill her, Chen stopped them, saying, "My brothers, forgive her for my sake! I'll give you a proper apology tomorrow." Turning to Ruihong, he said, "You'd better shut up. If you go on with your curses, even I won't be able to save you."

As she wept, she thought, "If I die, who will avenge my family? Let me swallow the humiliation for now, and die after I take my revenge." So thinking, she stopped cursing but stamped her feet and continued to cry. Chen consoled her with comforting words.

After they tossed all the corpses into the river and cleaned the boat, the men unfurled the sail again and went to a sandbar, where they took out the trunks and the baskets to divide the loot among them.

Little Four Chen said, "Brothers, there's no rush. Since it's the fifteenth night of the month, when the moon is at its fullest, let me hold a wedding ceremony before this night of reunion is over. We'll have a celebration feast before we take our time dividing everything up. Won't that be nice?"

"All right," said the men. Eagerly they opened several of the jars of fine wine Cai Wu had brought with him and set out the food. They then sat down in a circle in the cabin and lit the candles brightly. As they were drinking to their hearts' content, using Cai Wu's many silver wine utensils, Chen carried Ruihong out into the cabin, sat her down beside him, and said, "Young lady, a wonderful fellow like me and a beauty like you make a fine match. This is our wedding night. Let's be together until the end of our lives." Ruihong covered her face, weeping.

"Let each of us offer our sister-in-law a toast," said the thugs. They filled one cup with wine and held it to her. Little Four Chen took the cup and held it to her lips, saying, "Take a sip, just as an acknowledgement of my brothers' good will."

Ignoring his plea, Ruihong pushed his hand away.

Turning to the other men, Chen said, "I thank you all for your good wishes. Let me drink it up for her." So saying, he raised the cup and drained it in one gulp.

Little One Qin said, "You can't just have one cup, big brother. Drink two, so that both of you will live to a ripe old age." So saying, he offered another cup. Again, Chen finished it. Then he toasted each of the men in return.

After being plied with wine by the men for some time, Chen got quite tipsy. The men said, "While we drink to our hearts' content, we shouldn't be too hard on the newlyweds. Big Brother, you can withdraw now."

"In that case," said Chen, "you stay on. I'm going to excuse myself." He picked up Ruihong, took a lamp, and went into the back cabin. After he put Ruihong down, he closed the door and began to undress her. Ruihong was in no position to resist. He removed all her clothes, carried her to bed, and had his way with her. How tragic that a young lady of high status fell into a thug's hands!

> A violent storm ravaged a tender blossom;
> A wild wind destroyed the delicate bud.
> Far from being a night of nuptial love,
> It was a tussle between fated foes.

Let us leave Little Four Chen and come to the boatmen as they continued drinking in the cabin. Jam-packed Bai commented, "Brother Chen is now in paradise."

Iron Jar Shen said, "Yes, he's having a good time, but we're not all that happy."

Little One Qin asked, "Why should we be unhappy?"

Iron Jar Shen replied, "We did everything together, but he got himself the first prize. Tomorrow when we divide up everything, will he be willing to make some concessions?"

Scabby Li put in, "You say he's having a good time, I say that his joy will be our doom."

"Why is that?" asked the other men.

Scabby Li explained, "As the saying goes, 'If the weeds are not uprooted, they'll grow back again.' We killed her whole family. She will want to swallow us whole. How could she be happy as Brother Chen's wife? If she cries out for help when we get to a densely populated area, won't that mean the death of us?"

"You're right!" exclaimed the others. "Let's speak to Brother Chen tomorrow and bump her off. That will make a clean end of the business!"

"But after he enjoys her tonight, he won't be willing to kill her."

Bai suggested, "Let's not tell him. Let's do it quietly."

Scabby Li objected, saying, "If we bump her off on the sly, we'll damage our brotherly feelings. I've got an idea that can let us have it both ways: While he's asleep, let's open the trunks and baskets, divide everything up, and go our separate ways to enjoy what we have. Brother Chen has got himself a pretty girl. So let's give him a smaller share. If this whole thing is found out, he'll be the one to face the law. The rest of us will all be off the hook. If nothing is found out, it'll be his luck. In this way, no brotherly feelings will be hurt, and we won't come into trouble. Wouldn't that be nice?"

The other men said in chorus, "Great idea!" They stood up, opened the trunks and the baskets, and divided among them the gold, silver, clothes, jewelry, and wine utensils, leaving behind only a few items that no one found useful. Then they packed and closed the cabin door. As soon as the boat reached a thoroughfare, they got on shore and went their separate ways.

> As the treasures in the trunks were being shared,
> He enjoyed the beauty under the quilt.
> While the honey was harvested by others,
> The wild bee slept with the flower in his arms.

Little Four Chen gave Ruihong such undivided attention that he was totally oblivious to the conspiracy in the main cabin. When he rose late the next morning, he saw no one around. Thinking that the other men must still be sleeping off the wine, he went to the stern, but no one was there, either. Then he went to the front cabin, and not even the shadow of a man was in sight. He was appalled. "Where could they have gone?" he wondered. When he reentered the main cabin, he saw that all the trunks and baskets were open. He checked them one by one and found all of them empty except one, in which lay a few things and some books. It now dawned on him, to his mute indignation, that the other men had taken the loot and left. He thought, "I got it! They were afraid that because I kept the young lady, we would be found out eventually. So they've all quietly slipped away." Then another thought struck him: "I can't make the boat go all by myself. And staying here is no solution in the long run. This is a dilemma. If I go ashore to find someone to help me make it to a populated area, she may cry for help, and I'll be as good as dead. When I'm in such a fix, I can't keep her. Let me take out the weed by its root, so to speak." He picked up a broad ax and dashed into the back cabin.

Ruihong was still sobbing in bed. Though her face was awash in tears, the thug found her even more attractive. Wild with joy, he felt his arms and hands go limp. His murderous determination instantly melted away. The ax fell on the floor with a thud. He mounted her again. How tragic that the tender blossom was ravaged by a violent storm! After he had had his pleasure of her, he said, "Young lady, I know you must be tired. Let me get you something to eat, to make you feel better." He jumped up and went to the stern to light a fire and cook. But then suddenly he thought, "If I'm infatuated with this woman, I'll surely be bringing death on myself. But I don't have the heart to kill her. Oh well, just consider myself a luckless man. Let me also abandon this boat and go somewhere else for a living.

If, by any chance, I can make enough money to buy a boat, I'll get to live as well as before. She can be left here in the boat. If she's destined to live, she'll be rescued, and that'll be to my credit." But another thought occurred to him: "No, that won't do. If I don't do away with her, she'll be a source of trouble. But I won't use the sword on her. I'll leave her corpse whole."

He cooked himself some food and, after eating his fill, put together all of his savings and the few things the others had left him, wrapped them into a large bundle, and put it to one side. Then he found a rope, made a noose of it, and entered the cabin.

Afraid that he would come to rape her again, Ruihong had put on her clothes and was facing the wall, tears in her eyes, thinking of a plan of revenge. The thought that the thug would come back to kill her had never crossed her mind. (*Ruihong was one born to suffer.*)

In less time than it takes to narrate, the thug ran up to her, held up her head with his left hand, and slipped the noose around her neck. Before Ruihong could cry out, he gave the rope a mighty pull. In excruciating pain, Ruihong flailed her arms and legs and, after a few thumps of her body, she lay motionless and stiff in the bed. Believing she was dead, the scoundrel let go of her and went to the outer cabin to pick up his bundle and a short cudgel. Then he leaped onto the shore and went off in big strides. Truly,

> He gave up the pleasures of the pillow,
> And thought he got away from a source of trouble.

It so happened that Ruihong was not destined to die at that time, after all. Luckily, the thug had made only a single knot on the noose. Though Ruihong stopped breathing and fainted when he pulled at the noose, the knot came loose as soon as he let go of the rope. It was quite unlike the case of someone hanging to death, where the noose tightens as the body sinks. With the pressure around her neck gone, Ruihong regained her breath and gradually came back to consciousness, but she felt too weak to move, as if she had been overkneaded by a masseur. Panting for breath, she felt suffocated at the neck and managed by a prodigious effort to raise a hand and pull off the rope. In anguish, she sobbed and said inwardly, "Father! If you had listened to me, this would never have happened! There must have been bad blood between our family and this gang of thugs in a previous incarnation, or such a tragedy wouldn't have happened to us."

Bursting into another fit of sobbing, she thought, "I swallowed the humiliation in order to survive, hoping I could seek revenge and wipe out the humiliation, but the swine didn't mean to spare me, after all. I don't mind death, but how can I find peace in death when all this injustice remains unavenged?" As she pursued these thoughts, she kept sobbing and felt even more aggrieved. Suddenly, with a loud bang at the stern, the boat rocked to and fro a few times and her bed almost turned over on its side. The shock stopped her tears. When she strained her ears to listen, she heard a clamor of voices in the next boat. There was also the rhythmic chanting of the boatmen as they punted the poles, but all was quiet in the boat she was on. She wondered to herself, "Why are these thugs silent when their boat has been hit? Can those on the other boat be their accomplices?" Then she thought again, "Maybe that's a police boat. So they dare not protest." She wanted to cry out but was afraid that it was no use.

In this moment of uncertainty, she suddenly heard a big commotion on her boat and footsteps running into the rear cabin. Believing that the same gang of thugs was there again, she said to herself, "I'm going to die this time!" Then she heard voices say, "Which official's boat is this? It's been plucked clean! And everyone is gone!"

Realizing these were no robbers, Ruihong struggled up and cried, "Help! Help!"

As the crowd rushed over, they saw that it was a beautiful young woman. They helped her get down from the bed and asked her how she had been robbed. Before she could speak, tears streamed down her cheeks. After telling them her father's official title, where she was from, and how her parents had perished, she added, "Brothers, please pity one who has suffered so much and take me to the authorities and report the case, so that the murderers can be brought to justice. You'll be doing a good deed."

"So it's a young lady," said the crowd. "You must have had a hard time! But we're in no position to make any decisions. Let's get the Master here to talk to you." One of them hastened to get the Master. Before long, as a man entered the cabin, the crowd exclaimed, "The Master's here!"

Ruihong raised her eyes and saw that he was a well-dressed man of powerful physique. Since everyone called him "the Master," she thought he must be a man of some importance, and tearfully prostrated herself on the floor.

The man hastened to raise her to her feet, saying, "Why such ceremony, young lady? If you want to say something, please stand up and tell me."

Ruihong told him everything that had happened and added, "Please have mercy and help me in my distress. I will never forget your kindness, in life or in death."

"Don't worry," said the man. "The thugs shouldn't have gotten too far from here. Let us go with you to report to the authorities, so that the police can hunt them down. They will surely be caught."

Ruihong thanked him with tears in her eyes.

To his followers, the man said, "There isn't a moment to lose. Help Miss Cai to our boat, quick!"

As his followers came over to help her, Ruihong found her shoes, put them on, and went out the cabin door. She saw that the boat was a double-sail cargo boat of the largest kind. Once in that boat, she was led into a cabin to rest. The boatmen carried everything from the thugs' boat to their own before setting sail.

You may very well ask, who was that man? Well, he was named Bian Fu, a native of Hanyang Prefecture, owner of this huge boat built after he had amassed an impressive family fortune as a merchant traveling on the lakes and rivers. The boatmen were all his servants. Having just sold off all his stock of grain downriver, he was on his way home, laden with another shipment of goods. As the boat was sailing before the wind, suddenly a strong gust of wind blew it toward the shore. The helmsman had turned the rudder with all the force he could muster, but to no avail. The boat had slammed right into the stern of the thugs' boat. As the thug's boat was a government boat, the boatmen had been afraid that they would land themselves in endless arguments. Frantically, they had tried to turn the boat away, but, being stranded in a shallow spot, it would not budge despite all their tugging and towing. That was why they had been chanting in rhythm as they pooled their strength trying to maneuver the boat away from the spot.

Wondering why the boat was deserted, Bian Fu had told the boatmen to cross over for a look. Upon hearing that there was only a beautiful young woman asking for help, Bian Fu had had a wicked idea. With a show of sympathy, he had tricked her into his boat, and that was that. Helping her to seek justice from the authorities could not have been further from his mind.

On her part, after having gone through such a harrowing experience, Ruihong was looking for someone to whom she could pour out her tale of woe. Therefore, the moment she laid her eyes on Bian Fu, she felt as if she had met someone in her own family, and pleaded to him for help. His kind promise convinced her that he was full of good intentions. But after she boarded his boat and calmed down, she thought, "I shouldn't have come with this man. He is a total stranger to me. How can I expect him to go out of his way to help me? How can I follow him? He did promise to do all he could, but who knows if he means it or not. If he has wicked ideas, what's to be done?"

While these doubts were assailing her mind, Bian Fu came to her with a supply of fine food and wine. Ingratiatingly he said, "Young lady, you must be hungry. Please take some wine and food."

Her thoughts all on her parents, Ruihong had no appetite. Sitting by her side, Bian Fu plied her with wine, using honeyed words. After she took two small cups, he said, "I have a word of advice. I wonder if you would care to listen."

"Pray tell me."

"In a moment of indignation, I promised to go with you to report the case to the authorities, but I forgot about my boatful of merchandise. As I understand it, there's no telling how long a court case is to take. If it's going to drag on for half a year without a settlement, I won't be able to dispose of my goods. That will only spoil things for both of us. A better option might be for you to go to my home first. After I dispose of the goods, I'll get a small boat and come back here with you to deal with the case. I won't mind if the case drags on for years. And there's another thing: A single man and an unmarried woman going about together will surely invite gossip. Even though we are innocent, who would believe us? You know how rumors can fabricate things out of thin air. What's more, you have no relatives to turn to for help and nowhere to go. I'm just a lowly merchant, but my family circumstances are not bad. If you don't think it's beneath you, let's become husband and wife. As for the matter of revenge, I'll surely give those thugs a taste of whatever they did to your family. You just count on me. I'll have every one of them arrested to vent your spleen. What do you say?"

Ruihong was devastated. Her tears trickling down, she thought, "I'm born to suffer. I've again run into a bad man. But now that I'm already in his trap, there's no way I can get out of it." With a sigh, she thought, "Oh well, revenge for father and mother is more important than my suffering. Since I've already been defiled by that thug, I won't qualify as a chaste woman anyway, even if I die now. I'll take my own life after the revenge, to clear my name."

Her mind now made up, she replied tearfully, "If you are indeed determined to help me avenge myself, I will follow you. But I won't believe you unless you take an oath."

Thrown into raptures by these words, Bian Fu knelt down with alacrity and vowed, "If I, Bian Fu, do not avenge the young lady, let me drown in the river." Having said that, he rose and told the boatmen, "Moor the boat at the first village we come to and buy some fish, meat, and fruit for a wedding feast here in the boat." The wedding took place that very evening.

After a few days, they arrived in Hanyang. The fact of the matter was that Bian Fu already had a wife, who was a most jealous woman, and he stood in the greatest fear of her. Not daring to take Ruihong home, he found another place for Ruihong to stay. He instructed the servants not to breathe a word about this secret to his wife, but one of them, bent on currying favor with the mistress, reported everything to her. In a blaze of wrath, the woman wanted to confront her husband but then thought better of it. Instead of spending all that time and energy, she did not say a word about the matter in the open but quietly had a servant seek out a human trafficker and fixed a date on which to sell Ruihong.

On the appointed day, Mrs. Bian got her husband dead drunk, locked him up from the outside, and rode in a sedan-chair to Ruihong's place. The human trafficker, who had been waiting outside the door, followed her in. At the announcement that Mrs. Bian was there, Ruihong had no choice but to go out and greet her. The human trafficker was delighted that the young woman turned out to be such a striking beauty.

Switching on an obsequious smile, Mrs. Bian said to Ruihong, "My husband is so ridiculous in the way he does things. He married you and yet he dumped you in this place. This certainly doesn't look right! If outsiders get to know of this, they'll think I'm the one to blame. I just told him off, and here I am, to bring you home. You can pack now."

Without seeing Bian Fu, Rui Hong was full of misgivings and refused to go.

"If you don't want to live with us," said the woman, "at least stay for a short visit for just a couple of days, if only to oblige me."

This last argument made sense to Ruihong. Feeling she could not very well insist, she went into her room to pack.

As soon as she turned her back, Mrs. Bian settled a price with the human trafficker and told her servant to go outside and get the payment. Then she rented a sedan-chair and tricked Ruihong into it. The carriers tore along at top speed all the way to a deserted place by the shore, where the trafficker led her to a boat. Realizing that she had been the victim of an evil scheme, Ruihong let out wails of grief and was about to throw herself into the river when the trafficker pinned both her arms tightly, allowing her no room for movement, and pushed her into the cabin. The middleman and the sedan-chair carriers were then dismissed. The ropes tying the boat to shore were loosened and the boat got under way in full sail.

After selling Ruihong, Mrs. Bian took away everything in the room and locked the door before leaving. Bian Fu was fast asleep when she got home. She woke him up with a few slaps across the face and gave him a harsh lecture along with more hits and kicks. The commotion lasted for days on end, during which Bian Fu dared not even get a foot out the door. One day, seizing the first opportunity that presented itself, he went to Ruihong's place and gave a start when he found the door locked. When he learned upon inquiries of the servants that she had long been sold by his wife, he almost fainted from sheer rage. Later, because of his failure to avenge Ruihong, he did fall into the river and drown, just as he had vowed he would.

Bian Fu's wife was a loose woman to begin with. After his death, she indulged in even more debauchery. After she had spent all of the family savings, she was abducted by her lover and sold to a brothel. Clearly, heavenly retribution never misses its mark. There is a poem in testimony:

> To live and avenge her father, she swallowed the shame,
> Unsuspicious of the wicked schemes of the rake.
> Be warned: do not make vows that you cannot honor,
> For you will face retribution from heaven above.

While Ruihong cried with abandon in the trafficker's boat, the trafficker tried to calm her down with these words: "Do not cry. Where you're going, you will be well fed and well clothed, and you'll get to live a happy life. It's better than staying in the Bian family and taking abuse from that woman."

Ignoring him, Ruihong thought, "If I kill myself, my big job of revenge won't be done. But if I don't die, I'll turn into a whore." She turned these thoughts over in her mind a million times. Finally, the determination to take revenge won out. She decided to bear her suffering and see how things would develop before deciding on the next course of action.

Before long, darkness fell and the boat stopped at a mooring place. The trafficker tried to force her to sleep with him. She rejected him and cowered in a corner, fully clothed. As the man came to embrace her, she screamed, "Murder!" Afraid that he would get into trouble if people in the neighboring boats heard her, he quickly let go of her and dared not pester her again.

After arriving in Wuchang Prefecture, the trafficker sold her off to Mr. Wang, a procurer. In the brothel there were already three or four prostitutes, who, all dolled up and wearing heavy makeup, were leaning seductively against the door when Ruihong arrived. The sight of these coquettes further pained her. She thought, "Now that I've fallen into prostitution, seeking revenge is beyond any hope. I'm too ashamed to hang on to life." Thereupon she decided to die and refused to take on patrons.

Strangely enough, every time she was determined to die, a rescuer would come to her to keep her out of harm's way. (*Heaven keeps her alive to wreak revenge on the murderers.*)

Mr. Wang consulted his wife, saying, "Since she refuses to take on patrons, what's the point of keeping her? If she does something desperate, we'll be in big trouble. Let's dump her off on someone else and find a replacement."

As the saying goes, "Chances and coincidences make up this world." It so happened that a native of Shaoxing, a certain Hu Yue, came on the scene. Being a relative of the prefect of Wuchang, he was in the city to hit the prefect up for a contribution and, indeed, got quite a windfall. With his weakness for wine and women, he frequented the brothels in the vicinity of his lodging and, enamored of Ruihong for her unrivaled beauty, tried several times to patronize her. It was only because Ruihong threatened to kill herself that he did not succeed. Upon hearing that the procurer was trying to get rid of her, he offered a handsome price for her as a concubine. With a predestined bond between them, the procurer readily agreed to the match.

After bringing Ruihong to his lodging, Hu Yue prepared wine and food that very evening for a chat with Ruihong, but she just kept crying and refused to let him come near her. As she was beyond mollifying, Hu Yue grew desperate. He said, "Young lady, you were in a brothel. You refused to take on patrons because it is a base profession. But now that you are married to me, what more can you ask for? What can be so tragic as to make you cry like that? Tell me. If you have a problem, I can help you solve it and ease your grief. If it's something serious, the prefect is a relative of mine. I'll ask him to take on your case. Why make yourself so miserable?"

Impressed by his connection, Ruihong gave him an account of everything that had happened and added, "If you could help me hunt down my enemies and avenge me, I'd be happy to be your servant, let alone a concubine." With that, she broke down in another fit of sobbing.

Hu Yue said in response, "So, you're from a good family. How sad that you were hit by such disasters! But this is not something that can be done quickly. Let me have my relative issue an arrest warrant and raise a hue and cry everywhere. In the meantime, I'll go with you to the authorities in Huai'an and hunt down the thugs through their families. We'll surely get them."

Ruihong prostrated herself on the floor, saying, "If you would go out of your way to do this, I would repay you for your kindness life after life."

Raising her to her feet, Hu Yue said, "Since we are married now, what concerns you concerns me. Why say such a thing?" Thereupon they went to bed, hand in hand.

As it turned out, Hu Yue's sincerity was also all pretense. After having fobbed her off for a few days, he claimed that he had already asked the prefect to issue an arrest warrant. Giving credence to him, Ruihong was overcome with gratitude. After another few days, he rented a boat and set out on the return journey. Going downstream with a favorable wind, they reached Zhenjiang in less than ten days. There, he switched to a small boat to go home. Ruihong was bitterly disappointed that he never mentioned her case again. But, things having already come to such a pass, there was little she could do. She began to observe a sustained vegetarian diet and secretly prayed day and night to heaven and earth that her wish for revenge be granted.

After a few days, they arrived at home. The sight of a beautiful concubine filled Hu Yue's wife with jealousy. She often made scenes, but Ruihong never argued with her, nor did she let Hu Yue into her room, which consoled the woman to a slight extent.

There was a common practice in Shaoxing: those with money and ability would go to the capital to buy eligibility for appointments to posts normally awarded to clerks who passed all the required tests, so as to gain office at the county level.[3] This was a strategy popularly called "Flying over the sea." How did they do it? Generally speaking, after passing all the tests required for promotion to status as an official, clerks in a government ministry needed to wait, sometimes for years, for appointment to an official post. But those who bribed their way onto this list could jump the queue and gain a post in a matter of days, thus "flying over the sea." There were also those who, unable to do this on their own, acted in groups of four or five, so that after one of them landed a post, the others would split the benefits with him. Upon first assuming their posts, those who had thus flown over the sea, equipped with lavish gifts, would insinuate themselves into the favor of senior officials in the county, so that they could be assigned some official business. From whatever case they got to handle, however minor, they would extort bribes. When their notoriety began to spread, they would quietly desert their posts, knowing they would not be able to hold on to them any longer. Of ten officials who landed their posts in this way, only one or two would have a clean record and retain their integrity in office. Therefore it was said that over half of all county officials throughout the land were from Shaoxing.

After staying at home for more than a year, Hu Yue also thought of going to the capital to try his hand at this business. In addition, an acquaintance of his, an incumbent official, wrote him a letter, expressing willingness to give him a hand. Beside himself with joy, he prepared some money and packed for the journey.

Worried that his wife and concubine would not get along, he said to Ruihong that he wanted to take her with him, promising that he would seek a post in the place where disaster had befallen her family, so that he could have the murderers brought to justice. Having been duped once, Ruihong did not believe him, but she had been hoping for a chance to travel so that she might be able to do something about her plan of revenge. So she agreed. When his wife learned about this, she raised a rumpus and came to blows with him while heaping curses on him. But he turned a deaf ear to her. On a chosen auspicious day, he rented a boat and departed with Ruihong.

After a peaceful journey, they arrived in the capital. Having found lodging and settled Ruihong in, he went the next day to visit his acquaintance. To his dismay, the official had died of a sudden illness a month earlier. The entire family was in a frenzy, making preparations for escorting his coffin on a journey to his native place.

Upon learning that he had lost this backing, Hu Yue was so bitterly disappointed that he felt half his body go limp. He had brought only a small supply of silver. With this acquaintance dead and gone, how was he to get his hands on an official post? He thought of going back home, but was afraid of being scorned. In this quandary, he went to consult a fellow townsman who was in the capital for the same purpose. Without enough money to get what he wanted, the man began to weave lies, offering to act on Hu Yue's behalf and land a low-grade post for him, promising that if he ran out of money, he would try to borrow some. Destined to run into bad luck at this time, Hu Yue fell for the man's sweet talk and gave him the packet that contained all the silver he had on him. With Hu Yue's money, the man succeeded in landing himself a post and sneaked off like a puff of smoke to take up his post.

Hu Yue was now left with nothing but his bare hands. Running short of the daily necessities, he wrote a letter home, asking for money. Still angry with him, his wife stoutly refused to send him even a penny. Thus stranded in the capital, he fell into bad company and ran around day after day with a gang of hooligans wheedling money out of people.

One day, when plotting for a big job without coming up with an idea, he thought of presenting Ruihong as his sister and using her to ensnare a man. Afraid that she would reject his scheme, he said to her, trying to fool her, "I've been hoping that, after coming to the capital, I could get an official post so that I could track down your enemies. But I'm down on my luck. That acquaintance of mine died, and that cursed townsman of mine cheated me out of my money. Now that I'm stranded in this place, I'm really in a tight spot, and I can't raise any money to make the journey home. Yesterday I talked with my friends and came up with a plan. It may work."

"What plan?"

"I'll say that you're my younger sister and that I'm offering you up as a concubine. If someone should come to interview you, you just let him see you. After he coughs up the money, we'll give him the slip before the night is out. He won't be able to find us. On our way home, we'll stop at Huai'an first, send you home, and hunt down the murderers, so that I can put this weight out of my mind."

Ruihong was against the idea at first, but when she heard that he would send her to her own home, she gave her consent. Elated that she had agreed, Hu Yue told those ruffian friends of his to find a buyer. Truly,

> They laid out a trap
> To await a victim.

Our story branches at this point. In Wenzhou Prefecture, Zhejiang, there lived a scholar named Zhu Yuan. In his forties, he remained childless. His wife repeatedly urged him to get himself a concubine, but he said, "I'm a loser without a career. I don't want any concubine." In autumn that year, when the list of successful candidates at the local level of the imperial examinations was publicized, it turned out he had placed high on it. So he went to the capital to sit for the national level of the examinations. However, without sufficient blessing from the star of literary achievements, he failed the spring examinations and felt too ashamed to return to his native town. He stayed on in the capital and studied with several other examinees while waiting for the next round of the examinations. Upon learning that he had no male heir, these friends of his persistently advised him to take on a concubine. Following their advice, he asked a matchmaker to find one for him. As soon as his intention was known, the matchmakers spread the word among their circles and found several candidates within a matter of days for Zhu Yuan to see and pick, but none of them struck his fancy.

Having caught word of this news, Hu Yue's gang of hooligans pounced. Claiming that Ruihong's beauty was second to none since time immemorial, they urged Zhu Yuan to fix a date and take a look for himself.

As Ruihong's clothes were no longer as nice as they used to be, Hu Yue had the hooligans borrow some for her. After she was arrayed in finery, Zhu Yuan was brought in. Hu Yue stepped forward, exchanged greetings with him, and offered him a cup of tea before asking Ruihong to come out and stand by the screen.

As Zhu Yuan approached her, Ruihong turned sideways and dropped a curtsy, joining her hands at her right hip. Zhu Yuan hastened to return the greeting. Upon a closer look, he found her indeed a ravishing beauty and gave an inward cheer, "What a beauty!"

Ruihong was impressed by Zhu Yuan's refined air and graceful manners. She said to herself, "This gentleman is so good-looking and scholarly. Why should he be the luckless one to fall into this trap?" Feeling saddened, she turned back to the inner section of the house after standing for only a few moments.

"Sir, what do you think?" asked the gang of ruffians. "We didn't lie to you, did we?"

Nodding with a smile, Zhu Yuan said, "No, you didn't. You can follow me to my lodging and talk about the betrothal gifts. You can then bring her over on a chosen day." With that, he rose to go. The ruffians followed him to his lodging, where they settled on one hundred taels of silver.

Having heard about the many frauds and hoaxes in the capital, Zhu Yuan was afraid that he would fall into some trap and demanded that after he made the payment in the morning, the bride should be brought to him that very evening. When the ruffians relayed the message to him, Hu Yue gave himself up to thought. After a while, he hit upon a plan. Afraid that Ruihong would object, he told everyone to sit down while he himself went to talk to her.

"That scholar has taken the bait," he said. "But he insists that we take you to him the very day he makes the payment. That gives us too little time to play our game. We have to turn his trick against him and send you over as he says. There will surely be a feast. You take your time drinking. At about the fifth watch, we'll burst in on the two of you and wake up the local headman. We'll accuse Zhu Yuan of forcibly seizing a married woman. Then we'll take you back, threatening that we will report him to the authorities. Being a *juren,* he'll be afraid of putting his career in jeopardy. So he'll surely turn around and beg us to let him off. You and I get to return home in style. Won't that be nice?" (*Brothels in our day often resort to this trick. Be warned!*)

Displeased, Ruihong said, "I wonder what karmic sin I committed in my previous incarnation to deserve so much misery in this life! And now I'm part of this evil plot against another human being. I'm definitely not going."

Hu Yue said, "Wife, I didn't want to do this, but I don't have a choice. We'll have to do it the hard way. Do not turn me down!"

Ruihong turned a deaf ear. Hu Yue dropped on both his knees and pleaded, "Wife, I have no other choice. Please oblige me just this once. I won't ever ask you for a favor again."

Unable to fend him off, Ruihong gave in. Eagerly Hu Yue dashed outside to inform his friends, who all agreed that it was an ingenious plan, and so they gave their reply to Zhu Yuan accordingly.

On a chosen auspicious day, as soon as payment was made in full to Hu Yue, his friends demanded a division of the silver there and then. "Not so fast," Hu Yue protested. "We'll do this after the thing is done. What's the rush?"

By evening, Zhu Yuan had a servant rent a sedan-chair to bring Ruihong over to him. In the meantime, he gave orders for preparations of wine and food. Before long, Ruihong was brought to him. After an exchange of greetings, he led her into his room and told his servant to treat the matchmaker to wine and food. But let us leave the matchmaker there and follow Zhu Yuan and Ruihong into the brightly lit room where a feast had been set out. Upon a closer look by the lamplight, Zhu Yuan found Ruihong to be twice as attractive as before. In immense delight, he said, "Please sit, wife."

A bashful Ruihong turned sideways and sat down, not daring to say a word. Zhu Yuan had a page boy fill a cup of wine and, respectfully setting it down before her, said, "Young lady, please help yourself to some wine."

Ruihong did not reply, nor did she offer a toast in return.

Smiling ever so slightly at what he believed was her shyness, Zhu Yuan filled a cup for himself and sat down across the table. "Young lady," he continued, "you and I are already husband and wife. Why so bashful? Please take a sip. I'll finish my cup to keep you company."

As Ruihong kept her head down without a word in reply, Zhu Yuan thought, "She must be bashful because of the presence of the page boys." Forthwith he dismissed them, closed the door, and went to her side. "The wine must have gotten cold," said he. "I'll give you a cup of warmer wine. But don't disappoint me in my respect for you." He filled another cup with wine and handed it to her.

On top of her feelings of shame at his gesture, Ruihong was also suddenly seized with sadness as she recalled her parents' love for her and her current plight. Being stranded in this place, her body defiled, she was now forced to join an act of shameful deception without being able to carry out her plan of revenge. "Am I not a disgrace to my ancestors?" she thought. In gut-wrenching grief, she burst into tears.

Observing the tears, Zhu Yuan said softly, "Young lady, it is by the will of heaven that you and I get to meet over a distance of a thousand li. What makes you so sad? Are you worried about something that happened at home?" But he got no answer to his repeated questions. Noticing that she seemed to be in even greater sorrow, he continued, "Judging from the way you look, I believe there must be something bothering you. Please tell me. If I can be of help, I'll do the best I can." (*These are words Ruihong had heard all too often. One who has been tricked by a candy peddler will no longer believe sweet words.*)

Ruihong remained silent. At his wits' end, Zhu Yuan was reduced to drinking alone. After he finished eating and was in a semi-inebriated state, the night watch-drum struck twice. Zhu Yuan said, "It's late. Let's retire for the night."

As before, Ruihong paid no heed to his words. Feeling he could not very well press her, Zhu Yuan went to the desk, picked up a book, and sat down by her side to read.

Impressed by his attentiveness and his lack of any sign of anger at the way she ignored him, Ruihong started off on a new train of thought: "This scholar looks like a man of virtue. If I had met such a man in the beginning, I would have been avenged long ago. Hu Yue seems to be nothing more than a talker. If I rely on him, when will I ever be avenged? Now that he has received payment from this *juren* and sent me over here, why don't I turn his trick against him and stay with this scholar? My plan of revenge may work out with him."

As her mind revolved on these thoughts without coming to a decision, Zhu Yuan spoke up again, "Please go to sleep, young lady."

Purposely Ruihong continued to ignore him. Zhu Yuan went on reading. When the third watch was about to come to an end, Ruihong made up her mind. When Zhu Yuan again urged her to go to sleep, she said, "Now I'm yours."

Zhu Yuan smiled. "Do you mean to say you were someone else's?"

"Sir, you have no idea. I'm Hu Yue's concubine. Because he has fallen on hard times and gotten stranded in the capital, he and a gang of hooligans came up with this scheme to cheat you out of your money. They will soon barge in here to get me back and accuse you of forcibly taking an innocent man's wife. Then they'll extort money from you because, afraid of compromising your future, you may want to pay them to stay out of trouble."

Appalled, Zhu Yuan said, "This is shocking! If you hadn't told me, I would have fallen into their trap. But you're Hu Yue's concubine. Why do you tell me this secret?"

Ruihong replied tearfully, "I need to carry out a major plan of revenge. I believe you are a man of virtue who will surely avenge me. That's why I'm willing to submit myself to you."

"Tell me the injustice you have suffered. I'll certainly make every effort to avenge you."

When Ruihong sobbed out her tale of woe, Zhu Yuan also shed tears. As they were talking, the night watch-drum struck four times. Ruihong said, "That gang of ruffians will be here any time now. If you don't get away soon, you'll be in trouble."

"Don't panic. I have a friend who lives near here in a large house. We can spend the rest of the night with him. Tomorrow we'll move to a faraway place. There's nothing to worry about." He opened the door, quietly had a servant light a lamp, and they went to his friend's house. The friend was quite startled when, in answer to the knocking on the door, he saw Zhu Yuan at that time of the night with a beautiful woman who appeared to him to be of questionable background. After Zhu Yuan told him everything, that friend moved his own bedding to an outer room and gave his own room to Zhu Yuan. With the servants' help, all the pieces of luggage were carried into the house and stored in two empty rooms. Let us leave them there for the moment.

Back to the gang of ruffians. As soon as Ruihong mounted the sedan-chair, the gang forced Hu Yue into dividing up the money. They bought some wine and meat and ate and drank until the fifth watch. They then went to Zhu Yuan's lodging and stormed in with a cry. All they saw were two empty rooms. There was not even the shadow of a human being.

In astonishment, Hu Yue said, "They are gone. How did they know?" Turning to the other men, he said, "You must have ganged up with him on me. Give me back my money!"

Also turning hostile, the ruffians said angrily, "You sold your wife and now you try to rob us and accuse us of tricking you. We're not done with you yet!" (*He brought trouble on himself.*) They gathered all around him and beat him black-

and-blue. It so happened that the garrison troops passed by and took every one of them to the yamen. Under interrogation, they confessed to the fraud and were each given thirty strokes of the rod. The money was surrendered and then confiscated by the government. Hu Yue was sent back home under guard. There is a poem in testimony:

> He set a clever trap with the beauty as a bait,
> But the beauty was not of the same heart and mind.
> He lost the lady and got beaten in the rear;
> In his hand was nary a penny more.

After Zhu Yuan married Ruihong, they loved and respected each other and both felt like fish in water. In half a year, Ruihong got pregnant. Upon full term, she gave birth to a child, to Zhu Yuan's immense joy. He wrote a letter to his wife to tell her about the matter. Time sped by. When the child was one year old, it was time for the national-level examinations again. Day and night, Ruihong prayed to heaven that her husband would pass the examination, so as to help avenge the Cai family. When the list of successful candidates was posted, Zhu Yuan learned that he had indeed passed. He was sixty-fifth on the list and ranked in the third class at the palace examinations. He was therefore eligible for a post as a county magistrate. It so happened that the post of county magistrate of Wuchang was vacant. Zhu Yuan applied for that vacancy and said to Ruihong, "Wuchang is not far from where your enemies are. I'm only afraid they may have died. If so, you won't get to feel avenged. But if they're alive, I'll arrest every one of them, even if they fly to the sky, and offer their blood to your parents. (*The thugs* [Illegible.])

Ruihong said, "If you would take it upon yourself to do so, I'd be content even after I die."

Zhu Yuan sent a servant home to bring his family to Yangzhou and wait for him there so that they could go together to his new duty station. In the meantime, he waited for the letter of appointment from the ministry of personnel. A few days later, the letter came. He bade farewell to the imperial court and left the capital.

Most of those assigned to posts in the Wu and Chu regions hired boats at Zhangjiawan, Linqing, and traveled by water either directly to their duty stations or via their hometowns, whichever way was more convenient. To undertake the journey by boat all the way downstream was faster than to go by land and was less bumpy. The land route was all the more inconvenient for those traveling with families, especially when porters from government courier stations were not available.[4] Boats that had carried grains to the capital and were on the return journey downstream, unloaded, were sometimes rented out to officials. With an official sitting in the cabin, the boatmen would falsely claim that theirs was a government boat, so that they could carry tax-exempt merchandise. This was an old custom.

Now, Zhu Yuan and his concubine went to Linqing to rent a boat. After looking at a few without finding any to their liking, Zhu Yuan finally settled on one that looked nice enough. The boat owner gave him a name card and kowtowed to him. His head servant carried the luggage into the cabins and led the master and mistress into the boat. After burning paper sacrificial offerings to the gods, the boat owner directed the boatmen to set sail.

In the cabin, Ruihong noticed that the boat owner spoke in a Huai'an accent identical to that of Little Four Chen, ringleader of the gang of thugs. (*Her heart bent on revenge, Ruihong was always watchful. Otherwise, a boat owner's accent* ([Illegible.])) She asked her husband what the boat owner was called. Zhu Yuan checked the helmsman's name card and saw that it said "Boat owner Wu Jin." Both the surname and the given name being different, he should have been beyond suspicion, but the more Ruihong listened to his voice, the more it reminded her of Little Four Chen. Full of misgivings, she told her husband to summon the boat owner, ostensibly to give a few instructions. Peeping out from her hiding position, Ruihong found him the very image of Little Four Chen. Baffled by the difference in names, she wanted to ask, but there was no excuse to do so.

One day, it so happened that a boat carrying Zhu Yuan's mentor was moored next to them, so Zhu Yuan went over for a visit. In his absence, the boat owner's wife entered the cabin to visit with Ruihong. After tea was served, Ruihong saw that:

> She was not a striking beauty,
> But she had her share of charms.

Purposely, Ruihong asked the woman, "How old are you?"

"Twenty-nine."

"Where are you from?"

"I'm a native of Chiyang."

"Your husband doesn't sound like a native of Chiyang."

"He's my second husband."

"How old were you when your first husband died?"

"My first husband and I came here transporting grain. He suddenly fell ill and died. This second husband of mine is from Wuchang. He used to be a hired hand on the boat and was kind enough to help me with the funeral. I was alone and had no one to turn to for help. So I had no choice but to marry him. He adopted my first husband's name and took over the business."

Making a mental note of the information, Ruihong nodded imperceptibly and gave the woman a perfumed handkerchief by way of a gift. The woman left with profuse thanks.

After Zhu Yuan went back to the boat, Ruihong repeated the conversation to him, adding that Wu Jin was none other than Little Four Chen, ringleader of the gang.

Zhu Yuan said, "We must not act rashly while we're still on the river. Let's put up with him for now and start the legal proceedings after I take up office. We also need to find the other thugs through him."

"Yes, that will be the wisest thing to do. It's just that, as the saying goes, 'When enemies meet, eyes blaze with anger.' How am I going to get through the next few days?" How she wished that a gust of wind would blow her to Wuchang in the twinkling of an eye, like the one that blew Wang Bo to Prince Teng's Pavilion![5]

> Revenge had been on her mind for several years;
> To her regret, no chance had presented itself.
> Now that she met her foe on the same boat,
> She had to wait for a few more thousand li.

When Zhu Yuan's boat reached Yangzhou, his family had not arrived. So he had to moor at the pier and wait. Ruihong felt even more miserable. On the third day, they heard a commotion on the shore. Zhu Yuan learned upon inquiry that the boat owner was locked in a fight with two men. The boat owner was heard saying, "A fine thing you did!"

Zhu Yuan had been feeling helpless as he witnessed Ruihong in such agony. Now he had an opportunity to take the ringleader to task as a first case in his new job. (*A well-knit plot.*) He ordered the boatmen, "Bring them to me!"

As a matter of fact, the boatmen's politeness to the boat owner was in appearance only, and with good reason. After Little Four Chen had strangled Ruihong and abandoned the boat, he ended up in Chiyang for lack of a better place to go. It so happened that Wu Jin, owner of this boat, had needed help when escorting his shipment of grain to the capital, and he had taken Little Four Chen on board. Wu Jin's wife was a dissolute woman prone to having clandestine affairs, which could not have suited Chen better. And so they hit it off and carried on an affair throughout the journey. In fact, they became so inseparable that they began to loathe Wu Jin for being in their way. After they crossed the Yellow River, Wu Jin caught a cold. Little Four Chen feigned concern and bought medicine for him. Whatever its ingredients, the medicine proved to be so effective that Wu Jin died right after he took it. The woman gave Little Four Chen her private savings, but, to the boatmen, she claimed that she had to borrow Chen's money for the funeral expenses. After about two weeks, she married Chen, saying that she had to do so as payment for the debt. Even though she treated the boatmen to a fine feast to win them over, they remained resentful, which was why all the politeness was in appearance only. As soon as Zhu Yuan said, "Bring them to me," they eagerly dashed off to shore and brought the three men to the boat.

As the group of three knelt at the foot of the main mast, Zhu Yuan asked, "What was the fight about?"

The boat owner said, "These two used to be my partners on my boat. They stole my money and gave me the slip. I haven't seen them in two or three years. By heaven's will, I met them today, so I asked them for my money back, but they turned around and hurled abuses at me and fought me, two against one. Please stand up for me, sir."

Addressing the other two men, Zhu Yuan said, "What do you have to say for yourselves?"

They replied, "Nothing of the kind happened. He's lying."

Zhu Yuan pressed further, "You couldn't have come to blows for no reason at all?"

The two men said, "There *is* a reason. We were indeed his partners in the boat business, but he got infatuated with a woman. We were afraid that our business would suffer. So we took our share of the money and left to run our own businesses. We don't owe him a penny."

"What are your names?" asked Zhu Yuan.

Before the two men answered, Little Four Chen said, "One is Iron Jar Shen. The other is Little One Qin." (*This is the working of heaven.*)

Before Zhu Yuan had time to ask further, he felt a tug at his clothes from behind. He turned and saw that it was a maidservant. "The young mistress wants a word with you, sir," she said.

Zhu Yuan went into the rear cabin. Her cheeks awash in tears, Ruihong grabbed him by his sleeves and said under her breath, "Those two men were his accomplices. Do not let go of them."

"I see," said Zhu Yuan. "Things having gotten thus far, I must not wait until we arrive in Wuchang." Straightaway he wrote a name card and ordered that a sedan-chair be prepared for him. With the local headman's help, he had all three men trussed up. Then he went to see the prefect of Yangzhou for a report. After questioning him on more details, the prefect ordered that the three thugs be taken to the lockup to await interrogation the next day.

By the time Zhu Yuan returned to the boat, the boatmen had already heard that Little Four Chen was a member of a gang of criminals. They now acquainted Zhu Yuan with all the details of his murder of Wu Jin. Zhu Yuan, for his part, wrote a report stating the case, and delivered it to the prefect along with a request that the other members of the gang also be brought to justice. After reading the report, the prefect promptly issued an order for yamen lictors to bring Little Four Chen's wife to court.

The news spread throughout the city of Yangzhou. Murder mixed with adultery plus the presence of a female culprit were enough to attract a bustling crowd of spectators to the prefectural yamen as the trial began. Truly,

> Good news never leaves the house;
> Scandals travel a thousand li.

In court, the prefect ordered that the three thugs be brought from the lockup into his presence. The woman was also taken into the courtroom and made to kneel at the foot of the dais.

Surprised to see his wife there, Little Four Chen wondered to himself, "Why would a spouse be dragged into a case about a little fight?"

He was shocked when the prefect called him Little Four Chen instead of Wu Jin.

In most situations, truth is something one can scarcely get away from. Little Four Chen did not respond the first time his true name was called, but he did in resignation the second time.

With a scornful smile, the prefect said, "Do you remember what happened three years ago with Captain Cai? As the saying goes, 'The net of heaven may be of large mesh, but it lets nothing through.' What do you have to say for yourselves?"

Looking at each other in dismay, the three men found themselves unable to speak, as if their lips had been sealed with fish glue.

The prefect continued, "Where are the other accomplices: Scabby Li, Jam-Packed Bai, Savage Second Hu [sic], Crooked-Mouth Ling, and Toady Yu?"

Little Four Chen said, "I was there in the boat at the time, but I didn't get a penny. They took everything and fled. Ask the two of them."

Iron Jar Shen and Little One Qin said, "We did divide the money among us, but at least we didn't rape the young lady, as Little Four Chen did."

Knowing all the ins and outs of the case, the prefect said sharply, afraid of making Zhu Yuan lose face, "Stop the nonsense! I was only asking you where those other thugs are!"

Little One Qin said, "We went our separate ways after we divided up the money among us. I heard that Scabby Li and Jam-Packed Bai took up trading in floss with a merchant from Shanxi. Savage Second Hu, Crooked-Mouth Ling, and Toady Yu fled to Huangzhou and are making a living as boatmen. We haven't met since then."

The prefect called the woman up and asked, "You committed adultery with Little Four Chen, murdered your husband, and married him. These are all facts. You don't have anything to say to that, do you?"

The woman was about to deny the charge when the boatmen at the foot of the dais rose to testify. Their statements of the facts rendered her speechless. The indignant prefect ordered that the heaviest bamboo rods be used on all four of the accused. Each was given forty strokes until their skin ripped, their flesh was torn, and blood flowed out. Their confessions were recorded. The three men were sentenced to death by beheading and the woman to death by dismemberment. A cangue was put on each of them and they were taken to death row. A warrant was then issued for the arrest of Jam-Packed Bai, Scabby Li, and the others.

After disposing of this case, the prefect went personally to Zhu Yuan's boat to pay him a return visit and to show him the records of the proceedings. Zhu Yuan thanked him profusely. Ruihong also felt much relieved.

A few days later, Mrs. Zhu arrived. As Ruihong was introduced to her, the wife and the concubine felt favorably disposed toward each other. The boy's refined looks added to Mrs. Zhu's delight. After another few days, Zhu Yuan took up his office in Wuchang. On the third day, he dispatched lictors to hunt down Savage Second Hu and the others. Hu and Ling were indeed working as boatmen at the mouth of the river at Huangzhou and were easily apprehended and brought to court. According to their confession, Toady Yu had died of illness one year earlier. Jam-Packed Bai and Scabby Li were managing a store with a merchant of Shanxi in the provincial seat. Zhu Yuan had them sent to jail, planning to convict them later, after the arrest of the other members of the gang who were still at large. The provincial seat being not far from Wuchang County, the police brought back within a few days Jam-Packed Bai and Scabby Li, trussed up together. After obtaining their confessions, Zhu Yuan ordered forty strokes of the rod for each of them, put together a file, and sent lictors to take them to Yangzhou Prefecture to bring the case to a close.

In the three years Zhu Yuan served as magistrate, Wuchang County enjoyed such peace and order that no one pocketed anything found on the road and no dogs needed to bark at night. After he was promoted to be an imperial inspector, he was assigned on an inspection mission to the Yangzhou region. (*Enemies are fated to meet on a narrow road.*) Ruihong said to him, "That gang of murderers may still be in prison in Yangzhou. Since there hasn't been an execution there in the last few years, they must still be alive. After you go there, please bring that case to a close. I would like to offer their blood to my father and the two brothers, partly to demonstrate my devotion to them and partly to fulfill your promise. There's another thing: My father once had a maidservant called Bilian. When she was six months pregnant with my father's child, my mother raised objections and married her off to a Zhu Cai in the neighborhood. Later we learned that Bilian gave birth to a boy. Please find out for me if the boy is still alive. If so, he can take our family name to continue the Cai family line. This will be to your eternal credit." (*Ruihong is able to see the larger picture.*) Having said this, she gave way to her grief and cried as she prostrated herself on the floor.

With alacrity Zhu Yuan raised her to her feet and said, "I will keep these two things in mind. Once I'm there, I will surely get them done. I will write to you and let you know."

Ruihong thanked him heartily with another bow.

As an imperial inspector visiting the Huai and Yangzhou region on behalf of the emperor, Zhu Yuan was far from being just a magistrate arriving to assume office. Verily,

> His orders sent chills down one's spine;
> In gods and ghosts he inspired awe.

It being the middle of the seventh month before the usual time for carrying out death sentences, Zhu Yuan went first to Huai'an, where he asked the local officials to find Zhu Cai and Bilian. Indeed, they were found. The son, already eight years old, was a handsome boy. Because they were fulfilling the orders of the imperial inspector, the local officials went about this mission with the greatest zeal. The very day they found the boy, they gave him a bath in perfumed water and a change of clothes and shoes and sent him to the garrison, where he was to be granted free room and board. In the meantime, they reported in writing to the inspectorate.

Zhu Yuan gave the boy the name of Cai Xu [literally, "Continue"] and wrote a memorial to the emperor about Cai Wu's murder, adding, "Cai Wu, having rendered distinguished military service to the empire, must not be left heirless. I propose that his son Cai Xu be granted the status of heir upon his coming of age, and that Little Four Chen and the other murderers be executed after autumn."

The emperor granted his request. In the winter of that year, Zhu Yuan personally went to Yangzhou and had Little Four Chen, Wu Jin's wife, and the six others taken out of prison to the execution ground. All of them died, and a clean job it was. Truly,

> Good is returned with good,
> Evil is returned with evil.
> It is not that retribution is lacking,
> But one must wait for the right timing.

At Zhu Yuan's order, the executioners put the heads in a lacquer box. In the temple of the city god, Zhu Yuan erected a shrine to the memory of Captain Cai's entire family. With incense, flowers, brightly lit lamps and candles, and sacrificial offerings of pig, goat, and ox, he had the heads laid out in a straight line and wrote a speech for the memorial service. He then engaged eminent monks in the area to perform a forty-nine-day prayer service to deliver the dead souls from misery. He also made financial arrangements for Cai Xu and instructed the prefectural and county officials to take good care of him. The boy's mother, Bilian, was to live with him, to attend to the annual incense-offering ceremonies in honor of Captain Cai. Zhu Cai was given money so that he could get himself another wife. (*Good handling of the case. Zhu Yuan is a wise man.*)

After everything was done, Zhu Yuan wrote a letter home, sparing no details, and dispatched an able lictor to deliver it to Ruihong.

Upon learning from the letter that the Cai family now had an heir, that the murderers had all been executed, and that their blood had been used as sacrifice to the dead of the Cai family, she clapped a hand over her forehead in a gesture of joy and offered her thanks to heaven and earth. That very night, she bathed, changed her clothes, wrote a letter to thank her husband, and went to thank Mrs. Zhu. Once back in her own room, she bolted her door and cut her own throat with a pair of scissors. (*Even death is not enough to express her gratitude. To die so unflinchingly in a quiet moment is much more difficult to do than lay down one's life in hot-eyed excitement.*) Her letter said,

> From your humble concubine Ruihong:
> Though born into a military family, I am meek by nature and well trained in the
> female virtues. For a man, the most important virtue is righteousness; for a woman,

it is chastity. An unchaste woman is no different from an animal. My father, in relaxing his military vigilance, indulged in drinking. Flaunting his wealth, he caught the attention of robbers and died at their hands, along with my mother and brothers. I lived on in aching grief only because my personal sense of shame was of little importance compared to the cause of revenge for the whole family.

In the old days, General Li swallowed humiliation and surrendered to the Xiongnu in the hope of awaiting a chance to serve Han dynasty again.[6] I may be just a woman, but I had similar aspirations. Unfortunately I was repeatedly raped without being able to carry out my plans. Luckily I met you. You saved me from misery and gave me your love. On the very day we made each other's acquaintance, you promised to avenge me. By the compassion of heaven, you were soon given an official career. The criminals were brought to justice one by one and succumbed to the law of the land. Their blood was offered as sacrifice to the murdered. The Cai family line, already broken, has been resumed and the hereditary government emoluments will be restored. Your kindness to this declining family is as boundless as heaven and earth and beyond all comparison. Now that my wish for revenge has been fulfilled, it is time for me to die to show my gratitude to my ancestors in the netherworld, because I have brought disgrace to my family for losing my chastity and hanging on to a life of shame. My son, six years old now, enjoys the love of your principal wife and will certainly be successful. After I die, please remember me as if I were still alive. There being a limit to our marriage bond, I write you this letter instead of bidding you farewell face to face, to express my innermost feelings.

Mrs. Zhu was overwhelmed with grief upon learning of Ruihong's death. The funeral was held in grand style. The letter was sealed up and delivered to Zhu Yuan in his office. After reading it, Zhu Yuan collapsed to the ground in a flood of tears and fainted. Then he fell ill and stayed behind closed doors for several days. As the prefectural and county officials came to see him, he gave them a tearful account of what had happened. Everyone shed tears and praised Ruihong for her nonpareil chastity and filial piety. Of this, we need say no more.

Later, after Zhu Yuan returned to the capital upon completion of his mission, he rose on the official ladder until he became a three-region military coordinator.[7] Ruihong's son, Zhu Mao, passed the imperial examinations at an early age. He wrote a memorial to the emperor in praise of his birth mother, Cai Ruihong, for all the hardships she had endured, and requested that a memorial arch be built in her honor. The emperor granted the request. The arch in honor of her chastity and filial piety stands to this day. There is a poem in praise of her:

> *Wreaking vengeance is a man's mission,*
> *But a woman pursued it with grim will.*
> *How laughable those who die too readily!*
> *They accomplish nothing and die in vain.*

Du Zichun Goes to Chang'an Three Times

Those with deeper thoughts than feelings should seek the Dao;
Those with deeper feelings than thoughts easily go astray.
All seven emotions are hard to break with,
But waves in the river of love bring the most grief.

As the story goes, during the Kaihuang reign period [581–600] under Emperor Wen of the Sui dynasty, there was in Chang'an a young man, Du Zichun, who lived with his wife, Wei-shi, in the southern part of the city. The Du family had been in the salt business in Yangzhou for generations and had accumulated hundreds of millions of strings of cash and millions of acres of land.

Enjoying this immense wealth amassed by his forefathers, Du Zichun knew nothing about the hardships of farm work. Moreover, being a man of free and easy spirit, he eagerly imitated Shi Chong in extravagance and Lord Mengchang in largesse.[1] Behind his house [in Yangzhou] he built a garden with pavilions, to adorn which he bought prized flowers and exquisite porous rocks. And he purchased singing and dancing girls and bewitching women as concubines and put them in the secluded boudoirs. Every day he set out banquets in the garden to entertain guests. Won't you agree that Yangzhou is a glamorous place with an ample crop of frivolous and dissipated young men? With a moneybags like Du Zichun throwing money around, who would not want to seek his patronage? So, Du Zichun might not have had three thousand retainers [as Lord Mengchang had], but he had at least several hundred hangers-on. Those good-for-nothings were surely not content with enjoying his largesse within the confines of his residence. As was only to be expected, they urged him to find amusement outside. Being a man without a mind of his own, he saw no harm in obliging them. (*Young men, take warning!*) Behold:

With strong horses pulling light carriages,
They took to the roads for their spring outings.
Taking dogs, holding falcons on their arms,

They went on hunting trips, tramping through autumn fields.
They sought laughter in the pleasure quarters,
Sparing no expense on lavish gifts.
In gambling games they lost tons of money,
On painted boats they enjoyed the music of the flute.
Touring scenic spots, they wallowed in delight,
And they were masters of the houses of ill repute.

Du Zichun the spendthrift treated ingots of silver as so many clods of earth. His wife, Wei-shi, being a pampered young woman, also cared about nothing else but having the finest food and clothes. Before long, the piles of gold and silver in the house had vanished and the salt in the storehouse was sold out. His means exhausted, Du Zichun asked for loans hither and yon. In the city of Yangzhou, who did not know Du Zichun to be a man of wealth? No sooner had the subject been raised than people sent him money from all four directions, and he managed to maintain his lifestyle for a while longer. When no one was willing to lend him money anymore, he began to sell the land and rent out the houses. Alarmed at the way things were going, the debtors descended upon him, asking for repayment. The reed-covered islets in the river were sold off and so were the salterns on the seashore. But Du Zichun could ill bear to part with his own residence and the garden, though he did sell off clothes, jewelry, and household utensils. With his extravagant spending habits, what little money he got in exchange for these things disappeared in the time it took to drink a bowl of tea. Having grown up among piles of gold and silver, he could hardly get on with life when his hands, so used to the feel of silver, stayed empty for the briefest moment. He was not one to call it quits when what money he had on hand was used up. And so he could not do otherwise but sell his garden and his residence.

In most situations, when something is in ample stock, you believe that the supply will never run out. But once the supply begins to run short, you are surprised at how quickly you are left with nothing. After he sold the house, Du Zichun had spent all of the money before he had even vacated the premises. Now that he had been reduced to poverty, all his friends went to dig other gold mines. Who would come to fawn on him again? Even the male servants, seeing what a sorry state their master was in, either redeemed themselves or simply bolted away. None remained. The prettier maidservants were offered to debtors to set off the debts and the uglier and more stupid ones were sold off to pay for Du Zichun's daily expenses. With all of the servants gone, Du Zichun and his wife, in their forlornness, moved into the servants' quarters. Gradually, their clothes wore out and they ran short of rice. Not only did those who had been under his patronage not go to see him, he himself felt too ashamed to be seen in public, and stayed hidden at home. Truly,

Once the gold by his bedside was all spent,
The mighty hero lost all his luster.

Having been a person of consequence in Yangzhou for so long, Du Zichun felt too ashamed to stay on now that he cut such a sorry figure. Quietly he went to Chang'an, home of his ancestors, to seek help from his relatives. The Du and the Wei clans from Duling and Weiqu [in the suburbs] were the leading clans of Chang'an. Among the many members of the two thriving clans, there was no lack of officials and merchants who were in fact all relatives of Du Zichun, which was why he had thought of this idea. He did not expect them to give him gifts of money but only asked for loans to tide him over. But all the relatives said, "Zichun is such a spend-thrift! His fabulous family fortune all went down the drain. He will never return any-thing we lend him." So they said that they did not have any money for him. No one offered to help him out. However, among the closest of the close relatives, there were indeed some who gave him a few handouts, which did not go very far at all in satis-fying the needs of a prodigal spender like Du Zichun. For several days in a row, he ran around on a half-empty stomach in his search for help without getting anywhere.

It was a bitterly cold day in the last month of the year. A snowstorm had just cleared up. As Du Zichun happened to pass West Gate, without a cotton-padded coat nor anything in his stomach, a gust of west wind blew by and gave him goose bumps all over. Shivering with cold, he said to himself with a sigh, "Haven't I, Du Zichun, lived my life in vain? I have so many nice relatives, but now that I've come down in the world, they turn their backs on me. And those whom I patronized are acting the same way. What's the use of having relatives? What's the use of showing people kindness? I, Du Zichun, am a man of worth. Can it be that I will never rise again?" As he was mumbling to himself, an old man walked by. Hearing his sighs, the old man stopped and asked, "Why are you sighing so deeply, my good man?"

Du Zichun saw that the old man had

> *A ruddy complexion but hoary hair,*
> *Green eyes and thick eyebrows.*
> *His voice sounded like the striking of a bronze bell;*
> *His beard was a flowing skein of silvery threads.*
> *He wore a blue silk Tang-style headscarf,*
> *A dark brown Daoist robe,*
> *A silk belt around his waist,*
> *A pair of hemp shoes on his feet.*
> *He was either a Daoist immortal*
> *Or an elder of virtuous conduct.*

Du Zichun had no one on whom to unload all his pent-up grievances. Now that the elderly man had asked him, he eagerly poured out his tale of woe.

The old man replied, "As the saying goes, 'The ways of the world are snobbish; status determines your circle of friends.' When you were rich, naturally people cur-ried favor with you. Now that you've fallen on hard times, they turn their backs on you. What's so strange about that? However, everyone born into this world is destined for some happiness; every blade of grass has a root in the soil. Don't tell me there's no generous person willing to help you out. But how much silver would be enough for you?" (*An unusual question.*)

"Only three hundred taels would suffice."

The old man replied, laughing, "With your spending habits, three hundred taels won't do. More!"

"How about three thousand?" (*The figure jumps ten times. The answer is even more unusual.*)

Waving a hand, the old man said, "Still not enough."

"If I could have thirty thousand taels, I could go back to Yangzhou a rich man, as before. But no one will be that generous with me."

"This old man is not all that rich, but I make it my business to help people. Let me give you thirty thousand." So saying, he withdrew three hundred pennies from his sleeve. Giving them to Zichun, he continued, "This is just for you to pay for one meal. Tomorrow at noon, meet me at the Persian Guild in the West Market. Be there without fail!" Having said that, the old man went off.

Inwardly rejoicing, Zichun said to himself, "I've been running around day after day, begging for help, but no one is willing to help me out. I thought I was going to die of hunger. And now, here comes along a kind-hearted old man with an offer of thirty thousand taels. Isn't this a godsend? Let me buy some wine and food with the coins he already gave me and go to bed early for a good sleep, and then go to the Persian Guild to get the money at noontime tomorrow."

So he went to a tavern, gave all three hundred pennies to the owner, and ate and drank to his heart's content before he went back home to sleep. (*Still the behavior of one who knows nothing about frugality.*) Then another thought struck him: "I may be a clever man, but I just had a moment of foolishness. So many of my close relatives gave me the cold shoulder. Why would that total stranger offer me money? And thirty thousand taels is no joke. Even if they were made of stone, they would add up to quite a heavy load. How rich is that old man to be able to spare so much for me? Could he have just been trying to comfort me because I was sighing? Or he could have been playing a trick on me. How can I take him at his word? I shouldn't go tomorrow."

Then he started off on a new train of thought: "He did look to me like an honest man. I didn't ask him for money. He didn't have to offer me any. Why would he lie? Could he have given me the three hundred pennies as bait in an elaborate hoax? (*He called himself a fool, but these are not the words of a fool.*) I should go tomorrow."

And so he debated with himself whether to go or not. After another few moments of reflection, he burst out laughing, "Yes, that's it! He didn't mean thirty thousand taels, but thirty thousand pennies! They are thirty thousand all right. But, as the saying goes, 'One bite when hungry is better than one bushel when full.' Thirty thousand pennies would be more than thirty taels and would last me quite a few days. How can I not go?"

His thoughts all in turmoil because of the promised thirty thousand taels of silver, he did not get a wink of sleep throughout the night. When dawn was finally about to arrive, irresistible drowsiness overpowered him and he drifted off to sleep. By the time he woke up, it was almost noon. Hurriedly he rose, combed his hair, and washed. If he had known better, he should have saved a few pennies from the previous evening in order to buy breakfast. But he had been so used to spending money like water, so willful, and so upset whenever out of money, that as soon as he laid his hands on the three hundred pennies, they didn't mean much to him anymore. Also, in his delight at the prospect of getting thirty thousand taels, he wasn't going to take the trouble to count his pennies. Luckily, his stomach had recently grown used to being empty, so hunger did not bother him all that much.

Before he set out, he thought lightheartedly, "I don't have anything to do at home anyway, and the Persian Guild is within walking distance. What's the harm of taking this little trip? When I see the old man, I won't say a word about the silver. I'll just say I'm there to thank him for the money he gave me last evening. Wouldn't it be nice if we could both just have a tacit understanding without having to say everything out in the open?"

The Persian Guild was located in a building where those from foreign countries bearing tribute for the imperial court traded in pearls, jade, rhinoceros horn, jasper, and the like. Because each transaction there involved hundreds or thousands of taels of silver, the place came to be called the "Treasure Trove." With his heart set on the old man's silver and yet worried that he might have been lied to, Du Zichun was led by his languid feet, step by slow step, to the Persian Guild, while keeping a close lookout for the old man. (*Vivid.*)

When he was on the point of entering the building, he ran smack into the old man on his way out. Angrily, the old man said, "Why are you late for the appointment? I was here early in the morning and waited for you in vain as the sun gradually moved west. It was such a long wait! Don't you know the story about Zhang Liang meeting Mr. Yellow Stone on Yi Bridge at the end of the Qin dynasty?[2] Mr. Yellow Stone was to transmit to him a book on the art of war at the fifth watch five days later. Because Zhang Liang arrived late, the appointment was postponed for another five days. After one more postponement, Zhang Liang went to the appointed spot in the middle of the night. Only then did he receive the book *Three Strategies*. Later he assisted Liu Bang in bringing peace to the land and was enfeoffed as Lord of Liu. I may not be as great as Mr. Yellow Stone, but you are certainly no Zhang Liang! Do you suspect that I have no silver for you? Why should I go to all this trouble just to become an object of suspicion? Go home now. I have no money for you."

This last sentence gave Zichun such a shock that his face turned ashen. As bitter remorse swept over him, his arms sank like the broken wings of a stork. He thought, "I was that close to getting thirty thousand taels of silver! Luckless me! How could I have overslept! And now he changed his mind." But again, he thought, "If he could make another appointment, as Mr. Yellow Stone did, I'd be happy to bring my bedding over and wait here all night." Then another idea struck him, "If this old man really wants to give me money, why would he care so much about the timing? And why all this talk about that historical anecdote? Maybe he was just telling that story to cover his lack of money."

While Zichun was thinking these wild thoughts, the old man said, as if completely aware of what was going on in his mind, "I was going to reschedule with you and make you undertake a few more trips. But you suspect me of saying what I said because I have no money with me. Oh well, I do mean to perform a good deed. Why should I impose extra trips on you? Follow me inside."

Hearing that he was to get the silver after all, Zichun pulled himself together again, like a toy tiger that springs up at the touch of a button. Eagerly he followed the old man to the first room in the western corridor. The old man opened a closet and took out six hundred large ingots of silver, each weighing fifty taels, thus thirty thousand taels in all. Laying them out in front of Zichun in all their glittering splendor, he said, "Take them and do whatever you like with them, but do not disappoint me."

Won't you agree that Du Zichun was a brainless man? Without even asking the old man what his name was or where he lived, Du Zichun just joined his hands across his chest and said, "Many thanks!" (*Wonderful! Remarkable!*) He hired about thirty porters and had them carry the silver to his home.

The next morning, he rose bright and early, went out, bought a fine horse and a saddle, and had several suits of clothes made for himself in the latest fashion. To his relatives he said boastfully, "Had I been at your mercy, I would have died of hunger long ago. Well, what do you know? Heaven always leaves a door open. A kind-hearted man gave me tens of thousands of taels of silver. I'm about to set out on my journey back to Yangzhou as a salt merchant, and am here to bid you farewell. I've written a poem entitled 'Reflection.' Please kindly give your comments." The poem said,

> None answered my knocks at the stately gates;
> I endured all your insults and hostility.
> Off to Yangzhou I go now, astride a crane;
> Ask not how much I carry around my waist.

His relatives had been sneering at Du Zichun, the prodigal son. Little expecting that he would ever rise again in the world, they were quite embarrassed upon reading the poem. But then they thought, "In this whole city of Chang'an, there is no one able to give a donation of thirty thousand taels so readily. If there were such a man, wouldn't we know him? This can't be true." Some said he must have dug up silver buried by his ancestors. Some said, "He may have joined a gang of bandits in his desperation. He got the silver either by robbing traveling merchants or by stealing from treasuries."

Let us leave them in their speculations and come back to Zichun. With several fully loaded wagons, he left East Gate and set off for Yangzhou. When he arrived home after a few days, his wife, Wei-shi, went out to greet him and said, "Judging from the glow on your face and all that luggage, you must have brought back some money. Which relative gave it to you?"

Zichun replied with a radiant smile, "Not even one penny of these tens of thousands of taels is from a relative."

After he gave a full account of how he had sighed at West Gate and how he had received the gift of silver at the Persian Guild, Wei-shi said, "Such a kind person is indeed hard to come by in this world. Did you ask his name? We should return his kindness, even if we can only do so in our next lives."

Zichun froze. Eventually he said, "All I saw was the silver. I didn't even see the old man. I didn't ask. I'll remember what you just said and ask his name first the next time he gives me money."

Having heard that Zichun had hauled tens of thousands of taels of silver from Chang'an and was a rich man again, his former hangers-on swarmed to his house, all obsequiousness, like a flock of flies or an army of ants. They urged him to restore the former grandeur of his establishment and resume his pleasure-seeking ways. For one used to having millions of taels of silver at his fingertips, thirty thousand taels were all too insignificant. In less than two years, he spent them all. Gradually, he was reduced to selling his horse in exchange for a donkey, and then he sold the donkey and walked. Day after day, he bore the hardships of life. However, as the saying goes, one who sits idle can eat away a mountain of fortune; one who stands idle can eat his way into a hole in the ground. Without a source of income, how was he to get on with life? In regret, he said, "Of all the mistakes I have made, the worst was giving my relatives that poem 'Reflection' when I said good-bye to them before leaving Chang'an. It was all too clearly an announcement of severance of relations with them. How could I have the cheek to beg them again? Even if I do, they'll certainly reject me. Now I'm indeed a man without a home or country to call my own. What am I going to do?"

Wei-shi said, "If that old man who gave you money is still there, he may give you more, for all you know." (*Like husband, like wife.*)

With a scornful smile, Zichun said, "You and your fantasies! I have no idea if he's still alive, or if he's rich or poor. How can I expect more money from him! But my relatives are flesh and blood, after all. Those ties can't be cut. As they say, it's better to lean on someone who knows you than on a stranger. I see nothing else for it but to go to Chang'an and ask for help from my relatives." Indeed,

> To get on with his life,
> He had to have the cheek.

And so Du Zichun went back to Chang'an. In all humility, he approached his relatives again. To his dismay, they all said the same thing, as if by prior agreement: "Why don't you go to that number-one moneybags? How could we have the strength to raise you to your feet?" These sarcastic comments, with their sharp sting, were so unbearable that Zichun almost died of mortification.

One day, when passing West Gate, he ran into the old man again. Zichun was so overcome with shame that his face turned flaming red.

The old man said, "You look like someone in for a windfall. But why are you in such rags? You can't be down and out again?"

"I thank you so much, sir, for your thirty thousand taels of silver. I thought I would never be able to spend them all, but the moment I let some slip through my fingers, they were all gone. This must be an unlucky year for me, which is why I missed out on this good fortune and got myself into this sorry state."

"You have relatives throughout the city of Chang'an. Can there be no one to help you out?"

At the very mention of help from relatives, Zichun's brows contracted. "I may have lots of relatives, but they are, one and all, misers who hate to part with even one penny. They don't have even a fraction of your generosity."

"I should give you more, but you spent all thirty thousand taels in less than two years. If you live to be a hundred years old, where am I going to get more than a million taels for you? Don't hold me to blame!" So saying, the man raised his folded hands in a gesture of good-bye and went off in a westerly direction. Truly,

> In a fat year, prepare for a lean one;
> Men of today are no equals of the ancients.

After the old man was gone, Zichun said in lament, "My relatives sneer at me, and now even that elderly gentleman who pitied me most has also turned against me. Maybe he was so eager to be a great patron that he gave me thirty thousand taels without being able to afford it, and now he's also hard up. But other than him, to whom else can I go for help?"

He was thus talking to himself when the old man, who hadn't gone far, turned back again and said, "I've seen plenty of profligates, but none as bad as you are. Thirty thousand taels of silver were just like three pennies to you and went down the drain in the twinkling of an eye. Had I known you were such a spendthrift, I wouldn't have helped you. But apart from me, who else will? If you die of hunger and cold, won't my previous efforts have gone to waste? As the saying goes, 'If you kill, be sure you see blood. If you help, be sure you do a thorough job.' Well, what's a few taels of silver to me? Let me help you out, poor man!" From his sleeve, he withdrew another three hundred pennies and, giving them to Zichun, said, "Go buy some wine and food. At noontime tomorrow, meet me in the western corridor of the Persian Guild building as before. Since thirty thousand taels are not enough for you, I'm going to give you one hundred thousand taels this time. But be sure to come early. Don't make me wait for you again."

What a compassionate old man he was, giving one hundred thousand after he had already given thirty thousand! And what a thick-skinned man Du Zichun was, ready to take the gift again the next day!

Zichun was beside himself with joy at the old man's second offer of money—

seventy thousand more than last time. With both hands he took the three hundred pennies with a deep bow. Then, raising a hand in a gesture of farewell, he went off in big strides. He went straight to a tavern, where he stacked up the coins in a pile and gave all of them to the owner. Then he sailed up the stairs, picked a table, and sat down. When the waiter laid down wine and food, he fell to heartily, partly because he had not eaten since the day before, and partly because with one hundred thousand taels soon to be his, exceeding his wildest hopes, he had cast all worries to the winds.

Believing he had more money on him, the owner brought him more wine and dishes in a never-ending stream. Zichun thought that his three hundred pennies could cover every item in this repast. So he did not reject but ate and drank to his heart's content and gave the leftovers to the waiters.

Impressed by his extravagance, the waiters commented to each other, "This man is in rags, but he turns out to be such a generous patron!"

Zichun went downstairs. As he was on his way out, the owner said, "Please pay your bill first."

Convinced that his bill was less than three hundred pennies, Zichun said, "You keep the change."

The owner said, "What a scoundrel! You ate more than you paid for, and yet you talk so big!"

"I'm not to blame. It was you who served all that wine and food to me." As he turned to go, the owner went up and seized him. "What a fine thing to say! If I had served more, you would also have taken them for free, wouldn't you?

As they came to heated words, a few local residents passing by tried to calm them down. "How much does he owe you?" they asked the owner.

The owner did the calculations and said, "Two hundred pennies."

Zichun burst into hearty laughter. "The way he worked himself up, I thought I owed him tens of thousands of taels. So it's just two hundred pennies. That's a trifle. Why even bother to mention it?"

The owner shot back, "Yes, it's a trifle. You've got that right! So count out your money and get this thing over and done with."

"But I didn't bring much money with me today. I'll pay you tomorrow."

"I don't know you. Why should I give you credit?"

"Who in Chang'an doesn't know that I, Du Zichun of the south of the city, am the richest of the rich? What's two hundred pennies to me? I won't shortchange you, whatever the amount. If you don't trust me, I'll write a note for you. You can come to get the money from me tomorrow."

Hearing him call himself "the richest of the rich," everyone shook with suppressed laughter and looked him up and down. One of the onlookers in the back who had heard about him said, giggling, "So it's that profligate. I'm afraid he doesn't make the list of rich men anymore."

Having heard that remark, Zichun said, "Don't laugh at me, sir! I may not have the looks of a rich man today, but an acquaintance of mine will be giving me one hundred thousand taels of silver at noontime tomorrow. Won't I be a rich man again?"

Upon hearing this, everyone doubled up with laughter. They said, "Has this man taken leave of his senses? An acquaintance with a gift of one hundred thousand taels of silver indeed! Where is he?"

The owner said, "I don't care if you have a hundred or two hundred thousand taels. Just pay me two hundred pennies and be gone!"

"I'll pay you extra tomorrow, but I can't produce one more penny today."

"What a brute!" said the owner. "How can you eat without paying the bill?" He grabbed Zichun by his chest, ready to land a fist on him. As Zichun struggled in vain to free himself, a voice was heard saying, "Stay your hand! If you have a problem, why don't you talk it out?"

Opening his eyes wide, Zichun saw that the man threading his way through the crowd was none other than the old man he had met at West Gate. "The very person I want to see!" he cried out. "Let us hear your judgment, sir!"

The old man asked, addressing the owner, "Why are you grabbing this gentleman and making such a scene?"

"He refuses to pay me two hundred pennies for all the extra wine and food he had. I'm just asking him to pay up."

Zichun explained, "I paid him in advance the three hundred pennies that you gave me. He served me extra wine and food on his own initiative. What did I have anything to do with it? I said I would pay him more tomorrow, but he just doesn't listen and turns around and threatens to beat me. Sir, tell me, who is right?"

To the owner, the old man said, "Since he paid you before he began to drink, why did you serve him extra food? That was your own fault." Turning to Zichun, he continued, "Being as poor as you are, you shouldn't have run up such a large bill. Nothing more need be said. I've got two hundred pennies here. I'll pay the bill and make peace between the two of you." From his sleeve he retrieved the money and paid the owner, who thanked him profusely.

Zichun said, "Again you saved me, sir. I have nothing to repay you with. If you don't think it beneath you, may I treat you to three cups of wine here?" (*How is he going to pay?*)

The old man replied, smiling ever so slightly, "There's no need for that. I'll impose on your hospitality some other day." With a greeting to the crowd, he turned and went back the way he had come. Zichun also returned home.

That night, Zichun thought, "No one took pity on me in my poverty. Luckily that old man gave me thirty thousand taels of silver and now he promised me another one hundred thousand taels. If he hadn't come to settle the dispute earlier today, I would have come off badly in that fight in the tavern. As for tomorrow's appointment at the Persian Guild, I must go even if there's no money. What's more, he didn't lie last time. He can't lie this time either."

When the next day finally arrived, he headed straight for the Persian Guild building. The old man was already there. The old man led him into the west corridor, as before, and carried out two thousand shoe-shaped ingots of silver, totaling one hundred thousand taels. Offering them to Zichun, he said, "This silver is for you to use. But you must not spend them all in one go and come back to look for me again."

Zichun said thankfully, "If I go poor again, you need not take care of me anymore." Right away, he rented a horse and a wagon, loaded the money, said goodbye to the old man, and went off.

The truth of the matter is that cats prone to stealing chickens will not change their nature. Hardly had he deposited the money at home when he again went out to buy a saddled horse and have clothes made for himself. Then he went to bid his many relatives farewell, saying, "I thank you for having told me to go to that moneybags. Indeed he behaved like one. Without ado, he gave me another one hundred thousand taels. With this money comes my status in this city. However, wouldn't this born profligate Du Zichun bring disgrace to you, my honorable relatives? (*Comic.*) I'd rather go to Yangzhou and join in a partnership with salt merchants. Wouldn't that be a better way out?" There was all too clearly a sting in these remarks, to the mute anger of the relatives suffering such indignity from him.

With his horse and wagon, Zichun transported the one hundred thousand taels of silver back to Yangzhou. At the sight of the heavily laden horse and wagon, Wei-shi knew that he had brought back silver again. "So, did the old man at West Gate give you money again?" asked she.

"Who else but that old man?"

"Did you ask his name?"

His eyes popping, Zichun said, "Good gracious! I did remember to ask him, as you told me to, when he was carrying out the silver in the Persian Guild building. But he kept reminding me like an old woman to manage the money well and not to waste any. I had to say something in reply. And, with all that silver piled up on the ground, I had to rent a horse and a wagon, watch porters load the silver, keep an eye on the silver still on the ground, and put everything in order. I was just too busy to ask his name. But I do regret not having done that. If, by any chance, I slip back into my old ways and use up all the money, how am I going to face him again? I'm destined to die of hunger, after all!"

Wei-shi said, laughing, "Now that you have one hundred thousand, are you still afraid you'll become poor again?"

When Zichun first got the silver, the idea of practicing frugality did cross his mind, but after arriving in Yangzhou, his dissipate nature reasserted itself. In no time he forgot all about his humbler days. Those friends who fawned on him when he was rich and abandoned him when he was poor danced attendance on him again. Wei-shi, a rich man's daughter who had never had to worry about money, also let him have his way for appearances' sake. Indeed, the more money one has, the more uses one finds for it. Within three years, the one hundred thousand were clean gone.

In greater poverty than before, Wei-shi grumbled, "I told you to ask the old man's name, but you just wouldn't. And now, what do you have to say for yourself?"

Zichun rejoined, "Complaining doesn't help. He gave me thirty thousand and then one hundred thousand. Even if I did get his name, I couldn't go to him again. It's just that since I can't go to him or to my relatives, do I, Du Zichun, have to sit tight and wait for my death? The old family house in the southern part of Chang'an is worth more than ten thousand taels. My relatives all have their eyes on it. As poor as I am, I'm too ashamed to live in Chang'an anyway. Why do I need that house? As the saying goes, 'The property will last a thousand years, but not the owner.' I'd rather sell it, so that the money can pay for our daily expenses. Otherwise, we'll die of hunger right by the side of a granary, so to speak."

So Du Zichun was to go to Chang'an a third time. Wasn't he a born fool? There is a poem in testimony:

> *Do not presume that your gold will not run out;*
> *Once all spent, when will any come your way again?*
> *For ten years you were a generous patron;*
> *Who pities you when you travel far in search of help?*

After arriving in Chang'an, Du Zichun refrained from going to his relatives. He was even afraid of seeking out the old man. Instead, he lived in the family house in the southern part of the city and engaged a few well-known brokers for the sale of his ancestors' house plus the foundation. After both sides reached agreement on ten thousand taels of silver at the going price, he filled out the contract and asked the brokers to handle the sale. He thought that at that price, the money was his for the taking. But his relatives, knowing he was in dire straits, were bent on getting the best deal out of him, and refused to make an offer. All the brokers came to inform him that he did not have a buyer. With a sigh, he said, "I, Du Zichun, am a luckless one! For such valuable landed property, there is only a seller but no buyer. Maybe the brokers are not good enough. Let me go out and find a buyer myself."

He had barely reached the thoroughfare when he saw the old man approaching him. With alacrity he dived into a crowd, hoping he would not be detected. To his dismay, the old man grabbed him by his sleeve from behind and cried, "What an ungrateful man you are!"

At this accusation, Du Zichun felt so ashamed that he wished he could disappear.

"You totally forgot the day you sighed at West Gate!" said the old man. "I may not be rich, but I've given you tens of thousands of taels of silver. I don't expect any repayment, but how could you have dodged me without even a word of greeting? If I dumped the silver into the river, at least I'd hear a splashing sound in return!"

Zichun said apologetically, "Frugality is no virtue of mine, but I, Du Zichun, do know right from wrong. How would I not be grateful to you for your immense kindness? It's just that both times, I squandered away the money. I'm so ashamed upon seeing you that I wish I could drop dead on the spot. That's why I tried to dodge you. I'm not ungrateful by any means!"

"If so, this means you will come around and practice frugality. I'll help you once again."

"If I go back to poverty again this time, I'll take a vow to heaven."

The old man said affably, "There's no need for a vow. Just tell me what you are going to do with the money."

"My ancestors left behind a few salterns on the seashore, a few inns on busy streets in and outside of the city, a few reed-covered islets in the Yangzi River, and a few hundred *mu* of fertile land. These are all highly profitable properties. In my desperation for money, I pawned them off cheap. If I can have the money, I will redeem them all. In less than two years, I'll be a rich man. I will build poorhouses and free grave sites to support the old, raise the young, provide for orphans and widows, give homes to the homeless, and bury those without a grave. I will then be able to return to the right road." (*It is nothing but money that puts him on the right road.*)

"Since you're so determined, I will help you once again." Again the old man produced from his sleeve three hundred pennies, gave them to Zichun, and said, "At noontime tomorrow, see me in the Persian Guild building. The earlier, the better."

Having suffered humiliation at the tavern the last time, Zichun did not want to go there. Instead, he said good-bye to the old man and went directly back home. As he walked along, he thought, "I am too careless. The old man gave me money twice, but I didn't even ask his name. My wife grumbled endlessly for this omission. Tomorrow, I must not forget to ask."

At the first light of dawn, he went to the Persian Guild. After he sat a while at the door, the old man appeared, walking toward him. It was still early in the morning. The old man was pleased. "You came at a good time today," said he. "About all those plans you have for management of your properties, too little money won't do. I must give you three hundred thousand taels. It takes six thousand shoe-shaped ingots to make up the amount. Even counting them can take up a whole day. That's why I wanted you to be here early." With that, he led Zichun into his lodging in the western corridor and effortlessly carried out six thousand ingots. He offered them to Zichun and added, "This is all I have. If you become poor again, don't come back to me."

Thankfully, Zichun said, "May I ask your honorable name? And where is your honorable residence?"

"Why do you ask? Are you thinking of repaying me?"

"You gave me four hundred thirty thousand taels in total. How can I ever repay you, in my humble ways, for such immense kindness? If you need a house, the receipt of my sale is still in my sleeve. I'll gladly offer it to you."

"If I want your house, why don't I just hold on to my own money?" said the old man, laughing.

"When I was down and out, none of my relatives and friends gave me a helping hand, but you came to my aid three times. If I were a hopeless case, you wouldn't have been willing to give me so much silver. If you have any use for me, I'll be ready to go through water and fire, if need be."

Nodding his head, the old man said, "Yes, I do have a use for you, but the timing is not yet right. Three years after you've built up your family fortune again, go to Cloud Terrace Peak of Mount Hua and see me under the twin junipers in front of the shrine of Laozi." There is a poem in testimony:

> Four hundred thirty thousand is not a trifle;
> He still concealed his name this last time.
> On the appointed day on Cloud Terrace Peak,
> What use will he have for that insolent man?

Zichun transported the three hundred thousand taels of silver home. Indeed, this time, he mended his ways. Instead of buying a saddled horse, having new clothes made, and bidding his relatives farewell, he quietly rented a horse and a cart and started packing for his journey to Yangzhou. Still, news about his windfall shook the city of Chang'an like a bolt from the sky. As word spread around, his relatives said, "With three hundred thousand taels of silver, he's a rich man all right. Being relatives, we're duty-bound to give him a farewell dinner."

Some said, "We gave him the cold shoulder when he was poor. How can we treat him to dinner as soon as he lays his hands on some money? To switch from arrogance to humility so quickly will only make him look down on us."

But those for the dinner outnumbered those against. Failing to win the argument, those in the minority joined the larger group and carried wine and food out of the east gate of the city to offer Zichun a farewell feast. After the third round of wine, Zichun rose and said, "I'm much obliged to all of you, my honorable relatives, for coming to send me off. Let me improvise a song by way of offering you a toast in return. Please don't laugh at me."

You may well ask, what kind of a song was it? Well, it was one about a poor man seeking help but getting none. The relatives felt as if they were sitting on pins and needles, but they could not just stand up and go. It would have been better had they not gone to send him off so as to be spared the insult! The song went,

> I was born into a rich family;
> From childhood I wallowed in luxury.
> As I poured money down the drain,
> The family fortune melted away.
> With no money in my empty hands,
> With all my clothes in tattered rags,

I lamented my profligate ways.
What a laughingstock I became!

Nothing is more painful than to ask for help;
Nothing is sadder than to tell of such quests.
I went, heartsick, from mansion to mansion,
Without getting even half a penny.
If not for the kind old man of West Gate,
Who three times graciously came to my aid,
I would have died somewhere along the road,
A burden to you all, my dear kinsfolk.

After he finished singing, Zichun clapped his hands and burst into hearty laughter. "Farewell!" he said to them as he jauntily took himself off. He thought, "When I went to them as a poor man, they didn't offer me even a cup of tea, let alone wine. Now that I'm loaded with silver, they take the trouble to give me a feast and see me off as far as East Gate. So money is something one can't do without. How could I have squandered it all away!" He was overcome with emotion as he went along.

Upon his arrival in Yangzhou, Wei-shi thought, judging from the humbleness of his clothes and the horse and cart, that he was bringing back only what little money he had gotten from the sale of the ancestral house and didn't have enough to put on a great show. Little did she know that Zichun had vowed to the old man that he would manage the family estate well. Having seen through his snobbish relatives after the send-off feast, he had had a change of heart and was determined to politely turn away all those friends who fawned on him only when he was rich.

Gradually he redeemed at the original price the salterns, inns, islets, and rice fields that he had pawned off. Indeed, a large capital yields high returns. Within two years, he regained his fabulous wealth. He built charity institutions in regions astride the Huai River all the way to Guazhou. Each charity institution consisted of farmland, schools, and grave sites, all for free. Orphans, widows, the elderly, and the weak in need of support were given food and clothes. Teachers were engaged for those who wished to study, and the dead were encoffined and buried. People living far and near within a thousand li were overcome with gratitude to him. In fact, throughout the empire, people spoke of him in these terms of praise: "As soon as Du Zichun got back on his feet from dire poverty, he went on to do so many good deeds. Isn't he a born hero?"

Bearing in mind the old man's appointment with him, he handed over the management of the estate to his wife in the third year, saying, "On my three trips to Chang'an, if it hadn't been for the old man's help, I don't know where my pauper's bones would have ended up. He told me that after I built up the family fortune again, I should go to Cloud Terrace Peak on Mount Hua in three years and meet him under the twin juniper trees in front of the shrine of Laozi. He will need my service. It's been three years now. I must go."

Wei-shi said, "He did you such great kindnesses that he's like a parent of your rebirth. If he needs my service, I'll do the same, let alone you. What's more, even when you were away in those days of poverty, I was able to get by on my own. And now, with all this wealth, I won't be in want of food or clothes. Go ahead. Don't worry."

That very day, she prepared a send-off meal and accompanied him out of the west gate of the city. There, they drank a cup of farewell wine.

> *He bade his wife farewell with a bamboo-leaf cup*
> *To visit a sage on a lotus-blossom peak.*

After bidding Wei-shi farewell, Zichun went all alone on horseback to Mount Hua without taking any servants.

Of all the famous mountains of the land, the best are the following five: Mount Song in the middle, Mount Tai in the east, Mount Heng in the north, Mount Huo in the south, and Mount Hua in the west.

All five of these mountains are home to immortals. Of these five, Mount Hua is the tallest. It appears to be rectangular when seen from each of the four directions, as if it had been chiseled with knives and axes. Hence its popular name "Chiseled Mountain." Atop the mountain, there was a small, perilous, fifty-li-long trail that, overgrown with vines and kudzu, led to Cloud Terrace Peak.

Once there, Zichun raised his head and saw the twin junipers with dense canopy-shaped foliage. In between the two trees stood a blood-red gate that bore atop of it a horizontal board bearing the inscription in golden characters "Shrine of the Supreme Laozi."

It being the fifteenth day of the seventh month, the weather was still hot. Having just climbed up the mountain trail, Zichun was bathed in perspiration. He quickly wiped himself dry and, in all solemnity, went up and prostrated himself before the statue of Laozi. At this point, the old man emerged from inside. Arrayed in the finery of an immortal, he looked so very different from before. Behold! He wore

> *An exquisite Daoist green-jade hat,*
> *A crimson brocade feathered robe,*
> *A yellow silk ribbon around his waist,*
> *A pair of red-cloud shoes on his feet.*
> *He had a silvery flowing beard*
> *And speckles of white around his temples.*
> *A holy mist hovered around his fragrant sleeves;*
> *His eyes shone like glittering morning stars.*

From afar, the old man said, "So you indeed undertook the long journey to keep the appointment!"

Zichun walked up, bowed twice, and, keeping his head lowered, said, "You, sir, gave me rebirth. How could I fail to keep the appointment? But I wonder how I can be of service to you."

"I do need your service. Otherwise I wouldn't have asked you to come here in this summer heat." So saying, he led Zichun into the inner section of the temple where he tried to produce immortality pills. Zichun saw that in the middle of the central hall stood a furnace with nine statues of jade maidens standing around it.[3] To its left was a green dragon, and to its right, a white tiger. There was also a large vat more than seven feet high with a mouth more than five feet in width. It was filled to the brim with clear water. Under the western wall was spread a leopard skin. The old man told Zichun to sit down cross-legged on it against the wall, facing east, whereas he himself went out and reemerged with a pot of wine and a plate of food. You may wonder what that plate contained. Well, on the plate were three white stones. Zichun thought, "How can I eat a stone?" In fact, the stones had been cooked and had the delicious taste of taro. Hungry and thirsty after a long climb along the mountain trail, Zichun finished both the wine and the food.

By this time, the red glow of the sun was dying in the west and the afternoon dimmed into evening. The old man said, "I asked you to come here over such a long distance in the heat of summer just for this purpose: You must sit here, calm and composed, until daybreak. Everything you will see will not be real. Whatever the danger, however deep the suffering, you must bear them. Do not speak. (*The author is using this occasion to warn against speaking one's mind freely.*)

After these instructions, the old man went toward the alchemy furnace, but then he turned his head and said again, "You must not forget my warning. Do not make even one sound. Remember this well!"

Zichun gave the old man his promise. Hardly had he sat down and regulated his breath when a fifteen- to sixteen-foot-tall general wearing a phoenix-winged golden helmet and golden armor led four to five thousand soldiers to the hall, beating gongs, striking drums, shouting battle cries, and waving flags. "Who is this man sitting by the western wall?" said the general sharply. "How dare you not remove yourself from my presence? What's your name?"

Zichun paid him no attention.

Highly incensed, the general ordered that arrows be released against him. Some of the soldiers also threw knives at him, aiming at his back, and some tossed spears at him, aiming at his chest. What a terrifying sight! Recalling the old man's warning, Zichun refrained from making a sound. Unable to do anything to him, the general led his troops out. As soon as the gold-armored general was gone, a python more than ten feet long wrapped its tail around Zichun and shot forth its forked tongue right into Zichun's nostrils. At the same time, wolves and tigers pounced from above his head. Their howls and roars shook the valleys. Their fangs, as sharp as knives and saws, sank into him, inflicting wounds all over his body. Blood flowed all over the floor. Then a group of fearsome, hideous-looking demons with copper heads and iron horns hopped over to him. As he endured their taunts and teases, a sinister wind sprang up. The sky and the earth darkened. As a heavy rain came down in sheets, water accumulated on the floor and rose all the way to his chest. Then a deafening bolt came from right above his head. The sparks of fire that flew around lit up his hair. Keeping the old man's warning in mind, Zichun remained silent. Gradually the thunder rolled away, the rain let up, and the water receded.

Zichun said to himself in delight, "The sky has cleared up. There shouldn't be any more scares for me." At this point, the golden-armored general with his troops marched into the hall again. Pointing at Zichun, the general roared, "You, sorcerer of Cloud Terrace Peak, still refuse to tell me your name. Do you think there's nothing I can do to you?" Turning to his men, he ordered, "Go to Yangzhou at once and bring his wife, Wei-shi, here!"

Before the words were quite out of his mouth, Wei-shi was already there in the hall. She was pinned to the ground and given three hundred strokes of the rod. As her skin ripped, her flesh was torn, and her blood spurted, Wei-shi cried mournfully, "I may not be good-looking and virtuous, but I served you for so many years. How can you have no feelings for me? Please say something to save my life!"

Zichun thought, "The old man said that everything I see would not be real. This must also be unreal. What's more, he has done so much for me. He takes precedence over my wife, even if she's real."

As he remained silent, the general flew into a towering rage and cut Wei-shi to pieces. Meanwhile, Wei-shi lashed out at Zichun between her wails, saying, "I've been your wife for half my life, and all for nothing! How can you have the heart to allow this to be done to me? I will surely avenge myself of this injustice under the Nine Springs."

Zichun turned a deaf ear. The general said in wrath, "This scoundrel has already mastered sorcery to perfection. Why keep him? Kill them both!"

A soldier came up with a sword and, with one swing of the sword against Zichun's neck, he cut off Zichun's head. Having just put his family estate to order, Du Zichun now dies a violent death. How tragic! How pitiable!

> *Where did the roaming soul go?*
> *To whom did he leave his estate?*

With the strike of the sword against his neck, Zichun knew he was dead. A yaksha appeared by his side and took his soul into the hall of King Yama of Hell. "Du Zichun is a sorcerer on Cloud Terrace Peak," said the yaksha. "We brought him here so that he can go through every suffering until his body is rotten."

With one puff of karmic wind, Zichun resumed his former shape. His soul was then taken to the residence of Wang Quan, former assistant magistrate of Shanfu County, Songzhou, and he was reincarnated as Wang Quan's daughter. Prone to accidents and afflicted with all sorts of illnesses from birth, she never spent a moment of her life without acupuncture, moxibustion, or bitter medicinal broth. Gradually she grew into a beautiful girl, but she was a mute.

In the same county there lived a *jinshi* called Lu Gui. In admiration of her beauty, he sought her hand in marriage. The Wang family declined because she was a mute. Lu Gui said, "A wife needs only be good-looking and virtuous. It's all right if she doesn't speak. To be a mute is better than to be a long-tongued gossipy woman." So he offered betrothal gifts and brought her into his household. After the wedding, they lived in conjugal harmony. She bore him a son. One day, when the boy was an adorable two-year-old with well-marked eyebrows, bright eyes, red lips, and white teeth, Lu Gui remarked to Wang-shi as he played with the boy in his lap, "Isn't this boy adorable?"

Wang-shi smiled but said nothing.

In anger, Lu Gui said, "You've never made a sound in all the three years we've been married. All too clearly, you hold me in contempt. What love is there between us? Why would I want this son?" So saying, he took the boy by his feet and flung him against a rock. Poor thing! This beloved son became a mass of mangled flesh.

Forgetting that the mute daughter of the Wang family was his reincarnation, Zichun felt a surge of love and pity as he witnessed the boy's death. As a cry of lament escaped his lips, a flame flew out of the alchemical furnace and almost burned down the hall.

Dawn was drawing near at this time. The old man rushed forward, seized Zichun by his hair, and submerged him in the water vat. The fire went out a considerable while later.

The old man stamped his feet and said in lament, "Of the seven human emotions—joy, anger, sorrow, fear, love, hate, and desire, you have been purged of six, but love remains. If only you had put up with the agony a little longer, my pills of immortality would have been ready, and you could have risen to the sky with me as an immortal. I can go on making elixir, but when will you ever break free from your mortal incarnations? In this whole wide world, it's so difficult to find someone qualified to be an immortal! What a shame!'

Seized with remorse, Zichun went into the hall and saw that inside the furnace was an iron rod as thick as a man's arm. All the elixir was gone. The old man took off his clothes, jumped into the furnace, and, with a knife, scraped from the iron rod what little elixir remained. He served the powder to Zichun and told him to leave the mountain.

Prostrating himself on the ground, Zichun asked for forgiveness, saying, "I'm so worthless that I failed you, my mentor. I would like to take the Daoist order under your guidance. Please have mercy and keep me on this mountain."

The old man shook his hand in a gesture of refusal and said, "I cannot keep you here. Go home now. Not another word!"

"In that case, please allow me to mend my ways. I'll come to serve you again in three years."

"If you practice until you purge yourself of all emotions, you can attain the Dao in your own home. If you can't purge yourself of all emotions, what use is there in coming to me? Work hard!"

Thus ordered, Zichun took leave of him and went down the mountain.

A few days later, he arrived in Yangzhou. Wei-shi greeted him and asked, "What did the old man want of you?"

Zichun replied, "Oh well, I'm worthless. I failed him in his kindness."

When Wei-shi asked what had happened, he said, "He is one who has attained the Dao. He told me to watch the alchemist furnace and not to say a word. But in a moment of weak will, I let out a cry and ruined all the elixir that he had been trying hard to make over the past few decades. He said that if only I had endured for one more moment, his elixir would have been ready and even I would have become an immortal. Didn't I ruin both him and myself? So I'm home, to start all over again in self-cultivation."

"What made you cry out?"

After Zichun told her everything, husband and wife sighed deeply. Henceforth, Zichun banished all thoughts of the family estate from his mind and spent his days burning incense and meditating on ways to achieve immortality. To all orphans and widows he met, he gave donations of hundreds and thousands of taels of silver. Gradually he was left with less than ten percent of what he used to have, even though he had not fallen into dire poverty as before.

Three years elapsed in the twinkling of an eye. One day, he said to Wei-shi, "I'd like to go to Cloud Terrace Peak again to see that old man and achieve immortality. What remains of the family estate is all yours. You should have enough to live on. Just pretend that I'm dead. Don't think of me anymore."

Being someone also with a predestined bond with Daoism, Wei-shi did not have the slightest wish to keep him upon hearing of his decision to leave. She said only, "That old man gave you so much silver because he detected your potential as an immortal and therefore tried to enlighten you. How can you not know that?"

The next morning, when she was about to offer him a send-off toast of wine, she found only a poem he had left for her the night before. He had already gone quietly to Cloud Terrace Peak. His poem said,

> My sudden rises and falls were sneered at by all;
> My death and rebirth filled me with alarm.
> I now break free from the net of this mortal world;
> With a long, drawn-out sigh I join the clouds.

You may well ask, why did Zichun choose not to say farewell to Wei-shi face to face? It was because after three years of observance of a vegetarian diet, he was determined in his great faith to go from Yangzhou to Mount Hua on foot. Afraid that Wei-shi would send servants to keep him company and prepare a horse carriage for him, he deliberately left home quietly without her knowledge. Calluses had formed on his feet before he arrived in Huazhou. Once on top of Mount Hua, he went directly to the temple of Laozi and found the twin junipers in greater verdant splendor than before. There was no one in the hall, nor was there a shadow of the alchemy furnace.

With a sigh, Zichun said to himself, "It must be that I am not meant to be an immortal after all, which is why my mentor doesn't want to try to enlighten me anymore. Be this as it may, I have taken a vow. I can't just leave without even seeing my mentor. I'll die here rather than go back." And so he stayed on in the temple for three whole years, living on the products of the forest. Without ever seeing the old man again, he could do no more than kneel before the statue of Laozi, kowtow, and pray, saying, "Your humble disciple Du Zichun is a benighted mortal of the lower realm. As I chased profit and indulged in pleasures, my mentor in his compassion pointed out the right path for me. But because I failed to purge myself of the emotion of love, I was not able to achieve the Dao. I was sent back home for more self-cultivation, which I did unremittingly for three years. Here I am again in the temple, as unshaken in my faith as before. I have purged myself of all emotions, freed myself from all that occupies the six sensory organs,[4] and committed myself to inaction. I have cultivated my inner nature until all ties with the mortal world have been removed. I pray that my predestined bond with Daoism will begin early, that I attain immortality soon, and that these mortal bones will transcend the world and gain the right path to enlightenment."

As he was praying before the statue of Laozi, suddenly a man walked out from the back of the temple and exclaimed, "You are a sincere one!"

Hearing a voice, Zichun raised his head and whom did he see but the old man! In happy astonishment, he went up and kowtowed, saying, "I missed you so much, my mentor! I've been here for three years, hoping to see you. Why did I never get to see you even once?"

The old man said, smiling, "You and I have never been apart. How could you say you hadn't seen me for three years?"

"If you were here, why have I never seen you?"

"Look at the statue on the pedestal. Do you see any resemblance?"

Eagerly Zichun went up close to the statue of Laozi, peered intently, and found the statue to be the very image of the old man. Only then did he realize that the old man was none other than the Supreme Laozi. Prostrating himself on the floor, he asked for forgiveness, saying, "How was I to know with my mortal eyes? I only hope that my mentor would take pity on this disciple and impart the great Dao to me."

Laozi said with a smile, "I was afraid that your ties with the mortal world in which you lived for so long remained unsevered. So I created situations covering all seven human emotions to test you. Now that you have purged yourself of all emotions, there's nothing more for me to say. I recall that during the Han dynasty, Liu An, prince of Huainan, had his heart set on achieving immortality.[5] The Eight

Immortals were so moved by his sincerity that they descended to earth and helped him mix elixir. On the day the elixir was ready, the whole family rose to heaven. Even the dogs and the chickens that ate the leftover powder in the alchemy vessel followed them up to heaven. To this day, his roosters are still crowing in the sky and his dogs are still barking amidst the clouds. Now, if you become an immortal, how can your wife not achieve the Dao with you? I have here three divine pills for you. You can save one and go back home to feed it to Wei-shi, so that she can also extricate herself from the mortal world and ascend to heaven soon."

With another bow Zichun accepted the divine pills. He said, "When I fell on hard times and went to my relatives in Chang'an for help, they all called me a prodigal son. No one showed me compassion. I would like to go with my wife Wei-shi to Chang'an again, to turn our ancestral house into a temple in your honor. In the temple we will build a sixteen-foot gilded statue and offer incense. I will call my relatives together and enlighten them, so that they can break free from earthly temptations. Would you, sir, approve of my doing so?"

"Good," said Laozi in approval. "If you have this wish, I will show my magic power on the day the golden statue is completed and help you rise to heaven. You will still be in good time." Truly,

> He woke up from a ten-year Yangzhou dream,
> In which he won ill fame as the prodigal son.

Let us now pick up another thread of the story. After Zichun's departure, Wei-shi also devoted herself to the cultivation of the Dao and relinquished her luxurious style of living. She donated all of the family wealth and spent her days in a Daoist nunnery, living on alms. All the people of Yangzhou were puzzled by the behavior of this couple, with the husband away as a mendicant Daoist and the wife living a beggar's life.

One day, Zichun came back. Both he and Wei-shi having attained the Dao, they now had a tacit understanding and needed no verbal exchanges. After Wei-shi took Laozi's divine pill, they dressed themselves like Daoists begging for alms and went to Chang'an to see their relatives. Presenting them with a subscription book, Zichun explained his intention of turning his ancestral home south of the city into a temple to the Supreme Laozi and declared that he was therefore seeking donations of one hundred thousand taels of gold to build a sixteen-foot statue in the main hall. He exhorted them to give generously.

His relatives said, laughing, "Twice he gained windfalls and both times he fell into poverty again. But let's forget about that. Later, he did learn how to manage his money with the third windfall. And yet, after three years, he gave all that away. If he alone did that, fine. But that Wei-shi, instead of stopping him, donated everything that he had left her. (*Wei-shi transcends the mortal world and therefore can achieve the Dao.*) Maybe good fortune is simply not in their stars. That's why they end up in such a sorry condition. That ancestral house is worth ten thousand taels of silver. Why would they want to turn it into a temple and ask for donations to build a gold statue? They are such fools that even if they get the money, they'll lose it to some swindler. Why should we pay them any attention?"

They all closed their doors, saying they didn't want to meddle in something that did not concern them. Zichun and his wife returned home, smiling. The relatives offered no donation because they felt certain that Du Zichun and his wife would not be able to raise enough money for a gold statue. To their surprise, after half a month, Zichun went to their doors again with invitations that read:

"In an action that exceeded my capacity, I donated six thousand catties of gold to build a statue of Laozi. Thanks to help from all quarters, the statue has been completed and will be hoisted onto the pedestal tomorrow. I request the pleasure of your company at a humble meal to celebrate the occasion. Please do not turn down this invitation." (*Zichun already received the formula for elixir from Laozi. He asked for donations just for the sake of enlightening the public.*)

His relatives were all stunned. They marveled, "How could he have come up with so much gold? And how could the statue have been built with such divine speed?" With alacrity, they sent servants to make inquiries and learned that at the door of every relative and every family of upper or lower class throughout the city, there had been a Du Zichun on that day, delivering a letter of invitation. Upon hearing that there were so many replications of Du Zichun, they said, "Something is not right about this."

On the day of the ceremony, everyone made an appearance. The entire neighborhood was filled with a heaving mass of humanity. All the men and women of the city had turned out to offer donations. From afar, one could see that over the magnificent gate of the newly renovated house was a horizontal board that bore in gilded characters, each as large as a wicker basket, the inscription "Palace of the Supreme Laozi."

The gate led to halls and corridors that were no less majestic and eye-dazzling than the heavenly palace. Upon seeing the imposing sixteen-foot gold statue of Laozi in the main hall, Zichun's relatives said in amazement, shaking their heads and clicking their tongues, "So he did finish the grand project! But where did he get so much gold?"

At the sight of the large plate of vegetables and the vessel of wine in front of the statue, they thought, "This must be the meal he prepared. However well-cooked, there's so little of it, enough for only one person in one bite. How could he have issued invitations to so many people?"

Strangely enough, Zichun and his wife offered the food and wine to everyone who paid homage to the statue. Everyone partook of the meal and praised it for its delicious taste. While they were marveling, they saw that a shaft of divine light shone forth from the head of the statue and changed into three white clouds. On the middle cloud sat Laozi, on the left was Du Zichun, and on the right, Wei-shi. From the hall they rose into midair, more than a hundred feet above the ground.

Raising a hand, Zichun bade farewell to the crowd and said, "Mortals love money too much to know anything about the great Dao. But when the three disasters of war, famine, and plagues strike and the four elements of earth, water, fire, and wind wreak havoc, where are they going to dispose of their family fortune? Do not be miserly! Do not begrudge donations!"

As soon as he finished with this admonition, celestial music with *sheng* pipes and *xiao* flutes was struck up and echoed throughout the air. With banners and streamers leading the way and canopies bringing up the rear, the three of them rose slowly to the sky. All the people of the city, of both upper and lower classes, joined their palms and bowed toward the sky. There is a poem in testimony:

> *His fortune gone, he was poor but he cared not;*
> *Unflinchingly he set his heart on the Dao.*
> *A selfless man will attain the Dao in the end*
> *And climb the heavenly ladder on white clouds.*

Daoist Li Enters Cloud Gate Cave Alone

None believes stories about the immortals;
Who can elude the grip of fame and gain?
This story about entering Cloud Gate Cave
Sends sweet and cool breezes through the air.

Our story begins early in the Kaihuang reign period [581–600] under Emperor Wen of the Sui dynasty. There lived in the city of Qingzhou a rich man named Li Qing who owned dye mills that had been the Li family property for generations. Though only of trader status, the clan thrived and multiplied. All five to six thousand of its men were skilled workers able to make a living with their bare hands. With every family of the Li clan living in abundance, all and sundry far and near called the Lis "Half the Prefecture."

Being the oldest member of the clan, Li Qing was looked up to as its head. A kind and benevolent man, he treated everyone in the clan with equal affection and never played favorites, regardless of the degree of kinship. For this fact alone, everyone in the clan, old and young, male and female, held him in high esteem. Every time his birthday came around, members of this large clan strove to outdo one another in seeking exotic art objects, antiques, and fine silk to present to him, wishing him longevity. But he was a frugal man who cherished his good fortune. Loath to waste anything, he stored all the gifts in his cellar. Year after year, the gifts piled up until there were more of them than he could count.

There was one thing on which he did not begrudge spending money. What was it? Ever since childhood, he had been given to doing good works. He would donate thousands of strings of cash at a time to works of charity as well as to pursuits of the Dao and immortality. He would keep mendicant Daoist priests at home and learn from them ways to mix the elixir of immortality and to perfect the inner nature. Little did he know that these priests were no more than wandering swindlers out to cheat people out of their money. What real knowledge and scholarship did they have? He spent a prodigious amount of money on them without learning even one magic trick. Be all this as it may, he remained as faithful as ever. Every day, he burned incense, sat in meditation, and cultivated mental serenity in the hope of gaining immortality.

In the year of which we speak, he was exactly seventy years old. Two months before his birthday, his sons and grandsons began to consult one another, saying, "A seventy-year-old man is a rarity. This is no ordinary birthday. Let's find some unique gifts to wish him eternal youth."

Anticipating what the younger generations would be up to, Li Qing preempted them by setting out in advance a feast for each branch of the clan and issuing invitations one branch at a time. At the feasts he announced, "I am glad that you have all been working hard, making your own living. The gifts you give me every year must have come to almost ten thousand taels of silver in value. Clothes and utensils in this house have reached the height of lavishness. But, in fact, as I am given to Daoist pursuits, I have been wearing cotton clothes and observing a vegetarian diet for fifty years now. I have no use for items of luxury. I never turned down your gifts because I couldn't very well disappoint you in your generosity. All the gifts have been stored in the cellar. I haven't checked them, but I suppose most of them have decayed. This is a grievous waste of your money. Now, thanks to the gods in heaven who haven't summoned my soul, another birthday of mine is approaching. You must be planning for a birthday celebration, but that's against my inclinations. So I'm doing this in advance, to tell you to give up your plans."

"But ever since ancient times, a birthday celebration has been called a prolongation of life," they rejoined. "What's more, you will be seventy. How many people get to live that long? If we don't celebrate, how are we going to demonstrate our filial piety? This is a rare opportunity."

Li Qing said, "If you are not going to change your mind, how about giving me something that I want?"

Jubilantly, they said, "Of course! Just say the word!"

"I would like each of you to give me a hundred feet of a finger-thick hemp rope ten days before my birthday. That would add up to five to six hundred thousand feet. Won't that be a much more impressive prolongation of my life?"

Marveling at this strange request, they promised, "We will surely do as you say, sir, but why would you want ropes?"

Li Qing replied cheerfully, "I'll let you know when all the ropes are here. I must not blurt out anything at this moment."

Thus instructed, his sons and grandsons spread the word around, one to ten and ten to a hundred, and the ropes came in before the appointed day. They piled up on the ground until they formed a hill. But why would Li Qing need so many ropes?

The fact of the matter was that ten li south of Qingzhou stood a mountain called Cloud Gate Mountain. The top of the mountain looked like it had been cut in half by an ax. In the city, people living in houses facing south could see clearly every cloud and every bird that flew over the gap. Therefore the mountain was also called by the populace "Ax-Hewn Mountain." In the mountain was a large cave of unfathomable depth. Some curious people had thrown rocks into it but heard not a sound, which was why everyone thought it was bottomless.

After he received the ropes, Li Qing had two large wooden stakes and a winch put up right by the mouth of the cave. He then had a craftsman make a large sturdy bamboo basket. From a copperware store he bought several hundred copper bells of all sizes. Wondering what he was up to, the younger clansmen went to ask him. Only then did Li Qing give them an explanation:

"I did say that I would let you know in time. I won't leave without telling you about it. I have been attracted to Daoism ever since I was in my teens. More than fifty years have gone by, but I have made no progress. According to a geography book I often read, Cloud Gate Mountain contains the seventh cave dwelling of the immortals. I'm already seventy. I won't get to live for more than two or three years in this world. While I still have strong hands and legs, I want to put the hemp ropes you gave me to good use on my birthday. I'll tie one rope to each of the four corners of the bamboo basket, add one to the middle of the basket and tie the bells to the middle rope. I'll sit in the basket while you lower it slowly from the winch. If something should happen, I'll shake the middle rope, so that you can pull me up as soon as you hear the bells ring. If I'm predestined to meet immortals down there, I'll also come back to let you know." (*This promise to go back and let them know shows where his weakness lies: he hasn't broken all ties with the mortal world.*)

Before he had quite gotten the words out, the younger members of the clan all kowtowed and raised objections. "You must not do this!" they said. "That huge cave must be swarming with ghosts and spirits of the mountains and the trees, poisonous snakes, and grotesque beasts. The black vapor and the stench alone are enough to kill a human being. At your advanced age, how would you be able to deal with all that?"

"My mind is made up. I won't regret it, even if I die. If you object, I'll have to do it on the quiet and just throw myself down the cave. Without the ropes and the bamboo basket, I'll never be able to come out again."

An older and wiser member of the clan, knowing his stubbornness all too well, said, "The best way for us to show you respect is to do as you say. But this is such a momentous event. You must not go alone quietly. You must notify all the relatives so that we can go together to Cloud Gate Mountain to see you off. That way, people will spread the news with delight all over the four seas. Won't that be nice?"

Li Qing conceded, "That's not a bad idea."

The five to six thousand male members of the Li clan then told the other relatives to join them in sending Li Qing off. Even if each one notified only one person, that easily added up to ten thousand people.

When Li Qing's birthday arrived, all the relatives took along wine and food and, amid the music of the drum band, went with Li Qing to Cloud Gate Mountain. Almost all of the residents of Qingzhou turned out to watch. Before long, they reached the top of Cloud Gate Mountain. As they looked around, they were deeply impressed by the spectacular scenery. Behold:

> *The many peaks stand in a circle;*
> *The cliffs form a ring of screens.*
> *The flowing streams gurgle in the stillness;*
> *The rank weeds grow in abundance.*
> *Strangely shaped trees on the crags rise to the sky,*
> *Rare flowers on the rocks glow in the sunlight.*
> *Beyond the misty mountain path,*
> *A bridge, and wilderness that fades into a blue haze.*
> *Against the hills in the distance,*
> *Green pines sough, and water joins the white clouds.*
> *The air echoes with the dripping of dew;*
> *The rustle of leaves in the wind falls on the ears.*

When the bamboo basket and the ropes were all ready, members of the clan took turns offering Li Qing wine. An older one among them said, "Judging from the way you are so determined to attain the Dao, I believe you are destined to achieve immortality. You have nothing to worry about on your way there. But we must still exercise caution, so that we won't have regrets. No one has ever ventured into that dark cave. How can you take chances so lightly with your precious life? Since the bamboo basket and the ropes are ready, why don't we let down a dog first? If nothing happens to the dog, we'll let down a smart servant, so that he can see if there are any signs of immortals. After he comes up and describes what he has seen down there, we'll then let you down. Won't that be perfectly safe?"

Li Qing replied, "Thank you for the idea, but one who is determined to seek the Dao will move the immortals into taking him as a disciple only when he's ready to risk his life. This is said to be the seventh cave dwelling of the immortals. It doesn't have poison or arsenic. Why even try to test it? Having such doubts is a sign of a lack of Daoist faith. How would transcendence from the mortal world then be possible? I'm firm in my decision. I will make the trip. You need not worry. I've made up a four-line song by way of bidding you farewell. Don't laugh at me!"

His kinsmen said in unison, "Let's hear it!" The song Li Qing intoned is as follows:

> *With one foot already in the grave anyway,*
> *I'm not alone in waving a hand at Cloud Gate.*
> *How comic that old man of the flask![1]*
> *I still loathe the sight of hanging flasks at the market.*

Nodding their heads and sighing, the kinsmen managed to say these comforting words: "With your kind of determination, may you meet an immortal as soon as you're down there!"

"Thank you all for your kind wish. You will see if this old man is so destined." He bowed twice toward the sky, sat down in the basket, waved good-bye to all the kinsmen, and, without another word, cranked the winch and let himself down by the rope. All his kinsmen turned pale. Even onlookers unrelated to him were appalled. Shaking their heads, clicking their tongues, they said, "Why doesn't that old man just enjoy his otherwise peaceful life at home? Imagine having such fanciful ideas and going into such a deep cave to seek immortality! Isn't he courting death?" Yee! Now that he has been lowered into the cave, we wonder if he will ever return! Truly,

> All immortals had once been but mortals;
> But few mortals care to cultivate the art.

Li Qing went down for goodness knows how many tens of thousands of feet. When he felt that he had reached the bottom, he climbed out of the bamboo basket to look for signs of immortals. But all was dark at the bottom of the cave. He could make out nothing. And the ground was slippery and soft, as if with water. Before he had taken one step, he fell. He had just struggled up with all the strength of a seventy-year-old when he fell again, and he fainted away.

As for his kinsmen up there by the mouth of the cave, they waited until daylight faded to dusk without seeing the middle rope move or hearing the copper bells ring. They said, guessing, "The damp stench must have overwhelmed him." When they winched up the bamboo basket, they saw that it was empty. Li Qing was not there. In panic, they lowered the basket again. After waiting for a while, they pulled it up again, but it remained empty. Among the onlookers, some lamented, some laughed. In a flurry, they went their separate ways, leaving Li Qing's kinsmen around the mouth of the cave, crying with abandon. They lamented, "We tried so hard to stop him, but he just wouldn't listen and insisted on going down. Although it's not too bad to die at seventy, he should at least have left us his corpse, so that we could have him put in a coffin and buried him. Without a corpse, what are we going to do?"

None of the kinsmen did not shed a sad tear. One who was prone to taking a philosophical view of things commented, "Life and death are predestined. He is meant to die on his birthday today. If we had kept him at home, he would have died anyway. Since he got what he wanted, there should be no regrets. Even though we don't have his corpse, we still have his clothes and hats. It might be better for us to go home this evening and, tomorrow morning, bring a few Daoist priests with magic power here to call back his soul. The practice of burying only the clothes and hats of the dead began from ancient times. As far as I know, the Yellow Emperor, after rising to the sky at Lake Tripod upon gaining the great Dao, left behind a sword and two shoes, which were then put in a coffin and buried at Bridge Mountain.[2] Maybe the old gentleman has already become an immortal and wants nothing more than an empty grave from us. Isn't it foolish of you to cry like this around the cave?"

For lack of a better choice, the kinsmen followed his advice, wiped their eyes dry, put their things in order, and returned home. The next morning, they came back to the top of the mountain to call back the soul. They set up a shrine tablet to Li Qing's memory and put his coffin in a hall for all kinsmen to offer libations. After the forty-nine-day mourning period was over, they built a grave mound for a proper burial. Of this, no more need be said.

Now, back to Li Qing in his coma after his second fall. Immediately upon coming to a considerable while later, he rose to grope and peer about. It turned out that the bottom of the cave was only about ten feet wide. He did not see anything out of the ordinary in the rock wall all around him, and the mud under his feet was too slippery for him to move about freely. His only choice was to go back to the basket, sit down, and shake the rope to ring the copper bell, so that he could be winched up again. He groped around for the basket, but it was not there. He cried out, but got no response. He couldn't fly out of the cave, could he? Indeed, coming was no challenge, but going was out of the question. What was Li Qing to do?

In resignation, he sat down cross-legged on the ground. After goodness knows how many days, he found the thirst and hunger hard to bear. He recalled the story about a man in ancient times keeping himself alive by eating snow and chewing on a rug, but, there being no snow or rug around, he grabbed a handful of mud and swallowed it. As a matter of fact, when the door of a cave dwelling of the immortals was opened once every three thousand years, some mud would squirt out of the bottom of the cave. Called "blue mud," it was the stuff of which meals for the immortals were made. It was delectable enough and relieved thirst as well. After eating a few handfuls, Li Qing felt his strength coming back. When he resumed examining his surroundings, he saw, through a crack at the foot of the rock wall, a small cave less than two feet in height. He thought, "Sitting in the mud gets me nowhere. I'm as good as dead anyway. Whatever poisonous snakes or demons there are in that cave, I'd better climb into it and see for myself." By so doing, he was to enter another world when all looked dark and hopeless. He who had been driven to desperation was later to open an herb store. Verily,

> King Yama did not order that he die today;
> There surely was another way out of the cave.

Recklessly Li Qing crawled into the small cave. After crawling for about six or seven li, he gradually became aware that the ceiling had risen higher by more than two feet, but not enough for him to stand up and walk. So he continued crawling. Not knowing whether it was day or night, he took a nap when tired and had a few bites of the blue mud when hungry. After crawling for another twenty li or so, he saw a faint glimmer of light ahead of him. He thought, "Oh, I'm so glad there *is* an exit, after all." He ate more blue mud, pulled himself together, and pressed on until he was out of the cave. Beyond the cave stretched verdant wooded hills. Once out into this new world, he rose to his full height, planted his feet firmly on the ground, straightened his clothes, wiped his shoes clean, and said thankfully toward the sky, "Heaven be thanked for pulling me out of such a crisis today!"

After walking for fourteen or fifteen li along the main road, he began to feel the pangs of hunger. There was no peddler of food anywhere in sight. Even if there had been, he had no money on him, nor had he taken any of the blue mud from the cave. As he could hardly move another step, he saw by the roadside the clear green water of a spring flanked by chrysanthemums. He scooped up some water with both hands to drink. In fact, this was not water that could be had easily. Water from this spring, which the immortals called the "Chrysanthemum Spring," was the best tonic for longevity and freedom from illnesses. A few scoopfuls of it so refreshed Li Qing that he became swift of foot and nimble of hand.

Another ten li or so later, he suddenly caught sight of a glittering glazed roof looming atop the trees. Wondering what place this could be, he hastened in that direction and saw a temple with a red gate standing on top of a nine-tiered white marble terrace, with each tier more than ten feet high. There being no staircase, he had to pull himself up with all his might by the vines and the kudzu. Not daring to knock rashly on the closed gate upon reaching it, he waited with bated breath. After what seemed an eternity, a blue-robed boy opened the gate from inside and shouted, "Li Qing! Why are you here?"

With alacrity, Li Qing prostrated himself on the ground and said, "Li Qing, owner of dye mills in Qingzhou of the mortal world, is here in all temerity to beg that you accept me as your disciple. Dead or alive, I will never forget your kindness!"

The boy said, laughing, "Who am I to accept you as a disciple? I'll take you inside, so that you can speak to my master." With that, the boy went inside. Soon thereafter, he reemerged to take Li Qing inside. Once brought to the foot of the jade dais, Li Qing raised his head and saw that the hall was as magnificent as if it were a palace in heaven. Behold the grandeur of the palace:

> The vermilion roof sparkled in the sun;
> The green tiles shone under the rosy clouds.
> The grand glazed hall stood a hundred feet high;
> The white marble terrace was nine tiers tall.
> The carved beams were inlaid with hawksbill turtle shells;
> The engraved columns were adorned with coral.
> In the jade palace with gates made of shells,
> The flying eaves touched the floating colored clouds.
> Over the painted rafters of the jade towers and terraces
> Settled the blue mist of heaven.
> The winding railings were bedecked with agate;
> The thick curtains glittered with strings of pearls.
> Blue birds and black cranes danced in pairs;

White deer and red unicorns pranced in twos.
The fields were aglow with blooming flowers;
The woods were alive with the songs of birds.

Li Qing saw that in the middle of the hall sat a patriarch of the immortals, wearing a green jade lotus-shaped crown, a gold-traced feather cape, a yellow waist-band, and a pair of vermilion shoes. A *ruyi* scepter in hand,[3] he had the ethereal grace of one used to roaming the eight poles of the world. To his left and right, also facing south, four immortals were sitting on each side. Wearing robes of different colors, they all had the otherworldly air of immortals. In the hall swirled wisps of auspicious clouds amid air that was filled with the fragrance of incense. All was quiet and still in the solemn hall unsullied by the slightest mote of dust.

Li Qing stepped forward, kowtowed to each one of the immortals, and gave them an account of how he had risked death to find his way there.

The patriarch sitting in the middle said, "Li Qing, you were not supposed to come here. Why did you undertake such an unauthorized trip? I don't have a vacancy for you. You'd better go back now."

In tears, Li Qing said, "I've devoted myself all my life to the pursuit of the Dao without ever seeing any effect. And now, having so fortunately come to this heavenly palace and seen you, patriarch, how can I go back empty-handed? I'm already seventy years old. I won't have long to live anyway after I go back. I won't be able to make it back again. I'd rather die right here at the foot of the dais rather than go back."

The patriarch shook his head in refusal. The other immortals, however, pleaded on his behalf, saying, "Even though Li Qing shouldn't have come here, his sincerity is quite touching. If we don't take him, people will say that it's no use trying to attain immortality. In our belief, the first virtue is to redeem people from the mortal world. Let's keep him for now. We can always send him back if he proves to be impossible to teach."

Only then did the patriarch say with a nod, "All right. He can stay in the western side room for now."

Eagerly Li Qing said his thanks. As he proceeded to the side room, he thought, "If I don't have what it takes to be a Daoist, how could I qualify as a disciple of the immortals? Now, I promised my sons and grandsons that if I encountered immortals, I'd ask leave to go home and let them know. But the patriarch agreed to take me on board only because I pleaded desperately and the other immortals intervened on my behalf. How can I ask for a leave of absence? If I give them offense, they'll reprimand me for not having severed my bond with the mortal world. What am I going to do? Let me sit quietly for a while to set my mind at peace before I decide what to do next."

Li Qing had hardly sat down in the western side room when an old man came into the room and announced, "Preceptor Ding of the Bright Rosy Cloud Temple of the Penglai Mountains has just arrived.⁴ The Queen Mother of the West is inviting all sages to a grand banquet by the Jasper Pool."

Without ado, nine crane-pulled chariots lined up neatly outside the hall. The patriarch led the other eight immortals out of the hall. Li Qing joined the group of green-robed boys in seeing them off. Looking at Li Qing, the patriarch gave him these instructions: "Feel free to tour everywhere, but be sure not to open the north window. Mark these words well!" With that, he and the other immortals mounted the cranes and rose into the air amid clouds and the music of wind and reed instruments. But let us come back to Li Qing.

Looking out in three directions from the windows of the side room, Li Qing saw exotic birds that sang throughout the four seasons and rare flowers and grass that retained their color throughout the year. Indeed, there was more than he could ever see and more scenic splendor than he could ever enjoy. Gradually moving toward the north window that was closed, he thought, "Since all the three other windows can be used, why can't I open the north window? There must be something out of the ordinary about it that they don't want me to see. But they've all gone for a banquet so far away that they're not likely to be back any time soon. Let me quietly open it just for a little peek. They won't know."

He walked up to the window and gave it a gentle push. With a creak, the window swung open. As he peered around, he saw the most extraordinary thing: The entire city of Qingzhou lay under the north window. The houses in the city were clearly within view. Then he saw his own grand house in dilapidation and the houses of his close kith and kin also sadly in disrepair. Overcome with emotion, he moaned, "Oh no! This is what my clan has come to in the few days I've been away! As the saying goes, 'A family without a master is a house without a pillar.' Had I known this earlier, I wouldn't have come here and let my sons and grandsons do so badly as to bring disgrace to the clan!" Before he knew it, thoughts of returning home entered his mind. (*His ties with the mortal world keep him from attaining the Dao.*)

To his dismay, before his lament was over, the immortals were back. "Li Qing! Li Qing!" they called from the hall.

Quickly Li Qing closed the north window and went to the foot of the dais. The immortal occupying the middle seat said indignantly, "I told you not to sneak off and open the north window. You disobeyed my order and opened it. Then you groaned in regret, thinking of returning home. I didn't want to keep you precisely because your ties with the mortal world have not been severed. I can't keep you here. Go back now and be quick about it! Don't linger on in this cave!"

Unable to come up with an answer, Li Qing kept kowtowing and asking for forgiveness. Plaintively he said, "I went through goodness knows how many hardships on my way here. I missed death just by a thread. If I go back now, not only have my family pulled up the basket and ropes (*If the basket and the ropes had been there, he would have returned.*), but also, how can this old man again make it through the small thirty-li-long tunnel to the other cave?"

With a smile, the patriarch said, "You have nothing to worry about on that score. I will have someone show you another way out."

Relieved, Li Qing stood up, bowed his thanks, and turned to go. At this point, an immortal to the left of the patriarch mumbled something to him. The patriarch called out, "Li Qing, come back here."

Li Qing thought, "That immortal must have advised him to keep me, just as he did last time." Merrily he hastened back and knelt down to listen to the patriarch's order.

You may well ask, why did the patriarch call Li Qing back and what did he have to say? Well, the patriarch said, "I dismissed you, but what are you going to do without a means of livelihood? I have plenty of books on my bookshelf. Feel free to take one. If you want to make a living, just read the book. It has everything."

While promising that he would, Li Qing thought, "So the immortals know only about what goes on here. They know nothing about Qingzhou. My family wealth numbers in the tens of thousands of taels of silver. Even the birthday gifts the younger generations gave me are worth thousands of taels. Why would I have nothing to live on after an absence of a few days?" However, out of gratitude for their good will, he went to the bookshelf and picked the thinnest volume.

As he approached the patriarch to thank him, the patriarch asked, "Did you pick a book?"

"Yes, I did."

"All right. Go now!"

Li Qing was about to get out the door when an immortal to the right of the patriarch also mumbled something to him. The patriarch nodded and called out again, "Li Qing, come back here."

Li Qing thought, "So, that one must have advised him to keep me."

No, he had guessed wrong again. The patriarch said, "It's going to be a long walk before you reach home. After you arrive at home, you may not have anything to eat. You can eat here to your heart's content before you set out."

Immediately, a page boy presented Li Qing with two large taros. They were in fact boiled cobblestones as soft, tender, fragrant, and sweet as taros, and even more delicious than the blue mud of Cloud Gate Cave. Again he went over to say his thanks.

The patriarch said, "Li Qing, you will be back here again in only about another seventy years, but countless children's lives in Qingzhou will depend on you. You must do good works far and wide. Do not compromise your integrity. I have a prophetic quatrain for you that will do you good the rest of your life. Remember it well!" The quatrain said,

> Go when you see a rock;
> Ask when you hear clappers.
> Live next to where you see Jin;
> Flee upon the advent of a Pei.

Li Qing took another bow in acknowledgment of the quatrain. The page boy who had led him in was now told to show him out. You may wonder what kind of route it was going to be. Even though he might not need a hundred thousand feet of hemp rope, wasn't it still going to be a perilous journey? In fact, the page boy took him on an entirely different route. They walked around the compound and climbed up a hill at the back. At the sight of many people cutting white stones that appeared to be of the finest quality, Li Qing asked, "Why would the immortals need white stones?"

The page replied, "This is white marble. Another venerable gentleman will be arriving soon. So these people are told to make some white marble pieces ready for him, to make the tenth armchair."

"What's the name of that venerable gentleman?"

"What I told you is all we heard. I don't know more. Even if I knew, I couldn't tell you. My master will hold me to account if I reveal any divine secrets."

While talking, they walked for fourteen or fifteen li along a major thoroughfare flanked with tall ancient trees interspersed with exotic flowers. There were so many sights to see that Li Qing wouldn't have noticed if they had in fact covered more distance. When the road began to narrow after they passed another high mountain, the page pointed ahead with a hand and said, "The north gate of Qingzhou is less than ten li from here."

"When I came the other day, I went out by South Gate. Why am I taking North Gate today? I lived in Qingzhou for seventy years without knowing that Cloud Gate Mountain goes all around the city. So this is why I could see Qingzhou through that north window. But which road leads to the front of the immortals' residence and which one to the back? Please tell me, so that the next time I visit the patriarch, I can take the right road, to spare myself the trouble of descending into Cloud Gate Cave by rope."

Before he had quite gotten every word out, a tiger leaped out with a gust of wind and pounced on him. Scared out of his wits, he cried in dismay and fell backward on the ground. Poor thing!

> Before he achieved immortality,
> He was to end up in a tiger's stomach.

Storyteller, let me ask you something: According to an old legend, blue mud and white cobblestones were ambrosia of the immortals, out of the reach of mortal beings. Those lucky enough to taste them were immune to illnesses and safe from demons, tigers, and wolves. Li Qing had eaten these two kinds of food to his heart's content, and he had stayed in the immortals' cave dwelling. Even though he was sent back home because of his lack of unwavering faith, he was supposed to return to the cave in seventy years. He was no less than an immortal now. How could he have perished in the mouth of a tiger?

Dear audience, please be patient and let me take my time explaining it to you.

That tiger was no ordinary tiger that preys on humans. It was a divine tiger whose duty it was to stand guard for the immortals. The page boy sent it just to frighten Li Qing into forgetting the way he had come, not to take his life.

After being unconscious for some time, Li Qing gradually came to. Crying "Help! Help!" he slowly struggled up to a sitting position. The tiger and the blue-robed page boy had both disappeared. Stamping his feet, he exclaimed, "How horrible! That tiger must have carried the boy off to eat him! Poor boy!" But then he thought, "That boy serves the immortals. He must also be something of an immortal himself. How would a tiger dare hurt him? That's quite impossible! But why did he abandon me halfway instead of escorting me all the way home?"

Mystified, he scrambled to his feet and straightened his clothes. A sudden look back filled him with surprise. The road he had just taken was nowhere in sight. All that met his eyes were high mountains and steep cliffs. "How very strange!" he muttered. Afraid that another tiger would jump out and make a meal of him, he ran for all he was worth. After about four or five li, he came to a fork in the road. As there were no passersby who could give him directions and the day was far advanced by now, what was he to do if he took the wrong road and got lost? At a loss as to what to do, he suddenly caught sight of a large rock on one of the roads. The light dawned on him as he recalled the patriarch's quatrain, one line of which said, "Go when you see a rock." He thought, "So he was telling me to take this road."

After walking for another four or five li, he came into view of the north gate of Qingzhou. Once in the city, he found the streets vaguely familiar but the houses flanking the streets totally different from before. Puzzled, he tried to ask passersby, but he could not find anyone he knew. Gradually, evening closed in. He rushed home. To his surprise, his house had also taken on a new look. An imposing gateway arch flanked by high walls now stood where there had been none. He said to himself, "Could I have come by mistake to the prefectural yamen?" Upon a closer look, he thought, "This does look like a yamen, but, no! it is my house. It has certainly changed beyond recognition. I didn't spend that many days in Cloud Gate Cave, and I left the small cave earlier today. How could there have been so many changes? Could the prefectural government have turned my house into a yamen while I was away? But they should have asked the master of the house first. Too bad it's getting late. I'll wait until tomorrow and sue them. They should pay me at government price."

Without even one penny to pay for lodging at an inn, he took off one article of clothing and exchanged it for a string of cash. Still feeling full, he bought only one measure of wine. Then he went to bed, but his agony kept him awake all night. Tossing and turning in bed, he groaned and moaned in regret. But then he thought, "I shouldn't be blaming the patriarch. He did ask me what means of livelihood I would have after I went back and he told me to pick a book that would teach me how to make a living. And then, saying that I might not have anything to eat back at home, he gave me two boiled cobblestones. Didn't he foresee everything?" Reaching into his sleeve, he found to his delight that the book was still there, but he did not have the time to read it yet.

After daybreak, he settled his bill with the innkeeper and began to walk around the streets of Qingzhou. He did not see even one of his dye mills, let alone any member of his clan. Apologetically, he asked everyone he saw, but all of them shook their heads, pouted their lips, and said, "We've never heard of a Li Qing, or about anyone descending into Cloud Gate Cave." Li Qing was mystified. When afternoon gave way to evening, he had to go back to the inn to retire for the night.

The next day, he walked up and down the smaller lanes, still without encountering anyone he knew. Every person whom he approached to ask for information said the same things he had heard the day before. In greater bewilderment, he thought, "I was indeed surprised that the way out of the cave I took yesterday was somehow different from before. (*Wonderful.*) Could it be that (*Another twist.*) this is an altogether new Qingzhou? (*No, it is not.*) It's not the old Qingzhou, for sure. That's why I don't get to meet anyone I know. But there's only one Cloud Gate Mountain. There can't be a second one. Why don't I go out South Gate and up Cloud Gate Mountain for a look? If the mountain stays the same, then this should be the old city of Qingzhou. Let me take my time looking into the matter. I'll surely be able to get to the bottom of this mystery." So he hurried out of South Gate in the direction of Cloud Gate Mountain. Seeing a pavilion at the mountaintop, he thought, "This is all too clearly Cloud Gate Mountain, but I've never seen a pavilion here. Let me see what it's called."

Upon seeing the inscription "Rotten Rope Pavilion, built in the fourth year of the Kaihuang reign period [584]," Li Qing said to himself, "I know. In ancient times, there was a woodcutter who happened to see immortals at a game of chess. He stopped to watch. When the game was over, goodness knows how many years had gone by. The handle of the ax he was sitting on had rotten away. The story of the rotten ax handle is still being told today. Most probably, what happened was that after my children and grandchildren lowered me into the cave, they thought I met immortals. So they claimed that the ropes had rotten away and built this pavilion, calling it 'Rotten Rope Pavilion' just so that what happened could be spread far and wide as a nice story. It's written here 'built in the fourth year of the Kaihuang reign period.' Isn't it this very year? But how can the city have undergone such changes? Let me see what's up there."

There, by the mouth of the cave, stood a stone tablet that bore the inscription: "Spot where Li Qing's soul was called back." He gave a start. "I'm alive and well. I'm not dead. Why would they want to call back my soul?" Then he thought, "Ah yes. After they witnessed my descent into that scary cave, they raised the basket. Then, failing to see me, they thought I was dead and therefore set a tablet here to call back my soul." Then another thought occurred to him. "Yee! Could I be dead and it's just my soul that wandered to this place?" As doubts began to assail his mind, he could not come to a decision, thinking, "If they tried to call back my soul, they should have wanted to bury me, and what other burial place could there be but our ancestral grave site? Houses may change, but ancestral grave sites don't change, even in a thousand years. Why don't I go there to take a look? I may be able to come to the bottom of all this."

He went down Cloud Gate Mountain past East Gate and saw that, in the distance, the hill where the ancestral grave site of his clan was located resembled a flying green dragon coming down from the sky. He thought, "I remember that the *Book on Burials* says that a hill shaped like a flying phoenix or a crouching dragon will produce an immortal in a thousand years. Our family grave site does have the right feng shui features. But how come as soon as I met a few immortals—the only one in my family ever to do so—I was driven back home? I will never get to rise to heaven. I wonder who will do justice to the feng shui?" (*Someone already has.*)

At the ancestral grave, after making the obligatory bows twice, he saw that many of the green pines and white poplars, each so thick that one could barely get one's arms around it, had been cut down. The tombstones had either been knocked over or were broken. Overcome with sadness that the site was not at all what it used to be, he said with a sigh, "Can my offspring have all died out? Why doesn't any one of them come here to take care of the graves?"

Only one tablet remained standing. The inscription on it, barely legible, bore characters that said, "Tomb of Daoist Li Qing." He said to himself, "If they only had the soul to bury, this grave should be an empty one, with nothing more than some clothes and a hat. But the tombstone has been eroded badly by moss. It must not have been made in the fourth year of the Kaihuang reign period. I must have died long ago. It must be my soul that's wandering about in this place. Since the dead and the living are worlds apart, my kinsmen and my children don't get to see me. Otherwise, how can I not see even one out of the thousands and thousands of them?"

His mind filled with doubts, he felt as if he was in a daydream. "I don't even know whether I'm dead or alive. Where can I go to find out?" As he was wondering, his ears caught the faint sounds of a fisherman's drum and clappers. He walked up and saw that it was a blind old man singing in front of the Temple of the God of Eastern Peak and asking for money from the crowd gathered around him. At this point, Li Qing recalled the second line of the patriarch's quatrain: "Ask when you hear clappers." He thought, "Isn't this a fisherman's drum plus clappers? I'm supposed to ask him. Let me stand off to one side. I'll wait until everyone's gone before going over to ask."

The blind old man raised about ten pennies. No one else was willing to pay one more penny. One of the spectators said, "Why don't you start your story? We'll collect more money for you as you sing."

"That won't do!" said the blind man. "I'm blind. After I finish, you'll all scurry away. I won't be able to run after you."

"Nonsense!" said someone in the crowd. "You're a disabled man. If we take advantage of you, what kind of human beings are we?"

The blind man believed them. Striking his drum and his clappers, he began to chant the following quatrain:

> *Throughout summer, winter, spring, and autumn,*
> *Water flows east under Sunset Bridge.*
> *Where is the battle horse of the general?*
> *Weeds, wildflowers, and sorrows all over the land.*

After intoning the above quatrain, he launched into the story proper, which was about Zhuangzi lamenting over a skeleton. Being a story in the Daoist tradition, it appealed to Li Qing. He stepped forward and strained his ears to listen. The blind man talked for a while and sang for a while. When he came to the part about the skeleton growing flesh and skin, returning to the mortal world and jumping up from the ground, some in the audience laughed and some lamented. At the midpoint in the story, the blind man stopped playing his instruments, to wait until enough money was collected before resuming. This was a convention in storytelling. The audience was quite captivated when listening, but when it was time to pay up, they exchanged uneasy glances at one another and did nothing. Those who had no money on them made a few sarcastic remarks and walked off smugly. (*Such are the ways of the world. A storytelling session is no exception.*)

Only five pennies were collected this time. The one collecting the money was so upset that in an outburst of anger, he unleashed a torrent of abuse on the audience. One young man took it upon himself to accept the challenge and exchanged heated words with the collector. Insults flew thick and fast between them until, with neither yielding to the other, they came to blows. In their tussle, the fifteen pennies scattered over the ground. Most of the rest of the audience gave a cry and dispersed. Those who stayed went to separate the two locked in fight, leaving the blind man alone.

His heart going out to the blind man, Li Qing picked up the fifteen pennies from the ground and, handing them over to him, said with a sigh, "People are so heartless, and money is given such importance!" (*How true!*)

The money in hand, the blind man asked upon hearing his lament, "Who might you be?"

"I'm here to ask you for information. If you tell me what I'd like to know, I'll reward you with several tens of pennies."

"What is it that you want to know?"

"Do you know a Li family in the dye business in the city of Qingzhou?"

"I'm a Li. May I ask your honorable name?"

"I am Li Qing, seventy years old now."

The man burst out laughing. "You are making fun of a blind man. I'm no gullible young man. In fact, I'm a little older than you are. I'm seventy-six. My great granduncle was called Li Qing. How come you are also a Li Qing?"

Intrigued by his background, Li Qing said, trying another approach, "There are all too many people in this world who share the same surnames and given names. I wouldn't dare make fun of you, but what happened to that great granduncle of yours?"

"It's a long story. In the fourth year of the Kaihuang reign period under Emperor Wen of Sui, when that great granduncle of mine was also seventy, he wanted to explore a cave dwelling of the immortals in Cloud Gate Cave. So he got himself an ample supply of hemp ropes and was lowered into the cave. Now, won't you agree that it's not a cave anyone can descend into? Of course, he died. The fact of the matter was that our whole clan depended on his blessings. After he died, the family fortune went on the decline. And then a war broke out and wiped out the entire clan. I'm the only survivor, living proof of the retribution on my family. I have no children. I make a living by singing and telling stories."

Li Qing thought, "So they mistakenly thought I had died in Cloud Gate Cave." Aloud, he asked, "It couldn't have been more than one year since he went down the cave. How could the family have fallen into such poverty so fast? And how could the entire clan have died out, leaving only one?"

"My goodness! You must be talking in your dreams, sir! This is not the fourth year of Kaihuang. This is the fifth year of the Yonghui reign period [650–55] under Emperor Gaozong of the Tang dynasty. Emperor Wen of Sui ruled for twenty-four years and was succeeded by Emperor Yang, who, after ruling for fourteen years, was killed by Yuwen Huaji [d. 619]. Chaos broke out throughout the land. Then Emperor Taizong founded the Tang dynasty but yielded the throne to his father, who later came to be known as Emperor Gaozu [r. 618–26]. After nine years, Emperor Taizong himself succeeded the throne and ruled for twenty-three years [627–49]. The emperor currently on the throne is Emperor Taizong's son, now into the fifth year of his reign. This is the seventy-second year since the fourth year of Kaihuang. (*Just like the story about the Peach Blossom Spring, safe haven from the world.*)[5] I was only five when that great granduncle of mine died. I'm now seventy-six, and you said it was fast."

"As far as I know, there were five to six thousand men in the Li clan. In seventy-two years, they shouldn't have all died out, leaving you alone."

"You wouldn't have imagined it, sir. All the men in my clan had enough skills to make a living with their bare hands. But after Emperor Yang of Sui died, a Wang Shichong rose in rebellion. When he came to Qingzhou and saw the many able-bodied men in my clan, he conscripted them all. And that Wang Shichong was such a loser that he was defeated in every battle. His entire army perished, men and horses. If I were not a disabled man, I would not have survived." ([Illegible.] *like cattle . . . humans are the same.*)

Upon hearing this account, Li Qing felt as if he had just woken up from a dream or from a wine-induced sleep. All his misgivings vanished. Now he knew everything. He gave the thirty to forty pennies he had on him to the blind man. Without a word of explanation, he took leave of the blind man and went back into the city of Qingzhou.

As he walked, he thought, "As an ancient poem says, 'Seven days in the mountains/ A thousand years in the world.' So, such strange things do happen. The few days since I was lowered into Cloud Gate Cave in the fourth year of Kaihuang have actually been seventy-two years. It's the fifth year of the Yonghui period under emperor Gaozong of Tang now. Time in the mortal world goes by so quickly! Had I stayed longer there, even this city of Qingzhou would have vanished. Now my children and grandchildren have all died, and my great houses all belong to other families. Well, I don't mind that, but without even half a penny on me or any acquaintances to borrow from, how am I going to get by? Since I'm going to die anyway, why was the patriarch so determined to drive me back?"

After heaving a few sighs, he reflected for a while. Then light suddenly dawned on him. "How can someone wanting to achieve immortality be so stupid?" he thought. "Before I left, the patriarch said all too clearly that I might not have anything to live on after I went back home, and he told me to pick a book from his bookshelf. The book is still in my sleeve. Why don't I take it out and see what line of work I can engage in?"

You may well ask, what kind of a book was it? It was a book on pediatrics, with a few prescriptions in it. Now he understood. "The patriarch did tell me that in about seventy years, he would allow me to go there again. Now, seventy years in the mortal world is a long time, unlike time spent in Cloud Gate Cave. I've never even seen the inside of an herb store. At my age, how can I enter the medical profession so rashly? Nor do I have any money to buy the herbal ingredients. I'd better go to an herb store to consult an experienced physician before I decide what to do next."

He hadn't walked more than three hundred steps when he saw a whitewashed signboard on which was written, "Mr. Jin's ancestral family store selling dried processed medicinal herbs from Sichuan and Guangdong."

Li Qing's heart leaped for joy. "The third line of the patriarch's quatrain says, 'Live next to where you see Jin.' Now isn't this a Mr. Jin? People all say the immortals know everything in advance. How can I not believe that?"

In the store sat a young man about twenty, called Big Brother Jin. Li Qing hastened forward, chanted a greeting to him, and asked, "Do you accept cash only or do you allow credit?"

Big Brother Jin replied, "I take cash from ordinary customers, but physicians and owners of herb stores can get whatever medicine they need on credit because they are regular patrons. They can pay the bill once every quarter or every month. It's a half-credit, half-cash system."

Telling a lie, Li Qing said, "I'm a pediatrician. I've always carried a bundle and made the rounds of the villages. Now that I'm getting old, I'd like to open an herb store and have patients come to me. I wonder if I can rent a room somewhere. Could you please let me know? I'll buy my medicine from you."

"There's an empty room right next to my house. Didn't you see the sign 'For Rent' posted on the door? But it may be too small for you."

"I don't have a family. One room is enough for me. But I need to put up a sign at the door and I need medicine drawers and utensils inside, the way a physician's office should look. Where can I buy those things? Can I get them on credit as well?"

Big Brother Jin said, "I've got a lot of those in stock. I'll just lend them to you for now. You can pay me along with your medicine bills, after your business begins to pick up. Won't that be good for both of us?"

With Big Brother Jin helping him in everything, Li Qing settled down next to the medicine store. Recalling what he had said in derision of the "old man of the flask" as he bade farewell to his kinsmen on Cloud Gate Mountain, he thought, "I never thought I'd return today and become a physician, bearing out that prophecy." (*Nicely picking up an earlier thread.*)

In front of the door he hung up a horizontal board bearing the inscription "Hanging Flasks" and a vertical board bearing the inscription "Pediatrician Li, specializing in all kinds of difficult and complicated cases." The store itself was equipped with all the necessary furnishings. Indeed, when you have all the trappings ready, you've completed your Buddha's statue, as they say. Thus amply supplied with all the paraphernalia of a physician, Li Qing acquired the look of a professional practitioner of medicine.

It so happened that a sort of children's epidemic was going around the city of Qingzhou that year. Children of families rich as well as poor died instantly upon the slightest exposure to it. There were so few pediatricians to be had that physicians specializing in adult illnesses were also kept busy. But this was a sinister epidemic. Even medicine prescribed by the most famous doctors might just as well have been dumped right into the river. Helplessly, parents watched their children die. Old man Li Qing was the only exception among the doctors. He didn't need to go to the patient's home to take the pulse for a diagnosis. As soon as he was given a description of the symptoms, he would pick the first herbs that came to his hand and wrap up a packet of them for the patient. For each packet, he charged one hundred pennies, regardless of the differences in the prices of the herbs and their different levels of efficacy. To those who asked for two packets, he would say, "Why would you need a second packet of my medicine?" He would rather return the money and take the medicine back. Those asking for his medicine were skeptical, but, their children being in critical conditions, every one of them had no choice but to buy that one packet and try it out. Now, won't you be impressed by the wonders it worked? The moment the medicine was fed into the sick child's mouth, the symptoms were half gone. The moment the brew went down into the

STORY 38

stomach, the child completely recovered. If the child was already dead, the aroma of the brew alone was enough to bring the child back to life. Li Qing's fame spread throughout the city. All and sundry called him "One Packet Li." Goodness knows how many children he cured and goodness only knows how much money he made.

To my way of thinking, a bachelor like Li Qing shouldn't have too many expenses. After paying his rent, medicine, utensils, and furnishings, Li Qing should have had a great deal of money left. He could hardly let it rot at home, as he had done with all of his birthday gifts. Well, where he had sources of income, he also had channels for using them. Since his return, he had mended his ways. He used to save his money without spending much, but now, after paying Big Brother Jin for the furnishings and utensils in the store and the various dried and processed medicinal herbs, he kept for himself only enough money for his daily expenses and donated all the rest to the poor. (*Junping's fortune-telling and Li Qing's medical practice are the stuff of which legends are made.*)[6] Indeed, he did good works far and wide; his kindness knew no bounds.

Henceforth, his fame spread even wider. In the entire Qi and Lu regions, not only Qingzhou, those wishing to pursue the medical profession would, upon hearing of his name, come to honor him as a teacher, in the hope of learning some skills from him.[7] But they found that he never read medical books nor went to patients' houses to take their pulses. Every time someone came to him for a prescription, he took the payment, picked just a few different kinds of herbs, and offered the client one packet. In some cases where the symptoms were the same, he gave different prescriptions. In other cases where the symptoms were different, he gave exactly the same prescription. And yet none of his prescriptions failed to work, to the amazement of all and sundry. Unable to figure out any pattern, the students waited until he had a free moment and, in all humility, asked to be enlightened.

Li Qing said, "You were wondering why I give prescriptions without even taking the pulse. Well, diagnosis is based on observation, auscultation, asking about the symptoms, and feeling the pulse. These are seen as four steps that require great skill on the part of the physician. But it is also clear that taking the pulse comes last in the list. It is not of primary importance. In addition, children's pulses are different from adults'. Children are not yet fully developed in their vital energy and blood condition. What can we detect from their pulses? In brief, the cure is all in the mind. The best way is to use your mind to identify what is wrong. Rigid formulae for prescriptions won't effect a cure. When you watch me prescribe, you must try to figure out why I prescribe the way I do. Didn't the *Encyclopedia of Herbs* originate from our Shandong region? You must first familiarize yourself with that book and learn the properties of the herbs before starting to give prescriptions. First, distinguish between herbs that warm and those that cool, in accordance with the kind of predominant climate of the year. Second, dispense medicine with dry or wet properties in accordance with the geographic features of the place where the patient is. Third, be sure to know what kind of family the patient is from. Those

904

from rich families are, in most cases, more delicate and fragile. Those from poor families are tougher. So you need to adjust the herbs accordingly. Ask carefully about the symptoms to know what kinds of herbs to use, and then come up with brilliant ways to add to or detract from prescriptions given in medical books until the dominant and subsidiary elements reach the right proportions. When the right medicine is prescribed for the right illness, naturally the illness will go away. Therefore, the ancients compared the prescription of medicine to the design of military strategies. The strength of the medicine is not in the quantity but in the right mixture of herbs. Zhao Kuo, who read his father's book in vain and brought defeat on himself, is a negative example that should serve as a warning."[8]

The students bowed thankfully and withdrew, little knowing that Li Qing had in his possession a thin but divine book, a secret which he was not going to divulge for no good reason. Indeed,

> *The lives of sick children must be saved;*
> *Without the book, how was the old man to bring a cure?*

Time sped by. After Li Qing opened his herb store and started his medical practice in the fifth year of the Yonghui period under Emperor Gaozong of Tang, all too quickly six years elapsed and the five-year Xianqing reign period also came to an end. After the three-year Longsuo period, the two-year Linde period, the two-year Qianfeng period, the two-year Zongzhang period, the four-year Xianheng period, the two-year Shangyuan period, the three-year Yifeng period, the one-year Tiaolu period, the one-year Yonglong period, and the one-year Kaiyao period, twenty-seven years had gone by.

In the first year of the Yongchun reign period [682–83], an imperial decree was issued, announcing that the emperor would go personally to Mount Tai to offer sacrifices to heaven and earth in the tradition of Emperor Wudi of the Han dynasty. You may well ask, what was that all about? Well, of the five most famous mountains in the empire, Mount Tai is the most spiritual. Its top soaring into the sky, it is believed to be the origin of clouds and rain. When peace reigned in the land and crops thrived in favorable weather, a sagacious emperor would ascend to the top of Mount Tai to offer sacrifices to the gods of the mountain and inscribe on a tablet an ode to his own achievements to claim credit from heaven and earth. The characters carved into the tablet were all gilded with gold. The scrolls were placed in white marble boxes placed beside the tablets. It was the grandest event of the imperial court. The Lord on High is by no means easily deceived. If the ode deviated ever so slightly from the facts, a wild storm would spring up to put an abrupt end to the ceremony.

This ritual had not been initiated by Emperor Wudi of Han. In fact, seventy-nine generations of kings before the Great Yu had held such ceremonies.[9] In more recent history, the First Emperor of Qin[10] and Emperor Wudi of Han were the only two who did so. Why would emperors who accomplished this be called sagacious emperors? That was just to present a fake picture of peace and prosperity and mislead the public. In fact, the First Emperor of Qin was caught in a rainstorm and could do no more than take shelter under a pine tree. And Emperor Wudi sprained his ankle when descending the mountain. Therefore, after Emperor Wudi, not one emperor dared to hold sacrificial ceremonies there. Emperor Gaozong of Tang had already issued two identical decrees. This was the third. Qingzhou being on the way to Mount Tai, the prefect ordered every family to provide a corvée laborer to repave the roads in preparation for the emperor's advent. Being the owner of a store, Li Qing was also put on the list of laborers and urged to go.

After Li Qing began his medical practice, the pediatricians in Qingzhou were so ashamed of themselves that they all closed up their clinics and dared not stick their heads out again. So if Li Qing was to work on the roads as a corvée laborer, how was he to render service to sick children in cases of emergency? Therefore all the people of the city turned out to the prefectural yamen to plead for exemption on his behalf. They chose a few men who had a way with words as their representatives. Approaching the prefect, one of the representatives said, "Doctor Li Qing is ninety-seven years old. Being almost a centenarian, he is too weak to work as a laborer. We will be glad to make a financial payment on his behalf, so that an able-bodied young man can be chosen to take his place. If he gets to stay in his store, that would be a blessing to the children of the entire prefecture."

Li Qing had claimed that he was seventy the year he set up shop, which was why people thought he was now ninety-seven, but in fact he was already one hundred and sixty-eight years old. People older than seventy had always been exempted from corvée labor according to the law. Therefore the people of the city offered to pay for the hiring of a replacement so that he could stay in his store and practice medicine.

As it turned out, the prefect was a native of Lingnan [an area south of the Five Ridges in Guangdong and Guangxi], where people believed in witchcraft rather than medicine. He said, "Li Qing may be ninety-seven years old, but he must be healthy enough to work as a laborer. If he can prescribe herbs, why can't he work on the roads? Don't you know that Jiang Taigong, at eighty-two, went to the battlefield as an aide to King Wu of Zhou?[11] If Li Qing is a subject of the imperial court, he remains one unto death. Where can he hide? Granted that he cures sick children, he can't be the only pediatrician in a city as large as Qingzhou? I checked the records. He's been practicing medicine for twenty-seven years only. Before he came on the scene, had the children of Qingzhou died out? If I take only this name out of the list, how am I going to convince everyone of my impartiality?"

The other representatives also pleaded hard on Li Qing's behalf, but the prefect turned a deaf ear. At a loss as to what to do, they went in desperation to Li Qing's store to consult him about a more convincing argument to present to the prefect.

Li Qing said, "I'm ever so grateful to you for your kindness. As this old man sees it, it's all right not to plead again. This is such a trifle that there shouldn't normally be any difficulty approving the request. The prefect is so adamant just because the emperor himself is coming, rather than just a superior of his. So a mistake could cost him his head. He wants the people on the list to do the service themselves instead of hiring replacements, so that if something happens, it will be easier to establish accountability. This is what most officials are concerned about. He won't yield to more pleas. But judging from the way things develop, I believe that this decree may most likely also come to nothing. There was an identical decree in the second year of the Linde period and a second one in the first year of Tiaolu. This is the third time now. If the emperor didn't come the first two times, he may not come this time, either. I assure you that something will happen within five days to make the emperor revoke the decree. Let's all put our minds at ease and let the prefect do whatever he likes."

This speech took everyone by surprise. They said, "The prefect is going to sign the order any time now. The lictors will be going out in all directions to get the laborers. There's no time to lose! But this old man makes it sound as if nothing's going to happen. He will have to work as a laborer as long as the decree is in effect. We took the trouble of pleading on his behalf and offering to pay for a replacement, but he's all eagerness to do his duty. Maybe he has made so much money that he's looking forward to being paid two pennies a day by the prefecture!" With a sarcastic snort, they went their separate ways.

As it turned out, this time Emperor Gaozong was determined to go to Mount Tai for the ceremony. By his order, the officials of the ministry of rites had already drafted the protocol for the ceremony. The only remaining thing to be done was to choose an auspicious day for him to set out on the journey. But all of a sudden, the emperor suffered an attack of muscular dystrophy and could not even rise to his feet. How would he be able to undertake the journey for the grand ceremony? Within three days, the superiors of the prefect of Qingzhou transmitted to him the order to hold the previous imperial decree in abeyance. Only then did people of the city realize what divine vision Li Qing had, and their respect and admiration for him grew even more profound.

The Shandong region had an ample crop of Daoist magicians. The First Emperor of Qin, in his pursuit of the Dao, had sent Xu Fu to the Penglai Mountains with five hundred young boys and girls to pick herbs of immortality. That Xu Fu was a native of Shandong. Later, Emperor Wudi of Han, also devoted to Daoism, appointed Li Shaojun as General of Wencheng and Luan Da as General of Wuli, and prayed every day at the Skyward Terrace, the Bamboo Palace, and the Cassia Hall for immortals to descend to earth. Both Li Shaojun and Luan Da also came from Shandong. Therefore those in this profession passed on their knowledge from generation to generation. When these magicians saw that Li Qing—almost a centenarian, in medical practice for twenty-seven years since he was seventy—did not appear any older, but, in fact, looked even more hale and hearty than before, they surmised that he must have undertaken inner cultivation in the Daoist tradition.

And now, hearing that he was able to look into the future, they felt certain that he had attained the Dao and, like Dong Feng and Han Kang, was selling medicine under a concealed identity.[12] So they swarmed to Li Qing's store to honor him as a teacher of the mysteries of Daoism and to find out his true background. They pleaded time and again that he enlighten them on the great Dao.

Li Qing said in self-deprecation, "This old man has no foresight. I gave up all desires when I was thirty. I don't exert myself in anything I do. I only try to quietly conserve my energy, which may be why I stay free from illnesses."

Suspecting him of trying to hide the truth from them, the magicians said, "To achieve longevity is not that difficult, but to foresee what will happen in the future is no easy feat. What magic art do you have, sir, that told you the imperial decree would be revoked in five days?"

"I'm no immortal with clairvoyance. How can you not know the stories about Confucius making predictions at the sight of water lily seeds and a one-legged bird?[13] I just made a guess, using a children's song that I heard, and I happened to be right. Nursery rhymes are made without specific purposes but are in fact inspired by the essence of heaven and earth. If you follow the events they hint at, you'll find that facts will bear them out. After I first opened my store here, back in the fifth year of Yonghui [654], I heard a children's song during the Longsuo period [661–63]. You must also remember it. It said,

> Mount Tai is high; how many stories high?
> Mount Tai can be climbed, but that won't come about.
> Troops and horses are three times drafted;
> Each time they go circling around it.
> One and two and three times they try it;
> Again and again they do not make it.

"Sure enough, the first two times bore out that song. That was how I concluded that they wouldn't make it the third time, either. Older people have seen more and experienced more and therefore get to know a thing or two. It's not because of some magic art!"

Since he did not tell them what they wanted to hear and he was too busy with taking payments, prescribing medicine, and dealing with alms seekers, the magicians gradually went their own ways.

The next year, Emperor Gaozong died. Empress Wu Zetian ascended the throne, which she occupied for twenty-one years. The crown prince succeeded her and became Emperor Zhongzong. Six years later, Empress Wei rebelled against him. Emperor Ruizong exterminated her and sat on the throne for six years before Emperor Xuanzhong took over power. In the tenth year of the Kaiyuan reign period [713–42], forty-three years after the afore described events, Li Qing was now one hundred and forty years old, as was known to the entire city of Qingzhou. Partly because his medicine still worked wonders, partly because he looked the same as before—if not as an immortal who had attained the Dao, then at least as a venerable old man— he attracted a large following of students of medicine and Daoism as well as fans who just had faith in him. They all hated to leave him. Truly,

> *Immortals in fact live in the mortal world;*
> *Flesh and blood were formed in a previous life.*

Our story branches at this point. Emperor Xuanzong was also an admirer of immortals and revered Daoism. He had two mentors, a Heavenly Preceptor Ye Fashan and a Heavenly Preceptor Xing Hepu. Both having attained the Dao, they acted on behalf of the emperor and spent their days seeking out supernatural beings and imparting to the emperor their knowledge about inner alchemy, rejuvenation, and nourishment of the yin and the yang.

In the ninth year of the Kaiyuan reign period, the two heavenly preceptors Xing and Ye said to the emperor, "There are three immortals living in the mortal world. One is Zhang Guo, a native of Tiaoshan, Hengzhou. One is Luo Gongyuan, a native of Ezhou, and one called Li Qing, a native of Beihai. Even though they belong to the realm beyond the mist and clouds and have no interest in the riches and honors of the mortal world, they may be willing to come if the imperial court sincerely invites them."

Consequently, Emperor Xuanzong sent Xu Qiao, drafter of the grand secretariat, to invite Zhang Guo; Cui Zhongfang, director of the Office of Rites, to invite Luo Gongyuan; and Pei Wu, protocol officer of the grand secretariat, to invite Li Qing. After bidding adieu to the emperor, the three envoys left on their missions, each equipped with documents bearing the imperial seal. Of this, more later.

Having reached the end of his span of life in the mortal world and accomplished his mission, Li Qing, in his divine wisdom, was well aware of Officer Pei's imminent visit. Recalling the patriarch's quatrain, of which the fourth line was "Flee upon the advent of a Pei," he said to himself, "So I am supposed to flee, which means all too clearly that it's time for me to dissolve my body."

You may well ask, what does this mean? Well, on the day immortals attain the Dao, they inevitably have to depart from the mortal world. Some ascend to heaven in broad daylight. Some appear to die like ordinary people but they leave no remains in their coffins. This is called bodily dissolution, which is quite unique. All the five elements—metal, wood, water, fire, and earth—can be dissolved. Therefore mortal beings would not even know that someone among them was in fact an immortal.

Li Qing rose bright and early in the morning and told his disciples not to hang out his signboard, adding, "I'm not selling medicine today. I'll be bidding you farewell at the noon hour today."

Much taken aback, his disciples said, "You look perfectly fine, sir. Why talk such nonsense? What's more, we've been at your service for so long without ever having learned any of your secrets. How can you just go like this? Please stay until you have explained in detail all of your secrets. If you leave this world then, the

Daoist tradition will remain alive among us, and generations to come will know you as one who attained the Dao."

Li Qing replied with a smile, "I don't have any secrets to pass on to you, nor do I wish to be known by generations to come. My destined hour has come. You can't keep me. But since Big Brother Jin next door is not here, I'll have to trouble you to buy a coffin for me. After my last breath is gone, put me in it and nail the lid in. Do not wait until tomorrow. Give everything in this store to Big Brother Jin, to show my gratitude to him as a neighbor and as a client of his in these seventy years." (*Big Brother Jin should be in his nineties by now. Could he have lived so long because he benefited from his association with Li Qing?*)

The disciples forthwith went to carry out his orders. They bought a coffin and other items and accomplished their mission in the twinkling of an eye. Eighty-nine years old now, Big Brother Jin was still in robust health and walked as if on wings. He had amassed a large family fortune and had many children and grandchildren. Everyone called him Grandpa Jin. Li Qing, having watched him grow old from his youth, still called him Big Brother Jin. Big Brother Jin was not there that day because he had risen at the fifth watch that morning and gone to the countryside.

At the noon hour, Li Qing took a bath in perfumed water, changed into new clothes, and went into his room, closely followed by his disciples. Li Qing said, "You all go to the door. Let me sit quietly for a while to clarify my mind, so that my thoughts won't be all in a jumble at the last moment. When Big Brother Jin comes back, please bring him in, so that I can say farewell to him face to face. We've had such a long friendship, after all."

The disciples went out the door as he told them to and asked if Big Brother Jin had returned, but he had not. After a while, they returned to the room, only to find Li Qing already dead. Those disciples who had been with him for a long time burst into tears of sorrow, but there were also some despicable ones who looked around for money and valuables.

After all the racket died down, they put Li Qing in the coffin, as he had instructed. His corpse was also different in several ways from ordinary ones. As his hands and legs were crossed in front of his chest in the manner of a coiling dragon, how could he be lowered into the coffin like that? But when the disciples tried to pull his limbs straight, they found that the corpse was like a piece of iron that none could budge. In resignation, they lowered the corpse the way it was into the coffin, nailed the lid in, and let it stay in the room. Li Qing being a well-known name, news of his death immediately spread around half of the city of Qingzhou. His clients all came to pay their respects to him. Greeting the visitors and escorting them out, the disciples talked themselves dry in the mouth and bowed until they could not straighten up again. There is a poem in testimony:

> For a hundred years he mixed with mortals;
> In a trice he departed to ride the white clouds.

Where was his divine chariot?
He left only his herb mortar to his disciples.

In the meantime, Pei Wu, protocol officer of the grand secretariat, arrived in Qingzhou in a carriage provided by a government courier station. Having learned of his arrival, the prefect led the elders of the city to meet him, bearing incense and candles. Once in the main hall of the prefectural yamen, when the envoy read aloud the imperial decree, seeking the service of immortal Li Qing, the prefect professed ignorance and asked the elders of the city to enlighten him. They told him, "In Qingzhou, there is a pediatrician Li Qing, who died yesterday at noontime without illness at age one hundred and forty. Apart from him, we don't know of any immortal named Li Qing."

In astonishment, Officer Pei said with emotion, "I've undertaken such a long journey to deliver the imperial decree, in the hope of inviting the immortal physician Li Qing to the imperial court so that I don't let the emperor down. Unfortunately, he died yesterday, not earlier nor later. The emperor won't get to see him even once. Too bad there is no such predestined bond between them. I remember that Emperor Wudi of Han had heard of someone who had successfully turned out immortality pills and sent the grand master of the palace to ask him for the prescription. The man also died before the grand master arrived. Emperor Wudi wanted to kill the grand master for having gone too late and therefore failing to obtain the prescription. Luckily, Dongfang Shuo offered this advice, 'If that man had immortality pills, he must have taken some himself, so he shouldn't have died. Since he died, that means the pills didn't work. Even if Your Majesty got the prescription, it would not have done any good.' The emperor agreed. Luckily, our emperor, being wiser than Emperor Wudi of Han, will not do what Emperor Wudi wanted to do to the envoy, even without the advice of someone like Dongfang Shuo. But, since heavenly preceptors Xing and Ye called him an immortal, he should have lived as long as heaven and earth. How could he have died? If he died, he was no immortal. But one who died without illness at age one hundred and forty is hard to come by, even if he was not an immortal."

Then and there, Officer Pei ordered the prefect to have the neighbors write a deposition, describing Li Qing's daily activities, his ways of self-cultivation, and the circumstances and the hour of his death. Officer Pei would then present the deposition to the emperor by way of acquitting himself. (*In the end, even a real immortal would not be spared official formalities.*)

Not wishing to be remiss in his duty, the prefect summoned Li Qing's neighbors and told them to prepare a deposition, so that the imperial envoy could set out on his return journey.

Thus ordered, the neighbors left the prefect's presence. One of them said, "We are all too young to know the details of his background. How are we going to do this deposition? I understand that only Grandpa Jin got to know him when he first came. Grandpa Jin must know all about him. But he left for the countryside yesterday. He should be back either today or tomorrow. Let's ask him to write the deposition and go with him to submit it to the prefect."

The other neighbors all agreed. On their way home together, they ran right into old man Jin, with a large bag of herbs on his back. The neighbors stopped him, "All's well!" they said. "Grandpa Jin is back! If you hadn't gone to the countryside yesterday, you could have said farewell to your friend Doctor Li."

"Where did he go? Why should I say farewell to him?"

"He passed away at noontime yesterday."

"Nonsense! I met him at South Gate yesterday. How could you say such a thing to curse him?"

Startled, the neighbors said, "He died. How was it possible for you to see him? It must have been his soul you saw."

Old man Jin also gave a start. "I don't believe there can be such a thing!" Instead of returning home, he headed straight for Li Qing's store, only to see a coffin, Li Qing's disciples wearing mourning white, and many people paying homage to the departed. Shaking his head, old man Jin said, "This is unbelievable!"

The disciples went up to him, saying, "Our teacher passed away at noontime yesterday. Because you were not here, sir, we've kept the coffin in the room." Handing a list to him, they said, "All the things in the store are left to you as souvenirs."

Old man Jin took the list but did not look at it. He cried, "Did he really die? I still don't believe it!"

The neighbors said, "Grandpa Jin, tell us how you saw him yesterday."

"I left early yesterday morning. Before I was out of South Gate, I met a relative who insisted on treating me to breakfast. I wasn't able to take leave of him until quite a while later. When I reached the foot of Cloud Gate Mountain, it was already noontime. I saw a few kinds of good medicinal herbs and was picking them when I ran into a green-robed page boy walking with an incense burner in his arms. I didn't pay him attention, but before I went about sixty to seventy steps farther, I saw your teacher coming toward me. For some reason, his left foot had a shoe on, but his right foot was bare. I asked him where he was going. He said, 'There are nine of my mentors and fellow disciples in the Rotten Rope Pavilion on Cloud Gate Mountain, waiting for me to join them in their chat. I won't come back for a few days.' From his sleeve he took out a letter and a brocade bag that contained something like a jade *ruyi* wand, and told me to bring it back to the city and give it to a certain Officer Pei, so as not to hold up his official business. The letter and the brocade bag are still on me. How could he have died?" Having said that, he retrieved the two objects from his sleeve.

In the beginning, the disciples suspected Old Man Jin of playing tricks on them and refused to believe him. At the sight of the letter and the bag, they relented and said, "Let's not quibble about whether it was noontime or not, but our teacher never left this room. How could he have given these two objects to you? How strange!"

The neighbors chimed in, "This is really out of the ordinary. He had already passed away. How could he still be asking someone to deliver things for him? And he knew Officer Pei would be coming to invite him. Even a ghost would not have had such uncanny foresight. He must be a real immortal."

Old Man Jin asked, "What Officer Pei is inviting him?"

After the disciples told him about how the imperial envoy Officer Pei had come to invite Li Qing to the court and how the prefect, upon learning of his death, ordered a deposition from witnesses, Old Man Jin said, "I see. Since I have these two things from him, there's no need for a deposition. I'll go with you to see the prefect so that he can relay the message to the envoy."

The disciples and the neighbors followed Mr. Jin to the prefectural yamen. Carrying the letter and the brocade bag, Jin related to the prefect how he had met Li Qing the day before and how Li Qing had given him the two objects. In surprise, the prefect went with them to report to the envoy. Officer Pei, disappointed at the futility of the mission, had been urging the prefect to close the case for him, so that he could be on his way. Intrigued, the prefect and a large group of people came to him and presented him with a letter, saying that Li Qing had at noontime the day before asked Old Man Jin, a neighbor, to relay it to the envoy. Complying with their request to open the envelope, Officer Pei saw that it was a thank-you letter. It said,

> I have read in the upper realm Your Majesty's kind letter. With immortals in this world to protect the populace and ensure peace, Your Majesty should follow the examples of kings Yao and Shun in their nonactivity and emperors Wen and Jing in their prudence, and wait in patience for your destined hour to ascend to the divine realm. There is no need to practice austerities, suppress intelligence, and learn magic art from benighted men of the mountains. This humble subject, having just attained the Dao, is not yet a full-fledged member of the divine realm, but even the venerable immortal Zhang Guo and my fellow Daoist Luo Gongyuan would also rather return to their divine abode than serve Your Majesty for any sustained period of time in your esteemed court. In the olden times, the First Emperor of Qin issued an invitation to Anqi Sheng in his abode in the East Sea.[14] Anqi declined the invitation but asked the envoy to present a pair of red jade shoes to the emperor. However unworthy I am, I will not fail to return Your Majesty's kindness. I hereby humbly present to Your Majesty a green jade ruyi pin as a small token of my sentiments. Please accept it in all your graciousness.

Upon reading the letter, Officer Pei said in amazement, "As far as I know, immortals don't die. Those who die just dissolve their bodies. Why don't we open the coffin for a look? If it's empty, he's an immortal beyond any doubt. I can then go back to the court to report to His Majesty and solve the puzzle in everyone's mind."

The officials and people of the city all agreed. When the coffin in the store was opened, there, for all to see, were only a green bamboo cane and one shoe. The corpse was not there. It would have been all right if the coffin had not been opened, but as it was, an even more wondrous thing happened: a column of blue smoke rose toward the sky. Then the coffin rose into the air and disappeared from view. (*Even a coffin can fly. What Daoist art is this?*) Five different kinds of aroma filled the air all over the city and assailed the nostrils of everyone within a circumference of three hundred li. Officer Pei and the officials and populace of the city bowed toward the sky. Li Qing's letter and brocade bag were sealed up carefully and the envoy was sent off on his way back to the imperial court.

The next year, an epidemic went around the empire, sparing only those in Qingzhou who had smelled the aromas, bearing testimony to Li Qing's posthumous good works for the benefit of his native town. A shrine in his honor stands to this day on Cloud Gate Mountain and is never short of worshipers throughout the seasons. There is a poem that says,

> *A chess game led to a Rotten Ax Pavilion;*
> *Today, rotten ropes are seen on Cloud Gate Mountain.*
> *A hundred years go by in the twinkling of an eye;*
> *How foolish those fighting for fame and gain day and night!*

Magistrate Wang Burns Down Precious Lotus Monastery

Take the tonsure and wear a black cassock;
Offer incense and worship Buddha.
Refrain from furtive acts of disgrace;
They will defile your otherwise good name.
Keep a vegetarian diet,
Chant Buddha's name,
Read the sutras and meditate.
Living the carefree life of immortals,
You will not envy the well-to-do.

Once upon a time, in Gold Mountain Monastery of Hangzhou, there lived a monk, whose Buddhist name was Attaining Enlightenment. He took the Buddhist order at an early age and amassed quite a fortune. One day, he was walking down the street when he saw a beautiful woman. Thrown into raptures, he melted with desire. How he wished he could gather her in his arms and swallow her whole! After he had passed about ten houses, he still turned his head back to gawk at her, thinking, "I wonder which family that woman is from. If I could sleep with such a beauty for even one night, I would die content." Then he thought, "We monks are also mortal beings born of parents. Why should we stay away from women just because these few locks of hair have been shaved off? The great Buddha was ludicrous. If he wanted to be the patriarch of Buddhism, he should have been content with practicing abstinence himself. Why set this rule for all monks of later generations to observe? We are but mortal beings. How can we be expected to fight off our desires? And those officials who laid down the laws of the land in the old days were most abominable. They lived in grand style, going about in fine horse carriages in the company of beautiful women. If they got to enjoy themselves so much, they should have shown some compassion for ordinary folks and accumulated credit for themselves in the netherworld. And yet, they chose to make enemies of monks and enacted such unreasonable laws. Why should a monk who sleeps with a woman be put to the rod? Are we monks not made of flesh and blood? Cultivation of the spirit is a personal matter. Physical punishment is not the right way to do it." (*Why did you choose to be a monk in the first place?*)

Then he turned his anger on his parents: "If they couldn't provide for me, I should have died, and that would have been the end of it all. Why did they have to send me to this place? Look at me! I can't do a thing! With so much bitterness pent up in me, I'd better return to secular life, get myself a wife, and start a family. At least I would get to enjoy married life." But then he recalled how monks feed themselves without having to till the land, clothe themselves without having to weave, and live in magnificent buildings, doing nothing but burning incense and drinking tea. This easy life was something he was not ready to give up.

While thinking these wild thoughts, he dragged his feet listlessly down the streets until he found himself back at the monastery. His mind in a daze, he sat around, woebegone and glum. Before evening set in, he went to sleep, his heart still with the beautiful woman who was beyond his reach. As he heaved sigh upon sigh, sleep just would not come to him. After a few more moments of thinking, he said to himself with another sigh, "I don't even know her name or address. Am I not a fool to be having those flights of fancy?" Then another thought struck him: "Actually, there is an easy way out! With her small bound feet, she can't walk very far. She must be a resident of this neighborhood. I'll just spend a few days to go around and make inquiries. If I have a predestined bond with her, I may run into her again. Who knows? I'll then follow her quietly, remember where she lives, and have someone who knows her give me a hand. I must have her."

His mind thus made up, he waited for daybreak. After he rose, washed, and rinsed his mouth, he took out a brand new silk cassock that draped over the left shoulder and put on a pair of nice shoes and white socks. Thus done up in finery, he left his room and, as he happened to pass the hall of the Bodhisattva Guanyin, he thought, "Let me ask the Bodhisattva if I have a chance." He sank to his knees and prostrated himself twice. Then he took the pot containing divination slips and shook it a few times. One slip fell out. He picked it up and saw that it was divination slip number eighteen, inscribed with the words "The Very Best." There was also a quatrain that said:

> *With her predestined marriage bond with you,*
> *She'll meet you today, not by accident.*
> *Be ready for hard work, give up the idle life,*
> *And you will live better than ever before.*

Beside himself with joy upon reading this prophecy, he said to himself, "This divination says all too clearly that I will meet her any time now. I must not pass up this opportunity." With another two bows, he put down the pot and dashed off to the spot where he had seen her the previous day. There, a woman was walking slowly in his direction. Upon a closer look, he saw that she was none other than his sweet foe, and she was all alone. In happy astonishment, he thought, "The Bodhisattva's divination is indeed accurate. I'll surely get what I want."

He followed closely on the woman's heels. As she raised the speckled bamboo curtain of a side door and stepped in, she turned back, smiled flirtatiously at him, and beckoned him with a hand. The monk went into raptures. He took a glance all around him and, seeing no one in sight, eagerly raised the door curtain and went in to greet her. Instead of returning his greeting, she raised an arm and flicked her sleeve at his head, knocking down his monk's hat. Then she took a step forward and gave the hat a kick with her small pointed foot. As the hat rolled off to one side, she giggled mockingly.

Smelling the scent of musk, the monk said, "Young lady, don't make fun of me!"

As he picked up the hat and put it back on his head, the woman said, "Why are you, a monk, in my house in broad daylight?"

Attaining Enlightenment said, "You were kind enough to beckon to me. Why say such a thing?" Driven by his unbridled lust, he went forward to embrace her, not caring in the least if she was willing or not. As he pulled at her clothes, the woman said, laughing, "You bald rogue! Have you never seen a woman? How can you be such a boor! Follow me inside."

After many twists and turns, she led him into her room. They removed their clothes and lay down in bed. Their bodies had barely touched when a big man barged in, a steel ax in hand. "Where did this bald donkey come from?" he bellowed. "How dare you seduce a decent woman?"

Cowering with fear, Attaining Enlightenment fell on his knees on the floor and said, trembling, "This lowly monk is at fault. Please spare this unworthy life for Buddha's sake! After I return to the monastery, I will chant ten volumes of *The Lotus Sutra* to ask for blessings and longevity for you, sir!"

Turning a deaf ear to him, the man swung the ax right against his head and knocked him to the floor.

You may wonder if this blow of the ax killed Attaining Enlightenment or not. In fact, his thoughts were so occupied with the woman that it had all been a dream. Upon waking up with a start, the monk said to himself, frightened as he recalled how he was killed in the dream, "It's too dangerous to have clandestine affairs. I'd better not do anything of that kind. The best option is to return to secular life and live in peace." He began to let his hair grow long and then he married. After less than three years, he died of consumption. On the day he left the monastery, he wrote a poem that said:

> In youth I refused to take up the books;
> I forced myself to mortify my flesh.
> On snowy nights I sleep alone, my feet icy cold;
> On frosty days I shave my hair, with chills down my spine.

Kept apart from beauties in red towers,
I'm not allowed to cast them one little glance.
A sad ghost I will be after I die,
Groping in darkness in Western Paradise.

Even though he broke the commandments and returned to secular life, Monk Attaining Enlightenment got to preserve his reputation and his integrity. I shall now move on to a story about other Buddhist monks who violated the monastic commandments and caused a major scandal that brought disgrace to Buddha and to their monastery.

Where did the story take place? Well, it took place in Yongchun County, Nanning Prefecture of Guangxi. In the prefectural seat there was a Precious Lotus Monastery. Built in the Yuan dynasty, it acquired hundreds of houses and more than a thousand *mu* of land through the generations. With its abundant stock of funds and grains and ample supply of clothes and food, it was a monastery of fine, long-standing repute. The abbot, with the Buddhist name of Buddha Manifest, had under him more than one hundred monks, each with his own functions. Visitors were greeted by a monk, led into a cell for tea, and shown around the monastery. The tour would end with more tea and refreshments. Such was the hospitality of the monks.

Though they kept all visitors for tea, the monks in fact divided the visitors into different categories, giving favorable treatment to the rich and powerful. This need not be gone into at length, because, generally speaking, monks' offers of food, like Empress Lü's feast, are not to be lightly accepted.[1] Why? Even though they have taken the Buddhist order, monks pursue material gains with greater relentlessness than lay people. The pots of green tea and the refreshments are nothing less than bait. Rich or poor, visitors give donations in cash or in kind for what the monks claim to be projects to guild the statues of Buddha or to renovate the monastery. When they run out of worthy causes, they will ask for donations for oil for the lamps in front of the Buddha's statues. They treat generous givers as patrons who can be harassed again in the future, fawn on them in a thousand ways, and wheedle more money out of them from time to time. As for those who refuse to give, they accuse them of being misers and vilify them in a hundred ways behind their backs, even spitting when passing them on the streets. The greed of monks knows no bounds. Then there is also a category of people who never give their poor relatives a penny but, whenever the monks hit them up for a donation, readily part with their money. Aren't these fools who set their priorities all wrong? As the following poem attests:

Their largesse goes to Buddha, not to people;
They donate to monks, not to common folks.
If an order is set to works of charity,
The poor should be of first priority.

However, Precious Lotus Monastery was different. It did not solicit donations for its frequent renovations of its buildings. Therefore, people of all classes far and near had such respect for the kind monks of this monastery that they gave several times more generously than if solicited.

There was in the monastery a Progeny Hall, which was said to be most responsive to prayers for fertility. Indeed, those who prayed for sons had sons born to them; those who prayed for daughters had daughters born to them. You may well ask, why was it so responsive to these prayers? Well, on both sides of Progeny Hall were more than ten monks' cells, each furnished with a curtained bed. Healthy women in the prime of life were told to observe a vegetarian diet for seven days before going to say their prayers and to do divinations in the monastery. Those whose sacred wooden divination slips fell right-side up when tossed on the floor were allowed to spend the night there, one to a cell. Those who were not so fortunate were told that they were lacking in sincerity. The monks would repent on their behalf and have them come again for prayers after observing another seven-day vegetarian diet. Each cell was tightly surrounded by walls on all four sides. After their husbands and servants checked the rooms meticulously and made the selections, the women were taken into the cells at night. Their families and servants slept outside the doors to keep watch. Therefore no suspicions ever crossed anyone's mind. (*The divination slips could not be dispensed with.*)

After returning home, the women indeed would conceive, and the boys and girls they gave birth to were big and robust and free from illnesses. Such wondrous effects attracted women from families of scholars, officials, and ordinary folks, to offer their prayers for fertility in Progeny Hall. Even people from surrounding counties came. Every day, the monastery was inundated with bustling crowds of people. Prodigious amounts of donations were made. When the women were asked if the Bodhisattva was responsive that night, some said they dreamed that Buddha had sent them sons, some claimed they dreamed of arhats sleeping with them, some denied having dreams, and some were bashful and declined to comment. Some never went again, but others made more visits from time to time. (*This speaks volumes about these women's characters.*)

Now, just think: the Bodhisattvas themselves severed all ties of love and other human emotions when cultivating their own inner natures. How could they choose to busy themselves with matters relating to carnal desire out in the mortal world and send children via dreams to this temple every night? Wasn't that a whole lot of nonsense? But the people in that region had always been the sort that believed in witchcraft rather than in medicine. Therefore they easily yielded themselves to evil and, with total faith in the monastery, continued the practice in their delusion, sending their wives and daughters to the temple for the enjoyment of the villains. Truly,

They took poisonous weeds
For a miraculous cure.

For all their pretensions to modesty and politeness, the monks of this monastery were greedy, lustful, wicked, and evil to the last degree. The cells looked secure, but in fact they could be reached through hidden tunnels. After the evening bells were struck and the women had fallen fast asleep, the monks would go to take advantage of them. Upon waking up, the women found themselves already defiled. If they raised a clamor, they were afraid that their names would be sullied and therefore had to submit in humiliation. Partly because the women were in good health and the vegetarian diet cleansed their spirits and partly because the monks were young and robust and also gave the women expensive fertility pills, nine women out of ten achieved pregnancy. Those women with a sense of shame dared not tell their husbands and suffered in silence like a mute tasting bitter herbs. There were also debauched women who now had the pretext to go from time to time for enjoyment. And so the practice went on for years.

When those villains' evildoings reached their height, heaven sent an official along. Who was he? He was the new magistrate of the county, Wang Dan, a native of Jinjiang County, Quanzhou, of Fujian. Having passed the imperial examinations in early youth, he was a man with the sharpest intelligence. Knowing that this place, with ethnic tribes mixing with Han people, was the hardest to govern because the local customs were quite wild, he defied the local despots and eliminated all latent sources of evil after he assumed office. Within half a year, crimes declined and bandits and thieves lay low. The people of the county were delighted and impressed.

Upon hearing that prayers for fertility in Precious Lotus Monastery were most effective, Magistrate Wang did not believe it. He thought, "If the Bodhisattvas are responsive, prayers should be enough. Why make the women sleep in the temple? There must be something fishy. But, without any hard evidence, I must not make a rash move. I need to go there and see for myself before I do what has to be done."

On the day he chose, the first day of the ninth lunar month, he went to Precious Lotus Monastery to offer incense. When he and his retinue arrived, Magistrate Wang saw that by its whitewashed walls were planted tall locust trees and old willows. Over the vermilion gate was hung a horizontal board bearing in gilded characters the inscription "Precious Lotus Monastery." Opposite the temple stood a screen wall, along which were parked many empty sedan-chairs. The crowds of worshipers going in and out of the gate dispersed at the sight of Magistrate Wang. The sedan-chair carriers also busily moved their sedan-chairs elsewhere. Magistrate Wang told his followers not to disturb anyone.

Upon hearing that the county magistrate was there personally to offer incense, the abbot struck the bells and the drums, assembled the monks, and led them to the gate, where they dropped to their knees in a salute to the magistrate. Magistrate Wang did not dismount his sedan-chair until he came to the Hall of Sakyamuni, the main hall of the monastery. Magistrate Wang saw that it was indeed a magnificent monastery. Behold:

There are halls after halls,
Towers after towers.
Outside the Hall of Sakyamuni,
Rosy clouds hover over the red doors.
In front of the lobby,
An auspicious air shrouds the green tiles.
The junipers and the slender bamboo
Embower the painted and carved beams.
Green pines and ancient cypresses
Shade the winding balustrades.
Real Pure Land can hardly be found on earth;
Famous mountains under the sun swarm with monks.

While offering incense and paying homage to Buddha, Magistrate Wang inwardly prayed that he be allowed to purge this monastery of evil. After the prayer service was over, Abbot Buddha Manifest led the monks in bowing to the magistrate and invited the magistrate into his cell. After tea was served, Magistrate Wang said to Buddha Manifest, "I heard that under your leadership, all the monks of this monastery assiduously worship Buddha and practice the strictest austerities. Please give me a copy of your curriculum vitae. I will report to my superiors and request a government certificate of credence for you, to make you the prefectural director of religious affairs with lifelong tenure as abbot of this monastery."

Overjoyed at this unexpected good fortune, the abbot kowtowed gratefully.

Magistrate Wang continued, "I also heard that in your monastery, prayers for fertility are most effective. Is that true?"

"We have a Progeny Hall. It is indeed very responsive to prayers."

"Are there any required ceremonies?"

"There are no sutra-chanting ceremonies. The only requirement is that women who pray for fertility must be healthy and pious, and they must observe a vegetarian diet for seven days. When they pray before the Buddha' statue, those who get the right divination slips will rest in the cells on both sides. When their prayers are answered with dreams, they achieve pregnancy."

"But I'm afraid it's not appropriate for women to stay in a monastery," said the magistrate.

"The cells are very secure. One woman occupies one cell, and her own family members keep watch outside the door. No unauthorized person is allowed. There is no problem."

"I see. I don't have children yet, but my wife can't very well come."

The abbot said, "If you want children, sir, you need only offer incense and pray. Your wife can observe a vegetarian diet at home. That will also work."

"Don't the prayers work only if the women stay in the monastery? Why do you say that in my case, my wife doesn't have to come?"

"You, sir, are the head of a county with a large population, and you are also a champion of Buddhism. Your mind has a spiritual connection with heaven and earth. Yours is no ordinary case."

You may wonder why Abbot Buddha Manifest didn't want the magistrate's wife to come. As the proverb says, "A thief has a guilty conscience." With such goings-on in the monastery, he was afraid that Mrs. Wang would have a large retinue, and the more people there were, the more likely the shenanigans would be exposed. So he had to stop her. Little did he know that the magistrate was just putting on a show to sound him out.

"You do have a point," conceded the magistrate. "I will come another time to pray in all piety. But now I'd like to tour the grounds." So saying, he rose and asked the abbot to lead him to Progeny Hall via the main hall.

Hearing that the county magistrate was here, the men and women offering incense in Progeny Hall dispersed with alacrity.

Magistrate Wang saw that it was a grand three-section hall, splendidly adorned with carved beams and pillars, painted ridgepoles, and an ornate roof. In the middle shrine was the statue of a goddess with a jade necklace and a headdress glittering with pearls. Clad in an embroidered robe and a colorful cape, the statue had a child in her arms. On her side stood four or five other statues. That was the Goddess of Fertility. A yellow silk embroidered curtain hanging over the shrine was pulled apart and held in place by two silver hooks, one on each side. There were several hundred pairs of colored shoes donated for the statue of the goddess. Amid the proliferation of banners, flags, and canopies, the carved candles on the brackets flooded the room with light. The air was filled with thin wisps of fragrant incense from the incense burners. To the left was a statue of Fairy Zhang, god of fertility, and to the right was the statue of the god of longevity.

Magistrate Wang bowed to the statues and took a stroll around the hall before he asked the abbot to take him to the cells for women. The rooms were all well partitioned, with nice ceilings, flat floors, and neat curtained beds and chairs. Magistrate Wang looked closely without finding one crack anywhere. Indeed, even a mouse, a bug, or an ant would not have found a place to hide. Failing to find anything suspicious, Magistrate Wang went back through the main hall and mounted his sedan-chair. Again, the abbot led the monks out and knelt down outside the gate to see the magistrate off.

In his sedan-chair, Magistrate Wang gave himself up to thought. "Those cells are secure," he said to himself. "It doesn't look like there's foul play. But how can a statue made of clay and wood be so responsive to prayers? Can it be an evil god up to mischief?" Turning his thoughts this way and that, he suddenly hit upon a plan.

Back in the county yamen, he summoned a clerk and said to him, "You go quietly and find two prostitutes. Have them pose as married women and send them to Precious Lotus Monastery to stay overnight. Prepare one bowl of red ink and one bowl of black ink. Tell them that if men go to sleep with them at night, they are to paint the ink secretly on the men's heads. Tomorrow morning I'll go personally to the monastery to investigate. Do not leak this out to anyone."

Thus instructed, the clerk brought to his own home two prostitutes he knew, one called Zhang Meijie, the other Li Wan'er, and told them about what they were supposed to do. This being a mission entrusted to them by the magistrate, how could they decline? When evening finally came, the two prostitutes, now dressed like married women from decent families, rented two sedan-chairs. With servants following behind, carrying their bedding and a box containing the bowls of red and black ink, they went to Precious Lotus Monastery. The clerk picked two cells, made the necessary arrangements, and, leaving the servants there, went to report to the county magistrate. Before long, the monks sent a young acolyte to light the lamps and serve tea. That night, there were more than ten women praying for children. Who would take the trouble to check if the two prostitutes had offered incense or had tossed divination slips? Soon, the bells and the drums stuck, announcing the advent of evening. The women all went into the cells to retire for the night, with their family members keeping watch outside. The monks also went to their rooms and closed their doors, and we shall leave them for now.

Zhang Meijie closed her door, set her silver bowl of red ink by the pillow, trimmed the lamp, took off her clothes, and went to bed. Her mind preoccupied, she dared not fall asleep. From time to time, she took a peek from behind the bed curtain. At about the first watch of the night, when all was still, she suddenly heard a creaking sound on the floor in front of the bed. Thinking it was a mouse, she raised her head and saw that a piece of the floor board was slowly being pushed to one side. A man's head popped out from the hole. When the man drew himself to his full height, Zhang Meijie saw that it was a monk. Appalled, she thought, "So, these monks have been using such tricks to seduce innocent women. No wonder the county magistrate has devised this plan."

Not making a sound, she watched as the monk noiselessly went to blow out the lamp. Then he approached the bed, undressed, raised the bed curtain, and got under her quilt. As she pretended to be asleep, the monk mounted her, slowly raised her thighs, and began to have his way with her.

As if waking from a dream, Zhang Meijie said, "Who are you? How can you take advantage of the night and do such a vile thing to me?"

As she tried to push him off, the monk held her tightly in his arms and said, "I am a golden arhat, here to give you a son." So saying, he began to grow wild in his movements. This monk was quite a master in the art. Even an experienced prostitute like Zhang Meijie found herself no match for his prowess. Panting for breath, she reached out a hand, dipped her fingers in red ink in the silver bowl, and smeared the ink all over the top of his head while he was in a transport of joy. Thinking that she was caressing him, the monk suspected nothing.

After two such games, he rose, got off the bed, and gave her a packet, saying,

"These are pills to adjust your menstrual periods and improve your chances of conceiving. Take three maces each time with hot water early in the morning. Take one dose every day for several days in a row, and you'll surely have a safe pregnancy and an easy delivery." Having said that, he went off.

Tired by now, Zhang Meijian drifted off to sleep. But again, she felt a body pressing against her. That monk was even more of a boor. No sooner was he under the quilt than he spread her thighs and started his act. Taking him for the monk who had been there before, she pushed him and said, "Having done that twice, I'm tired. I want to sleep. Why are you here again? Don't you ever have enough?"

The monk said, "Young lady, you're mistaken. I'm a newcomer. I haven't even had a taste. How can you say I don't ever have enough?"

Frightened at the thought that the monks would be taking turns, she said, "I'm of a weak constitution. I'm not good at this sort of thing. Don't bother me like this."

"That's all right. I've got aphrodisiacs here. If you take the pills, you'll be able to enjoy the fun all night through." He produced from his clothes a paper packet and gave it to her. Afraid that the pills might be poisonous, Zhang Meijie did not dare take them. As before, she smeared his head with the red ink. This monk was more valiant than the previous one and he did not leave until the roosters crowed. The piece of the floor was then put back in place. Of this, no more need be said for now.

Let us come to Li Wan'er. She had just gone to bed when her candle was put out by a moth. She did not dare close her eyes, either. At about the first watch of the night, a rustling sound came from behind her bed. A man raised the bed curtain, got into bed, slid under the quilt, held her tightly in his arms, and kissed her on the mouth. Li Wan'er stroked his head and found that it was clean shaven. Being impatient by nature, she dipped her fingers into her bowl of black ink and smeared it all over his pate, saying, "Which hall of this monastery are you from?"

The monk gave no answer but started to do what he was there to do. That member of his was large and hard, like a spear or an iron staff. Being several years younger than Zhang Meijian and lustful, Li Wan'er was pleasantly surprised. She thought, "I've always heard that monks are masters of this art. I never believed that, but I now know it's true." Her desire stirred up, she strained to meet him. It was a joyous game of clouds and rain:

> He was a monk of the Buddhist order;
> She was a beauty from a brothel.
> The monk falsely claimed to be an arhat;
> The beauty disguised herself as a virtuous wife.
> One was like a much-used stone mortar
> That bore the pounding of many pestles.
> The other was like a new wooden stake

> *That stayed firm in the wind and the waves.*
> *One ignored the Buddhist commandments*
> *And enjoyed himself to the full.*
> *The other bore in mind the magistrate's words*
> *But still wanted to have a good time.*
> *It was like Ananda Buddha meeting the she-devil;[2]*
> *It was like Monk Yutong playing with Red Lotus.[3]*

No sooner was their game over than another man got into the bed and said in a subdued voice, "You've had enough fun. It's my turn now. Do I have to wait until you're all spent?"

The first monk gave a scornful snort and took himself off. The second monk, once under the quilt, gently caressed Li Wan'er all over her body. She feigned reluctance, but the monk said, kissing her on the mouth, "Young lady, he must have worn you out. I've got aphrodisiacs here to arouse you." With his tongue, he delivered a pill into her mouth. As soon as she swallowed it, she felt her nostrils assailed by an aroma and, dissolving in desire, found greater enjoyment in the movements.

However lustful she was, she dared not let the magistrate down. Again she dipped her fingers in the ink and caressed the monk's head, saying, "Nice shaven head!"

"Young lady, I am a tender and sensitive lover, nothing like those uncouth things. If you don't find me too unworthy, come visit often."

Li Wan'er faked enthusiasm. After the game of clouds and rain was over, he also gave her a packet of fertility drugs. They solemnly bade each other farewell when the roosters crowed. Truly,

> *A monk and a laywoman spent a night together,*
> *Hardly the union of a wedded couple.*

Let me come to the other branch of our story. After receiving the clerk's report that night, Magistrate Wang marched out of the yamen at the fifth watch the next morning with about a hundred police officers and militia equipped with ropes and weapons. Upon arriving at Precious Lotus Monastery, he ordered the men to lie in ambush on both sides and await further orders. As the sky was already turning light, the magistrate told the more than ten men with him to knock at the gate that remained closed.

Upon hearing that the county magistrate was there, the abbot, Buddha Manifest, hurried into his clothes, woke up more than ten young acolytes, and rushed out to greet the magistrate. Magistrate Wang did not dismount from his sedan-chair until he reached the main hall. Dispensing with the usual bows to the statue of Buddha, he went directly into the abbot's cell and sat down. After Buddha Manifest and the young acolytes kowtowed to him, he asked for a list of the names of all the monks for a roll call. The abbot had the acolytes strike the bell and the drum to assemble all the monks.

Upon waking up and hearing that the county magistrate was in the abbot's cell, doing a roll call, the monks hurried out of their beds and dashed there. When everyone was there, Magistrate Wang ordered that all the monks take off their caps. They all complied, without knowing why.

It would have been all right if they had not removed their caps, but as they did, there, for all to see, were two heads with red tops and two heads with black tops. At a sharp order from the magistrate, the four monks were trussed up and made to kneel down in front of the magistrate.

"Why is there red and black ink on your heads?" the magistrate asked the four of them.

Not knowing where the ink had come from, the monks looked uneasily at each other without coming up with an answer. The other monks were also mystified. As Magistrate Wang pressed them for an answer, those four said that it must have been a practical joke that fellow monks had played on them.

With a smile, Magistrate Wang said, "I will summon the jokesters to bear witness." Forthwith he told the clerks to bring the two prostitutes over.

Having been pestered by the monks all night, the two women were fast asleep. The clerk and the servants almost broke their own arms pounding the doors of the cells, and cried themselves hoarse before the two woke up. They then went into the abbot's cell and knelt down.

The magistrate said, "Describe what the two of you saw last night."

The two prostitutes told of how the monks had taken turns sleeping with them, how they had given them aphrodisiacs and fertility pills, and how the two of them had rubbed ink over the monks' heads. Then they produced from their sleeves the fertility pills and the aphrodisiacs and presented them to the magistrate.

Now that their secret was out, all the monks trembled with fear and groaned inwardly in despair. The foursome busily kowtowed and asked for forgiveness.

Magistrate Wang thundered, "You band of rogues! How dare you fool ignorant people in the name of gods and rape innocent women! What do you have to say for yourselves?"

The abbot had an idea. After telling the monks to kneel down, he said to the magistrate, "All of our monks are scrupulous in their adherence to the monastic commandments. These four are the only exceptions. I have reprimanded them time and again for their greed, lust, and their evil ways, but they turn a deaf ear to me. I was about to present Your Honor with a petition to be jointly signed by all the other monks, to request punishment for these four. Fortunately, Your Honor has caught them. They deserve death for their crimes. But the others are innocent. Please forgive them."

The magistrate said, "I heard that there were quite a number of women praying for children last night. There must be secret tunnels in the cells. Why did these four not go to the other rooms but choose to fall into my trap together? How can it be a coincidence?"

Buddha Manifest said again, "In fact, those two cells are the only ones with secret tunnels. There are no other secret tunnels leading to any of the other cells."

Magistrate Wang said, "This can be easily verified. Bring me all the women. If they haven't seen anything, the other monks' innocence will be established." Right away, Magistrate Wang had all the women in the monastery brought in for questioning. With one voice, they denied having slept with the monks. Knowing they were too bashful to come out with the truth, Magistrate Wang ordered a body search. It turned out that every one of them carried a packet of fertility pills.

Magistrate Wang burst out laughing. "If you didn't sleep with the monks, where did you get these fertility pills?"

As the women blushed in embarrassment, the magistrate continued, "You must have also taken the aphrodisiacs?"

The women grew even more fearful. None dared to answer.

Magistrate Wang did not pursue the matter further. He ordered the women to go home. Their husbands, watching the proceedings off to one side, were struck motionless with mortification. Sheepishly, they took their wives home. Of them, more later.

Lying through his teeth, the abbot said that the fertility pills found on the women had been given to them the moment they entered the monastery, but the two prostitutes insisted that they were given the pills after the act.

Magistrate Wang said, "The truth is already out. How can you still try to deny it?" He ordered that the officers and the militiamen tie up all the monks in the monastery except the attendants and two acolytes, who were young boys. Buddha Manifest tried to resort to force, but, noticing that the magistrate's men were all carrying weapons, he dared not make a move. In the meantime, Magistrate Wang told the clerk to take the two prostitutes home. He himself rose and mounted his sedan-chair. As the officers and militiamen escorting the monks walked at the head of the procession, they caused such a stir that local residents turned out en masse to watch.

Back in the yamen, Magistrate Wang called the court to session and ordered torture. The pain was too much for the monks, who were used to an easy life. As soon as the ankle-squeezers were put on them, they confessed. Magistrate Wang recorded their confessions and put them in prison. He then prepared the files and submitted them to his superiors. Of this, no more for now.

In prison, the abbot worked out a plan with the monks. To prison warden Ling Zhi, he said, "We did something wrong in a moment of foolishness. We are deeply remorseful. And now, all locked up here, we don't think we'll ever be set free. When we were arrested this morning, we didn't have anything on us. We have no money to spend. However, we've saved up plenty of money in the monastery over the years. If you could quietly let three or four of us go back to the monastery to bring money over here, you'll not only have your usual amount, but also an extra one hundred taels of silver." (*Nowadays, cases of prison-breaking abound. The government's severe crackdown on greedy, abetting prison wardens does not change the situation. If all dangerous criminals could be tried as soon as they were arrested and, if proven guilty of capital crimes, executed as soon as the trial was over, all worries about their imprisonment would be eliminated, and no prison wardens would be lured into breaking the law. Wouldn't that be a most efficient policy?*)

His greed stirring at the enticing promise, Ling Zhi said, "I'm in no position to decide for the many colleagues of mine. The one hundred taels will have to be distributed among us. What little share of it remains for me will be only nominal. If you could give two hundred taels to be shared among us, plus one hundred for me, I'll go with you to the monastery."

The abbot readily agreed. "Whatever you say. I won't say no to you!"

Immediately, Ling Zhi told the other wardens about it. Secretly they escorted four monks back to the monastery. A search throughout the cells turned up a prodigious amount of gold and silver, of which Buddha Manifest gave three hundred taels to Ling Zhi. As the wardens beamed with joy, the abbot said, "Please wait here a few more moments. Let me pack some bedding, so that the monks can sleep better at night."

The wardens said, "Good idea." So they let the monks do their own packing. The four monks put knives and axes and other weapons into the rolls of bedding. After everything was ready, they had an attendant hire a few porters, who carried the rolls of bedding into the prison. Then they bought wine and meat and plied all the wardens with wine until they were dead drunk. They then waited for dusk to fall before making their move and breaking out of the prison. Truly,

> *They bribed their way out of the jaws of death;*
> *They plotted to break through the gate of hell.*

Back to Magistrate Wang. Pleased at having uncovered the crime, he was sitting by the lamp, going over his report to his superiors, when a thought suddenly struck him: "With so many dangerous men in the prison, what's to be done if something untoward happens?" (*Heaven gave the magistrate this inspiration.*) Then and there he wrote an order for the lictors to summon all the officers back to the yamen and have them stay on guard, weapons in hand.

At about the first watch of the night, the monks in prison took out their knives and axes and, with a cry, cut down the wardens, opened the prison gate, set free all the felons, and stormed out of the prison, shouting, "Those who have suffered from injustice, now is the time to avenge yourselves! We only want to kill the county magistrate. We do no harm to the people. Those who yield to us will live! Those who block our way will die!" Their cries shook heaven and earth.

The officers on guard at the yamen quickly arrived. As they fought the monks at the prison gate, Magistrate Wang, having heard the news, immediately called a court session to order. Upon hearing about a prison-breaking operation, local residents also came with spears and knives to help the officers.

However hard they fought, the monks had only short knives and axes at their disposal. The officers, on the other hand, were equipped with long spears and lances. Suffering heavy casualties, the monks were not able to gain the upper hand. Knowing that they were fighting a losing battle, the abbot ordered everyone to stop and withdraw into the prison. After hiding the weapons, he claimed, "Only some ten people rebelled. They have all been killed. The rest of us have no intention of rebelling. Please take us to the yamen and allow us to explain." (*Buddha Manifest is as crafty as can be.*)

Knowing that the situation was now under control, Magistrate Wang told the clerks of the bureau of justice to lead officers to the prison for a search of weapons. When they brought all the weapons to the courtroom and displayed them, an incensed Magistrate Wang announced, "This gang of criminals committed monstrous crimes and resorted to rebellion when found out. If I hadn't taken precautionary measures, not only would I have been killed, but the people of the whole city would have suffered. They must be executed to serve as a warning!" He called the officers to him and, handing them the monks' weapons, gave these instructions: "Although those evil monks failed in this attempt, they will be up to mischief again in the future. It'll be hard to stay ahead of them. Now that they are guilty of prison-breaking, keep a few of them for questioning tomorrow and behead the rest of them. I'll wait for your report."

Thus instructed, the officers stormed into the prison, torches in hand. Seeing that things had taken an ugly turn, the abbot cried, "We were not part of the rebellion!" Before the words were quite out of his mouth, his head rolled to the ground. In an instant, more than a hundred monks were killed, their heads rolling on the ground like so many watermelons. Verily,

> Good and evil will get their retributions;
> You just have to wait for the right timing.

The next day, Magistrate Wang summoned the remaining monks for interrogation and asked how they had managed to hide so many weapons in the prison cells. They confessed that they had bribed Ling Zhi and the other wardens into letting a few of them return to the monastery and smuggle weapons into the prison. Having established the facts, the magistrate sent them back to prison. He then sent for Ling Zhi and the other wardens, but was told that they had all been killed in the commotion. Before the night was out, he wrote a report to his superiors for permission to burn down Precious Lotus Monastery. The report said,

> This court finds Abbot Buddha Manifest and the other monks guilty of insidious crimes. Wallowing in a sea of lust, they set traps to rape innocent women who prayed for fertility. They crawled through tunnels to force the pious women into adultery. Posing as Bodhisattvas descending from heaven and as arhats appearing to them in their dreams, the monks violated these women in the most abominable ways. Once

defiled, white silk can hardly ever be washed clean. Suffering humiliation in the dark night, they dared not speak a word. By my instructions, Li Wan'er and Zhang Meijie smeared their heads with red and black ink. Red symbolizes the abbot's lechery; black symbolizes the monks' hearts that are dyed as black as coal. Brought up in the halls of a Buddhist monastery, they suffered consequences of their own making. Fallen into debauchery, they harbored thoughts that can hardly be made public. Hiding knives and axes in their rolls of bedding, they who had renounced the world broke the law. Wielding weapons, they who had taken oaths of compassion resorted to violence. In the depths of the night, those protectors of the Buddhist doctrine forced open the prison gate. After the striking of the bells had subsided, those heavenly guardians fought their way out of prison. The fish slipped out of the net but remained defiant. The tigers broke out of the cage and preyed on men. For their defilement of innocent women, they will not be forgiven, even in death. For their killing of wardens and wounding of militiamen, they cannot be absolved of their crimes. Since prison-breaking and rape constitute serious offenses, execution by beheading befits the crimes. Abbot Buddha Manifest, being the ringleader, deserved a violent death. Precious Lotus Monastery, being a haven of evildoers, deserves to be burned down. Elimination of those criminals will ensure that Buddha's name is not sullied.

This report soon circulated among the populace of the city. Everyone applauded. Boys and girls born of women impregnated by the monks were disowned by their fathers. The older children were expelled and the newborns were drowned. Many of the women hanged themselves in shame. The morals of the local populace began to gain the right path. When word spread to other prefectures and provinces, orders were issued forbidding women to offer incense at monasteries. This explains why higher-up authorities still often issue similar bans today.

Magistrate Wang gained fame as a result and was promoted to be an imperial inspector. There is a poem in testimony:

> *Do not seek to have children by unnatural means.*
> *Let alone through adultery in a monastery.*
> *Have no more dreams of illicit unions;*
> *Clear and muddy rivers are not to be mingled.*

40

The God of Madang Conjures Wind to Blow Wang Bo to Prince Teng's Pavilion

A hill with hidden treasures acquires beauty;
Sand containing gold glitters in radiance.
A person endowed with talent
Stands out from others in speech and manners.

The above quatrain makes the point that since time immemorial, scholars who hide their aspirations and talent and bide their time have been compared to precious gold and jade buried in soil. After being unearthed, they will need to be carved and chiseled by skilled craftsmen into fine objects of art. Hence, scholar is not a word to be lightly thrown about to call just anyone. A scholar should be one with enough inward grace to match the beauty of the mountains and rivers under the sun. The speech of one with talent and learning marks him out from others. Hence, "scholar" is no ordinary word.

Storyteller, why all this palaver about talent and scholarship? Because I'm going to tell a story about a gust of wind that blew Wang Bo [648–75] to Prince Teng's Pavilion.

Our story takes place during the reign of Emperor Gaozong of the Tang dynasty. There lived in Longmen, Jinzhou [in Shanxi], a scholar named Wang Bo, courtesy name Zi'an. With his abundant talent, he was well versed in the nine classics and books of poetry since early childhood. At age thirteen, he took to traveling with his maternal uncle on the rivers and lakes. One day, en route from Jinling to Jiujiang, Wang Bo passed Mount Madang at the most inaccessible spot in Jiujiang. How do we know it was inaccessible? There is in testimony a quatrain titled "On Madang" by Lu Luwang:[1]

No mountain is more perilous than Taihang;
No water is more dangerous than Lüliang.

When you put the two together,
They add up to Mount Madang.

When Wang Bo's boat reached Madang, a sudden wind churned the waves. As the roaring waves leaped to the overcast sky and the boat rocked to and fro on the point of capsizing, everyone in the boat fearfully prayed to the river god for protection. Wang Bo was the only one who did not exhibit the slightest sign of fear. Sitting bolt upright, he continued to read his book aloud. In amazement, the boatman asked, "Every one of us in the boat is on the brink of death. Why are you alone so fearless?"

Cheerfully Wang Bo said, "How long I'm going to live is decided by heaven, not by the god of dragons."

Appalled, the boatman exclaimed, "How can you say such a thing!"

Wang Bo said, "Let me save my fellow travelers' lives." So saying, he asked for a piece of paper and a brush-pen, and wrote a poem. As soon as he tossed the paper into the water, the clouds dispersed, the fog lifted, and the wind and the waves died down. The poem said,

> *This sage of Tang is no mad man of Chu;[2]*
> *Nor are these waters the river of Miluo.*
> *In life I rely on my moral strength;*
> *Today I sit unruffled amid the wind and waves.*

Everyone on the boat congratulated him, saying, "You have such rare talent that you moved the river god. We survived thanks to you. Otherwise we would all have drowned."

Wang Bo rejoined, "Life and death are determined by heaven. There's no getting away from this fact."

Everyone was deeply impressed. A moment later, the boat moored by the shore. They saw that they were at Mount Madang. Everyone went ashore. Wang Bo also went ashore and strolled about by himself. He saw that by the roadside stood an old temple embowered in the verdant foliage of the pines and junipers. He went up for a look. Over the gate hung a vermilion board bearing in gilded characters the inscription "Palace of the Middle Source Built by Imperial Decree." Forthwith Wang Bo took out a brush and wrote a poem on the wall:

> *A lonely boat is moored at Mount Madang;*
> *Reed catkins flow down the stream along the bank.*
> *Suddenly I see a red gate standing ajar,*
> *Serene under shrouds of auspicious air.*

The poem finished, he went into the temple and looked around. It was indeed a splendid temple. How do we know this? There is a poem in testimony:

> *The green tiles rise unto the clouds;*
> *The vermilion gate opens unto the sun.*

A block of gold serves as the beam;
A thousand pieces of jade pave the roads.
The emperor penned the inscription;
Celebrities wrote on the tablets.
Blessed are the people and the empire,
With favorable weather for the crops.

Wang Bo went before the statue of the god, offered incense, and said prayers. After spending much time admiring the scenery of the river, he was about to return to the boat when he caught sight of an old man sitting on a rock by the water's edge. With green eyes, long eyebrows, flowing hair and beard, a fair complexion, and a refined air, he had the look of an immortal. Marveling at his appearance, Wang Bo straightened his clothes, stepped forward, and bowed to the old man.

"Might you be Wang Bo?" asked the old man.

Taken aback, Wang Bo said, "I've never seen you before, sir, and we can't be related. How do you know my name?"

"I've always known it!"

Realizing that he was not looking at a mortal being, Wang Bo went to stand by the rock, his hands joined across his chest in a gesture of respect. The old man asked him to sit down by his side. Wang Bo declined the offer, but in the end he sat down at the old man's insistence.

The old man said, "I understand that you wrote a poem in the boat. It was quite impressive. With your talent, why don't you go for worldly success? Why would you settle for a life of poverty and such wretched travel conditions?"

"I'm too impoverished and short of travel money to make my mark in the world. Being in such dire straits, I have no chance at worldly success."

"Mr. Yan, military governor of Hongdu [present-day Nanchang, Jiangxi], wishes to offer an ode to Prince Teng's Pavilion on the occasion of the Double-Ninth Festival, which is tomorrow. With your outstanding talent, why don't you go to him and present him with your writing? You may be paid several thousand taels of silver, and you may even acquire eternal fame."

"How far is it from here to Hongdu?"

"More than seven hundred li by river."

"It's too late now. How will I be able to make it overnight?"

"If you board a boat, I'll whip up a wind to fill the sail, to make sure that you arrive there tomorrow morning."

"May I make so bold as to ask if you are an immortal or a god?"

"I am the god of water of the middle source. The temple atop the mountain is dedicated to me."

Startled, Wang Bo bowed again and said, "This poor young student and humble mortal has given you offense. Please forgive me!"

"What kind of talk is this! If you receive payment for your writing after you get to Hongdu, you can share it with me."

"If I do receive payment, I wouldn't dream of keeping all of it for myself."

The old man said, laughing, "I was jesting."

In a trice, a boat appeared. The old man told Wang Bo to board it. With another bow, Wang Bo took leave of the old man and went on board. Scarcely had the ropes been loosened and the sail unfurled than an auspicious breeze arose, a halo floated about in the air, a red aura shrouded the bank, and a purple mist enveloped the pier. In awe, Wang Bo looked back toward the shore, but the old man had disappeared from view. Indeed,

> Amid the rustling sound of the wind,
> The waves rose and spouted high.
> The sail unfurled like a spreading wing;
> The boat glided like a shooting star.
> One turn of the head, and a thousand hills flashed past;
> One bat of the eye, and a hundred li went by.
> Before the roosters crowed at the crack of dawn,
> He had passed Poyang Lake in an instant.
> The night watch-drum had just been struck
> When he seemed to be approaching Hongdu.
> Indeed,
> When your time goes, ill luck follows on your heels;[3]
> When your time comes, good luck falls into your lap.[4]

Soon dawn arrived. From the stern, Wang Bo saw that, sure enough, he was in Hongdu. In happy astonishment, he told the boatmen, "Wait for me here." He hitched up his robe, went ashore, and went into the city at an unhurried pace. It was indeed a beautiful city, as attested by the following poem:

> Hongdu is a city most glamorous;
> Its households numbered in the tens of thousands.
> With green water, blue hills, and flowers galore,
> Its walls and towers lie shrouded in mist.

That day was precisely the ninth day of the ninth month. Upon arrival at the military governor's residence, Wang Bo saw that Governor Yan was indeed holding a feast in the main hall in honor of all the well-known scholars and officials in the lower reaches of the Yangzi River. The prefect officiated at the event and invited all to their seats around the table, which was laden with wine, fruit, and fine food. The guests sat down in the order of their status. The one sitting opposite Governor Yan was the new Academician Yuwen Jun of Fengzhou. At the table, there were also officials about to assume their offices and a few *jinshi* such as Liu Xiangdao and Zhang Yuxi.[5] All the hundred or so guests were distinguished scholars gifted in literary composition. As young as he was, Wang Bo sat at the end of the table.

A short while later, Governor Yan stood up and addressed the assembly of scholars in these words: "This pavilion built by a member of the royal family commands the best scenic view in Hongdu. I humbly invited all of you gentlemen here in order to solicit a piece of writing to be dedicated to this, Prince Teng's Pavilion. The essay chosen will be carved into a stone tablet for the benefit of generations to come, so as to preserve the glory of the name of this blessed place. Please do not turn down this request of mine!"

By his order, red-robed clerks brought out a brush-pen, an ink slab, and a piece of stationery paper. None of the famous scholars present dared take on the challenge. One yielded to another and so the writing implements passed from the head of the table all the way down to Wang Bo. Without any demurral, Wang Bo readily accepted them.

Turning up their noses at this youth, whom none of them had ever seen before, the scholars threw glances at one another in displeasure and whispered in one another's ears, "Whose son is that lad? What temerity!"

Commander Yan was also disappointed upon seeing Wang Bo accept the writing implements. He rose and went to a small room to relieve himself. Without saying anything out loud, he thought, "My son-in-law, Wu Zizhang, a native of Changsha, has peerless talent. I invited all these scholars because if they demurred, I could have my son-in-law write this piece, to bring honor to the family. Now here comes along this young lad with the audacity to insult all the famous scholars present. He doesn't even have a modicum of courtesy!" He told the clerks to watch what the young man wrote and come back to report to him.

A good while later, one clerk came and recited the first line the young man had written:

> *Nanchang of old, or Hongdu of today.*

Governor Yan said, "This is so mundane. Who couldn't come up with such a line!" Another clerk came in to recite:

> *Lies under the southern stars of Yi and Zhen[6]*
> *And adjoins the mountains of Heng and Lu.[7]*

Governor Yan said, "This is cut-and-dried stuff."
Another clerk came in and reported these lines:

> *It is girdled by three rivers and five lakes;*
> *It commands Chu and leads to Ouyue.[8]*

Governor Yan fell silent.
Another clerk came in and intoned:

> *Its many treasures are heaven's endowments:*
> *The aura of divine swords goes to stars Dou and Niu.[9]*
> *Its wealth of human talents are the earth's blessings:*
> *Chen Fan's respect for Scholar Xu is a case in point.[10]*

Governor Yan said, "His idea is similar to mine."

Another clerk came in with these lines:

> *Grand cities lie shrouded in mist;*
> *Great men race past like shooting stars.*
> *It stands where the central plains meet the southern regions;*
> *The host and guests are the elite of the southeast.*

In a flutter of excitement, Governor Yan thought, "This lad does have admirable talent."

Subsequent lines reported by clerks hurrying in and out of the room also impressed Governor Yan. Then another clerk chanted,

> *Sunset clouds fly with a lonely wild duck;*
> *Autumn water and the sky merge in one color.*

Involuntarily slapping the table, Governor Yan exclaimed, "This lad gets divine help in his writing. He is a genius!" He did what he was there to do and returned to the banquet table, where the guests had all turned pale.

Looking Wang Bo in the eye, Governor Yan said, "Your writing shows extraordinary talent."

As the governor invited him to take a seat of honor, Wang Bo said in demurral, "I'd better first finish the piece and ask for your comments and guidance." Soon his essay was completed. He presented it to Governor Yan, to the latter's great delight. The governor had an attendant pass the writing around the table. The scholars were so mortified that their faces all turned ashen. In their consternation, they dared not make even one comment.

The entire essay was later printed and is still on everyone's lips to this day.

Governor Yan took Wang Bo's hand and made the young man sit down by his side, saying, "This pavilion will enjoy eternal fame. Your essay will make this gathering known to generation after generation. All credit for the future renown of Hongdu's scenery goes to you. I will reward you handsomely." (*The old ways are so commendable.*)

While they were talking, a man suddenly stood up, left his seat, and said at the top of his voice, "This young boy is passing off as his own what was written by a now-deceased scholar. He is deceiving you all! This is plagiarism. And he is brimming with smugness, too!"

Wang Bo was flabbergasted. The governor raised his eyes and saw that it was his son-in-law, Wu Zizhang.

"This is an old piece of writing, long in my collection of books," said Zizhang.

"How do we know that for a fact?" asked Governor Yan.

"If you don't believe me, let me try reciting it from memory." There and then, Zizhang recited in the presence of all the guests the entire essay from beginning to end without making even one mistake. When he finished, all the guests turned pale. Governor Yan also grew apprehensive.

In this moment of suspense, Wang Bo said, quite unruffled, "Your memory is not any less remarkable than that of Yang Xiu, Cao Zhi, Mi Heng, and Zhang Song.[11]"

"It's an old essay. I've always been able to recite it."

Wang Bo continued, "If you say it's an old essay by a now-departed scholar, is there a poem attached to the end of it?"

"No," replied Zizhang.

Wang Bo rose, left his seat, and asked the scholars, "Is this essay really an old one or is it a new one? If old, does anyone remember the eight-line poem attached to the end of the essay?"

He asked the question time and again, but no one responded. Thereupon Wang Bo wrote the following poem on paper as fast as his brush could go:

> Prince Teng's Pavilion overlooks the river's islets;
> Guests depart amidst tinkling bells as song and dance stop.
> The morning South Beach clouds fly onto the painted beams;
> The dusk West Hill rain sprinkles through the beaded curtains.
> With lazy clouds in deep pools, the days pass idly by;
> As seasons change and stars shift, the years go quickly past.
> The prince of the pavilion—where is he now?
> The river beyond the railing—lonely it flows on.

Showing the poem to Governor Yan and the scholars as well as Wu Zizhang, Wang Bo asked, "Is this new or old?" After reading it, a shamefaced Zizhang sheepishly returned to his own seat.

The guests rose and said to Governor Yan, "Young Mr. Wang's writing and your son-in-law's memory are both unrivaled. What a match of talents!"

The governor said, "What you said is very true."

As Wu Zizhang and Wang Bo toasted each other in mutual admiration, everyone else around the table rejoiced. The party did not break up until late in the evening. After the guests departed, Governor Yan kept Wang Bo alone for a few more cups of wine.

The next day, Wang Bo took leave of his host. Governor Yan rewarded him with five hundred bolts of fine silk and some gold and silver wine utensils, altogether worth a thousand taels of silver. Bowing gratefully, Wang Bo took his leave and departed. Governor Yan had his attendants escort him down into the boat. The boatmen untied the ropes and got the boat underway. Wang Bo's ears came to be filled with the sound of water rushing by as rapidly as wind-driven rain.

The next morning, the boat was back at the foot of Mount Madang. The boat moored and Wang Bo went ashore. He carried the gifts from Governor Yan into the temple, laid them in front of the statue of the water god, and bowed in gratitude. When he rose, he noticed that the poem he had written on the wall looked as if the ink was still fresh, whereupon he added another poem to it:

> An all-night blissful wind sent the boat through the air;
> In a trice, it sailed all the way upstream.
> Thankful for the divine act, I hold on to my wish:
> To share your peace and quiet in my next life to come.

After writing the poem, Wang Bo went out the temple gate to buy sacrificial animals and wine to offer to the temple, but the boat had disappeared, as had the boatmen. When he was debating with himself as to what to do, suddenly an auspicious cloud and mist enveloped the temple. As a fragrant wind sprang up, he saw sitting on a rock an old man who was none other than the god of water he had seen two days earlier. Wang Bo went forward, bowed twice, and said gratefully, "You were so kind as to have helped me with a favorable wind that got me to Hongdu, where I received lavish gifts. I was about to buy sacrificial animals and wine to offer to you, honorable god, as a token of my gratitude."

The old man lowered his head and laughed. "What are sacrificial animals?" he asked. "I understand that they are either goat or oxen. On occasions that call for ceremonies, members of the nobility do not slaughter oxen without good reason, and highly placed officials do not slaughter goat without good reason. How can I accept such lavish offerings from you just for a little gust of wind that filled the sail of your boat? In my realm of water, ensuring the sanctity of life is a major virtue. I wouldn't take offerings that involve killing of life. And I don't want to put you to expense. I am delighted that you wrote about sharing my peace and quiet. But your span of life in this mortal world is not yet over. I will try to see you again in a few years."

Wang Bo kowtowed and said thankfully, "I will obey your order. But may I be told how much longer I can live?"

"The king of the netherworld is the one who determines the length of everyone's span of life. I dare not incur misfortune by divulging such a divine secret. But I can't do any harm by telling your fortune. From your appearance, I can see that you have a strong mind but weak bones. You carry an aura of refinement, but your constitution is feeble. In addition, your cranium is flat and your eyes are defected. For all your extraordinary talent, you will not attain high status. In fact, wealth and rank are matters predestined by heaven. How much one possesses, and whether one is a commoner or a duke or a minister, is determined by divine will. In the olden days, even the great saint Confucius, who is a model for kings and emperors, was not spared the misery of famine when he was in the states of Chen and Cai. These are cases of 'plants that flower but do not bear fruit.' You must make every effort to do good works. Heaven will bless you. Wealth or poverty and a life span long or short should not be matters of concern. Bear this in mind!" Having said this, he took leave of Wang Bo, but, after taking a few steps, he turned back and said, "I do have a favor to ask of you. When you pass by the temple of Changlu, remember to buy some paper coins and burn them for me."

"Why?"

"I owe the god of Changlu a small debt. Please pay it for me."

"It's not that I begrudge the money, but I just saw that the money donated to your temple is piled up as high as a hill. Why don't you use that to pay off your debt?"

"You have no idea!" said the old man. "The money there came from greedy people who ask for too much. They bring harm to others out of self-interest. They profit at the expense of other people and exploit others in the accumulation of their own wealth. When they happen to pass by my temple, they ask for undeserved blessings. Before the gods punish them, they make offerings to the gods because they feel uneasy in their own hearts. Their money is useless to me because it's all bribery. I wouldn't even dream of using it." (*A god who does not take bribes will not bless those who offer them. The greedy, be warned!*)

Again Wang Bo bowed in acknowledgment of the request, whereupon the old man vanished with a refreshing breeze.

Wang Bo was awestruck. He took along the lavish gifts he had received, left Mount Madang, and went to Changlu by boat. His mind occupied by the old man's comments that his flat cranium and the defects in his eyes meant that he was not destined for high status, he was in such low spirits that, upon reaching Changlu, he forgot about the divine old man's request. All of a sudden, a chilly wind sprang up. White-capped waves surged and flocks of noisy crows kept circling the boat. With the crows perching on the masts, the scull, and the stem, the boat could not move, to the consternation of everyone on the boat, including Wang Bo.

"Where are we?" asked Wang Bo of the boatmen.

A boatman replied, "We're in Changlu."

Only then did Wang Bo recall the river god's request. Immediately he burned incense and prayed silently to the river god, pledging to go ashore after the wind subsided to buy paper coins and pay the debt. After he finished saying the prayer, the crows flew away before the incense had even burned out, the wind died down, and the waves subsided, to the delight of everyone in the boat.

The next day, when the boat moored at the shore, Wang Bo bought one hundred thousand pieces of paper coins, returned to the boat, went back to the place where the wind had sprung up the previous night, and burned the paper coins before resuming his journey. Later, Mr. Luo Yin, visiting the place, wrote this eight-line poem:

> *The river god pitied the talented youth;*
> *His divine power quickened the young man's journey.*
> *In a fresh breeze, with the speed of thunder,*

The tablet was filled with beautiful lines.
The essay was to enjoy eternal fame;
His renown shook the two capitals.
Had it not been for the divine blessings,
Hongdu's scenery would not have been known far and wide.

Later, Wang Bo's father was assigned to office in a remote coastal area. Wang Bo went on horseback to see him and stopped at a government guesthouse for a little rest. He was about to ask a clerk something when he heard a man crying in the main hall, "Mr. Wang! I haven't seen you in a long time! What brought you here?"

Wang Bo gave a start. The man did look familiar to him. He must have seen the man somewhere but had forgotten his name. The man continued, "Have you forgotten, Mr. Wang? We met at Hongdu. I am Academician Yuwen Jun."

Overjoyed, Wang Bo adjusted his clothes and bowed. The academician asked Wang Bo to sit with him and ordered tea as they began to chat. After they finished the tea, Academician Yuwen said, "How delightful that gathering in Hongdu, and how sad this journey to the coast!"

"What brought you here, sir?"

The academician replied, "I had been an instructor before I was promoted to be a remonstrance official in the vice director's bureau of the department of state affairs. When the emperor of our Tang dynasty planned to send an expeditionary army to Korea, I remonstrated against the idea and ran afoul of the emperor, who then assigned me to an island in the sea. I've been traveling on this thousand-li journey all by my forlorn self. I never expected to be able to meet an acquaintance in this guesthouse. I've written a poem, 'On Exile.' Let me chant it for you." The poem said,

An exile a thousand li from home,
On the vast sea I float on a lonely boat.
The lakes abound in crops of lotus roots;
The island grows grains only as a supplement.
In hopes of returning to the mainland,
I collect prescriptions to cure miasma.
I see that those who hold their tongues
Manage to stay by the emperor's side.

Wang Bo said, "Providing frank admonitions against errors is the duty of everyone who serves the emperor. You may be an exile, but your repute as a loyal, outspoken official will live on to the end of time." Thereupon he intoned a poem by way of a response:

An official who cares only about his pocket
Does not deserve his title.
Frankness is to the empire's benefit;

To be punished for it is not shameful.
With each step of the journey to the sea,
The hair and the beard gain more frost.
A historian putting his brush to paper
Will also shed many a bitter tear.

That night, the two of them intoned poems until midnight and both stayed at the guesthouse. The next day, the academician set out wine for Wang Bo. On the third day, the academician asked Wang Bo to set out on their journeys together. As it suddenly began to rain, they had to remain in the guesthouse for shelter. They spent their days talking without ever getting tired. The sky did not clear until the fifth day. They then boarded a seagoing boat together and kept each other company when eating and sleeping.

When they were in the middle of the sea several days after the boat had set sail, suddenly a gust of howling wind whipped up tall waves. Like a leaf floating on the water, the boat looked like it was about to capsize. The boatmen were petrified with terror. Fear also came upon Academician Yuwen Jun. He said in lament, "On top of being exiled to a remote island in the sea, I also have to be caught in such a storm. Such is my fate!"

With unruffled composure, Wang Bo related how he had been caught in a storm at Mount Madang and what the river god had said to him both times they met, saying that, indeed, just as life and death were a matter of fate, wealth and rank were determined by the will of heaven, and that the storm should not be anything to worry about. After he finished talking, the waves went down and the wind subsided, to the joy of everyone in the boat.

All of a sudden, celestial music wafted within hearing. An auspicious five-colored cloud descended from heaven and floated on the surface of the water. As it approached Wang Bo in the boat, everyone was awestruck. In the cloud were seen banners and canopies, and crimson staffs and flags. There were two rows of fairies wearing brocade clothes, embroidered gowns, flowered hats, and vermilion robes. Several tens of fairy maidens stood in front in their finery, complete with jade pendants. A blue-robed girl at the front with a green tablet in her hand announced, addressing Wang Bo, "We are here by order of the goddess to summon you."

In amazement, Wang Bo asked, "Which goddess?"

"Wu Cailuan, noble jade maiden, goddess of water.[12] She lives amidst the verdant splendor of Penglai Island. The water god at Mount Madang is also there. It is on his recommendation of your unparalleled literary talent that we are here to invite you to the abode of the water goddess on Penglai, so that you can write on the wonderful scenery of Penglai. Please go quickly. The goddess's order must be obeyed."

"Humans and gods take different roads. How can I be summoned to see a goddess? I understand that life and death are determined by heaven, and the length of the span of life is determined by the king of the netherworld. How can a jade maiden summon me to compose a piece of writing? I'm not going."

The girl said, "If you don't go, the water god of the middle source will come for you."

Before she had quite finished, a dark cloud was seen coming from the southeast. When it reached the boat, there descended from it onto the surface of the water a divine being wearing a yellow turban and an embroidered battle robe and carrying a demon-subduing seven-star sword in his arm. He shouted at the top of his voice, "Wang Bo! I'm here by order of the fairy maiden of Penglai to take you there to write an essay. Why do you refuse to go? The water god of the middle source is also at Penglai for a gathering of the immortals. They've been waiting for you for a long time now. You are predestined to be an immortal. In your poem written in his temple, you promised to share his peace and quiet. How can you forget?"

Wang Bo thought, "The water god of the middle source of Mount Madang did say that he would meet me in the future on an island in the sea. Could this have been preordained?" Merrily he said, "I will be glad to go."

The divine being thereupon called over an attendant, who brought a horse to the boat. In his delight, Wang Bo thought that he was on flat land rather than a deep sea. He turned, bade farewell to the academician and everyone else in the boat, hitched up his robe, stepped onto the surface of the water, and climbed onto the saddle. Behold! dark clouds and a black fog blocked out the sky. Agape with astonishment, everyone in the boat, including Academician Yuwen Jun, looked for Wang Bo but failed to see him. In an instant, the fog lifted, the clouds dispersed, the wind abated, and the waves died down. Everyone else in the boat emerged unscathed. Only Wang Bo was gone, as an immortal. Talented poets have always been divine;

> The wind that blew him to Nanchang was no accident.
> Having composed the essay to Prince Teng's Pavilion,
> He followed fairies to be with the water god.

Notes

Foreword

1. Patrick Hanan, *The Chinese Vernacular Story* (Cambridge, MA: Harvard University Press, 1981), 121–22, speculates that twenty-two of the forty stories here may have been written by a single collaborator, a man known only as Langxian 浪仙, whose vision of life and writing was considerably bleaker than Feng's. Katherine Carlitz explores fiction from another collection attributed to this writer in her "Style and Suffering in Two Stories by 'Langxian,'" in *Culture and State in Chinese History: Conventions, Accommodations, and Critiques*, ed. Theodore Huters, R. Bin Wong, and Pauline Yu (Stanford: Stanford University Press, 1997), 207–35. For a general introduction to these collections, see Shuhui Yang, *Appropriation and Representation: Feng Menglong and the Chinese Vernacular Story* (Ann Arbor: Center for Chinese Studies, University of Michigan, 1998).

2. Tan Zhengbi 譚正璧, comp., *Sanyan Liangpai ziliao* 三言兩拍資料 (Materials on the "Three Words" and "Two Slaps" Stories), 2 vols. (Shanghai: Shanghai guji, 1980); Sun Kaidi 孫楷第, comp., *Xiaoshuo pangzheng* 小説旁證 (Marginal Comments on Fiction) (Beijing: Renmin wenxue, 2000). See also Patrick Hanan, *The Chinese Short Story* (Cambridge, MA: Harvard University Press, 1973).

3. About story twenty-seven, see Ann Waltner, "Writing Her Way Out of Trouble: Li Yuying in History and Fiction," in *Writing Women in Late Imperial China*, ed. Ellen Widmer and Kang-I Sun Chang (Stanford: Stanford University Press, 1997), 221–41.

4. F. W. Mote, *Imperial China 900–1800* (Cambridge: Harvard University Press, 1999),

851. See also chapter 29, "The Lively Society of the Late Ming," 743–75.

5. Mote traces the political decline of the late Ming in *Imperial China*, chapter 30, "The Course of Ming Failure," 776–810.

6. See note 2 above.

7. Patrick Hanan, trans., *Falling in Love: Stories from Ming China* (Honolulu: University of Hawai'i Press, 2006), xii.

Introduction

1. For a detailed discussion of the *Sanyan* and its influence on Chinese fiction, as well as a bibliography of relevant works, see Feng Menglong, *Stories Old and New: A Ming Dynasty Collection*, trans. Shuhui Yang and Yunqin Yang (Seattle: University of Washington Press, 2000), xv–xxvi, 778–94.

2. Lu Shulun, "Feng Menglong," in his *Feng Menglong sanlun* (Shanghai: Shanghai guji, 1993), 7.

3. Pi-ching Hsu, "Celebrating the Emotional Self" (PhDdiss., University of Minnesota, 1994), 48.

4. Quoted in Lu Shulun, "Feng Menglong," 92.

5. The facsimile edition of *The Complete works of Feng Menglong* (Feng Menglong quanji), published by Shanghai Guji Chubanshe in 1993, contains forty-three volumes that, when stacked together, are more than six feet high.

6. Patrick Hanan, *The Chinese Vernacular Story* (Cambridge: Harvard University Press, 1981), 80–81.

7. Hanan, *Chinese Vernacular Story*, 80–81.

8. The moralistic and didactic tone of the three *Sanyan* titles (*Illustrious Words to Instruct the World, Comprehensive Words to Caution the World,* and *Constant Words to Awaken the World*) can probably also be understood in the same light.

9. Y.W. Ma, "Feng Menglong," in William Nienhauser, ed., *The Indiana Companion to Traditional Chinese Literature* (Bloomington: Indiana University Press, 1986), 381.

10. Hanan, *Chinese Vernacular Story*, 104; and Patrick Hanan, *The Chinese Short Story: Studies in Dating, Authorship, and Composition* (Cambridge: Harvard University Press, 1973), 76–86.

11. In his "Preface to *Art Song Prosody*" (Qulü xu), Feng complains that "the most abused literary genres today are classical poetry and prose." In his preface to *Hill Songs,* he also says that "although there is an abundance of false poetry and prose, there are no false folk songs." See Guo Shaoyu, *Zhongguo lidai wenlun xuan* (Shanghai: Shanghai guji, 1979), 3:194, 231.

12. Cyril Birch, "Feng Meng-lung and the *Ku Chin Hsiao Shuo,*" in *Bulletin of the School of Oriental and African Studies* 18 (1956): 82.

13. Patrick Hanan, "The Nature of Ling Meng-ch'u's Fiction," in Andrew Plaks, ed., *Chinese Narrative: Critical and Theoretical Essays* (Princeton, N.J.: Princeton University Press, 1977), 87.

14. Hanan, "Nature of Ling Meng-ch'u's Fiction," 87.

15. David Rolston, *Traditional Chinese Fiction and Fiction Commentary* (Stanford, Calif.: Stanford University Press, 1997), 232. Rolston also says that the simulated storyteller can be seen "as a functional attempt to deal with the absence of the 'author' in early vernacular fiction."

16. The word *huaben* was adopted as the regular term for the traditional Chinese vernacular short story only in the twentieth century. On its early usage as simply "story," rather than "promptbook," see Charles Wivell, "The Term '*Hua-pen,*'" in David Buxbaum and Frederick Mote; eds., *Transition and Permanence: Chinese History and Culture* (Hong

Kong: Cathay Press, 1972), 295–306. The promptbook theory has been criticized from another angle: because professional storytellers were more likely to have relied on abstracts or notes in the classical language, the earliest extant *huaben* texts were perhaps also meant for reading, rather than reciting, as were their later imitations; see André Lévy, "*Hua-pen,*" in Nienhauser, ed., *Indiana Companion*, 443.

17. See W. L. Idema, "Storytelling and the Short Story in China," in *T'oung Pao* 59 (1973): 3, 35–39.

18. W. L. Idema, "Some Remarks and Speculations Concerning *P'ing-hua,*" reprinted in his *Chinese Vernacular Fiction: The Formative Period* (Lieden: E. J. Brill, 1974), 72.

19. See, for example, Yang Xianyi and Gladys Yang, trans., *The Courtesan's Jewel Box* (Beijing: Foreign Languages Press, 1981).

20. See Hu Wanchuan, "*Sanyan* xu ji meipi de zuozhe wenti," reprinted in his *Huaben yu caizi jiaren xiaoshuo zhi yanjiu* (Taipei: Da'an, 1994), 123–38.

21. Patrick Hanan points out in his *Chinese Vernacular Story* (1981) that twenty-two stories in *Xingshi hengyan* were probably authored by an associate of Feng Menglong's, named Langxian, including stories 6, 15, 16, 18, 20, 25, 26, 27, 28, 29, 34, 35, 36, 37 and 38 (120–39). However, in note 21 of his introduction to *Falling in Love: Stories from Ming China* (Honolulu: University of Hawai'i Press, 2006), he says that "the thesis of common authorship [of stories in *Xingshi hengyan* and *Shi diantou*] is far from proven, and I think it prudent here to consider the two sets of stories as by separate authors (xviii). Scholars generally agree that this group of stories were not authored by Feng but by a different hand. Feng, however, was still the chief editor, and must have had a voice in these stories in the collection, just as in any other preexisting stories in the *Sanyan* collections. For Feng's role as the chief editor and therefore the finalizer of *Xingshi hengyan*, see Shuhui Yang, *Appropriation and Representation: Feng Menglong and the Chinese Vernacular Story* (Ann Arbor: Center for Chinese Studies, University of Michigan, 1998), 15.

Preface

1. The Six Classics are *The Book of Songs, The Book of History, The Book of Rites, The Book of Music* (now lost), *The Book of Changes*, and *The Spring and Autumn Annals*.

2. Minister Bi is Bi Zhuo of the Eastern Jin dynasty, an excessive drinker. Chamberlain Liu may be Liu Ling, author of "Ode to Wine" and one of the Seven Sages of the Bamboo Grove of Western Jin dynasty, but Liu Ling had never attained the rank of chamberlain. Chamberlain Liu may also, in fact, be Wang Ji (589–644), chamberlain of the bureau of music during the Tang dynasty and author of "The Land of the Drunk."

3. "Broad Road" and "Drumming with an Earth Clod," originating respectively in the Spring and Autumn period and in the reign of the prehistoric sage king Yao, are both songs in praise of times of peace and prosperity.

1. Two High-Minded County Magistrates Vie to Take On an Orphan Girl as Daughter-in-Law

Story 1 has been translated as "Two Magistrates Vie to Marry an Orphaned Girl" by William Dolby in *The Perfect Lady by Mistake and Other Stories by Feng Menglong*, 114–43. London: Paul Elek, 1976.

1. In Buddhist belief, a *yaksha* is usually an evil spirit.

2. Pan An (247–300), or Pan Yue, courtesy name Anren, was a man of letters and an official in the Western Jin dynasty but is now better known as the man who personifies male attractiveness.

3. For more on Guo Wei, see story 15 in Feng Menglong, *Stories Old and New: A Ming Dynasty Collection.*.

4. For more on Qian Liu, see story 21 in Feng, *Stories Old and New*.

5. Sima Guang (1019–86) is the author of *Historical Events Retold as a Mirror for Government* (Zizhi tongjian, the first chronological general history of China from 403 B.C.E. to 959 C.E.). In his childhood, he saved a playmate

from drowning in a water vat by smashing the vat with a rock.

6. "Nine Springs" is a term for the netherworld.

7. Qu Boyu was a virtuous court minister in the state of Wei during the Spring and Autumn period.

8. The Dragon Diagram Hall (Longtu Ge) was established during the Song dynasty to house official documents and was staffed with various ranks of academicians. It was later incorporated into the Palace Library.

2. Three Devoted Brothers Win Honor by Yielding Family Property to One Another

1. Empress Wei murdered her husband, Emperor Zhongzong, in 710 and was killed in a coup later in the same year by Li Longji, who later became Emperor Xuanzong. Wu Sansi, Empress Wu Zetian's nephew, had an adulterous relationship with Empress Wei and was killed in 707 by Crown Prince Li Chongjun.

2. The poem "The Bush Cherry" in *The Book of Songs*, China's earliest poem collection (ca. 600 B.C.E.), uses the interdependence of a flower and its calyx as a metaphor for the closeness of brothers.

3. The Jie was an ancient ethnic group derived from the Xiongnu or Huns.

4. This is a reference to the fact that the kingdom of Wei, lasting through six rulers of the Cao clan (including Cao Cao who was posthumously recognized as the first emperor of the Wei), was wiped out in year 264 by Sima Yan, who founded the Jin dynasty in the following year.

5. Zeng Shen (505–435 B.C.E.), courtesy name Ziyu, a disciple of Confucius, was well known for his devotion to his parents.

6. Boyi, eldest son of the king of the state of Gu Zhu toward the end of the Shang dynasty, refused to take the throne after his father's death and, later, in protest against King Wu of Zhou for having overthrown Shang, starved himself to death.

7. "Hui" here can be and often is pronounced "Kuai" or even "Gui."

8. Liu Xiu (6 B.C.E.-57 C.E.), Emperor Guangwu of Han dynasty, wanted to marry his older sister to Song Hong, a married man, but the latter refused, saying that he could not abandon his wife whom he had married in his humble "chaff and husks" days before his rise to power.

9. One *jin* equaled 220 grams in the Eastern Han dynasty, when the story takes place, and 590 grams in the Ming dynasty, when the story was published.

10. In the Han dynasty, government officials were exempt from tax payments.

11. Shu Guang of the Western Han dynasty, after serving for five years as mentor of a son of Emperor Xuan (r. 73–48 B.C.E.), resigned from his post along with his nephew Shu Shou, the junior mentor.

12. Qi Xi, a court official of the state of Jin during the Spring and Autumn period, when submitting his resignation in the year 570 B.C.E., recommended to the king that Xie Hu, his personal enemy, replace him. After Xie Hu's death, the king asked Qi Xi to recommend another replacement, and he named his own son, Qi Wu. Hence Qi Xi's reputation for being able to shun neither his relatives nor his personal foes when making recommendations for official posts.

3. The Oil-Peddler
Wins the Queen of Flowers

This story has been translated as "The Oil Peddler Courts the Courtesan" by Lorraine Lieu and the editors, in *Traditional Chinese Stories: Themes and Variations,* ed. Y. W. Ma and Joseph S. M. Lau (New York: Columbia, 1986), by Yang Xianyi and Gladys Yang as "The Oil Vendor and the Courtesan" in *Lazy Dragon: Chinese Stories from the Ming Dynasty* (Hong Kong: Joint Publishing Co., 1981), and as "The Oil Seller" by Patrick Hanan in *Falling in Love: Stories from Ming China* (Honolulu: University of Hawai'i Press, 2006).

1. Pan Yue (247–300), courtesy name Anren, popularly known as Pan An, was a man of letters in the Western Jin dynasty and reputedly very handsome.

2. Deng Tong of the Western Han dynasty was a fabulously rich court favorite with the authority to mint his own money. But later he lost favor with the new emperor and died of hunger in prison.

3. Zheng Yuanhe and Li Yaxian are characters in "The Story of Li Wa" by Bai Xingjian (775–826) of the Tang dynasty.

4. According to legend, Zhao Gou, Prince Kang, later to be Emperor Gaozong of Southern Song dynasty, crossed the Yangzi River on a horse he found in a temple to flee from Jurchen soldiers, but once he was out of danger, he saw that the horse was made of clay.

5. Jin Wuzhu or Wanyan Zongbi, was the fourth son of Emperor Jin Taizu (r. 1115–22) of the Jin (Jurchen) dynasty. The Jin was overthrown by the Mongols in 1234.

6. Xishi, also known as Xizi, was a famous beauty of the state of Yue in the late Spring and Autumn period.

7. A "girl of stone" (*shinü*) is a woman with a hypoplastic vagina.

8. Sui He and Lu Jia were political advisers of great eloquence in the Western Han dynasty.

9. Granny Wang is a fictional character in *Outlaws of the Marsh* (Shuihu zhuan) and is also featured in *The Plum in the Golden Vase* (Jin Ping Mei), both full-length novels published earlier in the Ming dynasty.

10. According to legend, Xiaoji, son of King Wuding of the Shang dynasty, died in exile, a victim of his stepmother's machinations.

11. Shensheng, son of Duke Xian of the state of Jin in the Spring and Autumn period, was driven to suicide by Liji, Duke Xian's beloved concubine, who planned to have her own son designated as heir.

12. Benzoin is a hard fragrant yellowish balsamic resin from trees native to Indonesia, Vietnam, and other southeastern Asian countries.

13. This is a famous line by Liu Yuxi (772–842), poet and philosopher of the Tang dynasty.

14. The Clear and Bright (Qingming) Festival falls in early April and is the time for people to visit the graves of their ancestors.

15. The four treasures of the scholar's study are brush-pen, ink slab, ink stick, and rice paper.

16. Guan Yu (160–220), courtesy name Yunchang, was a valiant warrior in the Three Kingdoms period and a central figure in the folk pantheon. A complete translation of this phrase should be: ". . . in the pose of Guan Yunchang when he went valiantly, armed with a sword, and practically all by himself, to the enemy camp to attend a meeting that was clearly devised as a trap to capture him." There has been a whole array of popular stage versions of this story.

4. The Old Gardener Meets Fairy Maidens

This story has been translated as "The Old Gardener" in *Lazy Dragon: Chinese Stories from the Ming Dynasty*, 183–208

1. Zhang Hua (232–300) compiled the hundred-volume *Bo wu zhi* (only ten extant), which was filled with information about rare objects and stories about the supernatural.

Yu Shinan (558–638) was an eminent scholar and calligrapher in early Tang dynasty. In preparing for a journey to be undertaken by Emperor Taizong, court officials planned to bring along some books, but the emperor said, "There's no need to bring books, since Yu Shinan, the walking library, will be going with us."

2. Xiangzi is Han Xiangzi, one of the lengendary Eight Daoist Immortals.

3. Wang Ze was a soldier who rebelled in Beizhou, present-day Qinghe County in Hebei, and, in 1047, the seventh year in the Qingli reign period under Emperor Renzong of the Song dynasty, declared himself king. The rebellion lasted only sixty-six days. For a fictional account of Wang Ze by Feng Menglong himself, see chapters 30 to 40 in his *The Quelling of Demons* (Ping yao zhuan), 1620.

4. The Jasper Pool refers to the abode of the gods in heaven.

5. Liu An (179–122 B.C.E.), Duke of Huainan of the Western Han dynasty, was a devotee of alchemy and, as legend has it, rose to heaven and became an immortal, but in fact he died by his own hand after his armed rebellion against Emperor Wudi failed.

5. The Grateful Tiger Delivers the Bride at Big Tree Slope

Also entitled "A Tiger Makes a Match" and "A Tiger Repays an Act of Kindness." Story 5 has also been translated as "On Big Tree Slope a Faithful Tiger Acts Best Man" by William Dolby in *The Perfect Lady by Mistake*, 159–83.

1. According to *History of Eastern Han* (Hou Han shu), compiled by Fan Ye (398–445), a prefect called Liu Kun was such a good and upright official that the tigers in the area under his jurisdiction voluntarily crossed over to the other side of the Yellow River to keep the area safe.

According to *The Essentials of the Five Lamps* (Wu deng hui yuan), compiled by Pu Ji (1179–1253), Abbot Shanjue of the Tang dynasty had two tigers that served him as personal attendants.

2. Bian Zhuang, a valiant man of the state of Lu in the Spring and Autumn period, had killed two tigers at once. Li Cunxiao, an adopted son of Li Keyong (856–908), Duke of Jin, was also a valiant warrior strong enough to kill a tiger.

3. According to *Anecdotes of the Western Capital* (Xijing zaji), there was a Mr. Huang who, in his youth, knew how to subdue snakes and tigers. Later in his life, he lost his art due to excessive drinking, and fell prey to a tiger.

4. Annam Protectorate of the Tang dynasty was in present-day Vietnam.

5. An Lushan (703–57), a regional commander of the Tang army, rebelled in 755 and, after a series of victories, seized Chang'an, the capital, and declared himself Emperor Xiongwu of Yan. Two years later, he was killed by his son, An Qingxu.

6. A green dragon symbolizes luck, and a white tiger, misfortune.

6. Divine Foxes Lose a Book at Small Water Bay

1. An Lushan (703–57), a regional commander of the Tang army, rebelled in 755 and,

after a series of victories, seized Chang'an, the capital, and declared himself Emperor Xiongwu of Yan. Two years later, he was killed by his son, An Qingxu.

2. Youzhou in the Tang dynasty is present-day Beijing. Jizhou is present-day Ji County.

7. Scholar Qian Is Blessed with a Wife through a Happy Mistake

Story 7 has been translated as "The Perfect Lady by Mistake" by William Dolby in *The Perfect Lady by Mistake*, 15–16.

1. Xu Qian (1270–1337), known as "Mr. White Cloud," was a scholar who declined all offers of official posts and devoted his life to research and teaching.

2. Fan Chengda (1126–1193), sobriquet "Hermit of Rocky Lake," was a famous poet and a prolific writer, and was also a vice prime minister for a time.

3. Xi Shi, also known as Xizi, was a famous beauty of the state of Yue in the late Spring and Autumn period.

4. Cui Yingying is the heroine of the play *The West Chamber* by Wang Shifu of the Yuan dynasty.

5. Pan An (247–300), or Pan Yue, courtesy name Anren, was a man of letters and an official in the Western Jin dynasty, but is now better known as the personification of male beauty.

6. Cao Zhi (192–232), courtesy name Zijian, was a poet of prodigious talent of the state of Wei in the Three Kingdoms period.

7. The character "jun" in his name (Yan Jun) means "handsome."

8. Lord Guan is Guan Yu (d. 220), a sworn brother of Liu Bei who founded the kingdom of Shu in the Three Kingdoms period. Guan Yu is, to this day, revered as a central figure in the folk pantheon and is the embodiment of fidelity to commitments.

9. Chen Ping (d. 178), a major advisor to Liu Bang, the first emperor of the Han dynasty, was a tall and handsome man. On Pan An, see note 5 above.

10. Xun Yu (163–212), director of the Imperial Secretariat, used to wear perfume that

lingered in the air. Pan An (see note 5 above) was walking down the streets of Luoyang one day when a group of women danced around him and tossed fruit at him as a way to express their admiration.

11. Fan Li was a court minister of the state of Yue in the Spring and Autumn period. He had once lived as a hermit in Wujiang County. Zhang Han was a native of Wujiang County of the Western Jin dynasty, better known as the official who resigned from his post and returned to his hometown because he longed for the delicious flavor of the perch and water plants native to that region. Lu Guimeng (d. 881), a native of Wujiang County, was a hermit who never pursued an official career.

12. In a story written in the Tang dynasty, a man named Pei Hang bought an expensive jade pestle and offered it as a betrothal gift to Yunying, the woman he loved. Later, the husband and wife became immortals. According to legend, the Old Man Under the Moon, the god of marriage, has a bag full of red strings with which he ties predestined couples together by their ankles.

13. Wedding candles are candles with dragon and phoenix designs for use in the bridal chamber.

14. The Nine-Li Hills in Tongshan County, Jiangsu, is where Xiang Yu (232–202 B.C.E.), contender with Liu Bang for the throne, was ambushed and defeated.

Kunyang Gate, in present-day Ye County, Henan, is where Wang Mang (45 B.C.E.–23 C.E.) was defeated by Liu Xiu (6 B.C.E.–57 C.E.), founder of the Eastern Han dynasty.

15. The Duke of Zhou was a great statesman who consolidated the newly established Western Zhou dynasty and formulated the Rites, especially the wedding rituals.

16. Liuxia Hui, a court official of the state of Lu in the Spring and Autumn period, is known for his stoic indifference to sexual temptation. He once used his own body warmth to save a homeless woman from being frozen to death, but did not have relations with her.

17. The notorious prime minister Zhao Gao of the Qin dynasty demanded absolute

obedience by pointing at a deer and calling it a horse and killing everyone who disagreed.

18. Legend has it that Liu Yi, a scholar in the Tang dynasty, delivered a message to the dragon king of Lake Dongting from his third daughter, who, abused by her husband, the dragon of Jing River, asked for help from her father, the dragon king. The dragon king's brother killed the girl's husband, rescued her, and married her to Liu Yi.

19. According to the Ming dynasty novel *Romance of the Three Kingdoms*, after Guan Yu (160–220) surrendered to Cao Cao, with the two wives of his lord and sworn brother Liu Bei in his care, Cao Cao assigned Guan Yu and the two women to a single chamber in an attempt to disrupt the proprieties between lord and subject. However, Guan Yu never entered the chamber. Holding a candle, he remained standing outside the door throughout the night until dawn without showing the slightest trace of fatigue.

8. Prefect Qiao Rearranges Matches in an Arbitrary Decision

This story has been translated by Patrick Hanan as "Marriage Destinies Rearranged" in *Falling in Love: Stories from Ming China* (Honolulu: University of Hawai'i Press, 2006).

1. Zhao Feiyan (d. 1 B.C.E.) was a court lady in the service of Emperor Cheng (r. 32–7 B.C.E.) of the Han dynasty and was later made empress.

2. Xishi, also known as Xizi, was a famous beauty of the state of Yue in the late Spring and Autumn period.

3. According to the Ming dynasty novel *The Romance of the Three Kingdoms*, Zhou Yu (175–210), military adviser to Sun Quan of Wu, devised a plan to capture Liu Bei, Sun's rival, by offering him Sun's sister as wife so as to lure him to the Wu region to pick up the bride. But Liu Bei's military adviser, the great strategist Zhuge Liang, saw through the plot and beat Zhou Yu at his own game by having Liu Bei successfully take away the bride and return to his own territory safe and sound.

Zhou Yu led his troops in a chase, but was defeated by Liu Bei's general, Zhang Fei. This story is invariably cited in reference to situations whereby one ends up suffering a double loss through actions intended to produce a gain.

4. The Dragon Diagram Academy was established between 1008 and 1016 to house official documents. The title Dragon Diagram derives from an ancient legend about a dragon emerging from a river with markings on its back—markings that inspired the eight trigrams that became the basis of the *Book of Changes*.

9. Chen Duoshou and His Wife Bound in Life and in Death

This story has been translated as "The Couple Bound in Life and Death" by Jeanne Kelley, in *Themes and Variations*.

1. Sun Bin, a descendant of Sun Wu of *Sun Tzu's Art of War* fame, was a military strategist of the Warring States period (475–221 B.C.E.) and author of *Sun Bin on the Art of War*. Pang Juan was a jealous opponent of his.

2. Liu Bang (256–195 B.C.E.) was founder of the Western Han dynasty. Xiang Yu (232–202 B.C.E.), Liu Bang's rival, killed himself by the Wu River in present-day Anhui.

3. The demarcation line in the middle of the Chinese chessboard is called "the Chu-Han Boundary." Hence the reference to pawns crossing the river. Lady Yu, Xiang Yu's favorite concubine, sang and danced for him at Gaixia on the eve of the final battle between Xiang Yu, King of Chu, and Liu Bang, King of Han.

4. The Double Ninth Festival falls on the ninth day of the ninth lunar month. On this day, the Chinese tradition is to drink dogwood or chrysanthemum wine, climb up mountains, and deck the hair with dogwood sprays.

5. A "noodle-soup" feast is a celebration on the third day after a baby's birth, with noodles in soup as a token of longevity.

6. The Jade Emperor is the supreme deity in popular belief.

7. The kitchen god in Chinese folk mythology has a dark face because he oversees the smoky cooking stove.

8. According to the play *Thornwood Hairpins* (Jingchai ji) by Ke Danqiu of the Yuan dynasty, a girl called Qian Yulian in the Song dynasty entered into a betrothal with Wang Shipeng against the wishes of her stepmother. Later, when Wang Shipeng was demoted and sent away, her stepmother forced her to marry her rich nephew, Sun Ruquan, whereupon Qian Yulian tied a rock to herself and jumped into the Ou River. She was rescued and later married Wang Shipeng.

10. *The Liu Brothers in Brotherhood and in Marriage*

1. King Yao (pre-Xia era) is revered as a sage king. King Jie, the last ruler of the Xia dynasty, is traditionally considered a tyrant.

2. Mulan (Magnolia) was a girl who disguised herself as a man and went into military service in her ailing father's stead. See the first prologue story of story 28 in Feng Menglong, *Stories Old and New: A Ming Dynasty Collection*.

3. In the Ming dynasty, those serving in the military were partially subsidized by their own clans and were therefore entitled to travel back to their hometown once every few years to collect their due.

4. Song Yu (ca. 290–ca. 223 B.C.E.) said in one of his rhapsodies (*fu*) that a beautiful girl who lived next door to him stole furtive glances at him from over the fence wall for three years.

Liuxia Hui (Hui of Liuxia), a court official of the state of Lu in the Spring and Autumn period, was known for his stoic indifference to sexual temptation.

5. During the Spring and Autumn period, a man offered a piece of uncut jade to King Li of the state of Chu. The king did not take it, believing it was a piece of ordinary rock. After King Li was succeeded by King Wu, the man offered the jade to the new king but was again rejected. It was King Wu's successor, King Wen, who had the rock-like object cut open and found a piece of flawless jade inside.

11. *Three Times Su Xiaomei Tests Her Groom*

1. For more on Su Shi, see story 3 in Feng Menglong, *Stories to Caution the World: A Ming Dynasty Collection, Volume 2*.

2. For more on Wang Anshi, see stories 3 and 4 in *Stories to Caution the World: A Ming Dynasty Collection, Volume 2*.

3. For more on the friendship between Su Dongpo and Abbot Foyin, see story 30 in Feng Menglong, *Stories Old and New: A Ming Dynasty Collection*.

12. *Four Times Abbot Foyin Flirts with Qinniang*

1. "He" in this poem refers to Su Dongpo. Sima Yi (179–251), courtesy name Zhongda, was an able prime minister of the Kingdom of Wei and the grandfather of Sima Yan, who founded the Jin dynasty.

2. Yao Chong, courtesy name Yuanzhi (650–721), was a prime minister and a historian of the Tang dynasty.

3. For more on Su Dongpo, see story 11 in this collection and story 3 in Feng Menglong, *Stories to Caution the World: A Ming Dynasty Collection, Volume 2*. For more on his friendship with Abbot Foyin, see story 30 in *Stories Old and New: A Ming Dynasty Collection*.

4. Han E and Qin Qing were great singers in ancient times, according to *Liezi*, the Daoist classical work collected at the beginning of the Han dynasty, traditionally attributed to Lie Yukou of the Warring States period.

5. The four treasures of the study are brush-pen, ink slab, ink stick, and paper.

6. This is an allusion to Zhao Feiyan (d. 1 B.C.E.), who was a court lady in the service of Emperor Cheng (r. 32–7 B.C.E.) of the Han dynasty and was later made empress. She is said to have been so light and slim that she could dance on an outstretched palm.

7. In the rhapsody "Gao tang fu," attributed to Song Yu (ca. 290–ca. 223 B.C.E.), King Xiang of Chu slept in a dream with the Divine Maiden of Mount Wu.

13. The Leather Boot as Evidence against the God Erlang's Impostor

This story has been translated as "The Boot That Reveals the Culprit" by Lorraine Lieu and the editors in *Traditional Chinese Stories: Themes and Variations.*

1. For more on Emperor Taizu of the Song dynasty, see story 21 in Feng Menglong, *Stories to Caution the World: A Ming Dynasty Collection, Volume 2.*

2. Liangguang is now Guangdong and Guangxi.

3. Marshal Yang Jian was one of the Six Villains of Xuande mentioned above.

4. Lantian, in present-day Shaanxi, is famous for its jade.

5. Grand Preceptor Cai is Cai Jing, one of the Six Villains of Xuanhe mentioned at the beginning of the story.

6. Yang Shi (1053–1135), also known as Gentleman of Mount Gui, was a philosopher of the neo-Confucian school of principle.

7. According to "King Mu of Zhou, III" in *Liezi*, a woodsman in the state of Zheng forgot where he hid the deer that he had killed and thought he had dreamt about it. Another man heard about this, found the deer, and took it home. Then the woodsman remembered in a dream the place where he had hidden the deer and, in the same dream, also saw the man who got the deer. He sought out that man, and the two brought the case to court. When asked for his judgment, the prime minister said, "I can't tell what is dream and what is not."

8. Zhuang Zhou, or Zhuangzi (ca. 369–286 B.C.E.), was a Daoist philosopher. According to the book that bears his name, he once dreamed that he was a butterfly, which did not know that it was Zhuang Zhou. When he awoke suddenly, he found himself Zhuang Zhou again, but he did not know whether he was Zhuang Zhou who had dreamed that he was a butterfly, or a butterfly dreaming that it was Zhuang Zhou. For more on Zhuang Zhou, see story 2 in Feng Menglong, *Stories to Caution the World: A Ming Dynasty Collection, Volume 2.*

9. A cangue is a wooden collar, usually three or four feet square, used in ancient China to confine the neck and sometimes also the hands of convicts.

10. Xiao He (d. 193 B.C.E.) was an early lawmaker. When he was prime minister under the first emperor of the Han dynasty, he formulated the larger part of the Han penal code.

14. The Fan Tower Restaurant as Witness to the Love of Zhou Shengxian

This story has been translated as "Shengxian" by Patrick Hanan in *Falling in Love: Stories from Ming China,* 1–20.

1. The Winding Pond, a scenic spot in Chang'an (present-day Xi'an, capital during the Tang dynasty) no longer exists. The Golden Bright Pond, dug to the west of Bianliang (present-day Kaifeng) during the Five Dynasties period, no longer exists either.

2. Fanlou, Fan Tower, was a grand and famous restaurant in the Eastern Capital (present-day Kaifeng) in the Northern Song dynasty. It was rebuilt in 1988 according to descriptions given in *The Eastern Capital: A Dream of Splendors Past* (Dongjing meng hua lu), written in 1147 by Meng Yuanlao (1110–60).

3. The young lady of *Story of the Western Chamber,* a play generally attributed to Wang Shifu of the Yuan dynasty, is Cui Yingying, who has a clandestine affair with Student Zhang Sheng but is in the end happily united with him in marriage.

4. In the Song dynasty, grave robbery was a capital offense.

5. *The Book of Predestination* (Qian ding lu) is attributed to Zhong Lu of the Tang dynasty.

6. Bao Zheng (989–1062), as prefect of Kaifeng, gained such fame as a wise and fair dispenser of justice that stories about him abound

in folklore and traditional drama. But he could not have been involved in this case, because this story is supposed to have taken place during the reign of Emperor Huizong, who ruled from 1101–1125, after Prefect Bao had died.

15. In Eternal Regret, He Daqing Leaves Behind a Lovers' Silk Ribbon

1. Xingruzi is most probably a fictitious name.

2. Zhang Chang (d. 47 B.C.E.), who served as magistrate of the capital under Emperor Xuan (r. 73–49 B.C.E.), often painted his wife's eyebrows and is held up as an example of a loving husband. Sima Xiangru (179–117 B.C.E.), one of the most celebrated rhapsody (*fu*) writers in the history of Chinese literature, is also known for his romance with Zhuo Wenjun. The two eloped after their meeting. See the prologue story of story 6 in Feng Menglong, *Stories to Caution the World: A Ming Dynasty Collection, Volume 2.*

3. During the Clear and Bright Festival in early April, people visit the graves of their ancestors.

4. Zhao Mengfu (1254–1322) is one of China's greatest calligraphers and painters.

5. Lü Dongbin is one of the Eight Immortals in the Daoist legends.

6. Bodhidharma is reputed to be the first patriarch of the Chan (Zen) school of Buddhism in China.

16. In Defiance, Lu Wuhan Refuses to Give Up the Colored Shoes

This story has been translated as "The Rainbow Slippers" in *Falling in Love: Stories from Ming China.*

1. Xishi, also known as Xizi, was a famous beauty of the state of Yue in the late Spring and Autumn period.

2. Bianzhou is another name for Bianjing or Bianliang (present-day Kaifeng, Henan), the capital of the Song dynasty before it fell into Jurchen hands in 1127.

3. "Clouds and rain" is a metaphor for

sexual encounters. The term was first used in the rhapsody "Gao tang fu," attributed to Song Yu (ca. 290–ca. 223 B.C.E.).

4. A cangue was a wooden collar, usually three or four feet square, used in ancient China to confine the neck and sometimes also the hands of convicts.

17. Zhang Xiaoji Takes in His Brother-in-Law at Chenliu

1. In the year 220, Cao Pi (187–226) dethroned Emperor Xiandi (r. 190–220) of the Han dynasty and, claiming that Emperor Xiandi had abdicated the throne in his favor, proclaimed himself emperor and founded the Wei dynasty.

18. Shi Fu Encounters a Friend at Tanque

1. Deng Tong of the Western Han dynasty was an immensely rich court favorite, with the authority to mint his own money. But later in life, he lost favor with the new emperor and died of hunger in prison. This story is also told in story 9 in Feng Menglong, *Stories Old and New: A Ming Dynasty Collection.*

Zhou Yafu (d. 143 B.C.E.), prime minister under Emperor Jing of the Han dynasty, was implicated in a corruption case involving his son, and died in a hunger strike in prison.

2. The ten things to watch for are whether the silkworms are cold, warm, hungry, or full; whether they stay far apart from each other or huddle together; when they molt; when they wake up; and whether they eat quickly or slowly.

3. The eight rules to observe: 1. Keep the lights dim when the silkworms are molting. 2. Turn the lights bright when they are awake. 3. Keep the temperature warm when the silkworms are small and when they are about to sleep. 4 and 5. Maintain bright light and cool down the air when the silkworms are large and when they awake. 6. Make sure that the air is breezy when they feed. 7. Add leaves and feed them quickly when they are hungry; 8. Feed

them slowly and with thin leaves when they have just awakened.

4. The three situations are when the silk moths lay eggs, when the grubs are transferred onto bamboo trays, and when the silkworms are transferred to sheds where they can spin cocoons. The five places are where the silkworm raisers move around, where mulberry trees are grown, where the grubs are grown, where the silkworms' bamboo trays are laid out, and where the silkworms spin cocoons.

5. For the story about Yang Bao saving a siskin, see the prologue story of story 6 in this collection.

19. Bai Yuniang Endures Hardships and Brings about Her Husband's Success

1. The three cardinal guides are ruler guides subjects, father guides son, and husband guides wife. The five constant virtues are benevolence, righteousness, propriety, wisdom, and fidelity.

2. Liu Xiu (6 B.C.E.–57 C.E.), emperor of Han dynasty, wanted to marry his older sister to Song Hong, a married man, but the latter refused to abandon his wife, whom he had married in his humble "chaff and husks" days before his rise to power. In the Han dynasty narrative poem "Mulberry up the Lane," Luo Fu, a fair maiden, was picking mulberry leaves when a prefect passing by offered her marriage. She replied, "You have your own wife, Prefect, and I have my own husband."

3. Huang Yun, courtesy name Zi'ai, was a famous scholar in the Eastern Han dynasty. Upon hearing that the minister of education, Yuan Wei, wanted to marry his niece to him, he drove away his wife. For the story about Zhu Maichen and his wife, see the prologue story of story 27 in Feng Menglong, *Stories Old and New: A Ming Dynasty Collection*.

4. According to legend, the Weaving Maiden is a star on one side of the Milky Way, and her husband, the Herdboy Star, is on the other side. They get to meet only once a year, across a bridge formed by magpies, on the seventh day of the seventh lunar month.

20. Zhang Tingxiu Escapes from Death and Saves His Father

1. Qizi, whose advice to his nephew, the notorious King Zhou of the Shang dynasty, was consistently rejected, had feigned madness and worked as a slave but later regained eminence under King Wu of the Zhou dynasty. Wu Yun, courtesy name Zixu (d. 484 B.C.E.), was a member of the aristocracy in the state of Wu during the Spring and Autumn period. For a time, he was so impoverished that he had to beg for a living.

2. The four treasures of the scholar's study are brush-pen, ink stick, ink slab, and paper.

3. *Thornwood Hairpins* (Jingchai ji) is a play by Ke Danqiu of the Yuan dynasty. In the play, a girl called Qian Yulian in the Song dynasty enters into a betrothal with Wang Shipeng against the wishes of her stepmother. Later, when Wang Shipeng is demoted and sent away, her stepmother forces her to marry her rich nephew, Sun Ruquan, whereupon Qian Yulian ties a rock to herself and jumps into Ou River. She is rescued and later marries Wang Shipeng.

4. In this scene of the play *Thornwood Hairpins*, Wang Shipeng believes that his fiancée, Qian Yulian, has drowned and therefore holds a memorial service by the river in her honor.

21. With Her Wisdom Zhang Shu'er Helps Mr. Yang Escape

1. Pei Kai, courtesy name Shuze, was a handsome man of the Jin dynasty, known at the time as "the man of jade." Wang Yan, courtesy name Yifu, was a handsome man as well as a famous conversationalist, also of the Jin dynasty.

2. Wang Kai was a fabulously rich man in the Jin dynasty. For more on Wang Kai and his game of one-upmanship with Shi Chong (249–300) in showing off their wealth, see the prologue story of story 36 in Feng Menglong, *Stories Old and New: A Ming Dynasty Collection*.

3. The original Chinese text says "Rong County, Henan Prefecture" at this point but "Hejian Prefecture" toward the end of the story, when Yang Yuanli meets his uncle. There was

no Rong County in Henan, nor is Henan on the way from Yanzhou of Shandong to Beijing, but Qing County of Hejian Prefecture (in present-day Hebei) does lie on the way from Yanzhou to Beijing.

4. A *zhuangyuan,* as explained in the translators' note, was a *jinshi* who ranked first in the palace examination, in which the emperor interviewed those who passed the imperial civil service examination at the national level. A *huiyuan,* in the Ming and Qing dynasties, was one who came out first in the national-level examination held once every three years in the capital.

5. A green dragon symbolizes good luck, and a white tiger, misfortune.

22. With His Flying Sword Lü Dongbin Attempts to Kill the Yellow Dragon

1. Penglai Island is the fabled fairyland of the immortals in the Daoist belief.

2 Lord Donghua is an immortal in Daoist legends

3. Lü Dongbin is one of the Eight Immortals in the Daoist legends.

4. In the play *Yellow Millet Dream at Handan,* written by Ma Zhiyuan (1260–1325), Lü Dongbin was passing Handan after a failed attempt at the civil service examinations when he met Zhongli and achieved enlightenment through a dream that took no longer than the cooking time for a pot of millet porridge.

5. In the Daoist belief, there are twenty-four organs in the body corresponding to the twenty-four seasonal division points in the solar calendar.

6. Bai Juji (772–846) was one of the most influential poets of the mid-Tang. For more on Bai Juyi, see story 10 in Feng Menglong, *Stories to Caution the World: A Ming Dynasty Collection, Volume 2.*

7. Taiyi is a revered celestial god in the Daoist belief. In the Han dynasty, prayer services to the god Taiyi were held on the fifteenth night of the first lunar month of each year.

8. The First Emperor of the Qin dynasty (r. 246–210 B.C.E.), who unified China for the first time in history, was buried north of Mount Li in Xi'an, Shaanxi. Emperor Wudi of the Han dynasty (r. 140–87 B.C.E.) was buried at Mount Mao in Xingping County, Shaanxi.

9. Sakyamuni preached sermons at Holy Vulture Peak, Grdhrakuta, in ancient India.

10. According to the chapter "Zeyang" in *Zhuangzi,* two countries lived on the horns of a snail, one on the left horn, the other on the right horn. The two countries often waged warfare against each other over territorial disputes.

23. Prince Hailing of Jin Dies from Indulgence in Lust

1. Wanyan Liang (1122–61), emperor of the Jin dynasty from 1149 to 1161, was posthumously demoted to Prince of Hailing.

2. Xishi was a famous beauty of the state of Yue in the late Spring and Autumn period. Mao Qiang was another beauty of ancient times.

3. The Jasper Pool is a legendary abode of the gods at the top of the Kunlun Mountains in western China. Jade Maidens are maids who serve the gods.

4. Zhao Feiyan (d. 1 B.C.E.) was a court lady in the service of Emperor Cheng (r. 32–7 B.C.E.) of the Han dynasty and was later made empress.

5. Master Hemp Robe was a legendary fortune-teller with divine skills in the Song dynasty. He is said to have given advice to Chen Tuan, courtesy name Xiyi (d. 989), who is featured in story 14 in Feng Menglong, *Stories Old and New: A Ming Dynasty Collection.*

Bodhidharma (d. 536), born in India, was the founder and first patriarch of Chinese Chan (Zen) Buddhism.

6. It was a common practice for a married woman to have the fine hair on her face removed by twisting and untwisting thin threads alternately to pull it out.

7. Han Xin (d. 196 B.C.E.) was commander-in-chief under Liu Bang (256–195 B.C.), who later became the first emperor of the Han dynasty.

According to the play *Wu Yuan Plays the Xiao Pipe*, by Li Shouqing of the Yuan dynasty, in the Spring and Autumn period of the Zhou dynasty, Lord Mu of the state of Qin arranged a grand gathering of the lords of seventeen states at Lintong, where Wu Zixu of the state of Chu lifted a mighty cauldron in a show of strength. Lord Mu of Qin was so awestruck that he gave up his ambitions of annexation.

Prince Wuji of the state of Wei (d. 243 B.C.E.) stole the commander's tally and went to the rescue of the state of Zhao, which was under siege by Qin troops.

8. Sun Wu, author of *Master Sun's Art of War*, was a great military strategist of the late Spring and Autumn period.

Wu Qi (d. 381 B.C.E.) was a military strategist of the Warring States period.

Lu Jia was a political essayist at the beginning of the Han dynasty.

9. Hongniang is the personal maid of Cui Yingying, heroine of the play *The Western Chamber* by Wang Shifu of the Yuan dynasty. Hongniang plays a major role in bringing together Cui Yingying and her lover.

10. Xiao He (d. 193 B.C.E.), prime minister under the first emperor of the Han dynasty, formulated the larger part of the Han penal code.

11. Yang Xiu (175–219), courtesy name Dezu, was a fine scholar in the service of Cao Cao. He later died at Cao Cao's hands, a victim of his own cleverness, as described in *Romance of the Three Kingdoms*.

12. It was believed that dragons liked the meat of swallows.

13. Li Shaojun was a magician of the Han dynasty. After Imperial Consort Li died, Emperor Wudi missed her so sorely that Li Shaojun promised to summon her spirit. He made the emperor sit behind a gauze curtain in a dimly lit hall. Through the curtain, the emperor saw a beautiful woman resembling Consort Li sitting behind another gauze curtain some distance away.

14. Emperor Shizong (r. 1161–89) of the Jin dynasty was Wanyan Yong.

24. Emperor Yang of the Sui Dynasty Is Punished for His Life of Extravagance

1. "Jade Tree and Rear Court Flowers" is the title of a song composed by Chen Shubao (553–604), king of the Chen dynasty during the Southern Dynasties period. He was a talented poet but an incompetent ruler obsessed with feminine beauty. Jingyang Palace in the next line was his palace, located by Lake Xuanwu in present-day Nanjing.

2. Yun Dingxing was a high-ranking official in the court of Emperor Wen (r. 581–604) of the Sui dynasty.

3. Liu Wu, prince of Liang of the Han dynasty, had a fabulous garden located near Kaifeng of Henan.

4. Shudiao was a eunuch in the service of Duke Huan (d. 643 B.C.E.) of the state of Qi in the Spring and Autumn period.

5. Li Yuan (566–635) was to be the founder of the Tang dynasty.

6. Parts of the Grand Canal built by Emperor Yang of the Sui dynasty are still in use today.

7. Yu Shinan (558–638) was a famous calligrapher and scholar.

8. Zhao Feiyan (d. 1 B.C.E.) was a court lady in the service of Emperor Cheng (r. 32–7 B.C.E.) of the Han dynasty and was later made empress.

9. Peach Leaf was the name of a concubine of Wang Xianzhi (344–86), son of the famous calligrapher Wang Xizhi (303–61).

10. Zuo Fen, a consort of Emperor Wu of the Jin dynasty, was a talented poet, though of mediocre looks.

11. Zhang Lihua (d. 589), a great beauty, was a consort of Chen Shubao, king of the Chen dynasty. See note 1 of this story. She and another royal consort hid from the Sui troops in a well with the king but were captured. Zhang Lihua was killed, but the king was spared.

12. Han Qinhu was the one who captured the King of Chen and his royal consort, Zhang Lihua.

13. When leading the Sui army to bring down the Chen dynasty, Yang Guang had written an indictment against the king of Chen and had made 300,000 copies of it for circulation among the troops.

14. Guan Longfeng was a virtuous court minister under the despotic King Jie of the Xia dynasty. He remonstrated against the king and was killed.

15. The three sage sovereigns and five virtuous kings are legendary rulers of high antiquity. The three sage sovereigns are Fuxi, Suiren, and Shennong. The five virtuous kings are Huangdi (the Yellow Emperor), Zhuanxu, Di Ku, King Yao, and King Shun.

16. Dongfang Shuo (154–93 B.C.E.) was a man of letters of the Western Han dynasty. Stories about his wisdom abound. He once pleaded to Emperor Wudi on behalf of guards who stood in pouring rain.

17. In fact, the Labyrinth Compound was not in Chang'an but in Jiangdu, or present-day Yangzhou.

25. Mr. Dugu Has the Strangest Dream on His Journey Home

1. This is an allusion to a dream of the Daoist philosopher Zhuang Zhou or Zhuangzi (ca. 369–286 B.C.E.). According to the book that bears his name, Zhuang Zhou once dreamed that he was a butterfly that did not know that it was Zhuang Zhou. When he awoke suddenly, he found himself Zhuang Zhou again, but he did not know whether he was Zhuang Zhou who had dreamed that he was a butterfly, or a butterfly dreaming that it was Zhuang Zhou.

2. This is an allusion to a dream of Zhao Shixiong of the Sui dynasty on Luofu Hill in Guangdong. Under a blossoming plum tree, Zhao Shixiong dreamed that he shared wine with a woman emitting fragrance while green-robed children sang and danced around them. This allusion often appears in poems on plum blossoms. Luofu Hill is a scenic hill about which legends abound.

3. Bai Xingjian (775–826) was the younger brother of the great poet Bai Juyi. He passed the imperial examinations and acquired the *jinshi* degree in 807 and later held a number of official posts. He was also a prolific writer. The most famous of his works was "The Story of Li Wa."

4. The Fengtian incident occurred in 783. Taking advantage of Yao Lingyan's mutiny, Zhu Ci rebelled and proclaimed himself emperor. Emperor Dezong fled to Fengtian (in present-day Qian County, Shaanxi).

5. Bai Juyi (772–846) was one of the most influential poets of the mid-Tang dynasty. For more on Bai Juyi, see story 10 in Feng Menglong, *Stories to Caution the World: A Ming Dynasty Collection, Volume 2.*

6. Zhang Yanshang was a minister in the court of Emperor Dezong (r. 780–804).

7. Empress Dowager Hu was Hu Chonghua, consort of Emperor Xuanwu (r. 500–15).

8. Du Fu (712–70) was one of the most celebrated poets in the history of Chinese literature.

9. Fuxi was one of the legendary three sage sovereigns in high antiquity.

10. Liu Bei (161–223) founded the Shu Han kingdom of the Three Kingdoms period.

11. Princess Wencheng (d. 680) of the Tang dynasty married Songtsam Gambo (617?-50), king of the Tubo Tibetans, in 641.

12. For more about Sima Xiangru's elopement with Zhuo Wenjun, see the prologue story of story 6 in Feng Menglong, *Stories to Caution the World: A Ming Dynasty Collection.*

13. For more on Li Bai, see story 9 in Feng Menglong, *Stories to Caution the World.*

14. In the prose poem "Gao tang fu," attributed to Song Yu (ca. 290 - ca. 223 B.C.E.), King Xiang of Chu saw in a dream the Divine Maiden of Mount Wu and had a sexual encounter with her.

15. In fact, Dugu Xiashu had not yet won the *jinshi* degree at that time.

16. In fact, these lines are by Song Zhiwen (ca. 656 - ca. 713), another great Tang dynasty poet.

17. Before his rise to power, Su Qin (d. 317

B.C.E.) of the Warring States period was shunned by his kinsmen for returning home impoverished after a prolonged journey to find employment.

18. On Su Qin, see note 17.

19. In the Tang dynasty, Guanglu Grand Master was mostly just a prestige title.

26. Magistrate Xue Proves His Divinity through a Fish

1. Zhuangzi or Zhuang Zhou (ca. 369–286 B.C.E.) was a Daoist philosopher. According to the book that bears his name, he once dreamed that he was a butterfly, which did not know that it was Zhuang Zhou. When he awoke suddenly, he found himself Zhuang Zhou again, but he did not know whether he was Zhuang Zhou who had dreamed that he was a butterfly, or a butterfly dreaming that it was Zhuang Zhou.

2. The seventh day of the seventh month of the lunar calendar is a festival that celebrates the annual meeting across the Milky Way of the stars Herdboy and Weaving Maiden.

3. Sage Sun is Sun Simao (581–682), a famous physician and author of medical literature. Legend has it that he saved a snake that happened to be the Dragon King's son in disguise. The grateful Dragon King gave Sun Simao a thousand prescriptions.

4. Han Kang of the Eastern Han dynasty sold medicinal herbs in the Chang'an marketplace for more than thirty years without ever haggling over prices.

5. Dong Feng of the state of Wu during the Three Kingdoms period never took payment for his medical practice in the Lushan Mountains. He asked only that each patient plant an apricot tree for him. 100,000 apricot trees were planted in total. He exchanged the fruit for grain, which he then donated to the poor.

6. A green dragon symbolizes luck, and a white tiger, misfortune.

7. Dragon Gate Hill is located by the Yellow River near Hejin County, Shanxi. It is believed that carp gather there in the second and third months of the year when the tide is high. Legend has it that those carp that can jump over Dragon Gate Hill become dragons, hence the analogy of candidates passing the imperial examinations to carp jumping over Dragon Gate.

8. Marshal Zhai of the Western Han dynasty used to entertain many guests at home. After he was removed from office, his friends deserted him. After he regained office, however, they descended upon his door again, whereupon he wrote on the door a poem, including the line quoted above, to turn them away.

9. It was believed that if a cat jumped over a corpse, that corpse would sit up.

10. On Han Kang, see note 4 above.

27. Li Yuying Appeals for Justice from Jail

1. Shun, a legendary sage king in ancient China, is said to have suffered abuses in his youth from his stepmother. Mount Li, where Shun used to till the land, is most probably in present-day Jinan, Shandong.

2. Min Ziqian (536–487 B.C.E.), one of Confucius's students, had also suffered abuses from his stepmother, who gave her own two sons warm silk-floss-padded jackets in winter but gave him a jacket padded only with reed catkins. Upon learning of this, his father wanted to oust her, but Min Ziqian said, "If she stays, only one son suffers from cold. If she is gone, all three sons will suffer."

3. As explained in note 1 above, Shun often suffered from his stepmother's abuses in his youth. Once, when he was on top of the granary, fixing the roof, she took away the ladder and made his father set the granary on fire.

4. Shensheng (d. 656 B.C.E.), son of Duke Xian of the state of Jin in the Spring and Autumn period, killed himself after being slandered by Liji, his father's concubine, who wanted to make her own son the crown prince.

Boqi, son of Yin Jifu during the reign of King Xuan of the Western Zhou dynasty, was vilified by his stepmother and expelled from home.

5. In the Buddhist belief, a yaksha is usually a malevolent spirit.

6. Prince of Anhua of Shaanxi was Zhu

Zifan (d. 1510), who rose in armed rebellion in the year 1509. The emperor dispatched an expeditionary force led by Zhang Yong, a eunuch, to put down the rebellion.

7. The Avici Hell is the last and deepest of the eight hot hells in Buddhist belief.

8. "The Nine Springs" is a term for the netherworld.

9. On Mulan joining the army in her father's name, see the first prologue story of story 28 in Feng Menglong, *Stories Old and New: A Ming Dynasty Collection.*

Tiying was the daughter of Chunyu Yi of the Han dynasty. When her father was summoned to the capital, Chang'an, to be sentenced for a crime, she followed him there and submitted a request to the imperial court that she be allowed to work as a maidservant in a government institution to redeem her father. Emperor Wen eventually pardoned him.

10. The five internal organs are the heart, liver, spleen, lungs, and kidneys.

11. In the Ming dynasty, the five punishments were beating with a bamboo rod, flogging with a wooden stick, imprisonment, exile, and death. The four virtues are benevolence, righteousness, decorum, and wisdom.

12. In the Tang dynasty, two sisters named Dou of Fengtian County (in present-day Shaanxi) jumped to their death from a cliff rather than submit themselves to bandits.

Yunhua is unidentified.

13. This is a reference to stories about palace maids writing love poems on red leaves and letting them flow out of the palace ditches to reach the outside world.

14. In the *Book of Songs,* there is one poem about seven brothers blaming themselves because their widowed mother wants to remarry.

28. Young Master Wu Goes to a Tryst in the Next Boat

This story has been translated as "Wu Yan" in *Falling in Love: Stories from Ming China*

1. According to legend, the Old Man under the Moon, the god of marriages, has a bag full of red strings with which he ties would-be couples together by their ankles.

2. Bai Juyi (772–846) was one of the most influential poets of the mid-Tang dynasty.

3. He Yan, a native of the state of Wei in the Three Kingdoms period, was a handsome man with fair skin.

4. Xun Yu (163–212), director of the imperial secretariat, used to wear perfume that lingered in the air.

5. Pan An (247–300), or Pan Yue, courtesy name Anren, was a man of letters and an official in the Western Jin dynasty, but is now better known as the man who personifies male beauty. He was walking down the streets of Luoyang one day when a group of women danced around him and tossed fruit at him as a way to express their admiration.

6. In the prose poem "Gao tang fu" attributed to Song Yu (ca. 290–ca. 223 B.C.E.), King Xiang of Chu saw in a dream the Divine Maiden of Mount Wu and had a sexual encounter with her.

7. By the traditional Chinese method, one is considered one year old at birth and adds a year on each lunar New Year's Day. Thus, someone born in December is considered two years old one or two months later, on the lunar New Year's Day, which usually falls in January or February.

29. With His Passion for Poetry and Wine, Scholar Lu Scorns Dukes and Earls

1. Dong is Dong Zhongshu (179–104 B.C.E.), an important philosopher. Jia is Jia Yi (201–169 B.C.E.), a famous man of letters.

2. Liu Zhen (d. 217) and Cao Zhi (192–232), courtesy name Zijian, were both talented poets of the state of Wei during the Three Kingdoms period.

3. Li Qinglian is Li Bai (701–62), one of China's greatest poets. He called himself "Qinglian (Blue-Lotus) Recluse." Cao Zijian is Cao Zhi. See note above.

4. Historian Gao is Gao Qi (1336–74), a

poet and historian who served on the editorial board that compiled *History of the Yuan Dynasty.*

5. For the poem on peonies written by the great Tang dynasty poet Li Bai, see story 9 in Feng Menglong, *Stories to Caution the World: a Ming Dynasty Collection, Volume 2.*

6. Huishan Spring is located at the foot of Mount Huishan in Wuxi, Jiangsu.

7. The Prince of Huainan is Liu An (179–122 B.C.E.), who supported thousands of retainers and Daoists in his mansion. In folklore, he became an immortal and rose to heaven, but in fact he died by his own hand after his armed rebellion against Emperor Wudi of Han failed.

8. Xishi was a famous beauty of the state of Yue in the late Spring and Autumn period.

9. Usually, the table for the host faces west, and the table for the guest of honor faces east.

10. Oxheads are armed runners serving the king of hell. In the Buddhist belief, a yaksha is usually a malevolent spirit.

11. Gongyi Chang, one of Confucius's students, was once imprisoned under false charges, but Confucius believed Gongyi was innocent and married his daughter to Gongyi.

12. Xiatai is where King Jie of the Xia dynasty had imprisoned Chengtang or Tang, who later founded the Shang dynasty. Youli, in present-day Tangyin County, Henan, is where King Zhou of the Shang dynasty had imprisoned Ji Chang, whose son later founded the Zhou dynasty. Ji Chang was posthumously called King Wen.

13. Sun Bin, a descendant of Sun Wu, was a military strategist of the Warring States period and the author of *Sun Bin on the Art of War.* Sima Qian (145–86? B.C.E.) was a great historian and scholar who compiled *Shiji, Records of the Grand Historian.*

14. *Gongshi* in the Ming dynasty is equivalent to the term *gongsheng* (tribute student), referring to scholars recommended by local government for further studies at the national capital and subsequent admission to the civil service.

15. Boyi and Shuqi, poverty-stricken brothers in the Shang dynasty, were held up as examples of men of moral integrity.

16. Fan Li, after helping the king of Yue conquer the state of Wu in the Warring States period, became a rich businessman.

17. Zhang Shizhi was chief minister for law enforcement under Emperor Wendi (r. 179–156 B.C.E.) in the Western Han dynasty.

18. When greeting General Wei Qing (d. 106 B.C.E.), to whom every other court official showed the greatest deference, Ji An (d. 112 B.C.E.) just folded his hands in front of his chest and refrained from bowing.

30. In a Humble Inn, Mr. Li Mian Meets a Knight-Errant

1. For the story about Zhu Maichen's wife divorcing him, see the prologue story of story 27 in Feng Menglong, *Stories Old and New: A Ming Dynasty Collection.*

Jizi is Su Qin (d. 317 B.C.E.), who was shunned by his kinsmen, including his sister-in-law, for returning home impoverished after a prolonged journey to find employment.

2. Yang Guozhong (d. 756) was a power-abusing prime minister and cousin of Imperial Consort Yang.

3. For more on the story about Li Bai failing the examinations and translating the letter, see story 9 in Feng Menglong, *Stories to Caution the World: A Ming Dynasty Collection, Volume 2.*

4. Zhou Xing (d. 691), Lai Junchen (651–97), and Suo Yuanli (d. 691) were notoriously cruel and ruthless officials.

5. A yaksha is usually a malevolent spirit in the Buddhist belief.

6. An Lushan (703–57) rose in armed rebellion against the House of Tang in 755. For a fictional account of his adulterous relationship with Imperial Consort Yang, see the prologue story of story 19 in Feng Menglong, *Stories to Caution the World: A Ming Dynasty Collection, Volume 2.*

7. Yan Gaoqing (692–756), prefect of Changshan (present-day Zhengding, Hebei) and cousin of Yan Zhenqing (708–84), one of China's greatest calligraphers, was later killed by An Lushan as he tried to suppress An's rebellion.

8. The four treasures of the scholar's study are brush-pen, ink slab, ink stick, and paper.

9. On Su Qin, see note 1 above.

10. Nie Zheng (d. 397 B.C.E.) assassinated the prime minister of the state of Han and then killed himself.

Jing Ke (d. 227 B.C.E.) tried to assassinate the First Emperor of Qin but failed.

31. Regional Commander Zheng Renders Distinguished Service with His Divine-Arm Bow

1. Maitreya is Buddha of the Future, represented in temples and monasteries as the fat laughing Buddha with a cloth bag hanging from a pole.

2. In the Northern Song period (970–1126), Luoyang was called the western capital and Bianliang (present-day Kaifeng) the eastern capital.

3. Consort Yang, Yang Yuhuan (719–56), was a favorite consort of Emperor Xuanzong (r. 712–56) of the Tang dynasty. For more on Consort Yang, see story 9 and the prologue story of story 19 in Feng Menglong, *Stories to Caution the World: A Ming Dynasty Collection, Volume 2*.

4. Xi Shi was a famous beauty of the state of Yue in the late Spring and Autumn period.

5. Penglai Island is the fabled abode of the immortals.

6. Zhang Sengzhou (d. ca. 519) was a famous painter of the Liang dynasty (502–57) during the Southern dynasties.

7. Chong Shidao (d. 1126) later commanded troops in repelling the invading Jurchen army.

8. Dongchuan and Xichuan are eastern Sichuan and western Sichuan.

9. Wuzhu of Jin (d. 1148), or Wanyan Zongbi, was the fourth son of Ogda, Emperor Taizu of the Jurchen Jin.

10. According to another legend, when pursued by the Jurchens, Zhao Gou, Prince of Kang (later to become Emperor Gaozong, r. 1127–62), took refuge in a temple. After he crossed the river on horseback and threw off his pursuers, he found that the horse he was riding was the clay horse he had seen in the temple.

32. Scholar Huang Is Blessed with Divine Aid through His Jade-Horse Pendant

1. Penglai is the fabled abode of the immortals.

2. Pan Yue (247–300), courtesy name Anren and popularly known as Pan An, was a man of letters in the Western Jin dynasty and reputedly very handsome.

Wei Jie (286–312) was also an exceedingly handsome man, called by his contemporaries "man of carved jade" (*yuren*).

3. Monkey King, a much beloved character in the Ming dynasty novel *Journey to the West*, is able to change hairs on his body into bugs that put people to sleep.

4. Liang Hong and Meng Guang of the Eastern Han dynasty were a loving married couple even when they were in straitened circumstances.

5. Mr. Zhang is Zhang Junrui, a character in the play *The Story of the Western Chamber* that is generally attributed to Wang Shifu of the Yuan dynasty. Young Mr. Zhang scaled a wall to meet his lover, Yingying.

6. Song Yu (ca. 290–ca. 223 B.C.E.) said in one of his rhapsodies (*fu*) that a beautiful neighboring girl stole furtive glances at him from over the wall for three years.

7. Xiao He (d. 193 B.C.E.) helped Liu Bang found the Han dynasty. When Liu Bang was still contending with Xiang Yu of Chu for the throne, Han Xin offered Liu Bang his services, but, disappointed that his talent was not put to good use, Han Xin fled under the cover of night. Xiao He chased him and brought him back.

8. Officer Gu, a character in the "Biography of Wushuang" in *Taiping guangji* of the Song dynasty, is a champion of justice and doer of good deeds. The story has been translated by Dale Johnson as "Wu-shuang the Peerless" in *Traditional Chinese Stories: Themes and Variations*.

Xu Jun of the Tang dynasty acted on his friend Han Hong's behalf and took Han's wife back from General Shachili, who had forcibly seized her.

33. *Over Fifteen Strings of Cash, a Jest Leads to Dire Disasters*

The title of the Song dynasty version of the story is "The Wrongful Execution of Cui Ning." This story has been translated by Jeanne Kelly as "The Jest that Leads to Disaster" in Traditional Chinese Stories: Themes and Variations, and by Yang Xianyi and Gladys Yang as "Fifteen Strings of Cash" in Lazy Dragon, and by William Dolby as "A Joke over Fifteen Strings of Cah Brings Uncanny Disaster" in *The Perfect Lady by Mistake*.

1. Li Cunxiao (d. 894) was an adopted son of Li Keyong (856–908), whose birth son, Li Cunxu (885–926), founded the Later Tang dynasty. Li Cunxiao performed meritorious military service but was later framed and executed.

2. Peng Yue (d. 196 B.C.E.) helped Liu Bang found the Han dynasty but was later killed by Liu Bang. For an account of his tragic death, see story 31 in Feng Menglong, *Stories Old and New: A Ming Dynasty Collection*.

3. Liu Wu (d. 144 B.C.E.), prince of Liang of the Han dynasty, had a fabulous garden located near Kaifeng in Henan.

34. *For One Penny, a Small Grudge Ends in Stark Tragedies*

1. Lü Yan, or Lü Dongbin, is one of the Eight Immortals in the Daoist legends. For more on Lü Dongbin, see story 22.

Hedong, meaning "east of the Yellow River," is in present-day Shanxi. Yuezhou should be Puzhou, located in the southwestern corner of Shanxi.

2. Zhongli Quan, more commonly known as Han Zhongli, is also one of the Eight Immortals.

3. Sun is Sun Bin, a military strategist of the Warring States period. He was a descendant of Sun Wu and author of *Sun Bin on the Art of War*.

Pang is Pang Juan, an opponent of Sun Bin.

4. In the war between Chu and Han (206–203 B.C.E.), Liu Bang defeated Xiang Yu and founded the Han dynasty.

5. The "silencer" was an oblong piece of wooden board with which a magistrate trying a case struck the table, to frighten the accused with the noise.

6. Yellow Springs is the netherworld.

7. Liuxia Hui, or Hui of Liuxia, a court official of the state of Lu in the Spring and Autumn period, is known for his stoic indifference to sexual temptation. He once used his own body warmth to save a homeless woman from being frozen to death but did not have relations with her.

The man of Lu was a bachelor in the state of Lu during the Spring and Autumn period. He once refused to let in a neighboring widow who knocked on his door in a rainstorm, because he was afraid he might not be able to control himself.

35. *In Righteous Wrath, Old Servant Xu Builds Up a Family Fortune*

This story has been translated as "Old Servant Hsü" by John Kwan-Terry, in Ma and Lau, eds., *Traditional Chinese Stories*.

1. The three teachings are Confucianism, Daoism, and Buddhism. The nine schools of thought are those of the Confucians, the Daoists, the Yin-Yang, the Legalists, the Logicians, the Mohists, the Political Strategists, the Eclectics, and the Agriculturists.

2. In Chinese folklore, Zhong Kui is a deity who drives away evil spirits.

3. This is a reference to Peng Chong's servant Zimi. Peng Chong, Prefect of Yuyang, pledged allegiance to Liu Xiu, Emperor Guangwu (r. 25–57) of the Eastern Han dynasty, but later declared himself king of Yan. His servant Zimi killed him and his wife and offered their heads to Liu Xiu.

36. *Enduring Humiliation, Cai Ruihong Seeks Revenge*

1. Legend has it that Yidi is the one who invented the making of wine in China. When King Yu of the Xia dynasty was offered a taste of the brew Yidi had made, Yu commented after

taking a sip, "This is stuff that will ruin men and their countries." Henceforth he distanced himself from Yidi.

2. Wu Zixu (d. 484 B.C.E.) was an official of the state of Wu in the Spring and Autumn period. He died by his own hand at the order of the king of Wu, and his corpse was thrown into a river.

3. In the Ming dynasty, clerks working in government offices could take examinations conducted by the ministry of personnel once every three years. Those who passed three such examinations, after having served for a minimum of nine years, were eligible for appointment to posts at the county level, to be vice magistrates or county marshals.

4. In the Ming dynasty, according to government regulations, officials assigned to new duty stations must travel at their own expense rather than use the services of government courier stations.

5. For the story about the Tang dynasty poet Wang Bo traveling to Prince Teng's Pavilion, see story 40 in this collection.

6. Li Ling (d. 74 B.C.E.), a general, surrendered to the Xiongnu after losing a battle to them. In a letter to Su Wu (140–60 B.C.E.), who, as envoy from the Han emperor, was detained by the Xiongnu, Li Ling explained that he had surrendered in order to await more opportunities to serve the Han empire.

7. The three border regions in the Ming dynasty were Ningxia, Gansu, and Jizhou (in present-day Hebei).

37. Du Zichun Goes to Chang'an Three Times

1. Shi Chong (249–300) was a fabulously rich man. For more on his wealth and his precipitous downfall, see the prologue story of story 36 in Feng Menglong, *Stories Old and New*. Lord Mengchang (Tian Wen, d. 297 B.C.E.) was known for his generosity and maintained more than 3,000 retainers in his household.

2. Zhang Liang (d. 189 B.C.E.), courtesy name Zifang, was an adviser to Liu Bang, founder of the Han dynasty.

3. Jade maidens are maids who serve Daoist deities.

4. The six sensory organs are the eyes, ears, nose, tongue, body, and mind.

5. Liu An (179–122 B.C.E.), Duke of Huainan of the Western Han dynasty, was a devotee of alchemy and, as legend has it, rose to heaven and became an immortal. But, in fact, he died by his own hand after his armed rebellion against Emperor Wudi failed.

38. Daoist Li Enters Cloud Gate Cave Alone

1. "The old man of the flask" was, according to *Hou Han shu* (History of the Later Han Dynasty), compiled by Fan Ye (398–445), an old man who sold medicinal herbs in the marketplace. Each time he sold all his herbs, he would vanish into the flask hanging over his stall.

2. The Yellow Emperor is the legendary ancestor of the Chinese. Bridge Mountain is in Huangling County, Shaanxi, where the mausoleum of the Yellow Emperor is located.

3. A *ruyi* is usually an S-shaped wand or scepter, made of jade, that symbolizes good fortune.

4. Penglai is the fabled abode of the immortals.

5. Peach Blossom Spring is an isolated village described as a safe haven from the outside world in a story titled "The Peach Blossom Spring" by Tao Qian (365–427), courtesy name Yuanming.

6. Junping is the courtesy name of Yan Zun of the Han dynasty. Instead of pursuing a career in the civil service, he made a living as a fortune-teller in Chengdu. Every day, after he made enough money for his own sustenance for the day, he closed his shop and gave lectures on Laozi's *Daode jing*.

7. Qi and Lu are respectively the eastern and western parts of present-day Shandong.

8. Zhao Kuo (d. 260 B.C.E.), a general of the state of Zhao during the Warring States period, could talk glibly about military strategies, but once he took command of the Zhao army against the Qin, he was badly defeated. He him-

self died in a failed attempt to break through an enemy siege.

9. Yu of the Xia dynasty was a sage king who led the people in controlling floods and succeeded Shun as ruler.

10. The First Emperor of the Qin dynasty, named Ying Zheng (259–210 B.C.E.), unified China for the first time in history.

11. Jiang Taigong or Grandpa Jiang, popular name for Jiang Ziya, is a legendary character modeled upon Lü Wang, statesman and strategist who became adviser and prime minister to King Wen of Zhou at the age of eighty.

12. Dong Feng of the state of Wu during the Three Kingdoms period never took payment for his medical practice on the Lushan Mountains. He asked only that each patient plant an apricot tree for him. Ten thousand apricot trees were planted in total. He exchanged the fruit for grain, which he then donated to the poor. Han Kang of the Eastern Han dynasty sold medicinal herbs in the Chang'an marketplace for more than thirty years and never haggled over prices.

13. When King Zhao of the state of Chu was traveling across a river, his boat hit an object. He had someone ask Confucius what it was. Confucius replied that it was a water-lily seedpod and that only someone destined to be a hegemon could come by it. On another occasion, the king of the state of Qi sent someone to tell Confucius about sightings of a bird dancing on one leg. Confucius told him to have people prepare for a major rainstorm, because the bird heralded rain.

14. Anqi Sheng was a magician whose services were sought by the First Emperor of Qin. Called "the thousand-year-old man," he was said to have achieved immortality.

39. Magistrate Wang Burns Down Precious Lotus Monastery

1. Lü Zhi (d. 180 B.C.E.), wife of Liu Bang, the first emperor of the Han dynasty, once held a feast for all the court officials and killed those who tried to resist the offers of wine.

2. Ananda Buddha, cousin of Sakyamuni,

was once delivered by the latter from the temptations of a woman.

3. For the story about Monk Yutong playing with Red Lotus, see story 29 in Feng Menglong, *Stories Old and New.*

40. The God of Madang Conjures Wind to Blow Wang Bo to Prince Teng's Pavilion

1. Lu Guimeng (d. 881), courtesy name Luwang, was a famous Tang dynasty poet.

2. The mad man of Chu is Qu Yuan (340–277 B.C.E.), the model loyal minister in Chinese history. Frustrated because the king repeatedly ignored his advice, he drowned himself in the Miluo River.

3. Literally, "When your time goes, a thunderbolt will smash the stone tablet of the Jianfu Temple." This is from a Song dynasty story: When the famous essayist and poet Fan Zhongyan (989–1052) was prefect of Raozhou, a poverty-stricken scholar went to seek his help. Fan offered to make him one thousand rubbings of a Jianfu Temple stone tablet with inscriptions by the most popular calligrapher of the day, Ouyang Xun, for each would be worth a thousand in cash. On the very night before the rubbings were to be done, the stone tablet was destroyed by a thunderbolt.

4. Literally, "When your time comes, the wind will send you to the Pavilion of Prince Teng."

5. Liu Xiangdao (596–666), courtesy name Tongshou, was a scholar with a distinguished career in the imperial civil service. Zhang Yuxi is unidentified.

6. Ancient Chinese astronomers divided all the visible stars in the sky into twenty-eight constellations, which further form four major groups, each taking up one of the four quadrants of the sky. The stars Yi and Zhen belong to the southern group.

7. Mount Heng is southwest of Nanchang, Jiangxi, and Mount Lu is north of it.

8. The Chu region is present-day Hubei and Hunan. Ouyue is present-day Fujian and Zhejiang.

9. According to legend, Zhang Hua (232–300) saw an aura over Fengcheng that spoke of hidden precious swords. After he appointed Lei Huan prefect of Fengcheng, Lei dug up a pair of swords and presented one to Zhang, keeping the other for himself. After both men died, the swords were seen at Yanping Ferry, where they joined together and changed into two dragons.

The stars Dou and Niu belong to the northern group of stars of the twenty-eight constellations. See note 6.

10. Chen Fan (d. 168), when serving as the prefect of Yuzhang (in present-day Jiangxi), set out a couch for Scholar Xu Zhi's visit. After Xu Zhi left, Chen Fan respectfully hung the couch from a rafter.

11. Yang Xiu (175–219), Cao Zhi (192–232), Mi Heng (173–98, courtesy name Zhengping), and Zhang Song (d. 212) were all talented men with capacious and retentive memories.

12. Wu Cailuan was a native of Puyang County, Henan, of the Tang dynasty. She was believed to have become a Daoist immortal.

CPSIA information can be obtained
at www.ICGtesting.com
Printed in the USA
BVHW031047150620
581447BV00001B/3